Cost Accounting for Health Care Organizations

Concepts and Applications

Steven A. Finkler, PhD, CPA
Robert F. Wagner Graduate School of Public Service
New York University
New York, New York

AN ASPEN PUBLICATION®
Aspen Publishers, Inc.
Gaithersburg, Maryland
1994

Library of Congress Cataloging-in-Publication Data

Finkler, Steven A.
Cost accounting for health care organizations : concepts and
applications / Steven A. Finkler.
p.   cm.
Includes bibliographical references and index.
ISBN: 0-8342-0378-2
I. Title.
[DNLM: 1. Health facilities—Costs—Accounting. 2. Hospitals—
Cost of operation—Accounting. 3. Cost accounting. WX 157 F399c
1993]
HF5686.H7F56 1993
657'.8322042—dc20
DNLM/DLC
for Library of Congress
93-7175
CIP

Editorial Resources: Ruth Bloom
Library of Congress Catalog Card Number: 93-7175
ISBN: 0-8342-0378-2

Printed in the United States of America

1   2   3   4   5

To Charles T. Horngren

Whose path-breaking work
placing the focus of cost accounting
on management decision making
has influenced much of my life's work.

Table of Contents

Preface

Cost accounting has become a critical part of health care management in the past decade. As hospital prospective payment has taken hold, all health care organizations have increased their focus on the control of costs. All health care managers, not just accountants, are becoming more and more aware of the importance of understanding as much about costs as they possibly can.

There are a number of existing textbooks in the cost accounting field. However, these generic cost accounting texts focus primarily on manufacturing industries and only secondarily on service industries such as health care. As such, their emphasis is largely on the process of converting raw materials into finished goods. Determining the cost of work-in-process and by-products receives a great deal of attention in such books. There is a scarcity of cost accounting texts written expressly for health care.

This book provides a thorough coverage of cost accounting from a health care perspective. It covers all of the basic tools of cost accounting common to all industries, and uses health care examples. *Cost Accounting for Health Care Organizations: Concepts and Applications* focuses on costing issues and concepts peculiar to the health care field. The tools covered are all practical, although they are not all commonly used. Some approaches, such as learning curves, are commonly used in other industries but not in health care. It is my hope that readers of this book will see the value of some of these less frequently used techniques and adopt them for use in their organizations.

The main theme of the book concerns the generation of useful cost information to aid managers in making decisions. The contents are therefore oriented toward both current and future accountants who will generate the information, as well as all current and future health care managers who want to know the types of information potentially available.

Cost Accounting for Health Care Organizations: Concepts and Applications does not rely heavily on debits, credits, journal entries, and other technical accounting terminology. This was done intentionally to make it accessible to a wide range of readers. While it is expected that this text will be used by students and faculty in university programs in health administration (both undergraduate and graduate), it is primarily for individuals already working in the field of health administration. The need to get improved information to facilitate decisions is critical at all levels of management.

The types of managers likely to benefit from reading this book include chief executive officers, chief operating officers, directors of medical staff, chief nursing officers, vice presidents of patient care services, and directors of planning. The chief finance officer and other members of the finance departments of health care organizations will find much material that can immediately be used in their day-in and day-out activities. Heads of many other clinical and support departments would also find this book helpful.

One of the special features is its merging of concepts and applications into one text. Each chapter provides not only a conceptual discussion of the issues related to that chapter's topic, but also specific examples. Further, each chapter is followed by one or more articles that apply some of the material discussed in the chapter. Such readings should be viewed as an integral part of the book and its educational process.

Each chapter begins with a set of specific learning objectives listed for the reader. That list is followed by a set of key terms used in the chapter. Each of the key terms is shown in italics the first time it appears in the chapter, and all are defined in the glossary, which appears at the end of the book. Each chapter has exercises and questions for discussion. The solutions can be found in Appendix A at the end of the book.

The text is broken down into four parts. Part I provides the foundations of cost accounting. Part II addresses the use of cost accounting for planning and control. Part III provides additional cost accounting tools to aid in decision-making. Part IV discusses the latest trends and techniques in cost accounting.

Part I provides the reader with a solid foundation in the essentials of cost accounting. The chapters in this section provide an introduction to costing and cost definitions. Various approaches to product costing and cost allocation are discussed. Breakeven analysis is also covered in the section, as are techniques for making nonroutine decisions.

A primary focus of cost accounting is on developing information that managers can use for planning and control. Once the reader is familiar with the foundations of cost accounting provided in Part I, a number of specific tools for improved planning and control can be considered. That is the role of Part II of the book. The chapters in this section focus on forecasting and prediction of future costs, budgeting, flexible budgeting and variance analysis, and management control.

Part III addresses a number of additional cost accounting tools that can be helpful in generating management information for decision making. Specifically, there are chapters on cost accounting ratios, productivity measurement, inventory, uncertainty, information systems, and performance evaluation. The chapter on cost accounting ratios is a specific innovation of this book.

For the past decade, there has been a growing literature critical of current cost accounting practices throughout all U.S. industries. The concern is that costing has evolved primarily into a tool for external reporting of financial results rather than for the management of the organization. The concern has led to a movement to revise cost accounting practices drastically to make them more relevant. The criticisms of cost accounting and a number of suggested approaches for improvement are discussed in Part IV. The chapters in this part also examine activity-based costing, total quality management, and the future of costing.

The last chapter also provides a summary of the book. Some instructors may choose to assign this last chapter at the beginning of the course to provide an in-depth overview of the material. It can then be assigned again at the end to provide a review and to allow for integration of the great breadth of material covered in the book.

The development of this work was a major challenge. I have attempted to create a book that provides a thorough, clearly written, comprehensive coverage of cost accounting. However, I recognize that there is always room for improvement. Readers are encouraged to write to me to point out errors or unclear passages, or to suggest additional applications or other improvements. All contributions will be acknowledged in the next edition. Please write to me at Room 600 Tisch Hall, Robert F. Wagner Graduate School of Public Service, New York University, 40 West Fourth Street, New York, NY, 10012-1118.

Some of the material contained in the chapters of this book was adapted from articles written by myself and published over the past seven years in *Hospital Cost Management and Accounting,* and its predecessor, *Hospital Cost Accounting Advisor.*

My thanks go to the many individuals who helped me in the process of developing this book. I especially thank Thomas D. Gessel, Walter Jones, Robert Murphy, Ray Newman, and Michael Zucker for their in-depth reviews of a draft of the manuscript. Their helpful comments resulted in a number of improvements to the book. I am also extremely grateful to the students in my Fall 1992 Cost Accounting and Analysis class at New York University's Wagner School. Those students gave the book a valuable "test drive." Shari Faith Fisch, Linford Russell, and Kevin Sullivan made especially helpful suggestions as the course proceeded, and I thank them in particular.

Steven A. Finkler

Part I

Cost Accounting Foundations

Part I provides the reader with a solid foundation in the essentials of cost accounting. The chapters in this section provide an introduction to costing and cost definitions. Various approaches to product costing and cost allocation are discussed. Breakeven analysis is also covered in this section, as are techniques for making nonroutine decisions.

Chapter 1 is introductory in nature. The distinctions among financial, managerial, and cost accounting are explained. The chapter discusses the use of cost accounting for planning, control, and nonroutine decision making. The role of cost accounting for inventory costing and income determination is also introduced. The chapter stresses the importance of several particular issues in cost accounting: the role of human beings; the need to develop cost information not only for reporting, but also for management control; and the benefit/cost philosophy regarding the generation of cost information.

Chapter 2 provides basic cost accounting definitions. The concepts of full costs, average costs, cost objectives, direct and indirect costs, fixed,

variable, marginal, total, and joint costs are introduced. These concepts are then applied to marginal cost pricing and to the issue of departmental costing versus product-line costing.

Chapter 3 of the book discusses product costing in greater detail. Job-order and process costing are explained and contrasted. Standard costing systems and microcosting are also discussed in the chapter.

Chapter 4 addresses the complex issue of cost allocation. The reasons for allocating costs are explained, and guidelines for cost allocation are provided. Cost allocation techniques are discussed, including cost pools and cost bases. This chapter also reviews the institutional cost report. There is discussion of how cost allocation relates to standard costing and microcosting. The difficulties concerning allocation of joint costs are considered. The chapter ends with a discussion of the relative merits of ratio of cost to charges (RCC) costing versus relative value unit (RVU) costing.

Next, Chapter 5 addresses cost–volume–profit analysis. The relationship between fixed costs and volume is stressed. The discussion of breakeven analysis provides a number of examples of cost–volume–profit analysis. The underlying assumptions of breakeven analysis are examined. The chapter ends with a discussion of the use of breakeven analysis for decision making.

Chapter 6 is the last chapter in this section. It discusses the issue of developing cost information for nonroutine decisions. The identification of alternatives and the issue of relevant costs are considered. A number of examples are provided.

1

Introduction to Cost Accounting

Goals of This Chapter

---

1. Describe the purpose of cost accounting.
2. Distinguish among financial, managerial, and cost accounting.
3. Explain the use of cost accounting for planning and control, nonroutine decisions, inventory valuation and income determination, and required external reports.
4. Discuss the conflict between generating cost data for reporting versus for management planning, decision making, and control.
5. List several key characteristics of a good cost accounting system, and describe some difficulties in designing such a system.
6. Explain the importance of human motivation in cost accounting.

Key Terms Used in This Chapter

Accounting; congruent goals; control; cost accounting; cost accounting system; cost measurement; cost reimbursement; cost reporting; divergent goals; financial accounting; incentives; income determination; inventory valuation; managerial accounting; Medicare Cost Report; nonroutine decisions; period costs; planning; product costs; profitability analysis; strategic planning.

Note: Key terms appear in italics when first used in the chapter. All key terms are defined in the Glossary.

THE PURPOSE OF COST ACCOUNTING

From a narrow perspective, *cost accounting* is an element of financial management that generates information about the costs of an organization and its components. As such, cost accounting is a subset of *accounting* in general; accounting generates financial information for decision making. From a broader perspective, cost accounting encompasses the development and provision of a wide range of financial information that is useful to managers in their organizational roles. This book takes that broader perspective.

The user of financial information can make a wide variety of decisions based on that information. In fact, there is little reason to generate information other than to use it in a decision-making process. Even if the user of financial information does nothing after receiving it, the user may well have used the information to help decide that no change or action was required at that time.

The reader of this book should always bear in mind that the prime reason for undertaking any information-generating activity is so that an effective decision can be made. Often, the tools of cost accounting can be better understood if one first considers the types of decisions that might be made using the information. In order to aid in that process, each chapter of this book reprints several articles that provide an application of some of the elements discussed in the chapter.

Financial Accounting vs. Managerial and Cost Accounting

Accounting is often subdivided into two major categories: (1) *financial accounting* and (2) *managerial accounting.* This subdivision aligns itself with the two major classes of users of accounting information: (1) external users and (2) internal users.

Financial accounting provides information primarily for individuals or entities who are out-side of, or external to, the organization. These include banks, suppliers, in some cases owners, the government, and a range of others interested in the finances of a particular organization.

Information is conveyed to these users primarily by a set of financial statements—in particular, the income statement (or statement of activity or statement of revenues and expenses), the balance sheet (or statement of financial position), the cashflow statement, and the statement of changes in fund balances (or statement of changes in owner's equity). Statements prepared for external use (as noted above) often must follow prescribed and somewhat uniform presentation formats as required by the American Institute of Certified Public Accountants (AICPA); various levels of government; and other bodies, such as the American Hospital Association.

Internal users of financial information are the employees who manage the organization. Internal managers need a broad range of financial information to run the organization effectively. Managerial accounting generates any financial information that can help managers to manage better. Statements generated for internal use can take any form that management feels will communicate necessary or useful information. They have no mandated format and can vary greatly from organization to organization.

Figure 1-1 illustrates the position of cost accounting within the larger realm of accounting. Cost accounting is often considered to be synonymous with managerial accounting, but that is not a completely accurate portrayal. Cost accounting includes all of managerial account-

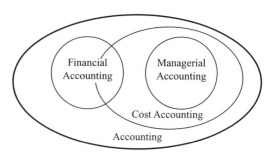

Figure 1-1 Position of Cost Accounting Within the Larger Realm of Accounting

ing, but it also focuses on certain elements of financial accounting that are closely related to *cost measurement* and *cost reporting.* For example, the generation of a hospital cost report for Medicare is technically part of financial accounting, since the report is generated for an external user—the Health Care Financing Administration (HCFA), which administers the Medicare program. However, because a Medicare Cost Report focuses largely on the calculation of costs, it is properly a part of cost accounting as well.

This book explains the tools of cost accounting so that they can be used for both internal management applications and external purposes. The reader should bear in mind that often the distinction between the two is hazy at best. Reports generated for external users may become valuable documents for use by managers. However, caution is required. Reports generated for external users often have to comply with mandates from the external users. For example, the government may regulate specific treatment of certain types of costs. Although that treatment may be appropriate for external users, it might be misleading for internal managers. The Medicare Cost Report is a good example. Many health care organizations must comply with reporting regulations in preparing this report, but that does not mean that the report must be used internally. There may be alternative approaches to determining costs that would give the managers more useful information for the decisions they must make.

Cost accounting information is useful for managers in a number of areas. Just a few specific examples are for the management of department-level costs, for pricing decisions in negotiations with health maintenance organizations (HMOs) and preferred provider organizations (PPOs), for purposes of *strategic planning,* and for *profitability analysis.* These examples are all discussed in Mark Toso's article, which is included in the Applications section of this chapter (Application 1-1). The remainder of this section focuses more generally on the use of cost accounting for *planning and control, nonroutine decisions, inventory*

valuation and *income determination,* and preparation of required external reports.

Planning and Control

One of the primary purposes for collecting cost accounting information is to allow managers to better plan and control the operations of the organization. The planning process ensures that the organization has the opportunity to determine its maximum potential. The control process then ensures that the organization has the opportunity to achieve that potential.

Planning means that the managers of the organization think through the implications of their actions before they act. For example, should the organization undertake a new service? Planning allows the managers to anticipate whether the new service is likely to make or lose money. By planning ahead, advantageous opportunities can be undertaken and problematic ones avoided.

Decisions will not always be based only on the accounting information generated. An organization might decide to proceed with a new service even if cost accounting information indicates that the service will likely lose $100,000 per year. There may be overriding societal issues that make the service still worthwhile. The health benefits to the community may be so great that the organization decides to proceed even at a loss of $100,000.

However, that does not mean that the cost information was not used for making the decision. Most likely, the information was used in two ways. First, the information was used to determine the size of the loss so a decision could be made regarding whether to offer the service. If the projection had been a $1 million or $10 million loss per year, the organization might have decided against the project, despite its health benefits. Second, the calculation allowed the management of the organization to know how much of a loss would need to be subsidized by other sources. The managers can now make plans to have an excess of $100,000 per year generated from other activities.

If such an excess is not generated, then the organization risks insolvency. However, the organization has not proceeded with implementation of the service without any information at all, just because it is an important health service for the community. The calculation of cost information has provided the starting point for the broader planning the organization must do to subsidize the new service and remain financially stable.

Will the plans actually work? That depends largely on how well the employees of the organization work to control operations and keep to the plan. Sometimes things will happen that the organization cannot control; for example, prices of supplies may rise. However, that does not mean that the organization must ever abdicate responsibility for control. Managers must work to keep the activities of the organization under control. If uncontrollable events occur, management need not be passive. It can take actions to respond to those events. It may be necessary to alter the original plan. The tools that allow managers to control ongoing activities and to respond in an effective manner when either controllable or uncontrollable events occur make up the control elements of cost accounting.

Nonroutine Decisions

Most organizations generate a substantial amount of routine information for running the organization on a day-to-day basis. Cost accounting, however, additionally provides the tools for making the nonroutine decisions that managers face from time to time.

The question of whether to add or delete a health care service, or whether to expand a health care facility, can have significant financial implications for the organization. The routine information generated as part of the everyday accounting process may not be adequate information for the manager to make such decisions. The cost accounting tools provided in this book are designed to provide the reader with the conceptual basis to generate the infor-

mation needed to make correct decisions in these cases.

Inventory Valuation and Income Determination

In many industries, inventory is a significant part of the productive process. As manufacturing firms produce their product, some costs are treated as expenses in the year the product is made *(period costs),* whereas other costs are not considered expenses until the product is sold *(product costs).* The timing of when costs are treated as expenses has a potentially dramatic impact on the value of the inventory asset on the balance sheet as well as on the net income (excess of revenues over expenses) reported on the income statement.

This is an example of cost accounting's crossover between financial and managerial accounting. The examination of the costs of production is clearly related to managerial accounting. The determination of inventory and expense values for creation of financial statements is part of financial accounting. Both elements are part of cost accounting.

Inventory valuation and income determination receive substantial attention in most cost accounting texts, but inventory is a relatively minor asset for most health care organizations. The primary issues related to inventory valuation and income determination concern inventory that is transformed in the manufacturing process from a raw material into a finished good. Such manufacturing transformation is extremely uncommon in the area of health care services, and therefore is not a major focus in this book.

Required External Reports

As noted earlier, many health care organizations have regulatory and contractual reporting requirements related to cost information. These requirements have significant impact on the types of cost information generated by the organizations. As one considers the various elements and approaches to cost accounting, one must balance the information between its strict internal uses—to enable the manager to run the organization more efficiently—and its external uses—to create the desired cost information for reporting purposes.

COSTS FOR REPORTING VS. COSTS FOR MANAGEMENT PLANNING AND CONTROL

The roles of cost accounting for external reporting and for planning and control do not always work comfortably side by side. Often, the mandated need for external reports predominates the accounting process, leaving managers with inadequate information.

Managers frequently complain of problems that are symptomatic of cost accounting systems that are designed for reporting purposes rather than for managerial use. For example, in many health care organizations, supplies and purchased labor services do not show up on departmental expense reports for the month used, but rather one or two months thereafter. The lag may not be consistent from month to month or from one type of item to another. Without a special study, there is no way to tell how much of a month's usage was included in the actual figure reported.

Reporting costs as an expense for a month other than the month the resource was actually consumed creates problems. Managers try to determine whether they used an appropriate amount of resources for the number and type of patients treated. However, if they cannot match a month's expense report with the resources consumed in that month, then they cannot accurately compare resource consumption to patient volume and mix. This can substantially impair the ability of managers to control costs.

Hospital financial managers usually have a justification for why things are done in a way that may not be most responsive to the managerial needs of department heads. Health care cost accounting developed with a focus on gathering information for *cost reimbursement* (an external

reporting function) rather than for management. Yet, the main job of the managers of the organization is to manage efficiently and effectively. External reporting is an ancillary function.

In this era when efficiency and cost-effectiveness are more of a concern than ever before, it is vital to examine closely the various elements of the organization's *cost accounting systems*. Even the most routine and mundane reports should be considered. Do they provide the information that a manager needs to make effective decisions and to control the operations of the health care organization, or are they designed for the convenience of external reporting? If they are for external reporting, then a thorough revision of such reports may be in order.

GOOD COST ACCOUNTING SYSTEMS

Application 1-2 at the end of this chapter is a review of an article by Robert Kaplan, a noted academic in the managerial accounting field. The theme of that article is that one cost accounting system may be insufficient. Rather than trying to develop a perfect cost accounting system, Kaplan proposes the use of several parallel systems providing cost information for different purposes. This raises a broader question: What constitutes a good cost accounting system or set of systems for a health care organization?

Ever since the introduction of prospective payment systems, there has been a clear and growing lack of satisfaction with the costing systems that hospitals have used over the last several decades. As a result, the last several years have been a bonanza for health care consultants—especially in the hospital field. A wide range of types of cost accounting systems have been installed, which have ranged from relatively modest cost to multimillion dollar systems. Yet, it is not clear that these new systems have been totally satisfactory or even more satisfactory than the systems they replaced. Horror stories of millions of dollars spent on systems work properly are becoming more and more common.

Perhaps one reason is that posed by Kaplan: we have expected one cost accounting system to be able to do more than it possibly can. There has been a great focus on the replacement of hospitals' cost accounting systems. Perhaps part of the solution is to view and install new systems oriented toward product costing as supplementary systems rather than replacements. It is difficult for any one system to serve the conflicting needs of allocating costs for external reporting, determining incremental costs for negotiating and decision making, and determining product costs for productivity measurement and cost control.

Another possible reason for problems with new systems is that cost accounting systems are being developed and installed without adequate specification. The definition of a "good cost accounting system" is difficult to pin down, because different health care organizations have different information needs. A good cost accounting system is one that is based on a knowledge of what information is needed, why it is needed, and what will be done with it once it is available.

Application 1-3 is an article by Bryan Dieter, "Understanding the Hospital Cost Accounting Process." By reading that article at this point and getting an overview of the process of cost accounting for health care organizations, one can begin to make the assessment of what information a good cost accounting system needs to provide.

Benefit/Cost Philosophy of Cost Information

We can set a minimum standard for a good cost accounting system. It should generate information that is more valuable than the cost of the system itself. This rule of thumb has always been a part of health care costing systems. Accuracy in cost measurement is desired, but must be balanced against the cost of acquiring the information.

Given the intense financial constraints faced by most health care providers, it is difficult to have enough resources—human and computer—to meet all the needs of a good cost accounting system. Any additional money spent on cost accounting must be able to show a return on the investment.

Clearly, there are substantial amounts of money at stake. If a health care organization uses new information to discover that a product line loses a lot of money, and if it can eliminate that product line, then the new information is quite valuable. If the same information were discovered about an integral service that cannot possibly be eliminated if the organization is to continue to exist, then the information is much less valuable.

It costs money to generate cost accounting information. The more complex the information, the more costly it is. Often, managers desire to use extremely accurate accounting information for making decisions. From an idealistic point of view, that makes perfect sense; from a pragmatic point of view, it is not always a sensible option.

When one decides to generate cost information, the benefit of the information to be generated should be weighed against the cost of the information. Sometimes an approximation, which is much less expensive to make than an exact calculation, will be perfectly sufficient for making a reasonable decision.

Wise use of the limited resources of an organization calls for the use of the least expensive adequate data for making a decision. When one decides whether to generate information, one should always consider what less costly information alternatives exist. Often, the less costly alternatives require substantially less time and effort; in general, one should tend toward use of these. More costly alternatives should be used only when their extra benefits exceed their additional costs.

THE HUMAN ELEMENT IN COST ACCOUNTING

Students of cost accounting often expect the sole focus to be on numbers—"How much does something cost?" However, the primary focus of cost accounting is first and foremost on people. The measurement of numbers is secondary. People are the essential ingredient in any organization; they are what makes things work. Unless we consider people, there will be no way to collect cost information and, more important, no way to control costs.

Determining costs can be a totally absorbing task. One risk in cost accounting is that we tend to lose touch with the various human beings who are involved in the different parts of the process. If we do not closely consider the individual people involved in the cost accounting process, we may calculate accurate costs, but we may be causing things to cost more than they should.

People who work within the health care industry often do so because of an underlying sense of altruism. They want to help society. They want to help individuals. However, that does not mean that the goals of individuals working for health care organizations are completely and uniformly the same as those of their organizations. For example, most employees of a health care organization would prefer a substantially larger salary than they are currently receiving. The organization might prefer lower salaries than it is currently paying. These divergent goals must be recognized by the organization (see Figure 1-2).

Cost accounting requires an explicit recognition of people and their goals and interests, as well as those of the organization. Application 1-4 at the end of this chapter discusses the human element in cost accounting. One recurring theme throughout this book is that managers must consider not just calculation of costs, but also the incentives and motivations of the people working for the health care organization. In cost accounting, we record the results of actions taken by people. Understanding their motivations and likely responses to incentives is essential to the design of an effective cost accounting system. It is necessary for the interests of the individual to be brought together, or become *congruent,* with those of the organization (see Figure 1-3). Individuals are more likely to act consistently in the organization's best interests if there is a system of *incentives* in place. The cost accounting system can help establish a framework of incentives.

In recording the cost outcomes, we must use care in making judgments about the performance of individuals. If employees are not competent or do not work hard, a signal of failure may be warranted. However, if a manager is both competent and hard working, the cost accounting system should not indicate poor performance by the individual, even if actual costs exceed expectations. Such an indication is more likely to be discouraging than it is to provide the individual with an incentive to work even harder. When people work hard and fail, they often question why they worked so hard. If you will be seen as a failure no matter how hard you work, why work hard at all? Thus, we must be extremely judicious in the design of cost accounting tools for evaluation. Understanding

---

DIVERGENT GOALS

Organization	Individual
Low Salaries	High Salary
Small Staff	Large Staff
Small Offices	Large Office

Figure 1-2 Divergent Goals. *Source:* Reprinted from *Budgeting Concepts for Nurse Managers,* Second Edition, by S.A. Finkler, p. 43, with permission of W.B. Saunders, © 1992.

CONGRUENT GOALS

Incentive Effect

Figure 1-3 Congruent Goals. *Source:* Reprinted from *Budgeting Concepts for Nurse Managers,* Second Edition, by S.A. Finkler, p. 44, with permission of W.B. Saunders, © 1992.

their likely impact on the human beings who work for the organization is a critical element of management.

Too often, organizations take their human resources for granted. Application 1-5 at the end of this chapter discusses how health care organizations can more explicitly account for the costs of their human resources.

SUGGESTED READING

Baptist, A.J., et al. January 1987. Developing a solid base for a cost accounting system. *Healthcare Financial Management:*42–48.

Burik, D., and D.L. Marcellino. January 1987. Successfully implementing a multihospital cost system. *Healthcare Financial Management:*50–54.

Cooper, R., and R.S. Kaplan. 1991. *The design of cost management systems: Text, cases, and readings.* Englewood Cliffs, N.J.: Prentice-Hall, Inc.

Counte, M.A., and G.L. Glandon. 1988. Managerial innovation in the hospital: An analysis of the diffusion of hospi-

tal cost-accounting systems. *Hospitals and Health Services Administration* 33, no. 3:371–384.

Eastaugh, S.R. November 1987. Has PPS affected the sophistication of cost accounting? *Healthcare Financial Management:*50–52.

Finkler, S.A. 1987. Costs for reporting vs. costs for management and control: Hospital implications. *Hospital Cost Accounting Advisor* 3, no. 6:1, 7–8.

Horngren, C.T., and G. Foster. 1991. *Cost accounting: A managerial emphasis.* 7th ed. Englewood Cliffs, N.J.: Prentice-Hall, Inc.

Jayson, S. September 1992. Focus on people—not costs. *Management Accounting:*28–33.

Mendenhall, S., et al. January 1987. Cost accounting in health care organizations: Who needs it? *Healthcare Financial Management:*34–40.

Mistarz, J. October 1984. Cost accounting: A solution, but a problem. *Hospitals:*96–101.

Tselepsis, J.N. May 1989. Refined cost accounting produces better information. *Healthcare Financial Management:*26–28, 30, 34.

EXERCISES

QUESTIONS FOR DISCUSSION

1. What is the prime reason for collecting cost accounting information?
2. Distinguish between financial and managerial accounting. Where does cost accounting come in?
3. Distinguish between planning and control.
4. What are some examples of nonroutine decisions?
5. Would Robert Kaplan contend that one good cost accounting system is the best approach, or that there should perhaps be

several systems, each addressing different needs?
6. In order to design a good cost accounting system, what do you need to know?
7. True or false: One should always develop the best cost accounting system possible, which generates the most accurate information. Why or why not?
8. Describe the conflict between the use of cost accounting to generate information for reporting and its use to generate information for management.
9. What is the relationship between motivation and incentives, and cost accounting?

Note: Solutions to the Exercises can be found in Appendix A.

Application 1-1

Reader's Forum: The Value
of a Cost Accounting System

Mark E. Toso, MSBA, CPA, is currently
President of TriNet Healthcare Consultants, Inc.,
Chelmsford, Massachusetts.

The question has been raised as to the value of a cost accounting system to a hospital. It has been asserted that management of a hospital is unlike the management of any other business and that hospital management cannot make decisions regarding a particular disease entity due to the interrelationship of hospital activities that support all disease entities. The cost/benefit of cost accounting information has been challenged due to the uniqueness of the hospital operation and the perceived inability of managers to demonstrate how the costs of implementing and maintaining a cost accounting system are offset by new revenues or cost reductions.

In order to address the broad issue of the value of a cost accounting system when managing a hospital, it is important to review the perceived uses of cost accounting information in a thoughtful and pragmatic manner. We can then make an assessment as to whether we, as health care managers, can use this information to achieve the goal of managing the hospital in a more effective and efficient manner—in decision making, planning and control, and profitability.

Source: Reprinted from Mark Toso, "Reader's Forum: The Value of a Cost Accounting System," *Hospital Cost Management and Accounting*, Vol. 1, No. 4, July 1989, pp. 5–7. Copyright 1989, Aspen Publishers, Inc.

Until the advent of the prospective payment system (PPS) in 1983, hospitals were paid for their services based on their cost; therefore, a hospital manager did not have to behave in the same way as a manager of a traditional business. Since 1983 the health care industry has evolved from being a regulated industry to one that is very competitive. The dominant theme has changed from one of growth for all hospitals to one of decline for inpatient hospital services. This has led to an emphasis on increased market share and to the reduction of operating costs.

The emphasis on controlling and understanding costs led to the development of cost accounting systems by numerous vendors and hospitals. These cost accounting systems accommodate detailed clinical and financial information collected at a procedural level. The clinical and financial data base can provide information which can be used for a variety of purposes:

- cost management at a departmental level
- pricing decisions with HMOs and PPOs
- strategic planning
- physician management
- profitability analysis

COST MANAGEMENT AT A DEPARTMENTAL LEVEL

The development of a cost accounting system requires the development of standards at a procedural level. The development of these standards, in turn, contribute to the development of flexible budgeting and productivity monitoring. These budgeting and monitoring tools help to manage operations in the context of declining inpatient services and payers who are adopting capitation systems similar to Medicare. The ability to adjust staffing and spending patterns based on volume and case-mix will become even more important as state regulators (Medicaid and Blue Cross) and HMOs/PPOs adopt case-mix payment systems similar to Medicare. Therefore, the departmental standards that are created by the development of the cost accounting system serve as valuable managerial tools.

PRICING DECISIONS WITH HMOs AND PPOs

Although most HMOs and PPOs have negotiated with hospitals on the basis of per diems or a percentage of charges, many are now beginning to adopt the case basis of payment. In addition, many payers are looking for specialized pricing for specific types of services (for example, children's hospitals and open heart surgery programs). In negotiations with HMOs and PPOs, as well as with other payers, it will be important to have the cost per case broken down between fixed and variable components for product-specific pricing analyses. In a cost accounting system the procedural cost information is broken down into a number of components of cost such as fixed and variable, salary and nonsalary, and overhead.

STRATEGIC PLANNING IN TODAY'S COMPETITIVE ENVIRONMENT

Hospital managers need to know how much it costs to deliver a specific service and/or product line. A hospital would not want to embark on an expansion of a service or product line that was losing a substantial amount of money. In fact, for the first time hospitals are beginning to close both services and entire facilities where volume is not sufficient to cover the costs of delivering the service.

Strategic financial planning is the theme of today's hospital planners. Financially driven strategic planning is based on the assumption that the planning efforts should improve the health care system's financial position. Strategic financial planning recognizes that health care systems are generally nonprofit and are often affiliated with a religious organization where financial performance is not the primary indicator of success; however, a health care system cannot achieve the organization's statement of purpose or mission unless financial viability is achieved.

PHYSICIAN MANAGEMENT

A cost accounting system will be of little value if physician input is not obtained. Assuming that physicians have been part of the process that developed the utilization standards for the case-mix measure employed by the cost accounting system, management has a powerful tool to control physician behavior. A cost accounting system will provide information to review physician efficiency through a comparison of individual physician treatment protocols for varying types of patients with protocols of other physicians at the same hospital or through other acceptable standards. Additionally, if the system can provide profitability analysis about a physician's clinical practice patterns, management can alter physician behavior based upon what the system has determined it can afford to pay. Managing average length of stay does not mean that the physician will release a patient before it is clinically appropriate; it does, however, make the physician aware of the financial realities management must deal with in order to maintain hospital viability.

PROFITABILITY ANALYSIS

A goal of the cost accounting system is to establish the costs of providing service by

- case type or DRG
- department
- specialty or product line
- physician
- patient

In addition, the cost accounting system would provide management with payer and net revenue information by the same categories mentioned above. This will allow hospital management to identify profit margins by payer, by physician, by service, or by product line and make the appropriate decisions about resource allocation based upon the goal of maintaining the financial viability of the hospital. This does not mean that because a specific procedure or case type is losing money that the procedure will no longer be provided or the case type no longer can be treated.

This information has to be used in the context of how the hospital operates all of its services. Cost accounting information does not replace management; rather, it provides a tool that allows management to understand how its hospital provides health care services. In a competitive environment it is critical for hospital managers to understand the hospital production function and to work with physicians to improve the quality of provided services while at the same time providing those services in a more effective and efficient manner. Cost accounting information provides hospital managers with the necessary knowledge to do this. In conclusion, there are several points which are important to mention:

- In today's competitive environment, hospitals that can control their costs will be the survivors. Market share is very important, but the realities of today's environment indicate that many hospitals will be downsizing, with financial performance as the most important variable. The only exception might be the large teaching hospitals, which have a different purpose and also have development capabilities that can raise substantial amounts of money.

- The cost of implementing a cost accounting system is declining every year. Hardware and software are available on mini-computers, microcomputers, or on in-house mainframe computers. Hospital management has now had the opportunity to work with this type of information over the last several years and it is beginning to utilize the information more effectively to make decisions and control hospital operations.

- Information is a very important strategic tool and cost accounting information provides management with information that will allow it to understand the actual costs of delivering services. If management does not understand the hospital production function, how can it make decisions that will reduce the cost of providing a service without having a negative impact on the quality of that service?

Application 1-2

iew of "One Cost System Isn't Enough"

Steven A. Finkler, PhD, CPA

In this article Robert Kaplan once again demonstrates that he is one of the leading "thinkers" in the cost accounting field. As managers and academics alike pick at cost accounting systems trying to make them do magic with a push here and a tug there, Kaplan cuts through to the essence that magic is not always possible.

Kaplan's point of view is clearly demonstrated by the title, "One Cost System Isn't Enough." Hospital managers can well understand Kaplan's perspective when he notes that "[e]ven the best designed and implemented operational control system. . . .can be useless for measuring product costs" (page 64). Prospective payment systems have caused us to evaluate hospital cost systems and they have clearly been found to be inadequate for product costing.

What is a surprise, however, is that Kaplan is addressing his comments primarily to the industrial manufacturing companies in this country. That group is, after all, the "expert" group of organizations from which hospitals want to obtain the holy grail with respect to adequate cost information. Yet, Kaplan's article makes

clear that industrial cost accounting systems have tended to be every bit as much a failure (if not more so) than hospital cost accounting systems. He explains why the failure has occurred and puts forth his approaches to a solution.

Cost accounting systems are needed for three primary purposes, according to Kaplan. These three purposes are (1) inventory valuation for financial reporting, (2) operational control of ongoing activities, and (3) product costing information for decisions about the mix of products to be offered. However, each of the three purposes has different information requirements. Often the requirements conflict, and cannot be simultaneously generated by the same costing system. Given the existence of conflict, which system will dominate?

According to Kaplan, cost accounting for inventory valuation will dominate because of the specific mandated demands of the financial reporting function. Kaplan's expectation that operational control and product costing will suffer as a result of the needs for inventory valuation are clearly based on a focus on manufacturing industries. In hospitals, inventory is clearly a much less important issue. However, hospitals have had their own set of mandated external financial reports (e.g., the Medicare Cost Report) which have generated similar costing problems. Given the major

Source: Reprinted from Steven A. Finkler, Review of "One Cost System Isn't Enough," by Robert S. Kaplan, *Harvard Business Review,* Vol. 88, No. 1, January–February 1988, pp. 61–66, published in *Hospital Cost Accounting Advisor,* Vol. 3, No. 12, May 1988, pp. 6–7. Copyright 1988, Aspen Publishers, Inc.

emphasis on costing systems in hospitals today, we should take care to examine Kaplan's treatise in order to avoid falling into many of the same traps that have been problems for industry.

For example, Kaplan cites the case of a chemical company that had an excellent product costing system. However, the system failed to provide information for motivation and evaluation of managers. In order to compete as industry costs dropped, the company shifted its cost accounting focus to cost centers. This allowed for better operational control. Unfortunately with the new system the marketing staff lacked the accurate product cost information needed for pricing. The problem was not that the new system didn't do what it was designed to do. The problem was that "[n]o single system can adequately cover all three functions. The demands of each differ in terms of reporting frequency, degree of allocation, nature of cost variability, system scope, and degree of objectivity" (page 62).

The article discusses in some detail the requirements of a cost accounting system for fulfilling the needs of each of the three key functions. One of the most important contrasts is the way that costs are allocated.

If a system is primarily to be used for inventory all costs must be allocated, and there is little causal relationship required. That is, as long as all of the costs are allocated to the various products, it is not vital if there is little or no cause-and-effect relationship between the allocated cost and each specific product. For operational control purposes, one should allocate only those costs that a manager can control.

For product costing all costs relevant to the product must be allocated. One of the rules of cost accounting cited in most major textbooks is that managers should be held responsible for only those costs that they can control. Yet hospitals, in an effort to know the total costs of operating the hospital, assign all costs to revenue departments. This cost allocation (step-down) process was mandated by Medicare. The cost information it yields aids in external reporting. However, the very system that helps us report costs for reimbursement clouds the information needed for operational control. Managers'

attention is taken away from direct departmental costs and shifts to overhead costs over which the managers have little, if any, control.

The changes currently being made to hospital cost accounting systems have the potential to do even more harm in terms of reducing the overall usefulness of the system. On the one hand, product costing is vital for an organization in an environment in which many of their prices are fixed by the government. The lack of ability to set prices is accompanied at least to some extent by the ability to modify the mix of services (product lines) offered. On the other hand, product costs may not fit into regulatory reporting regimens, and they may not help managers maximize the productivity of their departments.

To make matters worse, as Kaplan points out, standard costs are certainly not designed to allow managers to control what is happening, or to allow for accurate product costing. Standard costs are a method for inventory valuation. Therefore many hospitals attempting to install standard costing systems may not be improving their information at all.

Kaplan doesn't have all the answers by any means. His description of product costing calls for assignment of all costs systemwide to individual products, on a causal rather than arbitrary basis. He indicates that major product decisions (introduction, abandonment, etc.) are rare events, and therefore a thorough product costing need be done only once a year, in most cases. He notes that "[t]he annual product cost computation does not have to be part of the main financial accounting system, nor does it require a lot of time and money to develop and implement" (page 65).

We suspect that, at least in the case of hospitals, this underestimates the magnitude of the task. However, that does not take away from Kaplan's central theme:

> No single system can adequately answer the demands made by the diverse functions of cost systems. While companies can use one method to capture all their detailed transactions data, the processing of this information for diverse purposes and

audiences demands separate, customized development. . . . Of course, an argument for expanding the number of cost systems conflicts with a strongly ingrained financial culture to have only one measurement system for everyone (page 66).

This article is strongly suggested reading for all readers of *Hospital Cost Accounting Advisor.*

Application 1-3

Understanding the Hospital Cost Accounting Process

*Bryan B. Dieter, BA, is currently President
of The Decision Support Group, Inc.,
Pasadena, California.*

As more pressure is exerted on hospitals to negotiate prices, reduce costs, and market services competitively, the accurate identification of costs per service becomes imperative. Since hospital management is beginning to recognize this need, this article will not address the "current environment" and why hospitals need a cost accounting system, but will focus on where and how to begin the whole cost accounting process.

In theory, cost accounting is fairly basic: identify resources consumed in the production/provision of goods or services and the corresponding costs of those resources. Applying the theory to a real hospital setting can be complex and time consuming. However, if this is done properly, the resulting information will be extremely informative and applicable, giving administrators, financial managers, and department heads an edge in everyday decision making.

The implementation of a cost accounting system requires preparation that vendors do not generally cover when presenting system features. This article will cover some of the groundwork to be completed prior to and during

the course of a system installation, and features to look for in the selection of a system, to ensure that the information generated has a high degree of accuracy and proves valuable as a management tool.

THE CHARGE DESCRIPTION MASTER

The driving force of any cost accounting system is the hospital's charging mechanism, usually referred to as the charge description master (CDM). The CDM should be the initial focal point in the initiation of cost accounting. This is especially true since "fee for service" and cost-based reimbursement methodologies have encouraged manipulation of the CDM to maximize revenue. With the inception of the prospective payment system (PPS), there will be a shift from many departmental revenue centers to *one* revenue center—the hospital itself. As a result of this shift, the charge description master should soon be considered the *cost* description master. Therefore, the CDM should be reviewed to determine charges that must be added, deleted, or revised in order to accurately reflect the manner in which the services are provided.

Specifically, the charges should reflect resource consumption in the provision of service, and therefore the cost. A common comment from hospitals on recommended charging changes is, "We can't charge different amounts for those services since we won't be reimbursed for them." That may be true. However, you still need to identify which services vary from the standard and cost you more than they should. You may decide to establish new/revised charges and assign no dollar value to them, yet be generating the information necessary to monitor utilization and costs accurately.

Another consideration is whether or not, in marketing your hospital's services, you will be offering "packaged prices." If so, charges need to be established to monitor costs and revenue separately for those packages.

Some common revisions to CDMs include

- Routine services. Revise the room-charging mechanism to include patient acuity levels (staff utilization) identified in the nursing acuity system, e.g., establishing a charge for Med/Surg Unit 4E, Semiprivate, Level 2. The semiprivate and other occupancy designations should be retained to facilitate the allocation of overhead expenses.

- Surgical services. Common revisions to Surgical Services CDMs:

    Removal of charge explosion system, a system that generates charges automatically based upon customary resource utilization for the procedure performed. These systems usually charge all patients equally for the same procedure without regard for *actual* resources or services provided to the patient. This type of system does not allow for utilization/costs identification and monitoring by surgeon, surgical team, or anesthesiologist.

    Acuity-based room charges. Room charges should be based on the number of staff members involved in the procedure and the length of time for each case. Usually three or four levels of base charges (for example, 15-min., 30-min., or one hour minimum) and incremental charges (each additional one, five, or 15 minutes) are appropriate.

Capital equipment. Separate equipment charges should be established based on those pieces of equipment which are used only for specific cases. Costs should be determined by the frequency of use of the equipment and its rate of depreciation. Maintenance contract costs should be associated with equipment when possible.

Suture charges. The hospital should charge for sutures individually, yet in classifications based on type and cost (e.g., ophthalmic, strand, micro, wire).

Tray charges. Tray charges should be established for each type of tray since instrument and supply costs vary greatly.

Additional labor. Establish a charge for additional staff (usually R.N. or tech) who may float through the room during the procedure to provide assistance only as needed—usually an incremental time charge of 10 or 15 minutes.

After-hours or emergency charges. These charges would reflect pay differentials for overtime, on-call, and call back. This charge may also help to identify surgeons who routinely schedule at more costly times.

- Emergency room. ER visits should be acuity based and reflect time actually spent "hands-on" with the patient or on functions directly related to that patient (e.g., triage, arranging for transport/admission, paperwork, communication with outside agencies). Studies have shown little, if any, relationship between the amount of time a patient spends in the ER and the actual amount of staff time related to him or her.

- Laboratory. Establish stat charges to reflect cost increase over batched tests.

- Pharmacy. Establish administration mode charges (e.g., injectable, i.v.). These charges should reflect pharmacist time in preparation of the pharmaceutical. Charge separately for the actual drugs dispensed.

- Physical therapy. Charges should reflect both time and modality. The current charging system may not recognize the skill level and cost of staff involved or of supplies utilized in providing the various treatments.

- All departments. In all departments, review for duplicate and unused charges and delete them. Also, "miscellaneous" charges reflecting proportionately large amounts of revenue should be carefully researched to identify which services provided are being coded as "miscellaneous," and should be revised as necessary.

This is only a partial list of commonly suggested revisions to the CDM. The emphasis is on the importance of reviewing the CDM to ensure that charges *do* reflect resource consumption and, ultimately, costs. In addition, charges should be specific enough to result in equitable charges to patients based upon actual goods and services received and to diminish the occurrence of some patients subsidizing others.

DEPARTMENTAL GENERAL LEDGERS

The next step in the process is a review of the general ledger of each department by the materials manager, the accounting department, and each department head. This activity is essential to identify costs that may be accumulating in inappropriate natural classifications (subaccounts) or cost centers. The hospitalwide natural classification of expense categories should also be assessed to determine whether additional classifications should be added. For example, if the hospital groups labor costs into one or two categories designated "labor" or "salaries," it is recommended that they break them out into categories such as "management/ supervision," "technical/specialist," "RN," "clerical," etc. Another example is separating "radiology films" from "general supplies" in the radiology department and separating other specific, high cost supplies in other departments.

After the general ledger has been reviewed and revised as needed, the accounting department and each department head should review each natural classification *departmentally* to classify expenses as fixed, variable, or semivariable for each department. If the expense is semivariable, an amount or a percentage should be identified as either fixed or variable. This determination may initially be difficult, but on the "first cut," a best educated guess is usually fairly accurate. As more information is available, or as studies of each expense are completed, the amounts or percentages can be refined, thus making the information more accurate.

RESOURCE UTILIZATION STUDIES

To be conducted concurrently with the three steps outlined above are the departmental and service specific resource utilization/consumption studies. These studies identify the "standard" list of materials utilized in the provision of each service. The service referred to is any charge listed in the CDM. Many hospitals are currently grappling with the question, "Which services should be studied and to what level of detail should studies be conducted?" Generally, the 80/20 rule (80 percent of revenues or costs come from 20 percent of services—closer to 90/20 [sic] in actuality) is recommended in the selection of services to be studied specifically. An identification of direct labor (by classification), supplies, and equipment (minor and capital) utilized in the provision of each service selected for study would establish the *minimum* basis for meaningful cost accounting information. However, it is recommended that these studies be regarded as the groundwork and that cost accounting be a "living" system. Additional studies *do* improve the accuracy of the cost accounting information and can, in some cases, significantly alter the identified costs. Other cost classifications recommended for study include service contracts, professional fees, additional supply studies, purchased services, and rental/lease costs. Also, indirect cost studies should be completed where a relationship can be identified between an indirect expense and specific services/procedures.

The main intent in cost accounting is to quantitatively identify how each service benefits from each natural classification of expense. This is the most important point in understanding the cost accounting process. If this concept is understood, hospital cost accounting itself will be more easily comprehended, and the selection of a system becomes greatly simplified.

For the cost accounting system, a relationship needs to be identified between the services provided within each department and the expenses, both direct and indirect, incurred. For some of those expenses, the relationship is fairly clear— for example, R.N. and technical labor, physician fees (if service-specific), medical supplies, prostheses, radiology films, instruments (minor equipment), depreciation on movable equipment, and some maintenance contracts. For the other direct expenses where the relationship may not be as evident, discussions should be initiated or studies performed to determine the most accurate statistic for recognizing how each service benefits (whether equally or variably) from each expense (resource).

SELECTING A COST ACCOUNTING SOFTWARE SYSTEM

The next major step is the selection of a software system that will take the information you have developed and determine and maintain your cost-per-service information base. The development of a system internally is no longer a cost-justified alternative to purchasing a system, although it may have been the only viable alternative as recently as a year ago. Today, it could take more than two years and millions of dollars to develop a sophisticated system in-house, whereas there are excellent systems available for around $75,000. With numerous vendors, accounting firms, and consulting companies selling their systems and/or consulting services under the "cost accounting" umbrella, it is becoming increasingly difficult to understand the real features and applications of each

and how each differs operationally from the others.

There are some features which should be considered important in the selection of a system. Few, if any, systems will meet all of these criteria, but the goal in selecting a system should be to choose one that has the capability to meet your changing and increasingly sophisticated informational requirements in the future. Some recommended features of a cost accounting system include

- capability to handle and process detailed resource utilization studies for every natural classification of expense for all departments, direct and/or indirect (overhead)

- reconciliation of identified expenses to actual financial statements

- internal indirect cost allocations to both the departmental and service levels. This is very important, since the indirect expenses allocated to the departments often exceed their direct expenses. The allocation of these expenses to the departments and to the services is a critical point in monitoring full costing and is often not given the detailed review it deserves.

- ability to maintain a very large number of statistical bases for allocating costs

- updating of information quickly. The cost accounting system should interface with the other financial systems software operating on the same hardware, thus eliminating a second manual entry of current financial information.

- interface with the case-mix system. The cost accounting system should be able to pass cost information to the case-mix system (which ideally would accept five cost fields per service: direct, indirect, fixed, variable, and total) and accept information from the case-mix system to review profitability of service and cost variances from standard (by product line, case, physician, payer, etc.).

- budget system interface—preferably flexible product line budgeting

- support of multihospital users on the same system (if applicable)
- forecasting capabilities and "what-if" situation forecasting
- ability to support both standard and allocated costing methodologies for *all* services
- exception reporting—reports identifying new services on the CDM or costs which have not been accounted for
- variance reporting—reports comparing standard and actual costs and corresponding variances
- base data file—a file that contains resource utilization study information from national averages or standards, to be used to allocate costs to those services not directly studied
- grouping or "roll-up" feature—allows for easy comparison of departments and administrative responsibility areas as well as interhospital comparisons, etc.
- extensive security features—identifying and limiting users as desired
- data entry ease. A data entry person should be able to enter the information directly from input forms.
- general ledger reclassifications—should allow reclassifications inter- and intradepartmentally.
- support of fixed, variable, and semivariable classification of expenses by department
- rapid recalculation response time. You should be able to recalculate entire hospital information or each department individually.
- maintenance of the hospitalwide cost accounting information base within the singular system. The cost accounting system should support the whole hospital's cost information base. Avoid systems that have only the capability to maintain departments as separate entities.

The system you select should be designed and have the capability to support you as your informational needs become more refined. The system should not soon become obsolete or require a great deal of staff time to maintain. The system should have the capability of being fully operational within one month of installation, using whatever information you currently have available, and support future refinements. It should share information internally with your other financial systems and support both standard and allocated costing methodologies. Contrary to seemingly popular belief, a mini- or mainframe-based system does not have a longer implementation time frame than a PC-based system, and in some instances it is considerably less. There are currently one or two vendors who have systems that meet most of the selection criteria outlined. Most of them do not, and you should approach the selection process critically. Avoid "simple" systems designed mainly to generate consulting revenue.

USING CONSULTANTS

You may wish to use consultants to assist in the implementation of your system. If the system is designed well and has easily comprehensible input forms, consultants may not be necessary. However, a few who have had extensive experience in hospital cost accounting can facilitate a successful system installation, and you may benefit from their experience in conducting studies and assisting in the development of standards. Consultants would also expedite the installation, a very important consideration in generating timely information, and may also identify immediate cost-saving opportunities.

SUMMARY

Some hospitals today are actually faring well financially under PPS and are questioning the urgency of implementing a cost accounting system. The system would prove beneficial to those hospitals as well, since the information would allow them to review their margin per product line, DRG, or service. This would assist in making decisions about which services or products to promote through physician recruitment and marketing, and which services or products require further cost containment efforts, and in formulating "make or buy" decisions while recognizing and understanding the financial implications of each alternative.

As both a consultant to hospitals and a vendor, I find that hospitals are often misled by vendors as to the preparation and work required to properly implement a cost accounting system that will generate *meaningful* information. However, the implementation and monitoring of a properly developed cost accounting system will provide information valuable in containing costs, reviewing the profitability of services, and contracts. Accurate cost accounting information can also promote informed hospital leadership and assist in responding to today's health-care payment initiatives. A flexible, sophisticated system with standards developed "from the bottom up" will have the capability to continue to monitor cost behavior and profitability of service in any payment system, prospective or otherwise, that impacts on health-care providers in the future.

Application 1-4

The Human Element in Cost Accounting

Steven A. Finkler, PhD, CPA

Cost accounting is a field in which we often become buried in the numbers. Determining what something costs can be a totally absorbing task. One risk in cost accounting is that we tend to lose touch with the various human beings who are involved in the different parts of the process. If we don't closely consider the individual people involved in the cost accounting process, we may calculate accurate costs, but we may be causing things to cost more than they ought to.

GOAL CONGRUENCE

It is the basic nature of individuals, that their own personal goals will generally be divergent from the goals of the organization they work for. This does not mean that human nature is bad; just that there is such a thing as human nature and we are foolish if we refuse to recognize it as such.

For example, other things being equal, most employees of a hospital would prefer a salary that is substantially larger than what they are currently receiving. Most would be quite con-

tent if the hospital were to double their salary overnight. There's nothing particularly bad about such people or wrong in their wanting more money. In fact, ambition is probably a desirable trait among employees.

On the other hand, most hospitals are reluctant to provide employees with substantial raises, because they lack the revenues to pay for those raises. While the employees are not wrong to desire the raises, the hospital is not wrong to deny such raises. Inherently however, a tension or conflict exists.

Most hospital managers would like more office space. They would like nicer office space with new furniture and remodeled facilities. They would certainly like more staff to carry out their existing functions. Introductory economics books clearly indicate that society simply has limited resources. All organizations must make choices concerning how to spend their limited resources.

In fact, if we were to find a hospital in which the vast majority of managers were content with the size of their salary, office and staff, then we probably will have identified a hospital that is failing in its mission. Perhaps there is a small percentage of all hospitals that is so well endowed as to be able to provide all health services their communities could dream of, and

Source: Reprinted from Steven A. Finkler, "The Human Element in Cost Accounting," *Hospital Cost Management and Accounting,* Vol. 2, No. 10, January 1991, pp. 1–4. Copyright 1991, Aspen Publishers, Inc.

also provide their employees with all of their desires.

Perhaps. But for the at least ninety-nine percent of all hospitals with limited resources, providing unlimited amenities to employees certainly means some patient service limitations must be taking place. The hospital, in allocating its scarce resources, by giving in to the wants of its employees must place limits on the amount of health care services it provides. In most hospitals there are some concessions to employees, and there are some patient service limitations.

Thus we must face the fact that in the majority of hospitals, even where morale is generally excellent and is not considered to be a problem, an underlying tension will naturally exist. Even though the employees may want to achieve the mission of the hospital in providing care, their personal desires will be for things the hospital will not choose to provide.

Perhaps surprisingly, to a great extent it is the accountants of the hospital who have to deal with this divergence and develop means of creating congruency. The hospital must bring together the interests of the individual and the hospital so that they can work together. And cost accounting systems are one area in which we can work on creating that common bond of interest.

In the budgeting and costing process we are attempting to control the amount the organization spends. We don't want to measure costs just because it is nice to know what things cost. The reason we spend time and money on the measurement process is so that we have information for decision making and for control. But it is not the cost information which actually controls costs, it is the human beings involved in the process.

It is in the direct interests of the hospital for costs to be controlled. In order to be sure that the human beings will in fact want to control costs, we need to make sure that it is somehow in their direct best interests for costs to be controlled. The key is to establish some way that the normally divergent desires of the hospital and its employees become convergent or congruent. We want both the hospital and the employee to want the same thing.

Since congruent goals are not always the norm, and since divergent goals frequently exist, we need to formally address how convergence is to be obtained. Organizations generally achieve such convergence or congruence by setting up a system of incentives that make it serve the best interests of the employees to serve the best interests of the organization.

MOTIVATION AND INCENTIVE

Developing a set of incentives to motivate people is not something that most cost accountants are likely to think of as part of their job. However, since cost accountants are at least to some extent "cost managers," we must consider what things can be done to provide incentives to motivate managers to control costs.

In industry, one common motivating tool is the use of bonus systems. Since managers have many desires that relate to spending money (e.g., larger offices, fancier furniture, larger staffs) we need to develop formalized incentives to spend less money. For example, we can tell a manager that last year his department spent $200,000, and that next year his budget is $208,000 (a four percent increase). However, for any amount that his department spends below $208,000, he can keep 10 percent. So, if the department spends only $180,000, he gets a personal bonus of $2,800. The total cost to the organization is $182,800, including the bonus, as opposed to the $208,000 budgeted. The employee benefits and the organization benefits.

However, incentives are tricky to work with, as the federal government seems to find out every time it tries to control overall spending. When an incentive is given to accomplish one end, sometimes the responses to that incentive are unexpected. In the case of the federal government, we have found that DRGs, intended to reduce health care spending, increase spending on nursing homes and home care agencies. In the case of a 10 percent bonus on spending reductions from budget, a manager may have an incentive to treat fewer patients to keep costs down. If that also reduces revenue, the outcome may be very undesirable.

Hospitals are also concerned about the quality of care. If incentives cause managers to reduce staff to save money, that savings is not very worthwhile if it unexpectedly reduces quality of care.

These are not insurmountable problems. They merely point out some of the complexities in developing an incentive system. The quality issue requires that the hospital have a strong internal quality assurance program. Part of the bonus process would have to be restrictions on bonuses when quality of care has declined.

The volume-of-patients problem can be solved by making the incentive depend on a flexible budget, which adjusts automatically for changes in volume. For example, if a department has a budget of $104,000 of fixed costs, and $104,000 of variable costs, for a total budget of $208,000 (as above), then we could adjust the budget prior to calculating the bonus. If volume of patients drops by 10 percent, we would expect costs to fall by $10,400 (i.e. 10 percent of the variable costs). Therefore, costs should have been $208,000 less $10,400, or a total of $197,600. If actual costs were $180,000, the bonus would be based on the $17,600 difference between the flexible budget to $197,600 and the actual cost, rather than being based on the full difference between the original budget and the actual result.

A flexible budget adjustment should be particularly appealing to managers if workload is rising. It is hard to convince a manager that a bonus based on reduced costs will help him, if each year our patient volume increases, and costs rise with patient load. In the above example, suppose that the number of patients rises by 20 percent above expectations when the $208,000 budget was prepared. The flexible budget would allow the variable portion to increase by 20 percent, or a total of $20,800 ($104,000 × 20%). If actual spending is $220,000, which is $12,000 over budget, the manager will still get a bonus, since the flexible budget will be the original $208,000, plus $20,800 allowed for the volume increase, or a total budget of $228,800. The actual spending of $220,000 will result in a bonus of $880, even though spending went over the original budget.

This does not mean that bonuses are the solution to all motivational problems. Bonus systems have a variety of other problems as well. Some bonus systems reward all employees if spending is down. But, if everyone gets a bonus, then no one feels that individual actions have much impact. As long as they believe everyone else is keeping spending down, some individuals may feel that they don't have to work particularly hard to reap the benefits of the bonus. In that case, probably very few will work hard to control costs.

On the other hand, if bonuses are only given to some employees, it may create a competitive environment in a situation in which teamwork is needed to provide quality care.

There are alternatives to bonuses. For example, one underused managerial tool is a letter from supervisor to subordinate. All individuals responsible for controlling costs should be explicitly evaluated with respect to how well they do in fact control costs. That evaluation should be communicated in writing. This approach, which is both the carrot and the stick, costs little to implement, but can have a dramatic impact.

Telling managers that they did a good job and that their boss knows that they did a good job can be an effective way to get the manager to try to do a good job the next year. In the real world, praise is both cheap and, in many cases, effective. On the other hand, criticism, especially in writing, can have a stinging effect that managers will work hard to avoid in the future.

UNREALISTIC EXPECTATIONS

While motivational devices can work wonders at getting an organization's employees to work hard for the organization and its goals, they can also backfire and have negative results. This occurs primarily when expectations are placed at unreasonably high levels.

There is no question that many workers do attempt to *satisfice*—to do just enough to get by. One thing we use incentives to accomplish is to motivate those individuals to work harder. A target that requires hard work and stretching, but is achievable, can be a useful motivating tool. If the target is reached there might be a bonus, or there should be at least some formal recognition of the achievement, such as a letter. At a minimum, the worker will have the self-satisfaction of having worked hard and reached the target.

But all of those positive outcomes can only occur if the target can in fact be reached. Some organizations have adopted the philosophy that if a high target makes people work hard, a higher target will make them work harder. This may not be the case. If targets are placed out of reach, this will probably not result in people reaching to their utmost limits to come as close to the target as possible.

It may seem as if we are short-changing ourselves whenever a subordinate achieves a target. We may think to ourselves, "We set the target too low. Perhaps if the target was higher, this person would have achieved the higher target. Since the target we set was achieved, we really don't know just how far this person can go. We haven't yet realized all of the potential." The problem with that logic is that there are risks associated with failure.

If managers fail to meet a target because they are not very competent or because they do not work very hard, the signal of failure that we send is warranted. In fact, repeated failure may be grounds for replacement of that individual in that job. But if a manager is both competent and hard working, failure is not a message that we want to send. Even though our intent may be simply to encourage the individual to achieve even more, the signal of failure will be discouraging.

When people work extremely hard, and fail, they often question why they bothered to work so hard. If hard work results in failure to achieve the target, they think, "Why not ease off? If you're going to fail anyway, must it be so painful?" Thus we must be extremely judicious to ensure that all goals assigned to managers are reasonable, or results may be less favorable than they otherwise would be.

CONCLUSION

Accountants can prepare budgets and cost reports to their heart's content. However, it is usually other managers and workers who must be counted upon to make those plans become a reality. Why would they want to do that?

It may seem like a flippant question, but in fact it is both serious and critical. When we ask a manager to accomplish something, we must be concerned with whether there is any reason in the world that he would want to do it.

Perhaps he will do it out of loyalty to the organization. Perhaps he will do it out of fear of losing his job. Perhaps he will do it in the hope of earning a promotion. Perhaps he will do it because he's just such a good guy.

Getting an understanding of what people will want to do and what they won't want to do is important. And once we know what they won't want to do, we should carefully attempt to develop some clear motivational device that will give them an incentive to do what they otherwise might not want to. After all, how many of us would work if we didn't get paid at all? Paychecks are simply a bribe to get people to come to work. Once they are at work, we need to provide additional incentives to make sure that the hospital benefits from their efforts to the greatest extent possible.

Application 1-5

Cost Accounting for Human Resources in Hospitals

Steven A. Finkler, PhD, CPA

For a number of years academics have been preaching that hospitals would one day have to adopt cost accounting techniques widely used in industry. That would necessitate some form of product-line cost accounting. That future is now upon us. The majority of hospital cost accounting articles written in the professional literature today focus on the issue of implementation of hospital product-line cost accounting systems. The more futuristic of those articles talk about using totally computerized systems to track the actual costs of each patient. That prognostication is also becoming a current reality, with implementation of such systems already occurring on a pilot basis. However, one major innovation in hospital cost accounting is still on the drawing boards. That innovation is human resource accounting.

Human resource accounting has received much theoretical attention among academics, but is still used only infrequently in actual practice. However, as the costs of hospitals have come under closer scrutiny, it may be time for hospitals to start examining accounting systems that provide better cost information about the hospital's investment in human resources.

In principle, hospitals are well aware of a number of human resource costs. For example, nurses are rarely laid off when there is a decrease in workload, if the decrease is likely to be temporary. The costs of recruiting and training new nurses, were workload to subsequently pick up, might well outweigh the wages saved in the interim. Essentially, the hospital makes an investment in human beings very similar to the investment it makes in building and equipment. The hospital is no more anxious to throw away its investment in people than it is to throw away a new piece of equipment. Yet accounting methods related to that investment are very poor.

The problems in accounting for human resources stem largely from the CPA's conservative approach to accounting. Once we make an investment in the form of buying a machine, we have a high degree of confidence that it will last for its predetermined useful life. However, when we spend money to recruit and train a person, we have no assurance at all that he will not quit the next day, taking our investment with him. On the other hand, we have no guarantee that the machine will not become technologically obsolete and have to be thrown away after just a few months.

Realistically, people are a key resource to the hospital as an organization, and people make up a substantial portion of the annual costs of operating the hospital. As we strive to improve the

Source: Reprinted from Steven A. Finkler, "Cost Accounting for Human Resources in Hospitals," *Hospital Cost Accounting Advisor,* Vol. 2, No. 5, October 1986, pp. 1–3, 7–8. Copyright 1986, Aspen Publishers, Inc.

efficiency of hospitals in the light of prospective payment systems and to make rational decisions about the various product lines of the hospital, we must have accurate cost information. That point is well recognized. Less well recognized is the fact that typical cost accounting systems create distortions because of the timing of when various human resource costs are treated as expenses.

The theoretical underpinnings for human resource accounting argue that the reason we spend money developing human resources is to earn a return on that money. For example, we send employees to conferences and training programs to improve their ability to run the organization efficiently. Presumably, if we didn't send our employees to such sessions, they would lack certain skills, and the result would be a less efficient, more costly organization.

In fact, even if the session is in some ideal vacation spot and more class sessions are missed than attended, the resulting employee morale and good will may be sufficient to generate a positive employee attitude that results in a more productive employee. In other words, a hospital, like any other organization, invests money in its employees because this is viewed, in the long run, as a good investment for the organization.

Yet, we have no measure of any of this. All spending is immediately treated as an expense—implying no carryover benefit to future years. No measure is ever made of how much was invested, and as a result managers do not have information needed in the process of acquiring, developing, retaining, using, evaluating, and rewarding their human resources.

Thus, the key issue, from a theoretical perspective is how to decide how much of an expenditure on a human resource is an expense related to the current accounting period, and how much is an asset, which will yield benefits in future years. Furthermore, since assets are defined in terms of the organization *owning the rights* to future benefits acquired through an exchange, there is great question as to whether the hospital's financial statement will be able to record such assets, under Generally Accepted Accounting Principles (GAAP).

That roadblock, however, is not of great concern to us. In managing a hospital, we don't rely on the historical cost valuations of assets that appear in financial statements when making decisions. We are well aware of many of the limitations of GAAP. Neither should GAAP limitations with respect to human resource accounting prevent us from considering such issues in our decision-making process.

Thus, for internal cost accounting purposes, there is no reason that the costs associated with hiring and training an x-ray technician all need to be expensed in the current year as part of general radiology department overhead. Instead, these costs can be amortized over the average period of time that an x-ray technician stays with the hospital. And each year's amortization expense can be included with the cost of x-ray technicians, as a direct labor cost.

A HUMAN RESOURCES COST ACCOUNTING MODEL

There are actually a number of models that have been developed to deal with human resource accounting on a theoretical level. Dillard discusses each of the various methods at some length.[1] The model with the most direct practical application is the one developed by Eric Flamholtz. His model is basically a historical cost approach that provides for the identification and classification of human resource costs.[2] In his model, human resource costs are divided into acquisition costs and development costs.

Acquisition costs include not only recruitment but also selection, hiring, and induction-related expenditures. Recruitment costs include such things as advertisements, head-hunter fees, travel costs, recruiter salaries, and administrative costs related to recruitment. In the Flamholtz model, all of these costs would be assigned to the actual hirees. Our goal is to determine not the cost per interview but rather the cost of attracting the individuals actually hired.

Selection costs are those costs related to picking those individuals to hire out of all those responding to initial recruitment efforts. These costs are a result of the time-consuming task of evaluating candidates.

The costs of hiring and induction refer to getting the individual to the job. That includes such things as moving expenses, and help finding a home or a job for the new employee's spouse, as well as the processing of paperwork for the new hire.

The other major classification of cost besides acquisition cost is development cost. These costs may be broken down into three principal categories: orientation, off-job training, and on-job training. Although we generally think of assets as declining in value over time, we keep renewing the value of our human resources in hospitals, by adding to the amount of training. Thus, the existing asset coming into a year is amortized, causing a decline in the asset, but new development takes place, causing an increase in the value of the asset.

Orientation costs include the formal process of training. This includes learning the hospital policies and becoming familiar with the facilities of the hospital. It may take just a few hours to show a new employee around while it might take weeks or months of formal training before a person can begin a specialized job.

Off-the-job training may take the form of a specialized training session or a more broadly designed program to encourage employees to seek advanced professional degrees. Dillard notes typical costs for such development as the "salaries of the trainers and trainees, tuition, meals, travel, facilities costs, consulting fees, and material." It should be noted that off-the-job training can take place at the hospital, but not on the specific job.

In contrast, on-the-job training refers to learning on the actual job as opposed to formal training sessions. The cost that is generally most important in this phase is the employee's salary during the period before becoming productive. To the extent measurable, the costs of other employees who become less productive while teaching the new employee are a related cost. Once all of the costs of human resources are specified, they can be aggregated, and an asset value assigned to each employee. Past experi-

ence can then be used to determine the lifetime over which to amortize various classes of human resources.

In some cases an employee will leave before the costs related to him are fully amortized. This would result in the same type of write-off that would occur if we disposed of a machine at a loss. On the other hand, some employees stay longer than the average. There will be little if any amortization for these employees in the later years of their employment with the hospital. That will tend to balance out against the write-offs.

IMPLICATIONS OF HUMAN RESOURCE ACCOUNTING

The bottom line of all this is that the current-period costs of treating patients are distorted by expensing all investments in human resources. For efficient product-line decisions, we should have as accurate cost information as possible.

There are also side benefits of having this additional information. For example, even though managers realize that there are direct and long-lived benefits of investment in human resources, in hard financial times there is a tendency to cut back in this area. It is very much like spending money to maintain equipment. We know that a little oil today will save the engine five years from now. Yet, the oil is treated as a current expense, and in hard times there is a tendency to cut back on such routine maintenance.

By having a human resources cost accounting system, the shortsightedness of such an approach becomes far more apparent. If we continue to invest in our human capital, we will see an asset being maintained. If we cease making that investment, expenses will still stay high, since the asset base will continue to amortize. At the same time, we will see the declining value of our human resource assets.

Those interested in seeing human resources in action should obtain a copy of the annual report of the R.G. Barry Corporation and Subsidiaries. That company has been a pathbreaker in the use of human resource accounting.

NOTES

1. Dillard, J.F., "Human Resources Accounting," *Handbook of Health Care Accounting and Finance,* edited by William O. Cleverley. Gaithersburg, Md.: Aspen Publishers, Inc., 1982.

2. E.G. Flamholtz, "Human Resource Accounting," in *Handbook of Cost Accounting,* edited by Sidney Davidson and Roman Weil. New York, N.Y.: McGraw-Hill, 1978.

2

Cost Definitions and Applications to Departmental vs. Product-Line Costing

---

Goals of This Chapter

---

1. Provide definitions and explanations of basic cost concepts, including the following:
   - full cost,
   - cost objective,
   - direct costs,
   - indirect or overhead costs,
   - average costs,
   - fixed costs,
   - variable costs,
   - marginal costs,
   - joint costs,
   - opportunity costs, and
   - responsibility accounting.
2. Discuss the importance of marginal costs for decision making.
3. Explain cross-subsidization of costs.
4. Clarify the difference between true costs, economic costs, and accounting costs.
5. Discuss the implications of the long run versus the short run on the nature of fixed and variable costs.
6. Explain the historical focus of cost accounting on departmental costing, and the more recent trend toward product costing.
7. Introduce the concept of external (social) costs and externalities.

Key Terms Used in This Chapter

Accounting cost; average cost; cost center; cost objective; cost reimbursement; cross-subsidization; department; Diagnosis Related Groups (DRGs);

Note: Key terms appear in italics when first used in the chapter. All key terms are defined in the Glossary.

direct cost; economic cost; external (social) costs; externality; fixed cost; full cost; incremental cost; indirect cost; joint cost; long run; marginal cost; Medicare Cost Report; microcosting; opportunity cost; out-of-pocket cost; overhead cost; product-line costing; prospective payment systems (PPSs); relevant range; responsibility accounting; responsibility centers; revenue center; short run; support cost center; true cost; variable cost.

DEFINITION AND CHARACTERISTICS OF COSTS

There is a simple question that is often asked, but that never receives a simple answer: "What does it cost?" It seems to matter little whether we are asking, "What does it cost to treat an average Blue Cross patient," or "What does it cost to treat a specific type of Medicare patient," or "What does it cost to treat a patient at ABC hospital?" The best we seem to be able to get in response to such simple questions is, "It depends; why do you want to know?"

Full Costs, Average Costs, Cost Objectives, Direct Costs, and Indirect Costs

Unfortunately, the problem in responding to that simple question is that the measurement of cost is an extremely complicated issue. An appropriate measurement of cost for one analysis may be totally inappropriate for another. Suppose, for example, that a policymaker wishes to decide whether to allow a hospital to acquire and operate a new kidney treatment machine called a lithotriptor. One datum sought by the policymaker is the likely total cost that would be associated with lithotripsy. Another measure desired is the cost per patient for the service if the machine is acquired. If asked for the lithotripsy cost per patient, an accountant would rightfully answer that it depends.

The cost per patient represents the *average cost.* Average costs are the *full cost* of treating all patients divided by the number of patients. Full costs represent all costs associated with a *cost objective.* (The cost definitions of this chapter are summarized in Exhibit 2-1.)

A cost objective is any particular item for which we wish to know the cost. It may be a specific patient, a class of patients, a service, a department, or an entire organization. Before one can begin to measure cost, the cost objective must be defined. In this example, the cost objective is the full costs of the lithotripsy service.

Full Cost:
All costs
associated with lithotripsy

Next, we must decide if we are interested in *direct costs,* or both direct costs and *indirect costs* (or overhead costs). Direct costs are those that are clearly and directly associated with the cost objective. They are generally under the control of the manager who has overall responsibility for the cost objective. Other costs are indirect. For example, the depreciation on the lithotriptor machine and the salary of its operator are clearly direct costs. The salary of a security guard or medical records staff member are indirect costs.

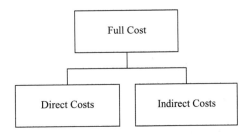

Line managers must carefully choose where to allocate their time in attempting to control costs. Indirect costs add a heavy burden to most departments. In reaction, some line managers spend inordinate amounts of their time fighting allocations of indirect costs to their departments. However, in many cases, line managers have little control over indirect costs—their time might be better spent attempting to control direct costs. In some cases, indirect costs may be controllable. The amount of laundry a department uses is one example; reprographics (photocopying) costs are another. In general, however, managers must make a careful judgment in determining the relative use of their time focusing on direct versus indirect costs.

The distinction between direct and indirect costs can become complicated. If the cost objective were the costs of the lithotripsy department, then a billing clerk in the finance department would be an indirect cost. The clerk

Exhibit 2-1 Cost Definitions

Accounting cost: A measure of cost based on a number of simplifications, such as an assumed useful life for a piece of equipment.

Average cost: Full costs divided by the number of units of service or patients.

Cost center: A unit or department in an organization for which a manager is assigned responsibility for costs.

Cost objective: Any particular item for which we wish to know the cost. It may be a specific patient, a class of patients, a service, a department, or an entire organization.

Direct costs: Costs clearly and directly associated with the cost objective. They are generally under the control of the manager who has overall responsibility for the cost objective.

Economic cost: The amount of money required to obtain the use of a resource.

Fixed costs: Costs that do not vary in total as the number of patients vary within a relevant range of volume or activity.

Full cost: All costs of a cost objective, including both direct costs and an allocated fair share of indirect costs.

Incremental or out-of-pocket costs: The additional costs that will be incurred if a decision is made and that would not otherwise be incurred.

Indirect or overhead costs: All costs that are not direct costs.

Joint costs: Costs that are required for the treatment of several or more different types of patients. The costs would be incurred unless the organization stopped treating all of those different types of patients.

Marginal costs: The change in total cost related to a change in patient volume or in services offered. These include variable costs and any additional fixed costs incurred because the volume change exceeds the relevant range for existing fixed costs.

Opportunity costs: A measure of cost based on the value of the alternatives that are given up in order to use the resource as the organization has chosen.

Relevant range: The expected range of volume over which fixed costs are fixed and variable costs vary in direct proportion.

Variable costs: Costs that vary in direct proportion with patient volume.

in the lithotripsy department would be a direct cost. The latter clerk is directly part of the lithotripsy department, and is under the immediate control of the department manager. However, if the cost objective were the total hospital-wide cost, then the billing clerk might also be considered a direct cost, whereas an outside independent auditor might be considered an indirect cost. On the other hand, if the cost objective were the direct care cost of a lithotripsy patient, then neither the billing clerk nor the lithotripsy department clerk would be direct costs.

You can see that it is extremely important to be careful in defining the cost objective before trying to calculate the cost. There will be times when a user is only concerned with direct costs. In such cases, the definition of which costs have been considered to be direct in the analysis must be made explicit to avoid confusion.

Full costs, however, include both direct costs and an allocated fair share of indirect costs. Determining a fair share of allocated costs is a difficult concept and will be addressed later. If the full costs are divided by the number of patients, the result is the average cost per patient.

Types of Costs: Fixed, Variable, and Marginal Costs

Full costs consist of both *fixed* and *variable* costs. Fixed costs are those that do not vary in total as the number of patients vary. Variable costs are those that vary in direct proportion with patient volume.

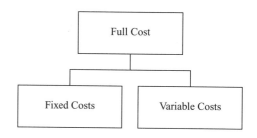

The definitions for fixed and variable costs assume that we are considering some *relevant range* of activity. It is not likely to be true that a fixed cost would remain the same over extreme variations in activity, but rather that it will remain fixed over some expected possible range of activity.

Suppose that a lithotriptor costs $1 million to acquire and install and has a five-year life. Assume that the machine is depreciated at a rate of $200,000 per year for five years. The annual depreciation cost of the equipment is a fixed cost because it will remain the same regardless of the number of patients who use it, within its capacity limitations. Further suppose that the labor and supplies needed to run the machine (the variable costs) are $200 per patient. What are the full costs of operating the lithotriptor machine? As we can see from Table 2-1, the full costs depend in part on the number of patients. More patients add more variable cost, increasing the full costs of the service.

What is the cost per patient treated (Table 2-2)? The average cost per patient is $400 if we have 1,000 patients. There are $200 of variable cost per patient plus $200 of fixed cost per patient (the $200,000 depreciation divided by

1,000 patients). The 1,000 patients represent 4 patients per day, 5 days per week, 50 weeks per year. What if we treat only 1 patient per day, or a total of 250 for the year? The variable costs are still $200 per patient, but the $200,000 of fixed costs are only shared by 250 patients, so they are $800 per patient ($200,000 ÷ 250 patients = $800 per patient). The average cost per patient is now $1,000 (the variable cost of $200, plus the fixed cost of $800) rather than $400. On the other hand, what if we treat 8 patients per day, or 2,000 for the year? The average cost would be only $300 per patient ($200,000 ÷ 2,000 patients = $100 of fixed cost + $200 of variable cost per patient = $300 average cost per patient). What is the cost per patient? *It depends on the volume of patients!*

The average cost is declining because of the fixed costs, not because of the variable costs. Variable costs do affect the full cost as volume changes. They do not affect the average cost as volume changes because each unit requires an equal amount of variable resources. Fixed costs, however, are shared as the volume of patients increases. The greater the volume, the more widely the fixed costs are spread, and the less cost for which any one unit is responsible.

Table 2-1 Full Costs of Lithotripsy. Acquisition cost = $1,000,000; expected useful life = 5 years; depreciation = acquisition cost ÷ life = $1,000,000 ÷ 5 years = $200,000 ÷ 1 year; variable costs = $200/patient.

Volume (A)	Fixed Cost (B)	Variable Cost Per Patient (C)	Total Variable Cost (D) = (A) × (C)	Full Cost (E) = (B) + (D)
250	$200,000	$200	$ 50,000	$250,000
1,000	200,000	200	200,000	400,000
2,000	200,000	200	400,000	600,000

Table 2-2 Average Costs of Lithotripsy

Volume (A)	Fixed Cost (B)	Fixed Cost Per Patient (C) = (B) ÷ (A)	Variable Cost Per Patient (D)	Average Cost (E) = (C) + (D)
250	$200,000	$800	$ 200	$1,000
1,000	200,000	200	200	400
2,000	200,000	100	200	300

To take this example one step further, suppose that a hospital has a lithotriptor and currently performs 1,000 cases per year at a cost of $400 per patient. A large organization approaches the hospital and offers to generate an additional 1,000 cases for the hospital but is willing to pay only $250 per case. Should the hospital accept the offer? At the current volume of 1,000 cases per year the cost per patient is $400. If volume were to expand to 2,000 cases per year, the cost per patient would be $300. The revenue per patient is $250. Nevertheless, the offer should be accepted. The loss for each of these additional patients will actually *increase* hospital profits.

That may not seem to make sense. Why should a hospital accept $250 to treat a patient at a cost of $300? The answer stems from the fact that *different cost measurement is needed for different questions and decisions.* Accountants not only tell you that the cost depends on issues such as volume; they also ask why you want to know what something costs. In this case, the hospital is already committed to having certain fixed costs. It owns the lithotriptor and will have $200,000 of depreciation regardless of volume. The extra 1,000 patients do not cause the fixed costs to rise. They only cause the variable costs to increase, at a rate of $200 per patient. This is less than the revenue rate of $250. For each of the additional patients, the hospital will receive $250 but will only spend an *additional* $200.

Note from Table 2-1 that the full costs rise from $400,000 to $600,000 if volume is increased by 1,000 patients—an increase of $200,000. Revenue would rise by $250 for each extra patient. The financial impact of accepting the extra patients can be seen as follows: .

Extra revenue: $250 × 1,000 patients	$ 250,000
Extra cost: $600,000 – $400,000	– 200,000
Increase in net income:	$ 50,000

Marginal Cost Pricing

Over the long run, average revenues must at least equal average costs for an institution to be able to replace its facilities and capital equipment, but in the short run, decisions should be made based on *marginal costs.* Marginal costs are defined as the change in cost related to a change in activity. Marginal costs are often referred to as *incremental* or *out-of-pocket costs.* If the added revenues exceed the added costs of treating additional patients, the health care organization will be better off to accept the offer and the patients.

Should the hospital always be willing to accept another lithotriptor patient for a revenue of $250, if variable costs are $200 per patient? No, it should not. Marginal costs are often equal to variable costs, but they are not synonymous with them. Suppose that the hospital already had 2,000 lithotripsy patients and was near the capacity of the machine. Extra patients might necessitate acquisition of an additional machine. In that case, the marginal costs would include not only the variable cost per patient, but also the cost of acquiring another machine. This might well exceed the additional revenue, and the offer would have to be rejected. In other words, *the cost to treat a patient is very situational.* It depends on volume. It depends on the decision to which the cost information relates. And it depends on the specific situation of an individual institution, such as whether it has substantial excess capacity or is near its full capacity.

CROSS-SUBSIDIZATION OF COSTS

Health care costing is far from perfect. This is largely because cost information costs money to collect. Logically, an organization does not collect information unless it is worth more than its costs. The introduction of *prospective payment systems (PPSs)* in the form of *Diagnosis Related Groups (DRGs)* has caused many hospital managers to begin to evaluate whether the value of accurate cost information has increased enough to make it worthwhile to devote additional resources to improve the accuracy of cost information. This new focus results largely from concerns about existing *cross-subsidization* between patients. Cross-subsidization is a situation in which some patients are assigned more costs than they cause the organization to incur and others are assigned less.

Suppose that a hospital had only two types of patients, A and B, with equal numbers of each type. And suppose that the *true cost* of treating an A patient were $5,000 and the true cost of treating a B patient were $15,000.

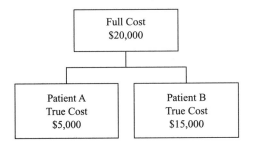

Quite a bit of costly detailed accounting would be needed to determine those costs. If the hospital were reimbursed for its costs, its income for each patient would be:

	Patient A	Patient B
Revenue	$ 5,000	$15,000
Cost	– 5,000	–15,000
Net Income	$ 0	$ 0

On the other hand, if we added up all of the costs of the hospital, and divided by the total number of patients, we could very simply determine that on average, each patient cost the hospital $10,000. If we allowed substantial averaging, some patients would be assigned more than their costs and others less.

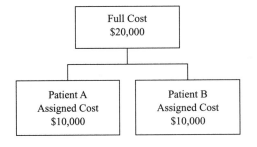

What would happen if the hospital received cost reimbursement, and it reported costs based on averages that included cross-subsidizations? If the hospital receives $10,000 per patient, instead of $5,000 per patient for half of its patients and $15,000 per patient for the other half, it would make no difference. The total revenue would be the same, and the cost and effort of obtaining more detailed, accurate information would be avoided.

	Patient A	Patient B
Revenue	$10,000	$10,000
Cost	– 10,000	–10,000
Net Income	$ 0	$ 0

If each payer pays for equal numbers of A and B patients, it would not matter to them either. For example, if Medicare, Medicaid, and Blue Cross each had beneficiaries, half of whom were A patients and half of whom were B patients, they would pay an average of $10,000 per patient whether they paid $5,000 for A patients and $15,000 for B patients, or $10,000 for each patient. Therefore, under *cost reimbursement,* for both hospitals and large payers, accuracy in cost finding was not crucial, and a number of cross-subsidizations in the process were acceptable if they saved substantial data collection cost. Under cost reimbursement, the health care organization is reimbursed for the costs it incurs to care for a patient.

There are, however, severe incentive problems with cost reimbursement. If two hospitals each performed open heart surgery and one had a cost of $15,000 per case, and another had a cost of $5,000 per case, they are each to be paid their cost, by those payers who reimburse costs. This gives no loss incentive to the high-cost producer and no profit incentive to the low-cost producer. How could the costs vary so widely? One possibility is reflected in the lithotriptor example above—if the fixed costs of expensive equipment are shared by a larger number of patients, the result is a much lower cost per patient.

Without a strong reason to do accurate costing, health care organizations are unlikely to be aware of what resources different types of patients really tend to consume. Many elements of the Medicare Cost Report lead to an averaging result, with cross-subsidizations between patients. In the case of open heart surgery, for example, the substantial fixed costs of the open heart surgery equipment (bypass pump, etc.) are often spread over all surgical patients based on the length of their surgery, rather than associating those equipment costs only with heart surgery patients. Such cross-subsidization was not viewed as a major concern in the past.

With PPSs in place, however, hospitals want to know what their costs really are for each type of patient. Knowing that the average cost per patient is $10,000 is now inadequate, even if average reimbursement is still $10,000! Suppose (in this rather extreme example) that because of cross-subsidizations all Medicare Cost Reports had shown all A and all B patients at one health care organization to have an average cost of $10,000, and therefore all DRG payment rates were set at $10,000.

	Patient A	Patient B
DRG Revenue	$10,000	$ 10,000
True Cost	−5,000	−15,000
Net Income	$ 5,000	$(5,000)

What incentive does that give hospital managers? If one group of their patients really costs $5,000 to treat, and the payment level is set at $10,000, managers will want to market that DRG vigorously. If another group of patients really costs $15,000 to treat, and the revenue associated with them is only $10,000, the hospital may want to discontinue treating those patients.

Under cost reimbursement, accurate cost measurement by type of patient did not really matter. Under PPS, with a fixed price per patient, there is incentive to treat only those patients who can be treated efficiently. This is likely to influence low-volume, high-cost producers in the direction policymakers would probably prefer. That is, low-volume programs have an incentive either to close or not to get started in the first place. But in order to make such decisions, the hospital must have accurate costing information that is free of the distortions caused by cross-subsidizations.

TRUE COST, ECONOMIC COST, AND ACCOUNTING COST

No hospital can really act in response to PPS incentives until they know the costs of treating different types of patients. Hospitals are now placing a greater focus on costing in general, and especially on product costing based on specific DRGs or DRG clusters. However, in the search for the true costs, we must bear in mind that cost information is costly. At some point, for management or for policy purposes, we must assess whether the benefit of more accurate data is worth the cost.

There has been much talk in the last few years of collecting true cost information for health care organizations. True costs, however, are largely an illusion. The notion that full and accurate accounting will result in the one true cost should have been at least partially dispelled earlier in this chapter. No matter how accurate accounting information is, there will always be different assessments of cost in different situations. Even beyond this, however, true costs do not exist because accounting can never do more than to crudely approximate economic cost.

The purest cost definition stems from the economist's concept of *opportunity cost*. Economics focuses on the allocation of scarce resources for alternative uses. Opportunity cost uses that focus by defining the cost of doing anything as the value of the forgone alternatives. If we buy a lithotriptor, and the resources devoted to that machine could have been used instead for a prenatal nutrition program, then the opportunity cost of the lithotriptor is the value of the prenatal nutrition program. The idea of choosing among alternative uses for society's scarce resources is quite useful for policy analysts.

The notion of *economic cost* is derived from the opportunity cost concept. Economic cost is defined as the amount of money that would be required to obtain the use of a resource. The amount paid for labor is an economic cost. If you offered less money, the labor would go to work in some alternative employment. Similarly, an economist's definition of capital costs would be the amount someone else is willing to pay to bid away your capital resources from you.

Thus, we have the opportunity cost concept, which economists would tell us yields a *true cost*. However, the opportunity cost is the value of the resource in each alternative use, and value is determined by the economic utility function of individuals. Calculation of value requires knowledge of the aggregate utility of all individuals in society (a social welfare function) for each possible alternative. However, economists have not yet derived a practical way to measure a social welfare function. Thus, that measure of true cost is out of our reach.

The economic cost measure is somewhat more restricted in scope than is the opportunity cost measure, but still requires us to measure what everyone else would have paid for each of the resources we use. Although that is more theoretically possible than the measurement of opportunity cost, it is obviously impractical. Thus, we will have to give up on any chance to collect true costs.

How about an accountant's definition of cost? Although it seems accountants using their own rules should be able to tell us the true accounting cost of various elements of providing hospital care, that is true only to a very limited extent. An accountant would start with the notion that resources are consumed and that the organization had to pay to acquire those resources. However, in contrast to economic costs, *accounting costs* are based on a number of simplifications.

Consider the measurement of capital costs for one year for a $1 million lithotriptor. The economic cost would be the amount someone is willing to pay us for the use of the machine for one year. An alternative economic cost measure would be to determine the market value of the machine at the beginning of the year and again at the end of the year. The decline in value represents the economic cost of having used the machine. In theory, one could obtain such appraisals for every asset, but in practice, it is unlikely that anyone would go to such extremes. An accountant would take a simplified approach of allocating the original amount spent to acquire the item over the years of its life. In this case, the cost for one year would be

the $200,000 of depreciation (assuming a five-year life with straight-line depreciation and no salvage value).

If we could determine the resources that have been consumed and match them with the amount that had been paid for those resources, we would have the accountant's true cost. It is not as pure a measure as the economist's true cost, but many would be satisfied with its degree of accuracy. Many researchers have used microcosting techniques in an attempt to come very close to measuring such a true cost. In doing so, the cost objective must be defined. One must be extremely explicit regarding whether one is interested in the true accounting marginal costs of some specific change in activities, or in the true accounting total costs of operating the health care organization, or in the true accounting average cost for treating a particular type of patient. The last is of most interest to policymakers and is unfortunately the most resistant to measurement.

Attempting to measure the true *total* costs is the easiest of the three. One can look at all of the dollars spent by the organization and use that as a measurement of cost. Unfortunately, that "cash basis" approach assumes that only things paid for currently are consumed this year. If nurses work to provide care this year but are not paid until next year, we have still used up the resources and should account for their cost. We can adjust, using accrual accounting, for such interyear problems. However, even using accrual accounting, when we look at the cost of capital, we must decide if straight-line depreciation is reasonable. Perhaps more of the equipment has been consumed in the first year than will be consumed in each of the latter years. Some accelerated method of depreciation might make more sense. We can never know exactly what part of the capital equipment has been consumed in the current year (unless we sell it at the end of the year). Therefore, *we will never have a true accounting cost,* even for the total cost of operating a hospital for a year.

Can we measure the true accounting marginal cost? If we add one more patient of a given type, what things change in the hospital? How much more labor? How many more supplies? If you could isolate every possible item of change and determine the amount of resources to be consumed, you could through a microcosting study determine an accounting measure of the true cost of the change. However, in practice this is harder than it sounds. Suppose that we add one patient, who uses some laundry. How much will the costs of operating the laundry department change? Will there be an extra two minutes or three minutes of laundry labor time per day? Will the extra time result in any overtime in the laundry, or simply less down time? Will the laundry machines need to be replaced one week sooner? Will housekeeping have to wash the floor in the laundry one more time? Will the laundry wear out and be replaced sooner? The actual determination of a true marginal cost is probably not possible. In practice, special studies usually hope for a reasonable approximation of true costs, making a variety of implicit and explicit simplifying assumptions along the way.

The calculation of the average cost per patient for a given type of patient, perhaps by payer class, is a particular concern for both managers and policymakers. It is also particularly difficult. In addition to the problems cited previously, a health care organization has a tremendous amount of joint cost. Once joint costs are introduced, there is little chance of determining even a nearly true cost.

Joint Costs

Joint costs are costs that are required for the treatment of several different types of patients. For example, suppose that a hospital performs bypass surgery, heart-valve replacements, and congenital defect heart repair.

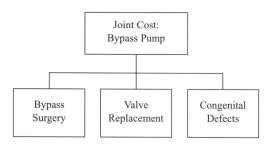

In order to do these three types of surgery, we must have a heart-lung bypass pump. If we were to discontinue performing bypass surgery, we would still need a bypass pump for valve and congenital surgery. Therefore, the opportunity cost of the bypass pump for bypass surgery is zero. Similarly, if we do bypass surgery, we will need the pump, so the opportunity cost of the pump for valve and congenital surgery is zero. Yet, we must spend a substantial amount on the pump or we can do none of the surgeries, so its cost can hardly be zero.

The cost of the pump depends crucially on why we want to know its cost. If we are committed to valve surgery, and want to know if it is financially worthwhile to keep doing bypass surgery, the correct cost for the calculation is zero. If we are trying to decide whether to do heart surgery of any kind, the cost of the bypass pump is what we would have to pay to acquire it, or what we can sell it for if we already have it. A serious measurement problem arises, however, if we decide to get the pump and do all three types of surgery, and then decide how much each type of surgery costs, including a "fair share" of the cost of the pump. The cost is a joint cost—no heart surgery can be performed without it. Any allocation becomes largely arbitrary; that is, there is no rational way to decide what part of the pump's cost should be associated with each type of surgery.

The degree to which allocation of joint cost is arbitrary can be seen more clearly if we look at a different type of joint cost: the salary of a hospital chief executive officer (CEO). How should that cost be shared among hospital patients? One way is to allocate an equal amount to each patient, on the grounds that every patient, no matter how sick, has benefitted from the presence and decisions of the CEO. Alternatively, we could argue that each patient day should be charged an equal share, on the grounds that the longer one is in the hospital, the more he or she benefits from leadership of the CEO. On the other hand, one could look at how the CEO spends his or her time and allocate costs to only patients in departments that have consumed an inordinately high proportion of the CEO's efforts.

The problem we are running into is a basic allocation dilemma. To derive a true cost, all costs should be assigned on a cause-and-effect basis. A patient who causes a resource to be consumed should be assigned the cost of that resource. Unfortunately, with truly joint costs, it is impossible to determine a cause-and-effect relationship. Academic accountants are largely in agreement that where no cause-and-effect relationship exists, *costs should not be allocated.*

The implications of the joint cost allocation problem are that there is no unique, true, average cost for a given type of patient. An average cost is derived from assigning all of the costs to all of the patients. If joint costs are not allocated, then the average costs for all patients will not add up to the full costs of the hospital. On the other hand, if the joint costs are allocated, they must be allocated based on one of a number of arbitrary bases, and therefore there is no one, true, average cost for any given type of patient. With a different allocation base, a different average cost would result.

So what does it cost? One might be tempted to say that no one really knows—and to be totally accurate, that would be correct. But in reality, we can make pretty good approximations of cost. The key question one should ask is whether we can generate estimates of cost that are useful for management decision making.

While we may never know the true cost, we probably can make substantially improved estimates of cost. Furthermore, if we are careful to define the reason we desire cost information, we can select the appropriate measurement of cost. It is true that there are no absolute solutions to the cost measurement problem. Nevertheless, it is also true that managers can probably make great strides if they have an understanding of the various types of cost information available.

THE LONG TERM VS. THE SHORT TERM

In health care administration, we frequently tend to deal with *short-run* and *long-run* issues.

How long, however, is the long run? This question is of considerable concern in trying to classify costs as being either fixed or variable. Break-even analysis (Chapter 5) relies on our being able to segregate fixed costs from variable costs. Flexible budgeting (Chapter 9) calls for us to plan ahead and evaluate actual performance based on which costs are fixed and which are variable. Pricing decisions for preferred provider organization (PPO) bids or health maintenance organization (HMO) contracts also call for intimate knowledge of which costs are relevant—that is, which costs will *vary* if we get the contract.

However, it is known that a cost that is fixed in the short run may well be variable in the long run. For example, suppose that a hospital has six different general medical/surgical units, each operating at an occupancy level of 85 percent. The amount of temporary agency registered nurse time used is likely to be strictly variable. Only if we encounter a short-term peak will we bring on more temporary nurses. On the other hand, the unit supervisors will be a fixed cost. Occupancy in each unit may rise to 95 or 100 percent, or fall to 75 or even 60 percent, but we will need a unit supervisor for each unit regardless of volume. The unit supervisor is a fixed cost, *at least in the short run.*

In the long run, unit supervisors become a variable cost. If we experience a decline in occupancy from 85 percent to 75 percent in each of the six medical/surgical units, we may decide to close down one unit next year, resulting in five units at 90 percent occupancy each, rather than six at 75 percent. In this longer run period, we are able to adjust (vary) the so-called *fixed* nurse supervisor cost. By eliminating one medical/surgical unit, we can eliminate one nurse supervisor. What is fixed in the short run becomes variable in the long run.

But how long is the long run? Depreciation on the hospital building is typically a fixed cost in the short run. If patient census declines during the year, we cannot adjust the depreciation on the building. Even for next year, if we close a medical/surgical unit and release a nurse supervisor, depreciation will remain unchanged. Depreciation will change only when the building is replaced—perhaps as a smaller building with fewer units. A period long run enough to allow some fixed costs to vary is not necessarily long run enough to allow all fixed costs to vary. In other words, the long run is not a single specific length of time.

In recording assets on the balance sheet, we seem to have less trouble with the short run and the long run. The short-run, or near-term, or current, or liquid assets are those with a lifetime of one year or the operating cycle, whichever is longer. The operating cycle is the time from payment of cash to acquire labor, supplies, and so on, until collection of cash from the sale of the services generated by use of the labor and supplies. In actual practice, except for a few industries with exceptionally long production cycles (such as forestry and liquor), we tend simply to use one year for the break between short term and long term.

It is clear from the example of the medical/surgical unit, however, that the short-term/long-term dichotomy used for financial accounting purposes is inadequate for describing the short run and the long run when it comes to fixed and variable costs. A simple definition of the long run is that it is the period of time when fixed costs become variable and can be adjusted for any given output level. For staff nurses, that may be a month or a quarter of a year. For a nurse supervisor, the long run might be next year. For depreciation on a brand new hospital building, the long-run period may be 40 or more years. It is an important part of the decision-making process to attempt to determine the long-run period for the various resources involved in the decision.

For example, in preparing a bid for an HMO contract, a hospital must determine the costs that are *marginal or relevant costs*—that is, the costs that will be incurred if the contract is undertaken, but not otherwise. In such a decision, we are interested with the costs that vary not simply with volume, but with the existence of the contract as well.

For example, reagents used for laboratory tests are variable costs in both the long and short runs. Performing more laboratory tests will consume more reagents. There is no ques-

tion that these are relevant costs to be considered in pricing the contract. Raw food materials would be a similar item. How about the labor to perform the laboratory test or prepare the food? Are those costs relevant to the contract? That depends on whether they are fixed or variable in the short run, with the short run being defined as the contract period. If they are fixed, and excess capacity exists, they are not relevant to the decision (see Chapter 6).

For example, if we must buy laboratory technician time in whole full-time equivalents (FTEs), and acceptance of an HMO contract would increase our productive time of one given laboratory worker from 76 percent to 78 percent, without increasing the number of FTEs or the cost of the laboratory workers to us, then that cost is not relevant to the contract. Certainly, we would try to build in that cost and try to recover it when we are trying to *sell* the contract, but for our own internal information, we know that we already have the labor necessary to perform the laboratory tests without spending any more than we would without the contract.

What about the machine that performs the laboratory tests? Again, assuming sufficient excess capacity exists, it is not a relevant cost. However, suppose that we are considering a five-year contract with the HMO. If the machine has seven years of useful life remaining, then it is a fixed cost throughout the short run (the five-year contract period) and is not a relevant cost. But suppose that the machine only has a three-year useful life before it will have to be replaced. What replacement machine will we buy?

If the answer depends on whether or not we have the contract, then the machine has become a relevant cost. If we would have to replace the old machine with a larger one if we have the HMO contract, the larger machine is a relevant cost. Not only that, but we must worry about the entire difference in cost to get the larger machine. If the HMO does not renew the contract, we will still have the larger, more expensive machine.

The machine example may not be representative of all situations. However, it should serve to make the point that we must consider the long run versus the short run in many decisions; we must be analytical about which costs are fixed and which are variable over the period to which a decision is related.

For the hospital that was rebuilt in 1982 and then had sharp reductions in occupancy (perhaps due to Medicare prospective payment), depreciation on the building should not play much of a role in considering alternative ways to fill empty beds in the next year, or the next five or ten years. On the other hand, for the hospital with a sixty-year-old facility and current plans for replacement in the near future, we need a different perspective. The long run is very short indeed when you are about to rebuild your entire hospital.

It is an easy trap to fall into to assume that reagents are always variable, and buildings are always fixed, and therefore reagents are always relevant and buildings never are. We often assume that the long run is far away. For health care organizations with old buildings or old equipment, the long run may be just around the corner. In decision making, we must always assess the period to which the decision is related. Costs that will differ over that period depending on what decision we make are short-term variable costs relevant to that decision, regardless of how long-term and fixed they become after the decision is made.

DEPARTMENTAL VS. PRODUCT-LINE COSTING

Most health care organizations are divided into *responsibility centers*. A responsibility center is an organizational unit for which a specific manager has authority and responsibility. Generally, responsibility centers in health care are either *cost centers* (often referred to as *support cost centers*) or *revenue centers*.

Managers of cost centers are held accountable only for their expenses, whereas managers of revenue centers are held accountable for both expenses and revenues. In order to determine the performance of the responsibility center and its manager, it is necessary to calculate the costs related to that center. This has given rise to costing in health care that focuses on the department. We are using the term *department* here to refer to any cost or revenue center. In practice, some departments, such as nursing in a hospital, may encompass a number of smaller responsibility units or cost centers.

Historically, health care reimbursement has been based on the costs patients incur in various departments. This has increased the focus on departmental costing. The introduction of PPSs, in the form of DRGs, has raised the possibility that a focus on the total cost by type of patient, rather than by department, might be appropriate. Such patient-oriented costing is referred to as *product-line costing*.

Departmental Costing

Invoices for services in health care—patient bills—generally show a charge for a set of independent services. The patient is charged for radiology services, pharmacy services, operating room services, and so forth. Cost accounting in health care developed in a way to determine the total costs of each department and then to assign those costs to each unit of service by the department.

For example, the radiology department would first determine its total costs. These costs would include the direct costs of technicians' salaries plus the specific materials used for each x-ray. They would also include the indirect costs within the department as well as those assigned to the department from other cost centers (Figure 2-1).

Then it would calculate a share of those total costs for each x-ray. The cost per x-ray would typically vary depending on the type; often, a special study might be done to find the relative costs of each different type of x-ray. Such a study might find that a wrist x-ray is twice as

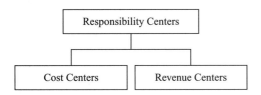

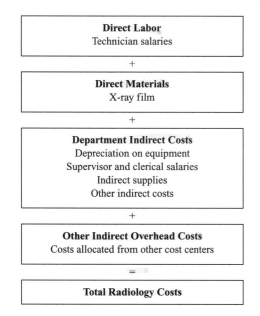

Figure 2-1 Total Radiology Department Costs

costly as an arm x-ray. The cost assigned to a patient would then depend on the number of each type of x-ray that the patient received.

Examples of departmental costing are provided at the end of the chapter in Application 2-1 for surgery costs and 2-2 for radiology costs. The reader is encouraged to review these applications for a more detailed perspective on departmental costing.

Product-Line Costing

The departmental approach to costing has long been the subject of some criticism. The method focuses on the department instead of the product. In most industries one of the most crucial pieces of information is the cost of the different products. The relationship between the product's price and cost is essential for understanding the financial impact different types of patients have on the organization.

This has traditionally been less relevant to health care organizations, where cost reimbursement predominated. In a cost reimbursement environment, knowing the specific accurate cost of each patient is less important

than one might expect. Although poor accuracy will mean that some patients are undercosted and therefore underreimbursed, other patients are overcosted and overreimbursed. As long as total reimbursements cover total costs, the accuracy of the costing can take a back seat.

On the other hand, under DRGs or other PPSs, accurate patient costing becomes much more important. Under PPS, the revenue for the patient is not merely a reflection of reported cost, but is instead a fixed amount. If the true underlying cost is substantially more than the revenue for a certain type of patient, the organization should know that. Similarly, if the cost is much less than the revenue, that would be of interest to managers. The efficient financial management of the organization therefore pushes much more strongly for product-line costing under a PPS system.

Consider the typical chest x-ray. Most health care organizations have a standard patient charge for a portable chest x-ray taken in the patient's room. One would think that departmental costing could be fairly accurate if patients are charged appropriately for the number of portable chest x-rays they have during their stay, at that standard charge. One should be able to build up to an accurate total measure of patient (product) costs by type of patient. In fact, that is probably not the case.

The building-up approach starts with costs that were calculated primarily for purposes of determining the costs of running the department, as shown in Figure 2-1. Those costs were not generated primarily to know the costs by type of patient. From a departmental perspective, it is probably adequate to know the average cost of a chest x-ray, but that information is insufficient for knowing the average cost of a chest x-ray for a specific type of patient!

Contrast a chest x-ray for a tuberculosis (TB) patient with that of a cardiac surgery patient. Suppose that TB patients are generally ambulatory. When the x-ray technician arrives with the portable machine, the patient easily moves to the position indicated by the technician, and the entire procedure takes six minutes. On the other hand, a cardiac surgery patient receives most of his or her x-rays following the surgery. The patient is likely to be in serious or critical condition, has a number of chest tubes and monitors, and is unable to aid the technician. It might take 30 minutes to take the x-ray.

From a departmental costing approach, the costs of these two types of patients can be averaged together to get the average cost per chest x-ray. That is the approach generally taken by health care organizations. This is comparable to General Motors assuming that there is an average radiator cost. Product decisions would be extremely difficult for General Motors under such an assumption. If the cost of radiators is averaged to find the average radiator cost, and the cost of engines is averaged, and the cost of fenders is averaged, what is the implication? Any car that uses an equal number of radiators, engines, fenders, and so on must have an equal cost. Therefore, the Chevette and the Cadillac both cost the same amount to produce!

Clearly, this is a ludicrous result. If the typical TB patient requires 6 minutes of labor and the typical cardiac surgery patient requires 30 minutes, then they are receiving different products from radiology, even if they are all called chest x-rays. From Table 2-3, we see that the cost of a TB chest x-ray might be $40, whereas the cost of a cardiac surgical patient's chest x-ray might be $52. They might each be assigned a cost of $46.

This approach is equivalent to General Motors assuming its costs are identical for all cars having an equal number of radiators, engines, wheels, and so forth. It is not commonly perceived as such because different patients consume different quantities of each service. Some patients consume three chest x-rays, whereas others consume only one, same is true of most services consumed in health care organizations. Therefore, it looks like patients are being uniquely costed under departmental costing.

How do we get around this problem? General Motors finds that it must know the cost of the radiator for each *type* of car. A Chevette radiator requires less metal and less labor to make than a Cadillac radiator. A TB chest x-ray requires less technician and machine time than a cardiac surgery chest x-ray. This product costing approach is discussed at some length in Application 2-3, where product costing is referred to as vertical costing, and departmental costing as horizontal costing.

Hybrid Approaches

Few things in cost accounting are totally black or white. The area of departmental versus product costing is no exception. Departmental costing may well be insufficient under PPS. But product costing that truly focuses on differential costs for different types of patients may result in tremendous data collection costs. In many cases, health care organizations try to seek a happy balance between the departmental costing needed for *responsibility accounting* (e.g., how well a cost or revenue center is doing) versus the product costing needed for effective product decisions (e.g., whether to discontinue offering a particular service).

Two examples of attempts to develop a hybrid approach are offered in Applications 2-4 and 2-5. Application 2-4 looks at costing out

Table 2-3 Chest X-Ray Cost

Chest X-ray	Tuberculosis Patient	Cardiac Surgery Patient	Average Patient
Technician labor @ $30/hour ($)	$ 3	$15	$ 9
X-ray film ($)	25	25	25
Other costs ($)	12	12	12
Total ($)	$40	$52	$46

nursing services for hospitals, which became a major focus of attention during the 1980s. Hospital nursing is a department that traditionally has had extremely poor costing. The total costs of any nursing unit are divided by the number of patient days of care to find an average cost per patient day. This is comparable to the chest x-ray example taken to an extreme. Although there may be different per diem rates for routine medical/surgical units as compared with intensive care units (ICUs), most hospitals typically have six or fewer nursing per diem rates for the entire hospital.

No one can really argue that all patients on a given nursing unit require the same amount of nursing care per patient day. However, under the departmental approach to costing, an average cost per patient day on the unit is quite reasonable. The total costs of the department are correctly captured, and they are assigned to the patients of the department.

From the point of view of understanding the resources that different types of patients really cause the institution to incur, however, this is a weak approach. Product costing that specifically tries to associate resources actually consumed by different types of patients could be much more useful for providing managers with information they can use in making decisions.

Application 2-4 considers nursing patient classifications in an attempt to divide patients into different types by intensity of consumption of nursing resources. The results are departmental in that they focus only on nursing department costs; however, they are product oriented in that they assign costs to different types of patients based on resource consumption by patient type.

Another area of health care costing that has had particularly poor costing under departmental approaches is the emergency services department or emergency room (ER). Many hospitals have standard charges for an ER visit across widely varying patient types. Application 2-5 looks at ER department costing. The approach taken in this application is to focus on the actual resources consumed by different types of procedures. Then the department can assess the consumption of different procedures by different types of patients.

The approach proposed in that article may not be a 100-percent pure *microcosting* approach to product costing (microcosting is discussed in Chapter 3). It still assumes that patients with different diagnoses will cost the same for a procedure of a given type. This is akin to assuming the cost of providing all chest x-rays is the same. However, the approach proposed is a major move away from the traditional ER departmental approach, which would not even consider the different types of procedures required for different types of patients.

The best solution for determining patient costs is not an easy one. The nature of costs is such that the more refined the analysis, generally the more costly it is. What we have been observing over the past decade is that since the advent of PPS, managers need better cost information to make correct decisions. As health care organizations try to evaluate their existing programs and services and consider the addition of new ones, they need to understand the financial impacts of the programs and services. This requires more accurate cost information.

It is unclear whether good management decisions require an extremely detailed microcosting, which would examine every single resource element consumed by each patient. True costs, as discussed earlier, will likely never be attainable. Managers using cost accounting information must constantly evaluate the trade-off between better cost information and the higher cost of generating that information.

The issues regarding product costing have been only introduced in this chapter. Chapter 3 looks at these issues in substantially greater depth.

EXTERNAL COSTS

Organizations usually measure costs by looking inward. In reality, however, organizations many times take actions that create externalities. An *externality* is a side-effect impact on someone not party to an action that results from that action. For example, when an industrial producer pollutes the skies, that pollution may not directly cost the company anything. However, the pollution has widespread side effects. These side effects, whether eye irritation or a higher incidence of cancer, create a wide variety of costs throughout society. Such costs are referred to as *external costs* or *social costs.*

Since most organizations do not directly consider the external costs they generate in their cost accounting systems, society often regulates actions that create externalities. The government may prohibit pollution and fine organizations that pollute. The fines are intended to translate the external cost into a direct internal cost that the organization will take into account in making its production decisions.

Not all externalities are costs. There may be positive externalities generating benefits to society. For example, when a hospital treats an indigent patient with a contagious disease, there are benefits to all individuals who might have caught the disease if the indigent individual had gone untreated. In this case, the hospital bears the direct costs of treatment, while individuals outside the hospital reap some of the benefits. Given that those benefits have a value to those individuals, society may be justified in taxing all individuals to subsidize care for the poor. Aside from issues related to morality or ethics, it may be directly beneficial to everyone to have taxes collected for that subsidy.

Managers of all health care organizations should be aware of the concept of externalities. In some cases, managers may need to be sensitive to the social costs that they are generating. At other times, it will be in the organization's interest to be able, if not to measure, then at least to identify the various external benefits it generates.

SUGGESTED READING

Baptist, A. 1987. A general approach to costing procedures in ancillary departments. *Topics in Health Care Financing* 13, no. 4:32–47.

Cleverley, W.O. 1989. Cost concepts and decision-making. In *Handbook of health care accounting and finance,* 2nd ed., ed. W.O. Cleverley, 99–116. Gaithersburg, Md.: Aspen Publishers, Inc.

Dieter, B. 1987. Determining the cost of emergency department services. *Hospital Cost Accounting Advisor* 2, no. 11:1, 5–6.

_____. 1987. Determining the cost of nursing services. *Hospital Cost Accounting Advisor* 2, no. 9:1, 5–7.

Finkler, S.A. 1986. Costing out the operating room: A case study. *Hospital Cost Accounting Advisor* 2, no. 2:1, 6–7.

_____. 1987. A microcosting approach. *Hospital Cost Accounting Advisor* 2, no. 12:1–4.

Hatoum, H.T., et al. 1988. Microcost analysis of the prescription dispensing process in an outpatient hospital pharmacy. *American Journal of Hospital Pharmacy* 45, no. 6:1328–1333.

Shafer, P., et al. 1987. Measuring nursing cost with patient acuity data. *Topics in Health Care Financing* 13, no. 4:20–31.

EXERCISES

QUESTIONS FOR DISCUSSION

1. True or false, and why: Clerks are always treated as indirect costs.
2. True or false: The cost objective is the budgeted cost that you are trying to achieve. Explain.
3. True or false: The relevant range refers to whether or not information is appropriate to a specific problem. Explain.
4. What are some things on which average cost depends?
5. Should short-term decisions be based on average or marginal costs? Why?
6. Is cross-subsidization of costs an aberration, or will it exist frequently?
7. Give an example of a joint cost (other than those suggested in the chapter).
8. Consider Applications 2-2 and 2-3. What underlying theme do they have in common?

Note: Solutions to the Exercises can be found in Appendix A.

PROBLEMS

1. Consider Applications 2-1 and 2-2. Select another department of a health care organization, and develop a departmental approach to costing for that department, similar to that used in those articles.
2. Consider Application 2-3. Select another area for a health care organization, and describe the various parts of a product costing oriented data collection.
3. Refer to Application 2-4. Use the acuity levels and hours of care for each acuity level as described in that reading. However, assume that total nursing costs were $167,744, and that there were the following number of patient days at each level:

Level	Patient Days
1	120
2	170
3	300
4	170
5	50

If a DRG 174 patient on average has a length of stay of 5 days, with 2 days at Level 1, and 1 day each at Levels 2, 3, and 4, what would be the nursing cost for a patient in that DRG?

Application 2-1

The Identification of Surgical Services Costs

*Bryan B. Dieter, BA, is currently President
of The Decision Support Group, Inc.,
Pasadena, California.*

The Surgery Department is generally one of the hospital's highest revenue-producing areas and also one of the most difficult in which to determine service-level costs. The services provided vary greatly depending upon each patient's condition, the surgeon's preferences, the hospital and surgery director's policies, and the anesthesiologist's practices. All of these factors can also impact upon the cost of providing services to each patient.

The most important mechanism for accurately identifying costs is a well-defined and representative Charge Description Master (CDM). The CDM should accurately reflect the resources utilized and the cost of services provided. It should be specific enough to promote equitable patient charges, yet not too cumbersome to use.

We will therefore begin with a review of an effective CDM. We aren't advocating this as the only acceptable methodology, but the charge structure discussed in this article has been implemented very successfully in a number of hospitals. More importantly, the charge structure and cost accounting methodology discussed can be applied in determining service-level costs in any well-defined CDM.

Source: Reprinted from Bryan B. Dieter, "The Identification of Surgical Services Costs," *Hospital Cost Accounting Advisor,* Vol. 2, No. 8, January 1987, pp. 1–5. Copyright 1987, Aspen Publishers, Inc.

THE CHARGE DESCRIPTION MASTER

In the past, charge structures for surgical services have been poor and frequently did not accurately represent resource utilization. Often, charges were grouped into gross categories, were generated through a charge-explosion system, or had no incremental time or acuity designations. A well-designed surgical services charge system should include

- acuity-related base and incremental time charges
- tray charges
- capital equipment charges
- suture and patient chargeable supply charges
- inpatient and outpatient designations

We will discuss the direct costing of these classifications of charges followed by various suggestions for allocating remaining direct and indirect expenses.

ESTABLISHING ACUITY-BASED CHARGES

In surgery, the acuity-related charges are not necessarily designed to reflect a patient's actual physical condition, but rather the acuity of the case from the standpoint of the surgery department itself—namely, how many and what type of staff are involved in the case and for how long. An example of acuity-related charges follows:

- Level 1—Base 15 Min. (1 RN for up to 15 min.)
- Level 1—Ea Add Min. (1 RN for each minute over 15)
- Level 2—Base 30 Min. (1 RN & 1 technician for up to 30 min.)
- Level 2—Ea Add 5 Min. (1 RN & 1 technician for each 5 min. over 30)
- Level 3—Base 1 Hour (2 RNs for up to 1 hour)
- Level 3—Ea Add 5 Min. (2 RNs for each 5 min. over 1 hour)
- Level 4—Base 1 Hour (2 RNs & 1 technician for up to 1 hour)
- Level 4—Ea Add 5 Min. (2 RNs & 1 technician for each 5 min. over 1 hour)
- Emergency Surgery—Base 2 Hours (2 RNs for up to 2 hours)
- Emergency Surgery—Ea Add 15 Min. (2 RNs for each 15 min. over 2 hours)
- Circulating RN—Each 5 Min. (1 RN for 5 min.)

In determining the base charges that would be most appropriate for your department, review your general staffing practices. The base charges that you establish should be related to your usual staff assignments. You may have as few as two or three levels, or up to ten or 12 depending upon your staffing patterns/requirements. The time designations (15 min., 30 min., 1 hour) associated with the base charges should reflect the mode, or the most frequent amount of time, for a case with that number of staff. A log or a record review will help determine what the base levels should be.

The incremental time charges are intended to account for those cases which exceed the mode. The emergency charge is designed to capture the expense for "on-call" and the pay differential for call-back. The base time for the emer-

gency surgery is usually set at a time which the staff may be guaranteed by contract if they are called in. If there is no guaranteed paid time for call-back, then a shorter base time may be appropriate for your hospital. You may encounter a situation in which your staff is called in for a procedure which takes only 20 minutes. However, the actual expense to the hospital is still for two RNs for two hours at time and a half. The charge structure should be able to reflect this actual cost. The 5-minute circulating charges are established for those instances when an additional nurse is required for only a limited portion of the procedure, perhaps to get the case started, or at a particularly difficult point in the procedure. This charge should be assessed only for the time actually spent by that nurse preparing for or assisting in the case.

These charges would account for the majority of the variable departmental labor per procedure. Additionally, a factor should be added to each base charge for turnaround functions related to opening up a room, cleaning up after a procedure, moving equipment, etc. These times could be determined from running a room log or from your productivity system if your hospital has one.

To determine the actual standard cost for each of your types of labor for each of your acuity levels, you could use the following formula (illustrated using Level 1 Base Charge):

Base Time 15 Min. + Turnaround Time 10 Min.	Number of Staff	Labor Cost/Hour	Standard Labor Cost
25 Min. ×	1 ×	$12.00 =	$5.00

For the purposes of cost accounting, it will be necessary to retrospectively estimate service volumes for the newly created charges. The easiest way to do this is to use work sampling. Select cases randomly from your surgery log book. You should select cases only from the period of time you have established as your base period for the cost accounting information. With the cases you select at random, you should assign each of them an acuity-based charge under the new CDM and the additional incremental time charges which would be associated with each case (the difference between the time allowed for in the base charge and the actual case time). You would then determine what percent of the total case volume each of the acuity charges represents. Then, using your total volume of cases over this same period of time, you would estimate what your case volume would have been for each acuity level during this base period of time. You will also have developed the volumes for the incremental time charges in this process.

You have now determined your service volumes for each of the labor-related charges and the times for each type of labor to provide each of those services. The next step is to allocate your actual expenses for each type of labor based upon the standard labor cost you identified for each charge. This is accomplished by multiplying the standard cost for each charge (as determined in the example above) by its corresponding volume. To determine your actual cost of providing these services during your base period of time, you would use this total standard cost information as a basis for allocating the actual expense from the general ledger.

It is important that whenever possible in the cost accounting process you keep the cost categories (i.e., RNs, techs, film, sutures, clerks, aides, housekeeping) separate with their own standard costs. There is significant value in not grouping expenses for allocation purposes. The major advantage is in providing department managers with utilization variance reporting by specific expense type. When you allocate an actual expense based upon the standard cost determined for that specific type of expense, you greatly increase the value of the cost accounting information. One of the primary purposes of implementing a cost accounting system should be to promote cost control at the department management level. The more finite the cost categories are, the greater the opportunity the department manager has to identify *specific* expenses that require additional cost containment efforts.

CAPITAL EQUIPMENT CHARGES

Capital equipment charges should be established for those major (as determined by cost) pieces of equipment that are used only for specific procedures. Examples include monitors, special lighting, scopes, saws, drills, and special tables. You should begin your determination of which pieces of equipment require charges by obtaining a copy of the department's capital assets report and identifying the use of each piece of equipment. This will also provide an opportunity to verify the listing and to correct or modify it as needed.

If your department hasn't used capital equipment charges in the past, you will need to have the surgery staff project as accurately as possible the service volumes for each of the charges you have established. The cost per use for these pieces of equipment is determined by dividing the depreciation of the equipment by the number of projected uses for the same period of time. Pieces of equipment which could be used interchangeably should be grouped together and one cost per use determined for the group. (See Table 2-1-1.)

Maintenance contract costs should be identified with the capital equipment the contracts are intended to cover. The costs for these contracts should be determined using the same methodology as for the capital equipment. They would then become a part of the cost for the capital equipment charge.

Table 2-1-1 Determining Monitor w/Recorder Capital Equipment Cost/Use

Number	Description	Annual Depreciation Cost	Annual Usage	Cost/ Use
15862	Cardiac Monitor	$1,100		
15863	Cardiac Monitor	1,100		
15866	Cardiac Monitor	1,100		
17415	Cardiac Monitor	1,260		
15881	Recorder	900		
15882	Recorder	900		
15883	Recorder	900		
		$7,260	2,500	$2.90

TRAY CHARGES

Determining the costs of trays is the most time-consuming and difficult task in identifying your surgery costs per charge. The concept is actually fairly simple: determine the replacement cost of the tray, multiply by the total number of that type of tray, divide by its expected life, and then divide by the anticipated number of times that tray would be used. The difficulty is in determining the replacement cost of the tray. Having spent many, many, many hours flipping through instrument catalogues, I've sworn never to undertake this venture again. A Kelly clamp is not *just* a Kelly clamp. It is certainly best left to the surgery staff, at least to identify catalogue numbers, so you just have to look up the prices.

Some may question the need to develop capital equipment and tray charges and argue for keeping the cost buried as an "other" expense. Yet, it makes a substantial difference in the identified cost for the acuity levels as well as in your review of costs by surgeon for providing each of your various surgical cases. All surgeons certainly do not use the same resources when performing similar cases. For apparently similar cases one surgeon may take longer and use a varying number and type of staff in addition to different equipment and supplies (chargeable and nonchargeable) and may request special and more expensive trays. If this information is buried in your "procedure based" charge system, you will not have the capability to accurately determine costs or provide *meaningful* product-line and physician-cost analysis.

SUPPLY COSTS

Patient-chargeable supplies are costed out at their actual purchase price. Any labor required will be accounted for in the acuity charges. In certain cost accounting systems, such as Hospital Cost Consultant's (HCC), you have the capability to reference these costs directly from your materials management system. This provides you with a much less maintenance intensive system.

Nonchargeable supplies should also have standards developed for their normal use. Items such as caps, gowns, shoe covers, masks, gloves, etc., can all be identified in relation to the acuity-based charges. Other nonchargeable supplies, not directly accounted for as a "standard" cost, are allocated to the acuity-related charges based upon the standard supply usage which was identified. In studies I have completed, a direct correlation has consistently been identified between a procedure's acuity level and length and its utilization of nonchargeable supplies.

OTHER DIRECT COSTS

You may wish to continue on and develop standards for other types of direct expenses. If so, it is worth the effort in most cases, since there truly can be benefits realized from continuing on to greater levels of detail, especially in the area of cost containment. However, it does require additional time, which many hospital staffs do not seem to have enough of lately. That brings us to "What happens with the other departmental costs?"

These costs, from the general ledger, need to be allocated to the procedures based upon a cost/benefit relationship. For example, if management labor is perceived as an expense from which all patients benefit equally, then this cost can be reasonably allocated only to each base charge. For monitoring purposes, you may also wish to keep these expenses separate from one another. This would give you the capability to monitor these "fixed" expenses on a per-procedure basis for the purpose of trend analysis and to identify possible methods of reducing your fixed expenses on a per-use basis.

INDIRECT EXPENSES

Indirect expenses are often grossly overlooked in determining procedure-level costs, primarily because most of the cost accounting systems available are inadequate in their ability to handle indirect costs. Indirect expenses will, in most cases, increase the total departmental expenses 40 to 110 percent over their direct general ledger costs. Grouping these expenses together and allocating them based upon one or two statistics only dilutes the accuracy of the information developed for your direct departmental expenses.

Some systems, such as the HCC System, allow for the development of standards for indirect as well as direct expenses. The HCC System also allows indirect expenses to be stepped down by natural classification of expense and does not require that each indirect department's expenses be stepped down in the same step.

In the surgery department this is helpful, since it allows the hospital to establish standard costs for housekeeping labor to turn around rooms after the surgical procedures, and even to develop standards for the specific housekeeping supplies that are used. It also allows you to allocate the other indirect costs of surgery based upon thousands of potential allocation statistics to improve the accuracy of the information. Some other examples include

- Personnel   The total labor time per charge
- MIS   Equally to each charge
- Building Maint.   Minutes per case
- Administration   Equally to each patient in base charge
- Admitting   Inpatient cases only
- OP Registration   Ambulatory cases only
- Materials Mgmt/   Number or cost of
  Purchasing   supplies

A future article in this series will focus specifically on the development of standards for indirect costs.

THE IMPORTANCE OF ACCURATE DATA

This article was intended to provide the reader with some thoughts on alternative methods of developing accurate procedure-level cost information. This data base of information will come to play an increasingly important role in the day-to-day operations of the hospital. If properly implemented, accurate cost accounting data can directly help you with management decisions intended to improve the financial performance of your hospital. It can also be very misleading if the information is inaccurate.

Many hospital management teams are implementing cost accounting in their hospitals to support product line and DRG analysis. That is indeed a very important use for the information, but too often too little attention is paid to how the building blocks of this aggregate information are developed. The adage "garbage in, garbage out" certainly applies to hospital cost accounting systems and methodologies. I am attempting in this series to provide *Hospital Cost Accounting Advisor* readers with some methods for developing more meaningful management tools. I also hope to encourage hospitals to step beyond the "good enough" attitude and establish more aggressive systems and data bases.

Application 2-2

Identifying Radiology Procedure Costs

Bryan B. Dieter, BA, is currently President
of The Decision Support Group, Inc.,
Pasadena, California

The Diagnostic Radiology Services Department is one of the more straightforward departments for identifying procedure level costs. As has been discussed in the preceding articles in this series, the initial focal point of the cost accounting process should be the Charge Description Master (CDM). The CDM should be critically reviewed to determine if your chargeable items *actually* reflect the resources utilized in providing each of your hospital's services.

This article is the fourth in a series intended to assist those involved in the hospital cost accounting process with determining procedure level costs in the major departments of the hospital. Our intent is also to promote discussion on the validity of the hospital's current CDM and to determine whether it is acceptable for what the hospital is attempting to accomplish. Do the CDM and the existing cost accounting methodologies support the accurate determination of costs and provide a sound basis for the analysis of your hospital's business?

For most hospitals, the CDM for Radiology Services is generally representative of the costs

incurred in providing procedures. Some key items to look for in your CDM include:

- *Charges for additional views.* The CDM should have charges to capture the cost of additional views of the same area. This does not include retakes of an original shot, but additional views to assist in the medical assessment of the patient.

- *Portable charge.* A charge should be available to capture the additional cost of procedures performed outside of the department. Charges should also be established for procedures performed in Surgery, since the resources for surgical x-rays differ from those for other departments.

- *Special equipment procedure charges.* If a particular procedure can be performed using two separate sets of equipment, and the rationale for using one rather than the other is medical, then you may wish to establish separate charges for the two sets of equipment. This will assist in product line analysis, especially if you plan on monitoring by physician. This additional information will support the analysis of physicians who routinely request more costly equipment.

CAPITAL EQUIPMENT USAGE

Identifying the cost of capital equipment per procedure is generally the most difficult part of cost accounting in the radiology department. At first this would appear to be the easiest process, not the most difficult. All that would seem to be necessary is to identify the depreciation of each piece of equipment for a given period of time and to divide by the volume of procedures provided in that period. The problem arises in matching procedures performed to the equipment actually used. As you go through this process, you will encounter many procedures that can be done in a number of rooms using different pieces of equipment.

There are a couple of ways that equipment can be tied to procedures. The most accurate is to begin with the capital assets listing and to identify for each piece of equipment which procedures, and what percentage of those procedures, are performed using that equipment. This tends to be a very tedious task and, while it does result in more accurate information, requires a labor-intensive effort.

The more common approach is to cost out the capital equipment of each radiology "room" and then to identify which procedures, and what percentage of each of these procedures, are performed in each room. This method is simpler than costing out each piece of equipment, but does sacrifice accuracy. Your decision to employ either method or a combination of them will depend primarily on the resources you have available to dedicate to the cost accounting process.

LABOR COSTS

The labor times to provide each of your chargeable procedures will generally come from your productivity management system. If you do not currently have productivity standards, a good starting point is your radiology department manager's estimates, industry standards (such as the ARA's), or a combination of multiple sources. It would be beneficial to work toward the development of more accurate man-agement engineered standards or studied labor times, preferably at the task level and staff level for each procedure. This provides the hospital with a more accurate basis for assessing costs. The detail also greatly improves the standards maintenance process by providing a more comprehensive review of the standards.

The labor standards are generally related to the time for the radiology tech to perform each procedure. To derive the standard cost, this time will be multiplied by the hourly rate for the techs. This will also become the basis for the allocation of the actual cost for technician labor. In every case, the actual departmental expenses should be allocated to the procedures based upon the standard cost identified. This methodology supports meaningful cost variance analysis.

Too many hospitals determine the standard cost for a particular expense, subtract that cost from the actual, and consider the difference another direct cost. This amount is then allocated to the procedures based on some other statistic. It doesn't make a lot of sense to spend the time to do standard costing and not use that as the basis to allocate the actual cost.

Often a relationship can also be identified between variable clerical staff functions and each of the procedures. In this case, the clerical variable labor cost should be allocated based upon the variable standard, and the fixed clerical labor cost will usually be allocated to each procedure equally. The department manager's cost is also allocated to each procedure equally, unless an actual and more accurate relationship can be identified.

SUPPLIES

Most of the general supplies used to provide radiology procedures are generally low cost, but should be identified as part of the resource utilization profile. However, the cost of the supplies to process the films (fixer, developer, etc.) are often substantial and should be measured. Often there are also office supplies which can be identified at the procedure level, for example, a jacket for the films, some forms, etc. All of these identified costs should be used as a basis to allocate their respective actual costs.

FILMS

Film costs are identified by size and number used per procedure. Some machines also use nondisposable cassettes and a cost per use should be determined for these. It is important to keep in mind the retake percentage. The department maintains statistics on the percentage of times that each of the x-rays is retaken. This percentage should be built into the standard film usage for each procedure. For example, if a procedure uses one 8 x 10 film and has a 5 percent retake factor, the standard film usage would be 1.05 films.

INDIRECT COSTS

The allocation of the indirect (overhead) costs to the departmental procedures is almost as important as the identification of the direct cost components. The emphasis in cost accounting is on determining a cost/benefit relationship between each chargeable item and each direct *and* indirect cost. That relationship is often more easily quantified for the direct departmental costs than for the indirects. However, standard costing and variable allocation statistics can be developed and applied for the allocation of the indirect costs. For example, benefits cost can be allocated to the procedures based upon the identified labor cost; purchasing and storeroom on identified supply cost or number of items; personnel on identified labor time; laundry and linen on a linen use study; part of housekeeping to the rooms based upon the actual time to clean each room, and the remainder can be allocated to each procedure equally.

These are only a few suggestions of possible allocation bases for identifying your indirect departmental costs at the procedure level. The cost accounting system that you use should have the capability to allow almost limitless standard cost or statistical basis development for allocating indirect departmental costs to the procedures.

Application 2-3

Cost Finding for High-Technology, High-Cost Services: Current Practice and a Possible Alternative

Steven A. Finkler, PhD, CPA

Economic theory indicates that the cost of producing a unit of a product or service will change as the volume produced changes. In large part this results from the sharing of the resources required in a set amount for production at any volume. In hospitals these "fixed costs" remain the same regardless of the number of patients treated, whereas according to economic theory the more patients, the less fixed cost any patient must bear.

In a free market environment a producer would be forced to cease production of any product produced at an uneconomically low volume. Such production would not spread fixed costs sufficiently and would therefore result in a high average cost. Producers operating at a sufficiently large volume would have lower unit costs, and therefore be able to undersell the low-volume, high-cost producers. Rather than cease business completely, a producer, knowing the average costs were high, could just stop producing a product.

In hospitals, cost reimbursement has somewhat restricted this free market mechanism. A hospital producing a low volume of product receives a higher price (reimbursement) and is thus enabled to keep producing the product inefficiently. The market mechanism does not force the hospital to produce at efficient volumes or cease production.

Hospital administrators and regulators alike are well aware of this, and have tried diligently to keep utilization of facilities high. Nevertheless, there have been persistent reports of underutilized facilities and excessive duplication of highly sophisticated, high-cost technology at too many hospitals.

PARADOX EXPLAINED

How does this apparent paradox arise? Apparently physicians have been quite willing to attempt to maximize utilization of facilities that they have. However, they have been reluctant to pass by some new technologies simply because there is a relatively low demand for them. Certainly there are medical justifications for these actions. Physicians would like the hospitals they are affiliated with to offer the highest possible quality of care, and bringing in new technology raises the quality of care.

In addition, the cost analysis of new technology has centered on direct cost and a "can we afford it" approach. Rather than look at the total

Source: Reprinted from Steven A. Finkler, "Cost Finding for High-Technology, High-Cost Services: Current Practice and a Possible Alternative," *Health Care Management Review,* Summer 1980, pp. 17–29. Copyright 1980, Aspen Publishers, Inc.

additional cost a hospital will incur in each department if a new program is added, the analysis typically looks at the new capital outlays. Capital costs, however, are but a small fraction of the overall costs of a hospital. Furthermore, the question of "can we afford it" depends a lot on who pays. Currently, 94 percent of hospital costs are paid by third party payers on cost-reimbursement systems.[1] The costs *can* be passed on to these third party payers, so the answer to the affordability question is often yes, irrespective of the potential demand for the service at that hospital.

As a result, hospitals offer high-technology, high-cost services at widely varying levels of utilization. Thus a major cause of different hospitals having different costs for the same service is simply the degree to which fixed costs are spread across patients.

Regulatory agencies have tried to combat the problem of inefficient production with a variety of flexible charging schedules based on different patient types. The aim of this approach is to cause hospitals to lose money on services offered inefficiently. Those hospitals would either have to become efficient or else cease production of the product to avoid such losses. The most recent program of that type is a project being tried in New Jersey that uses prospective reimbursement based on diagnosis-related groups.

A major problem these approaches have had is that they focus on prospective reimbursement of costs without in-depth investigation of appropriate cost data. Frequently, an average of charges made by hospitals for treatment of a patient type is used as the basis for the reimbursement rate for that patient type. Since charges are based on costs, this averaging should result in some average or reasonable cost for offering the service. However, cross-subsidizations within the hospital cost-finding system may prevent this method from reflecting the true economic costs of the patient type.

Cross-subsidies within the accounting system result from simplifications made to reduce the bookkeeping costs of data collection. The cost information produced is adequate for the uses for which the cost-finding system was designed.

However, there are problems when the data are used to determine a uniform cost per patient for a specific service at different hospitals with different levels of utilization. To improve hospital efficiency, regulators need estimates that give the cost per patient for a service at alternative volumes of production, based on economic resources utilized specifically for that service.

TWO APPROACHES TO HOSPITAL COST FINDING

Hospitals use cost information to establish rates, apply for cost-based reimbursement, and comply with governmental and hospital association reporting requirements. This has resulted in the compilation of different types of information than that used by most industries. However, current accounting literature has emphasized that there is not one "true" cost that can be measured;[2] different measures of cost are appropriate for different needs. Nevertheless, hospital information requirements have stressed cost-finding methods for both the control of departmental costs and external reporting needs, with only limited cost-finding efforts concerning economic resource costs by patient type.

Horizontal Cost Finding

The principal hospital form of cost finding will be referred to here as a "horizontal" system. The primary focus of such a system is on departmental costs.

Because the hospital is typically reimbursed based on the costs a patient incurs in various departments, rather than on the patient type, the costs of intermediate or departmental products are measured. (See Figure 2-3-1.) Even when attempts are made to reimburse hospitals based on patient type, the basis of the reimbursement is some averaging of the costs previously determined by this intermediate, product-oriented method. Thus hospital administrators would know the cost of the radiology or dietary departments or even the cost per X-ray or per meal served, but they do not readily know the total

HOSPITAL INDUSTRY

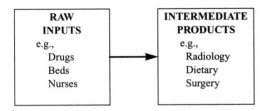

Figure 2-3-1 Horizontal Structure

cost impact of offering a specific high-cost, high-technology service. The administrators have no strong need for that information.

Under the horizontal system the cost for a final product (i.e., the patient treated) is derived by adding charges from each department for units of service the patient consumed from each department. Thus a typical chest X-ray would be charged at the same rate to a pneumonia, lung cancer or heart surgery patient, assuming the procedures required are the same in each case. No accounting is made of the fact that the addition of a heart surgery program may have increased X-ray volume to the point that an additional X-ray machine was purchased. The fixed cost of the additional machine is charged in equal shares to all patients having chest X-rays, not simply to the heart surgery patients. This method of cost finding would certainly pose a problem if a hospital must decide whether or not to offer a heart surgery program. That program should bear the cost of the new machine, a cost that would not otherwise have been incurred.

To a physician or hospital administrator, it is logical and natural to think of hospital products in terms of radiology and dietary because they are the traditional "cost centers" of the hospital. However, the physicians and administrators are well aware that they are not attempting to produce X-rays, but rather to treat a patient for an ailment.

Vertical Cost Finding

In contrast to horizontal cost finding, a vertical cost-finding system is oriented toward the cost of the final products or outputs. For exam-

ple, in an automobile factory, a vertical cost system would center on the car model. Different car models would use different raw material resources or inputs, and different costs would be accumulated for each model or final product. (See Figure 2-3-2.) Thus the auto manufacturer would know the cost of Model A, Model B and Model C. In the case of the hospital, a vertical orientation would lead to a greater focus on the costs for the type of patient treated.

Consider what the effect of horizontal cost finding would be on the auto manufacturer. It would cause him or her to think of costs in terms of radiator production or fender molding without respect to the car model for which the radiator is produced or the fender molded. The result would be an auto manufacturer well versed in the total cost of all radiators and fenders, and even the average cost of a radiator or fender.

However, the manufacturer would not know the difference in cost between a radiator for the Model A car and one for the Model B car. Such

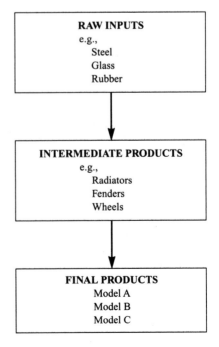

Figure 2-3-2 Vertical Structure

information is more readily provided by vertical cost finding. As a result of the lack of information imposed by the horizontal cost finding system, there would have to be substantial cross-subsidization between the different model cars when their costs were determined.

Comparing Two Cost-Finding Methods

Tables 2-3-1 and 2-3-2 serve to clarify further the distinction between vertical and horizontal cost finding. (All numbers in these and subsequent tables and figures are used for illustrative purposes and are not intended to represent actual costs.) Table 2-3-1 demonstrates the final product orientation of the vertical cost-finding structure. The cost of each final product is determined separately as a sum of the raw inputs utilized in its production. Note that inputs are calculated on a per car or model basis, and differ in cost for each model.

This contrasts with the horizontal cost-finding system depicted in Table 2-3-2. Note that the horizontal orientation is toward the total cost per month of each revenue center. From this the

hospital can calculate an average cost per unit of intermediate product (e.g., cost per meal served). The direct connection between inputs and final outputs or products is lost, although total overall costs of the hospital would be the same whether vertical or horizontal cost finding is used.

The examples posed by Tables 2-3-1 and 2-3-2 represent two hypothetical extremes. The vertical system is not likely to be able to give complete information about each car model. Allocations of joint costs may still be made in some arbitrary fashion. Similarly, the horizontal system will likely be adjusted for products which consume an inordinately weighted share of a department's economic resources.

However, these examples are not without some relevance. Consider the method by which operating room (surgery cost center) costs are assigned to patients. Total costs and total operating minutes are determined for the surgery center and an average cost per minute is calculated. Any procedure requiring 60 minutes is considered to be twice as expensive as a 30-minute procedure. Such a method ignores the possibility that there may be short procedures requiring expensive, sophisticated equipment and long

Table 2-3-1 Vertical Cost-Finding

| | Auto Industry | | |
| | Final Products | | |
Intermediate Products and Raw Inputs per Car	Model A	Model B	Model C
Radiator			
Labor	$ 20	$ 15	$ 30
Steel	20	18	33
Hoses	3	2	4
Total	$ 43	$ 35	$ 67
Engine			
Labor	300	250	500
Steel	860	750	990
Spark plugs	5	4	6
Total	1,165	1,004	1,496
Body			
Labor	400	300	600
Plastic	50	40	80
Metal	500	400	700
Total	950	740	1,380
Total Cost by Model	$2,158	$1,779	$2,943

Table 2-3-2 Horizontal Cost-Finding

	Raw Inputs for Month				*Intermediate Product Total Monthly Cost*
Intermediate Products	*Labor*	*Equipment*	*Supplies*	*Allocation**	
Radiology	$40,000	$20,000	$ 5,000	$3,000	$ 68,000
Dietary	10,000	2,000	60,000	4,000	$ 76,000
Surgery	80,000	30,000	10,000	8,000	$128,000

*Cost allocation from nonrevenue cost centers.

procedures which use much less costly resources. The horizontal cost-finding system cannot eliminate cross-subsidization because of the general averaging procedures which are used to find intermediate product costs, such as surgery minutes. An alternative cost-finding system, such as vertical cost-finding, would be needed to uncover the hospital's cost of offering the high-technology, high-cost service.

VERTICAL COST FINDING FOR A NEW PROGRAM

Vertical cost finding can be used for calculating the cost to the hospital of a specific new program or a specialized elective service, such as open-heart surgery. Open-heart surgery is used as the example here for two reasons. First, it emphasizes that the point of focus in vertical cost finding is the entire service. A hospital administration must decide whether or not to offer heart surgery rather than whether or not to have a heart bypass pump. Traditional hospital cost finding might point out only that the heart pump is a major expense of the surgery cost center. However, the surgery department would have neither the knowledge of the overall costs of treating heart surgery patients, nor the authority to make decisions regarding whether or not heart surgery should be performed. By looking at the costs of the entire heart surgery program, the administration can make a deci-

sion regarding the cost effectiveness of offering heart surgery based on the knowledge of its economic effect on the entire hospital.

The second reason that open-heart surgery is used as an example is that a new program or service is the prime target for an early battle between regulators and health care providers over appropriate cost data. Replacement of a worn-out X-ray machine is likely to receive rapid regulatory approval, since all short-term acute-care hospitals need a radiology department. Offering a new program, such as open-heart surgery, is likely to draw much greater public scrutiny regarding its cost effectiveness. Offering all elective services is not essential for the short-term, acute-care hospital to fulfill its basic role.

Note, however, that there are three major uses for the information that cost accounting can provide: (1) decision making, (2) budgeting and (3) control. The information needed for each of these tasks differs. In the open-heart surgery example only information needed for decision making is provided.

Furthermore, the value of the open-heart surgery program is not assessed, but its cost effectiveness for a given hospital is. Thus it may be found in the following example that any given number of heart surgeries should be produced at more or fewer hospitals. This article does not deal with the preferability of medical versus surgical treatment for heart disease.

Preliminary Steps of Vertical Cost Finding

Stated briefly, the problem is—What costs would a hospital incur if it has a program such as open-heart surgery, which it would not incur if it did not offer that service? In economic terms, what is needed is the marginal cost to the hospital of the entire heart surgery program and the cost for the specific volume of patients expected. Thus vertical cost finding will provide cost information appropriate to the anticipated utilization of heart surgery facilities.

The first step in vertical cost finding is to determine the exact production process for the program under consideration. The costs for a specific volume can be determined once the production process and input requirements are fully understood. It is possible, however, that the hospital will not know the exact volume of heart surgery procedures it will perform each year. It may want to know the costs for a wide range of volumes, in order to see at what level of utilization it becomes economical to offer a service. Governmental regulations, medical standards, experience of administrators and sampling techniques must be used to determine an estimate of input requirements at differing volumes.

To find the resource requirements of a program, the hospital must determine which departments come into direct contact with the program's patients. The flowchart in Figure 2-3-3 follows the patient through the hospital from admission to discharge. The flowchart serves as a basis to ensure inclusion of all costs. It includes patient movement, patient contact with hospital personnel and indirect inputs such as various overhead cost centers. Note that the latter is referred to as days of hospitalization or "routine care." This category includes a variety of items from heat and light to secretarial pools, record-keeping and parking lot maintenance. All factors of hospital operation must be considered for the effect the program would have on them.

Based on the flowchart, the cost elements of offering heart surgery might be broken down into the following groups: anesthesia, blood processing, cardiac catheterization, cardiac surgery intensive care unit, dietary, ECG [electrocardio-gram], inhalation therapy, laboratory, linens, medications, medical/surgical hospital beds, operating room equipment and supplies, operating room personnel, overhead and radiology.

Identification of Input Factors

Once such groupings are identified for which the addition, deletion or change in volume of the elective program would affect factors of production (resource utilization), all such input factors are identified. This identification of input requirement variation with volume is a crucial phase of the data collection. The input-output relationships for hospital programs are not well known. Ultimately, however, each input is the responsibility of some individual. These individuals should be called upon to identify the inputs that are required for each heart surgery patient and the amount of each input needed at different volumes.

The inputs must be identified as fixed or variable. As discussed earlier, this is a crucial factor in cost finding. Fixed inputs will typically be the physical environment (hospital rooms and surgery suites, etc.) and equipment required. Variable inputs will be supplies consumed by each patient, such as meals and medications. Some inputs will be semifixed. That is, they will be fixed for a given range of output, but when that range is exceeded, more of the input is needed.

It is relatively simple to calculate the program costs for an ongoing program at a specific volume because all inputs can be observed. In planning a new program or considering volume changes in an ongoing program, hospitals must estimate semifixed costs because the actual range for an input may not be known. While in some cases these inputs have a well-known, technologically fixed capacity, in other cases individuals will have to assess the capacity of inputs based on their experience and expertise.

For example, the head of the linen department can assess the effect of a new program or a volume change in an existing program on the capacity of autoclave (linen sterilization)

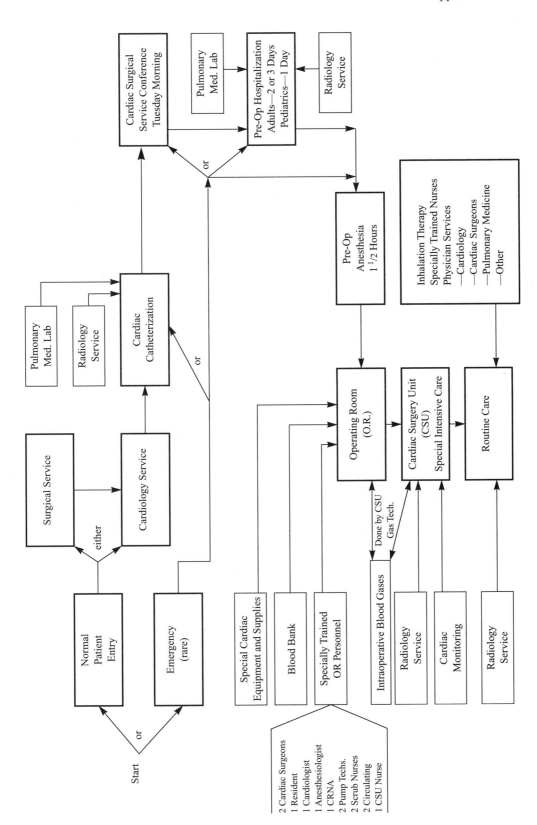

Figure 2-3-3 Cardiac Surgery Patient Flowchart

machines and the head of inhalation therapy can determine the capacity of respirator equipment.

Using the flowchart in Figure 2-3-3, the hospital administration can break the problem into manageable segments. For each cost element, the administration must determine what input requirements the addition of open-heart surgery places upon it. These input requirements should be divided into fixed, variable, and semifixed resources. The semifixed inputs must be identified for the volumes at which new increments are needed.

When the hospital administration determines input requirements, it is important that a systems approach be taken. That is, the administration should consider all inputs throughout the entire hospital system which might be affected by the program. These are called "relevant" costs. For instance, if offering heart surgery causes the capacity of the hospital's X-ray machine to be exceeded, then heart surgery must bear the entire cost of a new X-ray machine. Similarly, if the heart surgery program uses facilities that would otherwise be unused, there should be no cost associated with that use, since it is not a relevant cost for the analysis.

Once the input requirements are determined, their cost can be measured and the cost of heart surgery determined. However, the cost measurement can only be made after many conceptual issues are resolved. These issues include the distinction between use of long-run and short-run costs, historical versus replacement costs, treatment of overhead costs and discrete versus divisible labor inputs.

Cost Concepts

Long Run versus Short Run

The long run is defined as that period during which all factors of production can be adjusted for the desired volume of output. In the short run, plant and equipment are assumed to be set at a given level, and only certain operating expenses are assumed to be variable. (Actually, there is a continuum of intermediate "runs.")

For example, suppose a hospital decides to provide a program that requires 20 beds, and at the moment there are excess beds. In the short run, the extra cost of the service will include the staffing, but not the construction of the 20 beds. In the long run, new beds will have to be built if the hospital's overall volume for all services is growing. So the long-run cost of the elective product would have to include the entire cost of building the beds, because if the optional program were not offered, 20 fewer beds would have had to be constructed.

When a hospital determines whether long-run costs, short-run costs or those of some intermediate run are appropriate for use in an analysis, the key criterion is the time horizon of the decision's impact. If the decision is one that is expected to come up for review at frequent short-run intervals, an analysis of short-run costs may be adequate. Thus if a hospital is deciding the hours that a clinic should be open during the next month, the hospital would desire short-run costs. On the other hand, if the decision requires major capital expenditures and is the type that will only be made at long-term intervals, long-run costs are appropriate.

In the case of cost analysis regarding whether to add or delete a program such as heart surgery, major changes within the hospital are required to implement the decision. Once the decision is made, it is unlikely to be changed in the short run; it is intended to be a permanent decision. Thus the hospital considering offering heart surgery is interested in long-run costs.

Historical versus Replacement Costs

The accounting system records costs on a historical purchase price basis. Historical costs are generally used for reporting purposes outside of the hospital industry because such costs are considered to be objective and verifiable. Their use reduces the chance of tampering with data, and the user of the financial statements is thus protected from intentional misleading information about asset values. In periods of stable technology and no inflation, this would not result in serious distortions. However, in recent years there has been neither stable technology nor stable price levels.

Replacement cost tells what it would cost today to replace a building or a piece of equipment. If one views a program as a permanent part of the hospital product mix, then it is expected that equipment and buildings will have to be replaced as they wear out. Historical costs do not give information regarding how much it will cost to replace such facilities. While it is true that in the short run the hospital might be interested in only the cost of items to be replaced currently, for a long-run analysis the hospital must consider the cost of all assets utilized by a program since they will all have to be replaced at some time. Replacement costs are therefore more appropriate than historical costs for the open-heart surgery analysis.

Treatment of Joint or Overhead Costs

Joint costs represent a significant measurement problem. The current accounting techniques for hospitals treat this problem by allocating all overhead costs into the revenue-producing centers. Since such allocation procedures are arbitrary at best, they do not provide a good measure of the resources consumed by a specific program.

Fisher has noted that costs that are truly joint cannot be separated and assigned to the activities from which they arise. Since the hospital is interested in the economic cost consequences, arbitrary accounting allocations are inappropriate. Fisher gives an example of the joint cost problem when trying to assess the cost of a weapons system for the Defense Department:

> The operating costs of Headquarters, United States Air Force; the Air Force Academy; the Air Force Accounting and Finance Center; Headquarters, Air Force Systems Command; and the like, usually should not be allocated to Air Force weapon systems. These support activities are essentially independent of the Air Force's combat force mix. On the other hand, the costs of certain depot maintenance activities in the Air Force Logistics Command and of certain courses in the Air Training Command may be, and often are, appropriately identified as part of the incremental cost of a proposed weapon system.[3]

Similarly, for hospitals it is assumed that there is a basic mix of hospital products that require certain support facilities and personnel. None of these joint costs should be allocated to open-heart surgery in the sample analysis unless the amount of cost incurred changes because the heart surgery program is offered. This approach, if used for pricing all hospital products, would not allocate all costs and a loss would result. Here, however, the goal is not rate setting, but rather the determination of the incremental cost incurred by the hospital because it offers heart surgery. Thus for purposes of the vertical cost analysis, costs which would be incurred even if the service were not offered should not be considered part of the cost of the service under investigation, no matter how much the service utilizes those resources.

Divisibility of Labor Inputs

In general, personnel—including technicians, assistants and nurses—are cross-trained and can perform a number of functions. They can be shifted between tasks as needed. Labor inputs can generally be added or deleted in continuous increments as volume changes. Even though in fact there may be some discrete changes, one can gain a sufficiently close approximation using a smooth-change assumption.

In some cases, this is clearly inappropriate. For example, a heart-lung pump technician is a specialist whose duties may very well be clearly specified in a union contract. Such a technician might be idle when not assisting in open-heart surgeries, but will have to be paid during idle hours. In such cases, the technician is a dedicated resource and must be included as a large, discrete increment to costs. The same might be true to some extent for X-ray and medical supervisors, nurses, therapists, orderlies and some maintenance staff, because some of their functions do not change as volume increases. For example, the catheterization supervisor must regularly check the inventory of catheters regardless of annual patient volume.

Data Accumulation

Once the cost concepts are understood, the accumulation of data requires only a series of worksheets. Figure 2-3-4 presents the flow of such worksheets for open-heart surgery. For an understanding of the worksheets, follow Figure 2-3-4 starting with Worksheet A. Shown in Figure 2-3-5, this first worksheet is a diagram that plots the cost per patient in dollars on the vertical axis and the number of patients per year on the horizontal axes. In the heart surgery example, the sharp fall in the curve initially is due to the effect of spreading fixed costs over a greater number of patients. The slight jump in the curve results from the addition of semifixed inputs (primarily the addition of a second operating room and more intensive-care beds) at a volume of around 250 patients annually.

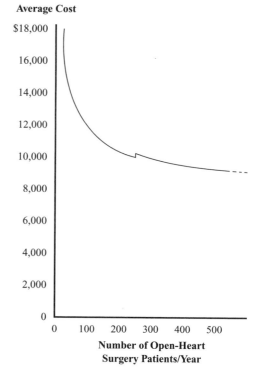

Figure 2-3-5 Worksheet A—Open-Heart Surgery, Cost per Patient at Different Volumes

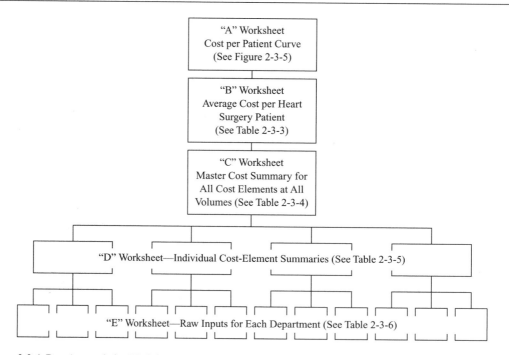

Figure 2-3-4 Data Accumulation Worksheets

Note that the curve in Figure 2-3-5 becomes very flat (horizontal) in the output range above 400 cases per year. This indicates that most economic savings from production at high volume are accomplished if at least 400 cases are treated each year. The curve will never become totally flat because some fixed inputs need not expand at all with volume, and the cost per patient of those inputs continues to decrease with volume. Eventually, however, these cost savings would be offset by such factors as travel cost and patient inconvenience, since large volume per center implies that fewer facilities at greater distances from each other would be needed to perform the heart surgery procedures. Patients would therefore have to travel farther to reach a center performing heart surgery procedures.

The source of the curve in Worksheet A is the average cost information from Worksheet B shown in Table 2-3-3. This worksheet is merely a summary table showing annual volumes and the average costs associated with those volumes. This information is taken directly from the last row in Worksheet C shown in Table 2-3-4. This worksheet is a summary by cost element and volume. For each possible volume of procedures, this worksheet records the cost from each cost element. These costs can be summed to give the total cost per heart surgery patient, given that a particular volume of such surgeries will take place.

The cost elements in Worksheet C are similar to currently used revenue centers. However,

Worksheets D and E (Tables 2-3-5 and 2-3-6) have accumulated data in such a way that each element's costs are related specifically to heart surgery. Furthermore, those costs are given for any desired volume of heart surgery.

Each row in Worksheet C comes from a cost-element summary in Worksheet D. Worksheet D cost-element summaries include equipment, nurses, supplies and construction costs. These costs are taken from individual Worksheet E tables. That is, there would be one Worksheet E table for each cost element's labor, another for each cost element's supplies, etc. The role of Worksheet E is to determine what raw inputs are needed, what the cost is per unit of input, whether the inputs are fixed or variable in nature, and what the costs of those inputs are at various volumes.

The flow of costs can be followed from one worksheet to another. For example, in Figure 2-3-5 the cost for each patient at a volume of 400 per year is slightly greater than $9,000. In Table 2-3-3 the cost is $9,177. This figure comes from the total of the 400 volume column in Table 2-3-4. And any cost element from Table 2-3-4, for example, operating room equipment and supplies, can be traced to Table 2-3-5. At a volume of 400, the cost per patient for this element is shown in Table 2-3-4 as being $935. In Table 2-3-5 this number is located in the totals column at a volume of 400. Note also in the totals column that costs do not consistently fall per patient as volume increases because of the addition of semifixed inputs at a volume of 250 patients. The supplies cost from Table 2-3-5 can similarly be traced from Table 2-3-6.

NEW PROBLEMS AND A NEW APPROACH

The currently practiced horizontal system of hospital cost finding has developed gradually over many years. Until now it has served as an adequate tool for the cost information needs that existed prior to the relatively recent severe inflation. But the continued rise of hospital costs, persistently greater than the rate of inflation, has created a need for a greater amount of cost find-

Table 2-3-3 Worksheet B—Average Cost per Heart Surgery Patient

Annual Patient Volume	Average Cost per Patient
50	$21,133
100	13,775
150	11,546
200	10,429
250	10,495
300	9,906
350	9,470
400	9,177
450	8,943
500	8,740

Table 2-3-4 Worksheet C—Master Cost Summary

	Average Cost Annual Cardiac Surgery Patient Volume									
Cost Element	50	100	150	200	250	300	350	400	450	500
Anesthesia equipment	$ 47	$ 33	$ 29	$ 25	$ 30	$ 28	$ 26	$ 25	$ 25	$ 24
Blood processing charges	325	325	325	325	325	325	325	325	325	325
Cardiac catheterization	1,813	1,242	1,074	994	943	908	880	857	842	826
Cardiac surgery unit	6,004	3,725	3,060	2,727	2,527	2,406	2,309	2,257	2,197	2,150
Dietary	96	96	96	96	96	96	96	96	96	96
ECG	5	5	5	5	5	5	5	5	5	5
Inhalation therapy	1,364	711	494	384	319	275	247	223	207	192
Laboratory	150	150	150	150	150	150	150	150	150	150
Linens	168	168	168	168	168	168	168	168	168	168
Medications	497	497	497	497	497	497	497	497	497	497
Med/surg hospital beds	1,116	1,116	1,116	1,116	1,116	1,116	1,116	1,116	1,116	1,116
Operating room equipment and supplies	1,374	1,083	985	935	1,020	983	956	935	919	906
Operating room personnel	6,923	3,840	2,880	2,412	2,691	2,380	2,156	2,001	1,891	1,792
Overhead	1,247	780	663	591	604	565	535	518	501	489
Radiology	4	4	4	4	4	4	4	4	4	4
Total	$21,133	$13,775	$11,546	$10,429	$10,495	$9,906	$9,470	$9,177	$8,943	$8,740

Table 2-3-5 Worksheet D—Operating Room Equipment and Supplies Cost Summary

Annual Patient Volume	Average Cost		
	Equipment	Supplies	Total
50	$584	$790	$1,374
100	293	790	1,083
150	195	790	985
200	145	790	935
250	230	790	1,020
300	193	790	983
350	166	790	956
400	145	790	935
450	129	790	919
500	116	790	906

Table 2-3-6 Worksheet E—Operating Room Supplies

Item	Unit Cost	Quantity	Cost
Sm. steri-drape	$ .66	3	$ 1.98
Lg. steri-drape	1.02	4	4.08
2 oz. irrig. bulb syringe	.46	3	1.38
Urine-meter	1.93	1	1.93
Foley	3.50	1	3.50
5 cc syringes	.08	3	.24
10 cc syringes	.09	3	.27
Needles—18 regular	.43	3	1.29
22 regular	.43	1	.43
22 spinal	.60	1	.60
19 spinal	.60	1	.60
Under H_2O drainage set	6.51	2	13.02
Magnet needle mat	.49	4	1.96
5705-36 argyle chest tubes	2.80	2	5.60
Curity pack	1.40	1	1.40
K 75 threeway stop cock	.20	2	.40
V-5404 McGan IV extension tubing	1.07	2	2.14
Salem sump tube	.98	1	.98
W1990 McGan additive cap	.23	2	.46
Surgical patties (cotton-aids)	26.00	1	26.00
Urine bag 950-18-19 cystie set	1.22	1	1.22
Etc.			720.52
Total			$790.00

ing based on program or product costs. To meet the demands of health systems agencies and to make cost-effective decisions regarding whether it is socially desirable to offer a program or product, today's hospital administrator needs a more vertically or program-oriented cost system than is currently in use.

NOTES

1. Gibson, R.M. and Fisher, C.R. "National Health Expenditures, Fiscal Year 1977." *Social Security Bulletin* 41:7 (July 1978) p. 7.
2. Demski, J.S. and Feltham, G.A. *Cost Determination: A Conceptual Approach* (Ames, Iowa: Iowa State University Press 1976).
3. Fisher, G.H. *Cost Considerations in Systems Analysis* (New York: American Elsevier, 1971) p. 73.

Application 2-4

Costing Out Nursing Services

Steven A. Finkler, PhD, CPA

As the nursing shortage has continued to persist, growing attention has been focused on the issue of the cost to provide nursing services to hospital patients.

The nursing shortage itself is curious in that it is not caused by a decrease in the number of available nurses. Actually there are more, not fewer, nurses working in hospitals than there were five or ten years ago. However, during that time period the demand for nursing care hours per patient day has increased—an increase that is not particularly surprising. One factor leading us in this direction is DRGs [diagnosis-related groups]. With DRGs having the impact of shortening length of stay, each day patients are in hospitals they tend to be sicker and require more care.

However, the nursing shortage has created havoc in many hospitals. There are instances in which the use of agency nurses has caused nursing departments to exceed their budgets by 20, 50, or even 100 percent. In this environment, there is clearly a need for improved approaches to finding the cost of nursing care for different types of patients.

Source: Reprinted from Steven A. Finkler, "Costing Out Nursing Services," *Hospital Cost Management and Accounting,* Vol. 1, No. 12, March 1990, pp. 1–5. Copyright 1990, Aspen Publishers, Inc.

WHY ARE CURRENT COSTING APPROACHES WEAK?

The essence of the problem requiring some special attention in the area of costing is that nursing costs are currently averaged into the per diem in most hospitals. As a result, all patients in a given unit of the hospital will receive the same daily charge for nursing care services, built into the per diem rate.

In terms of providing management with an understanding of the cost implications of different patients, this provides extremely poor information. It assumes that all patients consume exactly the same amount of nursing care, when we clearly know that different patients have different nursing requirements.

Why has costing for nursing care taken this direction to begin with? In order to charge different amounts to different patients, we must be able to determine different amounts of resource consumption. In some areas of the hospital, it would be virtually impossible to measure differential consumption. For example, how much of the chief financial officer's (CFO's) time is consumed by each patient? One would be hard pressed to show that different patients receive different amounts of benefit from the CFO. Even if they did, it would be impossible to measure.

In the case of nursing, however, different patients do consume different amounts of nursing resources. Nevertheless, until the decade of the 1980s, measurement of differential consumption was, if not impossible, at least too costly to consider. What hospital could assign an accountant to each nurse to observe how much of his or her time was being devoted to each patient?

Today, however, most hospitals have in place a working patient classification system. Such systems are required for hospital accreditation. Patient classification systems require rating patients based on their likely nursing resource requirements. Such systems will not be precisely accurate for each patient. Some patients will require more or less care than would be expected, based on their classification. However, if the system is functioning reasonably well, patient resource consumption will generally match that which is expected based on the classification system.

Patient classification systems can be the basis for a system that allows us to more accurately estimate the cost a hospital incurs for nursing care for different types of patients.

WHY CHANGE THE COSTING APPROACH?

The mere fact that we now have the ability to improve costing does not in itself explain why we would want to improve costing. What is to be gained from having a more accurate measure of the different costs of nursing care for different types of patients?

One argument that is sometimes offered is that separate costing for different types of patients will allow for variable billing. Instead of simply charging all patients the same amount per day for their nursing care, different patients will be charged different amounts, based on their resource consumption.

To the extent that all patients are paid on a prospective payment basis, such as DRGs, variable billing holds little appeal. Thus, for states such as New York and New Jersey, where every

patient is paid on a DRG basis, improving billing systems provides little support for refined costing. On the other hand, hospitals in most states still do charge at least some patients on a non-prospective payment basis. In those cases, variable billing may be a way to better justify hospital bills, and in some cases increase overall revenues to the hospital.

However, care must be exercised if the main focus of improved nurse costing is to change the billing system. On one hand, such a system is beneficial to nursing because it shows in a dramatic way the specific contribution that nursing makes to the overall revenue structure of the hospital. On the other hand, as many states move toward all payer DRG systems, variable billing for nursing services is a step in the wrong direction.

Revenue centers inherently give a department an incentive to generate more revenue by producing more output. Radiology departments have an incentive to take X-rays and lab departments have an incentive to perform lab tests. For prospective payment patients, however, extra services don't result in extra revenues. Thus we must exercise care not to create nursing as a new revenue center with an incentive to overprovide services.

However, the main benefit to improved costing for nursing services is that we can generate information for better management decisions. Is a particular service too costly? What price can be bid for an HMO or PPO contract? These are just a few examples of the types of questions that cannot be answered without reasonably accurate costing information.

Hospital costing has long been based on averages and cross-subsidizations. In the current environment, errors in our calculations of costs become more serious as negotiations for discounted prices become more intense. Thus, if we are mistaken about the resources that a particular class of patient consumes, the ramifications can be quite serious. Averaging of costs is less acceptable than it was in the past.

In addition, as costing becomes more specific and more accurate, not only are we able to deal better with our pricing problems, but we can be more efficient in our management of costs as well. Flexible budget systems can provide better analysis and control of costs, and productivity can be monitored better if we know more about our costs. Since nursing represents such a major component of overall costs, more accurate costing is clearly beneficial to improved management of the hospital.

SHOULD COSTING BE LINKED TO DRGs?

If hospitals are going to move in the direction of more accurate costing of nursing services, one of the critical questions is the determination of the categories for cost. Should we have one nursing cost for medical patients and another for surgical patients? Should we determine the cost for men as opposed to women, or for young people as opposed to old people? Should we have one nursing cost for each type of patient based on ICD code? Should we find the cost by DRG?

Currently we treat all patients as if they were the same for nursing care. If we change this, there is no inherent logical approach to take. The operating room charges patients based on the type of surgery. The lab charges are based on the type of lab test. For nursing there is no easy equivalent. We will have to do our costing based on the type of patient. The question is, how do we categorize patients into different types?

The nursing profession has argued against DRGs. Their contention is that DRGs are not natural groupings based on consumption of nursing resources. Several attempts have been made at such groupings. None of these groupings has been flawless or widely accepted. DRGs are a system for grouping patients that is in use nationwide. And, although not all patients within a specific DRG will consume the same nursing resources, we can find an average amount of nursing resources for each type of DRG.

For example, if our hospital uses a nursing patient classification system that has a scale from one to five, we can sample a group of patients from each DRG and find out, on average, how many days of the patients' stays were at level one, how many at level two, etc.

Thus, it seems that DRGs, although perhaps not ideal for this purpose in the eyes of the nursing profession, are an adequate categorization for the assignment of differential nursing costs. Many decisions are based on particular DRGs or clusters of DRGs, so DRG based cost information is valuable. Of course, in a particular hospital, an alternative choice may be made, if it provides information that is more useful for decision making.

AN APPROACH TO COSTING NURSING SERVICES

Nursing care costs consist of the staff costs of direct patient care, the staff costs of indirect patient care (supervisors, secretaries, etc.), patient care related costs (e.g., patient and unit supplies), and overhead (allocated from other departments).

We could try to determine the costs of each of these elements separately for each category of patient, or we can do the costing in some more aggregate fashion. Compromises between accuracy and the cost of refining cost information are always made. The challenge is to decide in any given environment which compromises are reasonable and which are not. We will start with the assumption that all nursing department costs are lumped together (substantial compromise), and later discuss possible refinements.

The key element that allows for improved costing of nursing services is the fact that nursing patient classification systems are currently in place in almost every hospital. Without such systems we know that different patients consume different amounts of resources, but we have no way to measure the differential consumption. With a classification system, once we have classified a patient, we have some idea about the nursing resources he consumes.

For example, suppose that we have the following patient classification resource guidelines:

Acuity Level	Hours of Care
1	2.8
2	3.5
3	4.5
4	5.9
5	8.4

In developing the patient classification system, various indicators are used to determine if a patient should be classified as a 1, 2, 3, 4, or 5. Once the patient has been classified, the classification system tells you how many hours of nursing care should be required to treat that patient in your hospital. In the above example, a patient classified as a 4 would typically require on average 5.9 hours of care.

Note that the scale is not linear. A patient classified as a 2 does not require exactly twice as many hours as a 1. A patient classed as a 4 does not consume twice as many hours as a 2. This complicates the calculation of cost somewhat. If the scale was strictly linear we could add up all of the values and divide into total nursing cost to get a cost per unit of patient classification. That is, suppose we had one patient day that was a 1, one patient day that was a 3, and one patient day that was a 4. The total of 1 + 3 + 4 is 8. If total nursing costs were $1,000, then the cost per patient classification unit would be $125 (i.e., $1,000/8). The cost for a patient day classified as a 4 would be $500 (4 × $125).

However, since the scale is not linear, it is necessary to use a relative value unit scale. We can let a patient classified as a 1 have a value of 1 on the relative value scale. Each other classification level would then be calculated in relative proportion to get a set of relative values. For instance:

$$\frac{\text{Level 2}}{\text{Level 1}} = \frac{3.5 \text{ hours}}{2.8 \text{ hours}} = 1.25$$

Therefore the Relative Value (RVU) for patient classification level 2 is 1.25, since that patient would consume 25 percent more nursing re-

sources than a patient with classification level 1. Continuing for all classification (acuity) levels:

Acuity Level	Hours of Care	RVU
1	2.8	1.00
2	3.5	1.25
3	4.5	1.61
4	5.9	2.14
5	8.4	3.04

If we were to assume the following information, we can apply this RVU system to develop cost information:

Total nursing costs: $129,548

# of Patient Days at each acuity level:	Level 1	100 days
	2	220 days
	3	350 days
	4	110 days
	5	40 days

The first step is to determine the total amount of work performed by the nursing department. This is done by multiplying the RVUs for each acuity classification level times the number of days at that level.

Acuity Level	Patient Days	× RVUs =	Total RVUs
1	100	× 1.00 =	100.00
2	220	× 1.25 =	275.00
3	350	× 1.61 =	563.50
4	110	× 2.14 =	235.40
5	40	× 3.04 =	121.60
	820		1,295.50

There were 1,295.5 units of nursing work performed. We can divide this into the total nursing cost to find the cost for each RVU of nursing work:

$$\frac{\text{Total Nursing Costs}}{\text{Total RVUs}} = \text{Cost per RVU}$$

$$\frac{\$129,548}{1,295.50} = \$99.99 \text{ per RVU}$$

Here we can see that the cost for a patient for one day with classification 1 would be $99.99. The cost for a patient with classification 4 would be $99.99 multiplied by 2.14 (the RVU for classification level 4).

How would you calculate the nursing cost for a patient from admission to discharge? Suppose that the average DRG 128 patient had a length of stay of 7 days, with two days classed as a 1, four days classed as a 2, and one day classed as a 4. The nursing cost for DRG 128 would then be:

Acuity Level	Patient Days	× RVUs ×	Cost/ RVU	=	Total Cost
1	2	× 1.00 ×	$99.99	=	$199.98
2	4	× 1.25 ×	99.99	=	499.95
3	0	× 1.61 ×	99.99	=	0.00
4	1	× 2.14 ×	99.99	=	213.98
5	0	× 3.04 ×	99.99	=	0.00
	7				$913.91

Would all patients in a given DRG be expected to consume the same resources? Not really, but we can still be confident that an approach such as this, on average, for any given DRG will give a much more accurate assignment of cost than simply assigning to every patient in a nursing unit the same per diem cost for nursing care.

Have we made any compromises in the costing? Yes. For example, we are implicitly assuming that all nursing costs vary in proportion to the patient classification system. Does that make sense? For example, will a sicker patient who requires more direct nursing care also require more indirect nursing care? More supplies? More overhead? These are empirical questions. The answer to them depends on the specific situation of your hospital.

It may well be that a simple per diem allocation is appropriate for costs such as overhead. Some costs such as unit supplies might also be best allocated on a per diem basis, while other costs such as patient specific supplies might well be best allocated using the RVU scale. How complex are we willing to make our costing system?

Obviously the best costing of nursing services requires direct continuous observation of each patient and assignment of actual resources consumed. We obviously are not going to go that far in our costing scheme. Patient classification systems, however, have placed us in a position to be able to substantially improve the assignment of nursing costs to patients in an economical way. The RVU system is quite simple and inexpensive, assuming that your hospital has a patient classification system. Whether it pays to go beyond that level of detail will vary from hospital to hospital.

Application 2-5

Cost Accounting for Emergency Services

*John Moorhead, MD, is currently Chair
of the Department of Emergency Medicine,
Oregon Health Sciences University,
Portland, Oregon.*

This article outlines an alternative approach to cost accounting in the emergency department. The system described provides a basis for product costing and management control to be used in the context of the overall planning strategy for the department.

The implementation of prospective payment systems has resulted in greater emphasis on planning and financial analysis at the hospital department level. Emergency departments have traditionally been viewed as loss leaders for hospitals, with operating losses balanced by the department's role as an admitting channel that provides opportunities for profits in other departments.

Financial management in any hospital department requires an initial statement of the goals and objectives of the unit, which are usually assigned to the department as part of the hospitalwide planning strategy. Although the emergency department appears to have the ability to attract patients autonomously, marketing plans—including pricing strategies—must support these assigned objectives.

Competition, particularly from freestanding clinics, has forced hospital managers to rethink their pricing strategies for emergency departments. The resulting management decision-making process for planning, budgeting, and control requires more specific cost information.

Cost accounting requires a definition of the product. It seems appropriate to consider the patient as the product in the emergency department, with the individual services provided (such as triage, nursing care, and ancillary tests) considered as intermediate products or, as Cleverley has defined them, service units.[1] The variety of products (combinations of service units) provided in the emergency department makes the process of determining service level costs potentially complex.

COST ELEMENTS

Managers must determine how many cost elements will make up the costed product. Costs that are generally of interest in this approach are the "direct" costs of providing care.[2] They are costs that can be traced to an individual patient's care and would not be incurred if the patient were not treated. Direct costs can be either fixed or variable, depending on the variability of expenses with relation to changes in volume. Due to the stand-by function of the emergency department, many of the costs are fixed.

Source: Reprinted from John Moorhead, "Cost Accounting for Emergency Services," *Hospital Cost Management and Accounting,* Vol. 1, No. 2, May 1989, pp. 1–7. Copyright 1989, Aspen Publishers, Inc.

The following cost elements are selected for this system:

1. direct labor: salaries and fringe benefits of direct care providers
2. indirect labor: salaries and fringes of administrative and support personnel, such as managers, clerical, and orderlies/aides
3. supplies: categorized as "major" or "minor"
4. department overhead: including capital, teaching, and support services
5. institutional overhead: administrative and support costs, such as plant operation, housekeeping, and laundry

Department managers must assign costs in each of these categories on the basis of volume (the same amount assigned to each patient) or acuity (patient-specific charges) using a criterion of fairness or usefulness in decision making. The total dollar volume is also an important consideration, because it would not be cost efficient to devote significant resources to the identification of patient-specific costs for line items with only a few dollars value, even if the information were potentially useful.

PATIENT CLASSIFICATION

One existing approach to the determination of emergency department patient-specific costs has focused on costing by diagnosis. This method utilizes average labor times per diagnosis to assign diagnoses to one of six or seven service levels, each of which represents a range of standard times. Thus the product is the patient with a specific diagnosis, and is assumed to comprise a relatively constant number of service units. As Dieter has pointed out, "[T]his approach will work, yet accuracy is lost when diagnoses are grouped."[3] He proposes a system for determining a separate cost for each diagnosis. This approach is appealing because of the similarity to DRG concepts, but fails for the same reasons. Providers have questioned the assumption of the constant profile of resources (by service units) required to produce a given product (patients with the same diagnosis) and thus cast doubt on the accuracy of this methodology.

This approach also lacks accuracy because it is based on the premise that making a diagnosis is the primary goal for providers in the emergency department. However, the main clinical objective for emergency department personnel is timely identification of problems and providing life-saving acute care. Thus when patients leave the department, at which time patients are classified and charges assessed, most patients do not have an accurate diagnosis, but simply a problem list and acuity rating. Patients with a headache, for example, may range from those with a simple tension headache, which is easily relieved in the department, to a patient with acute cerebral infarction who is unconscious and is admitted to an intensive care unit after multiple procedures. Attempting to account for this wide range of acuity by expanding the list of secondary characteristics (admitted vs. not admitted, etc.) makes the process too complicated.

A simpler approach allocates costs to nursing procedures by assigning a relative value to each task. By compiling a summation of relative values for a particular patient, an assignment can be made to a level of service. As labor-related costs account for the majority of the department's operating expenses, this process more accurately reflects the intensity of service provided to an individual patient and thus would appear to be a fair basis for charging. This system is a form of customizing the charges for individual patients by job order costing. As Horngren states, "job order costing is used by organizations whose products or services are readily identified by individual batches, each of which receives varying inputs of direct materials, direct labor, and factory overhead."[4] The emergency department is such an organization.

This system recognizes that intensity of direct service is the best measure of acuity and thus the most valid basis for differential charges. It is also most consistent with the objectives and process of providing emergency care (as outlined above). A further advantage is that the basis for the assignment of direct labor and some overhead costs is a classification (acuity) system based on resource utilization that can also form the basis for staffing needs and productivity assessment in the department.

THE NURSING ACUITY SYSTEM

The purpose of nursing acuity systems is to identify "by task the time required to provide care for the patients."[5] The most accurate method would be to measure the actual time spent with each patient. This is totally impractical in the emergency department. However, each nursing procedure can be assigned a predetermined relative value based on the time taken to perform that task. Initially the relative value might be assigned by the unit manager based on experience in that particular unit. A similar method is to poll each full-time staff nurse on the amount of time it takes him/ her to complete each procedure. One factor that has been found to influence these times is experience in the department. Units with quite low turnover have disregarded the lowest and highest times for each procedure (similar to the scoring system used to judge figure skating) when averaging the results from the survey. The most simple method would be to assign one relative value unit for each minute the procedure takes to perform. Like diagnosis costing, this method loses accuracy by averaging, but we feel it has a much narrower range than the diagnosis-based values.

The number of procedures performed in an emergency department makes this task initially appear complex and arduous. However, Baptist[6] has described a procedural costing method that can be used to "allocate the actual direct and indirect costs incurred by each revenue-producing cost center to the services it produced during a given base period." In this method only high volume procedures were selected for detailed cost analysis. The Pareto principle would support such a strategy, in that generally 20% of a department's procedures account for 80% of its output or costs.[7] The remaining procedures could be assigned an average relative value. Identification of these procedures can be accomplished from a review of historical billing data.

Cost information is of value only in that it helps in the decision-making process, and therefore the system should be as simple as possible. Thus, procedures that are identified as those provided to all patients are nondiscriminating and their costs should be allocated to overhead, which is assigned on a per patient basis.

Nursing procedures are particularly well documented in department procedure manuals and reviewed for all incoming staff as part of their orientation process. These form a standard treatment protocol for each service unit. Using time, or assigned relative value, and the nursing cost per minute or relative value, a standard cost is assigned to each procedure.

Table 2-5-1 is a sample of activities and their assigned relative values. Procedure times include preparation of equipment.

At this point there is a basis for cost determination and charge assignment. However, the basis for reimbursement from third party carriers is service levels. It is for this reason that the relative values need to be allotted to service levels. Department managers must determine how many levels of service will be needed to account for the variety of services provided in their particular department. A basic package of services could be bundled to make up the lowest level of service, with a corresponding time total and relative value units. This might consist of triage, initial nursing assessment, obtaining vital signs, patient teaching, and discharge instructions. If we use Table 2-5-1, this would be (2.8 + 5.5 + 3.1 + 6.4) = 17.8 minutes and a relative value of eighteen units. However, these services are provided to all patients and thus this information is of very little value in decision making. Thus, these procedures might more appropriately be assigned to overhead.

It is important to emphasize that these time ranges and relative values are subject to regular auditing procedures. The assigned times could vary by patient diagnosis or depend on how busy the department happens to be. For example, does the initiation of an intravenous line take the same amount of time in a busy department for a patient who is the victim of a major

Table 2-5-1 Sample of Activities and Assigned Relative Values

Activity	Definition	Time Allotted	Relative Value
Triage	Elicit the patient's chief complaint, complete triage form and turn into admitting	2.8 min.	3
Initial Assessment	Complete a brief history and physical to assess patient's chief complaint	5.5 min.	6
Vital signs	Take one set of vital signs	3.1 min.	3
I.V. start	Preparation and insertion of a peripheral I.V.	8.0 min.	8
Patient teaching/ discharge instructions	Review discharge instructions with patient	6.4 min.	6
EKG	Completion and transmission of an EKG	7.4 min.	7
Administration of medications (includes preparation)	po, ophthal, topical, rectal IM, SQ I.V. push, piggyback	3.2 min. 5.6 min. 6.2 min.	3 6 6
Venipuncture	Drawing labs by venipuncture	4.8 min.	5
Insertion of NG tube		8.7 min.	9
Gastric lavage for O.D.	Assisting M.D. with the insertion of the lavage tube, irrigation of the stomach, instilling the charcoal, removing the tube	36.8 min.	37

traumatic event as for the administration of cry-oprecipitate for a young hemophiliac with a hemarthrosis when the department is relatively quiet? The managers of each department will have to validate these times depending on the volume and kinds of patients that are treated there. This process should begin with the high priority procedures mentioned above.

A range of relative values will have to be assigned to each service level. Although most departments might have data showing historical volumes by service levels, the information will not provide enough detail for this system. Knowledge of the volume of patients treated at each relative value total will be necessary for department managers to determine a total of relative value units provided. To account for the effects of seasonality it is necessary to collect this data for a period of one year. It might suffice to collect information for one month each quarter but of course this method would lose accuracy. One might expect a bell-shaped distribution curve for relative value totals within and between levels.

DIRECT NURSING COSTS

Once the volume of patients treated at each total relative value level is known, it is simply a matter of multiplying the volume times the RVUs and adding to get a total number of relative value units provided in the year. Dividing budgeted annual costs for that category by the number of RVUs gives a cost per RVU. Adding all the costs assigned by acuity to the costs assigned from overhead by volume will give a basis for pricing. Table 2-5-2 provides a structure for determination of total annual RVUs. However, the annual RVUs for each service level have not been calculated.

Each of the seven service levels in Table 2-5-2 has a range of RVUs. A study of the average number of RVUs per patient in each service level must be undertaken. It is too simplistic to assume that the midpoint number of RVUs would accurately reflect the weighted average consumption. For example, in each service category, there might be a disproportionate share of

Table 2-5-2 Structure for Determining Total Annual RVUs

Service Level	RVUs	Annual Volume	Annual RVUs
1. Minimal	0	3000	0
2. Brief	1–3	5600	?
3. Limited	3–15	6500	?
4. Intermediate	16–30	7800	?
5. Extensive	31–45	4500	?
6. Comprehensive	46–60	930	?
7. Critical Care	over 60	170	?
Total Relative Value Units			?

patients near either the high or low end of the RVU scale for that service level.

To see this more clearly, consider a hypothetical example for service level 2, "Brief." The 5,600 annual cases for this service level could be composed of 1,000 patients consuming 1 RVU; 2,000 consuming 2 RVUs; and 2,600 consuming 3 RVUs—an average of 2.3 RVUs per patient. Alternatively, it might consist of the reverse: 2,600 with 1 RVU; 2,000 with 2 RVUs; and 1,000 with 3 RVUs—an average of 1.7 RVUs per patient. In neither case would an assumption of 2 RVUs per patient be accurate. The inaccuracy would be even more pronounced at higher service levels, which have broader RVU ranges.

INDIRECT NURSING COSTS

Using a "fairness" criterion it might be decided that costs will be determined by time for only direct patient functions (easily identified as benefiting an individual patient). It might be argued that indirect nursing activities benefit all patients and therefore could be assigned to overhead. Similar allocation is necessary for nonproductive time (meals, breaks, and personal activities), and time spent on unit-related activities that are necessary for the general management, coordination, and organization of the unit. Examples of these broad activity categories are published elsewhere,[8] but need local modification.

Engineering studies are therefore necessary to identify how much nursing time is devoted on average to each of these activity categories. Although formal time-motion studies are the most accurate determination, work sampling as described by Hagerty[9] has been found adequate to analyze these times.

Table 2-5-3 shows results from one department.[10]

Department managers will now have the necessary information on which to allocate direct labor costs to each service level. Total direct nursing costs are multiplied by the percent direct care and the resulting dollar amount is divided by the total number of relative value units produced annually.

For example,

budgeted direct nursing salaries	$796,374
multiply by 32.8%	$261,210
divide by RVUs	$x.xx/RVU

Thus, direct nursing care costs would be assigned to each service level on the basis of $x per relative value unit. The cost per RVU multiplied by the number of RVUs assigned to a procedure would determine the direct cost per procedure.

Unit managers will have to determine whether all costs will be allocated on the basis of acuity or just direct nursing costs. As Dieter states, "the allocation of indirect (overhead) costs is almost as important as the identification of the direct cost components. The emphasis is on determining whether a direct cost/benefit relationship can be determined between each chargeable and every direct and indirect cost, and if so, to quantify that relationship."[3] He continues, "[M]ost of the other expenses within the department can be directly related to the acuity of the patient." The total dollar amount in each category will determine the effect on

Table 2-5-3 Percentage of Time Spent in Various Activity Categories

Activity Category	Percentage of Time
Direct care	32.8
Indirect care	26.9
Unit related	20.3
Personal	20.0

patient charges if assigned to overhead or by relative value units. Allocation of categories with costs of $1 to $2 is less important than those with costs of $10 to $15. This assignment is arbitrary and should be made on the basis of fairness.

Nursing indirect and unit related costs would seem to vary by acuity and thus should be assigned on the basis of relative value units. Personal time is much less clear but the absolute dollar amount makes us favor including it with acuity based costs.

OTHER LABOR

Assignment of the costs associated with support staff on an acuity basis seems logical as are costs of managers allocated to overhead. The need for support staff is somewhat dependent on absolute volume but clearly determined by intensity of service provided. Managers' costs are fixed and assigning them on a relative value basis would not contribute to the decision-making processes within the department. Management is perceived as a service from which all patients benefit. Physician services are required by Medicare regulations to be priced and costed separately, and are therefore not included in these discussions.

MATERIALS

Most department charging structures are designed to capture material resource consumption through individual supply charges at least for "significant" items. "Significant" is usually defined on the basis of cost and thus would again be a direct variable expense to an individual patient. Examples of significant supply items are individual procedure trays. By definition these supplies would only be used in the care of service levels 4–7. This limited number of items can be listed on the billing form with charges passed through to the individual patient on the basis of the cost incurred to the department.

"Minor" supplies are a relatively small cost in actual dollars and are easily assigned to the acuity category. As Dieter explains, "[I]n studies I have completed, a direct correlation has consistently been identified between a procedure's acuity level and length and its utilization of non-chargeable supplies."[3]

DEPARTMENT AND INSTITUTIONAL OVERHEAD

Total costs assigned to the overhead category are divided by budgeted volume for the department to provide the basis for the basic charge per patient.

PRICING DECISIONS

Setting prices for services begins with a basic fee that encompasses a share of all costs assigned to overhead and thus is the same for each patient. The other component is a charge based on the assigned service level, which is determined by the total relative value of the procedures provided to that patient. It is this component which is of value in making a decision as to whether the department is better off with that particular category of patient. Of course, the costs only provide a basis for the prices. The goals, objectives, and philosophy of the department will also help to determine the absolute charge levels. For example department managers must consider the competitive nature of the local health care system. If competition from local free-standing urgency centers and prevalence of ED deductibles means that service levels 1–3 are price-sensitive, then charges in those levels must correspond to basic urgency care charges. However, price must be set at greater than variable costs so that the contribution margin is greater than zero. Some costs might be shifted to other service levels that are less price-sensitive.

Charge assignment using this system requires that individual procedures must be identified for each patient. This is usually done at the time of treatment. This form of charging has been criticized as being too complicated and time-consuming for nurses. However, I believe that this system reinforces the nurses' sense of accomplishment. It also allows nurses to look at these charges as more like professional fees, as the process identifies all services provided to individual patients. The development of this system is also facilitated by active involvement by the entire nursing staff. This kind of system has been well accepted by nursing units.

PRODUCTIVITY

Cost information is of value only as it aids in the management decision-making process.[2] Productivity is one parameter upon which decisions regarding the number and skill level of staff for hospital units are based. There is a very close tie between the cost accounting and the productivity management systems. "Ideally," according to Dieter, "these two systems share the same data base of standards for the labor components of cost per procedure."[3] With hospitals' market share of health services in decline, "the challenge for hospitals is to keep costs low while continuing to provide high quality patient care," argues Minyard, who goes on to say that some "argue that reducing the skill level may reduce the quality of care, which is likely to be any hospital's competitive edge in the future."[10] The system described above will provide the foundations for a productivity monitoring system and will allow managers to evaluate productivity as one basis for these staffing and pricing decisions.[11]

NOTES

1. Cleverley, W., "Product Costing for Health Care Firms," *Health Care Management Review,* 1987, 12(4), pp. 39–48.

2. Finkler, S., "A Microcosting Approach," *Hospital Cost Accounting Advisor,* 2(12), May 1987, pp. 1–4.

3. Dieter, B., "Determining the Cost of Emergency Department Services," *Hospital Cost Accounting Advisor,* 2(1), April 1987, pp. 1, 5–6.

4. Horngren, C., and Foster G., *Cost Accounting: A Managerial Emphasis,* 6th ed. Englewood Cliffs, N.J.: Prentice Hall, 1987, chapter 4.

5. Dieter, B., "Determining the Cost of Nursing Services," *Hospital Cost Accounting Advisor,* 2(9), February 1987, pp. 1, 5–7.

6. Baptist, A., et al., "Developing a Solid Base for a Cost Accounting System," *Healthcare Financial Management,* January 1987, pp. 42–48.

7. Keegan, A., "Saving Money throughout the Cost Accounting Installation Cycle," *Hospital Cost Accounting Advisor,* 2(10), March 1987, pp. 1–7.

8. Halls, B., "Utilization of Nursing Personnel: A Task-specific Approach," *Nursing Outlook,* 19(664), 1971.

9. Hagerty, B., et al., "Work Sampling: Analyzing Nursing Staff Productivity," *JONA,* 15(9), September 1985.

10. Minyard, K., et al., "RNs May Cost Less Than You Think," *JONA,* 16(5), May 1986.

11. Nauert, L., et al., "Finding the Productivity Standard in Your Acuity System," *JONA,* 18(1), January 1988.

3

Product Costing

Goals of This Chapter

1. Define alternative approaches to product costing.
2. Explain the key elements of process and job-order costing.
3. Describe the relative advantages and disadvantages of job-order and process costing.
4. Discuss the common use of hybrid alternative costing methods that fall between job-order and process costing.
5. Explain standard costs and provide an approach to standard costing for health care organizations.
6. Introduce the microcosting approach for situations that require extremely detailed and accurate costing.

Key Terms Used in This Chapter

Cost centers; direct costs; hybrid; incremental cost; indirect costs; job cost sheet; job-order costing; microcosting; overhead costs; patient classification system; per diem; process costing; product costing; product-line costing; relevant cost; responsibility accounting; service units (SUs); standard cost profiles (SCPs); standard costs; standard treatment protocols (STPs).

Note: Key terms appear in italics when first used in the chapter. All key terms are defined in the Glossary.

THE NEED FOR PRODUCT COSTING

The concept of *product costing* was introduced in Chapter 2. Whether the focus is on the department or a product line, ultimately all health care organizations need to assign a cost to each patient treated. This is generally accomplished through some form of *job-order* or *process costing* system. These approaches are discussed in this chapter.

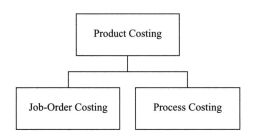

Regardless of which approach to product costing is chosen, there are a number of decisions that managers must make that require information about the cost of treating patients. Should a service be offered? Can we offer the service as cheaply as the competitor down the block? What is the minimum acceptable price for a product if it is to contribute to organizational profits? These are questions health care managers are asking today.

Product costing is also needed for external reporting. There has been a growing interest by parties external to the organization to know what it costs the organization to treat different types of patients. For example, health maintenance organizations (HMOs) would like to know hospital costs for each type of patient so that they can negotiate more effectively. The federal government would like to know costs by type of patient so that it can set Medicare Diagnosis Related Group (DRG) rates more effectively.

JOB-ORDER AND PROCESS COSTING

The major product costing approaches for accumulating costs and assigning them to products or services are process and job-order costing. Process costing is a system in which all units produced within a given time period are assigned the same cost. Job-order costing measures separately the cost of producing the units for each job.

Job-order costing is used in industries that produce products that consume different amounts of inputs. For example, a custom furniture manufacturer uses different amounts of labor, materials, and overhead for each job. At the other extreme, process costing is widely used when all products consume exactly the same inputs. For example, a soft-drink manufacturer uses virtually the same inputs for each can of cola produced. Many situations exist where products consume some resources in common but some that vary by the job. Cost accounting systems must be flexible enough to deal with such situations.

Table 3-1 shows a simple example of process costing for two surgical patients. Table 3-2 shows a simple example of job-order costing for the same two surgical patients. In Table 3-1, the

Table 3-1 Example of Process Costing for Surgical Patients

Cost Categories	$ Amount
Total nursing and technician labor: 10 hours @ $24	$ 240
Surgical supplies	2,260
Overhead costs (depreciation, administration, etc.)	500
Total costs	$ 3,000
Divided by number of patients	÷ 2
Cost per patient	$ 1,500

Table 3-2 Example of Job-Order Costing for Surgical Patients

Cost Categories	$ Amounts Patient A	Patient B
Nursing and technician labor:		
2 hours @ $20	$ 40	
8 hours @ $25		$ 200
Surgical supplies	260	2,000
Overhead costs (depreciation, administration, etc.)	250	250
Total costs	$550	$2,450

total costs for treating both patients are aggregated. Process costing assumes that all units of service consume equal amounts of labor, materials, and indirect costs. Therefore, the total costs of $3,000 are simply divided by the number of patients to find the cost per patient.

Table 3-2 uses the job-order approach. That approach requires a determination of the labor and materials used to produce each unit. Therefore, those costs are tracked individually for each patient. We note that Patient A consumed fewer hours of labor, and that each hour of labor consumed was less expensive than the labor consumed by Patient B. We also note that Patient A consumed fewer clinical supplies. The results show a stark contrast between the cost information yielded by process costing versus job-order costing.

Note that the overhead is allocated in equal amounts using the job-order system. Usually job-order will not be able to track the exact amount of overhead consumed to make each product. On the other hand, rather than splitting the cost equally between the two patients, it could be divided based on the length of the operating procedure, or on some other basis. Allocation of overhead costs is addressed in the next chapter.

It might appear from Tables 3-1 and 3-2 that job-order is clearly preferable because it gives more specific, accurate information. On the other hand, what if the consumption by all patients were nearly equal? Consider, for example, the data in Tables 3-3 and 3-4. In this case, we are considering the costs of doing a complete blood count (CBC) in a laboratory for

Table 3-3 Example of Process Costing for Laboratory Tests

Cost Category	$ Amount
Total technician labor: 1 hour @ $30	$ 30.00
Laboratory supplies	6.00
Overhead costs (depreciation, administration, etc.)	21.00
Total costs	$ 57.00
Divided by number of tests	÷3
Cost per test	$ 19.00

three patients. The process costing approach of Table 3-3 indicates that the cost per CBC is $19.

If we were to observe the laboratory labor constantly to determine the exact labor and materials for each test, we get the results from Table 3-4. We now find that there is no variation in supplies used, and only a very minor variation in the amount of labor used. Is it worth the extra cost of collecting job-order data for a type of product that basically is a constant, repetitive process?

Historically, health care organizations have used many elements of process costing in their accounting. For example, all patients receiving a chest x-ray may be charged the same amount. However, unlike the laboratory example in Table 3-4, in reality some patients probably consume far more technician time than others. Therefore, they should be treated in more of a job-order fashion to capture the cost of the true resources that they consume. The movement toward *product-line costing* in hospitals, popular since the advent of Medicare prospective

Table 3-4 Example of Job-Order Costing for Laboratory Tests

Cost Category	$ Amounts		
	Patient A	Patient B	Patient C
Total technician labor:			
19 minutes @ $.50/minute	$ 9.50		
21 minutes @ $.50/minute		$10.50	
20 minutes @ $.50/minute			$10.00
Laboratory supplies	2.00	2.00	2.00
Overhead costs (depreciation, administration, etc.)	7.00	7.00	7.00
Total costs	$18.50	$19.50	$19.00

payment using DRGs, is essentially a movement away from process costing and toward job-order costing. This is a recognition of the unique needs and resource consumption of each patient.

The advantage of using a job-order product costing system is that each patient will be assigned the cost of as many *direct costs* as possible on the basis of actual consumption. If a health care organization assigns inventory costs to patients based on their consumption of specific items, it is using at least some elements of a job-order system. This should improve the accuracy of costing. At the same time, improved accuracy often is associated with increased data collection costs.

In some cases, the higher costs of job-order costing are decreasing. For example, nursing is a particularly large part of overall hospital costs. Yet patient costing for nursing care historically has been very imprecise. This was the result of an inability to measure different patients' varying consumption of nursing inputs without incurring extreme measurement cost. To follow each patient or nurse and measure his or her input would be extremely costly.

The advent of *patient classification systems* in the 1980s now provides hospitals with a tool for improved product costing. A job-order approach can be taken whereby we could assign different nursing costs to different patients based on their daily patient classification. This would certainly provide a more accurate measure of the patients' relative consumption of nursing resources. And the cost to do so would no longer be prohibitive. This example is discussed specifically in Application 2-4.

In fact, few industries or organizations use exclusively process or job-order costing. Some *hybrid* system is usually established over time.

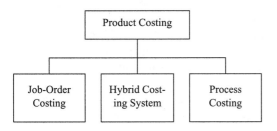

However, to establish a cost accounting system, one should first understand the rudiments of each of the two major approaches.

PROCESS COSTING

Many health care organizations adopted process costing because it is relatively inexpensive and generates information adequate for the organization's needs. Historically, decisions of whether or not to offer a service did not depend on knowing the true costs of the service. A process costing approach is excellent for assigning responsibility for costs. It is possible to evaluate the costs incurred in each *cost center* and to look to one individual who is responsible for that center and its costs.

A focus on the patient is less useful for *responsibility accounting*. Patients use services cutting across many cost centers. Therefore, if we try to determine why the costs for a patient are out of line, it is a more difficult process than trying to find out why a department's costs are out of line. Historically, health care organizations focused more on the responsibility issue than on the product costing issue. However, most industries do focus on product costing as well as on departmental costs.

As noted above, the classic example of process costing is the soft-drink manufacturer. All cans of cola appear the same to the customer. There is no reason to believe that any one can contains more or less ingredients or labor than any other. Nevertheless, we might actually produce some cans using labor at regular rates and others using overtime labor. We might make some cans of cola on a hot day when we have high air-conditioning costs in the factory and other cans on a cool day, when costs are lower. However, there is no significant advantage from costing out separately the cans made on the two days. Because each can of the product is essentially identical, and because we are likely to charge an identical price regardless of the difference in the cost of processing, it is adequate simply to aggregate all of the costs of all the units made and then determine an average cost. Before one requires more sophisticated, accurate, and costly information, it is necessary to specify the benefit to be received from such increased accuracy.

We would only need more exact data on the cost of specific cans if we were considering making a decision for which the data would be useful. For example, we might want separate cost data on different types of soft drinks that use different ingredients so we could actively market the least costly one or so we could discontinue any types for which the cost exceeds the selling price.

JOB-ORDER COSTING

In contrast to a process costing situation, such as a soft-drink producer, consider a custom furniture maker, designing and producing jobs to the specifications of their customers. A more refined costing system, called job-order costing, would be needed. If two tables are built—one a fine rosewood table built by the manufacturer's most skilled craftsmen and the other a cheap knotty pine workbench prepared by novices—we cannot reasonably total all of the costs of the two tables and divide by two. If we did, we would be misleading ourselves regarding the resources needed to make each table, and ultimately we would likely make poor managerial decisions regarding pricing our products and determining whether or not to offer certain products. Job-order costing tracks separately the cost of each job.

The extreme model of job-order costing for health care organizations is to treat each patient as a job. Each patient would have a cost sheet (see Exhibit 3-1) become a part of his or her medical record. The best way to understand the elements of job-order costing is to first start at this extreme. The degree of detail desired by any given health care organization can be based on a modification of the extreme position.

When a patient enters a health care organization, the production process for treating that patient begins. In other industries, the essential tracking document is called the *job cost sheet.* That form is used to accumulate all elements of materials, labor, and overhead consumed. In health care organizations, the medical record has served this purpose, however, from a clinical rather than financial perspective.

Supplies used are posted directly to the job cost sheet. In many health care organizations, supplies inventory is already on a job-order system basis using a sticker system. A sticker is placed on the medical record to indicate each supply item used. As individual items are posted to the job cost form, their dollar cost need not necessarily show up immediately on the form. The dollars can be added later. The most important element is to be sure that the resources consumed by each patient are associated with that patient. The accounting department can at a later date enter the costs of the resources consumed, whether supplies or labor. As computer applications expand in health care organizations, it is likely that many will adopt computer systems that automatically insert the cost as soon as the supply item is entered.

In addition to keeping track of supplies by patient, a job-order system requires that labor also be tracked by patient. Essentially, this means that each health care employee who has direct patient contact would have to keep a log of time spent with each patient, much the way that accountants and lawyers keep track of chargeable time to clients.

In organizations that have not kept such records, there is likely to be initial resistance to such a system. However, it is important that it be made clear that the goal is to ascertain what it costs to treat different patients so that those costs can be compared with revenue from those patients, rather than to punish workers for taking too long for a given task. Given the current financial environment, any technique likely to increase an organization's financial viability stands a very good chance of employee acceptance and support.

If a health care organization chooses to improve its product costing, it will likely move in the direction of job-order costing. However, it may improve costing gradually, rather than shifting to a new system all at once. Application 3-1 provides an example of job-order costing. Table 3-5 provides a summary of the advantages of process costing versus job-order costing.

Exhibit 3-1 Patient Cost Sheet

Patient Cost Sheet

Patient Number _____   Patient Name _____

Admission Date _____   Discharge Date _____

A. Direct Supplies

Date	Item Description	Item Code #	Comments	Quantity	Unit Cost	Amount

B. Direct Labor

Date	Employee Name/Title	ID#	Amount of Time	Hourly Rate Including Fringe	Amount

C. Ancillaries

Date	Department	Unit of Service	Quantity	Unit Cost	Amount

D. Overhead Applied

Date	Department	Overhead Basis	Overhead Rate	Amount

Table 3-5 Advantages of Process and Job-Order Costing

Advantage	Process Costing	Job-Order Costing
More detailed information		X
More accurate information		X
Less expensive system	X	
Less burdensome to maintain	X	
Usefulness for responsibility accounting	X	X
Better for decision making		X
Less potential employee resistance	X	

Even in a job-order system, some items will not be easily and directly assignable to specific patients. These items will constitute overhead. The overhead will have to be allocated to patients. This is often referred to as the application of overhead. Table 3-6 summarizes which costs are assigned on a specific basis to each unit of production versus on a broad average with each unit getting the same cost. For overhead, job-order costing generally uses the same averaging approach that process costing uses for all costs.

Not all costs are clearly *direct patient costs*. Some are *indirect* or *overhead* costs. If we are to accumulate and assign costs directly by patient as opposed to simply by department, there must be a way to allocate all costs to patients. This creates a problem because overhead costs often cannot be specifically associated with individual patients. In some cases, the costs are joint, such as the salary of an administrator who provides service to many patients. In other cases, the costs may be incurred specifically for one patient (fuel for heating a private room), but it would be too costly to measure and directly associate that cost with that individual. The allocation of overhead costs to patients is discussed in the next chapter.

Table 3-6 Comparison of Process and Job-Order Costing

	Costs		
	Labor	Materials	Overhead
Process	Averaged	Averaged	Averaged
Job-Order	Specific	Specific	Averaged

HYBRID APPROACHES TO PRODUCT COSTING

As mentioned earlier, most systems are hybrids rather than strictly process or job-order costing. Strict job-order costing requires having all supplies and labor in direct contact with the patient treated on a patient-specific basis.

How should we cost a patient's computerized tomography (CT) scan? Should we use process or job-order costing? If some patients consume far more time than others when receiving a CT scan, our costing will be far superior if we keep track of the differential resources used. With some system to record the time spent by each technician, this would not pose an overly burdensome task.

On the other hand, we would not likely put a laboratory on a job-order basis by patient. Thousands of identical blood tests are performed, and keeping track of the resources used for each test for each patient makes no more sense than keeping track of the cost of each can of cola.

If a patient receives both a CT scan and laboratory tests, should we measure the cost of treating that patient on a process (broad averaging) or job-order (specific detailed) basis? A key decision to be made by health care organizations is the level of detail desired. Where to draw the line between specific costs and the use of average costs is a decision that each health care organization must make in forming its own product costing system. Often, hybrids will allow some elements of a patient's cost to be accumulated on a process basis and other elements on a job-order basis.

The extremes of job costing and process costing are ideals that rarely find direct applicability. Consider, for example, Application 3-2 on product costing for the clinical laboratory. In that application, the laboratory cost for treating a diabetes patient consists of the costs for each type of test consumed. Taking a job-costing approach (Exhibit 3-2-2 in that application) adds up the quantity of each test for that type of patient. On the other hand, the cost for each test is calculated on a process costing approach. The labor and materials for all glucose tests are averaged to find the average labor and materials cost per glucose test. That is the same process approach as for a can of cola.

Also, the application article assumes all DRG 294 (diabetes ≥ 36 years old) patients consume the same quantity of each test. That is clearly a process costing approach for that class of patients. But the calculation of the costs of DRG 294 as distinct from patients in other DRGs is a job-order approach to product costing. Further, once the basic system described in the application is established, one could look at the specific tests for any one patient and develop a much more specific job-order cost.

The job-order costing concept of associating the cost of labor and supplies with individual patients is a simple one. The complex issue for each manager to determine is how much such data will cost, and whether they are worth the cost.

No matter what product costing approach is chosen, there will invariably be some averaging of costs. Process costing does its averaging over a large number of units (patients), whereas job-order costing uses a much smaller number. However, the Scinto article (Application 3-2) points out that even if job-order costing were undertaken to find the costs of one specific patient, the data used would already have some averaging in them—the average cost per glucose test, for example. Health care managers must make a decision as to how much averaging they are willing to tolerate. Stated another way, they must decide how much they are willing to pay to reduce the extent that averaging is used to determine product costs.

STANDARD COSTING SYSTEMS

Another approach to product costing is the use of *standard costs*. Standard costs are predetermined estimates of what it is expected to cost or what it should cost to produce one unit of a product. A standard cost for a health care organization would be the expected cost to treat a specific type of patient. Standards are deter-

mined by using historical results, time-and-motion observations, or theoretical calculations.

Up until this point, we have been considering product costing as a system to collect costs that are actually incurred. There are also times when an organization can benefit from knowing how much it *will* cost to treat patients. The development of standard costs can be a great aid to managers. They can use the information to make decisions concerning negotiations with other health care organizations or decisions concerning whether or not to offer a program or service. They can also be used to provide retrospective estimated information on what it is costing the organization to treat different types of patients without actually measuring the resources consumed by each patient.

Organizations that use standard costs develop a standard cost card for their products. Products may be patients, or they may be intermediate products such as laboratory tests or operations. Table 3-7 shows the elements of a standard cost card for a chest x-ray.

One example of a standard costing approach is provided in Application 3-2 (a clinical laboratory product costing). This type of approach has been formalized as a standard costing technique in a seminal health care product costing article by William Cleverley, reprinted at the end of this chapter (Application 3-3).

Table 3-7 Standard Cost Card for Chest X-Ray

Cost Category	$ Amount
Direct labor	
Technician: 18 minutes @ $30/hour	$ 9.00
Direct materials	
Film	25.00
Department indirect costs	
Variable costs per X-ray	4.00
Fixed costs: $60,000 divided by	
20,000 expected X-rays	3.00
Allocated overhead costs from other	
departments	
$100,000 divided by 20,000	
expected X-rays	5.00
Total	$ 46.00

The Cleverley Model

Cleverley proposed that health care organizations cost their products using a standard costing approach that is centered around *service units* (SUs), *standard cost profiles* (SCPs), and *standard treatment protocols* (STPs). In his system, he defines the treated patient as the product.

Cleverley points out that one of the chief problems in health care costing has been the definition of the product. For years, controversy existed over whether, from an accounting perspective, the product was the patient or the various services provided to the patient. However, under today's fixed pricing scheme (such as DRGs), there is greater agreement that the health care system product is in fact the patient.

Product costing provides inadequate information to managers because decisions often cannot be made with respect to one product. In many situations, we are unlikely to be able to retain some patients from DRG 36 (retinal procedures), while rejecting others. Similarly, as Cleverley points out, we are unlikely to discontinue DRG 36 while retaining DRG 39 (lens procedures). Therefore, there is an increasing focus on product lines, where groups of types of products are classed together for cost accounting purposes.

Each patient is treated by being given a variety of intermediate products or SUs. A particular type of laboratory test would be one SU. A day of nursing care at a certain intensity level would be another SU. For any given type of patient, we could design an STP, which would list all the intermediate products necessary to treat the patient. This STP could be prospective, identifying all the SUs one would expect a given type of patient to need, or it could be a tally sheet, keeping track of all the SUs a patient actually did consume.

If one were to predetermine an STP for each type of patient treated, and then actually track the SUs consumed, a rather sophisticated variance analysis would be possible, which would allow hospital managers to evaluate whether more SUs, or more expensive SUs, were being used than would be appropriate.

To optimize the decision-making capabilities generated by the SUs, they should be broken down into specific information about labor, materials, departmental overhead, and allocated overhead. To the extent possible, they should also be categorized as fixed or variable costs.

Standard treatment protocols identify the SUs needed to treat different types of patients (products). Thus, the anticipated cost of a class of patient can be determined because the STP will identify all of the SUs to be consumed in treating a class of patient. The SUs, in turn, consist of SCPs. Under the Cleverley system, for each type of SU, there would be an SCP. This SCP would indicate in fairly great detail all of the elements of cost for producing the SU.

Thus, the costing system starts with resources being consumed by the health care organization. This resource consumption is assigned to the various departments through a traditional responsibility center accounting system. Each department, in turn, assigns all of its costs to the service units that it produces. The SUs are assigned to patients, so that ultimately all of the costs of the organization are assigned to patients.

Such cost assignment assumes that all activities of the organization can be directly assigned to SUs that are directly assigned to patients. Obviously, that cannot account for many *indirect costs*. Cleverley contends that although currently only about half of all costs are directly assigned to patients, perhaps three quarters of all costs could be directly assignable with the SU concept. For example, dietary is currently an overhead item assigned as part of a per diem. Under a service unit concept, however, different types of meals (regular patient meal, salt-free meal, etc.) would be different service units, and patients could be assigned the exact dietary SUs they consume.

The overhead costs that still exist because of the indirect nature of the work performed (such as administration) would be allocated to departments as usual and would become part of the costs of each SU. (See Chapter 4 for a discussion of overhead allocation.)

Thus, the SCP for a given service unit would have the following components: direct labor, direct materials, departmental overhead, and allocated costs from outside the department. Each of these categories would be further divided between fixed and variable costs. In order to assign fixed costs per SU, it is necessary to estimate expected volume so that a cost per unit can be calculated.

Table 3-8 summarizes the Cleverley approach. An STP for a specific type of patient would first list all departments that produce intermediate products consumed by the patient. In Table 3-8, only one department is shown. Each intermediate product of each department represents an SU. Note that Patient Type A consumes 2 units of SU 15 from Department 1, 1 unit of SU 28, and 5 units of SU 43. Table 3-8 also shows the expected cost of each service unit broken down in detail.

The SCP for each SU for each department would need supporting detail to explain and justify the expected levels of cost to produce that SU. For example, Table 3-9 presents a standard cost break-down for Department 1, SU 43.

The cost for each SU is multiplied by the quantity of that SU consumed to get an extended cost. By considering the SCP for each SU, and the quantity of each SU for each department, we can build a total standard cost for treating a patient of a given type.

Under DRGs, where all patients of a given type pay the same amount, it is less important that a given patient's cost sheet shows the actual specific costs for that patient. However, it becomes more important to have a standard cost card showing the expected average consumption by a class of patients so that the price can be compared with the expected production costs of

Table 3-8 Cleverley Standard Costing Model—Standard Treatment Protocol, Patient Type A, Department 1 SUs

Service Unit	Quantity	Standard Cost Profile ($)		Extended Cost ($)
15	2	Direct labor	23.20	46.40
		Direct materials	11.20	22.40
		Department 1 indirect costs		
		Variable	5.24	10.48
		Fixed	7.40	14.80
		Allocated cost from other departments		
		Variable	9.25	18.50
		Fixed	4.20	8.40
28	1	Direct labor	41.20	41.20
		Direct materials	21.90	21.90
		Department 1 indirect costs		
		Variable	6.45	6.45
		Fixed	12.10	12.10
		Allocated cost from other departments		
		Variable	12.25	12.25
		Fixed	7.50	7.50
43	5	Direct labor	5.00	25.00
		Direct materials	4.50	22.50
		Department 1 indirect costs		
		Variable	3.00	15.00
		Fixed	2.50	12.50
		Allocated cost from other departments		
		Variable	10.00	50.00
		Fixed	2.00	10.00

Table 3-9 Standard Cost Card for Department 1, SU 43

Cost Category		$ Amount
Direct labor		
20 minutes @ $15/hour		$ 5.00
Direct materials		
Reagents	$ 3.00	
Other direct supplies	1.50	
Total materials		4.50
Department 1 indirect costs		
Variable (labor, supplies, other)		3.00
Fixed (supervisors, clerks, depreciation, supplies, seminars,		
dues, publications, etc.)	$125,000.00	
Divided by expected volume	÷50,000.00	2.50
Allocated cost from other departments		
Variable		10.00
Fixed	$100,000.00	
Divided by expected volume	÷50,000.00	2.00
Total cost per unit		$27.00

that type of patient. Based on such a comparison, a variety of decisions about the product can be made. This supports the type of costing approach presented by Scinto in Application 3-2.

Extensions to the Cleverley Model

There is little question that a standard costing approach such as that proposed by Cleverley will generate information for cost management that far exceeds the product (patient) cost information of a decade ago. Many consultants have different names for such standard costing approaches. The underlying concept proposed by Cleverley is fairly universal and has been gaining ever wider acceptance.

Standard costs are a tool widely used throughout most industries. Although health care has long contended that every patient is unique, and standards are not possible, the reality of reimbursement systems is that patients can be grouped together, at least for payment. Given that, health care managers have an obligation to group patients together for costing so that effective decision making can take place.

That does not necessarily mean that decisions can be made with respect to an individual DRG. As noted above, it may not be possible for a hospital to add or delete a DRG without considering the effect on other products offered. For example, open-heart bypass surgery and open-heart valve surgery go hand-in-hand. However, if valve surgery is starting to consume different SUs than those expected, or if the cost of a particular SU is changing, a cost information system should isolate that fact so appropriate investigation can take place.

One question that arises, however, is whether the approach outlined by Cleverley goes far enough to generate accurate information. For example, suppose that one type of service is a chest x-ray. The radiology department does many different types of x-rays.

Under the Cleverley approach, the cost of all chest x-rays would be tallied and would be divided by expected volume to generate a cost per chest x-ray. For each type of patient, we would determine how many of that SU are required, look at the SCP for the SU, and multiply the standard cost of the SU by the SU's volume to determine how much chest x-rays contribute to the total cost of treating that type of patient.

The problem with this approach (as was discussed in Chapter 2) is that it assumes that all chest x-rays are alike. That is an unreasonable assumption. It is better than assuming that all x-rays are alike, but not as good as identifying the differing costs for chest x-rays for different types of patients. In some cases, a patient will be reasonably ambulatory and can stand up and easily be positioned. In other cases, a patient may be postoperative, with chest tubes and other obstacles, and may take quite a bit of technician time in order to be properly positioned for the x-ray.

If we could argue that the degree of difficulty in taking a chest x-ray is fairly random across the patient population, we could probably ignore the variation from patient to patient. Any particular class of patient would have some complicated x-rays and some simple x-rays, and all in all it would balance out. Then, even though we speak of an STP, we would only expect the SUs listed in that protocol to be appropriate for a class of patients on average, not in each particular case.

However, if there are patterns that are associated with particular types of patients, then using one standard chest x-ray cost will cause a substantial costing inaccuracy. For example, if open-heart surgery patients are always difficult to x-ray for several days after their surgery, it is inappropriate to assign them the same average cost as is assigned to a type of patient that is never difficult to x-ray.

Thus, one refinement to the Cleverley system is to examine the variability within SUs. This does not necessarily mean that we have to collect cost information continuously on every SU. However, in the case of very common SUs where variability is likely, special studies to examine the underlying resource consumption of different types of patients are probably warranted. After all, many managers will be using the STPs and SCPs of patients for decisions such as negotiating prices with HMOs.

Another area for refinement of the Cleverley system is in the area of departmental overhead and fixed costs. Cleverley argues:

Departmental overhead consists of expenses directly charged to a department that do not represent labor or materials. Common examples might be equipment costs, travel allowances, outside purchased services, publications, and other small items. Usually these items do not vary with level of activity or volume but remain fixed for the budgetary period. If this is the case, assignment to an SCP can be based on a simple average.[1]

From this, Cleverley then divides such items by the number of SUs expected in order to arrive at a cost per SU. That cost is then part of the cost of each SU for the department.

This again is an oversimplification that can create substantial inaccuracy in costing. For example, consider the operating room. Very expensive pieces of equipment exist in the operating room to use with a very limited number of types of patients. The bypass pump and related equipment are used only for cardiac surgery. If such surgery is not performed, that equipment will not be needed by the operating room.

Therefore, that equipment should be considered a cost only of the SUs that relate specifically to it. Identification of fixed costs associated specifically with the patients who need such fixed costs can substantially enhance the accuracy of the standard costing system.

Thus, we note that use of a standard costing system such as Cleverley's is a big step forward for health care cost accounting systems. However, we must take care to realize that we are on a continuum, and that improvements toward the ideal (a perfectly accurate costing system) are generally possible, even though the ideal itself is probably not attainable.

Should we make every improvement toward the ideal? That depends on the cost of the extra information versus the degree to which that information will improve the accuracy of our cost measures. Finally, it also depends on what we intend to do with our cost measures, and what the impact of errors in our costing will be on the organization.

MICROCOSTING

Standard costs provide estimates of what costs should be for different types of patients. Although they can be reasonably accurate, if an application requires extremely specific and accurate product costing, one potentially useful approach is *microcosting*. Microcosting is the process of closely examining the actual resources consumed by a particular patient or service. Microcosting tends to be extremely costly and is generally done only for special studies.

The main thrust of a microcosting effort is to avoid arbitrary allocations as much as possible in collecting cost information for some particular purpose. In that way, the information generated is far superior for decision-making purposes. However, health care organizations have traditionally relied to a great extent on such allocations, which save a great amount of accounting time and effort, although they generate less informative data. A detailed view of microcosting is presented in Application 3-4 at the end of this chapter. Chapter 4 discusses cost allocation.

NOTE

1. W.O. Cleverley, Product costing for health care firms, *Health Care Management Review* 12(1987): 45.

SUGGESTED READING

Baptist, A. 1987. A general approach to costing procedures in ancillary departments. *Topics in Health Care Financing* 13, no. 4:32–47.

Bennett, J.P. September 1985. Standard cost systems lead to efficiency and profitability. *Healthcare Financial Management:* 46–48, 52–54.

Budd, J.M. 1988. How to determine standard costs. *Journal of Ambulatory Care Management* 11, no. 1:24–33.

Cooper, J.C. and J.D. Suver. April 1988. Product line cost estimation: A standard cost approach. *Healthcare Financial Management:*60,62, 64.

Finkler, S.A. 1979. Cost-effectiveness of regionalization: The heart surgery example. *Inquiry* 16, no. 3:264–270.

———. 1985. Job-order costing: Viewing the patient as a job. *Hospital Cost Accounting Advisor* 1, no. 5:1–5.

Horngren, C.T. and G. Foster. 1991. *Cost accounting: A managerial emphasis*. 7th ed. Englewood Cliffs, N.J.: Prentice-Hall, Inc.

Loeb, A.J. and K. Kahl. 1987. Microcosting pharmacy services: A basic approach. *Topics in Hospital Pharmacy Management* 7, no. 1:1–11.

Messmer, V.C. January 1984. Standard cost accounting: Methods that can be applied to DRG classifications. *Healthcare Financial Management:*44–48.

Nackel, J., et al. November 1987. Product-line performance reporting: A key to cost management. *Healthcare Financial Management:*54–62.

Schimmel, V.E., et al. 1987. Measuring costs: Product line accounting versus ratio of cost to charges. *Topics in Health Care Financing* 13, no. 4:76–86.

Smith, J.E., et al. 1988. Pharmacy component of a hospital end-product cost-accounting system. *American Journal of Hospital Pharmacy* 45, no. 4:835–843.

Sullivan, S. 1987. Product line costing for DRG profitability. *Hospital Cost Accounting Advisor* 3, no. 3:1–5.

EXERCISES

QUESTIONS FOR DISCUSSION

1. Distinguish between job-order and process costing.
2. If all patients getting a chest x-ray are assigned the same cost, is that job-order or process product costing?
3. What are the major strengths and weaknesses of job-order and process costing?
4. Is health care inherently more appropriately a job-order or process costing industry?
5. What is the prime difference between general product-costing and standard costing?
6. Describe the Cleverley product costing approach.

PROBLEM

1. Using the Cleverley approach discussed in the chapter and in Application 3-3, design an STP for a particular type of patient. List the SUs required for the STP, provide the SCP of each SU, and determine the standard cost for each patient.

Note: Solutions to the Exercises can be found in Appendix A.

Application 3-1

Job Order Costing in Physician Practice

Lorelei S. Cheli, BSN, MPA, is currently
Employee Wellness Director,
Medical Center of Ocean County,
Point Pleasant, New Jersey.

Changes in the reimbursement system for physicians' services, like those for hospitals, require the physician in private practice to examine cost issues. Traditionally, the physician in private practice has used a competition-oriented pricing called "going-rate" or "imitative pricing."[1] There is no rigid relationship between price, costs, or demand. Since costs have been difficult to measure, the going-price methodology has been thought to yield a price that is considered fair. A going-rate competition-oriented pricing strategy has been fostered by Medicare and private insurers whose reimbursement rate is based on usual, customary, and reasonable fees. This type of costing can no longer be used exclusively. Pressures from several different forces necessitate a more exacting means to measure costs in private practice.

Maximum allowable actual charges (MAACs) regulate the fee for services and procedures a nonparticipating physician can charge Medicare patients. These fees are considerably lower than those for non-Medicare patients. A focus on cost containment will continue and a physician who has a choice of serving Medicare or other patient types can make a practical deci-sion only if some form of cost information is available.

Current findings show that HMOs that have signed up Medicare patients have difficulty meeting their obligations. Costs have created problems for smaller HMOs. During 1987, 29 of the 159 HMOs (more than 18 percent) that contracted with Medicare later decided to get out of the Medicare market.[2] Some health plans still providing Medicare coverage are losing money, while others are reluctant to get involved. Economies of scale are an important factor in the success or failure of a group in the Medicare market. Smaller operations account for half of the HMOs that have withdrawn from Medicare. Location is an important factor, since Medicare payment rates tend to be lower in rural areas. Similarly, a physician contracting for a prospective payment with an HMO or Medicare through the MAAC reimbursement system encounters cost issues.

The nursing shortage is another factor in rising costs in private practice. In the past, many nurses chose office work and accepted lower pay scales to avoid hospital shifts and weekend rotation. Hospitals have taken several steps to lure nurses back to hospital nursing. Flexible scheduling and higher pay scales have created more competition for skilled office nurses. As a

Source: Reprinted from Lorelei S. Cheli, "Job Order Costing in Physician Practice," *Hospital Cost Accounting Advisor,* Vol. 4, No. 10, March 1989, pp. 1–6. Copyright 1989, Aspen Publishers, Inc.

result, higher hourly rates are being demanded by nurses employed in private practice settings.

A final area of concern is growing competition among physicians. Health care organizations now engage in competitive pricing by offering lower than average prices for certain services (e.g., "St. Louis Hospital guarantees lower rates for outpatient surgery"). Price advertising for private physicians is moving in a similar direction (e.g., cataract procedures). Physicians allocating funds for marketing and advertising need cost information to establish which market segments to target. A choice of patient type may be limited in certain specialties, but the location where services are performed should be considered.

Costs of personnel and overhead are important considerations when opting to perform procedures (e.g., flexible sigmoidoscopy) in the private office setting. The choice is often available to the physician and patient to use a hospital procedure room. The costs incurred by the private physician practice in offering the convenience of an in-office procedure should be carefully evaluated.

With the past payment structure, profits were large enough that no benefits were seen to measuring costs. A much simpler structure, with fewer alternatives for providing care and services, meant fewer choices on how to deliver care. This simplified system no longer exists. Physicians who do not examine the alternatives cannot satisfy patient needs as cost efficiently as possible and, in turn, meet their own financial goals.

Historical costs provide the basis for a framework for responsibility accounting that should be formulated for private practice. Historical cost records of any particular service or office procedure are rarely maintained. However, past material costs are easily obtained, and can be used in the process of establishing actual costs of any procedure or service.

In most private practice situations the person ordering supplies can pinpoint volume that was purchased on a monthly basis. Care must be taken in choosing a material purchase as a basis for measuring volume. For example, the number of throat culture media used per month would not be a good indicator of sore throat visits if the physician does not culture every sore throat. Each material must be viewed in relation to the practitioner's usual practicing habits.

Examining a material order for EKG mounts, where only one per cardiogram is used regardless of the practitioner, is a quick way to judge volume performed with no considerable error. Other services are not isolated as simply. To count these requires examining daily ledgers. One method would be to have the office person who gives the final bill to the patient, itemizing procedures and services, begin to maintain daily accounts.

Knowing volume of procedure types in itself is a valuable tool that private practices should have. Some practitioners can estimate the volume of some procedures. If the practice is highly specialized, this is obvious. Other more varied practices (e.g., internal medicine, general surgery, family practice) have less definitive information. Volume records enable the provider to predict employee needs and measure increases or decreases in demand. Volume records are a form of control on the physicians' habits for specific procedures. Variations in volume of any standard procedure performed per volume of patients can be reviewed. Volume also indicates which procedures or services a practice would most want to know costs for. Costs of other less frequently performed services could also be valuable, since these can incur greater costs because of their low volume.

To establish costs, a job-order costing system can be used to identify materials that are easily linked to a procedure. Different patient types typically require different materials and consume varying amounts of physician and nursing time. The job-order cost record will also serve a control function. Deviations can be investigated to determine underlying causes.

In a medical setting, as in industry, equipment and labor can cause deviations in standards. Patient type can also be isolated as a cause for deviation once standards are established. Medicare patients typically require more assistance from personnel and occupy examining rooms for longer periods of time than younger patients.

EKG JOB-ORDER COSTING EXAMPLE

Materials and labor can be directly isolated as elements of a specific treatment. For example, the direct materials and labor for an EKG might be

EKG Direct Materials

$ .09	Sigma Pads
.13	Mounts
.40	Pillow Case
.47	Gown
.40	Drape
.20	EKG Machine Paper
.13	Table Paper
$1.82	Direct Material Cost

EKG Direct Labor Cost

$2.26	Technician: 17 minutes @$8.00 per hour (perform and mount EKG)
3.20	MD: 4 minutes @$48.00 per hour (interpretation and report to patient). See appendix, p. 100.
$5.46	Direct Labor Cost

Overhead must also be allocated to each procedure to determine a close approximation of costs of different procedures. A medical practice incurs a substantial amount of fixed overhead independent of the type of procedures it performs. For a family practice these might include the following per year:

Fixed Overhead

$ 8,000	Malpractice and Other Insurances
36,000	Rent
1,668	Utilities
34,400	RN/Manager and Secretary
21,000	Benefits (Pension, Health Ins., SS)
	Office Equipment Depreciation
250	Reception Area $2,500/10 years
300	Clerical Equipment $6,000/20 years
250	Telephone $5,000/20 years
500	Copy Machine $3,000/6 years
1,300	Other
$101,868	Total Cost (approximately $102,000)

To apply this overhead, an application base must be selected to serve as a common denominator for all procedures. Each procedure is considered a cost objective that shares overhead expenses. The above costs are incurred on an annual basis independent of volume of procedures performed or hours of operation. If hours of operation are used as an application base, then for each hour of operation the overhead rate is $102,000/2,200 expected hours, or $46 per hour.

Increasing expected hours of operation would decrease the fixed overhead application rate, but would not necessarily generate the procedure volume needed to increase profits.

If volume of procedures is used as an application base, then for each procedure the overhead rate is $102,000/7,000 expected procedures, or $14.57 per procedure.

This volume is based on historical demand. If the practice is able to see greater volume within its current hours of operation, the fixed overhead per procedure can decrease.

EKG Fixed General and Direct Overhead

$14.57	Total budgeted overhead ($102,000/ 7,000 total budgeted procedures)
.33	EKG machine depreciation (Cost $2,000/10-year life = $200 per year divided by 600 budgeted EKGs)
$14.90	Overhead Cost
1.82	Direct Material Cost
5.46	Direct Labor Cost
$22.18	Total EKG Cost (materials + labor + overhead)

Medicare Patient EKG Profit

$29.80	Medicare MAAC reimbursement (as of January 1988)
–22.18	Costs (from above)
$ 7.62	Medicare Patient Profit

Non-Medicare Patient EKG Profit

$35.00	Charge to non-Medicare and other insurers BC/BS
–22.18	Costs
$12.82	Non-Medicare Patient Profit

SIGMOIDOSCOPY JOB-ORDER COSTING EXAMPLE

Materials

$1.16	Cidex ($6.95/6 current demand monthly)
.30	Gauze
.42	Gloves
.13	Table Paper
.42	Gown
.40	Drape
.40	Pillow Case
$3.23	Material Cost

Direct Labor Costs

$ 8.00	Technician Time (1 hour @$8.00 per hour set up, assist procedure, clean equipment)
16.00	MD Time (20 minutes @$48 per hour)
$24.00	Labor Cost

Fixed General and Direct Overhead

$14.57	Per Procedure
2.31	Sigmoidoscope Depreciation ($5,000 cost/5 years = $1,000/432 budgeted procedures)
$16.88	Overhead Cost
3.23	Material Cost
24.00	Labor Cost
$44.11	Total Sigmoidoscopy Cost

Medicare Patient Profit

$111.73	Medicare MAAC as of January 1988
−44.11	Costs
$ 67.62	Medicare Patient Profit

Non-Medicare Patient Profit

$130.00	Charge to non-Medicare patients, other insurers BC/BS
−44.11	Costs
$ 85.89	Non-Medicare Patient Profit

OFFICE VISIT INTERMEDIATE COST EXAMPLE

Direct material costs are usually minimal.

$ .83	Nurse Time (5 minutes @10.00 per hour)
12.00	MD Time (15 minutes @$48 per hour)
$12.83	Direct Labor Cost
14.57	Fixed General Overhead per Procedure
$27.40	Total Cost

Medicare Patient Profit

$ 25.00	Medicare MAAC as of January 1988
−27.40	Total Cost
$ −2.40	Medicare Patient Loss

Non-Medicare Patient Profit

$ 33.00	Charge to other non-Medicare patients as of January 1988
−27.40	Total Cost
$ 5.60	Non-Medicare Patient Profit

ALLERGY IMMUNIZATION COST EXAMPLE

Material, Labor, and Overhead

$ .19	Syringe
.13	Table Paper
16.00	M.D. Time (20 minutes @$48.00 per hour)
.83	Nurse Time (5 minutes @$10 per hour)
14.57	General Overhead
$ 31.72	Total Cost

Medicare Patient Profit

$ 7.00	MAAC
−31.72	Cost
$ −24.72	Loss

Non-Medicare Patient Profit

$ 10.00	Other Non-Medicare
−31.72	Cost
$ −21.72	Loss

Allergy Immunization costs without physician labor costs:

$ .19	Syringe
.13	Table Paper
.83	Nurse
14.57	General Overhead
$ 15.72	Total Cost

Medicare Patient Profit

$ 7.00	MAAC
−15.72	Cost
$ −8.72	Loss

Non-Medicare Patient Profit

$ 10.00	Other Non-Medicare
−15.72	Cost
$ −5.72	Loss

Clearly some procedures are distinguished as profit makers and others as losers. In each practice these can be isolated. Decisions as to which patient types and procedures to encourage cannot be based on profit motives alone. Certain services (e.g., allergy injections) cannot be labeled as procedures in the sense that they should be allocated the same overhead rate. An allergy injection requires that a physician be physically present in the facility should an emergency arise during the 20 minutes a patient is required to wait for a reaction. Rarely is the physician needed. To charge an allergy injection cost with 20 minutes of physician time along with overhead would result in a cost of $31.72 for an allergy injection. This is clearly not reasonable, since the physician during that 20-minute time period is seeing other patients.

USE VARIANCES

Job-order costing has its limitations in health care. While the concept is simple, complexities develop, and the demands on staff time to keep track of cost in itself must be considered. However, by initiating job-order costing, standards for direct labor and material or supply costs can be developed on appropriate procedures.

For example, an efficiency or use variance could be developed for Medicare patients versus the standard of non-Medicare patients. From job-order costing it is determined that, on average, Medicare patients will require two to three minutes more time with technicians to undress and receive the explanation of the procedure.

Time spent with physicians is usually two to five minutes longer for an EKG interpretation. There are several valid reasons for these unfavorable use variances. The elderly usually have a more complicated medical history, which in turn generates questions regarding medication and general condition. Often information must be given to a family member who coordinates the patient's care as well as to the patient. As the elderly in almost all health situations require more time from expensive personnel, Medicare should consider this as a real-cost item in setting their regulated reimbursement rates.

Whether Medicare allows for these differences or not, they are informative for the provider and should be calculated. For example, suppose that an EKG has a standard requirement of 17 technician minutes and 4 M.D. minutes. However, suppose that for Medicare patients, the actual average is 19 and 6 minutes, respectively. The following variances may be calculated.

Technician Time Use Variance

Actual Inputs × Std. Prices		Std. Allowed × Std. Prices
19 min × $.133		17 min × $.133
$2.53	−	$2.26 = $.27 U

M.D. Time Use Variance

6 min × $.80		4 min × $.80
$4.80	−	$3.20 = $1.60 U

Staff performance can be compared with co-workers in regard to use variance. The employee who spends more time than the standard should be evaluated to uncover the reasons. Motivation and competition among employees is an additional benefit to job-order costing. As staff members were asked to log their time for specific procedures, comparisons resulted. Who performed the fastest EKG, who disinfected and cleaned the sigmoidoscope the quickest, and who spent the most time talking to patients?

The dominant means of control in most private practice settings historically has been personal observation. The manager's perceptions of the relationship of inputs to outputs without any analysis of cost and benefits has guided decision making. With cost information on specific procedures acquired through job-order costing, performance of personnel, volume of procedures, and costs can be evaluated. Comparisons of performance from year to year through a budget system can evolve. Summarizing the past performance forces a budget-type planning of the future.

With every appointment scheduled, the future of a practice is being planned or budgeted. That budget must reflect a desirable mix of procedures or services to ensure a profitable outcome. With job-order costing the manager has a more accurate cost basis on which to budget patient types.

Appendix: Analysis of Physician Wage

Annual Salary Desired $105,600

Fees from hospital patients:

$	200	per day (5 patient visits at $40.00 per visit)
or	1,400	per week (7 days per week)
or	70,000	annually (50 weeks per year)
	−20,000	(estimated uncollected)
$	50,000	Total from hospital patients

$105,600	total income desired
−50,000	hospital income
$55,600	office income desired

Fees from office income:
28 office hours per week × 48 weeks =

1,350	hours per year
−200	(4 hours per week reading, education)
1,150	hours available

$55,600	income ÷ 1,150 hours per year = $48.34/hour
$ 48.00	approximate hourly rate

NOTES

1. P. Kotler and R. Clark, *Marketing for Health Care Organizations* (Prentice-Hall, Inc., New Jersey, 1987, p. 362).

2. "HMOs Hit Medicare Snags," *Physician's Washington Report,* March, 1988, p. 3.

Application 3-2

Product Cost Analysis in the Clinical Laboratory

*Leonard D. Scinto, MS, MPA, is currently
Director of Clinical Chemistry at St.
Joseph Medical Center, Stamford,
Connecticut.*

Cost accounting systems in health care organizations are primarily designed to provide organization-wide cost data to senior administration. A high tech department such as the clinical laboratory requires a different cost system: one that produces accurate data at the production cost level. It is important to recognize that neither system is superior to the other. Each system is necessary for effective and efficient management. They each provide different cost information since their products are different. The health care organization's products are discharged patients; a laboratory's products are test results.[1] The two cost systems are in reality one system, as shown in Figure 3-2-1. They should fit together well in order to derive the maximum information at all levels. The cost elements at the lowest level drive the system. It is at this level that laboratory managers manage production costs. A special cost model must be developed for this purpose.

The major controlling influence on costs produced within the clinical laboratory is the choice of laboratory instrumentation used at the workstation level. Laboratory instruments influence the two largest and important expenses in

any laboratory budget: labor and reagent test supplies. To determine the cost of a laboratory test on a specific instrument, a product costing method must be used. One such method in use

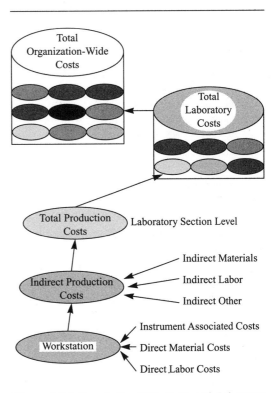

Figure 3-2-1 Organization-Wide Costs and Laboratory Costs

Source: Reprinted from Leonard D. Scinto, "Product Cost Analysis in the Clinical Laboratory," *Hospital Cost Management and Accounting,* Vol. 1, No. 7, October 1989, pp. 1–8. Copyright 1989, Aspen Publishers, Inc.

has been named the instrument cost accounting technique (ICAT).[2] This is the major method emphasized in the cost accounting guidelines developed by the National Committee for Clinical Laboratory Standards.[3] ICAT, which is based on standard cost accounting principles, examines the costs that are directly linked to the production of a laboratory test.

LABORATORY TEST COST CONSTRUCTION

Green and McSherry cite four major aspects of cost control systems[4]:

- cost data collected at the time the work is performed
- comprehensive cost data obtained from all inputs of the work process
- establishment of standard costs for these inputs
- monthly variance investigation of all relevant standard costs

Product cost analysis is the basic starting point for any cost accounting approach in the clinical laboratory. Figure 3-2-2 outlines the classification of laboratory costs. A micro-costing study is first performed to establish the prime cost of each laboratory test at the workstation level.

This part of the analysis deals with three prime cost aspects of laboratory analysis: instrument associated costs, direct material costs, and direct labor costs. Next, indirect production costs are determined for each test. These are specific for each laboratory section (chemistry, immunology, etc.), leading to a total production cost. Finally, general laboratory operating overhead costs are allocated to each test. The resulting product is the total laboratory cost for a particular test. This bottom-up cost analysis approach is illustrated in Figure 3-2-3.

To simplify the analysis of the three prime cost calculations, a PC-based worksheet (such as Lotus 123 or Microsoft Excel) is extremely

helpful. An example of such a worksheet is shown in Exhibit 3-2-1. The worksheet should be generically designed, so it can be used in any laboratory section to determine the costs associated with any instrument or test method.[5]

Instrument Associated Cost Analysis

The various entries on Part 1 of the test cost worksheet provide the basis for instrument associated cost calculations. This information is used in two equations to calculate the instrument's depreciation and maintenance costs per test. It is important not to overlook either of these items in any laboratory test cost analysis. Depreciation costs represent the reduction in value of the instrument as it ages and becomes obsolete. The method of depreciation I have used here is straight-line (the method in use at my hospital) although accelerated depreciation methods can be employed.[6] Maintenance costs involve the expense of cleaning, adjusting and repairing an instrument in order to provide optimal performance.

Test Material Cost Analysis

After each analyte under study has been listed on the worksheet, direct test costs are divided into four segments[7]:

1. the total number of patient tests performed
2. the cost of reagents per test
3. the cost of the test-associated disposables per test
4. the cost of any other instrument-related disposables per test

Laboratory activities and consumables to be considered in test performance analysis include some or all of the following[7]:

1. price per test kit or total reagent costs
2. number of tests per kit or total reagent volume

LABORATORY TOTAL TEST COST

$\|$

COLLECTION AND REPORTING COSTS	+	LABORATORY ADMINISTRATIVE COSTS	=	GENERAL LABORATORY OVERHEAD

include
- specimen collection and processing
- report delivery
- interpretive reporting
- data processing

include
- management salaries
- continuing education
- allocated hospital overhead
- quality assurance
- safety and infection control
- marketing
- communications (phones/fax/ modem)

+

TOTAL PRODUCTION COST (LAB SECTION LEVEL)

$\|$

INDIRECT MATERIAL COSTS	+	INDIRECT LABOR COSTS	+	OTHER INDIRECT COSTS	=	INDIRECT PRODUCTION COSTS

include
- general lab supplies

include
- supervision
- staff training
- overtime

include
- test method research and evaluation

+

INSTRUMENT COSTS	+	DIRECT MATERIAL COSTS	+	DIRECT LABOR COSTS	=	PRIME COST

include
- maintenance
- repairs

include
- reagents
- calibration

include
- pre-analytical, analytical, and post-analytical time

Figure 3-2-2 An Analysis and Classification of Laboratory Costs

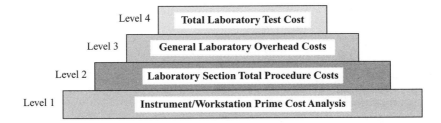

Figure 3-2-3 Laboratory Test Cost Tower: A Bottom-Up Approach. Laboratory test cost analysis is developed by tracing laboratory costs through each level in the tower from bottom to top.

Exhibit 3-2-1 Laboratory Test Prime Cost Worksheet

PART 1: TEST INSTRUMENT RELATED COSTS

Name: Ektachem-700 Chemistry Analyzer   Annual Quality Control Cost: $12,228
Manufacturer: Eastman-Kodak   Annual Maintenance Cost: $14,300
Purchase Price: $121,000   Study Period (Days): 60
Life Expectancy (Years): 10   Starting Date: 1/3/89
Annual Calibration Cost: $3,849   Completion Date: 3/3/89
Total Tests: 75,851

Instrument Cost Calculations (Per Test)

A. Depreciation Costs (Straight-Line) =

$$\frac{\text{Purchase Cost}}{\text{Life Span}} \times \frac{1 \text{ Year}}{365 \text{ Days}} \times \frac{\text{Study Period (Days)}}{\text{Total Tests}}$$

Calculation $0.03 Per Test

B. Maintenance Cost =

$$\frac{\text{Annual Maintenance Cost}}{365 \text{ Days}} \times \frac{\text{Study Period (Days)}}{\text{Total Tests}}$$

Calculation $0.03 Per Test

C. Calibration Costs =

$$\frac{\text{Annual Calibration Cost}}{365 \text{ Days}} \times \frac{\text{Study Period (Days)}}{\text{Total Tests}}$$

Calculation $0.01 Per Test

D. Quality Control Costs =

$$\frac{\text{Annual QC Cost}}{365 \text{ Days}} \times \frac{\text{Study Period (Days)}}{\text{Total Tests}}$$

Calculation $0.03 Per Test

TOTAL INSTRUMENT COSTS $0.10 Per Test

PART 2: DIRECT TEST MATERIALS COSTS

Test Name	Reagents	Test-Related Disposables	Instrument-Related Disposables	Total Tests	Material Cost (Per Test)
Glucose	$ 2,924.36	$100.84	$ 302.52	10,084	$0.33
BUN	2,709.28	96.76	290.28	9,676	0.32
Sodium	2,412.54	92.79	278.37	9,279	0.30
Potassium	2,558.92	98.42	295.26	9,842	0.30
Chloride	2,680.47	92.43	277.29	9,243	0.33
CO_2	2,244.24	93.51	280.53	9,351	0.28
Creatinine	2,090.66	95.03	285.09	9,503	0.26
Cholesterol	2,750.63	88.73	266.19	8,873	0.35
TOTALS	$20,371.10 +	$758.51 +	$2,275.53 ÷	75,851 =	$0.31

$$\text{Direct Material Costs Calculation (Per Test)} = \frac{\text{Reagents Costs} + \text{Test Disposables} + \text{Instrument Disposables}}{\text{Number of Tests}}$$

continues

Exhibit 3-2-1 continued

PART 3: DIRECT TEST LABOR

Time Segment	FTE Minute/Test	Annual Salary	Time Segment Labor Cost
Pre-Analytical	1.5	$27,740.00	$0.41
Analytical	1.0	$27,740.00	0.27
Post-Analytical	2.0	$27,740.00	0.55
Totals	4.5		$1.23

Direct Labor Cost Per Test Calculations:

Step One:

$$\frac{\text{Annual Salary}}{2{,}080 \text{ Paid Hours/Year}} \div 60 \text{ Minutes} = \text{Salary Cost/Minute}$$

Step Two:

Salary Cost/Minute $\times$ Minutes To Perform Test = Salary Cost/Test

Step Three:

Salary Cost/Test $\times$ 1.23 Fringe Benefit Factor = Total Labor Cost/Test

Calculations:

	Pre-Analytical	Analytical	Post-Analytical	Total
Step 1	$0.22	$0.22	$0.22	
Step 2	$0.33	$0.22	$0.44	
Step 3	$0.41	$0.27	$0.55	$1.23

PART 4: TOTALS

Test Name	Instrument Costs	Material Costs	Labor Costs	Test Prime Costs
Glucose	$0.10	$0.33	$1.23	$1.66
BUN	0.10	0.32	1.23	1.65
Sodium	0.10	0.30	1.23	1.63
Potassium	0.10	0.30	1.23	1.63
Chloride	0.10	0.33	1.23	1.66
CO_2	0.10	0.28	1.23	1.61
Creatinine	0.10	0.26	1.23	1.59
Cholesterol	0.10	0.35	1.23	1.68

3. number of controls run per test
4. number of calibrators run per test
5. single or replicate analysis per test
6. cost of disposable items used to perform the test
7. cost of specimen collection and processing
8. total number of tests performed during the study period.

The formula for direct materials per test is shown in Part 2 of the worksheet. The number of tests are divided into the cost of reagents, test associated disposables and instrument related disposables.

Direct Labor Cost

This is the total compensation required for personnel to perform all of the pre-analytical, analytical, and post-analytical steps of a test. The College of American Pathologists (CAP) Workload Recording Method, the only nationally recognized workload accounting system for clinical laboratories, was not developed for the purpose of test cost analysis, although many clinical laboratories use it for this purpose for lack of a better system. It was intended to be used to determine staffing needs as well as to measure productivity.[8] Consequently, it overlooks most (if not all) of the pre- and post-analytical steps in laboratory test production. These two steps are important labor intensive aspects of test analysis. They provide far more information on labor costs than a time study method that uses just the analytical phase in test production, as is the case in the CAP method.

Pre-analytical Time

This begins when the specimen arrives in the laboratory and continues up until the start of analysis. It involves activities such as specimen centrifugation, separation, and preparation. Since different staff members may be involved with various pre-analytical aspects, it is impor-

tant to accurately record the time and labor rate of each staff member.

Analytical Time

This is the analysis time required to perform all required procedures up to reporting of results. This is usually the least labor intensive phase, since most testing done in the clinical laboratory today is performed on microcomputer-directed high speed automated analyzers. Operation intervention in this phase is usually minimal.

Post-analytical Time

This accounts for the labor required to report results. This includes entering and verifying results in a computer, sorting, filing and telephoning reports. Time spent daily, weekly, and monthly performing instrument maintenance should be recorded in this phase.

The ICAT method calculates the full fiscal burden, not just productivity of a laboratory instrument or test method. The total number of full-time equivalents (FTEs) per minute required to produce a test and the total labor cost (annual salary plus fringe benefits) of personnel performing the work are determined for each of the three analytical time segments, as shown in Part 3 of the worksheet.

INDIRECT COSTS OF TEST PRODUCTION

These are costs that cannot be directly related to a test or the instrument required to produce the test. As illustrated in Figure 3-2-2, they include the cost of indirect labor, materials, and other items that cannot be directly charged to the laboratory test. These costs are commonly added on as a proportionate share to the direct costs associated with a particular test. Indirect production costs at the lab section level can be calculated out to a single per-test cost by dividing the section level's total indirect cost by the total number of tests performed in the section. This single per test cost when added to the prime cost will give the full production cost at the laboratory section level. Another tier of indirect costs is incurred at the department level. These costs include the collection and reporting of all laboratory tests as well as the allocated hospital overhead costs assigned to the laboratory department. Other indirect cost items that are important to consider in overall operations are listed in Figure 3-2-2. These are related to the nontechnical aspects of the production process: marketing, administration, and maintaining a safe and adequate work environment.

The general laboratory overhead can be converted to a per-test unit cost by dividing the total overhead cost by the total number of tests produced in all laboratory sections. The general laboratory overhead per test added to the full production cost (at the section level) ultimately yields the total laboratory cost per test.

TEST COST ANALYSIS AS A MANAGEMENT TOOL

Test cost analysis provides important financial information to laboratory managers. It can identify proper batch sizes to minimize waste, analyze the fiscal impact of a new proposed equipment purchase, and analyze the cost efficiency of existing instrumentation. Cost analysis provides managers with a rational mechanism for selecting the most cost-effective testing method among several new laboratory procedures, all claiming to be the least expensive to use. Laboratory budgeting becomes more effective with a cost analysis system in place. Managers who have accurate and timely test cost and workload information at their disposal are able to accurately project the effects of adding new or increased testing on staffing requirements, inventory, revenues, and expenditures.

Many laboratories have set testing charges based on a comparison with other laboratories in their market area. This method is highly unreliable. Total laboratory test cost can vary widely from laboratory to laboratory due to different methods, instruments, labor costs, and operating overhead. Laboratories using test cost analysis can identify actual direct supply and reagent costs, instrument costs, labor costs, and indirect overhead costs. Using total laboratory test cost, laboratory managers can assign a realistic charge for a test and method.

The establishment of the Prospective Payment System has given clinical laboratories a strong motivation for establishing true laboratory test costs. It has become increasingly important for clinical laboratories to focus on the actual costs of tests used to diagnose and monitor patients who are classified by DRGs. Clinical laboratory scientists and administrators working with various medical specialists are selecting the most sensitive and specific tests required to identify and monitor disease conditions within selected DRGs. Test choices are then grouped together to form a unique DRG-focused test panel. The test costs associated with this test panel are then calculated and can be rolled into other organization-wide costs to determine the fully loaded cost of a particular DRG category. Exhibit 3-2-2 shows the results of laboratory test costs for a new admission with diabetes.[9]

CONCLUSION

Every laboratory has a unique cost profile for the tests it performs. This is the result of different instruments, wage and benefit packages, employee productivity levels, and various costs associated with reagents, supplies, and overhead in a particular laboratory. Laboratories using idealized test cost data provided by a diagnostic manufacturer, which only include reagent and supply costs, will underestimate actual laboratory test costs by the exclusion of labor costs and other indirect expenses. The use of product cost analysis leads to improved management control by allowing laboratory managers to identify the optimal frequency and size of test runs, and efficient staffing for each workstation, as well as identifying and choosing economical reagents and testing supplies.

Exhibit 3-2-2 Laboratory Cost Analysis Worksheet for a Diabetes Admission

DRG 294, Diabetes ≥ 36 Years Old
Principal Diagnosis:
  Type 2 Diabetes Mellitus with Renal Manifestations
  Non-Insulin Dependent

	Direct Cost Per Test			Indirect Costs	
Test	Instrument Cost	Materials Cost	Labor Cost	Production Cost	Laboratory Overhead
Chemistry Profile					
Glucose	$0.10	$0.33	$11.01	$1.98	$4.06
BUN	0.10	0.32			
Sodium	0.10	0.30			
Potassium	0.10	0.30			
CO_2	0.10	0.28			
Chloride	0.10	0.33			
Creatinine	0.10	0.26			
Albumin	0.10	0.26			
Cholesterol	0.10	0.35			
Urine Creatinine	0.10	0.97	1.53	0.44	
Urine Microscopic	Manual	0.26	2.35	0.37	
Hemoglobin	0.15	0.14	1.10	0.75	
Hematocrit	0.15	0.14	1.10	0.75	
TOTALS	$1.30	$4.24	$17.09	$4.29	$4.06

DRG 294: LABORATORY TOTAL COST $30.98

The laboratory product cost analysis I have outlined here provides test costs and operation costs at various levels, beginning at the instrument/workstation, moving up to the section level, and ending at the laboratory department as a whole. The full laboratory test cost can then be used to determine the combined cost of a test profile for a specific DRG category. This laboratory DRG cost can then be used directly in the health care organization-wide cost system to monitor a full cost per patient admission.

In today's rapidly changing health care environment, clinical laboratory managers must be able to measure the actual cost of laboratory operations in order to make informed decisions and provide effective financial management of the clinical laboratory department.

NOTES

1. Patterson, P.P. Cost Accounting in Hospitals and Clinical Laboratories: Part 1, *Clinical Laboratory Management Review* 1988, 2(6):345.

2. Travers, E.M. and Krochmal, C.F. A New Way to Determine Test Cost Per Instrument, Part 1, *Medical Laboratory Observer* 1988, 20(10): 25.

3. National Committee for Clinical Laboratory Standards. *Draft Guidelines on Laboratory Cost Accounting.* Villanova, Pa., NCCLS, 1987.

4. Green, H.H. and McSherry, E. New case mix management tool for the DRG era, *VA Practitioner* 1985, 2:64.

5. Travers and Krochmal, p. 28.

6. Weston, J.F. and Copeland, T.E. "Managerial Finance," pp. 63–66.

7. Travers and Krochmal, p. 27.

8. College of American Pathologists, *Manual for Laboratory Workload Recording Method,* pp. 1–2, 1985.

9. Travers and Krochmal, p. 60.

BIBLIOGRAPHY

Dominiak, G.F. and Louderback, J.G., *Managerial Accounting.* Boston, Mass.: PWS-Kent Publishing, 1988.

Gore, M.J., Financial Management of the Clinical Laboratory: How To Improve Present Systems. *Medical Laboratory Observer,* 1988, 20(3):37–40.

Horngren, C.T., *Cost Accounting: A Managerial Emphasis,* sixth edition. Englewood Cliffs, N.J.: Prentice-Hall, 1986.

Horngren, C.T. and Sundem, G.L., *Introduction to Financial Accounting,* third edition. Englewood Cliffs, N.J.: Prentice-Hall, 1987.

Finkler, S.A., *Budgeting Concepts for Nurse Managers.* New York, N.Y.: Grune and Stratton, 1984.

Matz, A. and Usry, M.F., *Cost Accounting: Planning and Control,* seventh edition. Cincinnati, Ohio: Southwestern Publishing, 1980.

Sattler, J. and Smith, A., *Financial Management of the Clinical Laboratory.* Oradell, N.J.: Medical Economics, 1986.

Suver, J.D. and Neumann, B.R., *Management Accounting for Healthcare Organizations.* Chicago, Healthcare Financial Management Association, 1985.

Application 3-3

Product Costing for Health Care Firms

*William O. Cleverley, PhD, is currently Professor of Hospital
and Health Services, Administrative Division
at Ohio State University, Columbus, Ohio*

The implementation of the prospective payment system has brought enormous interest in cost accounting, and this interest is not limited to the hospital industry. The interest in developing sophisticated cost accounting systems is present in all sectors of the health care industry. Most, if not all, of this interest is a reflection of fixed prices for services and increasing economic competition among health care providers.[1]

This article identifies a framework for the discussion and development of cost accounting systems in the health care sector. Great reliance is placed on the similarities rather than the differences in cost accounting systems as they exist in industry. The framework requires two sets of standards, one relating to the production of departmental products, and one relating to the treatment protocol for defined patient categories.

RELATIONSHIP OF COST INFORMATION TO PLANNING, BUDGETING, AND CONTROL

Cost information is of value only as it aids in the management decision-making process.[2] Fig-ure 3-3-1 presents a schematic of the planning, budgeting, and control process in any business. Of special interest is the decision output of the planning process. This process should detail the products or product lines that the business will produce during the planning period.

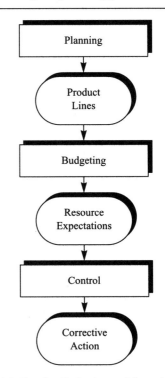

Figure 3-3-1 Planning, Budgeting, and Control Process

Source: Reprinted from William O. Cleverley, "Product Costing for Health Care Firms," *Health Care Management Review,* Vol. 12, No. 4, Fall 1987, pp. 39–48. Copyright 1987, Aspen Publishers, Inc.

Products and Product Lines

The term product or product line seems fairly simple and easy to understand in most business firms. For example, an automobile manufacturer produces cars. The finished car is clearly the product of the automobile firm. Individual types of cars may be grouped to form product lines such as the Chevrolet product line of General Motors.

Is the definition of a product as simple in the health care sector? Many individuals feel very strongly that products cannot be defined easily in health care firms. The major dilemma seems to arise in the area of patients versus products. In short, is the patient the product or is the product individual services such as laboratory tests, nursing care, and meals? In most situations the patient is the basic product of health care firms. This means that the wide range of services provided to patients, such as nursing, prescriptions, and tests, should be viewed as intermediate products and not final products. There is little difference between this situation and that in most manufacturing settings. For example, fenders are on one hand a product but they are really nothing more than intermediate products to the final product of a completed automobile. The automobile is sold, not the fenders. In the same vein, a treated patient, rather than an individual service provided in isolation, generates revenue. In short, a hospital that provided only laboratory tests would not be a hospital but a laboratory. One needs patients to be a health care provider.

Product lines represent an amalgamation of patients in a way that makes business sense. Sometimes people use the term strategic business units to refer to areas of activity that may stand alone. In this discussion a product line is a unit of business activity that requires a go or no go decision. In this context, a diagnosis related group (DRG) is not a product line. Eliminating one DRG is probably not possible, because that DRG may be linked to other DRGs within a clinical specialty area. For example, it may be impossible to stop producing DRG #36 (retinal procedures) without also eliminating other DRGs such as DRG #39 (lens procedure). In most cases the clinical specialty, such as ophthalmology, constitutes the product line rather than an individual DRG.

Budgeting and Resource Expectations

The budgeting phase of operations involves a translation of the product line decisions reached earlier in the planning phase into a set of resource expectations. The primary purpose of this activity is twofold. First, management must assure itself that there will be sufficient funds to maintain financial solvency. Just as individuals must live within their financial means so must any health care business entity. Second, the resulting budget serves as a basis for management control. If budget expectations are not realized, management must discover why not and take corrective actions. A budget or set of resource expectations can be thought of as a standard costing system. The budget represents management's expectations about how costs should behave given a certain set of volume expectations.

The key aspect of budgeting is the translation of product line decisions into precise and specific sets of resource expectations. Five basic steps are involved:

1. defining volume of patients by case type to be treated in the budget period;
2. defining standard treatment protocol by case type;
3. defining required departmental volumes;
4. defining standard cost profiles for departmental outputs; and
5. defining prices to be paid for resources.

The primary output of the budgeting process is a series of departmental budgets that spell out what costs should be during the coming budget period. In the development of a budget, the establishment of three separate sets of standards is involved.

Control

The control phase of business operations monitors actual cost experience and compares it to budgetary expectations. If there are deviations from expectations, management analyzes the causes for the deviation. If the deviation is favorable, management may seek to make whatever action created the variance a permanent part of operations. If the variance is unfavorable, action will be taken to prevent a recurrence, if possible. Much of the control phase centers around the topic of variance analysis.

COSTING PROCESS

Most firms, whether they are hospitals, nursing homes, or steel manufacturers, have fairly similar costing systems. In fact, the similarities outweigh the differences in most cases. Figure 3-3-2 provides a schematic of the cost measurement process that exists in most business firms.[3] This process consists of three activities: valuation, allocation, and product specification.

Valuation

Valuation has always been a thorny issue for accountants, one that has not been satisfactorily resolved even today. One need only see the current controversy over replacement costs versus historical costs to see the problem in full bloom. For discussion purposes, the valuation process has been split into two areas, basis and assignment over time. To some degree these two areas are not mutually exclusive and overlap with one

another. However, both determine the total value of a resource that is used to cost a final product.

The valuation basis is the process whereby a value is assigned to each resource transaction occurring between the entity being accounted for and another entity. In most situations this is historical cost. Once a value for a resource is established, there are many situations where that value will have to be assigned over time. Specifically, there are two major categories of situations. First, in many situations the value is expended prior to the actual reporting of expense. The best example of this is depreciation. Second are situations where expense is recognized prior to an actual expenditure. Normal accruals such as wages and salaries are examples of this category.

Allocation

The end result of the cost allocation process is assignment of all costs or values determined in the valuation phase to direct departments.[4] Two phases of activity are involved in accomplishing this objective. First, all resource values to be recorded as expense in a given period are assigned or allocated to the direct and indirect departments as direct expenses. Second, once the initial cost assignment to individual departments has been made, a further allocation is required. In this phase the expenses of the indi-

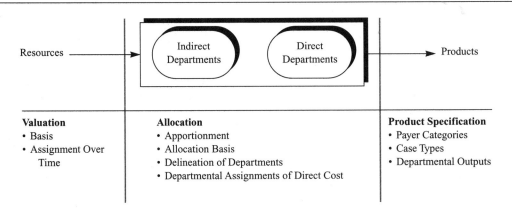

Figure 3-3-2 Cost Measurement Process

rect departments are assigned to the direct departments.

Using this framework for analysis, costing issues may be subcategorized. In the initial cost assignment phase, there appear to be two major areas that relate to the underlying costing process: assigning cost to departments and defining the indirect and direct departments. The first area concerns situations where the departmental structure currently specified is not questioned, but some of the initial value assignments may be. For example, premiums paid for malpractice insurance might be charged to the administration and general department or more directly to the nursing and professional departments that are involved. In the second area, the existing departmental structure may be revised. For example, the administration and general department may be split into several new departments such as nonpatient telephones, data processing, purchasing, admitting, business office, and other.

In the second phase of cost allocation, which consists of reassignment from indirect departments to direct departments, there are also two primary categories: selection of the cost apportionment method and selection of the appropriate allocation basis. Cost apportionment methods such as stepdown, double distribution, or simultaneous equations are simply mathematical algorithms that redistribute cost from existing indirect departments to direct departments given defined allocation bases. An example of the selection of an appropriate allocation basis for an indirect department might be square feet covered or hours worked for housekeeping.

Product Specification

In most health care firms there are two phases to the production (or treatment) process. Figure 3-3-3 provides a schematic of this process and also introduces a few new terms.

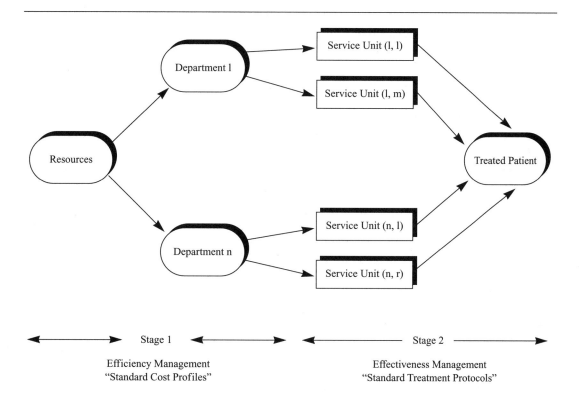

Figure 3-3-3 Production Process for Health Care Firms

In stage one of the production process resources are acquired and consumed within departments to produce a product that is defined as a service unit (SU). All departments have SUs but not all departments have the same number of SUs. For example, the nursing department may provide four levels of care, acuity level 1, 2, 3, or 4. The laboratory may have 100 or more separate SUs related to specific tests they provide. Not all SUs can be directly associated with the delivery of patient care. Some SUs may be indirectly associated with patient treatment. For example, the housekeeping staff may clean laboratory areas but there is no direct association of this effort with patient treatment. However, the cleaning of a patient's room is a housekeeping SU that could be associated with a patient.

The second production phase relates to the actual consumption of specific SUs in the treatment of a patient. Much of this production process is actually managed by the physician. This is true irrespective of the setting (e.g., hospital, nursing home, home health care firm, or clinic). The physician will prescribe the specific SUs required to effectively treat a given patient.

The lack of authority in this area complicates management's efforts to budget and control its costs. This is not meant to be a negative reflection of current health care delivery. Everyone would prefer to have a qualified physician directing care as opposed to a lay health care executive. This is perhaps the area of greatest difference between health care firms and other business entities. Management at General Motors can decide which automobiles will have factory-installed air conditioning and tinted glass. A hospital will find it very difficult to direct a physician to prescribe or not prescribe a given procedure when treating a patient.

Products to be costed may vary depending on the specific decision under consideration. At one level, management may be interested in the cost of a specific service unit or departmental output. Prices for some SUs, such as X-ray procedures, may have to be established, and management needs to know their costs. In other situations the cost of a specific treated patient or grouping of treated patients may be desired. For example, management may wish to bid on a contract to provide home health services to a health maintenance organization (HMO). It is important for them to understand what the costs of treating HMO patients are likely to be. Once the contract is signed, management needs to determine the actual costs of treating patients from the HMO in order to measure overall profitability from that segment of the business. Alternatively, a grouping of patients by specialty may also be necessary. A hospital may wish to know if it is losing money from treating a particular DRG entity or some grouping of DRGs, such as obstetrics.

STANDARDS DEVELOPMENT

The key to successful product costing systems is fairly simple to identify. Management must be able to develop and maintain two systems: standard cost profiles (SCPs) and standard treatment protocols (STPs).

Figure 3-3-3 illustrates the relationship between these two systems. The linking pin between the systems is the SU concept. In the simplest language, management must be able to know what it costs to produce an SU. It must also know what SUs are needed to treat a given patient.

Standard Cost Profiles

An SCP is not a new concept. It has been used in cost accounting systems in manufacturing for many years. There are two key elements to an SCP: the defined SU being costed and the profile of resources required to produce the SU.

As mentioned, the number of SUs in a given department may vary. Some departments may have one while others may have 100 or more. If the number of SUs is large there may be an unacceptable level of costing detail involved to make the system feasible. In these situations it may be useful to aggregate some of the different SUs. For example, the laboratory may have 1,000 or more tests to perform. It may make sense in this situation to develop cost profiles for only the most commonly performed tests and use some arbitrary assignment method for the remaining tests.

The SU does not have to be a product or service that is directly performed for a patient. Many of the so-called indirect departments do not provide services or products to the patient. Instead, their products or services are consumed by other departments, both direct and indirect.

It is also important to note that many indirect departments may have SUs that are directly provided for the patient. For example, the dietary department is often considered to be indirect because no revenue is billed for its product to the patient. However, a meal furnished to a patient is an SU that is just as direct as a laboratory test or a chest X-ray. Similarly, the housekeeping staff may provide cleaning services to a patient's room, and that cleaning service is a direct service consumed by the patient.

SUs may also be categorized as direct or indirect. A direct SU is one that may be associated with a given patient. An indirect SU is a service or product provided to another department as opposed to a patient. The differentiation between direct and indirect SUs is important not only in the development of SCPs but also in the development of STPs. Direct SUs must be identified when STPs are defined while indirect SUs need not be specifically identified, although some estimate of allocated cost is often required.

An SCP for a given SU should list the resource expense categories[5] of direct expenses, such as labor, materials, and departmental overhead, and allocated overhead. In addition, the SCP should ideally categorize the expense as variable or fixed. This separation is important to many areas of management decision making. Specifically, variable and fixed cost differentiation is critical to many incremental pricing and volume decisions. Variable and fixed cost differentiation is also important to flexible budgeting systems and management control.

Table 3-3-1 presents an SCP that will be used for discussion purposes. In the table, the SU being profiled is a regular patient meal provided by the dietary department. The total cost of providing one regular patient meal or SU #181 is $2.50. Variable cost per meal is $1.30 and average fixed cost per meal is $1.20.

In most situations direct labor will be the largest single expense category. In this example, this is not true because the direct material cost, mostly raw food, is larger. It would be possible, and in many cases desirable, to define direct labor costs by labor category. For example, in this case cooks, dietary aides, and dishwashers could be listed separately.

An important point to resolve is the division of cost into fixed and variable quantities. Table 3-3-1 indicates that .05 units of variable labor time are required per meal and .05 units of fixed labor are required per meal. A variety of methods that might be useful in splitting costs into fixed and variable elements is discussed in the literature. The fixed cost assignment is an average that is based on some expected level of volume. It is important to remember this point

Table 3-3-1 Standard Cost Profile for Dietary Department, Regular Patient Meal*

Cost Category	Quantity Required		Unit Cost	Variable Cost	Average Fixed Cost	Average Total Cost
	Variable	Fixed				
Direct labor	.05	.05	$ 6.00	$ .30	$ .30	$ .60
Direct materials	1	0	1.00	1.00	0	1.00
Departmental overhead	0	1	.50	0	.50	.50
Allocated costs						
Housekeeping	0	.1	1.00	0	.10	.10
Plant operation	0	1	.10	0	.10	.10
Administration	0	.02	10.00	0	.20	.20
Total				$1.30	$1.20	$2.50

* Expected volume = 1,600 SU #181

when developing SCPs. A decline in volume below expected levels will raise the average cost of production.

The third column in Table 3-3-1 is unit cost. This value represents management's best guess as to the cost or price of the resources to be used in the production process. For example, the dietary SCP indicates a price of six dollars per unit of direct labor. This value reflects the expected wage per hour to be paid for direct labor in the dietary department. Again, it might be possible and desirable to further break out direct labor into specific job classifications. This will usually permit better costing but it does require more effort.

Any fringe benefit costs associated with labor should be included in the unit cost. For example, the average direct hourly wage in the dietary department might be five dollars per hour, but fringe benefits may average 20 percent. In this case the effective wage would be six dollars per hour.

Departmental overhead consists of expenses directly charged to a department that do not represent labor or materials. Common examples might be equipment costs, travel allowances, outside purchased services, publications, and other small items. Usually these items do not vary with level of activity or volume but remain fixed for the budgetary period. If this is the case, assignment to an SCP can be based on a simple average. For example, assume that the dietary department expects to provide 200,000 regular patient meals next year. Furthermore, assume that the department has been authorized to spend $100,000 in discretionary areas that constitute departmental overhead. The average cost per meal for these discretionary costs would be $.50 and would be fixed.

Allocated costs are probably the most difficult to assign in most situations. In the dietary example only three areas are included, which is probably an understatement. A number of other departments would most likely provide service to the dietary department and would be included in the SCP.

There are two major alternatives to provide estimates of allocated costs in an SCP. First, individual costing studies could be performed and services from one department to others could be recorded. This process may be expensive and not worth the effort. For example, utility costs could be associated with each department if separate meters were installed. But the installation of these meters would probably not be an effective expenditure of funds, because costing accuracy would not be improved enough to justify the extra expense.

The second approach to allocating overhead costs would be a simple averaging method. All overhead costs might be aggregated and apportioned to other departments using direct expenses, full-time equivalents, or some other basis. This method is relatively simple, but its accuracy is suspect if significant variation in departmental utilization exists.

The best approach to costing is to identify as many direct SUs as possible. These SUs can be directly associated with a patient, and there are far more of these SUs than most people believe. For example, a meal provided to a patient is a direct SU that is currently treated as an indirect product in most costing systems. Laundry and linen departments have certain SUs that are directly associated with a patient, such as clean sheets and gowns. Housekeeping departments provide direct services to patients when they clean rooms. Administration and medical records departments also provide specific services to patients in the form of processed paperwork and insurance forms. When many of these costs that are currently regarded as indirect are reclassified as direct, there will be a substantially lower level of indirect costs requiring allocation. This system would improve the costing of patients, who are considered the product, and make the allocation of indirect costs less critical. Currently, indirect costs in many health care settings may be in excess of 50 percent of total cost. With better identification of services provided or SUs, the actual percentage could be reduced to 25 percent or lower.

Standard Treatment Protocols

There is an analogy between an STP and a job order cost sheet used in industrial cost accounting. In a job order cost system, a separate cost sheet is completed for each specific job, because each job may be different from jobs performed in the past and jobs to be performed in the future. Automobile repairs are an excellent example of a job order cost system. A separate cost sheet is prepared for each job. The cost sheet also serves as the bill or invoice to the customer.

Health care firms operate in a job cost setting. A patient's treatment may vary significantly across patients. The patient's bill may be thought of as a job order cost sheet. The bill reflects the actual services provided during the course of the patient's treatment. Of course, not all of the services provided are reflected in the patient's bill. For example, meals provided are rarely charged as a separate item.

In a typical job order cost setting, standards may not always be developed. When someone drops a car off for service, the dealer does not prepare a standard job order cost sheet. He or she has no incentive to do so because he or she expects the person to pay the actual costs of the service when he or she picks up the car. Otherwise, the dealer may retain the car as collateral.

A similar situation used to exist in health care firms. The client or patient would pay for the actual cost of services provided. Today this situation does not exist for many products. Health care firms are often paid a fixed fee or price irrespective of the range of services provided. Medicare's DRG payment system is an example of this type of payment philosophy.

Because the majority of revenue may be derived from fixed price payers, it is necessary to define STPs where possible. Table 3-3-2 provides an STP for DRG #208. This STP is intended to be used as an illustration only and should not be considered a realistic STP for DRG #208.

An examination of Table 3-3-2 shows that costs are again split into fixed and variable components. For example, this STP requires 25 patient meals at a variable cost of $1.30 per meal and a fixed cost of $1.20 per meal. The basis for these data would be the SCPs. In the dietary example, the split between variable and fixed cost is reflected in Table 3-3-1.

This separation of fixed and variable costs is extremely valuable for management in planning and control decisions. For example, if Medicare paid the hospital $1,400.00 for every DRG #208 treated, in the short run it would be financially wise to continue treating DRG #208 cases, because the payment of $1,400 exceeds the variable cost of $1,014.50 and therefore contributes to fixed costs.

Table 3-3-2 also depicts two areas where no actual quantity is specified. Pharmacy prescriptions and other laboratory tests are not individually identified. Instead the total cost of the services is shown with a separation into fixed and variable costs. Because of the large number of products provided in each of these areas, it would be impossible to develop an SCP for every possible laboratory test or pharmacy pre-

Table 3-3-2 Standard Treatment Protocol, DRG #208, Disorder of Biliary Tract

SU No.	SU Name	Quantity	Variable Cost/Unit	Fixed Cost/Unit	Total Cost/Unit	Total Variable Cost	Total Fixed Cost	Total Cost
1	Admission process	1	$48.00	$52.00	$100.00	$ 48.00	$ 52.00	$ 100.00
7	Nursing care level 1	1	80.00	40.00	120.00	80.00	40.00	120.00
8	Nursing care level 2	7	85.00	45.00	130.00	595.00	315.00	910.00
9	Nursing care level 3	1	110.00	45.00	155.00	110.00	45.00	155.00
29	Pharmacy prescriptions		38.00	19.00	57.00	38.00	19.00	57.00
38	Chest X-ray	1	12.00	8.00	20.00	12.00	8.00	20.00
46	Laboratory CBC	1	4.00	3.50	7.50	4.00	3.50	7.50
49	Other laboratory tests		85.00	55.00	140.00	85.00	55.00	140.00
57	Patient meals	25	1.30	1.20	2.50	32.50	30.00	62.50
65	Clean linen changes	5	.60	.50	1.10	3.00	2.50	5.50
93	Room preparation	1	7.00	3.00	10.00	7.00	3.00	10.00
						$1,014.50	$573.00	$1,587.50

scription. Some of the heavier volume laboratory tests or pharmacy prescriptions may be separately identified and costed. Table 3-3-2 indicates that a complete blood cell count (CBC) is a separate SU in the laboratory department.

Some of the items shown in Table 3-3-2 may not be reflected in a patient's bill. Patient meals, clean linen changes, room preparation, and admission paperwork processed would not usually be reflected in the patient's bill. In addition, separation of nursing care by acuity level may not be identified in the bill. Many hospitals do not distinguish between levels of nursing in their pricing structures.

The final point to emphasize is that not all SUs will show up in an STP. Only those SUs that are classified as direct will be listed. A direct SU is one that can be directly traced or associated with patient care. The costs associated with the provision of indirect SUs will be allocated to the direct SUs. The objective, however, is to create as many direct SUs as possible.

VARIANCE ANALYSIS

Variance analysis provides a useful summary of the health care production process. In general there are four types of variances that will be identified in the variance analysis phase of control given earlier systems of standards.[6] The four variances are price (rate), efficiency, volume, and intensity. The first three variances are a direct result of the development of the SCPs and result from departmental activity. A rate or price variance reflects the difference between the price actually paid and the standard price multiplied by the actual quantity used and may be expressed in the following way:

$$\left(\begin{array}{c} \text{Actual} \\ \text{price} \end{array} - \begin{array}{c} \text{Standard} \\ \text{price} \end{array} \right) \times \begin{array}{c} \text{Actual} \\ \text{quantity} \end{array}$$

For example, assume that the dietary department in Table 3-3-1 actually produced 1,500 patient meals for the period in question. To produce these meals it used 180 hours of labor and

paid \$6.25 per hour. The price or rate variance would be \$45.00, expressed as (\$6.25 – \$6.00) × 180 hours. This variance would be unfavorable because the department paid \$6.25 per hour when the expected rate was \$6.00. The actual quantity of labor used was 180 hours.

An efficiency variance reflects productivity in the production process. It is derived by multiplying the difference between actual quantity used and standard quantity by the standard price and may be expressed in the following way:

$$\left(\begin{array}{c} \text{Actual} \\ \text{quantity} \end{array} - \begin{array}{c} \text{Standard} \\ \text{quantity} \end{array} \right) \times \begin{array}{c} \text{Standard} \\ \text{price} \end{array}$$

In the example above, the efficiency variance would be \$150 unfavorable, expressed as (180 hours – 155 hours) × \$6.00. Standard labor is derived by multiplying the variable labor requirement of .05 by the number of meals produced, 1,500, to get 75 hours. The budgeted fixed labor requirement of 80 hours (.05 × 1,600 meals) is added to this figure. During the period 25 hours more labor than expected were used, resulting in the unfavorable efficiency variance of \$150.

The volume variance reflects differences between expected output and actual output. Volume variances exist in situations where fixed costs are present. If no fixed costs existed, resources required per unit would be constant. This would mean that the cost per unit of production should be constant. For most situations this is not a reasonable expectation, because fixed costs do exist. The volume variance is derived by multiplying the expected average fixed cost per unit by the difference between budgeted volume and actual volume and may be expressed in the following way:

$$\left(\begin{array}{c} \text{Budgeted} \\ \text{volume} \end{array} - \begin{array}{c} \text{Actual} \\ \text{volume} \end{array} \right) \times \begin{array}{c} \text{Average fixed} \\ \text{cost per unit} \end{array}$$

In the case of direct labor for the dietary department, the volume variance would be an unfavorable \$30, expressed as (1,600 meals – 1,500 meals) × \$.30.

The total of these variances equals the difference between actual costs incurred for direct labor and the standard cost of direct labor assigned to the SU, a patient meal in this example.

Actual direct labor ($6.25 × 180 hours)	$1,125
– Standard cost ($0.60 × 1,500 meals)	900
= Total variance	$ 225
Price variance	$ 45.00
Efficiency variance	150.00
Volume variance	30.00
Total variance	$225.00

The intensity variance results from the difference between the quantity of SUs actually required in treating a patient and the quantity called for in the STP. For example, if 20 meals were provided a patient categorized as DRG #208, there would be a favorable variance of five meals given the STP data in Table 3-3-2.

Intensity variances are generically defined in the following way:

$$\left(\begin{array}{c} \text{Actual} \\ \text{SUs} \end{array} - \begin{array}{c} \text{Standard} \\ \text{SUs} \end{array} \right) \times \text{Price per SU}$$

The intensity variance for this patient with respect to meals would be a favorable $12.50, expressed as (20 meals – 25 meals) × $2.50.

It may be useful to split intensity variances into fixed and variable elements. In this example, it is probably not fair to say that $12.50 was realized in savings because five fewer meals were delivered. Five times $1.30, the variable cost, may be a better reflection of short-term realized savings.

In addition to determining variances, it is important to specify the party responsible for the variances. After all, this is part of the basis for standard costing—being able to take action through individuals to correct unfavorable variances. It is clear that three variances—price, efficiency, and volume—will be isolated in the department accounts. However, the departmental manager may not be responsible for all variation, especially in the volume area. Usually, most departmental managers have little control over volume. They merely react to the services required from their departments.

The intensity variance can be largely associated with a given physician. Most of the SUs are of a medical nature and result from physician decisions regarding testing or length of stay. It may be very useful, therefore, to accumulate intensity variances by physicians. Periodic discussions regarding these variations can be most useful to both the health care executive and the physician. Ideally, physicians should take an active role in developing the STPs.

Using a standard costing approach based on SCPs and STPs is an effective way to assess planning decisions. It is also useful in control decisions. As prospective pricing and competitive discounting take on greater importance, so will standard costing in the increasing effort to contain health care costs while providing quality care.

NOTES

1. Cleverley, W. "Cost Accounting Pins a Value to DRGs." *Modern Healthcare* 14 (April 1984): 172–179.

2. Horngren, C. *Cost Accounting: A Managerial Emphasis.* 4th ed. Englewood Cliffs, N.J.: Prentice-Hall, 1977.

3. Cleverley, W. "Reimbursement Management." *Topics In Health Care Financing* 4 (Fall 1977): 13–28.

4. American Hospital Association. *Cost Finding and Rate Setting for Hospitals.* Financial Management Series. Chicago: AHA, 1968.

5. Lerner, W., Wellman, W., and Burik, D. "Pricing Hospital Units of Service Using Microcosting Techniques." *Hospital and Health Services Administration* 30 (January–February 1985): 7–28.

6. Suver, J., and Neumann, B. *Management Accounting for Health Care Organizations.* Chicago: Hospital Financial Management Association, 1981.

Application 3-4

A Microcosting Approach

Steven A. Finkler, PhD, CPA

In the current financial environment for hospitals, there has been general dissatisfaction with the cost accounting information traditionally available. This has led many hospitals to seek out new, computerized cost accounting systems. One approach that has been receiving growing attention in the research literature is the use of microcosting on either a regular or a special study basis.

Microcosting, sometimes referred to as component enumeration, is the process of closely examining the actual resources consumed by a particular patient or service. This may be done on an ongoing basis, either manually or by computer, or on a one-shot basis, typically manually.

The main thrust of a microcosting effort is to avoid arbitrary allocations as much as possible in collecting cost information for some particular purpose. In that way, the information generated is far superior for decision-making purposes. However, hospitals have traditionally relied to a great extent on such allocations, which save a great amount of accounting time and effort although they generate less informative data.

Source: Reprinted from Steven A. Finkler, "A Microcosting Approach," *Hospital Cost Accounting Advisor,* Vol. 2, No. 12, May 1987, pp. 1–4. Copyright 1987, Aspen Publishers, Inc.

DIRECT COSTS

The costs that are generally of interest in microcosting used for special studies are the "direct costs" of providing care. They are costs that are incurred in order to provide the care but that would not be incurred if the patient were not treated. This type of cost is often called the "relevant cost" or "incremental cost."

The classification of a cost as direct or indirect for a microcosting study depends to some degree on the number of patients. For example, one lab test can be performed with no addition of equipment, so equipment is not a cost of treating the patient in a special-purpose microcosting study. However, if the volume of patients and lab tests per patient rises beyond some level, additional equipment will be needed, and it becomes a direct cost.

Similarly, five minutes of extra nursing time for one patient will not have any impact on costs. On the other hand, one or two hours of extra nursing time per patient day for a number of patients will generate substantial additional costs. Those costs can be identified only by microcosting studies.

Suppose, for example, that two different types of patients are both classified by a patient acuity system as being at the most costly level for the unit, perhaps a 5 on a scale of 1 to 5. One type of patient might well consistently require a half hour or an hour more of care per patient day, unless we happen to have a really outstanding patient acuity system.

Note also that direct costs may be either variable or fixed. For example, suppose that we wanted to microcost the impact of AIDS patients' outpatient visits on the hospital. If the hospital has a clinic, labor costs (staff, physicians and nurses) may vary with volume, while space and equipment would not. In that situation, labor is a variable cost which is a direct increment resulting from patients' visits. If the clinic is already fully equipped and has sufficient capacity for the AIDS patients, then the depreciation and other fixed costs of the clinic would not be increased by visits by AIDS patients, at least in the short run.

However, if the volume of AIDS patients is so great that an additional clinic area must be added, the cost of acquiring the space and equipping it becomes a direct cost relevant to the AIDS patients, even though these items are fixed rather than variable costs.

The microcosting would have to include such fixed costs. To find the cost per AIDS patient visit, those fixed costs would have to be allocated. However, because the fixed costs were incurred specifically because of the extra patient volume due to the AIDS patients, the allocation is not an arbitrary allocation of a pre-existing joint cost.

Certainly, in setting a price for services, the hospital may choose to include a share of general overhead costs. However, since the same amount of joint costs would be incurred regardless of whether we choose to treat these additional AIDS patients or not, they are inappropriate information for making a decision as to whether we are better off with or without the AIDS patients.

COST MEASUREMENT

We frequently talk of using direct or incremental or relevant costs (see for example, "Cost Information for Nonroutine Decisions," *Hospital Cost Accounting Advisor,* Vol. 1, No. 3), but relatively little is written about how to obtain them.

The microcosting method calls for the development of a flowchart that identifies all of the activities that constitute the productive process of providing the care under investigation. Once the flowchart is developed, the direct variable and fixed costs are identified. The amount of resources consumed by each workstep in the process of providing the care is measured, and the costs of the components are determined.

Time and motion studies and work-sampling are often employed to determine the personnel time consumed by each workstep or element. This approach to costing is time consuming and therefore costly. However, it provides a very accurate measure of resources actually consumed and their cost.

The steps involved in microcosting are a) preparation of detailed flowcharts, b) description of the worksteps involved in each flowchart step, c) development of data collection instruments and a sampling plan, d) measurement of personnel time, disposables, and depreciation for each workstep, and e) assignment of dollar costs for the resources consumed in each of the worksteps.

Preparation of Detailed Flowcharts

In order to identify the resources consumed during a patient stay or visit, it is first necessary to make a flowchart of the patient stay or visit. First a generic flowchart documents the range of possible reasons for hospitalization. For each of those reasons, a separate flowchart must be created tracing the patient from admission to discharge. For each part of each of these flowcharts, the specific ancillaries consumed and other major resources utilized must be determined.

Staff in each of the various departments affected should be interviewed to verify the accuracy of the flowcharts.

Description of the Flowchart Worksteps

To measure the cost of the resources, it is necessary to detail the worksteps that make up each major step in treating the patient. Again, clinical staff should be interviewed to check the accuracy of the workstep definitions.

The resources consumed at each workstep must be analyzed to determine whether they are direct costs for the study patient group. For example, blood storage facilities are probably an indirect overhead cost that will not change because of the transfusions for any specific type of patient. On the other hand, the cost of intravenous lines are directly associated with the patient receiving blood.

Development of Data Collection Instruments

After the relevant worksteps have been identified, a set of data collection instruments should be developed. An instrument that divides each workstep into segmented, measurable units or work elements should be developed for each procedure. Each of these instruments will provide a structured record of the consumption of personnel time and supplies for each work element within the workstep. The level of detail of the worksteps can vary depending on the desired level of accuracy and detail in the microcosting results.

Measurement of Time, Supplies, and Depreciation

A cost-finding team should observe the various worksteps for which costs are to be estimated. Time and motion studies should be conducted of hospital personnel carrying out each step. Personnel should also be asked to estimate the length of time it takes them to carry out each task and then to monitor and record their own performance times. These data sources can then be used for cross-validation purposes.

At the same time observations must be made of the various supplies, equipment, and facilities that are used for each step of the process.

Assignment of Dollar Costs

Using the information obtained from the purchasing, payroll, and accounting departments, one can associate the costs of labor, supplies, and equipment with the amount consumed, as recorded in the data collection instruments discussed above. Costs are first determined on a per-unit basis. Costs for each workstep can then be determined by accumulating the cost of the units consumed in that workstep. All of the worksteps can be accumulated to determine the total costs of treating a patient in one hospitalization or clinic visit.

A MATTER OF DEGREE

The practical use of microcosting is a matter of degree. It is not simply a case of whether or not to microcost, but of how far to carry the microcosting process.

Microcosting is generally applied in rather limited situations, such as determining the cost of administering a particular drug or the cost of some other clinical intervention. This is because the required level of data collection detail for microcosting is substantial. In limited situations, microcosting can be carried out in great detail. Such detail may not always be necessary.

At the other extreme, aggregation of cost information may yield too little information to be of much use in making decisions, such as whether to try to attract a particular type of patient. For example, to assume, as many hospital cost accounting systems do, that all patients receive an equal amount of nursing care per day, is far removed from microcosting. We obtain very little information about the true cost of nursing resources for any particular type of patient.

However, if we were to study patient care for a particular type of patient, such as an AIDS patient, and determine that AIDS patients actually consumed 12 hours of nursing care per patient day in an ICU, while other patients with the same DRG received only six hours, we would be making a movement toward microcosting.

To determine whether the 12 hours of care for an AIDS patient day in an ICU are all RN care or are split in a measured proportion between RN and LPN would be a movement toward greater accuracy. To determine whether the RN care received by a patient was from a senior experienced nurse or a newly licensed RN would be a movement further along the microcosting continuum. To determine exactly which nurse delivered the care and what her hourly rate is would be a further movement. To determine how much time was spent by each specific nurse on each general type of activity (such as giving medication, bathing the patient, etc.) would be a further movement.

To determine the amount of time spent on each element of each activity would be a further movement along the microcosting continuum. For example, we could determine how long it takes to prepare a medication, how long to carry the medication to the patient's bedside, how long to insert an IV, and so on.

The more detailed we get in the microcosting process, the more expensive the costing effort. As a result, microcosting tends to be a matter of degree. One must use judgment in making the trade-off between the value of more precise information and the cost of obtaining it. It is inappropriate to use resources to gain a greater level of detail than is needed to adequately answer the questions that have been posed.

WHO SHOULD MICROCOST?

In some microcosting studies, a large accounting firm or other firm with expertise in industrial engineering techniques is hired to perform the time and motion studies and the remainder of the data collection. However, this is an expertise that will become more and more important to hospitals over time, and in the long run it is probably cheaper and more efficient for hospitals to develop a microcosting capability internally.

4

Cost Allocation

Goals of This Chapter

1. Define cost allocation, and explain why allocations are needed.
2. Describe the purpose of overhead application rates, and explain how they are calculated.
3. Explain the use of bases for allocation, the benefits of using bases based on budgets, and the benefits of using multiple bases in some cases.
4. Discuss the impact of alternative cost allocation approaches on employee motivation.
5. Address the problem of allocation of joint costs.
6. Provide a background on the traditional approach to cost allocation for health care organizations.
7. Discuss the use of relative value unit costing as an alternative to traditional ratio of cost to charges costing.

Key Terms Used in This Chapter

Actual costing; algebraic distribution; base; cost allocation; cost center; cost driver; cost finding; cost-objective; cost pool; direct distribution; direct labor cost; direct labor dollars; direct labor hours; double distribution; hourly rate; indirect costs; institutional cost report; job-order; joint costs; matrix distribution; normal costing; overhead; overhead application rate; per diem; process costing; product costing; ratio of cost to charges (RCC); reciprocal allocation; relative value unit (RVU); revenue centers; step-down allocation; surcharge; weighted procedure.

Note: Key terms appear in italics when first used in the chapter. All key terms are defined in the Glossary.

WHAT IS COST ALLOCATION?

Cost allocation refers to taking costs from one area or *cost objective* and allocating them to others. There are two primary types of cost allocation that concern us. The first is the allocation of *indirect costs* within a department to specific individual patients. For example, how much of the head nurse's salary should be assigned to each patient on a medical/surgical unit of a hospital? The second type of allocation is from one department or *cost center* to another. For example, in a hospital, housekeeping might allocate its costs to the various departments and cost centers that use its services. The housekeeping costs, once allocated to other departments, can eventually be allocated to specific patients.

Many allocated costs are referred to as overhead. *Overhead* refers to costs that are generally indirect and cannot be easily associated with individual patients, even by a *job-order* type of detailed observation and measurement. Overhead costs therefore require some form of aggregation and then allocation to patients. The previous chapter discussed alternative approaches to *product costing*. That discussion focused on the assignment of direct labor and supply costs to specific types of patients. If we are to accumulate and assign costs directly by patient as described in Chapter 3, there still must be a way to assign various overhead costs to patients.

In some cases, overhead includes *joint costs,* such as the salary of the health care organization administrator, serving many patients. Such costs are incurred for the benefit of all patients. However, no single patient has an impact on the total joint costs incurred. In other cases, the costs may be incurred specifically for one patient (e.g., the cost of heating a private patient room), but it would be too costly to collect the data needed to associate the cost directly with the individual causing it.

The goal of cost allocation is to associate costs as closely as possible with the patients who cause them to be incurred. In some cases, this calls for direct assignment of overhead to patients, whereas in other cases, some departments will have to assign costs to other departments first, before they are assigned to patients. In all cases, the benefits of more accurate assignment of costs to patients must be weighed against the cost of collecting such data.

All departments have direct and indirect costs. The direct costs are those that are directly related to the output of the department. For example, consider a laboratory. The technicians performing a test for a specific patient are providing direct labor that could be measured and specifically assigned to the patient. The reagents used to perform the test, the test tubes, and other specific supplies consumed in the testing process could also be measured and directly assigned to the patient. These represent the direct costs. They could be specifically measured in a job-order approach or averaged in a *process-costing* approach.

Within the laboratory, however, there are other employees who do not come into direct contact with the specific tests of individual patients. There is the laboratory manager, who is concerned with things such as scheduling the staff and dealing with the department budget. There is a secretary who handles correspondence. There is a clerk who orders supplies for all tests. Each of these individuals uses a wide array of clerical supplies and office equipment. These employees, supplies, and pieces of equipment are indirect costs.

There is no question that without such indirect costs the laboratory could not operate, and the individual patients' tests could not be performed. If one wants to know the full costs of providing care to a specific patient, one should assign or allocate an appropriate share of these indirect costs to the patient. However, it is much more difficult to match an individual patient with the indirect costs that the patient causes to be consumed than it is to match a patient with his or her direct costs. When a clerk orders supplies, how much of the time spent ordering should be allocated to any one test for any one patient? The indirect costs incurred *within* a department are often referred to as indirect care costs and are occasionally referred to as overhead.

This problem is further complicated by the fact that different departments or cost centers provide services to each other. Patients directly and indirectly receive the benefits of the housekeeping department. Housekeeping may clean a patient's room, providing direct benefit, and may clean the general areas of a hospital, providing an indirect benefit. It might be possible to measure the direct benefit as a direct cost. However, often the amount of direct housekeeping cost for any one patient is low relative to the cost of measuring it and assigning it directly to the patient. Therefore, all housekeeping costs are usually considered to be indirect to patient care. These costs are assigned to the various departments that consume housekeeping services. Each of those departments, in turn, allocates the housekeeping costs to the various patients cared for by the department.

This provides a mixture of process and job-order costing. All patients do not share housekeeping costs equally, as they would if a simple process-costing system were used. On the other hand, each patient does not receive a specific, unique amount of housekeeping cost, as he or she would if a strict job-order approach were used. This approach is viewed as being good enough, given the costs of more accurate data collection.

The process of allocating costs from department to department and then ultimately to specific patients has often been referred to as *cost finding* in the health care accounting literature.

DETERMINING OVERHEAD APPLICATION RATES

In order to assign costs from one area to another, it is necessary that there be a *cost pool* and a *base*. A cost pool is any grouping of costs to be allocated. A base is the criterion upon which the allocation is to be made. For example, we could choose to allocate costs *based* on patient days. In that case, the number of patient days would be the base. Alternatively, costs could be allocated based on hours. It is common to allocate housekeeping costs based on hours of service provided. The total number of hours of housekeeping service becomes the base. If

this base is divided into the total cost for providing housekeeping services, the result is a rate—in this case, a cost per hour of service.

For example, if there were 10,000 hours of housekeeping services, and a $100,000 cost for the housekeeping department, then the rate would be calculated as follows:

$$\frac{\text{Cost}}{\text{Base volume}} = \text{Rate}$$

$$\frac{\$100,000}{10,000 \text{ hours}} = \$10 \text{ per hour}$$

Each department would be allocated a housekeeping charge equal to its number of hours of housekeeping services consumed, multiplied by the $10 per hour rate. If total costs of a department were based on patient days instead of hours, those costs would be divided by the number of patient days to get a cost per patient day. Hospitals allocate many costs using a patient-day base. For example, if the $100,000 housekeeping cost were allocated to units based on a total of 25,000 patient days, the rate would be as follows:

$$\frac{\$100,000}{25,000 \text{ patient days}} = \$4 \text{ per patient day}$$

When rates calculated in this fashion are used to calculate product costs, they are referred to as *overhead application rates*. Each time a patient day is incurred, one would apply the rate to that patient. Suppose that housekeeping were allocated based on patient days and that the intensive care unit (ICU) had 200 patient days for the month. The overhead application rate of $4 calculated above would be applied to the 200 actual patient days for the unit, to get the housekeeping cost allocation to the ICU as follows:

$$\$4 \text{ per patient day} \times 200 \text{ patient days} = \$800$$

In addition to a patient's direct labor and supply costs, the patient would be assigned the rate for the specific overhead item being allocated. That is, the ICU could assign specific patients a cost for housekeeping, at a rate of $4 for each day the patient was on the unit. That would represent a relatively job-order approach to costing. If the ICU were to average its housekeeping allocation across all patients regardless of their length of stay, that would be more of a process-costing approach.

One reason to use application rates for overhead is to provide managers with information about product costs on an ongoing basis. Rather than waiting until the end of the year to determine the total amount spent on overhead, and then assigning that overhead to different patients, the development of overhead application rates can be used to provide management with information needed for price negotiations, evaluation of profitability of specific types of patients, and other important decisions.

Selecting the Base of Overhead Rates

Selection of the base to use is an important and difficult issue. It is critical to use a base that makes sense. If each department can affect the amount of housekeeping services it consumes, then it should be charged according to use.

Suppose that the common base for allocating housekeeping were square feet. A department with 20,000 square feet would be charged twice as much as one with 10,000 square feet. However, suppose that the smaller department requires that its wastebaskets be emptied more frequently and that its floors be washed twice as

often as other departments. These extra services consume housekeeping resources.

A more equitable base would be to allocate housekeeping based on the number of hours of service provided to each department. The accuracy of cost allocations would improve. Further, each manager would have a better idea of the resources that he or she causes the organization to consume.

On the other hand, it will require time and cooperation to track hours of service provided to each department. The housekeeping staff may feel that it is not worth the effort to keep such records. One must weigh the extra record-keeping cost against the advantages of the more accurate base. Further, even if it is worth the record-keeping cost, one must consider the political implications. If housekeeping does not want to do it, is it worth the battle? Perhaps yes; perhaps no. Thus, in the real world, there are sometimes obstacles to using the "best" possible base.

Exhibit 4-1 provides examples of different bases that could be used for several cost centers in health care organizations.

Use of Budgeted Rates

In most industries overhead application rates are budgeted based on an annual averaging process. This process consists of determining a base for the allocation (e.g., *direct labor hours*) and then dividing that base into a budgeted cost.

$$\frac{\text{Budgeted cost}}{\text{Budgeted base volume}} = \begin{array}{c}\text{Budgeted overhead}\\\text{application rate}\end{array}$$

Exhibit 4-1 Examples of Overhead Allocation Bases

Cost Center	Alternative Allocation Bases	
Laundry	Pounds	Pieces
Housekeeping	Square feet	Hours of service
Depreciation	Square feet	Construction cost
Employee benefits	Employees	Payroll dollars
Purchasing	Dollars purchased	Number of orders
Administration	Accumulated costs	Number of employees
Maintenance	Square feet	Work orders
Medical records	Patient days	Hours charted

The result is a budgeted cost per unit of the overhead base, or a budgeted overhead application rate. This rate is determined at the beginning of the year. Every time a unit of product (a patient in our case) consumes one unit of the base (e.g., a nursing hour of care), the product (patient) is charged the overhead application rate.

This allows for a determination of each patient's cost on an ongoing basis. Direct labor and supplies can often be observed on an ongoing basis. However, determination of the actual amount and cost of overhead consumed as it is consumed is much more difficult. Overhead might include costs such as heat and electricity, which cannot be determined exactly for a number of weeks at the earliest. Having a predetermined rate substantially simplifies the process of accumulating all the costs associated with a specific patient. On the other hand, it does increase the extent to which product costing is based on expected costs rather than on specific actual costs.

This approach is called *normal costing*. If the application rate is based on actual costs incurred, it is referred to as *actual costing*. In both approaches, overhead is assigned to each unit of the base consumed. If the rate is per patient day, then under normal costing, a budgeted rate is charged each time we have a patient day. Under actual costing, once the actual overhead costs and actual number of patient days are known, an actual rate per patient day is calculated and charged. The normal approach generates information much more quickly; the rate is set based on budgeted information, so one does not have to wait for actual information to be available. However, the actual approach is more accurate, because it does not rely on budgeted information, which is usually not a perfectly accurate prediction of what will happen.

Suppose that patient census varies from month to month. Fixed costs will remain constant. In months of low census, there will be fewer direct hours of care over which to spread fixed costs. In high-occupancy months, there will be more direct hours over which to spread fixed costs. Using actual costing, the result is

that the overhead rate will vary substantially from month to month. It will appear that the cost of treating similar patients is changing, when what we are really observing is the impact of a change in volume. Each patient is really consuming similar resources, whether treated in a busy or slow month. Normal costing eliminates this problem by applying the same rate in all months.

For example, suppose that annual fixed costs for housekeeping are $120,000, and variable costs are $20 per hour of service provided. On an annual basis, 12,000 hours of service are expected. The normal overhead application rate would be $30 per hour, as follows:

$$\text{Fixed costs} = \$120,000$$

$$\begin{aligned}\text{Total variable costs} &= \$20 \text{ per hour} \times 12,000 \text{ hours} \\ &= \$240,000\end{aligned}$$

$$\begin{aligned}\text{Total costs} &= \text{Fixed costs} + \text{Variable costs} \\ &= \$120,000 + \$240,000 \\ &= \$360,000\end{aligned}$$

$$\begin{aligned}\frac{\text{Normal overhead}}{\text{Application rate}} &= \frac{\text{Budgeted total cost}}{\text{Budgeted base volume}} \\ &= \frac{\$360,000}{12,000 \text{ hours}} \\ &= \$30 \text{ per hour}\end{aligned}$$

This rate would be charged to each department consuming housekeeping services. The rate would be constant all year. Suppose that in actuality the number of hours of service provided by housekeeping were as follows:

January	1,300	May	1,000	September	1,000
February	1,300	June	700	October	1,000
March	1,300	July	700	November	1,000
April	1,000	August	700	December	1,000

If all housekeeping costs were as expected, then actual costing would charge less per hour of service in busy months and more per hour in slow months. Consider the calculation of the actual application rate for January and July:

	January	July
Fixed cost		
$120,000 ÷ 12	$10,000	$10,000
Variable cost		
$20 × 1,300 hours	26,000	
$20 × 700 hours		14,000
Total Cost	$36,000	$24,000
Actual Overhead Application Rate		
Actual Cost ÷	$36,000	$24,000
Actual Base Volume	1,300 hours	700 hours
	= $27.69/hour	$34.29/hour

There is no conceptual basis for allocating $27.69 per hour of housekeeping service in busy months, and $34.29 per hour in slower months. This is simply a result of spreading fixed costs over units of service each month, instead of on an annual basis. Such allocation causes the fixed cost per hour of service, and therefore the overhead application rate to vary each month. The normal costing approach is preferred because it spreads fixed costs evenly throughout the year.

Selecting a Base

The first step in determining overhead application rates is to identify the most sensible base for allocating each overhead cost. The challenge is to assign overhead in a way that causes the minimum amount of distortion in the accuracy of product costing. In the case of the admitting department, assignments to patients based on the amount of time spent admitting the patient might make sense. This reflects a cause-and-effect relationship. The more admission personnel time consumed, the greater the cost the patient caused the health care organization to incur—therefore, the greater the cost that should be allocated to that patient.

But what about allocation of overhead such as administration, down-time, supervision, and depreciation? How can we allocate such costs? One way would be to take any department's indirect costs and assign them on either a

patient or patient-day basis. This would assume an equal assignment of overhead cost per patient or per patient day. However, most industries generally use the somewhat more refined technique of assigning overhead on the basis of either direct labor hours or *direct labor dollars.*

For example, suppose that 60 percent of all nursing hours worked are assigned by a job-order system directly to patients. The remaining nursing time includes nonproductive time as well as time doing general tasks at the nursing station, and so forth. The 40 percent remaining time that must be allocated may reasonably follow the same proportion as the 60 percent of time that was directly consumed by each patient.

Suppose, for example, that one patient consumed 10 direct nursing hours and another consumed 5 direct nursing hours. One approach to allocating indirect nursing hours would be to allocate them equally between the two patients. Alternatively, one could allocate the indirect nursing hours in the same proportion as the direct hours. Therefore, twice as much indirect cost would be allocated to the patient who consumed 10 direct care hours as to the patient who consumed 5 direct care hours.

One could make strong justifications for why the latter approach is more reasonable than an equal assignment per patient. It very possibly associates costs with patients who cause those costs to be incurred. Reasonable judgment must be used in the case of each overhead element to determine the appropriateness of different alternatives, such as assignment of cost per patient, per patient day, in proportion to direct labor hours, or in proportion to *direct labor cost,* and so forth. If there is a cause-and-effect relationship, we want that relation to dominate the allocation. That is, if a specific patient is the reason that certain costs are incurred, we want those costs ultimately to be assigned to that patient.

To have an accurate cost-assignment process, the application must result in assigning more overhead to the patients as they cause more overhead to be incurred. The key is to find ways to allocate overhead in a way that matches as closely as possible the changes in overhead costs incurred.

We may not be able to measure the amount of an overhead item used by each patient. But if we note that a certain overhead cost doubles when we double the number of nursing hours, then we would want to assign overhead to patients based on the number of nursing hours they use.

On the other hand, if a type of overhead item does not vary in any systematic manner with the number of nursing hours, we would want to find another basis for the allocation of that item. Perhaps the cost can be related to the patient's diagnosis, to the patient's age or sex, or to the number of hours the patient is on a monitor.

If job-order costing is used, the assignment of direct labor and direct materials is done on the basis of actual costs incurred. Thus, a high degree of accuracy is attained for direct costs. But even under job-order costing, overhead assignment is based on an application rate. That rate is based on an average. The use of an average inherently reduces the ability to assign to each patient the overhead that they caused to be incurred. Therefore, the focus of overhead application should be on the development of rates that will result in the highest possible degree of accuracy at a reasonable accounting cost. The more important it is to management to have an accurate cost of each product, the more overhead categories there will be, each using a different application base and rate. In this way, the overhead can be assigned as much as possible on a cause-and-effect basis.

The Steps in the Overhead Application Process

The process of application of overhead costs to units of production has been formalized into six steps.[1] For health care organizations, we can think of these six steps as

1. selecting a base for assigning costs to patients and/or departments
2. determining budgeted cost and volume
3. computing overhead rate
4. measuring the actual base
5. applying the budgeted overhead application rate to the actual volume, and

6. accounting for year-end differences between actual total overhead and the amount of overhead applied throughout the year.

Selecting a Base

The first step is to select an overhead cost application base. This base serves as the denominator of the fraction to be used to calculate the application rate. The base should be selected based on the existence of a cause-and-effect relationship between production volume and overhead costs. In addition, the base should be applicable to all patients.

Common industrial bases are direct labor hours, direct labor cost, and machine hours. Health care organizations could use hours or cost for staff as an application base along these lines. Other bases also could be developed if they result in a more accurate cause-and-effect relationship between overhead costs and volume of patients. Age, sex, and diagnosis were suggested above.

Determining Budgeted Cost and Volume

The second step is to determine a budgeted overhead cost and a budgeted volume of production. In the case of a health care organization, we would need to ascertain all departmental budgeted amounts that cannot be assigned to patients as either direct labor or direct materials. We would also need to estimate the expected volume.

Note that volume does not necessarily mean the number of patients. We are concerned here with the volume of the item used for the base. For example, each department would have to estimate the number of hours of housekeeping service that they expect to consume for the coming year, if the housekeeping base is the total number of hours of service.

Computing the Overhead Rate

The third step is computation of an overhead rate by dividing the total expected overhead cost by the total expected production volume. For example, if a health care organization expects to have overhead cost of $10 million and 500,000 nursing hours, then a rate could be developed by dividing the overhead cost by the nursing hours base to result in an application rate of $20 per nursing hour.

This rate is based on annual budgets. As noted earlier, the use of annual rather than monthly budgets smooths out some unwanted seasonal impacts. Similarly, use of monthly budgets for rate calculations would cause us to charge major maintenance costs only to patients treated in the month we plan the maintenance, rather than spreading those costs across all patients who benefit from them over the course of the year.

Measuring the Actual Base

The fourth step is to keep track of actual base data as the year unfolds. That is, we must track how many nursing hours are actually consumed for each patient or how many housekeeping hours of service are actually provided to each department.

We must make this measurement so that the predetermined overhead rate can be used to assign overhead costs. For example, once we know that there is an overhead rate of $10 per housekeeping hour, we must know the number of housekeeping hours in each department, so that we can assign an appropriate share of the housekeeping cost to each department.

Applying the Rate to the Actual Volume

The fifth step is to apply the budgeted overhead application rate to the actual units of the base consumed to determine the overhead applied. Thus, suppose that a specific department consumed 1,500 hours of housekeeping service. Since the application rate is $10 per hour, a total of $15,000 would be applied to that department ($10/hour × 1,500 hours). This application would generally be done monthly throughout the year.

Accounting for Year-End Differences

The sixth and final step is to account for any year-end differences between actual total overhead and the amount of overhead that has been applied to patients throughout the year.

Each month after actual overhead costs are accumulated, there will be an over- or underapplied amount. That is, we will have assigned too much or too little overhead cost. The over- and underapplied amounts will balance out by the end of the year if our predictions have been correct. If not, there will be a year-end variance between the amount of cost assigned and the actual amount. A variance is the difference between a budgeted or planned amount and the actual amount incurred. If an amount is spent that is greater than the budget called for, it is an unfavorable variance. (Variances are discussed in Chapter 9.)

If these variances are substantial, a normal costing system may not be desirable. It may be necessary to wait until year-end before applying overhead, and then use an actual overhead rate.

Year-end differences can arise for two main reasons. One reason is that the overhead department spent more or less money than expected. The other reason is that the consuming departments may have used more or less than expected.

For instance, suppose that a housekeeping rate of $10 per hour was predetermined based on an expectation of $100,000 of housekeeping cost, and 10,000 hours of service. The actual costs might have been $108,000, and the actual hours of service provided might have been 11,000. If $10 were assigned for each of the 11,000 actual hours of service, a total of $110,000 of overhead would have been allocated to the various departments that use housekeeping. This represents an overcharge of $2,000, given that only $108,000 of cost was incurred. The health care organization would have to make an adjustment for the $2,000 variance to ensure financial reports reflect actual costs.

There are many ways to make such an adjustment. One way would be to divide the $2,000 by the 11,000 actual hours. This would determine the overcharge per hour. Each department could then receive a credit based on the number of hours for which they were charged. Another approach would be to combine the variance with all other variances in the organization resulting from overhead applied, and make one average adjustment. Alternatively, the total of all such variances could simply show up as a specific item on the income statement.

It is important to note, however, that whatever approach is taken, it will not occur until the year is over. Meanwhile, the cost of patients will have been determined based on the overhead application rates. We will not wait until after the year is over to determine patient costs. Therefore, it is important to be as accurate as possible in determining the overhead application rates.

Multiple Bases

It is not necessary to assign all overhead costs using one application rate. Different departments can each have their own unique rate. In fact, within a department there can be different rates to allocate different types of costs.

Each rate should be based on a distinct *cost driver*. Cost drivers are those things that are most responsible for a cost being incurred. In the case of admitting, hours of personnel time may be the key cost driver. Therefore, the base might be the total hours of staff time in the department. Costs from that department would be allocated based on the amount of staff time consumed.

Some departments might need multiple bases and application rates. For example, radiology department supervision is a cost that might be considered to relate most closely to the number of x-ray technicians. In that case, we would want to assign overhead based on technician labor hours. This seems straightforward. We merely need to track the amount of technician time spent for each patient, and use a rate based on dividing radiology overhead by budgeted technician hours. However, there are many supply items (such as developing solution) that probably vary with the number of x-rays developed.

One might assume that the number of x-rays developed varies with technician time as well. That is true to some extent, but might be misleading. A difficult patient might take 40 min-utes to x-ray, even for just one image. Another patient might have 15 or 20 images taken in the same amount of time. The latter patient will consume more film and developing solution. The solution for this problem is to segregate indirect costs in a department into several groups, and use different application rates for each group. Thus, one overhead base might be technician time, and another might be the number of images. The more we isolate overhead and apply it based on a rational cause-and-effect relationship, the more accurate the overall costing will be. This is the basis for the activity-based costing (ABC) approach, which has recently been widely adopted in industry. That technique is specifically discussed in Chapter 17.

At all times, it is important not to lose sight of the reason for overhead application rates. We are attempting to arrive at an accurate product cost. Therefore, the items that constitute each department of the health care organization should be reviewed. What are considered overhead items? Could some of these overhead items perhaps be treated as direct labor or direct materials? Are there any cause-and-effect relationships that could allow us to establish an overhead application base that would more accurately assign resource consumption? It is by answering these questions that we are likely to improve the overall accuracy of our costing system.

COST ALLOCATION AND MOTIVATION

When one department in a health care organization allocates costs to another department, there exists a relationship much like two independent people buying and selling a service. However, because the buyer and the seller are both part of the same health care organization, special circumstances are inherent. This section focuses on some of the motivational problems in cost allocation between departments.

Suppose that a debate had arisen in your organization concerning laundry department cost allocations. Suddenly the laundry costs that were being assigned to various departments had risen dramatically, and the department heads were up in arms. "Why are we supposed to live within our tight budgets when the laundry department can spend whatever it wants?" they demand to know. "The laundry simply allocates its costs to the other departments. It seems unfair that laundry costs were being allowed to rise so much, and it seems unfair that the other departments were having unfavorable variances without having done anything differently or worse than they had planned."

Suppose that the operating room (OR) had recently shifted from reusable sheets and scrubs to disposable ones. Therefore, the OR was using substantially less laundry. Most of the laundry department costs were fixed costs. The reduction in volume of laundry reduced the total laundry department costs by only a minor amount. Therefore, the lower volume caused the cost per pound of laundry to rise. In fact, the laundry department had not spent "whatever it wanted," nor had it gone over its original frugal budget. It is possible, however, that when it became apparent that volume would be lower than expected, a new overhead application rate was determined. That rate, using nearly the same cost, but a lower base, would have to be higher. That higher rate would raise the amount of laundry cost allocated to other departments.

In essence, it was the action of the OR rather than overspending in the laundry that had created the problem. The laundry department was taking a lot of heat. The various laundry users were all above their budgets. And the OR was isolated from the storm it had caused.

Health care organizations that have cost allocation systems that allow departments to have poor financial results through no action on their own often have poor morale. Ideally, an isolated action on the part of the OR should not have an impact on the costs of the other departments using the laundry department.

In designing costing systems, we must be extremely aware of the incentives and motivational aspects of the system. Twenty years ago, many managers were held less accountable for the costs of their departments. That is no longer true. Old systems may well have built-in paradoxes that threaten the overall cost efficiency of the organization. Therefore, we must reexamine these old costing systems to determine not only if they generate accurate cost information, but also if they create perverse incentives.

Inequities in Interdepartment Allocation

Assume that the total costs of operating the laundry department are budgeted to be $100,000 per month. To simplify the argument to be presented, suppose that there are only three consumers of laundry: the OR, the nursing department, and the laboratory. The proportions of laundry to be consumed by the three departments are expected to be 25 percent, 70 percent, and 5 percent this year and every year. The OR consumes 100,000 pounds per month; the nursing department, 280,000 pounds per month; and the laboratory, 20,000 pounds per month.

If we agree that the long-run proportions of laundry will be constant, we could simply take the laundry costs each year and divide them among the three other departments on a 25 percent, 70 percent, 5 percent proportion. We could assign laundry costs without even measuring how much laundry came from each department. It certainly would seem fair, all other things equal, to expect the OR to be assigned $25,000 per month of laundry cost for its 25 percent consumption; the nursing department, $70,000 for its 70 percent consumption; and the laboratory, $5,000 for its 5 percent consumption. (Note that $25,000 + $70,000 + $5,000 = $100,000 total cost of operating the laundry.)

As long as actual consumption were close to budgeted consumption, we would have a system that was very cheap to administer. However, as soon as one department starts to consume substantially more than its normal proportion, there would be inequity. The other two departments would be paying for some of the laundry of the department that was increasing its proportion.

The solution to the inequity is to measure the amount of laundry consumed by each department each year and to charge accordingly. This represents current practice. Suppose the OR used 10,000 pounds less laundry than expected, and the nursing department used 10,000 pounds more than expected. If the total amount of laundry consumed stayed the same, then the OR would be assigned less of the $100,000 monthly cost and the nursing department more of it. This seems to be a stable and equitable system.

What happens when the OR reduces its consumption by 80 percent, with no change by the other departments? Total laundry consumption has now actually fallen by 80,000 pounds. The laundry is now cleaning 320,000 pounds per month instead of 400,000. Suppose that 10 percent of the laundry's costs are variable and 90 percent are fixed. The 20 percent decline in overall pounds (from 400,000 to 320,000) will result in only a 2 percent reduction of costs (10 percent variable multiplied by 20 percent volume decline). Thus, the laundry's costs fall to $98,000 per month.

The OR will be allocated a fair share of $6,125 ($98,000 × 20,000 pounds/320,000 pounds); the nursing department will be allocated $85,750 ($98,000 × 280,000 pounds/ 320,000 pounds); and the laboratory $6,125, the same as the OR, because it also uses 20,000 pounds. This represents a 14 percent increase in costs for the nursing department and a 23 percent increase for the laboratory. Are these increases fair, given that these departments have not changed their actions in any way?

That depends on whose responsibility the laundry department is. The laundry was designed to be a certain size in order to handle the needs of all departments, including the OR. If the OR originally intended to use disposables, the laundry would have been built smaller with less capacity and less fixed cost. Essentially, one could argue that part of the fixed capacity of the laundry should really be the responsibility of the OR.

Incentives of Allocation Systems

Ultimately, the question that we need to address is whether the cost allocation system in place causes individual department managers to make decisions that are in the best interests of the health care organization. Suppose that the OR had discovered that by buying a large number of disposable laundry items, they could

replace $20,000 of laundry department overhead allocation with $15,000 of outside purchases.

The OR department decision is clear-cut. They apparently can save the organization $5,000 by purchasing outside. The OR will probably be quite upset to find that their remaining 20,000 pounds of internal laundry has risen from a $5,000 cost to a cost of $6,125 (calculated above). Nevertheless, on a profit and loss basis, the department still comes out almost $4,000 ahead by using the disposables. They are buying the disposables for $5,000 less than they formerly paid the internal department, and the costs on their remaining laundry rose by $1,125. The net difference is still a savings of $3,875. They have clearly saved money for their department and the organization as a whole!

Not really. Actually, they have cost the organization additional money. Before, all laundry was done for a cost of $100,000 in-house. Now, the in-house laundry has total costs of $98,000 and the OR's purchases are an additional outlay of $15,000. The total laundry cost for the organization as a whole has risen from $100,000 to $113,000. The OR decision to buy disposables looks good to its department, but has caused total laundry costs to rise by $13,000 or 13 percent.

How can this be? In reducing their own total laundry costs from $25,000 in-house to $6,125 in-house plus $15,000 purchased, the OR has not taken into account the rise in costs from $70,000 to $85,750 in nursing and from $5,000 to $6,125 in laboratory. These two departments have seen their costs rise by $17,000, far more than offsetting the $3,875 savings in the OR.

This unfavorable result may occur whenever one department decides to use disposable laundry items, or an outside linen agency, or simply to have some documents photocopied across the street from the organization for a lower price than the in-house reprographics department charges. Clearly, there is a significant problem in the cost allocation system if what is good for one department is substantially bad for the organization as a whole. The underlying problem here is that all costs are being allocated as if they are variable, when in fact a substantial part of the costs of most health care organizations is fixed.

Behavior Neutral Allocations

The first element of the solution is for departments that provide services to other departments to segregate their costs into fixed and variable costs. Most new cost accounting systems that have been installed in the last five years, and that are being installed today, have the capacity to identify fixed costs as distinct from variable costs.

Once we know the budgeted fixed costs of a service department, that amount can be allocated in a lump sum to each department based on some long-run assessment of the proportion of service to be used by that department. In the above example, 90 percent of the laundry's $100,000 cost was fixed. Because the long-run expected utilization was 25 percent OR, 70 percent nursing, and 5 percent laboratory, the $90,000 fixed cost would be allocated to those three departments in that proportion. The fixed charge allocated to the OR would be $22,500, with $63,000 to the nursing department, and $4,500 to the laboratory.

The remaining costs for the laundry are variable. These costs should be charged to departments based on their actual consumption each month. The $10,000 of variable cost for 400,000 pounds is 2.5¢ per pound. If the nursing and laboratory departments use their budgeted number of pounds, 280,000 and 20,000 respectively, they will be charged $7,000 and $500 respectively. Thus, the total nursing charge will be $63,000 for long-term annual fixed costs plus $7,000 for current year variable costs, or $70,000 total, and the laboratory will be charged $4,500 of long-term annual fixed costs plus current year variable costs of $500, or $5,000 total. No action by the OR can have any effect on these amounts. If the nursing department or laboratory uses more or less laundry, its charge will go up or down by the variable cost of doing that laundry.

If a department such as the OR chooses either to go outside of the hospital to have its laundry done or to buy disposables, that is okay. However, it will reduce the charge to the department only by the variable costs. This is exactly the same amount as it reduces the cost of operating the laundry. The fixed charge will still be allocated to the department.

The OR is free to use only 20,000 pounds from the in-house laundry and to purchase disposables for $15,000 to replace its other 80,000 pounds of in-house laundry. However, if it does, the laundry cost to the OR would be the $22,500 long-term, annual fixed charge from the laundry ($90,000 total fixed cost multiplied by 25 percent) plus the current year variable charge from the laundry of $500 (20,000 pounds @ 2.5¢) plus the $15,000 outside purchase. This is a total of $38,000. This $38,000 is $13,000 more than the $25,000 the OR would spend if it uses the in-house laundry for the entire 100,000 total pounds (i.e., the $22,500 fixed charge plus the $2,500 variable charge for 100,000 pounds @ 2.5¢ per pound).

Note that the $13,000 loss to be suffered by the OR if they make the decision to buy disposables is *exactly the loss that the institution as a whole would suffer, as calculated earlier.* The nursing department and laboratory are no longer affected by the OR's decision. And the OR is no longer under the assumption that it is saving the hospital $3,875, when in fact it is costing the organization an extra $13,000. Under this approach, the impact seen by the OR as a result of its actions is exactly the same as the impact of those actions on the bottom line of the organization.

The key to making this work is to allocate costs based on two separate allocations. One allocation is fixed costs, which should be allocated in a lump sum based on a budget and should not depend at all on actual volume. The other allocation should be related to volume and should be the budgeted variable cost.

Use of Budgeted vs. Actual Costs

We noted above that the allocation of variable cost should be based on the budgeted variable cost. What if the actual costs of the laundry department differ from the costs budgeted for some reason other than a change in volume?

That really should be the responsibility of the laundry rather than of the other departments. The actual results for the departments other than the laundry should depend on their actions. They have no control over the laundry, and if its costs rise, they should not be held accountable unless they caused the cost increase by increasing their consumption of its services. Therefore, for both fixed and variable costs, the allocation should be based on budgeted fixed costs in total and budgeted variable costs per unit.

ALLOCATING JOINT COSTS

Another cost allocation problem relates to the allocation of joint costs. Joint costs are those that are incurred to provide services to more than one patient. Ideally, for costing purposes, each patient would have a direct cause-and-effect relationship with each cost incurred by the hospital. Costing could be done with the knowledge that all costs could be associated with individual patients that caused those costs to be incurred. Adding more patients or avoiding patients would have a direct, proportional effect on costs. In reality, that is not the case. Many costs are incurred to provide services to a group of patients. Any one patient has no effect on such costs.

Joint costs present accountants with difficult allocation problems. Although it is desirable to identify the costs incurred to provide care to each patient, one must carefully avoid making incorrect decisions on the basis of that full cost information. If costs are allocated to patients, a manager may mistakenly assume that those costs could have been eliminated if the patient were not treated. That is not true for joint costs; they would exist anyway.

Anytime there is a process that uses common resources for the benefit of different types of patients, joint costs will exist. Health care organizations consume many resources that are needed for the provision of care to all patients. The building, the chief financial officer, a scanner, and a myriad of other costs are not incurred

for any one specific patient, nor even for any one type of patient. If we were to eliminate treatment of any one type of patient, we would not eliminate any of these resources.

Should Joint Costs Be Allocated?

Once it is acknowledged that joint costs exist, the question arises as to why we might want to allocate them. Why not simply consider them to be general overhead costs not assigned to specific departments and patients? Horngren and Foster identify four principal purposes for the allocation of costs:[2]

1. as a guide for making decisions that affect resource allocation;
2. as a tool for motivation of both managers and employees;
3. for asset and income measurement for both internal and external reporting; and
4. for cost computation, justification, and reimbursement.

It would make accountants' jobs easier if there were a unique allocation that would always accomplish all four of these goals. However, that is not always the case.

In fact, the different purposes come sharply into conflict for most health care organizations. Cost reporting requirements have mandated cost allocations for joint costs. This has allowed reimbursement to take place because a cost is identified for each patient, including a fair share of all overhead costs. On the other hand, the allocation of joint costs to departments often runs counter to motivational goals because managers feel that they are being assigned indirect costs that they cannot control. Worse yet, if the health care organization makes decisions on the basis of the cost per patient, it may make the wrong decision if that cost includes an allocation of joint costs.

According to Horngren and Foster, "When all four purposes are unattainable simultaneously, the dominant purpose of making the allocation should guide the cost allocation."[3] When a large portion of health care organization costs were reimbursed on a cost basis, one could have argued that the reimbursement role was of overriding importance. Today, with the growing prevalence of prospective-based payments, that may no longer be the case.

The decision-making role is more important to health care organizations than it once was. Information is needed that will lead managers to make the correct economic decision. That decision-making role would tend to lead health care organizations away from allocating joint costs. One could argue for simply leaving the costs unallocated, and allowing the joint costs to reside in a nonrevenue center. When total health care organization costs are being determined, they would be added in. But for determination of the cost of any particular patient or type of patient, they would be excluded.

This is a controversial approach. Before concluding whether or not such an approach is reasonable, one should explore the topic of joint costs and better understand the process and approach of joint cost allocation. Once these approaches have been considered, an informed decision can be made regarding whether or not to allocate joint costs.

Methods for Allocating Joint Costs

The overriding principle to bear in mind in considering approaches for the allocation of joint costs is that all approaches are inherently arbitrary. No one patient type is more responsible for causing the health care organization to incur joint costs than any other. There is no "correct" allocation that will "fairly" cause costs to be assigned to each type of patient. Given that caveat, the common theoretical approaches to treating joint costs are based on patient price, physical measure, and no allocation.

Treating joint costs based on the price charged to the patient is one logical approach to the problem. Suppose that a department had joint costs of $1,000 and treated just two patients. Suppose that one patient is a type that is charged $10,000, and the other patient is a type that is charged $5,000 for the care provided. In that case, because the first type of patient is charged twice as much as the second type, one could assign twice as much of the joint cost to that patient type. In this example, $667 of joint costs would be charged to the first type of patient, and $333 to the second type.

This method of allocation would appear to have some merit. It is an objective method—it does not require any subjective value judgment. It also would seem to be fair. The type of patient that generates twice as much revenue bears twice as much cost. One might argue alternatively, however, that it would be fair to charge each patient type an equal $500. That would treat all patients alike. Why does a higher ultimate charging price imply that a patient consumes a proportionately higher amount of the joint cost item?

Despite this problem, the approach to costing that allocates costs based on relative prices is at least workable under a payment system such as Medicare Diagnosis Related Groups (DRGs), where the prices are predetermined regardless of the cost incurred. The method is more problematic for cost-reimbursement payment systems, because the price paid cannot be determined until after the cost has been allocated. The cost of the patient is an integral element of determining the price.

In such a case, the physical measure approach might be more useful. The physical measure approach uses some volume measure to determine the allocation of the joint cost. For example, hours of OR time is a common hospital tool for allocation of joint cost. The depreciation of the OR department can be charged to patients based on their relative consumption of the OR, as measured by the length of their surgical procedures.

In fact, that almost seems to have a cause-and-effect ring to it. It would appear that the patient who consumes more of the joint cost item is being charged more for it. However, if more is really being consumed, then the cost is not truly a joint cost. Consider the salary of the manager of the OR. That salary is a fixed cost regardless of the mix or volume of surgical procedures. Does the patient with a two-hour procedure really consume more of the manager's effort than one with a one-hour procedure? No. Therefore, allocation of that joint cost based on the measure of operation time is an arbitrary allocation. It is not based on cause and effect. However, it does allow one to allocate all of the manager's salary cost to all of the patients.

That allocation, however, does not tell anything about the true, underlying costliness of the different types of procedures. All that it accomplishes is assignment of all of the cost to all of the patients.

The final alternative approach of not allocating costs is the one most often put forth by academics. All of the allocation approaches merely cloud the issue. Yes, we can allocate the costs. And yes, the result is that all of the costs of the health care organization are therefore allocated to all of the patients of the health care organization. But what have we achieved in that process?

If we need information to make decisions, neither of the allocation approaches is satisfactory. Both of them imply things that are not true about the likely cost impact of changing volumes of patients. In order to make managerial decisions, one must know how costs are likely to vary based on the decision being considered. If the manager must decide whether to take actions that would increase the number of patients of Type A or of Type B, it is necessary to know the change in costs resulting from that decision. If joint costs are embedded in the average costs of each patient, the manager will have more difficulty making that decision correctly.

Furthermore, if the joint cost varies from budget, there are motivational problems that stem from embedding the joint cost in the cost per patient. Joint costs are often beyond the control of the manager. When costs rise and managers are held accountable even though they have no control over them, they will lose much of their motivation for controlling the costs that they can control.

In today's DRG environment, the decisions that managers make to improve the economic results of their health care organizations are of increased importance. Following the Horngren and Foster[4] logic, one could argue that because the role of joint cost allocation for reimbursement is now less important, and the role for

decision making is more important, focus should be shifting away from allocation of joint costs.

Realistically, few health care organizations will cease allocating joint costs completely; however, that is not being asked. The question is whether health care organizations will now move forward by reducing the extent to which joint costs are allocated in the costing done for internal management reports. There is no reason for managers to make decisions based on information in the mandated *institutional cost reports* prepared for outsiders. If decisions will be more reliable if they are made ignoring joint costs, then there should be a specific formal effort to generate "clean" information. That is, joint costs should be explicitly excluded from internal analyses so that the correct decision is more likely to be made.

Joint Costs and Multi-Institutional Health Care Organizations

Over the last several decades, there has been tremendous growth in multi-institutional health care organizations. Multihospital systems, national health maintenance organizations, and other types of health care providers have taken on a form that goes beyond a single institution in a single facility. The treatment of joint costs becomes a significant issue for such organizations.

Often multi-institutional systems have a central or corporate headquarters. This may create a layer of administration on top of the normal layers encountered in most health care organizations. Many of the activities of the headquarters may be focused on issues such as expansion and the future of the organization rather than on day-to-day operations.

Is it appropriate to allocate such overhead costs to individual institutions within the multi-institutional framework, and ultimately to patients? The same principles apply that have been discussed above. If there is a clear cause-and-effect relationship, then such allocation makes sense. For example, if the organization has a central laboratory or laundry that provides services to a number of its facilities, then certainly each facility should be paying for the resources it uses.

If there is no cause-and-effect relationship, then the allocation becomes arbitrary. Nevertheless, most multi-institutional organizations do allocate their corporate-level costs down to the various institutions. It is critical to evaluate these costs carefully when making decisions. If the costs are in fact joint costs that are not affected by a decision at any one facility, then the decision should not be influenced by those costs.

TRADITIONAL COST ALLOCATION FOR HEALTH CARE ORGANIZATIONS

The approach most health care organizations have been using for their cost-finding is the one mandated for use in Medicare cost reports, often called *institutional cost reports* (ICRs).

The ICR approach does incorporate some of the concepts discussed so far in this chapter. However, to a great extent, it represents a simplified approach that has historically been considered to be good enough. As you read about this approach, you will note that there are concepts of cost allocation that are ignored by the system. A more sophisticated system that generates more accurate patient cost information is feasible. Over time, one would expect to see more and more health care organizations adopting some more refined elements of cost allocation to improve the accuracy of their measures.

The ICR approach requires all resource consumption first to be associated with either a support cost center or a *revenue center*. For instance, housekeeping, dietary, pharmacy, intensive care, operating room, and coronary care are examples of cost and revenue centers. See Exhibit 4-2 for a more extensive list of examples of support and revenue centers. Each center accumulates its direct costs, such as labor and supplies.

The next step is to allocate all of the costs of the nonrevenue cost centers to the revenue centers. Revenue centers are the parts of the organi-

Exhibit 4-2 Examples of Cost Centers and Revenue Centers

Nonrevenue Centers (Support Cost Centers)	Revenue Centers
Administration	Blood bank
Admitting	Cardiology
Billing	Emergency department
Chaplaincy	Inhalation therapy
Communications	Labor and delivery
Dietary	Laboratory
Engineering	Medical/surgical supplies
Finance	Operating room
Housekeeping	Pharmacy
Infection control	Physical therapy
Information systems	Radiology
Legal services	
Maintenance	
Marketing	
Medical records	
Nursing department	
Payroll	
Planning	
Public relations	
Receivables	
Security	
Social services	

zation that specifically charge for their services. For example, patients are generally charged a specific amount for an operation, but not for building security. Revenue center managers are responsible not only for the costs incurred in their units or departments, but for the revenues as well. While this adds the burden of additional responsibility, it also adds benefits. If a unit or department is a revenue center, then it can point to an explicit measure of the financial contribution that it earns for the organization. The revenue it generates can be used as an argument for giving additional resources to the center to spend. Given their choice, most managers would want their departments to be classified as revenue centers.

How are health care organizations divided into cost centers that are revenue centers and cost centers that are not revenue centers? The key requirement for a revenue center is that it must be possible to measure different consumption of that center's services by different patients.

If patients consume different amounts of a resource, we need to have specific charges to reflect those differences. For example, if one patient had surgery and one did not, we need to be able to charge only the one who had surgery for the operation. We could use the number of surgeries as a base for determining a rate. Therefore, the operating room department is a revenue center.

Further, we would like to charge a greater amount to someone who had a more expensive operation than to someone who had a less expensive one. Therefore, instead of using the number of surgeries, we can search for an alternative base that would generate a rate that more accurately assigns costs to patients who cause them to be generated. Operating rooms often use the number of hours of surgery as their base for developing an overhead application rate. That rate is then charged to each patient according to the number of hours (or minutes) the surgery lasts. This will not be a precise measure of resource use, but will be a great improvement over the use of either a per diem approach (an equal cost assignment per patient per day) or an allocation based simply on an equal cost per operation.

Thus, departments that do not generate resource consumption that can be clearly associated with specific patients can be considered indirect departments. They generate only overhead costs and can be treated as cost centers only.

Why is nursing not a revenue center in most health care organizations? Clearly, different patients consume different amounts of nursing resources each day. Accurate product costing would require assignment of those different nursing costs to different patients. However, historically there was difficulty in measuring the amount of nursing resources each patient consumed; it would require an observer to follow each patient or each nurse and determine the amount. Thus, although much of nursing was a direct labor cost, it was too difficult and expensive to measure that cost. Therefore, it made sense to treat the cost as an indirect overhead, and there was no need to treat nursing as a revenue center.

With the widespread introduction of patient classification systems in the 1980s, this is no longer the case. Patient classification systems assign specific values to patients based on their severity of illness; for example, a scale of 1 to 5 might be used. Using the system, one could determine, on average, the amount of nursing resources consumed by a patient each day at each of the classification levels. It is now possible to approximate at least the amounts of nursing resources consumed by different patients based on their daily patient classification. However, most health care organizations still treat all nursing as an indirect cost to be allocated as an overhead item rather than as a direct cost, assigned specifically to each patient.

Why must the nonrevenue center costs be allocated to the revenue centers? Health care organizations get their revenues by charging for the services provided. When the prices or rates are set, the organization must consider all of its costs. Laundry is not a revenue center. It does not charge the patients a fee for its services. ORs consume large amounts of scrubs and sheets that must be laundered. If a hospital tries to set its OR prices high enough to recover the cost of OR direct costs, but it did not consider the indirect cost of the laundry it used, it might not recover all costs incurred by the organization. Therefore, in order to ensure that the organization sets prices high enough to recover all of its costs, the costs of the revenue centers must include all of the costs of the nonrevenue cost centers. This forces allocation of all costs, including joint costs.

Once all of the nonrevenue center costs have been assigned to the revenue centers, each revenue center can in turn assign its total direct and indirect costs to the units of service such as x-rays and laboratory tests that have been provided to the patients it has treated. One could then aggregate the costs assigned to a specific patient by each of the revenue centers to determine the total cost of treating that patient.

Even though Medicare now pays hospitals on the basis of DRGs rather than direct cost-reimbursement, the Medicare Cost Report is still completed by hospitals. The cost information from the report is used by the federal government in its process of setting national payment rates for each DRG. Similar ICRs are prepared by other health care organizations.

A Detailed Look at the ICR Approach

The steps in traditional cost-finding are examined briefly here to provide an understanding of the traditional cost-finding approach and its weaknesses. An additional and somewhat more detailed discussion of this approach is provided in Application 4-1.

Accumulate Direct Costs for Each Cost Center

The first step in the cost-finding process is to accumulate the direct costs of the cost center. For example, consider an OR.

Direct costs in the OR include salaries and wages for regular staff. This includes all supervisory and staff personnel who work in the OR and are included in the OR budget. The OR manager, scrub and circulating nurses, OR technicians, orderlies, and clerks and secretaries are all included. Employee benefits are also included in direct costs.

Other direct costs include the cost for supplies, seminars, agency per diem nurses, and all other items under the direct control of the OR department that are normally considered its direct costs. In this approach, all costs incurred directly within a department are considered direct costs, even though they are not direct patient-care costs.

Determine Bases for Allocation

The laundry department is an example of a nonrevenue cost center. Once its direct costs have been accumulated, they must be allocated to revenue centers. Each center that uses laundry should be charged for a portion of the costs of the laundry. In order to do this, the manager must first decide on the basis for the allocation. The selection of a base is a key element for any allocation process, as discussed earlier.

The cost of the laundry department could be charged in equal shares to each department that uses laundry. The base would be the number of departments. If 10 departments use laundry, each would be assigned one tenth of the laundry department costs. However, that would be quite unfair to departments that use relatively little laundry. Such an allocation would not be good enough.

Other approaches to allocating the cost of laundry would be on the basis of pounds of laundry or pieces of laundry. In fact, most health care organizations that have a laundry department assign laundry costs on the basis of the number of pounds of laundry. All dirty laundry is placed in a laundry cart that is weighed. Then total laundry costs can be allocated based on the share of total pounds of laundry consumed by each department. If there are 10,000 pounds cleaned, and a department consumes 2,000 pounds, it would be allocated 2,000/10,000 or 20 percent of the laundry department cost. The denominator is the total value of the base, and the numerator is the usage by the specific department.

Is that an appropriate basis for the allocation? It is not necessarily the best base. It would be more accurate to allocate costs based on the number of each type of laundry item. A laboratory jacket may be more complicated to sort and fold than a sheet. Although four laboratory jackets may weigh the same total amount as one sheet, they would undoubtedly require more labor than one sheet. Labor is one of the greatest expenses of the laundry department. Therefore, cost accuracy would improve if costing were done on the basis of the number of each type of laundry item. However, it would cost more to keep track of pieces than pounds.

Most health care organizations have decided that weight of laundry is a sufficient measure. It effectively assigns all of the costs of the laundry department to the revenue centers. And it uses an allocation basis that takes some, if not perfect, account of relative usage by different cost centers. In any event, the only perfectly accurate measurement would require one staff member to observe each patient constantly to see exactly what laundry he or she uses. That job-order approach would be prohibitively expensive.

Allocating fixed and variable costs separately would improve the process, as discussed earlier. It would avoid giving undesired incentives. However, ICRs do not generally report such split allocations, nor do they have provisions for using multiple bases to allocate differing types of costs from one cost center.

The problem of choosing the specific base is not limited to the laundry department. There are other cost centers that also have had to make choices. For example, any health care organization that has a building must allocate its annual depreciation to the various cost centers. That is usually done on the basis of square feet. A cost center that physically occupies many square feet would be charged more than one that has fewer square feet.

Actually, it costs more to build certain parts of a facility than it does other parts. For example, an OR may cost ten times as much per square foot as a patient room. By allocating an equal amount of depreciation per square foot, this means that too little is assigned to the OR and too much to medical/surgical patient rooms. Ultimately, this means that medical patients are overcharged, relative to their resource consumption, and surgical patients are undercharged. However, health care organizations generally have decided that an equal depreciation charge per square foot is sufficient. Recall that Exhibit 4-1 provides examples of alternative allocation bases.

Allocate from Cost Centers to Revenue Centers

All of the costs of the nonrevenue cost centers are allocated to the revenue centers using the allocation bases discussed above. Figure 4-1 provides a simplified example of what we are attempting to do with this allocation. In the figure, housekeeping and laundry are nonrevenue centers. Coronary care unit (CCU) and pharmacy are revenue centers. Each nonrevenue center must ultimately allocate all of its costs into the revenue centers.

Table 4-1 provides a simplified numerical example. As in Figure 4-1, housekeeping and laundry are nonrevenue centers, and the CCU and pharmacy are revenue centers. The first column in the table shows the direct cost incurred in each of the four centers. The next two columns show the allocation base and the proportion of the base related to each department.

Housekeeping cost will be allocated on the basis of square feet, and laundry on the basis of pounds. The table shows the percentage of all square feet that each cost center has, and the percentage of all pounds of laundry used by each cost center. The square feet in the housekeeping department and the pounds of laundry done for the laundry department are excluded because no cost center allocates its own costs to itself. Thus, housekeeping services are used 70 percent by the laundry, 25 percent by the CCU, and 5 percent by the pharmacy. Laundry ser-

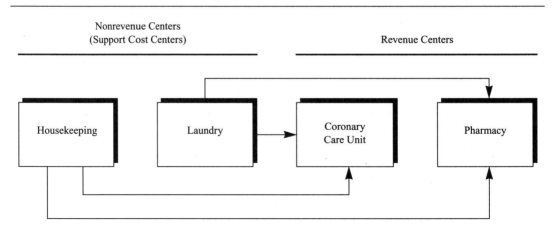

Figure 4-1 Allocating Costs to Revenue Centers

Table 4-1 Allocation Bases

		Allocation Statistics	
Cost Centers	*Direct Cost ($)*	*Housekeeping Square Feet (%)*	*Laundry Pounds (%)*
Nonrevenue			
Housekeeping	40,000	—	20
Laundry	60,000	70	—
Revenue			
Coronary care unit	500,000	25	10
Pharmacy	500,000	5	70
Total cost	1,100,000	100	100

vices are used 20 percent by housekeeping, 10 percent by the CCU, and 70 percent by the pharmacy.

There are several approaches to carrying out the actual allocation from the cost centers to the revenue centers. These approaches are the *direct distribution* approach, the *step-down* approach, and a group of more sophisticated multiple distribution techniques.

Direct Distribution. Table 4-2 shows an allocation of the direct costs to the revenue centers. The allocation in this exhibit is called a direct distribution. In the direct distribution method, nonrevenue center costs are allocated only to revenue centers. In making the allocation, a problem arises. Although 25 percent of the square feet are in the CCU, and 5 percent are in the pharmacy (see Table 4-1), if those percentages are used for the allocation, the full $40,000

of housekeeping cost would not be allocated. This is because 70 percent of the square feet is in the laundry, and no cost is being allocated to the laundry.

This problem is resolved by allocating to the revenue centers based on the remaining square feet after eliminating the nonrevenue centers. Since 30 percent of the square feet is in all of the revenue centers combined, and 25 percent is in the CCU, 25 percent divided by 30 percent gives the proportion of the housekeeping cost allocated to the CCU. Similarly, 5 percent divided by 30 percent gives the housekeeping cost allocated to the pharmacy; 25 percent divided by 30 percent multiplied by the $40,000 housekeeping cost results in the $33,333 of cost allocated to the CCU. Note in Table 4-2 that the housekeeping cost is reduced by $40,000 on the housekeeping line, and the allocation to the revenue centers increases on each revenue center

Table 4-2 Direct Distribution

		Allocation		
Cost Centers	*Direct Cost ($)*	*Housekeeping Square Feet ($)*	*Laundry Pounds ($)*	*Total Costs ($)*
Nonrevenue				
Housekeeping	40,000	(40,000)	0	0
Laundry	60,000	0	(60,000)	0
Revenue				
Coronary care unit	500,000	33,333	7,500	540,833
Pharmacy	500,000	6,667	52,500	559,167
Total cost	1,100,000	0	0	1,100,000

line, in the housekeeping column. Laundry costs are allocated to revenue centers in a similar fashion.

There is also an additional complexity because direct distribution fails to take into account that some nonrevenue cost centers provide service to other nonrevenue centers. Housekeeping cleans the laundry department. If all housekeeping costs went directly to revenue centers, none would be allocated to the laundry, and a distortion in costs would occur. The possible distortion is so great that a direct allocation to revenue centers only is not considered good enough. This method is generally not allowed for reporting purposes.

The Step-Down Method. Instead, an allocation approach called the step-down method is used. This is shown in Figure 4-2 and Table 4-3.

The step-down method requires the organization to allocate all of the cost of a nonrevenue cost center to *all* other cost centers (both revenue and nonrevenue). First, one nonrevenue center's costs are allocated to every other cost center. Then another nonrevenue center is allocated. As each center is allocated, its cost balance becomes zero, and it no longer is part of the process. In other words, no costs can be allocated to a cost center once it has allocated its costs. Note in Figure 4-2 that housekeeping would allocate costs to coronary care, pharmacy, *and* laundry. The laundry, however, would only allocate costs to coronary care and pharmacy. Therefore, some amount of distortion still remains in the allocation process.

Compare the results of the direct distribution method with the step-down method.

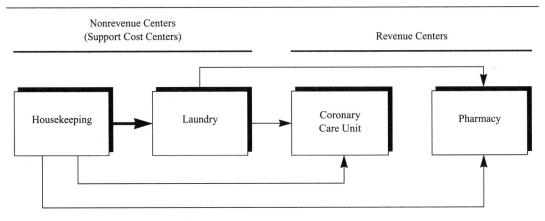

Figure 4-2 Allocating Costs to Revenue Centers by Step-Down

Table 4-3 Step-Down Distribution

| Cost Centers | Direct Cost ($) | Allocation | | | |
		Housekeeping Square Feet ($)	Subtotal ($)	Laundry Pounds ($)	Total Costs ($)
Nonrevenue					
Housekeeping	40,000	(40,000)	0		
Laundry	60,000	28,000	88,000	(88,000)	0
Revenue					
Coronary care unit	500,000	10,000	510,000	11,000	521,000
Pharmacy	500,000	2,000	502,000	77,000	579,000
Total cost	1,100,000	0	1,100,000	0	1,100,000

	Coronary Care Unit Cost	Pharmacy Cost
Step-down allocation	$521,000	$579,000
Direct distribution	–540,833	–559,167
Difference	($19,833)	$ 19,833

The direct distribution approach allocated a substantially different amount to each revenue center. The CCU's cost was reported to be $19,833 more under the direct distribution approach, whereas the pharmacy cost was reported as $19,833 less. Depending on the specific circumstances, the distortion caused by using direct distribution can be substantial.

Multiple Distribution. There are other more elaborate allocation approaches that eliminate most or all of the remaining distortion. The methods are the *double distribution* and the *algebraic* approaches. The latter is sometimes referred to as the *reciprocal* or *matrix distribution* approach. These rely on each cost center distributing costs to *all* centers, including all support cost centers. At the end of such a distribution, there will still be some remaining cost in the nonrevenue centers. Therefore, at least one more distribution must take place. The double distribution method uses a standard step-down approach for its second and final allocation of costs. The algebraic approach is based on solving a set of simultaneous equations. This generates the same result as an infinite number of distributions.

Although the allocation that results from use of such methods is more accurate, it is also more complicated to understand and implement. The hospital industry generally has considered step-down allocation to be sufficient. The specific steps of the reciprocal approach and its usefulness for both financial reporting and managerial decision making are discussed in Application 4-2. The reader is encouraged to refer to that application.

The Impact of the Order of the Step-Down

The use of step-down creates another problem. Should housekeeping be allocated before or after the laundry? The order of the allocation may affect the ultimate outcome. Table 4-4 changes the order of allocation. Laundry is now allocated using step-down before housekeeping is allocated.

Look at what happened to the ultimate cost in each revenue center.

	CCU Cost	Pharmacy Cost
Revised order of allocation	$549,333	$550,667
Original allocation	–521,000	–579,000
Increase/(Decrease)	$ 28,333	($ 28,333)

The total CCU cost has risen by $28,333, whereas the pharmacy cost has fallen by an equal amount. This is an extreme example, but it demonstrates the distortion possible by

Table 4-4 Step-Down Distribution with Altered Order of Step-Down Allocation

Cost Centers	Direct Cost ($)	Laundry Pounds ($)	Subtotal ($)	Housekeeping Square Feet ($)	Total Costs ($)
Nonrevenue					
Laundry	60,000	(60,000)	0		
Housekeeping	40,000	12,000	52,000	(52,000)	0
Revenue					
Coronary care unit	500,000	6,000	506,000	43,333	549,333
Pharmacy	500,000	42,000	542,000	8,667	550,667
Total cost	1,100,000	0	1,100,000	0	1,100,000

changing the order of allocation. In a perfect allocation system, the ultimate cost in each revenue center would remain the same regardless of the order in which the nonrevenue center costs are allocated.

Are the actual resources consumed by the organization any different because the order of allocation of nonrevenue centers changed? No. The same total amount of money was spent. The same resources were used. However, the cost of the CCU and the pharmacy can vary because of the accounting methodology used. With the more sophisticated algebraic approach, such variation in costs does not occur. However, the step-down method, as noted, has been considered to be good enough.

It is possible that the step-down method has allowed health care organizations to manipulate their cost reporting in an attempt to shift costs between revenue centers to increase reimbursement. For example, many hospitals have both inpatients and outpatients. Medicare inpatients are paid on a fixed DRG payment scale. Although it may change, at the date this book was written, outpatient payments for Medicare patients were not based on fixed DRG-type rates. If the order of the step-down causes more costs to be allocated to the outpatient areas and less costs to be in departments that treat predominantly inpatients, total reimbursement would rise.

An ICR Example

Part of an institutional cost report is reproduced here. This is from the type of report typically submitted to Medicare and Blue Cross. It shows how the step-down allocation appears for an actual organization. Exhibits 4-A-1 through 4-A-3 in Appendix 4-A present just a small portion of an ICR form. The actual report was nearly two inches thick. This form was submitted to Empire Blue Cross and Blue Shield, which acts as an agent for the Health Care Financing Administration (HCFA), the federal government agency in charge of Medicare. The institution's cost report is a public document. Exhibit 4-A-1 is the cover page of the report.

Exhibit 4-A-2 shows a portion of Worksheet B, Part I, of the report. This provides the allocation of general services costs. This part of the report, although much more complex, parallels the allocation process made in Table 4-3.

Notice that in the 0 column on the first page of this exhibit, there are $1,322,802 of costs in Row 17D for "nursing administration." These costs must be allocated. However, there are no costs in Rows 17E or 17F for "nursing services." Those costs have already been reclassified in an earlier section of the report. That reclassification placed the costs of nursing units directly into departments for which the hospital makes a per diem charge. This includes Line 25, "adults & pediatrics"; Line 26, "intensive care unit"; Line 27, "coronary care unit"; and a number of other departments. The hospital has more than 55 departments. The rest of the departments appeared on additional pages, not shown here.

Looking across all three pages from Exhibit 4-A-2, one can see the pattern created by the process, from which it earned the name "step-down" report. On the third page of Exhibit 4-A-2, Worksheet B, Part I, one can see in Column 17D that $2,297,296 is being taken out of nursing administration and allocated into the departments on Lines 25 through 39. Note that the $2,297,296 is greater than the original $1,322,802 of direct costs of nursing administration. That is because nursing administration has been allocated costs for depreciation, employee benefits, administrative services (other than nursing), plant operations, laundry, housekeeping, and cafeteria on the previous two pages. For example, there is a $21,838 allocation from housekeeping (Column 8) into nursing administration.

What is the basis for each cost allocation? Exhibit 4-A-3 provides the statistical basis for each allocation. This is Worksheet B-1 of the report. Notice in the headings for each column that the basis is given. For example, in Column 1, the basis for allocating the building depreciation is square feet. On the second page of the exhibit, laundry and linen are allocated based on pounds of laundry, and dietary is allocated based on meals served. On the last page of the exhibit, note that nursing administration is allocated based on time spent on supervision of nurses. A total of 10,000 hours of supervision has been used, and the amount of hours of supervision required by nurses in each of the departments is shown lower in that column. For example, the nurses in the adults and pediatrics department received 4,934 hours of supervision from the nursing administration department.

Worksheet B-1 (Exhibit 4-A-3) parallels the information shown in Table 4-1. However, in Table 4-1, percentages were used. In Exhibit 4-A-3, the raw numbers are shown. In order to determine what portion of nursing administration costs to allocate to subsequent departments in the step-down, one would have to determine what portion of nursing supervision total hours were consumed by each department. For example, since 4,934 hours of the total of 10,000 (both numbers are from Column 17D on the third page of Exhibit 4-A-2) were consumed by adults and pediatrics, 49 percent of the nursing administration costs should be allocated to adults and pediatrics (4,934/10,000 × 100% = 49%).

Looking back at the third page of Exhibit 4-A-2, we find that of the $2,297,296 in nursing administration, when it gets its turn to allocate, $1,133,486 has been allocated to adults and pediatrics (Line 25). If we divide $1,133,486 by the total of $2,297,296, we find that it is 49 percent. The portion of nursing administration that was consumed by adults and pediatrics has in fact been allocated to adults and pediatrics in the step-down process.

Allocating Costs to Units of Service

Up to this point, the discussion has focused on allocating all costs of the organization into the cost centers that are revenue centers. The next part of the cost-finding process centers on assigning each revenue center's costs to the units of service that it provides. For example, a laboratory assigns its costs to the various laboratory tests it performs; an OR assigns its costs to the surgical procedures that take place.

The choice of how to allocate costs to units of service requires an allocation base. In health care organizations, managers commonly think of bases such as the number of procedures, tests, treatments, or patients or cases.

However, these bases are sometimes referred to as being "macro" bases. In many instances, departments can more accurately assign costs to patients by using "micro" bases. For example, rather than assigning social services by the visit, it could be done by person-hours. Such a micro base results in a more direct association of resource consumption with individual patients. Table 4-5 presents examples of macro and micro allocation bases.

Table 4-5 Macro and Micro Allocation Bases

Department	Gross Production Unit (Macro)	Weighted Production Unit (Micro)
Operating room	Surgical case	Person-minutes
Anesthesiology	Anesthesia case	Anesthesiology-minutes
Postoperative rooms	Postoperative case	Person-minutes
Radiology	Examinations	RVUs
Laboratory	Tests	RVUs
Physical therapy	Modalities	Person-minutes
Isotopes	Treatments	RVUs
Blood bank	Transfusions	RVUs
Delivery room	Deliveries	Person-minutes
Social service	Visits	Person-hours
Emergency department	Visits	Person-minutes
Nursing	Patient days	Hours of care
Nursery	Patient days	Hours of care

Note: RVUs: relative value units
Source: Reprinted from *Understanding Hospital Financial Management* by Allen G. Herkimer, p. 93, Aspen Publishers, Inc., © 1986.

Using job-order costing from Chapter 3, the direct costs of providing services to patients would be specifically measured for each patient. Only the departmental indirect costs and the overhead costs from other departments would have to be allocated to the patients. However, health care organizations traditionally have used approaches for patient costing that are much more closely related to process costing. Specifically, there are four common approaches to allocating a revenue center's costs to units of service: the (1) *per diem,* (2) *surcharge,* (3) *hourly rate,* and (4) *weighted procedure* methods.

The per diem method is used if none of the other three methods reasonably applies. The major problem with this approach is that it assumes that each patient consumes exactly the same amount of resources per patient day. It takes no account of patient severity of illness or specific requirements. However, the cost-finding process has treated this approach as good enough.

The surcharge method is commonly used in the pharmacy and medical supplies cost centers. The revenue center compares its costs excluding inventory to the inventory cost and determines a surcharge. For example, if a pharmacy spends $10,000 on all costs except pharmaceuticals, and $100,000 on pharmaceuticals, then the surcharge would be 10 percent (i.e., $10,000 divided by $100,000). As each prescription is filled, the cost would be calculated as the cost of the drug itself plus 10 percent. The problem with this approach is that, in reality, just because a drug costs ten times as much to buy as another drug does not mean that it requires ten times as much pharmacist time to process. Some organizations overcome this problem partly by using a minimum charge applied to all drugs dispensed.

The hourly rate approach measures the amount of service a revenue center provides by time. This method is used by respiratory therapy, physical therapy, ORs, and recovery rooms. For example, an OR would divide its total cost (after the step-down allocation) by the total number of hours of procedures to determine a cost per hour. Sometimes the calculations are done in minutes, yielding a cost per surgical minute. The logic of this method is that longer operations consume more resources.

This method is very accurate for a service such as physical therapy, where there is generally only one therapist working with the patient. A problem that arises in using this approach in the OR is that an operation may have just one nurse, or may have two nurses, or two nurses and a technician. Also, the supplies and equipment used may not bear a direct relationship to time. It is possible that a two-hour operation might consume far more resources than a three-hour operation. This method, while not very good, traditionally had been considered to be good enough. In recent years, however, ORs have been trying alternative approaches. For example, many ORs keep track of person hours, rather than just surgical hours, to account for the number of staff members in the surgical suite.

The last method is the weighted procedure method (sometimes called the relative value unit or RVU method). This approach is based on a special study of the center's costs, which establishes a relative costliness of each type of service the center performs. This method is commonly used in departments such as laboratory or radiology, where there is a specific, limited number of services provided, and they are provided in similar fashion each time. A base value is assigned to one type of procedure, and all other procedures are assigned a relative value. Thus, if a blood gas is twice as costly as a complete blood count (CBC), the CBC might be assigned a value of 1.0 unit of work and the blood gas a value of 2.0 units of work. In any given month, the values assigned to all of the services provided can be summed and divided into the total cost of the revenue center. This yields a cost per unit of work.

For example, suppose that the total costs of the laboratory revenue center after the step-down allocation of nonrevenue center costs were $5,000. If the laboratory performed 300 blood gasses and 400 CBCs, it performed a total of 1,000 units of work (300 blood gasses × 2 units of work + 400 CBCs × 1 unit of work). Next, $5,000 divided by 1,000 units of work is $5 per unit of work. Therefore, the $5,000 total laboratory costs would be assigned at a rate of $10 per blood gas (2 units of work × $5 per unit) and $5 per CBC (1 unit of work × $5 per unit). The benefit of this approach is that it allows costs to be assigned without a micro-costing effort, even though the volume and mix of patients has changed.

A problem with this approach is that it relies heavily on the assumption that a blood gas is always twice as costly to perform as a CBC. This problem is exacerbated by the fact that many health care organizations use standard relationships based on a survey of institutions rather than on measurement of the relative costs in their own facilities. Because the personnel pay rates and the equipment used will vary from one organization to another, the relative relationships are not likely to be exactly the same at all institutions. However, in comparison to having an accountant observe the resources used each time a laboratory test is performed, it is considered to be good enough. It is clearly superior to the other approaches in use. These four methods are discussed in somewhat greater detail in Application 4-1. The RVU method is also discussed further below.

IS GOOD-ENOUGH COST FINDING GOOD ENOUGH?

For the first two decades under Medicare and Medicaid, the good-enough approximations that resulted from the traditional cost-finding and allocation approach discussed above were considered to be acceptable. Most large third-party payers—Medicare, Medicaid, Blue Cross, and private for-profit insurers—have a large mix of patients. If they are overcharged on one patient, they are likely to be undercharged on another patient. As long as the total costs are not overstated, overcharges and undercharges are likely to average out for large groups of patients. It would not be sensible for them to require health care organizations to spend substantially more money on improved cost accounting. They would then have to bear the cost of the improved cost accounting in addition to the costs of patient care.

With the introduction of DRGs, however, incentives have changed. Hospitals, in particular, are now at risk for the costs they incur. If patients cost more to care for than the DRG payment rate, the hospital suffers a loss. It has become of great interest to hospitals to have accurate methods for finding costs of specific types of patients. With a new type of DRG on the verge of being introduced for ambulatory care, and already introduced in some states for long-term care, improved costing is of interest in most health care organizations. Application 4-3 presents the results of a study intended to determine just how much distortion is created by the allocation process. That article reports significant distortions between ancillary costs and routine per diem costs.

To the extent possible, and still being mindful of the cost of collecting more accurate information, managers of health care organizations would like to improve on the good-enough approximations. They would like to eliminate the inaccuracies of using pounds of laundry instead of pieces or of using square feet instead of construction cost for depreciation. They would like to eliminate the distortions created by the order of allocation in the step-down process. They would like to remove the inaccuracies generated by weighted procedure, hourly, surcharge, and per diem assignments of cost.

Can this be done? Probably there will never be a 100 percent accurate costing system. As computer use in health care organizations increases, the potential exists to make great strides in accurate assignment of patient resource consumption. One immediate step that could be taken to improve costing is to use an algebraic or reciprocal solution to the allocation process, instead of step-down allocation. Step-down allocation is inherently flawed because it does not allow all cost centers to allocate costs to all other cost centers. This means that changes such as the order of allocating the departments can cause a distortion in the resulting costs in each cost center. If the consumption of each cost center's services by each other cost center was considered simultaneously (by inverting a matrix of equations) some distortion would be eliminated. That approach is discussed in Application 4-2.

RCC vs. RVU Costing

When attempts to collect cost information are made using the standard ICR-generated data, they are referred to as ratio of cost to charges (RCC) studies. For example, if one wanted to know how much it cost to do hernias, one could start by looking at all of the bills of hernia patients. However, charges are not the same as costs. Suppose that the charges for radiology services were $2 million, whereas the total costs for those services, as determined by the ICR process, were $1 million. Therefore, the ratio of cost to charges would be $1 million/$2 million, or $.50. One could then take the average radiology charge for a hernia patient and multiply by .50 to find the average radiology cost.

The problems with this approach are many. First, it assumes that the charge for each radiology procedure is double its cost. In fact, the charges for some might be more than double, and for others, less. Next, it relies on the entire cost-finding and allocation method described above. There are many reasons such an approach does not assign costs to a procedure that are an accurate reflection of resources consumed.

To overcome these problems, many health care organizations have started to use approaches such as the Cleverley model described in Chapter 3. Such approaches have been used not only for direct labor and materials, but also for overhead cost allocation. In developing such systems, the focus is on expanded use of the RVU approach.

An RVU approach performs a special study to determine the resources consumed by each activity (such as a service unit in the Cleverley model). The various activities (or service units) are then compared with one another, and a relationship is established. For example, suppose that a laboratory performed three types of tests, A, B, and C. A special study might find the following results:

Test	Cost	Volume	Total Costs
A	$ 5	5	$25
B	10	2	20
C	6	3	18
		10	$63

We now know the costs of each test. Suppose that in six months we determine that the laboratory spent $75, an increase of nearly 20 percent. Does that mean that the cost of each test has risen by 20 percent? Not necessarily. Perhaps we have done a greater volume of tests. Or perhaps the mix of tests performed has changed.

Suppose that we have done only eight tests in contrast with the ten done in the period when the special study was done, a 20 percent decrease in volume. Not only has the cost gone up, but the volume has gone down! How can we determine the cost of each test in this new period? We could do a special study, but it would be extremely costly to perform a special study every time we want to know current costs of each intermediate product. An alternative is to establish a relative value scale. The RVU approach establishes one item as the standard, given an index value of 1. It does not matter which unit is chosen, as long as everything else is compared to that unit. In our example, assume that Test A is the base unit assigned 1 RVU. Then Test B, which cost twice as much as Test A in the base period, would be assigned a value of 2, as follows:

$$\frac{\text{Test B base cost}}{\text{Test A base cost}} = \text{Test B RVUs}$$

$$\frac{\$10}{\$\ 5} = 2.0$$

Given that Test A cost $5 and has a value of 1, it makes sense that Test B, which cost twice as much, would have a value of 2. Similarly, Test C would be equivalent to 1.2 RVUs:

$$\frac{\text{Test C base cost}}{\text{Test A base cost}} = \text{Test C RVUs}$$

$$\frac{\$6}{\$5} = 1.2$$

We can use this information to determine the cost of each test in the subsequent period. We know that *total* costs have risen about 20 percent, and we know that total volume has decreased by 20 percent. We might expect a substantial increase in the cost per test. However, that does not consider case mix. Suppose that, in reality, the new patient volume is as follows:

Test	Volume
A	1
B	6
C	1
	8

Using the RVU system, we can convert this volume into RVUs as follows:

Test	RVUs	× Volume	=	Total RVUs
A	1.0	1		1.0
B	2.0	6		12.0
C	1.2	1		1.2
		8		14.2

Since the total cost of these 14.2 RVUs was $75, we can divide the RVUs into the total cost to find the cost per RVU:

$$\frac{\text{Total cost}}{\text{Total RVUs}} = \frac{\$75}{14.2} = \$5.28 \text{ per RVU}$$

We can now determine the cost for each type of test, without having to refer to charges or to cost information from the step-down report, as required by the RCC approach:

Test	RVUs per Test	Cost per RVU	Cost per Test	Volume	Total Cost
A	1.0	$5.28	$ 5.28	1	$ 5.28
B	2.0	5.28	10.56	6	63.38
C	1.2	5.28	6.36	1	6.34
				8	$75.00

Note that the total costs were $75, and the total number of tests was 8. However, even though total cost rose and volume decreased from the base period, the increase in the cost for each type of test was modest. Test A went from $5.00 to $5.28, Test B went from $10.00 to $10.56, and Test C went from $6.00 to $6.36. There was a substantial shift in mix toward the most expensive type of patient.

If the original study to establish the RVUs is done carefully, then the quality of the cost information can be substantially superior to that generated under an RCC approach. Note, however, that the RVU approach relies not only on the quality of the original data collection, but also on the relative stability of the interrelationships among products. The example above assumes that Test B has remained twice as costly as Test A. If there were a change in technology or procedure, that might not be the case, and the relative values would have to be adjusted.

Application 4-4 discusses one approach for developing an RVU system. Application 4-5 goes beyond this, discussing the results of a fairly sophisticated RVU system. In this latter application, the differences in costs found using an RCC approach versus an RVU approach are shown to be significant. The reader should carefully review these two articles to gain a better understanding of the contrast between RCC and RVU approaches.

It has become clear that the financial pressures on health care organizations are forcing them to try to develop more accurate sources of cost information by type of patient. This will inevitably lead to attempts to improve cost allocations. Application 4-6 gives an example of an attempt to allocate costs in the emergency department in a way that provides more useful data. The principles discussed in the first half of this chapter can serve as a guide for the revisions that must be made in the existing cost allocation systems described in the second half of the chapter.

NOTES

1. C. Horngren and G. Foster, *Cost Accounting: A Managerial Emphasis,* 6th ed. (Englewood Cliffs, NJ: Prentice-Hall, Inc., 1987), 98.

2. _____, *Cost Accounting: A Managerial Emphasis,* 7th ed. (Englewood Cliffs, NJ: Prentice-Hall, Inc., 1991), 458.

3. Ibid.

4. Ibid.

SUGGESTED READING

Braganza, G. 1982. Cost finding. In *Handbook of health care accounting and finance,* ed. W.O. Cleverley, 197–222, Gaithersburg, Md.: Aspen Publishers, Inc.

Broyles, R.W., and M.D. Rosko. Summer 1986. Full cost determination: An application of pricing and patient mix policies under DRGs. *Health Care Management Review* 11, no. 3:57–68.

Finkler, S.A. 1985. The future of product costing and cost allocation. *Hospital Cost Accounting Advisor* 1, no. 1:1, 3–4.

_____. 1985. The reciprocal method of cost allocation: A short term fix for DRG costing. *Hospital Cost Accounting Advisor* 1, no. 4:1, 7–8.

Hogan, A.J., and R. Marshall. February 1990. How to improve allocation of support service costs. *Healthcare Financial Management:* 42–52.

Horngren, C.T., and G. Foster. 1991. *Cost accounting: A managerial emphasis.* 7th ed. Englewood Cliffs, NJ: Prentice-Hall.

Stein, P. Fall 1990. Homogeneity—The key to cost allocation. *National Estimator:* 15–18.

Williams, S., et al. 1982. Improved cost allocation in case-mix accounting. *Medical Care* 20, no. 5:450–459.

EXERCISES

QUESTIONS FOR DISCUSSION

1. What are the two primary types of cost allocation?
2. Is cost allocation needed even if job-order product costing is being used?
3. What is an allocation base, and how is it used in setting allocation rates?
4. What are the advantages of using a budgeted rate rather than an actual overhead application rate?
5. What are the general steps in the overhead allocation process?
6. Is it possible for the consumption of housekeeping services by the nursing department to affect the overhead charges to the laboratory department?
7. Why would you want to avoid allocating joint costs, if possible?
8. What elements of the traditional institutional cost report system lead to inaccurate product costing?

Note: Solutions to the Exercises can be found in Appendix A.

PROBLEMS

1. The admitting department at Aspen Hospital processed 1,000 patients last month. A total of 2,500 admitting department personnel hours were consumed in processing the patients. The costs of the admitting department were $50,000. What are two possible allocation bases and rates?

2. Mr. Sic Lee's detailed medical records indicated that a total of 20 labor hours were directly used in providing his care. The cost of the labor was $380. It was expected prior to the beginning of the year that a total of 90,000 direct labor hours would be consumed by the health care organization's patients, at a cost of $1,350,000. The total overhead to be allocated to patients was expected to be $810,000.

   Determine the overhead to be assigned to Mr. Sic Lee based on the data given above. Solve this problem two ways. First, using a normal costing system, assign overhead on a basis of direct labor hours. Second, using a normal costing system, assign overhead on the basis of direct labor cost. Why might your results differ?

3. Use the information provided in Table 4-6 below. Allocate costs to the revenue centers using the direct distribution method.

4. Use the information from Problem 3. Allocate the costs using the step-down method.

Compare the results with Problem 3. Do they differ?

5. Use the information from Problem 3. Allocate the costs using the step-down method, but change the order of step-down from that used when you solved Problem 4. Do your results differ from those you found in Problem 4?

Table 4-6 Cost Base Information for Allocation

		Allocation Statistics	
Cost Centers	Direct Cost ($)	Maintenance Hours of Service (%)	Telecommunications No. of Phones (%)
Nonrevenue			
Maintenance	80,000	—	5
Telecommunications	40,000	15	—
Revenue			
Per diem	900,000	40	90
Operating room	300,000	45	5
Total cost	1,320,000	100	100

Appendix 4-A

Medicare Cost Report Excerpts

Exhibit 4-A-1 Institutional Cost Report—Certification

Provider No.
Period from 01/01/90 to 12/31/90

EICR—Empire Blue Cross and Blue Shield   Version: 91
In lieu of Form HCFA-2552-89 (12/89)   05/31

Worksheet

Hospital and Health Care Cost Report
Certification and Settlement Summary

Intermediary Use Only
__Audited   __Desk Reviewed

Date Received: ____
Intermediary No. ____

Part I—Certification

Intentional misrepresentation or falsification of any information contained in this cost report
may be punishable by fine and/or imprisonment under federal law.

Certification by Officer or Administrator of Provider(s)

    I hereby certify that I have read the above statement and that I have examined the accompanying cost report and the balance sheet and statement of revenue and expenses prepared by _____ (33-0194) (Provider Name(s) and Number(s)) for the cost report period beginning 01-01-90 and ending 12-31-90, and that, to the best of my knowledge and belief, it is a true, correct, and complete statement prepared from the books and records of the provider in accordance with applicable instructions, except as noted.

(Signed) _____
                    Officer or Administrator of Provider(s)

                _____
                Title

                _____
                Date

Part II—Settlement Summary

	Title V		Title XVIII		Title XIX
	1	A 2		B 3	4
1 Hospital		11639543		8958664	
2 Subprovider I		387055			
3 Subprovider II					
4 Swing Bed—SNF					
5 Swing Bed—ICF					
6 Skilled Nursing Facility					
7 Intermediate Care Facility					
8 Home Health Agency		1091713			
9 Comprehensive Outpatient Rehabilitation Facility (CORF)					
10 Total		13118311		8958664	

The above amounts represent due to or due from the applicable program for the element of the complex indicated.

Exhibit 4-A-2 Institutional Cost Report—Cost Allocation—General Service Costs

Provider No. _____
Period from 01/01/90 to 12/31/90
  Cost Allocation—General Service Costs

EICR—Empire Blue Cross and Blue Shield
in lieu of Form HCFA-2552-89 (12/89)

Version: 91
05/31
Worksheet B
Part I

	Cost Center Description	Net Exp. for Cost Allocation 0	Cap. Rel. Cost— Bldgs. & Fixtures 1	Cap. Rel. Cost— Movbl. Equipment 2	Employee Benefits 3	Subtotal 3A	Administrative & General 4	Operation of Plant 6	Laundry & Linen Service 7
	General Service Cost Centers								
1	Cap-rel costs—bldgs. & fixtures	10057369	10057369						
2	Cap-rel costs—movable equipment	8749151		8749151					
3	Employee benefits	23821018	48726	7411	23877155				
4	Administrative and general	21995738	2822931	3170817	2803776	30793262	30793262		
5	Maintenance and repairs								
6	Operation of plant	7187749	672903	522802	717424	9100878	1478574	10579452	
7	Laundry and linen services	1656701	79351	64221	201015	2001288	325139	128899	2455326
8	Housekeeping	4234204	98664	82461	709761	5125090	832648	160270	1601
9A	Dietary—raw food	1975372				1975372	320929		
9B	Dietary—other	3555271	280234	46609	686607	4568721	742257	455214	4234
10	Cafeteria		44201			44201	7181	71800	
11	Maintenance of personnel		209229	23035		232264	37735	339873	
15	Medical records and library	2076416	143892	112927	298081	2631316	427497	233739	
16	Social service	970843	30406	3235	178265	1182749	192155	49392	
17A	Medical supplies and expense	6898852		9358	11728	6919938	1124248		
17B	Central services & supply	756944	63375	103815	103435	1027569	166944	102946	
17C	Pharmacy	10220289	65672	349540	636502	11272003	1831306	106678	
17D	Nursing administration	1322802	124568	164432	103716	1715518	278712	202349	24826
17E	Intensive nursing care								
17F	General nursing service								
18	Visual aids	120322	32484	31911	20973	205690	33417	52767	
19	Non-physician anesthetists	307291			59946	367237	59663		
21	Int-res-sal & fringes (appvd.)	9139414	83103	34105	1738760	10995382	1786365	134993	
21A	Supervising MDs—teaching	4322807			843289	5166096	839310		
22	Int-res-other pgm. costs (appvd.)								
22A	Supervising physicians								
	Inpatient routine serv. cost centers								
25	Adults & pediatrics	30439700	2446206	558969	5175185	38620060	6274390	3973635	1333861
26	Intensive care unit	3095455	106906	186535	488044	3876940	629867	173659	229519
27	Coronary care unit	1358736	31214	238707	248574	1877231	304984	50704	37159
28	Surgical ICU	1526368	18470	15122	248104	1808064	293747	30003	124329
28D	Neo-natal intensive care unit	2137404	32934	76018	353233	2599589	422342	53498	63990
31	Subprovider I—psychiatric	3533373	299154	22919	694223	4549669	739162	485948	40907
33	Nursery	2230959	28490	11804	428740	2699993	438654	46279	136645
	Ancillary service cost centers								
37	Operating room	9535973	241366	619977	1082681	11479997	1865098	392077	342551
39	Delivery room & labor room	2741743	93769	57740	488056	3381308	549344	152319	
40	Anesthesiology	838627	17258	196344	83644	1135873	184540	28034	
41	Radiology—diagnostic	3137506	255126	785018	316845	4494495	730198	414429	26298
43	Radioisotope	629912	22972	56645	26622	736151	119599	37316	
43A	C.A.T. scan	124058	31537	67171	24045	246811	40098	51229	
44	Laboratory	7098960	335020	417404	1029069	8880453	1442763	544209	8387
47	Blood storing, process, transfus.	3127615	108834	68221	198256	3502926	569103	176790	
49	Respiratory therapy	1395321	8404	116276	186508	1706509	277248	13651	
50	Physical therapy	766384	50596	21374	145677	984031	159871	82188	9311
53	Electrocardiology	3044165	135753	266417	193500	3639835	591346	220519	5239
54	Electroencephalography	305469	83541	16529	57551	463090	75236	135705	
55	Med supplies chgd. to patients								

Exhibit 4-A-2 continued

Provider No. _____
Period from   01/01/90 to 12/31/90
        Cost Allocation—General Service Costs

EICR—Empire Blue Cross and Blue Shield
in lieu of Form HCFA-2552-89 (12/89)

Version: 91
05/31
Worksheet B
Part I

Cost Center Description	House-keeping 8	Dietary Raw Food 9A	Dietary Other 9B	Cafeteria 10	Maint. of Personnel 11	Medical Records & Library 15	Social Service 16	Medical Supplies & Expense 17A
General Service Cost Centers								
1 Cap-rel costs—bldgs. & fixtures								
2 Cap-rel costs—movable equipment								
3 Employee benefits								
4 Administrative and general								
5 Maintenance and repairs								
6 Operation of plant								
7 Laundry and linen services								
8 Housekeeping	6119609							
9A Dietary—raw food		2296301						
9B Dietary—other			5770426					
10 Cafeteria		480708	1207983	1811873				
11 Maintenance of personnel					609872			
15 Medical records and library				48458		3341010		
16 Social service				20014			1444310	
17A Medical supplies and expense								8044186
17B Central services & supply				16547				
17C Pharmacy				57914				
17D Nursing administration	21838			54053				
17E Intensive nursing care								
17F General nursing service								
18 Visual aids								
19 Non-physician anesthetists								
21 Int-res-sal & fringes (appvd.)	131026			209120	166579			
21A Supervising MDs—teaching								
22 Int-res-other pgm. costs (appvd.)								
22A Supervising physicians								
Inpatient routine serv. cost centers								
25 Adults & pediatrics	2953137	1410661	3544881	519725	352432	1521162	1049726	4334920
26 Intensive care unit	327566	44227	111138	38688	23404	172730	2166	409319
27 Coronary care unit		20951	52649	18674		101567	2166	142799
28 Surgical ICU	65513	19342	48605	21747	5507	125622	2166	327802
28D Neo-natal intensive care unit	131026			30572		75173	53728	143378
31 Subprovider I—psychiatric	494541	173575	436179	68078		153352		219633
33 Nursery	131026			35142		84862		24861
Ancillary service cost centers								
37 Operating room	196540			101251	4130			1097301
39 Delivery room & labor room	262053			45464				380993
40 Anesthesiology				11819	16520			170551
41 Radiology—diagnostic	163783			48222	8260			23127
43 Radioisotope				2679				
43A C.A.T. scan				2364				
44 Laboratory	98270			122998	8260			64750
47 Blood storing, process, transfus.				24505	8260			18501
49 Respiratory therapy				22220				42784
50 Physical therapy				15286	8260			578
53 Electrocardiology				29784				27754
54 Electroencephalography				5437				
55 Med supplies chgd. to patients								

Exhibit 4-A-2 continued

Provider No. _____
Period from   01/01/90 to 12/31/90
  Cost Allocation—General Service Costs

EICR—Empire Blue Cross and Blue Shield
in lieu of Form HCFA-2552-89 (12/89)

Version: 91
05/31
Worksheet B
Part I

	Cost Center Description	Central Services & Supply 17B	Pharmacy 17C	Nursing Adminis- tration 17D	Visual Aids 18	Non- Physician Anesthe- tists 19	I/R- Appvd. Sals. & Fr. Benefits 21	Super- vising Physicians 21A	Subtotal 25
	General Service Cost Centers								
1	Cap-rel costs—bldgs. & fixtures								
2	Cap-rel costs—movable equipment								
3	Employee benefits								
4	Administrative and general								
5	Maintenance and repairs								
6	Operation of plant								
7	Laundry and linen services								
8	Housekeeping								
9A	Dietary—raw food								
9B	Dietary—other								
10	Cafeteria								
11	Maintenance of personnel								
15	Medical records and library								
16	Social service								
17A	Medical supplies and expense								
17B	Central services & supply	1314006							
17C	Pharmacy		13267901						
17D	Nursing administration			2297296					
17E	Intensive nursing care								
17F	General nursing service								
18	Visual aids				291874				
19	Non-physician anesthetists					426900			
21	Int-res-sal & fringes (appvd.)		1740				13425205		
21A	Supervising MDs—teaching							6005406	
22	Int-res-other pgm. costs (appvd.)								
22A	Supervising physicians								
	Inpatient routine serv. cost centers								
25	Adults & pediatrics	859777	10875603	1133486	291874	356376	6224583	2225394	87855683
26	Intensive care unit	102630	418651	66851			722643		7349998
27	Coronary care unit	60247	39783	65932			361321		3136167
28	Surgical ICU	61852	386110	66622			173622		3560653
28D	Neo-natal intensive care unit	47221	23973	53297			583041		4280828
31	Subprovider I—psychiatric		148663	586270			430536	159697	8686210
33	Nursery		8428				197084		3802974
	Ancillary service cost centers								
37	Operating room	16547	30758	218243					15744493
39	Delivery room & labor room	5968	14252	106595			509135		5407431
40	Anesthesiology		113618				750798	107521	2519274
41	Radiology—diagnostic	14798	77224				375399		6376233
43	Radioisotope								895745
43A	C.A.T. scan								340502
44	Laboratory		89				422324	383590	11976093
47	Blood storing, process, transfus.		20					34241	4334346
49	Respiratory therapy								2062412
50	Physical therapy								1259525
53	Electrocardiology	14918	1857						4531252
54	Electroencephalography						93850	253887	1027205
55	Med supplies chgd. to patients								

Exhibit 4-A-3 Institutional Cost Report—Cost Allocation—Statistical Basis

Provider No. _____

Period from   01/01/90 to 12/31/90

Cost Allocation—Statistical Basis

EICR—Empire Blue Cross and Blue Shield
in lieu of Form HCFA-2552-89 (12/89)

Version: 91.02

05/31/91

Worksheet B-1

Cost Center Description	0	Cap-Rel Cost– Bldgs. & Fixtures (sq. feet) 1	Cap-Rel Cost– Movbl. Equipment ($ value) 2	Employee Benefits (Gross Salaries) 3	Recon- ciliation 3A	Adminis- trative & General (Accum. Cost) 4	Maint. and Repairs (sq. feet) 5	Operation of Plant (sq. feet) 6
General Service Cost Centers								
1 Cap-rel costs—bldgs. & fixtures		871246						
2 Cap-rel costs—movable equipment			7143229					
3 Employee benefits		4221	6051	122397259				
4 Administrative and general		244544	2588807	14372516	−30793262	189537921	244544	244544
5 Maintenance and repairs							622481	
6 Operation of plant		58292	426841	3677607		9100878	58292	564189
7 Laundry and linen services		6874	52433	1030429		2001288	6874	6874
8 Housekeeping		8547	67325	3638327		5125090	8547	8547
9A Dietary—raw food						1975372		
9B Dietary—other		24276	38054	3519637		4568721	24276	24276
10 Cafeteria		3829				44201	3829	3829
11 Maintenance of personnel		18125	18807			232264	18125	18125
15 Medical records and library		12465	92199	1528004		2631316	12465	12465
16 Social service		2634	2641	913810		1182749	2634	2634
17A Medical supplies and expense			7640	60117		6919938		
17B Central services & supply		5490	84760	530222		1027569	5490	5490
17C Pharmacy		5689	285381	3262790		11272003	5689	5689
17D Nursing administration		10791	134250	531663		1715518	10791	10791
17E Intensive nursing care								
17F General nursing service								
18 Visual aids		2814	26054	107509		205690	2814	2814
19 Non-physician anesthetists				307291		367237		
21 Int-res-sal & fringes (appvd.)		7199	27845	8913107		10995382	7199	7199
21A Supervising MDs—teaching				4322807		5166096		
22 Int-res-other pgm. costs (appvd.)								
22A Supervising physicians								
Inpatient routine serv. cost centers								
25 Adults & pediatrics		211909	456369	26528559		38620060	211909	211909
26 Intensive care unit		9261	152296	2501774		3876940	9261	9261
27 Coronary care unit		2704	194892	1274222		1877231	2704	2704
28 Surgical ICU		1600	12346	1271811		1808064	1600	1600
28D Neo-natal intensive care unit		2853	62065	1810718		2599589	2853	2853
31 Subprovider I—psychiatric		25915	18712	3558675		4549669	25915	25915
33 Nursery		2468	9637	2197774		2699993	2468	2468
Ancillary service cost centers								
37 Operating room		20909	506179	5549962		11479997	20909	20909
39 Delivery room & labor room		8123	47142	2501840		3381308	8123	8123
40 Anesthesiology		1495	160305	428771		1135873	1495	1495
41 Radiology—diagnostic		22101	640927	1624186		4494495	22101	22101
43 Radioisotope		1990	46248	136468		736151	1990	1990
43A C.A.T. scan		2732	54842	123258		246811	2732	2732
44 Laboratory		29022	340789	5275142		8880453	29022	29022
47 Blood storing, process, transfus.		9428	55699	1016284		3502926	9428	9428
49 Respiratory therapy		728	94933	956064		1706509	728	728
50 Physical therapy		4383	17451	746761		984031	4383	4383
53 Electrocardiology		11760	217516	991905		3639835	11760	11760

Exhibit 4-A-3 continued

Provider No. _____

Period from 01/01/90 to 12/31/90

Cost Allocation—Statistical Basis

EICR—Empire Blue Cross and Blue Shield
in lieu of Form HCFA-2552-89 (12/89)

Version: 91.02
05/31/91

Worksheet B-1

Cost Center Description	Laundry & Linen Service (Pounds of Laundry) 7	House-keeping (Hours of Service) 8	Dietary Raw Food (Meals Served) 9A	Dietary Other (Meals Served) 9B	Cafeteria (Avg. No. of Employees) 10	Maint of Personnel (Number Housed) 11	Medical Records & Library (% of Time Spent) 15	Social Service (Time Spent) 16
General Service Cost Centers								
1 Cap-rel costs—bldgs. & fixtures								
2 Cap-rel costs—movable equipment								
3 Employee benefits								
4 Administrative and general		42250			4393	18		
5 Maintenance and repairs								
6 Operation of plant								
7 Laundry and linen services	4600657							
8 Housekeeping	3000	182150						
9A Dietary—raw food			974351					
9B Dietary—other	7933			974351				
10 Cafeteria			203971	203971	22995			
11 Maintenance of personnel						443		
15 Medical records and library					615		10000	
16 Social service					254			10000
17A Medical supplies and expense								
17B Central services & supply					210			
17C Pharmacy					735			
17D Nursing administration	46518	650			686			
17E Intensive nursing care								
17F General nursing service								
18 Visual aids								
19 Non-physician anesthetists								
21 Int-res-sal & fringes (appvd.)		3900			2654	121		
21A Supervising MDs—teaching								
22 Int-res-other pgm. costs (appvd.)								
22A Supervising physicians								
Inpatient routine serv. cost centers								
25 Adults & pediatrics	2499317	87900	598562	598562	6596	256	4553	7268
26 Intensive care unit	430061	9750	18766	18766	491	17	517	15
27 Coronary care unit	69626		8890	8890	237		304	15
28 Surgical ICU	232961	1950	8207	8207	276	4	376	15
28D Neo-natal intensive care unit	119902	3900			388		225	372
31 Subprovider I—psychiatric	76650	14720	73650	73650	864		459	
33 Nursery	256038	3900			446		254	
Ancillary service cost centers								
37 Operating room	641853	5850			1285	3		
39 Delivery room & labor room		7800			577			
40 Anesthesiology					150	12		
41 Radiology—diagnostic	49275	4875			612	6		
43 Radioisotope					34			
43A C.A.T. scan					30			
44 Laboratory	15715	2925			1561	6		
47 Blood storing, process, transfus.					311	6		
49 Respiratory therapy					282			
50 Physical therapy	17446				194	6		
53 Electrocardiology	9816				378			

Exhibit 4-A-3 continued

Provider No. _____

Period from   01/01/90 to 12/31/90

Cost Allocation—Statistical Basis

EICR—Empire Blue Cross and Blue Shield
in lieu of Form HCFA-2552-89 (12/89)

Version: 91.02

05/31/91

Worksheet B-1

	Cost Center Description	Medical Supplies & Expense (Costed Reqstns.) 17A	Central Services & Supply (Costed Reqstns.) 17B	Pharmacy (Costed Reqstns.) 17C	Nursing Administration (Spvsn. of Nrs. Time) 17D	Visual Aids 18	Non-Physician Anesthetists (Assigned Time) 19	I/R-Appvd. Sals. & Fr. Benefits (Assigned Time) 21	Supervising Physicians (Salaries Rendered) 21A
	General Service Cost Centers								
1	Cap-rel costs—bldgs. & fixtures								
2	Cap-rel costs—movable equipment								
3	Employee benefits								
4	Administrative and general								261974
5	Maintenance and repairs								
6	Operation of plant								
7	Laundry and linen services								
8	Housekeeping								
9A	Dietary—raw food								
9B	Dietary—other								
10	Cafeteria								
11	Maintenance of personnel								
15	Medical records and library								
16	Social service								
17A	Medical supplies and expense	6837655							
17B	Central services & supply		448681						
17C	Pharmacy			7265140					
17D	Nursing administration				10000				
17E	Intensive nursing care								
17F	General nursing service								
18	Visual aids					10000			
19	Non-physician anesthetists						10000		
21	Int-res-sal & fringes (appvd.)			953				11444	
21A	Supervising MDs—teaching								2839477
22	Int-res-other pgm. costs (appvd.)								
22A	Supervising physicians								
	Inpatient routine serv. cost centers								
25	Adults & pediatrics	3684735	293580	5955182	4934	10000	8348	5306	1052211
26	Intensive care unit	347926	35044	229242	291			616	
27	Coronary care unit	121381	20572	21784	287			308	
28	Surgical ICU	278636	21120	211423	290			148	
28D	Neo-natal intensive care unit	121873	16124	13127	232			497	
31	Subprovider I—psychiatric	186691		81404	2552			367	75508
33	Nursery	21132		4615				168	
	Ancillary service cost centers								
37	Operating room	932719	5650	16842	950				
39	Delivery room & labor room	323849	2038	7804	464			434	
40	Anesthesiology	144970		62214				640	50838
41	Radiology—diagnostic	19658	5053	42286				320	
43	Radioisotope								
43A	C.A.T. scan								
44	Laboratory	55038		49				360	181369
47	Blood storing, process, transfus.	15726		11					16190
49	Respiratory therapy	36367							
50	Physical therapy	491							
53	Electrocardiology	23591	5094	1017					

Application 4-1

The Distinction between Cost and Charges

Steven A. Finkler, PhD, CPA

A popular topic recently has been the assessment of the economic efficiency with which hospital services are provided. For example, the literature on the economic effects of regionalization has been increasing.[1-4] More studies of economic impact have been appearing in medical journals as society's concern over health care costs has increased. Which services will be provided and where they will be provided are receiving greater scrutiny, and cost has become a major issue. Because the results of scrutiny, such as decisions regarding capital investment, have a direct impact on the medical community, medical researchers are taking an active part in assessing the economic efficiency of services and procedures, and practitioners are becoming concerned with the results of those studies. The medical researcher assessing financial information is entering the complex area of financial management. It is important that both the researcher and the practitioner be aware of some of the complications of hospital financial management.

Most studies of economic efficiency attempt to examine costs incurred under different situations. If a large number of hospitals with a wide range of volume for a particular service all have approximately the same cost per unit, one may conclude that volume does not have a significant impact on cost. However, these studies often use the charges that appear on patient bills as a proxy for cost. The terms cost and charges are used interchangeably in such studies, creating a serious problem in evaluating results because charges typically vary from actual costs. This paper traces the process by which hospitals find their costs and set their rates that determine charges so that readers of research on medical economic efficiency can determine whether charge information was used in studies where cost information would have been more appropriate, or vice versa.

THE ROOTS OF THE MISUNDERSTANDING

It is not surprising that many members of the medical community assume there is a close relation between costs and charges. Since most health organizations are nonprofit, it is logical to assume that price is set to be equal to cost. Furthermore, there has been substantial focus on the ills of cost-reimbursement systems such as Blue Cross, Medicare, and Medicaid because of the direct relation between cost and reim-

Source: Reprinted from Steven A. Finkler, "The Distinction between Cost and Charges," *Annals of Internal Medicine,* Vol. 96, No. 1, January 1982, pp. 102–109. Copyright 1982, American College of Physicians.

bursement. As costs rise, reimbursement rises automatically. There is minimal incentive to be efficient and control costs if all cost increases are automatically passed to Blue Cross or the government.

This example of passing on costs is an oversimplification of the cost-reimbursement mechanism, but is basically correct. Costs, after disallowance of specific items, are the amount that Blue Cross, Medicare, and Medicaid pay. However, none of those three groups pays the amount that is known as charges. Charges are list prices. The power of Blue Cross' size and the legal clout of the government entitle them to demand discounts off the list price. In fact, the discounts are so great that often Blue Cross, Medicare, and Medicaid pay less than the average cost.[5]

On the other hand, self-pay patients and private insurance companies other than Blue Cross have significantly less clout, and pay not only the costs they have incurred, but also make up any loss the hospital incurs when it gives substantial discounts to Blue Cross, Medicare, and Medicaid. Charges must be set high enough to make sure this compensation occurs.

Before getting into the specifics of the cost-finding and rate-setting process, an example may elucidate the basic distinction between cost and charges. Consider two automobile manufacturers with a similar line of cars. The first manufacturer, JM, is huge, selling 10 million cars. The second manufacturer, Kryler, is smaller, selling only 1 million cars. Both had been producing their cars for a cost of $4,200 each. Then the government introduced a law stating that a pollution control system must be developed. Each firm invested $1 billion to solve the pollution problem. To JM, this resulted in a cost increase of $100 per car ($1 billion ÷ 10 million cars). To Kryler, with its smaller volume of cars to absorb the development costs, this increased costs by $1,000 per car ($1 billion ÷ 1 million cars). JM cars then cost $4,300 to produce and Kryler cars cost $5,200 to produce. JM sold its new cars for $5,000. At this price they made a $700 profit per car.

If one asked a buyer of a JM car, "What did it cost?" the buyer would undoubtedly say,

"$5,000." However, we wouldn't expect the buyer to use the $5,000 price interchangeably with cost when cost was meant in the economic sense of the cost of production. Although we would never assume the purchase price to be equal to the production cost, we often make that assumption with respect to hospital services.

The Kryler car which is virtually identical to the JM car also had a price of $5,000. At this price they will lose $200 per car. Why didn't Kryler charge the production cost for the cars? At a $5,200 Kryler price, all customers would have purchased cars from JM. So Kryler was forced to charge only $5,000 and incur a loss.

One can think of Kryler as a low-volume producer of a medical service such as open heart surgery, and JM as a high-volume producer of open heart surgery. Kryler's cost per unit is much higher because of the need to spread fixed costs over fewer units. Examination of the price charged by the two gives no clue to the differences in production cost. Yet, while we wouldn't assume that the same selling price of two manufacturers means they have the same cost of production, we do make that assumption about hospitals.

This doesn't imply that hospitals are just like automobile makers. JM and Kryler are openly in competition. One earns a profit, the other loses money. Yet non-profit hospitals have been known to compete with each other. Furthermore, while some hospitals lose money, others (even if not making a net profit) must profit enough on the self-pay patients to make up for losses on Medicaid patients.

Unit costs are not always an inverse function of volume. Economic theory generally predicts that economies of scale will exist over a certain range of volume, but above that range diseconomies are expected. For example, in health care the regionalization process would at some point result in travel costs exceeding the savings of further regionalization. We neither support nor deny the existence of scale economies in the production of specialized health services; however, information about the price charged at medical centers with different volumes is inadequate to assess whether scale economies exist.

THE COST-FINDING PROCESS

In an economic sense, cost is represented by foregone opportunities. If we use a resource for one purpose, it cannot be used for another. We can think of cost in terms of the resources consumed. If one patient consumes more resources than another, we would say that the patient causes the health care institution to incur more cost.

For most studies of economic efficiency the cost in question may be thought of as marginal costs. A marginal cost is the extra amount of resource consumption incurred for providing a service as compared to the costs of not providing the same service. For instance, how much more will a hospital consume if it has a neonatal intensive care unit than if it does not? We can think of the marginal cost for an entire service, such as neonatal intensive care, or for an extra patient in neonatal intensive care.

The dollar measurement of resource consumption is difficult. Hospital costs are in fact frequently the charge of a producer from whom the hospital has purchased resources. For example, a bypass pump costing the hospital $80,000 to buy may have cost the vendor only $60,000 to produce. The vendor in turn has purchased the components elsewhere, so the pump cost includes charges of its vendors. Thus, the dollar measurement of actual resource consumption cost is quite complicated. However, we can distinguish between the cost to the hospital and the charges by that hospital. Economic cost will be used to refer to the price paid by the health care institution for the resources it consumes. It is conceivable that for some studies a researcher might wish to add to this other cost, such as increased travel for patients, visitors, and physicians. In other cases researchers may be more interested in vendor costs than hospital costs. The issue at hand is not what measure is appropriate for any study, but the idea that charges are not equal to, nor necessarily a good approximation of, what a hospital pays for the resources it consumes in providing services.

Studies of economic efficiency usually start with a definition of economic cost as being the price paid for the resources consumed. In comparing the cost of performing 100 open-heart operations at one location to the cost of 50 open-heart operations at each of two locations, the economic issue is whether the one, centralized high-volume location results in less total resource consumption than the total of the resources consumed by the two separate low-volume locations. In economic theory, the consumption would be less if some of the resources are fixed costs. A resource is a fixed cost if the amount consumed does not vary with volume. For example, if a bypass pump can handle up to 250 patients per year, the high-volume center might need one, whereas the low-volume centers would need one each. Total cost would be higher for two centers than for one, since two pumps are used instead of one. This assumes that extra costs of centralization such as increased travel do not more than offset the cost of the additional pump.

However, under the pricing system in health care organizations the patient charges at both the low- and high-volume centers will not reflect the difference in resource consumption of bypass pumps. The hospital cost accounting systems do not accumulate cost information by patient, but by department instead. In assigning resource consumption costs to departments, a large degree of accuracy is lost. Depending on the specific accounting procedure, costs may not be assigned to the department in which the consumption occurred.

Once the costs have been allocated to the various departments, they are assigned to units of service, which are used to allocate costs to individual patients. At this stage the association of actual resource consumption with the measured accounting cost becomes less precise. Not only may a department be attempting to assign a total amount of cost that is not representative of the resources consumed by that department, but it also may assign its costs to patients in a different proportion than their actual consumption of that department's services. Thus, what the health care organization calls the patient's cost is not the economic cost in the sense of the specific resources the patient consumed. Studies that have recognized this to be the case, either implicitly or explicitly, measured cost by directly examining resource consumption,[2-3, 6] a task that requires more time, effort, and cost than does use of charge data. The costs accumulated by the hospital cost accounting system will be called the accounting cost here.

DETERMINATION OF EACH DEPARTMENT'S COSTS

Most costs incurred by each department can be directly associated with that department. Most salaries and supplies are department specific. However, there is an element of cost that arises because of the services departments provide for each other. It is the cost of these services that is of particular interest.

For example, when a patient has a roentgenogram, all resources consumed in providing that roentgenogram are part of the patient's cost. One of the costs is the laundry expense of the laboratory coat worn by the technician. However, that cost is incurred in the laundry department and must be charged to the x-ray department. In a similar fashion, since patients do not come into direct contact with the laundry department, all of its costs must be charged to the various departments that utilize its services.

Ultimately, all costs must be assigned to the departments that charge the patients directly for their services. In a hospital, departments such as radiology, laboratory, and operating room are known as cost and revenue centers. Departments such as admitting, housekeeping, maintenance, and dietary are cost centers only. All of the expense of the cost centers must be assigned to the revenue centers. This allows the organization to accumulate all costs in the departments for which bills are issued, and determine how much it must charge to recover all of its costs.

To understand fully the problems of equating resource consumption with the patient generating that resource consumption, it is necessary to see how the cost allocation process works.

The commonest method for allocation is the step-down method. This method allocates the costs of one cost center to all other cost centers, both those that are and are not revenue centers. Once the costs have been allocated from a cost

center, it is deemed "closed," meaning that no other cost center can assign costs to it. After each cost center is allocated, there remains one center fewer in the analysis.

A "depreciation" cost center might seem reasonable, and depreciation would be the first center allocated. All departments consume some space, yet none provides any services to the building itself. If depreciation is allocated fairly to the departments there is no problem, but determination of a fair basis is a problem. Should depreciation be based on square feet or cubic feet? Are all areas of the building equally costly to build? Other cost centers cause similar problems. Should laundry department costs be based on pounds or pieces? Although such allocations usually are arbitrary, the process typically is not a major problem in cost determination.

A more serious problem is that of cost centers providing services to each other. The general administration departments service the housekeeping department, which in turn keeps the administrative departments clean. Which department is allocated first? The order of allocation can have a significant impact on which department ultimately bears the costs of the organization.

In Table 4-1-1 four departments are shown, two of which are revenue centers and two of which are not. Cost centers A and B each incur $100 of cost directly. The laboratory incurs $100 directly and medical/surgical incurs $500. Using some relatively fair allocation basis, we determine that 70% of center A's services are provided to center B, 25% to the laboratory, and 5% to medical/surgical. Cost center B does not provide any service to center A and only 20% of its efforts are for the laboratory. Most of center B's services (80%) are provided to medical/surgical. We would expect that most of center A's cost should wind up in medical/surgical, since 5% of center A's cost goes directly to medical/surgical, and 70% of center A's cost goes to center B, which allocates 80% of its cost to medical/surgical. Since 70% × 80% = 56%, and we have 5% directly from center A to medical/surgical, 61% or $61 out of center A's $100 should wind up in medical/surgical. Additionally, 80%

Table 4-1-1 Hypothetical Use of Cost Centers

| | Nonrevenue Cost Centers | | Revenue Cost Centers | | |
	A	B	Lab	Med/Surg	Total
Direct department cost	$100	$100	$100	$500	$800
Relative use of center A		70%	25%	5%	
Relative use of center B	0%		20%	80%	

Table 4-1-2 Hypothetical Allocations to Revenue Centers

| | Nonrevenue Cost Centers | | Revenue Cost Centers | | |
	A	B	Lab	Med/Surg	Total
Direct department cost	$100	$100	$100	$500	$800
Distribution of center A	−100	+70	+25	+5	
Subtotal	$ 0	$170	$125	$505	
Distribution of center B		−170	+34	+136	
Total		$ 0	$159	$641	$800

of center B's cost, or $80, should go to medical/surgical. Altogether, approximately $141 of the $200 total cost of centers A and B should wind up in the medical/surgical revenue center.

Table 4-1-2 shows what happens when we step-down from center A to B to the revenue centers. Center A is allocated in a 70%, 25%, 5% proportion to center B, laboratory, and medical/surgical, respectively. Center B, which then has $170 of cost because of allocations from center A, is allocated to laboratory and medical/surgical in a 20%, 80% proportion, respectively. The outcome is exactly what makes sense from an economic resource consumption perspective; $141 of cost centers A and B winds up in medical/surgical.

However there may be reasons for an organization to change the allocation order. Suppose for example that due to Medicare ceilings on the medical/surgical per diem reimbursement rate, the hospital cannot receive more than $600 in revenues for the medical/surgical cost center. The hospital will lose $41.

A restatement of the allocation order, going from B to A to the revenue centers, is shown in Table 4-1-3. Center B's cost is allocated to center A, laboratory, and medical/surgical in the 0%, 20%, 80% proportion that it provides service to those departments (Table 4-1-3). However, center A's cost must be allocated solely between laboratory and medical/surgical, since department B is already closed. Because center A provides 25% of its services directly to the laboratory, and only 5% of its services directly to medical/surgical, the allocation is on a proportion of 25 to 5. This result means that five sixths of center A's cost winds up in laboratory and only one sixth in medical/surgical, even though in reality center A primarily serves B and center B primarily serves medical/surgical. Since Medicare reimburses laboratory without a ceiling, and medical/surgical costs are now only $597, the hospital does not lose the $41 it would have lost by allocating center A to B first instead of center B to A. This process has been referred to as creative accounting.

Table 4-1-3 Hypothetical Distribution of Costs

	Nonrevenue Cost Centers		Revenue Cost Centers		
	B	A	Lab	Med/Surg	Total
Direct department cost	$100	$100	$100	$500	$800
Distribution of center B	−100	+0	+20	+80	
Subtotal	$ 0	$100	$120	$580	
Distribution of center A		−100	+83	+17	
Total		$ 0	$203	$597	$800

Although the example presents an extreme case, consider how many departments are in a hospital and that many of these departments provide services to several other departments. Since the hospital or other health care organization is more concerned with recovering its full costs than with assigning each department exactly the costs for which it is responsible, it would be reasonable to expect the organization to order the departments for step-down in an advantageous sequence.

In the management of a health care organization, securing maximum reimbursement is vital. However, researchers must be aware that this effort may result in cross-subsidization among departments. Ultimately, the cost assigned to the patient may be wrong due to allocation methods meant to secure maximum reimbursement rather than to accurately reflect resource consumption on a department-by-department basis. Because departments are closed to allocation progressively, even if there were no attempt to increase reimbursement some departments would not be able to allocate their expenses to the other departments that cause them to consume resources, leading to probable misallocation.

ALLOCATION OF DEPARTMENT COSTS TO UNITS OF SERVICE

Once costs have been assigned to departments, some measure of unit cost must be determined to use as a basis for rate-setting. For example, the laboratory must determine the cost

per blood gas test; the radiology department must know the cost per chest roentgenogram; the pharmaceutical department must know the cost per aspirin. These costs must be calculated in such a way that the total costs of the revenue centers (after receiving assigned costs from the nonrevenue cost centers) are allocated to the individual units of service provided. There are four basic methods for this allocation; each hospital will probably use all four, selecting for each department the most applicable method.

The Weighted Procedure Method

For routine tasks, the weighted procedure method is especially useful. Each product of a department is assigned a number of relative units. For example, in the laboratory each test would have a number assigned to it that represents its relative resource consumption. These weightings are based on consumption of supplies, equipment, and personnel. State hospital associations frequently compute a standardized set of relative value units that hospitals may refer to. The process requires evaluating how much time each procedure uses, such as direct production, preparation, evaluation, and supervision time. The cost of this time is based on the hourly rate plus fringe benefits of appropriate personnel. Total personnel cost is added to materials and equipment costs, consisting of overhead, equipment depreciation, and direct materials used. Once a total is determined for each procedure, all procedures are compared. One procedure, twice as costly as another, would be assigned a relative value twice as high as that of the other procedure. In this way a standardized list of relative values may be prepared. Different hospitals can assign their different costs using the standardized list as a basis for the relative resource consumption of each test.

A blood gas test might have a weighting of 40, whereas an acetone test might have a weight of 10. Thus, if a laboratory did 100 blood gas tests and 200 acetone tests, there would be a total of 6,000 relative value units (40 units × 100 tests = 4,000; 10 units × 200 tests = 2,000; 4,000 + 2,000 = 6,000). If the total cost of the laboratory (both direct costs and those assigned through the step-down process) were $1,200, the cost per relative value unit would then be 20 cents ($1,200 ÷ 6,000 total units). Therefore, the cost of a blood gas test would be $8 (40 units at 20 cents apiece) and an acetone test would be $2 (10 units at 20 cents).

The main problem with the weighted procedure method is the expense of performing the necessary observations of each procedure and then converting the various components into units suitable for assessing relative values. This procedure is so costly, in fact, that most hospitals use industry standards rather than computing the relative values themselves.

All institutions do not provide their services in exactly the same manner. In one hospital the pay scale for technicians is higher than another. Different hospitals use different machines for similar tests. Consider an example where a blood gas test is given 40 relative value units based on 10 units for labor, 20 units for equipment, and 10 units for a variety of other factors. If two hospitals have different pay scales, but exactly the same equipment, it is not possible for the labor cost to be exactly half as much as the equipment cost in both hospitals. However, the use of industry-wide standard relative value units per type of test implies that to be the case.

This problem results because the use of industry-wide relative value unit standards assumes all hospitals to be exactly the same. The resource consumption for each type of test is assumed to be the same in every hospital relative to all other tests in that hospital. That is, if a

blood gas test is twice as expensive as an acetone test in one hospital, it is twice as expensive as an acetone test in every hospital. This assumption is highly unlikely given the differences between hospitals. Yet, the cost to calculate the relative values separately in each institution would be excessive. Industry standard relative values are good enough for the main hospital cost accounting purpose, which is to allocate the costs of the departments to the patients. Slight misallocations between patients are tolerable, as long as all costs are distributed to the patients. But a researcher using this information must be aware that the cost for any type of patient, when measured in this way, is one step farther away from economic cost in the sense of resource consumption.

The Hourly Rate Method

The problems of using time as a proxy for resource consumption are even greater. The common approach for assigning costs of departments such as surgery, physiotherapy, inhalation therapy, and anesthesia is to accumulate all costs for the department and then divide by the total amount of service provided, using minutes or hours as a measure of service. If there are 60 hours of inhalation therapy during the month and the total costs of the department are $6,000, there is a cost of $100 per hour ($6,000 ÷ 60 hours).

In general this approach is reasonable if all patients tend to make use of the same resources. The chief problem, however, is when a department has a wide variety of resources available for use, but the patients' consumption of those resources varies widely. For example, a patient having an appendectomy does not require the equipment available in the operating room for use in open-heart surgery. Yet such patients are charged as much on a per-minute basis as the patient having open-heart surgery. Essentially, the operating room is a source of substantial cross-subsidization between patients requiring expensive equipment and those who do not.

Consider the implications of this subsidization in the regionalization debate. If 50 open-heart operations are done in a hospital per year, the hospital must acquire a significant amount of specialized equipment. Assuming that the average length of time of an open-heart procedure is 4 hours, then the 50 patients having heart surgery account for 200 hours of surgery time. If the hospital has three operating rooms, busy on average 8 hours per day, 5 days a week, 50 weeks per year, there are 2,000 hours of surgery. Patients having open-heart surgery are assigned only 10% of the cost for operating-room equipment that had to be added for them. Any estimation of the effects of regionalization on a service such as open-heart surgery is inaccurate if it uses the operating room cost assigned to the patient having heart surgery, instead of estimating the extra resources consumed. Clearly, no one wants to win the debate on regionalization based on misspecification of data. Thus, it is not possible to draw conclusions about cost in the economic sense of resource utilization if one uses cost data assigned on the basis of hourly usage.

The Surcharge Method

The third method for the allocation of department cost to patients also creates a gap between cost assigned and resources used. This method is commonly used by pass-through departments such as central supply or pharmacy. The main cost in these departments is for the supplies that they purchase, stock, and pass-through to the patient. The costs of the department, excluding the purchase price of items, to be passed through, are compared to the direct cost of the items passed through to determine a surcharge rate. For example, if the pharmacy department has a total cost for pharmaceuticals of $100,000, and has other costs, such as labor and overhead, of $50,000, then the surcharge rate is 50% ($50,000 ÷ $100,000).

The implications of this method are astonishing. A patient consuming an aspirin costing a penny would be assigned a cost of 1.5 cents for the aspirin and its purchase, stocking, and distribution. The patient consuming an expensive drug costing the hospital $10 would be charged $15. The discrepancy between the $1/2$ cent of labor and overhead to process the aspirin and the $5 to process the sophisticated medication may be partly offset by a policy to assign a minimum processing cost for each pill or drug, and then allocate remaining costs on a surcharge basis.

Per Diem

In departments or cost centers where these three methods are deemed inappropriate (such as in the maintenance, housekeeping, nursing, or dietary departments), total costs are divided by total patient days to determine a cost per patient-day, or a per-diem cost. Here the opportunities for cross-subsidization, or averaging across patients, become the greatest. Who pays for the availability of the defibrillator at the end of the hall: the patients who use it, those who are likely to use it, or everyone? If the cost is thrown into the per diem, everyone will pay based on their length of stay. It would seem that the patients highly unlikely to use the defibrillator are having too much cost assigned, whereas those likely to use it or actually using it are assigned too little cost. Nevertheless, such equipment ordinarily is accounted for on a per-diem basis.

SUMMARY OF THE COST-FINDING PROCESS

This entire cost-allocation process derives accounting costs rather than economic costs. In addition to the various issues just discussed, accounting costs differ from economic costs because by their very nature they tend to be average costs. The total cost for a department is divided by the number of units of service, to get an average cost per unit. As discussed earlier, however, economic cost is based on a marginal concept. Thus, if we asked the cost to do an additional roentgenogram, the economic cost would include only the extra or additional resources needed for that additional procedure. This cost would probably include no equipment cost, since the equipment already would be there. The accounting cost of an additional roentgenogram would be the average cost for roentgenograms of that type and would include a share of the cost of the machine. The correct choice depends on whether we are concerned with how many more dollars the hospital spends (economic cost), or with how much the hospital must collect for each roentgenogram if it is to break even (accounting cost). The key issue is awareness that accounting costs are significantly different in many respects from economic costs.

It is inappropriate to use the terms cost and charges interchangeably, and this section has reviewed the cost-finding process in hospitals because charges are not set until accounting costs are determined. As a measure of economic cost, we have used the concept of resource consumption. Studies of economic efficiency or cost-effectiveness take this approach. In assessing alternatives, we must consider the cost of the resources consumed under the various alternatives.

The cost-finding process is difficult. Starting out with a desire to determine the cost of resources consumed by each patient, one finds problems such as the desire to increase reimbursement based on costs, the need for expedient methods that are not costly in themselves, and theoretical problems regarding the actual consumption of services of jointly consumed resources. Of greater importance is the institution's goal of expedient methods for assigning costs to patients. This goal does not necessarily require that costs be assigned based on true resource consumption by the various patients. There is no requirement in health care cost accounting systems that a patient having open-heart surgery should be assigned 100% rather than 10% of the cost of specialized equipment. Cross-subsidization between expensive and less expensive patients has long been hospital practice. Accounting costs need not represent economic cost.

In light of this fact, we find that costs are not always allocated in line with resource consumption. Cost allocation to departments depends on how good the base is and the order of step-down. Reimbursement can vary greatly with the sequence selected. Allocation by the department to patients depends on the accuracy of the standard relative units used in a particular institution; the cross-subsidization that occurs in assignment of costs on a time basis; how seriously the surcharge method distorts cost allocated from true resource consumption; and how seriously the general averaging to get a per-diem rate biases costs upward or downward from the cost of resources actually consumed by a patient.

Thus, when one contrasts costs and charges, it must be clearly stated whether charges are being compared to the economic costs based on resource consumption or to the accounting costs based on the hospital's cost-finding system. In this paper, as in most research, economic costs are compared with charges. When accounting cost is used, it is only as a proxy for economic cost, and as the reader may have ascertained, a proxy of questionable value due to the potential differences between economic and accounting cost for a specific patient.

Determination of Charges

Charges are based on the rate-setting process. The first part of the rate-setting process, as described above, consists of converting resource consumption to department costs, department costs to a cost per unit of service provided, and assigning units of service to patients. Those costs form the foundation for cost-based reimbursement. With a few adjustments, reimbursers such as Blue Cross, Medicare, and Medicaid will pay those amounts. The cost-based reimbursement process applies to over half of hospital receipts coming from the government alone.[7]

MAKING THE NUMBERS COME OUT RIGHT

The process of setting charges is not complete at that point. What if a patient cannot pay his or her bill? Many patients are too wealthy for government assistance, but not wealthy enough to pay a $30,000 hospital bill, thus creating a "bad debt." If the hospital is not to lose money every year and eventually go out of business, someone must pay that patient's cost. Thus, patients are charged more than their cost, so that those who pay will cover the losses from those who do not.

There are other factors besides bad debts that cause charges to be greater than cost. Hospitals typically provide free service to families of staff physicians. Often educational programs such as preventive care, family planning, and childbirth classes are provided below cost as a community service. Additionally, Blue Cross in various states disallows some additional items. And Medicare and Medicaid sometimes impose maximum reimbursement rates. All of these factors must be compensated for, but government and Blue Cross will not bear a share of these costs. Therefore, less than half[7] of all patients must compensate for all of the debts, free service, community programs, and disallowed costs. The result is that charges may be substantially more than costs.

We have considered only the recovery of past costs. Yet for a hospital to survive, it must acquire equipment representing new technological advances, and it may need to expand services. At the least, it must replace equipment that wears out or becomes obsolete. New machines cost more than the old ones they replace, but accounting rules allow only the original cost of equipment to be included as a factor in cost calculations. If a hospital pays $50,000 for a roentgenographic machine, its cost is spread out over its lifetime, which may be 5 years. The cost of roentgenograms will be based on a machine cost of $50,000. But if we charge for roentgenograms based on that cost, how will the machine be replaced in 5 years when the same model costs $80,000 or $100,000 because of inflation? Charges must also include an element to cover expansion and replacement, and since only a small fraction of patients pay at the charge rate, the increase of charges over costs is substantial.

Essentially, the first rule of charges is to make the institution solvent. Given the various costs of the institution, including needs for replacement and expansion, and considering the

amount to be received by the reimbursers, charges must be set so that those who pay at the charge rate will make up any difference between total costs and reimbursement. Thus, the average charge is substantially higher than hospital measured costs.

GENERAL AGREEMENT ON RATES

The gap between economic cost and charges is great considering the differences between economic cost and accounting cost, and the need to set charges at a level higher than accounting cost, but the greatest factor in the distortion between cost and charges is the last step in the rate-setting process: comparison of costs to the community. Before final determination of rates, hospitals compare themselves to other hospitals to make sure their rates are in line with the general community. Why this process occurs is unclear, but there may be fear that utilization review committees or government regulators will seize price differentials as signs of inefficiency. Comparison may be made simply not to appear out of line or may relate to basic notions of supply and demand. If one hospital charges more for a major procedure than another, private insurance and self-pay patients will want to use the less expensive hospital. The hospital can ill afford to lose the business of the group that carries a substantial burden in assuring the solvency of the institution.

Whatever the cause, consensus pricing is widely practiced and the implications enormous. Consider a hypothetical example of two hospitals, each offering open heart surgery—one at a volume of 50 patients and another at a volume of 500. The low-volume hospital has a cost per patient of $5,200, and the high-volume hospital has a cost per patient of $4,300. This discrepancy occurs because there are fewer patients at the low-volume hospital to share a variety of equipment and other fixed costs relating to open-heart surgery.

Under a consensus approach to pricing, the low-volume hospital, if it found that the other hospital charged $4,500, would then set its charge at approximately $4,500. The high-volume producer charges $200 more than cost to recover debts and so forth. This rate leads to a loss of $700 per patient at the low-volume hospital, or a total of $35,000 ($700 × 50 patients). However, this loss is easily offset by increasing the charge in some area where the hospital is particularly efficient, or else by spreading the loss out over a very-large-volume service where it will have minimal effect—for example, 7 cents extra per laboratory test over the hospital's 500,000 volume of laboratory tests. Thus, a charge of $30.07 versus $30.00 for a particular laboratory test would cause much less public notice than a charge of $5,200 versus $4,500 for open-heart surgery.

This discussion is not meant to be an argument for or against regionalization. The numbers are hypothetical and do not make a case for the existence of economies of scale, but demonstrate that charge information cannot be used to prove that economies of scale do not exist. The intent is merely to show the fallacy of using charges to determine if regionalization reduces total resource consumption or cost.

This fallacy has sometimes been formally recognized in research, and sometimes ignored. Marty and associates[8] explicitly recognized the problem. However, they used data on charges and concluded from an examination of charge information that greater volume in itself does not lead to greater economy. This is a highly questionable conclusion to draw on the basis of charge information.

Joskow and Schwartz[1] briefly raise the issue that if charges are an accurate reflection of cost, certain results follow. However, their article does not discuss whether charges will bear any resemblance to cost. They support their contention of the relative insignificance of scale economies in open-heart surgery by citing the fact that in a study[1] examining open-heart surgery caseloads ranging from 60 to 600 patients per year, there was no significant difference in the bills. Given the consensus approach to setting charges, one would not expect to find any difference in the bills, regardless of how substantial the underlying cost differences may be.

The study of Hansing[4] has the same problem. He concluded that regression analysis did not show a fall in charges as volume increased. In fact, Hansing uses costs and charges interchangeably throughout his paper. Economic theory predicts a fall in costs as volume increases, spreading fixed costs over more patients. There is no theory to support expectations of a fall in charges as volume increases. Extreme care is required in drawing conclusions and making policy recommendations based on charge information if those policy decisions are to be based on the cost of providing the care, as opposed to the amount charged for the care. Indeed, it is risky to assume that there is a reasonable correlation between charges and economic cost.

Many studies of the economic efficiency of health care institutions take a social perspective.[1,4] What are the potential savings to society from a particular action such as regionalizing tertiary care? In free-market competitive industries we do not worry about efficiency from a societal viewpoint. An inefficient high-cost producer will be driven out of business by efficient competing firms (low-cost producers). However, in health care, reimbursement tends to be largely cost-based. High-cost producers may receive higher reimbursement rather than being forced out of business. Therefore, studies of economic efficiency in health care institutions tend to focus on the costs of that institution and, all things being equal, does it cost one institution more than another to provide the same service.

The use of charge data as a proxy for cost can lead researchers to draw unwarranted conclusions about economic efficiency, specifically in studies that contend they are comparing cost, when in fact they are comparing charges. In some cases researchers may well be interested in charge information directly. However, the research questions must be clearly delineated. For example, if a medical researcher were concerned with the economic impact of two competing treatments for a disease, he might be interested in the direct economic impact on patients to be treated for that disease. Charge information might be an appropriate measure. However, if a hospital charged substantially less than its economic costs for treating that disease, it would possibly increase charges for other patients. The total economic impact of the two alternative treatments on all patients might be better assessed by analysis of cost information rather than of charges. The researcher should carefully assess the appropriate data for the research question being posed.

SUMMARY OF THE PROCESS OF SETTING CHARGES

Charges are essentially list prices. Any organization has a right to set a price for its product or services. In the health care field, many purchasers of health care services get a substantial discount from the list price. In fact, they pay a cost-based reimbursement price that may be below average cost.

In determining a list price, profit organizations have often used an approach referred to as charging what the market will bear. If product A costs $100 to produce and can be sold for $150, it yields a $50 profit. If product B costs $120 to produce and can be sold for $125, then it yields only a $5 profit. There is no necessary relation between cost and price.

Nor is there a set relation between cost and price (charges) in health care. An initial difference between cost and price is built into charges to allow for expansion, replacement, bad debts, and disallowed (for reimbursement) costs. Then the resulting set of charges, which are already greater than cost, are adjusted to a community norm. This norm may be more or less than the economic cost or even the accounting cost for a specific patient.

CONCLUSION

In a non-profit organization, how can there be a difference between cost and charges? If there is not going to be a profit, won't prices (charges) be set so that they are exactly equal to cost? The answer is no; charges are not set equal to costs. In fact, they cannot be if the organization is to survive.

On average, charges must exceed costs because of the need for expansion and replacement of equipment and facilities, increasingly expensive due to inflation and technologic improvement. Charges must exceed costs to cover care to the indigent and courtesy care; costs of a community service; and items disallowed by Blue Cross, Medicare, and Medicaid. And, since the self-pay and non-Blue-Cross private reinsurers make up a small percentage of all patients, charges must be substantially above cost for those who do pay at "list price," since they alone must bear all of the costs and expansion and replacement needs not covered by Blue Cross, Medicare, and Medicaid.

Furthermore, charges are adjusted to get a desired rate structure usually based on community norms. The frequently stated Blue Cross position of paying the "lower of cost or charges" is a reflection of how commonly adjustments to the rate structure are made. Even though charges must be high enough to cover bad debts, expansion, replacement, and disallowed cost, Blue Cross's policy points out that there are likely to be situations in which charges are set lower than cost. And the very existence of paying "lower of cost or charges" is likely to lead to some manipulation of costs and charges to maximize reimbursement.

The gap between accounting costs and charges is potentially great, although in some cases it might be relatively small. There is also a gap between economic cost and accounting cost to contend with, whether that gap results from efforts to increase reimbursement or merely to expeditiously allocate cost. That gap is also potentially great, but in some instances might be small. Researchers attempting to assess economic efficiency must clearly defend their reason for believing these gaps are small if they use charges as a proxy for cost; otherwise, they should collect data on resource consumption and directly attempt to measure economic costs. Readers of research on economic efficiency should be aware of the complexity of the problems involved when costs and charges are assumed to be equal, so that they may make an informed evaluation of the results of such studies.

ACKNOWLEDGMENTS

Grant support: from the National Health Care Management Center at the Leonard Davis Institute of Health Economics, University of Pennsylvania; grant HS-02577 from the National Center for Health Services Research, Office of the Assistant Secretary of Health, Department of Health and Human Services; and the Accounting Department of the Wharton School, University of Pennsylvania.

NOTES

1. Schwartz W.B., Joskow P.L. Duplicated hospital facilities. *N Engl J Med.* 1980;303:1449–57.

2. Finkler S.A. Cost-effectiveness of regionalization: the heart surgery example. *Inquiry.* 1979;16:264–70.

3. McGregor M., Pelletier G. Planning of specialized health facilities: size vs. cost and effectiveness in heart surgery. *N Engl J Med.* 1978;299:179–81.

4. Hansing C.E. The risk and cost of coronary angiography: I. Cost of coronary angiography in Washington State. *JAMA.* 1979;242:731–4.

5. Berman H.J., Weeks L.E. *The Financial Management of Hospitals.* 3rd ed. Ann Arbor: Health Administration Press, 1976:61–4.

6. Harper D.R. Disease cost in a surgical ward. *Br Med J.* 1979;1:647–9.

7. Gibson R.M. National health care expenditures, 1978. *Health Care Financing Review.* 1979;1:1–36.

8. Marty A.T., et al. The variation in hospital charges: a problem in determining the cost/benefit for cardiac surgery. *Ann Thor Surg.* 1977;24:409–16.

Application 4-2

Using Reciprocal Allocation of Service Department Costs for Decision Making

Lawrence M. Metzger, PhD, CPA, is currently Associate Professor of Accounting at Loyola University of Chicago, Chicago, Illinois.

INTRODUCTION

The allocation of service department costs to other service and hospital production departments has long been a standard procedure in hospitals for such purposes as financial reporting, Medicare records, and other third-party reimbursement requirements. Traditionally, the most commonly used allocation method has been the step-down method. The purpose of this article is to describe the use of the reciprocal allocation method as an alternative to the step-down method for cost allocation purposes. The reciprocal method will not only serve financial reporting requirements but will also provide relevant and accurate information for potential decision-making situations.

STEP-DOWN ALLOCATION

Under the step-down method, service department costs are allocated in sequence to the departments they serve. The departments are ranked so that the cost of the one that renders service to the highest number of other departments is allocated first, and the cost of the one rendering service to the lowest number of other departments while receiving benefits from the highest number is allocated last. In essence, the step-down method is a one-way or one-direction allocation method.

This assumption of a one-way service between departments works well enough for financial reporting and in some cases represents the flow of the use of services quite well. For example, consider two service departments: medical records and the hospital cafeteria: While medical records personnel would indeed use the cafeteria to eat, it is unlikely that medical records directly services the cafeteria. In this case the step-down method is quite appropriate as an allocation method.

But there are also numerous situations in which service departments service or interact with each other simultaneously. Maintenance, for example, would service the cafeteria and maintenance personnel would eat in the cafeteria. The hospital power plant would serve the administration department, and the administration department would provide service to the power plant. Cafeteria personnel would also eat in the cafeteria, and the power plant would consume power to run its own operations. In effect these service departments consume part of themselves.

Source: Reprinted from Lawrence M. Metzger, "Using Reciprocal Allocation of Service Department Costs for Decision Making," *Hospital Cost Management and Accounting,* Vol. 4, No. 9, December 1992, pp. 1–6. Copyright 1992, Aspen Publishers, Inc.

Assigning the costs of support services to production departments can do more than determine costs. The allocation procedure can set up an internal market for the supply and demand of internally produced services. By charging for service departments' output, the hospital can

1. ration demand for user departments
2. provide signals on service department efficiency
3. facilitate comparison of externally supplied services

In general, the step-down method will not compute sufficiently accurate service department cost information for the uses listed above when extensive interactions exist among service departments; this is where the reciprocal method becomes valuable.

RECIPROCAL ALLOCATION

The reciprocal method is conceptually appealing because it recognizes the simultaneous interaction of service departments rather than the somewhat arbitrary, one-directional relationship the step-down method assumes. The accuracy and relevance of the reciprocal method derives from its recognition of the reciprocal relationships of costs among service departments.

Mechanically, the reciprocal method allocates the costs of service departments on a simultaneous basis. The method requires solving a series of simultaneous equations—generally as many equations as there are service departments. The calculations quickly become cumbersome, requiring the use of matrix algebra to solve. Until recently, this method was not practical due to the lack of readily available software to solve the equations.

The reciprocal allocation method can provide useful information for decision making when service departments

1. have variable costs
2. provide service to other service departments or to themselves

A service department's variable costs are those driven in the short run by a specific cost driver. For example, a portion of the power plant costs could be driven by, or variable with respect to, kilowatt hours consumed by the various departments. When there are variable costs in the service departments, the relationship between the cost and the other departments—both service and production—is more cause and effect than a pure allocation.

The true variable cost to operate such interacting service departments includes not only the direct variable costs of each department but a portion of the variable costs from the supporting departments.

EXAMPLE

The following example will develop the reciprocal model and show how its output can be used for both financial reporting and decision making. The example illustrates the relationships among four individual service departments in a particular hospital. The four service departments are the hospital's 1) power plant, 2) cafeteria, 3) administration department, and 4) maintenance department.

One advantage of the reciprocal method is that much of the information needed has already been determined for the other allocation procedures. The step-down method requires, at least in one direction, some measure of service department costs and cost drivers for allocation purposes. Statistical analysis— using such techniques as linear regression—can be used at relatively low cost to further refine the data for the reciprocal method.

For this example, statistical analysis has determined the variable costs of the four service departments and the relevant cost drivers for the past year. These data are shown in Table 4-2-1.

RECIPROCAL ALLOCATION
PROCEDURE

Matrix algebra will be used to calculate the reciprocal allocation values. (An in-depth dis-

Table 4-2-1 Summary of Costs and Cost Drivers

Department	Cost Driver	Cost Driver Level	Variable Cost
Power plant	Kilowatt hours	100,000	$ 600,000
Cafeteria	Number of employees	1,000	160,000
Administration	Payroll dollars	2,000,000	400,000
Maintenance	Number of work orders	100	200,000
Total			$1,360,000

cussion of matrix algebra will not be presented here. Refer to a business math book for an explanation of this procedure.) The mechanics of matrix algebra will be handled using the matrix inversion function on Lotus 1-2-3.

The following steps should be used when applying the reciprocal allocation method with Lotus:

1. Determine the percentage each department uses of the service provided by each service department, including the amount each service department consumes of its own service. These percentages would be based on the volume of the cost driver used by each department. These assumed percents are shown in Table 4-2-2.

For example, of the 100,000 kilowatt hours consumed for the past year, 15 percent was consumed by the power plant itself (S1), 8 percent by the cafeteria (S2), 10 percent by administration (S3), and 12 percent by maintenance (S4). The column labeled "Production" represents the combined percent usage of the cost drivers of all the production departments, examples of which include medical/surgical services, outpatient services, or the nursery. Production departments consumed 55 percent of the total kilowatt hours of power generated by the power plant. In a full allocation situation, the detail of this usage would be broken out by specific production department. Such detail is not necessary for this example.

The amount of the cost driver consumed by each department would be known from the already completed statistical analysis.

2. Set up simultaneous equations for each individual service department to solve for how much cost each service department will ultimately allocate. The equations consist of two parts: the first part is the known variable costs determined from the cost analysis shown above; the second is the percentage of services each service department consumed of itself and the amount of services allocated to it from the other service departments.

This information is provided by the figures in each column of Table 4-2-2. For example, the power plant (S1) allocates its own variable cost of $600,000 plus the amount it consumes of its own service (15 percent of itself) plus the 10 percent of cafeteria cost it consumes plus the 8 percent of administration cost it consumes and finally the 20 percent of maintenance cost it uses. The formulas for the power plant (S1) and the other service departments are as follows:

$S1 = \$600,000 + .15(S1) + .10(S2) + .08(S3) + .20(S4)$
$S2 = \$160,000 + .08(S1) + .05(S2) + .07(S3) + .08(S4)$
$S3 = \$400,000 + .10(S1) + .15(S2) + .08(S3) + .12(S4)$
$S4 = \$200,000 + .12(S1) + .10(S2) + .07(S3) + .05(S4)$

3. Set these equations up into matrix form. To solve them, gather all the unknowns on the left side of the equations and all the known values

Table 4-2-2 Percent of Total Cost Driver Consumed in Each Department

Department	S1	S2	S3	S4	Production	Total
Power plant (S1)	15%	8%	10%	12%	55%	100%
Cafeteria (S2)	10%	5%	15%	10%	60%	100%
Administration (S3)	8%	7%	8%	7%	70%	100%
Maintenance (S4)	20%	8%	12%	5%	55%	100%

on the right side. This procedure would yield the following:

$$+ .85(S1) - .10(S2) - .08(S3) - .20(S4) = \$600,000$$
$$- .08(S1) + .95(S2) - .07(S3) - .08(S4) = \$160,000$$
$$- .10(S1) - .15(S2) + .92(S3) - .12(S4) = \$400,000$$
$$- .12(S1) - .10(S2) - .07(S3) + .95(S4) = \$200,000$$

Expressing the above in matrix form yields the following:

$$
\begin{array}{ccc}
\mathbf{X} & \mathbf{S} & \mathbf{C}
\end{array}
$$

$$
\begin{bmatrix}
+.85 & -.10 & -.08 & -.20 \\
-.08 & +.95 & -.07 & -.08 \\
-.10 & -.15 & +.92 & -.12 \\
-.12 & -.10 & -.07 & +.95
\end{bmatrix}
\times
\begin{bmatrix}
S1 \\ S2 \\ S3 \\ S4
\end{bmatrix}
\quad
\begin{array}{l}
\$600,000 \\
\$160,000 \\
\$400,000 \\
\$200,000
\end{array}
$$

Expressed in equation form: $X \times S = C$. To solve for the values of S1 through S4, which represents the total costs to allocate for each department, solve for the inverse matrix of X and multiply the inverse matrix by the C matrix.

4. Enter the data shown in Step 3 for both the X matrix and the C matrix into the Lotus spreadsheet. Use the matrix inversion feature in the program to find the inverse of the matrix. The "/ Data Matrix Invert" command calculates the inverse of the X matrix.

The inverse matrix is as follows:

$$
\begin{bmatrix}
1.253 & .186 & .146 & .298 \\
.135 & 1.098 & .105 & .134 \\
.182 & .219 & 1.135 & .200 \\
.186 & .155 & .113 & 1.119
\end{bmatrix}
$$

5. Use the inverse matrix to calculate the reciprocal cost. This is determined by multiplying the inverse matrix by the matrix, which consists of the variable cost for each department (matrix C). This procedure is also available on Lotus with the "/ Data Matrix Multiply" operation. These amounts will be used for allocating the service department costs for reporting purposes.

The calculated reciprocal costs for each service would be:

S1:	$899,660
S2:	$325,374
S3:	$638,508
S4:	$405,466

These amounts represent the service department's initial variable cost, plus the amount allocated to each service department from the other service departments.

The allocation of the service department variable costs is shown in Table 4-2-3.

Notice that the total amount of cost allocated to the production departments equals the total original amount of service department variable cost: $600,000 + $160,000 + $400,000 + $200,000 = $1,360,000. So the reciprocal method has allocated the correct amount of cost for financial reporting purposes.

DECISION-MAKING ANALYSIS

In addition to the allocation information above, a key advantage to the reciprocal method is the data it can provide for decision making.

Table 4-2-3 Allocation of Service Department Variable Costs*

	S1	S2	S3	S4	Production
Initial cost	$600,000	$160,000	$400,000	$200,000	N/A
Assigned by S1	134,949	71,973	89,966	107,959	$ 494,813
Assigned by S2	32,537	16,269	48,806	32,537	195,225
Assigned by S3	51,081	44,696	51,081	44,696	446,956
Assigned by S4	81,093	32,437	48,656	20,273	223,006
Assigned out	(899,660)	(325,374)	(638,508)	(405,466)	0
Net cost assigned					$1,360,000

*Any small differences in totals are due to rounding.

Refer back to the inverse matrix. The numbers on the main diagonal (the line running from the upper left to the lower right) are called the reciprocal factors for the service departments. The reciprocal factor for S1 is 1.253; for S2, 1.098; for S3, 1.135; and for S4, 1.119. These factors tell us how much the total production of the service department will fall if the external demand (outside the service department) on the service department is reduced by one unit.

For example, a one-kilowatt-hour reduction in demand will reduce kilowatt-hour requirements in the power plant by 1.253 hours.

More information may be taken from this output. The next item that can be calculated is the charge rate. The individual reciprocal costs for each department divided by the total level of the cost driver used for each service will yield the charge rate for that particular service:

S1: $899,660/100,000 kwh   = $9.00/kilowatt hour
S2: $325,374/1,000 employees   = $325 per employee
S3: $638,508/200,000 payroll $ = $3.19/payroll dollar
S4: $405,466/100 work orders   = $4,055/work order

It turns out that the charge rate (for variable costs) is equivalent to the out-of-pocket or marginal cost of the service. So for the power plant, if the total demand by the production divisions were reduced by one kilowatt hour, the total variable costs in the system would fall by $9.00. This charge rate provides an accurate measure of the marginal cost of providing the service.

The charge rate has various uses. It can be used to help ration demand for user departments by providing relevant and accurate data for setting charge-back prices. Also, it can help measure service department efficiency by providing data that helps set standard costs for these services. In addition, if an outside bid to provide a service—such as power or a contract for maintenance—is received, the charge rate would be compared to the price quoted for the outside service.

More useful information may also be found in the reciprocal output. If a service department with reciprocal relationships is shut down, the number of units of service that would have to be purchased externally would be lower than the current production of the internal service department. When the units of service are purchased outside, the current reciprocal pattern of consumption is altered, because the remaining departments do not have to provide service to the external supplier.

Continuing on, dividing the total level of the service department cost driver by the service department's reciprocal factor provides information about the number of outside units that would have to be purchased if internal production were discontinued. Again using the power plant as the example: 100,000 kwh/1.253 = 79,808 hours. If the hospital discontinued internal production of power, 79,808 kilowatt hours of power would have to be purchased externally. The power plant consumes 20,192 (100,000 − 79,808) units of its own output.

It also turns out that dividing the reciprocal cost by the reciprocal factor will yield the total variable cost saved or avoided if this service is eliminated. This amount can be used along with the charge factor above to compare against alternative sources of this service.

In this example the results would be as follows:

S1: 899,660/1.253 = $718,005
S2: 325,374/1.098 = $296,333
S3: 638,508/1.135 = $562,562
S4: 405,466/1.119 = $362,347

For the power plant (S1), the total variable cost avoided if the power plant were shut down is $718,005.

SUMMARY

This article has provided a look into the use of the reciprocal method as an alternative to more conventional methods of hospital service department cost allocation methods. The reciprocal method can be used with readily available software and with data that are largely already known. This method will provide not only appropriate allocation values for financial reporting but data that can be used for hospital decision making. In the highly competitive and sometimes hostile environment in which hospitals now fight to survive, any additional relevant data—especially that generated at almost no additional cost—should be provided to managers to help in the decision-making process.

BIBLIOGRAPHY

1. Hay, L., Wilson, E. *Accounting for Governmental and Nonprofit Entities,* 9th edition. Boston, Mass.: Irwin, 1992.

2. Kaplan, R., Atkinson, A. *Advanced Managerial Accounting,* 2nd Edition. Englewood Cliffs, NJ: Prentice-Hall, 1989.

Application 4-3

The Accuracy of Cost Measures Derived from Medicare Cost Report Data

*John L. Ashby, Jr., MHA, is currently Senior
Policy Analyst with the Prospective Payment
Assessment Commission, Washington, DC.*

The Prospective Payment Assessment Commission (ProPAC) and other federal agencies have become increasingly reliant on Medicare Cost Report (MCR) data for evaluating prospective payment issues. However, little is known about the extent to which these data accurately represent the costs associated with treating Medicare beneficiaries—either in total or by DRG.

In late 1989, the Commission contracted with the Center for Health Policy Studies of Columbia, Maryland, for a major research project to assess the accuracy of cost measures that can be derived from MCR data. In the first component of the study, the effects of several changes in cost finding methodology were simulated. In the second component, aggregate and DRG-level cost estimates based primarily on MCR data were compared with values from hospital cost accounting systems.

The sample hospitals had fully implemented, state-of-the-art systems, and they had all invested heavily in terms of both capital expenditures and management staff time to obtain the most accurate cost measures possible for their own internal information needs.

For this reason, we believe that we assembled the best available "standard" against which to assess the accuracy of MCR cost measures.

BACKGROUND

The Medicare Cost Report was developed when the Medicare program began in 1965. Its main purpose was to determine the reimbursable cost of hospital provided services, as defined by Medicare, and to determine Medicare's share of these costs. When PPS was introduced in 1983, the MCR retained a critical role in determining Medicare cost-based payments for PPS passthroughs (principally direct medical education and capital), PPS-excluded units (principally rehabilitation and psychiatric services), and most non-inpatient services.

For nearly two decades, however, the MCR has also been used as a source of data to support research and policy analyses by HCFA, other federal agencies, and private researchers. The cost report provides the only national information available on the costs of providing hospital care specifically to Medicare beneficiaries. In

Source: Adapted from John L. Ashby, Jr., "The Accuracy of Cost Measures Derived from Medicare Cost Report Data," *Hospital Cost Management and Accounting,* Vol. 3, No. 10, January 1992, pp. 1–7. Copyright 1992, Aspen Publishers, Inc.

this role, the MCR is a vital information source for PPS policy development.

There are inherent limitations in using MCR data for policy analysis, however. First of all, the MCR defines both capital and operating costs according to Medicare reimbursement principles. While this is appropriate for determining cost-based payment, it does not necessarily provide an accurate measurement of the overall cost of providing patient care. Second, the Medicare program does not require either uniform accounting or uniform reporting of revenues and expenditures, and little is known about the effects of this inconsistency on the data available for policy analysis.

Potentially the most significant problem, however, is the extensive use of hospital charges in the Medicare cost finding process. Charges are used in the cost report to apportion costs among specific ancillary services, between inpatient and outpatient care, and between Medicare and other payers. Similarly, ProPAC and others use patient-specific ancillary charge data from HCFA's Medicare Provider Analysis and Review (MedPAR) file together with cost report data to estimate costs by DRG. These uses of charge data implicitly assume that hospitals price individual units of services according to the costs of those services. But hospitals actually consider a complex set of factors in developing their charges. Because PPS payments are no longer tied to costs, some hospitals may raise the prices of procedures commonly used by Medicare patients in PPS-exempt services, while others pursue the alternative strategy of raising the charges of procedures usually furnished for charge paying patient groups. There may be an attempt to raise rates on services that must be discounted to HMOs or PPOs, or to reduce the charges of services commonly used as benchmark prices in managed care contract negotiations. Most policy analysts agree that hospitals cannot be expected to price all of their services with an equal mark-up on costs when they must operate in competitive markets and accept widely varying payments for the same services. But it is nonetheless important to understand the impact of these management factors on the cost measures available for policy decision making.

OBJECTIVES AND METHODOLOGY OF THE STUDY

The primary objective of the study was to assess the accuracy of the hospital and DRG level cost measures that can be constructed using Medicare Cost Report data. In the longer term, the results of the study may also contribute to the process of modifying the cost report to enhance its usefulness in supporting policy decision making.

The study methodology consisted of two major components. The first component simulated the effect of four specific changes in MCR reporting approach:

- adding back certain cost elements that Medicare's reimbursement principles disallow for payment, but that widely recognized cost accounting methods would include in the overall cost of patient care;

- substituting a standard cost center configuration for the cost centers selected for reporting by hospitals;

- using standard statistical bases for allocating overhead costs to patient care services, in place of the statistical bases selected by hospitals; and

- using a multiple allocation system rather than a step-down procedure for allocating overhead

All of these changes, in theory, would improve the quality of the MCR cost data. However, this component of the study was not predicated upon the premise that current cost measures using MCR data are inadequate, nor would we assume that an alternative cost finding method that appears to produce more accurate cost measurements would necessarily be cost effective for implementation in the Medicare program. Rather, the study was primarily seeking information on the degree to which more advanced cost finding methods would affect cost data.

The second component of the methodology compared cost values based on MCR data with values from advanced hospital cost accounting and case-mix data systems. Separate simulations were done to test the advanced methods of measuring routine/special care costs and ancillary costs.

A sample of 73 hospitals was used for the first study component, but only 18 hospitals participated in the second component due to the complex nature of the data collection involved. The limited number of hospitals with systems passing the contractor's criteria for participation in the second component dictated a sample that overrepresents large, urban, and teaching hospitals. The most recent period for which a completed cost report was available was used for the analysis, generally fiscal year 1988.

RESULTS—COMPONENT 1

The first simulation tested the impact of adding back four specific non-allowable costs: interest on working capital, the administrative cost portion of malpractice premiums for self-insured hospitals, marketing costs, and recruitment costs. These are cost elements which seem clearly to be part of overall patient care expenses and yet have always been disallowed by HCFA. As seen in Table 4-3-1, interest on working capital raises total Medicare inpatient costs in the sample hospitals by 2.1 percent. The other three cost elements had small impacts, such that the sum of the four was 2.3 percent. This percentage factor equates to over $1 billion in total PPS payments.

Several other non-allowable cost elements that might potentially have been included in this analysis were omitted for various reasons. Some were excluded due to lack of consensus about their definition or appropriateness for recogni-

tion. The costs of bad debts and charity care were not measured simply because we had a better source of data for them from another project. Malpractice costs were not reallocated from the method used in the cost report because the disputes over this cost element have largely been settled by the courts. As such, it should not be a problem area in the future.

Table 4-3-2 summarizes the three simulations dealing with cost finding methodology. The three changes tested together raised the cost report estimate of total Medicare inpatient costs by an insignificant .1 percent. The simulations raised routine and special care costs (largely representing the nurse staffing on inpatient care units) by over 1 percent, but this was offset by a corresponding reduction in ancillary costs. The largest effects were seen in the area of pass-through costs, where the estimate of Medicare capital costs was increased by 4.4 percent and the estimate of Medicare's share of direct medical education costs was reduced by 3.2 percent.

By far the largest impact on the MCR cost measures resulted from using a multiple apportionment system (specifically matrix inversion) to allocate overhead costs to patient care services. This technique recognizes that departments can service each other (administration and housekeeping, for example), in contrast to the one-way allocation process of the MCR (which fails to account for housekeeping service to administration). Multiple allocation is responsible for almost all of the increase in the estimates of routine inpatient and capital costs, and these two effects are related. The more precise allocation tends to push more overhead costs into inpatient units, which in turn are more capital intensive than outpatient services.

The use of a standard cost center configuration and optimal bases for allocation (such as distributing housekeeping costs on the basis of hours of service provided to various patient care departments rather than the square footage of the units) had surprisingly little impact. Hospitals have considerable latitude in these areas, with cost centers selected at will and allocation bases changed with the approval of an HCFA fiscal intermediary. The small impact of standardizing cost centers and allocation bases suggests that

Table 4-3-1 Impact of Adding Back Select Non-Allowable Costs on Total Medicare Inpatient Costs

Cost Element	Increase in Costs (%)
Professional recruitment	.02
Administrative component of malpractice costs	.1
Interest on working capital	2.1
Marketing	.1
Total	2.32

Table 4-3-2 Percent Difference in Medicare Cost Estimates from Simulated Changes in Medicare Cost Report Cost Finding Technique

Cost Measure	Standard Cost Center Configuration	Optimal Statistical Bases	Multiple Apportionment	Combined Changes
Total Medicare inpatient costs	0.1%	–0.1%	0.4%	0.1%
Medicare inpatient routine and special care costs	0.3	–0.2	2.1	1.4
Medicare inpatient ancillary costs	–0.2	–0.1	–0.7	–1.0
Total Medicare outpatient costs	0.9	0.1	–1.0	0.3
Medicare capital costs	1.3	–0.4	3.4	4.4
Medicare direct medical education costs	–1.1	–0.4	–3.1	–3.2

these are not major avenues for hospital attempts to shift costs to passthrough areas. The study provided anecdotal evidence that the primary ways in which hospitals have acted to shift costs in recent years are redefining certain purchases from supply accounts to capital, and directly assigning personnel, supplies and capital (such as employing a housekeeper in the emergency room rather than the housekeeping department). These "cost allocation" maneuvers are hidden to MCR analysts, and determining their influence would require a virtual audit of a hospital's cost accounting system.

RESULTS—COMPONENT 2

Table 4-3-3 summarizes the differences resulting from MCR and hospital cost accounting techniques across all of the 40 DRGs analyzed, which accounted for more than three-quarters of all Medicare discharges. The MCR routine/special care cost estimates were found to be overstated by 12.6 percent relative to the hospital standard. Further, if it were possible to compare the MCR and hospital data strictly in terms of

Table 4-3-3 Percent Difference between MCR and Hospital Estimates of Aggregate Medicare Inpatient Costs

Medicare Cost Measure	Difference
Inpatient routine and special care costs	12.6%
Ancillary costs	–4.9
Total inpatient costs	4.4

Medicare allowable costs, this differential would have been slightly higher. The MCR estimates Medicare's share of "room and board" costs by calculating aggregate per diems for routine care and special care, and then multiplying these per diems by the applicable number of Medicare patient days. The hospital systems generally establish a standard per diem for each nursing unit, considering the average nursing acuity level of the patients treated by unit. In developing these standard per diems, the hospital systems generally employ multiple allocation techniques.

When the MCR routine/special care data were recalculated using patient-specific acuity data supplied by the hospitals, the discrepancy between the MCR and hospital values was narrowed to only 2.5 percent. This implies that Medicare patients may, on average, have lower nurse acuity than other patients. However, the study data only allow the conclusion that acuity-adjusted MCR data are closer to what the hospitals believe their true Medicare costs to be. The difference between the acuity-based and basic estimates probably reflects some combination of the original MCR cost estimates being too high to begin with and a real difference in average acuity.

While not measured directly as part of this study, the most common reason for the MCR routine cost estimates being too high before consideration of nurse acuity differences is thought to be that the costs of all pediatric patients are included in the calculation of average Medicare routine cost per day. Pediatric patients, who are eligible for Medicare only if they suffer from end stage renal disease, are significantly more expensive to treat on average than the aged patients who comprise the vast majority of the Medicare population.* Thus, inclusion of these patients biases the average per diem cost upwards.

It is interesting to note that most of the study hospitals opted to develop standard cost factors for each patient unit based on a retrospective analysis of acuity patterns rather than to continuously update their cost estimates with current acuity data. This was done to avoid the potential for nursing personnel to escalate their acuity ratings over time ("acuity creep") to support a contention that higher staffing levels are needed.

The MCR-based estimates of ancillary costs were found to be understated by 4.9 percent across all 40 DRGs, although if the comparison had been made strictly on the basis of allowable costs, this differential would be slightly smaller. The MCR methodology parallels that used by ProPAC and many other research groups. A ratio of costs to charges (RCC) was calculated for at least six cost center groupings in each hospital, and then these ratios were multiplied by DRG-specific patient charges supplied by the hospitals. Sophisticated cost accounting systems, on the other hand, typically estimate a standard cost for each service unit (lab tests, X-rays, surgical procedures, and so forth). With these data, the total cost of a patient stay can be calculated simply by summing the costs of the individual service units consumed by the patient, so that charge data are not involved.

MCR data produced ancillary cost estimates closer to the hospital standard when a single hospitalwide RCC was used rather than the customary 6 departmental RCCs. With this technique, overall ancillary costs were overstated by 2.2 percent rather than 4.9 percent, and the same pattern was observed in three-quarters of the study DRGs. In theory, the breakdown by department should offer greater precision. In practice, it may offer more opportunity for the effects of non-cost based pricing practices to influence the calculation.

When the two simulations—routine/special care costs and ancillary costs—were run together, the MCR methodology was found to overstate total Medicare inpatient costs relative to the hospital standard by 4.4 percent. Once again, an analysis based solely on Medicare allowable costs would have produced a slightly higher margin. This overall finding reflects the net effect of overstated routine costs and understated ancillary costs.

There was tremendous variation in the accuracy of MCR data (combined with patient-specific charge data) by DRG. As shown in Table 4-3-4A, there were four DRGs where the MCR data overestimated routine/special costs by more than 30 percent. In five DRGs, the discrepancy was less than 5 percent, while in two others (also shown in Table 4-3-4A) the MCR data understated costs by more than 10 percent.

For ancillary costs, the MCR-based estimate was understated by more than 10 percent in eleven DRGs, while costs were actually overstated for seven other DRGs. The four DRGs for which the overstatements and understatements were the greatest are shown in Table 4-3-4B. Costs for the most expensive of the DRGs analyzed, coronary bypass with cardiac catheterization, were found to be overstated by a substantial amount—19.4 percent. This may indicate that hospitals are inflating their prices by an above-average amount for some highly specialized ancillary procedures, such as perfusionist services, that are unique to open heart surgery. But it might also be caused by consistently higher mark-ups in the subset of sample hospitals that provide open heart surgery and other highly specialized tertiary services. This latter explanation is supported by other research.[1]

Because the overstated routine and special care costs tend to be offset by the understated ancillary costs, the variation in accuracy by DRG is somewhat less for total costs than was found for either of the two cost components independently. But it is still substantial. There are five DRGs where the MCR methodology overstated the standard cost by more than 10 percent, while it understated costs by at least 2 percent for five others. The four greatest overstatements and understatements are exhibited in Table 4-3-4C.

---

*A soon to be released study sponsored by the National Association of Childrens Hospitals and Related Institutions (Alexandria, VA) found that the nursing costs of treating a child are 26 percent higher than those of the average patient.

Table 4-3-4 Percent Difference between MCR and Hospital Estimates of Medicare Inpatient Costs, by DRG

A. Routine and Special Care Costs

DRG Name	Difference
Greatest overstatement	
Transurethral prostatectomy w CC	38.1%
Diabetes, age > 35	35.7
Transurethral prostatectomy, w/o CC	31.1
Medical back problems	30.1
Greatest understatement	
Major reconstructive vascular procedures w/o pump, w CC	−10.5
Circulatory disorders, with AMI-expired	−11.2

B. Ancillary Costs

DRG Name	Difference
Greatest overstatement	
Coronary bypass, w cardiac catheterization	19.4%
Major joint and limb reattachment procedures	10.3
Chemotherapy	7.2
Septicemia, age > 17	6.2
Greatest understatement	
Chronic obstructive pulmonary disease	−11.2
Angina pectoris	−11.5
Peripheral vascular disorders, w CC	−11.5
Circulatory disorders, w AMI, w/o CV complication, discharged alive	−11.9

C. Total Costs

DRG Name	Difference
Greatest overstatement	
Major joint and limb reattachment procedures	17.3%
Transient ischemic attack and precerebral occlusions	15.0
Coronary bypass, with cardiac catheterization	14.7
Medical back problems	10.2
Greatest understatement	
Cardiac arrhythmia and conduction disorders, w CC	−1.8
Circulatory disorders, with AMI, w/o CV complication, discharged alive	−3.5
Circulatory disorders, with AMI–expired	−6.6
Circulatory disorders, with AMI and complication, discharged alive	−8.2

IMPLICATIONS OF THE STUDY

Component 2 results are perhaps most important to consider first, because these results represent our best attempt to answer the basic question, "How closely do MCR-derived hospital cost estimates reflect a hospital's actual costs?" The results suggest that MCR data are reasonably reliable when they are used for their most common application, calculation of total Medicare inpatient costs. Even then, the cost report estimate may be overstated by several percentage points. The cost report's reliability is reduced considerably when routine inpatient costs and ancillary costs are analyzed separately. And cost report data, supplemented by charge data from the MedPAR system, are clearly not reliable or accurate for analyzing micro-level costs.

KEY FINDINGS

- The MCR was found to overstate Medicare inpatient costs by 4.4 percent. It overstates routine/special care costs by 12.6 percent, while understating ancillary costs by 4.9 percent.
- The large differential in routine/special care costs is believed to be due to a combination of inaccurate MCR cost finding (caused partly by combining pediatric and adult costs, which are substantially different) and Medicare patients having lower nursing acuity than other patients.
- There was tremendous variation in the accuracy of DRG-level cost estimates using MCR data and patient-specific charges, particularly for routine and ancillary costs measured separately. One of the least accurate DRGs was coronary bypass with cardiac catheterization, where ancillary costs were 19 percent overstated and the overall cost estimate was 15 percent too high.
- Standardizing cost centers and bases for allocation of overhead costs and using a multiple allocation technique changed the overall estimate of Medicare inpatient costs by only 0.1 percent. However, these cost finding refinements increased the estimate of Medicare capital costs by 4.4 percent (in a sample that overrepresents large, urban, and teaching hospitals).
- Adding back non-allowable cost elements that seem clearly to be part of overall patient care expenses increased the MCR estimate of Medicare inpatient expenses by 2.3 percent. Most of this was accounted for by interest paid on working capital.

The finding that MCR-derived ancillary costs are understated confirms the findings of another study by the Center for Health Policy Studies (conducted for the Assistant Secretary for Planning and Evaluation) which found that outpatient costs were overstated. This inpatient/outpatient cost relationship will be important in establishing the correct payment relationship as prospective payment methods are developed for various outpatient services. The nearly 5 percent understatement documented for inpatient ancillary costs, which encompass over three-quarters of total hospital ancillary costs, implies a much larger overstatement of outpatient costs.

The leading reasons for MCR routine and special care costs being overstated are that Medicare patients may have lower nurse acuity measured on a patient day basis than other patients and that pediatric costs are artificially raising the average Medicare per diem cost. Most observers believe that it would not be advisable for HCFA to require reporting of nurse acuity levels because it would add significantly to the hospital staff time required for reporting. Further, there are no generally accepted measures of nurse acuity and use of diverse methods would result in data of questionable validity in some cases. However, it would be possible for HCFA to modify its cost report format to document the routine cost of furnishing pediatric care so that these costs can be omitted from the calculation of the average Medicare routine per diem. If this were done, it would be necessary to develop a specific procedure for hospitals to document the routine costs of treating their few Medicare-eligible pediatric patients.

The Component 1 simulations of potential refinements in MCR cost finding technique make clear that the shortcomings of the cost report cannot easily be rectified. Standardizing both cost centers and allocation bases and introducing a more sophisticated allocation algorithm generally had minimal impact on Medicare cost estimates. In addition, two of the most significant effects were to raise the estimate of routine/special care costs (which the second component of

our study showed are already overstated), and to reduce the estimate of ancillary costs (which the second component showed are already understated).

The only compelling finding of Component 1 was that more sophisticated cost finding would raise the estimate of capital costs by about 4 percent. This finding may have some implication for capital payment policy, although it must be remembered that the sample for analysis overrepresented large, urban, and teaching hospitals. The study found direct medical education expenses to be overstated by about 3 percent, but the sample was inadequate for a comprehensive analysis of this cost element.

Advanced hospital accounting systems may potentially offer a useful source of data for specialized cost analyses. While this study found that only about 30 hospitals nationally had fully implemented, state-of-the-art cost accounting systems in early 1990, a number of others have probably come on line since then. Although the development of nurse acuity data is not necessarily consistent among hospitals, these data nonetheless show promise for improving DRG-level analyses. Hospital micro-costing of ancillary tests and procedures also varies in its sophistication from hospital to hospital, but on balance appears to provide superior data for DRG-level analyses compared to an RCC-based methodology.

NOTE

1. G.M. Carter and J.A. Rogowski, *The Hospital Relative Value Method As an Alternative for Recalibrating DRG Relative Weights* (Santa Monica, Calif.: RAND, 1993), 13–19.

Note: The author would like to thank Henry Miller, Ph.D., Brian Balicki, and other staff of the Center for Health Policy Studies, who performed this study under contract to Pro-PAC. The contributions of Steve Raetzman and Stuart Guterman in reviewing earlier drafts and monitoring project activities are also gratefully acknowledged. The opinions expressed in this article are not necessarily those of the Prospective Payment Assessment Commission.

Application 4-4

RVUs: Relative Value Units or Really Very Useful?

Kirk Mahlen was associated with
HBO & Co., Lexington, Massachusetts,
at the time this article was written.

By now, I'm sure that everyone involved in hospital finance has at least heard of the term "RVU." Yet, for many, doubts still exist as to what is actually involved in developing RVUs and effectively utilizing those values for procedure/patient-level costing. The purpose of this article is to provide an easy-to-understand, step-by-step example describing RVU development and use of RVUs in procedure/patient-level costing.

Given that everyone accepts the need to move away from RCCs as a costing method in the current regulatory environment, RVUs are an extremely cost-effective solution for improving the reliability and accuracy of cost data for many hospitals. With assistance from hospital department heads, it is possible to develop and maintain RVU cost information in most hospitals with a minimum of 1 FTE. While limited assistance and/or direction from an outside "expert" is certainly optional, it is strongly suggested in order to avoid certain pitfalls.

In addition to personnel resources, software will be required to facilitate the development and maintenance of procedure-level intermedi-

ate product costs. Suitable microcomputer software is available from several vendors at prices ranging from approximately $5–$10,000. This software should have the ability to convert cost data to RVUs. Ultimately, in order to be of any use in managerial decision-making, the RVUs must be utilized for procedure/patient-level costing and integrated with a comprehensive patient-level data base. From this, our goal is reasonably accurate and refined profitability analysis by, but not limited to, physician, specialty, payer, MDC, DRG, and product line. Adjusting for severity level and incorporating standard treatment profiles will further enhance this capability. For a relatively minor investment, RVUs provide a major improvement in the accuracy and thus, usability, of cost information for managerial decision-making.

PERFORMING THE MANAGEMENT STEPDOWN

It is likely that cost information will continue to be recorded in the general ledger (GL) by department and sub-account. Hospitals simply do not maintain procedure-level cost information as they do for gross charges. Under PPS, hospital net revenue is largely dependent on its case mix or DRGs. If we expand our interpretation of the

Source: Reprinted from Kirk Mahlen, "RVUs: Relative Value Units or Really Very Useful?," *Hospital Cost Accounting Advisor,* Vol. 4, No. 8, January 1989, pp. 1–7. Copyright 1989, Aspen Publishers, Inc.

basic accounting principle which maintains that we match revenues with expenses, then, under this new product-driven market, it becomes absolutely essential to accurately determine cost and profitability at the DRG or product level.

Obviously, cost at the DRG or product level should tie-back to the GL costs. This can be accomplished by first performing a management stepdown using existing GL department-level cost information and later allocating stepdown results to the procedure/patient level using RVUs. In order to reduce the potential for bias inherent in performing a single stepdown, the preferred method for performing the cost allocation would be simultaneous equations (provided the capability exists). For purposes of this example, I have chosen to utilize the single stepdown methodology due to relatively universal familiarity with its use.

[Note: Over the years the order of stepdown has been set by hospitals in a manner so as to optimize reimbursement. In the opinion of Hospital Cost Accounting Advisor, *use of stepdown for RVU costing is an easy—but unsatisfactory approach. Much effort and cost will be expended to develop RVUs that are "tainted" right from the start. For a small marginal increase in cost (relative to the costs of installing an RVU system) the reciprocal (or simultaneous equation approach) method of cost allocation can be used. (See* HCAA, *Vol. 1, No. 4, September 1985, for a discussion of this approach.) Such a method eliminates all distortions created by the order of the stepdown allocation. Editor.]*

1. We begin our simplified example with GL direct cost information for four departments:

Depts	Direct Costs
Hskpg	$ 1,000
Admin	2,000
Lab	5,000
X-Ray	4,000
Total	$12,000

2. Next, we refine our direct cost information by aggregating GL sub-account costs into specified expense classifications and performing any

management-defined adjustments and reclassifications that may be required. Salary, nonsalary, and capital expense classifications are frequently used:

Depts	Sal	Nonsal	Cap	Total
Hskpg	$ 600	$ 300	$ 100	$ 1,000
Admin	1,000	700	300	2,000
Lab	4,000	500	500	5,000
X-Ray	3,000	800	200	4,000
Total	$8,600	$2,300	$1,100	$12,000

3. Initially, this next step can be very time-consuming. Depending upon technique and the amount of effort expended, it can also be somewhat subjective. Here we identify components of cost and designate either a percentage or dollar amount of our direct costs as either fixed or variable. This is usually done through management consensus by examining GL departmental costs at the subaccount level of detail. Any subjectivity is significantly reduced as the hospital gains experience in using the data and refining fixed/variable assumptions. Unfortunately, in most cases, fixed/variable cost data is unavailable in the GL.

[Note: Although used infrequently by hospitals prior to the initiation of prospective payment systems, techniques such as linear regression can be used to take historical cost patterns (containing no fixed/variable cost distinctions) and estimate fixed and variable costs. There is substantial potential for improvement over subjective management estimates if one uses such techniques. See HCAA, *Vol. 1, No. 2, July 1985, or any currently used cost accounting text for further information. Editor.]*

Once the fixed/variable determinations are made, automated systems can be put in place to automatically calculate the fixed/variable cost components.

Depts	Direct Fixed			Direct Variable		
	Sal	Nonsal	Cap	Sal	Nonsal	Total
Hskpg	$ 300	$ 100	$ 100	$ 300	$ 200	$ 1,000
Admin	700	400	300	300	300	2,000
Lab	1,000	100	500	3,000	400	5,000
X-Ray	1,000	200	200	2,000	600	4,000
Total	$3,000	$ 800	$1,100	$5,600	$1,500	$12,000

4. In order to determine allocated direct and indirect costs for our two revenue-producing centers, it will be necessary to perform a management-defined cost allocation or stepdown. Before we can do this, it is necessary to develop allocation statistics for each overhead center and its components of direct cost. For obvious reasons, every attempt should be made to use those statistics which are most appropriate for accurate management cost allocation as opposed to Medicare or other third party allocation requirements:

Housekeeping (Sq. Ft. Cleaned)

Depts	Direct Fixed			Direct Variable	
	Sal	Nonsal	Cap	Sal	Nonsal
Hskpg					
Admin	20	20	20	20	20
Lab	40	40	40	40	40
X-Ray	40	40	40	40	40
Total	100	100	100	100	100

Administrative (Hours of Support)

Depts	Direct Fixed			Direct Variable	
	Sal	Nonsal	Cap	Sal	Nonsal
Hskpg					
Admin					
Lab	500	500	500	500	500
X-Ray	500	500	500	500	500
Total	1,000	1,000	1,000	1,000	1,000

[Note: A separate statistic can be created for each component of cost. The need for this is particularly obvious for capital costs.]

5. With appropriate software, we are now ready to perform the management stepdown for each overhead item and its components of cost from Step 3:

Departments' Housekeeping Allocation

Depts	Direct Fixed			Direct Variable		
	Sal	Nonsal	Cap	Sal	Nonsal	Total
Hskpg						
Admin	$ 760	$ 420	$ 320	$ 360	$ 340	$ 2,200
Lab	1,120	140	540	3,120	480	5,400
X-Ray	1,120	240	240	2,120	680	4,400
Total	$3,000	$ 800	$1,100	$5,600	$1,500	$12,000

Departments' Administrative/Final Allocation

Depts	Direct Fixed			Direct Variable		
	Sal	Nonsal	Cap	Sal	Nonsal	Total
Hskpg						
Admin						
Lab	$1,500	$ 350	$ 700	$3,300	$ 650	$ 6,500
X-Ray	1,500	450	400	2,300	850	5,500
Total	$3,000	$ 800	$1,100	$5,600	$1,500	$12,000

6. Finally, we are able to summarize allocated direct/indirect, fixed/variable, and salary/nonsalary/capital costs for our revenue producing centers. It is these components of cost that will ultimately be allocated to departmental procedures and patients based on RVUs:

Rev Depts	Direct Fixed			Direct Variable		
	Sal	Nonsal	Cap	Sal	Nonsal	Total
Lab	$1,000	$ 100	$ 500	$3,000	$ 400	$ 5,000
X-Ray	1,000	200	200	2,000	600	4,000
Total	$2,000	$ 300	$ 700	$5,000	$1,000	$ 9,000

Rev Depts	Indirect Fixed			Indirect Variable		
	Sal	Nonsal	Cap	Sal	Nonsal	Total
Lab	$ 500	$ 250	$ 200	$ 300	$ 250	$ 1,500
X-Ray	500	250	200	300	250	1,500
Total	$1,000	$ 500	$ 400	$ 600	$ 500	$ 3,000

[Note: The Indirect Fixed and Variable are the costs allocated from the nonrevenue departments in Step 5. Editor.]

DEVELOPMENT OF RVUs

1. RVUs are simply an expression of the relative cost of one procedure to another within a given department. As such, the first step in developing RVUs involves performing a cost study to determine variable intermediate product costs for significant procedures in the department to be studied. Most hospitals have chosen to use the 80/20 rule to study the 20% of a department's procedures which account for 80% of its reve-

nues or units. Since cost per procedure is generally not known prior to performing the cost study, it would not be available as an indicator in determining which procedures should be studied. The 80/20 rule is strictly arbitrary and can be adjusted or applied differently to each department. For example, in departments having a relatively small number of resource intensive procedures, it would be most appropriate to study all procedures. The exact cutoff should be determined based upon an examination and ranking of each department's procedures based upon either charges or units. Of course, there is nothing preventing the hospital from studying any procedure regardless of where it falls using an 80/20, 90/10, or 50/50 rule. The primary issue here involves the trade-off between the amount of resources committed to studying a given procedure and its relative significance.

The cost study is usually performed with short-term but extensive involvement on the part of hospital department heads. A procedure cost profile, similar to the example depicted below, must be developed for all procedures studied. Unstudied procedures are assigned costs using one of several default methods available.

Dept: Laboratory

Procedures	Unit Amt.	×	Unit Cost	Total Cost
CBC				
Technician	10 Mins	×	$.20	$2.00
Total Salary				$2.00
Needles	5 Units	×	$.05	$ .25
Paper	1 Sheet	×	$.25	.25
Test Tubes	2 Units	×	$.50	1.00
Total Supply				$1.50
Strep Screen				
Technician	5 Mins	×	$.20	$1.00
Total Salary				$1.00
Slides	58 Units	×	$.05	$2.90
Swabs	4 Units	×	$.025	.10
Total Supply				$3.00
Urinalysis				
Technician	15 Mins	×	$.20	$3.00
Total Salary				$3.00
Containers	1 Unit	×	$1.00	$1.00
Total Supply				$1.00

Dept: X-Ray

Procedures	Unit Amt.	×	Unit Cost	Total Cost
Chest X-Ray				
Technician	25 Mins	×	$.20	$ 5.00
Total Salary				$ 5.00
Film A	2 Units	×	$5.00	$10.00
Total Supply				$10.00
Head X-Ray				
Technician	60 Mins	×	$.20	$12.00
Total Salary				$12.00
Film B	1 Unit	×	$8.00	$8.00
Total Supply				$8.00

[Note: Even with RVUs some degree of cost inaccuracy will exist. For example, a chest x-ray is shown as taking 25 minutes in the example in this article. However, chest x-rays for some types of patients may usually take 10 minutes while chest x-rays for another type of patient may typically take 40 minutes. Use of the 25 minute RVU measure for all chest x-rays therefore creates its own distortion. Editor.]

2. We can now convert the cost data developed above to RVUs as follows

Lab	Costs			RVUs		
	Sal	Nonsal	Total	Sal	Nonsal	Total
CBC	$2.00	$1.50	$3.50	1.0000	.8182	.9138
Strep	1.00	3.00	4.00	5.000	1.6364	1.0440
Urin	3.00	1.00	4.00	1.5000	.5455	1.0444
Avg. Cst	$2.00	$1.83	$3.83			

X-Ray	Costs			RVUs		
	Sal	Nonsal	Total	Sal	Nonsal	Total
Chest	$5.00	$10.00	$15.00	.5883	1.1110	.8571
Head	12.00	8.00	$20.00	1.4116	.8889	1.1429
Avg. Cst	$8.50	$9.00	$17.50			

Sample RVU calculation for Lab-CBC where procedure cost is divided by the average cost for all procedures studied:

Sal	Nonsal	Total
2.00/2.00 = 1.000	1.50/1.83 = .8197	3.50/3.83 = .9138

COSTING AT THE PROCEDURE/ PATIENT LEVEL

We are now ready to allocate components of costs developed using the management step-down for each revenue-producing center to the procedure/patient level. Using our example, a comparison will be made between RCC and RVU costing for two patients. Before going further, however, I would first like to point out the following additional procedure costing methods which might be mixed and matched depending upon hospital needs, resource constraints, and applicability to certain departments and/or components of cost.

Units

Allocate a dollar value based on the number of procedure units. This might be most appropriate for the allocation of fixed capital costs. However, fixed costs allocated in this manner would not change with volume, thus creating problems of over or under applied cost as volume changes.

Multiply the number of units for each procedure by a specified ratio value (per diem cost).

Charges

Allocate a dollar value based on procedure charges. Multiply charges for each procedure by a specified ratio value (RCC). Because procedure charge information is readily available and hospitals are familiar with this type of costing for Medicare and other third parties, this method has become the method of choice by default. Obviously, after years of game playing with procedure charges, they bear little resemblance to cost. Cost may be somewhat accurate at the department level but there may be wide variations

in the accuracy of cost information derived at the procedure level using this method.

Cases

Allocate a dollar value based on the number of cases. Multiply the number of cases by a specified ratio value (per case cost).

Standard Costing

Multiply procedure volumes by the costs developed in the cost study.

EXAMPLE: RCC VS. RVU COSTING

Assumptions

1. Lab Total Cost = $6,500   Total Chgs = $13,000 RCC = .500
   X-Ray Total Cost = $5,500 Total Chgs = $ 4,000 RCC = 1.375

2. Department costs by component are taken from the management stepdown. (See Steps 5–6.)

3. Total weighted departmental RVUs are calculated by multiplying procedure volumes times the individual RVU values. (See Step 2.)

Lab	Units	Sal RVU	Total Sal RVU	Nonsal RVU	Total Nonsal RVU
CBC	5	1.000	5.000	.818	4.091
Strep	2	.500	1.000	1.636	3.272
Urinalysis	3	1.500	4.500	.545	1.636
Total	10		10.500		9.000
X-Ray					
Chest	3	.588	1.764	1.111	3.333
Head	1	1.412	1.412	.889	.889
Total	4		3.176		4.222

4. Total procedure costs for all procedures rendered during a specified period are determined by allocating the stepped down department costs for salary and nonsalary components based on

the Total Sal RVU and the Total Nonsal RVU above. Capital costs in this example are simply allocated to procedures based on number of units.

Lab	Direct Fixed			Direct Variable	
	Sal	Nonsal	Cap	Sal	Nonsal
CBC	$ 476.20	$ 45.26	$250.00	$1,428.00	$181.84
Strep	95.20	36.36	100.00	285.60	145.44
Urin	428.60	18.18	150.00	1,285.80	72.72
Total	$1,000.00	$100.00	$500.00	$3,000.00	$400.00

X-Ray

	Sal	Nonsal	Cap	Sal	Nonsal
Chest	$ 555.60	$157.90	$150.00	$1,111.20	$473.70
Head	444.40	42.10	50.00	888.80	126.30
Total	$1,000.00	$200.00	$200.00	$2,000.00	$600.00

Lab	Indirect Fixed			Indirect Variable		
	Sal	Nonsal	Cap	Sal	Nonsal	Total
CBC	$238.10	$113.65	$100.00	$142.86	$113.65	$3,090.36
Strep	47.60	90.90	40.00	28.56	90.90	960.56
Urin	214.30	45.45	60.00	128.58	45.45	2,449.08
Total	$500.00	$250.00	$200.00	$300.00	$250.00	$6,500.00

X-Ray

	Sal	Nonsal	Cap	Sal	Nonsal	Total
Chest	$277.80	$197.37	$150.00	$166.68	$197.37	$3,437.62
Head	222.20	52.63	50.00	133.32	52.63	2,062.38
Total	$500.00	$250.00	$200.00	$300.00	$250.00	$5,500.00

Patient Costing Using RCCs

	Units	Charges	× RCC	Cost
Patient 1				
Lab-CBC	1	$1,000 ×	.500	$ 500
Lab-Strep	2	5,000 ×	.500	2,500
Total Lab	3	$6,000		$3,000
X-Ray-Chest	1	$1,200 ×	1.375	$1,650
Total X-Ray	1	$1,200		$1,650
Patient 1 Total		$7,200		$4,650

	Units	Charges	× RCC	Cost
Patient 2				
Lab-CBC	3	$3,000 ×	.500	$1,500
Urinalysis	4	$4,000 ×	.500	2,000
Total Lab	7	$7,000		$3,500
X-Ray-Chest	2	$2,400 ×	1.375	$3,300
Head	1	400 ×	1.375	550
Total X-Ray	3	$2,800		$3,850
Patient 2 Total		$9,800		$7,350

Patient Costing Using RVUs

For purposes of this example, cost will be calculated for each department's total salary, non-salary and capital cost components only (from Step 5). In actuality, cost is calculated for each individual cost component including fixed variable and direct/indirect designations.

	Units	Procedure RVU	Total Dept. RVU	Total Dept. Cost	Patient Cost
Patient 1					
Lab-Salary					
CBC	1 ×	1.000 ÷	10.500 ×	$4,800 =	$457
Strep	2 ×	.500 ÷	10.500 ×	$4,800 =	457
					$914
Lab-Nonsalary					
CBC	1 ×	.818 ÷	9.000 ×	$1,000 =	$ 91
Strep	2 ×	1.636 ÷	9.000 ×	$1,000 =	364
					$455

Lab-Capital [(Units/Total Department Units) × Department Capital Cost]

CBC	(1 ÷ 10)	× $700	$ 70
Strep	(2 ÷ 10)	× $700	140
			$210

X-Ray-Salary					
Chest	1 ×	.588 ÷	3.176 ×	$3,800 =	$704

X-Ray-Nonsalary					
Chest	1 ×	1.111 ÷	4.222 ×	$1,300 =	$342

X-Ray-Capital				
Chest	(1 ÷ 4)	× $400	=	$100

Total Patient 1 Cost				$2,725

	Units	Proce-dure RVU	Total Dept. RVU	Total Dept. Cost	Patient Cost
Patient 2					
Lab-Salary					
CBC	4	× 1.000 ÷	10.500	× $4,800 =	$1,829
Urin	3	× 1.500 ÷	10.500	× $4,800 =	2,057
					$3,886
Lab-Nonsalary					
CBC	4	× .818 ÷	9.000	× $1,000 =	$364
Urin	3	× .545 ÷	9.000	× $1,000 =	182
					$546

Lab-Capital [(Units/Total Department Units) × Department Capital Cost]

CBC	(4 ÷ 10)	× $700		$280
Urin	(3 ÷ 10)	× $700		210
				$490

X-Ray-Salary					
Chest	2	× .588 ÷	3.176	× $3,800 =	$1,407
Head	1	× 1.412 ÷	3.176	× $3,800 =	1,689
					$3,096
X-Ray-Nonsalary					
Chest	2	× 1.111 ÷	4.222	× $1,300 =	$684
Head	1	× .889 ÷	4.222	× $1,300 =	274
					$958

X-Ray-Capital				
Chest	(2 ÷ 4)	× $400	=	$200
Head	(1 ÷ 4)	× $400	=	100
				$300

Total Patient 2 Cost	$9,276

SUMMARY PROFITABILITY ANALYSIS (RCC VS. RVU)

	Gross Charges	Ney Rev	RVU Cost	RCC Cost	RVU Profit	RCC Profit
Patient 1	$ 7,200	$ 4,200	$ 2,724	$ 4,650	$1,476	$ (450)
Patient 2	9,800	9,800	9,276	7,350	524	2,450
Total	$17,000	$14,000	$12,000	$12,000	$2,000	$2,000

As you might infer, the decision to use RCC vs. RVU costing will impact the accuracy of cost/profitability analysis not only at the patient level, but also by physician, specialty, payer, DRG, MDC, and product line. After years of so-called cost or charge shifting, which of the figures above would you prefer to rely upon for contractual negotiations, feasibility determinations, and other critical management decisions?

Application 4-5

Alternative Costing Methods in Health Care

*Leslie A. Davis Weintraub is currently a
Principal with Davis Health Strategies,
Sudbury, Massachusetts.*

*Richard J. Dube, MBA, is currently
Vice President of Finance at Anna Jaques Hospital,
Newburyport, Massachusetts.*

METHODOLOGY

The development of procedure level costs in a hospital can vary widely depending on the methodology used. Procedures, as referred to throughout the article, are the smallest level of detail maintained in a hospital's financial system (e.g., chest x-ray). Two common methodologies, both of which were involved in this study, are (1) ratio of cost to charges (RCC) and (2) relative value units (RVU). All data used in this study were developed at Framingham Union Hospital in Framingham, Massachusetts, a 311-bed general medical/surgical hospital. Fiscal year 1986 data only were used. The development of RCCs involved a breakdown of costs into five separate components, thus constituting five separate RCCs for each department. These categories were as follows:

- direct labor
- direct supplies
- overhead capital
- overhead labor
- overhead supplies

This five-tiered approach is somewhat more sophisticated than the traditional single RCC method. Two of the components of cost represent direct costs, while the other three are all indirect costs.

The relative value unit methodology in place at Framingham resulted from an in-depth cost accounting study performed primarily by the fiscal department staff with some outside consulting assistance. The procedural level costing study resulted in the development of eleven cost components, four of which are direct components of cost. The eleven components are

- direct variable labor
- direct fixed labor
- direct variable supplies
- direct fixed supplies
- direct capital
- support labor
- support supplies
- support capital
- overhead labor
- overhead supplies
- overhead capital

The hospital chose to distinguish between support departments and overhead departments as follows. Support departments are those such as housekeeping and dietary where a specific measurement of activity exists, allowing the department head some control over the usage of that department's services. Overhead departments include typical hospital overhead departments, such as fiscal services and depreciation, which are not usually considered within the department head's direct control.

The hospital's costing study involved determining the costs for all procedure charge codes. Once the data collection phase was complete, all data were entered into a procedure level cost management program for later integration with the hospital's mainframe cost accounting system. The hospital's cost accounting system allowed the hospital to store both departmental RCC cost values and procedural level costs as collected from the detailed study, hereafter referred to as RVU costs. The availability of these two variations of costing data allowed us to study the differences in the results of the two costing methods in much greater detail.

All data analysis was performed on the same group of patients, those treated at Framingham Union Hospital in fiscal year (FY) 1986. Preliminary analysis of the RCC/RVU cost comparison focused on an individual patient with costs detailed by department. Secondary analysis included a single DRG broken out by departmental costs. Comparisons at this micro level of detail proved to be unmanageable for a representative amount of data. Instead, we settled on examining all diagnosis related groups (DRGs) with greater than thirty cases. The number thirty was chosen as it represents a large sample size in statistical analysis. The resultant number of DRGs included in our cost comparison study was 87. These 87 DRGs represent 9,712 cases, or 74 percent of the hospital's total cases treated in FY 1986.

Statistical analysis was performed on these 87 DRGs for both sets of cost data so as to compare the statistical significance of the difference between the two methods. If the difference between the two costing methodologies was not found to be statistically significant for a particular DRG, then the two methods were considered comparable for that DRG. Conversely, if the difference was statistically significant, then the two methods were categorized as significantly different for that DRG. In order to determine statistical significance, the two-tailed t-test for paired observations was performed on each of the 87 DRGs. Additionally, confidence intervals were calculated for all DRGs in which the difference between the two costing methods was considered statistically significant. The confidence intervals were then assessed to determine the variation in the range of the interval, indicating either a tight or loose range. All statistical tests were performed at the 99 percent significance level or .01 significance. The 99 percent significance level was selected to assure statistical significance at varying sample sizes (number of cases of a DRG), as well as to maintain a high degree of accuracy.

FINDINGS

Results of the statistical analysis are outlined below. The analysis was performed on both total cost and direct cost for each DRG. Direct costs were analyzed separately so as to eliminate the influence of indirect allocated expenses and focus solely on direct costs. Prior studies on this topic have pointed to the possible influential effect of overhead allocation on the costing methodologies. Our goal was to eliminate that effect and compare the two methods. Direct cost analysis for the RCC method thus involved only the two direct cost components: direct labor and direct supplies. The RVU methodology analysis was limited to the four direct cost components; direct variable labor, direct fixed labor, direct variable supplies and direct fixed supplies.

When the difference between the methodologies was analyzed in terms of total cost, 29 DRGs fell into the category statistically significant, while for the other 58 DRGs the costing methodologies differential was not significant. Although these 29 DRGs only represent 33.3 percent of the total DRGs, they represent 58 percent of the total cases.

Additionally, they account for 40.3 percent of the total RVU costs and 41.2 percent of the total RCC costs. Lastly, they represent 40.7 percent of the net revenue. In comparison, a similar analysis performed with direct costs resulted in 38 DRGs in which the difference between the two costing methodologies was statistically significant. Representing 43.7 percent of the total DRGs, these DRGs constitute 65.8 percent of the total cases. The 38 DRGs account for 42.8 percent of the RVU costs and 44.2 percent of the RCC costs. These 38 DRGs also represent 43.8 percent of the net revenue of the 87 DRGs studied (See Table 4-5-1).

The analysis of direct costs resulted in a greater percentage of DRGs in which the difference between the two costing methodologies was statistically significant. One would expect this difference to occur, since direct costs do not include any overhead allocation. The allocation of overhead in the total cost methodology remains constant in both RCC and RVU costing. The equal elimination of overhead costs magnifies the difference between the methods, thus resulting in a greater number of statistically significant cases.

In order to assess the impact of the DRGs in which the difference between the two methods was deemed statistically significant, we decided to do some analysis on the basis of profitability.

The hospital is able to better assess the impact of the RVU methodology when profit/loss amounts are attached. The analysis focused on those DRGs with exceptionally high variances in total profit and profit per case between the two methods. Profit is defined as net revenue minus operating cost. The profit variance represents the difference in profit between the two costing methodologies. Another interesting observation involved DRGs that appeared to be profitable under one method, yet unprofitable under the other method. Once again the analysis was performed separately on both total costs and direct costs. Results are listed in Table 4-5-2.

Under the total cost analysis, four DRGs appeared profitable under one method and unprofitable under the other. DRG 391 (normal newborns) showed a profit of $69/case under the RCC method and a loss of $50/case under the RVU method. Although the total dollar amount of the variance is not particularly large, DRG 391 is the highest volume DRG in the

Table 4-5-1 Summary of Data

	Total Cost	Direct Cost
Number of DRGs where the difference between the two methods was statistically significant	29	38
Total number of DRGs in analysis	87	87
% significant DRGs of total DRGs	33.3%	43.7%
% significant cases of total cases	58.0%	65.8%
% significant DRG RVU costs of total RVU costs	40.3%	42.8%
% significant DRG RCC costs of total RCC costs	41.2%	44.2%
% significant DRG net revenue of total net revenue	40.7%	43.8%

Table 4-5-2 Total Cost Analysis

Profit per Case
DRGs with Positive versus Negative Profits

	RCCs	RVUs
DRG 24	($ 6)	$130
DRG 59	$190	($ 77)
DRG 124	($151)	$927
DRG 391	$ 69	($ 50)
DRG 374*	($190)	$ 51
DRG 379*	($ 51)	$ 86

Total Profit Variance
DRGs with > $100,000 Total Profit Variance

DRG 125	$123,346
DRG 373	($220,532)
DRG 391	$204,219

Profit per Case
DRGs with > $1,000 Profit/Case Profit Variance

DRG 1	($2,192)
DRG 124	($1,078)
DRG 125	($1,110)

*Denotes these DRGs are only statistically significant under the direct cost analysis.

analysis, with 1,706 cases. DRG 59 (tonsil/ade-noidectomy) presented a profit of $190/case under the RCC method, yet a loss of $77/case under the RVU method. Similarly, DRG 24 (sei-zure/headache) is unprofitable under the RCC method, with a loss of $6/case, and profitable under the RVU method, at a per case profit of $130. The fourth DRG in this category is DRG 124—circulatory disorders except AMI w/cath com dx. Here we found the largest total dollar variance, exceeding $1,000, with a loss under the RCC approach of $151/case and a profit under the RVU method of $927/case.

Continuing with the total cost analysis, three DRGs had a total profit variance of greater than $100,000. DRG 391 (normal newborns) had a positive profit variance of $204,219 and DRG 373 (vaginal delivery w/o com dxs) had a nega-tive variance of $220,532. As mentioned earlier, newborns are the number one volume DRG at Framingham Union. The other DRG with a total profit variance of over $100,000 is DRG 125 (circulatory disorders except AMI w/cath sim dx) with a positive variance of $123,346. When profit per case was analyzed instead of total profit, three DRGs had a profit per case vari-ance of greater than $1,000. DRG 125 was the only DRG with both a total profit variance over $100,000 and a per case profit variance of over $1,000. DRG 125 had a $1,110 profit variance per case. DRG 124 has a per case profit vari-ance of $1,078. Lastly, DRG 1 (craniotomy) had the highest per case profit variance of $2,192. A wide variation between the RCC and RVU method is apparent in a select number of DRGs, as displayed by significant profit variances. Total profit variance for the 29 DRGs selected in the total cost analysis was a negative $329,551 for a per case variance of ($59)/case. Similarly, the total profit variance for the 38 DRGs selected in the direct cost analysis was a negative $315,401 for a per case variance of ($49)/case.

The direct cost analysis resulted in precisely similar results for those DRGs with greater than a $100,000 total profit variance, as well as those DRGs with a per case profit variance of over $1,000. The only difference was seen in the analysis of DRGs with both positive and nega-tive profits according to the costing method selected. In addition to the four DRGs cited under the total cost analysis, two other DRGs fell into this category as well. DRG 374 (vagi-nal delivery w/sterilization or D&C) appears profitable under the RVU method at $51 profit per case and unprofitable under the RCC method with a per case loss of ($190). Also, DRG 379 (threatened abortion) shows a per case loss of $51 under the RCC method and a per case profit of $86 under the RVU method.

DISCUSSION

The traditional RCC approach has been accepted over the years as the standard method for cost determination. As hospitals began to shift toward strict cost containment with the advent of the prospective payment system (PPS), a more accurate method of cost determi-nation was desired. The RVU approach, or pro-cedural level cost determination, became the prevalent methodology for a select group of hospitals with the available resources. Proce-dural level cost development is a detail-oriented, time-consuming task that requires the assistance and cooperation of many individuals throughout the hospital. Subsequently, the associated cost can be very high. The results of such a study are generally accepted to be considerably more accurate than a ratio of cost to charges approach. The increased accuracy is attributable to the data collected in determining direct pro-cedural costs such as labor and supplies. Actual measurements are conducted to assess the labor time involved in performing each procedure and the associated supplies are directly assigned to the procedures as well.

Assuming that the RVU information is more accurately developed than the RCC data, we have demonstrated numerous examples where a large variance exists between the two methods. Significant differentials in profit occurred in large volume DRGs, which could have resulted in the hospital making strategic decisions on high volume DRGs on the basis of inaccurate information. The additional information gar-nered from the cost accounting study proved to be significantly different from the RCC data in 60 percent of the hospital's total cases. Alternatively, one could say that in 40 percent of the hospital's cases, the difference between RCCs and RVUs was insignificant and not worthy of the additional intensive data collection and analysis effort. Ultimately, the question becomes, "What level of information is necessary for the decision maker at the hospital to make critical decisions?"

Framingham Union feels they invested soundly in their cost accounting decision. As a result of the detailed RVU information, the hospital was able to realign its charge structure and conduct HMO negotiations based on accurate cost per case information. Currently, the hospital is using the data from the cost accounting study to develop a flexible budget. The future impact of the hospital's enhanced decision-making capabilities cannot be assigned a monetary value at this time; however, the hospital will continue to reap the benefits of the cost accounting data for years to come.

Even though the RCC/RVU differential was only statistically significant in 60 percent of the cases and not 99 percent, one inaccurate decision based on approximated RCC data could wreak havoc in the hospital's strategic financial plan. Inaccurate decision-making to any degree is best avoided. A small hospital, however, may not be able to cost-justify the expense of the cost accounting study when RCC data are readily available. Although RCCs are an approximation of true cost, they are a reasonable substitute, as evidenced by our study results, for 40 percent of the cases.

Each hospital must make an individual decision whether or not to invest in a cost accounting study based on the desired uses of the resultant information in ongoing hospital managerial decisions. RCCs are an approximation and lack the validity of RVUs. However, the hospital must be willing to make a significant investment in order to pursue the development of procedural level RVU costs. A number of methods exist to reduce the investment in a cost accounting study, including the use of short-cut techniques and national RVU standards. The varying degrees of data collection involvement will determine the actual cost of the study and must be accurately assessed when considering the RCC/RVU dilemma.

ACKNOWLEDGMENTS

The authors wish to give special thanks to Mr. Harmon Jordan, Director of Biostatistics, Mediqual Systems, Inc., for his assistance and guidance with the statistical analysis, and to Mr. John Nunnelly, Regional Vice President, HBO & Co., for his consultative assistance and guidance throughout the research process.

Application 4-6

Cost Allocation in the Emergency Department

*Martin S. Kohn, MD, FACEP, is currently the Chair of the Department
of Emergency Medicine at St. John's Episcopal
Hospital, Far Rockaway, New York.*

Methods of cost allocation are intended, as part of a management control system, to help collect data needed for the planning and control of financial entities. A properly designed system helps senior management set realistic goals and measure progress toward the goals. Hospital allocation systems tend to be peculiar because of the nature of health care reimbursement procedures.

Since it is a reasonable goal for hospitals to maximize third-party reimbursement for services rendered, the administrators will tailor allocation schemes to that end. An allocation system with a reimbursement maximization aim may make institutional sense, but it may provide incentives at odds with some of the fundamental clinical goals of hospitals.

The hospital emergency department (ED) seems to have been a place that has always defied financial analysis and management. Whether this absence of financial control has resulted from the ED's traditional role of providing emergency care to all comers, irrespective of the ability to pay, or because hospitals in

Source: Reprinted from Martin S. Kohn, "Cost Allocation in the Emergency Department," *Hospital Cost Accounting Advisor,* Vol. 4, No. 9, February 1989, pp. 1–6. Copyright 1989, Aspen Publishers, Inc.

general have only recently grappled with cost/revenue issues, is unclear.

It had been pretty well accepted that emergency departments lost money directly, but compensated by generating profits on the inpatients admitted through the ED. The perception that EDs did not have to stand on their own financial merits probably contributed to a lackadaisical approach. No effort was made to assess material and staffing resources used by patients (or categories of patients). Frequently, a flat average fee was charged to each patient to cover overhead and staffing costs. The patients might be charged individually for specific, identifiable supplies used during treatment.

The reimbursement methodology for many states has provided no incentive for hospitals to identify cost patterns. For example, in the regulated New York environment, the hospitals are reimbursed on formulas related to average costs. In a simplified description, Blue Cross, Medicaid, and Workers Compensation each consider the average cost of treatment for a patient covered under their programs, and calculate an average visit fee. The average is calculated on data from two years earlier, and is projected forward by allowing for inflation. The hospital then receives that fee for each covered visit, irrespective of the nature of the visit.

Medicare pays a fixed percentage of charges, as an interim payment for services rendered, which is supposed to approximate costs, based on data from two years earlier. A final settlement for outpatient services is completed after the year-end filing of a cost report.

The payment for each program is different, because of the nature of the patients, the kinds of services covered, and caps that may be imposed on certain expenses. An exception is the patient who is admitted to the hospital from the ED. Since admissions are reimbursed under a DRG scheme, there is no separate reimbursement for the ED component of such a visit.

An immediate peculiarity is already apparent. The patients who are usually most labor and supply-intensive in an ED are the patients who are admitted to the hospital. They may represent 10% to 30% or more of the ED patient volume. Yet, no revenue accrues to the ED for the management of its most expensive patients. To provide proper incentive and control, either appropriate revenue must be assigned to the ED for admitted patients, or appropriate costs from the ED should be allocated to the inpatient services. In the current environment, with very high hospital inpatient censuses, it has not been unusual for patients to spend several days in an ED, awaiting the availability of an inpatient bed. Under such circumstances, the absence of a reasonable allocation process can precipitate major cost/revenue discrepancies and management misdirection.

The "average" fee reimbursement system also limits the ability of hospital EDs to deal with competition. Urgent care centers (UCCs) or freestanding emergency centers (FECs) compete directly with EDs for the minor emergency patients. The UCCs attempt to provide care faster and less expensively than EDs. Part of the ability of UCCs and FECs to undercut EDs on cost is due to the typical ED cost allocation. With the standard fee being independent of service provided, patients with minor problems were clearly being overcharged. (While $75 for a severe asthma attack might be a bargain, $75 for a runny nose is clearly expensive.) The UCCs, by treating minor problems at prices more consistent with costs, are able to attract those patients from the EDs. Although one could argue that such patients should not be in the ED in the first place, the reimbursement mechanisms and cost allocations used depend on such minor emergencies for solvency. If, for example, the least seriously ill or injured 10% of patients leave the ED for a UCC, revenue is still down 10%.

In some instances, hospitals have set up charges that vary with the severity of illness or intensity of service for emergency patients. For example, in 1984, Lorain Community Hospital, in Lorain, Ohio, set up a graduated fee structure. Prior to the change, the charges were either $50 for a "minor" problem or $85 for a "major" case. With either fee, the charges for certain supplies were added on. In northeast Ohio, at that time, Blue Cross did not reimburse for emergency treatment of medical problems unless they resulted in hospitalization. The costs of most mild to moderate cases were paid out of pocket by the patients. Thus, a UCC with fees even slightly lower than the ED could be, and was, very competitive.

The fee gradation was loosely based on what was perceived as increasing utilization of nursing time. The allocation had to be approximated because of an absence of specific data. The specific charges for each level were derived by considering the estimated nursing time, and setting the requirement that total revenue had to match, or possibly exceed, revenue prior to the change. The charges also had to be within the bounds that insurance companies would accept for reimbursement. The result was a seven-level system, with charges ranging from $25 for the most minor problems (e. g., a cold) to $350 for a full cardiac arrest. In addition, a structure was instituted to allow for additional charges for each 15 minutes of intensive care nursing time above the amount allocated in the basic charge. Thus, by giving consideration to cost allocation, the ED at Lorain Community Hospital was able to restructure its charges to both compete effectively with UCCs (by advertising the reduced rates) and to receive appropriate reimbursement for its primary service objective, namely providing care for serious emergencies.

Although such a simple charge modification seems quite trivial, it is innovative enough that ED price adjustments merited front page coverage in the May 19, 1988, *Wall Street Journal.* Increased numbers of visits and increased profits were reported by hospitals that used graded charges. Such results, alone, would seem to be enough incentive to induce an administrator to refine cost allocation in the ED.

In New York, however, the "average"-cost-based method of third party reimbursement for emergency care removes most of the incentive. Also, New York Blue Cross plans, for example, pay for most of their clients' ED visits, so the attraction of a UCC's lower cost is blunted. However, the control and incentive parts of management remain. For example, would a decrease of two minor visits be offset by an increase of one visit resulting in an admission? On a strict ED revenue basis, the result would be a loss of two paying patients and a gain of one nonrevenue patient, since admissions are reimbursed as a DRG payment to the hospital. There should be an allocation method that reflects the benefit to the hospital without appearing to disadvantage the ED.

ANALYSIS OF A CURRENT ALLOCATION SYSTEM

To consider the ED allocation issue, a currently used system will be explored. The following issues will be considered:

1. Are the allocation bases rational?
2. Do the bases have any disadvantages?
3. Would a change in the allocation process provide benefit with a reasonable cost?

Fixed Overhead

Certain costs in the emergency department can be viewed as fixed. The largest of such costs would be depreciation for the building and capital equipment, administrative services and supervisory nursing services. Building depreci-

ation is assigned to the ED based on square footage as a fraction of the total hospital area. Equipment is depreciated against the actual cost of purchase. Supervisory nursing costs are assigned by actual hours of service, and administrative costs are assigned by historical patterns of the fraction of the administrators' time spent dealing with ED issues.

Currently, these costs are assigned equally to each patient, based on the year's budget for patient visits. A patient who spends 30 minutes in the ED, and utilizes 5 minutes of staff time, has the same fixed overhead allocation as a patient who spends three days.

Perhaps the overhead could be assigned by the time each patient spends in the ED. Technically, each patient's chart is supposed to have the time of arrival and the time of discharge written down. However, such notations are not always made, and when they are, the times don't always accurately reflect the useful time the patient spends in the ED. A four-hour stay could include two hours of waiting because the X-ray machine was being repaired. Thus, to be fair, the elapsed time would have to be evaluated to extract a useful "treatment time." Such a process would be cumbersome, expensive, and subjective—not desirable characteristics of a cost allocation process.

As it turns out, fixed overhead represents a small portion of the total costs of the ED, in the range of 5%. Such a ratio seems consistent with general experience. Thus, any elaborate method for fixed overhead allocation would have an undesirable cost-benefit ratio.

Variable Overhead

Like fixed overhead, variable overhead represents a small fraction of the total cost of the ED. Services such as laundry, housekeeping, power and miscellaneous supplies account for less than 5% of total costs. They are allocated to the ED, respectively, by pounds of laundry, hours of service, floor space and actual supply requisitions. Since the amount of money involved is relatively small, again, a complex patient allocation process is not indicated.

Variable Costs

Variable costs (salaries, pharmacy, laboratory, radiology, etc.) represent the largest fraction of ED expenses. Salaries for staff (including physicians) account for 90+% of variable costs. Salary expenses are allocated on a per visit basis, irrespective of the intensity or duration of service. A prorated allocation process makes sense when the reimbursement is independent of the actual service provided to the patient. However, it makes no sense in terms of trying to evaluate staff function.

If there were a change in patient characteristics, so that even a few more critically ill patients, requiring more personnel for more time, arrived in the ED, all that would be seen in cost data was that the average staff cost per patient increased. There would be no indication of the cause of the increase, and it could be interpreted as inefficiency on the part of the staff. Thus, even though a more sophisticated cost allocation system for salaries would not affect reimbursement for most patients, it would help interpret ED operations more effectively.

In addition, there is one group of patients whose care is reimbursed based on cost, namely, those covered by Medicare. Since the elderly patient often requires more attention and care than younger patients, a system that identifies intensity and length of care in cost allocation could result in increased reimbursement from Medicare. The much-discussed concept of ambulatory visit groups (AVGs) might reflect such differential costs.

As noted, other variable costs include laboratory and radiology. For the bulk of patients for whom reimbursement is independent of services rendered, the expenses for laboratory and radiology must be allocated to the ED. The allocation process is a prorated assignment based on total number of tests. If ED patients account for 10% of the total number of tests performed in the laboratory, then 10% of laboratory costs are allocated to the ED. The ratio is calculated on the basis of number of tests, and does not consider the cost of the test. An immunoglobulin electrophoresis has the same weight as a hematocrit determination. Since the bulk of ED patients have relatively minor problems, and the seriously ill patients have only basic diagnostic testing done in the ED, the ED utilizes the less expensive laboratory tests. Thus, allocating costs based on the fraction of total tests inflates the cost assigned to the ED.

From the point of view of the ED, such an allocation could be unfair, because the ED absorbs some of the costs generated by other parts of the hospital. However, the process could provide an advantage to the hospital. Because of DRGs, the hospital cannot be reimbursed for individual costs for inpatients. Thus, an allocation process that assigns some inpatient costs to outpatient areas, where they will be figured into a reimbursement rate, can benefit the institution. Again, we have a conflict between institutional financial benefit and the desire to provide useful data for management and control in the ED. The ED would benefit from data about actual laboratory utilization.

Since laboratory and radiology services are ordered, and recorded, by patient, the process of assigning the associated costs would be relatively straightforward. The cost data already exist, in some fashion, since they are used to determine Medicare reimbursement.

Admitted Patients

Patients admitted to the hospital through the ED generate no revenue for the ED visit, per se. Under the DRG system, the hospital is reimbursed for the admission, with no extra consideration for the time spent in the ED. To compensate for costs that are generated in the absence of revenue, ED costs for admitted patients are allocated to the inpatient services.

The allocation process is based on the percentage of total visits that result in hospital admission. For example, if 20% of ED patients are admitted to the hospital, then 20% of total ED costs are allocated to inpatient services. As with laboratory costs, the process could be seen as inequitable for the ED.

Patients who are admitted through the ED are the sickest, most resource-intensive of the patients treated in the ED. They consume far more than a prorated share of staff and supplies, so the allocation process reassigns less cost than is actually merited. Again, however, the process may be to the hospital's advantage. If higher costs were assigned to the inpatient services, it would not result in higher revenue, because of the DRG system. Leaving the costs in the ED results in higher reimbursement since the ED is an outpatient service.

Summary of Allocation Analysis

The currently used system for allocating ED costs has these advantages:

1. It is simple.
2. It helps maximize revenue for the institution by assigning what could be considered inpatient costs to the ED.

However, it also has disadvantages:

1. It does not provide data to help control and manage ED activities.
2. A variable cost allocation could be misinterpreted with respect to staff efficiency.
3. It offers a potentially inappropriate incentive. (Minimally ill patients produce a better bottom line than sick patients requiring hospitalization.)

Because of the peculiar reimbursement mechanism, the hospital has no incentive, and in fact, great disincentive, to alter its ED cost allocation process. However, a simple process that would allow managers to understand staff utilization (which represents the bulk of ED cost) is still desirable from the point of view of control and incentive.

ALLOCATION BY INTENSITY AND DURATION

The reality is that some patients require more time and attention than others. If the patient distribution changes, and there are a greater number of seriously ill patients, staff needs increase even in the absence of an increase in the total number of patients. Therefore, an allocation process that accounts for such variation will help identify trends, staffing needs, and operation efficiency in a way that the current system cannot.

Since staff costs represent over 80% of costs of emergency care, staff time spent with a patient seems a reasonable basis for assigning all costs. The sicker patient, requiring more staff, would also be likely to need more laboratory studies and more X-rays. Thus, staff time should also parallel other costs. For reasons already discussed, attempting to keep track of the time each patient spends in the emergency department is not useful. Although it would be helpful to know how much staff time is spent with each patient, such a process is too expensive and time consuming to be cost-effective.

However, grouping patients by categories would be a cost-effective and practical way of allocating starting costs. As was demonstrated at Lorain Community Hospital, referred to earlier, patients can be categorized by diagnosis and condition, in a way that reasonably predicts staff utilization. The number of categories depends on the precision you choose, and the time you have to spend. Four to seven categories seems to be common. A time-motion study can be undertaken to try to quantify the number of staff-hours consumed by patients with different diagnoses. Then the mean staff time for each diagnosis can be calculated, and the diagnoses grouped by range of staff time required (e.g., 0–5 min., 5–15 min., 15–30 min., 30–60 min., 60+ min.) in person-minutes.

Some information is available from organizations such as the Emergency Nurses Association about acuity ranking of patients. Such data can be used to verify your own conclusions, or to help get started in the process. After the categories are determined, then a weight can be assigned to each group, say in proportion to the average staff time in the category. In our example above, the mean time in each category would be (in minutes) 2.5, 10, 22.5, 45, and, say, 75. In our example, the weights would be 1, 4, 9, 18, and 30. Based on the number of patients in each category, and considering the total staff costs, the appropriate cost can be allocated to each patient.

For example, if there are 100 patients in each category, and staffing costs of $100,000, the cost per unit would be calculated as follows:

$$(1 + 4 + 9 + 18 + 30) \times 100 = 6,200$$

$$\$100,000/6,200 = \$16.13 \text{ per unit}$$

Then the cost per category would be as follows:

Category	Staff Cost
1	16.13
2	64.52
3	145.17
4	290.34
5	483.90

Then as each patient is categorized, based on diagnosis, the appropriate staff cost could be assigned. Such information would be very useful to the department director or others responsible for evaluating the ED. The result from ten fewer sore throat patients (category 1) and ten more cardiac arrests (category 5) would be readily apparent.

Allocation of costs for patients admitted to the hospital would then be based on the weight of the category. Most admissions would come from the higher categories, so clearly the amount of cost allocated to the inpatient services would be higher than under the simplistic prorated system. The allocation would more accurately reflect the ED's contribution to the admitted patient's care.

Even though such information would not be useful in hospitals in some states, with respect to reimbursement at present, it is still useful for operational purposes. In addition, considering recent trends, it is unlikely that the current ED reimbursement methodology will continue. There will be more and more pressure to reduce costs, which, in itself, will require better costing information.

There is nothing in the new process that prevents the hospital from continuing to generate reimbursement figures the way it has been doing. Since the reimbursement is based on average costs, none of the needed data have been lost. The hospital can continue to use its simplistic allocation process to its financial advantage, while also developing data systems that will help it understand its emergency department now, and be prepared for changes in the future.

SUGGESTED READING

Asunof, L., Business Bulletin, *Wall Street Journal*, May 19, 1988 CCXI(98), p. 1.

Sabin, M.D., and P.H. Wulf in *The Hospital Emergency Department—Returning to Financial Viability*. T.A. Matson, ed., American Hospital Association, Chicago, Ill., 1986.

Janiak, B. in *The Hospital Emergency Department—Returning to Financial Viability*. T.A. Matson, ed., American Hospital Association, Chicago, Ill., 1986.

5

Cost-Volume-Profit Analysis

Goals of This Chapter

1. Describe the relationship between costs, volume, and profits.
2. Explain the role of fixed costs in determining the average cost per patient.
3. Provide a tool for calculating the breakeven volume.
4. Explain how to apply that tool in cases of multiple products and/or multiple prices.
5. Point out a number of important assumptions inherent in breakeven analysis, which must be considered by managers.
6. Define and discuss mixed costs and step-fixed costs.
7. Consider the role of breakeven analysis in decision making.

Key Terms Used in This Chapter

Average costs; breakeven analysis; breakeven point; breakeven volume; ceteris paribus; contribution margin; cost-volume-profit; Diagnosis Related Groups (DRGs); fixed costs; joint costs; mixed costs; overhead costs; relevant range; semi-fixed costs; semi-variable costs; step-fixed costs; variable costs.

Note: Key terms appear in italics when first used in the chapter. All key terms are defined in the Glossary.

THE COST-VOLUME-PROFIT RELATIONSHIP

The relationship of costs, volume, and profits is one of the most essential in financial management. We have established in earlier chapters that there is no one unique answer to the question, "What does it cost?" The cost for anything depends on a number of factors. If we are dealing with the average cost, one of the most crucial of those factors is volume. Cost per patient cannot be estimated or measured without knowing the volume related to the cost. Profits consist of revenues minus expenses. Expenses represent expired costs. When an asset is acquired, it has a cost—the amount spent to acquire it. When the asset is consumed in the process of providing goods and services, it expires. Its cost becomes an expense. Therefore, the word *cost* often is used to refer to both assets, for example, inventory, and expenses, for example, supplies expense. It follows that, until we have information about costs, we cannot determine profits.

Why is this important? When organizations examine their total operations, or any given program or service, they must be able to anticipate likely profitability. Not-for-profit organizations cannot afford to run deficits continuously without encountering financial instability. Even not-for-profit organizations with substantial revenues from charitable donations have limits on how great their losses from operations can be.

This book does not seek to make normative judgments on whether health care organizations should only undertake profitable ventures. However, managers must be able to anticipate whether programs or services are expected to be profitable or lose money. Managers must also be able to estimate how great the profits or losses from a particular activity are likely to be. Financial solvency of the organization requires that there be an understanding of what losses are expected to be encountered, and how they will be offset. That information can be used by those who are in a position to weigh all factors in deciding what activities the organization should undertake or maintain.

If costs could be thought of as a constant amount per patient, determining profitability for any existing or proposed service would be quite straightforward. The revenue per patient could be compared to the cost per patient. If the revenue is greater than the cost, a profit will result. However, because the average cost depends on volume, the revenue per patient may be greater or less than the cost per patient, so profitability is uncertain.

The Role of Fixed and Variable Costs

The key element in *average costs* is the behavior of *fixed costs*. As discussed in Chapter 2, fixed costs are defined to be those costs that do not change in total as the volume of patients changes. Fixed costs can be thought of as a horizontal line on a graph. (See Figure 5-1.)

For any volume on the horizontal axis, the amount of cost will be $A. It does not matter if the volume is B, or less than B, or greater than B. The fixed cost will always be $A. This assumes that we stay within the relevant range. It is unlikely that fixed costs would remain the same at extreme values. However, within the range of volumes that might possibly occur for a program or service, one can generally assume that fixed costs are nearly constant.

In contrast, consider the *variable costs,* as seen in Figure 5-2. As the volume rises (moving to the right) on the horizontal axis, the costs rise on the vertical axis. Variable costs rise in direct proportion with volume. At Volume B, there are

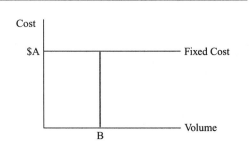

Figure 5-1 Graph of Fixed Costs. *Source:* Reprinted from *Hospital Cost Management and Accounting,* Vol. 1, No. 8, p. 1, Aspen Publishers, Inc., © 1989.

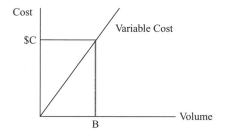

Figure 5-2 Graph of Variable Costs. *Source:* Reprinted from *Hospital Cost Management and Accounting,* Vol. 1, No. 8, p. 1, Aspen Publishers, Inc., © 1989.

$C of variable cost. If the volume were less than B, there would be less than $C of total variable costs, whereas if the volume were greater than B, the variable costs would be greater than $C.

The total costs at any volume can be determined by combining the fixed and variable costs for that volume. Figure 5-3 shows how the total costs would appear.

The average cost is found by taking the total cost at any volume and dividing it by the number of patients represented by that volume. This number will decline as volume increases.

For example, assume that fixed costs were $100,000, and that the variable cost per patient was $100. If there are 200 patients, the fixed cost would be $100,000, and the variable costs

would be $20,000 (i.e., $100 per patient multiplied by 200 patients). The total cost would be $120,000. The average cost would be $600 per patient. That represents the $120,000 total cost divided by the 200 patients. (See Table 5-1.)

However, if there were 400 patients, then the average cost per patient would be only $350. This is because the variable costs rise to $40,000 (i.e., $100 per patient multiplied by 400 patients). The fixed costs *remain the same* at $100,000. The total costs are therefore $140,000. Dividing that total by 400 patients, the average is found to be $350.

What is the essence of the reason for the drop in average cost from $600 to $350? It is because of the fixed costs. The fixed costs do not change in total. However, as volume increases, there are more patients to share those fixed costs. Therefore, each patient can be assigned a smaller share of the total. Average cost per patient decreases as volume increases because of the spreading of the fixed costs over a larger number of patients.

That means that costs per patient will tend to fall as volume rises. If revenue per patient were fixed, then it is possible that at low volumes the cost per patient would be higher than the revenue, and the program or service would lose money. However, at higher volumes, the cost per patient might fall sufficiently for the program or service to be profitable. That is why the expected volume becomes a critical focal point in analyses of services.

One of the most difficult tasks that cost accountants undertake is the determination of which costs are fixed and which are variable. Some expenses, such as depreciation, are clearly fixed. Other expenses, such as clinical supplies, are clearly variable. But many expenses do not neatly fall into one category or the other. Unless there are the unlimited resources necessary to study and examine closely each cost item for each unit or department, the health care organization will have to make some assumptions.

Assuming that clinical supplies are variable is a reasonable approximation, although there is probably a fixed cost related with maintaining an inventory of supplies. That inventory will

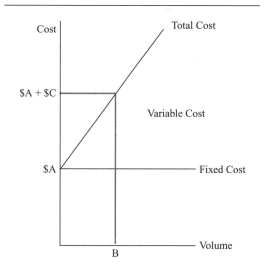

Figure 5-3 Graph of Total Costs. *Source:* Reprinted from *Hospital Cost Management and Accounting,* Vol. 1, No. 8, p. 2, Aspen Publishers, Inc., © 1989.

Table 5-1 Finding Average Cost

Volume (A)	Fixed Cost ($) (B)	Variable Cost per Patient ($) (C)	Total Variable Cost ($) (D) = (A) × (C)	Full Cost ($) (E) = (B) + (D)	Average Cost ($) (F) = (E) / (A)
200	100,000	100	20,000	120,000	600
400	100,000	100	40,000	140,000	350

probably be nearly the same at the beginning and end of each year, and can be ignored for practical purposes when deciding whether supplies are fixed or variable.

On the other hand, salaries are complex. They are neither strictly fixed nor strictly variable; they contain some fixed elements and some variable elements. This is discussed later in this chapter when mixed and step-fixed costs are addressed.

BREAKEVEN ANALYSIS

Breakeven analysis determines the volume at which a program or service is just financially self-sufficient. At lower volumes, losses would occur; at higher volumes, profits would be earned. Breakeven analysis is a managerial tool that is based on the relationships among cost, volume, and profit that were described above. The breakeven analysis technique provides managers with information regarding the financial viability of proposed and existing programs and services. The basic mechanics of breakeven analysis will first be discussed, followed by an extension of breakeven analysis to the Diagnosis Related Group (DRG) setting, where its use is even more imperative.

Basics

For a service or program that incurs any fixed costs, the cost per patient at low volumes is typically very high. As volume increases, these fixed costs can be spread over more patients, bringing down the average cost per patient. On the other hand, in many cases revenues will be a constant amount per patient. If we can deter-

mine the volume at which the average cost per patient is exactly equal to the revenue per patient, we have the volume at which we just break even.

In graphical form, the *breakeven point* is the volume, or breakeven quantity (BEQ), at which the total revenue and the total cost lines intersect (Figure 5-4).

In the graph, note that the costs start at a level higher than zero because there are fixed costs incurred regardless of volume. Revenues, on the other hand, start at zero. If there are no patients, there is no revenue. If the revenue per patient exceeds the variable costs per patient, there will be a volume at which the two lines intersect. The total cost line rises at a rate equal to the variable cost per unit. The total revenue line

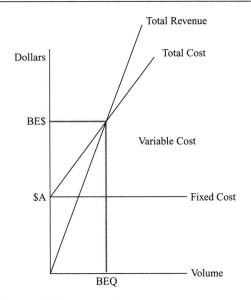

Figure 5-4 Breakeven Graph. *Source:* Reprinted from *Hospital Cost Management and Accounting,* Vol. 1, No. 8, p. 2, Aspen Publishers, Inc., © 1989.

increases at a rate equal to the revenues per patient. As long as the revenue per patient is greater than the variable cost per patient, the two lines must cross at some point. At that point, the *breakeven volume,* our revenues are exactly equal to our costs:

$$Revenue = Costs$$

Note, however, that the revenue per patient must exceed the variable cost per patient or there will always be losses. If the revenue is less than the variable cost, then each additional patient will cause losses to increase. If the revenue is exactly the same as the variable cost, then there will always be a loss equal to the fixed cost.

Even if the revenue is greater than the variable cost, that does not guarantee that a program or service will be profitable. It is possible that the volume that would be required to reach a breakeven point is so high that it is not practically feasible to attain it. For example, if fixed costs were $1,000,000 and the revenue per patient exceeded the variable cost per patient by only $1, the organization would need 1 million patients to break even. Therefore, it becomes important to have a way to determine how many patients would be needed to achieve a breakeven point.

As noted above, revenues are just equal to costs at the breakeven point. We can use this as a starting point to derive a formula mathematically for determining the volume that is necessary to break even. Costs consist of fixed costs and variable costs, so at the breakeven point, the following applies:

$$Revenues = Fixed\ costs + Total\ variable\ costs$$

Our revenues consist of the price per patient (P) multiplied by the number of patients (Q). (We can abbreviate fixed costs as FC.) Our total variable costs consist of the variable cost per patient (VC) times the number of patients (Q). Our equation thus becomes the following:

$$P \times Q = FC + VC \times Q$$

Our goal is to find the volume of patients at which we just break even, so we must solve the preceding equation for Q as follows:

$$P \times Q = FC + VC \times Q$$

$$P \times Q - VC \times Q = FC$$

$$Q \times (P - VC) = FC$$

$$Q = \frac{FC}{P - VC}$$

This equation or formula tells us that to find the volume at which we would break even, we simply need to divide the fixed costs by the price less the variable cost per unit. This should make intuitive sense. Suppose that you rented a machine for a fixed cost of $100, and produced a product with a variable cost of $3, which could be sold for $5. How many units of the product would you have to sell in order to cover your rental cost of $100? If we get $5 for each one we sell and the variable cost is $3, we are left with $2, which can be used to cover the fixed cost. We would need to earn $2 for fifty times to cover the fixed cost of $100. The difference between the price and the variable cost is referred to as the *contribution margin* (CM), because it is the amount that each extra sale contributes toward fixed costs and profits, after covering its variable costs. Our formula would look like this:

$$Q = \frac{\$100}{\$5 - \$3} = \$50$$

Breakeven Analysis for a New Service

The focus of breakeven analysis in health care has typically been based on the number of treatments, visits, or patient days. Patient days are in fact the statistic most central to a wide variety of cost calculations in hospitals.

However, under a prospective payment system such as *Diagnosis Related Groups* (DRGs), patient days are not an adequate measure for use in breakeven analysis. Whether a program earns enough revenues to cover its costs will depend on how many admissions there are for a given DRG, rather than on the total number of patient days for patients in that DRG. Extra patient days for the same number of admissions in a given DRG will generate no extra revenue, unless some patients are outliers. Therefore, we need to view breakeven analysis in a flexible way that can deal with visits and treatments, but can also encompass analysis under prospective payment systems such as DRGs.

Suppose that we are considering adding a new service to our hospital. For the moment, assume that all payments are based on DRGs and that all payers pay the exact same rate. These assumptions will be relaxed later. Assume further that preliminary analysis has provided us with the following data related to expected costs and the expected DRG reimbursement rate. (All numbers used in this and the subsequent examples are hypothetical.)

Type of Service	Reimbursement Rate	Program-specific Fixed Costs	Variable Costs
DRG 3	$1,000	$150,000	$800

Program-specific fixed costs would include items such as depreciation on equipment to be acquired for the service or salary supplements for program supervisors. Variable costs would include all costs that vary with the level of output, such as supplies and labor. According to our formula, this service would break even if it results in 750 admissions:

$$Q = \frac{FC}{P-VC} = \frac{\$150,000}{\$1,000-\$800} = \frac{\$150,000}{\$200}$$

$$= 750 \text{ Admissions}$$

It should be noted that no overhead costs were allocated in this calculation. This assumes that such overhead costs are joint; that is, that they will exist whether or not the new service is added. In that case, the new service should not include a share of those costs in its breakeven calculation because those costs would be incurred in any case.

Breakeven Analysis for Multiple Services

Continuing with the assumption that all payers pay based on DRGs, let's now extend the above example from one type of patient to multiple types of patients. Although this analysis is using DRGs as an example, the method presented applies broadly. Patients need not be grouped into DRGs. This method would apply equally to different types of home visits for a home health agency or different types of office visits for a physician's office practice. Further, although this example uses just three types of patients, this methodology applies equally well to 30, 300, or 3,000 types of patients.

Assume the data in Table 5-2. For this hypothetical hospital, all patients are either DRG 1, 2, or 3. The breakeven problem is now somewhat more complex. First, it is necessary to find an average price weighted for the proportion of patients in each of our DRGs.

Table 5-2 Hypothetical Cost Data for Multiple Types of Patients

Type of Service	% of Patients in this DRG	Rate of Reimbursement ($)	Program-Specific Fixed Costs ($)	Variable Costs ($)
DRG 1	25	500	50,000	300
DRG 2	35	2,000	100,000	1,200
DRG 3	40	1,000	150,000	800
		Joint Costs	500,000	
	100		800,000	

	Weighted % of Patients	Rate ($)			Weighted Revenue ($)
DRG 1	25	×	500	=	125
DRG 2	35	×	2,000	=	700
DRG 3	40	×	1,000	=	400
		Weighted average price			1,225

Next we must find variable costs weighted for the proportion of patients in each DRG.

	Percentage of Patients (%)	Variable Cost ($)			Weighted Variable Cost ($)
DRG 1	25	×	300	=	75
DRG 2	35	×	1,200	=	420
DRG 3	40	×	800	=	320
		Weighted variable cost			815

The last remaining step before calculating the breakeven volume of admissions is to determine the appropriate fixed cost. For the hospital as a whole to break even, it must cover all of its costs, including both program-specific fixed costs and hospital-wide joint costs. Therefore, the fixed cost figure is $800,000. Thus,

$$Q = \frac{FC}{P - VC} = \frac{\$800,000}{\$1,225 - \$815} = 1,951 \text{ admissions}$$

The 1,951 volume represents all admissions. Of that 1,951 total, 25 percent would be DRG 1 patients; 35 percent, DRG 2 patients; and 40 percent, DRG 3 patients.

This raises an interesting issue. In the previous example, only 750 DRG 3 patients were needed for that service to break even. However, 40 percent of 1,951 is 780. The DRG 3 breakeven volume has risen by 30 patients in this example. Why has this happened? It is because when one considers breakeven for the organization rather than one service, joint costs must be included. Joint costs were included in this multiple-service breakeven calculation.

Suppose the hospital could only expect 760 DRG 3 patients. From a financial perspective, should the service be continued? Absolutely. It is true that we need 780 patients in that DRG for the hospital to break even. However, as long as

there are more than 750 patients in the DRG, the hospital will be better off for having the service. The first 750 patients cover the direct fixed costs of the service. Each additional patient in the DRG will contribute toward joint fixed costs an amount equal to the difference between the price and the variable costs. In the case of DRG 3, the price is $1,000 and variable costs are $800. If there are 760 DRG 3 patients, the hospital will earn a contribution margin of $200 for each of the patients in excess of 750 patients, or a total of $2,000. This can go toward paying joint costs. (An underlying assumption for this analysis is that elimination of DRG 3 would not eliminate any of the joint costs.)

Breakeven analysis tells that we need 780 DRG 3 patients to break even. However, that information is different from the information needed to make a decision about discontinuing that product line. Recall that when working with cost accounting, it is often important to ask why a user needs to know the information. Knowing the breakeven point of a service so we can work to attain that volume is different from needing to know the breakeven point so that a decision to discontinue a service can be made. A constant theme of cost accounting is that there are different calculations of cost that are required when the information is used for different purposes. It is very important not to try to use information for a purpose other than the one for which it was designed. Doing so can lead to incorrect managerial decisions.

Breakeven All Services—Different Payment Rates

To complicate the above example further, suppose that, for each DRG, there were four classes of payers, as shown in Table 5-3.

In many cases, not only will a health care organization have more than one type of patient, but it will also have different revenue structures. The federal government regulations for paying for Medicare patients may differ from state government systems for Medicaid. The negotiated arrangements with Blue Cross may differ substantially from the practice for charging other insurance companies.

Table 5-3 Payment Rates for Different Types of Payers

Type of Service	Type of Payer	% of All Admissions	Payment Basis	Rate ($)	Fixed Cost ($)	Variable Cost ($)
DRG 1	Medicare	5	DRG rate	500	50,000	300
	Medicaid	8	Specified cost	300	50,000	300
	Blue Cross	10	Cost	400	50,000	300
	Other	2	Charges	600	50,000	300
DRG 2	Medicare	9	DRG rate	2,000	100,000	1,200
	Medicaid	10	Specified cost	2,200	100,000	1,200
	Blue Cross	12	Cost	2,400	100,000	1,200
	Other	4	Charges	3,000	100,000	1,200
DRG 3	Medicare	12	DRG rate	1,000	150,000	800
	Medicaid	10	Specified cost	900	150,000	800
	Blue Cross	14	Cost	1,000	150,000	800
	Other	4	Charges	1,100	150,000	800
					Joint 500,000	

Table 5-4 Weighted Averages

	Weighted Average Price				Weighted Average Variable Cost		
DRG 1							
Medicare	5% ×	$ 500	=	$ 25	5% ×	300	= $ 15
Medicaid	8% ×	300	=	24	8% ×	300	= 24
Blue Cross	10% ×	400	=	40	10% ×	300	= 30
Other	2% ×	600	=	12	2% ×	300	= 6
DRG 2							
Medicare	9% ×	2,000	=	180	9% ×	1,200	= 108
Medicaid	10% ×	2,200	=	220	10% ×	1,200	= 120
Blue Cross	12% ×	2,400	=	288	12% ×	1,200	= 144
Other	4% ×	3,000	=	120	4% ×	1,200	= 48
DRG 3							
Medicare	12% ×	1,000	=	120	12% ×	800	= 96
Medicaid	10% ×	900	=	90	10% ×	800	= 80
Blue Cross	14% ×	1,000	=	140	14% ×	800	= 112
Other	4% ×	1,100	=	44	4% ×	800	= 32
		Weighted Price $1,303				Weighted Variable Cost $815	

In cases with both multiple types of patients and multiple prices for each type of patient, breakeven analysis first requires that we find a weighted average price and weighted average variable cost. In this example, the weighted average is shown in Table 5-4.

The breakeven point in terms of total admissions is as follows:

$$Q = \frac{FC}{P - VC} = \frac{\$800,000}{\$1,303 - \$815} = 1,639 \text{ admissions}$$

For any given DRG, we could multiply total required admissions by the proportion of patients in that DRG to find the breakeven volume for that DRG.

CAVEATS

Breakeven analysis rests upon many assumptions, some of which are explicit and obvious to the cost accountant. However, some of the assumptions underlying the analysis are not as apparent. These latter assumptions might severely distort the results of an analysis if they are not given consideration. Many managers do not focus on these assumptions as much as they should when performing breakeven analysis.

Fixed Prices

Breakeven analysis assumes that the price (or set of prices for different types of patients and different payers) is *constant* as volume changes. In other words, volume increases are not accompanied by discounted prices, nor are price increases met with volume declines.

Most economists would argue that the world does not work that way. Volume increases result from price cuts. And few organizations can raise prices without expecting to lose customers to the competition.

One potential solution to this problem is the *relevant range* assumption used in breakeven analysis. It may be that our assumptions are not true regardless of volume (what fixed cost would be fixed if you tripled the number of patients?) but are true over the likely range of volumes under consideration. For example, 5 or 10 percent increases in volume might result from marketing efforts and might not require a price decrease to be achieved.

A manager working with breakeven analysis should critically examine price assumptions. Where did the predicted price come from? How sure are we that we can charge that amount and still achieve the volume we wish to attain? This requires an examination of the assumptions in the analysis after the answer is calculated as well as before! The breakeven point cannot be computed without first setting a price. However, once the breakeven volume is calculated, it is necessary to consider whether the resulting volume can realistically be achieved at the price in the analysis.

If the price that was used for the calculation appears to be unreasonable for the breakeven volume calculated, an adjusted price can be established that would be reasonable at that level. The breakeven analysis would then have to be repeated using the new price estimate.

Can we be sure that the price is correct or that the volume will be achieved? Marketing studies can provide us with some assurance, but we can never really be sure we are right. However, we can hope to avoid moving forward in situations in which we are obviously or very possibly wrong, but it takes self-discipline to review early assumptions at a very late point in the breakeven analysis.

Cost Measurement

There is an assumption in breakeven analysis that we have the ability to measure fixed and variable costs accurately. Realistically, many health care organizations do not have ongoing costing systems that generate variable and fixed cost breakdowns. Even those that do generate such information are not necessarily totally reliable.

Does it matter? It is critical that total costs be appropriately divided accurately into fixed and variable components before breakeven analysis is done. If too great a share of total costs is allocated to fixed costs, the breakeven point may well be understated and the profit per patient overstated. Such a result will, of course, have the potential to change decisions that are made as a result of the analysis.

For example, suppose that we are planning a new acquired immunodeficiency syndrome (AIDS) treatment center. We anticipate that the total costs will be $2 million per year if we have 100 patients, and we can recover an average revenue of $15,000 per patient from all sources.

What is the breakeven point in volume of patients?

If one half of the costs are fixed, the calculation is as follows:

$$Q = \frac{\text{Fixed cost}}{\text{Price} - \text{Variable cost per patient}}$$

$$Q = \frac{\$1,000,000}{15,000 - (\$1,000,000/100)}$$

$$= \frac{\$1,000,000}{\$15,000 - \$10,000} = 200$$

The profit or loss for each patient above or below that level would be the contribution margin of $5,000. On the other hand, if three-quarters of the costs are fixed, the breakeven point would be as follows:

$$Q = \frac{\$1,500,000}{\$15,000 - (\$500,000/100)}$$

$$= \frac{\$1,500,000}{\$15,000 - \$5,000} = 150$$

The profit or loss for each patient above or below that level would be $10,000.

Obviously, our ability to measure and/or predict costs and to identify them correctly as fixed or variable is an essential part of the process, and one cannot afford to use rough estimates except where absolutely necessary. In those cases, it should be recognized that the result is a rough estimate as well.

Another problem in this respect is the constancy of fixed costs. That is, if an item is fixed today, will it still be fixed in a month, six months, or a year? This largely is the issue of the relevant range discussed above. There is often a textbook assumption that problems under consideration have volume swings that are small, and that we can assume that variable costs are proportional and linear and fixed costs are fixed over the relevant range.

In real life, however, the range should be specified and examined. What possible ranges of activity levels are being considered? Will fixed costs remain fixed over that relevant range? Will variable costs continue to change in direct linear proportion to volume changes over that range?

The issue here is whether capacities of fixed items will be exceeded, requiring an expansion of fixed capacity at a new, higher level, and whether the volume of variable items purchased will change enough to have an impact on the price per unit. A particular problem in this respect is that in many analyses done at a health care organization, the relevant range will not be exceeded. Fixed costs will remain fixed, and variable costs will change roughly in direct proportion to volume. This lulls us into a sense of security, and we may fail to examine this issue in a case where the volume swings are wild enough to make such assumptions unreasonable. If a project does exceed the relevant range, adjustments can be made to account for what fixed and variable costs are in the range where breakeven, or some target profit, occurs.

Other Items Assumed Constant

A number of other things are assumed to remain unchanged in breakeven analysis. Unfortunately, breakeven analysis is a very static model in a very dynamic world.

For example, it is assumed that variable costs will remain as they are. Why shouldn't they? Perhaps because our suppliers raise their prices to us. Perhaps because our employees win bigger raises. We must also question how prices will change in response to changes in variable expenses. Suppose in the above example (using half of the total costs for AIDS patients as fixed) that variable costs rose 10 percent per patient and that revenues rose 10 percent per patient. The organization would be better off. The revenues would be rising $1,500, and the variable costs would only be rising $1,000. With the fixed costs still fixed, there would be a $500 extra contribution per patient.

On the other hand, what if variable costs rose $1,000 and prices rose $1,000? The contribution margin per patient would be unchanged; therefore, the breakeven point and profitability would stay the same. What if variable costs rose $1,000, but due to government set payment rates, revenues rose on average only $500? Obviously, the breakeven point would rise.

The moral, clearly, is that a part of the initial breakeven analysis should be consideration of what will happen over time as costs rise. Will prices exceed, keep up with, or lag behind the cost increases?

Another assumed constancy is the efficiency and productivity of the organization. In many cases, that may not be a bad assumption, since we are always talking about improving efficiency and productivity, but often we fail to realize those gains.

Nevertheless, if efficiency and productivity really do rise or fall, there will be a definite impact on costs. In many cases, cost changes resulting from increased inefficiency cannot be passed on in the form of increased prices. Will improved efficiency improve profits or result in lower revenues? That must be answered on a case-by-case basis. Certainly, it may affect decisions made using the breakeven information.

A final item of constancy is sales mix. When breakeven analysis is applied to a multiproduct organization as a whole (i.e., cutting across products), one of two assumptions must be made. Either we assume that the variable costs are a constant percentage of price across all products, or else we assume that constant proportions of each product are sold.

It is highly unlikely for a hospital or any health care organization to have a variable cost for each type of patient that is uniform across all types of patients. Hospitals are not like retail stores that can simply take the amount they pay for any item and double it to find the price.

Then how does one determine the breakeven patient volume for a hospital as a whole? The calculation requires a knowledge of the typical makeup (sales mix) of patients each year; for example, X percent of the patients are DRG 1, Y percent are DRG 2, and so forth. That is the approach used earlier in this chapter.

The breakeven calculation, using weighted average prices and variable costs, predicts the total number of patients needed to break even and the number of patients by type of patient. However, if the mix of patients changes, the entire calculation is thrown off. Therefore, such overall breakeven analyses must take account of likely swings in patient mix.

Cost Determinants

Breakeven analysis also generally assumes that volume is the only thing that affects costs. Realistically, even with constant efficiency and productivity, many factors other than volume have an impact on costs in an organization. Technology, equipment breakdowns, strikes, and personnel availability are just a few examples of items that can all affect variable and fixed costs.

Sensitivity Analysis

What can a manager do to protect against the impact of assumptions that turn out not to be correct? Throughout this section, actions have been suggested for incorporating improved information into the analysis. For example, if the relevant range is exceeded, revised pricing information can be reentered into the calculation.

However, that will not always be possible. At times, we may only know that it is possible that the assumptions may be incorrect, but we cannot know for sure the correct values until after the fact. One approach to be taken in such cases is sensitivity analysis.

This method requires you to consider the range of estimated possible actual values for the various components and to calculate the outcome under the various possible values. If the extreme results of the breakeven under the various alternatives (at both the high and low ends) still lead to the same management decisions (e.g., open the AIDS center), then the breakeven analysis can be used with confidence.

On the other hand, if one or the other extreme result for the breakeven analysis using the range of possible data values would cause a different management decision (e.g., do not open an AIDS center), then management must make a subjective assessment concerning the likelihood of various outcomes. For example, suppose that we are fairly certain that we can attract 175 AIDS patients. If the estimate that fixed costs would be $1,000,000 was correct (in the earlier example), then we would lose money. If the estimate of fixed costs at $500,000 was correct, we would make money.

Rather than just calculating once, we have considered a range of possible values for fixed costs. Since the results point us in opposite directions, we must decide how likely it is that the fixed costs will exceed $500,000. Is there a 50 percent chance that fixed costs will be as much as $1,000,000 or only a 5 percent chance?

Making subjective estimates is certainly difficult. In addition, the possible range of alternative values for each element of the calculation will add substantially to the level of complication of the simple breakeven tool. On the other hand, dealing with the complexity of reality head-on will probably result, at the very least, in fewer unpleasant surprises down the road.

MIXED COSTS AND STEP-FIXED COSTS

In the previous section, a number of potential problems with the use of breakeven analysis were discussed. These included problems related to multiple products, changing prices, changing costs, and uncertainty. Another specific problem relates to costs that are neither strictly fixed nor strictly variable

Breakeven analysis requires classification of costs into fixed and variable components. However, it may be that costs are neither fixed nor variable, but somewhere in between. Two common types of costs that do not neatly fit into that pattern are those that are *mixed costs* and those that are *step-fixed*.

Mixed costs, sometimes called *semi-variable costs,* are defined as costs that have both fixed and variable components. Electricity is a good example of a mixed cost. To some extent, electricity is fixed because there will always be some electricity that is used regardless of the number of patients. Hallway lights will always be kept on in most health care organizations. It does not matter if all patient rooms are occupied, or only a few. On the other hand, addi-

tional patients will certainly require the use of more electricity, so that portion is variable. Figure 5-5 shows a graphic representation of mixed costs. Note that the graph is similar to a variable cost graph, except that costs start at a higher level because of the fixed portion.

When one considers all costs for an organization or department, one is invariably dealing with mixed costs—there are some costs that are fixed and some that are variable. Compare Figures 5-3 and 5-5. The total cost line and mixed cost line are identical. In most health care settings, it is necessary to make a judgment regarding the portion that is fixed and then deal with the remainder as a variable cost. Dealing with mixed costs is of great importance in cost accounting and will be addressed further in Chapter 7.

Another variation from strictly fixed and variable costs is that caused by *step-fixed* costs. Figure 5-6 shows a step-fixed cost pattern. This is a situation in which costs are fixed over a range of activity that is less than the relevant range—commonly the case in health care. Step-fixed

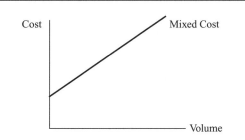

Figure 5-5 Graph of Mixed Costs

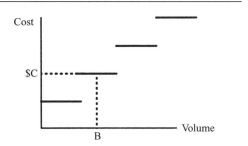

Figure 5-6 Graph of Step-Fixed Costs. *Source:* Reprinted from *Hospital Cost Management and Accounting,* Vol. 1, No. 8, p. 3, Aspen Publishers, Inc., © 1989.

costs are sometimes referred to as *semi-fixed costs*.

Many units or departments are staffed at a minimal level regardless of patient volume. For example, there may be 10 radiology technicians to handle a certain patient volume. If volume increases or decreases slightly, it will be more likely to affect the productivity of those 10 workers than to add or decrease costs. Each technician may have somewhat more or less down time between patients. If volume were to change dramatically, an additional technician might be added, or one might be laid off. In Figure 5-6, each horizontal line represents the addition of another staff member.

Supply items can easily be strictly variable. The number of dressings used will increase in direct proportion with the number of wounds dressed. Managerial costs can easily be strictly fixed. A manager receives the same salary regardless of department volume. But staff costs often will not vary patient by patient. Rather, there is no adjustment over a limited range of activity, and then a substantial change as a new staff member is added or removed, within the relevant range.

To some extent this situation is offset by the use of temporary staff members or overtime. Nevertheless, it represents an interesting problem for cost-volume-profit analysis. Application 5-1 explores the issue of step-fixed costs in greater depth.

USING BREAKEVEN ANALYSIS FOR DECISION MAKING

Breakeven analysis is obviously an aid in deciding whether or not to offer a service. However, it can be a valuable guide in helping management make other decisions as well. Suppose that projected admissions were below the breakeven point. Management could take a variety of actions ranging from cost cutting to marketing. Let us focus on the marketing alternative. If a hospital has substantial excess capacity, what patients would it try to attract?

The most profitable patients are those with the highest contribution margin. If we compare the extra revenue from an extra patient with the extra variable cost for that patient, the greater the difference, the better off the hospital is. Note that the key is not revenue; having high revenue alone does not create profits. The key is the contribution margin—the amount by which the revenue exceeds the variable cost.

In the multiple-patient breakeven example used in this chapter, the greatest difference between the revenue and variable costs is in the case of DRG 2, especially with respect to patients in the "Other" category, who generate a contribution margin of $1,800 per patient. Therefore, *ceteris paribus,* the marketing efforts of the organization should be oriented toward getting more DRG 2 "Other" patients. (See Table 5-3.)

However, care must be exercised in such analyses. Suppose that a hospital was nearly at capacity. If DRG 2 requires an average length of stay of 10 days, the contribution of the above patient would be only $180 per day. If either DRG 1 or DRG 3 had an expected length of stay of just one day, each extra "Other" patient would generate a contribution margin of $300 per day. Thus, the strategy for directing the marketing campaign may vary significantly depending on how close to capacity the organization is.

In situations in which a health care organization is near capacity of any resource (beds, operating room time, clinic visit capacity, etc.), contribution margin is no longer an adequate basis for decision making. Instead, one should use the contribution margin per unit of the most constrained resource. This concept is explored in more depth in Application 5-2.

SUGGESTED READING

Carney, K., et al. 1989. Hospice costs and Medicare reimbursement: An application of break-even analysis. *Nursing Economics* 7, no. 1:41–48, 60.

Cleverley, W.O. 1989. Break-even analysis in the new payor environment. *Hospital Topics* 67, no. 2:36–37.

Finkler, S.A. 1985. Using break-even analysis under DRGs. *Hospital Cost Accounting Advisor* 1, no. 1:1, 4–6.

Horngren, C.T., and G. Foster. 1991. *Cost accounting: A managerial emphasis.* 7th ed. Englewood Cliffs, NJ: Prentice-Hall.

Kohlman, H.A. April 1984. Determining a contribution margin for DRG profitability. *Healthcare Financial Management*:108–110.

Margrif, F.D. 1989. Getting to the bottom line. Hospitals' survival may hinge on the contribution margin. *Health Progress* 70, no. 6:42–45.

EXERCISES

QUESTIONS FOR DISCUSSION

1. True or false: Average costs fall as volume rises, as a result of fixed costs.
2. True or false: As long as the revenue per patient is at least equal to the variable cost per patient, the service or program will break even.
3. True or false: It is essential that breakeven analysis always consider all costs related to a program or service, including the joint costs.
4. What is the essence of using breakeven analysis for multiple services and/or multiple prices?
5. What are some assumptions underlying breakeven analysis that require consideration by a manager employing the technique?
6. Why is volume considered to be critical for any new venture?
7. When a health care organization tries to determine what type of patients it should attempt to attract, what is the most critical financial measure that should be considered?

PROBLEMS

1. Your hospital is considering adding a new service, which encompasses several DRGs. If you add the service, you will get patients in each of several DRGs for which you do not currently have any admissions. You are given the following data:

Estimated Number of New Patients	DRG	Reimbursement Rate ($)	Variable Costs ($)
150	4	400	100
100	5	600	500
250	6	200	100

There will be no fixed cost specifically associated with any one of the three new DRGs. The fixed costs for the new service that makes up these three DRGs will be $25,000. The joint overhead costs of the hospital are $500,000, currently being allocated to the hospital's three existing services. How many admissions in each of the new DRGs will be needed to break even on the new service?

2. (Note: This problem has been adapted from an earlier problem presented by Horngren,* which came originally from a CPA exam; refer to Application 5-1.) Aspen Hospital allocates overhead costs to departments such as pediatrics, maternity, psychiatric, and so forth. Aspen charges each separate department for common services such as meals and laundry and for administrative services such as billings, collections, and so forth.

For the year ended June 30, 1994, the operating room department at Aspen Hospital charged each patient an average of $1,650 per operation and had revenue of $2,656,500.

Expenses charged by the hospital to the operating room department for the year ended June 30, 1994, were as follows:

	Basis of Allocation	
	Operations ($)	Space ($)
Sanitation		112,800
Laundry	78,000	
Laboratory, other than direct charges to patients	97,800	
Pharmacy	83,800	
Repairs and maintenance	95,200	7,140
General administration		331,760
Rent		375,320
Billings and collections	90,000	
Bad debt expense	97,000	
Other	21,700	125,980
	563,500	953,000

*Horngren, C.T. and Foster, G. 1987. *Cost accounting: A managerial emphasis.* 6th ed. Englewood Cliffs, N.J.: Prentice-Hall, 1987:82–83.

Note: Solutions to the Exercises can be found in Appendix A.

The only personnel directly employed by the operating room are supervising nurses, scrub nurses, and circulating nurses. The hospital has minimum personnel requirements based on total operations. Hospital requirements beginning at the minimum expected level of operations follow:

Annual Number of Operations	Scrub Nurses	Circulating Nurses	Supervising Nurses
800–1,400	11	6	2
1,401–1,700	12	6	2
1,701–2,372	12	7	2
2,373–2,555	13	8	3

The staffing levels above represent full-time equivalents, and it should be assumed that the operating room always employs only the minimum number of required full-time equivalent personnel.

Annual salaries for each class of employee follow: supervising nurses, $68,500; scrub nurses, $59,000; and circulating nurses, $54,000.

The operating room has capacity for only 2,000 operations per year at the current time.

Calculate the minimum number of operations required for the operating room to break even for the year ending June 30, 1995. Patient demand is unknown, but assume that revenue per operation and costs remain at the same rates as last year.

3. (Refer to Application 5-2.) New Hospital has $200,000 of fixed overhead costs. It has the following three types of patients:

	Price ($)	Variable Cost ($)	Average Length of Stay (Days)	Average Length of OR Procedure (Hours)
DRG 1	8,000	7,700	2	1
DRG 2	2,000	1,000	3	4
DRG 3	5,000	3,000	8	7

When New Hospital plans its new marketing campaign, what type of patient should they try to attract, assuming:

1. They are not near capacity in any area.
2. They are nearly full and can take a limited number of additional patient days.
3. They have plenty of beds but are running out of operating room time.

Application 5-1

Using Breakeven Analysis with Step-Fixed Costs

Steven A. Finkler, PhD, CPA

In a recent issue of *HCMA* (Vol. 1, No. 4), a number of potential problems with the use of breakeven analysis were discussed. These included problems related to multiple products, changing prices, changing costs, and uncertainty. This article deals with one additional specific problem—step-fixed costs.

Breakeven analysis requires classification of costs into fixed and variable components. A contribution margin per unit is calculated (price minus variable cost). That amount represents how much money is available from each unit to contribute toward covering fixed costs, or toward generating a profit. The breakeven quantity is the minimal volume at which the total contribution margin from all units is sufficient to cover the fixed costs.

Thus, as long as cost behavior approximates that shown in Figure 5-1-1 or Figure 5-1-2, the model works. In Figure 5-1-1 we see that fixed costs stay constant as volume increases. For example, at a volume of B, costs would be $A. At any other volume, costs would still be $A. Variable costs increase in direct proportion with volume (Figure 5-1-2). At volume B, variable costs would be $C. At a volume lower than B,

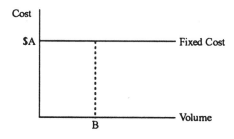

Figure 5-1-1 Graph of Fixed Costs

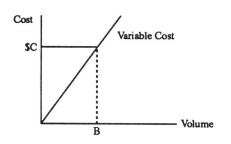

Figure 5-1-2 Graph of Variable Costs

costs would be less than $C. At a volume higher than B, costs would be greater than $C.

Fixed and variable costs can be combined in one graph by adding the fixed costs at any volume (e.g., $A) to the variable costs at that volume (e.g., $C), to determine the total costs ($A + $C) (Figure 5-1-3). The traditional breakeven

Source: Reprinted from Steven A. Finkler, "Using Breakeven Analysis with Step-Fixed Costs," *Hospital Cost Management and Accounting,* Vol. 1, No. 8, November 1989, pp. 1–5. Copyright 1989, Aspen Publishers, Inc.

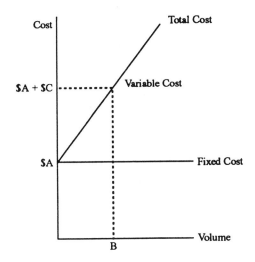

Figure 5-1-3 Graph of the Total Costs

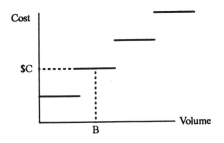

Figure 5-1-5 Graph of Step-Fixed Costs

chart can be determined (Figure 5-1-4) by adding revenue to the graph and then comparing the total costs to total revenue. The breakeven point occurs when the total revenue and total cost line in Figure 5-1-4 intersect.

Unfortunately, in most hospitals, the largest part of the hospital's costs—staffing—tends to be of a step-fixed nature, as shown in Figure

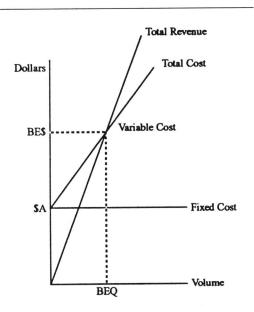

Figure 5-1-4 Breakeven Graph

5-1-5. Hospitals do not hire an additional hour of nursing time, or housekeeping time, or dietitian time, if there is one additional patient day. While these labor costs are not fixed over wide swings in volume, they are fixed over smaller volume changes. Therefore they are not really variable costs, nor are they really fixed costs. This article answers the question of how these costs should be treated in breakeven calculations.

A SIMPLISTIC SOLUTION

The approach often taken with respect to this problem is to ignore it. All costs are classified as either fixed or variable, and regular breakeven analysis (i.e., breakeven volume equals the fixed cost divided by the contribution margin) is applied. Implicitly or explicitly, the step costs are treated as being either fixed or variable.

In some cases this may create a reasonable approximation of reality. Suppose that we expect to have 6 hours of nursing care per 24-hour patient day. If agency nurses are hired on a daily basis, nursing labor will not be perfectly variable—it will not increase 6 hours for each extra patient day. First, agency nurses will be hired in 8-hour increments, not 6-hour increments. Second, the 6 hours needed are spread over a 24-hour day, not over a single 8-hour shift.

However, if nursing labor increases by 3 nursing shifts (i.e., 1 extra nurse per shift for 3 shifts) for each extra 4 patient days, then we can assume the cost to be variable without creating major errors in the analysis. (Note that 4 patient days @ 6 hours of nursing care per patient day implies a need for 24 hours of nursing care, or 1 more nurse per shift for that day.)

Even in this case, however, the error is somewhat greater than one might assume. If average daily volume on a unit rises by 1 patient, that would imply 365 additional patient days over the course of a year. Suppose that we have a nursing unit with 30 beds, and this year the unit had an average census of 20. At 6 hours per patient, that would require 120 nursing hours, or 15 nurses per day. For simplicity assume that 5 nurses work each of 3 shifts.

If our census were to rise next year to 21, what would happen to staffing? We would need an additional 2 hours of nursing care per shift. Would we float in a nurse or hire an agency nurse for each of the 3 shifts (pay for 24 hours because patient needs rose by 6 hours)? Probably not.

Our staffing guide might indicate that with a census of 18–22 we staff 5 nurses on each shift. Only if census fell below 18 would we float a nurse out, or if it rose above 22 would we add staff. Therefore, within that range the staffing is a fixed cost. At a census of 18 there would be 6,570 patient days per year, while at a census of 22 there would be 8,030 patient days per year. That range represents up to 1,460 patient days. Over that range staffing cost is fixed.

It is quite possible, however, that if census was 20 patients last year, it could conceivably fall to 16 or 17 patients per day on average this year, or it might rise to 23 or 24 patients. This implies a staffing range of 12 to 18 nurses for this unit per day (4, 5, or 6 nurses per shift). In dollar terms, this range would represent a very wide possible swing for a fixed cost. But to treat the cost as variable is not very satisfactory, since there is a substantial volume range in the middle over which the cost would be fixed.

In other areas of the hospital, the step nature of costs may be even more pronounced. For example, dietitians may prepare more or fewer meals, but only a substantial volume swing would result in a change in the number of employees in that department.

A More Useful Approach

An alternative approach to this problem, although it is somewhat more complicated, will provide a substantially improved calculation. This approach requires us to assume that we will require only the lowest staffing level possible, and to treat the step cost as a fixed cost. When the breakeven calculation is performed, the result may indicate a breakeven level at which the volume exceeds the capacity limits of the step cost item. In that case the step cost will have to be raised, and the breakeven recalculated, until a feasible solution is attained.

Example

Aspen Hospital is considering whether to open an outpatient lab. They are unsure how many tests would be processed by the lab, and would like to know the breakeven quantity. For this example we will assume that only one type of lab test is performed. That, of course, is highly unrealistic. The problem of multiple products has been widely discussed in the accounting literature (see, e.g., *Hospital Cost Accounting Advisor*, Vol. 1, No. 1, June 1985). However, in order to focus on the issue of step costs, we will not consider multiple products in the example.

Certain costs of the laboratory will clearly be variable, such as various chemicals and reagents used. Other costs will clearly be fixed costs, such as the salary of the laboratory administrator. Many other costs will be step costs, such as lab technician labor and some types of equipment.

We will assume that the variable costs per test are $.25. We will further assume that the fixed costs are $200,000 per year. In this simple example we will assume that labor has the following pattern:

Volume of Tests	Number of Techs
0– 5,000	.5
5,000–10,000	1.0
10,000–15,000	1.5
15,000–20,000	2.0
20,000–25,000	2.5
25,000–30,000	3.0
30,000–35,000	3.5

It is expected that lab tech salaries will be $25,000 including benefits.

Equipment related to this particular test has the following capacities:

Volume of Tests	Number of Sets of Equipment
0–13,000	1
13,001–26,000	2
26,001–39,000	3

The equipment for the test costs $30,000 per complete set. Aspen Hospital believes that on average they will receive $22 for each outpatient lab test performed. What is the breakeven volume?

The basic breakeven formula is as follows:

$$\text{Breakeven Quantity} = \text{Fixed Cost}/(\text{Price} - \text{Variable Cost})$$

Therefore, if we assume that there will be only .5 technicians and 1 set of equipment, the total fixed costs would be the $200,000 basic fixed cost, plus $12,500 for one-half technician, plus $30,000 for one set of equipment, or a total fixed cost of $242,500. The price is $22, and the variable costs are $.25. Therefore,

$$\begin{aligned}\text{Breakeven Quantity} &= \$242,500/(\$22.00 - \$.25)\\ &= \$242,500/\$21.75\\ &= 11,150 \text{ tests.}\end{aligned}$$

Unfortunately, when we examine our step cost items, we find that this volume is feasible with one set of equipment, but would require 1.5 technicians. Therefore, this is not a feasible breakeven solution.

The next step would be to recalculate the breakeven problem, using the staffing and equipment costs relevant at a volume of 11,150 tests. That is, we use the result from the first calculation to set the step costs for the next round of calculations. At a volume of 11,150 tests, we would need 1.5 technicians and 1 set of equipment. Therefore our new fixed costs are $200,000 plus $37,500 for 1.5 technicians plus $30,000, or a total of $267,500. Our breakeven calculation would be

$$\begin{aligned}\text{Breakeven Quantity} &= \$267,500/(\$22.00 - \$.25)\\ &= \$267,500/\$21.75\\ &= 12,300 \text{ tests.}\end{aligned}$$

[Note that the result of the calculation is actually 12,299. However, some rounding is appropriate as a reminder that in real life, things seldom work out exactly according to analyses.]

The breakeven quantity of 12,300 tests is a feasible result because it requires only 1 set of equipment and 1.5 techs, which is the amount that we have built into the calculation. If the breakeven result had been above 13,000, we would have had to recalculate fixed costs to allow for additional equipment and then perform the breakeven calculation again.

Starting the breakeven analysis under the assumption that all step costs will be at their minimal values is a valuable technique, because it prevents us from failing to find the lowest possible breakeven volume. In the situation of step costs, it is quite possible for there to be more than one breakeven point.

For example, in the above situation we now know that there is a feasible breakeven point at 12,300 tests. Suppose that instead of starting at the lowest level, we had assumed that actual volume would be 13,500 tests, and then tried to find the breakeven point around that level. If we were to try the breakeven model assuming staffing and equipment costs appropriate for 13,500 tests, the cost of two sets of equipment would have to be included. In many cases this might push the breakeven point to a higher level. For instance, at 13,500 tests the fixed costs would be $200,000 plus $37,500 for 1.5 technicians, plus $60,000 for 2 sets of equipment, or a total fixed cost of $307,500. Then,

$$\begin{aligned}\text{Breakeven Quantity} &= \$307,500/(\$22.00 - \$.25)\\ &= \$307,500/\$21.75\\ &= 14,140 \text{ tests.}\end{aligned}$$

We would wrongly be led to believe that there was no feasible solution unless we had over 14,000 tests, when in fact we are able to break even at a volume of 12,300 tests. This might incorrectly lead us to believe we can't achieve a breakeven without a volume higher than we can hope to attain. This creates an interesting paradox. Above 12,300 tests we are making money. However, if we exceed 13,000 tests we will start to lose money because of the $30,000 cost of the additional equipment. Should we allow our volume to exceed 13,000 tests? That depends on how much additional volume might be available. Clearly, however, the information about potential profits from 12,300 tests to 13,000 tests is more valuable than simply knowing that we are profitable above 14,150 tests. To get this information—i.e., the lowest feasible breakeven

point—we must start the calculations assuming the lowest steps on our step fixed costs. This approach to breakeven analysis might best be referred to as an iterative approach. It requires us to go around and around until we arrive at the best solution. Although it may seem to be a bit cumbersome, in an environment in which many of the costs we deal with are step costs, this method should substantially improve the accuracy and usefulness of breakeven calculation results.

Application 5-2

Alternative Contribution Margin Measures

Steven A. Finkler, PhD, CPA

One of the most basic concepts of cost accounting is the notion of a contribution margin: the revenue received for our product less the variable costs of producing the product. However, as a management tool the specific application of contribution margin is more complicated than might at first appear.

Specifically, in maximizing a health care organization's contribution margin, we must consider constrained resources. The specific constraint will impact on the relevant approach to using contribution margin. While the organization may well desire to maximize overall contribution margin, the approach to achieve that end will not always call for trying to treat patients with the highest contribution margin per patient, nor will it always call for focusing on the highest contribution margin percent.

BASIC CONCEPTS

Before addressing the problems that arise when we apply contribution margin to management decision making, we will first discuss the basic concepts of contribution margin.

Because certain costs of operating an organization are fixed, the profitability of the organization depends largely on the volume of services it provides. Each additional patient generates revenues, and also causes us to incur additional cost. As long as the extra revenue from an additional patient exceeds the incremental cost generated by that patient, the organization will be better off.

In a definition of contribution margin, the incremental cost is often referred to as the variable cost.

$$\text{Contribution Margin} = \text{Price} - \text{Variable Cost}$$

Since fixed costs must be paid in any event, the excess of the price over the variable cost provides extra money to the organization. That money can either be used to cover fixed costs or (if all fixed costs have been covered) it provides profits.

The general rule resulting from the concept of contribution margin is that from a financial viewpoint, the organization should proceed to do anything that offers a positive contribution margin. Inherently, such output improves the overall financial well-being of the organization.

Source: Reprinted from Steven A. Finkler, "Alternative Contribution Margin Measures," *Hospital Cost Management and Accounting,* Vol. 1, No. 5, August 1989, pp. 1–4. Copyright 1989, Aspen Publishers, Inc.

The concept is important because of the great extent to which costs are allocated in health care organizations.

It is frequently the case that additional services proposed by a hospital can only be offered at a loss, if average costs are compared to revenues. However, average costs include an allocation of fixed overhead. In many cases that fixed overhead cost will be incurred whether the new service is offered or not. All that is happening is that some of that cost is being shifted from elsewhere in the organization to the new service.

Since that shifting of cost makes other areas of the organization more profitable (or reduces their loss), that benefit should be considered before deciding the new service loses money and should not be undertaken.

We can overcome that cost allocation problem by evaluating the new service based on its contribution margin. If the additional revenues generated by the new service exceed the additional costs the organization incurs, then there is a positive contribution and the service should be offered. The profits of the organization as a whole will increase, even if the specific new service shows a loss.

In applying cost-volume-profit analysis in this way, one must be aware that often additional volume causes some fixed cost items to rise as well. The usual definition of contribution margin as being price minus variable cost is not quite correct. Actually, the contribution is extra revenue less extra cost. We must subtract all costs (whether fixed, step-fixed or variable) that will be incurred only if the service or the volume expansion is undertaken.

CONTRIBUTION MARGIN PER PATIENT VS. CONTRIBUTION MARGIN PERCENT

The concept of contribution margin is extremely valuable in helping management to make correct decisions about whether or not to offer a new service, or expand volume. For example, if an HMO offers to generate an increased volume for us, at a cut-rate (less than average cost) price, we can use this notion to determine whether or not such an offer is financially attractive in the short run.

In the long run we would like to avoid it, because it fails to provide enough money to replace plant and equipment. In the short run we are already committed to depreciation and interest on our existing plant, and any positive contribution margin is better than an empty bed. Some may disagree, saying that once price cuts are started there is no stopping them. In reality, however, the only way to avoid price cuts to gain volume is to either collude (which is illegal) or reduce industry capacity. Since cut-rate pricing doesn't allow enough money to replace plant and equipment, it eventually leads to a reduction in the number of beds, and that long-run capacity decrease will allow hospitals to stop offering discounts.

In dealing with short-run decisions, we are often faced with a specific offer, such as one from an HMO, in which the appropriate contribution margin measure is straightforward. For example, if they were to guarantee 100 normal birth deliveries at a fixed price per patient, we could compare that price to the incremental costs per maternity patient to determine profitability. The volume involved is also an important consideration. One more patient might just increase variable costs, while 100 more patients might necessitate a new monitor. In either case, however, the focus is the contribution margin per patient for the maternity patients involved.

Often, however, cost-volume-profit analysis cuts across patient types. Many organizations therefore focus on the contribution margin ratio. This ratio is the contribution margin divided by the price. Thus a patient with a price of $1,000, and variable costs of $700, would have a contribution margin of $300, or a contribution margin ratio of .3 ($300/$1,000), more commonly referred to as 30%.

Now the problems for management decisions may arise. Suppose that our marketing manager has identified three different types of patients for which we might have a chance of increasing volume. The question is which type should be the first priority of our marketing efforts. Assume the following information:

	DRG X	DRG Y	DRG Z
Revenue per patient	$1,000	$3,000	$9,000
Incremental cost per patient	$ 600	$2,400	$9,100
Contribution margin per patient	$ 400	$ 600	$(100)
Contribution margin ratio	40%	20%	–1%

Which of these three types of patients would we most like to attract? Without the benefit of contribution margin analysis, the marketing director would probably pursue DRG Z. After all, without doubt our revenues rise most rapidly as we attract more of that type of patient. And, given the underlying costs, we might even find that other hospitals won't fight particularly hard to retain them.

Marketing managers tend to be oriented toward revenues. Raising revenues is a key indicator of their success. However, revenues that are accompanied by substantial cost increases are not of financial benefit to the hospital. So an immediate benefit of contribution margin analysis is to steer us away from a revenue focus and toward a profitability focus.

But should we try to attract more of DRG X or DRG Y? A conflict between the two is readily apparent. DRG Y has the higher contribution margin of $600 per patient. DRG X has the higher contribution margin percent of 40% of revenues. Which is the more relevant measure to use in decision making?

THE ISSUE OF CONSTRAINTS

The answer to that question depends on constrained resources within the hospital environment. Some hospital managers do generally focus on contribution margin per patient, and some do focus on contribution margin percent.

If the hospital expects its total revenues to be constrained—for example, if it is in a state that has an overall budget cap on the hospital, then the best approach is that which maximizes the contribution margin percent. In other words, for every dollar that is received, you want to keep the largest amount of that dollar as contribution margin. Thus DRG Y patients, with their high contribution margin per patient, would be less desirable, because their high price would push us to the overall budget cap quicker than DRG X patients.

On the other hand, if there is no limit on the number of patients, or the amount of revenue, DRG Y would be preferable, because for every extra patient, the contribution margin increases by the largest amount.

However, neither of these approaches is adequate. Note that in the last paragraph we said "if there is no limit on the number of patients." However, often that will not be the case. There will be some constraining factor which places a limit on the number of patients in total or of a particular type.

For example, suppose that the hospital is nearly full. Then the number of patient-days available are limited. In pursuing patients we will need to know how much of the constraining factor they consume. Suppose for example, that DRG X has an average length of stay of 4 days, while DRG Y has an average length of stay of 10 days. Then we can calculate a contribution margin per patient day:

	DRG X	DRG Y
Revenue per patient	$1,000	$3,000
Incremental cost per patient	–600	–2,400
Contribution margin per patient	$ 400	$ 600
Divided by length of stay	÷4	÷10
Contribution margin per patient day	$ 100	$ 60

As you can readily see, if the number of beds (and therefore patient days available) is limited, the desirable marginal patient switches from DRG Y, at $600 per patient vs. $400 per patient, to DRG X, at $100 of additional contribution margin per patient day as compared to $60 per day. Thus the fact that the hospital is almost full has a direct bearing on what type of patient we want to try to attract.

The specific constraint that is most pressing is likely to differ in different institutions. For example, another hospital might have a low enough occupancy that patient days were not a crucial issue. For them, $600 per patient would be better than $400, even though the patient stays much longer. But what if that hospital has limited operating room capacity, and the DRG Y patient would consume more operating room hours? In that case we would want to market ourselves in such a way as to maximize the contribution margin per operating room hour consumed.

Whenever the hospital is going to make a formal effort to increase volume in some way and to increase contribution margin in total, some resource is likely to be constrained. Even if the hospital has plenty of capacity, a simple rule of getting the patient with the highest contribution margin is unlikely to be correct. This is because different patients are not likely to be equally easy to attract.

Suppose that the marketing department can attract two DRG X patients with the same cost and effort as it would take to attract one DRG Y patient. In that case the effort to gain $600 of contribution from a Y patient would be the same as the effort to gain $800 of contribution margin from the X patients. The constraining resource in essence becomes the time and effort of the marketing department.

In most hospitals multiple constraints will exist. Beds, and operating room capacity, and marketing efforts may all be constrained. From a mathematical standpoint, all of the constraints could be built into a model which is solved using linear programming.

However, that level of sophistication is probably unnecessary. It would, as a practical point, make more sense to simply focus on one or two of the most pressing constraints, and make sure that our efforts are in accord with maximizing contribution margin to the hospital given that constraint or those constraints.

For example, suppose that both our outpatient clinic and our inpatient beds were running at 90% of capacity. Suppose further that the contribution margin for inpatient care is substantially higher per hour of marketing effort than for outpatient care. In that case, marketing efforts should focus on filling the inpatient beds with patients having the highest contribution margin per patient day. When the inpatient side is full, the effort can swing over to the outpatient side.

Contribution margin analysis can be an extremely valuable management tool. The key to using it effectively, however, is to move away from the limited notion of attracting patients with the highest contribution margin per patient. In many respects that approach is as naive as trying to maximize revenue per patient regardless of cost. Instead, managers should consider the constraint in the organization that is most limiting, and assure that as we move toward the limitation imposed by that constraint, we are maximizing the contribution per unit of that constraining resource.

6

Costing for Nonroutine Decisions

Goals of This Chapter

1. Explain the role of cost information for making nonroutine decisions.
2. Discuss the concept and use of relevant costs.
3. Consider the role of nonfinancial issues in making nonroutine decisions.
4. Explain the irrelevant nature of sunk costs for decision making.
5. Discuss the impact of volume on decisions.
6. Discuss some examples of nonroutine decisions.
7. Define and discuss cost-benefit analysis and cost-effectiveness analysis.

Key Terms Used in This Chapter

Average costs; cost-benefit analysis; cost-effectiveness analysis; differential costs; direct costs; fixed costs; incremental costs; indirect costs; long run; marginal costs; nonroutine decisions; relevant costs; short run; total costs; variable costs.

Note: Key terms appear in italics when first used in the chapter. All key terms are defined in the Glossary.

COST INFORMATION FOR NONROUTINE DECISIONS

In the changing financial environment for health care organizations, managers are confronted with making more frequent decisions that go beyond the everyday routine in running a health care organization. Any one of these decisions can have important consequences for the finances of the organization. It is critical that managers choose relevant information for making these decisions.

It should be clear at this point in the book that there are many different measures of cost: *direct costs* and *indirect costs, average costs, total costs* and *marginal costs, fixed costs* and *variable costs*, and so forth. It is very easy to mistakenly use inappropriate information as the basis for a decision. Therefore, it is worth considering how to make sure decisions are based on information that is relevant to the specific decision.

Financial managers need to develop a method for analyzing cost information that will provide a sound basis for critical nonroutine decisions on problems such as:

- adding a new service;
- dropping an old service;
- expanding or cutting back a program or service;
- performing certain tasks, such as laboratory tests, in-house versus purchasing them from an outside company; and
- establishing charges for services to health maintenance organizations (HMOs) and preferred provider organizations (PPOs).

This chapter discusses how one can address such questions, considering only the costs relevant to the decision.

Identifying Alternatives

The first step in nonroutine decision making is to identify alternative courses of action. When organizations are in severe financial trou-

ble, they often find that they are able to drop services, cut staffing, and make a variety of changes that they would never have considered possible. One secret for avoiding getting into financial trouble in the first place is to consider a wide range of possible alternatives instead of accepting as fact that things must be the way they are. If alternatives are considered before a crisis is at hand, the solutions are often far more palatable and less traumatic than they otherwise might be.

In today's environment, problems and potential alternative solutions tend to be plentiful. Should a hospital open a home health agency or acquire a nursing home to benefit from the ripple effects of shorter length of stay? Should a hospital contract with an HMO to provide hospital services at a discount to fill currently empty beds? Should a health care organization open its own HMO? Should a hospital expand or close its outpatient clinic that currently loses money on each patient seen?

The first step is to realize that health care organizations are dynamic, changing institutions. Over time, managers should, on a regular basis, attempt to identify areas for possible improvement. This will automatically lead to a need to evaluate nonroutine decisions.

Defining Relevant Costs

Most health care organizations do not have trouble identifying problems and coming up with possible alternative solutions. The key issue in nonroutine decision making is correct identification of the costs that are relevant to the decision at hand.

The goal of using *relevant cost* information in the analysis is to show how financial results would differ for each of the alternatives. This will allow managers to select the best possible alternative. The first step is to consider what would happen if no action occurs and things continue as they are. That gives a baseline set of revenues and expenses.

Next, the revenues and expenses that would likely occur under each alternative must be considered. This may seem to be an overwhelming task. However, it is substantially simplified by the fact that some revenues and costs will remain the same regardless of which alternative is chosen. One key to understanding relevant costing is that costs and revenues common to all alternatives can be ignored. Selection of a superior alternative is based on the differences among alternatives rather than on the common costs or revenues.

At first glance, this would appear basically to require just an analysis of fixed and variable costs. If certain costs are fixed regardless of what we do, they are not relevant to the decision. They will be incurred regardless of which alternative is selected. The relevant costs (and relevant revenues) are the ones that will be different for each alternative. This is an oversimplification, as we will see later in this chapter.

Considering Nonfinancial Issues

Care must be taken in making decisions based on the relevant costing approach. Financial results are not the only data needed to make decisions about the services and programs offered by a health care organization.

Suppose that the analysis of costs indicated that open heart surgery loses money. It might still be in the best interest of a hospital to retain this service. Perhaps the prestige gained from having the service attracts both physicians and patients to some of the hospital's more profitable services. The profit gained on these services may more than offset the direct losses on open heart surgery.

However, even if it appears that a particular alternative action does not make sense from a broadly interpreted financial point of view, that does not necessarily mean that the course of action must be rejected. Health care organizations do not always have to make decisions on the basis of the best financial outcome. A health care organization may well decide that its mission requires certain services be offered, whether at a profit or a loss. However, the financial implications of such decisions should be clearly understood. Long-run survival of a health care organization can only be ensured if

areas generating losses are specifically identified and sources of philanthropy or profits that can offset those losses also are identified.

SUNK COSTS ARE IRRELEVANT

Suppose that you buy a piece of laboratory equipment for $100,000 to perform a certain test. The equipment can do 100,000 tests over its useful life. Suppose further that the other costs directly associated with each test are $4. Then, the day after you buy the machine, a new machine becomes available. This one also costs $100,000 and can do 100,000 tests over its lifetime, but it lowers the other costs per test from $4 to $2. The machine you just bought cannot be sold because it has suddenly become obsolete. You can continue to use the machine you just bought, or you can throw it away and buy a new one. If you throw it away, you will incur a loss of $100,000. What should you do?

The solution involves employing the traditional cost accounting rule, "It's no use crying over spilled milk" (alternatively referred to as, "Sunk costs are sunk"). The $100,000 spent yesterday has been spent, no matter what. The key in nonroutine decision making is to look to the future rather than the past. In the future, we can spend an additional $400,000 to perform tests using the old machine, or $100,000 to buy the new machine and $200,000 to perform tests using it, for a total of $300,000. Table 6-1 shows these calculations. From the table, we can see that the organization spends $100,000 less if it buys the new machine.

Of course, this does not figure in the cost of the old machine. That cost is a sunk cost. Whether you decide to buy the new machine or not, you will have spent $100,000 on the old

Table 6-1 Sunk Cost Example

	Keep Old Machine	Buy New Machine
Cost of new machine		$100,000
Cost of tests @ $4	$400,000	
Cost of tests @ $2		200,000
Total costs	$400,000	$300,000

machine (purchased just yesterday). Because that cost is the same under either alternative, it is not a relevant cost. If you keep the old machine, you will spend an additional $400,000. If you buy the new machine, you will spend an additional $300,000.

Table 6-2 repeats the example including the cost of the old machine. Note that whether or not we buy the new machine, we have incurred the cost of the old machine. The difference between the $500,000 total and the $400,000 total is still $100,000. Often the calculations in Table 6-1 are considered preferable to those in Table 6-2 because they stress that sunk costs are not relevant for making decisions.

In retrospect, buying the old machine had a bad outcome. It would have been cheaper to wait the extra day and buy the new machine. However, such decisions will often be made in an area of rapidly changing technology. Although it turned out to have a bad outcome (it cost you $100,000 for a machine that became obsolete a day later), it was not necessarily a wrong decision, assuming you could not reasonably have predicted how soon the new technology would become available.

It would, however, be both a bad outcome and a bad decision to fail to shift to the new technology now. To avoid explicitly recognizing the loss on the old machine, you would be incurring additional costs of $400,000 on top of the cost of the old machine, instead of additional costs of only $300,000 (including the acquisition cost of the new machine) on top of the cost of the old machine. Keeping the old machine costs a total of $500,000, whereas buying the new machine costs a total of only $400,000 including the cost of *both* machines.

Table 6-2 Sunk Cost Example, Including Sunk Costs

	Keep Old Machine	Buy New Machine
Cost of old machine	$100,000	$100,000
Cost of new machine		100,000
Cost of tests @ $4	400,000	
Cost of tests @ $2		200,000
Total costs	$500,000	$400,000

THE ROLE OF VOLUME

Many readers have heard the story of the dress manufacturer who says he is losing money on every dress he sells, but he isn't worried because he'll make it up in volume! That logic may, in fact, be quite correct.

Suppose that fixed costs are $5,000, and variable costs are $5 per unit. At 1,000 units, the total cost is $10,000, made up of $5,000 fixed cost plus $5,000 variable cost ($5 per unit times 1,000 units).

Fixed costs	$ 5,000
Variable costs	
1,000 units @ $5	+ 5,000
Total cost	$10,000

The cost per unit is $10 ($10,000 total cost divided by 1,000 units). At a price of $8 per unit, the manufacturer loses $2 a unit, for a total loss of $2,000.

Revenue 1,000 units @ $8	$ 8,000
Costs (from above)	−10,000
Loss	($ 2,000)

It would appear foolish to increase volume and lose $2 per unit on a greater number of units.

However, at 2,000 units, the total cost would be only $15,000 because the fixed costs do not rise.

Fixed costs	$ 5,000
Variable costs	
2,000 units @ $5	+ 10,000
Total cost	$15,000

At a selling price of $8 per unit, the revenues are $16,000 and a profit of $1,000 is earned!

Revenue 2,000 units @ $8	$ 16,000
Costs (from above)	−15,000
Profit	$ 1,000

This is not magic; it is simply relevant costing. The fixed costs are not relevant to the decision to increase production. The fixed costs of $5,000 exist regardless of volume (assuming we have not exceeded the capacity of our plant and equipment).

When we double production, variable costs double from $5,000 to $10,000. Thus, we can produce an extra 1,000 units for an extra cost of $5,000. The extra revenue is $8,000. The extra profit is $3,000. Because the only additional costs incurred are the variable costs, they are the only relevant costs that should be considered in making the decision.

Problems with Average Cost Information

The usefulness of average cost information is extremely limited in making nonroutine decisions. Average costs can be quite misleading because they are calculated at a particular volume. In the above situation, the original average cost was $10, while the price was $8. However, as volume increased, the average cost fell. At a volume of 2,000, the average cost was only $7.50. If we use the original average costs of $10 per unit as a basis for our decision making, we would tend to reject any output when prices are less than $10.

However, our problem with average costs goes beyond the fact that they change as volume changes. Suppose that volume rises from 1,000 to 1,500. Are the extra 500 units worthwhile?

Fixed costs	$ 5,000
Variable costs	
1,500 units @ $5	+ 7,500
Total cost	$ 12,500

At 1,500 units produced, the total cost is $12,500 ($5,000 fixed cost plus $7,500 variable). The average cost has fallen from $10 at production of 1,000 units to $8.33 ($12,500 divided by 1,500 units) at production of 1,500 units. If the price remains $8, which is less than the average cost of $8.33, what should we do?

Breakeven analysis, as discussed in the previous chapter, indicates that we would lose money at a volume of 1,500 units. (Q = breakeven point, FC = fixed costs, P = price, VC = variable costs.)

$$Q = \frac{FC}{P - VC}$$

$$= \frac{\$5,000}{\$8 - \$5}$$

$$= \$ 1,667$$

We need a total of 1,667 to break even. It would not be attractive to start this service knowing that volume would be only 1,500.

If we are already making 1,000 units, does it pay to produce 500 more? The extra 500 units are definitely profitable. Each unit generates $8 of revenues against only $5 of additional cost. The average cost of $8.33 is inappropriate for decision making because it includes and is influenced by fixed costs. If the extra production does not increase fixed costs, then only the variable costs should be considered. On the other hand, if additional fixed costs must be incurred, then they are obviously relevant to the decision and must be included in the analysis.

TERMINOLOGY FOR RELEVANT COSTING

In nonroutine decision-making, relevant costs are often referred to as *marginal, additional, differential,* or *incremental* costs. The advantage of using these terms is that they minimize confusion between the terms relevant cost and variable cost. Whereas variable costs are always relevant, relevant costs may also include other costs. The analysis should capture all costs that would change under a given alternative, even if they are previously defined as fixed costs.

Relevant costs are not categorized as fixed and variable costs, but rather as costs that would or would not change under each specific alternative. Therefore, using terms such as *incremental* costs more accurately describes the information relevant to the decision than does either *average* or *variable* costs.

EXAMPLES OF NONROUTINE DECISIONS

Adding or Dropping a Service or Program

Many services offered by a health care organization are essential to the basic functions of that organization. On the other hand, a service may exist because a small group of physicians was interested in it, or because it was viewed at one time as serving a particular need of the community, or because it was seen as a potential moneymaker.

Over time, the needs of the community may have changed, or expected profits for the service may never have materialized. Should the service be discontinued? Alternatively, should new services be added to a health care organization? The issues involved in these decisions are addressed in the following example.

Case Example: An Outpatient Clinic

Suppose that the fixed costs of operating an outpatient clinic are $500,000 and the variable costs are $20 per visit. At 10,000 visits per year, the average cost per visit is $70:

Volume (A)	Fixed Cost (B)	Variable Cost Per Visit (C)	Total Variable Cost (D) = (A)×(C)	Full Cost (E) = (B)+(D)	Average Cost (F) = (E)÷(A)
10,000	$500,000	$20	$200,000	$700,000	$70

If the average revenue received per visit is $50, the clinic is losing money. Perhaps the clinic should be shut down to avoid the current $200,000 annual loss.

One argument against closing the clinic is that the public must have access to care. If we view health care organizations as more than simply businesses, we may be willing to absorb the $200,000 loss for the good of the community. This is a reasonable philosophy, assuming we can ensure a $200,000 subsidy from either philanthropic funds or from profits generated elsewhere in the organization.

However, even a less benevolent organization should be cautious about a decision to close the clinic. Remember, relevant revenues and costs are those that would change based on a new alternative. Closing down the clinic is one of the alternatives. All revenues would be lost if the clinic closes. All variable costs could be avoided as well. However, it is unclear how much of the fixed costs, especially overhead, could be avoided.

This is an issue that requires close examination. It is likely that some fixed costs, such as annual capital expenditures to replace worn-out or obsolete equipment, could be avoided if the clinic is closed. On the other hand, some of the fixed cost undoubtedly covers depreciation on the building and an allocation of joint overhead costs from the parent organization.

To the extent that such costs would continue to exist, they are not relevant to the decision. To improve the bottom line, the amount of cost reduction must be greater than the revenue reduction. Consider the result if fixed costs of $300,000 remained if we shut down the clinic.

Currently, revenues are $500,000 (10,000 patients × $50), and costs are $700,000 ($500,000 fixed + $200,000 variable). If we close down the clinic, our revenues are $0 and our expenses are $300,000.

	Keep Clinic Open	Close Clinic
Revenues	$500,000	$ 0
Costs	−700,000	−300,000
Profit/(loss)	($200,000)	($300,000)

Thus, the organization will lose $100,000 *more* by closing down the money-losing clinic than it would by keeping it open.

Too often, in making nonroutine decisions to drop a service or program that is losing money, managers forget to calculate the portion of the loss that results from the allocation of overhead that would exist in any case. Clear thinking in this area is crucial to achieving financially sound decisions.

When you are considering adding a service or program, you must keep the same factors in mind. Generally, the calculation of whether a new service would be profitable includes consideration of all costs, including overhead. However, a correct decision on whether to add the service should be based only on the incremental costs. If the new service means more additional revenue than additional costs, the service should be added, even if according to traditional accounting methods it appears to produce a loss. The reason this makes sense is that when overhead is allocated to the new program or service, there is less overhead allocated elsewhere. If the revenues generated by the new service are greater than the incremental or added costs of the new service, then any losses it incurs will be more than offset by the increased profits of the other services—profits due to their lower overhead allocations.

The key question for this, and for all nonroutine costing decisions, is whether the organization will be more profitable if it accepts the proposed alternative than it would be if it did not. The average or full costs of the cost objective as determined by the accounting system are not as relevant to the decision as the amount by which the total revenues and total costs of the organization would change.

Expanding or Reducing a Service or Program

A more common problem for most health care organizations is deciding whether a service should be vigorously expanded or allowed to decline in volume. We can readily apply the dress manufacturer's logic regarding volume to the example of the outpatient clinic. What would happen if rather than closing the clinic, or leaving it as is, we expanded this service? Suppose that we could increase clinic volume by 100 percent—to 20,000 patients—by actively marketing the clinic, emphasizing its convenience, high quality, extended hours, and so forth.

The additional 10,000 visits would increase revenues by $500,000 (10,000 × $50), but would only increase costs by $200,000 (10,000 × $20). With 20,000 patients, the total costs are $900,000 and the total revenues are $1,000,000.

	Existing Volume	Expanded Volume
Revenues	$500,000	$1,000,000
Costs	−700,000	−900,000
Profit/(loss)	($200,000)	$ 100,000

Even though the average cost is initially $70 and the average revenue is $50, by doubling volume we can convert a $200,000 loss into a $100,000 profit. Prior to the expansion, we were losing money on every patient we saw (based on average costs of $70 and average revenue of $50), but like the dress manufacturer, we made it up in volume!

The key to the analysis is not the average cost, but the fact that each extra patient generates $50 in additional revenue but only $20 in additional cost. It is the incremental revenues and costs that tell us whether the expansion would increase health care organization profits. Application 6-1 provides an example related to expanding the quantity of services offered by a hospital.

In deciding to scale down services, we must use the same calculation. If we reduce our volume, we will not save the average cost for each unit of reduced volume. We will only save the variable costs generated by that unit.

When we consider adding or removing an entire service, we will often find that some fixed costs must be added, or can be eliminated, and these qualify as relevant costs. This happens much less often when we are merely changing the volume at which a service is offered. As a rule, unless the volume change is quite substantial, it will be the variable costs that are relevant to the decision. In the case of the clinic, it is likely that as the number of patients treated is reduced, revenues will decline proportionately ($50 per patient), but the only savings will be the $20 per patient variable cost.

Weighing the Make vs. Buy Decision

A classic problem in industry is whether to make certain products or parts or to buy them from an outside supplier. As financing systems are changing for health care organizations, this is becoming a more common problem in the health care industry.

The most frequently cited example is deciding whether a health care organization should perform all of its own laboratory tests or contract with an outside laboratory for some of the work. Qualitative issues are always a concern when we purchase from the outside. Will the tests be properly done? Will the results be available on a timely basis? Assuming we are satisfied on these points, the key financial consideration is differential costing. That is, which alternative will have lower costs?

The problem is somewhat complicated by whether we are considering a short-run or long-run decision. In the *short run,* many fixed costs already have been incurred and are no longer relevant. If we were to eliminate an existing laboratory, much of the overhead would remain.

In this case, the decision becomes a question of whether the prices offered by the outside organization are lower than the short-term incremental costs of producing the item in-house. In some cases, it may pay to maintain an internal laboratory but send certain tests out if the outside price is in fact cheaper than the variable costs associated with the test. In other cases, it may pay to close the laboratory. In all cases, however, we must be sure that the measure of cost for internal production is based on the money we spend to produce the item that we would avoid spending if the item is not produced. That is, do not consider internal costs that will be incurred in any case.

In long-run planning, we must consider the costs of replacing the plant and equipment. The outside bid must be matched against not only the variable costs, such as technician labor and reagents, but also the additional capital outlays.

It may well turn out that as long as we can continue to make use of the existing plant and equipment, it pays to perform laboratory tests internally. When the laboratory reaches an age at which the entire facility should be rebuilt, the appropriate decision may be to cease in-house production.

Establishing Short-Run Pricing

Another major area of concern for health care organizations is the appropriate price to charge a third party who controls the utilization of a group of patients. For example, suppose that an insurance company asks the health care organization to bid on a PPO basis for its business.

There is a great temptation to base the bid on average costs. All businesses fear that if any customers pay less than average costs, the organization will fail to recover the full costs of doing business. Certainly, if all customers but one pay exactly the average cost, and one customer pays less than the average cost, the organization will lose money for the year. On the other hand, if the only way to get some business is to bid less than average cost, and the capacity exists to handle that business, the organization will be better off to bid below average cost, as long as the bid will cover the incremental cost.

The bid represents the incremental revenue. The profits of the organization will increase any time it undertakes an alternative that generates incremental revenue that exceeds the corresponding increase in cost. One must keep in mind that the extra patients will not generate additional costs at a rate equal to average costs. They will generate additional costs at a lower rate, as long as some costs are fixed and do not increase with volume.

In the *long run,* health care organizations would not be able to afford to replace their plant and equipment if all payers paid something more than incremental costs but less than average costs. Thus, competition among health care organizations might inevitably lead to some of them being forced out of business. Although we may not be happy with that situation, we need to recognize that in the short run, our refusal to bid below average cost will cause the health care organization's profits to be lower or losses to be higher. In the current competitive environment, it is likely that another health care organization will cut its price to get the extra business. The organization that maintains prices based on average costs, paradoxically, is more likely to be the one forced out of business than the competitor that offers discounts in the short run.

There are factors that may militate against a short-run pricing strategy. For example, bidding low to get a new PPO contract may force you to lower the price you are currently charging other customers. The reduction of revenues from existing customers may more than offset the benefits from the new customer.

We have discussed here only a few of the potential nonroutine decisions that face health care organization administrators. The approach, however, is quite general. A simple test to see whether or not a rational decision is being made, in accordance with the concept of relevant costing, is to examine the effects on the profits of the health care organization. An alternative will sometimes be acceptable even if it generates revenues that are less than average costs. However, in all cases of alternatives that are acceptable based on relevant costing analysis, the total profits of the entire health care organization must be higher if the alternative is accepted than if it is rejected. Application 6-2 presents an application of relevant costing to privatization.

COST-BENEFIT AND COST-EFFECTIVENESS ANALYSIS

Managers and policy makers alike often look at nonroutine decisions in terms of whether they have a favorable cost-benefit ratio and/or whether they are cost-effective. This raises the question of what *cost-benefit analysis* (CBA) and *cost-effectiveness analysis* (CEA) are, and how they can be used to aid in making decisions. According to several leading authorities in this area, "Cost-benefit and cost effectiveness analysis have come to refer to formal analytical techniques for comparing the negative and positive consequences of alternative uses of resources. Often enshrouded in technical jargon and mathematics, CBA and CEA are really nothing more than attempts to weigh logically the pros and cons of a decision."[1]

CBA is often used in the public sector where there is no net income to serve as a guideline. The issue becomes one of determining whether the benefits of an action exceed its costs. If

$$\frac{\text{Benefits}}{\text{Costs}} > 0$$

then the project has a positive benefit/cost ratio and adds value to society. In order to determine

the ratio, it is necessary to assign values to both the costs and the benefits in monetary terms. In practice, it is difficult to assign monetary values to health care outcomes. We have trouble measuring the value of a life, and even more difficulty in measuring the difference in health outcomes that do not involve life or death.

CEA is not as ambitious as CBA, in that it does not require a measurement of the value of the benefits. Rather, it relies on using comparisons. One considers whether a project is cost-effective in comparison with some alternative approach. An approach that achieves a specific desired outcome for the least possible cost is considered to be cost-effective. If we do not have a comparison, we run into difficulties.

Consider, for example, a project that will save lives. If we know that we can save lives at a cost of $50 per life, would we consider that to be cost-effective? Certainly. However, in drawing such a conclusion, we are implicitly placing at least a minimum value on a human life by implying it is worth more than $50. This creates a difficulty in trying to establish a cut-off point. Is a project that saves lives at a cost of $10,000 per life cost-effective? How about $1 million? How about $1 billion?

Some might argue that there are many alternative options that could save lives for less than $1 billion per life saved. Therefore, the project that costs $1 billion per life is not cost-effective. In comparison with other alternatives, it costs more to accomplish its outcome of saving lives. The problem with assuming that $50 per life saved is cost-effective is that it puts a value on the benefit, rather than simply holding the benefit constant. A more CEA-oriented approach would consider different approaches to save a life, and find out which one costs least. That would be the cost-effective alternative.

Therefore, to operationalize CEA, one must compare alternatives that generate similar outcomes. For example, suppose that a hospital has been treating a certain type of patient using a particular approach. Now an alternative approach is suggested. Is the new approach cost-effective? We must first establish that the clinical outcomes are equal. Then we must show that the new approach costs less money than the old approach. If a new approach generates the exact same outcome for less money, then it is cost-effective.

Note how this avoids the problem of measuring the value of the benefits. Because we hold the benefits constant, any approach that costs less must inherently be superior to other approaches. In reality, however, it is difficult to find different techniques that yield the exact same health care outcomes.

Therefore, researchers often concentrate on alternative techniques that yield improved health outcomes at a lower cost. Suppose that a new approach can be shown to have a superior clinical result. If it is cost-effective to produce the *same* clinical result for a lower cost, then it must be cost-effective to produce an *improved* clinical result at a lower cost. This allows us to compare alternatives that have different costs and different benefits (levels of improved health), and to determine if one approach is superior, even though we are unable to assign a value to the benefits.

Will this approach work in all cases? No. It is possible for an alternative to yield an improved health benefit but to cost more. Will that approach be deemed cost-effective? No, even though the improved health may be worth the extra cost, it is not considered cost-effective because it costs more. CEA is limited to evaluating less costly alternatives with at least the same outcome. It cannot comment on the advisability of more costly alternatives that provide better outcomes.

Nevertheless, there are many areas that can be assessed using the CEA technique. Much of the discussion in this book focuses on measuring cost. Accountants must be able to help in the

next step—using the cost information for making decisions. An aid in doing that is the ability to take the CEA perspective. If an alternative is shown to be cost-effective, then we know that it is a superior alternative.

NOTE

1. K.E. Warner and B.R. Luce, *Cost-Benefit and Cost-Effectiveness Analysis in Health Care: Principles, Practice, and Potential* (Ann Arbor, Mich.: Health Administration Press, 1983), 46.

SUGGESTED READING

Brown, K., and C. Burrows. 1990. The sixth stool guaiac test: $47 million that never was. *Journal of Health Economics* 9, no. 4:429–445.

Cleverley, W.O. 1982. Marginal analysis in the health care industry. In *Handbook of health care accounting and finance,* ed. W.O. Cleverley, 169–184. Rockville, Md.: Aspen Publishers, Inc.

Finkler, S.A. 1985. Cost information for nonroutine decisions. *Hospital Cost Accounting Advisor* 1, no. 3:1–7.

Finkler, S.A., and D. Schwartzben. 1988. The cost effects of protocol systems: The marginal cost–average cost dichotomy. *Medical Care* 26, no. 9:894–906.

Goddard, M., and J. Hutton. 1991. Economic evaluation of trends in cancer therapy. Marginal or average costs? *International Journal of Technology Assessment in Health Care* 7, no. 4:594–603.

Horngren, C.T., and G. Foster. 1991. *Cost accounting: A managerial emphasis.* 7th ed. Englewood Cliffs, N.J.: Prentice-Hall.

Johannesson, M., and B. Jonsson. 1991. Cost-effectiveness analysis of hypertension treatment—A review of methodological issues. *Health Policy* 19, no. 1:55–77.

Warner, K.E., and B.R. Luce. 1983. *Cost-benefit and cost-effectiveness analysis in health care: Principles, practice, and potential.* Ann Arbor, Mich.: Health Administration Press.

EXERCISES

QUESTIONS FOR DISCUSSION

1. What are some examples of nonroutine decisions?

Note: Solutions to the Exercises can be found in Appendix A.

2. What is the goal of using relevant cost information? How are costs common to all alternatives treated?

3. Should sunk costs be carefully included or carefully excluded from a nonroutine decision analysis? Why?

4. Distinguish between cost-benefit analysis and cost-effectiveness analysis.

PROBLEMS

1. The Struggling Hospital has been pushed by its physicians to add an open heart surgery unit. This has always been resisted on the grounds that there was not adequate demand to make the unit financially reasonable. Under the DRG system, Struggling could expect to receive average reimbursement of $28,000 per open heart surgery for each of an anticipated 100 open heart surgeries per year. Incremental costs would be expected to be $30,000 per case, so a loss would be incurred.

   However, the prestige associated with offering open heart surgery would attract new affiliations. It is expected that 10 additional general practice physicians would join the staff and that each of these 10 physicians would generate 20 patients per year, spread across a wide variety of DRGs. Struggling has excess capacity and would welcome additional patients.

   It is expected that the average DRG reimbursement for these new patients would be $14,000. The average cost is expected to be $13,900. The average marginal cost is expected to be $13,200. Should Struggling add open heart surgery as a loss leader?

2. Wagner Hospital anticipates that it will have 50,000 patient days next year. This is substantially below its capacity of 70,000 patient days per year. The hospital has variable costs of $150 per patient day. Its fixed costs are $3,000,000 per year.

   a. Calculate the average cost per patient day for Wagner Hospital at a volume of 50,000 patient days and at 60,000 patient days.

   b. Assume that an HMO offers to generate 10,000 patient days per year. It currently sends no patients to Wagner Hospital. It is willing to pay a maximum flat amount of $180 per patient day. Assuming that its case-mix is similar to the current 50,000 patient days, should we accept its business?

Application 6-1

HMO Negotiations and Hospital Costs

Steven A. Finkler, PhD, CPA

During the decade of the 1990s, it is likely that more and more hospitals will come under pressure to negotiate arrangements with HMOs and PPOs. In some cases the financial impact of such arrangements (or the failure to make such arrangements) may be critical to organizational financial viability.

Often, however, hospitals enter into such arrangements without having thought through why they are making the arrangement, and what its long-term implications are. A recent study by Kralewski et al. reported a shocking finding when they noted that "The HMO knows as much (and often more) about the target hospital's cost structure as the hospital's management."[1]

If that conclusion is in fact true, it should be disturbing information for hospital managers. Negotiations with HMOs are inherently difficult. HMOs may have information about their own mix of patients that has critical financial implications. Such information may give them an edge to begin with.

If hospitals approach negotiating sessions with less information than their adversary in the negotiation it adds to the difficulties that al-

ready exist in arriving at an agreement fair to the hospital. If the HMO knows more about the hospital's own costs than the hospital knows, it removes any remaining bargaining chips the hospital may have.

WHO REALLY HAS BETTER COST INFORMATION?

Despite the claims that HMOs know more about costs than hospitals, the actual truth may be somewhat different. Perhaps HMOs just think that they know more.

For the most part HMOs get their cost information from hospital Medicare cost reports. Since these are public documents, they are easily obtained by the HMO. One can hardly assume, however, that with the hospital's cost report in hand, the HMO now knows more than the hospital. At the same time, hospital managers should realize that HMOs are likely to have some reliable sources of information.

Espionage

The Kralewski study of strategies employed by HMOs indicates that some unsophisticated industrial espionage takes place.[2] Most hospital managers would be quick to dismiss such a melodramatic possibility.

Source: Reprinted from Steven A. Finkler, "HMO Negotiations and Hospital Costs," *Hospital Cost Management and Accounting,* Vol. 3, No. 7, October 1991, pp. 1–4. Copyright 1991, Aspen Publishers, Inc.

However, it would not be surprising to find that HMOs have actually obtained some inside information that would give them an edge in the negotiations. Should the Chief Financial Officer conduct monthly lie-detector tests to see which finance department staff members are leaking information? Probably the place to look for leaks is in the medical staff.

The medical staff clearly has mixed interests. On the one hand they want the hospital to thrive. On the other hand, to the extent that members of the hospital staff are also members of an HMO, there is a clear conflict of interest. The conflict becomes severe if some of the physicians who practice at the hospital share in the profits of the HMO.

This is especially true for not-for-profit hospitals. They are prevented from treating physicians as partners who share in profits. Yet the for-profit HMO is not. That means that a reduction in hospital profits and increase in HMO profits benefits those physicians directly. The implication of this problem is that hospitals must be quite judicious in sharing cost information with physicians who are also HMO members.

Even with tight security over cost information, there is the potential for physician leaks of readily available information such as the way the hospital staffs units, or the usual occupancy of various special service units in the hospital.

The Cost Report vs. Marginal Costs

If HMOs are using the hospital's Medicare cost report, this may give the HMOs more information than a hospital manager would desire them to have. Nevertheless, it should put the hospital manager in control. Knowing what is reported as costs using the appropriate cost report methodology is very different from knowing the cost implications of an HMO contract. At best, cost reports use historical average cost information. HMO contracts, however, must be considered by the hospital on the basis of marginal or incremental costs.

To calculate whether an HMO contract is beneficial, the manager must consider the hos-

pital's financial position with the contract, and without it. In the simplest terms, what will be the total revenues and total expenses of the hospital if it has the contract, versus what will be the total revenues and total expenses of the hospital if it does not have the contract? The difference between these two calculations directly lets the manager know whether the hospital is financially better off with the contract or not.

The information needed to calculate such differences is not average costs, but rather marginal costs. The cost report may give an HMO a start in calculating marginal costs, but the hospital managers should be able to make much better estimates.

The hospital knows which units are nearly full and which are not. It knows how many more patients it can take with little or no increase in personnel costs. It knows a great deal about its fixed and variable costs. That information can be translated into approximations of marginal costs.

HMOs really cannot make good estimates of these factors. For example, based on a cost report an HMO may assume that all nursing salary costs are variable. In fact, each unit has a number of fixed personnel costs related to minimum staffing levels, head nurse salaries and clinical specialist salaries.

If the HMOs assume that all nursing unit personnel costs are variable, it will overestimate the marginal costs of the hospital. That would lead it to believe that the hospital has less room for negotiating than it actually has. It is interesting to note that the Kralewski study, which indicates that HMOs know more about hospital costs than hospitals do, is based on a study of HMOs. Perhaps HMOs don't know as much as they think.

Careful Preparation for Negotiations

If hospitals do have less information than HMOs, the only possible explanation is one of poor preparation. The Kralewski study did note that HMOs tend to have specific strategies for dealing with hospitals, while hospitals have not seemed to have strategies for dealing with

HMOs. One element of an overall strategy is the careful preparation of the financial information that forms the basis for any arrangement.

It is possible that hospitals have taken a more haphazard approach, deciding by the seat of their pants whether a contract seems financially advantageous or not. Such an approach would not seem to be in the best interests of hospitals that wish to survive in the long run.

How Low To Go

In dealing with an HMO, one question that hospitals ultimately face is how low to go. This is a difficult problem for the hospital. From a strict economic theory viewpoint, hospitals should be willing to take any additional business at any price that exceeds the marginal cost of the additional patients.

Some hospitals avoid the problem through a quick magic trick. They practice discounting through price illusion. This approach simply requires the hospital to negotiate its HMO prices as a percentage discount from charges. The benefit this has for the hospital is that once the HMO is firmly entrenched in the hospital, the hospital can raise its charges, thereby effectively recovering all or nearly all of the negotiated discount.

Given such a strategy, it would be understandable if hospital managers didn't spend much time getting too deeply involved in understanding hospital costs. However, HMOs are not likely to allow such price illusion to enter into their contracts.

The Long-Run Implications of Discounts

In trying to decide how low to go, the hospital must try to gain an understanding of why they are dealing with the HMO, and what the long-run implications are.

The most common reason to offer an HMO a discount is because there is overcapacity in the hospital industry, and the HMO promises volume. If the local hospital industry does have excess beds, and the HMO has alternatives, then hospitals are forced to negotiate.

This is not always the case. Sometimes a hospital may be the sole provider. Even if it has excess capacity, the HMO has little opportunity to steer patients to other facilities.

Sometimes there is little excess capacity. For-profit HMOs entered the New York City market with a flourish several years ago, but did not fare nearly as well as expected. New York City hospitals did not have substantial amounts of excess capacity. As a result, the HMOs did not obtain their normal discounts. They became a high-priced alternative to other types of insurance. In many markets the HMO reaction is to compete on the wide range of services they offer. However, in New York there are strong labor unions, and insurance coverage was already broad.

It is common, however, for HMOs to exist in markets that have a number of hospitals, each with excess capacity. In that case, what prices must hospitals offer, or can they afford to offer? Any price that is below charges, but above average cost, will yield a profit for the hospital.

Even if some of the volume offered represents individuals who currently would be patients of the hospital and who pay charges, the hospital should be willing to agree to a price that exceeds average cost. It is important to bear in mind that the appropriate calculation is not based on existing revenues, but on the revenues if the HMO provides the volume to the hospital, versus if the HMO takes the patients to another hospital.

What if the negotiations reach a point where the only agreeable price to the HMO is less than average cost? As long as it exceeds the marginal cost it is beneficial in the short run. This is because the fixed costs of the hospital will be incurred in any case. If the revenue exceeds the marginal costs of the patients, the short-run profit will increase.

What about the long-run profits? If patients are paying less than average cost, the hospital may find itself in a position where it cannot afford to replace its fixed facilities as they wear out over time. If the portion of patients not paying at least average cost grows, this could become a serious problem. It is unreasonable to expect that discounting below average cost can continue for an unlimited time period for that reason.

When HMOs provide volume to one hospital, they take it away from another. In markets with excess capacity, this creates severe financial problems for some hospitals. Over the long run, this is likely to cause a reduction in the number of beds in the community. As the excess capacity problem disappears, hospitals will have less need to offer discounts to HMOs. On the other hand, the reduction in capacity should make the system more efficient. With the remaining hospitals having high occupancy levels, their cost per patient should be lower.

Your hospital must base its plan on the approach that is most likely to allow it to be one of the ultimate survivors. This might well require deep discounts, well below average cost, in order to get HMO business. What if negotiations reach a point where the price would actually be less than the marginal costs of treating the patients? In that case the hospital may well decide not to deal with the HMO. Clearly, such a contract would mean that overall profits will decline, or losses will rise.

Nevertheless the hospital must take a long-term perspective. If it accepts losses in the near term, will that result in reduced competition? There may be times when it is worth accepting losses for a period of time. On the other hand, the hospital must be careful that it does not put itself in a position of being guilty of antitrust violations. Cut-throat pricing is not legal.

CONCLUSION

The most important conclusion to be drawn from this discussion about hospital costs and their role in negotiations with HMOs is that the hospital should develop a clear strategy for its relationships with HMOs. The hospital cannot negotiate effectively until it decides whether a relationship with an HMO is seen as a necessary evil or a mutually benefiting good. It must decide if its goals concern increases in profits, or simply maintenance of existing market share. It must determine whether the HMO has control over solely its patients, or its physicians as well. And the hospital must plan with care for the financial aspects of any negotiation.

NOTES

1. J.E. Kralewski, et al., "Strategies Employed by HMOs to Achieve Hospital Discounts: A Case Study of Seven HMOs," *Health Care Management Review,* Vol. 16, No. 1, Winter 1991, p. 14.

2. Ibid., p. 12.

Application 6-2

Privatization in Health Care Institutions

*Yehia Dabaa, MPA, is currently Clinical Research Assistant at
St. Luke's—Roosevelt Hospital Center, New York, New York.*

*Shari Faith Fisch, MPA, is currently associated with the
American Suicide Foundation, New York, New York.*

*Ellen Gordon, BS, is currently Assistant Vice President,
Moody's Investors Service, New York, New York.*

INTRODUCTION

In today's health care environment, hospitals provide services that may or may not be performed more economically by outside entities. This article concerns the relative benefits of privatizing an area of service or maintaining the status quo. A hypothetical case study of a non-routine decision is offered to help readers comprehend the benefits that may be realized and obstacles that may be faced in privatizing an area of service.

At the most basic level, privatization refers to an organization's shift from public to private ownership. Instead of being held accountable to the taxpayers, the organization is responsible to the stockholders. Advocates of privatization believe that it increases worker motivation to provide quality care. With increased health care costs, decreased government subsidies, slashed hospital budgets, and a myriad of constraints on resources, health care managers are looking to the private sector to lower costs and increase efficiency.

Source: Reprinted from Yehia Dabaa, Shari Faith Fisch, and Ellen Gordon, "Privatization in Health Care Institutions," *Hospital Cost Management and Accounting,* Vol. 4, No. 12, March 1992, pp. 1–8. Copyright 1992, Aspen Publishers, Inc.

PRIVATIZATION: INHERENT BELIEFS AND POSSIBLE GAINS

Some health care managers believe the health care market should distance itself from public, nonprofit organizational structures and rely more on the private sector. The reliance on privatization as a cure for the health care industry's upward-spiraling costs is due to ingrained beliefs about the nature of publicly owned entities and their privately owned counterparts. Many people believe public and nonprofit organizations permit bureaucratic malaise, which in turn promotes excess capacity, inefficient uses of resources, and technical obsolescence.

Advocates base their beliefs in the primacy of privatization and the inefficiencies of public and nonprofit organizations on a basic acceptance of the economic equation by which supply and demand is influenced by market forces. The market system—which involves buyers and sellers trading their goods freely—is a function of a capitalist economic system. Other aspects of capitalism include free enterprise, private ownership of capital, and free choice.

Advocates of privatization believe that the hospital's overhead allocation of indirect costs increases the prices of goods as compared to a natural supply-and-demand environment. Through overhead allocations, hospitals subsidize cost centers with inefficiently run areas because they need to include these departments in the overall organization. In situations where costs are subsidized, resources are not utilized to their peak efficiency and prices are kept higher than they would be under competitive market conditions. These price floors are not influenced by market demand and represent an imposed inefficiency in the public sphere. Inefficiencies of this kind in the private sector may result in an organization's inability to compete, and it may eventually go out of business. In a market situation, privatization would probably ensure that the most efficient method of production is used.

Other inefficiencies also exist. Under hospital control, a department may produce a good but otherwise have little autonomy. Hospitals allocate portions of fixed and indirect costs to various departments that are not controlled by the department manager. Lack of managerial control destroys the drive for innovation in the workplace, hampers the growth of technology, and limits the development of more efficient modes of production; management makes do with an overhead allocation system that functions as a deterrent to managerial excellence.

Many people advocate a return to a purer market equation. A competitive market would increase hospital efficiency, lower costs, and increase quality. Privatization is the call to arms of those advocating less administrative, legislative, and regulatory oversight and greater reliance on market forces.

THE ROLE OF COST ACCOUNTING AND NONROUTINE DECISION MAKING

Relying on market forces for a definitive assessment of the pros and cons of privatization does not necessarily answer all the needs of today's health care manager. Managers need more information about privatizing an area of service than can be contributed by supply and demand curves. In order to do a cost benefit analysis—in which the costs associated with all viable options are compared—managers must be sufficiently versed in cost accounting applications

and which costs are important for each nonroutine decision. When considering privatizing within a hospital environment, health care managers should carefully consider the nature of costs, whether they are fixed, variable, joint, sunk, direct, or indirect. For example, if one area of the hospital is privatized, hospital-incurred indirect costs and short-term fixed costs associated with the area in question will have to be reallocated to other hospital-wide departments; what may appear to be a cost savings may actually be a cost shuffling.

Within the framework of a nonroutine decision, health care managers need to identify the relevant costs (i.e., those that vary with the decision being made). Nonroutine decisions include the following.

- *Add/Drop*—adding or dropping a service. Overhead allocation of hospital indirect and joint costs should not be considered; they are not relevant to the decision to adopt a new service, because they are costs that are already incurred and they are not saved costs if management decides to drop a service.

- *Expand/Downsize*—expanding or limiting the scope of a service. All costs contingent on volume are relevant to this nonroutine decision. With this in mind, the fixed costs of providing the service are not relevant. When management decides to decrease or increase volume levels, costs of consequence are the variable costs associated with each patient and step-fixed costs associated with provision of service.

- *Make/Buy*—produce a product or service in-house or purchase it from an outside entity. If a good is produced in-house, relevant costs include capital costs and replacement costs of the fixed assets used in production, as well as all costs incurred from the production function. Managers should do a cost-benefit analysis where the measure of cost for internal production is based on the money we spend to produce the item that we would avoid spending if the item is not produced.

In most of these nonroutine decisions, joint costs (those that cannot be separated by usage) and common costs (those shared by all variables under consideration) are ignored, as are sunk costs (those associated with the original investment). Managers should attempt to avoid decisions based on irrelevant or inaccurate information. Further, irrelevant information may be misleading and lead to a wrong decision. Managers need to use critical thinking and look at all angles of a situation when doing these analyses.

THREE WAYS TO PRIVATIZE

Incorporating privatization into nonroutine hospital decision making requires an understanding of the privatization options available to health care managers. There are three ways for a publicly owned or operated organization to privatize: (1) contracting out, (2) hiring a private firm, and (3) consolidating production. Contracting out—one of the more conventional privatization methods—refers to the purchase of goods or services normally produced in-house from an outside, private company. For example, instead of manufacturing saline bags in-house, the hospital could contract with a privately owned company to provide for all its saline needs. When organizations contract out, short-run fixed costs remain, but all costs are variable in the long run; variable costs are saved in the short run but are replaced by the contract price plus ordering and carrying costs. The organization's overhead allocation costs remain the same, but department-wide indirect costs may decrease.

As with contracting for service, managers expect the costs associated with hiring a private firm to produce a desired good to be lower than those of producing it in-house. Public organizations hire private firms to manage various services or production processes. These private firms serve as consultants, lawyers, and other outside forces. For example, a private consultant may be hired to advise in-house production staff on saline production.

A third type of privatization relies on consolidating efforts among a number of public entities in a joint effort to create efficiencies of scale. Take, for example, a hospital that offers to produce saline for other hospitals in the area. The expected costs of using excess capacity to produce saline must account for a portion of fixed costs, the variable costs of production, and whatever profit margin is desirable and still within the competitive price range.

WHERE DOES PRIVATIZATION WORK BEST?

Privatization in the public/nonprofit sector works best when the area under analysis produces an actual product, as in the saline example above. The product can be compared on an equivalent level with any good in the free market. Costs relevant to the production function include production and carrying costs, and the managers must assess resources needed per volume level, and so on. The following case study illustrates the issues surrounding privatization and how cost accounting is used within the framework on a nonroutine decision.

CASE STUDY: WINTERPARK HOSPITAL

WinterPark Hospital is facing a problem experienced by many hospitals around the country. The facility was expanded in the early 1980s, when inpatient utilization was increasing and the hospital needed additional space. In an effort to remain competitive in its relatively affluent suburban service area the hospital constructed a facility twice the size of its original plant. WinterPark's resulting elaborate structure translated into high fixed costs. In particular, management projected that volume would increase significantly; consequently, a laboratory was built to accommodate this expected volume. Management's hope was to increase the number of lab tests performed as well as the complexity (acuity) of the tests performed.

In an effort to reduce the organization's overall costs, a special task force has been established to review hospital services and find ways to reduce costs. The hospital is examining many inpatient department revenue centers as well as numerous ancillary departments. The laboratory is the first department selected for review. The task force members hope to determine if the lab contributes to the hospital's bottom line and if they should consider contracting out for all or a portion of the tests performed by the lab. Qualitative issues are always a concern when purchasing from the outside, and the task force will have to evaluate if the tests will be properly done and available on a timely basis if they choose this alternative. However, if these conditions are satisfied, they intend to make differential costing the key financial consideration (i.e., which alternative will cost less to implement).

This analysis is separated into three components or scenarios: (1) base case—all tests are performed in-house, (2) close the lab and contract out for all services, and (3) retain "Not Complex" tests and "Complex" tests but contract with an outside firm for all "Very Complex" tests (the lab performs only these three types of tests).

Base Case Scenario: Keep Full-Service Laboratory

Under this scenario, total costs and total revenues must be examined. As presented in Table 6-2-1, fixed costs for the lab are $500,000. These costs include depreciation of the building and equipment, supervisors' salaries, four technicians, the fixed-cost portion of laundry and housekeeping departments allocated to the lab, and other indirect costs associated with performing laboratory services. In addition, fixed costs have been separated into program-specific fixed costs. As stated above, the lab performs three different tests, with a total of 10,000 tests annually. Test A constitutes 50 percent of all tests performed, while Test B and Test C represent 25 percent each. Joint costs are those required to perform several types of tests. It has been determined that joint costs should not be allocated when deciding whether or not to dis-

Table 6-2-1 Assumptions about WinterPark Hospital's Full Service Laboratory (Base Case Scenario)

Number of tests performed annually:	10,000
Types of laboratory tests performed:	
Not Complex	A—50%
Complex	B—25%
Very Complex	C—25%
Program-specific fixed costs (includes depreciation, supervisors' salaries, two technicians, laundry, housekeeping, and other indirect costs):	A—$250,000 B— 125,000 C— 125,000 $500,000
Price/reimbursement for all three lab tests:	$ 58.00
Joint costs (these are relevant in the decision to close the laboratory, although they are not relevant when reviewing each type of test)	$100,000

continue a service, primarily because these costs will exist even if Test A, for example, is discontinued. However, joint costs should be allocated when making resource allocation decisions and when calculating the cost of the entire department. Our cost objective (i.e., what we are trying to measure) is the cost of performing all three tests at the existing hospital lab.

Table 6-2-2 presents the costs of operating the lab. Total variable costs are $100,000, based on the number of tests performed and the variable cost per test. Total costs (fixed and variable) are $600,000. Total revenue for all tests is $580,000. This assumes that the hospital receives $58 per test.[*] Based on this calculation, the lab will lose $20,000 per year if they continue to perform all three tests in-house. More specifically, Test A produces a profit of $15,000 while Test B and Test C incur losses of $5,000 and $30,000 respectively.

As mentioned earlier, WinterPark expects to perform more Very Complex tests (Test C) than Not Complex tests (Test A). However, based on data for the past five years (which is reviewed

---

*Editor's note: It may be unrealistic to price all tests at the same rate. Bear in mind, however, that the objective of this case study is to focus on privatization and techniques to approach it. The specific data are of only minor significance.

Table 6-2-2 Base Case Scenario—Profits

COST OF OPERATING THE LABORATORY

Total Fixed Costs

	# Tests	% of Total	FC	VC
Test A	5,000	50%	$250,000	$ 5
Test B	2,500	25%	125,000	10
Test C	2,500	25%	125,000	20
	10,000		$500,000	

Total Variable Costs

	# Tests		VC		Total VC
Test A	5,000	×	$ 5	=	$ 25,000
Test B	2,500	×	10	=	25,000
Test C	2,500	×	20	=	50,000
					$100,000

Total Costs

	VC		FC		Total Costs	Average
Test A	$25,000	+	$250,000	=	$275,000	$55
Test B	25,000	+	125,000	=	150,000	60
Test C	50,000	+	125,000	=	175,000	70
Total cost					$600,000	

REVENUES—REIMBURSEMENT

	Price	# Tests	Total Reimbursement	Total Cost	Gain/(Loss)
Test A	$58	5,000	$290,000	$275,000	$ 15,000
Test B	58	2,500	145,000	150,000	(5,000)
Test C	58	2,500	145,000	175,000	(30,000)
Total revenue			$580,000	$600,000	$ (20,000)

Total revenue = $580,000
Total cost = $600,000
Loss incurred = $20,000

monthly) the hospital consistently performs twice as many Not Complex tests as either Complex or Very Complex tests.

Breakeven analysis determines the volume at which a program is just financially self-sufficient. In order to calculate the breakeven for multiple tests, the average price and the weighted average variable cost must be calculated.

WinterPark receives the same reimbursement (price) for each test; therefore, the weighted average price is $58. The variable cost per test, weighted by complexity, is $10. For the hospital to break even as a whole, it must cover all costs—including both program-specific fixed costs and hospital-wide joint costs. As shown in Table 6-2-3, in order to break even, the lab must

Table 6-2-3 Base Case Scenario—Breakeven

BREAKEVEN ANALYSIS

Weighted Average Variable Costs			Weighted Average Price		
50% ×	$ 5.00	= $2.50	50% ×	$58	= $29
25% ×	10.00	= 2.50	25% ×	58	= 15
25% ×	20.00	= 5.00	25% ×	58	= 15
		$10.00			$58

$$Q = \frac{\text{Fixed Costs}}{\text{Price} - \text{Variable Costs}}$$

$$= \frac{\$500{,}000 + \$100{,}000}{\$58 - \$10} = 12{,}500 \text{ tests}$$

BREAKEVEN FOR EACH TEST

Breakeven for Test A

$$Q = \frac{\$250{,}000}{\$58 - \$5} = 4{,}716 \text{ tests}$$

Breakeven for Test B

$$Q = \frac{\$125{,}000}{\$58 - \$10} = 2{,}604 \text{ tests}$$

Breakeven for Test C

$$Q = \frac{\$125{,}000}{\$58 - \$20} = 3{,}290 \text{ tests}$$

perform 12,500 tests annually. Of this total number, 50 percent would be Test A, 25 percent Test B, and 25 percent Test C. Although 50 percent of 12,500 is 6,250, when we consider performing Test A alone and calculate the breakeven, we determine that we only need 4,716 tests. This is because for any one service, joint costs need not be considered. The first 4,716 tests cover the direct fixed costs of the service, and each additional Test A performed contributes toward joint fixed costs in the amount equal to the difference between the price and the variable cost (contribution margin). If Test A volume will exceed 4,716, the test would be desirable as long as the lab operates and incurs joint costs anyway.

Based on this analysis, the lab incurs a loss of $20,000. And based on the breakeven analysis performed for the entire department, additional tests must be performed if the lab is to be self-sufficient. Clearly the lab is a necessary function of the hospital, which must provide lab services in order to service its patients' needs, and the hospital may decide to absorb this loss for the overall good of the organization. Many physicians may be discouraged from admitting patients to hospitals without full labs, because of the possible inconvenience of using an outside company. In this case the overall loss would be significant, because patient volume might drop, causing a greater loss.

Another alternative might be to keep the lab and increase the volume of tests performed. Although the hospital may have difficulty attracting patients due to the competitive environment, WinterPark might consider contracting with other nearby hospitals to perform their tests. The decision to expand these services will depend on the price received for performing them. While WinterPark needs to cover its variable costs, it should also consider covering a portion of its fixed costs to contribute to the bottom line. Additional capacity constraints must also be accounted for.

Scenario 2: Contract Out for All Lab Services

This alternative requires close examination, because even though it is likely that some fixed costs—such as annual capital expenditures to replace equipment as it wears or becomes obsolete—could probably be avoided if the lab was closed, other fixed costs would remain. Under the current arrangement, some of the fixed costs cover depreciation on the building and an allocation of joint costs from the entire organization.

The lab at WinterPark Hospital generates revenues of $580,000 and costs of $600,000. If we close the lab, fixed costs of $200,000 will remain (see Table 6-2-4). Thus, by closing the lab the hospital would lose more money than by keeping it open. In the short run the hospital has

Table 6-2-4 Scenario 2: Close the Existing Lab and Contract Out for All Tests

Relevant Costs and Revenues

Revenues	$0	(no tests performed)
Variable Costs:	$0	
Fixed Costs:	$200,000*	

If we close the lab entirely, the hospital will lose $200,000. This loss is $180,000 more than that of keeping the lab open.

*Includes depreciation on the building and fixed overhead allocated from other departments.

incurred many fixed costs already and they are no longer relevant, but the overhead remains. Based on this analysis, the task force has eliminated this alternative from its options.

Scenario 3: Retain Services for Test A and Test B and Contract Out for Test C

It is important to note that the lab has additional capacity to perform more lab tests and that the equipment is relatively new. Test C is a labor-intensive test, as reflected in the higher variable cost of $20. An outside company that specializes in this type of lab test recently offered to perform all Test C lab tests for $15 per test; the contract extends for five years but will adjust in price based on volume. This is $5 less than the hospital's current variable cost. Given the special nature of the test and the large volume this outside firm services, they can perform these tests at a much lower price. The task force was excited to learn that this test can be performed at a lower variable cost, but before making a final decision they wanted to know how this would affect the entire laboratory's profitability. As presented in Table 6-2-5, fixed costs for Test C would decrease from $125,000 to $75,000—a reduction of $50,000. The remaining $75,000 would be allocated to Test A and Test B, because these costs would still remain within the department. This will result in revised fixed costs of $300,000 and $150,000 for Test A and Test B, respectively.

Total revenues remain the same—$580,000—and total cost (including the lower variable cost associated with Test C) is reduced to $537,500. Therefore, the entire department would make a profit of $42,500. Reviewing the individual tests, however, reveals that Test A incurs a loss of $35,000 and Test B loses $30,000. These tests have more fixed costs allocated to them, so their losses rise. We have learned that careful review must be performed before services are purchased from outside the organization, because some fixed costs still remain and then must be absorbed by the entire department. In this example, the lower variable cost associated with Test C outweighs the additional overhead included in the fixed-cost component for the other tests performed.

Case Study Conclusion

The task force plans to recommend to the board of directors that the hospital accept the contract to perform Test C lab tests outside the hospital lab. However, the task force has requested that the laboratory personnel re-evaluate its fixed and variable cost components and review its cost structure to ensure that all direct costs are allocated correctly. The task force expected Test C, given its complexity, to account for greater fixed and variable costs. If these figures change, another evaluation of the cost differential is needed. The relevant costs in this example include the variable costs. The joint costs are not included, because we would not avoid these costs if Test C was not performed in the existing lab. As the lab continues to age, additional analyses will have to be completed to calculate the benefit of contracting out for the entire lab service. In addition, the hospital expects to evaluate the short run option of contracting with other hospitals to increase its existing volume and perhaps cover a greater portion of its fixed costs.

OBSTACLES FACED IN PRIVATIZATION

Like other management techniques, privatization has its supporters and opponents. Sup-

Table 6-2-5 Scenario 3: Retain Test A and Test B and Contract Out for Test C

COST OF OPERATING THE LABORATORY

Total Fixed Costs

	# Tests	% of Total	FC	VC	Revised FC
Test A	5,000	67%	$250,000	$ 5	$300,000
Test B	2,500	33%	125,000	10	150,000
Test C	0	0%	75,000	15	0
	7,500				

Test C fixed costs declined from $125,000 to $75,000 due to one less supervisor and one technician. Test C fixed costs that remain include equipment, fixed portion of allocated costs (laundry), and other fixed costs.

Total Variable Costs

	# Tests		VC		Total VC	
Test A	5,000	×	$ 5	=	$ 25,000	
Test B	2,500	×	10	=	25,000	
Test C	2,500	×	15	=	37,500	(payment to outside lab)
					$ 87,500	

Total Costs

	VC	Revised FC	Total
Test A	$25,000	$300,000	$325,000
Test B	25,000	150,000	175,000
Test C	37,500	0	37,500
Total cost			$537,500

REVENUES—REIMBURSEMENT

	Price	# Tests	Total Reimbursement	Total Cost	Gain/ (Loss)
Test A	$58	5,000	$290,000	$325,000	$ (35,000)
Test B	58	2,500	145,000	175,000	(30,000)
Test C	58	2,500	145,000	37,500	107,500
Total revenue			$580,000	$537,500	$ 42,500

Total revenue = $580,000
Total cost = $537,500
Profit = $42,500

porters believe that privatization of health care organizations could invigorate the market competition, lower costs, and improve quality and service effectiveness. Opponents, on the other hand, argue that very little is known about the effects of competition in the delivery of health care. Regardless of what the different parties believe, there are exogenous factors involved in accepting or rejecting this technique. Some of the factors impacting the privatization of health care providers include organization type and service provided, geographical location, union/employee rejection, and private providers chosen.

Organization Type and Service Provided

Successful applications of privatization principles are contingent on the type of organization and service provided. Privatization could work successfully in one market and fail in another. According to a number of sources, privatization leads to lower costs and improved cost control and service quality.[1] But the impact varies with the organization, and cost savings from the process of privatizing an area of service range from 10 percent to 60 percent.[2] As mentioned previously, production-oriented hospital services are easier to privatize than areas that are not quantifiable. Other issues that impact privatization include the organization's size, mission, and nonprofit or for-profit standing.

Geographical Location

The success or failure of privatization depends to a large extent on geographical location. One study showed that departments within a hospital increased the level of contracting out with a high level of return but another study indicated that there was a declining trend to contract out in county hospitals (some county hospitals apparently returned to public control after being privatized in the mid 1980s, due to substantial management fees charged by the private firms). Conflicting reports on the merits of privatization from broad-based studies overlook the differences in institutions located in different geographical areas, including differences in the cost of living, cost of supplies, base salaries, and qualified personnel available.

Union and Employee Rejection

Another issue of concern is the presence or absence of unions. Unions oppose privatization because they fear loss of power, and they could persuade employees and managers to oppose

this technique by predicting that privatization would result in employee lay-offs and the exploitation and loss of control of managers. They might also repeat the cliché, "If it was effective, it would have been adopted long ago" and argue that better options are available. Employee resistance to privatization can damn the project before it is even implemented. Further, political infighting by the institution's Board of Directors, managers, or trustees can undermine privatization efforts; people may feel that privatizing areas of service is not consistent with the organization's mission statement.

Choice of Private Providers

In addition to the financial aspects of privatization are the issues of the relative quality of care provided by private organizations and consumer access to health care. The general consumer may fear that private firms would be interested in money alone and not in the public well-being. This is expressed as a fear of declining access to health care, and deterioration in the quality of care provided. Many believe that the budget cutting and privatization in many countries has led to serious deterioration not only of health but of education, housing, nutrition, and other social services.[3]

Choosing providers plays an important role in whether privatization is accepted or rejected. The right provider could produce satisfactory results, which would encourage further privatization. The wrong provider could cause dissatisfaction or abolishment of the technique. This highlights the importance of controlling acceptable providers. Some public organizations fall into the trap of accepting a private provider who makes the lowest bid initially but who intends to raise prices or lower quality later. They also might err by accepting high initial bid prices in their eagerness for early success and quick implementation. Public organizations should select candidates with care, weighing political, social, and economic costs against benefits. Patient satisfaction with the private provider must be a high priority, because patients who are dissatisfied with a service or good may be reluctant to pursue treatment. In a time of intense competition among providers, hospitals cannot afford to lose customers who choose not to use or to underutilize the health care facility because of privatized services.

CONCLUSION

At first glance, privatization of hospital services seems to be a panacea for the current fiscal crisis faced by health care institutions, but privatization may not always be in the organization's best interest. Advocates believe that privatization will lead to increased competition, lowered costs, and improved services. But short-term realities may not mesh with long-term needs, and hospitals must assess the full impact of privatizing any area of service. The case for or against privatization is not clear. Privatization may mean lower costs and higher profits for the area of service in question, but institution-wide costs must also be considered in the cost-benefit analysis; increased allocations to other departments may make privatization more expensive than maintaining the status quo. Privatization is not necessarily a market cure, but it can spur on an institution that may be beset with bureaucratic inertia and a lack of efficient technological changes.

NOTES

1. M.A. Walker, *Privatization: Tactics & Techniques* (Vancouver, BC: The Fraiser Institute, 1988), 218.

2. Ibid.

3. L.B. Gardner and R.M. Scheffler, Privatization in health care: Shifting the risk, *Medical Care Review* 45, no. 2 (Fall 1988):215–253.

BIBLIOGRAPHY

Burke, M. "Hospitals Seize New Opportunities in State Privatization Efforts." *Hospitals* 66, No. 7 (5 April 1992): 50–52, 54.

Clarkson, K.W. "Privatization at the State and Local level." *Privatization and State-Owned Enterprises* 3 (1989):144–207.

Cox, W. "Privatization in the Public Service: Competitive Contracting and the Public Ethic in Urban Public Transport." In *Privatization: Tactics and Techniques* by M.A. Walker, pp. 200–237. Vancouver, B.C.: The Fraiser Institute, 1988.

Crowningshield, G.R. "Cost Accounting: Principles and Managerial Applications." 2:685–692, 1969.

Finkler, S.A. *Cost Accounting for Health Care Organizations: Concepts and Applications.* Gaithersburg, MD: Aspen Publishers, 1993.

Gardner, L.B., and Scheffler, R.M. "Privatization in Health Care: Shifting the Risk." *Medical Care Review* 45, No. 2 (Fall 1988):215–253.

LeTouze, D. "The Privatization of Hospital Pharmacy Departments." *Dimensions in Health Service* 66, No. 8 (November 1989):36–38.

Lutz, S. "Officials Weigh Taking Houston Hospital District Private." *Modern Healthcare* 22, No. 19 (May 1992):6.

MacAvoy, P.W. *Privatization and State Owned Enterprise.* Boston, Mass.: Kluwer Academic Publishers, 1989.

Neumann, B.R., Suver, J.D., and Zelman, W.N. *Financial Management: Concepts and Application for Health Care Providers.* Owings Mills, MD: National Health Publishing, 1988.

Scott, L. "Hospitals Sign More Contracts for Outside Expertise." *Modern Healthcare* (24 August 1992):51–72.

Smith, S.R. "Privatization in Health and Human Services: A Critique." *Journal of Health Politics, Policy & Law* 17, No. 2 (1992):233–253.

Terris, M. "Budget Cutting and Privatization: The Threat to Health." *Journal of Public Health Policy* 13, No. 1 (Spring 1992):27–41.

Walker, M.A. *Privatization: Tactics & Techniques.* Vancouver, B.C.: The Fraiser Institute, 1988.

Part II

Cost Accounting Information for Planning and Control

A primary focus of cost accounting is on developing information that managers can use for planning and control. Once the reader is familiar with the foundations of cost accounting provided in Part I, a number of specific tools for improved planning and control can be considered. That is the role of this part of the book.

The first chapter in this section, Chapter 7, focuses on the prediction of future costs. In order to plan for the future, it is essential to be able to anticipate what costs will be in coming periods of time. This chapter examines techniques for making such estimates. These range in sophistication from using groups of individuals to gain consensus based on opinion, to using regression analysis, curvilinear forecasting, and learning curves.

Chapter 8 discusses budgeting. The role of budgeting in health care organizations and the differing budgeting philosophies in different organizations are considered. The chapter also addresses the specific different types of budgets: master, long-range, operating, capital, cash, program, and special purpose. The chapter concludes with an examination of the negotiation and approval process for budgets.

Budgets are an instrumental planning tool. As actual events occur, they can become an excellent tool for control. The use of budgets for control purposes is discussed in Chapter 9. That chapter introduces the concept of a flexible budget and delves into several aspects of variance analysis.

Chapter 10 discusses management control. The nature of management control systems is addressed in detail. The chapter considers the management control process and the use of internal control systems. Key variables, transfer pricing, and management control of projects are all examined in the chapter.

7

Predicting Future Costs

Goals of This Chapter

---

1. Explain the use of groups of people for estimating costs in the absence of historical data.
2. Provide a tool for adjusting historical costs for the impact of changes in the price level (inflation).
3. Describe the linear regression technique of cost estimation.
4. Discuss alternative approaches to forecasting when a linear relationship does not exist.
5. Emphasize the importance of managerial judgment in estimating future costs.
6. Explain the role and usefulness of learning curves, and provide the essential tools for learning curve analysis.

Key Terms Used in This Chapter

Constant variance; cost estimation; curvilinear forecasts; Delphi; dependent variable; fixed costs; forecast interval; forecasting; independence; independent variable; indexing for inflation; learning curve; linearity; mixed costs; multiple regression; nominal group technique; normality; *R*-squared; regression analysis; seasonality; step-variable; *t*-test; trend; variable costs; Winters' forecasting method.

Note: Key terms appear in italics when first used in the chapter. All key terms are defined in the Glossary.

INTRODUCTION

Prediction of future costs is a problem commonly grappled with in health care organizations. Budgeting, discussed in the next chapter, relies heavily on the manager's ability to predict the expenses that will be incurred in the future. There are many different ways to approach prediction of future costs. These include

- using groups to make subjective estimates,
- using *regression analysis* to trend past costs into the future,
- using *forecasting* models to predict future volumes, and
- using *learning curve* methodology to incorporate economies realized over time from experience.

Most prediction of future costs is accomplished by using historical information projected into the future. This process has many difficulties and complications, which will be discussed in this chapter. However, even with these difficulties, at least the projection is based on a firm, historical foundation. Predictions are even more difficult to make in the absence of any experience or history. However, health care organizations have to make many such predictions.

Every time a new service or program is suggested, the financial evaluation is performed without any history. How can estimates be made in the absence of such data? To some extent, we can rely on engineering calculations. A determination can be made of exactly what resources should be required to treat a patient. However, even such a firm engineering calculation cannot tell the organization how many patients the new service will attract. Therefore, it cannot provide information about the total costs that will be incurred.

One solution to this problem is to base estimates on the collective opinion of groups of individuals with reasonable levels of experience, knowledge, and judgment. Such group forecasting is the topic of the next section of this chapter.

In cases where historical data do exist, the prediction problem is somewhat easier. Knowledge about the past is often an excellent starting point for predicting the future. If *trends* in volume over time lead one to expect volume increases or declines in the future, costs must be adjusted accordingly, because variable costs change proportionately with volume changes.

Predictions of future *fixed* and *variable costs* can be based on what costs were in the past. In using such data, however, we must be cognizant of the fact that the changes in cost from year to year come about not only because of the change in volume but also because of the general increase in the price level. In order to account for that increase in the price level, historical costs must be adjusted using price indices. *Indexing* past costs for the impact of inflation is considered after the discussion of using groups for estimating costs.

Even having segregated the portion of cost changes over time that are attributable to inflation does not totally remove the complexity in using historical information to predict the future. A 10 percent increase in volume will not lead to a 10 percent increase in costs if some of the costs are fixed. Those costs should not increase.

If we can readily identify the fixed costs and the variable costs, the forecasting problem is simplified. In reality, however, most organizations and departments have a complicated mix of fixed and variable costs. Any department can be viewed as having *mixed costs,* that is, costs that have fixed cost elements and variable cost elements mixed together. As volume increases or decreases over time, the fixed costs are expected to be constant, whereas the variable costs will be changing in response to the volume change. In order to predict future costs, one must therefore have a sense of how much of the mixed costs is fixed cost and how much is variable cost. Determining how to segregate mixed costs for making future predictions is one of the key focuses of this chapter.

The techniques used to segregate mixed costs are useful in that they allow for predictions that respond accurately to changes in volume. For annual predictions, such estimates are inexpensive and are often fairly accurate. However, these estimates depend on projections of patient volume. We need to have forecasting techniques that will allow accurate projections of patient volume.

Another forecasting issue relates to *seasonality* of patient flow. Many health care organizations have seasonal fluctuations in costs. For example, if a home health agency provides more home visits in winter months than in summer months, its costs will tend to be higher in the winter. Adequate planning requires managers to consider such fluctuations. In recent years, sophisticated computer programs have become available that allow for *curvilinear forecasts.* Such forecasts are based on curved lines. The curved lines allow the cost pattern projected to follow more accurately the busy and slow periods of the year. Curvilinear forecasting will be discussed in this chapter after the matter of mixed costs is resolved.

The last section of this chapter focuses on learning curves. Over time, organizations and individuals become more adept at doing repetitive tasks. They learn what works and what does not. Learning curve theory allows managers to incorporate that learning into cost estimates. The methodology considers how much less costly activities are likely to become over time as experience is gained. This knowledge will allow managers to ensure that the organization benefits from that organizational experience.

USING GROUPS FOR ESTIMATING COSTS

Accountants are most comfortable making forecasts and other estimates on the basis of solid facts. Historical data are often used as a foundation in making projections for the coming year. However, health care organizations have been entering into an ever-growing number of new ventures. It is common for there to be little or no historical data to draw upon in making such estimates. As a result, "seat of the pants" estimates dominate. There are techniques, however, designed specifically to help improve the accuracy of estimates when no specific historical information is available. The most common of these approaches are the *Delphi* and *nominal group techniques.*

In both approaches, a team or panel must be selected that consists of individuals who are likely to have reasoned insights with respect to the item being forecast. Although the health care organization may have no employee who has direct knowledge or experience, an attempt should be made to select a qualified group. Industrial experience has shown that by arriving at a consensus among a team of experts, subjective forecasts can be reasonably accurate. The experts do not have to be expert in the specific project, but in areas as closely related as possible.

The Nominal Group Technique

The nominal group technique is one in which the individuals are brought together in a structured meeting. Each member writes down a forecast. Then all of the written forecasts are presented to the group by a group leader without discussion. Once all of the forecasts have been revealed, the reasoning behind each one is discussed. After the discussions, each member again makes a forecast in writing. Through a repetitive process, eventually a group decision is made.

In the absence of such a group approach, an individual health care organization manager is often left alone to struggle through the process of developing a business plan, including the various necessary forecasts. It is efficient in many respects for one manager to be in charge of the development of a business plan. However, such an approach limits the availability of ideas.

By using a group approach, a number of individuals focus their attention on the same problem. Each person has a somewhat different perspective that influences his or her subjective forecast. Being exposed to competing forecasts and explanations of the reasoning behind them can be extremely helpful in providing the central planner with insights that had not already been considered. The underlying concept is that both the additional ideas and the discussion of the ideas by all members of the group will result in an improved forecast.

Obviously, there are weaknesses to the nominal group technique. One problem concerns lack of information. If different individuals base their forecasts on different assumptions, it may be impossible to reach consensus.

A more serious problem concerns politics and personalities. As members of the group defend their forecasts, extraneous issues having to do with whose idea it is may bias the group decision. Some individuals may be reluctant to share their ideas in public for a variety of reasons.

The Delphi Technique

The Delphi technique also employs a group, but it attempts to overcome the principal weakness of the nominal group technique. With the Delphi approach, the group never meets. All forecasts are presented in writing to a group leader who provides summaries to all group members.

For those forecasts that differ substantially from the majority—either high or low—a request is made for a written explanation of the reasoning behind the forecast. That information is also shared with group members on an anonymous basis. Then a new round of forecasts is made. This process is repeated several times, and then a decision is made based on the collective responses.

The weakness of the Delphi method is that it takes more time and requires written explanations. Rather than just being committed to attending one meeting, Delphi requires the participants to refocus their attention on the problem a number of times. Therefore, it places a greater demand on the time of the large number of individuals who are involved.

Nevertheless, Delphi has several particular advantages. By avoiding a face-to-face meeting, the technique avoids confrontation. Decisions are based more on logic than on personality or position. The dissemination of the respondent's underlying reasoning allows erroneous facts or assumptions that lie behind the forecast to be corrected.

These two methods both make use of the fact that individual managers cannot be expected to think of everything. Different individuals, bringing different expertise and different points of view to bear on the same problem, can create an outcome that is superior to that which any one of them could do individually. It is a cliché to say that two minds are better than one; nevertheless, in many forecasting instances, the Delphi and nominal group approaches can substantially improve the accuracy of forecasts and other estimates.

INDEXING FOR INFLATION

Many times historical information is available, and we do not have to rely on the Delphi or nominal group approaches. However, one of the biggest problems with historical data is that they are influenced by changes in price levels—namely, inflation. To make the data useful for estimating future costs, it is necessary to adjust, or index, the historical information for inflation.

Most people today are familiar with price indices. The Consumer Price Index (CPI) is reported each month, indicating the general rate of inflation for consumer purchases. In the health care industry, it is difficult to avoid price indices. For example, the majority of hospitals in the country receive Medicare payments based on Diagnosis Related Groups (DRGs). DRG rates are adjusted each year, based on a hospital market basket index. Price indices are used as a basis for adjusting various financial measures for the impact of inflation over time.

Indexing has a great number of potential applications, because accountants frequently use financial data from the past in their analyses in order to improve future managerial decisions and results. In a DRG environment with a growing emphasis on cost accounting, historical cost information is increasingly likely to form the basis for management studies. Yet, it is well known that historical financial information in general, and cost information in particular, are severely distorted by the impact of changes in the price level, or inflation. Thus, it becomes necessary to attempt to eliminate, or at least reduce, the distortion by accounting for the impact of changes in the price level.

It is especially important in areas such as cost prediction that we index for the impact of inflation. Simply comparing historical costs from different years will not provide a sound basis for predicting future costs. Any attempt to identify the cause of cost differences is clouded by the impact of inflation. Did that new, highly touted cost-saving device save money? It's hard to tell, because with inflation, costs went up anyway. Would costs have been even higher without the cost-saving device? To answer such questions, we would have to adjust for the impact of inflation on the cost. How much did our costs rise because of volume increases? Again, it is difficult to tell because the volume increases and inflation are mixed together. Thus, for the analysis to be useful, we must first adjust historical costs for the impact of those price-level changes.

Suppose, for example, that we wish to predict electricity costs for next year. Let's assume that for the Hypothetical Health Care Organization, electricity costs and patient-day volume over the last eight years were as follows:

Year Ending June 30	Electricity Cost ($)	Patient Days
1987	121,820	61,000
1988	140,636	63,000
1989	148,498	65,000
1990	175,327	70,000
1991	174,541	72,000
1992	190,504	76,000
1993	223,755	82,000
1994	228,959	80,000

These costs are assumed to represent the actual amounts spent by Hypothetical for electricity. However, the figures cannot be used for a meaningful comparison of true costs, because the dollar changed in value over this period.

Selecting an Appropriate Index

How can we adjust the costs so that they will all be comparable? We must use some kind of price index. We can choose from many different indices. As noted earlier, the most common of the price indices is the CPI. There are also wholesale price indices, general price deflators, hospital market basket indices, and a wide range of other general and specific measures.

Care must be exercised in selecting an appropriate index. Indices are generally averages. Some components of the index go up at a faster rate and others at a slower rate. For example, if we are trying to estimate fixed and variable costs for the entire health care organization, it would be a mistake to use the overall CPI measure. Health care costs have risen much faster than the CPI over the last several decades.

On the other hand, for estimating fixed and variable electricity costs, a measure specific to the health industry is probably also inappropriate, unless electricity costs were matching the rapid rise in overall health care organization costs over that period.

One alternative is to use a part of the CPI. The overall CPI measure considers the changing cost of a standard basket of typical consumer goods. The index was based at 100 for the 1982–1984 period, indicating that for those years, the basket of goods cost 100 percent of the average 1982–1984 cost. If the index today were 312, it would indicate that today it costs 312 percent of the 1982–1984 base period cost (or 3.12 times as much) to purchase the same basket of goods. The CPI, however, is broken down into a number of parts.

The CPI includes a medical care component that measures the change in price level in the medical care portion of the basket of goods. The medical care component of the CPI is subdivided into the following categories:

1. Medical care commodities
   - Prescription drugs
   - Nonprescription drugs and medical supplies
2. Medical care services
   - Professional services
     — Physicians
     — Dentists
     — Other professional services

- Other medical care services
  — Hospital and other medical care services
  — Hospital room charges
  — Other hospital and medical care services

Clearly, one must intelligently consider which index would be most likely to reflect the changes in the price level of the item being estimated. In the case of electricity costs, we can be very specific. Rather than even using a subcomponent of the CPI, we can use our past electricity invoices to determine the charge per kilowatt hour in each year. For electricity, this would be the best measure of changes in the price level.

Calculating the Inflation Adjustment

Suppose that kilowatt rates (determined by looking at old bills) were as follows for the past eight years, and for the coming year, 1995, based on approved utility rates:

Year Ending June 30	Rate Per Kilowatt Hour ($)
1987	.0700
1988	.0800
1989	.0820
1990	.0890
1991	.0890
1992	.0950
1993	.1051
1994	.1089
1995	.1132

To convert historical cost information into current dollars, multiply the historical cost by the current index value divided by the index value at the time the cost was incurred. For example, to convert the 1987 electricity cost into 1995 dollars, multiply the 1987 cost, $121,820, by the 1995 index of $.1132 divided by the 1987 index of $.0700:

$$\$121,820 \times \frac{\$.1132}{\$.0700} = \$197,000$$

The resulting figure is the adjusted value for the 1987 electricity expense. This process, if repeated for each of the years, would yield the following series of electricity costs, adjusted for the impact of changes in the price level:

Year Ending June 30	Electricity Cost ($)	Patient Days
1987	197,000	61,000
1988	199,000	63,000
1989	205,000	65,000
1990	223,000	70,000
1991	222,000	72,000
1992	227,000	76,000
1993	241,000	82,000
1994	238,000	80,000

Note that the index for 1995 was used for these calculations. This results in information already adjusted for the impact of inflation during next year. Generally, the index value for next year—of the CPI or hospital market basket, for example—will not be known until the end of next year. If you were to use the 1994 CPI for the calculation, the fixed and variable costs predicted for 1995 would be in 1994 dollars and would have to be adjusted upward for expected inflation before being used in a budget or plan for the fiscal 1995 year.

Health care organizations are sometimes caught between tides moving in opposite directions. For example, for hospitals, average length of stay over the last decade has been declining, leading to expected cost decreases, yet inflation keeps driving costs upward. Skillful management requires segregation of the impact of inflation so that cost-volume relationships can be understood and controlled.

COST ESTIMATION USING LINEAR REGRESSION

Even having adjusted historical information for the impact of inflation, *cost estimation,* or prediction of future costs, is difficult if some of the costs are "mixed" costs—that is, if some costs have a fixed cost element and a variable cost element mixed together. For example, total nursing cost for a hospital is a mixed cost. A substantial amount of nursing supervision is fixed, but floor staffing can be more readily adjusted to anticipated occupancy rates and is therefore a variable or *step-variable* cost. In any kind of planning for the future, it becomes quite important to have reasonable estimates of the portion of costs that is fixed and the portion that is variable.

A valuable technique for estimating costs is linear regression. Because regression analysis is often thought of as statistics or mathematics—fields that many managers shy away from—this technique has been underutilized in the health care field. Not all health care organizations use regression analysis, and even in health care organizations where accountants have made it a regularly used tool, department heads throughout the organization often have resisted adopting the technique. However, this technique will become more commonly employed as managers have to face ever greater constraints on costs. Given the widespread access to calculators and computers, using regression has become fairly simple. This section will demonstrate manually some of the necessary calculations. However, in the vast majority of cases, managers will use computers to do these calculations for them.

The linear regression technique uses past experience regarding costs to help predict future fixed and variable costs. The basic premise is that, over time, both costs and volume of output change. If a cost is a fixed cost, the change in volume will not cause it to change. Therefore, we can assume that any changes in cost that occur as volume of output changes are related to variable costs.

As a preliminary step, we should consider the impact of changes in the price level. Thus, for the analysis to be useful, historical costs must be adjusted for the impact of those price-level changes, as discussed above.

An Estimation Example Introduced

Suppose that we wish to predict electricity costs for a hospital for next year. Assume that patient days fell last year after a long period of steady growth. We expect patient days to fall by 4 percent next year. We do not expect electricity cost to fall by 4 percent, because we know that it has both fixed and variable elements. Fewer patient days mean less use of electrical equipment, but in the offices, hallways, cafeteria, and so forth, usage will not be affected.

If we knew the fixed and variable costs of electricity, we would be in a good position to predict costs for next year. The fixed costs would remain the same since changes in volume, by definition, do not affect fixed costs. The variable cost per patient day would then be multiplied by the expected volume of patient days to find the total expected variable cost. Adding the fixed and variable costs would give us our prediction of electricity costs for next year.

Historical information on electricity costs and patient-day volume, already adjusted for the impact of changes in the price level (i.e., inflation), are as follows:

Year Ending June 30	Electricity Cost ($)	Patient Days
1987	197,000	61,000
1988	199,000	63,000
1989	205,000	65,000
1990	223,000	70,000
1991	222,000	72,000
1992	227,000	76,000
1993	241,000	82,000
1994	238,000	80,000
1995	?	76,800

We would like to predict the electricity cost for 1995, yet we cannot immediately do that, because we do not know the fixed cost/variable cost relationship.

The High–Low Technique

One rather simplistic approach to this problem is to use a *high–low analysis* of past costs, selecting the highest and lowest volumes and looking at the cost difference between them.

Dividing the cost difference by the volume change yields a change in cost per unit change in volume. Using the above information, the lowest cost of $197,000 occurred in 1987, when the volume was 61,000. The highest cost of $241,000 occurred when volume was 82,000. The change in cost and volume between the high and low points can be shown as follows:

$$\frac{\text{High cost} - \text{low cost}}{\text{High volume} - \text{low volume}} = \frac{\$241,000 - \$197,000}{82,000 - 61,000}$$

$$= \frac{\$44,000}{21,000}$$

$$= \$2.095$$

The result, $2.095, represents the change in cost for each unit change in volume. Since fixed costs do not change as volume changes, this change in cost per unit change in volume must represent the variable cost. At a volume of 61,000 patient days, the total variable cost would then be as follows:

$$\text{Variable cost} = 61,000 \text{ patient days} \times \$2.095 \text{ per patient day}$$

$$= \$127,810$$

(The variable cost is actually $2.0952381; the use of $2.095 resulted in a slight rounding difference.) Since the total cost at that volume is $197,000, the fixed cost must be as follows:

Total cost	$197,000
Variable cost	−127,810
Fixed cost	$ 69,190

Note that we could confirm this by considering the costs for the high volume of 82,000 patient days. At that volume, the variable cost would be as follows:

$$\text{Variable cost} = 82,000 \text{ patient days} \times \$2.095 \text{ per patient day}$$

$$= \$171,810$$

Since the total cost at that volume is $241,000, the fixed cost must be as follows:

Total cost	$241,000
Variable cost	−171,810
Fixed cost	$ 69,190

Fixed costs are by definition fixed as volume changes. Therefore, the costs are the same at both the high and low volumes, except for the minor difference due to rounding.

This high–low method is very simple to operationalize. If we wish to know the costs next year if the volume is 76,800 patient days, we need merely to determine the total variable cost and add them to the fixed cost:

$$\text{Estimated cost} = \$69,000 + (76,800 \times \$2.095)$$

$$= \$230,104$$

Unfortunately, this method has a serious flaw. By using the extremes, it is likely to pick up an outlier as one of its two points. For example, suppose that an extreme heat wave caused an influx of patients suffering from heat-related problems. At the same time, electricity usage soared, because the hospital had to run the air conditioning 24 hours a day, and the electric utility briefly raised rates to try to reduce peak usage. Had those patients been spread throughout the year, the electricity cost would have been much lower. However, in this case, the heat demanded more electricity usage per patient day, and at a higher than normal rate per kilowatt hour. Using this unusual occurrence as a basis for our calculations can make the result very unrepresentative.

Figure 7-1 represents the pattern of usage and cost for electricity over a number of years, without an extreme outlier situation. In contrast, Figure 7-2 shows an outlier point that represents the impact of the heat wave discussed above. The high–low method essentially connects a line between the low and high cost points, assuming that the points in between will lie near to that line. As we can see, if one of the two points is an outlier, the results are quite misleading. All of the other data points are below the estimated line. The high–low method in this case would not lead to reasonably accurate cost estimations.

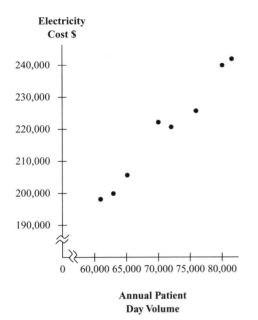

Figure 7-1 Historical Costs and Volume. *Source:* Reprinted from *Hospital Cost Accounting Advisor,* Vol. 1, No. 2, p. 4, Aspen Publishers, Inc., © 1985.

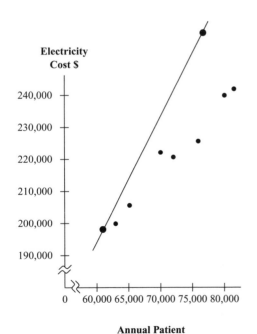

Figure 7-2 High–Low Method with Outlier. *Source:* Adapted from *Hospital Cost Accounting Advisor,* Vol. 1, No. 2, p. 4, Aspen Publishers, Inc., © 1985.

To avoid distortions caused by unusual outlier events, it is better to try to include all available information in the analysis and to exclude obvious outlier values. The high–low method can exclude obvious outliers, but it cannot benefit from the information that all the data points provide. The linear regression method can.

Using Linear Regression

The costs for electricity at various volumes have been plotted on the graph in Figure 7-1. The vertical axis represents cost (the *dependent variable*), and the horizontal axis represents the volume of patient days (the *independent variable*). The dependent variable is the one we are attempting to predict. Its value *depends* on the value of the independent variable. In other words, electricity costs depend on the number of patient days. In this particular situation, we would like to predict what costs will be next year if volume is 4 percent less than it was last year, or a total of 76,800 patient days.

The linear regression method essentially attempts to find a straight line through these historical points. Generally, it is not possible to go through all of the points with any one straight line. Therefore, we need to find a line that comes as close as possible to all of these points. The equation used to define a straight line is as follows:

$$y = mx + b$$

where y is the dependent variable, m is the slope of the line, x is the independent variable, and b is the point at which the line crosses the vertical axis, called the y intercept. (See Figure 7-3.)

If one knew the slope (m) and the intercept (b), then for any given x, the y value could be calculated. For example, suppose that a hospital had 81,000 patient days (x), the slope (m) of the cost line was $2.00, and the intercept (b) was $70,000:

$$y = mx + b$$
$$y = (\$2.00 \times 81,000) + \$70,000$$
$$y = \$232,000$$

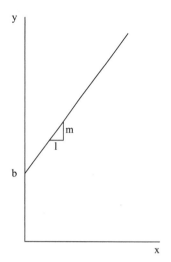

Figure 7-3 Graph of a Straight Line

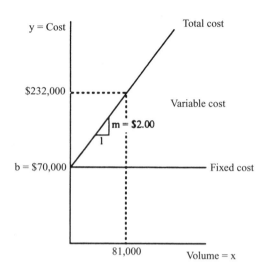

Figure 7-4 Graph of Total Costs

We can visualize this as simply the total cost line considered in Chapter 5. In Figure 7-4, the total cost line intersects the vertical axis at $70,000, the b value. The line increases at a rate of $2.00 per patient day, the slope or m value. (The slope is defined as the vertical rise in the line for each increase of one unit along the horizontal axis.) Note that the b value is identical to the fixed cost, and the m value is identical to the variable cost. If we can determine the b and m values, we will then be able to predict the cost (y value) for any given volume (x value). In this case x = 81,000, so we can determine that y = $232,000.

The information about the determination of a straight line provides the foundation for regression analysis. Linear regression, or "least squares," is an approach that uses a set of paired x and y values to generate an estimated line. That estimate yields values for b and m, allowing the user to predict the cost y for any value of x. In regression analysis, the traditional equation for a straight line is generally shown as

$$y = \alpha + \beta x$$

where α, the Greek letter alpha, is equivalent to b, and is referred to as the *constant*. Fixed costs do not vary with volume and therefore may be thought of as being constant. The Greek letter beta, β, is the same as m, and is referred to as the x coefficient. This is because it is multiplied by x. Since x is the volume, and β is equivalent to the variable cost, βx is the total variable cost. The total cost, y, is equal to the fixed cost, α, plus the total variable cost, βx.

We must realize that historical points probably will not all lie along a straight line. Therefore, regression analysis, in fitting the best possible straight line to the data, merely generates an estimate. The values for α and β are only approximately correct.

The goal of the linear regression process is to estimate a line that is as close as possible to the given data points. This is accomplished by locating the line where it is the least possible distance from the data points. During the calculations, the distance of each point from the line is squared so that the positive and negative values of points above and below the line do not offset each other. The line is located so as to minimize the sum of these squared distances. This gives rise to the commonly used name for linear regression, "minimization of least squares." Any line other than the regression line would have a larger sum of squared values. Therefore, it would be further from the historical data points. The least-squares derivation of α and β is based on the solution of two equations:

[1] $\alpha n + \beta(\Sigma x) = \Sigma y$ and

[2] $\alpha(\Sigma x) + \beta(\Sigma x^2) = \Sigma xy$

Note that n stands for the number of observations, and Σ, the Greek letter sigma, is a mathematical symbol representing the summation of a set of values.

The theory behind this calculation will not be discussed here. (The reader who is unfamiliar with linear regression is referred to any statistics text that covers regression analysis.) However, as a result of statistics, we are able to use a very straightforward method, simple linear regression, that takes into account historical information about volume and cost and uses it to establish a line that is a good estimator. The method is called "simple" linear regression because it uses one independent variable to predict one dependent variable. As we will see later, there is a statistical technique that uses more than one independent variable as a predictor for the dependent variable.

Using the electricity cost data provided earlier, we can calculate the elements needed to solve this equation. For the sake of keeping the example simple, both cost and patient day information will be provided in thousands. Although an actual manual calculation is shown below, in practice, computer programs are used. This example is provided for the benefit of readers interested in tracing through the underlying mechanics to improve their conceptual understanding (see Table 7-1).

From Table 7-1, we see the following:

$$\Sigma y = \$1,752$$
$$\Sigma x = 569$$
$$\Sigma x^2 = 40,899$$
$$\Sigma xy = \$125,527$$

There were 8 data points, so $n = 8$. We can now solve the two equations by substituting values:

[1] $\alpha n + \beta(\Sigma x) = \Sigma y$
$$8\alpha + 569\beta = \$1,752$$

[2] $\alpha(\Sigma x) + \beta(\Sigma x^2) = \Sigma xy$
$$569\alpha + 40,899\beta = \$125,527$$

Next, the first equation is solved for α:

$$8\alpha + 569\beta = \$1,752$$
$$8\alpha = \$1,752 - 569\beta$$
$$\alpha = (\$1,752 - 569\beta) \div 8$$
$$\alpha = \$219 - 71.125\beta$$

This value for α can be substituted into the second equation:

$$569\alpha + 40,899\beta = \$125,527$$
$$569 \times (\$219 - 71.125\beta) + 40,899\beta = \$125,527$$
$$\$124,611 - 40,470.125\beta + 40,899\beta = \$125,527$$
$$428.875\beta = \$916$$
$$\beta = \$916/428.875$$
$$\beta = \$2.136$$

This value for β can be placed into the expression for α as follows:

$$\alpha = \$219 - 71.125\beta$$
$$\alpha = \$219 - 71.125 \times \$2.136$$

Recall that for ease of calculation, we started with electricity cost and patient days in thou-

Table 7-1 Calculation of Least-Squares Values

Year	Electricity Cost (y) (in Thousand $)	Patient Days (x) (in Thousands)	x^2 (in Billions)	xy (in Billion $)
1987	197	61	3,721	12,017
1988	199	63	3,969	12,537
1989	205	65	4,225	13,325
1990	223	70	4,900	15,610
1991	222	72	5,184	15,984
1992	227	76	5,776	17,252
1993	241	82	6,724	19,762
1994	238	80	6,400	19,040
Totals (Σ)	1,752	569	40,899	125,527

sands. We can reconvert now by changing the $219 to $219,000, and the 71.125 to 71,125. It is not necessary to change the $2.136 value.

$$\alpha = \$219,000 - 71,125 \times \$2.136$$
$$\alpha = \$219,000 - \$151,852$$
$$\alpha = \$67,148$$

Therefore, our fixed cost is expected to be $67,148. The variable cost per patient day, β, is $2.136. (Note that there is a degree of rounding in these estimates.)

If we select any volume on the horizontal axis and go up to the estimated line, we can then go from the regression line across to the vertical axis to get a cost estimate. In the case of electricity, given a prediction of the number of patient days next year, we can get an estimate of total electricity cost (see Figure 7-5). Going up to the regression line from the expected volume of 76,800 places us at a point on the line that is equivalent to $231,127 of cost when we look across to the vertical axis.

Although no estimate or prediction of the future is likely to be absolutely accurate, this method minimizes the probability that there will

be a substantial difference between the prediction and the actual result. An underlying assumption in using regression analysis to predict future values is that the results of the past are a good indication of what will happen in the future. To the extent that the future differs from the past, the ability of regression to provide accurate information is limited.

Although this example demonstrates the actual process for calculating α and β, generally preprogrammed, hand-held calculators or computers are used to simplify the process. Using an inexpensive calculator designed to do linear regression or a computer with a statistics program, you simply input the historical information in the form of matched pairs:

> 61,000 patient days, $197,000 electricity cost
> 63,000 patient days, $199,000 electricity cost

This is continued until the volume and cost data for all years have been input.

Generally, the more years (i.e., data points) you use, the more reliable the result. However, if any major change has taken place (e.g., addition of a new wing) that would change fixed costs, then the data from before the change become less useful. You should not go back so far that you are using data not likely to be reasonably relevant today.

Once you have compiled all the information, follow the instructions for your specific calculator or computer software for regression analysis. When the regression computation has been completed, there are several alternative ways to proceed. One is simply to input the predicted volume (in this case, 76,800 patient days) and compute the predicted electricity cost for that volume. Alternatively, you can have the calculator determine the slope of the regression line and the vertical axis intercept.

In discussion of the high–low method, the issue of outliers was raised. That tends to be an extreme problem for the high–low method, because outlier information can dominate such analysis and badly distort the results. Because outliers make up, it is hoped, only a small portion of the data used for regression, they have less impact. Nevertheless, they should be considered. Application 7-1 addresses the issue of

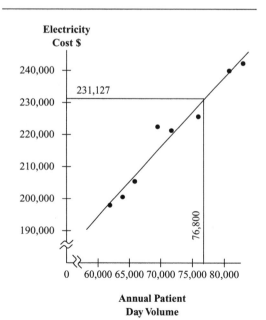

Figure 7-5 Using the Regression Line As an Estimator. *Source:* Adapted from *Hospital Cost Accounting Advisor,* Vol. 1, No. 2, p. 5, Aspen Publishers, Inc., © 1985.

outliers in regression analysis and appropriate approaches for dealing with them.

Multiple Regression

In some cases, one independent variable is insufficient to capture fixed and variable cost relationships. For example, a hospital's total nursing costs are probably related to patient days but are also related to the average severity of illness of the patients. Such additional factors can be addressed with *multiple regression* analysis.

This technique is very similar to simple linear regression, but it uses several independent variables to predict the dependent variable, whereas simple linear regression uses only one independent variable to predict the dependent variable. Thus, admissions, patient days, and average acuity could be used as independent variables in a multiple regression analysis to predict the fixed and variable elements of nursing cost. Multiple regression is easily accomplished using a microcomputer with appropriate software or using a somewhat elaborate hand-held calculator.

Although we have used electricity costs as an example, regression analysis is equally useful for estimating the fixed and variable cost for any cost objective. For example, we could use this approach to estimate aggregate amounts (such as total nursing costs, administration costs, maintenance costs, and housekeeping costs) or more detailed costs (such as the cost of a particular nursing unit).

The method is particularly flexible in that it will allow prediction of costs that can readily be segregated into fixed and variable components by other means as well as those that cannot. For example, it can separate total nursing costs into fixed and variable components. A manager could probably manually separate nursing administrators as fixed costs and staff nurses as variable to get this result. However, regression analysis will also separate the fixed portion of electricity cost from the variable portion—a task most managers would not otherwise be able to accomplish.

Regression Analysis Cautions

Regression analysis is a technique that is often used mechanically without being given adequate thought. It is important for managers to be cautious in the use of this tool. First, one should always ensure that the relationship between the variables makes sense. Second, the results should indicate that the independent variable is responsible for the variations in the dependent variable. Next, one should assess the significance of the independent variable(s). Finally, one should consider the reasonableness of the assumptions made in the analysis. Each of these four areas will be discussed.

Often, users of regression analysis simply assume, sometimes without even formally realizing it, that there are no problems related to these four areas. We will not go into a detailed examination of these technical statistical issues, but the reader should be aware of their existence and should try to make at least a casual effort to ensure that there are not serious problems with relation to any of them.

Plausibility

The cost estimation approach discussed uses an independent variable to predict cost, which is the dependent variable. However, just because the population in China is growing and the hospital budget is growing does not mean that the number of people in China is affecting the hospital's costs. If we used the population in China as an independent variable, it might seem to predict costs, but the prediction could not be assumed to be an accurate one, because there is no economic justification supporting the relationship.

This issue is referred to as plausibility. The relationship between the variables must make reasonable sense. There should be some reason that we believe that the independent variable is causal, that is, that it causes the dependent variable to vary.

Goodness of Fit

The ability of one variable to explain the variations in another is referred to as the "goodness of fit." If the independent variable rises and falls in some direct proportion with the dependent variable, there will be an excellent goodness of fit.

If the actual data points are not on the estimated line, it is likely that the future points will also not be on the line. The degree of goodness of fit is rarely perfect. The degree of historical dispersion is of interest because it gives a hint about likely future dispersion.

Some dispersion results because the independent variable is not a perfect predictor of the dependent variable. For example, more patient days cause the hospital to spend more on electricity. There may be other factors, such as the weather, the mix of patients, or the equipment used, that also affect electricity costs. Table 7-2 provides information for assessing dispersion.

The average value for the dependent variable ($\bar{y}$) is the basis for evaluation of dispersion. In the preceding example, the Σy was \$1,752,000 for 8 data points (see Table 7-2), so the average would be as follows:

$$\bar{y} = \Sigma y \div n$$
$$\Sigma y = \$1,752,000$$
$$n = 8$$
$$\Sigma y \div n = \$219,000$$
$$\bar{y} = \$219,000$$

If we compare each historical y value to the mean, $\bar{y}$, we have a measure of total dispersion. For example, in 1993, the actual cost was \$241,000, while $\bar{y} = \$219,000$. The total variation between the actual cost and the mean cost can be stated as follows:

$$y - \bar{y} = \$241,000 - \$219,000$$
$$= \$22,000$$

The regression result we calculated predicts that the cost for 1993 would be

$$y' = \alpha + \beta x$$
$$= \$67,148 + \$2.136 \times 82,000$$
$$= \$242,300$$

where we use a prime (′) to indicate a value generated from the results of the linear regression model. We now have three values for y, as follows:

y = one specific *actual* historical cost

$\bar{y}$ = the *mean* value of all the actual costs

y′ = one specific cost value *predicted* by the regression model

We have already noted that $(y - \bar{y})$ is the total variation between an actual cost and the mean cost. When we compare the three cost values, we note that $(y' - \bar{y})$ is the portion of the total variation that is explained by the independent variable, and $(y - y')$ is the unexplained portion:

Explained variation:
$$y' - \bar{y} = \$242,300 - \$219,000 = \$23,300$$

Unexplained variation:
$$y - y' = \$241,000 - \$242,300 = (\$1,300)$$

Total variation: $= \$22,000$

Table 7-2 Dispersion Information

Year	y ($)	$\bar{y}$ ($)	$y - \bar{y}$ ($)	$(y-\bar{y})^2$ ($)	y′ ($)	$y - y'$ ($)	$(y-y')^2$ ($)
1987	197,000	219,000	−22,000	484,000,000	197,444	−444	197,136
1988	199,000	219,000	−20,000	400,000,000	201,716	−2,716	7,376,656
1989	205,000	219,000	−14,000	196,000,000	205,988	−988	976,144
1990	223,000	219,000	4,000	16,000,000	216,668	6,332	40,094,224
1991	222,000	219,000	3,000	9,000,000	220,940	1,060	1,123,600
1992	227,000	219,000	8,000	64,000,000	229,484	−2,484	6,170,256
1993	241,000	219,000	22,000	484,000,000	242,300	−1,300	1,690,000
1994	238,000	219,000	19,000	361,000,000	238,028	−28	784
Totals (Σ)	1,752,000	1,752,000	0	2,014,000,000	1,752,568	−568	57,628,800

This division into the explained and unexplained variation allows for an assessment of how good the independent variable is at explaining why the dependent variable varies.

In order to assess the variation, the deviations for all data points must be taken into account. This is done by squaring the total deviation $(y - \bar{y})$ for each point, and then summing the squares. Thus, the sum of the squares of the deviations $[\Sigma(y - \bar{y})^2]$ represents the total variation. Similarly, the sum of the squares of the unexplained portion of the variation $[\Sigma(y - y')^2]$ can be calculated as well. (See Table 7-2.) This information can be used to calculate a measure of the goodness of fit.

Goodness of fit is measured by the coefficient of determination, referred to as the *R-squared*. Most calculators with linear regression capability will also calculate the *R*-squared. The *R*-squared value can range anywhere from a low of zero to a high of one. The closer the value to one, the better the equation is as a predictor. A value close to zero would indicate that our independent variable—volume of patient days in the above example—is not a good basis for predicting electricity costs.

$$R^2 = 1 - \frac{\text{Unexplained variation}}{\text{Total variation}}$$

$$= 1 - \frac{\Sigma(y - y')^2}{\Sigma(y - \bar{y})^2}$$

$$= 1 - \frac{\$57,628,800}{\$2,014,000,000}$$

$$= 1 - .0286$$

$$= .9714$$

In this case .97, or 97 percent of the total variation is explained by the independent variable patient days. This is an unusually high value for *R*-squared.

The coefficient of correlation, *r*, can be determined by taking the square root of *R*-squared.

$$r = \pm\sqrt{1 - \frac{\Sigma(y - y')^2}{\Sigma(y - \bar{y})^2}}$$

$$r = \pm .986$$

The value of *r* is either positive or negative, taking on the same sign as the β calculated earlier. The coefficient of correlation shows the direct relationship between the two variables. It can range from −1 to +1. The higher the absolute value, the greater the correlation. That is, if there is a high correlation, a change in the independent variable implies that there will be a change in the dependent variable. In the example, the correlation coefficient is .986, indicating that the line has a very good fit, and is therefore a good predictor of costs.

Independent Variable's Statistical Significance

In order for the independent variable to be responsible for costs, there must be a clear cause-and-effect relationship. More of the independent variable should result in more of the dependent variable. More patients should imply that more electricity is consumed. The regression analysis will indicate the slope of the estimated line. As discussed above, that slope represents the variable cost.

If the variable cost related to an independent variable is zero, the total costs will not vary as the independent variable changes. To ensure that this is not the case, a test is performed to ascertain that the value for the slope is indeed significantly different from zero. This is called the *t-test*. The *t* value of the slope measures significance. If the *t* value is greater than 2.00, then the slope is assumed to be statistically different from zero.

The *t* value or *t* statistic is calculated automatically by some calculators and almost all statistical computer programs. It consists of the value estimated for the slope or variable cost, divided by its standard error. In the above problem, the slope was 2.136, and the standard error of the slope was .116. Therefore, the *t* statistic was

18.4. This is greater than 2.0, indicating that the value is significantly different from zero.

Reasonableness of Assumptions

This last issue with regard to using regression analysis is often referred to as specification analysis. There are four elements of specification analysis: (1) *linearity,* (2) *constant variance,* (3) *independence,* and (4) *normality.* If the requirements of all four of these factors are met, then the resulting estimates are considered to be the best linear, unbiased estimates.

Linearity refers to a straight-line relationship. We are concerned with whether regression analysis, which projects a straight line, can reasonably estimate the relationship between the variables. It only makes sense to use a linear estimator if the relationship between the variables is linear. If one looked at the points on a scatter diagram, it should be reasonable to believe that a straight line could be an approximation. Look at Figure 7-1; it appears that a straight-line estimate would be reasonable. In contrast, look ahead to Figure 7-18, from the learning curve discussion later in this chapter (p. 284). Clearly, these points do not form a linear relationship, and a curved line must be used to estimate future costs. Linear regression analysis would be inappropriate. However, later in this chapter, we discuss both curvilinear forecasting and learning curves. Those are two examples of approaches that can be used if the relationship between the variables is not linear.

Constant variance refers to the fact that the scatter of actual historical data points around the estimated line should be fairly uniform. This is referred to as homoscedasticity. If for some reason the scatter of points are consistently near the regression line in some areas, and systematically further away in other areas (heteroscedasticity), it would indicate that the results are less reliable.

The third element of specification analysis relates to the independence of the residuals. The residuals are a measure of the distance from the regression line to each of the actual historical points. Each of these should be independent. If the residuals are not independent of each other,

a problem called serial correlation arises. This problem can also be identified by looking at the scatter and the regression line, or by using a test called the Durbin-Watson statistic. If there is serial correlation, the reliability of the results decreases.

The fourth element of specification analysis is that there is a normal distribution of historical points around the regression line.

Exhibit 7-1 summarizes the various concerns a manager must have in using regression analysis for cost estimation.

As a final note, it should be remembered that linear regression is simply a mechanical tool. It can only predict the future based on the past. The intelligence and judgment of a manager are called for to interpret the results. If there is reason to believe that the future will not be like the past, then the results must be adjusted. No tool can replace that element of managerial judgment.

FORECASTING

The cost estimation approach relies on a prediction of patient volume. Using that volume prediction, an estimate of costs is made. Therefore, an ability to forecast volume accurately is

---

Exhibit 7-1 Regression Analysis Cautions

Plausibility: The relationship between the variables should make sense.

Goodness of fit: The results should indicate that the independent variable is responsible for the variations in the dependent variable.

Statistical significance: The independent variable(s) should be statistically significant as measured by the *t* test.

Reasonableness of assumptions: One should consider the reasonableness of the assumptions made, specifically with respect to
- *linearity,*
- *constant variance,*
- *independence,* and
- *normality.*

essential to costing. This section first addresses some common approaches to forecasting. It then introduces an advanced, curvilinear approach. Finally, it discusses the critical role that managers play in the process.

Common Forecasting Approaches

The simplest approaches to forecasting are quite informal, "seat of the pants" type approaches. For example, next year can be assumed to simply be like the current year. Most managers try to be somewhat more sophisticated than that. Over time, trends may exist that would make it unlikely that this year will be a good reflection of next year. By taking more than one year's worth of data into account, forecasts are likely to give more accurate predictions.

Generally, forecasts are made using about five years' worth of historical data. This is not a hard and fast rule. However, using fewer than five years' of data prevents the forecast from being able to develop patterns fully. As one goes back further than five years, the data become less relevant because of changes in the way the health care organization runs. If one knows that there has been a dramatic change more recently than five years in some element that will affect the forecast, then fewer than five years' data can be used. If one knows that the health care organization or department has undergone no dramatic changes in the past ten years, then more than five years' of data can be used.

Forecasting Based on Averages

The simplest approach to forecasting using a series of historical data points is simply to take an average. The data for five years can be aggregated and divided by five to get an estimate for the coming year. Such an approach assumes that there is neither seasonality nor trend in the data. If the ups and downs over time are simply determined by random events, such an approach is reasonable. It must be noted, however, that the result is just a prediction for the year as a whole.

Forecasting can be much more useful if the forecasts are broken down by month. The same

averaging approach is possible using monthly data, except that it does not allow for longer and shorter months. The variation in months from 28 days to 31 days in length can create a problem. Also, if one is forecasting for a department that is only open weekdays, there is a variation from 20 to 23 possible weekdays per month. Thus, an average forecast based on annual data divided by 12 months would give an inexact result, even if there were neither trend nor seasonality. One would have to find an average forecast value per day (or per weekday) and apply that value to the number of days in each month in the coming year.

Such an averaging approach, however, assumes that there is neither trend nor seasonality—unlikely events for a health care organization. We will use several examples to consider the impact of trend and seasonality. For simplicity, we will use quarterly data for three years, even though one would generally use monthly data for five years.

Suppose that a health care organization needed to project patient days for the coming year in order to prepare department budgets. Suppose further that it had the historical patterns of patient days shown in Table 7-3 and Figure 7-6. From Figure 7-6, it is clear that there was an upward trend. If one were to take an average of the data points from Table 7-3, the

Table 7-3 Data with Trend

Quarter	Patient Days
1991–1992	
July–September	20,000
October–December	25,000
January–March	22,000
April–June	26,000
1992–1993	
July–September	24,000
October–December	28,000
January–March	29,000
April–June	33,000
1993–1994	
July–September	30,000
October–December	34,000
January–March	32,000
April–June	36,000

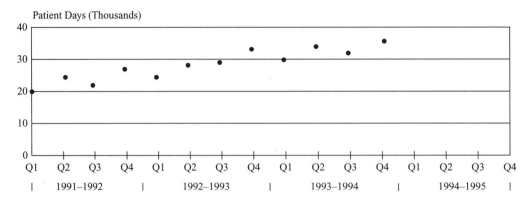

Figure 7-6 Graph of Data from Table 7-3. *Source:* Adapted from *Hospital Cost Management and Accounting,* Vol. 3, No. 2, p. 4, Aspen Publishers, Inc., © 1991.

resulting forecast is plotted on Figure 7-7 as a straight, horizontal line for the 1994 to 1995 year. That forecast makes little sense in the context of the observed upward trend in the scatter of the historical points for 1991 to 1994.

Using Linear Regression for Forecasting

As a result of the weakness of a simple average, linear regression is commonly used for forecasting. Regression can plot a single line that will provide a reasonably good predictor, based on existing data, for a trend. Figure 7-8 presents the forecast using a regression line. This is the same approach as used earlier to estimate a cost line.

Table 7-4 data present a different problem. Here, the data have a seasonal pattern, as can be

seen in Figure 7-9. Reviewing the graph in Figure 7-9, it is apparent that the winter months are busier than the summer months for this particular health care organization. A simple average would do little good. Taking an average would give the prediction for 1994 to 1995 shown as a horizontal line in Figure 7-10. This does not provide very much information about the seasonal cycle for the coming year. Using regression analysis, however, does not add substantially to the usefulness of the results, as can be seen in Figure 7-11.

Regression analysis assumes the use of a straight line for making the estimate. For a situation such as the trend observed in Figure 7-6, this worked out well. However, when there is a systematic pattern such as that observed in Fig-

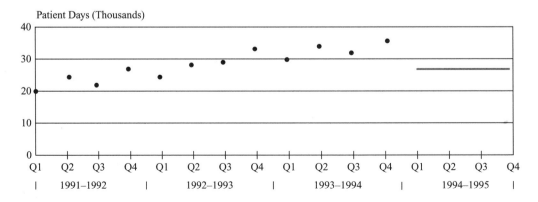

Figure 7-7 Forecast for Table 7-3 Data, Based on Average of Past Data. *Source:* Adapted from *Hospital Cost Management and Accounting,* Vol. 3, No. 2, p. 4, Aspen Publishers, Inc., © 1991.

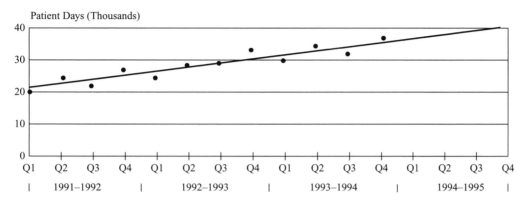

Figure 7-8 Forecast for Table 7-3 Data, Based on Regression Analysis. *Source:* Adapted from *Hospital Cost Management and Accounting,* Vol. 3, No. 2, p. 4, Aspen Publishers, Inc., © 1991.

ure 7-9, regression cannot capture that pattern. The regression analysis quarterly estimates for the coming year (Figure 7-11) lack the ability to capture the seasonal movement. This problem can be resolved by using *curvilinear forecasting.*

Curvilinear Forecasting

The limitation of regression is that it is based on a straight line. Seasonal patterns cannot be estimated well with straight lines. Curvilinear forecasting uses curved lines for making its estimates of the future. Because the forecast line can curve, it can more closely match a seasonal historical pattern. This results in a much more accurate forecast.

The method requires fairly sophisticated statistics and mathematics. Fortunately, however, computer software for curvilinear forecasting has become available that can be run on personal computers, making the technique available to most managers throughout the health care organization.

In using regression analysis, the optimal regression line is found by measuring the distance of the actual historical observations from the various alternative possible lines. The average distance that the actual points are away from the forecast line is measured in terms of the equation's standard deviation or average error. The optimal line is the one that is closest to all of the historical points (has the smallest standard deviation). Logically, this should then produce a prediction that is as close as possible in the future to what actually occurs. However, regression chooses its optimal line from among a series of straight lines.

Curvilinear forecasting allows the historical actual data to be compared with a much wider range of lines, including those that are curved. If a curved predictive line can be selected that is extremely close to the actual historical data, then the prediction should be extremely close as well.

For this example, we will use one of a number of forecasting programs currently available on

Table 7-4 Data with Seasonality

Quarter	Patient Days
1991–1992	
July–September	20,000
October–December	23,000
January–March	27,000
April–June	20,000
1992–1993	
July–September	21,000
October–December	25,000
January–March	29,000
April–June	20,000
1993–1994	
July–September	19,000
October–December	24,000
January–March	26,000
April–June	21,000

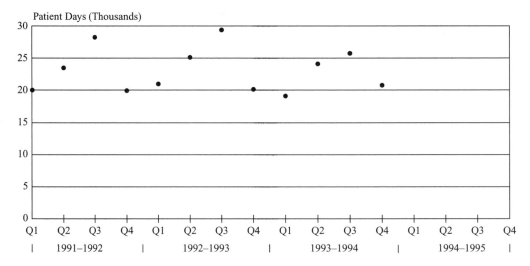

Figure 7-9 Graph of Data from Table 7-4. *Source:* Adapted from *Hospital Cost Management and Accounting,* Vol. 3, No. 2, p. 5, Aspen Publishers, Inc., © 1991.

the market. The program used, SmartForecasts II,* has a variety of different statistical models that yield curved lines. The novice can allow the model to forecast the future automatically, choosing the alternative statistical model that gives the best predictive power.

First, let's consider a forecast of the seasonal data in Table 7-3. We have seen in Figure 7-11 the predictions that would result from regression analysis. In contrast, look at the predictive (dotted) line in Figure 7-12. In this graph, time is on the horizontal axis, beginning with the

SmartForecasts II. Belmont, Mass: SmartSoftware, Inc. (800) 762-7899. As this book goes to print, an updated version, *SmartForecasts 3,* has become available.

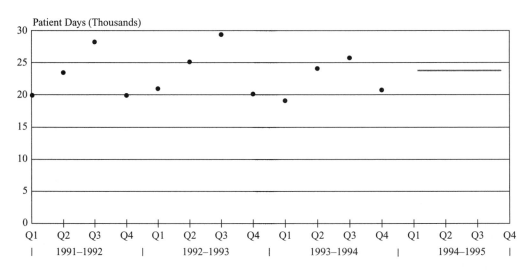

Figure 7-10 Forecast for Table 7-4 Data, Based on Average of Past Data. *Source:* Adapted from *Hospital Cost Management and Accounting,* Vol. 3, No. 2, p. 5, Aspen Publishers, Inc., © 1991.

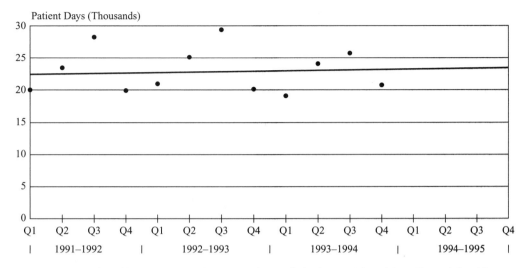

Figure 7-11 Forecast for Table 7-4 Data, Based on Regression Analysis. *Source:* Adapted from *Hospital Cost Management and Accounting,* Vol. 3, No. 2, p. 5, Aspen Publishers, Inc., © 1991.

first quarter of the 1991 to 1992 fiscal year, and ending with the last quarter of the 1994 to 1995 fiscal year. Patient days are on the vertical axis, as in the previous graphs.

The solid line in the graph in Figure 7-12 represents the actual historical data points connected from quarter to quarter. The dotted line is the forecast line. Table 7-5, generated by the

computer program, provides the forecast for each of the next four quarters, along with the lower and upper limits, for a range of possible outcomes.

For the forecast year, the dotted line in Figure 7-12 is bracketed above and below by a solid line that indicates a likely range or *forecast interval.* It is expected that 90 percent of the

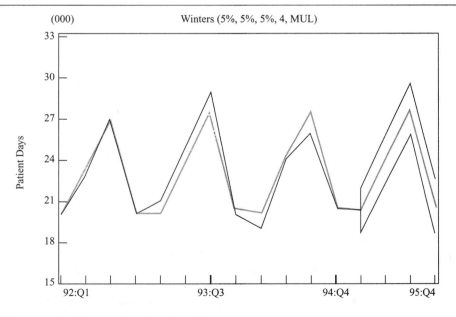

Figure 7-12 Forecast for Table 7-4 Data, Using Curvilinear Forecasting.

Table 7-5 Forecast and Forecast Interval Limits for Figure 7-12

Time Period	Approximate 90% Forecast Interval		
	Lower Limit	Forecast	Upper Limit
95:Q1	18656.190	20317.480	21978.760
95:Q2	22688.880	24377.600	26066.330
95:Q3	25892.970	27761.480	29629.990
95:Q4	18652.350	20651.630	22650.900

Table 7-6 Comparison of Results of Different Forecasting Methods

Method	Description	Results (%)
Winters'	Exponential smoothing with weights = 5%	(Winner)
Simple	Moving average of 4 periods	133
Single	Exponential smoothing with weight = 10%	179
Double	Exponential smoothing with weight = 10%	181
Linear	Moving average of 4 periods	190

time, the actual results for the coming year will remain within that range. Alternatively stated, in 9 out of every 10 predictions, the actual result will fall within the ranges outlined by the brackets. The forecast interval can be set at a higher or lower level if desired. For example, the range could be set at 99 percent, so that the actual result would only fall outside of the predicted range in 1 out of 100 predictions. However, the higher the percentage used, the wider apart the brackets would appear in Figure 7-12, and the wider apart the lower and upper limits of the forecast would be in Table 7-5.

It is interesting to examine the relationship between the actual historical data and the forecast line when extended back into the historical data. Unlike a straight regression line, which cannot possibly be very close to all the data points when there is seasonality, in this case the dotted line is extremely close to the solid line throughout the entire historical period.

The ability of the computer to select from among a variety of statistical forecast techniques and choose the one method that most closely follows actual patterns results in tremendous improvements in the accuracy of predictions. In this case, the *Winters' forecasting method* (as indicated across the top of the Figure 7-12 result) was the most appropriate. The computer compares several methods and selects as the winner the method that is closest to the historical data points. Table 7-6 indicates the comparison between the Winters' method, and other methods tried by the computer. The Winters' method is a curvilinear approach that is particularly adept at forecasting when the underlying data have a seasonal pattern. The per-

centages in the results column of Table 7-6 indicate how much farther away historical points were from the predictor lines using the other methods. (A discussion of the specific forecasting methods shown in Table 7-6 is beyond the scope of this book.)

Given that software programs such as these are relatively inexpensive (around $600), and are extremely easy to use, one cannot help but be impressed by the potential for improvements in a wide variety of forecasts throughout the health care organization. (Educators should note that SmartForecasts and similar software are generally available at substantially reduced rates for classroom and other educational uses.) Whether one is forecasting patient days, patient acuity, costs, or the number of chest tubes that will be used, the added sophistication can improve management and help conserve resources in many different departments.

Even in cases where regression analysis would seem to be adequate, the greater sophistication of curvilinear forecasting may be helpful. The data in Table 7-3 seemed to be treated adequately as a trend. What does a curvilinear forecast look like for the same data? Figure 7-13 is the SmartForecasts II forecast line for those data. Notice that the SmartForecasts forecast for the coming year is not represented by a straight line. The data, it turns out, have some seasonal patterns that were not immediately obvious. To the eye, it appeared to have the normal ups and downs of any trend pattern. The computerized forecasting model, however, determined that a curvilinear forecast would be more

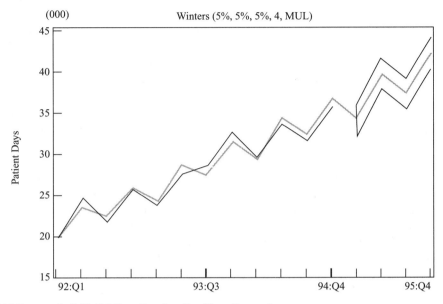

(000)   Winters (5%, 5%, 5%, 4, MUL)

Figure 7-13 Forecast for Table 7-3 Data, Based on Curvilinear Forecasting

accurate than a straight line. The historical data in this case indicate both a trend and a seasonal pattern.

Table 7-7 presents the forecast and 90 percent interval for the data. These results differ substantially from those predicted using the regression analysis. The forecasts based on Figure 7-8 would have been 36,682; 37,979; 39,276; and 40,573, for the four coming quarters, respectively. When one considers how closely the curvilinear forecast line is able to match up with the actual historical points in Figure 7-13, it is not hard to accept the curvilinear forecast as being more accurate than a linear regression result. Statistically, that fact is confirmed by the average forecast error of 1,180 using the Winters' curvilinear method, but 1,833 using linear

regression. The larger the forecast error, the greater the unexplained variation, and the weaker the likely accuracy of the forecast.

One of the more difficult aspects of health care forecasting is the combination of both trend and seasonality at the same time. This is not an unusual occurrence for health care organizations. However, for many noncomputer-based approaches to forecasting, it creates great difficulty. It is common to use regression analysis to identify the trend, then estimate the average percentage that a given month is above or below the trend each year, and project that average percentage into the future. That would have to be done separately for each month in the coming year—a somewhat complex process. However, as we have just seen, curvilinear forecasting can take account of both trend and seasonality automatically.

One additional advantage of the SmartForecasts software is that it recognizes the critical role that human beings must play in the forecasting process. Therefore, once the forecast is automatically made by the computer, the program allows for adjustments to be made to the result based on the input of the user. It is critical, regardless of the approach taken to software, that the experience, expertise, and

Table 7-7 Forecast and Forecast Interval Limits for Figure 7-13

	Approximate 90% Forecast Interval		
Time Period	*Lower Limit*	*Forecast*	*Upper Limit*
95:Q1	32471.270	34364.520	36257.780
95:Q2	38220.780	40056.750	41892.710
95:Q3	35689.680	37552.890	39416.090
95:Q4	40607.520	42569.820	44532.130

intuition of managers not be ignored in the forecasting process.

The Role of Managerial Judgment

Forecasting is often viewed as being a mechanical process. Historical data about the item being forecast are collected. The historical data points are averaged or entered into a linear regression or curvilinear model, and the forecast is generated. This approach is weak because it fails to incorporate all of the information that is available to the health care organization. It is limited by the inability to consider anything except historical information.

For example, consider the situation of a health care organization that is located in a growing community. To keep the example simple so that we can focus on the conceptual issue, assume that due to the continued growth in the community, patient days have been rising at a rate of 10 percent per year. Figure 7-14 shows what that historical pattern would look like plotted on a graph of patient days over time.

Suppose that the state were to adopt the DRG system for Medicaid payments, starting with the

coming year, for which a forecast is being made. The best estimates we can make are that this change in Medicaid reimbursement will lower the average length of stay organization-wide by 10 percent. What would the forecast look like for next year? Using a method that simply projects historical information into the future, the prediction would look like Figure 7-15.

Intuitively, we know that the projection in Figure 7-15 is incorrect. The various forecasting approaches are extremely useful for projecting into the future what has happened in the past. However, such mechanical tools have no ability to think. They cannot adjust to information that is not available to them. They merely take what is known from experience and assume that the future will be a reflection of the past.

Suppose that a health care organization department manager were told about the change in Medicaid, and asked to make a projection of patient days for next year. The result might be something like Figure 7-16. It makes sense that the decline in the average length of stay should have a negative impact, and we see such an impact in Figure 7-16. However, that graph is not correct either. The graph implies a 10 per-

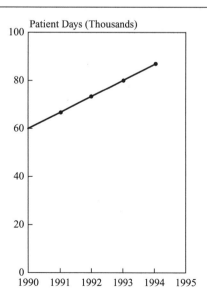

Figure 7-14 Historical Data for Years Ending June 30. *Source:* Adapted from *Hospital Cost Management and Accounting,* Vol. 3, No. 2, p. 2, Aspen Publishers, Inc., © 1991.

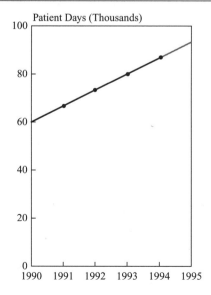

Figure 7-15 Formula-Based Projection of Past Experience into the Future. *Source:* Adapted from *Hospital Cost Management and Accounting,* Vol. 3, No. 2, p. 2, Aspen Publishers, Inc., © 1991.

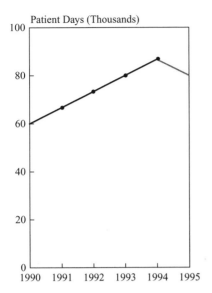

Figure 7-16 Judgmental Projection of Future. *Source:* Adapted from *Hospital Cost Management and Accounting,* Vol. 3, No. 2, p. 2, Aspen Publishers, Inc., © 1991.

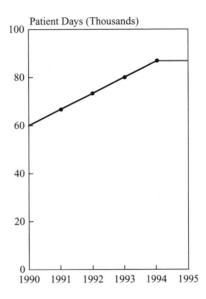

Figure 7-17 Projection Adjusted Based on Judgment. *Source:* Adapted from *Hospital Cost Management and Accounting,* Vol. 3, No. 2, p. 3, Aspen Publishers, Inc., © 1991.

cent decrease in overall patient days, but the Medicaid change is only decreasing the average length of stay by 10 percent. It is possible that there will be additional patients generating more patient days, as has been the trend.

Forecasting tools are probably better at projecting the past into the future than the manager is. In Figure 7-16, the manager has failed to account for the historical trend over time. On the other hand, the manager is more likely to be able to account for things that are happening currently. The mechanical method ignored that in Figure 7-15.

Figure 7-17 probably represents the most likely outcome. The graph in Figure 7-17 allows for a continual increase in patients, but with a decline in average length of stay. Figure 7-17 is likely to be the result of using a mechanical tool to project the past into the future, and then adjusting that prediction based on human intuition, knowledge, judgment, and experience.

The human role in forecasting should not be understated. This is one reason that it is inappropriate for the health care organization finance office to be making all of the forecasts for the various health care organization departments. If surgeons Jones and Smith take on a

new partner, volume could increase significantly. The operating room (OR) director can adjust the OR volume forecast to account for that. The finance office cannot, because it is unlikely to know about it. If Dr. Brown, our most productive heart surgeon, dies of a heart attack, again the OR would be more likely to be able to ascertain the likely impact on volume than would be the finance office. Certainly, no formula that predicts the future based on the past will be able to take that into account.

On the other hand, the finance office does have a significant role in the forecasting process. First of all, the finance office should be helping the various departments to use forecasting approaches that do a good job of projecting the past into the future. Second, it should be collecting data that can help managers make their judgmental adjustments to the results of the mechanical forecasting approaches.

For instance, data should be collected and disseminated on changes in third-party coverage, demographics, known shifts in patient mix, changes in accreditation standards or regulations, and so forth. Additionally, the finance office should suggest that each department consider changes in technology, availability of personnel, and any other factors that could work to make the future unlike the past.

Most importantly, the finance office should remind each department that it is the human manager of the department who has the critical knowledge base and intuition about that department, which is essential to forecasts that make sense. Arbitrary formula or computer-generated forecasts must be adjusted by the manager for the factors he or she knows that the formula or computer cannot have considered.

LEARNING CURVES

Many health care organizations are getting into new ventures such as home health agencies, off-site surgicenters, and health maintenance organizations (HMOs). Trying to predict the costs in areas where the organization lacks experience is always a difficult task. One complicating factor is the *learning curve* effect.

As employees and the health care organization itself become more familiar with a task or process, they become more proficient. The time taken to perform the task or process should decrease in response to this greater proficiency. For efficient management, it is important that this effect be considered in preparing an initial budget and subsequent budgets in the first several years of operations for any new service or venture.

Learning Curve Basics

A common budgeting problem is that once money is budgeted for a purpose, in future years, that amount is often taken for granted. New budget requests often come in for the old amount plus additions for inflation and new programs. Health care organizations often accept at face value that if it took three hours to do a task last year, it will take three hours to do that task this year.

That is generally not the case. Each subsequent year, it should take less time to perform the same tasks. This is not based on any presumption of inefficiency in earlier years, but simply on the fact that both workers and organizations learn from the process of making goods or providing services. If we continue to budget the same amount of time to do these tasks, we are automatically building some level of fat into the budget.

The learning curve effect was first widely noted during World War II, when there was an effort to determine how quickly and how many airplanes could be built. It was discovered that with each doubling of production, there was a systematic and *uniform* percentage reduction in the time required to build an airplane.

It was found that with every doubling of production, it took only 80 percent as much time per airplane as previously. Although airplanes are far different from patients, it has been found that the learning curve effect is widely applicable. What is especially astounding about the learning curve effect is that it is not dependent on having the same set of individuals do the work.

It is intuitively reasonable to conceive of an individual doing a task over and over and getting better at it. Therefore, most budget managers will readily accept the concept of a learning effect for an individual. However, it has been shown that over time the organization learns as well. Organizational learning may occur in areas such as better staffing approaches, better specific techniques for completing tasks, better training and supervision approaches, and so forth, resulting in a learning effect that goes well beyond the learning period for a new employee.

The learning effect is, however, subject to controlled processes, such as machines. Thus, if we were considering the total physician and nurse time needed for a health care organization's newly opened HMO, the learning effect would be very relevant. If we were, on the other hand, considering the technician time related to a computed tomography (CT) scan, the speed of the machine would have a limiting effect on the learning, unless the machine speed is totally controlled by the technician.

Calculations

To get a feel for the learning curve effect, we will perform some calculations using an 80 percent rate. This rate is the most widely used approximation. In different situations, the degree of learning will vary; that is, the 80 percent rate may not always be the most appropriate. However, the approach to the calculations is the same regardless of the rate used. Later, we discuss determination of the learning rate.

If we assume an 80 percent rate, learning curve theory projects that each time we double the cumulative total output to date, the labor cost per unit falls by 20 percent. For example, suppose that we were to open a new hospital clinic or an HMO. There would be new personnel, new forms, new procedures. What with all the usual initial foul-ups, the first patient examined by the nurse practitioner and then examined and possibly treated by the physician takes two full hours.

Treating just one more patient doubles the cumulative output level from one to two, and according to the learning curve effect, would take only 80 percent of 120 minutes, or 96 minutes. The personnel cost for treating the second patient is a full 20 percent lower than that for treating the first patient.

Doubling again requires us to see an additional two patients, to double the cumulative output from two to four patients. The costs will fall by 20 percent again. Learning curve theory says that it should take only 80 percent of 96 minutes each to treat the third and fourth patients, or 76.8 minutes per patient. Again, we have a substantial savings of almost 20 minutes per patient.

There has to be a catch. If the savings from additional patients are so great, why hasn't this been more obvious? The reason is that each cumulative doubling requires more and more patients. At first, we added just one patient to achieve a doubling. Next, we had to see two more patients to get a doubling. Next will be 4, then 8, then 16, and so forth. Over a period of many years, the cumulative total becomes so high that it would take many years to achieve a doubling.

At the same time that the doubling is requiring more and more volume, the savings in absolute minutes per patient is falling. Going from one patient to two, the required time fell from

120 minutes to 96, a 24-minute savings. Going from two to four, the time per patient falls from 96 to 76.8, slightly more than a 19-minute savings. Going from four to eight, the time per patient will fall to 80 percent of 76.8, or 61.4. This is a savings of only about 15 minutes per patient. Table 7-8 traces the effect of doublings up to 64 patients.

It is important to reemphasize that as the doublings take place, even though the learning rate remains the same, the number of minutes saved per unit for each doubling of volume decreases. Thus, we note in Table 7-8 that going from one to two patients reduces the time of the second patient by 24 minutes. However, going from 32 to 64 patients, the savings per patient is not quite eight minutes.

This gradual reduction in the rate of savings is referred to as the learning curve, and we often see the relationship graphed, as in Figure 7-18. It is quite clear from looking at this graph of Table 7-8 data that the big reductions in time take place early, and after a while, the curve nearly flattens.

Applicability of Learning Curves to Health Care Organizations

If the curve nearly flattens, what good is this concept to health care organization managers? In addition to using it for new ventures, we could use it to estimate costs for a low-volume

Table 7-8 Learning Curve Example. *Source:* Reprinted from *Hospital Cost Accounting Advisor,* Vol. 1, No. 9, p. 4, Aspen Publishers, Inc., © 1986.

Units this Batch	Cumu- lative Output	Average Time per Unit this Batch (minutes)	Time Reduction per Unit (minutes)
1	1	120.00	—
1	2	.80 × 120.00 = 96.00	24.00
2	4	.80 × 96.00 = 76.80	19.20
4	8	.80 × 76.80 = 61.44	15.36
8	16	.80 × 61.44 = 49.15	12.29
16	32	.80 × 49.15 = 39.32	9.83
31	64	.80 × 39.32 = 31.46	7.86

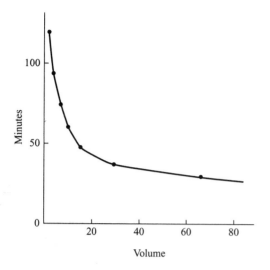

Figure 7-18 80% Learning Curve (Based on Table 7-8 Data). *Source:* Reprinted from *Hospital Cost Accounting Advisor,* Vol. 1, No. 9, p. 5, Aspen Publishers, Inc., © 1986.

procedure, such as open heart surgery. Many health care organizations that offer this service perform few operations in the program's start-up years. If there are 50 open heart procedures in the first year of the program, 50 more the next year, 100 the year following, and 200 the year after, we have 4 years of doubling the cumulative production. In each case, we should expect the labor time per operation to be falling.

This concept was developed originally for aircraft manufacture. Boeing might well turn out only 30 planes one year. Thirty more the next year would double production and bring down multimillion dollar costs by 20 percent. However, low volume is not the key to the learning effect. The concept is also applied in the microchip area, where hundreds of millions are turned out each year. The key to focus on is the *doubling* of production, not how great the total volume is.

An Example

Suppose that a hospital opens a new clinic and has 4,096 patients during the difficult first year. This represents quite a few doublings, from 1 to 2 to 4 to 8 to 16 to 32 to 64 to 128 to 256 to 512 to 1,024 to 2,048 to 4,096.

The costs will have fallen from 100 percent of the first patient, to 80 percent for the second, to 64 percent (80 percent of 80 percent) for the third and fourth, to 51 percent for the next 4, to 41 percent for the next 8, to 33 percent for the next 16, to 26 percent for the next 32, to 21 percent for the next 64, to 17 percent for the next 128, to 13 percent for the next 256, to 11 percent for the next 512, to 9 percent for the next 1,024, to 7 percent for the next 2,048. (Note the leveling off.)

By the end of the year, we clearly have an efficiently running clinic, with personnel costs per patient treated a mere fraction, about 7 percent, of the original cost. If the patient volume was constant throughout the year, then the 7 percent level was reached for the second half of the year, since we presumably treated 2,048 patients in the first half of the year and an equal number in the second half.

However, according to learning curve theory, which has been proven applicable in a wide range of industries, if we see another 4,000 patients next year, we will be doubling our cumulative production, and we should see costs fall by another 20 percent. That is, at the end of the second year, costs should fall by another 1.4 percent (i.e., 20% × 7%) of the original cost. That may not sound like much, but it really is.

Presumably at budget time, next year's budget request will be based on the costs after the shakeout period. However, according to this technique, there is still quite a bit of learning going on in the second year, and we should be able to treat this second set of approximately 4,000 patients for 20 percent less than the per-patient cost during the second half of the first year. Over the following 2 years at 4,000 patients per year, when cumulative output doubles again to approximately 16,000 patients, there should be another 20 percent reduction in labor.

In fact, if we have a new service that is growing rapidly, the doubling will come even more often. We might see 4,000 patients the first year, another 4,000 the next, and then 8,000 the following year. In that case, we should expect 20 percent reductions in the second year and again in the third year.

The Long Term and the Short Term

Over the long term, this approach becomes less important. If we have been giving patients IVs for the last 40 years, and if the hospital has had a fairly level patient population over that time, then there is still learning going on, but it is minimal.

If it would take another 40 years to double our cumulative number of IVs, then it will take those 40 years to get the next 20 percent savings. It is probably not worth trying to build into the budget any savings at all. On the other hand, if new tasks are being added to the nurses' duties, we should expect productivity to rise over time.

It is really when something is new and cumulative volume is doubling that the savings potential is the greatest. Health care organizations are currently entering so many new ventures, such as home health care, that in many cases, cumulative volume is doubling from year to year. It is in such cases that we must be most careful to use the learning curve to avoid poor cost estimation.

The Appropriate Learning Curve Rate

In many manufacturing industries, the learning curve has been solidly fixed as being 80 percent. However, it is conceivably possible for the rate to be as high as 100 percent (no learning takes place at all) or much lower than 80 percent (the rate of learning is high).

If we are to utilize this approach for budgeting, it would help if we could establish the learning curve for different types of activities. This would require collecting some time information during the early doublings. However, if the result is that the second-year labor budget may be set at a level 15, 20, or 25 percent lower, then the cost of collecting the data will certainly be worthwhile.

Linear regression can be combined with the use of logs to get a rather precise measure of the learning curve for various activities at a health care organization. However, there are simpler approaches we can use to get the same informa-

tion without having to resort to logs and regression analysis. Essentially, it is very easy to prepare a graph of the learning curve for any given percentage. Figure 7-19 represents the learning curves for 75, 80, and 85 percent. These can be constructed by simply starting with 100 percent and multiplying by the appropriate learning curve percentage over and over.

For example, to get the 75 percent curve in Figure 7-19 we would start with 100 percent, multiply by 75 percent to get a result of 75 percent for a volume of 2, then multiply that by 75 percent to get a result of 56 percent for a volume of 4, and multiply that by 75 percent to get a result of 42 percent for a volume of 8, and so forth.

Next, we have to collect actual data. Suppose that our observations indicated that the total time for the first unit was 90 minutes, for the next unit the time was 76 minutes, and then the average time was 61 minutes for the next 2

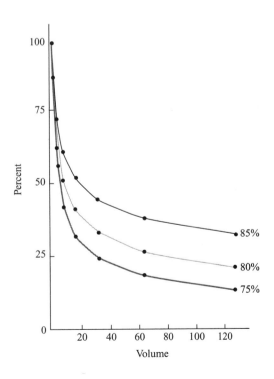

Figure 7-19 75%, 80%, and 85% Learning Curves (Based on 100%). *Source:* Reprinted from *Hospital Cost Accounting Advisor,* Vol. 1, No. 9, p. 6, Aspen Publishers, Inc., © 1986.

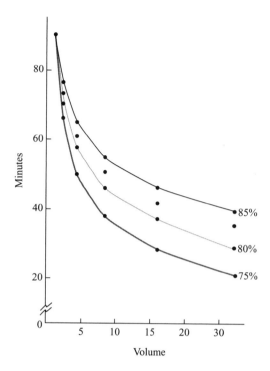

Figure 7-20 75%, 80%, and 85% Learning Curves (Based on 90 Minutes = 100%). *Source:* Reprinted from *Hospital Cost Accounting Advisor,* Vol. 1, No. 9, p. 7, Aspen Publishers, Inc., © 1986.

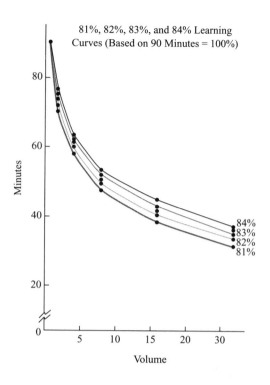

Figure 7-21 Precise Learning Curves. *Source:* Reprinted from *Hospital Cost Accounting Advisor,* Vol. 1, No. 9, p. 7, Aspen Publishers, Inc., © 1986.

units, 51 minutes for the next 4 units, 42 minutes for the next 8 units, and 36 minutes per unit for the next 16.

Since the first unit took 90 minutes, we can convert Figure 7-19 to Figure 7-20 by multiplying each percentage from Figure 7-19 by the initial 90 minutes for the first unit. That is, we are effectively making 90 minutes 100 percent of the time for the first unit of output. Then we would plot the data we collected. As you can see from Figure 7-20, the points of actual data collected fall between the 80 and 85 percent learning curves. If greater precision is desired, we can construct the appropriate graphs for 81, 82, 83, and 84 percent using the procedure described above.

Figure 7-21 presents that result. As you can see, the plotted points for the actual data collected most nearly approximates the 83 percent learning curve. That means that for future budgeting, we can anticipate that each additional

doubling of cumulative total volume should be able to be accomplished with 17 percent less labor.

As we strive for efficient management, we must plug up the traditional weaknesses in the cost control system. The learning curve is a tool that can be invaluable for accurate cost prediction. In that use, it can help prevent fat from accumulating in labor-intensive areas of health care organization operations.

SUGGESTED READING

Dennis, D.K. 1989. Estimating cost behavior. In *Handbook of Health Care Accounting and Finance,* 2nd ed., ed. W.O. Cleverley, 117–134. Rockville, Md.: Aspen Publishers, Inc.

Finkler, S.A. 1985. Cost estimation using linear regression. *Hospital Cost Accounting Advisor* 1, no. 2:1, 4–6.

———. 1986. The learning curve effect. *Hospital Cost Accounting Advisor* 1, no. 9:1, 4–7.

Hemenway, D., et al. 1986. Benefits of experience: Treating coronary artery disease. *Medical Care* 24, no. 2:125–133.

Horngren, C.T., and G. Foster. 1991. *Cost accounting: A managerial emphasis.* 7th ed. Englewood Cliffs, NJ: Prentice-Hall.

Michela, W. January 1975. Defining and analyzing costs— A statistical approach. *Healthcare Financial Management* 36–41.

Moses, D.O. Spring 1991. The impact of accounting procedures on learning rates. *The Journal of Cost Analysis* 10–39.

Smith, D.B., and J.L. Larsson. 1989. The impact of learning on cost: The case of heart transplantation. *Hospital & Health Services Administration* 34, no. 1:85–97.

Wright, T. 1936. Factors affecting cost of airplanes. *Journal of Aeronautical Sciences* 3, no. 2:122–128.

EXERCISES

QUESTIONS FOR DISCUSSION

1. What is the main difference between the nominal group and Delphi techniques? What are the pros and cons of each method relative to the other?
2. Why bother with cost indexation? Won't any prediction of future costs automatically trend in a factor for inflation?
3. What is the major goal of the linear regression approach to predicting future costs?
4. What is the major limitation of the high–low technique of cost estimation?
5. What is the primary difference between simple and multiple regression?
6. Many managers simply average historical data to get a forecast of future results. Is that approach adequate?
7. What is the principal advantage of curvilinear forecasting?
8. A carefully done computerized analysis should be sufficient for most forecasts? True or false. Why?
9. Is the learning curve effect related to improved productivity as employees or the organization gain experience?

PROBLEMS

1. Utryit Hospital has been using linear regression to estimate costs. It has been using patient days to predict electricity cost, but a recent study has indicated that different types of patients consume substantially different amounts of electricity. Therefore, it has decided to multiply its DRG case-mix index by the number of admissions to get a case-mix-weighted volume measure. The following information is available to you:

Year Ending June 30	Electricity Cost ($)	Case-Mix Weighted Admissions
1988	197,000	6,000
1989	199,000	6,400
1990	205,000	6,800
1991	223,000	7,000
1992	222,000	7,800
1993	227,000	7,600
1994	241,000	8,000
1995	238,000	8,000
1996	?	7,400 (expected)

Using a hand-held calculator that has linear regression capability, or a computer, use simple linear regression to estimate the electricity cost next year. Also compute fixed cost, variable cost per unit, and the R-squared for your forecast for the 1996 electricity cost. Does your solution agree with that in the chapter, which used patient days? Do you think your estimate is adequate?

2. The Invitro Hospital has this past year started performing a highly labor-intensive prenatal test for genetic illnesses. This chorionic villus sampling, or CVS test, requires a fair amount of laboratory technician labor.

In this first year, the hospital has done 256 such tests. Although the miscarriage rate is higher than for an amniocentesis, the CVS produces results at an earlier stage of pregnancy. This fact has led Invitro to project 768 tests for the coming year.

The head of the laboratory has included in the budget 721 hours of technician time to perform these tests, at a rate of $17 per hour including fringes, or a total of $12,257 for labor. He argues that in the first year of performing this test, the laboratory technicians spent an average of 56.3 minutes per test. Projecting this rate to next year's 768 volume would result in 721 hours required.

Intuitively, you know that the estimate is too high. Haven't the technicians improved their ability to do the test over the first 256 tests done? You ask for data on the time taken to do the first 32 tests and find that the technicians spent 100 minutes on the first test, 92 on the next one, 85 on each of the next 2, 79 on each of the next 4, 71 on each of the next 8, and 66 on each of the following 16. You also find out that the last 128 done each took 51.3 minutes on average.

How much should be budgeted for laboratory technician labor for next year?

Application 7-1

Regression-Based Cost Estimation and Variance Analysis: Resolving the Impact of Outliers

Steven A. Finkler, PhD, CPA

THE OUTLIER PROBLEM

The use of regression analysis in cost estimation has been discussed in *Hospital Cost Accounting Advisor* (Vol. 1, No. 2, July 1985). One issue not discussed in that article was the impact of outliers on the results. Clearly, outliers have the potential to throw off estimates significantly. Further, when those estimates are used as the basis for budgets, the problem caused by outliers extends into the area of variance analysis. Deciding whether a variance is large enough to warrant investigation becomes less clear-cut. This article focuses on resolving a number of problems resulting from outlier and other data that can distort a regression-based analysis.

Linear regression is often used for estimating future costs of hospital departments. Many departments are able to project changes in volumes of activity. However, a 10 percent increase or decrease in activity levels does not translate into a 10 percent change in costs. Some costs in each department are fixed, and will not vary either upward or downward with a change in vol-

Source: Reprinted from Steven A. Finkler, "Regression-Based Cost Estimation and Variance Analysis: Resolving the Impact of Outliers," *Hospital Cost Accounting Advisor,* Vol. 3, No. 4, September 1987, pp. 1–5. Copyright 1987, Aspen Publishers, Inc.

ume. Regression analysis uses historical information to evaluate the past changes in costs in relation to changes in volume. That information is then used to predict the likely future cost changes which would result from a given expected volume change.

When regression analysis is employed in cost estimation, the first step generally is to plot the points on a graph to allow for a visual inspection. Such an inspection has a number of benefits. First of all, the user can gain some insight as to whether a regression approach is appropriate. If the pattern detected shows seasonality, but no trend, then regression is probably a poor tool. However, if a trending effect is noted, regression analysis will generally give a superior prediction than less sophisticated estimating techniques.

Outliers are extreme data points that are sometimes caused by data collection errors or rare events. An advantage of a visual inspection of the plotted data points is that often outliers are readily apparent. For example, suppose that the data in Table 7-1-1 are being used to predict costs for the Operating Room Department for next year, when 8,550 hours of procedures are expected. These data have been plotted in Figure 7-1-1. Inspection of that figure shows that one outlier exists. The appropriate treatment of that outlier depends on what caused it.

Table 7-1-1 Operating Room Department Data

Year	Number of Surgery Hours	Cost
1980	7,300	$2,950,000
1981	7,550	3,100,000
1982	7,825	3,250,000
1983	8,200	3,610,000
1984	7,940	3,325,000
1985	8,120	3,256,000
1986	8,345	3,400,000
1987	8,450	3,458,000
1988	8,550	

If, for example, further investigation of the outlier shows that it was caused by a transposition error, then the data should simply be corrected. Perhaps the cost related to the 1984 observation was recorded as $3,610,000, but should have been $3,160,000.

On the other hand, it is possible that the outlier was not caused by any errors in calculation. Perhaps we simply had an extremely costly case-mix. Many of the patients that year had surgeries more costly than our normal average. This raises the question of whether that situation is likely to occur again. One possibility is that a specialty hospital in town that performs

only extremely costly surgeries closed their OR for six months for total renovations. Much of their normal patient load was handled by our hospital. Now that the renovation is over, such an occurrence is unlikely to be repeated for at least several decades. In that case, the outlier generates an erroneous implication about the probabilities of high-cost patients in the near future.

An alternative possibility is simply that the outlier represents a random occurrence which, given recent competition by outpatient surgery units for the less complex patients, is likely to occur from time to time. In that case, the outlier is relevant and should be retained. The key in determining whether to retain outlier data is the extent to which we believe that the data point is representative of a variation that may occasionally occur, versus the degree to which we believe that it resulted from an unusual event, and that it would be highly unlikely to occur again.

The impact of an outlier is generally to pull the estimated-line upward or downward, depending on whether it is above or below the bulk of the observations. It is also possible for the outlier to cause the slope of the regression line to change, particularly if the outlier occurs

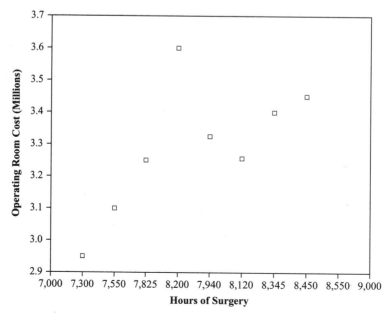

Figure 7-1-1 Operating Room Hours and Costs

farther away from the majority of the other data points (i.e., farther to the right or left along the X axis, as opposed to simply higher or lower along the Y axis).

A similar problem is raised by observations that are referred to as "influential points." An influential point is one that, because of its particular position among all of the data observations, happens to have a particularly strong impact on the results of the linear regression. This is more due to the nature of the regression process, than to anything particularly unusual with respect to the point itself. Influential points should often be removed from the data base in the same way that outliers are removed.

While outliers can often be determined by visual inspection, that is not the case with influential points. However, there are statistical techniques which can be used to check for both outliers and influential points. These techniques will not be discussed here because they are readily available in many statistical packages that would commonly be used for regression analyses, such as the Minitab software system.

Figure 7-1-2 shows the regression line based on all data points, including the outlier point. Figure 7-1-3 shows what the regression line would be if the outlier is eliminated from the data used for the analysis. Figure 7-1-4 compares the two regression lines. Note that there is a substantial difference between the lines.

This difference is particularly notable when we consider the value predicted for next year's cost based on the two regressions. When the outlier is included in the analysis, the regression analysis predicts costs to be $3,562,000 if next year's operating room activity level is 8,550 hours of surgery. In contrast, with the outlier removed, the predicted cost is $3,499,000, a difference of $63,000.

The benefits of removing an unwarranted outlier from the data are substantial. Not only is the predicted cost more accurate, but it is also subject to less random variability. In this particular example, the R-squared of the regression rose from .78 to .92 when the outlier was dropped, indicative of a better relationship between the independent and dependent variables.

Furthermore, the standard error for both the fixed cost (the Y intercept, or constant in the regression, may be interpreted as fixed cost in a cost-estimating regression analysis) and the variable cost (the X coefficient, or slope of the regression analysis, may be interpreted as the variable cost in a cost-estimating regression analysis) was halved. This implies a probability of less normal variation from the predicted cost.

Certainly, one would always prefer to have a more accurate estimate. However, in what specific way can that more accurate estimate be helpful? The remainder of this article focuses on one example, that of variance analysis.

VARIANCE INVESTIGATION

One of the most difficult decisions managers must make is whether or not to investigate a variance. Normal variations are likely to cause small favorable or unfavorable variances to occur in every budget. We have a few more patients or a few less patients. Patients are slightly more or less acutely ill than expected. Supply prices vary in some minor way from expectations. None of these variations warrants the time and effort of a thorough investigation.

Unfortunately, until the investigation takes place, one doesn't know if the variation was minor and did not really require investigation, or if the variance resulted from some major loss of control. Even if small in amount, the variance can be an early signal of a failure of management to exercise proper budgetary control, or of a marketplace shift of significant importance.

Thus, there is a desire to investigate variances, but this desire must be considered in light of the cost of the investigation. The benefits of any corrective actions that might be taken as the result of an investigation must be balanced with the costs of management time and effort to undertake the investigation.

The key question then becomes, when is a variance large enough to merit investigation? To some extent, managers must rely on their experience and judgment. Such judgment can always call for an investigation even if formal decision

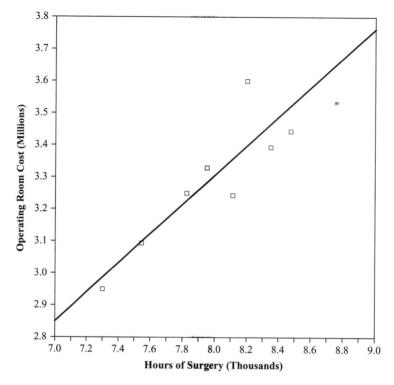

Figure 7-1-2 Operating Room Regression Results Including Outlier

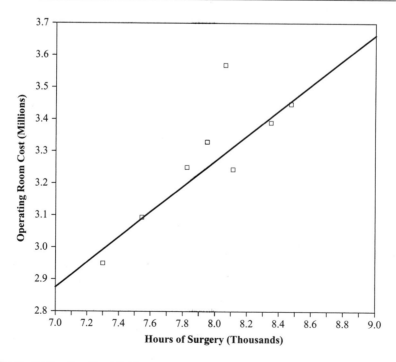

Figure 7-1-3 Regression Results without Outlier

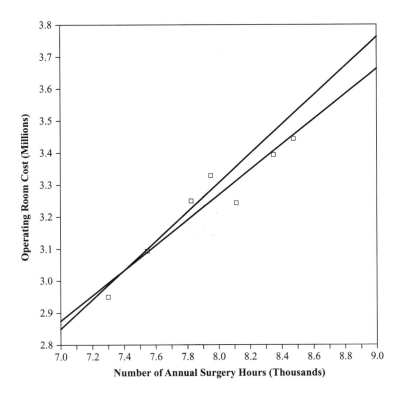

Figure 7-1-4 Regression Results Compared

rules would not. However, formal decision rules can be a great aid.

As variances become larger, there is a greater likelihood that there are problems that management should investigate. Therefore many hospitals may set a dollar or percent limit. If a variance is below the limit, no investigation is required. If the variance exceeds the limit, then an investigation is automatically undertaken. While such approaches are better than no decision rule, they fail to take into account the degree of probability that the variance indicates an "out of control" situation, as opposed to a simple random fluctuation.

If the budget is based on costs that were developed from a regression analysis model, then the model has considered the historical dispersion of costs. If the cost for an item typically fluctuates widely, then a somewhat large dollar amount variance might not be a particular concern. On the other hand, if historically fluctuations have been rather narrow, then a smaller variance might warrant attention.

Consider the example presented earlier in this article. Before the outlier was removed, the predicted cost for 1988 was $3,562,000. After the outlier was removed, it was determined that the predicted cost should be $3,499,000. Suppose that the department follows a rule that requires investigation of variances when they exceed the budget by more than one percent for the department as a whole. What would happen if the actual result was a cost of $3,590,000? (Note that this example looks at years in total for the sake of simplicity—actually, estimates should be made for each month, and variances investigated, when warranted, on a monthly basis.)

If the actual result is $3,590,000 and the budget was $3,562,000, the difference is only $28,000, which is less than one percent of the budget (one percent of $3,562,000 would be $35,620). Variance investigation might well not be undertaken. Had the budget been $3,499,000, the variance would have been $41,000, which would have warranted investigation. Thus there is a reasonable likelihood that a situation that might require investigation—and perhaps management intervention—might be overlooked.

In fact, because the estimate calculated without the outlier has smaller standard errors, the occurrence of a variance of any given dollar amount is less likely to occur randomly and therefore is more noteworthy.

While this discussion may make regression analysis appear a somewhat risky approach, the reader should be aware of the fact that the basic technique is extremely useful, and will often improve on the estimates and budgets prepared in its absence. Furthermore, many statistical packages are available that will aid in making the types of adjustments noted here.

8

Budgeting

Goals of This Chapter

---

1. Discuss the major purposes of budgeting.
2. Emphasize the importance of human actions for achieving budgets.
3. Discuss the long-range budget, the operating budget, the capital budget including time value of money issues, the cash budget and cash management, the program budget, and special purpose budgets.
4. Note the role of the negotiation and approval process in budgeting.

Key Terms Used in This Chapter

Accounting rate of return; annuity payment; breakeven time; budget; budgeting; business plan; capital budget; cash budget; compound interest; continuous budgeting; cost of capital; direct method; discounted cash flow; discounting; evaluative budgeting; float; future value (FV); hurdle rate; incremental budgeting; indirect method; internal rate of return; long-range (strategic) budget; negotiative budgeting; net present cost; net present value; operating budget; payback; planning; present value (PV); program budget; required rate of return; special purpose budget; time value of money; working capital method; zero balance account; zero-base budgeting.

Note: Key terms appear in italics when first used in the chapter. All key terms are defined in the Glossary.

INTRODUCTION

A *budget* is a plan. Budgets are generally formalized written documents. *Budgeting* is the process of developing a plan, implementing it, and attempting to control outcomes so that they conform to or exceed the results called for by the plan. Budgeting is an element of cost accounting, because much of the *planning* relates to costs the organization expects to incur.

Planning is an essential process for the efficient management of organizations. It allows one to think ahead about potential problems and either avoid them or develop potential solutions. Planning requires an ongoing effort, with plans being made and carried out, then the results evaluated, and the information from what actually happens incorporated into future plans to improve the accuracy of the planning process. As such, it forms a continuous loop of information (Figure 8-1).

Organizations have many different types of budgets. These include *long-range* or *strategic budgets, program budgets, operating budgets, capital budgets, cash budgets,* and *special purpose budgets.* This chapter discusses the planning aspect of all of these budgets and their role as elements of an overall, organization-wide master budget. The use of budgets to control results is discussed in the next chapter, which focuses on variance analysis.

THE ROLE OF BUDGETING

Budgets are the roadmap for where the organization is going. By following the budget, one is able to guide the organization in the direction required for achieving its goals and objectives. While poor budgeting will leave an organization that careens from crisis to crisis, efficient budgeting will allow managers to plan ahead and anticipate problems.

Managers generally do not like the constraints imposed by a budget. All organizations have limited resources, and budgets reflect those limitations. However, the existence of the budget allows all managers to understand those constraints and work within them. Without a

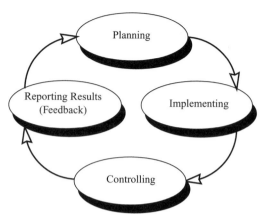

Figure 8-1 The Budget Process

budget, the organization could soon find itself spending beyond its means, with extremely negative results for the organization, its employees, and its patients.

Almost all organizations prepare budgets. This is not necessarily a voluntary process. For example, hospitals are only eligible for Medicare reimbursement if they have an annual budget. When budgeting is forced upon an organization, it may be of limited value. However, if managers accept the fact that the role of the budget is to place resources where they best accomplish the organization's goals, the process is likely to improve substantially the organization's overall ability to provide health care services.

Specifically, we can think of the budget process as serving the roles of

- forcing managers to plan ahead and consider alternatives,
- improving organizational communication and coordination, and
- providing a basis for evaluation of unit and managerial performance.

Forced Planning and the Evaluation of Alternatives

Efficient budgeting forces managers to plan ahead and anticipate problems. Allowing events simply to unfold does not in any way ensure that they will unfold in a manner that is advantageous to the organization. Such an approach means that the organization must constantly react to what is happening. Although flexibility of response is an attribute, response without a predetermined plan will not necessarily be efficient.

Having a plan allows the organization to consider in advance what might happen and what is likely to happen. For example, staffing based on likely patient volume will ensure that the appropriate staff is on hand as patients arrive. Furthermore, having a plan will allow the organization to react appropriately to staffing needs if events dictate. Many argue that being forced to consider what might happen and to plan how the organization will respond is the most valuable part of the budget process.

Part of forced planning is consideration of alternative available actions. In fact, the alternatives available for addressing problems are generally superior the earlier they are considered.

For example, if a machine is nearing the end of its useful life, a replacement can be planned. The planning process will likely include a thorough examination of alternative models of the new equipment, of alternative suppliers of it, and of the advantages of leasing versus purchasing the equipment. On the other hand, if the organization fails to plan for the equipment purchase, what will happen when the existing equipment breaks down and cannot be repaired?

Often, the answer is that replacement equipment will be acquired on a rush basis without a thorough review of alternatives. The cost of the equipment purchased is likely to be higher than it would have been, and the equipment purchased may not be the best for the job. The cost of the equipment was not put into the budget, which means that the organization did not make a conscious effort to reduce expenses elsewhere to allow for the purchase. The result is that spending will exceed the budget, possibly resulting in a financial crisis for the organization. All of these problems might have been minimized if the organization took the budgeting process seriously and planned ahead.

Communication and Coordination

In order for a health care organization to be successful, there must be a uniform sense of mission and direction. All employees must work toward common goals. The budget serves as the communicating device that lets everyone know what those goals are and how they are to be achieved.

Rather than allowing each individual to work independently on what he or she believes will be good for the organization, the budget serves the role of coordinating efforts to avoid work at cross-purposes. For example, when each department decides on its staffing, it needs to know how many patients to expect. If the marketing department is planning specific programs to attract certain types of patients, the patient care departments will be able to provide care more efficiently if they are aware of the planned marketing campaign. Otherwise, as patients unexpectedly arrive, overtime will be required.

The marketing department will have achieved its goal of generating more patients. However, there may be little financial benefit to the organization if higher overtime expenses are incurred. Communication throughout the organization is essential to efficient management of costs.

Evaluation

Did departments or managers perform as well as they should have? One of the difficult tasks of running any organization is evaluation of performance. Budgeting lays down a set of expectations. The actual results can be compared with these expectations to evaluate performance. The expectations should be reasonable and should be clearly conveyed to the manager.

BUDGETING PHILOSOPHY

When budgets are prepared, one would expect them simply to report financial expectations. That should be as nearly as possible a scientific task rather than a subjective one. In fact, however, different managers approach budget preparation with very different philosophical attitudes. These attitudes tend to be concerned primarily with two issues: (1) the proper way to motivate people and (2) the proper way to set an equitable level for a budget.

Motivation

Motivation and incentives are critical elements of any budget process. Human beings must carry out the budget, or it will not be achieved, regardless of how accurate forecasts have been. However, there is not universal agreement on what will best motivate people. There is agreement, however, that putting columns of numbers on a piece of paper will not accomplish the goals of the organization. Goals are accomplished by the efforts of people.

There must be agreement on the fairness of the budget and on the necessity for its constraints. The employees of the organization must feel that they are being treated equitably. Also, some reward or punishment must be associated with meeting or failing to meet the budget. Some organizations provide positive incentives, and others, negative. What is clearly agreed upon is that employees must have some personal incentive for wanting the goals of the budget to be achieved.

Some managers work from the philosophy that any budget that can be attained has not set a high enough goal. If managers can achieve the budget, why should they work even harder to surpass it? Therefore, only by setting a very difficult budget to achieve can one ensure that workers will maximize their efforts.

Other managers would argue that if the budget cannot be achieved, it guarantees failure. If managers become accustomed to failing to meet the budget, they will work less hard. Why kill themselves making the effort if they are destined to fail no matter how hard they work?

Most theorists agree that budgets should be set so that managers must work hard to achieve them, but that, in most cases, hard-working managers should in fact achieve their budgeted goals. Although some would argue that perhaps

the employees could have worked a bit harder and been a bit more efficient if the target were higher, the potential poor employee morale that could develop is not worth squeezing every last ounce of effort out of the staff.

Equity in Budgeting

A related issue is the process by which budgeted amounts are determined. Three common approaches are *incremental budgeting, negotiative budgeting,* and *evaluative budgeting.* Each approach attempts to develop equity in setting budgeted amounts.

The incremental approach determines how much more money an organization can spend in the coming year. For example, perhaps the finance office determines that revenue growth will be sufficient to allow expenses to rise, in total, by 5 percent. An incremental approach to budgeting would be to allow each department to raise its expenses by 5 percent. This is certainly the easiest way to approach setting budgets.

One might argue that the incremental approach is fair, because all departments are treated equally. No single department receives preferential treatment. On the other hand, this will only really provide equity if all departments have needs that are increasing equally.

Suppose that due to medical advances, more kidney stones are treated medically, and fewer surgically. If the medical and surgical units are both receiving 5 percent increases, then the surgical unit is being given a cushion. It has a decreasing demand for its services. In contrast, the units providing the medical treatment have a growing number of patients, but their resources are not growing as rapidly as their needs. Therefore, approaches other than simple incrementalism might be more equitable.

Negotiative budgeting would allow each unit or department to negotiate for its resources. This could conceivably send more resources to the areas that have greater need. Unfortunately, negotiation does not always take place based on objective arguments. It may depend substantially on politics and power. Therefore, negotiation also does not always yield equitable results.

Evaluative budgeting is based on the idea that each element of expenditure for each unit or department is explained and justified. Money can only be spent if there is a good reason for it. The benefits of each expenditure must be shown to outweigh the costs, and it must be shown that the approach taken is the best approach.

Few could argue with the equity of such an approach. However, the cost of implementing it is potentially enormous. It would be extremely costly to undertake such an approach. Some organizations do use a form of evaluative budgeting called *zero-base budgeting* (ZBB). Zero base considers not only the justification for each and every expenditure, but also alternative ways to provide the service, alternative levels of service, and even alternative service quality. ZBB is discussed further in Application 8-1.

THE MASTER BUDGET

An organization has many different types of budgets. Some budgets consider the next five years, others consider the life of a specific project, and others are concerned just with the coming year. Some budgets are income oriented, focusing on revenues and expenses on an accrual basis. Other budgets are cash oriented, focusing on inflows and outflows of cash. All of these budgets are brought together in the organization's master budget.

Some of the elements of a master budget will be qualitative in nature. For example, the long-term plan of an organization may discuss general direction, such as movement toward becoming a tertiary care center. In general, however, the elements of a budget should be as quantitative and specific as possible. A budget should not indicate that patient care will be provided at the lowest possible cost, but rather at a specified level of cost.

Consider, for example, going on a diet to lose weight. If there is a specific goal to work toward, such as losing 10 pounds, the diet is likely to work much better than if the diet is simply "to lose some weight" or even "to lose as much weight as possible." People accomplish more when they are working toward specific goals.

There is a great deal of complexity to putting together all of the pieces of a master budget, and making sure each element is accomplished in time for any calculations that must follow. To simplify this process, many organizations develop a budget timetable, such as the one shown in Exhibit 8-1. Such a schedule can help managers control the process, so that critical deadlines can be met.

Another aid in preparing budgets is the use of a budget manual. Such a manual provides detailed directions for managers to use in preparing each element of each budget. Budget manuals are discussed further in Application 8-2.

Exhibit 8-1 Sample Budget Timetable

ACTIVITY	RESPONSIBILITY	DEADLINES
1. Appointment of the budget committee	Chief executive officer	June
2. First meeting of the budget committee	Budget committee chair	July
3. Completion of budget foundations activities and communication to department heads	Budget committee	August 31
4. Completion of long-range and program budgets	Budget committee and subcommittees	September 30
5. Unit capital and operating budgets	Unit managers	October 15
6. Negotiation between unit managers and department heads	Department heads	October 22
7. Compilation of all unit budgets	Department heads	October 31
8. Development of cash budget	Chief financial officer	November 15
9. Negotiation and revision process	All managers	December 15
10. Approval and implementation	Board of trustees; all managers	December 16

THE LONG-RANGE BUDGET

The long-range budget is sometimes called the strategic budget or long-range plan. This budget is only prepared once every three or five years in most organizations. The goal of this budget is to lay out the general direction that the organization must take to accomplish its mission.

There is a tendency in the budgeting of many organizations to focus solely on the coming year's revenues and expenses (the operating budget). Often, preparation of that budget consists of simply adding an inflationary adjustment to a projection of the actual results for the current year. Such a budget does not allow for any growth by the organization.

Periodically, managers should look back on where their organization was five years ago, and contrast that to the organization's current position. Ideally, one would want to be able to point to a number of areas of significant accomplishment over that time period. However, if budgeting is done by merely projecting the current year into the coming year, it is unlikely that such growth and accomplishment will occur. The role of the long-range plan is to provide the thought regarding the major areas of change that are needed to arrive at that long-term growth.

The long-range budget should be reviewed annually to make sure that no major changes have taken place outside of the organization that would require a reassessment. However, the long-range budget should not be changed often. Once a direction is set, there should be stability in that goal, so that managers can move forward in that direction. If the major focus or direction is changed frequently, managers will never have an opportunity to provide substantial progress in any direction.

THE OPERATING BUDGET

The operating budget provides the plan for the revenues and expenses for the coming year. Some departments have responsibility for both, and budget accordingly. They are referred to as profit centers or revenue centers. Other departments are held accountable for only expenses; these are referred to as cost centers.

Revenues and Expenses

Expenses are the most common element of budgets. All departments incur expenses and must budget for them. Expenses generally consist of personnel costs and other than personnel services (OTPS) costs. All costs in the operating budget are current-period expenses. In contrast, costs incurred to acquire long-term assets are evaluated in the capital budget. Only the current-year depreciation portion of such costs are included in the operating budget.

The key starting point for preparation of both the revenue and expense portion of the operating budget is the volume forecast. Without having a projection of volume of service to be provided, it is impossible to estimate revenues or expenses. Revenues are generally paid for each patient or for specific services consumed by each patient. Many expenses are variable costs related to volume. Once a patient-volume forecast exists (see the previous chapter for a discussion of forecasting), it is possible for managers to determine revenues, appropriate staffing, and the needs for clinical and other supplies. That will allow preparation of the revenue, personnel, and OTPS budgets.

The process of developing an operating budget will vary somewhat from department to department. Essentially, however, one must consider each cost element and/or revenue source for the department or cost center. Personnel costs require determination of the specific number of hours of personnel required to provide the department's services. Given that no one works 365 days a year or 24 hours a day, the budget must plan for appropriate amounts of staff to cover all hours needed, including coverage for sick leave and vacations. In preparing the budget, the manager must be sure to take into account which positions are fixed regardless of volume and which positions vary with volume.

OTPS costs also may be either fixed or variable. The fixed costs tend to change from year to year due to inflation and/or judgmental decisions regarding appropriate levels of expenditure. The variable costs are budgeted to change in proportion with expected change in the volume of activity.

Sometimes operating budgeting has been criticized because it creates a focus on line-items of input instead of on what the organization is trying to accomplish. For example, a department knows the budgeted cost for technicians rather than the budgeted cost for a specific type of test it produces. One response to such criticism is the use of performance budgets that focus the information in operating budgets on what a department or organization is attempting to achieve. Application 8-3 presents a discussion of performance budgets.

The development of an operating budget is a topic that is too extensive to be adequately covered in this book. The reader is referred to specific readings on the topic, such as those listed at the end of this chapter.

Continuous Budgeting

One of the primary reasons for budgeting is to have a plan for the future. However, with an annually prepared budget, the time horizon of the plan shortens as the year goes by. A number of the weaknesses of the annual budget preparation system could be overcome by more frequent preparation of budgets. The *continuous budgeting* (or *rolling budget*) system has been gaining support as managers become aware of its advantages.

Under a continuous budgeting system, at the close of each month the annual budget is extended for one additional month. For example, once July has passed and the actual July performance is known, a budget is prepared for the next July. The following discussion assumes that the budget is updated continuously month by month, although some organizations perform continuous budgeting with quarterly rather than monthly updates.

There are four primary problem areas in the traditional approach of preparing budgets once a year:

1. time-management concerns,
2. attitudes toward the budget process,
3. accuracy, and
4. increasing myopia with respect to the future.

Continuous budgeting addresses each of these concerns.

Time Management

Traditional budgeting creates a serious disruption in work patterns; it is a major task, performed once a year. As a result, it inherently breaks the routine, preventing normal monthly tasks from being performed on a timely basis. The intensive annual period of budget preparation usually involves long overtime hours. The month following the budget preparation is spent trying to catch up with all of the postponed tasks.

In contrast, continuous budgeting is performed every month. By consuming one or two days of cost center or department managers' time each month, instead of two to three weeks all in one month, budgeting becomes part of the routine instead of a disruption in it. Managers can arrange their workload so that every month, they do a little budgeting. When budgeting is performed only once a year, there is little opportunity for a manager to accomplish routine tasks during the budget period. Essentially, continuous preparation of budgets allows managers to manage the time spent on the budget process.

Attitudes

Budgeting is generally viewed as a mammoth task, to be faced only with great reluctance. Cutting the proportions of the task down to size, by requiring a smaller (although more frequent) effort, can make budgeting a little easier to take. Essentially, this goes hand-in-hand with time management. If managers do not perceive budgeting as an overwhelming disruption in their job, but rather a normal, routine part of it, there is likely to be reduced antagonism toward the process, and as a result, a better effort.

Accuracy

When budgets are prepared annually, they often are based on hazy recollections of the year past. Previous months start to run together, with July and August being very much alike in our memory. The advantage of preparing a budget for next July immediately after this July has ended (or at least as soon as we can get our actual results for July) is that the chances are the budget for next July will be a more realistic and accurate reflection of the things that typically happen in July. It will capture the specific types of things that occur every July much better than we could hope for if we were to wait until March or April to start to prepare next July's budget.

Health care organizations using continuous budgeting generally only finalize the budget once a year. Thus, each month a budget is prepared for one month into the future, but once a year these budgets have to be grouped for the next year, and the normal annual review, negotiation, and approval process is undertaken.

This allows for added accuracy, because managers are not tied to their initial thoughts until the finalization process occurs. Thus, a budget can be prepared for July of next year. Several months later, that budget can be modified, adjusted, or corrected as new information dictates. This allows time for managers to think about their budgets and possibly to revise them as ways to improve operations are found. Under traditional budgeting, so much work is being done in such a short time frame that there is generally no time for reflection and well-thought-out revisions in the budget before it is finalized.

Myopia

One of the great benefits of budgeting is that managers can make better decisions if they can plan for the future. When workload is forecast for a year ahead, purchases can be made at volume discounts. Equipment and supplies can be bought at lower prices with six months of lead time, instead of being acquired at high prices as rush orders placed at the last minute.

With a traditional budget, our time horizon starts at about 14 months. If a fiscal year budget starting July 1 is prepared in April and finalized in May, we have a projection of the current May and June, plus all of the next fiscal year—a total of 14 months.

Managers can use this forecast for effective management. But by October 1, we can see only nine months into the future, and by January 1, only six months. Traditional budgeting results in a creeping myopia. Each month, we can see less far into the future. Efficiency of decision making decreases as uncertainty increases. Decisions that would be made easily in September will be postponed if they arise in March, because the manager lacks the information about future expectations.

Under continuous budgeting, creeping myopia does not occur. At all times, the organization has a time horizon of about one year.

Limitations of Continuous Budgeting

There are some limitations to the concept of continuous budgeting. If finalization occurs only once a year, then managers will be making decisions for the following year based on monthly budgets that have not been approved. On the other hand, if budgets are approved monthly, one year in advance (i.e., the January 1995 budget is approved in February 1994), we lose the advantage of being able to reflect and modify a budget before it is finalized. Nevertheless, use of continuous budgeting as a management tool has been gaining in popularity, and we are likely to see increased use of continuous budgeting in the future.

THE CAPITAL BUDGET

The capital budget is used to plan for the acquisition of assets with lives that are greater than one year. Health care organizations have long had separate capital budgets. Rather than include capital items in the routine operating budget, they are segregated, requiring separate justification. Until quite recently, however, there was little incentive to apply sophisticated analytical techniques to their evaluation. This is because even under DRGs, capital costs were often paid on a cost reimbursement basis. Recent changes in Medicare reimbursement for capital costs, building them into DRG rates, will have a dramatic impact on the tools that hospitals must apply to their evaluation of capital budget requests. This will likely affect other health care organizations as well in the future.

Therefore, health care organizations will have to take a much more business-like approach toward their capital acquisitions. This will require much greater use of *time value of money* tools such as *net present value* (NPV), *internal rate of return* (IRR), and the relatively new approach, *breakeven time* (BT).

The capital budget often deals with large amounts of money and major organizational commitments. The analysis of capital budget acquisitions has become one of the main areas of decision making for managers. Therefore, this section deals with the capital budgeting process at some length.

What Are Capital Items?

Capital budgeting relates to assets that have lifetimes that extend beyond one accounting year. From a theoretical point of view, if an item has a two-month useful lifetime, it would be a capital item if it is used partly in one year and partly in the next. Suppose that a 50¢ ballpoint pen was used partly in the last month of the year and partly in the first month of the next year. For a correct matching of revenues and expenses, half of the cost of the pen should be allocated into the first year, and half of the cost should be allocated into the second year. That will ensure that measurement of income for each year is accurate.

In practice, however, it would be too expensive to keep track of the cost of the 50¢ pen over a two-year period. Pragmatically, it makes sense to simply charge the entire 50¢ to one year— generally the year in which the pen is first placed into service.

It is always important to bear in mind that the benefits of accurate cost information should exceed the costs of collecting that information. Therefore, inexpensive items are often treated as operating expenses. Each health care organization establishes a dollar cutoff. Below that level, all items are treated as being operating expenses rather than long-term or capital assets.

When capital items become more expensive, however, it becomes worthwhile to track them carefully, assigning their costs into the appropriate years in which they are consumed, to avoid generating a material misstatement of fixed asset balances and of the excess of revenues over expenses.

Why Have Separate Capital Budgets?

The matching of revenues and expenses may explain why some assets must be treated as capital items and depreciated over their useful lives. Why, however, is it necessary to have a separate budget process for such items? Inclusion of capital assets in the normal operating budget would understate their net benefit. Their entire cost would appear in the current year because the full asset is purchased in the current year. However, only current-year revenues appear in the operating budget. Since capital items will be used in future years as well, their benefit (future revenues) would not be fully measured in the one-year operating budget.

It is quite possible that the organization would reject a capital item because of its high cost, when in fact it is a sensible investment if considered over its entire lifetime. By segregating the items into a separate capital budget, we can consider their full benefits in comparison to their full costs.

The separate evaluation of capital budget items has other advantages as well. Often capital acquisitions are extremely expensive. They also commit the organization for a long period of time. The higher the investment, the greater the effort that should be made to evaluate the appropriateness of the investment. Decisions made to expand a building or acquire major equipment lock in substantial amounts of money and have ramifications well beyond the current year. Since the organization will have to live with these decisions for a long period of time, extra scrutiny is warranted.

The Role of Regulation

The historical place of the capital budget has also depended to a great extent on the regulations in place. As long as Medicare and other payers reimbursed organizations directly for their capital costs, there was an inevitable impact on the capital budgeting process.

Should a $600 item be treated as an operating expense or a capital expense if it will last for ten years? Theoretically, it is a capital item because it provides benefits in more than one year. But each annual depreciation charge of $60 is so small that one would prefer to expense the item. However, suppose that revenues were paid on a DRG basis for operating costs, but on a pass-through basis for capital costs. In other words, in addition to the DRG payment, the hospital also received an amount that reimbursed the cost of capital items. By classifying the item as a capital expense, the total revenues received by the organization would be higher over the asset's lifetime than if it were classed as an operating expense.

In such a case, it is clear that hospitals would have an incentive to keep their dollar cutoffs very low for classifying items as capital assets. Changes in Medicare reimbursement have removed at least part of that incentive. Reimbursement of capital costs by Medicare is being phased out and merged into the general DRG payment. If hospital revenues are not made specifically on the basis of the amount spent on capital items, then the hospital must find efficient methods for evaluating whether or not to acquire capital items based on their inherent financial attractiveness. Of course, other factors may come into play as well. A critical piece of medical equipment may well be purchased regardless of its financial consequences. Nevertheless, it will be helpful to the organization to be aware of the financial implications of capital assets required.

Capital Budget Evaluation

There are three widely used major classes of evaluation for capital expenditures: (1) the *pay-back* method, (2) the *accounting rate of return* method, and (3) a group of *discounted cash flow* methods.

Payback

The payback method focuses on the fact that an organization must recover the amount it has invested in a project. After that point, all receipts in excess of operating expenses represent a profit for the organization. The sooner that point is reached, the better off the organization is.

Consider the following pattern of annual cash flows for three different investments of $1 million:

	Investment A	Investment B	Investment C
Start	($1,000,000)	($1,000,000)	($1,000,000)
Year 1	10,000	150,000	900,000
Year 2	10,000	150,000	150,000
Year 3	10,000	900,000	150,000
Year 4	3,000,000	0	0
Total	$2,030,000	$ 200,000	$ 200,000

For simplicity, assume that all cash inflows are received the last day of each year. According to the payback method, Investments B and C each have a payback period of three years because they have recovered their investment by the end of that year. Investment A has a payback of four years. Therefore, Investments B and C are each superior to Investment A, and they are equally attractive.

This is an unwarranted conclusion. The payback method has the advantage of focusing clearly on risk. The longer it takes to earn back an invested amount, the riskier it is. However, the method has the disadvantages of not focusing on the timing of cash flows, and not considering overall profitability of investments.

In the case of Investments B and C, the profits from both investments appear to be identical. Each of the two investments of $1,000,000 has earned a return of $1,200,000, leaving a profit of $200,000 after repaying the initial investment. However, the timing of the cash receipts is substantially different in these two projects. Investment B receives relatively little cash in

Years 1 and 2, whereas Investment C receives the bulk of the money in Year 1. That means that the health care organization making Investment C would receive a large amount of money in Year 1 that could be used for another project, or at least earn interest in a bank account. Therefore, it is really superior to B. The fact that the payback method does not note that superiority is a clear weakness in the method.

Another problem is that the method is so engrossed in focusing on the minimum possible length of time until a project repays its initial investments, it provides no consideration of the overall profitability of the project. Consider Investment A. In Year 4, this investment has a cash inflow of $3 million. The profit from this investment far exceeds that of the other two investments. However, under the payback method, it is considered to be an inferior investment to B and C because it has a longer payback period.

This example has been made fairly extreme so that the conceptual problems with payback are clear. In practice, it might not be readily apparent that one is selecting an inferior investment when using the payback method. Many businesses, largely concerned with the risk of new investments, use the payback method as their primary evaluation tool for capital asset acquisitions. In doing so, they risk making a poor investment choice.

Accounting Rate of Return

The accounting rate of return (ARR) method calculates the profitability of an investment by considering the profits it generates as compared with the amount of money invested. A typical formulation for this calculation is as follows:

$$ARR = \frac{\text{Average annual profit}}{\text{Investment}}$$

The higher the rate of return, the more profitable the investment. For example, suppose that a new lithotriptor (kidney stone) machine cost $1 million and had a ten-year life. Suppose further that the profits from the use of the machine were $100,000 per year. Then the ARR would be calculated as follows:

$$ARR = \frac{\$100,000}{\$1,000,000} = .10 \text{ or } 10\%$$

It is sometimes argued that the machine wears out over time. By the end of the ten years, the machine may be obsolete and have no remaining value. One could take the investment value at the beginning and end, and divide by 2, to get an average investment. If one were to calculate the ARR based on the *average* amount invested over the ten years, then the calculation would be as follows:

$$ARR = \frac{\$100,000}{(\$1,000,000 + \$0)/2} = .20 \text{ or } 20\%$$

Many object to this approach on the grounds that the organization really has to invest a full $1 million of its money and should earn its return on its entire investment.

Another problem is that, like the payback method, this method ignores the timing of cash flows. Since the focus is on the average profits over the lifetime of the project, it does not matter in this technique whether all or nearly all the profits are earned in the beginning or end of the investment's useful lifetime.

The method is superior to payback because at least it considers the entire set of profits over the lifetime of the investment. This method would not ignore the Year 4 profits of Investment A from the payback example. On the other hand, it would still consider Investments B and C to have the same profitability. It cannot distinguish the advantage that Investment C had because of its earlier cash inflows.

Discounted Cash Flow

To overcome the limitation of the payback and ARR methods, there exists a class of capital budgeting evaluation approaches that use *discounted cash flow* (DCF) analysis. This means that future streams of cash are converted into their value today. This process is called discounting.

Once future cash payments and receipts are discounted to the present, they can be reasonably compared with each other in order to assess the investment's financial performance. The concept of the time value of money, and the most common discounted cash flow techniques, are discussed next.

Time Value of Money

The time value of money is directly related to when the money is paid or received. Money at different points in time has a different value. One of the most direct ways to think of this issue is to consider whether you would be willing to lend $10,000 now to someone you really trust, if they promise to pay you the $10,000 five years from now. That does not seem to be a very good investment.

Money is intrinsically valuable. If you do not lend it for five years, you could spend it and enjoy the use of whatever items you buy. Or you could use it to pay off your loans, thus saving yourself the interest that you would otherwise have to pay on those loans. Or you could invest it, earning an increase in the total amount of money you have.

Clearly, having $10,000 today is better than waiting five years and then having $10,000. At a minimum, $10,000 today could be fully invested in government-insured securities so that you would have more than $10,000 in five years. Why would anyone lend it at a 0 percent interest rate?

While few managers would lend their own money on an interest-free basis, many managers see no problem with investing $10,000 of a hospital's money in a machine that generates a cash return of $2,000 a year for five years. The organization will break even because it will recover its initial investment of $10,000. Will it really break even, however? If it invests $10,000, and merely gets that $10,000 back in the future, it is losing money, because it gave up use of the $10,000. Just as an individual would not consider it wise to lend money merely to recover that same amount of money, the same thing holds true for organizations.

If an amount of money is invested at the beginning of a project or investment, that is referred to as the *present value* (PV). If it were invested at a particular interest rate *(i)* for a number *(N)* of time periods, it will grow to be worth some amount in the future, referred to as the *future value* (FV). The value will grow in a compounded fashion. Not only will the original investment earn a return, but any earnings along the way will earn a return as well. Most readers are familiar with the concept of *compound interest* from their own investments.

An amount of money received in the future can be converted to an equivalent amount of money today by reversing that compounding process. The reversal or unraveling of the compounded earnings over a period of time is called *discounting*. When one takes the cash receipts of the future and calculates their equivalent PV, that is referred to as a process of DCFs.

In some cases, the cash flows that are discounted to the present are not received at just one point in time in the future. An investment will likely yield returns each period over its lifetime. These returns may differ each year, or they may be the same. If the periodic payments are constant in value, they are referred to as *annuity payments* (PMTs). A PMT is simply a cash flow of a constant amount paid at evenly spaced periods of time (such as annually or monthly).

DCF analysis calls for considering the full financial impact of an investment, including the effects of the time value of money. Generally, these approaches take into account the profits of the investment over its lifetime and the timing of when cash is paid and received. It is not simply how much cash one receives that is critical, but also *when* one receives it.

DCF analysis does not focus simply on periodic profits, but rather on cash flows themselves. One investment might earn revenue that is received in cash immediately, whereas another might earn revenue that becomes a receivable for a period of time. The revenue that is received immediately can immediately start earning interest for the organization. The revenue that becomes a receivable cannot earn any interest until it is received. Therefore, in DCF analysis, the net income of each period is not the primary focus, but rather the cash that is spent or received in each period. However, because the analysis accounts for all cash spent and received over the entire lifetime of the investment, it ultimately accounts for all of the profits of the investment as well.

The actual calculation of cash flow discounting is based on mathematical formulas. These formulas were developed from the basic concepts of compound interest. The most fundamental of the formulas is the following:

$$FV = PV \times (1+i)^N$$

For example, if one invested $100 for two years at 10 percent interest compounded annually, what would one have at the end of two years? One could manually take 10 percent of the $100 investment ($10), the return for the first year, and add that to the original investment of $100. In the second year, there would be $110 invested. Ten percent of that is $11. At the end of two years, there would be $110 plus $11, or a total of $121. An alternate way to express this is the following:

$$FV = PV \times (1+i)^N$$
$$FV = \$100 \times (1+10\%)^2$$
$$FV = \$100 \times (1.10)^2$$
$$FV = \$100 \times (1.21)^2$$
$$FV = \$121$$

The process of using formulas was simplified when tables were developed to aid in the process. Appendix 8-A provides a set of PV and compound interest tables. Table 8-A-1 provides factors to use to find the PV of an amount to be paid or received in the future. Table 8-A-2 shows the amount that a dollar today would compound to at various interest rates and various amounts of time into the future. Table 8-A-3 provides factors for calculating the present value of an annuity, and Table 8-A-4 provides factors for determining the compounded value of an annuity in the future. In the tables, each column represents a different interest rate, and each row represents a time period. To solve the

above problem, we replace the following equation

$$FV = PV \times (1+i)^N$$

with

$$FV = PV \times (\text{factor from table})$$

Looking at Table 8-A-2, the compounded value of $1, in the 10 percent column and 2-year row, we find a factor of 1.210. Therefore,

$$FV = \$100 \times 1.210$$

$$FV = \$121$$

In using tables, it is critical to match the interest rate and the compounding period. A 12 percent rate for 1 year uses the 12 column and the 1 row. A 12 percent annual rate compounded monthly for 1 year uses the 1 column and the 12 row, because the interest rate is only 1 percent per month, and there are 12 months.

Today, many hand-held calculators can be used for time value of money calculations. The use of formulas and tables for these calculations has become less common because of this low-cost, easier approach. Note that calculators can deal with any interest rate, whereas tables, such as those in Appendix 8-A, are generally limited to just a selection of rates.

The two most common DCF techniques are NPV and IRR. We will also consider the net present cost and breakeven time approaches.

Net Present Value

When the future cash flows of a project are discounted to the present, the calculated result is the PV of those cash flows. The NPV is the difference between the PV of the cash inflows and the PV of the cash outflows:

$$NPV = PV \text{ inflows} - PV \text{ outflows}$$

Investments are profitable if the NPV is a positive number. That would mean that the value of what is received is greater than the value of what is spent.

In order to take the PV of a future cash flow, it is necessary to state an interest rate to be used for the calculation. That interest rate becomes the *required rate of return* or *hurdle rate* for the calculation. If the PV of the inflows is greater than the PV of the outflows, that means that the project earns a rate of return greater than the required rate of return. In that case, the investment is attractive.

In order to calculate the NPV, one must make estimates of the expected cash inflows and outflows of the project. Because that calls for forecasting, there is a degree of uncertainty. Even if the NPV indicates a profitable investment, the manager must exercise caution. Many organizations select a high hurdle rate to compensate for the risk that is taken when money is invested based on uncertain forecasts of the future.

Net Present Cost

Many health care investments do not result in new streams of revenue. A hospital may be faced with an investment decision, such as which of two different types of patient monitors to purchase. If we assume that the monitors will both do the job effectively, questions regarding the timing and total amount of payments become important. The hospital might even be faced with two different ways to acquire the exact same monitor.

Suppose that one way to buy a monitor is to pay $50,000, all at the time of purchase. Another way to pay for the monitor is on an installment basis, at a rate of $11,800 per year for five years, with each payment coming at the end of the year. The total cost per monitor under this arrangement would be $59,000. Which investment approach is less costly?

In order to compare the projects, it is necessary to find the PV of all of the costs related to the investment. In the direct purchase arrangement, that value is simply $50,000. In the installment approach, it is necessary to take the PV of the five payments of $11,800 each. If we were to use an interest rate of 10 percent, then the PV of five payments of $11,800 each at 10

percent per year would be $44,731. This could be determined using a calculator with

$$i = 10\%, N = 5, \text{PMT} = \$11,800: \text{Compute PV.}$$

Alternatively, we could calculate this using Table 8-A-3, as follows:

PV = PMT × (factor from Table 8-A-3)
PV = $11,800 × 3.791
PV = $44,734

(Note that using the tables introduces a minor rounding error.)

In other words, paying $59,000 on an installment basis is equivalent to paying $44,731 today. That is substantially cheaper than paying $50,000 today! To understand that this is correct, consider what would happen if one invested $44,731 today in a bank account paying 10 percent interest and each year withdrew the $11,800 needed for the installment payment.

Opening balance	$44,731	
Add Year 1 interest	4,473	(10% of opening balance)
New balance	$49,204	
Less installment 1	(11,800)	
Balance at end of 1st year	$37,404	
Add Year 2 interest	3,740	(10% of balance end of first year)
New balance	$41,144	
Less installment 2	(11,800)	
Balance end of 2nd year	$29,344	
Add Year 3 interest	2,934	(10% of balance end of 2nd year)
New balance	$32,278	
Less installment 3	(11,800)	
Balance at end of 3rd year	$20,478	
Add Year 4 interest	2,048	(10% of balance end of 3rd year)
New balance	$22,526	
Less installment 4	(11,800)	
Balance end of 4th year	$10,726	
Add Year 5 interest	1,073	(10% of balance end of 4th year)
New balance	$11,800*	
Less installment 5	(11,800)	
Balance end of 5th year	$0	

---

*$1 adjustment for rounding.

The initial investment of $44,731 turns out to be sufficient to make the five annual payments of $11,800. Even though the total amount paid, $59,000, is substantially more than the outright purchase price of $50,000, it is really less expensive. Putting aside $44,731 today would do the trick, as opposed to an outright payment of $50,000. This is because *when* money is paid is as important as how much!

Another critical factor is the interest rate. If the interest rate were higher or lower, the *net present cost* of the installment method would change. For example, at a 14 percent rate, the present value is $40,510. At an 8 percent rate, the present value would be $47,114. What interest rate is appropriate?

If the health care organization has $50,000 available for the current purchase, then an appropriate interest rate would be the rate that could be earned if that money were invested instead of used for the purchase. If it could invest in a CD at 10 percent, then it could invest the $44,731 at that rate and could use the other $5,269 for some other purpose, or it could invest it also. If the organization would have to borrow money to purchase the equipment, then the interest rate that would be charged to them would be an appropriate rate. The selection of appropriate interest rates to use for discounting is discussed further below.

In this example, it was assumed that the monitors were identical, and it is only the timing and amount of payments that differ. If different monitors were being considered, the problem becomes more complex. One must be careful to consider different operating and repair costs for the different monitors when estimating the amount and timing of the cash flows.

Internal Rate of Return

The IRR method is an alternative to NPV. Rather than starting with a hurdle rate and seeing if the project exceeds it, the IRR method is used to determine the rate of return that the investment earns. This is accomplished by finding the rate at which the PV of the inflows is exactly equal to the PV of the outflows.

Once the IRR is known, the organization would know the highest rate of interest that it could afford to pay if it has to borrow the money for the investment. If it pays an interest rate that is greater than the IRR, it would lose money on the investment. Many hand-held calculators designed for business use are capable of determining the IRR for an investment.

Breakeven Time

The BT concept measures the amount of time before the PV of the cash inflows is at least equal to the PV of the cash outflows. It is common for most investments to begin with a cash outlay. It then takes some time before the cash inflows are great enough to cover those outlays, on a PV basis. The sooner this occurs, the sooner the investment is profitable. Investments that become profitable more quickly are preferred to those that take more time.

It is contended that this approach encourages the rapid development of new technologies. By emphasizing the need for rapid breakeven, it pushes the organization to develop the new technology quickly. This in turn should lead to a distinct marketing edge. Thus, those projects that will need years of slow development are put aside. There is a good chance they will not be competitive by the time they are fully developed in any case. Those investments that can be placed into service and run at a good volume quickly are more likely to be financially beneficial, and under this evaluation approach, are more likely to be accepted by the organization. To operationalize this method, it is necessary to calculate the NPV each period, until the result is zero or positive.

Selecting Appropriate Discount Rates

The recent changes in Medicare reimbursement for capital will have dramatic effects on the way that hospitals plan their capital acquisitions in the future. The techniques of capital budgeting that have held less value for health care than other industries will become more commonly used. One of the inherent elements of time value of money calculations is that they all assume an implicit interest rate. The selection of that rate is worth some thought and discussion.

The NPV method discounts future cash flows back to a PV. In order to do so, one must decide on a discount or hurdle rate. If the project yields a negative net PV, it is unacceptable because it is earning a return that is less than the hurdle rate.

Internal rate of return is a good method for comparing different projects or investments to determine which ones are superior to others. However, it still does not resolve the question of how good a project must be to be good enough. For that decision, one still must know the organization's minimal acceptable discount rate.

The Minimal Acceptable Rate

The required rate of return for organizations is dependent on two factors. One factor represents the normal return for the cost of capital, and the other factor represents the risk of the project.

The *cost of capital* represents the cost to the organization of the money used for the capital acquisition. This is often represented by the interest rate that the organization pays on borrowed money.

In most industries, different projects often use different discount rates to allow for the differing levels of risk involved. For example, if an oil company builds a new refinery to replace an old one, the risk is low. They know what is involved in building and operating the refinery. On the other hand, if they are drilling for oil, there is great risk that they will not find oil. Therefore, a high-risk premium must be built into the model. The challenge for health care managers is to determine the appropriate rate to cover the cost of capital, and the appropriate rate to cover the risks of the project.

Cost of Capital

One might not think that determining the cost of capital for use in investment analysis would

be complex. However, there is substantial controversy over how to go about setting this rate.

One proposed approach to determining this rate is to use the organization's cost of marginal funds. If the project requires the organization to issue a bond at a 9 percent rate, then that rate is appropriate. If the project is smaller, and the money would be borrowed from a bank at a 10 percent rate, then that rate would be appropriate. If money is on hand, and it can only be invested at 7 percent, then that would be the appropriate cost of capital.

The criticism of this approach is that the project becomes extremely dependent on timing. If a project is proposed when the organization is cash rich, it only needs to earn 7 percent. If it is proposed when the organization must borrow from a bank, it must earn 10 percent. This says little about the relative merits of the project. One project that earns a 9 percent return might be rejected at a time when we need to borrow from a bank. Another project that earns only 8 percent might be accepted several months later if it is proposed at a better point in the organization's annual cash cycle.

An even more extreme potential problem concerns the use of donated capital. Given that gifts do not require any interest payments, is it appropriate to say that any project proposed right after the organization receives a charitable donation should need to earn only 0 percent? This seems quite inappropriate.

As a result of these problems, a number of other alternatives have been proposed. One approach is to use the average rate on the organization's long-term debt. Thus, if the organization has a bond outstanding that has an 8 percent interest rate, that rate could be used for all future projects.

The objection to this approach is that it is based on historical rates rather than current rates. Future projects use new money that generally requires new borrowing. Why should the high or low interest rates of the past influence the decisions made today?

Another alternative is to estimate an average cost of all money for the current year. For example, suppose that we expect to have the following amounts available for investment: $8 million to be borrowed from the bank at 8 percent; $1 million available from operations, which could otherwise be invested at 6 percent; and $1 million in charitable gifts with no interest cost. The average interest rate could be calculated as follows:

$$
\begin{array}{rcll}
\$\ 8,000,000 & \times & 8\% & = & \$640,000 \\
1,000,000 & \times & 6\% & = & 60,000 \\
1,000,000 & \times & 0\% & = & 0 \\
\hline
\$10,000,000 & \times & ? & = & \$700,000 \\
\hline
\end{array}
$$

$$\$700,000/\$10,000,000 = 7\%$$

This approach would argue that any project that can return more than 7 percent would be acceptable.

There is some logic to this approach, because it treats all projects the same, regardless of the specific point in time that they are proposed. It also makes sense because it uses the current cost of capital rather than a historic one.

However, it does have one serious flaw. It treats donated capital as part of the general cash available for investment. In doing so, it holds the projects financed with the donated capital to the same *profit* standards as the other projects. In essence, the donated capital brings down the average cost of capital for all projects. Is that desirable?

One might infer that the reason charitable donations are made is so that the organization can do things even if they are not profitable. To the extent that this is the case, projects should probably be evaluated on their business merit separately from their social merit.

Consider the average cost of capital without the donated money:

$$
\begin{array}{rcll}
\$8,000,000 & \times & 8\% & = & \$640,000 \\
1,000,000 & \times & 6\% & = & 60,000 \\
\hline
\$9,000,000 & \times & ? & = & \$700,000 \\
\hline
\end{array}
$$

$$\$700,000/\$9,000,000 = 7.8\%$$

Using this information, one could argue that all projects must earn at least 7.8 percent to be suitable as an investment, based strictly on their financial merits. A project earning 7.2 percent that has no particular social contribution would

not be accepted under this approach, because it does not earn a high enough return to cover the weighted average cost of borrowed money and foregone interest.

However, a project that only returns 2 percent, but that is very valuable to the health care of the community might be accepted. It would first be rejected on business grounds. However, it would then be evaluated on social grounds. Since the charitable funds have not been relegated only to projects earning 7 percent or more, they are now available for projects such as this one. In fact, they might be used on projects that have no return at all. In order to maintain the flow of charitable donations, it is important to bear in mind the purpose behind the donation. That purpose is probably not for maximizing the organization's profits.

Risk Factors

So far we have considered only the portion of the discount rate that relates to the cost of capital. It is also necessary to take into account the risk premium.

What types of risks do health care organizations have with their investments? There is the risk that the patient volume will not be as great as expected, and the investment will lose money rather than make money. There is the risk that inflation will be high, and it will cost more money to replace the asset when it is used up than it cost to acquire it. There is the risk that government regulations will change. The revised regulations might make the item nonreimbursable or paid at a lower rate. These are just a few examples of the most common risks facing most health care organizations.

Suppose that for every ten new services a health care organization offers, seven earn about what is expected; one earns about 20 percent above expectations; one earns about 20 percent below expectations; and one is a disaster, losing half of the investment. Obviously, the one poor project would not be undertaken if it could be identified in advance. The reality is that all ten projects look good, or they would be avoided. However, the reality also is that things sometimes do not turn out as expected, even if a careful investment analysis is done.

How will the health care organization recover the loss from the one poor project? Each of the projects must be expected to return more than enough to justify itself. That way, each of the successful projects can contribute to cover the loss on the unsuccessful one, and overall the organization will not lose money. In this case, for nine successful projects to cover a 50 percent loss on one unsuccessful project, each would have to have 5.5 percent extra added to their discount rate (5.5% × 9 projects = 50% on one).

Another risk factor relates to inflation. If the investment returns enough cash to cover just its cost and the cost of capital, how will it be replaced at the end of its lifetime? Undoubtedly, inflation will drive up the cost of the replacement. If we expect the annual inflation cost to be 4 percent, we must add that cost to the discount rate.

That assumes we are dealing with a not-for-profit organization. For-profit organizations must include a higher rate for inflation. This is because the government only allows depreciation based on historical cost rather than replacement cost. The government will perceive the inflation premium as being profits. It will tax those profits. Therefore, the for-profit health care organization must build in a high enough factor to be able to cover the impact of inflation, after paying taxes.

Depending on the type of investment, government regulation may be a minor or a major factor. If the organization makes an investment in a service with the chance that the government will stop paying for that service or will cut payment rates, it must take that risk into account. Such a risk premium is largely arbitrary. It is a best guess by the manager as to what represents a fair premium for the risks being taken. That depends on the likelihood of negative changes taking place and their potential magnitude.

The Total Rate

The total discount rate should reflect both the cost of capital and the risk premium. Undoubt-

edly, many managers will look at this rate and be surprised at how high it is. Rates of 15 to 20 percent would not be particularly shocking. In corporate industry, rates up to 25 or 30 percent are not uncommon. It is important that managers make the decision about the rate carefully. Setting the rate too low will result in the acceptance of poor projects that will contribute to the financial stress that many health care organizations are already experiencing.

Capital Budgeting and Income Taxes

As sophisticated capital budgeting techniques become more widely used in health care organizations, one factor that will require consideration is the role of income taxes. This affects not only for-profit health care organizations, but also not-for-profits that have or are considering for-profit subsidiaries or ventures.

Time value of money techniques that are widely used for valuing capital acquisitions or major project investments rely on cash flow information. The analyses consider how much cash flow comes and goes during each time period of the project or asset life. However, for taxable entities, cash flow is affected by income taxes. The income tax payments reduce the cash flow available to the organization.

Horngren and Foster pose three questions that must be examined when considering the income tax implications for capital budgeting:

- What income tax rate applies in each year of the project?
- Which cash inflows (outflows) are taxable (tax deductible)?
- What differences exist in tax rates and tax deductions among projects set in different jurisdictions (states, countries, and so on)?[1]

If one asks these three questions and incorporates the answers, the analysis is far more likely to generate a result that will lead managers to make correct investment decisions.

The Role of Depreciation in Capital Budget Analysis

Depreciation is a peculiar item for capital budgeting. Correct investment decisions are based on cash flows. Depreciation in general is not a cash flow. It is an allocation of a cost to acquire a multiyear asset into each of the years of the asset's life.

For capital budgeting purposes, we generally want to stay away from depreciation because it can be misleading. One machine might be purchased with full payment in the first year. Another might be paid in installments over its lifetime. Both machines will have the exact same depreciation each year. However, the timing of the cash payments to acquire the machine has a definite impact on the profitability of the project. Therefore, basic capital budgeting considers that cash flow occurs when cash is paid to acquire the asset rather than the annual depreciation charge.

To some extent, health care organizations have long had to modify this principle. If depreciation is reimbursed, then that depreciation is essential for calculating the cash flows from the investment. Note, however, that it is the *cash inflows* that are affected by the annual depreciation charge, not the cash outflows.

However, depreciation does have an additional impact on cash outflows if one considers income taxes. Depreciation represents a tax deduction. As such, it reduces the cash outflow. Therefore, it is important for for-profit organizations to take into account the factors that affect depreciation. These factors are the length of the useful life used for depreciation, the pattern of depreciation each year, and the total amount of depreciation allowed.

The real useful life of capital assets generally is substantially longer than the life used for tax calculations. Therefore, the revenue stream that is used to calculate cash inflows will have a different number of years from the period over which the asset's depreciation has an effect on tax deductions. The shorter the allowable life for tax purposes, the faster the depreciation will take place. This will give bigger deductions in the early years and smaller ones in the later years. That, in turn, will reduce taxes more sooner and less later. Such a pattern will increase the NPV of the investment.

Similarly, if the asset can be depreciated on an accelerated basis—higher deductions in the early years of the allowable depreciable life and smaller ones later—then the NPV will be improved. Most fixed assets qualify for the modified accelerated cost recovery system (MACRS) approach for federal income taxes. That method allows for greater writeoffs in earlier years.

Of course, the more that can be depreciated, the higher the NPV as well. For example, whether the expected salvage value can be depreciated or not, over the life of the asset, the total depreciation will be the same. However, the timing will differ. If you depreciate the full value including any salvage and later sell the asset for the salvage value, you must pay the government taxes on the selling price. However, the effect is to defer the cash outflow to the government.

Consider a $1,000 machine with a salvage value of $200 at the end of its useful life. If you deduct the full $1,000 and then sell the machine for $200, you must pay tax on that $200 of income. The result is a $1,000 deduction and a $200 revenue, or a net of $800. This is the same as if you only took depreciation of $800. However, the depreciation deduction is taken before the item is sold. Therefore, the tax savings from the extra depreciation will occur early, and the extra taxes on the sale will occur later. The effect is that the government will be allowing you to pay less taxes early and more later. This is equivalent to an interest-free loan.

Calculating the Effect of Taxes

The important element to keep in mind is that if you are taxable, capital investments should be evaluated on an after-tax cash flow basis. The time value of money calculations—whether NPV, IRR, or some other DCF approach—all evaluate cash flows. However, the cash flows must be adjusted for the tax payments that will be made each year.

Ultimately, we want to evaluate the entire set of cash flows related to the investment. Taxes are one of those cash flows. Taxes are calculated largely on a profit and loss basis, rather than a cash flow basis. The accrual basis of accounting used by health care organizations will lead to a number of tax implications that do not match up directly with cash flow.

For example, revenues will be considered for tax purposes when they are earned, not when they are received. But NPV only looks at revenues in the period the cash is received. Therefore, the organization may well incur expenses that are paid on a cash basis and then pay taxes in cash and still not have received the related revenues in cash. This can have a definite negative impact on the NPV result.

Managers should always be cautious in calculating NPVs. The methodology is sophisticated, but its results are only as good as the data being used. Health care organizations, with their long not-for-profit traditions, are in a position of particular vulnerability when it comes to taxes. Tax calculations are not routine, especially for not-for-profit organizations entering for-profit ventures.

Political Issues and Capital Budget Analysis

Although the DCF techniques are strictly analytical tools, one would be foolish to ignore the political realities of most health care organizations. The ultimate decision is only partly based on analysis and is partly based on issues such as mission, corporate culture, and just plain politics.

In an ideal world, one might argue that the ultimate decisions would be based solely on patient needs, within the limited resources the organization has available. Given that we do not live in an ideal world, one might question the wisdom of analytical approaches such as those discussed here. Some might argue that only academics are interested in tools such as those described above.

In fact, however, the trend is toward greater use of such analytical tools. Even if the ultimate decision takes into account political realities, it is likely to be at least tempered by the information that can be generated by DCF analysis. As the reimbursement systems start to remove the protective shield of reimbursement for all capital costs, it becomes ever more important for health care organizations to make their decisions with at least an understanding of the financial consequences of their capital asset investment decisions.

THE CASH BUDGET

Health care organizations have long known the importance of cash budgeting. Since health care organization financial statements are generally prepared on an accrual basis, profitability is not a reasonable measure of cash flow. Budgeting for cash inflows and outflows becomes a critical area for the ultimate financial stability and survival of the health care organization. With the introduction of Financial Accounting Standards Board Statement No. 95 on cash flows, greater attention is expected to be placed on cash flows by most health care organizations. For health care organizations under financial pressure, cash budgeting becomes critical.

Primary Reasons for Cash Budgeting

In good times, we want to understand cash flows to be able to anticipate cash available for investment or for expansion of patient care services. In bad times, we want to be able to anticipate our ability to meet legal obligations such as payroll, taxes, interest payments, and payables to suppliers.

Even if times are neither particularly good nor bad, health care organizations can best use their resources if they have good planning. Anticipating cash flows due to factors such as the months bond interest payments are due, when we have seasonal peaks in costs, and the lag until patient and third-party payments catch up with cost peaks is vital to efficient cash management.

There is a cliché that banks only like to lend money to people who do not need it. Certainly, it has been shown that banks only like to lend money when they feel reasonably assured that they will be able to be paid back. The current environment is one in which many bond-rating agencies are reviewing their ratings of hospital bonds. Hospital failures or bond defaults have been increasing. This pattern will undoubtedly make banks more cautious in their relationships with all health care organizations. However, careful advance planning, showing forecasts of when cash will be needed and when it can be repaid, is likely to enhance a health care organization's chance of being able to borrow money when it needs it. Cash budgeting has a variety of other benefits, such as helping the planning of expansions or equipment replacements as well as repayment of bond principal.

Techniques for Cash Budgeting

Although the existence of a cash budget is typical in health care organizations, alternative techniques do exist for the preparation of the budget. The three most common approaches are the *indirect method,* the *working capital method,* and the *direct method.*

The indirect method starts with the operating budget for revenues and expenses. This becomes an approximation of the cash flow for the year. Adjustments are then made for cash flow differences from net income. This method follows the cash flow statement that is included with the health care organization's audited financial statements. Obviously, however, this would be a prospective plan, whereas the financial statements contain the retrospective actual results.

Exhibit 8-2 gives an example of the indirect method for cash budgeting. In this approach, net income is increased by depreciation and other noncash expenses, such as amortization. This is because they are subtracted to arrive at net income, but they are expenses that do not consume cash.

Net income is then further adjusted for changes in working capital accounts. For exam-

ple, an increase in accounts receivable is indicative of fewer revenues being received in cash than the revenue line on the income statement implies. Therefore, increases in accounts receivable would be deducted from cash. The cash budget would then be further adjusted for anticipated cash flows such as borrowing, repayment of debt, or purchases of buildings and/or equipment. As one can see from Exhibit 8-2, these are often classified as cash flows from investing and financing activities.

The primary advantage of the indirect method is that it tends to parallel the financial statement presentation. To the extent that a health care organization's management believes that the cash flow statement it presents to the public is clear and complete, a similar approach would be useful for internal information. On the other hand, financial statements are generally summarizations of detailed data. It is not at all clear that the summarized data suitable for users of financial statements are sufficient for internal management purposes.

The working capital approach is useful if one views cash as being relatively less important and overall working capital as being more important. It changes the focus from cash to the changes in working capital (i.e., the changes in the net difference between current assets and current liabilities).

In the working capital approach, each month begins with the ending working capital from the previous month, to which income for the month is then added, and adjustments are made for other receipts and disbursements. This produces an ending working capital balance. Exhibit 8-3 provides an example of the working capital method.

As one can see from Exhibit 8-3, net income must still be adjusted for income items that do not affect current assets and current liabilities, such as depreciation. However, there is no need to make an adjustment for changes in working capital accounts, as in Exhibit 8-2. Even though accounts receivable increases do not generate cash flow, they do not have to be subtracted because they do represent an increase in a working capital account.

Exhibit 8-2 Cash Flow Budget: Indirect Method

Cash flow from operations		
Budgeted net income (revenues – expenses)		$1,000,000
Add items not requiring cash outflow		
Depreciation	$ 400,000	
Amortization	150,000	550,000
Deduct items not generating cash		
Increase in accounts receivable		(80,000)
Net cash flow from operations		$1,470,000
Cash flow related to investing activities		
Equipment acquisitions	$(300,000)	
Net cash flow from investing activities		(300,000)
Cash flows related to financing activities		
Mortgage	$ 300,000	
Principal payments on debt	(500,000)	
Net cash flow from financing activities		(200,000)
Net budgeted cash flow		$ 970,000

Exhibit 8-3 Cash Flow Budget: Working Capital Method

Beginning working capital		$ 300,000
Budgeted net income (revenues – expenses)		1,000,000
Add net income items not requiring working capital change		
Depreciation	$400,000	
Amortization	150,000	550,000
Other receipts		
Mortgage		300,000
Other disbursements		
Principal payments on debt	$500,000	
Equipment acquisitions	300,000	(800,000)
Ending working capital		$1,350,000

Depending on changes in working capital accounts, such as receivables, the change in cash can be calculated. This method is of limited use in health care organizations, where significant changes in working capital occur. Unlike an industry that has quite stable levels of inventory, receivables, and other working capital items, health care organizations may well have significant fluctuations, particularly in receivables and payables.

The direct method requires a detailed forecast of all accounts that will change that involve cash. This method is probably the most complicated of the three because of the level of detail, but it is essential for generating the information that is most useful.

The simplest way to approach cash budgeting using the direct method is to examine all of the journal entries that involve cash and categorize the different other accounts that change as cash changes. This will establish the lines that must appear on the cash budget. The next steps will be to estimate the inflows and outflows for each line.

Usually, health care organizations will modify this basic approach to give additional useful information. For example, Table 8-1 groups receipts by payer and groups disbursements into broad categories.

In this table, the budgeting is being done on a monthly basis. Because of the importance of meeting payrolls and other expenses on a timely basis, most health care organizations will prefer to plan for cash flows and to monitor cash on a more frequent basis than annually or quarterly. Therefore, a budget such as the one shown in Table 8-1, can be extremely useful.

Table 8-1 assumes that the organization desires to keep a $10,000 minimum balance on hand at the end of each month. This amount becomes the beginning balance budgeted for each month. Adding this to cash receipts gives a projection of cash available. Subtracting cash disbursements gives a tentative month-end balance. If the balance is above the desired $10,000, money can be invested. If it is below $10,000, then plans to borrow money must be made. The hardest element of cash budgeting is forecasting the cash flows.

Forecasting Cash Inflows

The cash budget obviously follows the operating budget in terms of timing of preparation. We must know the expected number and type of patients to be able to predict patient receipts. In the case of cash receipts and cash disbursements, experience is often an excellent guide to future patterns. We should be attempting to understand the cash flows of the past to predict the coming cash flows.

Additionally, it is important that we make the effort to recognize the variability in patient flow throughout the year. Seasonal factors are not

Table 8-1 Cash Budget for One Quarter

	January	February	March
Beginning cash balance	$ 10,000	$ 10,000	$ 10,000
Budgeted receipts			
Medicare	$130,000	$135,000	$120,000
Medicaid	70,000	95,000	70,000
Blue Cross	70,000	85,000	90,000
Other insurers	62,000	45,000	40,000
Self-pay	40,000	43,000	40,000
Philanthropy	5,000	5,000	9,000
Other	8,000	10,000	9,000
Total receipts	$385,000	$418,000	$378,000
Cash available	$395,000	$428,000	$388,000
Less expected payments			
Labor costs	$160,000	$170,000	$180,000
Suppliers	35,000	45,000	55,000
Capital acquisitions	10,000	15,000	20,000
Payments on loans	170,000	170,000	170,000
Total payments	$375,000	$400,000	$425,000
Tentative cash balance	$ 20,000	$28,000	$(37,000)
Less amount invested	(10,000)	(18,000)	28,000
Plus amount borrowed			19,000
Final cash balance	$ 10,000	$ 10,000	$ 10,000

only important for clinical areas that must deal with staffing. Such factors are equally important for cash flow. Forecasting techniques that can refine our predictions from month to month within the year are vital. (Forecasting was discussed in Chapter 7.)

Knowing patient volume in any given month is a key factor, but just as important is up-to-date information on payment lags by different payers. This is an especially difficult problem because the various government payers tend to change the promptness of payment from time to time. A five- or ten-day slowing of cash receipts from Medicare or Medicaid can have a tremendous impact on cash flows throughout the year.

A general budgeting rule is that once budgets are created and approved, we live with them for the year. Clinical department heads may provide explanations of why actual results vary from the budget, but the initial budget is still left intact. This generally holds true even if the budget is adjusted monthly for variance analysis purposes based on actual workload volumes so that actual costs are compared with a flexible budget. (See Chapter 9.) Increases in workload this month do not result in increases in the budget for future months within the year. This fixed approach may be inappropriate for cash budgets, however.

For the cash budget to be a useful tool, it should reflect coming cash flows as accurately as possible. If we realize midway through the year that Medicare has slowed its payments, a revised budget should be prepared to show the expected cash flows each month after that change. It would not serve us to run out of cash in a month due to a lag that is known but not included in our static projections.

Forecasting Cash Outflows

Choosing When To Pay

Predicting cash outflows is more complicated than inflows because of the element of choice. With cash inflows, we will always try to receive them as fast as possible. There is no choice concerning whether we should attempt to bill as

quickly as possible or to collect as quickly as possible. With outflows, a decision must be made concerning when payments will be made.

Clearly, there are some payments that have known, determinate payment dates. We will want to meet payroll and tax payments on or by the due date. Other payments, however, may lag a bit beyond the due dates. Good cash management dictates that we will not be late on payments that accrue interest costs in excess of our bank borrowing rate. There is no reason to pay 18 percent per year interest and penalty on a bill if we could borrow the cash from the bank for 12 percent to pay the bill.

Many of our suppliers will wait a bit for their payments. If our delay causes vendors to raise prices to us, we need to be cautious in planning our payments to them. On the other hand, if industry-wide delays in payments cause prices to everyone to increase, there is no need to be the only organization paying on time. In fact, assessing payment patterns of other health care organizations in the geographic area is a critical factor. Although we want to pay promptly enough to maintain our creditworthiness with suppliers, there is the fundamental choice of paying late. Evaluation of the benefits and costs of late payment is essential to the cash budgeting process.

Anticipating Cash Needs

Working from an operating budget, the health care organization should be able to anticipate what the annual cash needs will be. Just as with receipts, knowing the seasonal patterns for the health care organization will substantially improve our ability to budget cash. Care must be exercised, because cash payments will not necessarily be as dependent on seasonal swings as cash receipts are. For example, vacations may result in a roughly constant payroll, with people taking off during slow periods. On the other hand, payroll increases should be anticipated in some months as a result of peak patient volumes and overtime.

The level of detail of the cash budget is a critical factor to anticipate. Obviously, bond payments or payments for major purchases must be isolated and carefully considered for timing. Should routine monthly expenses be aggregated or treated individually? This largely depends on the degree to which we treat different payees differently. Because we will want to be sure to meet payroll on time, we would tend to isolate payroll in our projections. If there are some suppliers that we feel must be paid within 30 days, whereas others will wait 90 days for payment, we should try to create two separate lines on our cash budget. By knowing which vendors are paid fairly currently and which we wait to pay, we will be better able to anticipate cash needs as purchases are made. For example, if we start to buy a greater proportion of our supplies from a vendor who accepts slow payment, we can review our budget and anticipate lower cash outflows in the coming month and higher flows several months later.

The Planning Period

Health care organizations generally prepare cash budgets on a monthly basis. This is common to many other industries, although in some, such as banking, daily budgets are common. If Thursdays are payday in a particular community, the bank must plan to have more cash available on Thursdays than on other days of the week, so that paychecks can be cashed. It would not make sense for a health care organization to plan cash for the coming year on a daily basis. There are too many uncertainties.

On the other hand, if cash is a major concern, it might not be a bad idea to try to plan cash on a daily basis for each coming week or month as we go. In the New York City area, hospitals are having tremendous financial problems primarily due to low payment rates, which are set by the government for all payers. It is not uncommon to look at year-end statements for hospitals in New York and observe substantially less cash on hand than enough to cover expenses for one day. In such cases, continuous careful planning of day-by-day and week-by-week cash receipts and payments is critical.

At the other extreme, cash budgeting should also be done for long periods of time, such as 10 to 20 years. It is true that the longer the time period of the cash forecast, the less detail (and probably less accuracy) we will have. Nevertheless, capital projects, debt repayments, and the like require that we consider a lengthy time-frame.

A 20-year projection will allow the health care organization to begin to question whether enough cash is being generated each year to meet substantial needs well into the future. Without such long-range cash budgets, as the future approaches, problems may be encountered due to failure to plan now. Long-term cash budgets can help plan for new long-term financing, liquidation of long-term debt, and cash available for future capital projects.

Managing the Cash Budget

The plan is the critical starting point in cash management. However, the plan itself will be inadequate if it is not actively managed. How does one manage a budget that seems to rely primarily on whether the other health care organization budgets come out as expected? For instance, if we have fewer patients than expected, we will have less cash inflow. There is little that the cash manager can do to increase patient volume.

Having little to do is still more than having nothing to do. For starters, cash managers should be analyzing actual cash behavior patterns to be able to identify areas of cash receipts where our expectations are not being met and areas of cash expenditure where expectations are being exceeded. Patient receipts may decline because we have fewer patients. It is important, however, to determine whether in fact we have as many patients as expected, but cash receipts are down because our collections efforts are deteriorating.

To the extent that cash results differ from projections as a result of controllable activities that do not take place as budgeted, there should be a formal mechanism for passing along to appropriate individuals an indication of the impact on the cash budget of their department's activities.

As mentioned earlier, the cash budget or at least a forecast should be prepared showing revised cash results based on updated information and year-to-date results. This will allow us time to make whatever managerial decisions are necessary to respond to cash shortages.

One area of cash management that has the potential to aid health care organizations is an increased understanding of the impact of *float* on payments and collections. In particular, when the organization makes payments, the checks drawn do not clear the bank immediately. This means that the funds are still available to the organization for a period of time. By studying the patterns of float that exist, the health care organization can take better advantage of float.

Float typically results from delays in mailing or delivering checks after they have been drawn, the time the checks are in the mail, the time it takes the recipients to process and deposit the checks, and the time from deposit at the recipient's bank until disbursement by your bank. This period can be very short (payroll checks cashed at your bank the day they are drawn), or it can be quite lengthy.

For example, a health care organization can overdraw its account without penalty if it has calculated the time period from when checks are drawn until they clear, and sufficient funds are in the bank when the checks clear. This is especially true for health care organizations that use electronic transfers for much of their receipts. Checks can be drawn with the knowledge that it may take a week on average for them to clear, if we know that within that week we will receive an electronic transfer that will be available to the account immediately.

Consider the alternative impact of covering all checks as written versus investing money at an 8 percent rate during the float period. Suppose that each month disbursements average $15 million. Suppose further that most disbursements are in the mail for two days and then are processed for one and a half days on average. Suppose also that it takes one and a half days for the check to clear the banking system. This is a total of five days of float. The two days in the mail is conservative, but longer mail delays are offset by payroll checks disbursed directly. The one and a half days for processing may be long for some large vendors, but typical when all payments are averaged.

If we earn interest on that $15 million at 8 percent per year for five days per month, we would earn about $200,000 of extra interest, as compared to having the money in a noninterest-bearing checking account awaiting disbursement. In fact, it is possible that the health care organization could even increase float by drawing checks on distant banks, increasing the time the checks are clearing in the banking system. For example, payroll checks could be issued on a distant bank, and wire transfers could be used to cover the checks several days after they are issued.

Short-Term Cash Management

Cash is held by health care organizations primarily for day-to-day transactions, for safety, and for psychology. Clearly, we need cash today to pay the bills that we need to pay today. Cash balances are held to cover unexpected cash needs. However, that can be minimized if the health care organization has a good working relationship with a bank, so that borrowing would be possible on short notice. The psychology factor refers to the fact that some people feel more secure to see that there is money in the bank. However, peace of mind can be expensive. Investing cash and earning interest or paying off loans and reducing interest may be a better way to achieve long-term piece of mind.

Short-term cash management is concerned with issues of day-to-day prediction and management of cash inflows and outflows. The management of cash depends on how much cash the health care organization wants to keep in the bank. One option is to maintain the smallest possible balance without being overdrawn. Another choice is to keep an adequate balance to cover a bank's compensating balance requirements for loans outstanding and for loan privileges. Either of these two approaches requires daily transfers to cover the activity of the day. Alternative approaches keeping more money in the bank include having enough money to cover daily activity or an even higher amount great enough to cover not only activity but also contingencies.

It is important that the health care organization make some choice among these possibilities, or that it define some other specific guideline. There are pros and cons for any given desired indicator for how much cash should be in the bank. It is important, however, that management make a decision as to what indicator makes the most sense for the organization, and then manages cash in accordance with that indicator.

For instance, suppose that a nursing home has decided that to be reasonably safe, it wants to have enough cash for each day's activity plus a $50,000 contingency. That goal should then be met. Since there are some days (e.g., payday) when checking activity is great and other days when it is slow, active management is needed to keep the cash balance moving up and down as the different days' needs require. Failure to manage cash actively will likely mean that too much cash will be kept in the checking account to cover activity on high cash-use days. This implies a high opportunity cost.

Managers need to work weekly in anticipation of daily receipts and timing of disbursements. They also need to work actively on daily cash management. Obviously, the extent to which this is done will depend on the size of the health care organization. For example, New York University Medical Center spends approximately $500 million per year. That means that on average, nearly $2 million are spent on each working day. However, some days might see only $500,000 of spending, whereas others would see $5 million or $10 million. The need to know the cash in the bank at the end of each day for loan and investment decisions is clear-cut.

Smaller health care organizations do not have as many dollars in daily changes in their cash balances and investments. At the same time, smaller amounts of interest saved or earned may be just as meaningful to the small organization, on a relative basis. Ensuring that borrowing will take place when needed, and at minimal levels, and that excess cash is invested are important to all organizations.

Zero Balance Accounts

One tool for cash management that is becoming more common is the *zero balance account* (ZBA). Instead of using one main account for most cashflows, separate accounts are maintained at the bank for each major source of cash receipt and for major types of payments. The maintenance of separate accounts allows the cash manager to track money coming in closely by source. Similarly, payments can be tracked by type. This allows each stream of cash to be forecast and tracked on a more accurate and simple basis than when the funds are immediately commingled.

With ZBAs, at the close of each day, the bank, using computer technology, automatically transfers all positive or negative balances into one master concentration account. Any borrowing or investing of cash can then be done against that one account.

Cash has always been an important part of health care management. However, in the last few years, the focus on cash has increased. Fortunately, computer advances in banks as well as improved attention on the part of managers can result in significant savings from improved management of cash receipts and disbursements.

PROGRAM BUDGETS

In order to accomplish the organization's long-range plan, it is often necessary to carry out specific programmatic changes in the organization. For example, the long-range plan may call for growth, by adding five major new programs, at a rate of one per year. At the time the long-range plan is created, it would not be possible to create a specific, detailed budget for all of the costs and revenues related to each program that will be introduced in the next five years. In fact, the long-range budget may call for the rapid introduction of new technologies as they develop. The specific technologies may not exist when the long-range plan is made. Therefore, there is a need for a specific program budget that will provide the information necessary to introduce new programs.

One program budget will be created for each new program. Program budgets consider the likely revenues and expenses related to the program over a period of years. This allows the organization to determine whether there will be a financial benefit or loss from the program. Operating budgets look at revenues and expenses, but only for a period of one year. Capital budgets look at specific investments in assets with a life of more than one year. Cash budgets look at cash flows. Program budgets combine all of these elements for a specific program or service. They consider all revenues and expenses, the full life of capital assets involved, and the cash flow implications.

Program budgets in recent years have been referred to commonly as *business plans*. A business plan considers all of the financial implications of a proposed venture to determine its financial feasibility. Business plans are addressed further in Application 8-4.

SPECIAL-PURPOSE BUDGETS

A budget is a plan. There are no specific forms that are always used in preparing a budget; there are no specific rules. As part of managerial, rather than financial, accounting, there are no generally accepted accounting principles. The goal is to develop a set of information that will be useful to managers in their management of the health care organization. As such, we can prepare a budget for anything for which a plan is needed. When a budget does not fall into any of the categories described above, it is referred to as a special-purpose budget.

For example, suppose that an organization decided that it would like to provide screening for high blood pressure at a local shopping center. The goal would be to help improve the health of the community by identifying cases of hypertensivity and, at the same time, promote the organization in a highly visible manner. How much would it cost to provide the screening?

Would the organization have to charge money to cover the cost of the test? If so, how much?

These questions could be better addressed if the organization had a budget for the screening activity. If this is a spur-of-the-moment idea, then it is not already accounted for in the operating budget. A special-purpose budget must be prepared that considers all of the personnel, supply, and equipment costs; malpractice insurance implications; and so on.

It is possible that the organization may decide to offer the tests at cost, or it may budget a profit or a loss. If a loss is budgeted, there must be some decision regarding whether that loss will be subsidized by the organization or how else it will be covered. Special-purpose budgets can be very useful because they allow the organization to have the flexibility to act quickly to undertake activities that cannot be anticipated well in advance.

THE NEGOTIATION AND APPROVAL PROCESS

Budgets are often prepared by the managers of the departments throughout the organization. This ensures that the budgets are based on realistic information and expectations. The budgets are submitted to the finance department of the organization, which compiles the various components into the master budget. This budget must be approved before it can be implemented.

Often, however, the budgets submitted as pieces do not form a feasible master budget. The spending requests of the departments may total to more than the total available revenue. If a deficit is unacceptable, some changes will have to be made in the budget. Even if the budget presents a balanced operating picture for the current year, cash requirements may exceed projected cash inflows. In either case, changes would have to be made to either elements of the operating budget or the capital budget or both.

The changes are often made through a process of negotiation back and forth, as the organization's top managers try to find the areas where budget cuts would do the least damage. It should be kept in mind that budgets, like all of cost accounting, involve human beings. Therefore, the persuasiveness, power, and other personal characteristics of the individuals negotiating will have an impact on the outcome. Ultimately, a budget is decided upon and is presented to the organization's board for approval. Even at that stage, the budget might be sent back to the managers for additional changes.

Once the budget is finally approved, it must be implemented. Managers must review the budget as approved and begin to carry out whatever activities are necessary (hiring staff, letting staff go, etc.) to comply with the budget. After the budget is in place and the new year begins, managers will start to receive feedback as actual results are known. This feedback will require investigation to understand the causes of any differences between the plan and the actual results. Techniques for such investigation are the major topic of the next chapter.

NOTE

1. C.T. Horngren and G. Foster, *Cost Accounting: A Managerial Emphasis,* 7th ed. (Englewood Cliffs, NJ: Prentice-Hall, 1991), p. 705.

SUGGESTED READING

Bender, A.D. December 1991. Budget model can aid group practice planning. *Healthcare Financial Management* 50–59.

Berman, H.J., and L.E. Weeks. 1982. *The financial management of hospitals.* 5th ed. Ann Arbor, Mich.: Health Administration Press.

Clark, C.S., and M.A. Kleiman. 1992. Tools of financial analysis: Risk, return and incremental analysis. *Topics in Health Care Financing* 19, no. 1:26–33.

Collins, F., et al. 1987. The budgeting games people play. *The Accounting Review* 62, no. 1:29–49.

Cook, D. May 1990. Strategic plan creates a blueprint for budgeting. *Healthcare Financial Management*, 20–27.

Covert, P. 1982. Expense budgeting. In *Handbook of health care accounting and finance,* ed. W.O. Cleverley, 261–278. Rockville, Md.: Aspen Publishers, Inc.

Dillon, R.D. 1979. *Zero-base budgeting for health care institutions.* Gaithersburg, Md.: Aspen Publishers, Inc.

Esmond, T.H. 1990. *Budgeting for effective hospital resource management.* Chicago: American Hospital Association.

Finkler, S.A. 1992. *Budgeting concepts for nurse managers.* 2nd ed. Philadelphia: W.B. Saunders.

_____. 1986. Zero-base budgeting for hospitals. *Hospital Cost Accounting Advisor* 2, no. 5:1, 4–6.

Horngren, C.T., and G. Foster. 1991. *Cost accounting: A managerial emphasis.* 7th ed. Englewood Cliffs, N.J.: Prentice-Hall, Inc.

Kershner, M., and J. Rooney. 1987. Utilizing cost information for budgeting. *Topics in Health Care Financing* 13, no. 4:56–66.

Newton, R.L. May 1981. Establishing a rolling budgeting process. *Hospital Financial Management*, 54–56.

Plomann, M.P., and T. Esmond. October 1984. Using case mix information for budgeting. *Health Care Financial Management*, 30–31, 34–35.

Ryan, J.B., and M.E. Ward, eds. Fall 1992. Capital management. *Topics in Health Care Financing* 19, no. 1.

Straley, P.F., and T.B. Schuster. Fall 1992. Evaluation criteria: A framework for decision making. *Topics in Health Care Financing* 19, no. 1:14–25.

Suver, J.D. 1989. Zero-base budgeting. In *Handbook of health care accounting and finance,* 2nd ed., ed. W.O. Cleverley, 311–332. Gaithersburg, Md.: Aspen Publishers, Inc.

EXERCISES

QUESTIONS FOR DISCUSSION

1. What are three major roles played by budgets?
2. In preparing budgets, to what extent must human behavior be considered?
3. What are the advantages of continuous budgeting?

4. What is the focus of a long-range budget?
5. In what ways is zero-base budgeting useful?
6. What is the operating budget?
7. What are the purposes of the long-range budget?
8. What are program budgets?
9. Why are program budgets needed in addition to the ordinary operating budget?
10. What is a capital expenditure, and why is a separate capital budget needed?

Note: Solutions to the Exercises can be found in Appendix A.

11. Is the financial stability of an organization ensured, as long as it is making a profit? Explain.
12. What does "time value of money" refer to?
13. What are the problems with the payback method?
14. What is the difference between revenues and cash receipts?
15. Why is cash flow important?

PROBLEMS

1. Finkler Hospital has decided that there is a pressing need in its community for open heart surgery. Prepare a ZBB decision package. Include an analysis of at least several different alternative levels of capacity or effort.
2. New Hospital decides to invest $10,000 of excess cash in an investment yielding 6 percent per year. How much will it have at the end of five years, (a) assuming annual compounding and (b) assuming monthly compounding?
3. Mr. Rich has offered to give The New Nursing Home $100,000 today, or $300,000 when he dies. If the nursing home earns 12 percent on its investments, and it expects Mr. Rich to live for 12 years, which alternative should it take?
4. New Home Care Agency expects to make average pension payments of $10,000 a year for 25 years for a staff nurse who just retired. If the agency's discount rate is 12 percent, what is the maximum lump sum amount that the agency should be willing to pay today to have an independent insurance company assume the burden of future payments?
5. *Net Present Cost.* New Hospice is building an extension. They can use single-pane glass windows that cost $100 each, or they can buy double-pane windows that cost $150 each. The windows should last 20 years before they have to be replaced. The hospice expects that heating costs will be lower by $5 per year for each double-pane window they buy. The hospice can borrow or invest money at 10 percent. Which type of window should they buy? What would your answer be if the interest rate was 6 percent? Why did changing the interest rate change the answer?

6. Below are the projected revenues and expenses for a new clinical nurse specialist program being established by a hospital. Nurses would provide education while the patient is in the hospital, and home visits after the patient is discharged, on a fee-for-service basis. Should the hospital undertake the program if its required rate of return is 12 percent?

	Year 1	Year 2	Year 3	Year 4	Total
Revenue	$100,000	$150,000	$200,000	$250,000	$700,000
Costs	150,000	150,000	150,000	150,000	600,000
	$(50,000)	$0	$50,000	$100,000	$100,000

7. Unified Path gives a $93,000 grant to Care for the Homeless at the start of their year on January 1. To expand its activities, Care for the Homeless also convinces the city, state, and county governments to give it additional funds for the year. The city will give it $24,000, the state will give it $88,000, and the county will give it $50,000. The city pays its share in equal monthly installments, after the month has ended (the payment for January arrives in February, and so forth). The State pays 50 percent in the first month of the year, and the balance equally over the remaining months. The county pays 10 percent of its outstanding balance each month, with any balance paid in the last month. Prepare a cash budget for January, February, and March, showing just the cash inflows for each month.

Appendix 8-A

Present Value and Compound Interest Tables

Table 8-A-1 The Present Value of \$1. $P_{N,i} = 1/(1+i)^N$

N	0.5	1	1.5	2	3	4	5	6	7	8	9	10	12	15
1	.995	.990	.985	.980	.971	.962	.952	.943	.935	.926	.917	.909	.893	.870
2	.990	.980	.971	.961	.943	.925	.907	.890	.873	.857	.842	.826	.797	.756
3	.985	.971	.956	.942	.915	.889	.864	.839	.816	.794	.772	.751	.712	.658
4	.980	.961	.942	.924	.888	.855	.823	.792	.763	.735	.708	.683	.636	.572
5	.975	.951	.928	.906	.863	.822	.784	.747	.713	.681	.650	.621	.567	.497
6	.971	.942	.915	.888	.837	.790	.746	.705	.666	.630	.596	.564	.506	.432
7	.966	.932	.901	.871	.813	.760	.711	.665	.623	.583	.547	.513	.452	.376
8	.961	.923	.888	.853	.789	.731	.677	.627	.582	.540	.502	.467	.404	.327
9	.956	.914	.875	.837	.766	.703	.645	.592	.544	.500	.460	.424	.361	.284
10	.951	.905	.862	.820	.744	.676	.614	.558	.508	.463	.422	.386	.322	.247
11	.947	.896	.849	.804	.722	.650	.585	.527	.475	.429	.388	.350	.287	.215
12	.942	.887	.836	.788	.701	.625	.557	.497	.444	.397	.356	.319	.257	.187
13	.937	.879	.824	.773	.681	.601	.530	.469	.415	.368	.326	.290	.229	.163
14	.933	.870	.812	.758	.661	.577	.505	.442	.388	.340	.299	.263	.205	.141
15	.928	.861	.800	.743	.642	.555	.481	.417	.362	.315	.275	.239	.183	.123
16	.923	.853	.788	.728	.623	.534	.458	.394	.339	.292	.252	.218	.163	.107
17	.919	.844	.776	.714	.605	.513	.436	.371	.317	.270	.231	.198	.146	.093
18	.914	.836	.765	.700	.587	.494	.416	.350	.296	.250	.212	.180	.130	.081
19	.910	.828	.754	.686	.570	.475	.396	.331	.277	.232	.194	.164	.116	.070
20	.905	.820	.742	.673	.554	.456	.377	.312	.258	.215	.178	.149	.104	.061
25	.883	.780	.689	.610	.478	.375	.295	.233	.184	.146	.116	.092	.056	.030
30	.861	.742	.640	.552	.412	.308	.231	.174	.131	.099	.075	.057	.033	.015
35	.840	.706	.594	.500	.355	.253	.181	.130	.094	.068	.049	.036	.019	.008
40	.819	.672	.551	.453	.307	.208	.142	.097	.067	.046	.032	.022	.011	.004
50	.779	.608	.475	.372	.228	.141	.087	.054	.034	.021	.013	.009	.003	.001

i

Note: N = number of discounting periods, i = percent interest rate per discounting period.

Table 8-A-2 The Compounded Value of $1. $A_{N, i} = (1 + i)^N$

N	0.5	1	1.5	2	3	4	5	6	7	8	9	10	12	15
1	1.005	1.010	1.015	1.020	1.030	1.040	1.050	1.060	1.070	1.080	1.090	1.100	1.120	1.150
2	1.010	1.020	1.030	1.040	1.061	1.082	1.103	1.124	1.145	1.166	1.188	1.210	1.254	1.323
3	1.015	1.030	1.046	1.061	1.093	1.125	1.158	1.191	1.225	1.260	1.295	1.331	1.405	1.521
4	1.020	1.041	1.061	1.082	1.126	1.170	1.216	1.262	1.311	1.360	1.412	1.464	1.574	1.749
5	1.025	1.051	1.077	1.104	1.159	1.217	1.276	1.338	1.403	1.469	1.539	1.611	1.762	2.011
6	1.030	1.062	1.093	1.126	1.194	1.265	1.340	1.419	1.501	1.587	1.677	1.772	1.974	2.313
7	1.036	1.072	1.110	1.149	1.230	1.316	1.407	1.504	1.606	1.714	1.828	1.949	2.211	2.660
8	1.041	1.083	1.126	1.172	1.267	1.369	1.477	1.594	1.718	1.851	1.993	2.144	2.476	3.059
9	1.046	1.094	1.143	1.195	1.305	1.423	1.551	1.689	1.838	1.999	2.172	2.358	2.773	3.518
10	1.051	1.105	1.161	1.219	1.344	1.480	1.629	1.791	1.967	2.159	2.367	2.594	3.106	4.046
11	1.056	1.116	1.178	1.243	1.384	1.539	1.710	1.898	2.105	2.332	2.580	2.853	3.479	4.652
12	1.062	1.127	1.196	1.268	1.426	1.601	1.796	2.012	2.252	2.518	2.813	3.138	3.896	5.350
13	1.067	1.138	1.214	1.294	1.469	1.665	1.886	2.133	2.410	2.720	3.066	3.452	4.363	6.153
14	1.072	1.149	1.232	1.319	1.513	1.732	1.980	2.261	2.579	2.937	3.342	3.797	4.887	7.076
15	1.078	1.161	1.250	1.346	1.558	1.801	2.079	2.397	2.759	3.172	3.642	4.177	5.474	8.137
16	1.083	1.173	1.269	1.373	1.605	1.873	2.183	2.540	2.952	3.426	3.970	4.595	6.130	9.358
17	1.088	1.184	1.288	1.400	1.653	1.948	2.292	2.693	3.159	3.700	4.328	5.054	6.866	10.761
18	1.094	1.196	1.307	1.428	1.702	2.026	2.407	2.854	3.380	3.996	4.717	5.560	7.690	12.375
19	1.099	1.208	1.327	1.457	1.754	2.107	2.527	3.026	3.617	4.316	5.142	6.116	8.613	14.232
20	1.105	1.220	1.347	1.486	1.806	2.191	2.653	3.207	3.870	4.661	5.604	6.727	9.646	16.367
25	1.133	1.282	1.451	1.641	2.094	2.666	3.386	4.292	5.427	6.848	8.623	10.835	17.000	32.919
30	1.161	1.348	1.563	1.811	2.427	3.243	4.322	5.743	7.612	10.063	13.268	17.449	29.960	66.212
35	1.191	1.417	1.684	2.000	2.814	3.946	5.516	7.686	10.677	14.785	20.414	28.102	52.800	133.176
40	1.221	1.489	1.814	2.208	3.262	4.801	7.040	10.286	14.974	21.725	31.409	45.259	93.051	267.864
50	1.283	1.645	2.105	2.692	4.384	7.107	11.467	18.420	29.457	46.902	74.358	117.391	289.002	1,083.657

Note: N = number of compounding periods, i = percent interest rate per compounding period.

Table 8-A-3 The Present Value on an Annuity of $1 per Period

$$P_{N,i} = \frac{1 - [1/(1+i)^N]}{i}$$

N	0.5	1	1.5	2	3	4	5	6	7	8	9	10	12	15
1	.995	.990	.985	.980	.971	.962	.952	.943	.935	.926	.917	.909	.893	.870
2	1.985	1.970	1.956	1.942	1.913	1.886	1.859	1.833	1.808	1.783	1.759	1.736	1.690	1.626
3	2.970	2.941	2.912	2.884	2.829	2.775	2.723	2.673	2.624	2.577	2.531	2.487	2.402	2.283
4	3.950	3.902	3.854	3.808	3.717	3.630	3.546	3.465	3.387	3.312	3.240	3.170	3.037	2.855
5	4.926	4.853	4.783	4.713	4.580	4.452	4.329	4.212	4.100	3.993	3.890	3.791	3.605	3.352
6	5.896	5.795	5.697	5.601	5.417	5.242	5.076	4.917	4.767	4.623	4.486	4.355	4.111	3.784
7	6.862	6.728	6.598	6.472	6.230	6.002	5.786	5.582	5.389	5.206	5.033	4.868	4.564	4.160
8	7.823	7.652	7.486	7.325	7.020	6.733	6.463	6.210	5.971	5.747	5.535	5.335	4.968	4.487
9	8.779	8.566	8.361	8.162	7.786	7.435	7.108	6.802	6.515	6.247	5.995	5.759	5.328	4.772
10	9.730	9.471	9.222	8.983	8.530	8.111	7.722	7.360	7.024	6.710	6.418	6.145	5.650	5.019
11	10.677	10.368	10.071	9.787	9.253	8.760	8.306	7.887	7.499	7.139	6.805	6.495	5.938	5.234
12	11.619	11.255	10.908	10.575	9.954	9.385	8.863	8.384	7.943	7.536	7.161	6.814	6.194	5.421
13	12.556	12.134	11.732	11.348	10.635	9.986	9.394	8.853	8.358	7.904	7.487	7.103	6.424	5.583
14	13.489	13.004	12.543	12.106	11.296	10.563	9.899	9.295	8.745	8.244	7.786	7.367	6.628	5.724
15	14.417	13.865	13.343	12.849	11.938	11.118	10.380	9.712	9.108	8.559	8.061	7.606	6.811	5.847
16	15.340	14.718	14.131	13.578	12.561	11.652	10.838	10.106	9.447	8.851	8.313	7.824	6.974	5.954
17	16.259	15.562	14.908	14.292	13.166	12.166	11.274	10.477	9.763	9.122	8.544	8.022	7.120	6.047
18	17.173	16.398	15.673	14.992	13.754	12.659	11.690	10.828	10.059	9.372	8.756	8.201	7.250	6.128
19	18.082	17.226	16.426	15.678	14.324	13.134	12.085	11.158	10.336	9.604	8.950	8.365	7.366	6.198
20	18.987	18.046	17.169	16.351	14.877	13.590	12.462	11.470	10.594	9.818	9.129	8.514	7.469	6.259
25	23.446	22.023	20.720	19.523	17.413	15.622	14.094	12.783	11.654	10.675	9.823	9.077	7.843	6.464
30	27.794	25.808	24.016	22.396	19.600	17.292	15.372	13.765	12.409	11.258	10.274	9.427	8.055	6.566
35	32.035	29.409	27.076	24.999	21.487	18.665	16.374	14.498	12.948	11.655	10.567	9.644	8.176	6.617
40	36.172	32.835	29.916	27.355	23.115	19.793	17.159	15.046	13.332	11.925	10.757	9.779	8.244	6.642
50	44.143	39.196	35.000	31.424	25.730	21.482	18.256	15.762	13.801	12.233	10.962	9.915	8.304	6.661

i

Note: N = number of discounting periods, *i* = percent interest rate per discounting period.

Table 8-A-4 The Compounded Amount of an Annuity of $1 per Period

$$A_{N,i} = \frac{[(1+i)^N - 1]}{i}$$

i

N	0.5	1	1.5	2	3	4	5	6	7	8	9	10	12	15
1	1.000	1.000	1.000	1.000	1.000	1.000	1.000	1.000	1.000	1.000	1.000	1.000	1.000	1.000
2	2.005	2.010	2.015	2.020	2.030	2.040	2.050	2.060	2.070	2.080	2.090	2.100	2.120	2.150
3	3.015	3.030	3.045	3.060	3.091	3.122	3.153	3.184	3.215	3.246	3.278	3.310	3.374	3.473
4	4.030	4.060	4.091	4.122	4.184	4.246	4.310	4.375	4.440	4.506	4.573	4.641	4.779	4.993
5	5.050	5.101	5.152	5.204	5.309	5.416	5.526	5.637	5.751	5.867	5.985	6.105	6.353	6.742
6	6.076	6.152	6.230	6.308	6.468	6.633	6.802	6.975	7.153	7.336	7.523	7.716	8.115	8.754
7	7.106	7.214	7.323	7.434	7.662	7.898	8.142	8.394	8.654	8.923	9.200	9.487	10.089	11.067
8	8.141	8.286	8.433	8.583	8.892	9.214	9.549	9.897	10.260	10.637	11.028	11.436	12.300	13.727
9	9.182	9.369	9.559	9.755	10.159	10.583	11.027	11.491	11.978	12.488	13.021	13.579	14.776	16.786
10	10.228	10.462	10.703	10.950	11.464	12.006	12.578	13.181	13.816	14.487	15.193	15.937	17.549	20.304
11	11.279	11.567	11.863	12.169	12.808	13.486	14.207	14.972	15.784	16.645	17.560	18.531	20.655	24.349
12	12.336	12.683	13.041	13.412	14.192	15.026	15.917	16.870	17.888	18.977	20.141	21.384	24.133	29.002
13	13.397	13.809	14.237	14.680	15.618	16.627	17.713	18.882	20.141	21.495	22.953	24.523	28.029	34.352
14	14.464	14.947	15.450	15.974	17.086	18.292	19.599	21.015	22.550	24.215	26.019	27.975	32.393	40.505
15	15.537	16.097	16.682	17.293	18.599	20.024	21.579	23.276	25.129	27.152	29.361	31.772	37.280	47.580
16	16.614	17.258	17.932	18.639	20.157	21.825	23.657	25.673	27.888	30.324	33.003	35.950	42.753	55.717
17	17.697	18.430	19.201	20.012	21.762	23.698	25.840	28.213	30.840	33.750	36.974	40.545	48.884	65.075
18	18.786	19.615	20.489	21.412	23.414	25.645	28.132	30.906	33.999	37.450	41.301	45.599	55.750	75.836
19	19.880	20.811	21.797	22.841	25.117	27.671	30.539	33.760	37.379	41.446	46.018	51.159	63.440	88.212
20	20.979	22.019	23.124	24.297	26.870	29.778	33.066	36.786	40.995	45.762	51.160	57.275	72.052	102.444
25	26.559	28.243	30.063	32.030	36.459	41.646	47.727	54.865	63.249	73.106	84.701	98.347	133.334	212.793
30	32.280	34.785	37.539	40.568	47.575	56.085	66.439	79.058	94.461	113.283	136.308	164.494	241.333	434.745
35	38.145	41.660	45.592	49.994	60.462	73.652	90.320	111.435	138.237	172.317	215.711	271.024	431.663	881.170
40	44.159	48.886	54.268	60.402	75.401	95.026	120.800	154.762	199.635	259.057	337.882	442.593	767.091	1,779.090
50	56.645	64.463	73.683	84.579	112.797	152.667	209.348	290.336	406.529	573.770	815.084	1,163.909	2,400.018	7,217.716

Note: N = number of compounding periods, *i* = percent interest rate per compounding period.

Application 8-1

Zero Base Budgeting

Grace Phelan, RN, MSN, MPA, is currently
Supervisor of the Education Center, New York University
Medical Center, Cooperative Care, New York, New York.

Zero base budgeting (ZBB) is a concept that challenges the traditional incremental budgeting approach and changes the way managers view the budgeting process. It assumes that no products or programs are sacrosanct and forces managers to evaluate what they are doing.

This article will explore what zero base budgeting is, how it differs from traditional techniques, and its advantages and disadvantages. It will also describe the essential components of the ZBB process—the development of decision packages and the ranking process. Prerequisites to implementing a ZBB approach in an institution will also be identified. Finally, an example of decision packages will be offered.

The incremental budgeting approach that is widely used in organizations bases its current budget on last year's budget. Added to last year's budget are the expected increases for wages and materials as well as increases for programs and products that will be added or expanded. Only in rare cases will managers propose voluntary reductions in the budget. Opponents of the incremental approach stress that this technique is based on several assumptions that may not necessarily be valid. Cheek

states that these assumptions include that all activities making up the previous budget

1. were essential to achieving the organization's objectives, strategies and mission,
2. must be continued during the current year and are more urgent than newly requested programs,
3. are now being performed in the best, most cost effective manner and
4. will continue to be cost effective and necessary in the coming year thus requiring budget increases only for labor and materials inflation[1]

All of these possibly erroneous assumptions have the potential for inflating a budget.

In addition, these techniques may foster infighting, since there are limited funds available for distribution. Obsolete or ineffective programs or projects may be funded at the expense of newer ones that might contribute more to the organization's goals. There is more emphasis on the "bottom line" than on the efficient use of the organization's scarce resources. Additionally, top management is often forced to make a decision regarding funding without the information needed to make an informed, intelligent one. Instead of cutting marginal programs, there may be an arbitrary percentage cutback across departments when there are deficits.

Source: Reprinted from Grace Phelan, "Zero Base Budgeting," *Hospital Cost Management and Accounting,* Vol. 1, No. 9, December 1989, pp. 1–6. Copyright 1989, Aspen Publishers, Inc.

The traditional incremental approach also tends to minimize the step of planning as an integral part of the budgetary process by not relating expenses to the organization's goals and objectives. For these reasons, some managers are looking for better approaches to the budgeting process.

ZBB addresses many of the shortcomings inherent in the traditional approach. A concise definition is given by Phyrr:

> an operating planning and budgetary process which requires each manager to justify his entire budget request in detail from scratch (hence zero base) and shifts the burden of proof to each manager to justify why he should spend any money at all. This approach requires that the alternatives be identified in "decision packages" which will be evaluated by systematic analysis and ranked in order of importance.[2]

The key concepts in this definition include shifting the responsibility for budgeting from higher level managers and administrators to the managers who will be responsible for adhering to it. In addition, managers will be forced to make decisions regarding their priorities. Finally, the development of decision packages with alternatives and the ranking process allow top management to have the information they need to make better decisions when approving the budget.

DECISION PACKAGES

The development of decision packages is a cornerstone of the ZBB system. A simple definition of a decision package is "an incremental budget request which identifies and describes a level of funding for a specific activity."[3] Top management needs to determine who will develop the decision packages that will be ranked for allocation of funding. The best way to logically identify this is to review the organizational chart. A good rule of thumb is to identify at what level the information needed to make an informed decision can be obtained. In addition, managers who are responsible for adhering to the new budget should be the ones who develop it. These managers could be heads of departments or revenue or cost centers. Larger departments or centers can be divided into smaller, more manageable units. Identifying this level needs to be individualized for the organization and flexibility may be needed initially.

Once the level at which the decision packages will be developed is selected, individual managers will need to identify the specific focus of the decision packages for their departments. Prior to the development of the packages, guidelines from top management regarding industry trends and the economic forecast, as well as the expected increases for wages and materials, need to be given. This will permit managers to maintain consistency in budget preparation.

The focus of decision packages can take several different forms, such as

- people
- projects/products
- cost/revenue centers
- capital expenditures
- line items (such as advertising, travel)

In addition, effort should be concentrated on areas over which the manager has some control. To develop a decision package in which the organization has a legal mandate or contract and which does not allow for any change is futile.

To initiate the process, it is a good idea for the manager to identify what his department's current activities are. To this, he should add new services and/or products that are projected for the budgetary cycle.

After identifying what the topics are, the manager then needs to brainstorm alternate ways of performing them. There are several ways to look at alternatives. The most common are

1. identify different ways to do the activity and
2. identify different levels of function and their impact on quality

Phyrr and Cheek, two authors who have written texts on ZBB, suggest that one should first determine alternative ways to perform the activity and select the best option. The rationale for this is that generally these options are mutually exclusive (e.g., you could hire someone to do the job or you could contract out or automate or select another option). In most cases, you will need to select one option. Managers preparing decision packages need to identify alternative ways to perform the activity so that top management can analyze and rank which method is the most appropriate, considering the organization's goals, objectives, and fiscal condition. After the best way to perform an activity is selected, one can move on to identifying different levels of activities.

In addition, managers also need to identify the impact that these different levels of effort/output have. If 1 FTE [full-time equivalent] does 5, does it necessarily mean that 2 FTEs produce twice as much? Identifying varying levels of effort and their related output will provide those responsible for ranking with the information needed to make intelligent and informed decisions. Dillon offers the following example as a suggestion. There may be three levels you can look at:

1. minimal level, which indicates the necessary resources that allow the department to function at the minimal level
2. incremental level, which illustrates the incremental and total cost of providing the service at the current level
3. improvement level, which shows any cost for improving the present functioning level[4]

Consider the following alternatives for providing pre-operative education for patients participating in a pre-admission surgical testing (PST) program:

- pre-operative education at the time of PST either individually or in groups (This could be provided for all patients or selected groups. This education could be provided by either the nursing staff in the PST unit or nurses specially trained in patient education.)

- pre-operative education done on admission or the evening prior to surgery (This could either be done individually or in groups. This education could be provided by the primary nurse or by specially trained nurse educators.)
- no pre-operative education

All of the options (except the last) may be viable. They are each associated with different costs and benefits. Delineation of this information is needed for the organization to determine the best option for them.

This step encourages managers to use their creativity and ingenuity. Ideas may be generated that never would have surfaced. In addition, the person who has both the knowledge and the responsibility for the smooth and efficient operation of the department is the one who is identifying the various decision packages.

The decision packages that are developed should have a consistent format. The format varies with the organization, but in general the information includes the following:

- topic or title
- purpose
- cost
- benefits
- alternatives
- consequences of not performing

Caution should be exercised so that the amount of information contained in the decision package is not overwhelming. This aspect is especially important for the ranking process.

RANKING

After the decision packages are developed, the next step is ranking them. Ranking is the process that allows the organization to decide where to allocate its resources. According to Dillon, there are two criteria that are used in the ranking process to determine the importance of a project. These are the contributions that the decision package makes to the objectives of the department and the amount of funding that is necessary for the decision package.[5]

The initial ranking should be done by the manager who develops them. He has information and expertise that are important in prioritizing. In addition, since ZBB relies heavily on the participation of lower level management in the development of packages, not to involve them in the ranking process would be demoralizing, in addition to wasting their expertise.

After being ranked by the developer, packages from several decision units should be collated and ranked by higher levels of managers. At each level, decision packages from units are weighed and ranked. This continues until there is a single ranking for the organization. Ranking is done by "listing all the packages in order of decreasing benefit to the company."[6]

Organizations need to have a good grasp of how ranking will be done. A good starting point, once again, is to look at the organizational chart.

At higher levels there may be problems with the volume of packages. The number of packages in large organizations may be overwhelming. Proponents of the process suggest that there are two ways to handle this potential problem. They are to limit the number of packages that are ranked by

1. establishing cutoff expenditures levels and
2. limiting the number of levels of consideration[7]

In establishing a cutoff point, one would more closely examine packages below a particular cutoff level. The underlying rationale is that highly ranked packages are critical to the organization's survival. Although these packages may not be as carefully scrutinized, these packages still need to be presented to those responsible for ranking. This permits them to see the entire picture and also allows them to reinforce that this is where the resources should be allocated.

The cutoff level, which could be stated either in dollar or percentage terms, would be higher at higher levels of the ranking process. For ex-

ample, at the initial level it might be 60% of the total budget while at the highest level it might be 75%. This minimizes the number of packages that will be carefully examined. Those above (priority packages) will receive only a cursory review while those below will be carefully scrutinized. One problem that has been identified with using this technique is that some managers will try to manipulate the system by placing programs that are important to the organization or those that are legally mandated below the cutoff level while placing discretionary packages above. The rationale is that important or mandated packages will be analyzed and approved regardless of their placement and that packages above the cutoff will generally face less demanding scrutiny. Using this approach may facilitate the approval of marginal programs.

Higher level managers need to be cognizant of this potential problem. In addition, it also emphasizes the importance of even a cursory review by higher managers of all decision packages.

The second suggestion to deal with the number of packages is to limit the number of rankings. According to Dillon, reducing the number of ranking levels from 5 to 3 should result in significant savings of time since ranking and reranking take significant time and effort.[8] He cautions, however, that the savings in time can be offset by decreased information for and input by top management.

Key questions that need to be answered include

• who should rank?
• should it be an individual or group process?
• what type of technique should be used (e.g., single or multiple criteria)?

Decisions on these questions will need to be made by top management. Emphasis should be on the development of a system in which the ranking process will result in a single ranking, which will best reflect programs that have been prioritized for achieving the organization's goals. Funding for particular programs is done on the basis of the ranking process.

PREREQUISITES

Prior to the implementation of ZBB in an organization, there are several prerequisites that need to be met. First, top managers need to be committed to the concept and must believe that this is the best way to prepare budgets. Administrators who provide "lip service" only will doom the system to failure. There will need to be a concerted effort to involve managers at varying levels and initially funds will need to be allocated for training. Unless top managers are committed, ZBB should not be adopted.

Another important prerequisite is that the organization should have clearly defined goals and objectives. If decision packages are to be developed and ranked they need to have a standard against which they will be measured. The contribution of the decision package to the department's and organization's goals is an essential component of the ranking process.

Finally, the organization must be willing to allocate resources of time, money, and patience during the program implementation phase. Managers need to be involved in education programs explaining the process. Knowledgeable consultants or staff need to be available to assist with the inevitable questions that will arise. In addition, managers need to be able to discuss their questions, problems, and concerns. It is human nature to protect what is ours. ZBB may arouse these protective instincts and these feelings need to be recognized and addressed.

ADVANTAGES

The primary advantage of ZBB is that this process enables the organization to allocate its scarce resources to programs that will best enable it to meet its goals. The establishment of these goals and objectives forces the organization to focus its efforts. Reduction in budget will not be arbitrary but based on priorities. Inefficiency can be identified and eliminated.

Another advantage is the involvement of lower level managers. These managers who are accountable for adhering to the "bottom line" have a voice in the budgeting process. They are encouraged and even forced to use their creativity. They are required to analyze the functioning of their departments. They are given the opportunity to defend expenditures for their department and to explain what they would be able to do with either more or less money.

Finally, the development of decision packages gives top management information for the "total picture" and, hopefully, improves the quality of decisions regarding resource allocation. According to Finkler, the development of alternatives may be the greatest advantage to ZBB. He states that

> in forcing managers to say not what they could do without—the answer to which is nothing—but rather what they would do without if their budget is cut, we are in a superior position to evaluate the impact of budget cuts on various departments. By forcing those advocating new projects to consider various decision packages, we no longer wind up with an all-or-nothing approach to new services and programs. Instead, we are able to evaluate alternative volume levels, alternative quality levels, alternative luxury levels (e.g., new buildings in marble or concrete), and alternative approaches (e.g., fixed installation vs. mobile installation of new technologies).[9]

One final advantage is that since programs are already prioritized, if funding levels change, it is easy to identify which programs to add or delete.

DISADVANTAGES

Although ZBB has many advantages, it is not a panacea. Among the most frequently mentioned disadvantages is the amount of time it takes to prepare decision packages and rank them. Initially, managers need to be oriented to the concept. In addition, it does take time to prepare, evaluate, and rank the packages. Proponents of ZBB argue that this is time well spent in planning and problem solving. In addition, they state that although the time spent preparing the initial budgetary cycle under ZBB may seem excessive, it takes less time in subsequent years.

Another disadvantage is that managers can play games with ZBB. Although it is harder to hide slack or inefficiencies, it is not impossible. An example has already been mentioned in the section on ranking. ZBB can be manipulated, although the potential for manipulation may be minimal when compared with other approaches.

Suver and Brown also identify other potential problems, including the review process itself. They state that "few organizations have individuals with sufficient knowledge of all of the areas being reviewed to make the tough minded and intelligent decisions needed."[10]

Another problem that was identified is that some departments were unable to determine the exact costs of some programs because some budget unit costs encompass many functions and it was difficult to determine what portion of the cost should be allocated to what function.[11] In addition, the amount of information that is provided may be overwhelming.

Some experts suggest that ZBB be done on a rotation basis (e.g., every five years). Although this may have some advantages, you lose some of its advantages. Inefficiency and complacency can easily take hold in such a system.

Suver and Brown offer two alternatives that encompass some of the advantages of ZBB but minimize its disadvantages—performance auditing and the sunset concept.

The objective of performance auditing is to "review the effectiveness, efficiency and the economy of an activity."[12] Unlike ZBB, it does not include ranking or need to be done annually. Suver and Brown also state that performance auditing allows for a more in-depth manage-ment review because all of the activities do not have to be reviewed at one time. The sunset concept has as its basis that funding for programs or projects will cease after a certain date unless they can pass careful scrutiny, similar to programs under ZBB. This review process should allow outdated or inefficient programs to be eliminated.

Both these programs may have some merit in minimizing the problems associated with ZBB, while retaining some of its advantages.

[**Editor's Note:** For an additional perspective on zero base budgeting, see *Hospital Cost Accounting Advisor,* Vol. 2, No. 5, October, 1986.]

NOTES

1. L. Cheek. *Zero Base Budgeting Comes of Age.* New York: AMACOM, 1977, p. 3.

2. P. Phyrr. "Zero Base Budgeting" (unpublished speech delivered at International Conference of the Planning Executive Institute) New York, May 15,1972, quoted in L. Cheek, *Zero Base Budgeting Comes of Age.* New York: AMACOM, 1977, p. 12.

3. R. Dillon. "Zero Base Budgeting: An Introduction." *Hospital Financial Management,* 7 (November, 1977) p. 10.

4. Ibid., p. 11.

5. Ibid., p. 11.

6. P. Phyrr. "Zero Base Budgeting," *Harvard Business Review,* 48 (November/December, 1970) p. 16.

7. Dillon, p. 11.

8. R. Dillon. *Zero Base Budgeting for Health Care Institutions.* Rockville, MD: Aspen Publishers, Inc., 1979, p. 94.

9. S. Finkler. "Zero Base Budgeting." *Hospital Cost Accounting Advisor,* 2 (October, 1986) p. 6.

10. J. Suver and R. Brown. "Where Does Zero Base Budgeting Work?" *Harvard Business Review,* 55 (November/December, 1977) p. 82.

11. Y. Bhada and G. Minmier. "State of Georgia: Zero Base Budgeting." Bedford, England: Case Clearing House of Great Britain, p. 6.

12. Suver and Brown, p. 82.

Application 8-2

Developing and Using a Budget Manual

Steven A. Finkler, PhD, CPA

Today's hospitals have complex budgeting procedures that are generally performed by managers throughout the organization, who complete a series of forms. Budgeting is a fairly recent addition to the hospital management process. Prior to the introduction of Medicare, just a quarter-century ago, most hospitals did not have formal budgeting procedures. Over the last twenty-five years the hospital budgeting process has been constantly changing and developing.

Today, the budgeting performed in most hospitals is stable enough to allow them to develop manuals to guide the process. The complexity of the budget process necessitates the use of manuals—yet many hospitals have not yet documented their budget process in manual form. The reason for this lapse may be that the managers who could prepare the manual aren't aware of the need for it.

However, the budget process in most hospitals has become increasingly decentralized. The basic elements of the budget are prepared by individuals who are not necessarily comfortable working with financial information and who could benefit greatly from a manual. This is especially true with new managers of clinical de-

partments, who often have no background in the budget process.

WHAT IS A BUDGET MANUAL?

Willson defines a budget manual as "an orderly presentation of directives, instructions, or facts concerning a given activity or repeated procedure."[1] Most hospitals have, at least, a set of written directions for filling out various forms. Without a formal manual, however, a manager may not be able to acquire an adequate understanding of the budget process.

A budget manual should provide a comprehensive portrait of the budget process. It should not be limited only to the information a manager needs to complete a specific form. Managers' dissatisfaction with budgeting may be attributed largely to their lack of information about the entire process. Factors that seem unfair when taken out of context may seem reasonable when viewed as part of a larger picture.

Therefore, the most important element of a budget manual is not the specific instructions it contains but the overview it provides to every manager about the organization's whole budget process.

Budgeting has acquired a mysterious aura in many hospitals—a mystique that tends to be destructive. Instead of focusing on a common ef-

Source: Reprinted from Steven A. Finkler, "Developing and Using a Budget Manual," *Hospital Cost Management and Accounting,* Vol. 4, No. 7, October 1992, pp. 1–4. Copyright 1992, Aspen Publishers, Inc.

fort to best serve the hospital's patients, managers vie for maximum resources. The best way to create a cooperative effort is to share information openly.

Managers at all levels of the organization should understand that the hospital has a long-range plan and that it has established priorities to help it move in that direction. They should also understand that the hospital reviews its environment to ensure that the approved budget reacts adequately to the threats and opportunities the organization faces.

A budget manual can convey the complexity of the budget process while also simplifying it. Managers who find themselves buried in forms that must be completed for their unit's or department's operating budgets may feel that the process is unduly complicated. If they are given a wider perspective on the process, however, they are more likely to understand how their particular pieces fit into the larger picture. The interrelationships between the operating, capital, and cash budgets can be explained to help line managers understand the rationale for what they are doing and why a process of negotiation is often necessary.

Willson asserts that preparing a specific manual of budget procedures offers the following advantages:

- it clearly defines authority and responsibility in budget matters
- it promotes standardization and simplification because, presumably, the best procedures for developing the budget or plan are stipulated and a uniform or standard format for presenting the plan is identified
- it encourages coordinated effort by identifying what procedures should be followed and by whom
- it provides a convenient reference guide when questions of procedures, format, or responsibility arise
- it permits better supervision, because supervisors do not have to spend time explaining procedures that are covered in the manual

- it assists in the training of new employees and in transfer of duties because many phases of the job have been described in writing
- it assists in "selling" the budget by explaining the advantages of the procedure[2]

As noted above, however, an additional important advantage of a budget manual is that it communicates the entire budget process, providing each manager with an understanding of the overall budget framework.

WHAT GOES INTO A BUDGET MANUAL?

In describing the budget process, budget manuals should start with a clear statement of the objectives of the hospital's budget process. Although budgets are required by federal regulation in order for the hospital to be eligible for Medicare payments, the other expected benefits of the budget process should be noted as well. These might include such issues as Board mandates for balanced budgets, requirements imposed by bond covenants, or the need to reach certain profit levels to provide for future expansion.

Next, the lines of responsibility for the budget should be clearly stated. The Board's role in approving the budget should be explained, as well as the roles of the CEO, CFO, and other hospital managers. The authority of various managers and their responsibility for budget preparation should be explained, including specification for which managers are responsible for preparing what parts of the budget and who has the final authority over the amounts that will appear in the approved budget.

The manual should include descriptions of specific procedures to be performed by all managers with budget responsibility throughout the organization. All necessary budgeting forms should be contained in the manual, along with instructions for completing them so that managers do not have to figure out how to fill them out or try to learn it from the previous occupant of a position. Furthermore, procedures in such areas as budget review and revision should be explicitly described.

The manual should include a time schedule for budget preparation that establishes when various tasks must be undertaken and completed. It will be especially useful for managers to observe the overall schedule rather than to know only their own deadlines. They are more likely to recognize that their deadlines are reasonable if they are aware of the critical timing involved in bringing the various pieces of the budget together.

A discussion of departmental interrelationships is a critical aspect of the budget manual. Budgets should not be considered secret documents. Sharing information between cost centers will result in a more accurate budget than if each manager keeps within his or her own domain. For example, if the operating room is considering a new procedure that will shorten the length of stay of a specific type of patient, the med/surg units should be informed so that they can reduce their expected number of patient days.

Hospital budgeting is a dynamic process; over the last several decades it has been subject to continuous modification and improvement. Therefore the budget manual should be prepared in a looseleaf format, which allows specific revisions to be made without redoing the entire manual. Further, managers will pay closer attention to new procedures as they review each change before entering it into their budget manuals.

WHO DOES WHAT?

One of the major potential benefits of the budget manual is its capacity to convey to each manager what his or her specific budgeting responsibilities are. For each element of the budget, there should be a section specifying who is responsible for what activities, how they are to be carried out, and when they must be done.

Conveying this information can, of course, be somewhat complex. One approach is to simply specify who does what as the manual progresses

and various procedures are described. While this does provide the necessary information, it means that managers must frequently review the entire manual to locate their required activities. A more workable approach is to create a set of *responsibility charts*. Each chart shows all of the budget responsibilities for one specific job title. An alternative is a chart for each type of budget that lists the functions allotted to each job title.

DEVELOPING A BUDGET MANUAL

The development of the budget manual is a major undertaking, and hospital financial managers should not attempt to carry the full burden. It will be easier to develop the manual—and the results will be enhanced—if the tasks are divided among a larger number of people.

While financial managers may need to coordinate the process, widespread participation makes sense. Managers are more likely to want to use the manual, and more likely to accept its usefulness, if they have contributed to its development.

The hospital's budget committee should assume the role of making budget goals and objectives explicit. The financial managers should develop explanations of the various elements of the hospital's master budget and how they interrelate. Each cost center, however, should have the primary responsibility for drafting the parts of the manual concerned with budget preparation in its own area.

As the parts of the manual are prepared, drafts should be widely circulated to generate as much feedback as possible. During this process, suggestions will probably be made that will impact not only the manual but the budget process itself. The preparation of a budget manual invariably results in managers' taking an in-depth look at how the budget is currently prepared in each cost center. Things that have previously been accepted as fact are likely to be questioned, resulting in improvements to the budget process.

Further, managers will gain insights about the entire budget process as the manual takes shape.

They will learn how their pieces fit, which will also lead to suggestions that could improve the process. Thus manual development is not simply a codification of existing budget policies and procedures but also provides for refinement of the process.

Once drafts have been reviewed and revisions to the budget process made, the final manual must be reviewed and approved by the top management team. Then a list of the individuals (and their positions) who should receive a manual can be made and copies produced and distributed.

UPDATING THE MANUAL

Revision of the budget process should not be limited to the period when the manual is being prepared. As the hospital changes over time, or as regulations and reimbursement policies change, it will be necessary to revise budget procedures. The manual should occasionally be reviewed to ensure that it is up to date. We have already noted that a looseleaf format allows for easy insertion of changes. One department should be responsible for making sure the manual is properly maintained.

Willson suggests that

- all revisions should be handled on a systematic, scheduled basis
- any changes should be coordinated with all affected units
- typically, users will forward suggestions for change; *all* the procedures should be periodically reviewed for currency and applicability
- preferably, the revision should indicate the date it was made and the issue it supersedes
- it may be helpful to indicate (by, for instance, an asterisk) a segment that has been modified
- the procedure-issuing organization should maintain in its files the background of the change (i.e., the reasons, who suggested it)
- most important, manual changes do cost money, so the necessity of each change should be considered carefully.[3]

NOTES

1. J.D. Willson, *Budgeting and Profit Planning Manual,* Second Edition. Boston: Warren, Gorham & Lamont, 1989, p. 46–1.
2. Ibid, p. 46–2.
3. Ibid., p. 46–11.

Application 8-3

Performance Budgeting

Steven A. Finkler, PhD, CPA

Hospital managers have become more and more familiar with budgeting ever since Medicare was introduced in 1965 and required an annual budget as part of the reimbursement eligibility requirements. However, the process has been one of gradual evolution. Over the years budgeting has become increasingly decentralized, with cost centers throughout the hospital taking on an increasing role in the development of their own budget.

The introduction of performance based budgeting is the next step in the evolution of budgeting as a valuable managerial accounting tool in hospitals. Performance based budgeting evaluates the activities of a cost center in terms of what the center accomplishes, and the costs of that accomplishment. It is an approach to budgeting designed specifically to evaluate the level of performance of managers and cost centers in situations where traditional budgeting has been found to be inadequate.

BACKGROUND

In any situation in which there is not a perfectly engineered relationship between inputs

Source: Reprinted from Steven A. Finkler, "Performance Budgeting," *Hospital Cost Management and Accounting,* Vol. 2, No. 2, May 1990, pp. 1–8. Copyright 1990, Aspen Publishers, Inc.

and outputs, performance budgeting may be found to be useful. Rather than just evaluating how much output is produced along one dimension, such as patient days, performance budgeting allows the organization to define the various elements of performance that are important, and to assess managers and departments by their accomplishments in terms of the types of performance important for those departments. Each department can have its own set of performance criteria.

A classic example of why performance budgeting was developed is the case of a city parks department. How can one evaluate whether the parks department has an appropriate budget? Lawns must be maintained, bushes trimmed, and litter cleaned. Yet there is no clear output measure for the parks department.

Certainly, one could argue that the New York City Parks Department maintains 20 parks, just as we could define the number of patients or patient days for a hospital. However, if the parks department starts to perform their work in a shoddy manner, but still (after a fashion) maintains 20 parks, it is difficult to evaluate their budget performance. Their budget was for the maintenance of 20 parks and 20 parks were maintained.

Budget systems need to evaluate the level of quality of output as well as simple measures of whether something was done or not. In the current hospital environment in which we hear more and more about the quality/cost trade-off, we need tools to better examine that trade-off.

Hospitals have many situations similar to the parks department. For example, what do the administrative departments produce? How about planning, legal, finance, quality assurance, and so on? In many cases these departments have costs that do not vary with patients or patient days. These are discretionary (as opposed to engineered) cost centers. There is no clear relationship between inputs and outputs, and such centers always pose a problem for budgeting.

The radiology department has a clearly specified output. They produce x-rays of various types. If costs rise we can readily assess whether volume has risen. But if legal costs rise for the hospital it is much harder to relate this directly to current patient volume.

However, the performance budgeting issue is broader than just looking at discretionary cost centers. Radiology departments may reduce their costs per x-ray, but is such reduction accomplished through greater efficiency, or through reduced patient care? Perhaps the quality of each x-ray will decline, resulting in a need for more x-rays. For a patient reimbursed under a DRG system we will earn no additional revenue for an extra x-ray. But the radiology department will look good if it is evaluated based on the cost per x-ray.

Similarly, the nursing department may reduce their cost per patient day. Is that efficiency or reduced direct patient care, and therefore reduced quality of care? Performance budgeting is a technique that will help us to make that evaluation.

THE PERFORMANCE BUDGETING APPROACH

The main concept in performance budgeting is to define the output of each department in some specific way so that it can be more easily evaluated.

The simplest form of performance budgeting is flexible budgeting, which has become very popular in recent years. In flexible budgeting, a cost center is evaluated based on the volume of output and the appropriate cost to produce that output. The key to flexible budgeting is recognition that some costs are fixed and some are variable. As volume of work increases, the fixed costs need not rise, but allowance must be made for the variable costs associated with increases in production.

Thus performance measurement would consist of assessing whether fixed costs remained fixed, and whether the variable cost per patient was in line with expectations. Such flexible budgeting is only the simplest form of performance budgeting, because it relies so heavily on the common measure of output—typically the patient or the patient day.

Contrast this with the productive process of departments such as planning or legal services. Trying to evaluate these departments based on some measure of variable cost per patient is unrealistic. This makes budgeting and evaluation quite difficult.

The chief problem with respect to budgeting for the nonpatient care departments is that in many cases we have difficulty defining what they do. If you don't define what they do, you can't measure how much of it they do. As a result, we have trouble understanding the fixed/variable cost relationship. Furthermore, fixed costs tend to play a much more significant role in many of these departments. Finally, the departments themselves tend to have greater control over their volume of work produced. Thus the key is to develop some measures on which to evaluate the performance of each department.

Performance does not have to be measured by just one indicator. Nor is the question of defining performance limited to the nonpatient care departments. For instance, the radiology department may be evaluated not only on the cost per x-ray, but also on the number of x-rays that had to be retaken because the first image was inadequate.

In the case of a parks department, how might one establish the performance of the department, other than simply the number of parks maintained? We could measure the number of acres of lawn mowed, and the number of times during the summer that the parks department mowed the lawn. We could measure the number of square feet of paths resurfaced during the year. We could measure the number of pieces of equipment maintained (such as lawn mowers), and the average number of pieces unavailable due to mechanical problems. We could measure the number of baseball fields maintained. We could measure the number of complaints about how the parks are maintained.

There is no question that it will take some thought to come up with a good set of performance measures for each hospital department, especially the nondirect patient care departments. For example, are complaints an appropriate measure for a given department? If the patients complain about the food, is it because the quality or taste is bad, or simply that the patient is on a salt free diet and doesn't like it? However, for a department such as dietary, increases in the number of complaints may well be a significant performance measurement statistic.

Assuming that the number of complaints is decided to be a relevant factor in assessing the performance of a department, are we interested in complaints from physicians (there are too many times they have to wait for a second x-ray because the first was not done properly)? Or are we interested in complaints from patients (this place is incompetent, they can't get an x-ray done properly, and I'm going to tell all my friends)?

THE PERFORMANCE BUDGETING TECHNIQUE

Suppose the operating budget for the Office of the Chief Executive Officer (CEO) of HCMA Hospital were $500,000 for the coming year, as follows:

CEO Salary	$150,000
Other Staff Salaries	250,000
Travel	30,000
Supplies	20,000
Overhead	50,000
Total	$500,000

Certainly, trying to assess the performance of the CEO and his immediate staff is a particular challenge for a hospital. In most hospitals there would be great difficulty in attempting to evaluate the various aspects of the CEO's performance. What elements of a hospital's performance are within the control of the CEO and what elements are not?

Certainly, this is not meant to say that the CEO is not evaluated by the board. But that evaluation is generally in terms of the overall performance of the hospital. That may not be a particularly valuable approach.

The hospital may, due to demographics and the regulatory environment, be doomed to a less than wonderful existence. The best manager in the world, doing the best job in the world, may not be able to have more than a marginal positive impact on this. In other cases, hospitals have positive demographics and may do well despite an average or below average management team.

Fantastic managers can improve results somewhat, and poor managers can create poor results. However, more often than not there are existing environmental circumstances that have a tremendous impact on how a hospital fares, at least in the short run. How then can we evaluate a CEO's performance? Performance budgeters would argue that we should first categorize the various major elements of the CEO's job. For example some of his effort should go to external fund-raising. Some effort should go to general public relations and image building. Some effort should go to controlling hospital expenditures. Some effort should go to increasing the patient volume. Some effort should go to expanding the services offered by the hospital. Some effort should go to general supervision of the other hospital managers. Some effort should go to long range planning. Obviously, there are other factors that might be considered as well.

None of these elements are what would be considered engineered costs. Simply adding 10% to the budget of the Office of the CEO will not automatically result in a 10% increase in any or all of the factors we have listed as being important parts of the CEO's job. Performance budgeting therefore requires that a judgment be made concerning how much effort the CEO should devote to each of these areas.

One possible allocation of the CEO's time might be as follows:

Fund-raising	20%
General public relations and image building	10%
Cost control	20%
Increasing the patient volume	20%
Expanding services offered	5%
General supervision of other hospital managers	20%
Long range planning	5%
Total	100%

By planning this as a budget at the start of the year, it provides a plan of how the CEO's time should be spent, and of what areas are deemed to be either the most important, or else the most in need of the CEO's efforts.

However, there is no reason to believe that all resources within a department should necessarily be allocated in the same fashion. In order for administration to achieve its overall goals, it may well be that the CEO will devote relatively more time to fund-raising and less time to general supervision of managers than is the case for the CEO's staff. Thus we might have a time allocation for staff as follows:

Fund-raising	5%
General public relations and image building	5%
Cost control	25%
Increasing the patient volume	25%
Expanding services offered	5%
General supervision of other hospital managers	30%
Long range planning	5%
Total	100%

Similarly, other line items within the administrative budget would have to be allocated to the various activities of the department based on their relative required inputs. For example, travel costs are probably related primarily to fundraising and general public relations, and to a lesser extent to the other areas, as follows:

Fund-raising	50%
General public relations and image building	30%
Cost control	5%
Increasing the patient volume	5%
Expanding services offered	5%
General supervision of other hospital managers	0%
Long range planning	5%
Total	100%

Supplies are probably difficult to track, but there may be some particular area or areas that command a higher resource level. For example, fund-raising and public relations may consume the bulk of the supplies used, as follows:

Fund-raising	30%
General public relations and image building	30%
Cost control	8%
Increasing the patient volume	8%
Expanding services offered	8%
General supervision of other hospital managers	8%
Long range planning	8%
Total	100%

Overhead is probably difficult to assign on any rational basis. Therefore an even allocation across all activities is probably as good as any other.

Fund-raising	14%
General public relations and image building	14%
Cost control	14%
Increasing the patient volume	14%
Expanding services offered	14%
General supervision of other hospital managers	14%
Long range planning	14%
Total	100%

Whether this list is a complete list of the activities of a typical CEO's office, or the allocation for each of the resources is appropriate, is not important to this example, which demonstrates the approach of performance budgeting. These percents are not based on scientific study, and hospitals using performance budgeting would have to make their own decisions concerning appropriate focuses of attention, and appropriate time and resource allocations.

What is important to understand is that we are essentially taking a department with no visible direct output—the Office of the CEO does not treat patients—and we are defining the activities of that department. This in turn will allow us to measure the amount of output of the department, and ultimately the performance of the department.

We can now convert the original operating budget into an activity budget, which is a midway point in the development of a performance budget. This basically requires us to restate the original budget into budgets for each activity. This is accomplished as shown in Tables 8-3-1 and 8-3-2.

Table 8-3-1 presents a summary of the percentage allocation for each cost item to each activity. Thus every line item category within the original operating budget has been assigned to activities based on what we decide is a reasonable expectation. All of these percentage allocations were shown above. For example, travel was primarily allocated to fund-raising and public relations above, and we see that relationship on the travel line and fund-raising and public relations columns in Table 8-3-1.

Table 8-3-2 takes the total cost for each line item and multiplies it by the percentages in Table 8-3-1 to determine the budgeted cost for each activity for each line item. For example, Staff Salary is budgeted at a total of $250,000. Of that amount 5% is allocated to fund-raising. So 5% of $250,000, or $12,500, appears on Ta-

ble 8-3-2 in the Staff Salary row and Fund-Raising column.

We can now assess the total budgeted cost of each of the major activities. It is expected that the office of the CEO will spend $70,643 on fund-raising efforts, and $49,643 on public relations. In contrast, $102,743 will be spent on each of cost control and increasing patient volume activities, and $113,743 will be spent by this office on managerial supervision.

Are these amounts an appropriate allocation of these resources? Compare the bottom line of Table 8-3-2, which gives the total for each activity, with the right hand column of Table 8-3-2, which gives the total by line item from the original operating budget. The original operating budget appears to be primarily a fixed discretionary budget over which the organization has little control. However, the bottom row shows us that we are making implicit choices about the allocation of resources within the department to different tasks. The organization does in fact have substantial ability to modify how these re-

Table 8-3-1 Summary of Percentage Allocation to Activities

Cost Item	Activity							
	Fund-Raising	Public Relations	Cost Control	Patient Volume	Services	Super-vision	Planning	Totals
CEO Salary	20%	10%	20%	20%	5%	20%	5%	100%
Staff Salary	5	5	25	25	5	30	5	100
Travel	50	30	5	5	5	0	5	100
Supplies	30	30	8	8	8	8	8	100
Overhead	14	14	14	14	14	14	14	100

Table 8-3-2 Allocation of Expenditures to Activities

Cost Item	Activity							
	Fund-Raising	Public Relations	Cost Control	Patient Volume	Services	Super-vision	Planning	Totals
CEO Salary	$30,000	$15,000	$ 30,000	$ 30,000	$ 7,500	$ 30,000	$ 7,500	$150,000
Staff Salary	12,500	12,500	62,500	62,500	12,500	75,000	12,500	250,000
Travel	15,000	9,000	1,500	1,500	1,500	0	1,500	30,000
Supplies	6,000	6,000	1,600	1,600	1,600	1,600	1,600	20,000
Overhead	7,143	7,143	7,143	7,143	7,143	7,143	7,142	50,000
	$70,643	$49,643	$102,743	$102,743	$30,243	$113,743	$30,242	$500,000

sources are spent. One could decide relatively greater efforts should be made in one area and less in another.

Note however, that we still have not fully developed a performance budget. The Allocation of Expenditures to Activities (Table 8-3-2) is a very valuable plan, and it helps us to decide if we are planning to proceed in the most appropriate manner. It does little, however, in terms of determining after the fact if resources were allocated according to the plan.

Table 8-3-3 presents the next step, the actual performance budget. In this table the activities have been moved from the top row to the left side of the table. For each activity we must tackle the difficult task of quantifying output. This is particularly difficult for some, but not all, non-direct patient care departments. Certainly, dietary can measure their output in terms of meals and radiology can measure output in terms of x-rays. How can the CEO's office measure its output? The example chosen here is probably one of the most difficult departments for the application of performance budgeting.

At first thought many will argue that the output of the CEO's office can't be quantified. However, that is not a reasonable conclusion. Hospitals, after all, are not really trying to produce patient days or discharged patients. The real product of hospitals is improved health. However we cannot readily measure improved health, so we fall back on proxies such as patient days to measure output. Without some measure of output we can't measure productivity. We can't see if the cost per unit of output is at a reasonable level.

If the hospital as a whole can use patients or patient days as a proxy to measure output, each department can find a range of proxies to measure its output as well. Some of the measures will appear to be crude proxies at best. Certainly, however, patient days is a crude proxy for improved health, and yet it is a very useful one.

What are some potential output measures for the efforts of the CEO's office? In finding such measures, the first step was taken when we assessed the primary activities of the office. By splitting the overall operating budget for the department into fund-raising, public relations, cost

control, increased patient volume, expansion of services, managerial supervision, and long-range planning, we laid the groundwork for the evaluation. Each of these areas likely has some key tasks associated with it that can be measured.

For example, fund-raising requires a great deal of thought, and thought is difficult to measure. However, the thought must be put into practice to achieve anything. What activities will occur? Perhaps the hospital's fund-raising campaign for the coming year consists of a series of 50 personal visits by the CEO to philanthropists. And suppose that while many philanthropists will turn us down, a total of $2,000,000 is expected to be raised.

We can see on Table 8-3-3 that the output measures for fund-raising are the number of visits and the amount of money raised. The budgeted amount is 50 visits and $2,000,000. The total cost for these activities comes from Table 8-3-2. The average cost merely requires division of the budgeted cost by the budgeted output.

Note that there are two performance measures related to fund-raising: the cost per visit and the cost per dollar raised. Both of these measures are likely to be of interest. For a particular philanthropist not known for giving to hospitals, is the visit worthwhile? Or does the cost of the visit exceed that philanthropist's possible contribution? For the program as a whole, is the payback in dollars raised per dollar invested appropriate? Perhaps we would earn more per dollar invested in fund-raising by writing a letter to each of our past patients. Thus we are generating information that provides the potential to improve the planning aspect of budgeting substantially for many departments that have difficulty focusing on the tasks they will be performing, and on the possibility of alternatives that might be better.

For public relations, the most obvious measure is public appearances and speeches. The direct benefit of such appearances is quite hard to measure. However, at least we can use a performance budget to determine the cost of such appearances and then assess whether the cost is reasonable, or whether it makes it too costly a use of the CEO's time.

Table 8-3-3 Performance Budget

Type of Activity	Description of Output Measure	Amount of Output Budgeted	Total Cost of Activity	Average Cost
Fund-Raising	Visits to Philanthropists	No. of visits Funds raised	50 visits $2,000,000	$ 70,643	$1,413/visit $.035 cost/$1
Public Relations	Appearances Speeches	No. of appearances No. of speeches	120 appearances 40 speeches	49,643	$414/appearance $1,241/speech
Cost Control	Meetings Reduce cost Reduce LOS	No. of meetings Reduction in cost/P.D. Decrease in avg. LOS	40 meetings $22/patient day .15 days/patient	102,743	$2,569/meeting $4,670/$ reduction/P.D. $684,953/day reduction in avg. LOS
Increase Patient Volume	Meetings Discharges	No. of meetings Increase in discharges	20 meetings 400 discharges	102,743	$5,137/meeting $257/discharge
Expand Services	Meetings New Services	No. of meetings No. of new services	30 meetings 4 services	30,243	$1,008/meeting $7,561/service
Supervision	Meetings	No. of meetings	100 meetings	113,743	$1,137/meeting
Planning	Meetings	No. of meetings	25 meetings	30,242	$1,210/meeting
Total				$500,000	

The appearances by the CEO are not the only things that impact on the image of the hospital. The performance budget is not a budget of all monies spent on image building, but rather a budget of how this particular department allocates some of its resources in that area. If all departments in the hospital had performance budgets, we could aggregate all efforts on image building. For example, a campaign by the nursing department to have nurses give brochures and talks to patients about all the latest sophisticated facilities in the hospital would be an image building effort.

For most of the remaining items, the CEO and his or her staff will have meetings with various managers to discuss the specific activity. Therefore, the most common measure will be the number of meetings held. To some extent this is valuable. If the CEO doesn't cause the meetings to happen, then the specific actions that must result from the meetings won't happen. Meetings are not sufficient for cost control, but they are probably necessary.

On the other hand, meetings are really a measure of inputs rather than outputs. Wherever possible we should attempt to quantify the outcomes resulting from the meetings. For example, how much did the cost per patient day decline; how much did the average length of stay decline? How much new volume resulted from the meetings? How many new services were added this year? And in each case, what was the cost of the efforts of the CEO's office with respect to those results?

Interpretation of the budgeted average cost per unit requires some care. Why are some meetings more expensive than others? In some cases the meeting might require just the CEO or one staff member. In other cases the meeting will require more individuals from the CEO's office. In some cases the meetings occur on the spur of the moment, while other times the meeting may reflect hours or days of preparation.

On the other hand, looking at the budgeted cost per unit of each activity, it may become apparent that the original budget doesn't make sense. Perhaps the CEO thought that public relations would take only 10% of his time. Looking at the performance budget in Table 8-3-3, however, it becomes apparent that he expects to make 120 appearances and 40 speeches. The problem here is not that the cost per appearance or per speech is too high, but just the reverse. Is it realistic to be able to make so many appearances and speeches, while consuming only 10% of his overall time? Therefore, examination of the unit costs may lead to a reevaluation of the basic percentage allocations to different activities. Either more time will have to be devoted to public relations and less to other areas, or else the CEO will have to plan to make fewer appearances and speeches.

Clearly, there is a wealth of information to be gained from performance budgeting. It is a tool that is likely to improve both the planning and control processes in hospitals substantially.

Application 8-4

Developing a Business Plan

Steven A. Finkler, PhD, CPA

Hospitals are rapidly becoming involved in starting a variety of new ventures. This is really nothing new for hospitals, which have had a history of adding new programs and services. However, the hospital fiscal environment has changed so dramatically that the financial success (or at least financial feasibility) of new projects requires far greater scrutiny than was formerly the case. As a result, the decision to start a new venture requires thorough analysis and a carefully designed plan.

A business plan is necessary to assess the feasibility of a proposal, and to set goals and objectives, forecast revenues and expenses, plan marketing efforts, and actually get the proposal successfully implemented.

For the last few years articles in a variety of magazines and journals, and speakers all over the country, have sent a consistent message to hospital managers: a hospital is a business. That message has had a substantial impact on the way that hospital managers view the organizations that they manage. However, even when we choose to treat a hospital as a business, and to manage it in a businesslike fashion, we generally accept the overall mission and direction of the hospital. As a result, few managers have actually sat down and developed an overall business plan for their organizations.

Few financial managers have experience that can help them develop a business plan for a new project, service, or venture. If we are indeed to manage the hospital as a business, we need to view proposed change in a clear, highly evaluative manner. This article discusses some issues that must be addressed in order to develop a solid business plan for any aspect of a hospital's existing or planned services.

DEFINITION OF A BUSINESS PLAN

In its simplest terms, a business plan is like any comprehensive budget. It has an element of long-range planning. That element defines where the organization is and where it would like to go. The environment must be recognized, with opportunities as well as competition and weaknesses clearly spelled out. Like the program budget element of a long-range plan, the business plan must specify how we are going to get to where we want the organization to be. The goals and objectives, as well as the specific detailed approaches to accomplish them, must be clearly spelled out in quantified terms.

Source: Reprinted from Steven A. Finkler, "Developing a Business Plan," *Hospital Cost Accounting Advisor,* Vol. 3, No. 10, March 1988, pp. 1–6. Copyright 1988, Aspen Publishers, Inc.

THE ELEMENTS OF THE BUSINESS PLAN

The Program in Health Policy and Management at New York University has recently developed a series of executive education programs for hospital managers on the topic of development of business plans. According to their approach to this topic, the key elements of a business plan are the analysis of feasibility, marketing concerns, financial analysis, implementation, and follow-up.

FEASIBILITY

Determining the feasibility of a business plan, in the most general terms, is one of the first key elements in establishing the plan. Obviously, the ultimate feasibility of the plan cannot be determined until all of the pieces of the business plan are in place. However, it is not worth the effort of detailed financial and marketing planning if the underlying concept for the new program or service is clearly not sensible or feasible upon a more surface-level evaluation.

Basic Questions

The first step of the feasibility stage should be to ask the key players (proponents) a series of questions about the project. While these questions may vary according to the specific project, in general terms we can include the following:

- Why do we want to do the project?
- What specific services will be covered by the project?
- Why are the services covered by the project needed?
- What experience and expertise does our organization have in providing similar or related services?
- Who will provide the expertise we lack?
- What major classes of resources will be needed for the project?

- What major sources of capital financing are available?
- Should the project be handled as a joint venture? If so, joint with whom? What do we want from a partner?
- What regulatory or other restraints exist?
- What data will be needed for the final decision?
- What impact will tax laws have?
- What are the risks? Are we willing to take those risks?
- How much top management time will the project consume? Can our organization afford that level of commitment to this project?

The reasons for many of these questions are reasonably straightforward. We must know whether our interest in the project is based on providing increased community service, or based on generating profits to subsidize the other areas of community service we already provide. Alternatively, the goal may be to provide profits for expansion of other services. The ultimate decision on whether to go ahead will rest largely on what it is that motivates the project in the first place.

An understanding of the nature of the services to be provided, and why they are not already provided, is crucial. More often than not, the reason that a service is not offered is because it cannot be offered at a profit. If a large profit can easily be made, why isn't someone already doing it and making the profit? There may be satisfactory answers to these questions. But they are hard questions (often demoralizing) and they must be addressed at a very early stage in the analysis of the project. The answers to questions such as these should be included in the narrative of the plan. Sometimes other hospitals have avoided undertaking a program because they know we have the expertise or we have unique access to new technological innovations. Thus, a project may be desirable exactly because we have the experience, expertise, and resources. On the other hand, if we are lacking in any of these areas, we face the problem of obtaining such expertise. That should always raise a warning flag, because it is easiest to fail when you attempt to do something you don't know a whole lot about.

Often projects look fantastic in the absence of capital costs. Some projects may well be able to use idle facilities. Often, however, as one gets very deeply involved in a project it becomes apparent that the resources required are substantially greater than those anticipated at first. The sooner the major classes of resources can be identified, the quicker the project feasibility can be assessed.

The issue of whether to approach a project as a joint venture is one of the most crucial aspects of the business plan. One should be extremely clear in identifying exactly why there is a need to use the joint venture form. A casual approach may well turn out to generate a costly mistake for both parties. In general, each partner expects to get substantial benefits from the joint venture. Such an approach can only be successful if the benefits that accrue from the project are great enough to make both partners better off. If either partner's expectations of improvement are based upon a sacrifice by the other partner "for the common good," an unhappy result can be expected. Sometimes there is no choice. The partner has the dollars or the expertise that we lack. Sometimes the benefit is that risk can be shared. Whatever the reason for promoting the joint approach, extreme care and early evaluation of the potential problems of a bad marriage must be considered.

New projects, programs, services, and ventures always seem to be time sinks. The organization and management of the new concept must receive adequate attention for success to be possible. If the management talent is not on board, it must be determined where it will come from. If the managers who will direct the process (including top management) are not enthusiastic, the chances of success are substantially lowered.

Many of these questions tend to be answered implicitly by managers in the planning process. However, explicit attention in the form of written analysis of these questions in the plan is the best way to assure that satisfactory answers have really been achieved.

Often the answers to questions such as these are not encouraging. In some cases they are devastating. It should be borne in mind at all times that a decision to abort a proposed program or venture is not a defeat or a disaster. There is no shame associated with project feasibility exploration and determination that a proposal is not feasible.

Often programs are pushed through by their proponents to avoid "failing." However, the ultimate outcome of undertaking a program that cannot succeed is always worse than the costs of aborting the project at a very early stage. Organizations should develop ways to find out as many of the answers of basic questions (such as those posed above) as early as possible so that the sunk costs invested are as low as possible.

It is easy in economic theory to say that sunk costs are sunk and that we should never go forward with a poor proposal just because we have already made a major investment in it. Nevertheless, human nature is such that the lower the investment, the easier it is to abandon the idea.

One aid to such wise abandonment is an organizational statement that makes it clear that there are more poor ideas than good ones, but that we can only find the good ones by exploring a wide range of ideas. Therefore there should be positive reinforcement associated with all ideas—even those which do not pan out.

Basic Strategies

Having answered the basic questions, including but not limited to those discussed above, the next step is to undertake several basic strategies. Specifically, these concern demand analysis, competitive strategy, and competitor strategy.

Demand analysis is essential because any new venture can only succeed if the product being offered is something for which there is a need. Assessment of whether there are adequate customers to support the service is obviously crucial. Too often, however, hospitals fall into the trap of performing supply analysis in its stead. Projections are made based on how fast the new service can be geared up and what capacity will be available. Contrary to the adage, however, that a bed built is a bed filled, there is no reason to believe that just because a hospital has capacity for some new service, there will be a demand adequate to fill that capacity.

The issue of demand analysis flows into the concepts of competitor and competitive analysis. Once the demographics are understood in terms of how many buyers there are, and who they are, the hospital needs to consider how it can win those customers. This issue is far more complex than simply devising a good advertising campaign. It is far better to start by designing a product that will be well received than by designing the product in a vacuum and then trying to convince the customers the product is what they need.

Thus, competitor and competitive analysis require the hospital to assess how its product can be differentiated from that offered by the competition in such a way as to make it more desirable. The attributes of the product or service must be carefully considered, so that the hospital provides what there is a real need for, rather than the product it would be easiest to provide.

Often demand analysis and competitor/competitive strategy requires the efforts of a consulting firm, as the types of activities to be undertaken are beyond the normal scope of activities of hospital managers.

MARKETING

Once the hospital has addressed a basic set of questions, and considered the issues of demand and competitive position, it can turn to the issues of marketing and financial analysis. This assumes that we are still interested in the project. If we are being careful in the first steps, there is a high likelihood that many proposed projects will never reach this marketing analysis stage. The area of marketing can really be thought of from two very distinct perspectives: internal marketing and external marketing.

Internal Marketing

The vast majority of new ventures, programs, or services cannot possibly succeed without the support of a wide range of individuals throughout the hospital. Adding a home care service may seem to be totally distinct, requiring just the input of top management. However, in the long run the success of a new home care venture will hinge substantially on referrals from physicians and nurses throughout the hospital.

Therefore, the business plan must contain as one element an approach for the project advocate to gain support for the project from superiors, subordinates, and peers. Going about obtaining such support is largely a matter of organizational behavior, and as such is beyond the scope of this publication. However, recognition of this issue is crucial to ultimate success.

External Marketing

Marketing more traditionally is thought of as focusing on external elements—in particular the customer, but in some cases an intermediary. Hospitals have considerable familiarity with the intermediary notion, since they have long focused on the physician who brings in patients, rather than simply thinking in terms of patients alone.

The external marketing effort requires some market research and a media communication plan. Note that at times in developing a business plan it may seem that duplicative work is taking place, while in fact we are merely carefully laying the foundation for success.

Demand analysis has told us a lot about the potential volume for our new service. However, do the customers read the paper or watch television? Should we be attacking the market directly or through trade associations of intermediaries? These various aspects can be worked on either by marketing managers who are employees of the hospital, or by outside consultants.

FINANCIAL ANALYSIS

Financial analysis remains the last crucial test of whether the business plan should be completed and the project undertaken. There are a number of elements of a thorough financial analysis:

- reimbursement issues
- cost-effectiveness analysis
- forecasting (utilization, revenue, and expenses)
- capital budget development
- operating budget development
- break-even analysis
- cash flow projections
- net present value evaluation
- development of pro forma financial statements
- ratio analysis of pro formas
- sensitivity analysis

The reimbursement issues may be quite straightforward in some cases, when we are simply adding an internal service. If we are planning to open a home care service, or a long-term care facility, the problems become far more complex. Medicare and Medicaid rules for hospital payment differ substantially in these other areas. Furthermore, depending on the type of service being considered, the demographic breakdown in terms of payer mix may or may not be crucial to the success of the project.

As we commence a new service or program, there is a tendency to try to give the program advocate as much of what he wants as is possible. On the other hand, there is no better time to assure that the program is operated in an efficient manner than at the commencement. Any inefficiencies that exist in the beginning are very difficult to purge. Therefore, part of the plan effort should be devoted to assuring that a variety of alternative approaches are considered and that we wind up with the most efficient selection of equipment, configuration of labor and capital, and operating and information systems.

Forecasts can be crude or sophisticated. We are fortunate to be working in an era when microcomputers are becoming more and more useful to managers for a wide range of tasks. For example, forecasting future utilization or costs in an environment with seasonal fluctuations is complex. Yet in the last few years rather inexpensive (under $1,000) microcomputer software packages that employ sophisticated statistical

techniques (in ways easily accessible by unsophisticated users) to forecast effectively in complex environments have become available.

As a result, many of the forecasts used in business plans can be more than simply a seat-of-the-pants guess. The biggest hurdle in the process is determining useful historical data upon which to base the future forecast. A common contention is that with a new service everything is new, and therefore there is no basis for forecasting.

In many cases, however, close examination will show that this is largely untrue. A new outpatient pharmacy may seem to lack any historical data. On the other hand, our internal records can tell us how many prescriptions a pharmacist can fill per hour. Thus, our expense forecast can have some substantial historical base. Our medical records can give some historical data on the likely number of prescriptions to be filled per patient discharged. In the case of an outpatient lab, similarly, the hospital has access to information regarding the number of tests required prior to admission and after discharges. It is true that all forecasting involves making a guess about the future. However, we should strive to understand the likely success of a project, by making our guesses as accurate as possible.

For readers of this publication, it should be apparent that the business plan cannot be complete without development of a detailed capital budget, operating budget, cash flow budget, and break-even analysis, as well as a net present value (or internal rate of return) analysis. Although it is traditionally the domain of financial management, a great deal of this process should be handled by the project advocate.

It is true that there are some elements of this detailed financial planning that will be beyond the technical financial skills of the variety of clinicians involved in new programs. However, to have an ultimate proposal that everyone agrees is a fair assessment requires a mutual sharing of information. By including clinicians in the detailed financial planning, it is far easier to have agreement on problems such as those caused by a positive operating budget result but an insurmountable cash flow problem.

A very valuable element of a business plan is the development of pro forma financial statements, both for the project and for the organization as a whole. Such statements can give a very good feel for the impact of the program on the organization. Furthermore, they allow for development of ratios, which can be very good indicators of needed changes in the plan.

For instance, if the receivables turnover ratio projected is inadequate, it may point out a need to develop some improved approaches to collecting revenues faster. Thus, one should bear in mind that throughout the development of the plan it may be necessary to retreat, make changes, and then follow through on their implications.

Sensitivity analysis can be particularly useful in developing the plan and making final go/no-go decisions. What if revenues are only 90 percent as good as expected? What if they are only 75 percent as good? What if expenses run 10 percent above budget? Using a computer spreadsheet to develop the financial elements of the plan can allow for a final acid test. That is, before deciding to go ahead or not, we can determine just how far off our projections can be, and still have an acceptable venture.

IMPLEMENTATION AND FOLLOW-UP

The plan, presumably approvable if the prior elements have been completed with satisfactory results, is still not complete. Two vital elements remain before a plan should be considered ready for final review and approval. These are implementation and control.

Approving a project that has the ingredients for success does not put the hospital in the position to have a success. That requires implementation of the plan as envisioned. Furthermore, as the plan is fully implemented and begins operations, the process must be subject to ongoing control. That control must include not only analysis of results but also the power to make any changes needed to keep the program on track.

Too often, once a plan is approved, many of those involved turn away and move on to other things. In reality, however, many crises are yet to come in implementing and operating the new program. A specific plan for implementation and a specific plan for control are essential to success, and therefore should be detailed in the business plan. If they are not, then there is inadequate commitment to the program, and it should not be undertaken.

9

Flexible Budgeting and Variance Analysis

Key Terms Used in This Chapter

Acuity variance; budgeting; contribution margin; control chart; control limit; controllable; flexible budget; quantity (or use) variance; market share variance; market size variance; patient care variance; patient-mix variance; price (or rate) variance; productive versus nonproductive variance; revenue variance; uncontrollable; variance; variance analysis; volume variance; worked versus paid variance.

Note: Key terms appear in italics when first used in the chapter. All key terms are defined in the Glossary.

INTRODUCTION

Health care organizations have made tremendous strides in recent years in the area of *budgeting* and *variance* reporting and analysis. Budgeting improves outcomes by forcing the organization to consider alternative approaches and plan ahead for the coming year. Variance analysis is also essential for the management control function. The difference between a budgeted amount and the amount that actually results represents a variance. Managers investigate variances to determine their causes. Actions taken in response to variances can often dramatically improve the future operations of a health care organization.

Some variances are *controllable*. Managers can take actions to correct elements of operations that are out of control. This will help avoid unfavorable variances in the future. The primary focus of variance analysis should not be on assigning blame for overspending. Rather, the goal is to uncover the cause of problems that create overspending, so that the problems can be minimized in the future.

Other variances are not controllable. For example, the cost of an expensive essential supply item may have increased substantially and unexpectedly. Even if the organization cannot avoid the higher expense of the supply, variance information is essential to the overall management and well-being of the organization. It may be necessary to revise plans, for example, reduce costs in areas that are somewhat more discretionary to offset the higher expense for this essential supply item.

Such reductions may not seem fair to managers of the discretionary areas whose expenses are revised downward. However, the overall financial stability of the organization dictates that variances not be ignored. Overspending in some areas without offsetting reductions in others will lead to negative year-end results. Managers must consider the magnitude of the variances and decide whether the organization can sustain such negative results without making midstream changes.

Historically, variance analysis has focused on comparisons of actual results and budgeted expectations for each line in the budget of each cost center in the health care organization. Such comparisons are generally provided to managers for the current month and cumulatively for the year to date.

In the past decade, in an effort to understand variances better and to improve managerial efficiency in correcting the underlying causes of variances, there has been a movement toward a variety of improvements in variance analysis. For example, in Application 9-1, Kropf provides a method for calculating physician cost variances. This looks at each physician's variance attributable to the mix of patients and to the cost of treating those patients. Many health care organizations have started to use such physician variance analyses as a cost control technique. In Application 9-2, Minogue and Vogel discuss improvements in variance analysis for pharmacy departments.

A major recent improvement in health care variance analysis has been the introduction of *flexible budget variance analysis*. This approach places emphasis on the volume of patients actually treated by the health care organization. A budget is created based on an anticipated patient volume. If that volume is not attained, it may be misleading to compare the actual revenues and expenses to that original budget. Flexible budgeting adjusts the budget based on the actual patient volume. Flexible budget variance analysis calculates variances based on the adjusted flexible budget.

This chapter starts with a conceptual discussion of the traditional and flexible budget approaches to variance analysis. It then provides examples of calculations of variances. Next, the chapter focuses on the use of variance analysis for management control. Budgets are simply plans that are carried out by people. It is vital to consider the people in the process and their motivations and incentives. Unless people are willing to make an effort to meet the budget, it has little chance of being an effective management tool.

The final section of this chapter deals with *revenue variances*. Inherently, a cost accounting text is primarily concerned with expenses rather than revenues. Variance analysis traditionally has been used primarily for consideration and control of expenses. However, the tool does have significant potential application for understanding and controlling variations in revenues of health care organizations.

TRADITIONAL VARIANCE ANALYSIS

The traditional health care organization variance report is a line-by-line comparison of budgeted and actual expenses for each department or cost center of the health care organization. The report typically shows monthly activity and year-to-date cumulative results. An example of such a variance report is shown in Table 9-1.

In the table, we can see that a comparison is made for each line of the original budget for this cost center. Managers are held accountable for explaining why variances arose. For example, in Table 9-1, we can see that regular salaries for this general surgery unit were budgeted to be $38,320, but were actually $43,082. The unfavorable $4,762 is 12 percent over the budget. Why did that happen?

There are many possible causes of variances. More staff may have been needed because there were more patients or because the patients were sicker than expected. There may have been an outbreak of the flu, causing much higher than expected sick leave among the staff. Perhaps the variance was attributable to a raise given to staff that was higher than expected. It is possible that an employee resigned and was replaced by a new employee at a higher salary. It is possible, however, that there were inefficiencies. Late arrival and long coffee and lunch breaks translate into more staff hours.

The manager has a difficult job of determining which of these and many other possible factors were responsible for what portion of the variances. In most cases, variances are not the result of one cause, but rather of many different factors that interplay, sometimes combining to result in a large variance and sometimes offsetting each other, masking true underlying problems.

Variance analysis is not performed by the financial departments for the line departments of health care organizations. Accountants can measure the amount of the variances, but they cannot explain their causes. Such explanation requires investigation by someone knowledgeable about the department. Further, it requires the experience and judgment of a manager who understands the many specific details and factors that affect the spending of each department. Therefore, variances are analyzed and explained by cost center managers.

However, as noted earlier, the focus is not on blame. Organizations that use variance analysis to assign blame for poor outcomes rather than primarily to improve future outcomes risk poor morale, which is likely to have a negative impact on overall long-term cost control. The focus of variance analysis is to allow us to control better those costs that are controllable and to be aware of unexpected increases in noncontrollable costs.

Traditional variance analysis is not an excellent approach to understanding the spending of health care organizations. By providing managers with just the difference between actual and budgeted costs for each line item, even an experienced unit or department manager does not know where to begin investigating. However, mechanical accounting calculations could subdivide the variance into a number of elements. This can help managers to understand and explain the causes of variances.

We can look at the portion of each line-item variance caused by paying a higher price than expected for a resource versus the portion caused by using more of the resource. We can look at whether we used more per patient or had more patients. We can look at whether we used more per patient because the patients were sicker than expected. As we mechanically subdivide the variance, we make the manager's job easier, we tend to improve the accuracy of the explanations of the causes of variances, and we improve the organization's ability to control its costs. Flexible budget variance analysis provides the tools to make these subdivisions in each line-item variance.

Table 9-1 Sample Variance Report: General Surgery Cost Center

Account No./Description	This Month			Year-to-Date		
	Actual	*Budget*	*Variance*	*Actual*	*Budget*	*Variance*
311. Revenue						
010 Routine	148,607–	146,843–	1,764	1,310,469–	1,321,584–	11,115–
020 Other	2,459–	2,056–	403	20,277–	18,493–	1,784
(a) Total operating revenue	151,066–	148,899–	2,167	1,330,746–	1,340,077–	9,331–
611. Expenses						
010 Salaries—regular	43,082	38,320	4,762–	341,418	344,886	3,468
020 Salaries—overtime	729	972	243	7,344	8,748	1,404
030 FICA	2,922	2,621	301–	23,252	23,587	335
040 FICA	284	253	31–	2,253	2,276	23
050 Life insurance	91	81	10–	726	733	7
060 Other fringes	141	162	21	1,446	1,461	15
(b) Total employment costs	47,249	42,409	4,840–	376,439	381,691	5,252
300 Pt care supplies	2,012	1,998	14–	16,257	17,981	1,724
400 Office supplies/forms	438	579	141	6,040	5,213	827–
500 Seminars/meetings	135	50	85–	480	447	33–
600 Noncapital equip	250	74	176–	532	666	134
700 Maintenance repair	32	67	35	610	600	10–
800 Miscellaneous	—	48	48	381	432	51
900 Interdepartmental	582	530	52–	4,926	4,770	156–
(c) Total materials & supplies	3,449	3,346	103–	29,226	30,109	883
(d) Total operating costs (d = b + c)	50,698	45,755	4,943–	405,665	411,800	6,135
(e) Contribution from operations (e = a + d)	100,368–	103,144–	2,776–	925,081–	928,277–	3,196–
(f) Contribution % of revenue (f = (e/a) × 100)	66.44%	69.27%	2.83%–	69.52%	69.27%	0.25%

FLEXIBLE BUDGET VARIANCE ANALYSIS

The traditional approach to variance analysis suffers from a fatal flaw: it fails to account directly for the impact of volume changes on cost. Based on the discussion in earlier chapters, it should be obvious that as the volume of patients rises, variable costs must rise. Just as obviously, if volume falls, we would expect that variable costs will fall.

Suppose that a cost center actually incurs salary costs of $110,000, but the budget was only $100,000. There is a $10,000 unfavorable (U) variance.

Budget	Actual	Variance
$100,000	$110,000	$10,000 U

The cost center spent $10,000 more for labor than had been budgeted. Are labor costs out of control? Does the cost center manager need to take strong actions to prevent the excessive use of labor hours from continuing in future months?

The difficulty in answering these questions is that the $10,000 variance has been calculated without consideration of the patient volume. Suppose that 1,000 patients had been anticipated, but there were actually 1,200 patients treated. If some of the labor costs are variable, we would expect to spend substantially more than $100,000 because the volume has increased by 20 percent. It would be desirable to have a system that automatically segregates the portion of the variance that is simply attributable to changes in volume. The manager would then be able to investigate more easily the causes of the remaining portion of the variance.

Flexible Budgeting

A flexible budget is one that is adjusted for volume. An initial budget is based on an anticipated volume of activity. In preparing the budget, one could also prepare alternate budgets based on a range of possible volume outcomes. Thus, we could plan a budget assuming 1,000

patients, but also create alternate budgets showing the expected costs for 800, 900, 1,100, or 1,200 patients. Each of these would be considered to be a flexible budget based on the costs that we would expect to incur at the specified volume.

In preparing flexible budgets, it is essential to bear in mind that fixed costs do not vary with changes in volume, and variable costs do vary with volume. Therefore, the reason for different budgets at different volumes is because variable costs rise or fall with volume. This means that a flexible budget system must develop each budget based on a knowledge of which costs are fixed and which are variable.

A Naive Approach to Flexible Budgeting

Some health care organizations recognize the problems of comparing actual results with the original budget. However, rather than determining the underlying fixed and variable cost relationships, they attempt to solve the problem by treating all costs as if they were variable.

A naive approach to creating flexible budgets would allow all items in a budget to rise by 10 percent if volume is up by 10 percent. The problem with this overly simplistic adjustment is that fixed costs should not be rising at all as volume increases.

Such a budget adjustment is excessively lax. Once managers realize how that system works, they will know that there is substantial slack in their budgets during periods of rising volume. It will not take managers long to find ways to spend that slack, or, if a bonus system is in place, the resulting bonuses will be unduly generous.

On the other hand, what would happen when volume was lower than expected? Unlike the traditional system, which fails to require a manager to generate any cost reduction when volume falls, a naive approach to flexible variance analysis will assume that both variable and fixed costs will fall in proportion to volume reductions. Therefore, it will call for too much of a cost cutback.

Such naive approaches appear attractive for several reasons. First, they flex the budget with volume changes. Second, the simplicity of increasing or decreasing the budget by the same percentage as the change in volume appears to make sense at first glance. Finally, they do not require accurate breakdowns of which costs are fixed and which are variable. However, such approaches do not provide accurate information to managers.

Workable Flexible Budgets

A workable flexible budget system must first be able to identify which costs are fixed and which are variable. It must then use that information to allow volume changes to affect the variable costs in the budget, while leaving the fixed costs unchanged.

Most health care organizations that use flexible budgeting do not calculate a series of hypothetical flexible budgets at different potential volumes of activity. Instead, they wait until after an accounting period (such as a month) has ended, and then measure the actual volume. Based on that specific actual volume, a flexible budget can be developed.

The difference between the total budget for the line item and the flexible budget is referred to as a *volume variance* because it is attributable to a change in volume. The flexible budget is compared with the actual costs incurred to determine the extent of the remaining variance. If that variance is substantial, managers would need to investigate it and attempt to explain what caused it. Note that the volume variance is part of the total variance for that item, as is seen in Figure 9-1. The total variance has been divided into two parts, referred to as the flexible budget variance and the volume variance.

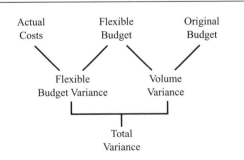

Figure 9-1 The Flexible Budget and Volume Variances

Determining whether a cost is fixed or variable is not always easy. In health care organizations, a great part of the overall cost is represented by staffing, which may well be neither strictly fixed nor strictly variable. Staffing may be fixed up to a point, and then require an incremental increase. For example, a unit may need seven nurses on a shift unless volume rises or falls by 500 patient days, at which point another nurse must be added or removed. Obviously, trying to build such patterns into a variance analysis system creates substantially increased complexity. As with all elements of cost accounting, you must consider whether the extra benefit of improved information is worth the cost of the higher level of sophistication.

At a minimum, however, one would want to examine each line item of each cost center budget and decide whether the resources represented by that line primarily are fixed or variable in nature. It might be worthwhile to restructure budgets to show staff that is fixed on a separate line from staff that varies with volume. Variable staff need not vary patient by patient. However, unlike managers and super-visors, they would be a category of staff that can be increased or decreased in response to changes in patient volume.

Price and Quantity Variances

The use of a flexible budget allows the organization to calculate mechanically the portion of each line-item variance caused simply by changes in volume and the remaining portion caused by other factors. This still does not bring health care organizations to the level of variance analysis sophistication utilized in most industrial organizations.

Flexible budget variance analysis calls not only for adjusting the variance for volume, but also for dividing that flexible budget variance into the portion that results from the price of the inputs, as opposed to the portion resulting from the quantity of input used to produce each unit of output. These *price* (or rate) and *quantity* (or use or efficiency) *variances* represent the next level of sophistication. (See Figure 9-2.)

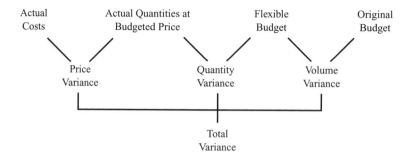

Figure 9-2 The Price, Quantity, and Volume Variances

Essentially, we can break down any variance into three main causes: more or fewer units of activity (patients, lab tests, etc.) than expected; higher or lower price paid for resources consumed; or more or fewer resources consumed per unit of activity. The first type of variance is automatically segregated by use of a flexible budget approach, which subdivides the total variance into a volume variance and an additional unexplained portion. In Figure 9-2, the volume variance is the difference between the original budget and the flexible budget. The additional, unexplained portion can also be segregated into a price variance by comparing the actual costs with the actual quantities at the budgeted price, and into a quantity (or use) variance by comparing the actual quantities at the budgeted price with the flexible budget.

A number of health care organizations have begun to move in this direction. The benefit from expanding the level of detailed information is that it is easier to isolate problem areas. Small variances can be quickly disposed of, and managerial attention can focus on the more serious problems. The implications for action differ substantially if it is the purchase price of a supply rather than the amount of the supply used that is creating a supply cost variance. Furthermore, by having more detailed variances, one quickly can determine whether it is in fact the price of a resource or the quantity consumed that requires investigation.

At times, variances will tend to offset each other. If the volume of patients is declining while the cost per patient is rising, the total line-item cost will show little variance. Adjusting for volume, as discussed above, will remove that problem. However, if the price of inputs is falling while the quantity used per patient is rising, the two effects can offset each other. Even with a volume-adjusted variance, we will not detect the increasing consumption per patient.

By dividing the variance for any line item into the portion attributable to the price of the inputs and the portion due to the quantity of inputs consumed, our ability to detect problems and control them is greatly enhanced. The cost of such information is not substantial, because this form of variance analysis requires only information that is readily available in the health care organization accounting system, and the costs of calculating and reporting the additional variances are minimal.

Overhead Variances

The above discussion of volume, price, and quantity variances generally is applied to direct labor and direct materials. Obviously, actual overhead costs will also vary from budgeted costs on frequent occasions. It is necessary to consider variances related to both variable overhead costs and fixed overhead costs.

Variable overhead costs are similar to direct labor and direct materials in many respects. A volume variance can be calculated. Greater volume would likely result in greater variable overhead costs and, therefore, a volume variance. In some instances, a price and quantity variance can also be calculated. These are often called spending and efficiency variances.

Calculating such variances requires knowledge of the price and quantity of inputs used per unit of output. These are often not known independently. For example, for 1,000 laboratory tests, we might expect to have $5,000 of variable overhead costs made up of many items. However, by the very nature of indirect costs, we do not know the quantity of each indirect item per unit of output. If we did, we could treat them as direct costs. Therefore, we can often calculate only a volume variance and flexible budget variance for variable overhead costs.

Fixed overhead costs represent a different problem. There can be no volume variance for fixed overhead costs. By definition, fixed costs are fixed; they do not vary with volume. Therefore, for any fixed costs, whether they are overhead costs or direct costs, the expected costs for the actual volume would be identical to the expected costs for the budgeted volume.

In some cases, it may be possible to determine price and quantity variances for fixed overhead costs. For example, if a department expects to have one manager and one supervisor, it must be determined whether variances arise because of a change in the number of managers (a quantity variance) or because of a change in the rate paid to managers (a price or rate variance).

The Acuity Variance

The *acuity variance* represents the amount that spending differed from expectations because the severity of patient illness differed from expectations. If patients are sicker than expected, it will generally require more resources to treat them.

The quantity variance represents all factors that result in consumption of more input per unit of output than budgeted. For example, if we use more hours of nursing care per patient day than the amount budgeted, we will have a variance. What does that variance represent? To some extent, it may represent an inefficient staffing pattern or perhaps inefficient work methods employed by our nursing staff. Perhaps coffee breaks and lunch breaks are gradually becoming longer. On the other hand, it may represent an increase in the average severity of illness, or acuity, of our patients. If the goal of more sophisticated variance analysis is to generate accounting reports that guide and direct managers as to where their variance investigation efforts should go, then it would be extremely useful to be able to quickly identify the degree to which variances are the result of sicker patients as opposed to inadequate managerial supervision and control.

Health care organizations that have functioning patient classification systems can translate patient acuity levels into required hours of patient care. Using that information, the quantity variance can be subdivided further into the portion caused by an unexpectedly high or low average patient acuity level as opposed to the portion caused by other factors. This is shown in Figure 9-3.

In this figure, the price and volume variances are unchanged. However, the quantity variance has been subdivided. Part of it is now isolated as

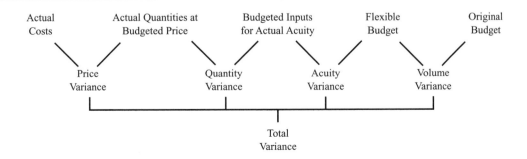

Figure 9-3 The Price, Quantity, Acuity, and Volume Variances

an acuity variance, and the other part is a remaining quantity variance. The key to this calculation is that the flexible budget provides for budgeted quantities of resource inputs at the expected acuity level. It is flexible in that it bases these budgeted resources on the actual volume of output. In contrast, the "actual quantities at budgeted price" category in the figure represent the actual quantities and actual acuity level.

A new category is placed between the actual quantities at budgeted price category and the flexible budget category: the "budgeted inputs for actual acuity." This category maintains the use of budgeted prices, as does the category to its left. It also maintains the use of the actual output volume, as does the category to its right. This category is differentiated in that it uses the quantity of input that would have been budgeted per unit, had the actual acuity been known.

In a sense, this new category is a type of flexible budget. The flexible budget provides the budget for the actual amount of output. The "budgeted inputs for actual acuity" category provides the budget for the actual amount of output at the actual acuity level. The difference between this category and the flexible budget is called an acuity variance, because the only difference is the use of the budgeted acuity versus the actual acuity. The difference between this category and the actual quantities at budgeted price category is referred to as the quantity variance, because it represents quantity of inputs consumed that is different from what would be expected for the actual volume of output at the actual acuity level.

The Worked vs. Paid Variance

Another issue that creates difficulties in the area of variance interpretation is the fact that not all hours that are paid for are actually worked. In calculating the labor cost budgeted per patient day versus the actual labor cost per patient day, the personnel cost includes the total cost, not just the portion for time worked. This means that a share of sick leave, vacation, holidays, and so forth is included in the cost per unit of activity.

Essentially, when one notes from a quantity variance that we are using more labor per patient, that could mean more direct care hours, or it could mean more sick leave than expected. Obviously, these two possibilities have very different implications for the organization. The potential diversity of possible causes of quantity variances makes the manager's job of investigation and interpretation of variances more difficult.

For the health care organization as a whole, the proportion of paid versus worked time might be quite predictable. However, for a given department, if one employee breaks his or her leg and goes on disability for two months, substantial department budget variances will be generated. The department will pay for the replacement employee and may also be charged for the sick leave payments to the employee who is out for two months. Such variances will not be explained by volume variance analysis, or by price, or acuity variance analysis. They will reside as an unexplained portion of the quantity variance.

If we further subdivide the quantity variance into two segments, we can isolate the portion of the variance that results from an unexpected level of paid but not worked time. The remaining quantity variance can be more directly considered and investigated for possible out-of-control situations. At that point, it will have been isolated from any portion caused by acuity and from any portion caused by paid but not worked hours. This will enhance the manager's ability to consider both why the paid but not worked portion has varied and why the paid and worked portion has varied.

At the current time, not many health care organizations formally make this calculation. However, as the use of computers at the level of the cost center continues to grow, it is likely that managers will start to make such computations to aid in their analyses of variances.

The Productive vs. Nonproductive Variance

Even having segregated the paid but not worked and acuity components from the quantity variance, it would be theoretically possible to subdivide the quantity variance further. Specifically, we could look at worked hours in terms of whether they are productive or nonproductive hours. By this, we are not referring to inefficiencies, but rather to the fact that employees may attend in-service education programs or for some other reason be away from their clinical or staff position.

If the number of hours spent at work but not "on the job" differs from expectations, that will send us a message different from that if nonproductive time was paid but not worked. It will also send a message different from that if the time was worked on the employees' usual tasks.

For example, in a nursing unit, if we spend fewer hours than expected providing care to each patient, we may have a quality of care concern. On the other hand, if a quantity variance was really caused because we spent fewer hours than expected in inservice education or at conferences, we might feel very different about the variance and about the need to investigate the variance. Data to calculate such a variance may be somewhat harder to obtain than data for the earlier variances, but it should be available within most health care organizations.

The Patient Care Variance

The last variance we should consider is the extent to which paid, worked, productive time is actually spent in the process of direct patient care. For example, suppose that a nursing department paid for exactly the expected number of labor hours, and staff worked exactly the expected number of hours and had exactly the expected amount of paid but nonproductive time (such as conferences). There still are questions. Did the patients receive the expected amount of direct care? Was there a higher level of nondirect patient care time and a lower amount of direct patient care time per patient day? (This might be due to poor scheduling, poor employee attitude, or time-consuming patient-chart documentation problems.)

Unlike all of the other variances discussed to this point, there are very considerable data collection obstacles with respect to calculating this variance. As with the other variances discussed above, we are not proposing the determination of new, additional variances. The entire process merely consists of dividing and subdividing the difference between actual and budgeted costs into smaller, more clearly defined segments.

This variance, however, requires that we be able to know how much of any given workday is actually devoted to direct patient care. In some departments, those data might be obtainable. For example, in the operating room, we could track the percentage of hours that each employee is actually in surgery. Although there are clearly important indirect tasks that must be undertaken, it would be valuable to be able to monitor the proportion of direct time and indirect time.

On the other hand, for many departments, such as routine nursing care units, such a determination would involve a tremendous data collection effort. Therefore, it is unlikely that any health care organizations would spend the resources to calculate this *patient care variance*. The cost of doing so would be too high relative to the value of the information obtained.

Health care organization budgeting and the control of budget results has changed dramatically in the years since the advent of Medicare. The advent of Diagnosis Related Groups (DRGs) is likely to push the process even further. Many of the variances discussed above are not calculated currently in many health care organizations. They do for the most part, however, represent workable ways to improve managerial capabilities for controlling the organization.

CALCULATION OF VARIANCES

The above discussion provided the conceptual basis for variances based on volume, price, quantity, acuity, not-worked time, and nonproductive time. This section of the chapter extends the discussion by giving a numerical example of the calculations that might be employed to determine the more widely used of those variances.

Assume that Florence Nightingale was the nursing supervisor for the Fourth Floor West Medical/Surgical Unit of The Getuwell Hospital. For the month just ended, she had budgeted for 450 patient days. She had planned to pay for 7 hours of RN nursing care per patient day at a rate of $20 per hour including benefits. Actual results for the month indicated total spending for nursing salaries for the unit was $98,700, considerably above the $63,000 (450 patient days × 7 hours per day × $20 per hour) budgeted. These data are summarized as follows:

The Getuwell Hospital
Fourth Floor West
Medical/Surgical Unit

Budgeted patient days	450
Budgeted RN hours per patient day	7
Budgeted RN hourly pay rate	$ 20
Budgeted total RN cost	$63,000
Actual total nursing salaries	$98,700

Why did the unit go so far over budget?

Florence determined that there were actually 500 patient days, and that 4,700 nursing hours were paid for during the month (9.4 hours per patient day on average). She also knew that the raise that went into effect at the beginning of the month would drive all wages up by $1 per hour, so she was not surprised to find that the average wage rate including benefits was $21 per hour.

The Getuwell Hospital
Fourth Floor West
Medical/Surgical Unit

Actual patient days	500
Actual RN hours per patient day	9.4
Actual RN hourly pay rate	$ 21

Calculating the Traditional Variance

The traditional variance report might look like this:

	Actual	**Budgeted**	**Variance**
RN salaries	$98,700	$63,000	$35,700 U

Typically, year-to-date information would also be provided, but for simplicity's sake we will not report it here.

In order to simplify the calculation of variances, we will introduce arithmetic notation as we proceed. The first items are as follows:

- bQo: The *b*udgeted *q*uantity of *o*utput (in this case, patient days).
- aQo: The *a*ctual *q*uantity of *o*utput.
- bPi: The *b*udgeted *p*rice of *i*nput per unit of input (in this case, nursing rate per hour).
- aPi: The *a*ctual *p*rice of *i*nput per unit of input.
- bQi: The *b*udgeted *q*uantity of *i*nput per unit of output (in this case, number of nursing hours per patient day).
- aQi: The *a*ctual *q*uantity of *i*nput per unit of output.

From the information given in the example, we know the following values for these six items:

bQo:	450 patient days
bPi:	$20 per hour
bQi:	7 hours per patient day
aQo:	500 patient days
aPi:	$21 per hour
aQi:	9.4 hours per patient day

The traditional variance simply requires comparison of the budgeted and actual amounts, as follows:

$aQo \times aPi \times aQi = 500 \times \$21 \times 9.4 =$	$ 98,700
$-bQo \times bPi \times bQi = 450 \times \$20 \times 7.0 =$	63,000
RN labor cost variance for Fourth Floor West Medical/Surgical Unit	$ 35,700

This variance would be referred to as an unfavorable variance because more money was spent than was expected. That does not necessarily mean that the manager or unit performed badly, nor does it mean that the variance was bad for the organization. The extra patients may justify the extra spending. In fact, they might generate enough extra revenue to make this a good event for the organization. However, accountants refer to spending in excess of budget as being an unfavorable variance.

Calculating the Volume Variance

In the past decade, many health care organizations have adjusted their variance reports to allow for the impact of volume changes. It does not make much sense to hold a manager responsible for keeping to a fixed budget when activity levels are increasing. Variable costs will drive up actual expenditures even if the manager does an exceptional job of controlling costs. Similarly, we would not want to reward a manager for exactly achieving a fixed budget if the volume of activity declined. Costs should have declined as well.

If the RN staffing is considered to be a variable cost, then a change in patient days would be expected to change the required amount of nursing care. As a result, the actual amount spent for 500 patient days should differ from the budget for 450 patient days.

One approach taken by many health care organizations is to treat the actual volume as if it were the budgeted amount. For instance, we would have the calculation below:

$aQo \times aPi \times aQi = 500 \times \$21 \times 9.4 =$	\$ 98,700
$-aQo \times bPi \times bQi = 500 \times \$20 \times 7.0 =$	70,000
RN labor cost variance for Fourth Floor West Medical/Surgical Unit	\$ 28,700

In this calculation, the budgeted cost has effectively been revised to \$70,000, and the unit manager is no longer responsible for the portion of the cost increase that is attributable to higher volume.

While that is a step in the right direction, constant changes in the underlying budget are not desirable. For instance, if volume decreases, we do not simply want to reduce the amount available for each department to spend. We also want to flag the fact that volume decreased so that the appropriate manager can focus on that specific issue. If patient days are decreasing while admissions are constant, that may be good. However, if admissions are declining, then revenues will fall as well. We do not want that fact to become buried.

Therefore, a preferable approach for volume changes is to isolate (rather than eliminate) the portion of the variance due to volume of activity changes. The one traditional variance can be subdivided into two parts, as follows:

Volume Variance

$aQo \times bPi \times bQi = 500 \times \$20 \times 7.0 =$	\$ 70,000
$-bQo \times bPi \times bQi = 450 \times \$20 \times 7.0 =$	63,000
RN labor cost volume variance for Fourth Floor West Medical/Surgical Unit	\$ 7,000

Variance Other Than Volume

$aQo \times aPi \times aQi = 500 \times \$21 \times 9.4 =$	\$ 98,700
$-aQo \times bPi \times bQi = 500 \times \$20 \times 7.0 =$	70,000
RN labor other variance for Fourth Floor West Medical/Surgical Unit	\$ 28,700

Total Variance for RN labor cost for Fourth Floor West Medical/Surgical Unit — \$ 35,700

This approach to variance measurement leaves all of the original information intact, yielding the traditional variance total of \$35,700, but also giving more information for management by subdividing the traditional variance into two pieces.

It should be noted, however, that a volume variance only arises to the extent that costs are variable. That does not mean that costs must be strictly variable—we do not expect to hire nurses by the patient day. However, the cost item being evaluated must vary at least in some rough proportion to the output measure being used as the volume base. To adjust the budget of a fixed cost item as volume changes is just as misleading as failing to adjust the expected cost of a variable cost item as volume changes.

Calculating the Price and Quantity Variances

Once the traditional variance has been subdivided into two pieces, we can move forward in improving the variance information. The next step is to divide the portion of the traditional variance attributable to causes other than volume into its price and quantity subcomponents.

This step, used by some but not most health care organizations, is widely used in industry.

As noted above, $28,700 of the total variance is caused by something other than the increase in patient days from 450 to 500. The two principal components of this $28,700 variance are related to the price we paid for the inputs and the amount of input used for each unit of output. These subcomponents are referred to as the price or rate variance, and the quantity, use, or efficiency variance.

Using the notation developed above, we could calculate the *price, quantity,* and *volume variances,* as follows:

Price Variance

$aQo \times aPi \times aQi = 500 \times \$21 \times 9.4 = \$ 98,700$
$-aQo \times bPi \times aQi = 500 \times \$20 \times 9.4 = \underline{ 94,000}$

RN labor price variance for Fourth Floor West Medical/Surgical Unit $\underline{\$ 4,700}$

Quantity Variance

$aQo \times bPi \times aQi = 500 \times \$20 \times 9.4 = \$ 94,000$
$-aQo \times bPi \times bQi = 500 \times \$20 \times 7.0 = \underline{ 70,000}$

RN labor quantity variance for Fourth Floor West Medical/Surgical Unit $\underline{\$ 24,000}$

Volume Variance

$aQo \times bPi \times bQi = 500 \times \$20 \times 7.0 = \$ 70,000$
$-bQo \times bPi \times bQi = 450 \times \$20 \times 7.0 = \underline{ 63,000}$

RN labor cost volume variance for Fourth Floor West Medical/Surgical Unit $\underline{\$ 7,000}$

Total (Traditional) Variance $\underline{\underline{\$ 35,700}}$

Note that the price variance is derived by comparing all actual information to information that contains actual results except for the budgeted price. Thus, the only difference between the top row and bottom row in the price variance calculation is the budgeted versus actual price, yielding a price variance. In the quantity variance calculation, only the quantity of input per unit of output varies.

The level of detail yielded by this industrial model of variance analysis is far superior to the traditional model used in health care, in terms of orienting managers toward problem areas for investigation. However, in health care organizations, a number of different factors may be responsible for the quantity variance.

Calculating the Acuity Variance

One particular concern in health care organizations is that the output is not a standardized product. We can treat exactly the same number of patients or patient days, but if the mix of patients is such that they are more acutely ill, they may require more resources. Therefore, it is quite beneficial to be able to factor out the portion of the quantity variance that results from the level of patient acuity or severity of illness.

In order to proceed, it is necessary to have a patient classification system in place that can reasonably predict the patient care hours staffing requirements at different acuity levels. Most hospitals and many other health care organizations have implemented such systems during the past decade.

Suppose that, in our example, we determined that our actual incurred acuity level would have called for The Getuwell Hospital to pay for 8.6 hours of nursing care per patient day, rather than the originally budgeted 7.0. Thus, we know that at least a part of the quantity variance was attributable to sicker patients, rather than to lax control. How much of the quantity variance is attributable to unexpectedly high patient acuity? In order to do this calculation, we need to add the following additional notation:

- $bQibA$: The *b*udgeted *q*uantity of *i*nput per unit of output, at the *b*udgeted *a*cuity level (budgeted amount of nursing hours per patient day based on a budgeted patient acuity level).
- $bQiaA$: The *b*udgeted *q*uantity of *i*nput per unit of output, at the *a*ctual *a*cuity level.

From the information given in the example, we know the following:

$bQibA$: 7 hours per patient day
$bQiaA$: 8.6 hours per patient day

We can now subdivide the quantity variance into two parts, as follows:

Acuity Variance

$aQo \times bPi \times bQiaA = 500 \times \$20 \times 8.6 =$	\$ 86,000
$-aQo \times bPi \times bQibA = 500 \times \$20 \times 7.0 =$	70,000

RN labor acuity variance for Fourth Floor West Medical/Surgical Unit	\$ 16,000

Remaining Quantity Variance

$aQo \times bPi \times aQi \quad = 500 \times \$20 \times 9.4 =$	\$ 94,000
$-aQo \times bPi \times bQiaA = 500 \times \$20 \times 8.6 =$	86,000

RN labor quantity variance for Fourth Floor West Medical/Surgical Unit	\$ 8,000

Total Quantity Variance	\$ 24,000

Apparently, two thirds of the quantity variance in this example was attributable to the unexpectedly high level of patient acuity. Since the patient acuity level is not a factor under the control of unit managers, we would want to separate the variance caused by such acuity changes. The separation generates information that is far easier to interpret than the aggregated information would be.

The framework generated in this section is represented in Exhibit 9-1. Note that the total of the variances shown in Exhibit 9-1 should always equal the original traditional variance for any line item. This process of variance analysis does not create new variances; it merely subdivides a line-item variance into subcomponent parts for superior analysis.

Exhibit 9-1 Formulas for Price, Quantity, Acuity and Volume Variances

Price Variance

$aQo \times aPi \times aQi$
$-aQo \times bPi \times aQi$

Quantity Variance

$aQo \times bPi \times aQi$
$-aQo \times bPi \times bQiaA$

Acuity Variance

$aQo \times bPi \times bQiaA$
$-aQo \times bPi \times bQibA$

Volume Variance

$aQo \times bPi \times bQi$
$-bQo \times bPi \times bQi$

VARIANCE ANALYSIS AND MANAGEMENT CONTROL

What do variances tell the manager? What do they mean? When and how should managers respond to variances? Once variances have been calculated, managers should use them to control the organization. The relationship between variances and management control is the topic of this section of the chapter.

Generally, one can expect that there are three possible reactions to a variance. One reaction is simply to ignore it. The variance may be deemed to be the result of a random event. One would probably expect to spend a little more or less than the budget each month for many types of expenses. A second reaction would be to adjust the budget or the budgeting process to reflect more accurately what it must cost to carry out a particular task. It may be clear that the budget was in error. The third possible reaction is to take actions necessary to alter performance. The second and third actions can only be taken if the variances are investigated to determine their causes.

Controllable vs. Uncontrollable Variances

Demski breaks down variances into those that are *controllable* and those that are *uncontrollable*.[1] In his scheme, variances that create a need to correct the budget are the result of either prediction error or modeling error. A prediction error might include unexpectedly high price increases or fewer than expected patient admissions. A modeling error might include a poor estimate of how long it takes to draw blood from each patient.

Variances that require changes in performance would include either implementation or measurement errors. An implementation problem means that the employees of the organization did not carry out the tasks as expected by the organization. This requires working with the employees to change their behavior. A measurement problem means that the amount of cost assigned to an area was incorrect. For example, the operating room did not use more supplies than expected in a given month, but a purchase of a three-month supply of an expensive item was all charged to the month it was purchased instead of being charged as the supply was used. The cost reported was measured improperly.

According to Demski, uncontrollable variances are the result of random error and should be ignored. For example, if there is unusually high sick leave due to a virus that attacks the health care organization staff, the month's employment costs will be higher than expected. The policy of ignoring such variances would seem to be extreme. One should at least attempt to determine that the variance is in fact not controllable. Gradually rising sick leave might indicate a controllable morale problem.

Basic Control Principles for Variances

Variance reports should be provided to managers on a timely basis in an understandable format and should give managers a perception of fairness.

Some health care organizations still prepare variance reports on a quarterly basis, with the report generated near the end of the subsequent quarter. If a manager received information about January in May or June, there is clearly no sense of urgency and little sense of importance associated with the document. Review of such document in July or August is likely to tell little about what went wrong in January. Whatever went wrong is likely to have repeated itself for half the year. Timeliness of reporting is essential if the process is to be taken seriously and to yield control benefits.

Most variance reports contain a wide range of abbreviations and assumptions. Variance reports tend to be ongoing. Thus, new managers are likely to receive monthly reports that lack definitions and explanations. In an effort to show that they are in fact capable of performing in their new management position, they are unlikely to admit to not understanding a routine report. Therefore, the finance personnel of the organization should be sure that all managers have the definitions and explanations needed to read and interpret variance reports adequately.

Health care organizations should have a mechanism for various managers to explain why they feel that charges to their department are unfair. It is difficult to generate the motivation for managers to control costs if they believe that the costs ultimately assigned to them are not fair. If managers are held accountable for costs that are not within their control, they often lose the incentive to attempt to control the costs that are. There should be a formal mechanism to call for comments and to make changes so that ultimately managers feel they are working in a fair environment.

When To Investigate Variances

It is wasteful to have managers unnecessarily investigate variances. Variances should only be investigated when there is something to gain from the investigation. Most often, small variances will occur just due to normal random fluctuations. Sometimes, however, there will be a need to take corrective action. Therefore, the health care organization must decide in what instances the variance warrants an investigation and in what instances the variance should be ignored.

One approach frequently taken is simply to assume that managers know enough to know when to investigate variances. Such an approach assumes that the same causes of variances keep recurring, leading one to wonder why they are not corrected. Further, it does little to help the new manager.

A more helpful approach is to plot variances on a graph over time. This allows the manager to spot unusual trends that might be cause for concern. For example, look at what happens in Figure 9-4. It is not hard to tell that the manager needs to take a close look at this situation. The random ups and downs have been replaced by an upward trend.

Another option is a *control chart* approach. In such an approach, a graph is used with upper and lower limits. If a variance exceeds the upper or lower *control limits*, the manager should investigate the variance. See, for example,

Figure 9-5. In September, the variance was above the control limit, and investigation would be required.

An important issue is where to set the control limits. How high is high? How low is low? To set the limits too far from the budget would allow correctable variances to continue unnecessarily. To set the limits too close to the budget would cause the manager to spend time needlessly trying to find causes that do not exist.

Some organizations in industry use a formal statistical measure for determining when to investigate variances. One such approach would be to determine a normal expected variation. No one expects to come in exactly on budget. Once this variation is determined, a standard deviation can be calculated. A rule often used in industry is to investigate any variance that is more than three standard deviations away from the expected reasonable variation.[2] Statistical ap-

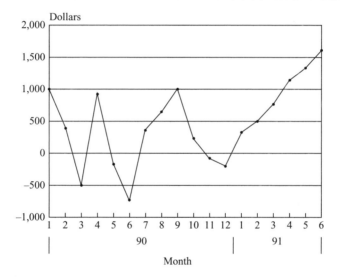

Figure 9-4 Variances Over Time. *Source:* Reprinted from *Hospital Cost Management and Accounting,* Vol. 3, No. 3, p. 3, Aspen Publishers, Inc., © 1991.

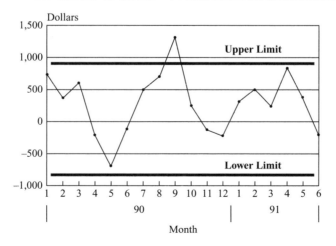

Figure 9-5 Variance Control Limits. *Source:* Reprinted from *Hospital Cost Management and Accounting,* Vol. 3, No. 3, p. 3, Aspen Publishers, Inc., © 1991.

proaches to determining when to investigate variances are discussed further in Skantz's article, Application 9-3 at the end of this chapter.

Such arbitrary rules are of questionable value, since they do not measure how costly it is for the manager to investigate the variance, nor how costly it will be for the health care organization if it fails to correct behavior that should be changed. Another problem is caused by the fact that variances may simply be caused by a large random event. Major investigation is not needed if the cause of the variance is simply an outlier. Application 7-1 at the end of Chapter 7 addressed the issue of outliers and variance analysis.

Control Limits Based on Cost Analysis

An alternative approach to statistical guidelines such as a set number of standard deviations is to calculate formally the costs of making an investigation and the costs if behavior needs to be corrected. In this approach, if one investigates, there may be no problem (just random events), or there may be a problem. The same holds true if one does not investigate.

Therefore there are four possibilities:

1. Investigate and find a problem.
2. Investigate and find no problem.
3. Do not investigate. It turns out there is no problem.
4. Do not investigate. It turns out there is a problem.

The cost for each of these four possibilities should be estimated. For example, suppose that it would normally take the pharmacy manager one day to investigate a variance fully. Suppose that the cost to the health care organization of the pharmacy manager is $400 per day including benefits. Suppose that when there is a problem, on average, it causes the health care organization to lose $5,000 per month, if it is not uncovered and corrected.

If we investigate, either there is no problem, or there is a problem and it is corrected. In either case, there will be no loss in the coming month, but there will be an investigation cost of $400. If

we do not investigate, there may be no problem, and because we did not investigate, no cost. However, there may be a problem that costs $5,000. The cost associated with the four possibilities listed above are shown in Figure 9-6. Taking the investigation route is the cautious approach. We avoid the risk of a possible $5,000 loss. Still, we always spend $400. Perhaps we should not investigate, and the cost will be $0.

The decision to investigate depends on how likely it is that there will be a problem. Suppose that there is a 20 percent chance that there is a problem. In that case, on average, there will be a problem one time out of five. Investigating all five times would cost $2,000. Having an undetected problem one time out of five costs $5,000. In that case, it pays to investigate.

This can be used to establish the control limits. Suppose that an observed variance of $5,000 implies that there is a 20 percent chance that there is a problem. The manager should investigate because spending $2,000 on investigation is cheaper than spending $5,000 on a problem.

Suppose that a $3,000 variance implies that there is a 10 percent chance of a problem. In that case, if we investigate ten times, we are likely to find a problem once. Ten investigations cost $4,000 ($400 per investigation). One problem costs $5,000. We should investigate a $3,000 variance.

Suppose that a variance of $2,000 implies that there is a 5 percent chance that there is a problem. A 5 percent chance means that there would be a problem once in every 20 times that we observed a $2,000 variance. That means that there would be a cost of $8,000 to investigate the 20 occurrences. One problem costs $5,000. It does

	Cost	
	Problem	No Problem
Investigate	$400	$400
Do Not Investigate	$5,000	$0

Figure 9-6 Payoff Matrix for Variance Investigation

not pay to investigate. The likely costs of investigation outweigh the likely costs of the problem. Therefore, we would not investigate a $2,000 variance.

Somewhere between $2,000 and $3,000 there is a variance for which the costs of investigation will just offset the costs of an out-of-control situation. That would be used as the control limit. The manager would investigate variances above the limit, but not those below the limit.

This is a rational approach that can be quite helpful to managers. The main weakness of this approach is that the manager must subjectively be able to know, from the size of the variance, how likely there is to be a problem. The advantage is that, ordinarily, even if the manager knows there is a 10 or 20 or 30 percent chance of a problem, that does not indicate whether it is worthwhile to investigate the variance. This approach does.

Reacting to Variances

It is appropriate to assign responsibility for variances to managers. It is less useful to assign blame. People are not perfect. If we allow for imperfections, people will try to correct their errors. When we try to require perfection, the response can be dysfunctional behavior.

For example, if there is extreme pressure to meet the budget, it may well be met, but in a costly manner. Quality of care may suffer, or an expected favorable supply variance may be converted to physical supplies hoarded in the department against the day when an unfavorable variance might be anticipated.

It is important always to bear in mind that we are dealing with human beings. Any approach to dealing with variances must consider the likely reactions of the various employees of the health care organization.

REVENUE VARIANCES

Product costing has changed the focus of health care organizations from procedures to patient groups. There is less emphasis on departments and increased emphasis on the cost of patients across departments. One goal of the increased emphasis on product costing is to focus on the profitability of different types of patients. This requires an understanding of both the expenses and revenues generated by different groups of patients.

For example, we can use DRG cost information to generate a set of revenue or sales variances. These variances can help managers understand what elements of health care organization activities are causing total health care organization revenues to differ from expectations. Specifically, revenue variances can focus on the total health care organization demand in a given geographic region, a health care organization's share of that total demand, its mix of patients, and the prices for each class of patient.

Focus on Contribution Margin

Although the title and topic of this section refers to revenues, all of the variance analysis calculations that follow will focus on *contribution margin:* revenue minus variable cost. The reason for this is that revenue is not a goal in and of itself. Increasing revenues by having more patients with low or even negative contribution margins will not serve the health care organization well.

We do not want to develop a managerial accounting system that gives wrong signals to health care organization managers. Shifting the mix of patients away from low-revenue patients and toward high-revenue patients may seem positive. However, it is only positive if the variable costs associated with the high revenue are low enough to improve the overall contribution margin.

For example, would you rather have five patients with reimbursement of $1,000 each and variable costs of $600 each, or five patients with reimbursement of $5,000 each, and variable costs of $4,900 each? Although the revenue in the latter case is $25,000 in contrast to $5,000, after deducting the variable costs associated with the patients, we are only left with a total contribution of $500 in the latter case, whereas we earn $2,000 of contribution in the former instance.

Use of Budgeted Variable Costs

In calculating the contribution margin (revenue minus variable cost), it is necessary to use some measure of variable costs. As our patient mix changes, some costs (the variable ones) change and others (fixed costs) do not. As product costing systems are being adopted by health care organizations, identification of fixed and variable costs throughout the health care organization is becoming more common.

In the calculation of revenue variances, it is important that the measure of variable cost used be a standard or budgeted cost per unit rather than an actual cost. The budgeted contribution margin is based on budgeted costs. That creates no controversy. One might expect that the actual information used for comparison with the budget would be based on all actual information, including actual variable costs. That, however, will unduly complicate the results and make variance interpretation unnecessarily difficult. When calculating the actual contribution margin for this variance analysis, we use the actual price but the budgeted variable cost per unit.

Keep in mind the fact that the health care organization will be calculating its usual variances for expenses, as discussed in the earlier sections of this chapter. If actual variable costs differ from budgeted costs, those differences will show up in the expense variance calculations. Here we would like to develop a framework for the calculation of variances arising as a result of revenue factors: the price charged, the mix of patients, and the number of patients. Therefore, to keep the analysis clean, it is appropriate to use the budgeted variable costs for all revenue variance calculations.

This does not mean that the contribution margin (i.e., the price minus the variable cost) will not change in our analysis. It will if prices change. However, since this analysis is for revenues rather than expenses, the contribution margin need not be influenced by underlying changes in the variable cost per unit from the budgeted variable cost level.

We will use an example for the remainder of this section of the chapter. The numbers used will be highly simplified. However, once the model is laid out, it can be applied to a more realistic set of numbers, with the only difference being increased time for computations.

Suppose that the health care organization's contribution margin for the last month was budgeted at $800,000, but in fact turned out to be $1,010,000. What is the underlying cause for this $210,000 favorable variance? What things occurred that led to this variance? Were they within or beyond our control?

There are four key pieces of information that are needed to calculate a complete set of variances. For each of the key elements, both budgeted and actual data are needed. If some of this information is not available, a simpler model that requires less input but yields less information can be developed.

The four key information items are the expected number of patients for the entire community, our health care organization's share of those patients, our health care organization's patient mix, and the weighted average price for each type of patient.

The most difficult information to obtain will be that related to the budgeted and actual total number of patients in the community. After the complete model, including that information, is developed, the modifications needed to eliminate that information will be discussed.

The Original Budgeted Contribution Margin

The original budgeted contribution margin of $800,000 will be referred to as the original static (unchanging) budget. This amount consists of a summation of the budgeted total volume of patients in the community, multiplied by our health care organization's market share, multiplied by the contribution margin for each type of patient, weighted for our case mix.

For example, suppose that we expect all of the health care organizations in our area (based on marketing demand studies) to have a total of

3,200 patients for the month in question. That establishes the budgeted size of the market. Suppose further that we expect to get 10 percent of this market.

In this simplified example, assume that we only admit two types of patients, which we will call DRG 1 and DRG 2. (You could choose some method other than DRGs for identifying your patient mix.) Extending the model from 2 DRGs to 470 would only require a greater number of computations.

In our example, we expect three quarters of our patients to be DRG 1 patients, and one quarter to be DRG 2 patients. We expect the contribution margin of our DRG 1 patients to be $1,000 each and the contribution margin of our DRG 2 patients to be $7,000 each.

The budgeted contribution margin for the health care organization consists of the weighted sum of the budgeted contribution margin for each of our types of patients. Assume the following information:

Budgeted total number of patients	3,200
Our budgeted share of market	10%
DRG 1 patients	75%
DRG 2 patients	25%
DRG 1 contribution margin	$1,000
DRG 2 contribution margin	$7,000

The budgeted contribution margin would be as follows:

DRG 1: Budgeted market volume × Budgeted share × Budgeted DRG 1 proportion × Budgeted DRG 1 contribution margin

+ DRG 2: Budgeted market volume × Budgeted share × Budgeted DRG 2 proportion × Budgeted DRG 2 contribution margin

or,

DRG 1:	3,200 ×	10% ×	75% ×	$1,000 =	$240,000
+ DRG 2:	3,200 ×	10% ×	25% ×	$7,000 =	560,000
Original budget contribution margin					$800,000

As noted above, the calculations here consist of the total volume multiplied by our share of the market, multiplied by the proportion in the given DRG, multiplied by the contribution margin for the DRG, and finally summed for all DRGs. As noted above, the actual contribution margin was $1,010,000. This is $210,000 more than the original budget contribution margin. We would like to know the underlying causes of this favorable total variance.

The Market Size Variance

The first of the variances that can be calculated is the *market size variance.* This variance will tell us if the reason that our revenues and contribution margin changed was simply due to a greater or smaller number of patients in the community than expected. In order to calculate this variance, we need all of the budgeted information from the original budget contribution margin, and we need to know the actual number of patients admitted to health care organizations for the month.

If that information can be obtained, the calculation is fairly straightforward. We replace the budgeted volume of patients for the community with the actual volume of patients, and calculate a new value for the contribution margin. This new value can be referred to as the *market size flexible budget.* This contribution margin projects a budgeted value for the health care organization, based on the *actual* size of the market. Suppose that, in our example, the actual number of patients was 4,000 for the community for the month.

The market size flexible budget contribution margin can then be calculated as follows:

DRG 1: Actual market volume × Budgeted share × Budgeted DRG 1 proportion × Budgeted DRG 1 contribution margin

+ DRG 2: Actual market volume × Budgeted share × Budgeted DRG 2 proportion × Budgeted DRG 2 contribution margin

or,

DRG 1:	4,000 ×	10% ×	75% ×	$1,000 =	$300,000
+ DRG 2:	4,000 ×	10% ×	25% ×	$7,000 =	700,000
Market size flexible budget contribution margin					$1,000,000

The difference between the original budget contribution margin of $800,000 and the market size flexible budget contribution margin of $1,000,000 is $200,000 favorable (F):

Original budget contribution margin	$ 800,000
– Market size flexible budget contribution margin	– 1,000,000
Market size variance	$ 200,000 F

This variance is simply the result of more patients admitted to area health care organizations and can be referred to as a market size variance.

The Market Share Variance

The next variance that can be calculated is the *market share variance.* This variance is based on the fact that we may not actually realize the percentage of total community admissions that we expect. For instance, suppose that we actually only achieve an 8 percent share of the total number of patients admitted. We can calculate a new contribution margin that we will refer to as the market share flexible budget contribution margin. This amount is the expected total health care organization contribution margin, given the actual share of the market realized and the actual market size. We can calculate the market share flexible budget contribution margin as follows:

	Actual		Actual		Budgeted		Budgeted
DRG 1:	market volume	×	Actual share	×	DRG 1 proportion	×	DRG 1 contribution margin
+ DRG 2:	market volume	×	Actual share	×	DRG 2 proportion	×	DRG 2 contribution margin

or,

DRG 1:	4,000	×	8%	×	75%	×	$1,000	=	$240,000
+ DRG 2:	4,000	×	8%	×	25%	×	$7,000	=	560,000
Market share flexible budget contribution margin									$800,000

The market share variance can then be calculated by comparing the market size flexible bud-

get contribution margin with the market share flexible budget contribution margin:

Market size flexible budget contribution margin	$1,000,000
– Market share flexible budget contribution margin	– 800,000
Market share variance	$ 200,000 U

Apparently, we had a $200,000 unfavorable variance because we did not maintain our share of the total community demand for health care organization services.

Note that in this particular example, the total size of the market expanded; thus, the health care organization would be expected to gain patients and profits. However, the share of the market obtained by the health care organization declined. We did achieve our targeted number of patients. Without analysis such as this, it might not become apparent that, although we had the expected number of patients, we did not share in the benefits of the expanding number of patients. Other health care organizations in the community captured the entire growth in the number of patients. A clear message for our marketing efforts comes forth from the analysis.

The Patient-Mix Variance

Another element in explaining the overall difference between the expected and actual contribution margin is our mix of patients. We may capture an increasing share of an increasing market, but unless we have a favorable mix of patients, profits may suffer.

In this example, we will assume that in actuality, 68.75 percent of our patients were DRG 1, and that 31.25 percent of our patients were DRG 2. In order to calculate a *patient-mix variance,* it is first necessary to establish a patient-mix flexible budget contribution margin, as follows:

	Actual		Actual		Actual		Budgeted
DRG 1:	market volume	×	Actual share	×	DRG 1 proportion	×	DRG 1 contribution margin
+ DRG 2:	market volume	×	Actual share	×	DRG 2 proportion	×	DRG 2 contribution margin

or,

DRG 1:	4,000	×	8%	×	68.75%	×	$1,000	=	$220,000
+DRG 2:	4,000	×	8%	×	31.25%	×	$7,000	=	700,000

Patient-mix flexible budget contribution margin $920,000

This patient-mix flexible budget contribution margin represents the expected contribution margin, given the actual patient mix, our actual share of the market, and the actual market size.

A patient-mix variance can then be calculated by comparing the market share flexible budget contribution margin with the patient-mix flexible budget contribution margin:

Market share flexible budget contribution margin	$800,000
– Patient-mix flexible budget contribution margin	– 920,000
Patient-mix variance	$120,000 F

In this case, the variance is favorable. Why? Our DRG 1 patients yield an expected contribution margin of $1,000 each, whereas our DRG 2 patients yield an expected contribution margin of $7,000 each. Even though we had exactly the same number of patients as expected (the increase in the size of the market was offset by our decreased share), we were better off because we had more of the patients with a higher contribution margin.

The Price Variance

The last of the variances to be calculated relates to the price charged for each patient. Going into a year, we have an expected average reimbursement level for each type of patient. Suppose that the expected price for DRG 1 was $4,000, and variable costs for DRG 1 were expected to be $3,000, yielding a contribution margin of $1,000.

It may be that we expect all DRG 1 patients to pay $4,000. It is more likely, however, that the $4,000 represents a weighted average revenue expected to be received from all payers. Private insurers might pay $5,000, Medicare might pay $4,000, and an HMO might pay a negotiated $3,500.

The purpose of these calculations is to yield useful information for managers to use in making decisions. Therefore, the price focus should be based on average expected receipts, not on gross charges. Given the changes possible in our mix of payers and the rates various payers are willing to pay, at least a part of our shift from budget to actual contribution margin will be resulting from shifts in the realized average price for each DRG.

Suppose in our example that the DRG 1 price stays exactly as expected. However, the DRG 2 average price received rises from $25,000 to $25,900. DRG 2 has an expected variable cost of $18,000. Thus, the DRG 2 contribution margin has risen to $7,900. We can now calculate an actual contribution margin. It should be noted that this actual contribution margin allows for actual prices, actual mix of patients, actual share of total community patients, and actual total community volume of patients. However, it is not a true actual contribution margin, as it is based on budgeted variable costs.

In order to calculate a price variance, it is first necessary to calculate the actual contribution margin (using budgeted variable costs) as follows:

DRG 1:	Actual market volume	×	Actual share	×	Actual DRG 1 proportion	×	Actual DRG 1 contribution margin
+DRG 2:	Actual market volume	×	Actual share	×	Actual DRG 2 proportion	×	Actual DRG 2 contribution margin

or,

DRG 1:	4,000	×	8%	×	68.75%	×	$1,000	=	$ 220,000
+DRG 2:	4,000	×	8%	×	31.25%	×	$7,900	=	790,000

Actual contribution margin $1,010,000

A price variance can then be calculated by comparing the patient-mix flexible budget contribution margin with the actual contribution margin:

Patient-mix flexible budget contribution margin	$ 920,000
– Actual contribution margin	– 1,010,000
Price variance	$ 90,000 F

The variance is favorable, as we would expect, given the increase in the price and contribution margin for DRG 2 patients.

The Total Variance

As variance analysis becomes more detailed to yield more information for managers, it should not change underlying relationships, but rather should merely provide more useful information concerning them. Originally, we noted that the expected contribution margin was $800,000, and the actual contribution margin (calculated using standard or budgeted variable costs) was $1,010,000, generating a favorable variance to be explained of $210,000. How does that compare to the detailed variances discussed?

As can be seen from the calculation below, we have merely identified the components of that variance.

Market size variance	$200,000	F
Market share variance	− 200,000	U
Patient-mix variance	+ 120,000	F
Price variance	+ 90,000	F
Total variance	$210,000	F

However, in subdividing the variance, managers can begin to identify strengths and weaknesses and plan for improved actions. Note that the total favorable variance is the sum of the favorable variances, less the unfavorable variance.

No Market Size Data

The piece of information most difficult to obtain is total market size. Even if estimates can be made based on marketing studies of the total likely demand, it is not at all clear that information will be readily available after the fact on what demand actually turned out to be for the entire community.

Only if admission rates are generally available on a timely basis can the market size variance be determined. Furthermore, if we cannot determine market size, we cannot determine a market share variance either.

On the other hand, we can still measure the patient-mix and the price variances. We can also calculate a volume variance. The volume variance represents the part of the difference in total health care organization contribution margin caused by the difference between the expected and actual number of patients. The volume variance essentially is a combination of the share and size variances.

Our formulas would be revised as follows:

Original Budget Contribution Margin

DRG 1:	Budgeted patient volume	× Budgeted DRG 1 proportion	× Budgeted DRG 1 contribution margin
+ DRG 2:	Budgeted patient volume	× Budgeted DRG 2 proportion	× Budgeted DRG 2 contribution margin

Volume Flexible Budget Contribution Margin

DRG 1:	Actual patient volume	× Budgeted DRG 1 proportion	× Budgeted DRG 1 contribution margin
+ DRG 2:	Actual patient volume	× Budgeted DRG 2 proportion	× Budgeted DRG 2 contribution margin

Patient-Mix Flexible Budget Contribution Margin

DRG 1:	Actual patient volume	× Actual DRG 1 proportion	× Budgeted DRG 1 contribution margin
+ DRG 2:	Actual patient volume	× Actual DRG 2 proportion	× Budgeted DRG 2 contribution margin

Actual Contribution Margin

DRG 1:	Actual patient volume	× Actual DRG 1 proportion	× Actual DRG 1 contribution margin
+ DRG 2:	Actual patient volume	× Actual DRG 2 proportion	× Actual DRG 2 contribution margin

Our calculation of variances would become the following:

The Volume Variance

Original budget contribution margin
− Volume flexible budget contribution margin
─────────────────────────────
  Volume variance

The Patient-Mix Variance

Volume flexible budget contribution margin
− Patient-mix flexible budget contribution margin
─────────────────────────────
  Patient-mix variance

The Price Variance

Patient mix flexible budget contribution margin
− Actual contribution margin
─────────────────────────────
  Price variance

The Total Variance

Volume variance
+ Patient-mix variance
+ Price variance
─────────────────────────────
  Total variance

These revenue variances can be helpful to managers in marketing, controlling the organization, and making a number of decisions about products and services offered.

NOTES

1. J. Demski, *Information Analysis* (Reading, Mass.: Addison-Wesley, 1972), 223–224.
2. S. Moriarity and C.P. Allen, *Cost Accounting,* 3rd ed. (New York: John Wiley & Sons, Inc., 1987), 848.

SUGGESTED READING

Chow, C.W., and K. Haddad. August 1989. Beware of pitfalls when evaluating standard cost variances. *Healthcare Financial Management* 84–86.

Cleverley, W.O. 1989. Cost variance analysis. In *Handbook of Health Care Accounting and Finance,* 2nd. ed., ed. W.O. Cleverley, 145–156. Gaithersburg, Md.: Aspen Publishers, Inc.

Cooper, J.C., and J.D. Suver. February 1992. Variance analysis refines overhead cost control. *Healthcare Financial Management* 40, 42, 46.

Deisenroth, J.K., et al. 1989. Flexible budgeting. In *Handbook of Health Care Accounting and Finance,* 2nd ed., ed. W.O. Cleverley, 247–268. Gaithersburg, Md.: Aspen Publishers, Inc.

Dieter, B. 1987. Flexible budgeting in health care. *Hospital Cost Accounting Advisor* 3, no. 3:1, 7–8.

Finkler, S.A. 1986. Cost accounting for human resources in hospitals. *Hospital Cost Accounting Advisor* 2, no. 5:1–3, 7–8.

_____. 1985. Flexible budget variance analysis extended to patient acuity and DRGs. *Health Care Management Review* 10, no. 4:21–34.

_____. 1990. Control aspects of financial variance analysis. In *Health services management: Readings and commentary,* 4th ed., eds. A. Kovner and D. Neuhauser, 149–166. Ann Arbor, Mich.: Health Administration Press.

_____. 1991. Variance analysis: Part I, extending flexible budget variance analysis to acuity. *Journal of Nursing Administration* 21, no. 7/8:19–25.

_____. 1991. Variance analysis: Part II, the use of computers. *Journal of Nursing Administration* 21, no. 9:9–15.

Horngren, C.T., and G. Foster. 1991. *Cost accounting: A managerial emphasis.* 7th ed. Englewood Cliffs, N.J.: Prentice-Hall.

Lohrmann, G.M. January 1989. Flexible budget system: A practical approach to cost management. *Healthcare Financial Management* 38, 40, 44–47.

Minogue, S., and D.P. Vogel. 1989. A contemporary approach to budget variance analysis: A pharmacy application. *Topics in Hospital Pharmacy Management* 9, no. 2:1–10.

Ramsey, L.P., and R.S. Cantrell. January 1985. Investigating cost variances using control charts. *Healthcare Financial Management* 61–62.

Saliman, S.Y., and W. Hughes. October 1983. DRG payments and net contribution variance analysis. *Healthcare Financial Management* 78–86.

Skantz, T. 1986. Statistical cost control: A tool for financial managers. *Hospital Cost Accounting Advisor* 2, no. 4:1–5.

Suver, J.D., et al. September 1984. Variance analysis: Using standards to predict recognized nurse staffing patterns. *Healthcare Financial Management* 48–50.

EXERCISES

QUESTIONS FOR DISCUSSION

1. If a variance is found to be noncontrollable, is there any need to do anything other than explain its cause?

2. The major problem with traditional variance analysis is that it focuses on trying to assign blame for spending more than the budgeted amount. True or false? Explain.

3. What is a flexible budget?

Note: Solutions to the Exercises can be found in Appendix A.

4. What are price, quantity, and volume variances?

5. Will the price, quantity, and volume variances total to an amount greater than, the same as, or less than the variance using traditional analysis?

6. Not all variances should be investigated. Managers should be selective in deciding when to investigate a variance. True or false? Explain.

7. What are the possible subdivisions of the quantity variance that might provide additional insight into the underlying cause of a variance?

PROBLEMS

1. *Revenue Variances.* Assume that the following information is known about the budget for Kovner Hospital:

Budgeted patient volume:	500
Budgeted patient mix	
DRG 1	50%
DRG 2	30%
DRG 3	20%
Budgeted contribution margin	
DRG 1	$500
DRG 2	200
DRG 3	400

You also know the following actual results:

Actual patient volume:	450
Actual patient mix	
DRG 1	65%
DRG 2	20%
DRG 3	15%
Actual contribution margin	
DRG 1	$475
DRG 2	250
DRG 3	470

Calculate the price, mix, volume, and total variances. Do the price, mix, and volume variances add information to the total variance?

2. Dr. Jones is a surgeon who operates on patients in two different Diagnosis Related Groups, DRG A and DRG B. Dr. Jones has been pressing the hospital for more perks.

He claims we cannot afford to lose him now that he has become so cost-efficient. As evidence of his improved efficiency, he points out that in March, he operated on 13 patients. The total cost of treating the patients was $97,000. In April, he operated on 13 patients. The total cost of treating the patients was $92,700. According to Dr. Jones, he has generated a total cost savings of $4,300. Although Dr. Jones admits that his patient mix did change somewhat from March to April, he is sure the case-mix change was not what accounted for the bulk of the cost decrease for the patients he treated.

Your investigation determines that in March, he treated 5 DRG A patients with an average cost of $4,200 and 8 DRG B patients with an average cost of $9,500. In April he treated 6 DRG A patients and 7 DRG B patients. Costs in April for Dr. Jones' patients were $4,600 for DRG A and $9,300 for DRG B. Although the April cost for DRG A patients had risen, Dr. Jones points out that costs for the higher volume, higher cost DRG B patients had fallen.

Use the physician cost variance approach discussed in Application 9-1 at the end of the chapter to develop a case-mix variance and a cost variance so we can better understand the impact of the changes in Dr. Jones' practice from March to April. What other information would be of interest in this particular case?

3. Statistician's Hospital has decided that variances that are within two standard errors of the budgeted or expected value need not be investigated because they are quite likely to occur simply as a matter of chance. However, if the variance is more than two standard errors, either plus or minus, there is a significant chance that a control problem exists. Investigation is required.

Statistician's has applied this concept quite widely. They examine patient days by DRG. They also examine all line-item cost variances from budget in this manner. Statistician's receives most of its revenues under prospective payment systems. Therefore, control of ancillary usage has become particularly important. They are just beginning to use this approach for control of ancillary usage.

Assume that last year is considered to be a period during which particular effort was made to control ancillary usage. As a result, we are willing to accept last year's results as a reasonable standard of performance. Assume further that last year, there were eight patients in DRG XXX (this unrealistically low number of patients is used to ease your calculations), and that the number of laboratory tests for each of the eight patients in this DRG was as follows:

Patient #	Number of Tests
1	15
2	28
3	21
4	40
5	33
6	29
7	22
8	36

Calculate the standard error based on this test group from last year. Suppose that in the first month of this year, the average number of laboratory tests per patient was 35. Is the resulting deviation from the standard great enough to warrant investigation?

Application 9-1

Physician Cost Variance Analysis under DRGs

*Roger Kropf, PhD, is currently Associate
Professor, Health Policy and Management Program at the
Robert F. Wagner Graduate School of Public Service,
New York University, New York.*

Cost variance analysis can be used to improve management's understanding of how the cost of treating patients admitted by individual physicians is changing over time. It is an alternative to two other common methods of assessing physician behavior with respect to patients of varying case-mix.

The first of these common methods is examination of the costs incurred by the individual patients of each physician. This approach is time consuming and doesn't focus the manager's attention on those physicians whose costs are changing. The second is to start by examining high-cost and/or low-profit DRGs and study only physicians whose patients fall into those DRGs. Because patients in only a few DRGs are examined, the manager may not see the overall direction of the physician's costs, either upwards or downwards.

The cost variance analysis method presented in this article provides information on trends (as well as absolute variance amounts) which is not provided by the other two approaches.

Table 9-1-1 shows the number of cases admitted and the average cost per patient for a physician during January–June and July–De-

cember of 1985. In order to study the effect of case-mix, the data are presented by DRG. For this example, only four DRGs are shown. The method can easily be extended to all DRGs.

The total operating costs incurred in the treatment of patients admitted by this physician dropped by $10,243.99 or approximately 5.5 percent, while the total number of patients treated dropped by 11 percent.

These two percentages do not adequately describe what has occurred, however. The effect of a drop in admissions on costs will depend on whether admissions are reduced in high- or in low-cost DRGs. While total costs are going down, an increase in the use of resources for low-cost DRGs could be masked by decreases in the admission of patients in high-cost DRGs.

The question that needs to be raised is the extent to which the variance in cost between these two periods was due to changes in case-mix (the number of patients in each DRG) and the extent to which it was due to changes in the cost of treating the average patient in each DRG. Other possible causes for the variance will be discussed later in this article.

PHYSICIAN COST VARIANCE

The physician cost variance is the difference in the cost of treating the patients admitted by a

Source: Reprinted from Roger Kropf, "Physician Cost Variance Analysis under DRGs," *Hospital Cost Accounting Advisor,* Vol. 1, No. 12, May 1986, pp. 1, 3–5. Copyright 1986, Aspen Publishers, Inc.

Table 9-1-1 Number of Cases and Operating Cost per Case, R. Smith, MD, 1985

		PRIOR PERIOD January–June					CURRENT PERIOD July–December		
	Cases		Operating Cost Per Case		Total Cost	Cases		Operating Cost Per Case	Total Cost
DRG 1	24	×	4,365.88	=	104,781.12	16	×	4,815.88	= 77,054.08
DRG 2	9	×	4,863.75	=	43,773.75	10	×	5,073.75	= 50,737.50
DRG 3	7	×	2,645.47	=	18,518.29	8	×	2,962.93	= 23,703.44
DRG 4	4	×	4,638.40	=	18,533.60	5	×	4,777.55	= 23,887.75
	44				$185,626.76	39			$175,382.77

	Total Operating Cost
January–June	$185,626.76
July–December	$175,382.77
Increase/(decrease)	($10,243.99)

physician between the current and a prior period. The variance can be expressed in total dollars or as a percent of prior period costs. The physician cost variance in this example is a negative $10,243.99 or 5.5 percent.

In order to interpret the meaning of the variance, it must be broken down into a number of other variances, as shown in Table 9-1-2.

CASE-MIX VARIANCE

This variance summarizes the effect of changes in the number of patients in each DRG. The effect of changes in cost per DRG is removed by using the current cost in both parts of the equation (see equation 1 in Table 9-1-2, as well as Table 9-1-3). The case-mix variance is a negative $25,712.81, which is two and one-half times the physician cost variance and 14 percent of the total operating costs in the prior period.

COST VARIANCE

This variance summarizes the effect of changes in the costs incurred by patients in each DRG. The effect of changes in the volume of patients in each DRG is removed by using the prior volume of patients in both parts of the equation (see equation 2 in Table 9-1-2, as well as Table 9-1-3). The cost variance is a positive

$15,468.82, which is one and one-half times the physician cost variance and 8 percent of the total operating costs in the prior period.

INTERPRETATION

Table 9-1-4 shows a number of cost ratios that are useful in interpreting the meaning of the cost variances.

The analysis shows that the change in case-mix was more important than the change in the cost per DRG in determining the magnitude of the drop in total operating costs. The case-mix variance was 166% of the cost variance and 251% of the physician cost variance.

On the other hand, the cost variance is positive, showing that the costs incurred by the patients admitted by this physician are increasing. If the number of patients admitted by this physician increases in the next period, management may see an increase in total costs.

Admissions may, however, continue to drop, resulting in even lower total costs while the costs incurred in treating the remaining patients continue to rise.

FURTHER ANALYSES

Since managers have a very limited amount of time to examine the reason for variances, es-

Table 9-1-2 Physician Cost Variance Analysis, R. Smith, MD, 1985

Physician cost variance = case-mix variance + cost variance
($10,243.99) =   ($25,712.81)   + $15,468.82

Where
(1) Case-mix variance   =

Σ(Current volume per DRG × current cost per DRG)
Minus
Σ(Prior volume per DRG × current cost per DRG)

Case-mix variance = $175,382.88   – $201,095.58
                    =   ($ 25,712.81)

(2) Cost variance   =

Σ(Prior volume per DRG × current cost per DRG)
Minus
Σ(Prior volume per DRG × prior cost per DRG)

Cost variance   = $201,095.58   – $185,626.76
                   = $ 15,468.82

Table 9-1-3 Calculation of the Case-Mix and Cost Variances

(1) Case-Mix Variance

	Current Volume		Current Cost		Total Cost
DRG 1	16	×	4,815.88	=	77,054.08
DRG 2	10	×	5,073.75	=	50,737.50
DRG 3	8	×	2,962.93	=	23,703.44
DRG 4	5	×	4,777.55	=	23,887.75

Σ(Current Volume × Current Cost) = $175,382.77

	Prior Volume		Current Cost		Total Cost
DRG 1	24	×	4,815.88	=	115,581.12
DRG 2	9	×	5,073.75	=	45,663.75
DRG 3	7	×	2,962.93	=	20,740.51
DRG 4	4	×	4,777.55	=	19,110.20

Σ(Prior Volume × Current Cost) = $201,095.58

Case-Mix Variance = $175,382.77 – $201,095.58
                   = ($25,712.81)

(2) Cost Variance

	Prior Volume		Current Cost		Total Cost
DRG 1	24	×	4,815.88	=	115,581.12
DRG 2	9	×	5,073.75	=	45,663.75
DRG 3	7	×	2,962.93	=	20,740.51
DRG 4	4	×	4,777.55	=	19,110.20

Σ(Prior Volume × Current Cost) = $201,095.58

	Prior Volume		Prior Cost		Total Cost
DRG 1	24	×	4,365.88	=	104,781.12
DRG 2	9	×	4,863.75	=	43,773.75
DRG 3	7	×	2,645.47	=	18,518.29
DRG 4	4	×	4,638.40	=	18,553.60

Σ(Prior Volume × Prior Cost) = $185,626.76

Cost Variance = $201,095.58 – $185,626.76
               = $ 15,468.82

---

tablishing priorities is important. This physician's situation might be examined further if it is part of a continuing trend of both higher costs and lower admissions or if an examination of the net revenues received from the physician's patients shows a significant and negative effect on the hospital's profits.

In addition to looking at the revenues received from this physician's patients, one could analyze the effect of changes in input costs and the volume of inputs consumed on changes in cost per case. The cost variance described in this article includes the effect of changes in both the cost of inputs and the volume of inputs con-

Table 9-1-4 Physician Cost Variance Analysis Cost Ratios

	Ratio
Case-mix variance/prior period operating costs	(14%)
Cost variance/prior period operating costs	8%
Case-mix variance/cost variance	(166%)
Cost variance/case-mix variance	(60%)
Case-mix variance/physician cost variance	251%
Cost variance/physician cost variance	(151%)

sumed. For example, the same number of nursing hours may have been used to treat patients, while nursing wages increased substantially between the two periods. The action required by management obviously differs substantially depending on whether input costs are rising or whether the physician is increasing the quantity of inputs used for a given type of patient.

We have also assumed that the severity of illness of the patients treated has remained constant and had no effect on the resources consumed. The physician may have been treating fewer patients in a DRG, for example, while those patients were sicker and required additional resources. If data are available on severity of illness as well as on the volume of inputs and the cost of inputs consumed by patients in each severity category, this issue can be pursued.[1]

LIMITATIONS

The method described in this article attributes all of the costs incurred by a patient to the physician who admitted the patient to the hospital. A number of other physicians may be responsible for treating the patient during a hospital stay, and the responsibility for ordering services may shift to another physician as the condition of the patient changes. The method is likely to be most useful, therefore, in describing the effect of physician referrals to the hospital, rather than in accurately estimating the effect of physician treatment patterns.

In hospitals where the vast majority of care is ordered by the admitting physician, the physician cost variance analysis suggested will indicate the effect of ordering and practice patterns on hospital costs.

Managers need to examine the changes in costs incurred by physicians. Looking at data on the costs of treating the individual patient is too time consuming. Data aggregated by DRG do not reveal how the behavior of individual physicians is affecting costs.

By carrying out a physician cost variance analysis, managers can gain some understanding of how changes in the costs attributed to specific physicians are related to changes in case-mix and the cost per patient.

NOTE

1. For a discussion of the use of patient acuity or severity in cost variance analysis, see Steven A. Finkler, "Flexible Budget Variance Analysis Extended to Patient Acuity and DRGs," *Health Care Management Review* (Fall, 1985), pp. 21–34.

A Contemporary Approach to Budget Variance Analysis: A Pharmacy Application

Sharon Minogue Holswade, MBA, is currently Vice President of Clinical Services at Robert Wood Johnson University Hospital, New Brunswick, New Jersey.

David P. Vogel, MS, is currently Director of Pharmacy at Robert Wood Johnson University Hospital, New Brunswick, New Jersey.

In most hospitals, the pharmacy department manager routinely evaluates monthly expenses as they compare to budgeted expenses and explains significant variances. This exercise can be either fruitful or frustrating, depending on a number of variables. These variables include the manner in which the budget was created, the availability of substantial detail in support of expense lines, and the knowledge of the pharmacy manager concerning the factors that can cause fluctuations in expense, particularly drug cost.

A number of articles have been written in an attempt to assist pharmacy managers with budget variance analysis. Excellent analyses of factors affecting budget variance have been written by O'Byrne[1] and Buchanan[2] in this journal. Other articles provide helpful insights to the manager relative to the other two variables. Buchanan,[3] Miller,[4] and Williams[5] have suggested thoroughgoing approaches to projecting realistic budgets. Hunt,[6] Nold,[7,8,9] and Mehl[10] have suggested approaches to data collection that help to support and explain variations in expenses during the year. The present authors will

Source: Reprinted from Sharon Minogue and David P. Vogel, "A Contemporary Approach to Budget Variance Analysis: A Pharmacy Application," *Topics in Hospital Pharmacy Management*, Vol. 9, No. 2, August 1989, pp. 1–10. Copyright 1989, Aspen Publishers, Inc.

make some recommendation regarding these variables in the discussion that follows; however, the reader is encouraged to review the articles just cited to supplement our comments and to enhance his or her understanding of budgeting and budget variance analysis.

THE PROBLEM WITH THE TRADITIONAL APPROACH TO VARIANCE ANALYSIS

Until January 1987, monthly budget variance analysis at the Robert Wood Johnson University Hospital (RWJUH), as at many others, resulted in a report comparing actual expenses to budgeted expenses when an individual variance was greater than 5% and more than $1,000 over budget or under budget. The report listed the relevant line items, the amount of the variance, and a brief explanation of the variance.

Explanations were relatively straightforward. For example, some annual or quarterly payments were budgeted monthly, creating wide variances in both directions. Expenses for newly approved positions or market adjustments in salary were not added to the budget, resulting in salary variances. Seasonal availability of pharmacy students as *per diem* employees created wide variances in full-time-equivalent positions (FTEs) and salaries in certain months. An unexpectedly high turnover of pharmacists created variances in the form of advertising expenses.

The most significant pharmacy expense variances, however, were the most difficult to explain. These expenses were drug and IV costs. For variances in these expenses the explanation frequently included some reference to change in volume or activity as a justification. It was very difficult, however, to quantify the change in activity. The use of percentage changes in admissions or patient days as an indicator of volume or activity never seemed to be sufficient to explain the percentage increase in expense. This was true because it is not possible to correlate an admission with the type of pharmacy resources consumed. For example, a 20% increase in admissions relating to maternity might affect the pharmacy budget very little, while a 5% increase in oncology admissions may have a significant budget impact.

This problem with pharmacy variance analysis was common to many departments with significant direct patient care responsibilities. In the traditional approach to hospital budgeting and budget analysis at RWJUH, many departmental activity levels were not integrated in such a way as to correspond to monthly expense levels. Activity reports typically relied on traditional measures such as visits, procedures, and admissions, but this type of measure is not always indicative of the activity experienced by the department. For example, a first visit to a physician may consume one hour of time, while a revisit may consume fifteen minutes. To count these simply as two visits does not reflect the resources consumed to provide these services. Similarly, there is a substantial difference in resource consumption between the preparation and dispensing of one dose of IV chemotherapy versus the preparation and dispensing of a 24-hour supply of oral propranolol.

A CONCEPTUAL CHANGE

In late 1986 it was determined that a new method of variance reporting should be established that would address the explanatory deficiency of the traditional system. The new system would incorporate department-specific workload data that would be weighted to reflect resource consumption and departmental expenses more appropriately. The weighted workload data would be totaled and divided into departmental expenses that vary with activity to establish a unit cost for producing one unit of activity. In theory this number should remain constant, regardless of changes in volume or activity at the departmental level.

The goals of the new system would be to: (1) relate variances in departmental expenses more closely to actual changes in activity; and (2) produce reports that were easy to prepare in a minimum of time and that could be easily read and interpreted by a wide range of individuals, including senior administrators, finance officers, and board members.

The outcome of implementing this concept was a new report entitled the relative unit cost (RUC) report, which would be completed each month by departmental managers and submitted in lieu of the traditional budget variance report. The administration felt that implementation of this report could be made with minimal impact on management time, since the necessary data were already available and the education of staff would not be a restrictive variable.

A different approach to this problem was described by Coarse[11] in 1985. He thoroughly described the concept of flexible budgeting but did not make any reference to its implementation or use in his own institution. He did acknowledge that "its use [in hospitals] is not widespread. This is partly due to its complexity and partly due to lack of understanding of its basic elements by hospital managers, including pharmacy managers."[12] In contrast, the approach implemented at RWJUH is markedly less complex, an attribute that has substantially affected its success and acceptance.

THE RELATIVE UNIT COST REPORT

The RUC report is a one-page cumulative summary of cost and activity data for an entire year. It must be completed and submitted with two supporting documents: a workload statistics report and a RUC variance report. The RUC report (Table 9-2-1) contains two fixed columns with comparative data. One column has the previous year's monthly averages; the other column contains budget data for the current year. A third column for use in variance analysis contains adjusted budget data. The remainder of the columns on the form contain data for each month, as well as a year-to-date (YTD) column.

For the pharmacy department there are only five reportable lines of data in each column: total numbers of orders, total weighted activity units, the ratio of actual activity units to budgeted activity units, the salary cost per activity unit, and the nonsalary cost per activity unit. These five pieces of data can be calculated from two sources: departmental workload statistics and the monthly budget report from the finance department. The RUC report is customized for each department and may contain other relevant lines of data for other departments.

The preparation of the November 1988 RUC report of the pharmacy department will be explained in detail to illustrate how the report is used.

Workload Activity

The first step in the preparation of the monthly RUC report is to collect and total relevant workload statistics. The November 1988 Pharmacy Statistics Report is shown as Table 9-2-2. Statistics are collected only for the six activities shown, which represent over 90% of the department's workload related to drug distribution. There are some activities, most notably clinical activities, for which monthly statistics are not collected. It is important to note that at this point the purpose of the collection of these statistics is to measure relevant changes in activity, not to measure total productivity. Therefore, statistics that were not readily available and those that were not expected to have a significant impact on total weighted units were not collected. This approach is consistent with the project's goals of simplicity and ease of use.

Each activity is then weighted according to its relative consumption of time. The numbers used are modifications of national standards as

reported as an output of PharmaTrend and its precursor productivity monitoring systems.[13,14]

One way in which our statistics and weights differ from PharmaTrend is that new order and refill line items are counted rather than the total number of doses dispensed or charged. A new order or refill order represents one complete dispensing function, irrespective of the number of doses dispensed. Even in the unit dose drug distribution system, doses are dispensed as a 24-hour supply that often contains more than one dose and occasionally more than four doses.

For each activity the number of orders multiplied by its weight equals a number of activity units. The net total of all activity units is the basis for measuring all changes in activity and comparing them to changes in cost.

The total number of statistics is given for both the current year and the same month of the previous year. This comparison shows relevant changes in specific activities that will eventually be reflected as one net change in activity in the RUC report itself. Thus this required appendix to the RUC report becomes an important backup reference document that is easily accessible in case questions arise concerning fluctuations in departmental activity.

In the example (Table 9-2-2) total parenteral nutrition (TPN) orders were significantly lower in November 1988, while chemotherapy orders were significantly higher. Non-IV new orders and refills were relatively higher in 1988, but IV orders were unchanged. The preparation of peritoneal dialysis manifolds is listed only as a current year statistic because it represents a new service initiated in August 1988. While it is appropriate to account for new services in this manner, potential users of this system are cautioned not to add statistics for services that have been provided throughout both reported years, but for which statistics are only now relevant and/or available. Statistics can be added for these activities if the previous year's data are accessible. Alternatively, statistics for these activities can be collected for one year prior to their incorporation into the reporting mechanism. Actual and budgeted costs per activity unit will decrease in both years once these statistics are added; however, this has no relevance to ex-

Table 9-2-1 Relative Unit Cost Report for November 1988

Department	1987 average	1988 budget	Adjusted unit cost	Jan	Feb	Mar	Apr	May	June	July	Aug	Sept	Oct	Nov	Dec	YTD
PHARMACY																
No. of orders	78,993	255,938		84,446	80,672	84,600	78,036	83,372	81,596	85,713	90,141	80,064	85,838	83,301		83,434
Total weighted units	249,209			273,395	256,108	269,465	246,846	265,770	256,786	277,204	288,233	262,303	281,562	271,664		268,121
Ratio of activity to budget	1.09	1.03		1.07	1.00	1.05	0.96	1.04	1.00	1.08	1.13	1.02	1.10	1.06		1.05
Salary																
Cost per activity unit ($)	0.32	0.33	0.39	0.34	0.34	0.35	0.36	0.35	0.38	0.40	0.37	0.39	0.37	0.42		0.37
Nonsalary																
Cost per activity unit ($)	1.21	1.21		1.19	1.22	1.53	1.26	1.34	1.39	1.12	1.39	1.31	1.11	1.24		1.28

Table 9-2-2 Pharmacy Department Statistics for November 1988

Activity	Weight (minutes)	Weighted 1987 volume	1987 activity units	Weighted 1988 volume	1988 activity units
New orders	3.0	25,673	77,020	28,106	84,318
Refill orders	2.0	33, 375	66,750	36,538	73,076
IV admixtures	5.0	17,335	86,675	17,340	86,700
Hyperalimentation (TPN)	20.0	725	14,500	458	9,160
Chemotherapy	20.0	314	6,280	818	16,360
Peritoneal dialysis manifolds	50.0			41	2,050
Total workload units			251,225		271,664

pense analysis. It is still the relative difference between actual and budgeted costs per activity unit from month to month that is important to monitor.

Workload Activity Compared to Budget

The next step in preparation of the monthly report is to transfer the total number of activities (orders) and weighted activity units from the statistics report (Table 9-2-2) to lines 1 and 2 of the November column of the RUC report (Table 9-2-1).

The total number of activity units in November (271,664) is divided by the budgeted monthly activity units (255,938) to produce a ratio of 1.06. (The determination of the budgeted activity units will be described later.) This ratio essentially reports that pharmacy workload was 6% over budget in November.

Salary Cost and Nonsalary Cost per Activity Unit

The total salary expenses ($114,100) and nonsalary expenses ($336,863) for November, as reported by the finance department, were each divided by the number of workload units (271,664) to produce a dollar cost per unit of activity ($0.42 and $1.24, respectively). These two numbers are entered on lines four and five of the RUC report. They are then compared to budgeted standards, and any difference becomes the basis for variance explanations.

There are a number of difficulties with using these gross ratios, but they can be effective indicators of expense-activity relationships in spite of their limitations. Salary expenses are typically step-variable in nature. That is, they remain fixed over a range of activity levels. Expenses are adjusted up a step or down a step by adding or subtracting FTEs if activity routinely exceeds the upper limit or falls below the lower limit of the activity range. As a result, budgeted cost per activity unit for salaries actually reflects a range that extends from a higher cost per activity unit when workload is low and a lower cost per activity unit when workload is high. This fact is frequently used as a valid explanation in the variance analysis.

At RWJUH, drug and IV costs account for 98% of all nonsalary costs in pharmacy. Therefore, these costs were our focus when determining an appropriate method to compare nonsalary costs to activity. The total cost per activity unit does reflect some expenses, such as advertising and travel, that are not workload volume-related and should not change at all with activity. However, these expenses are fixed and contribute so little to the total that their inclusion does not affect any interpretation or evaluation of the numbers.

Actually, on a "micro" level, changes in drug and IV costs are not directly proportional to changes in the activities that are reflected by pharmacy statistics. Changes in IV or non-IV orders can involve products that cost less than $1.00 per order or more than $100.00 per order. On a "macro" basis, however, the authors have found that changes in drug and IV costs are relatively proportional to the net change in activity. At a cost of $1.21 per activity unit, the ingredients for an average 24-hour unit dose supply would cost from $2.24 to $3.36 (weighted at 2 to 3 units per activity); the ingredients of an average IV would cost $6.05 (weighted at 5 units per activity); and the ingredients for an average total parenteral nutrition preparation or chemotherapy preparation would cost $24.20 (weighted at 20 units per activity). Although these numbers are not likely to be absolutely accurate, they are not bad approximations. They do provide a mechanism to account for a substantial portion of the changes in drug cost in relation to activity. The routine collection of detailed drug use data allows detection of the increased use of drugs whose cost substantially exceeds these averages. For example, a marked increase in the use of IV immunoglobulin during 1988 was cited to explain some of the excess of actual cost per activity unit over the budgeted cost per activity unit.

The last step in the preparation of the RUC form itself is to change the figures in the year-to-date column to reflect new averages that include the current month. After the first three or four months of the year, these year-to-date numbers provide a broader perspective on activity and expense trends compared to budget.

Variance Report

The last step in preparing the monthly RUC report is to document the variance analysis on the second supplementary form, the variance report. Exhibit 9-2-1 shows the variance report for November 1988. Budgeted versus actual cost per unit of activity for both salary and nonsalary costs is shown in the left-hand column. The narrative documents actual over-budget dollars but does not go any further if cost per activity unit is not over budget. If that amount is over budget, then further explanations are necessary. Significant increases in non-activity-related expenses, such as advertising or travel expenses, are exceptions and must always be explained.

The finance report, internal pharmacy drug use reports, and other available information are used to investigate increases in cost per unit of activity. The use of drug cost documentation to explain variances has already been mentioned. The pharmacy department maintains detailed monthly drug use data on 98 drug entities (16% of the formulary) that account for 81% of all drug costs. These data have been sufficient to explain all noticeable variances in actual versus budgeted drug expenses.

The finance report (i.e., expense report) can also help to explain significant variances. For example, one of the detailed line entries on the November finance report showed that the cost of sick-time buy-back payments was charged to the department in November. This figure represents an annual expense that was budgeted over the entire year. Thus this information on the finance report was used to explain a salary variance of $0.05 per activity unit in November (see Exhibit 9-2-1).

If some explanations keep appearing each month and represent permanent changes to departmental expenses, the administration may choose to establish an adjusted budget cost reflecting this change. For example, approved but unbudgeted new positions or salary increases may qualify for such an adjustment. Such an adjustment for salary unit cost appears in column 3 of Table 9-2-1. Although the original budget remains unchanged, monthly variance analysis becomes more efficient because only differences between actual cost and adjusted budget cost must be explained.

Budgeting with the RUC Report

The budgeting process takes on a new look when the data provided by the RUC report are used. Budget dollars can be projected more accurately on the basis of activity projections. For example, 1989 budget preparation materials included a projected increase of 3.2% in admissions for 1989. The RUC reports documented increases in pharmacy activity that were proportional to increases in admissions by factors of 1.96 in 1987 and 1.45 in 1988. Based on an av-

Exhibit 9-2-1 Relative Unit Cost Report Variance Analysis

DEPARTMENT: PHARMACY

	November	
	Budget	*Actual*
Salary	0.39	0.42
		−0.05
		0.37
Nonsalary	1.21	1.24
		−0.09
		−0.01
		1.14

Pharmacy activity was 6% over budget in November. Salary expenses are $19,028 over budget. Salary expenses for Nov. include $13,537 in sick-time buy-back expenses; this is equal to 0.05 per activity unit. Salary cost per activity unit is otherwise under budget.

Nonsalary expenses are $29,217 over budget. Of this amount, $19,000 is attributable to the increase in activity. If unbudgeted inflation (@7.6% = 0.09 per activity unit) and unbudgeted inventory control computer expenses (@0.01 per activity unit) are considered, nonsalary costs are under budget.

erage of those two results, the increase in projected 1989 admissions was multiplied by 1.75 to yield an estimated increase in pharmacy activity of 5.6%. As a result, nonsalary costs for 1989 were calculated first by multiplying 1988 activity units by 1.056. This number was then multiplied by the average cost per activity unit for 1988 ($1.27), adjusted to $1.34 to reflect an estimated inflation factor of 5.4%. The result was the total projected nonsalary budget for 1989. If the budget is approved, the RUC report budget column for 1989 should reflect these calculations.

An additional modification to the budget projection should be made if any drug cost increases are anticipated to be significantly higher on a cost-per-dose basis than the averages referred to previously. For example, in 1988 a budget adjustment of $100,000 was added for tissue plasminogen activator (TPA), increasing the cost per unit activity by a factor of 0.03. Similarly, if any major decreases in high-cost drug use are anticipated, an adjustment to the budget projection should be made.

The new salary cost per activity unit will be determined on the basis of the approved number of FTE positions, which may increase, decrease, or remain the same as a result of the budgeting process. The new salary cost per activity unit may also reflect an adjustment for planned salary increases in the year to come.

RESULTS AND CONCLUSIONS

The relative unit cost report took approximately six months to develop and implement. Since its implementation the report has been invaluable in correlating activity to expenses throughout all departments. Monthly variance reports have become more specific and credible. The report has also served as an educational tool. Staff members have an increased understanding of departmental operations in relation to finance, and staff confidence with respect to dealing with finance has grown as a result.

In the pharmacy department for each of the last two years, the report documented an increase in activity that was significantly different from increases as measured by patient days or admissions. Total pharmacy activity units increased by 9.4% from 1986 to 1987, while admissions increased by 4.8% and patient days increased by 6.2%. Similarly, total pharmacy activity units increased by 8.0% from 1987 to 1988, while admissions increased by 5.5% and patient days increased by 5.8%. These data confirm subjective impressions that the increase in volume at RWJUH has been concentrated in highly resource-intensive cases: cardiac surgery, trauma, cardiology, and oncology. Objective documentation of these impressions is invaluable with respect to justification of resources and expenses to the administration.

By utilizing additional available data the system can be refined or expanded as management requires. Productivity monitors can be introduced through the addition of FTE positions or productive hours. Changes in units produced per productive hour or FTE can be an informative workload measure for the department. At RWJUH these indicators are currently being monitored and evaluated for eventual inclusion in the RUC report. Other modifications will be analyzed in an attempt to increase the sophistication of the report without jeopardizing its simplicity, its ease of interpretation, or its contribution to the efficient use of valuable administrative time.

The system described in this article has proven to be a valuable tool for management. Since it correlates relevant departmental data into a simple format, it has provided the management of RWJUH with a financial tool that reflects departmental operations more effectively than did the traditional budget variance reporting system that it replaced.

NOTES

1. A. O'Byrne. "Budget Monitoring: Understanding the Concepts." *Topics in Hospital Pharmacy Management* 3, no. 4 (1984): 33–41.

2. C. Buchanan. "Budget and Financial Reporting." *Topics in Hospital Pharmacy Management* 6, no. 3 (1986): 29–52.

3. C. Buchanan. "Selecting a Method to Forecast Drug Costs." *Topics in Hospital Pharmacy Management* 4, no. 4 (1985): 21–32.

4. R.F. Miller. "Forecasting Drug Costs." *Topics in Hospital Pharmacy Management* 3, no. 4 (1984): 42–48.

5. R.B. Williams. "Preparing the Operating Budget." *American Journal of Hospital Pharmacy* 40 (1983): 2181–2188.

6. M.L. Hunt. "Use of Financial Reports in Managing Pharmacies." *American Journal of Hospital Pharmacy* 41 (1984): 709–715.

7. E.G. Nold. "Developing a Data-Collection System." *American Journal of Hospital Pharmacy* 40 (1983): 1685–89.

8. E.G. Nold. "Financial Analysis." *American Journal of Hospital Pharmacy* 40 (1983): 1975–1979.

9. E.G. Nold. "Developing Reports." *American Journal of Hospital Pharmacy* 40 (1983): 1968–1975.

10. B. Mehl. "Indicators To Control Drug Costs in Hospitals." *American Journal of Hospital Pharmacy* 41 (1984): 667–675.

11. J.F. Coarse. "Flexible Budgeting for Hospital Pharmacists." *Topics in Hospital Pharmacy Management* 4, no. 4 (1985): 9–20.

12. Ibid., 9–10.

13. M.H. Stolar. "Description of an Experimental Hospital Pharmacy Management Information System." *American Journal of Hospital Pharmacy* 40 (1983): 1905–1913.

14. A.L. Wilson. "PHARMIS: A National Pharmacy Workload and Productivity Reporting System." *Topics in Hospital Pharmacy Management* 7, no. 1 (1987): 65–72.

Application 9-3

Statistical Cost Control: A Tool for Financial Managers

Terrance R. Skantz, PhD, is currently Associate Professor of Accounting at Florida State University, Boca Raton, Florida.

The Medicare prospective payment system (PPS) is forcing hospital managers to reexamine their methods of cost control. Since PPS provides the same payment for any case classified in a given diagnosis-related group (DRG), this becomes a natural unit of analysis. In other words, cost control techniques will revolve around each of the 467 DRGs specified by PPS. One can expect that cost accounting techniques will be revised to provide information useful to managers in pinpointing areas that need investigation.[1] Statistical cost control is an excellent candidate for enhancing the success of the financial manager's control of resource utilization.

COST CONTROL AND CRITICAL VARIABLES

It is well recognized that success in any business endeavor depends largely on careful monitoring and controlling of critical variables. For example, in pharmaceutical firms, finding new products (drugs) is critical. Thus, careful monitoring of research, development, and clinical testing is essential.

In cost control situations, the problem is to identify the key variables that trigger cost incurrence. Two critical variables in a hospital setting are (1) patient days and (2) ancillary services. These variables deserve careful monitoring by financial managers. It will be necessary to set standards or targets for these two variables for each DRG. Depending on the volume of cases for a given DRG, weekly or monthly reports comparing actual with standard performance should be prepared. Although this paper focuses on patient days as a critical variable, the same cost control method applies to any factor that can be classified by DRG or any other relevant unit of analysis.

INVESTIGATION OF DEVIATIONS FROM STANDARD

A key question facing financial managers is whether to investigate deviations from the targets or standards. It is costly to conduct investigations. The time of the financial manager and other personnel is a valuable commodity. It will not be cost effective to investigate all departures from standard. Some method of choosing significant deviations is necessary. Three methods

Source: Reprinted from Terrance R. Skantz, "Statistical Cost Control: A Tool for Financial Managers," *Hospital Cost Accounting Advisor,* Vol. 2, No. 4, September 1986, pp. 1–5. Copyright 1986, Aspen Publishers, Inc.

are possible: (l) judgment of the financial manager, (2) an arbitrary rule such as "investigate any deviation in excess of 10 percent from standard," and (3) statistical control, a method based on the statistical behavior of the critical variable for the DRG in question.

Judgment Approach

This method requires the manager to have an intimate knowledge of each DRG. He or she would have to know if a deviation from standard is large enough to justify investigation or whether it arises from a normal situation. It is quite unlikely the manager will have this knowledge, since the DRG classification system is new, and the financial manager will have little prior experience. Indeed, as discussed in a later section, the first step in the application of the statistical cost control method is to determine the range within which the critical variable should fall under acceptable operating conditions.

Arbitrary Rule

This method probably suffers from more drawbacks than the judgment approach. It will be demonstrated later that equal deviations from standard for a critical variable may require different responses for different DRGs. Thus, a single arbitrary rule could be inferior to a judgment approach. Multiple arbitrary trigger points, e.g., 10 percent for some DRGs and 5 percent for others, is simply the judgment approach but with fewer options. Unless there is some prior experience, there is no basis for setting the cutoff points.

Statistical Cost Control

Common sense indicates that different DRGs will exhibit different frequency distributions for the values of the critical variable and that the size of the deviation from standard necessary to trigger an investigation will differ as a result. This is exactly what the statistical method takes

into account. Discussed below are the two steps involved when using this method. First, one must provide a statistical description of the acceptable or "in-control" distribution of the critical variable (length of stay). Second, current results are monitored through a sampling procedure and compared with the in-control distribution in order to decide whether to investigate.

Describing the Acceptable Distribution

As a starting point, the financial manager must describe the acceptable average (or standard) length of stay for each DRG category as well as the acceptable variation around this average. Data from a representative period, possibly the most recent six months, should be used for this phase. It is very important that only properly classified cases be included in the analysis, since the results must be representative of the DRG in question.

Table 9-3-1 demonstrates how one calculates the necessary statistics. The number of cases is small, only for illustration. As shown in equation 1, the mean (or average) length of stay for the five cases is 2.20 days. This mean, denoted $\overline{X}$, is the standard length of stay for this DRG.

Next, a valid measure of acceptable dispersion is needed. For statistical reasons, it is assumed that the typical cost control situation will involve finding the average length of stay for all cases (a sample) during some monitor period and comparing this sample average with the standard length of stay.[2] In these cases, the appropriate measure of dispersion is the standard error of sample means, not the standard deviation of the sample.

The calculation of standard error is shown in two steps.[3] First, the standard deviation is found by subtracting the mean from each case (Table 9-3-1, column c), squaring this difference, and summing these squared deviations (column d). Then, as shown in equation 2, an average of these deviations is found by dividing by one less than the original number of cases. The square root of this average is the standard deviation. Second, as shown in equation 3, the standard error is found by dividing the standard deviation by the square root of the sample size. Notice

Table 9-3-1 Calculation of Mean and Standard Deviation

(a) Patient	(b) (X) Length of Stay	(c) (X − X̄) Deviation from Mean	(d) (X − X̄)²
1	1.5	−.70	.49
2	2.4	+.20	.04
3	3.0	+.80	.64
4	2.3	+.10	.01
5	1.8	−.40	.16
Total	11.0	0	1.34

Equation 1.

Mean $= \bar{X}$

$=$ Sum of Observations/Numbers of Observations

$= 11.0/5$

$= 2.20$

Equation 2.

Standard Deviation $= S$

$= \sqrt{(X - \bar{X})^2 / (\text{Number of Observations} - 1)}$

$= \sqrt{1.34 / (5 - 1)}$

$= .58$

Equation 3.

Standard Error $= s_e$

$=$ Standard Deviation $/ \sqrt{\text{Number of Observations}}$

$= .58 / \sqrt{5}$

$= .259$

---

that during the analysis phase, one might find that the mean and dispersion are simply unacceptable. For the time being, however, we are taking these as measures of acceptable performance.

Table 9-3-2, Part A, provides a more realistic set of statistics for two DRGs. The mean length of stay, 1.376 days for DRG 159 and 3.695 days for DRG 160, is the goal or standard for these DRGs. The standard error is .356 days for DRG 159 and .739 days for DRG 160. The larger the standard error, the more dispersion we can expect for a given DRG. More specifically, the standard error is a measure of expected dispersion in sample averages around the mean length

Table 9-3-2 Statistics for Length of Stay (Patient Days)

		DRG 159	DRG 160
Part A:	Test Period:		
	Mean (Standard), X̄	1.376	3.695
	Standard Error, s_e	.356	.739
Part B:	Monitor-Period:		
	Sample Average	2.090	4.409
	Deviation from Standard	.714	.714

of stay and provides a statistical basis for judging if a deviation from the standard (mean length of stay) is unusual.

Since sample averages are normally distributed,[4] the standard error and the mean length of stay allow us to describe completely the variable's distribution. Figure 9-3-1 illustrates why this is true. The familiar bell-shaped (or normal) distribution has 95.44 percent of the area within two standard errors of the mean. For DRG 159, this implies that approximately 95 percent of all cases require a stay between .664 and 2.088 days from admission to dismissal, or a range of 1.424 days. For DRG 160, however, the range is 2.956 days (2.217 to 5.173). Of course, the area represented by any other range of length of stay is also known from standard statistical tables.

If this average and deviation are acceptable, then it follows that a 20 percent deviation from

DRG 159

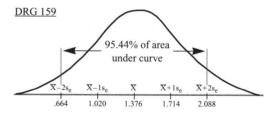

DRG 160

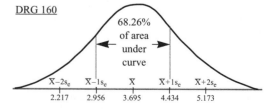

Figure 9-3-1 Distribution of Length of Stay When Conditions Are Under Control

the standard length of stay for DRG 159 (or .275 days) is more likely than a 20 percent deviation for DRG 160 (or .739) days. For DRG 159, a .275 day deviation is equal to 77 percent of one standard error ($.275/.356 = .77$) while a deviation of .739 days for DRG 160 is equal to one standard error.

Comparison of Actual to Standard Performance

The problem facing the financial manager is to decide whether a deviation from standard is due to random events or if there has been a real change in the process of caring for patients. A random deviation is due to the nature of the DRG. (The standard error measures in statistical terms this expected, unalterable dispersion.) On the other hand, an undesirable shift or change in the care process that increases the length of stay should be investigated and corrected.

Knowledge of the mean and standard error for a DRG gives the manager a rational basis for this investigation decision. Consider the case shown in Part B of Table 9-3-2, where there was an equal departure from standard for both DRGs during the monitor period. For DRG 159, the deviation is slightly *more than two* standard errors above the expected value of 1.376. The chance of a deviation this large or larger is about 2.3 percent *if things are running correctly*. This is the percent of the area under the distribution in Figure 9-3-1 to the right of the value 2.088. For DRG 160, the deviation is slightly *less than one* standard error above the expected value. The chance of a deviation this large or larger is approximately 16 percent.

A manager with limited time and resources would probably be wise to investigate DRG 159 and try to correct the problem. Since there is only a 2.3 percent chance that the length of stay was generated by an "in-control" situation, the manager concludes that a real change in the care process has occurred. It could take weeks to determine exactly what is wrong. But the financial manager can proceed with greater confidence that there is a correctable problem and that costs

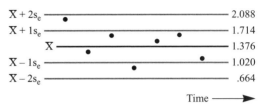

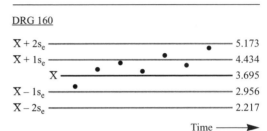

Key: ● Represents monitor period sample averages.

Figure 9-3-2 Cost Control Charts

will be reduced when the source of the deviation is finally discovered.

Another way of viewing this situation is the cost control chart. Figure 9-3-2 provides a chart for DRGs 159 and 160. Notice that the bands around the standard are equal to one standard error. The upper and lower limits are set by the financial manager based on his or her judgment. For example, the policy may be that any observation outside of two standard errors requires an investigation. The fact that there are lower as well as upper limits emphasizes that both negative and positive performance deserves investigation. Positive performance would be encouraged and could lead to a new lower standard and probably a new standard error.

An advantage of the control chart is that it allows the manager to track the performance over time. Trends might be revealed. Truly random deviations should be scattered around the standard. A trend up or down may signify a slow shift in the patient care process. Intervention may be necessary in these cases even though the pre-set limits have not been exceeded. Figure 9-3-2, for example, reveals a random scatter over time for DRG 159 but shows a disturbing upward trend for DRG 160. Notice that even with statistical methods, professional judgment is still critical.

COSTS AND BENEFITS OF ALTERNATIVES

Statistical cost control is a method for rationalizing one aspect of the financial manager's decision process. It provides an excellent basis for serious cost control/monitoring. After time, however, one additional consideration might be included in the analysis—the question of costs and benefits associated with the decision alternatives at hand.

For example, the cost of not investigating deviations (allowing them to continue) is the additional costs associated with excessively long patient stays. The hospital would need to know how costs are affected by patient days. (This illustrates why one chooses a "critical" variable for analysis, i.e., a variable tied closely to cost incurrence.) Thus, a cost-effective investigation policy would tend to investigate relatively small deviations if the cost of serving a patient day is high. A successful investigation would elimi-

nate these high costs. Setting an effective investigation policy based on cost-benefit and statistical considerations is very complex. Most hospitals would probably find the simpler statistical model preferable, since it will be much easier to implement. Once this technique was fully operational, additional cost-benefit factors could be incorporated.

NOTES

1. See Victor C. Messmer, "Standard Cost Accounting: Methods That Can Be Applied to DRG Classifications," *Healthcare Financial Management,* January 1984, pp. 44–48.

2. If the investigation decision is made on a case-by-case basis, certain assumptions about the distribution of the critical variable are necessary. These assumptions are liable to be unrealistic. The use of sample averages rather than case-by-case results avoids these assumptions.

3. Computer packages are readily available to calculate all the statistics discussed in this paper.

4. The size of the sample must be large, around 30 cases, for the normal distribution to hold. Smaller samples use the t-distribution, which approaches a normal distribution as the sample size increases.

10

Management Control

Key Terms Used in This Chapter

Accounting controls; administrative controls; bonding; budgeting; control; critical path; expense center; goal congruence; internal control; investment center; key variables; matrix management; planning; profit center; programming; responsibility center; revenue center; transfer pricing.

Note: Key terms appear in italics when first used in the chapter. All key terms are defined in the Glossary.

INTRODUCTION

Cost accounting is a broad field covering all financial aspects of *planning* and *control*. One subset of cost accounting is the area of *management control systems*. Control is the process of attempting to ensure that desired results are achieved. Management control systems are formalized systems used by an organization's management to ensure that its mission and specific goals are accomplished as effectively and efficiently as possible. This is an area in which health care organizations will likely increase their level of sophistication dramatically in the next five to ten years.

A great deal is written on the topic of planning; relatively less is said about the issue of control. Nevertheless, most organizations do establish control systems. At the very least, these systems generate variance reports that allow managers to determine whether the organization is in control or if some elements of its operations are out of control. Such reports were discussed in the preceding chapter. However, the elements of management control are much broader than analysis of variances. This chapter focuses on the various other elements of management control systems.

There are many elements of a control system designed to keep control over the organization and its results. Checks and balances exist to prevent fraud and embezzlement. Computer security controls exist to prevent alterations or accidental loss of critical information. And, as mentioned above, variance reporting systems exist to report on the organization's ability to keep actual results close to the budget. Much of this focus, however, is on technical details and tends to overlook the most important key to control. According to Horngren and Foster, control "Systems exist primarily to improve the collective decisions within an organization. Because decisions entail human behavior, our emphasis rightly belongs on human rather than technical considerations."[1]

Management control systems comprise a field that includes topics such as systems for collecting accurate financial and cost information, systems to resolve conflict among needs, the programming process and program analysis, budgets, control of operations, measurement of output, performance reporting, and performance evaluation.

If an organization decides to give managers a bonus if their department operates at or below budgeted expenses, that bonus system is a management control system. Its intent is to cause the individuals working for the organization to act so as to maximize the organization's best interests. Management control systems attempt to make what is in the best interests of the organization also be in the best interests of the individuals working for the organization.

IS MANAGEMENT CONTROL A SCIENCE?

The field of financial accounting is based more on an agreed-upon set of rules than a science. How about management control systems? Do they offer more theoretical support and scientific evidence than simply a set of Generally Accepted Accounting Principles? According to two noted authors in the field of management control, Anthony and Young,

> management control principles are tentative, incomplete, inconclusive, vague, sometimes contradictory, and inadequately supported by experimental or other evidence. Some of them will probably turn out to be wrong. Nevertheless, they seem to have sufficient validity so that it is better for managers to take them into account than to ignore them. Most importantly, they seem to work in a considerable number of actual organizations.[2]

Therefore, management control is hardly a science, but there has been enough evidence of the value of such systems that health care managers should learn about them and consider the cases in which they might prove useful.

RESPONSIBILITY CENTER ORGANIZATION FOR MANAGEMENT CONTROL

The focus of management control systems is on influencing the actions of individuals within the organization. We wish to have a system in place that automatically leads people to take the appropriate actions to keep the organization moving toward meeting its objectives. The objectives of the organization should be established through a strategic planning process. Because the focus of management control systems is on the actions of individuals, the starting point in establishing those systems is the *responsibility center.*

The responsibility center is the smallest organizational unit in any organization. It constitutes a group of individuals who have the responsibility for performing some task. Several responsibility centers are aggregated to form larger responsibility centers.

For example, any given nursing unit may be treated as a separate responsibility center. Several nursing units may come together to form a larger responsibility center. Thus, the sixth floor medical/surgical unit may be joined by fifth floor and fourth floor medical/surgical units to form an overall medical/surgical responsibility center. This overall medical/surgical responsibility center is brought together with other nursing responsibility centers to form the nursing department, which is itself a responsibility center. The nursing department is brought together with other departments ultimately to form the entire organization as one responsibility center. In a multi-institutional system, that responsibility center will ultimately be merged with others (see Figure 10-1).

This responsibility center arrangement is obvious and second nature to most health care managers. However, it holds the key to the establishment of all management control systems. Different responsibility centers have the ability to control different types of financial elements.

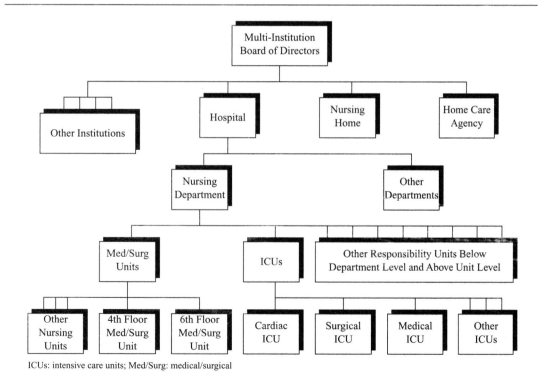

ICUs: intensive care units; Med/Surg: medical/surgical

Figure 10-1 Layers of Responsibility Units

To achieve the best result, we need to develop a set of control systems that assigns responsibility to each center based on the financial elements it is uniquely in a position to control.

In order to accomplish this, responsibility centers are classified as being

- *revenue centers,*
- *expense centers,*
- *profit centers,* and
- *investment centers.*

Revenue centers, in the management control systems sense, make up only a very small number of responsibility units in health care organizations. These revenue centers are responsible primarily for revenue generated rather than costs. The fundraising department of an organization would be a revenue center, because the primary focus in evaluating the department is on how much philanthropic funds are raised.

The most common responsibility unit in an organization is the expense center, more commonly referred to as a cost center or a support cost center. A cost center has an expense budget and is responsible for controlling its costs.

Next most common is the profit center. A profit center is responsible for both revenues and expenses. Health care organizations have referred to profit centers as revenue centers, emphasizing the fact that a specific charge for such centers will appear on patient bills. When one hears the term revenue center in a health care organization, one should assume that the center also has responsibility for its expenses.

If prospective payment systems (PPSs) become the dominant payment form, many of these profit (revenue) centers will likely become simply cost centers. Just as General Motors classifies the steering wheel department and the radiator department as cost centers, so will health care organizations classify laboratory and radiology. If we are not charging the patients on a piecemeal basis for the various individual services they consume, there is little reason to assign a portion of the overall revenue for each patient to individual responsibility centers.

The investment center is a responsibility center that not only controls its revenues and ex-penses, but the level of capital investment as well. Control systems must be established in such a way that those who have control over their investments are also evaluated on the basis of how well those investments fare. Approaches to achieve such evaluation are discussed in Chapter 16.

The mere establishment of cost centers or profit centers is only the starting point in establishing a management control system. For example, sutures are one item that appear under the operating room cost center. However, the manager of the operating room may not be able to control the price paid for sutures. Prices are more likely under the control of the purchasing department. We must develop a set of systems within the responsibility center structure that will allow for proper motivation through proper assignment of responsibility. The development of a management control system for a responsibility unit is discussed in Application 10-1 at the end of this chapter.

THE MANAGEMENT CONTROL PROCESS

In many organizations, management control systems develop informally over time. Even organizations that have not specifically set out to have a management control system are likely to have at least an informal one. Everyone knows where the power is in an organization, and everyone reacts to that power. However, a more formalized, intentional system may well yield more positive results both in terms of outcomes and employee morale. A formal system includes

- programming,
- budgeting,
- operating measurement,
- reporting and evaluation, and
- feedback and correction.

Programming is the process of deciding what major programs the organization will commence in the future. For example, a long-range plan may project the programs to be introduced over the coming five years. This is an important aspect of control, because it provides a framework in which the organizational movement and growth is controlled over that period. Without control over such programs, it would be difficult to ensure that the new programs that are added will move the organization in the direction of its mission and objectives.

Budgeting provides a more specific and detailed level of plan. It is one of the most important control characteristics. If we think of the control mechanism of the human body, there is a budgeted temperature. If we vary from that temperature, the body puts into play a variety of control mechanisms designed to get the system back under control. First, however, you must be able to define what a controlled state is. The body temperature should be 98.6 degrees. The organization should be following its budget. If we veer from the budget, we have a signal that we must investigate, determine if we are out of control, and take measures to reinstate control.

During routine organization operations, activity is measured. Such measurement provides the raw data to report on how the organization is faring. The management control system must ensure that adequate and accurate data are accumulated to meet the needs of management.

The management control process must take the operating data and generate a set of reports. These reports, in turn, must be evaluated. Such reports and evaluation allow for coordination and control of current activities, determination of how good a job individual managers are doing, and determination of how well a program or service is doing. Essentially, this reporting function lets us know if the organization is moving toward its goals and objectives.

The final step in the process is feedback and correction. A management control system has stopped one major step too short if it simply reports and evaluates. The final key is to use the information thus gained to improve future outcomes.

The Human Factor

Management can achieve little in an organization unless the workers of the organization are willing to cooperate and help it to achieve its goals and objectives. To evaluate the efficiency of the workings of the management control system, it is vital to consider whether the health care organization's employees are in fact working in its interests.

The first step is to determine the organization's interests. In order to make that determination, it is necessary to take stock of what the most important goals are. For example, are the most overriding goals for the organization financial, such as making a $3 million profit to allow for future expansion? Or is the most important goal providing an increasing amount of service? Or is the key goal related to increasing the reputation of the organization for patient care?

Obviously, it will be difficult to have an effectively working control system unless we have thought through what is most important for the organization to accomplish. Once the goals are specifically determined, they can be communicated. Once the organization's employees understand what the goals are, they can work toward accomplishing them. The control system can help the organization ensure that they will be accomplished.

This is achieved largely by creating *goal congruence*. Goal congruence means that the goals of the employees and the goals of the health care organization are the same. Inherently, individuals want to do what is in their own best interests. The goals of the organization and its employees normally diverge, at least to some extent. This is true even if people go into health care based on a strong sense of a desire to serve people and to improve the health of society.

Employees want higher salaries, larger offices, fancier furniture, and more staff. The organization wants them to get by with lower salaries, smaller offices, existing furniture, and less staff. Neither side is necessarily wrong in its attitudes or behavior. It is just a fact that human beings will have their own agendas, which are not 100 percent identical with those of their employer.

One can simply say that the employee is being paid, and therefore should do what is in the organization's best interests. On the other hand, one can be more realistic and predict what behavior is likely to occur. If employees are unlikely to do what is in the organization's interests without some additional incentive, then that incentive should be provided, assuming that it is not too costly. The costs of any management control system should always be weighed against its benefits.

The management control system should ensure that goal congruence exists. That is, there should be some systematic approach taken to cause employees to want to accomplish the organization's goals. Usually, this is accomplished by the creation of some system of motivation. Through motivation systems, employees are given incentives to want to accomplish the organization's goals.

Formal vs. Informal Control Systems

Most organizations will establish a network of formalized elements of an overall control system. Additionally, there are informal elements that should not be overlooked because they can have a critical impact on outcomes.

Formal control mechanisms include features such as

- an annual employee review prior to determination of raises,
- specific rules regarding requirements of an individual's job,
- quality review to ensure maintenance of an acceptable level of patient care,
- variance reports with justifications and explanations, and
- checklists to ensure compliance with government regulations.

The various formal controls comprise one means to make sure that goal congruence is accomplished. Suppose the organization needs to comply with certain regulations. By having a checklist that must be completed, the employee has an incentive to make sure that compliance has been achieved. If the checklist is not completed, or is completed inaccurately, the employee's job is being risked.

Informal controls are also important in accomplishing the organization's goals. The fact that most people working in health care organizations have entered the field to help people gives them a common bond or set of values. Patient care quality is a goal that most employees want to achieve. Peer pressure on those providing less than excellent care represents an informal control system.

Informal controls also work through shared loyalties and organizational norms of behavior. Attitude is essential to accomplishing objectives. Thus, money that the organization spends on an employee picnic or on an employee drama group may seem like a fringe benefit. In reality, however, it tends to build the team philosophy that the organization needs in order to have loyal workers.

Furthermore, attitudinal changes can have dramatic long-run impacts. Even as some employees leave and new ones arrive, the new workers learn the organization's "work culture" from the other employees and tend to adhere to it. Once developed, a positive attitude can be self-generating over time.

Merging Goals

Goal congruence is needed to get employees to work toward the organization's goals. The ultimate in goal congruence, however, is not to design incentive systems that get employees to do things they otherwise would just as soon not do. The ultimate accomplishment would be to get the employees to adopt the organization's goals as their own.

It is very important for the organization to work on developing a sense of personal value and achievement from the attainment of the organization's goals. Department managers should want to achieve budget goals because it gives them a personal sense of accomplishment to do so. When the employees of the organization start to feel a personal sense of well-being from meeting some target or goal of the organization's, then the control system is working as efficiently as possible.

How can this merging of goals be accomplished? There are no pat answers. The approaches of team building mentioned earlier are a start. A formal set of mechanisms such as letters or certificates of achievement can help to develop this attitude. A program of management education that clearly imparts to the employees the organization's positive attitude toward them can help. Open lines of communication are critical. The employees must share in all of the good and bad events so that they start to empathize with the organization.

There should be a formal policy, starting at the top and working down through the organization, in which each level of management tries to determine what it could do to make the employees in the next level down associate more closely with the success of the organization. Only by formal attention and by open discussions between levels in the hierarchy can there be progress in achieving a situation in which employees are willing to "go that extra mile" for the organization.

How, then, can we determine if a health care organization has an effectively working management control system? First, we should determine whether the system is based only on technical details or whether it recognizes the central role that human beings play in accomplishing the goals of the organization. Second, we should evaluate the organization's performance with respect to its most important goals.

Are the stated goals being achieved? If not, is it at least partly because employees did not provide the necessary concerted effort to accomplish them? If so, what measures can be taken to generate a greater desire on the part of the employees to accomplish the goals and objectives of the organization? If the goals of the organization are being achieved, then it is highly likely to be the result, at least partly, of an efficiently running management control system. Such systems can be effective at controlling costs, as discussed in Application 10-2.

KEY VARIABLES

One element of a management control system is the identification and monitoring of a set of *key variables*. These variables represent measur-

able factors that can change rapidly and have a significant impact on the results of the organization. Health care financial managers should attempt to establish and monitor a set of such variables.

For example, the most important key variables for hospitals in the past were patient days, census, and occupancy. Given the cost-reimbursement systems of the past, it was vital to keep the hospital full. The more patient days, the greater the contribution to overhead and ultimately to the well-being of the hospital. Obviously, as PPSs account for increasing proportions of a hospital's patients, merely keeping the hospital full is no longer enough. Turnover becomes crucial as well.

The development of a set of key variables requires some thought, as they will not necessarily be developed as part of the financial accounting system of the organization. Many managers mistakenly think of profits or revenues as being key variables. Certainly, they are key measures of how successful the organization has been. However, revenue and profit represent key results rather than key variables.

A management control system should generate information to help managers control ongoing operations. It is preferable to get early warning signals of problems that require attention to response, rather than to wait for the key results to develop.

We need to identify factors that are measurable that may be indicative of developing problems. For example, under PPSs, a crucial key variable is admissions. Each admission leads to an additional fixed revenue payment. If admissions suddenly dip, quick action is needed. We must determine why admissions are down—is it a temporary or permanent situation? Can marketing efforts in a particular area reverse the trend? Should we be laying off personnel in certain areas?

The key variable will not provide the information needed to answer these questions. Knowing that admissions are down does not tell us why they are down. The key variable alerts us to a potential problem that must be investigated. Waiting until year-end would show reduced revenues and possibly large losses. We would undoubtedly find out that admissions were down. The crucial aspect is to discover potential problems as early in their development as possible.

We could probably list 15, 20, or even 30 factors that could vary and might be classified as key variables. However, most health care organizations would be better off monitoring just a few—perhaps five or ten of the most volatile and most important variables.

For example, the average age of affiliated physicians is obviously quite important to the long-term success of a hospital. If the age is creeping up, it means that we are failing to recruit young physicians who can replace older physicians when they retire. Down the road, a series of retirements could have dramatic negative impact on admissions. Thus, as part of the management control system, we would want to monitor average affiliated physician age. However, it does not qualify as a key variable, because it is unlikely to change dramatically in a short period of time. Key variables are items we would want reports on at least monthly, if not more frequently.

On the other hand, a hospital's average length of stay for its patients might well be considered a key variable. If the average length of stay for the hospital's patients in aggregate starts to inch up, the organization may well be headed for trouble.

In fact, under Diagnosis Related Groups (DRGs), each hospital may well have some particular DRGs that make a profit and some that lose money. Some measure of the hospital's case-mix is certainly in order as a key variable.

A simple approach to developing a case-mix key variable measure would be to select 20 or 30 of the highest cost-per-case or highest volume DRGs and to determine which of those are profitable and the percentage of total admissions that those DRGs represent. For example, suppose that the 20 DRGs that account for the most revenue per DRG account for half of all hospital revenues. Suppose further that only 8 of the 20 DRGs are profitable, but those 8 account for 30 percent of both admissions and revenues.

We can establish the percentage of admissions represented by those eight DRGs as a key variable. It is easy to determine frequently what percentage of admissions is represented by those eight. If the percentage starts to fall, we would need to investigate immediately. A variety of more sophisticated case-mix index measures could be developed to serve as key variables if this approach is inadequate.

Finding a good set of key variables takes some thought. The number of applications by prospective students is a key variable for a university. The length of the back-order log is a key variable for manufacturing firms. For a home health agency, the weekly number of visits is a key variable.

For hospitals, some additional potential key variable areas include measure of

- the actions of competitors,
- regulatory changes,
- actions by payers such as employers or insurers,
- technological change,
- the local economy, and
- physician affiliation trends.

As one can see from this list, some of the information desired may come from external sources. Nothing in our accounting system will describe the actions of competitors. However, that information must be generated by the management control system.

If the hospital down the block opens a home health care agency, it is possible that it will have little effect on us. On the other hand, if it opens a health maintenance organization (HMO), eventually (perhaps gradually at first), it will start to siphon hospital admissions away from us via the primary care network established with the HMO.

We should be aware of moves with potentially negative implications as soon as possible. On the other hand, we should also be aware of targets of opportunity. Competitors' actions may lead us to believe an advantageous merger would be possible. Again, key variables should serve as early warning signals for such possibilities.

Regulatory changes and actions by payers are obviously crucially important. We should be trying to monitor not only the actions of these parties, but their plans as well. Thus, a monthly report of key variables should include discussions of new managed care organizations in the planning and any other changes in the works that may affect us down the road.

Technological change is ever present in the medical environment. Sometimes the changes require major capital outlays, and can be carefully monitored in the annual preparation and approval process for the capital budget. On the other hand, some changes are more subtle—for example, occurring only in the operating room. These subtle changes, however, can often affect operating room costs, length of stay, and other hospital costs. Therefore, managers should require reports whenever changes are made that might have a significant impact on costs.

They say everyone talks about the weather, but no one does much about it. Few health care organizations can do much about the local economy, but it is still worth thinking about. When a steel mill closes down, few people leave immediately, and patient volume is not likely to plummet overnight. In fact, it is often the case that health insurance benefits continue for two or three months after such a closing. The impact is felt later—when the benefits run out, and the population starts to move away. However, the adjustment process will probably be a difficult one, and the planning for lower long-term admissions and lack of insurance coverage should start as early as possible. Thus, the local economy can indeed be a crucial key variable.

Earlier, we stated that the average age of affiliated physicians was important but not really a key variable. On the other hand, physician affiliation trends may be important enough to warrant being considered a key variable. If physicians were to suddenly start leaving the hospital, that could be a serious problem. However, other key variables—such as those focusing on admissions, competition, or the local economy—might give us information about the underlying problem.

As you can see, it will take some effort to collect key variable information. We should be judicious in deciding how many and which items constitute key variables. At the same time, it should be apparent that key variables can provide extremely valuable information for the management of a health care organization.

INTERNAL CONTROL SYSTEMS

One aspect of the general area of management control is referred to as *internal control.* Internal control systems have two primary purposes. The first is to provide systems to protect the assets of the organization. The second is to promote efficiency so that resources are used as effectively as possible. This section discusses the basic fundamentals of internal control systems.

In the decade of the 1990s, Certified Public Accountants (CPAs) have stepped up their examination of internal control systems as part of their annual audit because of the passage of the Statement on Auditing Standards (SAS) Number 55. This standard, *Consideration of Internal Control Structure in a Financial Statement Audit,* became effective for all audits of financial statements for periods that began on or after January 1, 1990.

The impact of SAS 55 is that internal controls will be reviewed to a much greater extent than previously, as part of the CPA's audit each year. For example, the accounting firm of Grant Thornton notes in a bulletin to its staff,

> The principal effects of SAS 55 on our practice will be to require documentation of our understanding of a client's control structure (i.e., control environment, accounting system, and control procedures) and our assessments of control risk, regardless of the extent (if any) to which we intend to "rely" on such controls.[3]

There is no doubt that, although this ruling is directly aimed at what CPAs do, it will indirectly have a dramatic impact on the work that organizations must do in the area of internal control. Organization systems will have to improve to pass the increased scrutiny of the outside auditors. Further, organizations will most likely be asked by their auditors to provide substantial information about their internal control systems or else face substantial increases in audit fees (or both). In light of these impacts, it is worthwhile for organizations to review their systems, make improvements where possible, and be especially careful to document all aspects of their control systems to reduce problems and costs during annual audits.

Controls are often referred to as "accounting and administrative" controls. *Accounting controls* (sometimes referred to as "preventive" controls) are *before-the-fact* controls. These controls are sometimes aimed at preventing employee misuse of assets (such as embezzlement and fraud). However, they are also aimed at preventing suboptimal use of resources where no wrongful intent is involved. Because of the before-the-fact nature of accounting controls, they are often viewed as having the greater impact on controlling intentional misuse of resources. For example, a system that requires all narcotics supplies be kept under lock and key and that also requires signatures when narcotics are withdrawn for use is a before-the-fact accounting control.

In contrast, *administrative controls* are those that tend to be *after-the-fact* controls. Administrative controls are often referred to as feedback systems. Such controls allow us to take corrective actions to avoid losses in the future, based on observed problems in the past. Administrative controls are often viewed more with respect to inefficiency than intentional misuse of resources.

For example, a system of standard costs for each DRG would be an accounting control. By having a projection of what it should cost to treat a given type of patient, we have information that helps to prevent unlimited spending. This is before-the-fact information. In contrast, the variance reports, which compare actual results to budgeted results, represent administrative controls.

Accounting and administrative controls work together to ensure that the organization does not incur losses that are avoidable. Control systems should provide procedures and records that ensure that management is in control of key decisions. According to the American Institute of Certified Public Accountants, control should include four key areas:

1. There should be a system of management authorization, and key activities should not be able to occur without such authorization.
2. Once authorization occurs, financial transactions should be recorded in a manner to allow for preparation of financial statements, and to allow for adequate accountability for assets.
3. Access to assets should be limited to those having the authorization of management.
4. Existing assets are compared to assets per the organization's records from time to time and differences are reconciled.[4]

Distinctions between accounting and administrative controls are not critical. The important issue is to have a full range of controls to protect the interests of the organization. Also, it is important for the controls to work together. For example, we could total the patient identification numbers for all patients discharged on a given day or week or month. This total is referred to as a *hash* total. It is simply a control number. There is no inherent need for this total, and it is used only for control. We could then total the patient numbers from all bills issued for patients discharged on that day or week or month. The two totals should agree. If they do not, it is possible that we have failed to bill one or more patients. The focus is not on total billings, but simply on a check to assure that all patients have been billed.

Elements of an Internal Control System

There are a variety of elements that, added together, provide an organization with a good system of internal control. The first critical element is that there be a workable audit trail. Additionally, Horngren has noted that an internal control system should have reliable personnel with clear responsibilities; separation of duties; proper authorization; adequate documents; proper procedures; physical safeguards; *bond-*

ing, vacations, and rotation of duties; independent checks; and cost/benefit analysis.[5] Each of these is discussed in turn.

Audit Trail

The first element in accounting control is to establish a clear audit trail. Each element in the accounting system should be able to be traced back to its source.

The audit trail starts by having a chart of accounts that describes the types of financial transactions that should result in an entry to any particular general ledger account. There should also be documentation of the types of documents that come from outside the system, then exist in the system, and then are used for creating a financial transaction entry. There should also be formal procedures concerning whose authorization is needed for various decisions.

Finally, there should be documentation of how financial transactions flow from the initial entry of the transaction to the ultimate summary report. Any number on a summary report should be able to be traced back to the individual items that constitute the total. This will allow discrepancies to be traced back, ultimately, to the initial recording of the transaction. Of course, it is implicit that examination for discrepancies takes place, causes of the discrepancies are determined, and follow-up action occurs.

Reliable Personnel

There is a schizoid nature to internal control. We work hard to create infallible systems that catch the errors that individuals make. However, ultimately we have to count on individuals to carry out those systems. If we have a process of recording information where human errors commonly occur, internal control can correct for those errors by requiring that a second person review all documents for omissions and other errors. How do we know that the second person is doing his or her job?

If an organization hopes to have accurate records and a system that protects assets, it must be able to trust its employees. They should be both capable and trustworthy. Organizations must walk a tightrope as they hire employees to work throughout the accounting system. If we hire employees who are not qualified, we run the risk of high error rates, which may be very costly. If we hire overqualified employees, we will at a minimum be paying more than we need to for the job. Worse, they may become bored and error-prone.

One important response to the issue of qualified, reliable employees is that supervision is critical. Once we have established procedures that include various checks and balances, we need to observe the working of the system to be sure constantly that the prescribed procedures are in fact being followed. All levels of employees should be held responsible for complying with the appropriate control procedures for their jobs, whether it is a second signature before the issuance of large amounts of cash or correct use of a time-card machine.

Separation of Functions

There is a variety of potential control problems that are solved by appropriate separation of authority in the organization. These problems include theft of accounts receivable receipts, other embezzlements, theft of assets, and hidden inefficiencies.

The first element of separation is that the individual who keeps records on an asset should not have physical or custodial control over that asset. For example, the individual who disburses cash should not be the one who does any bookkeeping. The person who receives payments from self-pay patients should not be the one who updates the patients' receivables records.

It is also important that those who authorize the use of assets not be those who actually disburse those assets. For example, the person who authorizes payments to a vendor for supplies should not also be the person who issues and signs the check for payment. An individual who receives patients' checks should not be the one to authorize patients' accounts as being uncollectable.

Another aspect of separation is that the operations of the organization should be kept separate from the accounting of the organization. For example, the central supply department should not take the inventory in the central supply area for accounting purposes. Accountants from outside the central supply area should perform the count to gain an independent view of the inventory on hand. Similarly, time clocks, if used, should be placed under the supervision of someone not from the department(s) of the employees using the time clock.

Proper Authorization

Having proper authorization for expenditures is one of the prime approaches to keep money from being spent on things that are not deemed appropriate. For example, air travel may be generally authorized only for coach fares. Another example would be that supplies must be acquired through the purchasing department rather than being ordered directly by clinical departments.

It is possible to have two types of authorization. One type is general authorization. General authorization is a standing approval of certain actions. Such authorization is usually written. General authorization may contain limits and prohibitions. The other type of authorization is specific authorization. Specific authorization would require an individual to override the general authorization when exceptions are made.

Adequate Documents

To ensure that we can control all financial transactions, sufficient documentation must be kept. This is becoming a growing problem as the age of computerization progresses. Many organizations do not cut payroll checks for all employees. Some employees have their pay directly deposited into their bank accounts. Third-party health care payers do not want hard-copy bills—they want electronic transfers of information.

Nevertheless, it is important to the organization's system of internal control to have some definite information on what financial events have taken place. The information should be recorded as soon as an event occurs and it should completely record what has occurred. In addi-

tion, it should be as free from potential manipulation as possible.

In the case of payroll checks, hard-copy pay stubs should still be generated for the employees. In the case of computer billing, copies of the billing tape should be maintained, including the supporting documentation for the bills. Whenever possible, documents should be prenumbered and used in consecutive order.

Proper Procedures

Industrial techniques of specialization and routine are widely used in the clinical areas of organizations. There is a certain way to perform many clinical tasks, and we try always to follow that procedure. Accounting should similarly have standard operating procedures. Often these can be codified into a procedures manual.

Doing things by the book may seem rigid to some employees, but it has an important goal. If we follow proper procedures, we are likely to reduce the number of errors. Less time will have to be spent correcting those errors. Furthermore, following specific procedures should result in doing things in an efficient manner. Less time spent doing various activities will mean that money is saved.

By the same token, the "book" should not be stagnant. Accounting controls and procedures should themselves be subject to review and updating. The goal of the control system is to save the organization money by being prudent and by being cost-effective. Over time, we may be able to find ways to accomplish our desired control more efficiently. The objections most people have to "doing it by the book" arise when the book does not make sense. That usually means that certain procedures have become outdated.

In the past decade, there has been a growing focus on total quality management (TQM) and continuous quality improvement (CQI). Essentially TQM and CQI call on the organization to control operations more efficiently, getting things done correctly the first time instead of having to expend resources correcting errors. TQM and CQI are modern manifestations of the need to exercise management control throughout the process of generating and providing goods and services. Do it by the book, and keep the book constantly up to date. They may be old-fashioned, but they are two good approaches to ensuring the achievement of TQM and CQI. TQM and CQI are discussed further in Chapter 18.

Physical Safeguards

Physical safeguards are obvious controls that are too often underused. Cash and blank checks should obviously be kept locked when not in use. Back-up copies of computer records should be maintained in a separate location and should be updated frequently. Controls over the disbursement of inventory should be used to protect it.

Nevertheless, all organizations fall into bad habits. Unfortunately, a review of all physical safeguards usually takes place only after a major loss. A review of compliance with the organization's physical safeguards certainly should be undertaken at least annually.

Bonding, Vacations, and Rotation of Duties

Bonding of employees against embezzlement and fraud is vital to help protect the organization against large losses. However, such insurance is not adequate by itself. Often it will pay only for losses above a certain level. Additionally, proof of losses is difficult, and proof of the party responsible is even more difficult. Bonding is a good administrative control. Nevertheless, once again, administrative controls work best when combined with accounting controls.

What preventive controls go hand-in-hand with the bonding of employees? One approach is mandated vacations and rotation of staff. Many types of embezzlement require constant supervision by the embezzler. If money is being stolen from the accounts-receivable cash stream, checks received later are often used to cover the cash that has been taken. In turn, those checks will have to be covered at a later date. Similar issues can arise on the payables side.

By requiring vacations, we move another employee into each role periodically. That provides an opportunity for discrepancies to be uncovered. Similarly, a formal rotation system establishes the fact that no employee will be doing exactly the same job year after year. Even rotating employees from handling a task for the patients whose name falls in the first half of the alphabet to handling the same task for those whose name is in the second half provides a degree of control. Further, these controls serve not only to discover problems, but to prevent them as well.

It has been shown that temptation levels and embezzlements rise when the employee feels that the system cannot catch the theft. If employees know that they must take a vacation, and if they know that they will be rotated out of the job periodically, there is a greater expectation of getting caught, and therefore a lower rate of actual commissions of crimes.

Independent Check

We have noted at several points that the control system should not be stagnant. We should be reviewing and evaluating the system. This review should try to find ways to improve the reliability of the controls and to reduce their cost. These reviews should be undertaken by internal auditors who work for the organization but do not work on a regular basis with the departments they are reviewing. It is important to use internal employees for the review because they are likely to have a good, in-depth understanding of the operations of the organization.

Outside independent auditors should also be reviewing the control system. They have the benefit of experience from reviewing many other control systems. This can help them offer suggestions for improvement. They also have the benefit of not having been involved in the design of the control system in place. That allows them to see flaws in the system that someone very close to it would probably not notice.

Organizations should demand substantial comments on their internal control system from the independent auditor. These comments should aid the organization in improving its system and ultimately in saving more money than the increased audit costs.

Cost–Benefit Analysis

Systems can become quite elaborate. The more careful we are to ensure that our system catches all problems, the more it costs. We must bear in mind that we want our control systems to be cost-effective. We should not spend more on the systems than they are worth. We should also be aware that no matter how careful we are with our control systems, fraud and embezzlements can still take place, especially if several employees collude.

Horngren sums up this issue well:

> No framework for internal control is perfect in the sense that it can prevent some shrewd individual from "beating the system" either by outright embezzlement or by producing inaccurate records. The task is not total prevention of fraud, nor is it implementation of operating perfection; rather the task is designing a cost-effective tool that will help achieve efficient operations and reduce temptation.[6]

Legal Considerations Concerning Internal Control

Often organization managers focus on internal control as a tool of efficiency. By having adequate systems, we can avoid waste and provide care to patients at a lower cost. This is certainly a vital aspect of internal control. However, legislators are less concerned with efficiency of organizations than they are with prevention of abuses.

In an attempt to reduce abuses in firms, the Foreign Corrupt Practices Act (FCPA) was passed in the 1970s. The act, poorly named, relates to all public companies. It requires maintenance of a system of internal controls and maintenance of accurate accounting records. It has been noted that "The biggest impact of the FCPA has been the mandatory documentation of the evaluation of internal control by management."[7] In other words, it is incumbent upon management to review its system, be explicit in the cost–benefit tradeoffs made that limit the system, and evaluate the extent to which the internal control system works.

TRANSFER PRICING

In industry, one of the most difficult management control problems relates to *transfer pricing*. Transfer prices are the amounts charged to one responsibility center for goods or services acquired from another responsibility center in the same organization. Determining the amount to be allocated from one cost center to another has definite motivational impacts that require formalized management control.

For example, suppose there is no housekeeping charge, or one fixed housekeeping charge to various departments, regardless of their consumption of the services of the housekeeping department. Managers will have an incentive to overconsume the services of the housekeeping department because the cost of additional services is zero. The manager consuming the service is unrealistically appraising the cost of the extra service because there is no extra cost to the user department.

On the other hand, if departments can charge each other whatever they would like, that also may be unfair, especially if a manager must purchase the service internally. For instance, suppose that all reproduction (photocopying, printing, etc.) must be done within the organization. A manager who can find an outside source that is less expensive could rightfully object to such a price.

The general principle of management control with respect to transfer prices is to attempt to use market prices when they are available. When they are not available, managers should generally be charged an annual share of the fixed costs of the service department plus the variable costs for the services consumed. In that way, incremental services can be purchased at their incremental cost to the organization. This will generally cause managers to make wise resource allocation decisions. A more detailed discussion of transfer pricing is contained in Applications 10-3 and 10-4.

MANAGEMENT CONTROL OF PROJECTS

Most discussions of management control focus on continuing operations. One less discussed but quite important area is management control of projects. A project tends to be a one-shot occurrence rather than a continuing operation. As a result, projects are often a disruption and, to a great extent, an added burden for a manager without any relief from routine activities. Additionally, the management of a project requires substantially different focus and approaches than the management of daily activities. Consequently, it is worthwhile to consider specifically some aspects of project management.

This section focuses on some aspects of why project control is different from control of routine operations and on the organization of the entity managing the project. Then it addresses the management control process, specifically the planning process; implementation of the project; and final evaluation of the project.

Why Projects Are Different from Routine Operations

Anthony and colleagues define a project as "a set of activities intended to accomplish a specified end result, of sufficient importance to be of interest to management. The project ends when that result has been attained or, in some cases when the attempt is abandoned."[8] The most common types of special projects in organizations are major facilities modifications, ranging from modernizing a patient waiting area to constructing an all-new facility to replace an 80-year-old building.

To some extent, controlling a project is easier than controlling day-in and day-out activities because of the existence of an explicit, clear-cut objective. In routine activities, organization managers are balancing organizational financial well-being, patient well-being, and employee morale all at the same time. Different objectives create conflict, and it is difficult to steer a steady course when different people in the system have substantially differing personal goals.

Projects tend to avoid those problems to some degree. Although it is still important to maintain quality (often construction quality, rather than direct patient care quality), financial control (to complete the project within a budget), and employee morale (to make sure the project is completed satisfactorily), the bottom line is still very clearly defined. A project almost always has a determinable objective and completion point. The focus of completing the project rarely falls from view, and the manager simply must determine how best to get to that completion point.

Of course, getting there is not all that simple. The work to be done to complete the project successfully is not standardized; the work has peaks and slow periods, there is a greater degree of uncertainty than in routine operations, and developing a project team that functions as a unit is a major difficulty.

Standardization of Tasks

The work performed to get to the completion of the project is almost by definition not the type of work the organization's employees perform on a routine, day-in and day-out basis. Therefore, the work is less standardized than most work that goes on in the organization setting. As unique as each patient in an organization might be, there is a clear organization, with various individuals having clearly defined job duties.

When organization employees start to get involved in facilities planning, for example, the mere fact that they currently use existing facilities gives them little basis for really designing new facilities. In fact, even construction workers brought in from the outside to perform much of the actual work are unlikely to work in the same standardized fashion organizations generally expect from their own employees. Because every project tends to be somewhat different, it is difficult to set work standards. A ratio of three nursing hours per patient day in a particular unit may have a much greater degree of reliability than do the work requirements on a project.

As a result, as the work is planned, it is necessary to anticipate a greater possibility of variation from expectations and, therefore, possible cost overruns. Yet, the fact that the type of work needed to complete a project is out of the ordinary, nonroutine, and, therefore, not standardized is just one of the problems in controlling projects. Another major issue is the fact that most projects tend to have peaks and valleys in required work effort.

Peaks and Valleys

Projects, especially those that require construction, tend to be difficult to manage partly because they do not tend to occur at a smooth pace throughout the project. There tends to be a flurry of activity when the project is first proposed and planning begins. However, that flurry of activity requires substantial time effort from only a few organization managers. As the planning process gets more and more detailed, the staff to handle the work must be increased. During the construction phase, a great influx of workers enter the organization, but the impact of dislocations on existing personnel cannot be overlooked without creating serious problems in the organization's continuing operations. Part of managing a project includes efforts to make sure that the requirements for managing ongoing operations do not change substantially.

Uncertainties

The biggest headache in project management generally tends to surround the issue of uncertainties. "If everything goes according to plan" is one of the most common phrases used in the early stages of project management, whereas "everything went according to plan" is one of the least heard phrases at the end of a project. "Expect the unexpected" is a requirement for project management, and a often a way for managers to try to avoid ulcers.

No matter how intelligent or competent an organization manager is, there is no substitute for experience. Managers must accept that if their jobs relate only to routine operations, they will not have the experience with special projects to anticipate the types of obstacles that will occur. Even if the organization has a manager whose main function is to move from special project to special project, there are elements of projects that cannot be accurately determined in advance.

For example, when the workers begin to add a sub-basement for the new lithotriptor, will the digging process reveal sand or bedrock? Will the supplier of key materials have a strike that will throw the entire project off schedule? Will a materials component expected to save time and money prove unsuitable during installation, resulting in the loss of time and money? Will the weather be particularly bad at a point when outside work is necessary?

Certainly, we can anticipate that problems will arise and build slack into the process. Project managers should consider not only the project completion date if everything goes according to plan. A crucial aspect coming out of the uncertain nature of the process is to consider the impact if various things go wrong. The most critical junctures, where a day or a week lost will create substantial setbacks for the project, are the ones where the most effort is then needed to develop fall-back alternatives in advance, in case something goes wrong.

Project Team Relationships

Frequently, a project team is formed that includes both organization employees and outsiders. Often, this creates conflict over issues such as who is in charge and what the responsibilities are for each involved individual. Furthermore, when working with unfamiliar people, we lack the knowledge we have from working with people over a period of time. Different individuals are motivated by different things and have different strengths.

Organization of the Project

A variety of approaches can be taken in forming the basic organizational approach to the project. The best approach for any given organization will depend to a great extent on the specifics of both the project and the personnel currently available in the organization.

One approach is to have the entire project performed by current organization personnel. Alternatively, an outside contractor can be hired and given full responsibility. Some combined effort between internal and outside personnel is common. On some occasions, an entirely new organization may be formed for the specific purpose of managing the project.

When projects are carried out by an internal team, it is common practice to form a *matrix management* structure for controlling the process. When the project is primarily run by an outside contractor, that contractor will likely have its own management control system. However, controlling contractual relationships raises its own set of problems. We first consider the matrix management issue and then discuss relationships with contractors.

Problems of Matrix Structure

The nature of a matrix structure is an organizational relationship in which a manager must draw upon a variety of organization personnel who do not directly report to him or her. That is, personnel from other responsibility centers report to the project director during the project as well as to the manager heading their permanent responsibility center. In order to coordinate a project, someone must be in charge of it. Inherently, this requires the matrix approach. Obviously, however, whenever someone must report to two different supervisors with two totally different objectives, conflict arises.

To some extent, matrixing occurs in most organizations. It is not uncommon for there to be several different vested interests within an organization tugging on one manager for a share of that manager's limited resources. Product-line management of health care services has made matrix management common in many health care organizations. Anthony and colleagues describe the situation of matrixing in project management "as one in which managers responsible for end products obtain a *substantial fraction* of the resources needed to do their jobs from other responsibility centers."[9]

The problem that arises because individuals are called upon to be responsible to two different bosses is not insignificant. For the project manager, it is a special problem because the project will come to an end, and then the various individuals involved will revert to having to answer to only one boss. When conflicts arise, the project manager is generally in the more difficult position because the individuals from other responsibility centers realize they will have to live with their direct department head long after the project is over.

To make matters more difficult, the role of the project manager not only encompasses planning, but also coordination and problem solving. Coordination of various individuals coming from different parts of the organization is a complex task. The fact that much of the contact between the project officer and these individuals comes when problems are arising can create an atmosphere of tension.

One solution to these problems used in some organizations is the reassignment of individuals from their own responsibility center to the project team for the duration of the project. This eliminates much of the conflict arising from having two different bosses or from being involved in solving the project manager's problems. Once reassigned, people are more apt to treat the problems as being their own. The problem with this approach, of course, is the loss of the various individuals from their normal activities for the duration of the project.

Relationships with Contractors

Even if a decision is made to have almost all work done by one outside contractor, there will still need to be an organizational liaison between the organization and the contractor. The nature of that relationship depends largely on whether the contractual agreement calls for payment based on a fixed-fee or a cost-based amount. Clearly, the incentives for the contractor, and therefore the management control exercised by the organization, must differ substantially depending on which of these two types of contracts is in place.

Fixed-fee contracts obviously put the organization in a position of less risk. Many of the uncertainties surrounding the project become less significant if the contractor, rather than the organization, bears the risk. Such an arrangement may be particularly useful if the contractor, from his or her experience on similar projects, has a much better perception of the likely uncertainties and their implications than the organization has. On the other hand, once a fixed-fee contract has been signed, the contractor has a strong incentive to provide the bare minimum product that will be accepted. Quality control by the organization takes on far more importance than in a cost-based contract, in which the contractor can pass along the cost of a higher quality job.

Thus, in a fixed-contract situation, it is quite important for the organization to be able, in advance, to specify clearly the exact job that it wants done. The organization must be able to draw up (perhaps with the help of independent outside architects and engineers) detailed specifications, to ascertain whether the specifications are being met, and to determine as the project progresses whether the described specifications will actually meet the organization's needs. Even if the contract is based on a fixed amount, it should be noted that if the organization decides to make changes as the work progresses, the contract will be renegotiated and the actual final cost of the project will rise.

Cost-based contracts place the organization at much greater risk. However, if the specifications for the project cannot be clearly defined, or if the contractor cannot predict with sufficient reliability the outcome of some uncertainties, a cost-based contract may be necessary. While the contractor might be willing to offer a fixed-fee contract, there may be built in such a substantial amount to protect the contractor from losses due to uncertainties that the organization is better off taking the risk themselves. The cost-based contract has the advantage that changes made during the process do not require renegotiation of the entire contract as they would with a fixed-fee contract.

Regardless of the type of contract to be used, the organization must assure itself of the capabilities of the contractor to perform the work. The best contract in the world will not make up for the long-range problems associated with a poor job.

Planning, Execution, and Evaluation

A project tends to be a one-shot occurrence rather than a continuing operation. As a result, projects are often a disruption for a manager, and to a great extent an added burden, without any relief from routine activities. Additionally, the management of a project requires substantially different focus and approaches than does management of daily activities.

Planning a Project

Before getting far along with a project, managers must accept the fact that few projects turn out anything like the original plan. It is hoped the final result will be better than the original plan, but in any case, it will likely be substantially different. As a result, managers should focus on planning as a process, rather than development of one specific plan. An anticipated degree of flexibility is a necessity.

As a result, care must be exercised not to define all the specific details of the project at too early a point. Anthony and colleagues suggest that

> Schedules, resource requirements, and budgets [be] prepared as close to the inception of work on the project as is feasible. If they are prepared earlier than is necessary, last-minute changes in the project specifications, newly acquired information about the nature of the work to be done, or more recent estimates of unit costs may require that the work be redone, with a consequent waste of some of the earlier effort.[10]

In planning for a project, the first step is to specify clearly the organizational relationships. A great deal of time and effort is also required to delineate the expected time required for completing each aspect of the project. Based on those relationships, we can develop the control systems that will be used. Finally, costs must be estimated.

Establishing Organizational Relationships

Management control is an area of managerial or cost accounting in which human behavior is far more important than the budgeted numbers. Without individuals working toward the interest of the organization, little can be accomplished. Projects represent a particular organizational problem because the relationships tend to be relatively short term and because, frequently, the relationships are not made explicitly clear.

Thus, one of the most important features required in order to be able to control a project is the establishment of clear lines of authority and responsibility. Furthermore, the level of autonomy for each manager should be specified to the degree possible so that each one knows the types of decisions he or she can make independently, as opposed to having to seek prior approval.

Checks and balances should be built into the organizational structure from the beginning of the project. There should be thought prior to beginning the project as to who will inspect the quality of the job and review the project costs as they are incurred. All parties should explicitly acknowledge the role of those individuals, so that they do not feel that an outside snooper, with no business in being around, is looking over people's shoulders.

Conflict is inherent in projects, for a variety of reasons. Careful planning of organizational relationships in advance can help to keep this conflict within a reasonable level.

Time Management

Many details must be specified for the actual project to be accomplished. However, aside from the industrial engineering department of the organization, most of the organization's managers will not have to be too finely involved in many of the technical aspects. Nevertheless, control of the time aspects of the project is crucial and is one of the key management control issues in the entire process.

Projects often result in dislocation of departments or patients. In some cases, units are closed down, with a resulting substantial, albeit temporary, loss in revenue. Any deviations in the completion of tasks can result in substantial, costly delays in project completion. In an environment in which many things are done stat, such delays can present a frustrating obstacle.

To help manage the time aspects of projects, several techniques are available. The two most commonly discussed in the operations literature are the program evaluation and review technique (PERT) and the critical path method (CPM). The approach taken by these two methods essentially is to lay out all of the tasks that must be undertaken and attempt to find possible bottlenecks in the process.

Usually in a project, a number of things can be done simultaneously. However, somewhere along the way, certain parts of the project must be completed before other parts can begin. These methods allow predetermination of those spots, so that planning can be employed to minimize delays at those points.

In working with methods such as PERT and CPM, commonly referred to as network analysis models, a diagram is generally prepared. On the diagram, lines are drawn indicating the work that must be done. Several activities may begin at the same time independently of each other. These activities would be represented by separate lines emanating from the starting point (see Figure 10-2).

On the diagram are points indicating the completion of various subtasks. (See Figure 10-3.) The points are often referred to as milestones. The line that connects one milestone to another represents the activities that must be undertaken to reach that milestone, and the time period re-

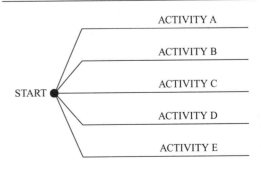

Figure 10-2 Project Activities. *Source:* Reprinted from *Hospital Cost Accounting Advisor,* Vol. 2, No. 8, p. 7, Aspen Publishers, Inc., © 1987.

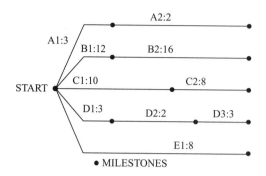

Figure 10-3 Project Milestones. *Source:* Reprinted from *Hospital Cost Accounting Advisor,* Vol. 2, No. 8, p. 7, Aspen Publishers, Inc., © 1987.

quired for each activity is also indicated on the diagram. For example, Step D1 takes 3 days and must precede Steps D2 and D3, which take 2 days and 3 days, respectively.

At some point, several sets of independent activities must all be completed before the next activity can begin. At that point, those separate lines come together (Figure 10-4). If the activities represented by one of the lines coming together have required 28 days (Activities B1 and B2 in Figure 10-4), while the other activities joining at the end of B2 require fewer days (Activities C and D in Figure 10-4), then the 28-day line becomes the critical factor.

A day lost on the C or D line will not hold up the project. However, a day lost on Activity B will directly delay the entire project. The difference between the 28 days for the critical activity and the amount of days required for each other activity is called the "slack" for the other activities.

The critical activities, referred to as the *critical path,* are often indicated in a bold line to draw attention to the importance of that activity (Figure 10-5). A number of software packages exist for determining the critical path in projects too complex to be charted and analyzed by hand.

Management control of the critical path has obvious implications. Several days lost in the critical path holds up the entire project and can be quite costly. In fact, attention should be paid to possible ways to shorten the critical path and thereby reduce overall time for the entire project.

Without the critical path, managers risk spending time trying to shorten activities that would have little impact on the overall project, while ignoring the really crucial activities. Note that the crucial activities may not be those that seem to be the most important elements of the project. To be crucial, they need simply be the activities that create bottlenecks that slow the entire process. Similarly, it rarely pays to incur the cost of speeding up areas that have slack, but it might be worthwhile to make efforts, even at an extra cost, to speed up the critical path. CPM and PERT are discussed in greater detail in Chapter 14.

Control Systems

Organization project control requires frequent reporting. Unlike routine operations where

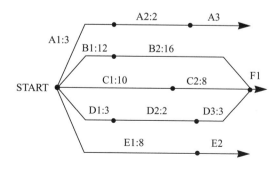

Figure 10-4 Interdependent Activities. *Source:* Reprinted from *Hospital Cost Accounting Advisor,* Vol. 2, No. 8, p. 7, Aspen Publishers, Inc., © 1987.

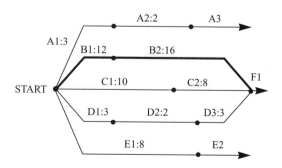

Figure 10-5 Critical Path. *Source:* Reprinted from *Hospital Cost Accounting Advisor,* Vol. 2, No. 8, p. 7, Aspen Publishers, Inc., © 1987.

monthly, or perhaps even quarterly, reports of results are adequate for control, events that need specific management attention can happen rather quickly. The project can get out of control in weeks or even days if the organization does not develop a set of control systems to provide reports frequently.

Are resources arriving on time? If not, are they resources that relate to areas that have slack, or are they for a critical path activity? Are overruns occurring on a particular activity? Why? Can we avoid additional overruns in that area by making some kind of basic change in approach or design?

To be able to answer questions such as these, it is vital to have a variety of management reports. In order to get information quickly, we frequently will have to do without fully costed information. Thus, it may be more valuable to know simply the amount of lumber used than it would be to know its cost if we have to wait longer to get that information.

Designing the types of reports that will be issued and deciding on their frequency are key elements of the planning process for a project. For ongoing operations, many reports are developed as the need arises. With projects, the flexibility to add needed reports is certainly valuable, but to the extent the reports needed can be anticipated, our control process will be considerably stronger.

Cost Management Planning

One of the most difficult aspects of management control for projects is control of costs. Organization managers are conditioned from working on fairly predictable events, despite the inherent uniqueness of each patient. In aggregate, we can predict the cost of a given volume and case-mix of patients. Furthermore, if the volume increases, driving up costs, in many cases the increased volume is accompanied by increased revenues. Certainly, there is room for improvement in these estimates for day-to-day organization operations, and the movement to PPSs has served to push us toward greater control of resources used for a given volume and case-mix. However, with projects, the uncertainties play an even greater role.

To a great extent, organization managers really have no choice but to rely on the experience of the contractor they select. As discussed earlier, the work to be done is less standardized, and the uncertainties are greater. These elements combine to make prediction, and therefore control of costs, more difficult.

In fact, not only must we deal with the unknown costs of certain anticipated events, we must deal with the unknown costs of events that are unanticipated. As Anthony and colleagues point out with regard to what they call *unknown unknowns*, "Their actual costs may range from zero, if none of them actually occur, up to any amount whatsoever. There is no definable upper limit. The most the estimator can do is to include a contingency allowance for these cost elements."[11]

Controlling the Project Work

If the project has been well planned, control actions needed during the actual work will be minimal. Management control is needed for intervention to the degree necessary to move the various individuals involved toward the ultimate outcome.

As with management of routine operations, what is needed during the execution of the project basically is a good word to those doing a good job and additional direction to those doing a sub-par job. The control systems established during the planning stage should generate a sufficient flow of information to allow managers to be able to spot any problem areas as they arise.

If the problems are greater than can be handled with additional direction to the individuals involved, the lines of authority already developed become crucial. Someone must be in a position to take charge and make the determination of what must be done to put the project back on track.

The speed with which problems are detected often dictates the amount of corrective action required and the cost of that corrective action. As a result, the evaluation process is vital, not so much for providing information for an after-the-fact post-mortem, but for providing project managers with the information they need to make decisions and take actions during project implementation.

Evaluation

In order to evaluate performance, it is necessary to compare actual results against some standard. However, projects are often, by their very nature, nonstandardized. Nevertheless, during the planning stage, costs will have been estimated, as will the number of hours of work and pounds of raw materials. Furthermore, the critical path part of the planning process will have provided a number of milestones. Thus, we must evaluate the project's process not only in terms of resource consumption, but along time dimensions as well.

To the extent that the performance analysis is developed to assess the quality of the performance of individuals associated with the project, it is important to make sure that the reports segregate those things that are controllable from those that are not. One of the elements of such separation is to compare actual results to some flexible budget measure. That is, actual costs should always be compared to what it should have cost for what was actually done, as opposed to being compared to the cost originally budgeted.

NOTES

1. C.T. Horngren and G. Foster, *Cost Accounting: A Managerial Emphasis*, 6th ed. (Englewood Cliffs, N.J.: Prentice-Hall, Inc., 1987), 373–374.
2. R.N. Anthony and D.W. Young, *Management Control in Nonprofit Organizations*, 3rd ed. (Homewood, Ill.: Irwin Press, 1984), 3.

3. Grant Thornton, *Accounting and Auditing Bulletin 90-21* (May 21, 1990), 1.
4. Auditing Standards Executive Committee, American Institute of Certified Public Accountants, *Statement on Auditing Standards No. 1—Codification of Auditing Standards and Procedures* (New York: American Institute of Certified Public Accountants, 1973), 20.
5. Horngren and Foster, *Cost Accounting: A Managerial Emphasis*, 919–922.
6. *Ibid.*, p. 922.
7. *Ibid.*, p. 915.
8. R. Anthony, et al., *Management Control Systems*, 5th ed. (Homewood, Ill.: Irwin Press, 1984), 794.
9. *Ibid.*, p. 799.
10. *Ibid.*, p. 804.
11. *Ibid.*, p. 810.

SUGGESTED READING

Allcorn, S., and J.R. Gardner. 1989. Internal auditing services. In *Handbook of health care accounting and finance*, 2nd ed., ed. W.O. Cleverley, 373–406. Gaithersburg, Md.: Aspen Publishers, Inc.

Anthony, R.N., and D.W. Young. 1988. *Management control in nonprofit organizations*, 4th ed.. Homewood, Ill.: Irwin Press.

Dodd, E.S. 1988. A quantum leap in hospital responsibility reporting, *Hospital Cost Accounting Advisor* 4, no. 3: 1–5.

Eccles, R.G. 1985. *The transfer pricing problem.* Lexington, Mass.: Lexington Books, D.C. Heath and Company.

Finkler, S.A. 1988. Management control systems: An overview. *Hospital Cost Accounting Advisor* 1, no. 5:1, 6–8.

Grazier, K. 1986. Cost accounting for hospital-owned HMOs. *Hospital Cost Accounting Advisor* 1, no. 10:1–5.

Jaspan, N. and W. Nagel. 1989. *Loss prevention.* In *Handbook of health care accounting and finance*, 2nd ed., ed. W.O. Cleverley, 407–440. Gaithersburg, Md.: Aspen Publishers, Inc.

Ross, G.H. November 1990. Revolution in management control. *Management Accounting*, 23–27.

Young, D.W. 1984. *Financial control in health care: A managerial perspective.* Homewood, Ill.: Dow Jones-Irwin.

EXERCISES

QUESTIONS FOR DISCUSSION

1. Is management control a clear-cut area based on generally accepted principles or one that relies to a greater extent on common sense and flexibility?

2. How are responsibility centers classified? What is the goal of such classification?

Note: Solutions to the Exercises can be found in Appendix A.

3. What is the primary focus of management control systems?
4. Give an example of a formal and an informal management control.
5. Give three examples of key variables for an emergency department.
6. What are the goals of an internal control system?
7. What are the elements of an internal control system?

PROBLEM

1. One year ago, University Hospital and nearby Women's Hospital merged. As part of the merger, University Hospital eliminated its small maternity service, and Women's Hospital eliminated most of its internal laboratory. The two hospitals are both owned by one parent organization, yet they remain distinct profit centers, with an "each tub on its own bottom" philosophy.

   A problem recently arose when Women's Hospital demanded a price reduction for the laboratory work associated with an amniocentesis. This procedure is performed at Women's on a regular basis, but after the merger, the laboratory work for it has been performed at University.

   However, Women's had recently found that an independent laboratory would do the work for $250, as compared with the

$300 University was charging. Although the total dollars involved were not substantial (Women's only had about 300 amniocenteses per year), all agreed that an important policy issue was involved and that resolution should be sought.

   A joint oversight committee of the two hospitals found that the direct incremental costs of performing the amniocenteses were $200 in labor and supplies. In addition, University was charging $60 for overhead that would be incurred whether or not the amniocentesis laboratory tests were done at University, and $40 for profit. It was also found that Women's was currently making a $70 profit on the entire procedure but could raise that profit by $50 if it could get the laboratory work done for $50 less.

   How much would the transfer price be under

   • full charges,
   • variable costs,
   • market price, and
   • negotiated price?

   How much profit does each hospital make under each alternative? How much do the combined hospitals make under each of the above alternatives? What would happen if Women's purchased from an outside laboratory for $250?

Application 10-1

Developing a Planning and Control System for a Responsibility Unit

Steven A. Finkler, PhD, CPA

As hospitals diversify more and more, they are creating a wide variety of new responsibility units. The basic conditions which existed many years ago have changed. As a result, the systems in place for controlling the operations of routine hospital departments may not be the most appropriate systems for controlling all responsibility units. This article discusses some of the key issues to be considered in designing control systems for such units.

The role of a planning and control system is to help the manager responsible for the system to make appropriate plans for that unit as a part of the whole, and to control operations in such a way as to keep as closely to an approved plan as possible. A well-developed system should be able to generate better plans and decisions as well as to improve managerial actions during the year. Such a system should help the unit and its manager act in the best interests of the organization.

According to Dermer, a planning and control system should "(l) arouse the managers so that they are motivated to contribute to the organization's mission; (2) guide the appropriate behavior by constraining or influencing them as

required; (3) help them accomplish the task requirements by either drawing attention to or helping them solve problems of planning, decision making, and controlling their sphere of responsibility; (4) provide a fair basis for evaluation; and (5) develop in them the capacity to learn and to do more. And, if the process is to be adaptative, feedback from the key variables measured must provide the input for system adaptation and evolution." [Jerry Dermer, *Management Planning and Control Systems,* Homewood, Ill.: Irwin, Inc., 1977, p. 176.]

Dermer's approach to achieve those goals for a planning and control system is based upon a series of factors that should be considered by the system's designer:

- the strategic mission of the organization
- the expectations for the responsibility unit
- the causal factors that influence success
- the key variables for the unit
- a normative system which can plan for and control the key variables
- the system gap
- organizational constraints and resources
- implementation
- evaluation based on feedback and redesign

Each of these factors will be discussed.

Source: Reprinted from Steven A. Finkler, "Developing a Planning and Control System for a Responsibility Unit," *Hospital Cost Accounting Advisor,* Vol. 2, No. 12, May 1987, pp. 1, 6–7. Copyright 1987, Aspen Publishers, Inc.

Obviously, the hospital's mission must be the starting point. Perhaps one of the key management weaknesses in hospitals is that personnel are promoted from clinical positions in a responsibility unit to management positions without hearing a discussion of the hospital's mission. It is often taken for granted that they know the mission; yet a clinician's view of the obligations, responsibilities, and goals of the organization may differ substantially from the perception of the hospital's board and top management.

A difficulty in designing a control system around the hospital's mission is that the stated mission of the hospital may well not be in terms of specific quantifiable measures. However, since hospitals tend to measure their success in quantifiable terms—revenue growth, profits, patients treated, and so on, the measurable goals used in your hospital to evaluate its overall success should be considered in designing the system of each individual unit within the hospital.

This leads into the issue of understanding the expectations the hospital has for the specific responsibility unit under consideration. In order to design a system to control the behavior of a unit in a manner that the hospital will find desirable, it is first necessary to determine exactly what behavior the hospital would find desirable. Is the unit supposed to be making a profit? Is it supposed to be capturing a growing share of the market? Is it supposed to generate high levels of patient satisfaction? Obviously the objectives will vary substantially from unit to unit. A new venture may be aimed at making profits. On the other hand, an admissions department will never generate a profit, so we must find other measures of the adequacy of its performance.

The next step in the design process is to determine the causal factors that influence the success of the unit. Causal factors are the elements which impact on a key result we hope to accomplish. For some units, dollars spent on advertising result in increased revenues and increased profits. Thus, the advertising budget would be a causal factor. But we could certainly think of responsibility centers where advertising would have little direct impact on the results of the unit.

The causal variables are often financial in nature—advertising, pay rates, bonuses; but often they are not directly financial. For example, a participatory system for a unit may increase employee job satisfaction to the point of lower turnover, resulting in lower costs. Thus issues such as the participatory setup are relevant financial management concerns, not because they are inherently financial, but because they ultimately impact on the hospital's costs of operation.

Nor do we always maximize a causal variable. For example, the amount of labor input may have a causal affect on quality, and quality may affect our reputation, which in turn affects admissions. Yet there will be a limit on the amount of labor we use, as a point of diminishing returns is reached, with the extra inputs costing more than the various benefits they generate.

Once we have a perspective on what the hospital is trying to accomplish, and what it would like a specific unit to accomplish, the causal variables can be used to establish a set of key variables for the unit. Key variables (discussed at length in *Hospital Cost Accounting Advisor,* Vol. 1, No. 6) are the most important of the causal variables. It is these variables which require planning and the highest levels of control.

The key variables are those which are measurable, which indicate critical elements in the unit's functioning, and which should be monitored to allow quick action to correct an out-of-control situation. There is some controversy over whether variables must be controllable to fit into the key variable category, but in many cases they need not be. For example, patient days and acuity are often not controllable by a nursing unit. However, they may be critical for staffing. If both patient days and acuity are falling, a nurse manager should be taking actions to reduce staffing and the associated costs. Thus, a control system would need to generate information about these variables on an extremely current basis.

As one can see, however, the focus of designing a system for a unit is first to determine the types of information that would be most useful for that unit, rather than simply supplying all units with generic information of varying levels of value to different units.

A normative system which can plan for and control the key variables represents an ideal. It is effectively the ideal system that would ensure available information about the key variables, perfect management to act in response to the information, and appropriate resources to carry out the system without glitches.

In reality, however, there will be a system gap, and it is quite important to recognize this in the system planning stage. The system gap is the difference between the ideal system and what is currently available. The difference between what currently exists and the normative ideal should be carefully evaluated. Only in that way can we move as close as possible to the ideal.

The movement toward the ideal is accomplished by considering organizational constraints and resources and redefining the system in light of them. In other words, a gap exists, and we need to see the impediments to removing the gap, as well as the resources available to us. The best possible control system, given the limitations of our organization, can be developed only if we establish an ideal system and back away from it, but only as much as is absolutely necessary.

Even the ideal system will be of little value to the unit and ultimately to the hospital unless it is implemented. The system as designed needs to have specific steps for implementation clearly laid out. Giving a system to a unit manager for implementation, without a detailed specific implementation plan, will probably result in key features of the plan never being implemented. The system will not work well as a control system, and the system itself, rather than the way it has been implemented, will be blamed. Therefore, it is vital that careful planning in developing a system not stop one step short. An implementation plan is essential to gain the benefits of the system design.

The final element in a planning and control system is feedback. Evaluation of how a system is working and redesign of the system are best done fairly soon after implementation. As time goes by, the system becomes an accepted part of life, whether it works well or poorly. The success of the system is vital in many respects. First of all, obviously, we want the system to work in the unit in which it has been installed. If it is not working properly when installed, this should be promptly corrected so that the unit can function in a controlled manner. Secondly, we want to evaluate the success of the planners. Systems to control the hospital's operations are crucial, and should be planned by people who can design and carry out a successful system. Thirdly, we want to learn from our mistakes and plan future unit control systems better. Without a review of the success of our systems as we install them, we will simply repeat our mistakes over and over.

Cost Control Systems

Steven A. Finkler, PhD, CPA

All hospitals need to control costs. To help organize for such control, cost control systems can be invaluable. Barfield, Raiborn, and Dalton define a cost control system as "a logical structure of formal and/or informal activities designed to analyze and evaluate how well expenditures were managed during a period."[1] Such a system requires a specific management effort—first, to put it into place and then to monitor costs.

THE THREE STAGES OF COST CONTROL

There are three principal focal points for a cost control system: control before expenditures are made; control during the process of making an expenditure; and control after the expenditure has occurred. We can think of these three elements in terms of

- planning
- monitoring
- feedback

Source: Reprinted from Steven A. Finkler, "Cost Control Systems," *Hospital Cost Management and Accounting,* Vol. 3, No. 11, February 1992, pp. 1–5. Copyright 1992, Aspen Publishers, Inc.

Planning: Before-the-Fact Control

Before-the-fact control entails the planning process. Its focus is on prevention of problems, rather than diagnosis or cure. In making plans for a hospital for the coming period of time it is essential that managers focus specifically on the issue of cost control.

A focus on cost control means more than simply producing the smallest possible budget. If budget reduction is achieved by fiat—simply declaring that spending is reduced by 5 percent or 10 percent—the potential of cost control will probably not be achieved. It is more likely that there will be cost overruns.

Cost control must come about by management effort to determine places where one can reasonably spend less money. The item of expenditure that is being reduced must be identified, and the reasoning behind the assumption that the organization can live without that spending must be clear. That is why before-the-fact cost control efforts should begin before the annual budget process.

These cost control efforts should take place when managers can take some time to reflect on the way that services are provided, and can carefully assess the impacts of changes in operations. Budget time is a hectic period when new volume and patient mix information is often just translated into a new budget based on constant assumptions about the way that care is provided.

Before-the-fact planning for control of costs should not be limited to a focus on operations and budget preparation. It also requires specific input in the form of policies and specified objectives. In order to have managers make reasoned decisions about where costs can be cut and where they cannot, or even more pertinently, where they must be cut, managers must have specific organizational guidance. That guidance comes in the form of specific, well-communicated objectives, and specific formal policies. Such objectives and policies may be both quantitative and qualitative in nature.

Monitoring: Control During the Expenditure Process

All costs should be monitored as they take place. Hospitals tend to rely too heavily at times on variance reports, which are not generated until well after a result occurs. It is the job of managers to be aware of problems as they arise, and to take corrective action. In the majority of cases, by the time a significant controllable variance is reported on a management report, its cause should already have been corrected.

Managers must know that this is a direct part of their responsibility. In hospitals, with so many clinical managers, the primary focus is on the delivery of patient care. As a result, unfavorable budget variances are often dealt with only when necessary—certainly after the fact.

Hospitals need to train their management team that ongoing control will minimize unfavorable variances, and in the long run reduce the amount of effort needed, rather than increasing it. Putting a process back in control as soon as it slips out of control is easier than dealing with it after a long time period has elapsed. The result of such ongoing management is to ultimately make the managers' jobs easier, while saving the hospital resources.

Feedback: After-the-Fact Control

After-the-fact control relates to both the use of variance reports to quickly identify any problems that managers were unaware of and did not act to correct as they occurred. This form of control is also vital to the improvement of future plans and results. It constitutes the critical element of feedback.

In addition to being useful for controlling current expenditures, after-the-fact control forms the main basis for responsibility accounting. Managers are held accountable by a comparison of their expected results with those that actually occurred.

THE ROLE OF HUMAN BEINGS IN COST CONTROL SYSTEMS

It is apparent that cost control systems cannot work independently of the hospital's people. It will take changes in human behavior to make cost control a functioning, ongoing part of a hospital's management process. Barfield, Raiborn, and Dalton refer to this as a need for cost consciousness. In their words,

> Cost consciousness refers to a companywide attitude about the topics of cost understanding, cost containment, cost avoidance, and cost reduction. Individual employees, with similar goals and objectives, collectively compose the organization. The ways in which costs can be controlled by an organization inherently consider the set of attitudes and efforts of the individual employees of that organization.[2]

It is readily apparent that some of the "soft" areas of managing an organization are in fact essential. The development of team spirit and an atmosphere of community become essential if one is to create the attitudes needed to control costs.

There is no way to measure the financial benefits of a hospital employees' picnic. Nor is there any direct measure of the payback for dollars spent on most management development programs. However, there is a clear need for the hospital to design a set of programs that will in-still in managers an understanding of the impor-tance of cost control, and a desire to work for the organization to control costs.

The remainder of this article focuses on the concepts of cost understanding, cost contain-ment, cost avoidance, and cost reduction.

COST UNDERSTANDING

In order to be able to control costs, managers must be able to understand them. Specifically, a major concern is whether managers have a good understanding of what costs are controllable, and what costs are not controllable, and of the things that are likely to cause the actual costs in-curred to differ from expectations.

The most obvious causes of variations be-tween a planned result and an actual result are changes in the work performed. If there are more patients, or sicker patients, or a different mix of the types of patients, that will impact on the cost of providing care. This assumes that some costs are variable, which is certainly the case. Hospitals should attempt to introduce flex-ible budgets that account for the volume of pa-tients at a minimum. Over time hospitals should be attempting to enhance their systems by al-lowing them to flex for the type and acuity of patients, as well as number of patients.

In addition there are other factors that Bar-field, Raiborn, and Dalton indicate can impact on an understanding of why costs might differ from expectations. These include cost changes as a result of unexpected inflation, the impact of technology, changes in supply and demand, changes in competition, changes due to season-ality, and changes in quantities purchased.

At this juncture, virtually all hospitals antici-pate and plan for inflation. However, few are able to accurately prognosticate the exact im-pact of inflation for an organization or its de-partments. To the degree that inflation differs from expectations, it will be a culprit in skewing results away from plans. Of course, the most ob-vious and significant inflationary impact is if salary increases are granted that differ from those expected when budgets were prepared.

Hospitals are among the organizations most significantly impacted by technology change. To some extent this can be anticipated and planned for. On the other hand, some changes are so dramatic and rapid that they distort the results for the current period as compared to the plan. Managers should develop an attitude of examining each element of new technology to determine if it can in some way reduce costs. Often technology is simply a cost add-on, while the existence of the technology might allow for revisions in operating procedures that would al-low for cost savings.

Supply and demand are economic concepts that certainly do affect hospitals. Prices charged for care may often not move in direct relation to the laws of supply and demand. Often, however, the prices the hospital pays for the things it ac-quires do change in such proportion. This is seen clearly in the cost of hospital workers. In some parts of the nation the worst of the nursing shortage has passed. In other areas there has been and continues to be a shortage of all health workers. Changes in the supply of workers, for better or worse, can have a dramatic impact on actual costs.

The health care industry has been growing in-creasingly competitive. Hospitals must contend not only with price pressure from HMOs and PPOs, but also with competition from clinics and free-standing surgery centers. Changes in competition should be anticipated to the extent possible. However, often there are unexpected surprises, and these may require a response from the hospital. Even if the hospital chooses not to respond, the actions of the competitor may have an impact on the volume or costs of the hospital.

Seasonality is a problem that hospitals are fa-miliar with and tend to plan for. Hospitals are adept at knowing how many and what types of patients are likely to arrive at different times of the year. Are they equally adept at having main-tenance done on equipment when it is relatively likely to be less needed? Are there formal schedules to take advantage of purchases that may be cheaper at certain times of the year? Seasonality presents a definite opportunity for cost control if managers understand its nature, and how it can impact on costs.

Quantity purchasing presents the opportunity to gain price discounts. Most hospitals will formally consider that in doing their inventory planning. But plans do go awry when something is needed on a rush basis. In those cases, given the life and death nature of hospitals, immediate, high-priced orders are often placed. Such events are likely to occur. Does the hospital have a policy regarding how large an order should be made when a rush order is placed? If the rush order includes only the specific needed item, it adds one additional purchase. If the rush order can be combined with the next scheduled normal purchase, it may only move up the date of an order, rather than adding an extra one.

The concept is that by thinking about control of costs, one can start to develop additional specific areas where costs can be controlled. In order to do that, managers must take the time to understand costs, and their behavior, to the greatest possible extent.

COST CONTAINMENT

The concept of cost containment is that increases in costs over time are constrained to the greatest degree possible. It should become a clear mission in each department to focus on each element of cost, and to plan on how the cost of that item can be prevented from increasing over time, or kept to the minimum possible increase.

There is often a presumption that if inflation is 5 percent, it is only fair and reasonable to allow budgets to rise by that amount. Such presumptions are responsible for unneeded increases in costs. Many costs of a hospital are fixed. For a relatively new building, the depreciation cost for the building itself is unlikely to increase. A presumption of a 5 percent hospital-wide cost increase would be unwarranted. Similarly, if the hospital has outstanding a substantial amount of long-term debt at a fixed interest rate, those costs would not automatically increase each year.

The same logic holds true within departments. The fact that most costs may go up each year does not justify an assumption that all costs will rise. By granting across-the-board inflation increases, the organization is allowing each department to find some ways to expand their overall consumption of resources, without explicit justification.

On the contrary, some costs might be expected to decline each year. A manager's need for an administrative library may decline after the first few years in which a library is initially built. A department that allows a certain amount per employee for attending seminars may find that at some point it is cheaper to bring speakers to the hospital, rather than sending staff to meetings. Thus, overall training costs might be expected to hold steady or decline at some point.

Competition at times creates difficult situations for hospitals. At other times, however, it can create advantageous situations. Competition among hospital suppliers can lead to cost reductions, as price wars break out among the suppliers. Often the hospital can only take advantage of such competition by periodically pricing-out alternative suppliers.

As with understanding costs, the constraint of costs requires managers to allocate time to think about the issue of cost constraint. Managers must attack this problem at a time of the year when they can review each element of their operations and fully understand why some costs do rise over time, and why some costs might not have to rise over time.

COST AVOIDANCE

While cost containment focuses on stemming the increase in costs, cost avoidance requires managers to innovatively find ways to totally avoid spending money on some things. This is harder than simply identifying things that should not go up in cost. It requires the absolute elimination of spending on certain proposed items.

The only way to accomplish cost avoidance is with a critical review of every proposed expenditure, and a requirement that managers be able to justify the benefit received from each and every new expenditure. Not only should one be able to justify the proposed expenditure, but also to explain that there is no adequate, less expensive alternative.

Once a cost is added to a department, it becomes very difficult to eliminate. An enhancement which is nice, but which the hospital has survived for years without, becomes an inviolate essential once it has been added. Since cost reduction is the most difficult aspect of cost control, it is best to avoid costs in the first place until there is a truly pressing reason why the hospital must incur them.

COST REDUCTION

As noted above, cost reduction is probably the most difficult aspect of cost control. It is easily accepted by most managers that they must understand the behavior of costs. Cost containment—restraining the increase in costs—is something that all managers realize they must face. Cost avoidance is unpleasant, but every manager has had resource requests denied. Cost reduction, however, asks the managers of the hospital to actually find ways to make do with fewer resources.

How can a department use fewer hours of staff time per patient? How can it absolutely reduce the amount of electricity used? Is there a way to save water by shifting to restricted flow shower heads?

Cost reduction often focuses on personnel. Can the organization get by with fewer people? In most manufacturing concerns, there is a fairly direct engineered relationship between inputs and outputs. It takes just so much labor to build a certain type of machine. Hospitals are faced by a much greater challenge. There are no clearly defined appropriate amounts of labor needed for patient care.

Yet that does not justify long-time assumed relationships in terms of required personnel. As the practice of medicine keeps changing over time, there must be a continuing reassessment

of how to do things differently, better, and at less cost.

One of the most difficult aspects of cost control is being tough-minded. In organizations such as hospitals, especially, it is attitude that often determines which costs cannot be avoided and which can be. On the other hand, being overly tough-minded can result in deteriorating morale. As discussed earlier, the human element is critical to the cost control equation. Cost cutting is not ruthlessness. Rather it is rational behavior in a world of competition and limited resources. Progress must constantly be made.

Managers should be trained to perceive the need for such control of costs. Unless a unified commitment from managers is made for a cost control system, attempts at cost containment, cost avoidance, and especially cost reduction are doomed to fail.

THE ROLE OF MANAGEMENT

The issue of cost control systems should make clear to every manager that it takes a lot of time to manage well. Managers can only manage efficiently if they allocate their scarcest commodity, time, carefully.

The role of management is not to do the routine, or repetitive. Managers' greatest contribution is in the area of making decisions, and doing the out-of-the-ordinary. Time must be devoted to determining how to change the current equilibrium, rather than how to maintain it.

In order for a cost control approach to be successful, managers clearly must devote a lot of time to examining, questioning, justifying, and challenging how and why money is spent in their department. One of the most difficult challenges faced by any hospital is to convince their managers to develop an approach to management that allows enough time for these activities, which require thought.

Changing the status quo is difficult. It is much easier to simply sign vacation approvals, and review purchase requisitions, than to critically review the ways things have always been done. One must force oneself to set aside the time to take on that difficult process. But it is essential to do this for significant cost control gains, and hospitals must convey that essential nature to all of their managers.

NOTES

1. J. Barfield, C. Raiborn, and M. Dalton, *Cost Accounting: Traditions and Innovations,* West Publishing Company, New York, 1991, p. 523.
2. *Ibid.*

Application 10-3

Competitive Pricing Models
for Intra-Hospital Services

*James D. Suver, DBA, CMA, FHFMA, is currently
Professor of Health and Public Administration at
the University of Kentucky, Lexington, Kentucky.*

The increased emphasis on *bottom line* results of health care providers is forcing managers to consider internal profit center concepts to improve performance. An internal profit center approach encourages managers to maximize the difference between revenues and expenses for individual departments. This approach is generally effective for services sold outside the hospital. However, dysfunctional results can occur when services are provided between hospital profit centers. What happens, for example, when a lab sells services to internal and external profit centers, when a hospital-owned HMO is evaluated as a profit center, or when a freestanding clinic is owned by the hospital? Should there be a lower price for internal users or should all services be priced based upon full cost? The price established for the service would decidedly influence the profit and performance measurements reported. Consider what happens when physicians are treated as profit centers. The revenues received from the DRGs would be compared with the costs incurred in providing the services. The costs of the resources used by the physician would heavily influence the profit reported by him. In such cases, the impacted parties would have different outlooks on what would be a fair price. A faulty internal pricing policy can result in inefficient allocation of resources, poor motivational environment, and ineffective decision making.

Basically, a problem occurs when materials or services are *sold* between profit centers in the same organization. Each manager acting in his own best interest would like to pay the lowest price for purchased items and sell his output at the highest price. A pricing policy that recognizes this conflict is essential to effective decision making.

INTERNAL PRICING TECHNIQUES

In accounting technology, internal pricing techniques are categorized as *transfer pricing policies*. An effective transfer pricing policy maximizes goal congruence. "Goal congruence" refers to a process in which an individual maximizing his own gain also maximizes the gains to the organization. This is easier said than done. All of the various techniques that have been used have deficiencies. Each of the major pricing techniques will be discussed in detail in the next section.

Source: Reprinted from James D. Suver, "Competitive Pricing Models for Intra-Hospital Services," *Hospital Cost Accounting Advisor,* Vol. 1, No. 11, April 1986, pp. 1, 3–4. Copyright 1986, Aspen Publishers, Inc.

COST-BASED PRICES

The most commonly used transfer price is one based on cost. This can be either a full cost or a variable cost. A cost-based approach does not provide a profit margin to the selling department. Clearly, a manager of a selling division who is evaluated on bottom-line performance does not like this kind of policy. However, there are more serious problems. Services that are provided at full cost provide no incentive to the selling department to control expenses. Since the selling department cannot make a profit, it can obtain a surrogate benefit by padding overhead costs. Cost control can be achieved only through careful budget analysis and strict expenditure controls. A full-cost transfer pricing policy can also lead to passing on inefficiencies and may create a noncompetitive price for the service.

The opposite of a full-cost pricing model is one based on variable costs. Variable costs are the out-of-pocket costs incurred in providing the service. Theoretically, the use of a variable-cost pricing model will lead to an optimal decision about whether to purchase a service internally or externally. Consider, for example, the decision on whether to provide a lab test internally or purchase it from a free-standing clinic. The relevant data are:

Internal Variable Costs	$ 8.00
Internal Full Cost	18.00
Free-Standing Clinic Price	15.00

Based on a full cost of $18, it would appear that the service should be purchased externally at $15.00. A profit center manager in the health care organization would clearly prefer to buy at $15 instead of $18. But what is the impact on the entire organization? The organization is now incurring out-of-pocket costs of $15 instead of only the $8 from using internal sources. This assumes the overhead costs would be incurred by the hospital in any case. The organization would seem to have a problem in "goal congruence." The individual manager, if he has a choice, will buy externally, yet the organization from a total bottom-line approach will be worse off. Other factors, such as capacity of the producing de-

partment or product quality, can also influence the decision. These will be discussed later in this article.

MARKET-BASED PRICES

If a competitive market price exists for the output of the producing department, this price can also be used for internal pricing decisions. The use of a market price fits quite well with the profit center concept and makes profit-based performance measurement appropriate for many departments in the health care provider.

In the previous example, the buying department would pay a maximum of $15 for the internal service. With the full cost at $18, the producing department must find ways to reduce its costs or show a negative bottom line. Even with the negative bottom line, the organization as a whole is better off if the purchase is internal. Use of a market price for all internal transfers would ensure that the final price would also reflect market conditions and that internal inefficiencies are not simply passed onto the cost of the product.

The use of a market-based internal price requires that certain policies govern actions between internal divisions:

- The buying department must buy internally when the producing department meets the market price and wants to sell internally.

- The buying department is free to purchase externally if the producing division does not meet the external price.

- The producing division can reject internal sales if the manager believes there are more profitable revenues to be earned externally.

- An impartial arbitration/appeal process must be established to resolve conflicts when they occur.

NEGOTIATED MARKET-BASED PRICES

In most cases, an external market price represents the maximum amount that a purchasing department should pay for an internal service. Because of reduced administrative costs, guaranteed volume and other cost-avoidance aspects of internal purchasing, it may be possible to justify a lower price. In such cases, the best possible approach may be a negotiated market price, with the producing and purchasing departments agreeing on the price to be established.

A negotiated market price is also the best avenue to take when there is no external market price or when there is idle capacity in the producing division. In the case of the former, the producing division must receive a price that is sufficient to encourage it to offer the internal service. When there is idle capacity, the producing division should not expect to receive full market price. A price approaching the lower limit of the variable cost will more accurately reflect the opportunity cost of not selling the service.

Opportunity costs are usually defined as the potential benefit given up when one option is selected over another. For example, when a producing department is operating at full capacity, the selling of a service internally reflects the market price given up by not selling externally. When the producing department has excess or idle capacity, there are no lost external sales, and the only costs involved would be the incremental or variable costs of producing one more service.

GENERAL FORMULA FOR TRANSFER PRICING

In most cases, the formula for transfer pricing can be expressed as:

Transfer price = variable costs per unit of service
+ opportunity cost per unit of
service on external sales.

Given the data used earlier, the following transfer prices could be calculated:

Variable Costs	$ 8.00
Internal Full Costs	18.00
Free-Standing Clinic Price	15.00
Opportunity Costs = 15 − 8 = 7	

Case 1—Producing department has no idle capacity.

Transfer price = 8 + 7 or $15.00

Case 2—Producing department has excess capacity.

Transfer price = 8 + 0 or $8.00

It is doubtful that the producing division would want to sell at this price, but from an overall hospital perspective, the $8 would be correct. A negotiated market price approach may be the most appropriate method in this case.

NO EXTERNAL MARKET SALES

For some services there may not be an external market. In these cases, the market price approach will not be effective. Some type of cost-based approach must be used if the profit center concept is to be used. Potential methods would include variable costs plus a contribution margin or variable costs plus a flat sum equal to a share of fixed costs.

In all cases, standard costs rather than actual costs should be used in the transfer price negotiations. This can at least prevent the automatic transfer of inefficiencies to the purchasing department.

The use of a profit center concept can lead to better decision making by pushing the decisions down to lower levels in the organization. This means that the transfer of services between internal profit centers results in a keen interest in the prices paid for such services. One manager's gain is another manager's loss. Therefore, an effective transfer pricing system must be established to award sub-optimization and maximize the overall provider's gain. The concepts explained in this article offer the opportunities to establish such a system.

Transfer Pricing in the Hospital-HMO Corporation

Kyle L. Grazier, DrPH, is currently Associate Professor and Director of the Sloan Program at Cornell University, Ithaca, New York.

More and more hospitals are reorganizing and restructuring their operations to include alternative delivery and financing systems. The most common expansion has been the ownership or operation of an HMO. The first article in this three-part series (*Hospital Cost Accounting Advisor* 1:10) discussed the issues involved in an effective cost accounting system and the identification of fixed and variable costs within such a corporate structure. In this article, transfer pricing of goods and services between the HMO and hospital will be addressed.

GOAL CONGRUENCE

Given the decentralization of decision making inherent in a restructured hospital-HMO delivery system, there are many opportunities for the transfer of goods and services, and thus "selling" and "buying" among profit centers of the organization. Difficulties often arise from dissatisfaction among the participating managers with regard to those transfers. Properly established transfer prices increase the probability that the incentives for the managers of each di-

vision—or in this case, the HMO and hospital—will coincide with the goals of the overall organization.

FINANCIAL ACCOUNTING ENTRIES

In discussing goals and managerial incentives, it is clear that it is the cost accounting and control focus which is of interest here, not financial accounting. It should be noted, however, that in accounting for the consolidated entity, "any goods and services transferred within the enterprise and not yet sold to outsiders should be carried at cost."[1] Thus, transfer prices in excess of cost must be eliminated when periodic consolidated financial statements for external financial reporting are prepared.

TRANSFER PRICING METHODS

From a managerial and cost control viewpoint, transfer prices need to be such that they give the manager an incentive to work in the overall organization's best interests. This will occur only if the price allows the manager's part of the overall organization to be financially successful. But setting proper transfer prices is easier said than done. There are several methods,

Source: Reprinted from Kyle L. Grazier, "Transfer Pricing in the Hospital-HMO Corporation," *Hospital Cost Accounting Advisor,* Vol. 1, No. 11, April 1986, pp. 1, 6–8. Copyright 1986, Aspen Publishers, Inc.

each of which utilizes a different basis for calculation, but none is considered the one and only correct method. Each has its advantages and disadvantages, and the time required to utilize the various methods must be considered to determine the practicality of a particular method for the particular management situation. Pricing on the basis of full charges, variable costs, and market prices spans a wide range of sophistication, theories, and time. As in the determination of fixed and variable costs, the manager's assessment of appropriateness is far more critical than the numerical calculation.

To illustrate the different methods, consider the following data. Hospital X, an 800-bed teaching hospital, now charges third parties $400 per day for inpatient room and board services. The hospital averages 85 percent occupancy, with few Medicare patients and about 20 percent Medicaid patients. The financial manager has determined that approximately $50 of the $400 is fixed costs and $250, variable costs; $100 is profit. Another hospital nearby (Hospital Y) charges $350 per day to its private patients and a local HMO's patients.

The new HMO manager for Hospital X has determined that she will need 1,000 patient days over the first year of operation. Although the HMO is a wholly owned subsidiary of the hospital corporation, she must procure the lowest reasonable inpatient rates for her enrollees, regardless of source. This is required if she is to break even by year's end, and if the HMO's premiums are to be competitive with other plans in the area.

TRANSFER PRICING USING FULL CHARGES

Initially, the financial manager of the hospital is likely to suggest the use of full charges as the basis for the transfer price. Charges per unit of service or product are set, and do not require additional computation or management time.

Under the full charges method of transfer pricing, the hospital would charge the HMO $400, the same as for other third party payers. The hospital operations manager would benefit

from the $400,000 in increased revenues as beds are filled by the HMO's patients, but the HMO manager would be foolish to accept Hospital X's rate when her performance appraisal is based on profits. Hospital Y's rates save her $50,000 per year in inpatient charges. Thus, the corporation may stand to lose the improved occupancy and increased revenues to its hospital from its HMO due to the incongruence in objectives.

TRANSFER PRICING USING VARIABLE COSTS

Variable costs are commonly suggested as the basis for transfer prices in manufacturing, where there has been a longer history of setting variable and fixed costs than in hospitals and HMOs. As noted in the first article in this series (*Hospital Cost Accounting Advisor* 1:10), there are inherent difficulties in calculating the fixed and variable costs in health care systems in general. But even if variable costs could be identified more easily, as in some manufacturing settings, there are difficulties in using variable costs as a basis for transfer pricing. The problems are the same as in the use of full charges: incongruence in incentives.

The "buying" manager would be pleased by a price that excluded the associated fixed costs. In our sample setting, the HMO manager would pay only $250,000 for the needed 1,000 days. However, the "selling" or producing manager would not be able to cover the fixed costs of the product through the sale of the services; if evaluated on the basis of profits, he would surely seek another buyer who could at least recover the $50,000 in fixed costs, if not contribute to profits. The results of an improperly set transfer price would be seen in a corporation that fails to reduce inventory or fill its hospital's beds, with its HMO buying services from the competition.

TRANSFER PRICING USING MARKET PRICES

The most appealing theoretical basis for transfer prices is market prices. Under this system, the buying or selling manager would determine the going rates in the community for all transfer products. These rates then become the transfer prices between divisions in the corporation. Using the data provided here, the HMO manager would obtain a market price of $350 per day from Hospital X, and still purchase in-house. The hospital's financial manager would have made a profit. The corporation would have utilized unused capacity and improved the profits of its HMO.

How often prices are changed or which markets are included or excluded is subject to negotiation among the parties. Theoretically, the managers are content: if each were buying or selling at the perfect market price, then each would be indifferent as to whether the goods or services were being provided inside or outside the organization.

Market transfer prices are not, however, without their disadvantages. Few markets are perfectly competitive; often one seller or buyer can exert an inordinate influence on supply or demand in the market. Market prices also demand the manager's time, in that the market must be assessed as to not only the going prices, but also the comparability of the products. Finally, there must also be decisions on whether to use short-run or long-run market prices as a basis; the existence of "sale" prices can pose difficult decisions as to what time period to use to "average" the market prices.

OTHER ALTERNATIVES

There are other alternatives to setting transfer prices on the basis of charges, variable costs, or market prices. Full standard costs or a full cost plus some margin are sometimes used, although deficient in their resultant incentives. Standard variable costs as transfer prices have some advantage over full costs, but have the same disincentives for the producer manager as do variable transfer costs. Standard variable costs often are modified by adding a margin based on expectations of future demand rather than actual demand. Multiple transfer prices are another alternative; here a high price might be recorded in

the supplier's accounts but a lower price in the buyer's account. The managers are able to meet management objectives but the corporation as a whole risks losing the cost controls in buying and selling that the cost accounting system was designed to address.

AN INITIAL ANALYSIS

While market prices appear to be the most appealing in their ability to properly motivate managers, they are costly in time and effort. Given these difficulties, it may be time-efficient to perform an initial analysis of the total outlay costs of a product, say a bed-day from the hospital, and the opportunity costs to the corporation of transferring the product internally.[2] The opportunity costs can be viewed as the foregone profits from charges received from other payers outside the corporation.

Accountants most often record only the outlay costs (approximated here by variable costs), but transfer prices need to accommodate the opportunity costs as well. In a perfect market, opportunity costs equal market price minus outlay costs. For example, if Hospital X has no excess capacity—operations are at 97 percent occupancy—and a perfect market exists, the transfer price of the bed-day would be the outlay costs ($250/bed) + market price ($400) – outlay cost ($250)—or in other words, the market price, $400. If there were excess capacity—with occupancy only 60 percent of its 800-bed capacity—there would be almost no opportunity costs of selling internally to the HMO. In this case, the outlay costs per unit—$250—would be the appropriate transfer price.

Two final points warrant comment. First, opportunity costs are not always known or calculable; there is seldom certainty that a hospital will have a paying client. They are estimates, and benefit from sensitivity analysis (to be discussed in the next article). Second, the outlay costs and the opportunity costs change depending on the volume of bed-days requested at any point in time by the HMO. The resultant market and transfer prices, in turn, are dependent upon volume, as well; this illustrates the need to have a schedule of transfer prices rather than one transfer price that ignores timing or volume.

It should be clear from this brief discussion that determining market prices and transfer prices can take considerable time. The value of that time depends, of course, on the extent to which goal congruence among various divisions and the corporation is required for effective functioning.

The energy exerted on development of an effective transfer pricing mechanism must be governed by the goals of the overall organization. Hospital-owned and operated HMOs offer new challenges to those responsible for the financial and managerial controls of the organization. Appropriate transfer prices can enhance or undermine the goals of the organization and its managers, and for that reason deserve considerable thought and attention.

NOTES

1. C.T. Horngren, *Cost Accounting, A Managerial Emphasis,* Fifth Edition, Englewood Cliffs: Prentice-Hall, Inc. 1982, p. 643.

2. Adapted from C.T. Horngren, *Cost Accounting, A Managerial Emphasis,* Fifth Edition, Englewood Cliffs: Prentice-Hall, Inc. 1982, p. 637.

Part III

Additional Cost Accounting Tools
To Aid in Decision Making

The reader who has completed Parts I and II of this book now has a solid foundation in the basics of cost accounting and the essential tools for planning and control. There are a number of additional cost accounting tools that can be helpful in generating management information for decision making. Part III examines a number of those tools.

Chapter 11 discusses cost accounting ratios. Most financial managers are familiar with the use of ratio analysis for financial statement evaluation. This chapter explains ways that cost information not generally shown on financial statements can be converted to ratios to improve managers' decision-making capabilities.

Productivity measurement is the topic of Chapter 12. As the need for efficiency in the provision of health care services has increased, there has been a growing focus on productivity. This chapter provides the manager with the tools needed to address the issue of productivity.

Chapter 13 considers cost issues related to inventory. All health care organizations tend to have some inventory. Although the amount held is much less significant than in many other industries, there are a number of important inventory issues in health care. The chapter not only

addresses the costing of inventory but also methods to minimize costs related to inventory.

Uncertainty is a problem for most health care organizations. Even using the forecasting and cost estimation techniques of Chapter 7, we are unlikely to have a perfect prediction of the future. Chapter 14 considers a number of techniques designed to aid managers in making decisions when uncertainty exists. The techniques discussed in Chapter 14 include expected value analysis, simulation, network cost budgeting, and linear programming.

The last decade has seen a revolution in the capabilities of computer systems. Chapter 15 considers the role of information systems in costing. Considerations in designing computerized cost accounting systems are discussed. The chapter also considers the potential problems that arise as managers start to do more and more of their own computing.

The final chapter in Part III is Chapter 16, which looks at performance evaluation and incentive compensation. The chapter considers issues related to determining whether a manager did a good job and whether a unit's performance was satisfactory. Creating compensation incentives is also a major focus of the chapter.

11

Cost Accounting Ratios

Goals of This Chapter

1. Review the concept of ratio analysis as applied to financial statement information.
2. Introduce the use of ratio analysis for cost accounting information.
3. Provide examples of several possible types of cost accounting ratios.

Key Terms Used in This Chapter

Decision ratios; financial ratios; general information ratios; monitoring and control ratios; ratio analysis; ratio.

Note: Key terms appear in italics when first used in the chapter. All key terms are defined in the Glossary.

INTRODUCTION

Ratio analysis is a widely used managerial tool. In the health care industry, there have been many articles written on the topic of *ratios*.[1–5] Specific ratio data are available from several sources, such as the Healthcare Financial Management Association's Financial Advisory Service, which provides subscribers with ratio information from a large group of hospitals.[6] However, the focus of ratio analysis has been on information from financial statements. It is suggested here that ratios built around cost accounting information can provide valuable tools for improved management of health care organizations.

FINANCIAL RATIOS

Financial ratios have often been a useful tool for people outside of an organization to use in assessing the organization's financial condition. Financial ratios are based on information contained in financial statements. They provide a financial indication by dividing one number by another. Most financial ratios are calculated using information from the organization's financial statements. For many health care organizations, financial statement information is readily available to the public. Ratios are commonly taught in business school programs as being a part of any thorough financial statement analysis.

Some ratios, such as the widely used current ratio (current assets divided by current liabilities), are used as indicators of the organization's ability to meet its short-term obligations. In addition to such "liquidity" ratios, solvency (also called leverage or capital structure) ratios, efficiency (also called activity) ratios, and profitability ratios have been developed. The key ingredient to most of the frequently used ratios is that they can be prepared from information contained in the organization's annual financial statements.

Ratios are generally used as a basis for comparison. Any one ratio provides limited information. Knowing that the current ratio is 2 (implying $2 of current assets for every $1 of current liabilities) may be more informative than knowing that current assets are $1,832,000, while current liabilities are $916,000. However, it would be even more helpful if there were something against which to compare that value of 2.

Organizations compare their own ratio values for trends over time. In addition, they compare their values with those of specific close competitors. It is also common to compare values with groups of other organizations or even the industry as a whole.

Financial ratios have long been used by financial analysts, stockholders, banks, suppliers, bond raters, regulatory bodies, and others outside of the organization. Over time, it has become apparent that ratios are useful for internal purposes as well as for external analysis. Ratios have become a common managerial tool for understanding and improving the financial performance of organizations.

Financial statement information is valuable in that it lends itself to interorganizational comparison. While many not-for-profit health care organizations do not release their financial statements, a great deal of financial statement information is readily available. Bond prospectuses contain financial statements. Tax returns for not-for-profit organizations must be filed annually. They contain financial statement information and are open for public inspection. Many trade associations, such as the American Hospital Association, collect financial statement data and then distribute comparative data to their members.

Financial statement data are not ideal. Even when prepared in accordance with Generally Accepted Accounting Principles, financial statements are notoriously poor at recording the impact of inflation and the value of intangible assets. Further, when used for ratio analysis, the impacts of alternative accounting principles reduce their comparability.

For example, inflation causes land and buildings to be understated in value on the financial statements; the good or bad will of a health care organization due to its relations with employees and suppliers is ignored; and inventory values may vary substantially depending on whether last-in, first-out or first-in, first-out inventory accounting systems are used for inventory costing. As a result, ratios based on financial statements have many weaknesses. (See the discussion in Application 11-1 for a more detailed discussion of these problems.) Nevertheless, their value is great enough that they are widely used despite their limitations.

DEVELOPMENT OF A NEW SET OF RATIOS

There is no inherent need to limit ratio analysis to information from the financial statements. In fact, there is good reason to use other information. Managers can use internal management data, not just financial statement information.

A ratio is simply one number divided by another. Any two numbers that can be compared to give a useful piece of information can be a ratio. The most commonly used health care industry ratio, in fact, does not come from financial statements. That ratio is the occupancy rate, which is simply filled beds compared with total beds. Similarly, most hospitals collect ratios such as the number of employees per occupied bed.

The number and accuracy of cost accounting reports has increased in recent years. Managers can make maximum use of the cost accounting information available by creating and using ratios from nonfinancial statement data. The time is right to develop a new branch of ratio analysis: ratios based on cost accounting data.

Using internally available data limits the ability to compare your health care organization with other similar organizations. Not as much of the internal statistical information is publicly available, as with financial statement data. However, such ratios will give a more accurate picture of your current standing, and it will still allow for comparisons over time.

Cost accounting ratios can become extremely valuable tools. They do not have any of the problems inherent in financial statements. The data used in preparing them do not have to follow the rigid requirements of Generally Accepted Accounting Principles. Any desired adjustments can be made to adjust the ratios for inflation, and so forth.

What, then, are the five key cost accounting ratios? There is no unique correct list of the most valuable financial ratios or the most valuable cost accounting ratios. Any two numbers can be compared to form a ratio. Certainly, the current ratio and the debt to equity ratio are commonly considered to be valuable financial ratios for health care organizations, but one would be hard pressed to identify the five key financial accounting ratios. The same holds true for cost-accounting–based ratios. There are no indicators that can be assumed to be the *most* valuable.

What then are *some* potentially valuable cost accounting ratios? This chapter will attempt to identify several such ratios. As cost accounting information improves further over time, it should be possible to add other ratios to our base of management information.

Each manager working in his or her individual organization is in the best position to determine what information would be useful to him or her. Given that a ratio is simply one number compared to another, the key is to think of the relationship between any two numbers and the interesting or valuable information that relationship might yield.

SOME COST ACCOUNTING RATIOS

We can loosely group cost accounting ratios into three categories: (1) *general information ratios,* (2) *monitoring and control ratios,* and (3) *decision ratios.* The distinction between these categories is not clear-cut, and certain ratios could be classified in several categories.

General Information Ratios

Some cost accounting ratios would fall into the classification of providing general information for managers. The following are examples:

$$\text{Fixed to total cost ratio} = \frac{\text{Fixed cost}}{\text{Total cost}}$$

$$\text{Variable to total cost ratio} = \frac{\text{Total variable costs}}{\text{Total cost}}$$

The ratio of fixed cost to total cost and the corresponding ratio of variable cost to total cost are good examples of ratio information that managers should have as background data in the running of the health care organization. As cost systems improve, our ability to monitor the fixed/variable split should improve. As prospective payment systems alter the health care system, keeping track of fixed costs as a portion of the total will help in developing preferred provider organization (PPO) bids, health maintenance organization (HMO) price schedules, and so forth. Similar splits should be maintained for controllable versus noncontrollable costs and direct versus indirect costs.

Another valuable ratio that often cannot be calculated from financial statement information is the portion of total expenses that are labor related. This ratio could be made even more valuable by a split between labor considered to be fixed and labor considered to vary with occupancy levels.

$$\text{Labor to total cost ratio} = \frac{\text{Labor costs}}{\text{Total costs}}$$

One potential problem with a national prospective payment rate that is uniform for all discharges for a given DRG is that there may be underlying, geographically induced differences in health care organizations. Ratios are quite flexible and can provide information about many questions. For example, it would be possible to aggregate all costs related to weather conditions, such as heat and snow removal, and compare those costs to total costs, costs per discharge and so forth. Such a series of ratios could be used for better understanding the relative impact of such costs on health care organizations in different parts of the country.

$$\text{Geographic cost ratio} = \frac{\text{Geographic-specific costs}}{\text{Total costs}}$$

Monitoring and Control Ratios

It is difficult to draw hard-and-fast distinctions among classes of cost accounting ratios. However, we might think of this next group of ratios as being useful to monitor and control the specific, ongoing operations of the health care organization.

One cost accounting ratio that many health care organizations have long used is the cost per patient day. This ratio, total cost divided by total patient days, must be considered cautiously. As patient days fall, will costs fall by the cost per patient day? Probably not, since many of the costs of the health care organization are fixed.

$$\text{Cost per patient day} = \frac{\text{Total cost}}{\text{Patient days}}$$

A more useful piece of information is the variable cost per patient day. This ratio would describe how much costs would fall for each patient day reduction. As cost accounting systems improve, these data should become available. Under prospective payment systems, a day reduction in length of stay should be valuable for the health care organization, but we should know how valuable.

$$\text{Variable cost per patient day} = \frac{\text{Total variable costs}}{\text{Patient days}}$$

Under prospective payment systems, the fixed revenue rate tends to shift our focus from patient days to discharges. Thus, we should pay attention to the cost per discharge. A rise in this ratio would be an early indicator of control problems that will later appear in variance reports.

$$\text{Cost per discharge} = \frac{\text{Total cost}}{\text{Discharges}}$$

On the other hand, changes in the cost per discharge may simply reflect a change in the case-mix of the health care organization. Therefore, we should calculate the ratio that compares the total costs of the health care organization to some case-mix adjusted measure of discharges.

$$\frac{\text{Cost per case-mix}}{\text{adjusted discharge}} = \frac{\text{Cost per discharge}}{\text{Case-mix index}}$$

Suppose that we had costs last month of $2 million and we discharged 800 patients. The cost per discharge ratio would be $2,500, as follows:

$$\text{Cost per discharge} = \frac{\text{Total cost}}{\text{Discharges}}$$

$$= \frac{\$2,000,000}{800}$$

$$= \$2,500$$

This might be alarming if we expected to have a cost per discharge of $2,350.

Suppose, however, that we expected to have a Medicare-weighted case-mix of 1.10, and we actually had a patient mix of 1.18. This higher weight would lead to increased revenues, but how well have we done on the cost side?

The *expected* case-mix adjusted cost per discharge ratio would be $2,136, as follows:

$$\frac{\text{Cost per case-mix}}{\text{adjusted discharge}} = \frac{\text{Cost per discharge}}{\text{Case-mix index}}$$

$$= \frac{\$2,350}{1.10}$$

$$= \$2,136$$

In fact, the *actual* cost per discharge of $2,500, when divided by the actual case-mix index of 1.18, yields an actual case-mix adjusted cost per discharge of $2,119, as follows:

$$\frac{\text{Cost per case-mix}}{\text{adjusted discharge}} = \frac{\text{Cost per discharge}}{\text{Case-mix index}}$$

$$= \frac{\$2,500}{1.18}$$

$$= \$2,119$$

Thus, actual cost per discharge adjusted for case-mix was $2,119. These costs were actually slightly below the $2,136 that would have been expected, rather than well over expectations. The cost per discharge class of ratios can be quite useful as a cost monitoring and control tool. In addition to adjusting for case-mix, a series of ratios could also be developed incorporating patient acuity or severity, if your health care organization maintains such data.

As we explore the range of cost accounting ratios, one ratio leads to the next, and the possible variations multiply. Once we have considered cost per discharge, it becomes obvious that the relationship between cost and revenue is quite important to monitor.

$$\frac{\text{Revenue to cost}}{\text{per discharge ratio}} = \frac{\text{Average revenue per discharge}}{\text{Average cost per discharge}}$$

We can use either absolute cost per discharge or case-mix weighted. We can use average cost or some measure of variable cost per discharge. We can look at all revenues or revenues for a class of patients, such as Medicare patients or Blue Cross patients, or patients for a given DRG.

Over time, it is likely that health care organizations will begin to adopt the standard cost practices of industry. The result will be a standard cost to treat a patient with a particular diagnosis. Standard cost ratios will compare actual costs for treating a group of patients to the standard cost. If quality is maintained, a low ratio is desirable. These ratios will likely eventually be refined to the detailed level of standard cost such as for an operation or the respiratory therapy component of a patient's care.

$$\text{Standard cost ratios} = \frac{\text{Actual costs}}{\text{Standard costs}}$$

Decision Ratios

Although the above ratios lend themselves well to helping to monitor the operations of the health care organization, we also need information to make decisions about particular services and product lines that the health care organization offers. In the past, few health care organizations had any real capacity to measure costs of patient groupings and have any confidence in the meaningfulness of the cost data. More and more health care organizations, however, are developing systems to measure the costs of treating patients in specific DRGs or DRG clusters, or other types of groupings.

The ratio of reimbursement to cost for any given product line is an example of a decision ratio of obvious interest.

$$\text{Reimbursement to cost} = \frac{\text{Reimbursement}}{\text{Cost}}$$

In some cases, such information would be used to determine if certain services should not be offered. In other cases, such ratios could be used to indicate where the organization should be spending most of its marketing efforts.

Exhibit 11-1 presents a summary of the cost accounting ratios suggested in this chapter. The reader should bear in mind that these are just a few of the many possible such ratios. Applications 11-2 and 11-3 provide additional examples of cost accounting ratios.

COMPARISONS

It was noted earlier that financial ratios are often used in comparisons. An organization may track its own ratios over time or may compare itself to a specific close competitor or to all firms in an industry. With cost accounting ratios, making comparisons is somewhat more difficult.

It may be possible to identify a specific organization to use for comparison. Both organizations can then agree to collect information for specific ratios and to share that information. Definitions of the ratios can be agreed upon in advance. It must be noted, however, that competing organizations are unlikely to want to

share proprietary internal information. It is more likely that an organization in another geographic market might be willing to share information. However, the change in locale may have an effect on the ratios that must be taken into account.

Getting industry-wide information is an even more challenging problem. However, there are some private services that collect such information and then make it available to participants.

Exhibit 11-1 Examples of Cost Accounting Ratios

General Information Ratios

$$\text{Fixed to total cost ratio} = \frac{\text{Fixed cost}}{\text{Total cost}}$$

$$\text{Variable to total cost ratio} = \frac{\text{Total variable costs}}{\text{Total cost}}$$

$$\text{Labor to total cost ratio} = \frac{\text{Labor costs}}{\text{Total costs}}$$

$$\text{Geographic cost ratio} = \frac{\text{Geographic-specific costs}}{\text{Total costs}}$$

Monitoring and Control Ratios

$$\text{Cost per patient day} = \frac{\text{Total cost}}{\text{Patient days}}$$

$$\text{Variable cost per patient day} = \frac{\text{Total variable costs}}{\text{Patient days}}$$

$$\text{Cost per discharge} = \frac{\text{Total cost}}{\text{Discharges}}$$

$$\text{Cost per case-mix adjusted discharge} = \frac{\text{Cost per discharge}}{\text{Case-mix index}}$$

$$\text{Revenue to cost per discharge ratio} = \frac{\text{Average revenue per discharge}}{\text{Average cost per discharge}}$$

$$\text{Standard cost ratios} = \frac{\text{Actual costs}}{\text{Standard costs}}$$

Decision Ratio

$$\text{Reimbursement to cost} = \frac{\text{Reimbursement}}{\text{Cost}}$$

As more cost accounting ratios are identified as being potentially useful, trade associations or for-profit ventures can start collecting and disseminating that information.

At a minimum, health care organizations can start to make useful comparisons by tracking the value of key ratios over time. For example, Figure 11-1 shows two ratios tracked over a five-year period. The numbers in the figure have been adjusted for changes in price levels (i.e., inflation). One ratio shown on the graph is the unadjusted cost per discharge. Notice how that has been sharply rising over time—a potential cause for concern. However, also plotted is the cost per discharge adjusted for case-mix. As one can see, the changes in this measure have been modest. The two lines together inform the user that cost per discharge has been rising but primarily because the complexity of the cases has been rising rather than because some underlying lack of cost control exists.

This graph demonstrates the potential usefulness for tracking ratios over time, and for considering several ratios in conjunction. Over time, the demands on managers for constantly improved information will quite possibly lead to significant expansions in the use of cost accounting ratios.

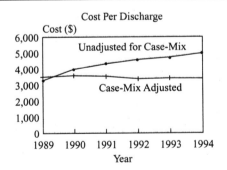

Figure 11-1 Cost Accounting Ratios over Time

NOTES

1. M.G. Choate and K. Tanaka, Using financial ratio analysis to compare hospitals' performance, *Hospital Progress* 60, no. 12 (December 1979):43–58.

2. S.R. Eastaugh, Financial-ratio analysis and medical school management, *Journal of Medical Education* 55, no. 12 (December 1980):983–992.

3. S.A. Finkler, Ratio analysis: Use with caution, *Health Care Management Review* 7, no. 2 (Spring 1982): 65–72.

4. G. Sadleback, Financial manager's notebook: Financial ratio analysis, *Healthcare Financial Management* (January 1983):61–62.

5. J.T. Whitman, Ratio analysis—Indispensable management aid, *Hospital Financial Management* 33, no. 9 (September 1979):74.

6. W.O. Cleverley, *Financial Report of the Hospital Industry.* Westchester, Ill.: Healthcare Financial Management Association (annual publication).

SUGGESTED READING

Choate, M.G., and K. Tanaka. 1979. Using financial ratio analysis to compare hospitals' performance. *Hospital Progress* 60, no. 12:43–58.

Counte, M.A., et al. 1988. Using ratios to measure hospital financial performance: Can the process be simplified? *Health Services Management Research* 1, no. 3:173–180.

Eastaugh, S.R. 1980. Financial-ratio analysis and medical school management. *Journal of Medical Education* 55, no. 12:983–992.

Finkler, S.A. Spring 1982. Ratio analysis: Use with caution. *Health Care Management Review* 7, no. 2:65–72.

———. 1985. Cost accounting ratios. *Health Care Organization Cost Accounting Advisor* 1, no. 4:1, 3–6.

———. 1985. Health care organization key variables. *Health Care Organization Cost Accounting Advisor* 1, no. 6:1–4.

Sadleback, G. January 1983. Financial manager's notebook: Financial ratio analysis. *Healthcare Financial Management*, 61–62.

Snook, I.D., Jr., and W.B. Sudell. 1975. Financial ratio analysis: A quick simple test. *Hospital Financial Management* 29, no. 6:16–19.

Whitman, J.T. 1979. Ratio analysis—Indispensable management aid. *Hospital Financial Management* 33, no. 9:74.

EXERCISES

QUESTIONS FOR DISCUSSION

1. What types of comparisons are useful for ratio analysis?

2. Why would there be an advantage to cost accounting ratios if extensive financial statement ratios are available?

3. What are some major issues that cost accounting ratios can address?

4. Assume that you are a hospital pharmacist. What are some cost accounting ratios that might be useful to you?

―――――

Note: Solutions to the Exercises can be found in Appendix A.

PROBLEMS

1. Consider the examples given in Applications 11-2 and 11-3. Design a set of new cost accounting ratios for a health care organization. Provide hypothetical data and calculate the ratio values. Explain the managerial value of each of your ratios.

2. Aspen Hospital actually had total spending of $6 million and 2,000 discharges for the month of May. The case-mix index of discharged patients was 1.4. Managers at Aspen expected the case-mix adjusted cost per discharge to be $2,000. Were costs higher or lower than expectations? By how much?

Ratio Analysis: Use with Caution

Steven A. Finkler, PhD, CPA

Health care management literature has recently contained a number of articles extolling the virtues of ratios and exhorting the health care manager to use ratio analysis to compare the institution over time with itself and with its peer group.[1-3] It is time to step back and question the serious limitations of ratio analysis when removed from the textbook and put into use. In some ways it is almost sacrilegious to be critical of ratio analysis for health care management. Recent years have seen a constant effort to develop the use of modern management techniques in the health care area. Ratio analysis is certainly used in industry in general. In fact, few managers would consider ratios to be a controversial topic—they are merely one more tool for the aware manager.

Yet ratios can be misleading. They can obscure relationships and confuse the manager if they are used without a full understanding of the implicit assumptions made by ratio analysis. Two of the principal problem areas that have led numerous managers to draw incorrect conclusions from ratio analysis results are: (1) inflation, which significantly distorts ratios and

makes their interpretation highly questionable; and (2) trends, which in themselves are not important, although the underlying cause of trends should concern the manager.

An extra degree of understanding is needed so that ratios may be used with enough care to be of value to managers. Note, however, that given financial information currently available in the health care field, reasonable comparisons among institutions are quite difficult and in many cases not possible.

That is a strong assertion and one that will not be likely to please those individuals and groups with a vested interest in ratio analysis. Many health care consultants provide a ratio analysis service. Is the product they sell something of value to the health care manager? If the ratio analysis consultants cannot overcome the difficulties raised below, they must either attempt to hide these limitations from their clients or disclose them and risk the loss of substantial amounts of lucrative business.

RATIOS AND INFLATION

Inflation creates a complicating factor in the use of ratio analysis. It distorts the ratios themselves and, without the exercise of some care, can distort the interpretation of observed trends.

Source: Reprinted from Steven A. Finkler, "Ratio Analysis: Use with Caution," *Health Care Management Review,* Vol. 7, No. 2, Spring 1982, pp. 65–72. Copyright 1982, Aspen Publishers, Inc.

Cause of the Distortion

Financial statements prepared in accordance with Generally Accepted Accounting Principles (GAAP) are primarily oriented toward historical cost information. Balance sheets based on GAAP must show assets at their cost, as opposed to some measure of their current value. If the hospital owns a piece of vacant land that doubles in value, the financial statements will show it at its old cost, rather than its new market value. This tends to make financial statements misleading. Yet to show the assets at their market value would require an appraisal. Because appraisers generally cannot agree exactly on an asset's value, accountants show the assets at their cost (less accumulated depreciation) until they are sold or otherwise disposed of.

The accounting profession has been studying this problem and is beginning to establish new rules. The process is a difficult one, and the debate consumes volumes. There are two principal alternatives, both of which have weaknesses. The price level adjustment approach would take the historical cost and adjust it upward based on the increase in a representative price index. Unfortunately, individual assets rarely change in value by the same amount as any price index, which is a broad average. The second alternative is replacement cost, which would value an asset at the cost to replace it. The problem there is a return to subjective estimates of what it might cost to replace the asset.

The advantages of the methods have been discussed.[4] However, for the present and the foreseeable future, hospital financial statements will remain on a historical cost basis. Given that the financial statements are used for preparing the ratios, if the statements are distorted, the ratios are distorted. Given the inflation of the last 15 to 20 years, there are significant distortions on the balance sheet.

The Current Ratio Example

Hypothetical data are presented in Tables 11-1-1 and 11-1-2 for a hospital for two years, 1980 and 1975. The current ratio is the most commonly used ratio to assess the liquidity of the firm, a key measure of financial viability.

Using the Table 11-1-1 data, the current ratio is as follows:

$$\text{current ratio} = \frac{\text{current assets}}{\text{current liabilities}}$$

$$\text{1980 current ratio} = \frac{10,363,274}{10,055,417} = 1.03$$

$$\text{1975 current ratio} = \frac{7,187,753}{6,518,896} = 1.10$$

The use of ratios to signal trends flashes a warning. The current ratio has fallen significantly from 1975 to 1980. Or has it?

Consider the effect of the last-in first-out (LIFO) method of inventory accounting. Briefly, LIFO is an acceptable form of valuing inventory at cost, but it assumes that the more recent purchases of inventory are consumed prior to older purchases. During inflation, this method funnels recent, higher-priced purchases into the income statement (thus maximizing cost and therefore reimbursement), but at the same time it leaves older, lower-priced purchases on the balance sheet.[5]

The result is that the balance sheet inventory figure stated at cost for a firm on a LIFO system will become more distorted each year that inflation persists. Assume that at the start of 1977 the hospital owns 1,000 bags of saline solution purchased for $5 per bag. In 1977 an additional 20,000 bags are purchased at $6 apiece, in 1978 an additional 20,000 bags are purchased at $7 apiece, in 1979 an additional 20,000 bags at $8 apiece and in 1980 an additional 20,000 at $9. Each year consumption equals 20,000 bags. At the end of 1980 the balance sheet would show inventory of 1,000 bags worth $5 each. However, the value is really $9 each. Thus inventory is stated at $5,000, but is actually worth $9,000, a significant understatement in the value of the inventory.

This is a byproduct of the historical cost method. Under LIFO, the historical cost of the inventory is $5,000, even though its value is

Table 11-1-1 Hypothetical Consolidated Balance Sheet for Hospital *A* for the Years Ended 1980 and 1975

	1980	1975
Current assets		
Cash	$ 506,226	$ 557,240
Short-term investments	485,995	443,980
Accounts receivable net of uncollectable accounts	8,078,653	4,825,104
Estimated retroactive receivables—third party	83,883	139,428
Due from other funds	89,455	218,770
Inventories at cost	589,387	498,001
Prepaid expenses	152,549	87,746
Other accounts receivable	251,919	379,016
Other current assets	125,207	38,468
Total current assets	10,363,274	7,187,753
Noncurrent assets		
Board-designated investments	3,822	200,728
Property, plant and equipment, net of accumulated depreciation	20,498,986	17,053,958
Marketable securities and investments	2,494,769	2,973,426
Estimated reimbursement—due from third parties		
Long-term investments	308,353	
Deferred expenses	28,088	64,000
Construction in progress	269,032	712,678
Funds held for expansion	—	268,775
Total noncurrent assets	23,603,050	21,273,565
Total assets	$33,966,324	$28,461,318
Current liabilities		
Accounts payable	$ 3,883,148	$ 2,872,733
Accrued expenses	2,362,883	1,442,125
Current portion of long-term debt	393,665	191,258
Demand note payable	452,753	1,060,468
Due to other funds	2,051,046	312,897
Due to third-party agencies	869,973	573,549
Other current liabilities	41,949	65,866
Total current liabilities	10,055,417	6,518,896
Noncurrent liabilities		
Deferred revenue	99,038	94,500
Due to other funds	303,091	303,091
Reserve for self-insurance	477,448	—
Long-term debt due after one year	6,053,618	3,270,364
Other noncurrent liabilities	156,900	107,324
Total noncurrent liabilities	7,090,095	3,775,279
Fund balance	16,820,812	18,167,143
Total liabilities and fund balance	$33,966,324	$28,461,318

Table 11-1-2 Hypothetical Operating Information for Hospital *A*

	1980	1975
Total operating revenues	$97,290,300	$68,169,100
Total operating expenses	98,406,850	69,995,000
Total operating income	$(1,116,550)	$(1,825,900)

$9,000 and even though the 1,000 saline bags on hand may actually have been purchased in 1980, and even though the bags purchased for $5 were physically consumed years ago. This perfectly allowable accounting system is sometimes referred to as accounting magic, or creative accounting.

Consider the implication for the current ratio. Assume that the hospital in Table 11-1-1 records inventory on a LIFO basis and that inflation in the prices of inventory items has been 15 percent per year for the five years from the end of 1975 to the end of 1980. On a compounded basis, that means that an inventory item purchased in 1975 for $1.00 would have cost $2.01 in 1980. The inventory value shown for 1980 could be understated by almost 100 percent. If this were approximated by adding the 1975 inventory cost to the stated 1980 inventory cost, it would yield an approximation that is not unreasonable given some of the effects of LIFO accounting. In that case the 1980 current ratio would be 1.08; that is, it would be almost the same as 1975, and there would be much less impression that any deleterious trend had developed.

Should downward trends in the current ratio be ignored? No. However, users of ratios should adjust for the current value of the inventory if it is based on the LIFO method.

The Rest of the Iceberg

In a sense the current ratio is the tip of the iceberg, because it makes use of only one asset that is likely to be distorted, inventory, and then only for a firm on the LIFO method. The full iceberg comes into view when one begins to look at ratios that include noncurrent assets as well as current assets.

Exhibit 11-1-1 defines a number of commonly used ratios that are likely to be affected by the impact of inflation. The noncurrent assets are likely to distort a great deal. The value of land, buildings, equipment and investments becomes radically altered during periods of inflation. These ratios are not a comprehensive listing of

Exhibit 11-1-1 Financial Ratios Most Distorted by Inflation (besides the current ratio)

Capital Structure

$$\text{Percentage of assets financed by total liabilities} = \frac{\text{total liabilities}}{\text{total assets}}$$

Activity

$$\text{Total asset turnover} = \frac{\text{total operating revenue}}{\text{total assets}}$$

$$\text{Fixed asset turnover} = \frac{\text{total operating revenue}}{\text{net fixed assets}}$$

$$\text{Current asset turnover} = \frac{\text{total operating revenue}}{\text{current assets}}$$

$$\text{Inventory turnover} = \frac{\text{total operating revenue}}{\text{inventory}}$$

Profitability

$$\text{Return on assets} = \frac{\text{operating income} + \text{interest}}{\text{total assets}}$$

Other

$$\text{Viability} = \frac{\text{total liabilities}}{\text{total assets}} \times \frac{\text{operating expense}}{\text{operating revenue}}$$

all ratios distorted by inflation, but they can serve as examples of the problems to be encountered. Table 11-1-3 calculates the ratios displayed in Exhibit 11-1-1 for 1975 and 1980, based on the hypothetical information in Tables 11-1-1 and 11-1-2.

Percentage of Assets Financed by Total Liabilities

The purpose of this ratio is to show the extent to which the hospital has to borrow to finance its asset base. The ratio should be as small as possible, inasmuch as it is preferable for liabilities to be small, relative to the value of the as-

Table 11-1-3 Ratios Based on Hypothetical Example

	1980	1975
Percentage of assets financed by total liabilities	.50	.36
Total asset turnover	2.86	2.40
Fixed asset turnover	4.12	3.20
Current asset turnover	9.39	9.48
Inventory turnover	165.07	136.88
Return on assets	−.03	−.06
Viability	.51	.37

sets. In Table 11-1-3 the ratio has increased from .36 to .50. Is this indicative of an unfavorable trend? Not necessarily.

The largest single asset group is property, plant and equipment, net of depreciation. In both years, it represents well over half of total assets. This category is also likely to represent costs far different from the current value of the assets.

A better ratio to use here would compare the current value of assets to liabilities. Although accounting rules prevent reporting the financial statements on a current value basis, they do not prohibit the use of current value estimates for internal management uses. Assume that the replacement value of the property, plant and equipment in this example was approximately $42 million in 1980 and $22 million in 1975. This ratio would then become .31 in both 1980 and 1975. No change in the ratio would have occurred over the five-year period. The implications of this ratio, adjusted for the effects of inflation by using current values in both years, are far different from those cited above when using an unadjusted ratio.

A ratio similar to percentage of assets financed by total liabilities is the debt-to-equity ratio. This ratio compares total liabilities to total fund balances. Although financial statements rarely say so explicitly, the total fund balance is simply total assets minus total liabilities. Therefore the equity, or fund balance, is calculated from balance sheet historical-cost asset information. This ratio must therefore be adjusted by subtracting liabilities from assets adjusted to current value to get an appropriate fund-balance value for the equity portion of the ratio.

Total Asset Turnover

This ratio indicates how much revenue is generated relative to the assets used; thus the more revenue per dollar of assets, the better the financial position of the hospital. Table 11-1-3 shows that a favorable trend exists, with the ratio having increased from $2.40 of revenue per dollar of assets employed in 1975 to $2.86 of revenue per dollar of assets employed in 1980.

However, assets are unadjusted for the distortions of inflation. Assume once again that property, plant and equipment have current values of $22 million in 1975 and $42 million in 1980. This adjustment alone would show that when revenue is compared to the value of the assets that are being employed, the ratio is 2.04 in 1975 and 1.75 in 1980. That means that the trend is an unfavorable one, not favorable as indicated by the unadjusted figures. Once again, other assets such as inventory and investments would have to be adjusted as well as plant, property and equipment to be able to calculate meaningful ratios.

Fixed Asset Turnover

This activity ratio seeks to focus on how well the hospital employs its noncurrent assets. Together with the current asset turnover ratio below, they provide a detailed breakdown of the total asset turnover ratio. Because property, plant and equipment is a much greater proportion of noncurrent assets than it is of total assets, the distortion will be even greater here. Making the same adjustment as before, to bring property, plant and equipment to current values, this ratio changes from 3.20 and 4.12 in 1975 and 1980, respectively (a favorable trend), to 2.60 and 2.16 in 1975 and 1980, respectively (an unfavorable trend).

Current Asset Turnover

The principal current asset that requires adjustment for inflation is inventory. The current asset ratio, intended to compare the amount of current assets needed to generate revenue, will be affected by the inventory distortion, if there is any. For a firm on a first-in first-out (FIFO) inventory accounting system, the inventory will be only slightly undervalued, and the ratio will be approximately correct without current value adjustment, although such adjustment will improve the accuracy of the ratio by at least some small amount. If the inventory is maintained on a LIFO basis, the same distortions will occur here as did in the current ratio.

Using the same inventory adjustment that was used for the current ratio, the current asset turnover ratio changes from 9.48 and 9.39 in 1975 and 1980, respectively (almost no trend), to 9.48 and 8.96 in 1975 and 1980, respectively. Thus an unfavorable trend is exposed, which would have otherwise gone undetected.

Inventory Turnover

The implications of adjusting the current asset turnover ratio are even more greatly magnified when ratios designed to focus on inventory activity are considered. The inventory turnover ratio compares current revenues to investment in inventory. Unadjusted, a favorable trend is clearly apparent. Each dollar invested in inventory supported $165.07 of revenue generation in 1980, as compared to $136.88 in 1975. But this may be a fiction of the accounting system used. If the firm were using LIFO, making the same correction as earlier, the ratios would be 89.47 in 1980 and 136.88 in 1975.

Note how misleading ratio analysis can be. If two firms were identical according to the financial statements, but one used a LIFO system and the other a FIFO system (something only noted in the footnotes to the financial statements), their inventories could in fact have widely differing values, and their true financial trends could be totally opposite from each other. In other words, for the LIFO firm one could totally misinterpret the ratios unless they are adjusted to reflect the current value of the inventory instead of the historical cost.

Return of Assets

Obviously, if assets are understated the return on assets will be overstated. The key to be aware of here is that the return measured by this ratio is the return on the amount originally invested

in assets, unless adjustment to current value is made.

Viability

Using the viability index defined here, a low ratio is desirable. A low ratio implies high assets relative to liabilities and/or high revenue relative to expenses. An adjustment for inflation is required to avoid undue alarm. Of the four factors, assets are the most largely affected by inflation without automatic adjustment. That is not meant to imply that the other three factors are not severely affected by inflation. They are. However, as most revenues, expenses and liabilities increase due to inflation, their inflated amounts are channeled directly into the financial statements. Assets, however, are locked in at their historical cost. Thus the financial information concerning assets is the most out of date and therefore misleading.

If the data are adjusted to reflect the assumptions made above about inventory and property, plant and equipment values, the viability index ratio for both years can be recalculated. The results are ratios of .31 and .32 for 1980 and 1975, respectively. Thus the impression of decreased viability given by the unadjusted ratios in Table 11-1-3 may simply reflect the fact that the ratio acknowledges inflation's impact on three factors considerably more than on the fourth. The value of the ratio as a tool is considerably weakened by the impact of inflation unless that fourth item, assets, is brought closer in line with the other three by adjusting to some estimate of current value before calculating the ratios.

Implications for Internal Ratio Analysis over Time

The problems caused by inflation are not insurmountable when it comes to evaluating one given institution over time. An effective manager should have a good idea of the replacement value of the resources of the organization. Certainly, fire insurance must be based on replacement cost rather than historical cost. And the manager knows at least roughly the current price of inventory, the current value of land and so forth.

If the manager makes an annual practice of preparing a set of financial statements based on replacement cost, then it is a relatively simple matter to determine ratios over time that are comparable. Simply use these internal financial reports based on replacement cost, instead of the official GAAP-prepared statements when the ratios are calculated.

Implications for Interorganization Comparison

The problem of comparison among organizations is much more severe. Rarely is sufficient information given in an annual report for a manager to make a reasonable estimate of the current value of items on the financial statement of other organizations.

For large publicly held corporations in for-profit industries, this problem has been overcome. Such corporations are now required to include price level adjustment and replacement cost information in their annual reports. Given this information and a bit of numerical manipulation, the ratios—adjusted for the impact of inflation—can be calculated for a variety of companies over time and used for reasonable comparison of those companies.

Most health care organizations do not fall under the rules requiring that disclosure. That means that it probably is not possible to make reasonable comparisons across institutions. Frequently that comparison has been the major thrust of attention on ratio analysis. Is your institution in trouble? Compare yourself to the industry average and find out!

It is not clear, however, how there can be a benefit from a comparison of pears with an average of apples and oranges. If the ratios are not inflation adjusted, they make no sense for interim comparison. This is a problem for which a solution has not been presented by proponents of ratio analysis.

An Example Not Given

It might seem desirable at this point to take Tables 11-1-1 and 11-1-2 and restate them based on adjustments for inflation that occurred during that period. Then a new set of ratios could be calculated, and the reader would be dazzled by the substantial difference between the Table 11-1-3 ratio comparisons and the resulting new ratios reflecting the impact of inflation.

The logical way to restate Table 11-1-1 would be to use price-level adjustments. Using government indexes one could restate numbers in current terms, but that contains the strong assumption that all assets related to health care are equally affected by inflation. If the medical-care component of the consumer price index rises 75 percent over that five-year period, then it must be assumed that land, buildings, inventory, investments and so forth have all increased at a 75 percent rate. This is obviously not the case, since the index is based on a weighted average of different rates of price increase for different items.

Even if it were possible to separate the index into a separate rate for each various type of asset, one would not be much better off, since land has increased in price by different percentages in different geographic locations—even from one town to the next.

Replacement cost information is a much more reasonable approach to the problem. However, only the managers of an institution can get a reasonable estimate of replacement costs. The balance sheet simply does not give an external user the detailed information about specific individual assets that is needed to make an informed estimate of replacement costs. To restate Tables 11-1-1 and 11-1-2 would imply that the reader can adequately make an adjustment to the financial statements of any organization. Because these data are generally not available, except for the manager's own institution, Tables 11-1-1 and 11-1-2 have not been restated.

TREND ANALYSIS

One of the principal uses for ratios is to compare an institution with itself over time. Trend analysis can be quite useful in discovering potential problems in their early stages. Ratios based on a manager's own institution over time can be adequately adjusted for inflation.

In general, this analysis can be quite helpful, but its principal limitation is that it focuses on how much relationships change, instead of how or why they change. For example, consider a hospital with a current ratio, adjusted for inflation, of 1.7 in 1975, 1.9 in 1976, 2.1 in 1977, 2.4 in 1978, 2.8 in 1979, 2.4 in 1980 and 1.8 in 1981. What does this trend tell us? The hospital had growing liquidity and therefore improving financial health from 1975 through 1979. In 1980 liquidity started to fall, and it dropped severely in 1981. Is the hospital in trouble? Has something gone wrong?

Not necessarily. Consider a hospital raising funds for a major expansion and putting those funds in a short-term money market fund until construction is to begin. In 1980 construction starts, and in 1981 the bulk of the construction takes place. The current ratio merely showed the accumulation of current assets in anticipation of the project, followed by their planned expenditure.

On the other hand, consider a current ratio pattern as follows: 2.4 in 1975, 2.2 in 1976, 2.0 in 1977, 1.9 in 1978, 1.7 in 1979, 1.6 in 1980 and 2.2 in 1981. This trend might indicate a health care organization with increasing liquidity problems. Was 1981 a turnaround year? The ratio increased sharply in 1981. Perhaps cost-cutting measures had been undertaken, and the situation turned around. Or perhaps things have become so desperate that the organization is selling off some of its fixed assets to generate sufficient cash to survive a little while longer.

Of course these examples are so extreme that one would anticipate that the organization's manager would know what was happening. The point, however, is that the ratios can lead one to draw a conclusion exactly opposite from what really happened. And presumably ratios are most useful when they tell about something not already known.

What if the stability of these two hospitals relative to the industry norm was assessed? If the industry average was 2.0 in 1981, it can be concluded that the healthy institution that just laid out a substantial amount for expansion (ratio 1.8) is in trouble and that the hospital really in trouble but selling off assets (ratio 2.2) will look healthy. At the very least, one will not be able to distinguish the extent to which the latter hospital has turned around a viability problem and is improving versus the extent to which the problem is worse and has led to a fixed asset liquidation for temporary survival.

The problem is the simplistic approach of how much things have changed instead of why they change. A current ratio, inflation adjusted, that hovers at 2.0 year after year would provide no signal to the manager. But if every year there were $100,000 transferred from endowment fund income to the general fund and this year the endowment fund is only earning $10,000, there is a problem.

One way to overcome this problem is to be sure to use a broad enough variety of ratios. If long-term assets are being sold to improve the current ratio, then the total-liability-to-total-asset ratio will become worse. Unfortunately, some ratios tend to carry more weight than others, and even though many things affect the current ratio and can mask underlying problems, it remains a key focus. Also, it is not clear which ratio could inform the manager that endowment income was crucial for a safe current ratio and that endowment income was down this year.

A second approach to this problem is greater reliance on the statement of changes in financial position (often called the statement of sources and uses of funds, the statement of sources and uses of working capital or the statement of changes in working capital). This statement must be included along with a balance sheet and statement of revenues and expenses (income statement) to receive an opinion from a Certified Public Accountant on an organization's financial statements. It focuses on the sources and uses of current assets. Unlike the current ratio, which only gives an indication of the amount of change in current assets and current liabilities, this financial statement details what caused the change in these items. For example, one major source of current assets listed would be endowment fund income. A manager would quickly see that this number must be carefully monitored during the year because of its ultimate impact on working capital.

Any manager concerned enough to be interested in the current ratio should take the next step and carefully review the statement of changes in financial position, not only to see what has happened in the past, but as a better indicator of the future.

Ratios are a useful managerial tool, but their value has been substantially overstated. Especially during inflationary periods, their use requires a great deal of caution. In general, ratio analysis has been offered without qualification regarding its limitations. The risks and dangers of using ratio analysis evoke the cliche about the danger of a little knowledge.

At the very least, users of ratios should be aware of two points. First, ratios describe relationships between numbers, but not how those relationships came about nor whether there is reason to believe the relationship will persist. The focus is on how much, rather than how or why. Second, ratios are generally calculated from financial statement data prepared with GAAP. This implies use of historical cost rather than current cost. Therefore all distortions inherent in financial statements during inflationary periods will be inherent in the ratios, although perhaps not as obvious. These distortions are probably great enough that the usefulness of ratios based on GAAP financial statement numbers must be seriously challenged.

NOTES

1. R. Caruana and G. Kudder. "Seeing Through the Figures With Ratios." *Hospital Financial Management* 8:6 (June 1978) pp. 16–26.

2. R. Caruana and E.T. McHugh. "Comparing Ratios Shows Fiscal Trends." *Hospital Financial Management* 10:1 (January 1980) pp. 12–28.

3. W.O. Cleverley and K. Nilsen. "Assessing Financial Position With 29 Key Ratios." *Hospital Financial Management* 10:1 (January 1980) pp. 30–36.

4. B.R. Neumann and A.L. Friedman. "Should Financial Statements Disclose the Cost of Replacing Hospital Assets." *Health Care Management Review* 5:1 (Winter 1980) pp. 49–58.

5. S.A. Finkler. "LIFO Inventory Accounting." *Hospital Financial Management* 10:1 (January 1980) pp. 38–44.

Application 11-2

Cost Accounting Ratios

Paul Selivanoff, CPA, is currently Vice President and Chief Financial Officer at Central Texas Medical Center, San Marcos, Texas.

James R. Gravell, MBA, CPA, is currently Chief Financial Officer at Medical Center Hospital, Punta Gorda, Florida.

The cost accounting ratios described here are being used at Florida Hospital. We hope readers will find them interesting and useful.

LABOR BENEFITS FACTOR

The purpose of the Labor Benefits Factor is to relate wage-related benefits such as overtime, on-call time, shift differential, worker's compensation, travel allowance, and training to the actual wage dollars paid. This computation is useful in determining the labor cost of a specific procedure when microcosting.

Example

Salaries and Wages Expense:	$1,000
Overtime Paid	100
On-call Time Paid	10
Shift Differential	70
Worker's Compensation	20
Paid Days Off	100
FICA Taxes	70
	$370

Labor Benefits Factor = 370/1,000 = .37 or 37%

Source: Reprinted from Paul Selivanoff and James Gravell, "Cost Accounting Ratios," *Hospital Cost Accounting Advisor*, Vol. 1, No. 10, March 1986, pp. 5–6. Copyright 1986, Aspen Publishers, Inc.

This factor, based on historical expenses in the department being analyzed, shows that for every one dollar of wages paid, an additional 37 cents is paid in benefits. It can be used in microcosting or estimating costs during budgeting for a new position. We have found it varies widely, depending on the personnel mix within each department.

AVERAGE COST PER PROCEDURE

This crude measure is useful for analyzing gross changes in case mix or resource consumption. One of our directors, who didn't have the benefits of a cost accounting system, used this to flag variances in his general ledger. Changes in the average cost over time could be caused by changes in case mix or in the individual cost of the items. This measure won't tell you which is responsible, but it is useful in providing some way to track cost over time. Any group of cost items can be tracked and analyzed using this method. It works as follows:

$$\text{Average Labor Cost per Procedure} = \frac{\text{Total Wages}}{\text{Total Procedure Volume}}$$

$$\text{Average Materials Cost per Procedure} = \frac{\text{Total Materials}}{\text{Total Procedure Volume}}$$

COST ACCOUNTING ACCURACY INDEX

The Cost Accounting Accuracy Index provided a needed tool to give management an indicator of the changes in accuracy of the cost information we supplied over the entire length of our implementation, which is phased and includes the use of RCC, Relative Value Unit, and 80/20 Microcosting. As we microcost more and more procedures, we intuitively understood the accuracy of the cost information would increase, and we expressed this using an accuracy index computation as follows:

Accuracy Index = (dollars costed using RCC × .50)
    + (dollars costed using RVU × .75)
    + (dollars costed using microcosting
        methods × .90)
    ÷ total cost in the hospital

Using this index, which ranges between 50% and 90%, we are able to show management how the accuracy of the cost data is increasing with each report we present during the implementation phase.

The accuracy ratios—.50, .75, and .90—were developed from a statistical comparison of the difference in costs obtained at the procedure level under each methodology and include an adjustment for our confidence limit. It is beyond the scope of this document to present the exact statistical model used. A hospital might use these accuracy ratios as standards or develop their own using their own model if they desired. The focus is not on the ratios, but on the change in accuracy over the time period of the implementation. We see this as an excellent tool to show management the benefits they are receiving through increased accuracy.

VARIABLE COST PER PATIENT DAY

Another way to examine variable costs is to look at the difference in costs between two or more years adjusted for changes in patient volume and inflation. This model shows how the computation might work:

Variable Cost per Patient Day
    = (last year total cost – this year total cost)
    ÷ (last year patient days – this year patient days)
    × regional or national inflation adjustment factor

NURSING HOURS PER PATIENT DAY

The nursing hours per patient day can be used as an inflator/deflator for comparisons between nursing units or as a measure of relative acuity/management efficiency over time for a single department. As patient acuity increases, the nursing hours per patient day should increase. In addition, management and staffing efficiency could also cause a decrease/increase.

$$\frac{\text{Nursing Hours}}{\text{per Patient Day}} = \frac{\text{Nursing Hours}}{\text{Patient Days}}$$

A Variation:

$$\frac{\text{Nursing Hours}}{\text{per Patient Day}} = \frac{\text{Nursing Wages}}{\text{Patient Days}}$$

Application 11-3

Cost Accounting Ratios

James J. Donbavand, BBA, MBA, is currently Manager
of Information Analysis and Planning at
The Methodist Hospital, Houston, Texas.

Although the concept of fixed and variable costs is fairly well understood in industries that have worked with these concepts over the years, I have found the distinction to be a difficult one to make in hospitals. While an acceptable definition can usually be arrived at with a department manager, I believe a method of validating the reasonableness of the results of a cost study in the hospital departments is a tool most financial managers will find useful.

The sample ratios presented here (Exhibit 11-3-1) are designed to look at either detail or summary level expense variances in relation to revenue variances. For example, registered nurse expense in the sample department is approximately 77.7% variable, while the head nurse is a purely fixed expense.

In comparing these ratios for this department for several full years, a certain trend or level

should become apparent. Another useful application would be the comparison of like departments.

The objective here (as is usually the case with ratio analysis) is not to definitively measure a financial concept but to understand it better to be able to work with it. I would like to point out that while other possible ways of measuring variability do not work because of the impact of inflation on costs, this method will work if the traditional fixed budget has been prepared well.

As a final note, although different departments will have varying ratios of cost-to-charges (RCC), the charges *within* a department for its services are usually well enough correlated to the approximate cost of the individual services that the variance of revenue (actual to budget) can serve as an indicator against which to measure expense variability. Therefore, where a ratio exceeds 100%, that category may be assumed to be 100% variable with the excess categorized as an inefficiency variance.

Source: Reprinted from James J. Donbavand, "Cost Accounting Ratios," *Hospital Cost Accounting Advisor,* Vol. 1, No. 10, March 1986, pp. 6–7. Copyright 1986, Aspen Publishers, Inc.

Exhibit 11-3-1 Sample Ratios

RATIO ANALYSIS

	Budget	Actual	Percent Increase
Revenue	$1,000,000	$1,180,000	18.0
Visits	20,000	22,000	10.0
Salary			
RN [registered nurse]	$250,000	$285,000	14.0
LPN [licensed practical nurse]	200,000	210,000	5.0
Head nurse	30,000	30,000	-0-
Ward clerk	70,000	75,000	7.1
Total	$550,000	$600,000	9.1
Non-salary			
Medical supplies	$90,000	$105,000	16.7
Other supplies	10,000	11,000	10.0
Drugs	25,000	28,000	12.0
Rent	40,000	40,000	-0-
Depreciation	8,000	8,000	-0-
Total	$173,000	$192,000	11.0
Total Department Expense	$723,000	$792,000	9.5

Acuity Index	$\frac{\text{Revenue Variance}}{\text{Volume Variance}}$	$\frac{18.0}{10.0}$	=	1.8%
Variability Ratios RN	$\frac{\text{RN Salary Expense Variance}}{\text{Revenue Variance}}$	$\frac{14.0}{18.0}$	=	77.7%
Head Nurse	$\frac{\text{Head Nurse Variance}}{\text{Revenue Variance}}$	$\frac{0}{18.0}$	=	0%
Total Salary	$\frac{\text{Total Salary Variance}}{\text{Revenue Variance}}$	$\frac{9.1}{18.0}$	=	50.5%
Medical Supplies	$\frac{\text{Medical Supplies Variance}}{\text{Revenue Variance}}$	$\frac{16.7}{18.0}$	=	92.8%
Total Expense	$\frac{\text{Total Expense Variance}}{\text{Revenue Variance}}$	$\frac{9.5}{18.0}$	=	52.8%

12

Measuring Productivity

Goals of This Chapter

1. Define productivity measurement.
2. Differentiate between total productivity measurement and partial productivity measurement.
3. Provide tools for productivity analysis.
4. Consider the measurement of indirect costs as part of the productivity measurement process.
5. Introduce the concept of discretionary costs.
6. Consider the problems related to controlling discretionary cost.
7. Explain the use of efficiency and effectiveness for assessing the productivity of discretionary cost departments.

Key Terms Used in This Chapter

Committed costs; cost accounting ratios; direct costs; discretionary costs; effectiveness; efficiency; engineered costs; index of labor hours; index of output; indirect costs; partial productivity; productivity; productivity measurement; total productivity; work measurement; zero-base budget.

Note: Key terms appear in italics when first used in the chapter. All key terms are defined in the Glossary.

INTRODUCTION

One concern of many health care organizations today is *productivity*. As financial resources become more and more constrained, productivity improvements represent one way of cutting fat rather than lean. The last chapter introduced the notion of *cost accounting ratios*. Productivity is an example of the area where the use of cost accounting ratios provides information for improved management of health care organizations. As financial constraints continue to mount, productivity becomes an ever-increasing concern for health care organizations. Cost accounting, as a field oriented toward generating information for decision making and performance measurement, has begun to focus attention on the problems related to *productivity measurement.*

The area of productivity measurement, however, remains somewhat of a mystery in many industries, not just health care. In health care, the difficulties are compounded by problems related to quality and output measurement. Productivity represents the measurement of inputs required to produce an output. However, outputs have always been difficult to define in health care. Proxies such as visits, treatments, patient days, and discharges have been used.

Although one could take a complete course of study in the field of productivity, this chapter introduces and highlights key issues. As is the case in many areas of cost accounting, the human role is essential in productivity. It is the action of employees that determines, to a great extent, how productive the organization will be. Application 12-1 at the end of this chapter considers a participative management approach to productivity. Such a tact is likely to have a greater chance of success than simply designing productivity tools and imposing their use.

PRODUCTIVITY DEFINED

The most common productivity measure is output per labor hour. That is, for each hour of labor input, what quantity of goods or services is produced? This will measure just part of the organization's productivity. It fails, for example, to account for the amount of capital equipment used in producing the output. In more general terms, we can define productivity as simply being the ratio of any given measure of output to any given measure of input over a specified time period.

Thus, we can look at either *total productivity,*

$$\text{Total productivity} = \frac{\text{Total outputs}}{\text{Total inputs}}$$

or we can look at some *partial productivity* subpart of that total:

$$\text{Partial productivity} = \frac{\text{Total outputs}}{\text{Partial inputs}}$$

It should be noted, however, that there is no correct result for these ratios. There is no absolute standard for the correct level of productivity. Therefore, these ratios must be used as a basis for comparison. A health care organization can compare itself with others but would probably do best to focus on the changes in its own productivity ratios over time.

In measuring productivity, we have the option of either stating the results in dollar terms or physical units. For example, while we could measure a health care organization's dollars of revenue per labor hour, we might also wish to determine how many patients are treated per hour. In general, the total productivity ratio is measured in dollar terms, whereas partial productivity ratios are more frequently given in physical units.

THE TRADITIONAL APPROACH TO MEASURING PRODUCTIVITY

In many industries, the product being produced is made in a repeated process. The same product is made over and over, and it is relatively easy to identify which resources were used to make which products. For any given product, the total inputs and their cost can be accumulated for a period such as a month and divided by the total units produced to find the cost per unit. If the cost per unit can be reduced, productivity will rise.

In the health care field, there are several obvious limitations of that approach. First, the product varies considerably. A hospital will likely treat patients from several hundred different Diagnosis Related Groups (DRGs), and within DRGs there is substantial variation among patients. Furthermore, we do not just keep producing. If we have extra labor and materials at a slow point in a factory operation, we can produce some extra units to lower the cost per unit. In a health care organization, we can only work with the patients we have. That sometimes means unavoidable down time (and lost resources) waiting for the next patient.

Additionally, it is difficult to assign costs of most departments directly to patients of any given type. Although cost accounting systems are moving in the direction of direct association of costs with patients, it is not clear that resource inputs will ever be assigned to patients with the same degree of accuracy and detail as is possible in a factory process that produces only one given type of product.

Thus, we run into problems of productivity measurement. Should we measure productivity as the cost per patient day, or the cost per discharge, or the cost per hour of surgery? All of these measures are flawed in the same way. They are unlikely to tell us how our productivity is changing because there is no assurance that the output measure is constant. As the clinical mix of patients changes, the inputs required for patient days, discharges, or hours of surgery change as well.

THE TOTAL PRODUCTIVITY RATIO

A health care organization's total productivity (P) can be expressed by the following ratio:

$$P = \frac{\text{Outputs}}{\text{Supplies} + \text{labor} + \text{capital} + \text{overhead}}$$

This ratio is particularly useful when expressed in dollar terms because it shows the financial benefits of improved productivity. For example, suppose that a clinic handled more visits per labor hour this year than last year. The partial productivity of visits per labor hour has increased, but has the clinic benefited financially? That would depend on two things. First, what happened to the revenue per patient? Second, what happened to the cost per labor hour?

Even if the revenue per patient were constant, and even if the clinic treated more patients per labor hour, it may have a worse financial outcome. This could occur if the cost of the labor hours rose faster than the increase in the number of treatments per labor hour or if the clinic used more supplies and equipment per labor hour. Total productivity avoids that measurement problem.

Using the total productivity measure, we find the dollar value of outputs as compared with the dollar cost of inputs. Thus, the increase in wages or the price of supplies are considered in this measure, as well as the quantity of inputs consumed.

In most industries, the output is measured by multiplying the units produced by their selling price. This uses units produced rather than units sold because the focus of productivity is on production rather than sales. However, for a health care organization, the number of unbilled patients at the end of each year is likely to be approximately the same, and we can generally ignore the problem of stockpiling output. Therefore, we could express total productivity as follows:

$$P = \frac{\text{Operating revenue}}{\text{Supplies} + \text{labor} + \text{capital} + \text{overhead}}$$

We must exercise caution to keep our unit of evaluation constant over time. When we are dealing with partial productivity measures, such as treatments per hour, this is generally not a problem. However, when using dollar amounts, we run into the problem of inflation. To make the productivity measures comparable over time, we would have to keep the calculations in constant dollars (see Chapter 7 for a discussion of indexing for inflation).

A more difficult problem concerns the potential for changes in quality. Productivity measures implicitly assume that quality is held constant. Obviously, it is incorrect to consider a reduction in hours per treatment to be a productivity gain if it was accomplished by reducing quality. Similarly, the basic total productivity ratio is inadequate to segregate the impact of case-mix changes from the impact of productivity changes.

THE PARTIAL PRODUCTIVITY RATIO

The partial productivity ratio is a measure of output compared with a partial measure of input. As discussed above, the number of patients treated in a clinic, per labor hour, would be a partial productivity ratio.

The advantage of the partial approach is that it allows us to focus on what is happening with just one part of our input picture. However, that, in turn, can lead to problems if we substitute one form of input for another.

For example, suppose that we were to replace some registered nurses (RNs) with licensed practical nurses (LPNs). The LPNs might well be less efficient than are the RNs in that it may take them more hours to provide the same level of care. Using a partial productivity measure, the extra labor hours will make it appear as if our productivity has decreased. However, if the cost of LPNs is sufficiently less than that of RNs, then the cost of treating patients may in

fact have decreased, and productivity improved (assuming quality remains the same). Despite the potential substitution problem, partial productivity measures are widely used.

A Partial Productivity Measure Example

Suppose, for the sake of a simple example, we consider the technician labor hours necessary for a computed tomography (CT) scan. Table 12-1 provides us with baseline information and data for the current period. The baseline data may represent actual results from an earlier period or may be based on engineered standards.

In this example, we are assuming that CT scans come in only two types, head and body. The baseline output is 220 hours, made up of 100 head scans at 1.0 hour each (on average) and 80 body scans requiring 1.5 hours of technician time each (on average).

Using the same level of productivity, the actual volume for the current period, 120 head scans and 70 body scans, should have consumed 225 hours. In fact, we performed the scans in the current period using a total of only 215 hours. Productivity measures can be calculated without determining how many actual hours were spent on each product. Thus, we have no break-down of the 215 actual technician hours between head and body scans. A special study could be performed if we were particularly concerned with the relative costliness or efficiency with which the different types of CT scans were performed.

However, from Table 12-1, we can calculate several statistics without a break-down of labor

Table 12-1 Labor Hours for CT Scan

Scan Type	Baseline			Current Period		
	Labor Hours per Scan	Number of Scans	Total Hours	Actual Number of Scans	Actual Labor Hours	Current Volume × Base Period Hours
Head	1.0	100	100	120	N/C*	120 × 1.0 = 120
Body	1.5	80	120	70	N/C*	70 × 1.5 = 105
Totals		180	220	190	215	225

*N/C = Data not collected.

hours by scan type. The current period *index of output* is 102.3 percent:

$$\text{Index of output} = \frac{\text{Actual output hours}}{\text{Baseline output hours}} \times 100\%$$

$$= \frac{225}{220} \times 100\%$$

$$= 102.3\%$$

That indicates that our output increased by 2.3 percent over the base period. The *index of labor hours* is 97.7 percent:

$$\text{Index of labor hours} = \frac{\text{Actual labor hours}}{\text{Baseline labor hours}} \times 100\%$$

$$= \frac{215}{220} \times 100\%$$

$$= 97.7\%$$

That indicates that we actually worked only 97.7 percent as many hours in the current period as in the baseline case.

The *index of output per labor hour* compares these first two indices. It is 104.7 percent:

$$\begin{matrix}\text{Index of output} \\ \text{per labor hour}\end{matrix} = \frac{\text{Index of output}}{\text{Index of labor hours}} \times 100\%$$

$$= \frac{102.3}{97.7} \times 100\%$$

$$= 104.7\%$$

That is, our output in the current period per labor hour is 104.7 percent of that in the baseline period. Alternatively stated, we have a productivity gain of 4.7 percent in the current period.

In an environment of inflation, regulation, and technological change, it is hard to keep track of whether things are improving in terms of productivity. The advantage of using calculations like those in this example is that it provides management with information in constant terms. The partial productivity measure demonstrated ignores the impact of anything except

the amount of output being generated by an hour of labor input. We get a concrete measure of simple productivity changes.

We can, of course, create any number of partial productivity measures throughout each health care organization. Even further, we can move a step closer to total productivity without moving all the way. In the above example, after finding the partial productivity gain of 4.7 percent based on time taken to produce the output, we could then bring the cost of labor into the calculation.

For example, if the wages of technicians have increased by 4 percent while we have a partial productivity gain of 4.7 percent, then we would have a .7 percent productivity gain, net of the increased cost of labor. Thus, we know that the changes made in the way we provide CT scans have resulted in labor-hour savings that are more than enough to offset the labor salary increases. Although the .7 percent net productivity gain may seem very small, it should be considered in light of the fact that the revenue per unit of service is also likely to be rising over time.

However, it is very difficult to bring revenue into the calculation unless you use a total productivity ratio. In a total prospective payment system, we cannot really assign revenue to individual intermediary services, such as a CT scan. Even if we have patients who are paying charges based on individual services, those charges cover not only labor, but equipment and overhead as well, making any attempt to calculate the labor portion of the revenue increase an almost hopeless task. However, partial productivity measures in themselves are quite useful for labor negotiations, for monitoring of continued efficiency of operations, and for identification of places to improve the operations of health care organizations.

PRODUCTIVITY AND INDIRECT COSTS

Another alternative to the traditional comparison of total cost of inputs divided into total output is to develop a productivity measure that is based on a comparison of *direct costs* and *indirect costs*. A number of departments in health care organizations utilize some resources in direct patient contact and other resources indirectly. The operating room of a hospital is a typical example. Although the patient hours in surgery are logged, and direct patient care is rather easily measurable, there are a number of other activities that must be performed to prepare for the patient, and other required activities after the patient has been taken to recovery.

Clearly, there may also be inactive, unproductive time by personnel in the operating room, but there is also some productive time that is not direct patient care time. The same thing holds true for all departments that measure their direct patient care activity in time, such as respiratory therapy, physical therapy, and so forth.

The question is whether there is a relationship between the hours of direct patient care time and indirect, but productive, time. If there is, then we can monitor the relationship on a monthly basis to ascertain whether productivity is being improved or at least maintained.

For example, suppose that we found that respiratory (inhalation) therapists needed 30 minutes of indirect time for each 1 hour of therapy. The indirect time might include reviewing the patient chart, gathering supplies and/or equipment, walking to the patient room, walking from the patient room, making entries in the patient chart, and replacing and restocking supplies and equipment. Additional indirect time might include scheduling and other necessary administrative activities.

If we divide the required indirect time by the direct time, we determine that the expected indirect time is 50 percent:

$$\frac{\text{Indirect time}}{\text{Direct time}} = \frac{30 \text{ minutes}}{60 \text{ minutes}} \times 100\% = 50\%$$

If we performed a study of what our inhalation therapists do and found that the 30 minutes of indirect time was a reasonable level for a 1-hour therapy session, then we could establish it as a standard.

Suppose that we have in fact done that. Our indirect standard rate would be 50 percent of our direct rate. In future months, we could add 50 percent to the direct patient care hours to determine the total care hours. Then we could examine the actual total hours to assess our productivity.

A complexity, however, is that we will pay for more therapist time than simply the direct care time and the standard indirect time. There will be vacation, holiday, and sick leave. There will be hours spent on in-service education. There will be days when we are overstaffed, and there will be normal slack time between patients that cannot be used productively.

Of course, we would like to reduce overstaffing, and we would like to reduce the slack time between patients. Suppose that, in an initial month under the new productivity measurement system, we have 800 hours of direct therapy time. Our 50 percent indirect standard would dictate that we should expect also to have 400 hours of indirect time for a variety of necessary, although not direct patient contact, activities:

$$\begin{array}{rl} 800 & \text{Direct hours} \\ \times\ 50\% & \\ \hline 400 & \text{Required indirect hours} \end{array}$$

Thus, our productive time would be 1,200 hours, including both direct and indirect.

If we actually paid for 1,500 hours, we could divide the 1,200 productive hours by the 1,500 total hours to get a productivity level:

$$\text{Productivity level} = \frac{\text{Productive hours}}{\text{Total hours}} \times 100\%$$

$$= \frac{1{,}200}{1{,}500} \times 100\%$$

$$= 80\%$$

Note, this will not give us the traditional productivity measure in terms of cost per unit. Rather, it will give us a percentage. In this case, the productivity level is 80 percent. Perfection would be 100 percent. To attain the perfection level of 100 percent, we would not only have to have wasted no time and had no slack or overstaffing, but we also would have to have no sick time, holidays, or vacation.

If we used this productivity measure, we would want to track the percentage over time.

Our concern would not be with achieving the 100 percent ideal, but rather would focus on tracking increases and decreases in the percentage from our starting point of 80 percent.

For psychological reasons, we may not like using the measure in this form because it requires that no one take vacations or holidays in order to be fully productive, and that is unreasonable. We might prefer to develop a normal rate for nonproductive time. For example, we might note that vacations, sick leave, and holidays are scheduled to be 12 percent of worked hours. Additionally, in-service education might be scheduled at a rate of 2 percent of worked hours. The two factors combine to a total of 14 percent.

In that case, suppose that in the above example, we paid for 1,500 hours, of which 1,200 were worked. In addition to the 1,200 worked hours, we should have an additional 14 percent, or 168 paid hours for vacation, holiday, sick leave, and in-service education (1,200 × 14% = 168). That would make a total of 1,368 hours that have been accounted for:

```
   800   Direct hours
 + 400   Required indirect hours
 + 168   Vacation, sick-leave, holiday, and education
 ─────
 1,368   Total
 ═════
```

Using this approach, we could define 1,368 paid hours as 100 percent, rather than using 1,200 as 100 percent.

We still have not reached 100 percent productivity because we actually paid for 1,500 hours. If we divide the 1,368 hours calculated by the 1,500 hours actually paid for, we have a productivity measure of 91.2 percent:

We would then monitor that level over time.

One problem with attempting to build in a percentage for vacation, sick leave, and so forth is that those items do not tend to be taken evenly throughout the year. We may have a month in which no one takes vacation or education time. Thus, we will not spend any actual hours on those activities, but an allowance for them will be built into our productivity measure. The result will be a misleadingly high productivity. Conversely, in months when a lot of vacation is taken, our 14 percent allowance will not be nearly enough. As a result, we will pay for far more hours than are worked, and will show a very low productivity.

It would probably make more sense to eliminate vacations, holidays, and education from the actual hours and from the calculation. We would still want to leave sick leave (except for long-term disability) in the calculation if we believe that it is at least partly controllable. Suppose, in the earlier example, that of the 1,500 paid hours, 150 hours were for vacations, holidays, and education. The adjusted actual paid hours for our productivity measurement would be 1,350 (i.e., 1,500 paid hours less 150 hours of vacations, holiday, and education).

Our direct hours are still 800, and indirect hours are still 400. Although we expect all vacations and holidays to be taken, there is no reason to believe that sick leave must be taken. We could argue that a 100 percent productivity level would require no sick leave. If so, then we should divide the 1,200 total direct and indirect productive hours by the 1,350 adjusted actual hours to get the productivity level. In this case, it would be 88.9 percent:

$$\text{Productivity level} = \frac{\begin{array}{c}\text{Productive hours}\\ \text{(direct + indirect)}\\ \text{+ vacation, holiday, etc.}\end{array}}{\text{Total hours}} \times 100\%$$

$$= \frac{1,368}{1,500} \times 100\%$$

$$= 91.2\%$$

$$\text{Productivity level} = \frac{\begin{array}{c}\text{Productive hours}\\ \text{(direct + indirect)}\end{array}}{\begin{array}{c}\text{Adjusted hours}\\ \text{(actual total − vacation,}\\ \text{holiday, and education)}\end{array}} \times 100\%$$

$$= \frac{1,200}{1,350} \times 100\%$$

$$= 88.9\%$$

The exact approach we take is largely a matter of preference. Each organization should make its own decision, and then be consistent across departments and over time. However, it should be made clear that it is unrealistic to expect to achieve a 100 percent productivity level and that the use of the measure is for comparison over time. Certainly, if we can reduce the overstaffing and slack time between patients, we can improve the productivity measure—we can move closer to 100 percent. Also, if sick time can be reduced, the productivity measure is also likely to rise. However, given some of the uncontrollables (such as patient flow into the organization), it may not be possible to achieve a 100 percent productivity.

On the other hand, if we can develop ways to reduce indirect time, it is possible to see steady increases in productivity—even above 100 percent. Suppose for example, that we were to automate patient records with a completely computerized system. It is conceivably possible that the time recording patient information could drop substantially. If so, the indirect time per patient might fall by enough to drive productivity above 100 percent.

In that case, once the new system is well established, we would probably want to develop a new, lower standard for indirect time, because it is the equipment, rather than superlative worker effort, that is resulting in the high productivity. If, however, our workers simply reorganize their efforts to be more productive, there is no reason we cannot continue to show productivity above 100 percent without rebasing it.

Another problem that must be considered is the fixed/variable nature of indirect costs. Suppose that, due to technological improvement, we are able to reduce the length of time that the average operation takes from 2.0 hours to 1.8 hours. What impact will that have on indirect costs? We must exercise care. If we had performed an operating room study similar to that described for respiratory therapy, we would have developed a relationship between hours of operations and indirect hours. For example, we might have determined that for every 100 hours of surgery, we use 30 hours of indirect time,

preparing for the surgery and taking care of necessary steps after the surgery:

$$\frac{\text{Indirect time}}{\text{Direct time}} = \frac{30 \text{ hours}}{100 \text{ hours}} \times 100\% = 30\%$$

Thus, we have a relationship of 30 percent indirect hours.

In a month with 3,000 hours of surgery, we would expect 900 hours of indirect productive time:

3,000	Direct hours
× 30%	
900	Required indirect hours

If we actually paid for 3,900 hours (after subtracting vacations, etc.), we would say that we were 100 percent productive. However, what happens if technology allows us to shorten the average operation by 10 percent as suggested above? If we had 2,700 hours of operations, should we have only 810 hours of indirect time (2,700 direct hours × 30% indirect factor)?

Some types of indirect activities will tend to vary with the number of patients rather than the length of procedure time. Preparing an operating room, recording a patient's treatment on his or her chart, or walking to a patient's room to administer a treatment will not change because of the underlying change in the length of the treatment.

How can we handle this problem? One approach would be to fall back on the more traditional productivity measure, which simply looks at the cost per unit produced. However, if we do that, we lose track of the valuable information generated by having an expected relation between direct and indirect costs. Bear in mind that in the more typical instances where direct hours per patient or per operation are fairly stable, the productivity measure discussed in this section yields a lot of information about how the indirect costs are changing.

A more sensible approach is to monitor some productivity measure of direct costs. For example, we should keep track of the average hours of surgery per patient or average hours of respiratory therapy per treatment. If these measures start to fall, that is a sign of increasing productivity in the area of direct costs. However, it also is an indication that the indirect cost relationship to direct costs should be reevaluated.

Alternatively, some health care organizations will likely start to have their clinicians log their hours for various activities. The benefit of such logging would be that not only would we have a continuously updated relationship between direct and indirect productive hours, but we would also have a continuously updated relationship between worked hours that are direct, indirect, and nonproductive.

MANAGING DISCRETIONARY COSTS

One of the major challenges of management is control over *discretionary costs.* These are costs incurred in departments that are essential to the organization but that do not have simple input–output relationships. Productivity in such instances is extremely difficult to assess. Examples of such departments include personnel, marketing, legal, finance, administration, housekeeping, security, and plant operations. There are many other such departments throughout most health care organizations. Additionally, most departments will have some costs that are discretionary, such as consultants and in-service education. How can one determine an appropriate amount to budget for such departments? One can logically classify health care costs as falling into three broad categories: engineered, committed, and discretionary.

Engineered costs are those for which there is a specific input–output relationship. More patient days require more meals from the dietary department. More x-rays require more sheets of x-ray film. Generally, such relationships can be readily observed. Engineered costs normally include the direct materials and direct labor cost.

In health care, even direct labor is not a clearly engineered relationship. For example, more patient days will undoubtedly call for more hours of direct nursing care. A hospital may have an accepted standard number of hours of nursing care per patient day. However, that standard is not really based on industrial engi-neering requirements as much as it is based on negotiation about what amount of care is needed to produce acceptable care. If the number of hours of care per patient day were cut, there probably would be just as many patient days produced. On the other hand, the quality of each patient day might well decline.

Engineered costs can be controlled by using flexible budget variance reports. The concept of a flexible budget is that there is a direct relationship between inputs and outputs. If the number of patient days increases, then the cost for meals, x-rays, and nursing will increase as well. Thus, variance reports that allow for the impact of changes in volume on output should be satisfactory for controlling such costs.

Committed costs are those costs that cannot be changed in the short run, such as during the coming year. An example would be the depreciation cost on a nursing home building. Similarly, long-term leases, depreciation on equipment, insurance, and some interest are costs over which managers have little current control. Costs that will become committed require careful scrutiny by the organization. Generally, they are reviewed as part of the capital budget process. Once committed to, however, they tend not to vary from year to year. Fluctuations in the volume of services provided will often have no effect on such committed costs.

Discretionary costs are those that are incurred, typically each year, in an amount that is approved as part of the normal budget process. However, there is not a clear relationship between the volume of services and the amount of cost that must be incurred. Managers must make a decision regarding the level that is deemed to be appropriate. As a result, these costs are sometimes referred to as managed costs.

Health care organizations tend to accept the activities of the various discretionary departments as being appropriate at a particular level of service. The accepted budget is generally the result of a negotiated process. Once the budget is approved, it does not vary with volume the way that a flexible budget would. Is the level accepted for the budget adequate for the department to get the job done? Is there too much money in the budget for the department? Is the department's productivity improving or declining? These questions are typical problems for discretionary costs, for which there is no easy answer as to how much is enough.

Keeping Discretionary Costs under Control

There are a number of differences between the nature of engineered costs and discretionary costs. Horngren and Foster cite differences in terms of typical inputs, process, outputs, and the level of uncertainty.[1]

While the inputs that make up engineered costs consist of both physical and human resources, discretionary costs are predominantly for human resources. The productive process in departments whose costs are engineered is often readily observable and repetitive. On the other hand, the productive process in discretionary departments is similar to a black box, with activities being nonroutine, nonrepetitive, and hard to quantify.

Just as the process of discretionary departments may be hard to define clearly, so are the outputs. Whereas an engineered cost department produces some measurable output, capable of being evaluated in terms of revenue production, and to some extent quality, the discretionary cost departments often are producing information. The outputs of such departments defy measurement and are hard to value. Quality measurement may also pose a problem.

For example, if the legal department loses a malpractice law case, is it because they did a poor job or because the case was not winnable? Was their decision to go to court rather than to settle a good decision with a bad outcome or a poor judgment call on their part? Were the legal resources devoted to the case too little to be able to make a winning case, or too much for a case that could not be won in any event?

As the above example demonstrates, not only is there difficulty measuring the value and product of a discretionary cost center, there is great uncertainty involved as well. The productive process of an engineered department is often

straightforward. Certain inputs will result in the production of certain outputs. In the case of discretionary costs, we may not know the result or output until after all the inputs are in. The lawsuit is an excellent example of the type of gambles that are taken by discretionary cost centers.

Zero-Base Review

The budget for discretionary costs is generally based on a negotiation. The simplest form for such a negotiation process to take would be to focus on the requested increment over the prior period. Typically, the increment consists of salary increases, general increases to cover the cost of supply price increases, and an increase to cover the costs of specific new projects. The problem with such an approach is that it never leads to examination of the base upon which the budget is being increased. Over time, there may be aspects of the discretionary cost department that have a lower priority than they once did. However, they are never removed from the budget.

At the other extreme are *zero-base budgets* (sometimes referred to as "zero-based budgets"). This well-known technique requires that all costs be justified. This is an expensive and time-consuming practice. Although some would suggest using this approach annually, in health care organizations, departments rarely undergo such a thorough review more often than perhaps once every five years.

Zero-base budgeting is more than just a review of the specific items proposed in the budget. It also represents a philosophy of exploring alternatives. First, the objectives of the department are determined, then alternative ways to achieve those objectives are explored. This includes alternative levels of output, alternative ways to perform the function, and even alternative levels of quality.

Zero-base budgeting is probably most effective in terms of discretionary costs. Because these costs do not have a clear relationship between inputs and outputs, they are inherently more subjective than engineered costs. As such, an approach that forces consideration of the benefits and costs of alternative levels of effort and alternative approaches can be extremely useful.

A difficulty to overcome is the natural vested interest that each department head has in spending the resources currently allocated to the department. It is a rare manager who would willingly restructure his or her department at a much lower level of expenditure. Nevertheless, with proper supervision and managerial commitment, zero-base budgeting can actually result in major structural downsizing of departments that have not been reviewed in a number of years.

One of the problems with the incremental approach to budgeting is that there is always an assumption that each department could probably make do with less, but that too great a cut would affect volume of services and revenues. Desperate times often result in across-the-board cuts of 10 percent. However, although a 10 percent cut might severely affect an engineered cost department, some discretionary cost centers might handle a 40 percent reduction in spending with far less organizational impact.

The bottom line of zero-base budgeting is that it is important to understand what types of objectives are being accomplished by discretionary cost centers and what resources are being devoted to the accomplishment of the various objectives. This will allow a prioritization, so that the organization will be able to evaluate the likely impact of substantial increases or decreases in the resources allocated to the discretionary center.

Work Measurement

Another approach to dealing with discretionary costs is to perform a review of activities with the hope of converting a discretionary cost center into an engineered cost center. The focus here is that some departments appear to be discretionary because their costs do not vary with the organization's volume of service provided. However, that does not mean that there is no input–output relationship. It merely means that one must be more careful in defining the output of the department. If the center can be converted into an engineered cost center, then the produc-

tivity tools discussed earlier in the chapter could be applied.

Work measurement is a technique that evaluates what a group of workers is doing and attempts to assess the number of workers needed to accomplish the task efficiently. For example, is the cost of the central supply department related to the number of patients? Clearly, it is to some extent. More patients will mean a greater volume of supplies flowing through the organization. However, would one treat that department's budget as a flexible one, increasing with each extra patient day? Probably not.

In all likelihood, the central supply budget will be viewed as a discretionary cost. On the other hand, the labor cost of that department might vary considerably based on the number of packages received and unloaded each month. In that case, the number of packages unloaded might be used as an output measure.

An even more extreme example is the mail room. Certainly, it would be hard to try to relate mail room costs with patient days. On the other hand, it could be related to pieces of mail sent out and pieces of mail received and sorted.

Thus, with the proper measurement of the type of work being performed, it might be possible to reclassify many costs as being engineered. In that case, the control of those costs may become more manageable.

The Problem of Discrete Costs

In the effort to reclassify some costs as being engineered costs, one sometimes runs into problems of the discrete nature of individuals. Suppose that a nursing home employs ten workers in central supply. The department could be viewed as a discretionary center with a requirement for ten employees. Work measurement, however, would determine how many packages each employee unloads. A cost per package could be determined.

Such an approach would imply that we can hire or fire employees as needed on a per-package basis. Obviously, the labor costs will not be that variable. However, the question must be asked regarding exactly how discrete the costs are. Must we hire ten full-time workers? Would it be possible to hire eight full-time workers and fill in the rest with part-time workers? Such an approach might result in using part-timers only when we are very busy. The result might be that only nine and a half full-time equivalents (FTEs) would be needed instead of ten. On the other hand, part-timers might make errors in stocking supplies that would more than offset the savings.

The nursing home must make a decision regarding the appropriate approach to staffing each department. Such decisions may well be reevaluated from time to time. For example, as the number of legal issues rises, it may be more efficient to hire a full-time lawyer than to pay an outside law firm for half of the time of one of their lawyers. A nursing home may decide to contract out for all legal work, eliminating the law department. That might be costly in busy legal times, but it means that there would be no permanent staff to carry at times when there is little legal work. That would shift a fixed legal cost into being variable with the amount of work to be done. Thus, by thoroughly reviewing the nature of costs, the organization has some ability to shift costs between being engineered or discretionary and between being fixed and variable.

Efficiency and Effectiveness

In order to deal with the various peculiarities of discretionary cost centers, one approach is to concentrate on the *efficiency* and *effectiveness* of the departments in the use of discretionary costs. The definition of effectiveness is whether or not the organization accomplishes its desired goal. A set of goals or objectives should be established for a discretionary cost center. After the fact, there should be measurement to see if those goals and objectives were met. If so, the department is effective. On the other hand, efficiency refers to the amount of resources used to accomplish the result. For any given result that occurs, the organization should be attempting to minimize the cost of resources required.

The terms *effectiveness* and *efficiency* are often grouped together under the general heading of cost-effectiveness. This relates to whether

costs were minimized for the desired outcome. The problem with the use of cost-effectiveness is that it is an aggregate measure. It looks at the attainment of objectives and their cost together. By looking at efficiency and effectiveness, one can assess two things individually: (1) whether or not the goals were achieved and (2) the cost of what was actually achieved.

There are a number of different approaches to ensuring the efficiency and effectiveness of a discretionary cost department. These include a thorough review of all budget elements, such as the zero base review discussed earlier; development of monitoring tools for assessing efficiency and effectiveness; introduction of competitive market forces; leadership; a formalized spending approval mechanism; and promotion of an organizational culture.[2]

Monitoring Tools for Efficiency and Effectiveness

The evaluation of discretionary cost centers is generally quite subjective. Since there is no engineered relationship between inputs and outputs, there is no clear-cut amount of output to be measured. As a result, most health care organizations do not evaluate the productivity of discretionary cost centers on the basis of quantitative information, as they would other cost centers. As long as the discretionary center does not spend over its budget and seems to get its job done, its performance is judged to be adequate. It is possible, however, to quantify much of what is done by discretionary cost centers, to allow for a better monitoring of their efficiency and effectiveness.

Consider a personnel department. Personnel is an excellent example of a discretionary cost center—its activity is not related to volume of service, much of its cost is for human resources, and there is no well-known relationship between the size and resources of the personnel office and the amount of work it performs.

Efficiency and effectiveness ratios can help monitor the productivity of such a discretionary cost center or department. Horngren and Foster noted, "What is the optimal amount of resources to spend on the personnel function in an organization? How can top management assess whether a personnel department is increasing the efficiency and effectiveness of its operation? Few organizations ask such questions, in part due to the difficulty of answering them."[3] They discuss a variety of ratios to use in approaching this problem. For example, to monitor the productivity of the hiring function of a personnel department, one could use the cost per hire, the acceptance ratio, and the average time to fill each vacant position. These are examples of cost accounting ratios. (See the previous chapter for a discussion of cost accounting ratios.)

The cost per hire is the total hiring cost divided by the total number of hires. To calculate this, one would have to allocate the total costs of the personnel department among the various major responsibilities of the department. While such divvying up of department costs would take some work, it is a valuable exercise, because it provides a much better indication of what the discretionary cost center is doing and how much each element of its activities costs.

The cost per hire, for example, would include the costs related to vacancy advertisements, employment agency fees, personnel time for interviewing and processing potential candidates (including nonpersonnel-department workers), travel costs, and moving costs.

The acceptance ratio is the number of candidates who accept job offers divided by the number of jobs offered. The average time to fill vacancies is the average time between when the personnel department is authorized to recruit for a position and when the new employee begins work.

We can think of cost per hire, acceptance ratio, and average time to fill positions as being measures of efficiency. However, they provide inadequate information, unless we can also consider effectiveness. Are we accomplishing what we want to? It might be easy to improve efficiency (lower the cost per hire) if one allows effectiveness to fall. What represents effectiveness in the case of a personnel department? It is not just hiring people, but hiring the right people.

A health care organization would hope that the personnel department hires people who do not quit in three months or have to be fired. We would want to hire people who are capable enough to merit promotions over time. Horngren and Foster[4] suggest the following as two possible measures of effectiveness: (1) the retention ratio and (2) the promotion-to-manager ratio.

The retention ratio would compare the number of people hired in a preceding year who are still with the organization to the total number of people hired that year. Obviously, we would want to break down this ratio, and probably the efficiency ratios, into categories. A hospital might want specifically to segregate nurses, because of the nursing shortage of the late 1980s, which continued into the 1990s for many health care providers. Thus, the personnel department might calculate the retention ratio for nurses and the retention ratio for all other employees. In all likelihood, even more subdivisions of the ratio would be desirable.

The promotion-to-manager ratio would divide the total number of employees hired in a given year who have been promoted by the total number of employees hired in that year. Note that for both the retention and promotion ratios, there is a lag. The report of ratios this year concerns the effectiveness of hiring practices in prior years. However, these ratios are better measures of the quality of the hiring practices than is simply the cost per individual hired.

The ratios related to hiring represent only one of the various functions of personnel departments. Personnel departments are only one of the discretionary cost areas of health care organizations. There is no single master list of ratios to be calculated for a personnel department or for any other discretionary cost center. However, the ratios discussed here should give the reader the starting point for developing measures for efficiency and effectiveness.

Comparison of Measures

Measuring these quantitative statistics is not sufficient to monitor efficiency and effectiveness. The cost per hire, by itself, does not tell us much about the efficiency of the personnel department. How much should it cost per hire? In order to improve the usefulness of such measures, it is necessary to compare the results either to the department itself over time or to other similar organizations.

Tracking discretionary cost centers over time is the minimal comparison that should be made. Is the personnel department improving its own level of efficiency and effectiveness over time? Is it at least holding the level at a constant? Health care managers would certainly want to track the results of the various efficiency and effectiveness measures from year to year.

The monitoring process can be substantially enhanced by comparing the discretionary cost center's results to those of other similar organizations. Health care organizations have been very effective at generating cross-sectional data for their use. Interfirm comparisons are always subject to problems of noncomparability. Other organizations may be larger or smaller. They may have more or less of a teaching function. They may be more or less urban.

Nevertheless, such comparisons tend to be very useful in establishing relative efficiency and effectiveness. For example, as the nursing shortage became more severe, each hospital's own cost per hire ratio probably jumped substantially. By being able to identify this as an industry trend, the personnel department could better explain its decreasing efficiency rating. Further, by comparing itself with other hospitals, it could determine if its cost per hire is rising more or less drastically than that of other hospitals.

Many discretionary cost center departments have trade associations. Some of the data needed for efficiency and effectiveness measures are available through such associations.

Competitive Market Forces

Another mechanism for controlling the costs of discretionary cost centers is to make them subject to market forces. For example, suppose that the internal copying center in a health care organization is allocating a charge of six cents per copy to departments for their duplicating. If a copy center across the street can produce copies for five cents each, the internal center is charging above-market prices.

The health care organization could allow various departments the choice of using the internal department or going outside for their duplicating. This would force the internal department to become more efficient.

There are potential negatives with this approach. For one, an internal department may have to be maintained for confidential document copying. If the total internal volume falls due to departments using the outside center, the internal cost per copy will rise due to fixed costs being spread over lower volume.

A key question remains, however. Why should an outside copy center, which earns a profit, be able to charge less than an internal department, which does not have to earn a profit? Using market prices as a maximum can push discretionary centers to be more efficient.

Leadership

The subjective nature of much of what goes on in discretionary cost centers increases the importance of having strong leadership. By having such departments headed by a charismatic leader, the employees are more likely to devote themselves to the job. A hard worker who is a good leader can generate hard work from the department's employees.

In contrast, if a discretionary department is headed by a lifetime bureaucrat who believes in making work, not waves, then the department will take on that personality. The costs will tend to rise, rather than the output.

Spending Approval Mechanism

One of the problems of discretionary cost centers is that their costs tend to creep up gradually over time. Since there is no explicit measure of output in many cases, there is a greater need to scrutinize new costs.

To deal with this issue, a formal system can be put into place for approval of adding positions, filling vacancies, upgrading positions, or authorizing overtime. By requiring someone from outside the department to review these spending decisions, there is a better chance of fairly questioning the purpose and need for the expenditures.

This section suggests a number of different approaches that can be taken to managing discretionary costs. The most important point is that one should not assume that they are not manageable. A reasonable amount of effort should be able to bring such costs into a framework of control, in which their productivity can be monitored.

NOTES

1. C.T. Horngren and G. Foster, *Cost Accounting: A Managerial Emphasis,* 6th ed. (Englewood Cliffs, N.J.: Prentice-Hall, Inc., 1987), 379.
2. Adapted from Horngren and Foster, *Ibid.,* 381.
3. *Ibid.,* 388–389.
4. *Ibid.,* 389.

SUGGESTED READING

Bolster, C.J., and R. Binion. 1987. Linkages between cost management and productivity. *Topics in Health Care Financing* 13, no. 4:67–75.

Chizever, S.D., ed. 1989. Hospital productivity [special issue]. *Topics in Health Care Financing* 15, no. 3.

Choich, R., Jr. May 1988. Relationship of productivity analysis to departmental cost-accounting systems. *American Journal of Hospital Pharmacy* 45, no. 5:1,103–1,110.

Finkler, S.A. 1986. Productivity measurement. *Hospital Cost Accounting Advisor* 1, no. 8:1–4.

Hemeon, F.E., III. 1989. Productivity, cost accounting, and information systems. *Topics in Health Care Financing* 15, no. 3:55–67.

Horngren, C.T., and G. Foster. 1991. *Cost accounting: A managerial emphasis*. 7th ed. Englewood Cliffs, NJ: Prentice-Hall.

Kingsley, D.B., and J.E. Wivell. 1989. Standard cost accounting and productivity systems—An integrated approach. *Journal of Social Health Systems* 1, no. 2: 5–11.

Serway, G.D., et al. 1987. Alternative indicators for measuring hospital productivity. *Hospital & Health Services Administration* 32:379–398.

Van Bodegraven, A. 1989. Developing and using standards for work performance. *Topics in Health Care Financing* 15, no. 3:13–26.

EXERCISES

QUESTIONS FOR DISCUSSION

1. According to the text, what is the most common measure of productivity?
2. What is the difference between total productivity and partial productivity?
3. What are some difficulties related to measuring productivity in the health services area?
4. Can productivity of indirect costs be measured? If so, how; if not, why not?
5. How can you determine if the relationship between direct and indirect costs needs to be reevaluated?
6. What are some examples of discretionary cost centers or departments in health care organizations?
7. Distinguish between engineered, committed, and discretionary costs.
8. Why is control of discretionary costs difficult?

9. What are efficiency and effectiveness? How can those concepts be used to control discretionary costs?
10. Consider a discretionary cost center or department (other than personnel services) and design a set of efficiency and effectiveness ratios to monitor productivity for that cost center or department.

PROBLEMS

1. The Hung Ri Hospital recently bought new equipment for the kitchen with the hopes of increasing food worker productivity. Based on the cost of the equipment and its lifetime, it has been estimated that the investment will be worthwhile if we can improve productivity by 5 percent.

    Last year, before undertaking the purchase, a special study was conducted. Its results indicated that it took 15 minutes to prepare a standard meal, 18 minutes to prepare a low-sodium meal, and on average 24 minutes to prepare meals with other special

Note: Solutions to the Exercises can be found in Appendix A.

requirements. Last year, we prepared 200,000 standard meals; 40,000 low-sodium meals; and 50,000 other special meals. This year, we prepared 170,000 standard meals; 45,000 low-sodium meals; and 60,000 other special meals. The total time for the food workers this year was 76,500 hours. Using a partial productivity ratio, determine if we achieved the desired 5 percent productivity gain.

2. Suppose that the direct time in a laboratory was 27,000 hours of labor, and that a study indicates that indirect time is generally required to be 33 percent of direct time. During the year, excluding vacations, holidays, and education time, the laboratory department paid for 40,000 hours of labor. How productive was the department in terms of its total use of direct and indirect costs?

Application 12-1

Productivity Management:
A Model for Participative Management
in Health Care Organizations

*Newton Margulies, PhD, is currently Professor and Director of
Executive Education, Graduate School of Management at the
University of California—Irvine, California.*

*John F. Duval is currently Vice President of the University Medical Center
and Assistant Clinical Lecturer at the University of Arizona
College of Medicine, Department of Pathology, Tucson, Arizona.*

In recent months the issue of improving the productivity of America's work force in both the service and the manufacturing sectors has received considerable attention. In the health care area, the pressures of spiraling medical costs, the problems associated with government-sponsored reimbursement and the high costs associated with labor and labor-intensive industries have prompted management within the health care community to investigate various approaches to improving productivity.[1,2]

Since 1965 there have been many attempts to slow the upward spiral of health care costs. Professional standards review organization (PSRO) legislation, certificate-of-need legislation and congressional mandates for an ongoing appropriateness review of existing services are all attempts of government-imposed limitations on reimbursement.[3] These programs, however, have not been targeted at the largest single cost to hospitals—labor. In spite of the high technology associated with modern health care delivery systems the industry remains labor intensive. A full 60 percent of hospital costs are labor related.[4]

LACK OF COMMITMENT TO PRODUCTIVITY THINKING

The principal difficulty encountered by hospitals in addressing the question of productivity is that productivity analysis in health care stands as a relatively underdeveloped management tool.

Productivity analysis is a relatively new idea in the health care field. Prior to 1965, and the enactment of Medicare and Medicaid legislation, productivity improvement received minimal attention. However, the current cost of inflation in the health care industry, contributed to in part by the Medicare and Medicaid legislation, has created concerns for productivity that can no longer be ignored by health care administrators.[5] Despite these concerns and in the face of increasingly scarce resources, many hospitals have not yet established productivity tracking systems or methods for measuring and analyzing potential areas for productivity improvement.[6]

Multiplicity of Activities

Within the hospital environment, the flow of services administered to the patient comes from a variety of disciplines: professional, allied pro-

Source: Reprinted from Newton Margulies and John F. Duval, "Productivity Management: A Model for Participative Management in Health Care Organizations," *Health Care Management Review,* Winter 1984, Vol. 9, No. 1, pp. 61–70. Copyright 1984, Aspen Publishers, Inc.

fessional, technical and nonprofessional. In many instances, in order to provide one service several other services must be integrated and coordinated. The complexity of the situation serves to complicate the organizational environment, thus making the job of identifying a specific work unit as a focus for productivity analysis an extremely difficult task.

Product Search

Many of the activities in health care are service related and have no readily measurable product. An example would be the social services component. It is difficult to measure a product in a department where not only the needs of the client are changing, but where the nature of the client is changing also. However, the intangible quality of the output may not preclude some productivity analysis. It has recently been argued that productivity measures are not only possible but necessary.

Units of Work Activity

Difficulty in defining units of work activity follows the problems encountered with measuring a physical product forthcoming from a given service. In order to quantify output, one must first be able to define it. This problem seems to be an ongoing one in many health care service departments.[7]

In an effort to resolve this problem, many productivity measures have been developed, but they may not reflect the product or service. Medical record labor hours per discharge unit, nursing labor hours per patient day, radiology labor hours per patient day, radiology labor hours per procedure and laundry labor hours per 100 pounds are just a few examples. A common problem exists in many of these measures. For example, nursing labor hours per patient day are aggregate statistics that yield no information on the amount of productive, relative to nonproductive, time that is being spent on the job. Because of this the statistic is of limited value. In radiology, if the number of procedures and total labor hours is known, the productive time per paid labor hour (or something proportional to it) can be computed.

A number of traditional methodologies have been used to evolve viable work standards in developing the various productivity measures. Most of the methodologies are derived from historical data standards, estimated standards, time standards (stopwatch studies) and standard data standards (College of American Pathologists standards).[8] All of these methodologies are used to arrive at work standards through which individual or group productivity can be measured.

These traditional methodologies make some common assumptions about the worker, most of which are closely aligned to McGregor's managerial philosophy which he labeled Theory X.[9] Theory X and its counterpart Theory Y were identified by McGregor as being the two basic sets of assumptions on which managers base their style. Theory X assumes that the worker is lazy, self-seeking, motivated only by monetary incentives and must be controlled by management in order to work toward organizational goals. Theory Y assumes that the worker is capable of self-direction and self-control and will integrate his or her efforts with organizational goals. Theory X's approaches to productivity analysis tend to view the worker as being incidental to the study; therefore, little attempt is made to involve the worker in the decision-making processes that guide the study or interpret its outcome. These approaches are clearly less than ideal because they do not make use of the wealth of information about the work place that is available from those who perform the work functions directly.

Although there is still a good deal of merit in the traditional approaches to developing productivity/work measurement systems, the value position reflected in the Theory X assumptions may be detrimental to the development of viable and useful productivity improvements.

PARTICIPATIVE MANAGEMENT

Over the last decade, and more recently due to the publicity of the Japanese participative management success, there has been a tendency for American management to more seriously consider the merits of participative management.[10–12] Many organizations have initiated, in a variety of forms, approaches to facilitate greater participation among workers. To be sure, not all organizations have met with instant success but enough have experienced significant increases in morale and productivity to support the notion of participative management. There is a growing body of empirical research that supports the premise that the success of these approaches may rest with the quality and abilities of management and not with the employee.[13] The core issue may simply be education in the broadest sense. It is not realistic to expect employees (or managers) to enthusiastically participate in management processes when, for the most part, they do not have the necessary skills to perform such activities. The success of participative programs rests in management's commitment to educate themselves and their employees in how to participate and how to engage with employees in collaborative problem identification and resolution.

AN APPROACH TO PRODUCTIVITY MEASUREMENT

In developing a cohesive approach to the development of participative productivity measurement systems, management must not only commit itself to supporting such efforts, but must also commit itself to the careful mapping of strategies by which to accomplish them. Figure 12-1-1 represents the theoretical construct that provides the framework for the development of participative management systems. The model is described in two phases. *Phase I* represents the necessary education and management support needed to prepare the worker to participate in such an effort. This phase identifies the critical components required to develop an environment that facilitates participative management activities. *Phase II* represents a means by which participative methods can be put into operation in developing productivity tracking systems. Specifically, those steps and components are identified that facilitate the development of

accurate activity standards to be used in the tracking and evaluation of productivity.

PHASE I: PREWORK

Management Support

The initial ingredient, and perhaps the most significant factor, in developing any participative system is the strong program support of key management personnel. Enthusiasm and encouragement of management can provide the impetus for initiating and sustaining the program. Participation is often threatening to many managers. This subtle resistance can provide obstacles for the implementation of participative mechanisms.

Financial Support

Participative management practices cost money, primarily in terms of invested worker and management time. Remember that management time is spent in both active participation and administration of the program. An example of how quickly participation time can accrue is reflected in the use of quality circles—a participative quality control technique.[14] Quality circles generally consist of eight to ten members representing a cross section of their respective organizations who meet for one hour a week. The purpose of quality circle meetings is to discuss ideas and problems affecting the work place. For a group of ten members, the cumulative time consumed by group meetings equates to 13 personnel weeks a year. Thus management must be aware of the magnitude of the commitment that it is making. Such commitments are generally based on the assumption that the long-term benefits provided to the organization by worker participation will outweigh the costs encountered in initiating and maintaining participative programs.

Attitudinal Support

In order to successfully implement participative management programs, managers must

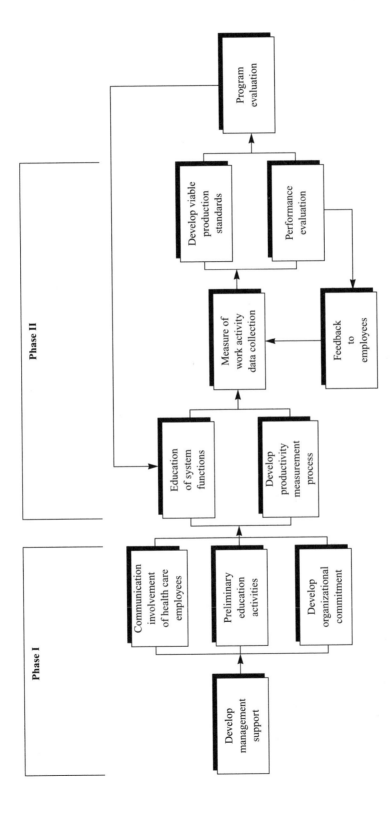

Figure 12-1-1 Phasal Model for Productivity Improvement

learn to participate with the employee and encourage the rank and file to participate in the organizational decision-making process. Management must demonstrate an active willingness to work toward participation and to leave old management styles behind. The core of a participative management program, whether aimed at productivity problems or any other work place difficulty, can only further the improvement of management–worker relations.[15–16]

Structural Support

The final element required to support the worker in the implementation of participative programs is structural in nature. Management must make provisions for the necessary organizational structural changes required to facilitate the participative process. Provisions may include changing official lines of communication, worker participation in various meetings, establishing internal resources to facilitate the process, or they may include the actual restructuring of the physical environment, for example, where people sit and the types and location of offices.

Educational Support

The role of education and training in participative management is usually underemphasized. Because of the newness of the participative approach, few workers or managers have had the opportunity to be exposed to participative skills. Bluntly stated, management and workers alike must develop the appropriate participative skills before they can be expected to participate effectively. Of particular importance is the inclusion of middle managers in retraining and educating in participative skills. Since middle management is the critical interface in linking the organizational goals established by top management with the participation of workers, adequate training of these individuals is almost requisite for program success. This need is underscored by the fact that many middle managers have developed their management skills and styles in authoritarian work environments.[17]

Marketing of Participation

The implementation of participative management styles, independent of their long-range goals, generally requires the expenditure of additional effort on the part of both management and workers. The added responsibilities coupled with the stresses introduced into the work place by the changing of roles can generate a good deal of resistance to participatory programs.[18] For this reason it is critical that a well planned marketing program be developed to inform and educate the participants in participative management programs on the use of such programs and the potential benefits that might be reaped by all involved.

Marketing support of participative productivity measurement, like any participative program, is important because it helps provide momentum to such programs. While this fact may be obvious, it is important to note that these programs are not self-perpetuating. In order for participative programs to be successful, they must be nurtured and supported by ongoing educational and marketing efforts, which are necessary to effect attitudinal changes in the work place.[19]

PHASE II: APPLICATION

Phase II of the model specifically addresses the application of the arguments made in Phase I to the development of a productivity tracking system.

As shown in Figure 12-1-1 Phase II employees have already been provided with the necessary skills to prepare them to participate in the program. Theoretically the worker now has a sound enough knowledge base and appropriate communication channels to permit the introduction and implementation of the factual phase of the program.

Introduction of the Productivity Measurement System

The introduction of the productivity tracking system is a critical step in the flow of the model with respect to the means by which the introduction is handled. Throughout Phase I, management has taken steps to develop a foundation of trust and communication to support worker participation. In the introduction of the productivity measurement system to the worker, this trust must be maintained by openly communicating the processes and methods by which the system will be developed, what the system will ultimately measure and what the goals of the system are. The authors' experience has been that the participants must have a comprehensive knowledge of what it is they are participating in in order to be effective. Too much information may be better than too little.

Education on System Function and Worker Responsibilities

Following the introduction of the system, the employee–manager discussions help to develop the specifics of how the participative program will be designed. Early formulation of roles, responsibilities, employee–manager interaction, schedules for meetings and relevant others who need to be involved provide important formulations of the program format.

Measurement of Work Activity

The actual measurement of work activity is where all the previous activities identified are molded into a cohesive effort. Employees are asked for their substantive input into developing the method and measurement system. By identifying and measuring the time to complete the various tasks in their respective workdays, the employees are providing data on work activities that reflect a quality and depth not readily available to management.

If program development has progressed smoothly to this point, the data collection phase generates a "sense of mission" that contributes to the enthusiasm and quality of the measurement. Participants now regard the program as a joint venture between management and employees, and this commonality of purpose can ensure the accuracy and adequacy of the data

forthcoming from the productivity analysis. Once the participants have developed a sense of involvement, participation and "ownership" of the program, the more accurate the information will be and the more likely that even better productivity criteria will be formulated.

The measurement of work activity and the source via the process described previously provides the basis for the evolution of viable worker productivity standards. The substantive data provided by the employees allow for the informed establishment of a system of activity standards against which individual and departmental performance can be tracked and evaluated.

Feedback

Finally the model incorporates the necessary feedback loop. Feedback essentially follows two routes; both routes flow back to the employees, one route being performance evaluation and appraisal of the function, and the other being feedback on how well the individual is functioning within the framework of the work unit.

As experience with the implementation of quality circles has shown, commitment on the part of management to worker participation can be a motivating force to maintain system viability.[20] This two-channel communication facilitates the expansion of the management–worker dialogue into other facets of the organization's performance. It also fosters a climate of trust and collaboration throughout the organization.

HOW THE MODEL WORKS

To illustrate how the model (Figure 12-1-l) operates to use participative methods to develop productivity tracking systems, the following section describes a specific case in which the fundamental principles and many of the mechanics of the model were used.

Background

The University of California Irvine Medical Center (UCIMC) is a large acute care facility in

Orange, California. In addition to providing general acute and psychiatric care, the hospital serves as a poison, burn and trauma center, and provides other services for central Orange County.

In May 1981 top management targeted the Department of Respiratory Therapy at UCIMC as the unit within the hospital where productivity tracking measures would best be initiated. Respiratory Therapy, a unit of the Department of Medicine, Pulmonary Division, employs 45 full-time equivalents, inclusive of support and clerical personnel, and provides approximately 30 different services to the patient population. Patient service areas within the department are divisionalized by medical specialty and are geographically dispersed throughout the hospital's grounds. Reflecting this fact, the department's structure is organized around its patient mix with the major structural divisions being adult and neonatal respiratory therapy. In addition there is a small ancillary materiel management group that supports the other divisions. With patient care being the primary mission of the department, the focus of the productivity study was specifically on the adult and neonatal divisions.

The Environment

At the time of the productivity study, three major destabilizing factors were at work that adversely affected the environment within the department. First, the manager of the department was relatively new and on arrival had instituted a variety of different and generally more stringent policies that created dissatisfaction among department personnel. Second the department was working under relatively high workloads. This, coupled with a relatively understaffed condition, contributed to a stressful, low-morale climate within the department. Finally several members of the department's rank and file were active in union activities and continually attempted to recruit new members, which generally created significant peer pressure adding to an already stressful situation.

All of these factors contributed to the destabilization of the environment into which the pro-

ductivity study was to be launched. The principal impact of this destabilization was that a general sentiment of mistrust was widespread among employees and among the management personnel ranks.

Groundwork

Prior to the initiation of the actual program development, a good deal of time (four weeks) was invested in studying the number of both the inputs into and the products forthcoming from the department activities. Careful identification of the flow, types and number of services was also carried out in order that instruments could be designed to effectively measure the therapists' activity levels.

Additionally, during this period careful observation and documentation were made of potential destabilizing factors so that when the actual work activity measurement segment of the productivity study was introduced, the marketing program could target those specific problems most likely to impact data gathering and program development.

Throughout the preliminary and operational periods of the productivity study, strict neutrality was maintained by the study coordinator so as not to be identified with either management or labor. Given the existing environment in the department, it was felt that this approach would be most expeditious in bridging the gap between the various participants.

Work Activity Measurement Inventory

Based on the information gathered during the preliminary phase, the Work Activity Measurement Inventory (Exhibit 12-1-1) was designed as the productivity study's principal data collection vehicle. The inventory measured the time required for procedure delivery, inclusive of cleanup and charting, and was filled out by all line therapists on a daily basis during the productivity study period. The format of the inven-

Exhibit 12-1-1 Worksheet Productivity Tracking

Date: _____   Current Classification: _____

Work Period: DAY,   PM,   NIGHT   Start Time _____   "S" If done with Student
(circle one)   Stop Time _____   Work Area Code

PROCEDURE	TIME REQUIRED*								COMMENTS**
	1	2	3	4	5	6	7	8	
Aerosol									
Aerosol Continuous									
Bedside Spirometry									
Blood Gas Analysis									
Blood Gas Puncture									
Bronchoscopy—Biopsy									
Bronchoscopy—Diagnostic									
C.P.A.P. (Check)									
Incentive Spirometry (Check)									
Incentive Spirometry (Set-up)									
Hydro Room									
I.P.P.B.									
Optimal PEEP Study									
Postural Drainage									
Therapist Stand-by									
Ventilator—Continuous (Check)									
LB-3									
CPR									
Volumes & Capacities									

* Please enter time at beginning of set-up and at end of clean-up or charting.

** Please note any incident or peculiarity which affects time required for completion of a procedure or which affects patient care.

Work area codes:
Burn ICU 1   Surgical ICU ....
CCU 2   Tower ....
Clinics............................. 3   3rd Floor ....
Emergency Room 4   4th Floor ....
Mental Health 5   5th Floor ....
Out Buildings 6

tory also allowed the documentation of shift to shift variations in completion time, the effects of teaching responsibilities on procedure completion time and any effects caused by the geographical constraints of particular work areas within the hospital.

The introduction of this data-gathering instrument to department personnel followed a two-step format. In order that imperfections in the instrument, and the marketing program designed to introduce it, could be identified and corrected, the inventory was first tested with the working supervisors. This test introduction lasted two weeks. During the two-week period the supervisors completed the inventory daily and closely monitored the effectiveness of the marketing activities and the quality of the data forthcoming from the inventory. Additionally, feedback on the inventory was continually solicited in order that needed changes could be effected prior to implementation of the department-wide study.

In general, this approach to developing productivity standards was well received by the supervisors. An unforeseen benefit was that the data gathered from the supervisors provided an excellent baseline against which the line therapists' responses could later be compared for accuracy.

The second step in the format was the marketing and introduction of the inventory to the line therapists. Because of the number of persons involved, and in order to maintain consistency of information, the marketing of the productivity study took the form of several large group meetings during which the basic philosophy behind the study, the role of the therapists in the study and the potential long-range impacts of a productivity tracking system in the department were discussed. Because of the limited amount of resources available for use in support of the study, continuing education of the therapists in the various aspects of participative management skills was handled on an informal basis. This approach proved to be inadequate because it was extremely difficult to meet with all the therapists, individually or in groups, due to the constraints of their normal workday. The lack of formal training in participative methods had adverse effects on the process: in essence participants had to learn by trial and error, which presented a serious obstacle to program implementation.

Data Collection

Following the introduction of the inventory, the study moved into a six-week data collection phase. During this period the therapists completed and handed in the inventories daily. The data were then compiled in a central log to be used later in the development of time standards. Incoming data were compared with the preliminary test study results and with stop-watch measurements, which were carried out for selected procedures. Although some variations did occur, possibly due to individual measurement differences or other unidentified factors, on the whole the data compared quite favorably.

Time Standard Development and the Activity Reporting System

Following the data collection phase, the time data for all the procedures provided by the department were compiled and their respective means computed. The mean completion time for a given procedure was then adopted as the time standard for that procedure.

The time standards developed in the productivity study were incorporated into a computer-assisted, three-step, productivity tracking system. Daily activity was documented by the individual therapists at the end of their shifts. The data were then compiled by the shift supervisor. Totals for each 24-hour period were then entered into the computer (PDP 1134, Digital Equipment Corporation). The computer compiled daily and monthly personnel power use reports which documented total department activity and productive time (time spent in delivery of procedures for which the medical center would be compensated) in terms of minutes worked per paid personnel hour by the therapists (Table 12-1-1).

Table 12-1-1 Computer Summary: Productivity Tracking

*** DEPARTMENT OF RESPIRATORY THERAPY ***

WORK FORCE UTILIZATION STATISTICS
MONTHLY REPORT FOR JAN

Treatment	Total Treatments	Total Work Minutes
(1) Aerosol	1774.0	30158.0
(2) Aerosol Continuous	2598.0	20056.6
(3) Bedside Spirometry	158.0	1422.0
(4) Blood Gas Analysis	2051.0	15382.5
(5) Blood Gas Puncture	405.0	5670.0
(6) Bronchoscopy—biopsy	3.0	507.0
(7) Bronchoscopy—diagnostic	8.0	560.0
(8) C.P.A.P.	37.0	185.0
(9) C.P.R.	20.5	1230.0
(10) Hydro Room	6.5	390.0
(11) Incentive Spirometry-—check	1460.0	9373.2
(12) Incentive Spirometry—set-up	194.0	2677.2
(13) I.P.P.B.	792.0	15285.6
(14) LB- End Tidal CO_2	84.0	789.6
(15) Optimal PEEP Study	4.0	240.0
(16) Postural Drainage	1269.0	18527.4
(17) Therapist Stand-by	84.5	5070.0
(18) Ventilator Continuous	2033.0	16894.2
(19) Volumes and Capacities	247.0	2544.1
Total Treatments Delivered—	13228.5	
Total Minutes Worked—	146962.39	
Minutes Worked per Paid Hr. This Period	34.39	

KEY LESSONS TO DATE

In reviewing and reflecting on the experience of the productivity study approach, when used in an actual work environment, the following important learnings emerged.

1. The need for a formal training program in participative skills, involving both management and workers, to support the activities in the study was clear. In the case study formal training was substituted with informal group meetings. Although these proved useful, the episodal nature of the contacts did not provide adequate reinforcement to ensure an optimal response from the workers.

2. Effective marketing of the program through discussion and supported by formal education and training is critical.

3. Successful change programs must rely on informed and motivated persons within the organization if the results are to be maintained. Although outside consultants are often useful in the preliminary stages of analysis, designing the program and executing the initial efforts of organizational change, consultants cannot sustain the organization's efforts over time. The maintenance of change falls on the internal resource persons within the organization. Those internal resources do not develop spontaneously; individuals must be trained, developed and given the legitimacy to perform required tasks.

4. Organizational change is more likely to meet with success when key management persons are involved and support the change process. Planned change must have the support and understanding of management and other key personnel if it is to pro-

ceed smoothly and produce enduring effects. Although there may be exceptions, change without support of key management is generally at a great disadvantage. Basically there is no substitute for the positive boost that an informed and sophisticated management can provide.

5. Organizational change is best accomplished when persons most likely to be affected by the change are brought into the process at its inception. Change is generally threatening, but much of the anxiety and uncertainty can be reduced by early involvement of participants.

For the most part, sudden and unexpected change creates and intensifies resistance to it. Involving persons early in the change process not only acclimates them to the idea of change, but permits them to influence those changes that will affect their jobs, relationships and personal satisfactions.

6. Given the feelings of threat and paranoia brought on by organizational change, honest and open communication about change plans is imperative for the overall and ultimate success of the program.

The experience described in this article rekindles and supports the notion of participative management as a vehicle for productivity improvement. It seems abundantly clear, however, that management support, organizational preparation and a long-term perspective are necessary for successful implementation of this approach.

NOTES

1. J. Maron-Cost, "Productivity: Key to Cost Containment." *Hospitals* 54, no. 18 (1980):77–79.
2. W.A. Michela, "Numerous Productivity Indicators Analyzed." *Hospitals* 52, no. 23 (1981):62–69.
3. M.C. Burkhart and M. Schultz, "Management of Health Service Delivery and Professional Productivity: A Case Study Model." *Public Health Reports* 94 (July–August 1978):326–331.
4. Maron-Cost, "Productivity: Key to Cost Containment."
5. Ibid.
6. M. Mannisto, "An Assessment of Productivity in Health Care." *Hospitals* 54 (September 16, 1980):71–76.
7. Ibid.
8. Maron-Cost, "Productivity: Key to Cost Containment."
9. D. McGregor, *The Human Side of Enterprise.* New York: McGraw-Hill, 1960.
10. "The New Industrial Relations." *Business Week* 2687 (May 11, 1981):84–98.
11. "A Try at Steel Mill Harmony." *Business Week* 2694 (June 29, 1981):132–136.
12. C. Deutsch, "Trust: The New Ingredient in Management." *Business Week* 2695 (July 6, 1981):104–105.
13. C.G. Burck, "What Happens When Workers Manage Themselves?" *Fortune* 104 (July 27, 1981):62–69.
14. E. Rendall, "Quality Circles—A 'Third Wave' Intervention." *Training and Development Journal* 35 (March 1981).
15. "The New Industrial Relations."
16. Deutsch, "Trust: The New Ingredient in Management."
17. Burck, "What Happens When Workers Manage Themselves?"
18. "The New Industrial Relations."
19. Ibid.
20. Rendall, "Quality Circles."

13

Inventory

Goals of This Chapter

---

1. Discuss periodic versus perpetual methods of accounting for inventory.
2. Explain the specific identification; first-in, first-out (FIFO); weighted average; and last-in, first-out (LIFO) methods of measuring inventory costs.
3. Consider the long-run implications of using LIFO costing.
4. Explain the economic order quantity (EOQ) technique.
5. Examine the question of logistics in health care organizations.
6. Assess the role of just-in-time inventory for health care.
7. Explain the key issues of inventory costing for manufacturing, including an explanation of raw materials, work in process, finished goods inventory, period versus product costs, variable versus absorption costs, equivalent units of production, and spoilage/waste.

Key Terms Used in This Chapter

Absorption costing; carrying costs; conversion cost; cost drivers; cost of goods sold (CGS); direct costing; economic order quantity (EOQ); equivalent units of production; finished goods inventory (FGI); first-in, first-out (FIFO); inventory costing; just-in-time (JIT); last-in, first-out (LIFO); logistics costs; ordering costs; period costs; periodic; perpetual; prime costs; product costs; raw materials inventory (RMI); safety stock; specific identification; stockouts; variable costing; weighted average; work in process (WIP).

Note: Key terms appear in italics when first used in the chapter. All key terms are defined in the Glossary.

INTRODUCTION

For most health care organizations, inventory represents a relatively small part of total assets on the year-end balance sheet. Purchases of supplies are often dwarfed by labor costs. A product is generally not produced and stored until sold, the way it is for manufacturers. Services provided by health care organizations are usually consumed immediately by patients. Nevertheless, issues related to inventory have become important to the financial success of health care organizations.

As health care organizations have worked harder and harder to be cost conscious and efficient, inventory management has received a great deal of attention. Holding inventories for less time, avoiding purchases of unneeded items, applying uniform price codes to inventory items, and reducing inventory damage and obsolescence have been topics of concern.

The costs of inefficient decisions concerning when to buy inventory items and how much to buy can become significant. Also, health care providers must be able to assess the cost of their inventory items on hand and consumed.

This chapter begins with a discussion of issues related to the measurement of inventory cost. It then proceeds to address issues related to the minimization of costs related to having inventory. That discussion includes not only the traditional *economic order quantity* (EOQ) technique, but also addresses *logistics costs* more broadly, and the popular *just-in-time* (JIT) inventory technique imported in the 1980s from Japan.

The last section of this chapter addresses issues of inventory costing for health care manufacturers. Although only a small minority of health care organizations are manufacturers, some health care providers do manufacture a product that is later sold. In such instances, determining the cost of the product is a more complicated procedure. The determination of which costs to assign to inventory and how to do it has significant ramifications for the organization's reported profits and assets.

INVENTORY COSTING

The accounting process of *inventory costing* has not received much attention at many health care organizations around the country. However, the movement toward greater efficiency has made this a more important issue. The cost accounting process can contribute to efficient cost management in the area of inventory.

This section addresses two issues. The first relates to tracking inventory. How does the organization determine how many units have been used and how many units are on hand at the end of the year or at any interim point in time? Next, this section considers how one determines the cost of the units of inventory that have been sold and the cost of the units on hand.

Perpetual vs. Periodic Inventory

The most fundamental element of inventory accounting is establishment of a *perpetual* or *periodic* system of inventory accounting. Perpetual and periodic inventory accounting relate to how the organization keeps track of the inventory it purchases.

Inventory tracking is based on a fundamental equation:

$$\begin{array}{ccccc} \text{Beginning} & & & \text{Units} & \text{Ending} \\ \text{inventory} & + \text{ Purchases } & - & \text{sold} & = \text{inventory} \\ \text{(BI)} & \text{(P)} & & \text{(S)} & \text{(EI)} \end{array}$$

The amount of inventory an organization starts with, plus the additional amount it acquires, less the amount sold, represents the amount still on hand. Suppose that you start the year with 10 bags of saline solution, and during the year you purchase 20 additional bags. If 25 bags are used in treating patients, how many remain?

$$\begin{array}{ccccccc} & \text{(BI)} & + & \text{(P)} & - & \text{(S)} & = & \text{(EI)} \\ \text{If:} & 10 & + & 20 & - & 25 & = & ? \\ & & & \text{Then:} & \text{EI} & = & 5 \end{array}$$

There are 5 bags left at the end of the accounting period.

The perpetual inventory method requires the organization to keep a running, continuous record of the receipt of inventory items and their use. There is a starting balance. Then, on a daily basis, items are counted when they enter the inventory, and they are counted when they are used. At the end of any day, one knows exactly how much inventory is on hand. This is generally considered to be a highly accurate, informative, and costly approach to inventory accounting.

Supermarkets that use uniform price code (UPC) scanners are generally using a perpetual system. Because they know at any point in time exactly which items have been sold, they can afford to keep less of any particular item on the shelf. The risk of running out is lessened if you always know how much you have. Reordering can be timed more precisely. This means that they have less cash tied up in any one type of inventory item. In the case of a supermarket, it also means that there is room to stock additional items on the shelves, possibly increasing sales. In the case of a health care organization, it would mean needing less storage space for inventory items or the ability to stock a greater range of inventory items.

In the perpetual system, a physical count of inventory is taken once a year to confirm the perpetual records and to allow adjustments for any losses that have occurred due to breakage, shrinkage, obsolescence, or theft. The magnitude of problems of that sort is determined by the difference between the amount that should be on hand according to the perpetual records, and the amount shown to be on hand based on the physical count.

The alternative to the perpetual system is the periodic system of inventory accounting. In this system, a specific tracking of inventory does not take place. From a reporting perspective, the accountant simply adds the beginning amount of inventory to the purchases of inventory to find the total amount that was available for use. At the end of an accounting period, the remaining inventory is counted. This amount is subtracted from the amount available in order to calculate how much inventory was used.

If we started with 10 bags of saline solution, and we purchased 20 bags, we would know that we had 30 bags available, but under the periodic system, we would not keep track of how many we used. The year-end inventory count reveals that five bags are left on hand. Therefore, we can deduce how many were used:

$$
\begin{array}{c}
(BI) + (P) - (S) = (EI) \\
\text{If:} \quad 10 + 20 - \;? \;= \;5 \\
\text{Then:} \quad S = 25
\end{array}
$$

We believe that 25 bags have been used. However, we do not know if patients received them or if they were stolen or thrown away.

The periodic system of accounting for inventory is generally much less expensive than perpetual inventory accounting. While it is less expensive, it provides less information on an ongoing basis. Other approaches must be developed to inform managers of the appropriate time to reorder inventory, given that we will not know how much inventory we have at any particular point in time. Furthermore, at year-end, there is no way of knowing the amount of lost or stolen inventory, because the manager has no way of knowing how much inventory should have been on hand. For some types of inventory items, computerization has brought down the cost of perpetual inventory substantially.

In a health care organization, some types of inventory generally will be maintained on a perpetual basis, and some types on a periodic basis. The more expensive the item, the more critical the item with respect to outage problems; the easier the item is to track on a perpetual basis, the more it makes sense for the organization to use a perpetual system.

For example, heart valves and other implants are generally quite expensive. Often, they have a limited useful lifetime, after which they would have to be discarded. It would not make sense to overstock. At the other extreme, being out of stock might cost a life. In such a case, we would expect to use perpetual inventory. In some cases, such as with respect to narcotics, perpetual inventory is often mandated by law. For other items, the health care organization might well use periodic accounting, for example, for Band-Aids—a low-cost, high-volume item. Even if a department were to run out of Band-Aids, we could make do for a short period by moving supplies around among departments, and reordering would not take long.

Health care organizations should certainly pause every four or five years to reconsider their inventory method. Which items are recorded using a periodic approach and which using a perpetual system? Why was the existing choice made in each case? Do the reasons still stand? Perhaps technology in inventory management has advanced enough to allow for more perpetual inventory record keeping on a cost-effective basis. The health care organization management should assess the extent to which shifting certain types of inventory to a perpetual system could yield improved control of inventory and, therefore, reduced costs.

Specific Identification, FIFO, Weighted Average, and LIFO Costing

Whether the health care organization chooses to use perpetual or periodic inventory, it must still make a decision concerning how to allocate inventory costs between the income statement and balance sheet. The manager must determine the cost of the items that were used, and the cost of the items still on hand at any point in time.

There are four methods that are generally allowed for use in making this allocation. They are

1. *specific identification*
2. *first-in, first-out (FIFO)*
3. *weighted average*
4. *last-in, first-out (LIFO)*

The specific identification method assumes that each unit of inventory is identified, perhaps using a serial number. We can keep track of each unit when it is received and when it is sold. Therefore, at the end of an accounting period, we know specifically which units are still on hand and which have been sold. We are able to

identify for the financial statements the actual cost of the units on hand and the actual cost of the units that have been used. This method is often associated with perpetual inventory, since we are likely to use a perpetual system if we are tracking each individual item.

The FIFO method assumes that as we acquire inventory, we always use the oldest inventory first. For example, pharmaceuticals often have expiration dates. Therefore, the units received with an older shipment are generally used before those from a newer shipment. This minimizes the amount of past-expiration date pharmaceuticals, which have to be discarded.

The weighted average method assumes that all of the specific type of inventory in question gets mixed together and is unidentifiable. Therefore, we simply total the costs and total the number of units, and we find an average cost per unit. Suppose, for example, that the health care organization keeps a liquid chemical in a large tank. Once new chemical is added to the tank, there is no way to determine if we are using old or new chemical; it has all mixed together.

The LIFO method assumes that the very most recent acquisitions of inventory are always used prior to inventory acquired at an earlier date and still on hand. This method makes sense in cases where new purchases of inventory are piled on top of old purchases, and inventory is used from the top of the pile.

The choice of inventory method in a stable price environment would probably depend on the method that most closely follows the movement of inventory in the organization. For most health care organizations, the vast majority of their inventory is most sensibly accounted for on a FIFO basis. In order to avoid date expiration, spoilage, and just plain wear and tear, most inventories should normally be moved in an orderly fashion with the oldest inventory used first.

In inflationary periods, however, we have an additional concern. The flow of inventory becomes a critical issue for costing. Even if we have identified how much inventory was used and how much inventory is left, we do not have enough information to prepare financial statements. It is necessary for us to know which inventory was used and which remains, given that not all units had the same purchase cost.

Assume the following simple information from Table 13-1 in order to understand the key issue. We start the year with no inventory, and during the year, we purchase 10 units of an inventory item on January 15 for $10 each and another 10 units of the same item on July 15 for $12 each. The total we have spent to acquire inventory is $220, as shown in the table.

Assume that we use nine units in our treatment of patients during September, and end the year with 11 units still in inventory. How much did the units that were used cost? What is the value of the units that remain?

If we followed reasonable logic, we will have used the nine units purchased in January. Therefore, the cost of the inventory used is $90 (9 units @ $10). The remaining inventory should show up on the balance sheet:

Inventory Balance
End of Year

1 unit @ $10 =	$ 10
10 units @ $12	120
Total inventory	$130

Thus, we end the year with inventory having a cost of $130.

While this use of FIFO is logical and sensible, it is not necessarily in the best interests of the health care organization. Suppose that instead of using FIFO, we had calculated the cost of the units used and of the units left on a LIFO basis. In that case, we will have used nine units purchased in July. The cost of the nine units used will be $108 (9 units @ $12). The remaining inventory would show up on the balance sheet as follows:

Inventory Balance
End of Year

10 units @ $10 =	$100
1 unit @ $12	12
Total inventory	$112

Now the cost of the inventory is $112 instead of $130.

This has certain tax advantages. If a for-profit health care organization were to report expenses of $108 instead of $90, its costs of doing business would be $18 more. Therefore, its profits from its operations would be $18 less, so there would be less profits to tax.

Another crucial issue for health care organizations, however, is that even if they are not-for-profit, this same calculation can work to their advantage. If the patient care for any patients is paid for on a cost-reimbursement basis, then the use of LIFO results in a higher cost and, therefore, a *higher* reimbursement. In our example, this means that by reporting costs of $108 instead of $90, we could increase our cash flow from reimbursement by as much as $18!

One might question whether this potential benefit, while significant, is enough to warrant using our newest inventory before our earlier purchases. However, that is not a relevant argument, because of the existence of periodic inventory.

Under periodic inventory, we never really know which units have been sold. By taking a physical count of our inventory, we know how much inventory has been used, but not which specific units. Therefore, the decision regarding which units have been used and which remain is always based on an assumption. In describing LIFO and FIFO, we did not say the methods describe the order in which inventory is used. We defined them based on the order in which inventory is *assumed* to be used.

Thus, when one uses FIFO inventory costing, one is assuming that the organization is logically using the oldest inventory first. When one decides to use LIFO inventory costing, one assumes that the most recent acquisitions are the

---

Table 13-1 Inventory Information: Inflation Example

	Quantity	Unit Cost ($)	Total Cost ($)
Beginning inventory	0	0	0
January 15 purchase	10	10	100
July 15 purchase	10	12	120
Total cost			220

first ones used. There is no need to prove that this is in fact the case.

It would be possible to use LIFO costing, which assumes that we had used the July purchases in September and kept the earlier January purchases on hand. We could do this *regardless* of whether or not that is in fact what happened! By using LIFO, we are not saying that we actually used the last-in inventory first. We are simply saying that our costing is based on an assumption that the last in are used first.

To make this point as clear as possible, in the above example, let us assume that the nine units were used in March, rather than in September as the example originally stated. Thus, we have the following:

> Purchase ten units in January.
> Use nine units in March.
> Purchase ten units in July.

Under LIFO, which units were used in March?

If we record our inventory on a perpetual basis, we would record the use of inventory in March, and therefore would be obliged to show the January, low-cost items as having been used. However, with record keeping on a LIFO *periodic* basis, we would show that the units used up in March of this year were the ones that were not acquired until July—after the point in time that we used them!

Clearly, there is a fiction here. How can we use up units before we have even acquired them? Physically, this would not be possible. However, from an accounting point of view, it is perfectly possible. We simply wait until the end of the year, then apply the LIFO inventory method by assuming that those items bought closest to the end of the year were the first ones consumed during the year.

Thus, health care organizations can continue to use their regular inventory processing methods. Inventory can flow through the health care organization in its normal manner, which will generally mean that we physically use up the oldest inventory first. However, in accounting for it, we will *assume* that something different happened.

Does this mean that perpetual inventory is an inappropriate method for health care organizations to use? Not at all. A health care organization can use perpetual inventory as a managerial tool for internal control purposes. However, for purposes of financial statement preparation and cost reporting, we would want to use periodic bookkeeping.

Long-Term Impact of LIFO Costing

If a health care organization were to report costs of $108 instead of $90 because of the use of LIFO inventory reporting, what would happen during the next year if the remaining 11 units were used? That question has a variety of interesting ramifications. Let us first consider it assuming that there is no replacement of inventory, and then we will relax that assumption.

If there is no replacement of inventory, and if we use all remaining 11 units, their cost would be the $112 that we had in inventory at the end of the previous year. Had we instead used FIFO during the previous year, our ending inventory that year would have been $130. This means that during the second year, our cost reported on LIFO would be $112 instead of $130. Our costs would be $18 lower on LIFO. All the benefits gained from higher reimbursement in the previous year would be lost.

However, in the meantime, we would have had the use of $18 one year sooner. The effect of LIFO during inflationary periods is to provide an interest-free loan for one year, at the very least. (This only works to the extent that the organization either receives cost reimbursement for some of its patients or else is a for-profit organization that can reduce its tax payments to the government.)

The assumption that inventory will not be replaced is quite unrealistic. Additional inventory will be purchased, and during inflation, it will be purchased at ever higher prices. Suppose that during this second year, another ten units are purchased at a price of $14 each. What would be the cost of the 11 units used during the year?

Regardless of which inventory method we are using, we have the following:

Original purchase:	10 units @ $10
Next purchase:	10 units @ $12
Second-year purchase:	10 units @ $14

If we were using FIFO inventory accounting, in the first year, we would have sold nine units that each cost $10, for a total cost of inventory used of $90. During the second year, we would assume to use the one unit remaining from the very first purchase, which cost $10, and we would assume to use the next ten units purchased, each of which cost $12.

FIFO
Second-Year Sales

Original purchase:	10 units @ $10	Last unit from this purchase
Next purchase:	10 units @ $12	All of these units
Second-year purchase	10 units @ $14	None of these units

The total cost for the units used in the second year would therefore be $130 (one unit @ $10 plus 10 units @ $12). Note that we say "assume to use," since it does not matter which units are actually used when.

On the other hand, with LIFO, in the first year, we assumed use of nine of the units purchased for $12 each, for a cost of $108. We were left at the end of the year with ten units that cost $10 each and with one unit that cost $12. Which 11 units would be used in the LIFO calculation during the second year?

LIFO
Second-Year Sales

Original purchase:	10 units @ $10	None of these units
Next purchase:	10 units @ $12	Last unit from this purchase
Second-year purchase	10 units @ $14	All of these units

First, we would assume to use the last ones in; those purchased during the second year for $14 each. Next, we would assume to use the last one purchased in the previous year, which cost $12. Thus, the cost under LIFO would be $152 (i.e., 10 units @ $14 plus 1 unit @ $12). This is $22 more than the cost under FIFO.

That means that not only would we not have to repay the interest-free loan from the first year, but we would actually add to it! Each year, as long as prices continue to rise due to inflation, LIFO will continue to provide a higher cost than FIFO, resulting in higher reimbursement and/or lower taxes.

What happens when the rate of inflation declines rather than rises? A decreasing rate of inflation is like a speeding car that starts to slow down. The car is no longer moving forward as fast, but it is still moving forward. LIFO loses its advantage over FIFO only when the rate of inflation is actually negative. As long as the inflation rate in the price of inventory items acquired is any positive amount, LIFO is advantageous.

What if the health care organization expects new technology to make some inventory items cheaper over time? In some industries, such as the calculator business, some inventories are maintained on a LIFO basis because inflation drives up prices, but other types of inventory items are kept on a FIFO basis because technology drives down their prices. It would be hard to argue, however, that all health care organization inventory items are falling in price over time. Therefore, it seems hard to justify why any health care organization would keep all of their inventory on a FIFO basis.

In the long run, LIFO presents health care organizations that receive cost reimbursement on any of their patients with a way to improve current cash flow. To the extent that the improved cash flow comes from tax savings, there is one catch. The price of this cash flow is lower reported earnings. By reporting higher expenses and lower income, one can pay less in tax. However, one must actually report lower income.

In the case of cost reimbursement, even this problem is somewhat mitigated. To the extent that higher reported expenses result in higher cost reimbursement, LIFO does not cause reported income to be lower because there is additional revenue. However, patients paid on a fixed-price basis, such as Medicare Diagnosis Related Group (DRG) payments, will neither generate extra revenue nor extra cash as a result of higher reported expenses. Therefore, net income will be lower.

Is it worth the price to have lower reported income (because of higher reported expenses not fully offset by higher reported revenues)? It is if the result is not true higher expenses while improving cash flow. In other words, we pay exactly the same amount for the inventory we purchase, we just report some of it as an expense in an earlier period.

Cash flow is the essence of LIFO. It generates a long-term, growing, interest-free loan that, for all intents and purposes, is never repaid. Were it to be repaid, we still would have had the use of money interest-free for long periods of time.

Objections to LIFO Costing

Many health care organizations do not use LIFO costing for their inventory. Most large corporations adopted it in the late 1960s or early 1970s. By the late 1970s, the health care industry was one of the few industries resisting this change. Why?

Certainly, one might argue that there is extra bookkeeping cost involved in using LIFO. However, that argument is a weak one. All that is necessary is a modest, once-a-year adjustment to inventory values. One might argue that inflation is not the concern it once was. That too is a weak argument, unless one really believes that we will enter a period of actual deflation (not a period of decreasing rates of inflation). Any inflation at all means there is some LIFO benefit.

Last, one might argue that health care inventories are not significant enough really to benefit from use of LIFO. There is an easy way for each health care organization to assess the accuracy of that argument. Simply take an old set of financial statements and compare it to a new one to see how much the value of year-end inventory has grown over the last 10 or 20 years.

Some of the difference in inventory value is attributable to increased patient volume, but a substantial amount is due to increasing prices. Prices for health care inventory items have certainly more than tripled in the last 20 years. If we assume a tripling, this means that a balance sheet showing $3 million of inventory on a

FIFO basis might well only show $1 million had it been on a LIFO basis for the last 20 years. Had that difference been reflected in higher cost reimbursement, that would currently represent a $2 million interest-free loan. The loan would have started out modestly and grown over the years. Now is as good a time as any to begin to earn an interest-free loan if you are not already earning one.

One note for those who believe that this is a waste of effort (as many believed 20 years ago): Medicare is now on a DRG system, which does not base operating payments on any one specific health care organization's cost. Therefore, if a LIFO health care organization were to decide not to replace its inventory, its interest-free loan would not have to be repaid to Medicare. The Medicare portion of the loan became a permanent gift to the health care organization when DRGs were adopted. If other payers eventually go onto prospective payment, those health care organizations using LIFO will not only have used a large amount of money interest-free for a period of years, they will also wind up never having to repay the principal amount.

MINIMIZATION OF INVENTORY COSTS

The minimization of costs related to inventory has become a management focus in most health care organizations. While the earlier discussions in this chapter focused on determining the costs of inventory, this section considers how to minimize costs related to having inventory. Specifically, this section discusses a model for inventory management called the economic order quantity (EOQ) technique. It then considers other issues related to logistics costs in health care organizations. The section concludes with a discussion of the just-in-time (JIT) inventory approach and its role in health care organizations.

The EOQ Technique

The management of inventory costs is inherently a problem area for health care organizations. The more inventory acquired at one time, the greater the investment (and therefore interest cost) and *carrying costs* (such as storage). On the other hand, keeping only a small amount of inventory on hand increases the number of times we must order inventory and the related *ordering costs.* The fact that ordering costs and carrying costs tend to work in opposite directions dictates the need for a formalized, quantitative approach. The types of costs related to inventory are summarized in Exhibit 13-1. These costs are discussed below.

EOQ is the most widely used quantitative technique for management of inventory ordering and carrying costs. EOQ is a mathematical approach that balances the various costs related to inventory in order to determine an optimal solution. That solution dictates to the manager the optimal number of units to order for a specific supply item each time it is ordered. The technique also allows the manager to determine when and how often to order the specific inventory item.

Carrying Costs

One of the costs that is considered by the model relates to the costs of carrying inventory. Carrying costs are divided into two major classes: (1) capital costs and (2) out-of-pocket costs.

The capital cost represents the fact that once we pay for inventory, we have tied up funds that

---

Exhibit 13-1 Examples of Inventory-Related Costs

1. Purchase Price of Inventory
2. Carrying or Holding Costs
   A. Capital costs
      1. For required inventory
      2. For safety stock
   B. Out-of-pocket costs
      1. Insurance and taxes on inventory value
      2. Cost of annual inspections
      3. Obsolescence and date-related expirations
      4. Damage, loss, and theft
3. Ordering Costs
   A. Labor of employee placing order
   B. Shipping and handling charges
   C. Errors in orders

---

could otherwise be earning interest. Alternatively, we could have used those funds to reduce the amount we have borrowed. In either event, there is a definite interest-related opportunity cost resulting from tying up our funds in inventory.

Out-of-pocket costs include such expenses as insurance on the value of inventory, annual inspections, and obsolescence or date-related expiration of inventory. They also include damage to inventory and loss or theft. Obsolescence, date-related expiration, damage, loss, and theft are sometimes referred to as risk factors related to inventory.

Ordering Costs

A second major cost related to inventory is the cost of placing orders. The more frequently we order inventory, the less we keep on hand, but the more we spend on placing orders. Shipping and handling charges are likely to be higher in total. More hours of purchasing department labor will be required. More mistakes are likely to be made by suppliers, resulting in more time to correct improper shipments.

If we sum the costs of ordering and the costs of carrying inventory, we have the total costs related to the inventory. Figure 13-1 shows the impact of ordering costs, which rise in total as the number of inventory orders placed per year rises, while the carrying costs of inventory fall. The key problem is to find the point at which the total costs are minimized, Q*. That point is defined as being the EOQ.

Total Costs

Since the minimization of inventory costs calls for a mathematical optimization technique, it is convenient to express the various factors that must be considered in terms of formulas and symbols. We will let S stand for the cost to carry one unit of inventory for a year. This includes both the capital and out-of-pocket carrying costs.

If we multiply the cost of carrying one unit for a year times the number of units on hand for the year, we will have determined the carrying cost. However, the number of units on hand will

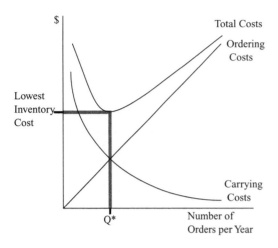

Figure 13-1 Inventory Ordering and Carrying Costs. *Source:* Adapted from *Hospital Accounting Advisor,* Vol. 2, No. 3, p. 3, Aspen Publishers, Inc., © 1986.

vary. Each time we order and receive inventory, our inventory level will be high. Right before we reorder, our level will be low. Thus, in order to calculate the total carrying cost, it is necessary to multiply the cost to carry one unit, S, by the *average* number of units in inventory.

Q will stand for the number of units of inventory we order at one time. Thus, in its simplest form, we will start with Q units and use them until none are left, and then order and receive Q additional units. This ignores the issue of a *safety stock,* which will be discussed later.

If we presume that we use inventory in even amounts each day, we can assume that on average, we will have Q/2 units of inventory. That is, we start with Q and end up with zero. The average would be (Q + 0)/2, or simply Q/2. For example, if we order 100 chest tubes, and use one per day for 100 days before receiving the next shipment, on average, we will have had 100/2, or 50 chest tubes on hand.

We can then calculate the carrying cost as being the cost to carry one unit, S, times the average inventory, Q/2:

$$\text{Carrying cost} = \frac{Q}{2} \times S = \frac{QS}{2}$$

Ordering costs will consist of the cost of placing each order multiplied by the number of or-

ders. If we let A stand for the total number of units needed in a year, then A/Q will tell us the number of orders we will have to make. Allowing P to stand for the costs related to placing each order, we can express the total ordering cost as the number of orders times the cost per order, or as follows:

$$\text{Ordering cost} = \frac{A}{Q} \times P = \frac{AP}{Q}$$

The total cost of carrying and ordering inventory, TC, can then be expressed as follows:

$$TC = \frac{QS}{2} + \frac{AP}{Q}$$

Graphically, this is the total cost line in Figure 13-1. Note that this does not include the cost of the inventory itself.

Calculating the EOQ

You may note from Figure 13-1 that the total cost line decreases, reaches a minimum, and then increases. Because we want to find the lowest cost, we want the minimum point on the curve. Finding extreme points on curves—minimums and maximums—is a common mathematical problem. In this case, we can state the formula to solve for this optimal point, Q*, as follows:

$$Q^* = \sqrt{\frac{2AP}{S}}$$

For example, suppose that Efficient Hospital needs to order 1,000 chest tubes each year at $10 per tube. Assume that the interest rate is 8 percent. The capital carrying cost per unit would be 8 percent of $10, or 80¢. Assume that additional out-of-pocket costs, including the impact of the value of inventory on insurance, the cost of inventory damage while on hand (mistakenly opened items), the opportunity rent cost, and so forth, add another 50¢ to each unit we have on hand on an annual basis. The total carrying cost would then be $1.30 per unit.

Assume that the ordering cost, including the labor in our purchasing department, the shipping and handling charges, and so forth, are estimated to be $12.74 per order. What is the optimal number of chest tubes to order at one time?

In this problem, A = 1,000 tubes per year, P = $12.74 per order, and S = $1.30. The optimal order size would be as follows:

$$Q^* = \sqrt{\frac{2 \times 1,000 \times \$12.74}{\$1.30}}$$

$$= \sqrt{19,600}$$

$$= 140 \text{ Chest tubes per order}$$

Note that at this number of tubes per order, excluding the purchase price of the inventory itself (which is presumed to be the same regardless of how many we buy at a time—we will relax that assumption later), the total ordering and carrying cost would be as follows:

$$TC = \frac{QS}{2} + \frac{AP}{Q}$$

$$= \frac{140 \times \$1.30}{2} + \frac{1,000 \times \$12.74}{140}$$

$$= \$91 + \$91$$

$$= \$182$$

It is not coincidental that the ordering cost equals the carrying cost. Figure 13-1 makes clear the fact that the total cost is minimized at the point where these two costs intersect or are exactly the same!

Relevant Costs

As is true with most cost accounting problems, one of the key concerns is that we include in our calculation only costs that are relevant for that specific calculation. Suppose the costs of purchasing chest tubes include the following items: the purchase price, shipping and handling, telephone call to place order, inventory

taxes, salary of receiving dock supervisor, insurance on inventory, warehouse rental, and capital cost. The relevant costs are those that we would expect to vary with the amount of inventory on hand at any time, the costs that would vary with the number of units purchased, and the costs that would vary with the number of orders placed in a year.

Inventory taxes (where applicable) and insurance on inventory are items that would vary with the number of units in inventory at any time. The capital cost, which depends on the purchase price, would vary with the size of the order, as would shipping and handling. The costs of the telephone call to place the order would vary with the number of orders.

The cost of the receiving dock supervisor is unlikely to vary with either the size or number of orders, and thus would not be a relevant cost. Also, in the short run, the cost of storing the inventory is not likely to change. On the other hand, if we could use some of our inventory storage space for offices by reducing the number of units in inventory, then the equivalent rental cost for such offices might reasonably be considered an opportunity cost and could be counted as part of the out-of-pocket carrying cost of the inventory.

Real-World Complications

Restrictions on Order Size. The EOQ model assumes that units can be acquired individually. That is not always the case. Some items may well be packaged in such a way that the supplier will only provide round quantities or even dozens.

This does not create a significant problem. To find the least-cost solution, you must still solve the EOQ model for the exact quantity that would minimize the cost. Then you must find the closest amount that can be ordered, both above and below the EOQ. For instance, suppose that chest tubes were only sold by the dozen. Our EOQ was 140. We would have to use the total cost formula to solve for TC at 11 dozen (132) and 12 dozen (144). Whichever of these two alternatives is less costly would be the optimal result.

Note that even though 144 is closer to 140 than 132 is, we cannot assume that 144 is the optimal result, because of differences in the behavior of ordering costs and carrying costs. In this particular problem, for 132 units the total cost is as follows:

$$TC = \frac{QS}{2} + \frac{AP}{Q}$$

$$= \frac{132 \times \$1.30}{2} + \frac{1,000 \times \$12.74}{132}$$

$$= \$85.80 + \$96.52$$

$$= \$182.32$$

For 144 units, the cost is slightly less:

$$TC = \frac{QS}{2} + \frac{AP}{Q}$$

$$= \frac{144 \times \$1.30}{2} + \frac{1,000 \times \$12.74}{144}$$

$$= \$93.60 + \$88.47$$

$$= \$182.07$$

Note that, in either case, the variation from the EOQ is so small that the extra cost is very minor.

Quantity Discounts. Until now, we have worked with the assumption that there is one price for each type of inventory. Realistically, volume discounts may apply. The impact of such discounts is to reduce the costs of buying larger quantities because the higher carrying costs are offset by lower prices for the inventory itself. Furthermore, if the purchase price is lower, the capital costs for carrying the inventory also would be lower (recall the capital cost is the interest rate times the purchase price).

In order to determine the optimal order quantity, we would first calculate the EOQ as we had done before. If discounts are available for purchases of larger quantities than the EOQ we have calculated, we must consider the costs related to those larger quantities. However, in

such a case, we would never purchase more than the minimum needed to get the price break. Suppose, for example, that the price for chest tubes was as follows:

Quantity Ordered	Price
1– 99	$10.10
100–199	10.00
200 and over	9.98

Recall that the EOQ was calculated to be 140. We must now consider whether it would be worthwhile to purchase 200 at a time rather than just 140. Two steps are necessary. First, we must calculate the total cost of purchasing 200 units, considering the fact that the capital cost is 8 percent of $9.98 rather than 8 percent of $10. Thus, the annual carrying cost will fall from $1.30 per unit to $1.2984 per unit. The total cost of this alternative would be as follows:

$$TC = \frac{QS}{2} + \frac{AP}{Q}$$

$$= \frac{200 \times \$1.2984}{2} + \frac{1,000 \times \$12.74}{200}$$

$$= \$129.84 + \$63.70$$

$$= \$193.54$$

The next step that must be taken is to subtract from the cost we have calculated for purchases of 200 units the total extra discount we would receive over the course of a year. In this example, we purchase 1,000 tubes a year. An extra discount of 2¢ above the discount available at the EOQ would result in a savings of $20. This would bring down the cost of the 200 alternative from $193.54 to $173.54. This latter figure is below the $182 cost of the EOQ, so it does pay to buy the larger quantity.

Uncertain Conditions and Stockouts. Until this point, the discussion has assumed that we will use the inventory in an even fashion and can receive new inventory exactly when we need it. Realistically, uneven patterns of usage might result in an increase in the rate that we use inventory, which might cause us to run out.

There is also the possibility that for some reason the supplier will have a delay in delivering the items we order. We must allow for problems that might arise in shipments.

Figure 13-2 shows a typical inventory usage pattern, assuming that inventory is consumed evenly over a period of time. In this figure, it is assumed that we purchase 90 units and completely use them up over the course of a month. Three months are shown on the graph. When would we order more inventory? Clearly, you cannot wait until the last day of the month, or you will have no inventory for the start of the next month. We must calculate the point at which an order must be placed.

If we use 90 units over a typical 30-day month, then we are using inventory at a rate of 3 units per day. If it takes 10 days to place an order and receive shipment, then an order should be placed 10 days before the end of the month. Alternatively, since we know that it takes 10 days for the order to be received, and we use units at a rate of 3 per day, we should order when there are 30 units left on hand. We can formalize this by calculating when the number of units on hand equals the following:

$$\frac{\text{Units used for a time period}}{\text{Days in time period}} \times \begin{array}{c}\text{Days from order}\\\text{until receipt}\end{array}$$

For example,

$$\frac{90}{30} \times 10 = 30$$

We need to order when there are 30 units left.

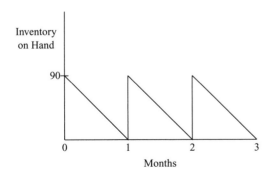

Figure 13-2 Inventory Usage over Time

This, however, assumes that we are comfortable having inventory arrive just as it is needed. What if a shipment is delayed for some reason? In any type of business, *stockouts* can be costly, perhaps even causing production to cease for several days. In a health care organization, the potential negative implications of running out of certain items are obvious. As a result, it is usually necessary to maintain a safety stock—some minimum level of inventory you attempt always to maintain on hand. This inventory would be dipped into only when an event arises that, in the absence of a safety stock, would have resulted in a stockout. Inventory should, of course, be rotated to protect freshness, so the safety stock does not consist of the same physical items from year to year.

How much safety stock is appropriate? An optimal policy requires a balancing of the cost of a stockout with the cost of carrying extra inventory. The cost of the safety stock consists of the carrying cost of that many units. Because the safety stock is supposed to stay at a fixed level, there are no ordering costs, and because it is not supposed to be depleted, there is no need to take an average number of units. The full safety stock level, multiplied by the carrying cost per unit, gives the carrying cost for the safety stock.

Calculating the cost of outages is, of course, much more difficult. If the supply would not result in a life-threatening situation, it might suffice to consider the marginal costs of delaying an operation by a day (and thus keeping the patient in the hospital, consuming resources, for an extra day). In that case, the cost to the hospital might be $300. Suppose that for a particular inventory item, we believe that there is only a 10 percent chance that we would have a stockout that would result in a one-day delay. A 10 percent chance, applied to a $300 cost, means that we would have an expected $30 loss in any given year. That loss can be compared with the extra carrying cost of a safety stock sufficient to avoid stockouts.

In another case, the risk of a stockout might be less serious—we might be required to purchase an item from a local retail pharmacy at a retail price. The cost of running out in that case would be minor. On the other hand, if the chance of a stockout might result in loss of life, a safety stock is almost certainly warranted.

When to Reorder. Knowing when to reorder does not require any special skill. We should know how long it takes to receive an order from the time we place it. Then we should order early enough so that the new shipment will arrive right before we run out, or just as we reach our safety stock.

If we know the precise rate of usage of an item, we can reorder automatically. On the other hand, if the usage is variable, it will probably be necessary to have routine examinations of stock and inventory reports to purchasing so that the order may be placed at the appropriate time.

Storage Constraints. An uncommon, but possible, problem that might arise would be an EOQ that is so large that we have no room to store the inventory. If we are constrained in that way, it would pay to order as close to the EOQ as possible. Looking at Figure 13-3, we can see that if Q' is our capacity limit (so that we cannot possibly buy more), it would not pay to buy any less than Q' because total costs rise as we move to the left (to lower quantities).

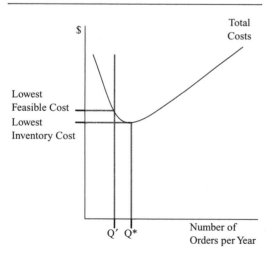

Key: Q* = economic order quantity with no constraints
    Q' = economic order quantity with capacity constraints

Figure 13-3 Optimal Ordering with Constrained Capacities. *Source:* Reprinted from *Hospital Cost Accounting Advisor,* Vol. 2, No. 3, p. 6, Aspen Publishers, Inc., © 1986.

A question that arises, however, is whether or not it pays in such a case to rent additional storage space. This may be addressed in a straightforward manner. The total ordering and carrying cost at Q' would have to be compared with the EOQ. If we could rent space for less than the difference in the two total costs, it would make financial sense to rent the space.

For example, suppose we could only store 25 chest tubes at a time. The total cost of the 140 EOQ is $182, as previously discussed. The total cost of ordering 25 at a time would be as follows:

$$TC = \frac{QS}{2} + \frac{AP}{Q}$$

$$= \frac{25 \times \$1.30}{2} + \frac{1,000 \times \$12.74}{25}$$

$$= \$16.25 + \$509.60$$

$$= \$525.85$$

As we can see, at such small volumes, the cost per order raises the total costs substantially: $525.85 is $343.85 more than the cost at the EOQ. Thus, if we could rent space that would allow us to store the extra 115 chest tubes (so we could order 140 rather than 25 at a time) for less than $343.85, it would pay to do so.

Inventory models are a part of any efficient management operation that invests dollars in inventory. Health care organizations have often considered their inventories to be of nominal value. However, the financial situation faced by many health care organizations is such that it is becoming time to adopt such tools if they are not already in place.

Logistics Cost Issues

Logistics costs exist in health care organizations, as they do in all industries. A wide variety of supplies must be stored, handled, and delivered throughout each organization. A variety of equipment must be owned and maintained. Facilities need to exist to handle the day-to-day patient flow and to cope with peak demand periods.

Basic Logistics Concerns

The techniques of controlling inventory costs by using methods such as the EOQ model are well established. However, the EOQ model does not answer all of the questions related to the logistics of acquiring inventory and ultimately getting that inventory to the patient. For example, EOQ does not determine whether inventory should be stocked in one central supply area or distributed into smaller supply centers spread throughout the organization.

Having inventory spread into a number of decentralized storage areas will likely result in having a number of minimum stocks instead of just one. As a result, the aggregate minimum amount of inventory (across all storage locations) will clearly rise because each location will desire a safety stock. As a result, the cost of carrying the inventory will rise as well. The amount of storage space consumed will also likely rise. On the other hand, the costs of distributing the inventory may decline because of fewer rush deliveries of a specific item to a department. Also, the various departments may be better served by the increased control and improved inventory availability generated by having a supply of inventory in their department where they can closely monitor it.

The area of logistics includes the costs related to acquiring inventories, transporting them, storing or warehousing them, distributing them, and carrying them. It also includes decisions regarding the capacity levels for which the organization prepares itself.

There are a variety of trade-offs that must be considered in making decisions that affect the logistical operations of the organization. If we expand our capacity for outpatient surgery, we will have a greater investment in both equipment and fixed staff. If we do not expand our capacity, we may lose elective surgery cases to competitors.

Higher levels of availability for service translate into higher levels of patient service and higher cost. Similarly, the decision to rapidly expand our product-line as new technologies and treatments become available will raise costs but have positive benefits in terms of our physi-

cian and patient base. Alternatively, specialization in fewer products will reduce our capabilities to serve all potential patients but also reduce the total logistical costs. Tyndall has identified a series of factors that must be identified for an organization to evaluate the trade-offs between the costs and benefits related to logistics:[1]

- Identifying cost drivers, or the structural determinants of the company's logistics activities, and their behavior....
- Measuring cost drivers in sufficient detail so as to understand cause and effect....
- Measuring the interaction of cost drivers (e.g., determining whether they reinforce or counteract each other).
- Identifying the specific service levels that matter to customers and measuring their value.
- Recognizing the correct trade-offs among the logistics costs and the service criteria.
- Evaluating these, both as a whole and incrementally, to contain costs.

A Reevaluation of Logistics

The logistics in place in most health care organizations developed gradually during a period of cost reimbursement. Many things that are taken for granted as being efficient may well be efficient only as long as costs can be passed along to patients or third-party payers.

Health care organizations have begun to react to this by reducing the variety of items stocked in inventory and, to some extent, inventory levels. However, it is appropriate to reevaluate a range of logistical support systems based on the current reimbursement environment.

Specifically, one might want to ask the following questions:

1. Can we provide logistical support in a different way that will allow us to get more admissions?

2. Can we provide logistical support in a different way that will allow us to discharge patients sooner?
3. Can we provide logistical support in a different way that will reduce costs that are no longer paid under cost reimbursement systems?

In evaluating logistics with respect to these three questions, the factors cited by Tyndall may be of some assistance.

The first factor is the identification of *cost drivers*. That is, the logistics responsible for the generation of costs. For example, suppose that laundry is collected from and distributed to departments once a day in your organization. More frequent collection and distribution would tend to require more labor circulating through the organization. On the other hand, it would possibly reduce the amount of linen inventory that the organization must own. The frequency of laundry collection is a cost driver.

Another example of a cost driver would be who cleans the operating rooms after surgery. They might be cleaned by the operating room department staff or by the housekeeping staff. It may be more efficient from one perspective to use housekeeping staff because of less duplication of personnel. On the other hand, there may be quicker turnaround in the operating room if its own staff does the cleaning. Clearly, not all logistics issues relate to inventory.

The second factor noted by Tyndall was measurement of the cost drivers to understand cause and effect. As we consider our existing logistical arrangements and alternatives, we would like to know the cost impact. For example, if all departmental inventories are stocked from central supply daily, how much more expensive is that than if they are stocked weekly? Note that such calculations are two-sided. Extra labor is involved in frequent stocking. On the other hand, if supplies are restocked frequently, there is less need for large duplicative, safety stocks throughout the organization.

Not only do individual logistical actions tend to have cost increases and decreases, but there are likely to be interaction effects. As Tyndall noted, these interactions may reinforce or coun-

teract each other. For example, keeping larger safety stocks is one cost driver. We may want large safety stocks for some medical/surgical items because of the high risk associated with running out of those items. The larger the safety stock, the higher the cost. At the same time, decentralizing the supply function also inherently increases the minimum inventory level. Thus, these two cost drivers reinforce each other, both raising the cost and reducing the likelihood that the organization will run out of the supply item in question. Alternatively, however, some cost drivers may counteract each other. As noted earlier, for example, restocking frequently will tend to offset the need for maintaining large inventory safety levels.

Perhaps the most crucial element in the reevaluation of each organization's approach to logistics is understanding which factors are important to the customer. In the traditional manufacturing setting, we may worry only about quality and service—items that are important to the customer from his or her own perspective. In health care organizations we must certainly worry about such factors, but we must also worry about additional factors related to issues such as the speedy treatment and discharge of the patient.

Some of the most obvious logistical issues in this regard were quickly noted by health maintenance organizations (HMOs) in their early days. HMOs found that patients admitted to hospitals on Fridays had longer lengths of stay than those admitted on Mondays. Very little diagnostic activity occurred over the weekend, causing length of stay to be expanded. From the hospital's perspective, longer length of stay due to low ancillary activity levels on weekends was not as much of a problem under cost reimbursement as it is today. Many, if not most, hospitals have already reacted to this problem by better management of preadmission testing, admission planning, and improved weekend ancillary utilization.

However, it is likely that there are still areas of logistical support where bottlenecks occur. Such bottlenecks may extend length of stay and, thus, are very important to uncover and possibly correct.

We say "possibly" correct because the issue of logistics is, when all is said and done, one of trade-offs. When we note that absence of an x-ray technician on a Sunday may extend the length of stay of a patient, we must consider the cost of the technician as well as the cost of the extra day. It is possible that we may overreact to the movement toward shorter length of stay. Suppose that the technician is earning $150 per day (including benefits). Perhaps we will have to pay overtime to have him or her work that day. That brings the cost up to $225.

If the presence of the technician reduces one patient's length of stay by one day, is it worth the $225 added labor cost? That probably depends to a great degree on issues such as marginal cost and occupancy level. If the hospital is full, and we must turn away an additional patient because of the extra day of stay for the existing patient, it would very possibly make sense to have the technician on that day. On the other hand, if we have extra capacity, the marginal cost of keeping the patient an extra day may not be substantial. Certainly, it may be less than the $225, in which case, it would not necessarily make sense to have the technician on that day.

Essentially, improving logistical services may make it possible for us to treat more patients, to treat patients and discharge them more quickly, or to treat patients more efficiently and less expensively. Increased logistical services, however, come with their own price tag. Whether logistical support should be improved, reduced, or simply reconfigured must be determined by each health care organization individually. Logistics are discussed further in Application 13-1.

Just-in-Time Inventory

In the last decade, there has been a growing focus on the concept of just-in-time (JIT) inventory, as the manufacturing sector of the United States strives to compete with its international competition. The growing discussion has led some health care managers to start to question whether or not the method is really workable for health care organizations.

What are the elements of JIT inventory? What are its strengths and weaknesses? Does it have any applicability to the health care industry? These are the questions that will be addressed below.

The Basic Philosophy of JIT

According to Henke and Spoede,

> In the ideal, the just-in-time (JIT) operating philosophy calls for raw materials and partially processed goods to be delivered precisely at the times—and to the locations—they are needed . . . at exactly the time required to meet customer orders. JIT philosophy seeks to minimize those costs associated with handling and storing inventory that add no value to the product, and to thereby reduce the cost per unit.[2]

Obviously, it is unrealistic to believe that health care organizations ever will be able to receive inventory exactly when needed. That could only happen if the organization could plan the use of each inventory item. However, that does not mean that the entire JIT philosophy need be rejected. Perhaps health care organizations can learn to develop a nearly just-in-time approach to managing inventory.

Essentially, the goals of JIT are for user organizations to reduce their warehousing cost, handling costs, obsolescence losses, and interest costs. Although health care organizations do not generally have warehouses, they do in fact devote substantial amounts of space to inventory. This space is taken up both in central supply areas and in smaller storage locations spread throughout the organization. If inventory quantities can be reduced, the organization can often find valuable uses for the vacated space. Reduced handling, avoidance of obsolescence, and reduced interest costs would obviously benefit health care organizations.

Can JIT Work in Health Care?

In industry, the main arguments for having large stores of inventory supplies relate to being able to provide customers what they want when they want it. Large stocks avoid the necessity of stopping the production process when you run out of a given supply.

The theoretical ideal of JIT cannot be accomplished in factories, let alone health care organizations. The concept that every item arrives exactly when needed requires a high level of coordination at various levels, which is not likely ever to be accomplished. The application of JIT really centers on how close one can come.

However, attempting to come close is not without its costs and problems. No matter how hard an industry works to coordinate its needs with its supplier, there will invariably be problems with implementing a JIT system. Whether in industry or hospitals, the workflow will not necessarily proceed in an orderly manner. There will be peaks and valleys in demand. Failure to perfectly anticipate peaks will mean that some orders will not be filled because of lack of inventory.

Of course, in most industries, that will only result in a lost sale and perhaps an angry customer. In the health care industry, it may result in loss of life. Therefore, health organizations will always have to maintain at least some inventories of some items. However, not all inventory items are critical to life. It is likely that a careful review of all health care inventory and supply purchases would indicate that a large percentage of items—perhaps over 90 percent—are not life-essential.

How much canned food inventories does a hospital maintain? How much housekeeping cleaning fluid? Many inventory items are not clinical care supplies. Even the majority of clinical supplies could probably arrive an hour or two late without causing a crisis.

JIT assumes that the producer (e.g., hospital) forms close working relationships with its suppliers. Deliveries are made on a very timely basis. Such relationships are hard to develop and are not likely to be error-free. However, to the extent that they are gradually built and improved over time, the possibility of ever-decreasing inventories on hand does exist.

It is important to bear in mind that JIT systems are never assumed to be easily and perfectly implementable. The ideal of JIT is never achieved in reality. Virtually all organizations do maintain at least small levels of safety stock, but even with those safety stocks, outages do occur. Health care organizations that choose to implement some version of JIT must be aware of this and must make careful plans. What will be done to get more of a critical item when an outage occurs and the supplier cannot provide the item?

Lending arrangements with other institutions must be established. From a competitive point of view, it may be very difficult to make such arrangements. Perhaps the arrangement can be made with an institution in a location sufficiently far away as not to be a direct competitor. The problem with that approach, however, is that it increases the time until the critical item can be obtained.

Part of the issue of whether JIT can work is how important it is for the organization to make it work. What are the potential payoffs from a smoothly working system? It would seem essential that any health organization considering the implementation of JIT first establish the current total costs of all of their inventories. That should include ordering costs, storage, interest, and so forth.

That total cost should be compared with a perfectly working JIT system. The basic costs of the inventory itself remain. In fact, they may be higher because the organization is likely to lose at least part of the benefit of quantity discounts. The cost of special orders should also be considered. Even under a fully functioning JIT system, crises will arise that will necessitate rush orders. The difference between a JIT system that works and one that does not is not the absence or presence of rush orders. It is whether rush orders are filled quickly enough to meet the organization's needs.

Once the costs of the perfect JIT system are known and compared with the costs of the current system, the organization has a starting point to evaluate the possible benefits of JIT. It is important to bear in mind, however, that at least part of those possible benefits will never be achieved, and many of them may not be achieved in the early years.

Experience has shown that there are significant difficulties in getting JIT systems up and running. Many unexpected supply distribution problems arise. These result in running out of supplies, losing potential customers, and increasing the size of protective stockpiles by managers distrustful of the system.

Given the uncertainties, it would make sense for health care organizations to undertake JIT only if the potential savings were deemed to be so significant that it would be worth the great effort involved. While JIT may make sense for some, the reality is that most health care organizations are probably not good JIT candidates.

Health care represents one of the industries for which JIT is perhaps *least* applicable. Henke and Spoede note,

> JIT works best in repetitive industries and is not appropriate in a fixed continuous process environment or in plants that produce relatively small quantities of fairly unique products.... Job-shop plants, even though they need help controlling inventory and quality, generally cannot benefit from JIT.[3]

They contend that the job-shop type of organization must have greater protective inventory of every type because of uncertain demand. That protective inventory offsets the benefits of JIT. That would certainly apply to health care organizations.

Hospitals in some ways represent the most extreme example of a job shop. Each patient represents a new and unique job. Certainly, many patients use common inputs. Further, it is likely that the hospital can fairly confidently predict the usage of certain supplies on a daily basis. Like a restaurant that does not know which items on the menu will be most popular, history can provide a great guideline of likely needs. Nevertheless, it is the unique, rather than common, needs of the different patients that are the key. The problem does not arise from the demands for a common supply used by nearly all patients. The problem is due to the need for a

specific item that might only be called for once a month but, on the other hand, might be needed twice in one day. The random nature of patient illness places a great burden on hospital inventory management.

It seems a shame to determine that a new idea, receiving great attention nationwide, probably just does not provide much help to the health care industry. However, the reality is that it is not the reluctance of health managers to change that is the problem in this case, but rather the inapplicability of the methodology. The total use of JIT inventory probably does not make sense for health care organizations.

However, almost all industries, *including health care,* have attempted to carry out the underlying principles of JIT. The EOQ approach attempts to determine when and how much inventory should be ordered to minimize total costs related to inventory. JIT is really just a new twist on that old theme. JIT raises the question of whether it is possible to work closely with suppliers to alter some of the variables in the EOQ model.

Perhaps rather than rejecting JIT out of hand, health care managers should rethink their current ordering policies with an attempt to move somewhat toward JIT inventory in the areas that are noncritical and where the greatest possible benefits are most likely to accrue with the lowest risk. Application 13-2 reviews a book on the topic of zero inventory levels.

INVENTORY ISSUES RELATED TO HEALTH CARE MANUFACTURING

Issues related to manufacturing are not of major relevance for most health services providers. Although many argue that the provision of health care services has much in common with manufacturing, it lacks one key ingredient in most cases. The ingredient that separates manufacturing from service is the production of a product for sale at a later date.

However, some health care organizations do stock inventory. For example, a firm may prepare surgical trays for different operations. The firm would buy the various elements needed for all operations and then organize the items on trays for specific operations. These trays can then be sold to hospitals. Such an organization would have a finished product that would be stocked as inventory.

This section addresses inventory costing issues related to health care manufacturing organizations.

Types of Inventory

Figure 13-4 presents the basic flow of inventory through a manufacturing organization. In manufacturing processes, organizations begin with purchased supplies that must be processed into a finished product. The original supplies are referred to as *raw materials inventory* (RMI). These materials enter into the production process. If units of product are started but are unfinished at the end of an accounting period, they are referred to as *work in process* (WIP). Not only materials, but also labor and overhead become part of WIP. When the WIP is completed, it becomes *finished goods inventory* (FGI).

The combined value assigned to RMI, WIP, and FGI would appear on the balance sheet as an asset at the end of the accounting period. The cost of any finished goods that have been sold becomes an expense on the statement of revenues and expenses. Therefore, finding the cost of FGI and the *cost of goods sold* (CGS) is a major reporting function of cost accounting for manufacturing organizations.

Period Costs vs. Product Costs

All manufacturing costs are divided into either *period costs* or *product costs*. A period cost is one that is automatically considered to be an expense relating to the accounting period in which it is incurred. A product cost is associated with the product being sold. It does not become an expense until the product is sold. Product costs are those costs that are directly related to the production of the product, and period costs are all other costs.

Period costs are relatively easy to handle because 100 percent becomes an expense at the end of the accounting period. Costs such as advertising and general administrative expenses fall into this category.

Product costs are assigned to units produced. These costs include direct labor and direct materials used in making the product. They also include a wide range of overhead items, such as factory supplies and depreciation on factory buildings and equipment. Labor and overhead costs are referred to as *conversion costs*. That is because they represent the amount it costs to convert raw materials into finished goods. Labor and raw materials are referred to as *prime costs*.

Suppose that 100,000 units were manufactured during a year and that factory depreciation for the year was $1 million. If all of the units were sold, then there would be a $1 million depreciation cost as part of the CGS expense. What if only half of the units were sold? Then CGS would include only $500,000 of depreciation, while the other $500,000 would be considered to be part of the value of finished goods inventory and would be treated as part of the inventory asset. In other words, inventory at year-end for a manufacturer does not only include the value of inventory purchased. It also includes the value added in the form of labor and overhead.

Variable vs. Absorption Costing

A major controversy in inventory costing relates to whether product costs should be determined on an *absorption costing* or *variable costing* basis. The absorption costing approach considers all direct and indirect manufacturing costs to be assigned to the product. The costs are essentially absorbed by the product as it is produced. Variable costing only assigns variable costs to the product. Variable costing is sometimes referred to as *direct costing*. The contro-

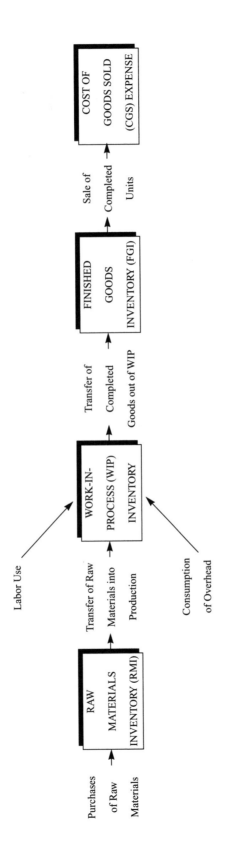

Figure 13-4 Manufacturing Inventory Flow

versy is over the appropriate treatment of fixed factory costs.

In both methods, direct materials and direct labor are considered to be part of the cost of the product. If you make fewer units, you use less materials and labor, and if you make more units, you use more materials and labor. Such costs are added to the WIP as it is worked on, and become part of the FGI value. Even though the labor and supplies have been used and paid for, they are not treated as expenses until the units of product are sold and become a CGS. Similar treatment exists for all variable factory costs in addition to labor and materials.

Fixed factory costs are treated differently under the two methods. Absorption costing allocates the fixed costs to the units produced. The portion of the fixed costs allocated to units that are sold become an expense in the current year. The portion of the fixed costs allocated to units in inventory remain an asset until that inventory is finally sold. Under variable costing, all fixed costs would be treated as if they were period costs. They would be charged off as an expense in the year incurred instead of waiting for sale of the inventory.

Clearly, the choice of variable or absorption costing can have a dramatic impact on the balance sheet and income statement (statement of revenues and expenses) of the organization. Suppose that factory depreciation was $1 million, and only half of the product made was sold. Under absorption costing, the expenses would include only $500,000 of depreciation. The other $500,000 would be in the value of the inventory. Under variable costing, the expense for the year would include the full $1 million, and none of it would be in the inventory. Profits would be reported at a lower value (due to the higher expense), and inventory on the balance sheet would be reported at a lower value (due to lack of inclusion of depreciation as part of the inventory value).

Which method is correct? Some believe that absorption makes more sense, because the units produced but not sold by the end of the year certainly did benefit from the building. Therefore, some depreciation cost should be allocated to them. Others argue that absorption costing cre-

ates perverse incentives by allowing the product cost to vary from year to year in response to changes in production volume.

Consider the fact that during a recession, sales tend to decrease. Suppose that 100,000 units are normally produced and sold, at a cost of $1 million of labor (a variable cost), $1 million of materials (a variable cost), and $1 million of depreciation (a fixed cost). Under absorption costing, the units each cost $30 to produce:

$1,000,000	Labor
1,000,000	Materials
+1,000,000	Overhead
$3,000,000	Total product cost
÷ 100,000	Units
$ 30	Per unit

If sales are expected to fall to 50,000 units during a recession, the organization could make 50,000 units. In that case, the cost per unit would be $40:

$ 500,000	Labor
500,000	Materials
+1,000,000	Overhead
$2,000,000	Total product cost
÷ 50,000	Units
$ 40	Per unit

This means that not only will sales fall, but the cost per unit sold will rise, making the organization even less profitable.

If managers do not want to appear to be unprofitable, they could raise production rather than lower it. For example, suppose that they produced 200,000 units. The cost per unit would be $25:

$2,000,000	Labor
2,000,000	Materials
+1,000,000	Overhead
$5,000,000	Total product cost
÷ 200,000	Units
$ 25	Per unit

As units are sold, they would be less expensive, and the profit decline from reduced sales would be partially offset by the lower cost per unit.

Is this improved profit desirable for the organization? Almost certainly not. The cost per unit is varying because of the amount of fixed depreciation per unit. However, the total depreciation of $1 million has not changed. The organization does not save money at the higher volume. However, it does increase its investment in inventory. By making more units, the organization is currently spending money on labor and supplies to produce units that it cannot sell. The opportunity cost of the money needed to pay for the labor and supplies (paid interest expense or lost interest earned) is a burden on the organization during a period of low sales.

If a variable costing approach were used, then the $1 million of expense would be an annual period cost. It would be charged as an expense regardless of how many units were made and regardless of how many units were sold. The product cost per unit of production would be $20 ($10 of labor per unit + $10 of materials per unit) regardless of the number of units sold. The managers would have no perverse incentive to produce more units when sales are lower. Rather, they would produce fewer units, reducing the organization's opportunity costs.

Although there is much support for variable costing, financial statements are generally reported on an absorption costing basis. However, for generating useful management information, cost accountants would be wise at least to prepare an alternate calculation each year showing inventory and profits on a variable costing basis.

Equivalent Units of Production

The allocation of absorption costs among WIP, FGI, and CGS is straightforward if all unsold units are finished. However, it can become particularly complicated if some units are only partly completed at the end of the accounting process. The WIP inventory must be assigned a value. It has more than the raw inventory cost but less than the value of a unit of finished goods.

Assigning value to WIP inventory is accomplished by calculating *equivalent units of production*. This method consists of evaluating how complete the units are and then converting them into an equivalent amount of finished units. For example, if 100 units are half complete, they are treated as if they were 50 complete units. The calculation of equivalent units can become quite complicated. The units may be half complete in labor but three quarters complete in terms of materials. Also, there may be units in different stages of the productive process.

The reason that this calculation is needed, however, is because of the essence of process costing. The costs incurred must be allocated among the units produced to determine the cost per unit. Total labor costs, for example, cannot be divided by 50,000 complete plus 50,000 partly complete units to find a cost per unit. If labor was divided in that case by 100,000, it would understate the labor cost per unit, because it would be treating it as if the labor produced 100,000 complete units, when it did not. If the 50,000 partly completed units had already received half of their labor, they have used the same amount of labor as 25,000 complete units. Therefore, dividing the total labor cost by 50,000 complete units plus 25,000 equivalent units will provide a more accurate measure of the labor cost per unit for each unit in inventory, as well as for each unit sold.

Another problem related to equivalent units is that costs are not constant. The cost of raw materials or labor may change during the accounting period. This raises a question as to how to treat the units that are still unfinished at the end of the period. One approach is to assume that the first units started were the first ones finished. Therefore, the first units should be assigned the earliest incurred costs, and the unfinished units should be assigned the most recently incurred costs. That is referred to as a FIFO (first-in, first-out) equivalent units of production method. Another alternative is to assume that all costs for the period are averaged together, and each unit's cost is based on the average cost of the resources used. That is referred to as the weighted-average equivalent units of production method.

Spoilage and Waste

A last issue related to manufacturing is concerned with spoilage and waste. This issue is important for all health care organizations. In factories, the loss of raw materials is a major concern. Units that must be disposed of not only mean that the raw material is lost, but any conversion costs related to those units are also lost. Health care organizations also are subject to the problem of lost resources due to less than satisfactory production.

When a second x-ray must be taken because the first did not provide a clear picture, that represents wasted resources. If a patient needs a second operation because of postoperative bleeding after the first operation, that may also represent a failure in the original instance. Some organizations have adopted slogans such as, "Do it right the first time, every time."

The key issue is that higher quality sometimes does not mean higher total costs. Managers must be aware that although efforts to reduce errors may increase the cost of each patient a little bit, the potential savings from avoiding having to do something over may offset a large part, if not all, of the costs of improving the original quality level.

It is unlikely that health care organizations will ever be able to eliminate totally the need to redo procedures. In manufacturing, the concepts of normal and abnormal spoilage have been developed. A certain level of spoilage is unavoidable without incurring unacceptably high quality control costs. Therefore, there is an expectation of some "normal" spoilage. If the waste level exceeds that expectation, it is referred to as "abnormal" spoilage. Such spoilage requires management to determine its cause and undertake actions to avoid such high levels in the future. Readers interested in the specific accounting methods for recording spoilage should refer to a cost accounting textbook that focuses predominantly on manufacturing companies.

NOTES

1. G.R. Tyndall, Logistics costs and service levels: Evaluating the trade-offs, *Journal of Cost Management for the Manufacturing Industries* 1, no. 1 (Spring 1987): 50–56.

2. E.O. Henke and C.W. Spoede, *Cost Accounting: Managerial Use of Accounting Data* (Boston: PWS-Kent Publishing Company, 1991), 78–79.

3. *Ibid*, 86.

SUGGESTED READING

Baptist, A. 1987. A general approach to costing procedures in ancillary departments. *Topics in Health Care Financing* 13, no. 4:32–47.

Finkler, S.A. 1985. Job-order costing: Viewing the patient as a job. *Hospital Cost Accounting Advisor* 1, no. 5:1–5.

Hall, R.W. 1983. *Zero inventories*. Homewood, Ill.: Dow Jones and Irwin.

Hopson, J.F., et al., 1990. Simplifying the use of the economic order quantity formula to control inventory cost. *Journal of Cost Management for the Manufacturing Industry* 3, no. 4:8–13.

Horngren, C.T., and G. Foster. 1991. *Cost accounting: A managerial emphasis*. 7th ed. Englewood Cliffs, N.J.: Prentice-Hall.

Kowalski, J.C. November 1991. Inventory to go: Can stockless deliver efficiency? *Healthcare Financial Management*, 20–34.

Nackel, J., et al. November 1987. Product-line performance reporting: A key to cost management. *Healthcare Financial Management*, 54–62.

Schimmel, V.E., et al. 1987. Measuring costs: Product line accounting versus ratio of cost to charges. *Topics in Health Care Financing* 13, no. 4:76–86.

Sullivan, S. 1987. Product line costing for DRG profitability. *Hospital Cost Accounting Advisor* 3, no. 3:1–5.

Torre, C.J., Sr. 1992. Planning and implementing systems integration for material management and accounting. *Journal of Healthcare Materials Management* 10, no. 2:30, 32, 34.

EXERCISES

QUESTIONS FOR DISCUSSION

1. What is the difference between periodic and perpetual inventory accounting?
2. What are the particular benefits of using the LIFO inventory system during periods of inflation?
3. Does switching from FIFO to LIFO inventory accounting require a change in the flow of inventory?
4. What are the factors considered by the EOQ inventory approach? What is the essence of the technique?
5. What relevant costs must be considered in an EOQ analysis?
6. What are some real-world issues that complicate the EOQ calculation?
7. What are some examples of logistics costs?
8. Can a manager minimize all logistics costs?
9. Does application of just-in-time inventory require zero inventory levels?
10. Can JIT work for health care organizations?
11. What are the three major classes of inventory for manufacturing organizations?
12. What is the difference between period and product costs?
13. Is the issue of absorption versus variable costing relevant to most health care concerns?

PROBLEMS

1. *An Economic Order Quantity Problem.* The E.O. Queue Hospital is trying to determine how many bedpans to buy at a time. They use approximately 2,000 per year. Each bedpan costs the hospital $4. The hospital calculates their capital cost at a rate of 10 percent of the purchase price. Additional carrying costs are 60¢ per unit. Every time the hospital places an order for bedpans, the labor cost in the purchasing department is $16, the shipping and handling cost for the order is $20, and other costs related to making an order are $4.

(a) What is the economic order quantity?
(b) Suppose that they could get a 10¢ discount per bedpan if they order at least 1,000 at a time. Should they take advantage of this discount?

2. If a nursing home buys 500 syringes for $8 each, then uses 500, and then buys 500 more for $9 each, what is the cost of the syringes used, and what is the value of the ending syringe inventory?

3. Aspen Surgical Supply Services provides prepared surgical trays to hospitals. Each year, they have product-related overhead costs of $500,000. The average cost per tray for variable components is $600. In 1993, they prepared 10,000 trays and delivered 9,000 to customers. In 1994, they expect to prepare 14,000 trays and deliver 9,000 to customers. What is the cost of goods sold expense charged to 1993 and 1994 under absorption costing? Under variable costing? Are they more profitable in 1994, assuming their selling prices have remained the same?

4. Aspen Surgical Supply Services provides prepared surgical trays to hospitals. At the end of the year, Aspen had 200 trays that had been started but not completely put together. Half of the trays had one quarter of the labor completed and half of the various supplies filled. The other half had three quarters of the labor and 90 percent of the supplies. For these 200 trays, the average labor cost per tray was $20, and the average supply cost per tray was $580. How many equivalent units were complete for labor? How many equivalent units were complete for supplies? What was the value of this work in process inventory?

Note: Solutions to the Exercises can be found in Appendix A.

Application 13-1

A Review of "Logistics Excellence"

Steven A. Finkler, PhD, CPA

Elsewhere in this issue of *Hospital Cost Accounting Advisor* (HCAA) there is an article on reappraising the impact of logistics on your hospital. In part that article referred to work by Gene Tyndall published in *The Journal of Cost Management.* Tyndall and John Busher have more recently written an article on logistics excellence in *Management Accounting.*

Busher and Tyndall begin their focus on logistics excellence by bemoaning the relative invisibility of the logistics profession in most organizations. As they note, "logistics has its own society, its own terminology, and its own business purpose. The fact remains, however, that unlike marketing, manufacturing, or finance, logistics is not a household word. The purview of logistics seems different in every company, regardless of its products, services, or industry."

The authors are convinced that logistics, despite its relative anonymity, serves a key role in the competitive edge and survival for most organizations. Further, they agree that logisticians "have allowed our basic purpose—getting the right product to the right place, at the right time,

at the right cost, and in the right condition—to remain virtually unchanged." Nevertheless, with the recent Japanese influence on efficient methods of production (zero inventories, just-in-time production, and so on), an examination of efficient logistics management is in order.

The article notes that the basic problem faced by logistics managers has not changed. In order to maximize revenues, there is a desire to provide high inventory stock levels and customer service. Such actions eliminate disruptive outages of inventory and help assure customer satisfaction. On the other hand, they raise costs. (These issues are discussed at more length in the article on logistics in this issue of *HCAA*.) However, the article by Busher and Tyndall primarily details ten principles of excellent logistics management.

Busher and Tyndall have researched the area of logistics and have attempted to pinpoint the success factors for logistics management. Despite the differences in the job function for logistics across organizations, they feel that these ten factors that make the logistics function operate smoothly are universal:

- Link logistics to corporate strategy.
- Organize comprehensively.
- Use the power of information.
- Emphasize human resources.

Source: Reprinted from Steven A. Finkler, Review of "Logistics Excellence," by John R. Busher and Gene R. Tyndall, *Management Accounting,* August 1987, pp. 32–39, published in *Hospital Cost Accounting Advisor,* Vol. 4, No. 1, June 1988, pp. 7–8. Copyright 1984, Aspen Publishers, Inc.

- Form strategic alliances.
- Focus on financial performance.
- Target optimum service levels to improve profitability.
- Manage the details.
- Leverage logistics volumes.
- Measure and react to performance.

The first of the principles is to link logistics to corporate strategy. According to the authors, this is the most important factor for achieving the potential of logistics for profit improvement. Most hospitals do have a mission. The degree to which hospitals develop strategic plans to accomplish the mission is less broadly applied, but is becoming more common as time passes. However, the actual linkage of logistics support to accomplish the strategic plan is probably not common. Yet it makes excellent common sense. By specifically examining changes in logistics to accommodate the hospital's strategic plans, managers might well come up with significant benefits.

The second principle concerns organizing comprehensively. According to Busher and Tyndall, determination of appropriate logistics levels and provision of services according to those levels require a close degree of coordination. If the responsibility for logistics functions is widely split, duplication of effort and suboptimal results will occur. Hospitals shouldn't feel alone, however, if they don't group logistics functions together. According to the article, few firms do group the functions together, even though this is recommended.

The use of information is a very sensible principle. Because of advancing computer technology, information actually has declined in cost over the last decade. As new cost accounting systems are installed, hospital managers should consider the implications for generating information that could be channeled to the correct managers to result in improved logistics management.

The principle of formation of strategic alliances does not represent an internal Machiavellian philosophy of management. Rather, it points out the need to explore external relationships between suppliers and the organization. Hospital supply firms (largely in an effort to guarantee their market share) have developed sophisticated systems for improving the flow of their product to meet hospital requirements.

One of the interesting facets of the article is that the authors rarely refer to minimizing the cost of logistics. Rather, they focus on the realization of the full profit potential of logistics. This is perhaps the most significant part of the article—that logistics is not simply a cost we must bear, but can be used to help the organization, in our case the hospital, to operate in such an efficient manner as to be able to realize improved profits.

Busher and Tyndall refer to their principles as "uncommon sense." They feel that most of the ten points are taken for granted as existing, when in fact they don't. They believe that following their ten points will lead to substantial improvements in market share and growth in assets and profits.

Application 13-2

A Review of "Zero Inventories"

Steven A. Finkler, PhD, CPA

Inventories do not make up a major part of hospital assets, because they receive relatively little attention. However, they are subject both to large potential waste and to management control techniques. In an environment of limited resources, it is in the hospital's interest to focus on any area where costs can be controlled without negative impact on quality.

A recent article in *Hospital Cost Accounting Advisor* focused on the economic order quantity technique as one way to avoid undue inventory costs. Most hospitals have also taken actions to reduce waste generated by opened and unused supply items. A relatively new approach to controlling the various costs associated with inventory is the zero inventory technique, widely used in Japan and discussed by Robert W. Hall in his book *Zero Inventories*.

The zero inventory approach is more of a philosophy than a specific technique. As Hall rightfully points out, *"Zero Inventories* connotes a level of perfection not ever attainable in a production process" (p. 1). One cannot expect to actually achieve a zero inventory level in any industry. In the hospital industry there are obvious

reasons why a "just in time" approach to inventory might have disastrous consequences.

However, as Hall also notes, "the concept of a high level of excellence is important because it stimulates a quest for constant improvement through imaginative attention to both the overall task and to the minute details. That leads to practical actions which break out of previously accepted tracks of thought about production.... *The goal of stockless production is to find practical ways to create the effect of an automated industry which will come as close as possible to this concept of ideal production.* It is not an end in itself because the pure ideal cannot be literally attained. It is a guide to constant improvement, by big steps and small ones, to bring ourselves ever closer to the ideal. It causes us to see problems we never before recognized and to develop better and better techniques to solve them. It constantly promotes the simplest, least costly means for every possible aspect" (pp. 1–2).

Hall clearly has his feet planted solidly on the ground. The realistic underpinning takes away much of the reader's initial skepticism, which comes from the mere name, zero inventories. Many of the concepts presented in the book appear inapplicable to hospitals at first glance. For example, planning production to execute a level schedule sounds impossible for hospitals

Source: Reprinted from Steven A. Finkler, Review of *Zero Inventories,* by Robert W. Hall, Homewood, IL, Dow Jones and Irwin, 1983, published in *Hospital Cost Accounting Advisor,* Vol. 2, No. 10, March 1987, pp. 7–8. Copyright 1987, Aspen Publishers, Inc.

with variable demand. However, hospitals can learn a great deal in scheduling clinic visits and other areas where some patient flow control is feasible.

In fact, the orientation of the book toward identification of problem areas, adapting the organization for flow and flexibility, and monitoring quality provides useful insights for improving the efficiency of any organization.

The book is not at all aimed at the hospital industry. It basically provides an overview of the philosophy and approach that have made Japan a leading industrial nation. The goal of the book is to help U.S. industries learn elements of the Japanese system that can improve their operations. As a result, the hospital manager reading the book will have to deal with the language of manufacturing, assembly line, and production. However, the book sets forth many valuable approaches, and translating the concepts to the hospital industry will be quite worthwhile.

14

Dealing with Uncertainty

Goals of This Chapter

1. Provide tools for improving management decisions that depend on uncertain future events.
2. Introduce and explain the expected value technique.
3. Explain the technique of simulation analysis.
4. Describe and provide examples of network cost budgeting.
5. Introduce linear programming as an aid in management decision making.

Key Terms Used in This Chapter

Critical path; event; expected value; linear programming; network cost budgeting; objective function; outcome; probabilistic estimate; sensitivity analysis; simulation; slack time; state of nature; subjective probability; what-if analysis.

Note: Key terms appear in italics when first used in the chapter. All key terms are defined in the Glossary.

UNCERTAINTY

Health care managers make many decisions after first making financial estimates. Potential revenues and costs are predicted based on a number of calculations, and decisions are made based on the results of those calculations. Inherent in such estimates is a degree of uncertainty.

Often, managers know that there are different possible *events* that may occur—they cannot know for sure in advance, however, which event will happen. Yet decisions are made based on the selection of one of the possible events. There are a number of decision analysis techniques available to help improve the predictions made and used for decisions. This chapter addresses four prominent approaches: (1) *expected value,* (2) *simulation,* (3) *network cost budgeting,* and (4) *linear programming.*

THE EXPECTED VALUE TECHNIQUE

Expected value analysis is a technique that estimates the costs or revenues based on the likelihood of each possible *outcome.* The key focus of expected value analysis is on the possible events that might occur. Management can take actions to affect outcomes, but events are defined as occurrences that are beyond the control of managers. For that reason, events are sometimes referred to as *states of nature.*

For example, a person who received trauma to an arm may or may not have a broken arm. The state of nature is either that the arm is broken, or it is not. A physician must decide whether to order an x-ray of the arm. It may well be that only 10 percent of such cases have broken arms. Invariably, however, the physician will order the x-ray to avoid the negative consequences of failing to order the x-ray in the event it turns out that the arm is broken.

There has been much debate on whether our society overconsumes clinical diagnostic services—using them even if there is a very low probability that they will find a positive result. That will *not* be the subject of this discussion. Rather, we will focus on managerial decisions

that must be made without knowing the true state of nature that currently exists or that will come to exist in the future. We will do this to attempt to find optimal solutions in the face of incomplete information.

An Expected Value Example

There are many potential examples of situations where alternative events might occur. One situation would be planning for a new service, without knowing for sure how many patients the service will attract. For example, suppose a hospital is considering buying a new lithotriptor (an expensive machine for treating kidney stones). Based on physician estimates of demand, we expect to use the machine on 1,000 patients per year. Calculations based on payment rates and operating costs indicate that the service would be profitable at that volume. However, there is the possibility that a nearby competitor will also buy a lithotriptor. In that event, demand at our hospital would probably be only 700 per year. Because there would be fewer patients sharing the cost of the machine at that volume, it is determined that money would be lost.

Certainly, one could make arguments for having the machine even if it loses money. It might enhance the hospital's reputation. It might allow the hospital to meet the demands of physicians who will otherwise refer all of their kidney patients to another facility, not just those patients who need lithotripsy.

Here, however, we want to focus on the financial calculation with respect to the lithotripsy patients themselves. Other factors can be taken into account in making the ultimate decision. However, the decision maker must have a reasonable idea regarding whether the new service will directly make or lose money.

Should the manager assume 700 patients or 1,000 patients? Some managers might tend to be conservative, calculate as if the worse event occurs, and, therefore, use the 700 estimate. Other managers might look to the most likely result. What if there is only a 25 percent chance that the other hospital will buy a lithotriptor? In that case, the manager might use the 1,000 for the calculation, if that is what will probably happen. Neither of these approaches is optimal.

The Expected Value Concept

Expected value is a methodology that finds a middle ground between the two extremes. It does not rely on either event but rather on a combination, or weighted average, of the two. The weighted average to be used must be based on a combination of the likely gain or loss in each event and the probability of that gain or loss occurring.

At first, one might object to this. We are fairly certain that one or the other event will occur, not somewhere in between. Either the other hospital will buy a lithotriptor, or it will not. Volume will be very close to 1,000, or close to 700, not somewhere in between.

That is true. However, from the viewpoint of maximizing the financial results of decisions, in the long run it still makes sense to undertake the weighted average approach. The reason is that over the course of time, any health care organization will make a large number of decisions. It can never predict totally what events will occur, but it must make decisions anyway. The best strategy is to approach the decisions so that *on average,* over the long run, the financial results are maximized. To understand this, we must consider some basics of probability theory.

Probability Theory

Consider a dice game. In dice, any one of the six sides can come up. The chances of any particular side coming up are 1/6. Over a large number of bets, each side of the die will come up an equal amount of times. Therefore, if you bet $100 on one die coming up number 1, you would probably lose, because there is a 5/6 chance some other number will come up.

In fact, if you bet six times on number one, you would win once, and lose five times, on average. We say on average, because in just six rolls of the die, all six could come up number

one, or number one might never come up. However, with a larger number of rolls, and a balanced die, you would win one time out of six, on average.

If the payoff was based on an amount equal to the amount bet, you would expect to lose $400 over every six bets placed. That is because you would lose $100 five times and win $100 once, for a net loss of $400.

Would you ever bet on a die? That depends on a number of other factors. Suppose that when you lose, you lose your full $100. However, when you win, what if the payoff is $1,000, rather than the $100 you bet? This totally changes the game. Now, the chances are that you will lose $100 five times, and win $1,000 once, for a net win of $500! The amount of the payoff is extremely important and must be taken into account.

That is a problem with the conservative approach of assuming that there will be 700 lithotripsy patients or the alternative approach of considering that 1,000 patients is most likely, and therefore should be used in the estimate. Before such a decision can be made, there must be some understanding of the payoff. How much will we lose at 700 patients, and how much would we make at 1,000 patients?

Equally important is the probability of each event occurring. Earlier, we noted that if the payoff just equals the $100 bet, you would lose $400 on every six rolls, on average. Suppose, however, that the die we use has three ones, and one two, one three, and one four. The probability of a one occurring has risen to 3/6. Fifty percent of the time, a one should come up on the die, because half of the sides have a one. If you bet $100 six times, and the payoff was $100 for a win, then you should lose three times and win three times, and just break even. You no longer expect to lose $400, even though the payoff is the same as the bet. The probability of winning has changed and must be taken into account.

Given that the payoff rates and the probability of an event occurring are variables, the decision of whether or not to make a bet is complex. Simple decision rules, such as avoiding the lithotriptor if there is a possibility of the 700 patient volume or accepting the lithotriptor because there will probably be 1,000 patients, are poor. They do not consider the payoffs *or* the probability of each event occurring.

Using Expected Value

According to Horngren and Foster, "An expected value is a weighted average of the outcomes with the probabilities of each outcome serving as the weights. Where the outcomes are measured in monetary terms, *expected value* is often called expected monetary value."[1] In order to compute the expected value, it is first necessary to establish a probability distribution for the possible states of nature. For example, suppose that there is a 25 percent chance that the competitor will buy a lithotriptor and a 75 percent chance that it will not, if we buy one. Further, suppose that the profits from 1,000 patients are expected to be $50,000, whereas the loss related to 700 patients will be $150,000. We can restate this as follows:

	Lithotriptor Project	
	Probability	**Payoff**
We buy/they buy	.25	($150,000)
We buy/they do not buy	.75	50,000
	1.00	

Note that the total of the probability column must always equal 1.0.

The expected value of this proposed project can be measured by multiplying each probability by the expected payoff and summing the results:

We buy/they buy	.25 × ($150,000)	= ($37,500)
We buy/they do not buy	.75 × 50,000	= 37,500
Expected value		= $ 0

In this case, the large potential loss is so great that it just offsets the benefit from the probable gain, and the expected financial result is zero. In that case, there is not expected to be a financial gain from the undertaking. However, the hospital might be happy to take on the machine to keep physicians happy and improve the overall hospital reputation and service to the community.

Bear in mind, however, that the machine will result in some financial impact: either there will be a $150,000 loss, or there will be a $50,000 profit. However, over a large number of projects with this set of characteristics, we can expect to just break even—losing on some and gaining on others.

Taking Risk into Account

One problem with this approach is that it assumes that investors are risk-neutral. Essentially there are two components to this issue. One is that you do not mind losing if you are likely to win an equal amount. The other is that the potential size of the loss is not a major concern.

Consider the latter issue first. In the above example, the potential loss is $150,000, whereas the potential gain is only $50,000. Some managers may be reluctant to risk such a large potential loss for such a small potential reward. Even though the gain is more likely than the loss, and even though mathematically there will be no loss on average, managers may feel that they should not undertake any projects that bear the potential of a large loss.

In terms of the first concern, the risk-neutral perspective is that the probability of the large loss is really quite small. That small probability offsets the potential large size of the loss. In the long run, with enough bets, you come out even. Many managers might argue, however, that there is no assurance that the dice will roll our way. Certainly, with a large enough number of investments (bets), things should even out. However, we may not invest enough times. We may run a series of losses and be fired before the laws of chance turn our way.

From such a perspective, it makes sense to demand a risk premium. That is, rather than being neutral, one might decide that a project must have a positive expected value to be accepted. This will represent a reward for being willing to accept the risk of losses. The size of the risk premium should be determined after considering the magnitude of the potential loss in comparison with the magnitude of the potential gain.

The Full Range of Possible Events

In making decisions based on expected value, one should also attempt to consider all possible states of nature that might occur. In our lithotriptor example, we have treated the problem as if the only possible events are that we buy the unit or not, and that if we buy the unit, the competition may or may not buy it.

We have only evaluated two options. We buy it, and they do not, or we buy it, and they also buy it. See Figure 14-1 for the options we have considered. Presumably, we have implicitly assumed that if we do not buy the machine, there is no change from our current status. Given that decision making only considers change from the status quo, that seems to be reasonable.

However, there is a flaw in the logic. If our hospital does not buy the lithotriptor, there are still two possible outcomes: (1) we do not buy, and the competition does not buy; and (2) we do not buy, but the competition does buy. All possible events must be considered in the expected value analysis.

Subjective Estimates

What are the chances that the other hospital in town will buy a lithotriptor even if we do not? We can only guess at that. However, we have also guessed at the probability that they would buy one if we did. We must recognize the fact that all of these estimates are based on *subjective probability.* When we roll a die, we know

that there is a 1/6 chance of each side coming up. Assuming it is a fair die, the probabilities are known with certainty. In situations facing managers, we often do not know with certainty what the probabilities are.

There may be situations in which we know with a high degree of confidence what will happen. History may provide information that convinces us that there is a 30 percent chance of one event and a 70 percent chance of another. More often than not, however, managers must use their knowledge, experience, and judgment to make a best guess about the likelihood of each event.

One reason that risk aversion is common, and that managers demand a risk premium—a positive rather than zero expected value—is the nature of subjective probabilities. We might have the odds wrong. It is true that having the odds wrong can work for you as well as work against you. However, there is always the risk of unknown negative factors that were not taken into account in determining the probabilities. Therefore, many organizations demand a substantial positive expected value to move forward with a project.

In the lithotriptor example, suppose that we believe that if we do not buy a lithotriptor, there is a 50 percent chance that the other hospital will. Why might we believe that there is a higher likelihood that they will buy the machine if we do not than there was if we did buy it? Before we only estimated 25 percent, whereas now we estimate 50 percent.

Perhaps we think that they might buy it to compete directly with us, but there is a low

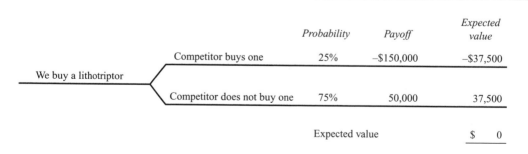

		Probability	Payoff	Expected value
We buy a lithotriptor	Competitor buys one	25%	–$150,000	–$37,500
	Competitor does not buy one	75%	50,000	37,500
	Expected value			$ 0

Figure 14-1 Original Lithotriptor Purchase Alternatives and Expected Value. *Source:* Reprinted from *Hospital Cost Management and Accounting,* Vol. 4, No. 2, p. 4, Aspen Publishers, Inc., © 1992.

chance (25 percent) of that occurring. However, if they have the lithotripsy market to themselves, it is more likely to be profitable. Therefore, they are more likely to make the investment.

Suppose we calculate that if they buy the lithotriptor and we do not, we will lose some of our current patients. As a result, we will have lower profits by an amount equal to $30,000. On the other hand, if neither buys the machine, there will be no financial effect. In that case, the options and expected values would appear as in Figure 14-2. Note that this figure provides a more comprehensive look at all of the possible events that might occur. In looking at Figure 14-1, we were blinding ourselves to a possibility that might occur and might have a negative impact on the hospital.

Although Figure 14-1 indicates there is no expected profit from buying a lithotriptor, the expected value analysis in Figure 14-2 reveals that the hospital may still have a clear financial interest in buying it. It turns out that if the hospital does not buy it, it has a negative expected value!

In other words, if we buy it, we might make money or lose money. If we do not buy it, Figure 14-2 reveals that we will either have no financial effect or have a loss. The expected value

of not buying the machine is a loss of $15,000. This is based on the 50 percent chance that the competitor will buy the machine, inflicting a $30,000 loss on our hospital. It is easy to see why it is necessary to be inclusive in considering all alternative events that might occur. Preparing a decision tree of the possible outcomes, such as appears in Figure 14-2, can help us visualize whether all alternative possibilities have been considered.

Sometimes appropriate decisions result in favorable outcomes; sometimes they do not. Let us change the probabilities that we have been using. Suppose that the probabilities in our example were as follows:

	Competitor buys	Competitor does not buy
We buy	10%	90%
We do not buy	80%	20%

Based on this, we can recalculate our expected values. (See Figure 14-3.)

In this situation, we find that if we buy the lithotriptor, there is an expected increase in profits of $30,000. This expected value has increased from the zero value that we calculated

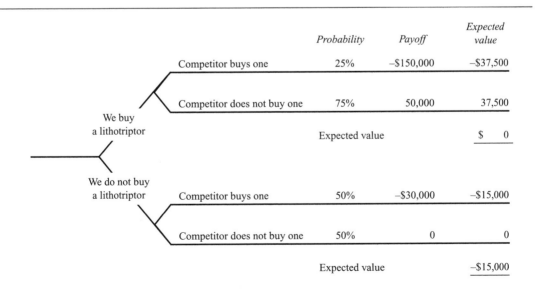

	Probability	Payoff	Expected value
Competitor buys one	25%	−$150,000	−$37,500
Competitor does not buy one	75%	50,000	37,500
Expected value			$ 0
Competitor buys one	50%	−$30,000	−$15,000
Competitor does not buy one	50%	0	0
Expected value			−$15,000

We buy a lithotriptor

We do not buy a lithotriptor

Figure 14-2 Expected Lithotriptor Purchase Alternatives and Expected Value. *Source:* Adapted from *Hospital Cost Management and Accounting,* Vol. 4, No. 2, p. 5, Aspen Publishers, Inc., © 1992.

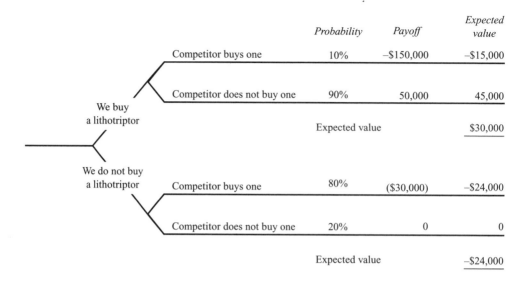

		Probability	Payoff	Expected value
Competitor buys one		10%	–$150,000	–$15,000
Competitor does not buy one		90%	50,000	45,000
We buy a lithotriptor	Expected value			$30,000
We do not buy a lithotriptor	Competitor buys one	80%	($30,000)	–$24,000
	Competitor does not buy one	20%	0	0
	Expected value			–$24,000

Figure 14-3 Expected Values Based on New Probability Estimates. *Source:* Adapted from *Hospital Cost Management and Accounting,* Vol. 4, No. 2, p. 6, Aspen Publishers, Inc., © 1992.

earlier, because the example now assumes that there is an even smaller chance of the competitor buying a lithotriptor if we do. On the other hand, if we do not buy the machine, the expected value is a loss of $24,000. This is because we have increased the likelihood that they buy it if we do not.

What would the correct decision be for our hospital? We expect to make a profit if we buy it, and to lose money if we do not. The analysis clearly indicates that it is a good decision to buy the machine. What if we buy it, and the competitor also buys one?

In that case, we will not attain our volume of 1,000 patients. There will be only 700 patients, and we will lose $150,000. The good decision will have yielded a very bad outcome. Nevertheless, it was the right decision to make.

If managers worry too much about bad outcomes, they will become frozen, unable to make decisions. There will invariably be some bad outcomes. Failing to act is not an insurance policy against bad outcomes. In this example, failing to buy the machine likely would have resulted in the competitor buying it. Failure to act probably would have cost the organization $30,000. If we buy it and they do too, the outcome will be even worse. However, it will be a

relatively unlikely event. In the long run, if our ability to make subjective estimates is at all reasonable, the good results will outweigh the bad ones by a substantial amount.

The Value of Additional Information

This raises the question, however, of whether we have the ability to make good predictions. Managers should be reasonably capable of making subjective estimates, which are not wild guesses but rather predictions founded in experience.

The specific percentage chance the competitor will buy a lithotriptor is unknown. However, from experience, we probably know with a great degree of certainty how often our competitor follows us in a new costly technology and how often it does not. We probably also know from experience how often the competitor has forged ahead if we have not aggressively adopted new technology.

Nevertheless, sometimes it is worthwhile to acquire additional information. Perhaps a consultant can provide us with additional insight about the profitability of running the machine or the probability of demand really being 1,000 as opposed to 900 or 1,100. Perhaps we can hire someone to tell us with greater certainty what our competitor's plans are likely to be. How much is that information worth?

Right now, Figure 14-3 would result in our buying the machine and having an expected value of $30,000. If we knew for sure what our competitor would do if we bought the machine, how would that change things?

In this Figure 14-4, we change the payoffs to what they would be if we could make our decision after we knew what the competitor would do if we bought. To decide how much the information is worth, we will have to use our subjective probabilities. For example, we will assume that there is a 10 percent chance that the perfect information will tell us that the competitor will buy the machine if we do and a 90 percent chance that the perfect information says that the competition will not buy if we do.

If we knew for sure that they would buy the machine if we did, we would not buy it, so instead of losing $150,000, we would have a zero loss. If we knew for sure that they would not buy it if we did, we would then buy it and have a $50,000 gain. Thus, the expected value of our buying the machine would be as follows:

$$
\begin{array}{llr}
& 10\% \text{ of a } \$0 \text{ payoff} & = \$ \quad 0 \\
+ & 90\% \text{ of a } \$50,000 \text{ payoff} & = \underline{\quad 45,000} \\
& & \underline{\underline{\$45,000}}
\end{array}
$$

This is a $15,000 increase over the expected value in Figure 14-3. That is the value of the perfect information. Our expected value rose

because with perfect information, we can be sure to avoid the very bad outcomes. We would pay up to $15,000 to learn our competitor's true intentions.

Unfortunately, perfect information is not generally available. However, one must consider whether there is some way that some additional information could be obtained. If so, then it is worthwhile to try to estimate whether the value of the additional information would exceed the cost of obtaining it.

Another Expected Value Example

Expected value theory does not only relate to new projects such as a lithotriptor. The concepts apply equally to the routine, ongoing services of the health care organization.

For example, suppose that we are planning the staff level for the emergency room (ER). The ER managers know that it is most economical to staff the ER at just the level needed to provide care to all patients who arrive. Extra staff would mean wasted resources. Staff will be available and paid, but not have patients to treat. However, if the ER is short of staff, it will likely need to keep some staff members on overtime shifts, creating more cost than if adequate staffing had originally been planned.

An expected value calculation could be developed that shows the staffing cost at various assumed numbers of patients. For example, we might assume the following distribution and payoff:

		Probability	Payoff	Expected value
	Competitor buys one	10%	0	0
We intend to buy a lithotriptor				
	Competitor does not buy one	90%	50,000	45,000
	Expected value			$45,000

Figure 14-4 Expected Values with Perfect Information. *Source:* Reprinted from *Hospital Cost Management and Accounting,* Vol. 4, No. 2, p. 7, Aspen Publishers, Inc., © 1992.

ER Cases	Probability	Cost/Patient ($)		
		Low Staff	Medium Staff	High Staff
20,000–25,000	.10	50	60	70
25,001–30,000	.40	55	50	60
30,001–35,000	.35	60	50	55
35,001–40,000	.15	70	60	50

The cost per patient is minimized when the staffing pattern is correct for the volume of patients. Low staffing with low volume results in a $50 cost. Moderate staffing with moderate volume also has a $50 per patient cost, as does high staffing with high volume. If volume is high, and staffing is too low, costs are high for overtime. If volume is low, and staffing is high, cost per patient is high due to overstaffing. Using expected value analysis (see the expected value problem at the end of this chapter), one could determine the optimal staffing pattern.

This is just one example. However, there are many situations in the routine operations of health care organizations in which expected value analysis could be useful to managers. Two additional examples are provided in Applications 14-1 and 14-2.

SIMULATION ANALYSIS

Health care planning often relies on a series of best estimates. Managers are aware that each estimate is uncertain. Rarely are projections right on target, but it is hoped that no one error will be extremely large. Hospital managers generally rely on that fact when they place their confidence in an overall projection for a new project or a routine operating department budget. Even small errors, however, can result in projections being way off the target, because of a compounding of errors.

If one estimate has a possible plus or minus margin of error of 10 percent and is used to predict another number, a compounding of errors occurs. The normal variability of the final number estimated increases because of the potential error already built into earlier estimates. Although errors in estimates may compound each

other, such compounding is rarely accounted for by health care managers. This may be because managers are unaware of such compounding of errors or because the calculations required to consider the impact are complex. Simulation analysis is a tool that can take the various errors in all the estimates into account and provide managers with the likelihood of actual results being substantially different from the budgeted projection.

A Simulation Example

Suppose that a hospital were considering opening a home health agency. It is only willing to undertake this venture if it is expected at least to break even. It is hoped that a positive profit will result.

In preparing a plan for the home health agency, volume is clearly one of the critical factors. It is unlikely that any hospital would undertake a new venture without estimates of the number of new patients. The relationships between fixed costs, variable costs, and volume are fundamental to determining whether the service is likely to break even, to be profitable, or to lose money.

However, forecasting volume accurately is difficult for ongoing services. It is even more difficult for new programs that the hospital has no experience on which to rely. Few managers would expect their volume forecast to be right on target. If it is reasonably close, most managers would be content. For new projects, such as a home care agency, many managers would insist on a margin for safety, just in case the venture does not turn out exactly as was forecast.

A question that arises, however, is whether managers fully consider how far the actual result is likely to vary from the expected one. Suppose that the volume forecast was developed by assuming that the agency would draw its patients primarily from hospital discharges. The volume estimate for the home agency was prepared by estimating the number of the hospital's discharges who would be likely to need home care, the amount of home care they would need, and the portion of the discharges the hospital could capture.

In that case, the estimate is really based on a number of underlying projections. First, how many patients will the hospital actually discharge in the coming year? Second, what portion of the discharges will need home care? Third, how much home care will they need? Fourth, what percentage of the home care patients from our hospital will we capture as our market share?

Suppose that the hospital managers estimate that there will be 10,000 discharges, 10 percent of the discharges will need home care agency visits, the average number of visits will be 5, and the hospital will capture 40 percent of the possible market. This would yield an estimated number of home care visits of 2,000 (10,000 × 10% × 5 × 40%) for the first year of operations. A manager might feel conservative in requiring that the venture be undertaken only if it breaks even at no more than 1,600 patients. That leaves a 20 percent margin for error.

If the volume required to break even is calculated to be 1,200 patients, the manager is likely to feel quite secure in going ahead with the agency. The predicted volume is 2,000. A 20 percent error would only lower volume to 1,600. The breakeven point only requires volume of 1,200. Clearly, this project is likely to make money.

Is that calculation adequate? What if each of the variables estimated is a 20 percent overestimate? Suppose that after starting the home care agency, the hospital were to have 8,000 discharges, only 8 percent of them need home care, they average only 4 visits per patient, and only 32 percent of the patients use the hospital's agency. In that case, how many visits will there be? There will be only 819 (8,000 × 8% × 4 × 32%)! Even though no element fell by more than 20 percent, the compounding effect is a decrease of nearly 60 percent in the number of patients.

To make matters even worse, a variety of other elements need to be estimated in addition to patient volume. What will the mix of patients be? What government reimbursement rates will be in effect? What will be the prices of supplies? Labor? How much labor will be needed per visit? How much equipment will be needed, and what will it cost? What will the bad debt expense rate be? These represent just some of the types of items that must be estimated with no real history to use as a basis. If the various costs are each 20 percent higher than expected, and/or the reimbursement is 20 percent less than expected, the magnitude of the compounding will be much greater than already cited. The potential variability is enormous.

On the other hand, how likely is it that the hospital discharges will really be 20 percent below expectations? Quite unlikely. The implication of compounding errors is not that no project should be undertaken because of uncertainty and the risk it creates. However, managers need to use tools that can aid them in the process of determining how likely it is that a bad outcome will in fact occur.

Sensitivity Analysis

One approach to this problem is *sensitivity,* or *what-if, analysis*. This approach, usually using a computer, allows the manager to consider various possible actual results and see their impact on the projection. This will tell a manager how sensitive the profits of the venture are to any given change in one or more variables.

A computer model would be constructed that would calculate project results. This model might be as simple as a Lotus 1-2-3* template that calculates the profits of the project based on input values for each revenue and expense item. Changing the predicted number of discharges has an impact on the number of home care patients, which has an impact on revenues, which has an impact on profits.

Using such a model, the manager can ask, What if the number of discharges falls 20 percent? What if the number of visits per patient is only four? What if the number of discharges falls 20 percent *and* the number of visits per patient is only four?

---

*Lotus 1-2-3 is a registered Trademark of the Lotus Development Corp.

This approach requires management judgment in determining a reasonable set of what-if assumptions. If the manager believes that it is quite unlikely that the hospital's discharges would fall below 9,500, then that would be the lower limit used in the sensitivity analysis. On the other hand, if the manager has little feeling for the market share that the hospital will be able to capture, that variable will be allowed to range more widely in the analysis.

This approach is very useful for managers and can provide them with either a sense of comfort or information that will alter a decision to go ahead with a project. Suppose that the manager changes the model to assume that everything that reasonably could go wrong does go wrong. If the results still indicate a profit, or only a borderline loss, then the manager can go ahead with the project with the knowledge that large losses or total project failure are quite unlikely. On the other hand, if the estimate indicates a large loss, then the manager must reconsider whether the organization is willing to take the risk of the loss.

Probabilistic Estimates

Sensitivity analysis is based to some extent on the notion of probabilistic estimates. A *probabilistic estimate* is based on a manager's subjective estimate of what is most likely to occur. The most likely outcome is generally the one that the manager has used to make the original estimates for the projection.

In making a projection, the probabilistic (i.e., based on probabilities) nature of the estimate is often ignored. Even in sensitivity analysis, probability is primarily kept in the background. In the what-if analysis, the manager considers outcomes that have a reasonable likelihood of coming true and implicitly discards outcomes that have an extremely low probability. However, the probabilistic nature of the analysis is kept at an implicit level.

This limits the usefulness of sensitivity analysis. It can help a manager get a sense of the likely possible range of outcomes. The manager

can assume that everything that might go wrong will go wrong (or everything that might go right will go right) and find the extremely unfavorable (or extremely favorable) result. However, this falls short because it does not give the manager a sense of how likely or unlikely the result is to occur.

Once the manager starts to assume unexpectedly unfavorable outcomes for various individual variables, it becomes difficult to gain a sense of how likely it is that all of these variables might actually go wrong. That is where simulation analysis can help the manager.

The Simulation Technique

A simulation model is much like a template used in a sensitivity analysis. The full set of calculations is structured. However, the simulation goes further in generating a value for each variable in the model. These values are placed into the model, and a result is calculated; this is done many times. The key to the simulation is that the value chosen for each variable is based on a probability distribution.

In other words, managers must indicate how likely they believe a variable is to take on a variety of different values. For instance, suppose that the manager has the following belief regarding the number of hospital discharges for the coming year:

Number of Discharges	Probability of Occurring (%)
9,250	5
9,500	15
9,750	20
10,000	30
10,250	15
10,500	10
10,750	5

These beliefs represent the manager's subjective probability based on experience combined with any information available about the number of discharges in the past years. The simulation model will select each of the above values on a random basis, adjusted for probability.

The Simulation Process

The way this is done can be visualized by using a simple analogy. Consider a hat with 100 slips of paper in it. There will be 5 slips with the value 9,250. There will be 15 slips with the value 9,500. There will be 20 slips with the value 9,750, and so forth. The number of slips with each value corresponds to the probability of that value occurring.

When someone selects a slip from the hat, the chance that it will be any of the numbers from the above table will exactly match the manager's subjective estimate of the probability of that number of discharges actually occurring in the coming year. This process must be done for each variable in the model. The probabilities must be estimated for the percentage of discharged patients needing home care. The probabilities must be estimated for the number of visits per patient. The probabilities must be estimated for the percentage of discharged patients needing home care that use our service. The probabilities must also be estimated for the average reimbursement rates, for the mix of patients, for the cost of supplies per visit, for the cost of labor, for the cost of fixed cost items, and so forth.

In selecting a value for each variable, the simulation takes an approach different from what most managers are likely to take. It does not assume that everything that could go wrong does go wrong. It bases each variable's outcome on the likelihood of outcomes for that variable. In other words, most of the time when one variable goes wrong, another variable is likely to go right.

What are the chances that everything goes wrong at once? The more variables there are, the less likely that is to happen—but it could. That is why simulation models are not generally run only 1 time, or 10 times, or even 100 times. It is common to run simulations at least several thousand times. The results generated by the simulation are then shown as a range and a frequency. For instance, managers might decide they want to know the likelihood that the project results will fall into the following ranges:

	$ Range
Gain	> 100,000
Gain	50,000 to 100,000
Gain	25,000 to 49,999
Gain	10,000 to 24,999
Gain	1 to 9,999
Loss	0 to 10,000
Loss	10,000 to 24,999
Loss	25,000 to 49,999
Loss	50,000 to 100,000
Loss	> 100,000

The simulation model results would indicate the number of times (and, if desired, the percentage of times) that the simulated results fell into each category. Running the model only once or a few times will lead to unsatisfactory results. There are many possible outcomes, and a few trials may not give a fair reflection of the likelihood of any particular outcome. That is why simulations are rarely performed unless a computer is available.

The specific result for the home health agency example that we have been using will, of course, depend on all of the variables involved and the subjective probability of the outcomes for each individual variable. A simulation report might appear as in Exhibit 14-1.

The frequency column indicates the number of times in 10,000 trials that the results came out within a particular profit range. The probability that the profit or loss will fall in any specific range is also given. The last column is the cumulative probability. Note that the table indicates that there is a 71 percent probability that the home health agency will be profitable, and an 82 percent chance that it will either be profitable or suffer only a modest loss.

What about the possibility of everything going wrong that could go wrong? That possibility does exist. In fact, there were 18 simulations in which the losses exceeded $100,000. However, when one considers that those were 18 chances out of 10,000, the likelihood is remote. It is substantially less than a 1 percent chance. On the other hand, there is a 3 percent chance of losses greater than $50,000, and a 9 percent chance of losses greater than $25,000.

Exhibit 14-1 Sample Simulation Report

Outcome ($)		Frequency*	Probability (%)	Cumulative Probability (%)
Gain	> 100,000	283	3	3
Gain	50,000 to 100,000	1,431	14	17
Gain	25,000 to 49,999	2,451	25	42
Gain	10,000 to 24,999	1,631	16	58
Gain	1 to 9,999	1,282	13	71
Loss	0 to 10,000	1,084	11	82
Loss	10,000 to 24,999	922	9	91
Loss	25,000 to 49,999	645	6	97
Loss	50,000 to 100,000	253	3	100
Loss	> 100,000	18	0	100

*Out of ten thousand trials.

Implementing Simulation Results

Ultimately, the simulation results must be used by the manager in making a decision. In the example we have used, should the project be undertaken? That is a difficult question. The project will most likely be profitable. Are the potential profits great enough and likely enough to persuade the hospital to take the risk of possible losses? That depends to a great deal on the specific philosophies of individual health care organizations.

Some organizations are more willing to be risk takers than others are. Relatively profitable health care organizations can afford to take a number of risks. Even if a few projects fail, the profits from the successful ones will outweigh the losses by a substantial amount. Very unprofitable organizations can also afford to be risk takers. They must find some profitable ventures to get themselves out of a cycle of annual losses. If the ventures succeed, they will become less unprofitable. If the ventures fail, it will only hasten the inevitable.

Health care organizations that are in the middle of those two extremes are in a more difficult position. The expected value of the home agency in the example is positive. There is a substantially greater chance of gain than loss. Investing in such opportunities over time should lead to profit increases. On the other hand, three times out of ten, there would be losses on the

new venture, given expectations similar to the hypothetical information provided in Exhibit 14-1. Politically, such failures may be so unpalatable that they will make managers reluctant to act in the overall financial best interests of the organization. The results from Exhibit 14-1 could be used to calculate an expected value, using the frequencies generated by the simulation.

Limitations of Simulation Analysis

There are three primary concerns about the use of simulation analysis. The first is that it might be prohibitively costly. The second is that the model may be built incorrectly. The third is that the probability estimates may be incorrect.

Cost was a major problem as recently as ten years ago. To run a complicated model thousands of times was prohibitively costly. In recent years, however, computer power has increased in a geometric fashion. It has now become relatively inexpensive to run simulations, and there are many software programs available that simplify the process. Moriarity and Allen noted, "The cost of computer time to run a simulation is now usually nominal ($10 or less for several thousand trials)."[2]

The need to set up the model correctly is important but really does not add to the complexity of planning a new venture or preparing a budget. In any case, the specific calculations that need to be made must be carefully laid out to result in a correct analysis.

A greater concern is the subjectivity of the projections. Ultimately, we cannot get around the fact that the simulation analysis rests on the subjective probabilities assigned by the person developing the simulation. In some instances, rather than rely on just one person, it may be desirable to bring together a committee of individuals and have them arrive at a consensus set of probabilities.

Such probabilities may still not be correct. However, experienced hospital managers often have a good sense of the likelihood of different occurrences. A committee is likely to arrive at an even more sensible conclusion because more people bring more information into the analysis. When a committee's consensus is combined with the simulation approach, predictions are likely to improve dramatically.

Despite the limitations of simulation noted above, the reader should keep one essential point in mind. The simulation avoids ignoring the possibility of unfavorable outcomes compounding other unfavorable outcomes. At the same time, it improves on sensitivity analysis by not treating the "all things go wrong" situation as if it was just as likely to occur as the originally projected result. Using simulations is likely to enable hospital managers to substantially improve the accuracy of their decisions.

NETWORK COST BUDGETING

Network analysis is a popular management tool used primarily for planning and controlling nonroutine, complex projects. It also may be beneficially used for some ongoing activities in many organizations. Using arrow diagrams, a *critical path* is found that determines the shortest time for project completion. An article that discussed one network technique, program evaluation and review technique (PERT), is reviewed in Application 14-3. It is possible to enhance the value of network analysis by connecting it directly to costs and budgeting. Network cost budgeting refers to combining the

techniques of network analysis with cost accounting to generate the most cost-effective approach to the project.

In network analysis, it is often assumed that the network is laid out in an optimal fashion. However, it is clear that networks do not indicate the *only* time lines that are possible. By using overtime or extra staff, it is often possible to reduce the amount of time needed. Such time reductions are often associated with extra cost, but that cost may be justified if other benefits result.

For example, suppose that a hospital plans to construct and open a new clinic or surgicenter. Once opened, the new facility is expected to yield profits for the hospital. Each day of delay in opening the unit means lost profits. If the unit can be opened earlier by adding extra construction crews, it may be worth the extra cost.

Therefore, a technique is needed to match the potential benefits of shortening the project time with the additional costs that would create. Network cost budgeting is a technique designed for working out those calculations. Moriarity and Allen, who call this approach PERT/cost budgeting, cite its potential usefulness for projects such as "constructing a new manufacturing facility, undertaking a major research project, developing a new product, or instituting a major new marketing campaign."[3]

Network Analysis

A network uses a diagram to show the relationships in a complex project. Arrows are used to represent specific activities that must be done. It is possible to have many activities all begin from one point and take place at the same time. The crucial aspect of network analysis is identifying those activities that must be completed before some other activity or activities can commence.

Figure 14-5 presents an example of a simple network diagram. For the example, assume that a hospital has determined midway through the year that revenues are below expectations and that a financial crisis is anticipated. A decision is made to select five departments that have the potential for budget cuts that would at least partly offset the crisis.

However, rather than blindly cutting the budgets for those departments, a zero base review will be conducted in each one. In a zero base review, all expenditures of a department must be justified. The budget is not based on an increment over past approved budgets. Instead, each element of the budget is reviewed and its role determined. If the element is not considered vital for carrying out the mission of the department, or if it carries out a portion of the mission that is considered expendable, then the element is subject to being eliminated. Based on the information from that review, a determination would be made concerning how much to cut from the operating budget of each department. The elements of the review are modeled in the network in Figure 14-5. (Note: special projects for which network analysis is useful do not always concern mortar and bricks.)

In Figure 14-5, each activity starts at a numbered point. The number is shown in a circle. Each activity has a number at its start and at its completion, and the activity can be identified by those two numbers, such as Activity 1-2 or 2-4. An alternative presentation is to place each activity in a "node" as in Figure 14-6, and refer to it by the name or description in the node.

The Critical Path

A critical path is always found as an element of network analysis. In fact, one widely used network approach is called the critical path method (CPM). In order to find the critical path, it is necessary to determine the expected length of time for each activity. In this example, it is assumed that an initial plan was developed as follows:

- Develop an audit plan, assign staff, schedule audits: 31 days.
- Audit Department A: 22 days.
- Audit Department B: 15 days.
- Audit Department C: 13 days.
- Audit Department D: 9 days.

- Audit Department E: 19 days.
- Review audit results: 31 days.
- Make budget modification decisions (top management), hear appeals, make final decision: 31 days.

Note that all days are shown, including weekend days. In this plan, however, it was not assumed that any work would take place on weekends.

It was decided that there would be two teams of auditors. The fastest approach would then be to have one team audit A and then E, while the other team audited B, C, and D. The critical path for the project is shown in bold in Figure 14-7. One route or path through the network is 1-2-3-5-6-7-8. The total days for that path are 130. In this simple example, there is only one other path through the network. That is 1-2-4-6-7-8. Adding up all of the days along that path comes to a total of 134 days, or nearly four and a half months.

The critical path is determined by totaling the days required for each possible route through the network and finding the longest one. Recall that all of the tasks must be undertaken. Therefore, the project can be achieved in no less time than the time it takes for the longest path.

Benefits of Planning

There is always a temptation, especially in times of crisis, to get to work—determine what must be done, and do it without wasting any time. Planning takes time. Developing the initial estimates of time for each activity and putting it together into a plan will take hours, days, or longer. However, this example demonstrates some of the advantages of having a plan.

Many activities are generally done a certain way. If someone is told to undertake an activity, he or she is likely to do it in the usual way. Conducting a zero base budget review requires a careful audit plan. Meetings must be held to determine goals of the audit and to plan specific audit activities. Auditors and departments must schedule mutually convenient times for the audit. These tasks make up Activity 1-2. In a pe-

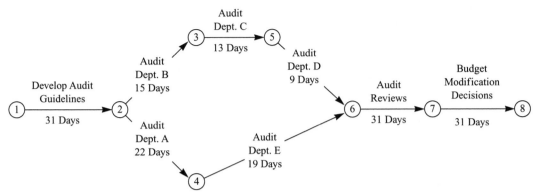

Figure 14-5 Network Analysis Example. *Source:* Reprinted from *Hospital Cost Management and Accounting,* Vol. 3, No. 6, p. 3, Aspen Publishers, Inc., © 1991.

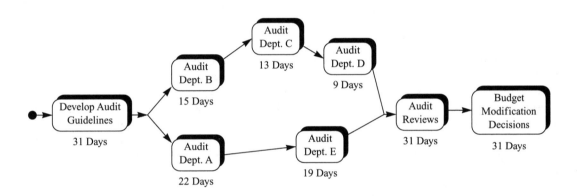

Figure 14-6 Network Analysis Using Nodes. *Source:* Reprinted from *Hospital Cost Management and Accounting,* Vol. 3, No. 6, p. 3, Aspen Publishers, Inc., © 1991.

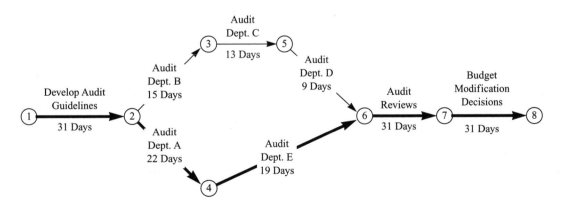

Figure 14-7 Critical Path Indicated in Bold. *Source:* Reprinted from *Hospital Cost Management and Accounting,* Vol. 3, No. 6, p. 3, Aspen Publishers, Inc., © 1991.

riod of noncrisis, getting this activity completed over the course of a month might be quite reasonable. However, in a crisis, that might be considered quite unreasonable.

A review of this plan by top management may result in better communication of exactly the extent to which they consider this to be a priority. If the activity is important enough, then the individuals involved will be told that they should put other work aside temporarily. Necessary meetings should be held immediately, rather than at some mutually convenient time over the next few weeks. Audits should commence as soon as the auditors are ready. Reviews of audit results for Departments A, B, and C should be done while audits for D and E are taking place. Reviews of audit results for D and E should be done immediately upon the conclusion of the audits and should in no case take longer than one week. Decisions should be made and appeals heard also within one week.

A revised network appears in Figure 14-8. The new critical path is only 65 days long, or slightly more than two months. Over half of the project time has been eliminated simply by indicating its priority. This reflects the significant benefits that can be obtained by creating and reviewing a plan prior to starting work on a project.

Working Time vs. Slack Time

These modifications reflect one important distinction in network analysis. Some time allocated to a project is actual working time. However, much time in any project is waiting time. Waiting time between activities is clearly identified in network analysis.

For example, in Figure 14-7, Activities 2-3-5-6 take 37 days, whereas Activities 2-4-6 take 41 days. That means that if 2-3-5-6 are done as expeditiously as possible, at the end there will be a 4-day wait while 2-4-6 catches up. Those 4 days are referred to as *slack*. A delay in the completion of 2-3-5-6 would have no impact in delaying the overall project. However, even a one-day delay in 2-4-6 would delay the project. That is why the critical path line goes through those ac-

tivities. Figure 14-9 shows the revised network, with indications of slack time.

Within an activity, there may also be waiting or slack time. In the original example, it was assumed that Activity 1-2 required scheduling meetings and then waiting until the meetings take place. Then work takes place on an audit plan. Then the actual audits are scheduled. Then there is waiting until the audits take place. All of that waiting time is occurring on the critical path. The total Activity 1-2 initially required 31 days including slack. When the priorities were communicated indicating the importance of the project, its time came down to 10 days without eliminating any work.

The solution to the problem of slack time within an activity is to break the activity into a number of smaller activities. Then each waiting period would be explicitly indicated in the plan. If the project has enough importance, those people reviewing the plan will indicate its priority and shorten or eliminate those waiting periods. However, in the absence of a formalized plan that specifically shows the waiting periods, they might go unrecognized and might slow completion of the project considerably.

Consideration of Costs

An underlying assumption of network analysis is that finding the critical path and minimizing it also minimizes costs. Further, knowing which paths have slack and allowing that slack also keeps costs down—no overtime is spent to complete an activity in the minimal number of days if that activity has several slack days. However, cost minimization is not necessarily optimal. It may be beneficial to push a project through faster, even if at a higher cost.

The cost function for projects may often be U-shaped. That is, to get the project done in an extremely short time period requires very high costs. These often appear in the form of labor costs for extra workers or for overtime. As the time allowed for the project increases, costs fall dramatically. If the project drags out for a long time, costs begin to rise again. Individuals spend more time on a very long project than on

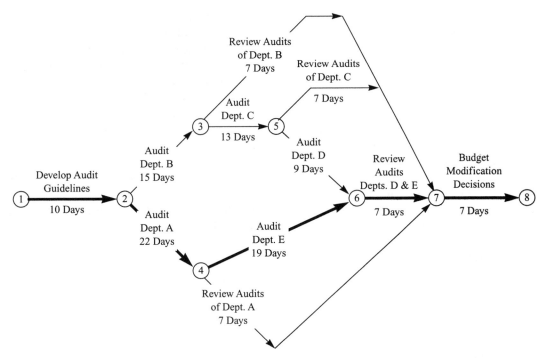

Figure 14-8 Addition of Simultaneous Tasks. *Source:* Reprinted from *Hospital Cost Management and Accounting,* Vol. 3, No. 6, p. 4, Aspen Publishers, Inc., © 1991.

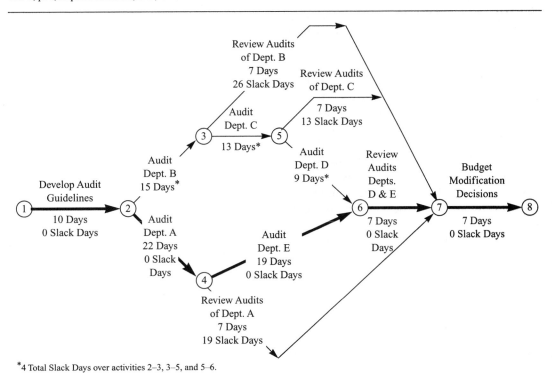

*4 Total Slack Days over activities 2–3, 3–5, and 5–6.

Figure 14-9 Adding Slack to the Analysis. *Source:* Reprinted from *Hospital Cost Management and Accounting,* Vol. 3, No. 6, p. 4, Aspen Publishers, Inc., © 1991.

a moderate one, if only to refamiliarize themselves with the project and its status.

The enhancement that network cost budgeting adds to network analysis is the determination of the optimal time and cost budget for the project. The first step in this process is to determine the "least cost, least time" to complete each activity. That is, first one must determine the lowest cost for an activity, and then one must determine the fewest possible days for the activity within that cost. In many cases, there is only one number of days for which the least cost is attainable. In many cases, however, it may be possible to do an activity at the lowest cost over a range of possible days. In those cases, we want to find the fewest possible days for accomplishing the activity at the lowest cost. We will assume that the example shown in Figure 14-9 presents the least cost, least time for each activity.

The next step is to determine the critical path based on those times. There is a focus on the critical path, because network cost budgeting focuses on the impact of shortening projects. The project can only be shortened by decreasing the time required for an activity on the critical path. The critical path 1-2-4-6-7-8 was indicated in Figure 14-9.

Next, the accountant must determine how much extra it would cost to shorten each activity by one day. In most of the activities, such cost will represent the cost of additional personnel or the cost of weekend or other overtime work. Recall that the days shown in this network include weekends, but assume they are not worked. By working a six- or seven-day week during the project, or by working 12 hours a day instead of 8, or by hiring additional staff, some activities (perhaps most activities) can be completed in a shorter number of calendar days.

The Network Cost Calculation

In order to carry out this process, the hospital's accountants will have to review each activity and the various individuals involved. However, the calculations often are not compli-

cated. Activity 1-2 requires a fair amount of meetings for planning activities. Which members of the meetings are paid an annual salary with no overtime, and which individuals will be paid overtime? What is the extra cost per overtime hour? How much overtime would have to be worked to reduce the activity required time by one day? This process must be done for each activity.

Once that is completed, we can determine which activity is the least costly to shorten by one day. For example, suppose that the following information was calculated for Activities 1-2 and 2-4 on the Figure 14-9 critical path:

Activity 1-2

Original Days:	10
Extra cost for 9 days:	$ 800
Extra cost for 8 days:	1,100
Extra cost for 7 days:	1,100
Extra cost for 6 days:	NF*

Activity 2-4

Original Days:	22
Extra cost for 21 days:	$400
Extra cost for 20 days:	400
Extra cost for 19 days:	400
Extra cost for 18 days:	400
Extra cost for 17 days:	600
Extra cost for 16 days:	600
Extra cost for 15 days:	NF

Once the cost per day reduction is known for each activity, the next step would be to determine the benefits of a shortened project and compare the costs of the least costly way to reduce one day with the benefits of such a reduction.

The Network Benefit Calculation

What are the benefits of shortening a project? If we are planning to open a clinic, benefits would be the daily profits once the clinic is opened. What are the benefits in the example

---

*NF stands for "not feasible" and indicates that it is not possible to reduce this activity further, even at additional expense.

that has been discussed in this section? The goal is to reduce unnecessary costs in the current-year budget. With each passing day, the five departments, A, B, C, D, and E, spend money on items that may be eliminated once the project is completed.

In order to compare the costs of a faster project with its benefits, we need to know the benefits. In order to determine the benefits in this case, it will be necessary first to complete the project and see how much the budgets are cut. We are caught in a circle. However, it is reasonable for an estimate to be made of the anticipated budget savings. Suppose that it is *hoped* that $1,200 per day of spending can be cut from the five departments over the remainder of the year, and *expected* that at least $1,000 per day can be cut. The sooner the project is completed, the sooner the hospital will begin saving at least $1,000 per day.

Each day that the critical path can be reduced produces an anticipated benefit of $1,000. Therefore, overtime and other measures should be used to reduce the critical path, as long as the extra cost for each day the project is reduced is less than $1,000.

In Activity 1-2, one day can be saved for $800. The time for that activity should therefore be reduced by one day. However, reducing that activity by another day would cost an additional $1,100. Therefore, the activity should not be reduced by two days.

In Activity 2-4, there could be a reduction of up to six days. The first four cost an extra $400 each, and the next two cost an extra $600 each. However, it is important to remember that reductions in days are only effective as long as they are on the critical path. The first four days that Activity 2-4 is shortened will make both Paths 1-2-3-5-6-7-8 and 1-2-4-6-7-8 have an equal total number of days. There will no longer be any slack in the 1-2-3-5-6-7-8 path.

The implication is that before one shortens Activity 2-4 by a fifth day, the extra cost of reducing Path 2-3-5-6 by one day must be considered. It will be necessary to reduce both 2-4-6 and 2-3-5-6 by one day to save a day on the total project. The combined cost may exceed the $1,000 benefit.

Further Complications

Another problem to consider is the selection of which activities to shorten. For instance, does it make more sense to shorten 2-4 or to shorten 4-6 by a day?

In certain areas of the network, this is not a problem. If only one path is over part of a network, we want to shorten all activities along that part of the path as long as the benefit exceeds the extra cost. Therefore, Activities 1-2, 6-7, and 7-8 should all be shortened as much as possible. Each of those activities is on the critical path, and each one occurs at a point in the network where there is only one activity at a time.

In the case of Activities 2-4 and 4-6, it is more complicated. Before deciding to reduce 2-4 by four days, as we did above, we must consider whether it would have been cheaper to reduce Activity 4-6 instead. Similarly, once Path 2-4-6 has been reduced by four days, it will be the same length as 2-3-5-6. Additional reductions would have to take place on both paths to save any project time. Therefore, we will have to find the lowest cost to reduce one day from either 2-4 or 4-6 and combine that with the lowest cost to reduce one day from among Activities 2-3, 3-5, and 5-6.

The concept of network cost budgeting is not new, but it has not been widely used in health care organizations. It is a technique that has significant potential benefit for bringing the length of projects under control.

The introduction of computer software that makes network analysis on personal computers possible has increased the accessibility and usefulness of this technique.

LINEAR PROGRAMMING

Linear programming is a mathematical technique that allows the user to maximize or minimize the value of a specific objective in a constrained environment. For example, one might want to maximize profits or minimize costs. Alternatively, one might want to maximize quality or the number of patients treated. A wide variety of objectives can be defined, as long as one has a way to measure the objective chosen. Quality maximization, for example, might pose a problem due to the difficulty of developing a useful quality measure.

Unconstrained maximization or minimization is rarely a realistic goal. Minimized costs would be zero. However, we never expect an organization's costs to be zero. We want to minimize the costs, given that the organization treats a certain number of patients of a certain type. Similarly, we may not want to maximize profits if it means eliminating a certain service currently offered. For example, a hospital may have a community program that it feels is necessary to meet its mission. It might not give up that program, even though profits would be higher. The hospital wants to maximize profits, subject to the condition that the program be maintained.

Constraints generally exist and must be considered as we attempt to maximize or minimize our objective. In fact, there are often numerous constraints. A nursing home has a limited number of beds. An ambulatory surgery center has a limited number of operating suites. It would not make sense to spend money on marketing efforts to attract more patients if no capacity existed to treat them.

The more complex an organization is, the more difficult it becomes to determine exactly how to maximize objectives. Suppose that a health care organization wants to maximize profits. What is involved? Patients are treated, revenues are earned, and costs are incurred. However, there are many interrelationships among patients. If we decide to do coronary artery bypass graft surgery, then we will have a bypass pump. That pump is needed for heart valve surgery. If we eliminate the bypass surgery, we are constrained to keep the pump unless we eliminate valve surgery. Health care organizations have many similar, complicated constraints.

There are often too many interrelationships to consider simultaneously without being overwhelmed. The organization may treat hundreds of different types of patients, using hundreds of different types of resources. Revenues and profit margins vary greatly over the different types of patients.

Given all of these various issues to consider at one time, how can one make effective decisions? Linear programming develops a series of equations based on the stated objective and subject to its various constraints. The equations are solved simultaneously (using a computer program) to determine the optimal allocation of resources. The more accurate the equations are that state the existing relationships, the more accurate the resulting model and its solution will be.

Developing Equations

The first equation to be developed is the *objective function*. This equation states the relationship between the objective and the other variables in the process. Selecting the objective is not a simple task. In fact, there exists a substantial body of literature aimed at determining whether health care organizations maximize revenues, profits, costs, prestige, volume of patients treated, quality, or some other objective.

However, it is not necessary for health care managers to discover some underlying truth about the organization's objective function. Financial necessities are such that individual health care organizations will probably be able rather easily to set their objective function, *for the purposes of developing a linear programming model,* as either profit maximization, or achievement of a target level of profit, or breakeven, and so forth. Bear in mind that regardless of the objective chosen, it can be tempered to meet the mission of the organization by the various constraints that will be added to the model.

For example, if a hospital wanted to maximize revenue, the equation would set revenue equal to the sum of the price of each product multiplied by the units of each product. If we only offered three products—DRG 1, DRG 2, and DRG 3—the revenue would equal the DRG 1 rate times the number of DRG 1 patients, plus the DRG 2 rate times the number of DRG 2 patients, plus the DRG 3 rate times the number of DRG 3 patients. Thus, the objective would be to maximize revenue, where revenue is defined as follows:

> Revenue = DRG 1 rate × # of DRG 1 patients
> + DRG 2 rate × # of DRG 2 patients
> + DRG 3 rate × # of DRG 3 patients

Increasing the number of patients in any of the three DRGs would increase the total revenue and would apparently make the hospital more profitable. However, we also want to know the average length of stay (LOS) of each type of patient, and the maximum number of patient days that can be attained given the hospital's number of beds. Suppose, for example, that DRG 1 patients have a LOS of five days, DRG 2 patients have a LOS of ten days, and DRG 3 patients have a LOS of seven days. Suppose further that the hospital has 100 beds available for 365 days per year, or a total of 36,500 patient days at full capacity. Then five times the number of DRG 1 patients plus ten times the number of DRG 2 patients plus seven times the number of DRG 3 patients cannot exceed 36,500. Thus, we have developed the equation for a constraint:

> 5 × # of DRG 1 patients
> + 10 × # of DRG 2 patients
> + 7 × # of DRG 3 patients ≤ 36,500

If the hospital board is firm in a feeling that DRG 3 is so vital to the community interest that it must be offered whether or not it earns a profit, then a constraint can be established that sets the output level of DRG 3 greater than a certain level, such as zero:

> # of DRG 3 patients > 0

Given the probable fixed costs that will be incurred once we decide to offer some positive amount of a particular service, merely setting the level greater than zero will probably cause the organization to be fairly aggressive in terms of offering the service, and thus satisfy the mission of the hospital. On the other hand, if we want to guarantee some level of service for that DRG, such as 1,000 patients or more per year, the constraint can simply be established at that level:

> # of DRG 3 patients ≥ 1,000

Additional constraints also will have to be established, many of which typically involve cost. If we are maximizing revenues, it is likely that the objective is constrained by the fact that we must at least break even. Therefore, a constraint would be that revenues must exceed the sum of all costs. Note that a successful linear program would have to include detailed information with respect to fixed and variable costs. The linear programming model would need that information so that it could mathematically take into account the impact of treating just one more patient of a given type.

Just as a baker cannot bake a cake without flour, eggs, and water, linear programming cannot do its job without a solid cost accounting information system. The goal of linear programming will be to assimilate a huge amount of information and to provide guidance as to what actions to take to achieve the hospital's objective, given the available information. In no way does linear programming substitute for a cost accounting information system that can provide both full and incremental cost information with respect to each of the various products being evaluated. Linear programming in conjunction with such information, however, can substantially improve outcomes.

The full set of equations that are required, in general form, are listed below. Computer programs can do all of the processing necessary to solve the equations. The main focus of the financial manager should be on developing a good understanding of the relationships that must be expressed as equations. To the extent that aid is needed in setting up these equations, operations management consultants and/or texts should be used.

The generic format of the equations is as follows:

$$\text{Maximize: } R = p_1 x_1 + p_2 x_2 + \ldots + p_n x_n$$

$$
\begin{aligned}
\text{Subject to:} \quad & a_{11}x_1 + a_{12}x_1 + \ldots + a_{1n}x_n \le b_1 \\
& a_{21}x_1 + a_{22}x_2 + \ldots + a_{2n}x_n \le b_2 \\
& a_{m1}x_1 + a_{m2}x_2 + \ldots + a_{mn}x_n \le b_m
\end{aligned}
$$

where p_1 = the price of the first product, x_1 = the output level for the first product, n = the number of variables or products, and m = the number of constraints, or in more general terms,

$$\text{Maximize: } R = \sum_{j=1}^{n} p_j x_j$$

$$\text{Subject to: } \sum_{j=1}^{n} a_{ij} x_j \leq b_i$$

Once the equations have been specified and the data input into a computer, a solution will be generated. The solution will tell the optimum mix of patients. This mix may at first seem totally unrealistic, for example, telling you to specialize in all of one type of patient. However, it should be realized that even if a solution seems unreasonable, it can point you in the proper direction.

Many software programs for linear programming provide a great deal more information in addition to simply recommending a certain level of output for each type of patient. For example, the opportunity cost is generally shown also; that is, if we treat one less patient of a given type, we are shown how much that will affect the stated objective. We are given information on which constraints are binding and which are not. Often, you can see what the impact would be of relaxing a constraint.

There is no doubt that linear programming is complex, even with the aid of a computer. Specifying the objective, determining the equations for the constraints, interpreting the results, and implementing the results all require a great deal of effort. Furthermore, a good cost accounting system is a prerequisite. However, if all these hurdles can be overcome, linear programming can significantly improve decision making for the health care organization.

Application 14-4 provides further discussion on the topic of linear programming.

NOTES

1. C.T. Horngren and G. Foster, *Cost Accounting: A Managerial Emphasis,* 7th ed. (Englewood Cliffs, N.J.: Prentice-Hall, 1991), 648.
2. S. Moriarity and C.P. Allen, *Cost Accounting,* 3rd ed. (New York: John Wiley & Sons, 1991), 183.
3. S. Moriarity and C.P. Allen, *Cost Accounting,* 428.

SUGGESTED READINGS

Horngren, C.T., and G. Foster. 1991. *Cost accounting: A managerial emphasis.* 7th ed. Englewood Cliffs, N.J.: Prentice-Hall.

Marsh, J.J. 1989. Management engineering. In *Handbook of health care accounting and finance.* 2nd ed. Ed. W.O. Cleverley, 665–684. Gaithersburg, Md.: Aspen Publishers, Inc.

Moriarity, S., and C.P. Allen. 1991. *Cost accounting.* 3rd ed. New York: John Wiley & Sons.

Neumann, B.R., and J. Kim. 1985. Use of prediction simula-

EXERCISES

QUESTIONS FOR DISCUSSION

1. Can managers take actions that affect events?
2. Does an expected value represent the most likely outcome?
3. True or false: A rational decision maker would always want to undertake a proposed project with a positive expected value.

Note: Solutions to the Exercises can be found in Appendix A.

4. In expected value calculations, how reliable are the probabilities used?
5. How much would you be willing to pay to get information that improves your subjective probability estimates?
6. If a simulation analysis is well designed, does it matter how many times the simulation is run?
7. What problem is created by the compounding of errors?
8. What are some limitations of simulation analysis?
9. What is network analysis?

10. What is network cost budgeting?
11. What is linear programming?
12. Is the potentially large number of equations that must be solved in linear programming a computational roadblock?

PROBLEMS

1. Determine the optimal staffing pattern, using expected value analysis, for the problem posed in the Expected Value section of this chapter, pages 523–524.

2. Calculate the expected value for the simulation results reported in Exhibit 14-1. Assume that actual results fall at the midpoint of each range. Use $150,000 as the largest average loss or gain.

3. Design a network cost budget. Show an initial plan, and then revise it to reduce the period of time needed. Explain how each time savings is achieved. Show the critical path. Show slack. Prepare a separate calculation that shows a cost-benefit analysis for reducing the time to accomplish the task.

Decision Analysis and Capital Budgeting: Application to the Delivery of Critical Care Services

Donald B. Chalfin, MD, is currently Director of the Surgical Intensive Care Unit at Winthrop-University Hospital, Mineola, New York and Assistant Professor of Medicine, SUNY at Stony Brook, Stony Brook, New York.

Rising health care costs, prospective payment and Diagnosis Related Groups (DRGs), along with the growing concern over the inability to deliver high quality care, have forced clinicians and administrators alike to examine the ways in which we allocate scarce resources and budget limited expenditures. In light of this heightened cost consciousness, a great deal of attention has been focused on the disproportionate share of resources used in intensive care units (ICUs). Specifically, ICUs account for only 5 percent of all hospital beds, yet they consume nearly 20 percent of all hospital budgets.[1,2] At the same time, many issues have been raised concerning the cost effectiveness and the efficacy of intensive care. In view of this and in view of the growing national proliferation of ICUs, hospitals are now exploring alternative solutions to the treatment of the critically ill.

Recently, hospitals have explored the use of intermediate care ("step-down") units in lieu of ICUs.[3] Step-down units (SDUs) can be viewed as hybrids between ICUs and the standard hospital beds or wards, both in terms of the scope of services provided and the severity of illness of the patients who are treated. SDUs usually exist in conjunction with ICUs and are reserved for patients who require less intervention than the standard ICU provides but who nonetheless need closer monitoring and more therapeutic support than is available on the general medical or surgical floor. SDUs (or similar variants) have become popular because of the perception that many patients who are admitted to ICUs can be treated just as effectively in less aggressive and thus less costly settings. Thus, the issue of whether or not a hospital should build a step-down unit represents a timely and important capital budgeting decision that is well suited to formal modeling techniques.

METHOD OF MODELING: DECISION ANALYSIS

Formal decision analysis and its systematic approach to the "quantification of uncertainty" provides a valuable framework to study the general issue of capital budgeting and the specific question of whether or not to build a step-down unit. Decision analysis originated from the fields of operations research, economics, and mathematics and was first applied to military and business problems.[4] Over the past decade, decision analysis techniques have been used with increasing frequency in clinical medicine and have also been applied to problems involving cost effectiveness and cost-benefit analysis.[5-8] Decision analysis is based upon the explicit stipulation of all possible events along with their associated probabilities of occurrence. A complete discussion of the methods and techniques of decision analysis is beyond the scope of this article and can be found elsewhere.[9,10] In general, however, decision analysis models provide both a quantitative and a qualitative assessment of the problems under study along with an accurate estimation of expected outcome and thus, an optimal and logical solution. The assessment is quantitative because it incorporates a precise "valuation" of the underlying utilities (e.g., dollars, years of survival) for each of the possible outcomes, given a specific course of action. Additionally, every valid and viable model yields significant qualitative insight with respect to each individual process which comprises the "structure" of every problem. In order to effectively formulate a model and determine the appropriate "heuristic" approach, each component of every situation, along with all underlying assumptions about every possible alternative must be rigorously reviewed prior to its inclusion into the model.

DECISION ANALYSIS: STRUCTURE AND STEPS

The basic component of any decision problem structured under formal decision analysis is the decision tree. The decision tree, essentially, is a method in which all alternatives for any problem under analysis are explicitly stipulated, along with each of the possible subsequent outcomes. From this, quantitative expected values for each of the problem options can be determined, thereby leading to an informed choice.

Several sequential steps are crucial in the construction of every decision analytical model:[9]

1. *Creation of the decision tree.* Includes the actual formulation of the decision problem, assignment of probabilities, and determina-

tion of appropriate outcome values or measures.
2. *Expected value calculations.* A numerical determination for each of the decision alternatives.
3. *Selection of the alternative with the highest expected value.*
4. *Sensitivity analysis.* Testing the conclusions and the "robustness" of the model in terms of how variations in the underlying assumptions (e.g., probability and utility assessments) would alter one's choice among the alternatives.

The following case study involving capital budgeting illustrates the basic science and steps of decision analysis and its direct application to budgeting problems. It focuses on whether or not a particular hospital should build a brand new step-down unit or expand its ICU. SML-TREE, a commercial software package specifically developed for medical decision analysis, will also be used to demonstrate one of several invaluable decision analysis computer programs.

CASE STUDY: CASHEN MEDICAL CENTER

For this case study, several facts and assumptions must be noted prior to construction of the formal model. It is also important to note that all of the figures and statistics represent hypothetical values, as the purpose of this example is to demonstrate the appropriate use of decision analysis in long-term capital budget preparations.

Cashen Medical Center (CMC), a 500-bed community hospital, has decided that a dire need exists to expand its critical care services, because its current 10-bed ICU is always completely full. It has determined that only two possibilities are feasible:

1. expansion of the current 10-bed ICU to 15 beds
2. construction of a new 10-bed SDU

Either of these two options is acceptable to the medical and nursing staffs.

The annual fixed maintenance costs for either alternative that CMC has projected (in present dollars) are as follows:

ICU expansion	$2,500,000
SDU construction	$4,000,000

Both of these projected costs include all expenditures for all equipment associated with a properly functioning unit (monitors, ventilators, etc.). For the purposes of simplicity, we will assume that the initial construction costs for both of these options are insignificant.

CMC receives all of its reimbursement according to DRGs for its particular state. Like most other hospitals in the nation, CMC has determined that it loses significant amounts of money on all patients who require special services such as ICUs or SDUs. Because of economies of scale, CMC has determined, based upon statewide data, that projected losses for the expanded ICU or the new SDU will be directly linked to each unit's occupancy rate over the course of a one-year period. The projected losses are as follows:

Expanded ICU. CMC will lose $1,500,000 if the average annual ICU occupancy falls below 80 percent of capacity, or below 12 beds. If occupancy falls below 60 percent, or below 9 beds, CMC will lose $2,500,000. Above 80 percent occupancy, losses will amount to $150,000.

Step-down unit. CMC projects that if SDU occupancy falls below 80 percent, or 8 beds, they will lose $500,000. If occupancy falls below 60 percent, or 6 beds, they will lose $1,250,000. Above 80 percent occupancy, losses will amount to a mere $75,000.

CMC has determined that each scenario has an associated probability of occurrence:

Occupancy rate	Expanded ICU	New step-down unit
80% or greater	0.30	0.15
Between 60% and 80%	0.20	0.45
Less than 60%	0.50	0.40

(Note that the sum of all probabilities for all events must equal 1).

To simplify matters, CMC expects that the losses and the resultant probabilities will remain constant from year to year.

The Decision Tree Structure for Cashen Medical Center

In the initial step of the problem, the two decision alternatives, along with all possible chance events, are carefully delineated in the basic tree structure with the appropriate decision tree notation (see Figure 14-1-1).

This figure carefully illustrates the choices that are available to CMC. The box in the figure is the conventional symbol for a *decision node,* which is the point in the tree where a choice among the possible alternatives must be made. Each alternative is represented by a line that is attached to the box.

As previously stated, both decision alternatives—the expansion of the ICU or the construction of the SDU—are subsequently associated with three unique and mutually exclusive possible outcomes which are controlled by chance, or probability. Thus each alternative is termed a *chance node,* which is depicted in decision trees as a circle. All possible chance events, in this case the three possible rates of occupancy, are connected to the chance nodes by lines (see Figure 14-1-2).

At this juncture in the creation of the decision tree, the appropriate probabilities are assigned to each of the chance events (see Figure 14-1-3). It is important to reiterate that the sum of all probabilities for all chance events must add up to 1.

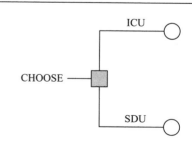

Figure 14-1-1 Basic Decision Tree

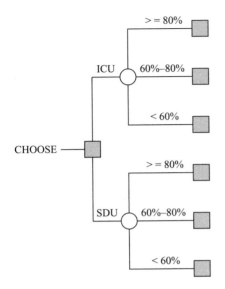

Figure 14-1-2 Decision Tree with All Chance Events

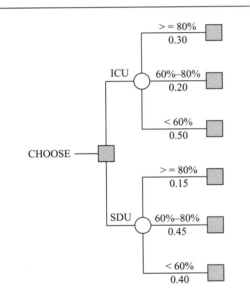

Figure 14-1-3 Decision Tree with All Probabilities

The final aspect in the construction of any decision tree is the assignment of valid "utility" measures to each of the possible outcomes. Very often, this is one of the most difficult steps in decision analysis because of multiple subjective influences that are often present. For this problem, the outcome measures will be the sum of all costs and expenditures for each of the projected rates of occupancy.

Table 14-4-1 shows the specific outcome values that were used. The costs consist of the sum of the annual maintenance costs ($2,500,000 for ICU expansion and $4,000,000 for SDU construction) plus the projected losses for each of the three occupancy rates.

Figure 14-1-4 thus consists of the final decision tree, complete with all of the probabilities and associated costs for each respective branch.

The Baseline Analysis and Solution

The next step in decision analysis is to determine the expected value for each possible choice. In this step, the tree is "averaged out" or "folded back"[9,10] by sequential multiplication of the outcome measures and their respective probabilities. The resultant values are then summed and then the alternative with the highest expected value is ultimately chosen.

In the case of CMC, since the medical and the nursing staffs find the ICU and the SDU option equally acceptable, the administration wants to opt for the cheapest choice: the one that will minimize expenditures and losses. The expected values for the total expected costs for each alternative are as follows:

1. ICU Expansion:
    Expected costs =
    $$(0.30 \times 2,650,000)$$
    $$+ (0.20 \times 4,000,000)$$
    $$+ (0.50 \times 5,000,000)$$
    $$= 795,000 + 800,000 + 2,500,000$$
    Expected costs = $4,095,000

Table 14-1-1 Outcome Values

Choice	Outcome (occupancy)	Costs ($)
ICU expansion	80% or greater	2,650,000
	60% to 80%	4,000,000
	less than 60%	5,000,000
SDU construction	80% or greater	4,075,000
	60% to 80%	4,250,000
	less than 60%	4,500,000

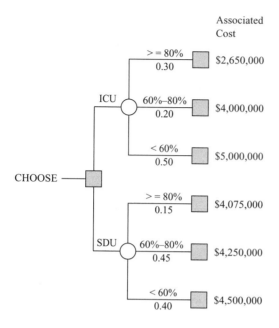

Associated
Cost

ICU
>= 80%   0.30 $2,650,000
60%–80%   0.20 $4,000,000
< 60%   0.50 $5,000,000

CHOOSE

SDU
>= 80%   0.15 $4,075,000
60%–80%   0.45 $4,250,000
< 60%   0.40 $4,500,000

Figure 14-1-4 Decision Tree for Cashen Medical Center

2. SDU Construction:
   Expected costs =
   $$(0.15 \times 4,075,000)$$
   $$+ (0.45 \times 4,250,000)$$
   $$+ (0.40 \times 4,500,000)$$
   $$= 611,250 + 1,912,500 + 1,800,000$$
   Expected costs = \$4,323,750

Given the indifference of the medical and nursing staff with regard to the alternatives, and seeing that the costs of a new step-down unit exceed the costs of an expanded ICU by \$228,750, the Cashen Medical Center administration should elect to expand the current ICU.

Sensitivity Analyses and Threshold Determinations

The final phase in any decision analysis is perhaps the most crucial, for it establishes the strength and "validity" of any particular model, especially in situations where the underlying probability and outcome measures are subject to considerable variation. Sensitivity ("what-if") analyses allow one to vary the underlying assumptions and to study how one's choices may

be altered. Threshold determinations show points, for any variable or set of variables, where no meaningful difference exists between any two choices. Many methods, such as multi-way analyses and Monte Carlo simulations, are available for sensitivity and threshold analysis, but these are beyond the scope of this article. For the CMC example, it is obvious that all of the probabilities along with all of the costs can be varied. Additionally, some of the underlying assumptions, such as the stipulation concerning the negligible construction costs for both units, further lend themselves to rigorous sensitivity analysis. To illustrate the basic concepts and their application to capital budgeting, sensitivity analyses and threshold analyses will be performed on two variables: (1) the annual maintenance costs of the ICU and (2) the annual maintenance costs of the SDU.

One-Way Sensitivity and Threshold Analysis

Often enough, analysts are interested in how a change in just one variable affects a final decision, both in terms of the magnitude of change and the ultimate choice. One-way sensitivity analyses permit an analyst to test conclusions by calculating the expected value over a wide range for the variable under question.

ICU Annual Maintenance Costs

The baseline value that the CMC administrators assigned to the expanded ICU was \$2,500,000. However, some of the administrators questioned this value because it relied upon several conditional assumptions. As a result, CMC believes that the decision should be tested over a wide range of costs for the expanded ICU: for \$0 to \$10,000,000. Figure 14-1-5 displays this analysis over this range.

As the figure shows, the threshold for the value of the annual ICU maintenance costs is \$2,728,750. At this value, with all other variables being held constant, there is no difference between expanding the ICU or building a new

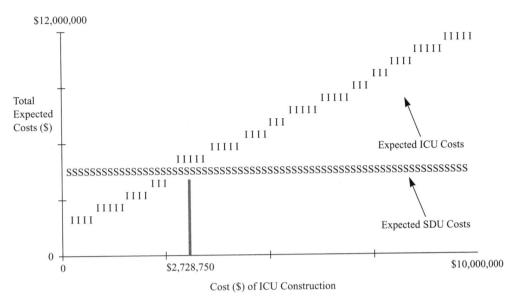

Figure 14-1-5 Sensitivity Analysis on the Costs of ICU Expansion

SDU (assuming that the decision makers exhibit risk averse behavior). Above this value, the costs for ICU expansion will exceed the costs for a new SDU, hence CMC should proceed with plans to construct a new SDU. Below this value for ICU maintenance costs, it is cheaper to expand the ICU and thus CMC should shelve the SDU plans.

SDU Annual Maintenance Costs

In the second one-way analysis, SDU maintenance costs will also be varied from $0 to $10,000,000, as shown in Figure 14-1-6.

In this analysis, with ICU maintenance costs and also other variables held constant, the threshold for SDU maintenance costs is $3,771,250. Above this value, CMC should expand the ICU because it represents the less expensive option. Below this, CMC should elect to build a new SDU because of the lower total expenditures.

Two-Way Sensitivity Analyses

One-way analyses are helpful in analyzing isolated changes. However, they often do not depict realistic situations, for most problems and decisions involve multiple concurrent variations. Hence multiway analyses serve the purposes of determining the change in decisions when several underlying variables are simultaneously altered. For this case study, a simplified two-way analysis will be performed, as changes in both ICU and SDU costs will be studied. Table 14-1-2 and Figure 14-1-7 show the results of this analysis. Note, in Table 14-1-2, that for each of the last five alternatives the SDU cost exceeds the ICU cost threshold by $1,271,250.

Two-way sensitivity analyses implicitly involve threshold determinations, for they show, given the value of a certain variable, what the value of another variable would be at the thresh-

Table 14-1-2 ICU Cost Threshold

SDU Costs ($)	Threshold of ICU Costs ($)
0	Not found
2,000,000	728,750
4,000,000	2,728,750
6,000,000	4,728,750
8,000,000	6,728,750
10,000,000	8,728,750

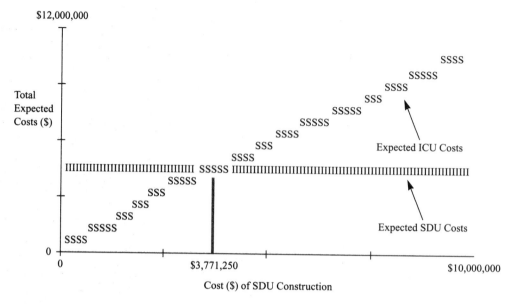

Figure 14-1-6 Sensitivity Analysis on SDU Maintenance Costs

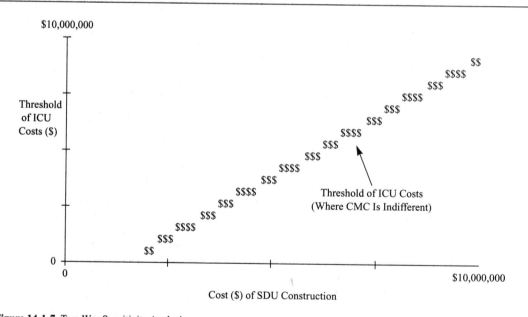

Figure 14-1-7 Two-Way Sensitivity Analysis

old, or the point of indifference between two decision alternatives. In this case study, CMC should proceed with the SDU construction if the SDU costs are less than the ICU costs plus $1,271,250. Similarly, they should elect to expand the ICU if ICU costs fall below SDU costs by the same amount.

CONCLUSIONS

The purpose of this paper was to demonstrate how formal, quantitative decision analysis can be used in problems of capital budgeting and how commercial decision analysis software, which generated all of the graphs and studies, can be used for these purposes. For the case study that was presented, the baseline analysis showed that both the expanded ICU and the new SDU would lose money. Yet given the underlying assumptions and constraints, budgetary losses would be minimized with the expansion of the current ICU from 10 to 15 beds. It must be reiterated, however, that this example was greatly simplified in order to illustrate the usefulness of decision analysis for important and timely health care problems. Specifically, it did not incorporate future value or inflation, and assumed that initial construction costs for both of the projects were equal and negligible. Dollar losses for each of the occupancy rates were simplified into only three strata. Furthermore, the assumption that the medical and the nursing staffs would be indifferent with regard to the choice between the alternatives is perhaps unrealistic.

Accurate decision analysis involves a significant investment of time and human resources. Painstaking attention must be given to the collection of data in the determination of the baseline probabilities for all chance occurrences and appropriate outcome measures must be rigorously sought. More generally, decision analysis models must closely represent the way in which people solve problems and search for solutions if its methods and conclusions are to become invaluable aids in the capital budgeting and other decision making processes.

NOTES

1. C. Bekes et al., Reimbursement for intensive care services under diagnosis-related groups. *Crit Care Med* 1988; 16:478.

2. M.R. Chassin, Costs and outcomes of medical intensive care. *Med Care* 1982; 20:165.

3. R.C. Bone and R.A. Balk, Noninvasive respiratory care unit: A cost effective solution for the future. *Chest* 1988; 93–390.

4. J.P. Kassirer, The principles of clinical decision making: An introduction to decision analysis. *Yale J Biol Med* 1976; 49:149.

5. D.F. Ransohoff et al., Prophylactic cholecystectomy or expectant management for silent gallstones. *Ann Int Med* 1983; 99:199.

6. J.P. Hollenberg et al., Cost-effectiveness of splenectomy versus intravenous gamma globulin in treatment of chronic immune thrombocytopenic purpura in childhood. *J Pediatr* 1988; 112:530.

7. S.D. Roberts et al., Cost-effective care of end-stage renal disease: A billion dollar question. *Ann Int Med* 1980; 92:243.

8. J. Tsevat et al., Cost-effectiveness of antibiotic prophylaxis for dental procedures in patients with artificial joints. *AJPH* 1989; 79:739.

9. H.C. Sox et al., Medical decision making. Boston: Butterworths, 1988.

10. M.C. Weinstein et al., Clinical decision analysis. Philadelphia: WB Saunders, 1989.

Application 14-2

Decision Analysis for the Hospital-HMO Cost Accounting System

*Kyle L. Grazier, DrPH, is currently Associate Professor
and Director of the Sloan Program at Cornell
University, Ithaca, New York.*

As has been discussed in the preceding two articles in this series, the cost accounting system is a decision-support system.* The decisions surrounding the hospital-HMO relationship often have profit/loss dimensions and as such warrant some investment in the ability to define, identify, and analyze costs. In the first article in this series, the fixed/variable cost decision illustrated the need for and use of a well-designed cost-accounting system. In the second article, the issue of the basis for and method of transfer pricing—the setting of prices for services exchanged within an organization—was examined from a cost accounting perspective.

The management decisions related to these two issues are often complicated by environmental uncertainties. This article presents decision-analysis methods of varying complexity which make that uncertainty explicit, quantify it where possible, and then utilize it to improve cost accountants' and managers' decisions.

Source: Reprinted from Kyle L. Grazier, "Decision Analysis for the Hospital-HMO Cost Accounting System," *Hospital Cost Accounting Advisor,* Vol. 1, No. 12, May 1986, pp. 1, 6–8. Copyright 1986, Aspen Publishers, Inc.

*Kyle Grazier, "Cost Accounting for Hospital-Owned HMOs," *Hospital Cost Accounting Advisor,* Vol. 1, No. 10, pp. 1–4; Kyle Grazier, "Transfer Pricing in the Hospital-HMO Corporation," *Hospital Cost Accounting Advisor,* Vol. 1, No. 1, pp. 1, 6–8.

DECISIONS UNDER UNCERTAINTY

Seldom is there certainty in management decisions. Managers attempt to cope with this inevitable uncertainty in various ways. Some managers surround themselves with support staff and computer systems, to improve their access to information about their environment, and to increase its accuracy. Others rely on heuristics or rules of thumb gleaned from their experience to provide them with the appropriate decision. Others attempt to systematically analyze and evaluate their own subjective estimates of the likelihood of certain events occurring, given several assumed scenarios.

The effectiveness and efficiency of these managers depend on their ability to incorporate the unknown into predictions of results. The methods used to accomplish this task range in sophistication from the simple rule of thumb to the complex computer-based mathematical simulation. The choice of techniques is dependent upon the financial and other resources of the user, the importance of the decision, and the impact of an error in that decision.

DECISION MODELS

Most decisions can be dissected along many dimensions: into quantifiable and nonquantifiable components; into alternatives, events, probabilities of events occurring, outcomes, and the utility of those outcomes; into risk/reward or payoff matrices. The extent of dissection and the choice of dimensions describe the decision-analysis technique.

Decisions involving prediction of behavior, especially of cost behavior, can be as simple as quantifying those parameters for which costs can be assigned and discarding those for which quantification is not feasible. Assumptions can then be made as to the linear nature of past costs, and the decision maker can predict that future costs will follow the same pattern as past costs.

A more complex method using, once again, prediction of costs as our example, permits additional refinement to the analysis. In brief, the steps include:

1. defining the objective of the decision maker
2. defining the alternative actions
3. defining those events that are subject to uncertainty
4. assigning probabilities to those events
5. calculating the expected value of each particular course of action
6. choosing the alternative that best meets the original objective.

An example will illustrate this process.

The first step in this process is to make explicit the decision maker's objective: in this case, to minimize the total future costs to the organization of additional HMO inpatients.

In our example, organizational costs of HMO patients include some fixed and some variable costs, some of which are offset by revenues from HMO premiums charged to the patients. We will assume for this example that the marginal costs or net costs to the system vary according to the number of employers to whom the hospital's HMO is marketed. Therefore, if the HMO is marketed to one employer, the net costs are $50 per patient day; if to five employers, the net costs are $30 per patient day.

The management actions under consideration are to market to one employer the first year (A1) and to market to five employers the first

year (A2). The relevant events that might occur and that are subject to uncertainty relate to inpatient demand by the HMO patients. The manager's analysts have determined (for simplicity's sake) that there are only two possible levels of inpatient demand by the HMO enrollees: 1,000 patient days (E1) and 5,000 patient days (E2). The manager assigns probabilities to the occurrence of these two events: $P = .6$ (for E1) and $P = .4$ (for E2).

As illustrated in the payoff table, there are four potential outcomes to this decision; these are represented by the cells of the table. In this case, the payoff table indicates possible costs. The amounts within the cells indicate the expected payoff in choosing each alternative, given the assigned probabilities for demand. They are calculated as follows:

probability × value of the event × net unit
cost of the alternative = payoff

Payoff Table

Alternatives	Events	
	E1 $P = .6$	E2 $P = .4$
A1—one employer ($50/day)	$30,000	$100,000
A2—five employers ($30/day)	$18,000	$ 60,000

For example, cell one's value is calculated as $50/patient day × 1,000 patient days × .6 = $30,000. These cell values are known as expected monetary values, but payoffs can be represented in nonmonetary, or "utility" terms as well.

On the basis of the payoffs, the manager could then decide which alternative best meets her objective for minimizing costs. Given the occurrence of either demand scenario, it appears that alternative two, marketing to five employer groups, meets the objective function of the decision maker, since it would have a lower cost no matter whether E1 or E2 occurs.

SENSITIVITY ANALYSIS

Sensitivity analysis is a form of decision analysis which lies somewhere between the two previous examples in its complexity. It answers the question "what if?" by allowing variations in the inputs to the analysis so that the effects of these variations can be seen. Sensitivity analysis can be viewed as an independent technique or as an adjunct to the above methods of analysis. It will be described here using the issue raised in the first article in this series: that of identification of the contribution of the HMO's patient costs to total costs to the organization.

In that article, regression analysis was cited as one means to assist the cost accountant-manager in this analysis. Sensitivity analysis permits the user to use those same regressions to answer different questions, questions that directly address the issue of uncertainty of the data input to the analysis. As noted in that article and in earlier issues of *Hospital Cost Accounting Advisor,* analysis is only as good as the data on which it is based. The ability to systematically vary the data items within a range believed by the manager to be likely, permits a much more sophisticated decision. Let us illustrate, using a simple regression rather than a multiple regression, so that a two-dimensional graph can be used.

Recall that the equation for the simple regression was as follows: a + bX = Y, where a = fixed costs per unit, b = variable costs per unit, X = volume of units, and Y = total costs.

Since cost accounting systems are decision-support systems, the manager can use these regressions to evaluate outcomes of her decision through varying inputs, such as the X variable. This manipulation can allow answers to "what if" questions related to changes in volume. Through the simple assignment of different values to the X variable, the manager can determine if there is a volume level which, if achieved, signals a reevaluation of the assigned fixed costs.

Figure 14-2-1 shows a changing relationship between fixed costs and variable costs as volume increases. At point A, variable costs start to become a larger proportion of total costs. As this relationship continues, it may behoove the manager to consider changing the fixed costs.

For instance, labor costs may be the primary source of the variable costs. If labor costs get

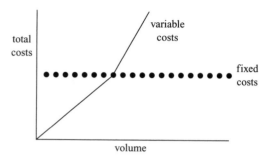

Figure 14-2-1 Relationship of Total, Variable, and Fixed Costs and Volume

too high, the manager may decide to buy some labor-saving equipment, thus increasing her fixed costs, and changing the proportion of total costs accounted for by the variable costs.

Sensitivity analysis permits analysis at this level and can improve the decision, often quite simply.

In the case of transfer pricing, analysis of the implications of changing the pricing structure or the basis for the pricing could better prepare a manager for the outcomes of her decision. For example, sensitivity analysis can allow the manager to test out the effects of different pricing levels. If market prices change, what would be the total costs to the department? Such "what if" analysis is often simple, yet effective.

When any analysis is chosen for a decision, cost-benefit assessments must be made. For most decisions, sensitivity analysis is systematic, thorough, and inexpensive. It can also help determine those instances in which more expensive analysis may be warranted.

For instance, using the transfer price example once again, sensitivity analysis on the changing market prices and their effect on departmental costs may signal to the manager a level of prices in the market, below which the department might not be able to cover its costs.

For instance, the hospital laboratory now charges the hospital's HMO $10 for a particular laboratory service. The market price for that test is also $10. The rumor is that the outside labs, the market, are about to lower their charges to $8 per service. Upon doing a sensitivity analysis on the effect of different prices on laboratory profits, the manager discovers that the market price of $8 would severely hinder the laboratory's ability to turn a profit. A decision would have to be made as to whether to offer the service below costs to the HMO, to no longer offer the test to the HMO at any price, or to attempt to negotiate a higher-than-market price from the HMO. Because this decision is a particularly crucial one for the laboratory, the manager might decide to hire a consultant or assign a staff person to study all the ramifications of the issue in more depth—a much more costly alternative. In this case, initial inexpensive sensitivity analysis has helped determine the need for more complex and/or costly analysis.

Sensitivity analysis and decision analysis are merely additional tools for the manager, just as the entire cost accounting system exists to aid in the operations and planning of an organization. Managers interested in learning more about decision analysis and its many techniques can refer to the bibliography below.

BIBLIOGRAPHY

Horngren, C.T. *Cost Accounting: A Managerial Emphasis,* 5th ed. Englewood Cliffs, N.J.: Prentice-Hall, 1982.

Raiffa, H. *Decision Analysis. Introductory Lectures on Choices under Uncertainty.* Reading, Mass.: Addison-Wesley, 1968.

Warner, D.M., et al. *Decision Making and Control for Health Administration.* 2nd ed. Ann Arbor, Mich.: Health Administration Press, 1984.

A Review of
"Using PERT in the Budgeting Process"

Steven A. Finkler, PhD, CPA

Many hospital managers have experienced a situation in which they have commenced a year without having already received an approved budget for that year. The budgeting process is becoming ever more complex and time-consuming. Delays in meeting budget preparation and approval deadlines are becoming more common. While most efforts have gone into developing a budget process that will yield the needed data for revenue and spending decisions, somewhat less time has gone into making sure that the process itself is efficiently managed. Metzger has focused in on this problem by considering the use of Program Evaluation and Review Technique (PERT) for budgeting.

Many readers may be familiar with PERT as a technique widely used for planning major projects. If the hospital adds a new wing, the construction team will probably use a PERT chart to help determine what part of the job must be done when. The key is to understand which task absolutely must be done before other tasks can commence (roadblocks or bottle-

necks) and to understand how long various parts of the job will take. In planning out the process, the most efficient (often the shortest) path can be determined.

The application of this technique to budgeting, however, is rather innovative. Yet, as the author points out, budgeting is a complex and time-consuming process. It does require a careful plan and a detailed schedule. The more complicated it becomes, the more value can be obtained by using a method that focuses on the time to complete a set of tasks.

Metzger explains that PERT requires three things to be useful. First there must be an ability to separate the activities involved. Each activity would represent a part of the overall project. In a hospital we can certainly envision the preparation of the budgets from each department as being separate activities. Combining the various budgets is an activity. The various layers of approval, and/or revision also represent activities.

Next PERT requires that we be able to order the activities. Which must come before the others? Some activities are simultaneous, while other activities cannot start until others are finished. That is certainly the case in hospital budgeting.

Finally, PERT requires that there be an estimate of how long each activity will take. In fact, PERT often uses three estimates for each activi-

Source: Reprinted from Steven A. Finkler, Review of "Using PERT in the Budgeting Process," by Lawrence M. Metzger, in *Journal of Cost Management for the Manufacturing Industry,* Vol. 3, No. 4, Winter 1990, pp. 20–27, reviewed in *Hospital Cost Management and Accounting,* Vol. 2, No. 10, January 1991, pp. 4–5. Copyright 1991, Aspen Publishers, Inc.

ty: a pessimistic estimate, an optimistic estimate, and a most likely estimate, which is derived by combining the first two. One can imagine that many hospitals probably use an optimistic estimate throughout the process. Being forced by a methodology to consider three different estimates may by itself improve the reliability of any budget schedule generated.

The article provides a detailed example applying PERT to a budget process. Information is provided on how to identify activities. Also, an explanation is given about optimal approaches for the determination of pessimistic and optimistic time estimates.

PERT is operationalized by use of a diagram with a starting point and branches. Metzger leads the reader through the construction of a PERT diagram for his budgeting example. This includes a discussion of some fairly technical dos and don'ts to ensure that the diagram is readable as well as consistent. For example, it wouldn't make much sense to say that projected workload levels are needed to calculate staffing, and staffing is needed to calculate labor cost, and labor cost is needed to estimate revenues, and revenues are needed to estimate workload. This is circular, and cannot be calculated, since workload is needed at the beginning, but is not determined until the end. Proper construction of the PERT diagram will ensure that no such illogical requirements are built into the budget process.

One of the major benefits of PERT analysis is that it will identify the "critical path." This is defined as "the series of activities in the network that will take the longest time." It is this path that determines the shortest total time for the entire process. It also identifies the areas that are most critical to keeping the entire budget process on time. Delays in other areas will not be critical, while a delay along the critical path will inevitably delay the entire process.

By the same token, once the critical path is known, attention can be focused on shortening the time for the items along that path. There may be 500 activities in the budget process, but perhaps only 25 of them lie along the critical path. With the focus on that path, the entire process becomes more efficient.

Throughout the entire diagram, we also indicate the earliest time that any element can begin, and the latest time that it can safely be completed without jeopardizing the entire process. This allows for quite a bit of efficient monitoring and control of the process. Metzger notes that PERT budgeting also "helps a manager think through the budgeting system systematically . . . provides a compact summary of the project in a form suitable for review by the various departments . . . [and s]ince the PERT network is helpful in identifying related tasks and their time/sequence relationships, responsibilities can be better assigned and resources used to better advantage."

We find this innovative approach to hold great potential merit. The budget process in hospitals is becoming unwieldy. There are too many details to easily be managed. This tool can help to put hospital management back in control of the process.

Application 14-4

Decision Making under Uncertainty: A Linear Programming Approach

*Jennifer L. Rosenberg, MPA, MBA, is currently
Territory Manager for Lederle Consumer,
Wayne, New Jersey.*

The management process is in essence a process of decision making. Rarely is a decision made with an outcome already known. Under certain conditions predictions can be made, but these predictions are assumed to be imperfect. More often decisions are made in uncertain times. Horngren defines uncertainty as the "possibility that an actual amount will deviate from an expected amount" (p. 615). Uncertainty means that an organization will be faced with multiple and often conflicting objectives, some conflicting with the objectives of the organization itself.

A decision model is a formal method used by organizations for measuring the effects of alternative actions that will be made in uncertain conditions. A cost-volume-profit model is the most obvious example of a decision model used to make decisions for planning and control as it relates to the interrelationships of factors affecting profits, particularly cost behavior at various levels of volume.

Generally, decision models contain each of the following:

Source: Reprinted from Jennifer L. Rosenberg, "Decision Making under Uncertainty: A Linear Programming Approach," *Hospital Cost Management and Accounting,* Vol. 1, No. 3, June 1989, pp. 1–5. Copyright 1989, Aspen Publishers, Inc.

- objective function (also called choice criterion)—some quantity that the decision maker would like to either maximize or minimize
- a set of actions to be considered
- a set of all possible relevant events that can affect the outcomes (also known as states or states of nature)
- a set of possible outcomes that measure the predicted consequences of the various possible combinations of actions and events

Decision models usually fall under the larger category of constrained optimization models. Because these models do not include information that cannot be quantified, these models do not provide the absolute solution to a problem. Rather, it is an efficient way of producing the optimal answer to a proposed problem.

A linear programming (LP) decision model is concerned with how to best allocate scarce resources to attain a chosen objective. LP models are designed to provide a solution to problems where the linear assumptions underlying the model are reasonable approximations. All linear programming models have two common features: (1) the decision to be made is subject to constraints; and (2) there is some quantity to be maximized or minimized. There are generally three steps in solving an LP problem:

1. Determine the objective function.
2. Determine the basic relationships.
3. Compute the optimal solution.

Two aspects of using LP are especially difficult to define. First, it is difficult to express the objective in a format suitable to be solved by an LP approach. Second, reliable estimates of the information inputs used in the LP model are not always easily obtained.

Linear programming has been used in a wide range of business problems. Transportation, resource allocation, personnel scheduling, and health planning are all settings in which LP has been used. Obviously, linear programming is not appropriate for all types of business problems. Hill describes four criteria for the use of linear programming:

1. The problem must be sufficiently complex that a simpler or even intuitive approach is unacceptable.
2. The problem's solution must be rewarding or practical enough that the added benefits of a linear programming analysis are worth the costs of the extra effort required.
3. It must be possible to describe the problem in quantitative terms.
4. All the mathematical relationships must be linear.

When there are only two or three variables in the objective function and a minimal number of constraints, methods that do not require the aid of computerization may be used. These methods include the spreadsheet method, the graphical solution method, and the trial-and-error method. Real situations are generally more complex and more than three variables are involved. In such cases, the "simplex method" must be used.

A spreadsheet method is useful when the user is interested in manipulating data in the model. In situations in which the user needs to find the optimal solution, software such as VINO or "What's Best!" must be utilized. (Eppen, 1987)

In the *spreadsheet method,* formulas are developed that represent the objective function and the constraint functions. Parameters are computed from the formulas and the decision

variables that are entered into cells in the spreadsheet. If the user is interested in a "what if" analysis, the user will enter predetermined variables into a specified cell and the formulas will be replaced with specific values. The result will be the optimal solution for the value entered. (See Example 1.)

The *graphical solution method* provides an easy way of solving linear programming problems with two decision variables. Using an xy graph, the optimal solution must lie on one of the corners of the "area of feasible solution," which is an area contained within the bounds created by the intersection of numerous lines representing the decision constraints. (See Example 2.)

The *trial-and-error solution method* uses coordinates of the corners of the area of feasible solutions to locate the optimal solution. (See Example 2.)

The *simplex method* utilizes standard computer software packages based on a systematic algebraic way of examining the "corners" of an LP constraint. The optimal solution is reached by solving a series of linear equations. Each corner represents a possible solution and can be represented in tabular form, known as the simplex tableau. By performing iterations on each corner or tableau, the optimal solution is reached when no further improvement can be made on a previous iteration.

EXAMPLE 1: SPREADSHEET METHOD—ASSIGNMENT OF NURSES TO DEPARTMENTS WITH VARIABLE DEMAND

The Director of Nursing at Busy Hospital is trying to determine how to staff nurses in Pediatrics. There are 6 shifts per day as follows:

Shift	Starting Time	Ending Time
1	Midnight	8 AM
2	4 AM	Noon
3	8 AM	4 PM
4	Noon	8 PM
5	4 PM	Midnight
6	8PM	4AM

The supervisor knows the minimum number of nurses required for each time slot:

Time	Minimum number of nurses required
Midnight–4 AM	8
4 AM– 8 AM	12
8 AM–Noon	20
Noon–4 PM	20
4 PM–8 PM	17
8 PM–Midnight	8

The Director of Nursing, faced with the nursing shortage, would like to minimize the total number of nurses required for this department.

The objective function would then be

$$\text{Min. } N1 + N2 + N3 + N4 + N5 + N6$$

where $N1$ = number of nurses working shift 1
         $N2$ = number of nurses working shift 2
         .
         .
         .
         $N6$ = number of nurses working shift 6 (See Table 14-4-1.)

The decision constraints would then be:

$$N1 + N6 < 8$$
$$N1 + N2 < 12$$
$$N2 + N3 < 20$$
$$N3 + N4 < 20$$
$$N4 + N5 < 17$$
$$N5 + N6 < 8$$

Nursing Staffing Symbolic Spreadsheet

I	II	III #	IV #	V #	VI
Shift	Start Time	Nurses Start	Nurses Work	Nurses Required	Extra Nurses
1	12 AM		0	8	
2	4 AM		0	12	
3	8 AM		0	20	
4	12 PM		0	20	
5	4 PM		0	17	
6	8 PM		0	8	

Column VI will contain the # of nurses working less the number of nurses required to give a slack amount.

Table 14-4-1 Objective Function

Shift	Mid– 4 AM	4 AM– 8 AM	8 AM– Noon	Noon– 4 PM	4 PM– 8 PM	8 PM– Mid
1	N1	N1				
2		N2	N2			
3			N3	N3		
4				N4	N4	
5					N5	N5
6	N6					N6

Column III will contain optimized decision values.

Two versions of the optimized spreadsheet are shown below:

Nursing Staffing Value Symbolic Spreadsheet

I	II	III #	IV #	V #	VI
Shift	Start Time	Nurses Start	Nurses Work	Nurses Required	Extra Nurses
1	12 AM	8	8	8	0
2	4 AM	4	12	12	0
3	8 AM	16	20	20	0
4	12 PM	9	25	20	5
5	4 PM	8	17	17	0
6	8 PM	0	8	8	0

TOTAL NURSES = 45

Nursing Staffing Value Symbolic Spreadsheet

I	II	III #	IV #	V #	VI
Shift	Start Time	Nurses Start	Nurses Work	Nurses Required	Extra Nurses
1	12 AM	5	8	8	0
2	4 AM	12	17	12	5
3	8 AM	8	20	20	0
4	12 PM	12	20	20	0
5	4 PM	5	17	17	0
6	8 PM	3	8	8	0

TOTAL NURSES = 45

The manager can now decide based on non-quantitative information in what shift to place the 5 slack nurses.

A "what if" analysis would be possible in this situation. For example, the nursing requirements might be changed due to the addition of extra beds. In this case the same spreadsheet could be used with column V altered accordingly.

EXAMPLE 2: GRAPHIC SOLUTION METHOD—PRODUCT MIX ASSESSMENT, OUTPATIENT LABORATORY

The outpatient laboratory at Busy Hospital performs two major tests—hematology and chemistry. The laboratory administrator is trying to decide which service to promote in order to achieve the maximum profits. Profits have been determined to be $5 for hematology tests and $4 on clinical chemistry tests.

The laboratory functions in the following way: Samples are collected in department 1 and processed in department 2. Labor requirements for the tests are as follows:

	Hematology	Chemistry
Department 1	1	1
Department 2	3	2

The supervisors of the two departments have estimated the following number of hours will be available during the next months:

Department 1	1000 hours
Department 2	2400 hours

The outpatient laboratory has taken advantage of a reagent contract available from the distributor of their hematology instruments. This places a limit on the amount of this reagent that can be purchased per month and therefore a limit on the number of tests that can be performed. It has been estimated that these constraints will limit potential services to 600 hematology tests per month.

The Linear Programming Model

Objective: Maximize Profits
In mathematical terms:

$$\text{Maximize } 5A + 4B$$

where   A = number of hematology tests
and   B = number of clinical chemistry tests

so that

$$A + B < 1000 \text{ (labor constraint, Department 1)}$$
$$3A + 2B < 2400 \text{ (labor constraint, Department 2)}$$
$$A < 600 \text{ (reagent constraint)}$$

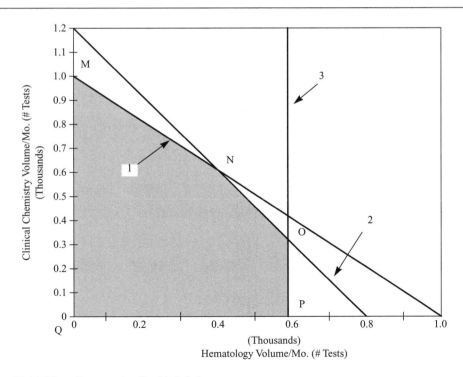

Figure 14-4-1 Linear Programming Graphic Solution

In the graph in Figure 14-4-1, Line 1 represents the Department 1 constraint, Line 2 the Department 2 constraint, and Line 3 the reagent constraint. The shaded area represents the area of "feasible solutions" which contains all the possible combinations of A and B that satisfy the constraints.

In the graphic solution, the optimal solution must lie on one of the corners of the "area of feasible solutions." In general, the optimal solution will be the point that lies on the border of the "area of feasible solutions" that is farthest from the origin, in this case (600, 400).

Therefore, in order to maximize profits the laboratory administrator should opt to perform 600 clinical chemistry tests and 400 hematology tests in the next month.

The above example, although extremely simplistic in nature, demonstrates the value of linear programming. Had the laboratory administrator chosen to maximize profits on the basis of profit per test alone, the optimal solution would never have been reached since the optimal solution designates performing a greater volume of clinical chemistry tests (the choice with the lower contribution margin).

TRIAL AND ERROR METHOD

1. Using the graph, choose all corner points.
2. Determine which point gives the highest total profit.

Point M (0, 1000):   Total Profit = $5(0) + $4(1000) = $4000
Point N (400, 600): Total Profit = $5(400) + $4(600) = $4400
Point O (600, 300): Total Profit = $5(600) + $4(300) = $4200
Point P (600, 0):   Total Profit = $5(600) + $4(0) = $3000
Point Q (0, 0):   Total Profit = $5(0) + $4(0) = 0

This reaffirms the conclusion that the optimal solution is 400 hematology tests and 600 clinical chemistry tests (Point N).

Obviously, linear programming models have limitations. As discussed above, all relationships involved in the problem must be linear. Furthermore, all variables and constraints must be described with absolute certainty. Finally, these models do not take into account variables that cannot be quantified. Therefore, users must take the "optimal" solution derived from linear programming as the best mathematical solution and not necessarily the best overall solution. Formal models such as LP are important, however, because they provide users with a means of eliminating inconsistencies.

Understanding how linear programming models work is extremely important for accountants and other management professionals. Because data from accounting is a vital input into linear programming, poor accounting data will affect the objective function or the area of feasible solutions, resulting in faulty decision making.

BIBLIOGRAPHY

Eppen, G.D., et al., *Introductory Management Science,* 2nd Edition. Englewood Cliffs: Prentice-Hall, Inc., 1987.

Hill, P.H., et al., *Making Decisions: A Multidisciplinary Introduction.* Reading: Addison-Wesley Publishing Company, Inc., 1979.

Horngren, C.T., and G. Foster, *Cost Accounting: A Managerial Emphasis,* 6th Edition. Englewood Cliffs: Prentice-Hall, Inc., 1987.

Turban, E., and N.P. Loomba, eds., *Cases and Readings in Management Science.* Plano: Business Publications, Inc., 1982.

15

Information Systems for Costing

Goals of This Chapter

1. Discuss various considerations in designing computerized costing systems.
2. Consider the various pros and cons of individual managers developing their own computer applications.
3. Provide applications readings that discuss the issue of the costs of computerized systems, and more broadly, the development of cost accounting software.

Key Terms Used in This Chapter

Cost accounting system; management information system.

Note: Key terms appear in italics when first used in the chapter. All key terms are defined in the Glossary.

INTRODUCTION

The last decade has seen a growing rate of development, adoption, and implementation of computerized *cost accounting systems.* The impact of prospective payment and managed care has led to an ever-increasing focus on the profitability of individual Diagnosis Related Groups (DRGs) or patient types, and ultimately a "product-line" perspective. This product-line perspective has in turn caused managers to need more timely and accurate information about the resources consumed by each product line.

CONSIDERATIONS IN DESIGNING COSTING SYSTEMS

In the haste to develop new systems, the goals of the cost accounting system are often overlooked. One must first decide what questions exist, and then design or acquire a system that will provide answers to those questions. The type of automated cost accounting system developed depends substantially on the type of information that management feels it needs, the reports that are to be generated on a regular basis, the use for such reports, and the type of information needed on an irregular basis. Exhibit 15-1 summarizes key questions that should be asked and answered before an information system is designed and implemented.

The issues related to the type of information, the reports, and the use of information are critical issues that must be addressed by the organization and its managers. It does not matter whether the system is being designed internally

---

Exhibit 15-1 Questions for Designing Information Systems

1. What information is needed?
   - For regular reports
   - For special reports
2. When is information needed?
3. How much detail is needed?
4. How should information be presented?
5. Have all managers been surveyed for their input?

---

from scratch, or being purchased off the shelf, or being purchased from an organization that will tailor the system specifically for the organization. One of the biggest risks in adopting a computerized cost accounting system is that the organization's managers will assume that outside experts can adequately determine the organization's needs.

Few organizations have the software development skills and capabilities to design their own cost accounting system. However, it is rare to find an outside contractor that is able to acquire the understanding of the organization in enough depth to design a system adequately without significant direction by the organization's management. If management hopes that the system will be satisfactory once installed, it must accept the burden of determining what its needs really are before the system is designed and put in place.

Cost accounting systems generate information for a variety of purposes. First, we are interested in being able to make appropriate reports for external users—that is, knowing what something costs simply so we can convey that information to those outside the organization. These reports are made to third-party payers, the Internal Revenue Service, the American Hospital Association, and so forth.

However, we also want information to ensure that the health care organization is functioning in a controlled manner. We must carefully determine the information needs we have to ascertain whether we are treating patients in a cost-effective manner. These needs are changing dramatically. No longer do we need simply to control the cost per x-ray; we must also control the number of x-rays for a patient of a given type. Health care organizations calculate variances based not only along the lines of price, efficiency, and volume, but also along the lines of case-mix or patient acuity or severity. Cost information is also needed for discrete changes: new services, new projects, new ventures, joint ventures, discontinuation of services, and so forth.

The information needed to address these areas must be carefully considered and specified in advance to avoid creating a very expensive but useless albatross. Essentially, managers should first decide in detail the type and amount of information they need. Too often, systems are installed, and then managers try to use the available reports from the new system—reports that do not directly address their needs.

It is particularly important to poll managers throughout the organization. The installation of a cost accounting system often requires a major time commitment by all managers throughout the organization. Unless all managers are given a chance to specify their needs, they are unlikely to believe that the system will benefit them. Unless they feel a potential benefit, they will resent the time required and will resist the effort. This can potentially doom the project before it gets off the ground.

When Is Information Needed?

Not only are the types of reports and their contents important; their timing is crucial as well. Information is costly to generate. The primary reason new costing systems are needed is to generate information for decision making. Often, elaborate accounting systems that can generate enormous amounts of information are installed, but the systems are so cumbersome that the needed information is generated in a report long after the decision point has passed.

Managers must consider the trade-offs between a huge system that offers every piece of information desired and a leaner system that can respond quickly to calls for information. However, for a high enough price, one can get both completeness and responsiveness.

How Much Detail Is Needed?

The level of detail and accuracy to be generated should be considered. More is not necessarily better. The more detailed and accurate the reports, the more they cost for data collection, recording, and report generation. The closer we want to come to knowing the true costs of providing a treatment, the more we tend to have to spend to generate that information.

The simplest cost accounting approach is to divide the total costs of the organization by the total patient days and arrive at a cost per patient day. This provides little detail. It is an extreme that has never been considered to be minimally acceptable. However, in response to greater information needs, we run the risk of moving to the other extreme. As health care organizations pour millions of dollars into new *management information systems* and cost accounting systems, we should not lose our common sense. Information should never be collected if the cost of the data collection exceeds the benefit from the improved decisions made based on the availability of that information. Application 15-1 addresses the issue of the cost of cost accounting computer systems.

How Should Information Be Presented?

As health care organizations adopt computerized cost accounting systems, one risk they encounter is potential information overload. Managers may want to be able to have highly detailed information on any elements of routine operations that are out of control. On the other hand, if you have to wade through detailed information on all elements that are under control to find the one that is out of control, the system is useless. Thus, exception reporting—highlighting areas that deviate from expectations—is an essential part of an efficient cost accounting system.

Cost accounting systems tend to be very complex. Yet it is not only the complexity that tends to create problems. A major problem is created by a system that does not respond to the needs of managers throughout the organization. The only solution to that problem is to take time before the system is designed to determine exactly what you want from the system. The design of new cost accounting systems is discussed at length in Applications 15-2, 15-3, 15-4, and 15-5.

THE RISKS OF DO-IT-YOURSELF COMPUTING

Computers are becoming more and more like telephones. Everyone has one on his or her desk, and everyone uses one as a routine tool for daily activities. This is certainly becoming true of health care managers, especially financial managers. However, just like a telephone, you can dial a wrong number. With a telephone call, you find out right away that you have reached the wrong party; with a computer, the error may be more subtle, and in many ways more expensive. This section focuses on some of the risks of developing your own computer programs and analyses.

There is no question that there is a temptation to do your own computing. The frustration managers have with information systems departments has always been great. Getting useful data analyses on a timely basis from information systems departments is a problem common to most industries. The inexpensive cost and ready availability of personal computers has placed great temptations for many managers to do more and more of their own computing.

One potential problem caused by such temptation is an inordinate amount of time wasted by noncomputer experts reinventing the wheel and spending countless hours at their personal computer performing tasks that do not require their own particular expertise. Anyone who has become hooked on computers knows how addictive and time-consumptive they can be.

A more serious problem is that few noncomputer experts really know how to avoid the many pitfalls common to computing. Certainly everyone learns quickly enough to save their work and to make frequent backups—one or two disasters teach all users that lesson. However, like the telephone call, we are all too aware when a file with a week's worth of work is accidentally erased. Similarly, over time, we learn to improve the documentation of our files, so that after a month or two, we can still understand what we were attempting to do, or, at the very least, we can still locate the file. Unfortunately, those sorts of problems really represent the obvious, proverbial tip of the iceberg.

Potential Danger Areas

A variety of dangers exist when one does one's own development of computer applications, even if using a standard software package such as Lotus 1-2-3.* These dangers include lack of adequate quality control, lack of generalizability, program instability over time, and lack of organizational access.

Quality Control

The first and perhaps most important risk is that of inadequate control over quality. In the traditional setting, one individual (or group) prepares the software application while another uses the result. The user often looks at the results with a questioning mind. We all know the saying, "To err is human, but it takes a computer to really foul things up." After hours toiling at the computer developing an application, the user's ability to question the results seems to disappear. After looking at the screen for so long, there seems to be a tendency to assume that it must be right. If the programmer is the end user of the information, final review for reasonableness of the results often never takes place. We have removed the check in a system that depends on checks and balances.

Novices at computer application development tend to underestimate how likely errors are. Even accountants, normally having a full understanding of the likelihood of errors in any accounting process, tend to fail to audit their own computer work. There is a common failure to test adequately, or even test at all, new applications before beginning to rely on their output.

Part of the impact from failure to test adequately could be minimized if each program at least contained a variety of validation checks and other built-in quality control measures. For example, in a spreadsheet, the computer can automatically foot and crossfoot, a simple, but often skipped, safety check to ensure that the range of rows and columns has been properly specified.

---

*Lotus 1-2-3 is a registered trademark of the Lotus Development Corp.

Even with such built-in checks, there is no assurance that the raw data have been input properly unless the data are verified. That task is second nature to a management information systems department, and yet often is skipped by end users doing their own computer work. A missed decimal sign can easily result in an unlocated error and the generation of data used throughout the health care organization to make a major decision based on false information.

The use of audit trails and operating controls would probably be required by financial managers in the work of their staff, but often fall by the wayside in their own work. A user of the application software should be able to trace backward through the calculations to the raw data, and the raw data should be traceable through the calculations to its impact on the final results. Additionally, there should be formalized procedures to ascertain that all data have been entered and validated, processing has completely taken place, and results are examined.

The bottom line is that even top financial managers are likely to make errors. If the information to be generated is likely to have an impact on decisions (and why waste time generating it if it will not?), then it should have the same types of controls one would desire if it were prepared by someone else. Even if it does have controls, the system is inherently weaker because the developer can never have the same clear eye for reviewing the output that he or she would have if someone else developed the analysis.

Generalizability

Users have a tendency to make their applications more rigid than necessary. For one user, that is often not a problem. However, when a department head develops an application template that is intended for use by a number of other individuals, problems begin to arise. For example, the Director of Nursing Services might develop a budgeting program for use by all nursing supervisors. However, in designing the spreadsheet template, it is possible that there will be inadequate development in the model to handle all of the specific problems that will arise for each individual user.

Information systems department personnel are trained to consider the design requirements to meet the needs of all likely users. They have a tendency to ask more pointed questions about who will use the software and how it will be used, rather than simply plunging ahead with the information at hand. As a result, a program that seems to work when viewed by the developer may be quite limited when applied to the intended purpose.

Program Stability

Most programs developed by users tend to be static. That is, they act over time as if the information required by the program were stable. In some cases, that is reasonable—only the data change when the model is used at a later date. However, in some cases, underlying assumptions also change. For example, suppose that a calculation of total personnel costs depends in part on occupancy levels. If we pull out the application template a year after it was developed to update personnel costs for wage increases and changes in benefits rates, we may fail to realize that the results will be incorrect unless we update the occupancy rate as well.

Programs generated by information systems departments tend to take into account all variables that may change over time. In fact, programs may be linked into on-line mainframe databases in such a way that they are automatically updated every time they are used, without requiring any action by the user. With programs developed by the ultimate user, such updating features are rarely employed, or in many cases, even feasible.

Organizational Access

Another problem with information systems being developed by the ultimate user is that it tends to create private rather than public data sources. Even though the developer may from time to time share information for a specific purpose, in general, effort has gone into developing a resource that is not generally available. This may create substantial duplication of effort by different department heads, or it may simply cause information not to be circulated to all who might find it useful. Obviously, this makes the information more costly to obtain on a per-use basis, because its benefits are not shared by as many individuals.

An additional problem is that systems developed by users make the organization more dependent on a specific individual. Organizations should have systems that can continue to operate in the event that an individual is disabled or leaves the organization. Even if neither of those events occurs, as people change positions within the organization, it makes transitions far more difficult.

The potential dangers of internally generated software applications are summarized in Exhibit 15-2.

Advantages of Self-Generated Computer Applications

The potential problems should not overshadow the fact that there are some advantages of having direct control over the computer system. There is an industry-wide shortage of competent information systems personnel. If a user can satisfactorily overcome the potential problems, the number of computer specialists needed by the organization can be reduced.

Additionally, a fair amount of communication time is eliminated. The specific detailed requirements of the system are immediately transferred from the end user of the software directly into the computer. This saves numerous phone calls, conferences, miscommunications, and so forth.

Another advantage to preparing your own program is that you will not waste time developing a system too complicated to use yourself.

Sometimes information systems departments get so carried away with the development of a system that it becomes too complex for the end user actually to use. It would be an interesting study to examine how much software is developed and then never really implemented because, despite all the time and effort devoted to its development, the ultimate user just cannot make it do what he or she wants it to do. Sometimes, a user-developed program is so much simpler that it is more likely to be used and to provide benefits to the organization.

The final advantage concerns the ability to control your own destiny. Accountants have in many respects lost control of accounting data to information systems experts. The general ledger is no longer the accountant's domain, but rather that of the people who input the data and print the output. Having the ability to do your own programming also gives you the ability to get the data you want when you want it, independent of the schedules of another department. There is a level of independence achieved by doing your own programming. The value of that independence should not be underestimated.

Exhibit 15-3 summarizes the advantages of self-generated computer applications.

Finding a Balance

The first step in finding a balance between the benefits of users developing their own systems and the problems created by such development is to assess the level of risk that such development creates. If the developer is the only one who will use the information generated or system developed, the level of exposure is limited. If several others will use the system but are aware of its intent and limitations, the risk is

---

Exhibit 15-2 Potential Danger Areas in Designing Your Own Software Applications

1. Lack of adequate quality control
   - Failure to test new applications adequately
   - Inadequate validation checks
   - Inadequate verification of data input
2. Lack of generalizability of application programs
3. Program instability over time
4. Lack of widespread organizational access

Exhibit 15-3 Advantages of Self-Generated Computer Applications

1. Reduces need for computer specialists
2. Saves communication time
3. Avoids unduly complicated systems
4. Provides better control of timing of data generation

somewhat greater, but still contained. If the information will be used for decisions that affect the entire organization, or if many individuals will use the system, the risk created by errors in the system, or a miscommunication regarding the system's capabilities and output, are magnified considerably.

For the more confined use, one approach that may prove adequate is to establish formalized training programs on system documentation, validation, testing, audit trails, and so forth. Frequently, these programs can be planned and taught by members of the information systems department. Obviously, this is a delicate issue, and it must be made clear to that department that there is no long-term intent to supplant them. On the other hand, they must be made aware of the reality of computers becoming as commonplace as hand-held calculators. The competition from users developing their own programs may in many ways lead to a greater incentive for the information systems department to provide high-quality service.

As the exposure becomes greater because of broader use of the information or system, more controls are necessary. It might be appropriate to require additional training in terms of problem definition and system development. Additionally, some review by the information systems department of all finished programs or spot audits of some programs might be appropriate.

For more broadly used information and systems, some additional institutional control is probably required. In fact, where the exposure is greatest, the benefits of normal checks and balances may outweigh the inconvenience costs of using the information systems department or an outside software vendor.

SUGGESTED READING

Boze, K.M., et al. 1992. Planning for a computerized accounting system. *Journal of Accountancy* 173, no. 6:45–51.

Burik, D., and L. Carls. 1987. Health care cost accounting: Finding the systems solution. *Topics in Health Care Financing* 13, no. 4:48–55.

Davis, G.B. 1988. Information systems: To buy, build, or customize? *Accounting Horizons* 1, no. 1:101–103.

Finkler, S.A. 1991. Variance analysis. Part II, The use of computers. *Journal of Nursing Administration* 21, no. 9:9–15.

Hemeon, F.E., III. 1989. Productivity, cost accounting, and information systems. *Topics in Health Care Financing* 15, no. 3:55–67.

Horngren, C.T., and G. Foster. 1991. *Cost accounting: A managerial emphasis.* 7th ed. Englewood Cliffs, N.J.: Prentice-Hall.

Hunton, J.E., and H.M. Courtney. 1992. How to match computers and accounting software. *Journal of Accountancy* 173, no. 6:54–57.

Keegan, A. 1987. Saving money throughout the cost accounting installation cycle. *Hospital Cost Accounting Advisor* 2, no. 10:1–7.

Kerschner, M., and E.L. Loper. 1987. Enhancing cost accounting efforts by improving existing information sources. *Topics in Health Care Financing* 13, no. 4:10–19.

Okulski, J.S., and T.K. Shaffert, eds. 1987. Information systems for the changing environment. *Topics in Health Care Financing* 14, no. 2.

Patterson, P. 1992. Computers bring cost accounting within OR's reach. *OR Manager* 8, no. 3:1, 6–7.

EXERCISES

QUESTIONS FOR DISCUSSION

1. What is the greatest mistake an organization can make in acquiring a computerized cost accounting system?

2. In planning a computerized costing system, are you likely to be better off if the process is kept to a relatively small number of individuals or if all managers are involved in system specification?

3. What are some essential issues that must be resolved as the system is designed?

4. What are some of the risks encountered when managers throughout the organization design and use their own computer templates?

Note: Solutions to the Exercises can be found in Appendix A.

Application 15-1

Saving Money throughout the Cost Accounting Installation Cycle

Arthur J. Keegan, MBA, is currently Vice President of HBO & Company, Atlanta, Georgia.

Almost every hospital financial information system installed in America today is obsolete and fails to properly match revenue and expenses. A hospital's laboratory used to be both a revenue center and a cost center. Today, with DRGs and capitated HMOs, the laboratory is just a cost center and the patient is the revenue center. In the good old days, the job of the hospital's financial information system was to take revenue from the patient billing system and match it to expenses in the hospital's general ledger. Now the flow reverses, and expenses must be taken from the general ledger and matched to patients' bills.

Unfortunately, the designers of the last generation of hospital information systems built the expense and revenue matching as a one-way street. Revenue can flow to expenses, but expenses can't flow to revenue.

Matching hospitalwide expenses to the patient requires some of the information processing techniques developed by cost accountants. So it is no surprise that when the Healthcare Financial Managers Association recently surveyed health care CFOs they found that the most important DP systems application for the next

three years will be cost accounting. Most of the hospital executives buying cost accounting services in the next three years will be first-time buyers with no experience in purchasing this type of software. The techniques laid out here will help them to select a system that offers the features they need at a reasonable price.

Always keep in mind that there are two major cost components in purchasing any software—the cost of installation and the costs of maintenance. The cost a novice buyer is most likely to overlook is the cost of maintaining the system after the software is installed. Only by minimizing the combined cost of installation and maintenance can a CFO ensure getting the best deal for the hospital.

Cost accounting systems that have low installation costs may be expensive to maintain, while a system that is more expensive to install may be much less costly to maintain over the long haul. The cost-conscious CFO must estimate maintenance costs when selecting a system.

THE COST ACCOUNTING INSTALLATION CYCLE

The cost accounting installation cycle starts with a definition of the general features of a costing system and ends with a fully installed

Source: Reprinted from Arthur J. Keegan, "Saving Money throughout the Cost Accounting Installation Cycle," *Hospital Cost Accounting Advisor,* Vol. 2, No. 10, pp. 1–7. Copyright 1987, Aspen Publishers, Inc.

and maintainable system. Choosing the various stages in between is an arbitrary process that no two people would ever agree on. Based on my experience as a teacher of cost accounting and as an installer of these systems, I split the installation process into the following seven steps.

- Step 1: Goal setting and general outline
- Step 2: Selecting the software
- Step 3: Finalizing the design
- Step 4: Measuring costs
- Step 5: Test driving
- Step 6: Feedback
- Step 7: Maintenance

The particular order of the steps can vary from system to system, but all steps are necessary to get a costing system in and off the ground. The costs of each step will vary according to the system chosen. Generally speaking, a greater investment in design simplifications and careful installation can lower the costs of maintenance. Designing in complexity will raise maintenance expenses.

Figure 15-1-1 shows a general curve of the work hours used during the installation cycle. The commitment normally peaks in Step 4—measuring the costs. This is the time when the most intense work is done on the system. Yet, in the long run, more hours will be devoted to maintaining the system (Step 7).

In selecting a system, it is wise to take the long view and make sure whatever is designed is not a monster to maintain—devouring resources in a time when most health care organi-

zations have precious few hours to spare. Trading off a few more installation dollars for long-term savings in maintenance is good business.

STEP 1: GOAL SETTING

Poor planning raises the cost of installation. Abe Lincoln once said that if he had six hours to chop down an apple tree, he would spend four of the hours sharpening the ax. (He promptly forgot this advice, and sent thousands of untrained youths off to die at Bull Run.) Let's not make the same mistake. An extra hour of preparation can save a hospital staff hours of time redirecting efforts in midstream and redoing half-finished work.

The first step in planning is to learn the link between cost accounting accuracy, system timeliness, and the cost of the system. One of these factors cannot be changed without affecting at least one of the other two.

Increasing the accuracy without lengthening the time to get a report increases the cost of the system. Increasing the frequency of reports without lowering the accuracy increases the cost of the system. All cost savings eventually mean reducing accuracy or timeliness. In discussions with the Controller of a major Fortune 50 corporation, which has cost accounting needs similar to those of a hospital, I learned that this corporation spends in excess of $8,000,000 per year on what its controller thinks is a reliable, timely, and accurate costing system. I know of no hospital or hospital system willing to devote even $5,000,000 annually to cost accounting, so hospitals are accepting a much lower level of accuracy than a Fortune 50 corporation.

When you have mastered the relationship between cost, accuracy, and timeliness, it will be easier to make decisions on whether increased levels of accuracy or timeliness are worth the cost.

Next, decide whether the main goal of the system is product costing or management costing (i.e., internal control). Product costing systems are designed to determine the cost of delivering the hospital's services to patients.

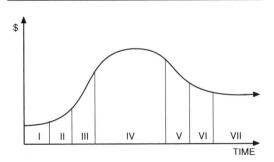

Figure 15-1-1 A Cost Profile of the Cost Accounting Installation Cycle

These systems are often less elaborate than management costing systems and are less costly to install or maintain. Product costing systems do not support the flexible budgeting and management control provided by management costing systems.

Management costing systems are more elaborate, complete, and expensive than product costing systems. These systems focus mainly on properly modeling the cost behavior of service-producing departments and reporting deviations from expected levels of expenditure. Management costing systems often include standard costing features. It is easy to think of them as a very detailed, flexible budgeting system.

If internal control—management costing—is the key feature of the costing system, other managers outside the finance department must be involved in the goal-setting stage. Once the choice of the mix of product costing and management costing features is made, the following general features should be considered and reviewed for their impact on system cost:

Departmental Cost Pools

Choosing the number of departments in the hospital to cost greatly affects the cost of the system. For product costing, the choice is usually limited to patient service departments, while management costing focuses on all expense generating areas. Do not do all departments at once. Use a reasonable method to select the key departments. Later, when things are less hectic, the uncosted departments can be added to the system. Go for the big payoffs during installation.

Cost Elements

Another general design feature is how many cost elements or micro costs make up a costed item. Some sample cost elements are variable direct salary, fixed salary, variable departmental overhead, or fixed general overhead. The more cost elements, the greater the cost of maintaining the system. Many hospitals set up more cost elements than they can afford to maintain, getting little useful information for their efforts. Clear thinking and economy here can pay off.

Direct vs. Indirect Costs

The definition of direct costs, like beauty, seems to be in the eye of the beholder. It generally means costs that can be traced to an individual patient's care. Choose a definition that can be consistently applied to the departments chosen to cost. Beware of accounts like supplies that share the same account number but are a direct cost for one department and overhead for another.

Fixed and Variable Costs

Getting consensus here is difficult, and a general rule better be developed first. Remember, most managers believe "Fixed cost equals me and variable costs equals you." Hospitals, like the local firehouse, have a lot of fixed labor. Beware of thinking of labor as highly variable.

Reporting

Before looking at systems, it is wise to determine the style and frequency of reports needed. Developing pro forma reports before buying a system is a wise investment. It will save time that could otherwise be lost in dealing with suppliers who lack the reporting features needed. Frequency of reporting—timeliness—affects the cost of the system.

Once a general decision is made on system function, emphasis on management and/or product costing, and general system features, the hospital can shop for suppliers.

STEP 2: SELECTING THE SOFTWARE

The cost of cost accounting software is *not* the cost of the cost accounting system. Do not lose sight of the difference between the price of the software and the cost of the system. The cost of the system includes design, installation, and maintenance costs on top of the price for software. Relatively inexpensive software that is costly to maintain and install is no bargain.

Most hospitals require assistance in installing the software. Sometimes installation services are packaged in with a software sale, and sometimes they are sold separately. All the selection criteria below apply equally well to a full system supplier or a separate installer.

System Functionality

Determine whether the supplier sells primarily a product costing or a management costing system, and compare the system's general characteristics to the hospital's initial design.

Supplier's Experience

Obtain precise data on number of installations, years in the business, and quality of references. A supplier's reputation is a critical asset. Talk to someone who dropped the system if you can—every supplier loses some customers.

Service/Support

Find out if the supplier has regional or national service. Determine the ratio of service people to clients. What level of service is included in licensing fees and what service is charged at hourly or daily rates?

Cost Pools

All software has limits, and design decisions must be made. Make sure the vendor supports the number and types of cost pools the hospital plans for.

Cost Elements

Make sure the cost elements desired by the hospital are supported by the software. Some

systems are restricted to as few as three elements of cost, while others allow an almost uncountable number. More cost elements still mean more maintenance costs, and sometimes mean slower response time.

Integration

Find out if the supplier has successfully integrated its cost accounting system with general ledger, billing, and payroll systems similar to the hospital's. Poor integration delays installation, reduces usefulness of the costing system, and raises the cost of maintenance.

Simplicity vs. Complexity

More complex software is not necessarily better. Accuracy has a higher cost of maintenance. Flexibility has more benefits than complexity.

System Speed

Inspect the costing system's response time. Determine how fast it generates test reports. Time can be money. Waiting six hours for a report may be unacceptable.

Updating Procedure

Check out how quickly and easily the system can be updated. Look at monthly processing and when reports can be run. Review the steps to changing a cost weight, changing a costing method, or adding a new procedure to cost.

License or Sale

The hospital should know if it owns or licenses the software. If the hospital merges with others, can it add other providers to its license agreement? Make sure the hospital gets all software enhancements released within six months of the installation date.

Price

Price is always important. For the same features, the lower the better. If possible, don't pay all of it until the system works.

These are the general concerns in purchasing costing software. Depending on a hospital's specific goals, other concerns may be more important. One goal may be to select a product that runs on certain hardware. Hardware restrictions significantly narrow the field of selection.

STEP 3: FINALIZING THE DESIGN

Selecting the cost accounting system software sets limits on what the system can do. Any software chosen will probably not do everything the hospital initially wanted to do. After software selection, a design should be set. This step should involve all the departments to be costed.

The big decisions in this step are how many items to cost and in how much detail they should be costed. The hospital at this stage will learn that all the knowledge needed for installing a cost accounting system does not reside in the accounting department.

Successful costing means properly describing how services are produced—the production function. The clearer the description of how a procedure is produced, the easier and cheaper it is to cost that procedure. The managers in charge of producing services can effect significant savings in installing a costing system. See Exhibit 15-1-1 for a sample production function.

One rule often used to reduce installation time is Pareto's principle (the "80/20" rule). This rule states that generally 20 percent of a department's procedures account for 80 percent of its output. Using this precept can limit precise costing to only the services most often used. Do not apply it blindly. Be on the lookout for different production methods in the same department.

Exhibit 15-1-1 Sample Production Function

Procedure: Liver Scan

Labor Components

Person	Activity	Time	Cost
Technologist	Prep.	15 min.	$2.90
Aide	Prep.	2 min.	.25
Aide	Transport	14 min.	1.75
Technologist	Injection	5 min.	.97
Technologist	Treatment	15 min.	2.90
Transcriptionist	Transcription	4 min.	.60
			$9.37

Supplies

Item	Cost
8 × 10 Film	$ .89
Processing chemicals	.09
Radionuclide	11.75
Gloves	.40
Syringe	.20
	$13.33

Total $22.70

Applying Pareto's principle to the radiology department will often result in overlooking angiographic procedures. Angiography uses a much different production process than routine diagnostic radiology, and is very resource-intensive.

At this stage, the number of cost components should be selected. This is very important if standard costs will be used in the system. For example, should direct labor be divided into just two components—fixed and variable—or should a labor component exist for each salary code or even for each job code? Critical to this decision is how many cost components the organization can afford to maintain. Don't set up a system that is detailed beyond a reasonable maintenance effort.

Overhead cost assignment to procedures is important for product costing but less critical for management costing. Spending a lot of time on overhead issues for a management costing system is a waste of time.

This step of the cycle is complete when decisions are reached on the actual procedures to cost, the description of the production functions, the number and kinds of cost elements, and exactly how overhead is to be costed. The scene now shifts to the various hospital departments where costing will take place.

STEP 4: MEASURING COSTS

After maintenance, this is usually the most costly step in the installation cycle. The hospital CFO should make extra effort to reduce the costs of this step.

Here the hospital's cost accountants get down and dirty and measure the cost of producing services. The purpose of this step is to translate costs from the general ledger format to the individual procedures.

Before the general ledger costs can be assigned to procedures, they first have to be mapped to the cost elements. In other words, individual salary accounts have to be mapped to either fixed or variable salary or some other cost elements. Many methods exist for this mapping, and they can be broken down into four general categories, from least costly to most costly.

Declaration

This method is the least costly and requires the department manager to assign accounts directly to a cost component. Each salary account is declared either fixed or variable, likewise with nonsalary and departmental overhead. Although it seems crude, it probably is the most cost effective and should be used as often as possible.

Inspection

This method requires assigning costs to fixed and variable based on reading contracts and purchase orders. Items that are fixed charges become fixed costs, and items whose cost varies with volume purchased are variable. In this method, salaried employees' wages are assigned to fixed expenses, while hourly employees' wages are considered variable.

Observation

Observation means going in and watching the services being produced. Observational techniques include work sampling, logging work time, regression analysis, and many others. These techniques are largely used for measuring direct labor inputs.

Engineering

Engineering techniques are used when cost standards or normative costs are to be set. The engineer determines what the costs should be after modeling the production process. These are the most expensive techniques, and should be reserved for areas of highly repetitive work or for areas that have a high potential for staff reduction.

A hospital will use a combination of declaration, inspection, observation, and engineering techniques for tracing costs to products. The techniques will be chosen based on the item to be costed.

A common problem in this stage in hospitals is that hospital departments produce more than a single output, and a weighting scheme is developed to allocate departmental cost pools to outputs. This can be done simply and cheaply by using the procedure charge as the allocation statistic or a Ratio of Cost to Charges method (RCC Method).

While RCCs are relatively inexpensive, they can be unacceptably inaccurate, since most hospital charges bear no relation to costs. Therefore, labor content, nonlabor content, and overhead must be estimated for each procedure. One way to save money is to rely on published standards or the department directors' best intuition. It appears that investing in detailed studies only yields a good payback for direct labor in high revenue areas. Overhead and nonlabor are economically costed by using descriptive measures.

Because of 19 years of Medicare cost reporting, the techniques for overhead costing are highly developed in the hospital industry. Realistically, sophisticated overhead costing adds very little punch to a managerial or product costing system. For management purposes, allocated overheads are usually uncontrollable while for product purposes marginal costs without fixed overhead are much more meaningful than full costs. Be wary of investing many of a hospital's scarce accounting resources in improving overhead costing.

The way to save money in the fourth step is to limit the number of costs you measure by engineering or observational techniques. Use as much descriptive costing material as meets the hospital's accuracy goals, and don't waste a lot of time on overhead.

STEP 5: TEST DRIVE

When Step 4 is done, the hospital can address two major issues. Does the output make sense, and how often should the hospital fire this sucker up? If the output looks funny, this is the best time to fix it.

First, audit all the costs. On a test basis, the cost accountants should make sure that they can trace inputs through to outputs. Beware of accepting a system with "black boxes" where numbers go in, magic takes place, and numbers come out. Black boxes can be expensive to fix if their designers accept jobs in the fast food industry.

After correcting all the problems that are obvious to the accounting office, design standard reports and determine how often they should be distributed. Because of generally poor inventory accounting in hospitals, costing reports are best done on a quarterly basis.

Skipping Step 5 can result in tremendous credibility problems. Department managers are usually very wary and anxious about the output of the cost accounting system. Trashy output is all they need to ignite a major rejection of the system and the loss of all investment up to this point.

STEP 6: FEEDBACK

Once the hospital's cost accountants finish tuning the system, feedback should be sought from the costed departments. The next step is to ask managers to sign off on the costing work

done in their departments and affirm that the work is accurate.

The benefit here is reinforcing the ownership of the data by the department managers. A lack of credibility is one of the best ways to waste a hospital's investment in cost accounting. Department managers need to be treated as intimate partners in the cost accounting cycle.

Also, involvement of departmental managers will lower the cost of maintaining the system. Managers who are well versed in the operation of the costing system will be able to alert the hospital's cost accountants to changes in the production process, emergence of new procedures, and changes in the fixed or variable nature of departmental costs. Involving the departmental managers allows the accountants to leverage off other experience and expertise and save money.

STEP 7: MAINTENANCE

This is where most of the money will be spent in a cost accounting system, because maintenance expense occurs every year the system is in operation. A small percentage savings here can mean big dollar savings over long periods of time. Therefore, an overriding concern in all decisions made during the installation should be the impact of that decision on the costs of maintaining the system.

One rule of thumb is that if a hospital cannot afford two people trained in how to run and maintain the cost accounting system, it should not go ahead with the system. Having only one "expert" in the system means when the expert goes, so goes the expertise. As Saki said "She was a good cook, as cooks go, and as cooks go, she went." Job opportunities are expanding rapidly for trained hospital cost accountants.

Given the complexity of these products, there will always be many decisions that are not well documented except in the head of the user. A second trained user will provide a check against undocumented modifications.

Develop a schedule of periodic maintenance and revision. Using the costing system for budgeting will increase the necessity of keeping all its information up to date. Departments should be put on a schedule of review with the more significant ones being reviewed more frequently than the less important ones.

Maintenance and updating will always need to be done when a production function changes. Switching to unit dose in pharmacy or primary nursing on a nursing unit requires changing the cost accounting data. Large variances in last year's unit cost and this year's cost is a dead giveaway of changing production functions.

It can't be said often enough: The best way to save money is save money on maintenance. Do not avoid maintenance, but keep the system simple enough for easy maintenance. Having only one employee versed in the system is not a money saving step; it is a prelude to disaster.

Common sense and proper planning are the sure way to keeping a cost accounting installation on track and under budget. Spend a little extra time sharpening your ax before cutting the costs of cost accounting.

Application 15-2

Cost Accounting Software Design

Randall C. Stephenson, MS, is currently
Marketing Director at First Data Corporation—
Health Systems Group, Norcross, Georgia.

Effective October 1,1983, when the Medicare program began paying hospitals for inpatient services under its new Prospective Payment System (PPS), hospitals began to experience a critical need for accurate cost information. Perhaps the single most important impact of prospective pricing will be to change the role that cost management plays in the overall financial management of a hospital. The achievement of positive financial results under such a system requires that management have a detailed knowledge of costs and the variables that influence them. These include

- patient case-mix and acuity
- labor productivity
- physician practice patterns
- capacity thresholds
- input-output relationships

A thorough understanding of these factors is required for management to initiate actions that will provide a positive contribution to the hospital's financial results.

Source: Reprinted from Randall C. Stephenson, "Cost Accounting Software Design," *Hospital Cost Accounting Advisor,* Vol. 1, No. 6, November 1985, pp. 1, 4–7. Copyright 1985, Aspen Publishers, Inc.

Old hospital costing methodologies are based upon top-down allocation routines, in which costs are determined on an average basis for whole products or groups of services. These techniques do not produce cost information at a level of detail that can support marginal cost analysis, competitive pricing and bidding, performance monitoring based upon variance analysis, or product-line decision making.

The dynamics of the industry necessitate innovative decision making by hospital executives to effectively manage the delivery of health care services. Experience has shown that accurate and detailed cost information has a wide variety of management applications in hospitals, including the following areas:

- product-line profitability analysis (case mix)
- flexible budgeting and control
- strategic planning
- department cost variance analysis
- decision support/modeling
- trend analysis

To address the need of hospitals to access timely and accurate cost accounting information, Management Science America (MSA) has developed software that enables hospitals to make use of proven "bottom-up" cost accounting techniques. The MSA Health Care System consists of three primary modules that are organized and integrated to fully support a hospital's varied uses of cost information. The three modules are Health Care Costing, Health Care Accounting, and Case-Mix Management. Their functions are summarized in Exhibit 15-2-1.

In developing a health care cost system a number of distinct, yet interrelated requirements for a cost accounting system must be recognized. Hospital managers at all levels of the organization will require concise, meaningful, and timely cost information to understand and control the costs for which they are responsible. Cost information must be organized to support management decision making throughout the organization. The cost accounting system must have the flexibility and adaptive structure to meet the specific and varying needs of strategic analysis and planning. Patient services must be appropriately and consistently costed on a timely basis by DRG or other appropriate product-line classification. To the extent possible, the hospital cost accounting system should be integrated with existing financial systems to ensure cost-effective operation.

The general design of the MSA system is derived from job costing systems that have evolved over the years in industry. (See *Hospital Cost Accounting Advisor*, Vol. 1, No. 5 for a discussion of job costing.) The job costing model is appropriate for a hospital because it can recognize the following factors that are inherent in providing patient care services:

1. Each patient's treatment is uniquely defined and modified to meet the patient's specific needs and the varying conditions of that patient.
2. Patient treatment and care can be defined as a number of service units, which are similar to component parts. The total treatment of a patient can be defined as a list of service units provided, that is, a bill of services.
3. The individual service units provided are fairly uniform in nature and for the purpose

Exhibit 15-2-1 Features of the MSA Health Care System

Health Care Costing Module

- defines products and product structure relationships at the procedure, subprocedure, or service unit levels
- establishes and maintains rates for labor, material, and overhead categories
- defines and maintains up to 16 cost elements for each product or service
- simulates the impact of changes in cost variables at any level
- provides extensive where-used reporting and same-as-except-for capabilities to reduce the clerical effort required to define and maintain cost standards
- supports engineering (microcosted), relative value unit (RVU), and average costing techniques

Health Care Accounting Module

- measures departmental performance in up to 16 cost categories
- calculates major operational variances based on volume changes and efficiencies
- provides statistical and cost information
- integrates with general ledger systems for management reporting

Case-Mix Management Module

- provides standard reporting on the basis of Diagnosis Related Groups (DRGs) or other user-defined product groupings
- provides utilities for ad hoc reporting online
- provides extensive outlier, net income, profitability, physician, and patient demographic reporting capabilities
- supports marginal cost analysis using standard cost profiles and detailed cost elements from the Health Care Costing Module

of costing can be defined in terms of standard cost units.

HEALTH CARE COSTING

The Health Care Costing Module identifies the cost of procedures and services performed throughout the hospital. Standard cost information is maintained at a detailed level in this module, and this information can be readily accessed and used by the other system modules.

The objective of the module is to develop a standard cost profile for each of the procedures or services performed throughout a hospital. These standard cost profiles can be developed for both charge items (e.g., discrete items or services typically detailed on the charge description master file or your hospital's patient accounting system) and service unit items (e.g., patient-oriented services that are not typically part of the patient billing process, but can be used as a means of assigning and transferring costs to patients as services are provided). An example of a service unit item might be a medical records chart workup or an admissions workup.

The module develops procedure-level or service-unit-level standard cost profiles using a mix of engineered (microcosted), relative value unit, and average costing techniques. This feature of the system facilitates the use of the 80/20 rule as it applies to cost accounting for hospitals. Experience has shown that in most hospital departments, a relatively small percentage of services performed will typically account for a majority of the department's costs.

For such high-volume, high-contribution procedures, a hospital may deem it appropriate to use microcosting (engineered costing) techniques to ensure data accuracy and reliability. The module enables hospitals to develop and maintain itemized procedure-level schedules of material costs, or *bills of material*. It also keeps track of where and by whom labor effort is expended as products, procedures, and services are delivered to patients. This information is referred to as a *routing*, which is the series of tasks done in a specific sequence by different people at different work centers. Through the use of these bills of material and standard routing concepts, a hospital can engineer (microcost) standard cost profiles for those items for which a high degree of costing accuracy is required.

Other services or products may make only a small contribution to a department's overall operation, and hence may be less critical from an accuracy standpoint. Microcosting techniques can be combined with RVU and average costing techniques to arrive at an overall costing solution that is both accurate and cost-effective.

The module enables hospitals to define and maintain up to 16 cost elements for each item to be costed. Cost elements in this case refer to components of the total standard cost of an item, identifying details such as direct labor, materials, fixed and variable overhead, and so on. These cost elements are user controlled and can be tailored to meet your hospital's specific needs. For example, you may need to define a unique cost element for depreciation or fringe benefits. Or you may wish to track indirect materials or indirect labor as separate cost elements. One key design feature is that costs are always tied to their origins in the general ledger. For example, a fixed cost element remains a fixed cost whether it is viewed as part of a DRG's total cost or part of a product line's total cost: Fixed or variable costs are clearly identifiable as such at any product level. This gives you a tremendous advantage in marginal cost analysis and competitive pricing.

In today's environment, modeling and cost simulation capabilities are more critical than ever. This system keeps track of the quantity and unit cost of inputs by using a bill of material. Six months later if the quantity consumed or unit cost of one of these inputs changes, the hospital doesn't have to recalculate the entire cost. It just changes one number on the bill of material for that product, and the system does the rest.

You can also input *new* cost factors (e.g., change the basis for cost allocation) and perform a cost rollup to see the impact on the overall cost. The ability to perform cost simulations enables administrators to determine the impact of changes in a wide range of cost factors. You can see the impact of anticipated changes for factors as simple as a payroll rate change or as complex as volume and method changes. If a factor has an impact on the cost of a procedure, material, patient, DRG, or service, the impact of that change can be modeled to aid in analyzing the results.

Users can develop, store, and maintain standard cost profiles using full absorption costing techniques. These fully absorbed cost standards can be used in the process of measuring and analyzing product-line profitability. Simultaneously, standard cost profiles can also be developed and stored from direct costing efforts for the purpose of support marginal cost analyses. Thus, one cost data base can be used to support the varied requirements of profitability analysis, competitive bidding and pricing analyses, and managerial decision support. The ability to use one common data base maximizes user flexibility and minimizes user maintenance requirements.

HEALTH CARE ACCOUNTING

With the Health Care Accounting Module, you can accurately and fairly measure performance in each department. Using procedural-level standards and statistical information about actual services provided, variances are calculated. Since costs are developed by element in the Health Care Costing Module (e.g., direct labor, direct supplies, depreciation, and variable overhead), the information sent to General Ledger can produce variances such as the following:

- volume variance
- patient mix (case-mix) variance
- labor rate variance
- labor efficiency variance
- material price variance
- material usage variance
- overhead spending variance
- overhead utilization variance

The ability to calculate and report variances at this level of detail can assist you in your effort to increase managers' understanding of their role in the cost management process. When cost variances are analyzed in terms of the components listed above, your managers can understand the cause and effect relationship that exists between their day-to-day decision-making efforts and the bottom line financial performance of the hospital. In addition, you can hold managers accountable only for those items that they control or influence. In short, the Health Care Accounting Module can be used to enhance your hospital's overall management control effort.

CASE-MIX MANAGEMENT

Today, case-mix management systems are recognized as invaluable tools in analyzing clinical, marketing, and financial trends in the health care environment. The Case-Mix Management Module provides you with the tools to analyze patient and product-line trends. This module will handle such tasks as identifying patient demographics in each DRG or the resource consumption profiles by DRG and by physician.

The Case-Mix Management Module is built around a matrix concept, as shown in Exhibit 15-2-2, which relates service programs of a hospital to its operational units. Service programs are defined using diagnostic groups of patients, medical organizations, or even specific physician groups. Operational units are groups of revenue centers as defined by aggregations of specific charge codes. Each cell in the matrix could contain information such as revenue or cost, or a service statistic such as patient days or number of procedures.

The Case-Mix Management Module is directly interfaced to the Health Care Costing Module, and can use the cost element data from the costing module. Because of this interface, the case-mix reports reflect standard cost data as opposed to cost data calculated by cost-to-charge ratio methods. This design feature is a significant advancement over older case-mix systems, where costs are based entirely on ratio of cost to charges or other top-down methodologies. The ability to utilize detailed procedure-level standard cost data in the Case-Mix Management Module means you can now engage in marginal cost analyses by program or product line, for the purpose of competitive bidding and pricing analyses.

Exhibit 15-2-2 Example of the Matrix Concept

		Facility A								
		Inpatient								
		Adult								
		Cardiology				Orthopedics				
			Surgery				Surgery			
		Medicine	Bypass	Other Open Heart	Other Surgery	Medicine	Hip Replacement	Other Joint Repl.	Other Surgery	
Patient Data										
Nursing Services	Medical									
	Surgical									
	ICU									
	CCU		■							
	•									
	•									
	•									
	Nursery									
	Neonatal ICU									
Ancillary Services	Radiology									
	X-ray					■				
	CT Head									
	CT Body									
	CT Combined									
	Ultrasound									
	Operating Room									
	Less Than 1 Hour									
	•									
	•									
	•									
	Use of Pump									
	ECG									
	EEG									
	EMG									
	Physical Therapy									

- charges
- costs
- statistics
- procedures
- diagnosis
- demographics
- charge items
- physicians

Source: Reprinted from *Hospital Cost Accounting Advisor,* Vol. 1, No. 6, p. 7, Aspen Publishers, Inc., ©1985.

Application 15-3

An Integrated Planning and Management Control System for Hospitals

*Robert F. Raco, BS, is currently President and
Chief Executive Officer of Transition Systems,
Inc., Boston, Massachusetts.*

*Peter W. VanEtten, MBA, is currently
Chief Financial Officer at Stanford
University, Stanford, California.*

An integrated planning and management control system for hospitals has been developed by the New England Medical Center (NEMC). This system is designed to enable hospitals to

- understand their product lines and their true costs
- develop realistic, flexible cost standards and financial plans for those product lines
- measure performance against those plans and implement management control strategies which will ensure that the plans are met
- develop effective marketing strategies by modeling alternative internal and external scenarios
- analyze the incremental costs and profitability of current—and future—product lines within the context of the hospital's specific marketplace

The system is designed within a framework that views hospital activity as a two-stage production process.

Source: Reprinted from Robert F. Raco and Peter W. VanEtten, "An Integrated Planning and Management Control System for Hospitals," *Hospital Cost Accounting Advisor,* Vol. 1, No. 7, pp. 4–7. Copyright 1985, Aspen Publishers, Inc.

In the first stage, hospital resources are converted into intermediate products comprising the individual procedures and services provided in the patient care areas, such as x-rays, laboratory tests, nursing care hours, and operating room time.

In the second stage of the hospital production process, the intermediate products are grouped or bundled to produce the final products—treated patients, or "cases." These final products are typically defined according to DRGs, but may also be defined according to any classification scheme deemed appropriate (e.g., severity of illness, disease staging, MDCs, ICD-9-CM, or a combination of these grouping approaches).

The distinction between the two production stages is important. First, the two distinct stages reflect the acknowledgment that the ultimate products of the patient-care process are the treated patients, while the individual services rendered during the treatment cycle are intermediate products. Second, the splitting of the process into two stages reflects the difference in control and management focus.

In the first stage, production occurs and is controlled in the cost center; the focus within each center is on the efficient production of the intermediate products and the control of unit cost. The second stage, however, is generally controlled by the physician. Thus, the focus of the second stage is on the number and mix of intermediate products "bundled" to produce final products.

NEMC's system consists of three integrated systems that provide software to support the management of the two production stages: Department Cost Manager, Clinical Cost Manager, and Clinical Financial Manager.

Department Cost Manager (DCM)

DCM focuses on the control and management of costs associated with intermediate products. DCM enables hospital managers to identify intermediate products, develop standard costs, perform variance analysis and marginal cost analysis, and simulate changes in department costs.

Clinical Cost Manager (CCM)

CCM is a planning, control, and intervention system that focuses on costs associated with the hospital's end product, or patient case. CCM enables managers and physicians to define the hospital's end products (using any of several case classifications), develop standard treatments and protocols for those classifications, cost out hospital case-mix, and perform variance analysis for cost, revenue, and profitability.

Clinical Financial Planner (CFP)

CFP is a financial modeling system that enables managers to perform a broad range of budgeting, planning, and simulation functions.

As a decision-support tool, it can be used to model a variety of user-defined activity, cost, and revenue scenarios to determine their profitability. CFP is also used to develop the hospital budget, establish new standards for intermediate product costs and treatment protocols, and project the effect of different marketing strategies.

Information to support these systems is fed from the hospital's existing operational and financial databases through interfaces. Interfaces have been designed to transmit data to these three systems with minimal or no changes to a hospital's current systems and/or operations.

Figure 15-3-1 presents an overview of the flow of information among these three systems and the base information systems. Note that the only required hospital feeder systems are General Ledger, Medical Records, and Billing. Optional feeder systems include Payroll and Materials Management as well as department-specific systems (e.g., Nursing Acuity, or Operating Room Information System).

This article focuses on the Department Cost Manager. Clinical Cost Manager and Clinical

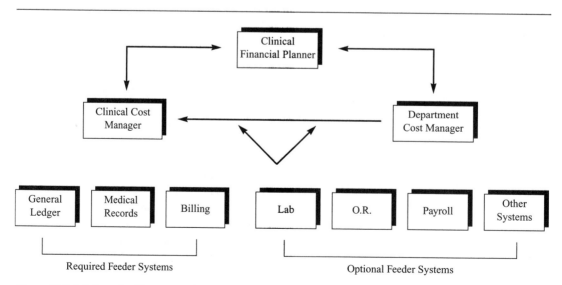

Figure 15-3-1 Information Flow among the Three Management Systems

Financial Planner will be discussed in Applications 15-4 and 15-5.

DEPARTMENT COST MANAGER (DCM)

DCM is a management control system for use primarily by direct (ancillary and routine) hospital departments. DCM's methodology views departments as cost centers rather than revenue centers (since end products, not intermediate products, generate revenue—particularly under a prospective payment system).

DCM focuses on the control and management of costs associated with intermediate products—procedures and services—that make up the end product or patient case. As a management tool, DCM performs the following functions:

- identifies intermediate products
- builds a standard cost for each intermediate product
- simulates changes in standard unit costs, department budgets, and staffing
- reports cost variances by product and department
- performs marginal cost analysis

In the DCM *product identification* process, the user selects and groups procedures and services into definable intermediate products. DCM's approach is based on the assumption that a relatively small number of procedures and services make up a high percentage of volume and cost. DCM interfaces directly with the hospital's database, which allows the user to complete this grouping and selection process online.

DCM's *product costing* process builds standard costs for each intermediate product. Within this framework, DCM identifies each department's direct costs by labor, supplies, and direct overhead components, distinguishing between fixed and variable costs. Because DCM is based on true cost accounting methodology, it can be applied to all hospital ancillary and routine departments.

DCM offers *department cost simulation* within the standards building process. By changing relative value units (RVUs) associated with each cost type, or changing labor productivity goals, overtime rates, wage rates, and so on, the user can model standard costs, department budgets, and staffing.

Variance analysis is a powerful DCM function and an effective mechanism for management control. Through variance analysis, DCM explains the difference between budgeted and actual costs by subdividing the variance into its component parts. By identifying these component causes of variance (volume and mix, utilization, and direct overhead variances), DCM provides clear definitions of cost accountability. Managers can thus be held responsible for costs they truly control.

DCM also provides information for *marginal cost analysis*. Because DCM distinguishes between variable and fixed costs, a hospital can estimate the effect of a projected change in volume on department costs. Such marginal cost data are also useful for determining the costs of additional cases or new programs. Other uses of DCM's marginal cost information include profitability analysis and more accurate pricing.

The DCM system includes these modules:

- Product Identifier
- Interface
- Standards Builder
- Reports

Product Identifier Module

Users define intermediate products by selecting and grouping hospital procedures and services in an on-line process. The end result is a defined, manageable number of intermediate products.

Assuming that, in general, a relatively small number of procedures and services make up a high percentage of volume and cost, Product Identifier allows users to select the exact volume percentage that will account for that small number of specific, individual intermediate products. The remaining low volume procedures and services can be grouped into one or more "other" intermediate product(s). Subsequent standard cost development and cost analysis then focuses on the specific intermediate products.

The product identification process is based on data that are fed directly from hospital volume and cost-related systems through the DCM interface table. This interface function minimizes the need for user input and allows the user to perform product identification on-line.

Interface Module

This module represents the interface between DCM and the hospital's database for volume, cost, and variable labor statistics.

An essential byproduct of the product identification process is the volume conversion factors that map the hospital's procedures (e.g., billing data) to the newly established intermediate products. The user can enter a multiplication or division factor for each procedure code to spread that procedure's volume to the products. These conversion factors become part of the interface table.

The user provides cost information to the interface table by specifying the unique feeder systems and account codes to be used for obtaining each department's costs and variable labor hours. As in procedure volume conversion, the user specifies any conversion arithmetic required for these cost and variable labor feeder keys.

All of this information becomes part of an interface table that is used to map hospital feeder data to intermediate products and departments. This key interface table is repeatedly used in building standard costs, generating cost variance reports, and so on.

If the user does not want to use volume and cost data provided through the Interface Module, DCM offers an override capability. This function allows the user to enter alternate data for standards development. The override capa-

bility has two primary purposes: to account for unforeseen changes in volume and cost after standard costs have been developed, or to enter information that cannot be accessed through feeder system interfaces (e.g., new procedures or departments).

Standards Builder Module

This module develops detailed cost standards by intermediate product. The key to this process is DCM's ability to associate intermediate products and their respective volumes with budgets and user-defined RVUs. Cost standards are built by cost type and cost category.

DCM defines nine specific cost types:

1. Variable Labor
2. Variable Supplies
3. Variable Other
4. Fixed Direct Labor
5. Fixed Direct Equipment
6. Fixed Direct Facilities
7. Fixed Direct Other
8. Variable Indirect
9. Fixed Indirect

DCM allows the user to establish a virtually unlimited number of categories within each cost type. Categories are subclassifications of cost types. For example, the variable labor cost type for nursing could be subdivided among R.N., L.P.N., and Nurse Technician categories. Unit cost standards would subsequently be developed separately for those and any other defined categories.

RVUs by cost type/category form the foundation for building cost standards. In an on-line process, the user defines RVUs for each product. RVUs represent minutes for variable labor but can represent *any* weighting scheme for all other cost types. Product volumes, combined with RVUs, yield a weighted volume for each intermediate product. The total budget for each product's cost type (or category, if applicable) is then spread back to the intermediate products according to the weighted volumes.

The Standards Builder Module provides additional functional information for variable labor costs. Standards Builder not only distinguishes among the various types of variable labor hours (e.g., worked hours, overtime hours, and vacation/sick/holiday hours) but also generates productivity measures in the form of standard ratios based on these different types of hours. The standard ratios can then be compared to actual ratios to monitor productivity.

The Standards Builder Module is designed to allow both "build-up" and "back-in" methods for establishing budgets and staffing levels for variable labor costs. Calculations for both methods are based on the given number of "specified work hours" to produce the products (as established by the weighted volume data described above—minutes × volume).

The *build-up method* determines the required variable labor staffing and budget given user-defined labor productivity goals and wage rates. The user establishes how many FTEs and dollars are needed by projecting certain labor ratios and salary rates against the given number of specified hours.

The *back-in method* develops labor standards and productivity measures based on an already set amount of FTEs and labor budget. The user "backs in" to labor productivity standards given certain parameters for overtime salary rates, vacation/sick/holiday percentage of regular paid hours, and so on.

Reports Module

DCM's cost variance and statistical reports can be generated at multiple levels, ranging from the whole hospital to a group of departments or to a specific cost category within a specific cost type of one department.

A user can obtain both single entity reports (which report one department or a group of departments combined into one total) and multiple entity reports (which report two or more departments separately on the same report). Single entity reports are most useful to a department manager. Multiple entity reports are more likely to be used by a higher level manager or administrator responsible for more than one department.

DCM variance reports explain cost variances from budget and thus provide direction for a hospital concerned with cost control. While a hospital cost center manager in the past has had access to the center's total variance (total budgeted cost less total actual costs), DCM can provide a variance analysis explaining changes in

- product volume
- product mix
- labor efficiency and price
- supplies utilization
- direct overhead utilization

The real power of this variance breakdown is that it allows for better cost control through identification of costs in categories linked with specific responsibility levels. Activity (volume and mix) variances are primarily the responsibility of physicians or case managers. Variances related to cost per unit (labor, supplies utilization, and direct overhead) are the responsibility of the cost center manager. Thus, DCM variance analysis allows for clearly defined accountability for both favorable and unfavorable variances from budget and will significantly aid the cost control process.

Application 15-4

Clinical Cost Manager

Robert F. Raco, BS, is currently President and Chief Executive Officer of Transition Systems, Inc., Boston, Massachusetts.

Peter W. VanEtten, MBA, is currently Chief Financial Officer at Stanford University, Stanford, California.

Clinical Cost Manager (CCM) is one of three systems that make up an integrated planning and management control system for hospitals. An overview of the three systems and a discussion of the Department Cost Manager (DCM) appeared in Application 15-3.

This system uses a framework in which hospital activity is viewed as a two-stage production process. In the first stage, resources are converted into intermediate products such as x-rays and lab tests. In the second stage, the intermediate products are grouped to produce the final products—treated patients, or "cases."

The goal of CCM is to provide the hospital with the management tools needed to treat its patients more cost effectively. This is accomplished by monitoring and controlling intermediate product utilization. Thus, while DCM assists in the management of intermediate product unit costs, CCM focuses on controlling the number of intermediate products used for patient cases.

CCM's primary functions are

- identification of end products (patient cases)

- development of standard treatment protocols
- periodic management and physician reporting for a retrospective analysis of case treatment performance

Unlike most other case management systems, CCM

- uses true economic costs (those provided by DCM) for case-mix costing. It is not limited to the use of charges or ratios of cost to charge.
- performs detailed case variance analysis (profitability, revenue, and cost).
- reports information using a flexible hospital-defined roll-up structure, by clinical subspeciality, physician, DRG or any other case-mix/severity grouping methodology.

ROLL-UP STRUCTURE

Figure 15-4-1 illustrates a typical hospital roll-up structure. The highest level in a hospital roll-up is the hospital. The first level of branches may represent attending physicians or the major clinical divisions (sometimes called departments)—Medicine, Surgery, and so on.

Source: Reprinted from Robert F. Raco and Peter W. VanEtten, "Clinical Cost Manager," *Hospital Cost Accounting Advisor,* Vol. 1, No. 8, pp. 4–7. Copyright 1986, Aspen Publishers, Inc.

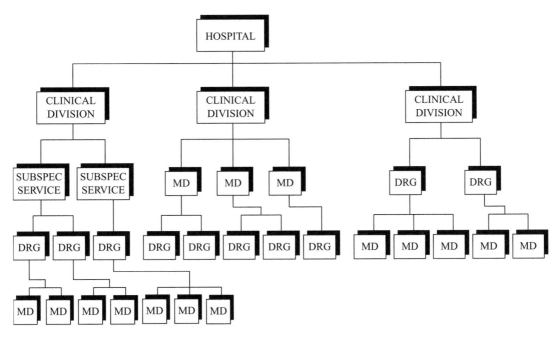

Figure 15-4-1 A Typical Hospital Roll-Up Structure

Each of the major branches, called "components," may have a different detail branch structure beneath it.

All CCM functions are based on patient-level data oriented to the patient *encounter* or *case*. Patient encounter data can be grouped into specific subsets, depending upon the clinical service, the physician, the DRG, and so on. This organizational hierarchy, or roll-up structure, allows CCM to sum the patient level data to mirror the clinical control structure.

A hospital can create multiple roll-up structures to characterize its organization from different functional views, and each roll-up can have as many as nine levels.

For example, instead of viewing profit, revenue, and cost only according to a clinical division structure (as shown in the example), the hospital might also want to aggregate all patient cases along a DRG or Principal Diagnosis structure to have a programmatic view of profit, cost, and revenue. These flexible, user-defined roll-up structures allow a hospital to define and group patient case activity from many different views at many different levels.

PRODUCT IDENTIFICATION MODULE

This module is used to identify end products, or case groupings. CCM's product identification is based on the following principles:

- Only those specific end products which represent a significant proportion of the hospital's cost and case load need to be identified. CCM enables the hospital to determine the breakpoint at which it is no longer meaningful to identify individual case types.
- Case-mix measures for product identification should be flexible (DRGs, severity of illness, etc.).
- Different grouping methodologies should be available for different clinical services in the hospital. (For example, DRGs could be used in Surgery while severity of illness is used in Medicine.)
- The user should be able to define and classify outlier cases, with specific ranges for outlier classification based on either charge

or length of stay. The objective is to remove cases with atypical resource utilization from case groupings. This will avoid skewing the treatment protocol and permit the user to focus on the resource-intensive cases.

The Product Identification Module generates reports that display case volume, average LOS, charges, costs, and cumulative percentages. This information helps the user to identify those specific end products which represent a significant proportion of the hospital's costs and those which can be grouped into an "other" category.

Statistical measures are also provided to evaluate the homogeneity of case costs within end product categories and to assess the efficacy of creating outlier categories:

- *Standard Deviation (SD)* is a measure of the spread of a distribution around the average (mean). The cost +/– one SD includes the cost of 67 percent of the cases; +/– two SD, 95 percent of the cases. The goal is to have the ratio of SD to the mean as small as possible.
- *Reduction in Variance (RIV)* is a measure of the amount of variability (of cost) that has been removed as a result of dividing a large group of cases into smaller, more homogeneous subgroups (i.e., dividing all cases for a clinical division into DRGs, or further refining it by creating outlier categories). The goal is to have RIV as near to 100 percent as possible.

Through an iterative report production process, different ranges for outlier categories can be evaluated. More homogeneous end product categories are created if standard deviations decrease and RIV increases.

In addition, alternative case-mix measures (Severity of Illness Index, Disease Staging, Patient Management Categories, etc.) can be compared with DRGs for end product identification. Key criteria include the number and percentage of end products that account for 80 percent of cost (the smaller the number of end products,

the better) as well as the statistical measures, SD and RIV.

Product identification is completed with the development of a customized interface that assigns the hospital's own end product classification system to patient encounter records. This information is in turn translated to roll-up structure groupings through online processing.

TREATMENT PROTOCOL DEVELOPER

This module develops a standard of resource utilization for each end product identified. Treatment protocols are developed in two steps or processes:

1. For each end product, the historical utilization of intermediate products per case is calculated. This historical standard represents the actual practice patterns at the user's hospital and as such is an internally generated treatment protocol.

2. Based on this historical data, the user can initiate a "clinical planning and budgeting process." Utilization history reports display historical end product volumes and intermediate product utilization with trends over time. Essentially, these reports show the "historical" treatment protocol, and they serve as an input form for projecting the new treatment protocol.

These reports are used in conjunction with the Clinical Financial Planner's (CFP) activity, cost, and revenue modeling capability to produce a clinical plan/budget. The resultant intermediate product utilization budget replaces the historical data as the treatment protocol. (CFP will be discussed in more detail in Application 15-5.)

External comparisons of treatment protocols with other CCM users offer a hospital a second way to "engineer" treatment protocols and an opportunity to go beyond currently available length of stay and charge comparisons.

Physicians from different institutions can compare intermediate product utilization and outcomes for case products. They can construct treatment protocols that represent preferred practice patterns— the most cost-effective ways of caring for particular patients. The results of this process are normative treatment protocols. (NEMC plans to offer a comparative database in the future to those users who would like to participate. Comparisons of the costs of intermediate products from DCM could also be included.)

REPORTS MODULE

CCM receives information on each case from feeder systems (ADT, Medical Records, Billing, and optional specific systems) and stores this information in several files:

- The demographic file includes demographic information on the patient.
- The encounter and procedure files contain the specific statistics (e.g., LOS) and clinical information (e.g., DRG) for each episode of hospitalization. (Outpatient encounter data are stored in a more aggregate form.)
- The utilization file contains the quantity and type of intermediate products used.

CCM generates cost and revenue for cases using intermediate product costs from DCM and revenue modeling from CFP. CCM identifies costs in a variety of ways for end products, using variable and fixed, direct and indirect, labor and supplies, and other categories.

On a monthly basis and for multiple roll-up structures, cost, revenue, case volume, and intermediate product utilization statistics are summarized. Each "location" in the roll-up structure has an actual and a protocol summary, which CCM uses to calculate profitability and variances for reports.

CCM profitability reports are structured to give the user information not only on the hospital's "bottom line" (net operating margin), but also on marginal costs and profitability. Profitability reports are produced for end products at any level of the roll-up structure.

CCM variance reports show the difference between budget and actual profitability, revenue, and cost. These variances can be caused by many factors that are under the control of diverse groups within the hospital. For instance, variances may be due to the actual volume of end products or mix of end products differing from budget (the activity variance), or actual utilization of intermediate products may differ from the treatment protocols (the utilization variance). These factors are primarily controlled by physicians. On the other hand, the actual unit cost of intermediate products may differ from the budget. Managers of the intermediate product departments are responsible for these variances.

CCM reports separate those variances which are under the control of the clinical divisions and physicians from those under the control of direct and indirect hospital departments. It does so by "transferring" the cost of the intermediate product to the end product at the budget standard variable cost, for both the budget and actual calculations. Variances due to actual intermediate product unit cost differing from budget are always identified separately on CCM reports.

CCM uses the variable cost (that cost which varies directly and proportionately with volume) to calculate clinical activity and utilization variances. Therefore, these variances reflect cost changes that should be expected to occur given the associated changes in clinical activity.

CCM provides detail variance reports that explain how case volume and case mix contribute to the activity variance. It also shows how both specific intermediate product departments and intermediate product usage contribute to utilization variances. CCM reports also show how individual physicians' practice patterns differ from treatment protocols by DRG and on aver-

Application 15-5

Clinical Financial Planner

*Robert F. Raco, BS, is currently President and
Chief Executive Officer of Transition Systems,
Inc., Boston, Massachusetts.*

*Peter W. VanEtten, MBA, is currently
Chief Financial Officer at Stanford
University, Stanford, California.*

Clinical Financial Planner (CFP) is one of three systems that make up an integrated planning and management control system for hospitals. An overview of the three systems and a discussion of the Department Cost Manager (DCM) appeared in Application 15-3. A discussion of the Clinical Cost Manager (CCM) appeared in Application 15-4.

CFP is a financial modeling system that offers a broad range of budgeting, planning, and simulation features. It links the intermediate product and end product production processes, allowing the examination of the interrelationships between clinical, operational, and financial activities of the hospital.

CFP allows the evaluation of the operating and financial impacts of alternative internal or external scenarios. The system encourages the exploration of strategies that affect case mix, number of intermediate products used per case, unit cost of producing intermediate products, and revenue generated by patient care. It also allows the examination of changes in the external environment of the hospital. CFP has a wide variety of strategic planning and decision-support applications, using either a top-down or bottom-up approach. For example, users can

- ask "what if?" questions at the clinical service, DRG, physician, and cost center levels to determine the effects on activity, cost, and profits
- estimate the financial and operating impact on the hospital of new programs or services
- calculate the cost of procedures for HMOs and PPOs
- evaluate the effect of changes in reimbursement or payer mix
- gather data for the establishment of cost-containment incentive systems for physicians or department managers
- understand the financial contributions of each case type or clinical subspecialty to the hospital
- simulate the impact of alternative wage and salary programs and inflation scenarios

CFP enables a user to test the impact of changes in a variety of parameters:

- activity
- cost
- revenue

Source: Reprinted from Robert F. Raco and Peter W. VanEtten, "Clinical Financial Planner," *Hospital Cost Accounting Advisor,* Vol. 1, No. 9, pp. 1–3, 7–8. Copyright 1986, Aspen Publishers, Inc.

The simulation process begins with *making assumptions* for a particular set of data. Each time a user creates a set of assumptions, it is assigned a unique "Assumption I.D." and is retained in the system.

A set of assumptions may be changes in numbers of cases for particular clinical services or physicians. It may be changes in labor cost factors for specific departments. It may be changes in payment rates from third party payers.

In short, there are a multitude of cost, revenue, and activity scenarios that can be simulated with CFP.

This diversity of possible scenarios is a function of two factors:

- the specific *variables* that can be simulated
- the *levels* at which the simulation is targeted

For example, an increase in cases (the variable) in the Department of Medicine (the simulation level) could be selected for examination.

Flexibility is further enhanced by the ability to simulate one or more sets of assumptions at the same time to create a new "merged" scenario. Since profit is calculated by merging cost and revenue at a specific level of activity, CFP enables a hospital to model *profitability.*

CFP serves as a useful decision-support tool because of these flexible multilevel modeling capabilities.

ACTIVITY MODELING

This module links clinical activity to demand for hospital resources (intermediate products) by case group. Patient activity can be modeled at any level within the hospital-defined roll-up structure (see the section on roll-up structures in Application 15-4 on Clinical Cost Manager).

The variables that can be simulated include

- case volume
- payer mix
- intermediate product utilization per case

COST MODELING

This module derives its cost data from the Department Cost Manager (DCM) (see Application 15-3), which determines fixed and variable labor and nonlabor cost components for each intermediate product and department.

The specific variables that can be simulated for cost *differ according to cost type:*

- Variable *labor* costs can be modeled by changes in productivity, the hospital's salary and fringe benefit programs, vacation/sick/holiday and overtime rates, and so on.
- Variable *supplies* and variable *other* costs can be modeled by changes in utilization and inflation.
- Fixed *labor* costs can be modeled by changes in the hospital's salary and fringe benefit program, staffing levels, and so on.
- Fixed *equipment* costs can be modeled by changes in price indices, the stock of equipment due to additions and retirements, and so on.
- Fixed *facilities* costs can be modeled by changes in price indices, the stock of facilities due to additions and retirements, and so on.
- Fixed *other* costs can be modeled by changes in utilization and inflation.

The cost detail captured by DCM allows CFP to simulate at three descending levels of cost:

- cost type within hospital (e.g., variable labor for the hospital)
- cost type within department (e.g., variable labor for a hospital lab)
- cost category within cost type within department (e.g., variable labor for lab techs in a hospital lab)

REVENUE MODELING

This module determines the gross and net revenue generated by clinical service, DRG, or physician based on the number of cases, hospital resources used, the payer mix, and the reimbursement environment. The system replicates hospital-specific reimbursement structures. The payer mix is case group specific. Among the factors that can be manipulated by the user are

- payer mix by clinical service, DRG, or physician
- intermediate product pricing
- free care and bad debt assumptions
- other hospital specific reimbursement parameters

For Medicare prospective payment, CFP can simulate changes in over 20 DRG factors, such as outlier payment, national and regional rates, and education factors.

CFP modeling offers multilevel simulation capability with a top-down approach. Assumptions at a particular level are spread downward and applied to affected lower levels in the roll-up structure. At the same time, CFP permits making simultaneous multilevel assumptions, because it possesses the logic to resolve discrepancies that might occur.

BUDGET DEVELOPMENT

One of the most useful applications of CFP is its contribution to the *budget development* process. A hospital develops its budget based on the best strategic and realistic assumptions for the following year. Using CFP's multilevel, multivariable modeling capabilities, the user can experiment with a variety of assumptions and scenarios to come up with hospital budgets for cost, revenue, and patient activity.

Once those budgets are set, CFP sends volume and cost information back to DCM to update intermediate product standards and budgets for the coming year; and sends patient activity information back to CCM to update patient case protocols and case volume budgets.

After the new fiscal year commences, CFP can model cost, revenue, and activity with the updated cost standards and case protocols passed back from its two companion systems.

Department Cost Manager, Clinical Cost Manager, and Clinical Financial Planner together represent a highly functional product-line management system that provides flexibility to define—and redefine different levels of product lines for the hospital. The true costs of these product lines can be determined—not only total cost, but also incremental costs—a critical factor in program planning and pricing.

The modeling capabilities can serve as the base for determining specific pricing strategies and seeing how those decisions, as well as changes in clinical practice and resource utilization, reimbursement scenarios, and cost inflation, will impact the hospital's bottom line. These profitability analyses can be performed for multiple organizational views of the hospital, either from a programmatic or from a clinical division standpoint.

Variance analysis shows throughout the year how close the hospital is to planned profitability, and allows the hospital to discover the reasons for a variance. This system creates a cost accountability structure that will help the hospital to bridge its clinical and financial operations.

16

Performance Evaluation and Incentive Compensation

Goals of This Chapter

1. Discuss the use of responsibility centers to aid in performance evaluation.
2. Consider the reason for decentralization and the strengths and weaknesses of decentralization.
3. Define and discuss responsibility accounting.
4. List the characteristics of sensible performance measures.
5. Discuss alternative performance measures for investment centers, including return on investment (ROI), return on assets (ROA), and residual income (RI).
6. Review alternative incentive compensation approaches, including bonus systems and executive incentive plans.

Key Terms Used in This Chapter

Bonus system; cost center; decentralization; incentive plan; investment center; profit center; profit-sharing plans; residual income; responsibility accounting; responsibility centers; return on assets; return on investment; revenue center; stock option plan; support cost centers.

Note: Key terms appear in italics when first used in the chapter. All key terms are defined in the Glossary.

INTRODUCTION

A critical aspect of control is performance evaluation. This chapter focuses on issues related to the evaluation of the performance of both organizational units and their managers. It also considers various techniques aimed at providing incentives to improve the performance of the organization's employees.

RESPONSIBILITY CENTERS

Health care organizations have long used the cost accounting approach of *responsibility centers* for the measurement of organizational performance. This has been done through the use of *revenue* and *support cost centers*. This section addresses the conceptual issues that underlie responsibility centers and their use for performance evaluation.

Decentralization

The use of responsibility centers arises because of the need to decentralize authority within every large organization. Some degree of autonomy must be delegated downward within health care organizations, in order for them to be able to run efficiently. It is impossible for top management of most health care organizations to make all of the decisions that are needed to carry out the organization's activities. Some degree of delegation of authority is essential.

The normal progression of most organizations is toward a greater degree of *decentralization* of power and authority as the organization grows over time. Large size creates a problem for tight control. No one person, or small group of managers, can have the physical capacity to supervise all activities and make all decisions directly in a large organization. Therefore, authority is delegated.

Some health care organizations are relatively centralized, whereas others are relatively decentralized. Even though some delegation is unavoidable, different organizations will keep relatively more or less control within top management. To a great extent, the degree of decentralization rests on the confidence top management has in the management team throughout the organization and on the quality of the performance measurement system in place.

Delegation creates a need for a system of performance evaluation. How can top management ensure that the actions taken by lower levels of management are appropriate? The better the system of evaluation, the more assured top management is that they will be aware of any problems that arise. That can allow for a greater degree of decentralization.

The Pros of Decentralization

The need for responsibility centers and some degree of centralization is clear. No one can make all the decisions that must be made in a health care organization. However, there are a number of additional advantages of decentralization. (See Exhibit 16-1.)

One of the most prominent advantages of decentralization is that it enhances the development of management talent within the organization. Managers in a decentralized environment are forced to develop skills as decision makers and problem solvers. This allows the organization to have a better sense of who has the necessary abilities and talent to be promoted in the organization and allows those basic abilities and talents to be cultivated and enhanced through experience. Lower level managers often have better morale if they are in positions of greater authority, and their performance levels are likely to be higher, than if all decisions are made for them.

Another key reason for having high degrees of decentralization is that it puts the power for decision making at the level where the best in-

---

Exhibit 16-1 Advantages of Decentralization

1. Development of management talent
2. Decisions made by those with best information
3. Ability to manage by exception

formation is available. As information about individual units and departments moves up through the organization, it tends to become distorted and dated. The manager on the scene is the most likely to be able to make a timely and informed decision.

A final significant advantage of decentralization is that it allows the health care organization to manage by exception rather than by rule. General rules are adequate in most cases. However, when exceptions arise in which rules are not likely to lead to the best outcome, there is a need to be able to have an exception to the rule. Centralized organizations tend to fear any exceptions, and rules are almost always enforced. Decentralized organizations have the flexibility to relax the rules when appropriate.

This highlights one of the most significant issues with respect to centralization. Does top management believe that lower levels of management are sufficiently intelligent and capable to determine when it would be best to allow an exception? Is the damage done by keeping to the rules all the time more or less than the damage done when exceptions are inappropriately allowed to take place?

The Cons of Decentralization

Decentralization is not without its weaknesses. (See Exhibit 16-2.) One weakness relates to the costs of training managers to handle authority. Another problem relates to the need for communication channels. Decentralization must also deal with errors made by managers. Still another problem involves conflicting goals and interests. Finally, decentralization requires a sophisticated reporting system. Each of these weaknesses is discussed below.

In order to minimize bad decisions, organizations must be committed to providing managerial training if they wish to be decentralized.

Exhibit 16-2 Disadvantages of Decentralization

1. High training costs
2. Need for rapid communication
3. Need to cope with errors
4. Conflicting goals and interests
5. Need for sophisticated reporting system

Managers have to learn how to make decisions. They must learn many issues related to the exercise of authority. All of this learning requires a costly investment in management education. Many top managers feel such an investment is well justified, whereas others do not.

In a decentralized organization, management must know what is going on as soon as possible. Even though lower level managers make decisions, top management wants to be informed of what is happening in the organization. Top management must be able to find out about any incorrect decisions and make adjustments quickly. Therefore, there must also be an ongoing investment in communication channels, which must be maintained over time. However, a centralized organization may need channels of communication even more than a decentralized one. In centralized systems, there is a need to feed information up and decisions down through the organization with a minimum of lost time.

One of the most difficult elements of decentralization is the realization that when authority is given to lower level managers, they will make some mistakes. Health care organizations must decide whether the mistakes will be more than offset by the benefits of decentralization.

Another problem of decentralization relates to the fact that each organization will generally have a mission statement and a number of goals and objectives to support that mission. As more and more managers have the authority to make decisions, the possibility exists that their decisions may vary from those needed to carry out the organization's stated goals and objectives.

A special concern is that individual managers will undertake activities that enhance their own performance at the expense of the organization as a whole. For example, if the radiology department is evaluated on the basis of its profits, then its manager may want to increase volume, thus increasing revenue assigned to the department. If the volume increase is for inpatients covered by the Diagnosis Related Group (DRG) system, the radiology department may show higher profits, but the organization will have higher expenses without any additional revenues. There must be some way to ensure that such conflicts between what's good for the manager and what's good for the organization are minimized.

Essentially, to minimize the negative impacts of decentralization, there must be a sophisticated reporting system. Such a system must focus on the issue of *responsibility accounting.*

Responsibility Accounting

Responsibility accounting is an approach in which specific units are established. Accounting information is then gathered for each unit. That information is then used to report on the performance on each specific unit and its manager. Reports are generated in a responsibility accounting system and generally reflect the costs and possibly the revenues and profits of a unit.

In a decentralized system, the budget acts as a tool of authorization. Each manager with budgetary responsibility is given a level of authority by that budget. It is important that managers take part in preparing the budgets that they must follow. That will help to ensure that the managers accept the budget and attempt to implement it. It is also important that managers be evaluated based on their performance with respect to the budget or plan.

Evaluation Reports

In some responsibility accounting systems, a single report that includes all costs is issued for each unit. In other systems, two reports are issued: (1) one for the performance of the unit and (2) one for the performance of the manager. In either case, the key focal point for managerial performance evaluation is the portion of the unit's costs that are controllable.

The basic premise of reporting for responsibility units is that responsibility should be equal to control. Managers must be accountable for the things that they can control but should not be accountable for things over which they have no control.

Defeating the Purpose of Decentralization

The role of decentralization is to place control at the point where costs are incurred. That should allow the manager who is at the point where costs can be controlled to have a greater freedom to take the actions necessary to control those costs. Most health care organizations do track actual costs versus budgeted costs for each responsibility unit. A problem often arises, however, from failure to delineate the budgeted and actual costs by the degree of controllability. It must be kept in mind that evaluations of responsibility centers should focus on human beings. We want to motivate managers to perform to their best ability. Some system must be derived to give managers the appropriate incentive to perform to their best ability in achieving the ends most desired by the organization.

Types of Responsibility Centers

To achieve the goal of providing proper incentives, responsibility centers are generally divided into *cost centers, revenue centers, profit centers,* and *investment centers*. Cost centers are responsible for costs only. Revenue centers are responsible for revenues only. Profit centers are responsible for both costs and revenues. Investment centers are also responsible for the source of funds used by the center.

Cost centers allow the manager to have the authority to incur costs. However, in cost centers, there is neither the authority nor the responsibility to control revenues. In many cases, revenues are not generated by cost centers. For example, the security, housekeeping, and medical records departments of hospitals do not generate a revenue stream. Therefore, their managers are evaluated based just on their control of costs of the department.

Over time, it is possible that some centers will start to have control over the generation of revenue, whereas other units will lose that control. For example, if a nursing home establishes a home care agency, it will likely be a profit center, because the revenues of the agency will be under the control of that responsibility center. On the other hand, many current revenue centers in hospitals are starting to lose their *bona fide* claim to being a revenue center. This is especially true in states like New York, where all inpatients are paid on a DRG basis. In such a situation, hospitals need to reevaluate exactly what degree of control any individual responsibility center has over revenues.

Developing Sensible Performance Measures

According to Barfield and colleagues,

> Managers will normally act specifically in accordance with how they are to be measured. Thus, performance measurements should have the following characteristics: (1) they must be designed to reflect organizational goals and objectives; (2) they must be specific and understandable; (3) they must promote harmonious operations between and among units; and (4) if financial they must reflect an understanding of accounting information.[1]

Managers can be expected to react rationally. That means that their behavior will make sense, based on how they are evaluated and rewarded. This issue is discussed in Application 16-1. However, that does not mean that evaluation must be based on strictly quantitative grounds. A number of qualitative measures, although subjective, may also be useful. Such measures can evaluate general competence, decision-making ability, problem solving, and so forth, based on a supervisor's observations.

Nevertheless, many managers are likely to respond better to concrete, quantitative measures of performance. Such measures create a specific goal to work toward and allow the manager to know how well he or she is doing. Quantitative measures, however, are not necessarily mutually exclusive. A problem often encountered is that by evaluating a manager based on only one principal measure, he or she may be given an incentive to act in a suboptimal fashion. Using several quantitative measures may get a more well-rounded and desired performance.

For instance, if profits are the sole measure of center performance, there may be a tendency to defer routine maintenance. Other discretionary costs may likewise be shifted to the future, raising short-term profits but creating long-term problems. Health care organizations should try to avoid these problems by carefully establishing several different performance measures, each of which ensures that managers work to achieve those ends that are in the best interests of the organization.

In the end analysis, there is no unique approach to the establishment of performance measures for responsibility units. However, given that almost all health care organizations must be decentralized to some extent, we must work toward creating a system of controls that gives managers incentives to act in the best interests of the organization.

EVALUATING INVESTMENT CENTERS AND THEIR MANAGERS

As health care organizations attempt to maintain financial stability, many have begun to invest in a variety of ventures to earn profits for the parent organization. However, net income may be an inadequate measure of the performance of an investment. Furthermore, the widely used *return on investment* (ROI) measure may give managers the wrong incentives. Alternative approaches, such as *return on assets* (ROA) or *residual income* (RI), may be better ways to evaluate managerial performance and to provide desired incentives in the area of investments.

Investment Centers vs. Profit Centers

At first thought, it would seem to be appropriate to evaluate a venture on the basis of the profits it generates. Such an approach, from a management control system point of view, calls for the establishment of the venture as a profit center. Profit centers, discussed earlier, focus on the revenues, expenses, and net income generated. Profit centers fail to account for the amount of capital the organization has tied up in the particular venture and may be a poor measure of the competency of the investment's management.

For example, if one were to have a personal investment choice between two projects, one of which would yield a profit of $100 and the other, a profit of $150, the latter investment would seem to be more lucrative, other things being equal. However, other things are not always equal. If the first venture requires an initial investment of $1,000 to generate the $100 profit, and the latter requires a $2,000 investment to generate the $150 profit, we would come to a different conclusion. In the first case, $100 is a 10 percent return on the original $1,000 investment:

$$\text{ROI} = \frac{\text{Net income}}{\text{Investment}} = \frac{\$100}{\$1,000} \times 100\% = 10\%$$

In the second case, $150 is only a 7.5% return on the $2,000 investment:

$$\text{ROI} = \frac{\text{Net income}}{\text{Investment}} = \frac{\$150}{\$2,000} \times 100\% = 7.5\%$$

The first investment is better, even though its profits are lower, because it requires a substantially smaller investment. Profits alone are not the key measure to performance. Profits must be viewed in relation to the amount invested.

To evaluate the investment adequately requires some type of measure that accounts for capital as well as profits. The measurement of capital costs is what differentiates an investment center from a profit center. Three common measures used to bring the investment into the evaluation are return on investment, return on assets, and residual income.

Return on Investment

Return on investment, or ROI, is the most frequently referred-to measure of performance for an investment. This measure is a ratio that divides the amount of profit by the amount of investment. Just as an individual would measure the success of a personal investment, so an organization would use ROI to measure the yield re-

ceived relative to an amount of money invested. If a hospital were to spend $1 million to establish an off-site surgery center, the ROI would show the return relative to that investment. This measure can therefore be a good indicator of how successful a particular invest-ment is.

However, this approach is not very good at providing managers with motivation to act in the best interests of the organization. Managers should always be evaluated based on matters that are within their control, as was discussed earlier. Suppose that a health care organization were to enter into a venture that requires a $1 million investment. Suppose further that the organization were to use $1 million of its own funds and that the annual income is $70,000, yielding an ROI of 7 percent:

$$\frac{\text{Net income}}{\text{Investment}} = \frac{\$70,000}{\$1,000,000} \times 100\% = 7\%$$

Alternatively, assume that the organization borrows $900,000 at an interest rate of 10 percent and invests only $100,000 of its own funds. In this latter instance, the $90,000 of interest expense (10% of the $900,000 borrowed) overwhelms the $70,000 of profit from operations, leaving a loss of $20,000. The $20,000 loss on a $100,000 investment is a negative ROI of 20 percent:

$$\frac{\text{Net income}}{\text{Investment}} = \frac{(\$20,000)}{\$100,000} \times 100\% = (20\%)$$

(Note that the ROI is calculated on the $100,000 invested by the organization, not the $1 million full cost of the venture.)

In these two scenarios, the ROI outcome was very different. The difference was the result of the decision of whether to invest the organization's own money or to borrow some of the money for the investment. Who makes that decision? The person who makes that decision has a substantial amount of control over the resulting profit and ROI. In both scenarios, the manager's control of operations was identical. However, with either profit or ROI as a tool for evaluation, the performance of the manager would be rated substantially differently. That is only justified if the manager made the decision over the source of the $1 million used for the project.

Generally, the manager who operates the investment does not control the source of the financing for the investment. That decision is made higher up within the organization. Whenever a manager is given a set of resources with which to work but does not control the source of those resources, ROI will not be an appropriate measure of performance.

Return on Assets

What alternative to ROI is available? Return on assets, or ROA, is often offered as a solution. If a venture requires the use of $1 million, then the manager should be evaluated based on the profits as compared with the $1 million in assets invested rather than with the amount of the organization's own money that it supplied. Using this approach, whether the organization puts up $1 million or only $100,000 will have no effect on the manager's evaluation, because the assets are $1 million regardless of their source.

Further, in order to ensure comparability, profits are used ignoring interest expense. That way, the profits and the investment are both numbers that are independent of the decision to borrow money. In the above example, suppose that net income were compared with profits, without ignoring interest expense. When no money was borrowed, ROA would be as follows:

$$\text{ROA} = \frac{\text{Net income}}{\text{Total assets}} = \frac{\$70,000}{\$1,000,000} \times 100\% = 7\%$$

When money was borrowed, ROA would be as follows:

$$\text{ROA} = \frac{\text{Net income}}{\text{Total assets}} = \frac{(\$20,000)}{\$1,000,000} \times 100\% = (2\%)$$

However, if the number used for net income ignores interest, then regardless of the investment decision, the ROA before interest expense would be as follows:

$$\text{ROA} = \frac{\begin{array}{c}\text{Net income}\\ \text{before interest expense}\end{array}}{\text{Total assets}}$$

$$= \frac{\$70,000}{\$1,000,000} \times 100\% = 7\%$$

The method is superior to ROI for the evaluation of the manager who does not control investment decisions but otherwise is responsible for the venture. However, both ROI and ROA discourage managers from undertaking ventures that are lucrative but not quite as lucrative as current investments.

For example, suppose that a hospital does not borrow any money and has a series of investments that have an ROI and ROA of 28 percent. The hospital might be quite pleased with any projects that have a return of 15 percent or more. What will a manager do if given the option of investing in a project with a likely 22 percent return?

From the hospital's point of view, this would be a desirable venture. However, if the manager is evaluated based on either ROA or ROI, adopting a 22 percent return project in addition to existing projects yielding an average return of 28 percent will lower the overall weighted average return to a level below 28 percent. It would be in the manager's interest to avoid any new project that yields less than 28 percent. Thus, under either ROA or ROI, the manager does not have an incentive to do what is in the organization's best interest.

Residual Income

An approach developed to overcome that problem is called residual income. In this approach, the health care organization would define a minimum desired return, such as the 15 percent described in the above example. All potential investments would be "charged" that 15 percent as a condition to determine whether the investment should be undertaken. Any profits left after that 15 percent charge would be accumulated as the residual income. The residual refers to the amount left after the base charge. The higher the total residual income, the better the performance evaluation of the manager.

This approach has an advantage over ROI in that the base charge can be applied to the entire asset base, regardless of whether the source of the assets is debt or equity. Further, because there would be some leftover profits on an investment with a 22 percent return, the manager would have the appropriate incentive to undertake such an investment.

The various evaluation alternatives are summarized in Exhibit 16-3.

Additional Considerations

In using any of the measures described above, a great amount of care must be taken to avoid having managers "game" the system. For example, it is very tempting for a manager to use cash to pay off liabilities at the end of the accounting period, even if those liabilities are not yet due. Although interest will be lost on the cash disbursed from the interest-bearing bank account, if the investment or asset base used for the calculation is simply total assets, the payments will reduce the base. When net income is compared with a smaller base, the ROA ratio rises. Similarly, if the base charge in the RI method is applied to a smaller base, the RI will be higher. Thus, it often makes sense to have current liabilities automatically subtracted from

assets in calculating the base in order to avoid such perverse incentives.

Similarly, fixed assets create a problem. As such assets depreciate, the investment base declines, and the ROI, ROA, and RI all rise. This can give managers incentives to postpone needed plant replacements and technological improvements.

This points up the fact that all of the measures require some budgeting approach rather than simply a maximization philosophy. Inherently, some ventures will always be more profitable than others, regardless of the skill of the manager. In any investment, we want to reward managers for doing particularly well with what they have. Thus, we should anticipate what the ROI, ROA, or RI should be and set that as a goal. Managers should be rewarded for their results relative to that goal. Furthermore, other objectives should also be included in any final evaluation. Thus, there should be at least a qualitative assessment of whether a manager is sacrificing the long-run well-being of the organization for short-run results.

CREATING COMPENSATION INCENTIVES

Many health care organizations are beginning to consider arrangements to enhance employee performance. Primarily, these revolve around

Exhibit 16-3 Primary Evaluation Alternatives

$$\text{Net income} = \text{Revenues} - \text{expenses}$$

$$\text{Return on investment (ROI)} = \frac{\text{Net income}}{\text{Investment}}$$

$$\text{Return on assets (ROA)} = \frac{\text{Net income}}{\text{Total assets}}$$

$$\text{ROA before interest expense} = \frac{\text{Net income before interest expense}}{\text{Total assets}}$$

$$\text{Residual income (RI)} = \text{Net income} - (\text{net income} \times \text{minimum desired return})$$

bonus systems that affect many employees and executive *incentive plans* that affect only a few employees. Exhibit 16-4 summarizes the various approaches to incentive compensation.

Bonus Systems

Employee bonus payment is one method to provide an incentive to employees to improve their performance. Historically, bonuses were rarely paid in health care organizations, largely because many third-party payers disallowed bonuses in calculating costs for reimbursement.

One by-product of prospective payment systems, and DRGs in particular, is that there is less emphasis by payers on how health care organizations spend their money. For example, under prospective payment systems, the payment per hospital discharge is the same, regardless of how that money is spent. That payment methodology has prompted a number of hospitals to offer to share savings with employees in the form of a year-end bonus in order to generate incentives to reduce hospital costs.

The bonus approach is almost the direct opposite of what historically has been observed in health care organizations. Many worked under the approach that if a department came in under budget at the end of the year, the budget must have been too liberal, and the next year's budget was cut accordingly. In such an approach, no sharing of savings takes place. There is no direct reward, such as a bonus; nor is there any indirect reward, such as increased staffing for the following year.

Exhibit 16-4 Incentive Compensation Approaches

1. Bonuses
   A. Based on individual merit or bonus pool shared by all employees
   B. Based on fixed goal or tied to volume of output
2. Letter evaluating performance
3. Executive incentive compensation payments
   A. Profit-sharing plans tied to stock price or to profits
   B. Cash or stock options

Given such a system, why should a manager even try to spend less than the budgeted amount? It is not uncommon to see a flurry of buying activity near the end of the fiscal year, as managers actually try to spend any remaining amounts in their budget to avoid budget cuts in the next year. Such behavior is clearly counterproductive to the organization's financial well-being.

Too often in budgeting, we lose track of one of the essential ingredients: human beings. We treat budgets in a very mechanical way. Yet the key to having a budget work is to make sure that the individuals within the organization have been given a set of incentives that make it in their own best interest for the budget to work. Bonuses are often used in organizations because they can give individuals incentives to take actions that are in the interests of the organization.

Types of Bonus Arrangements

Bonuses may be classed into two primary categories, although a wide variety of hybrid arrangements exist, and in fact may be more common than either extreme. One approach is a system based on individual merit. The other approach is one in which all employees share in a bonus pool regardless of their individual performance.

The use of a system based on individual merit presents the opportunity for the greatest increases in efficiency. Such a system gives employees a clear signal that what they do counts.

One of the principal problems with such a system is that a great administrative burden is placed on the organization if each individual (or even just each manager) is to be evaluated. Not only is it quite time consuming, it also opens the organization up to significant morale problems if the bonuses assigned are not deemed to be fair. Jealousies may be created that are so counterproductive as to offset much of the cost-saving benefit of the system.

The approach of sharing an organization-wide bonus pool across all employees is certainly easier to manage. Generally, the organization sets a system-wide target, and if expenses are below that target, part of the savings are allocated to a bonus pool that is shared across all employees. In some cases, the pool is divided equally per employee, in some cases, an adjustment is made so that those with greater seniority get a greater share, and so forth.

Such arrangements result in fewer people who are not getting any reward, and thus tend to be viewed with significantly less animosity. However, such an approach certainly does not solve all the problems. Those who make an outstanding effort often feel slighted because they see less productive workers sharing in the fruits of their superior efforts. Furthermore, because the direct link between one person's performance and that person's reward is removed, each individual can relax more and rely on the efforts of others. When each individual feels that his or her actions can have little, if any, impact on the ultimate bonus, all individuals have less incentive to find more efficient methods for the organization.

Linking Bonuses with a Flexible Budget System

Regardless of the approach taken to determining who gets how much bonus, it is essential that bonus systems be linked somehow to the volume of activity. If a nursing home spends 5 percent less than budgeted, but admissions and revenues have fallen 15 percent, there is little cause for celebration. In a system-wide evaluation, that is usually obvious.

Often, however, bonuses are rewarded on a department-by-department basis. Because prospective payment systems make it quite difficult to divide revenue rationally among departments, bonuses are often rewarded based on comparisons of budgeted and actual costs. In such an approach, it is crucial to adjust the budget for actual volume before comparing with actual costs. Otherwise, we may fail to reward a department appropriately for handling increased workload with minimal increases in resources, and we may erroneously reward a department that failed to cut variable costs in proportion to a decline in workload.

Quality Concerns

The use of a financial reward directly tied to each individual's behavior is a powerful moti-

vating tool. In fact, it may be too powerful a tool. There is great concern that the use of bonuses will lead to the cutting of quality of care. In considering a bonus system, any health care organization must specifically address the issue of how quality of care will be monitored and maintained.

Alternatives to Bonus Arrangements

There are alternatives to bonus systems that do not require the major effort of establishing a bonus system or create as much risk of reducing quality of care.

Probably the simplest of these would be to have each individual in the organization who has responsibility for a budget be evaluated in the form of a letter from his or her direct superior. Such a letter need merely indicate an awareness that a particularly good job, or poor job, was done with respect to controlling costs and meeting the budget.

This approach is obvious, simple, and usually highly effective, yet it is rarely employed. Bonus systems are a strong prescription and may be called for in some situations. However, we should not overlook the availability of some over-the-counter approaches that may be cheaper yet still strong enough to do the job.

Executive Incentive Plans

Incentive plans are a widely used approach to make it pay for executives to do what is best for the organization. In corporate industry, incentive plans are generally tied either to the value of the company's stock or to its profits. Obviously, for not-for-profit health care organizations, there is no publicly traded stock; therefore, that does not present a good option. The focus tends to be on profits. However, for proprietary health care organizations, especially the large chains, stock-based incentive plans are an option. Both approaches are discussed below.

Eligibility for Executive Incentive Compensation

Although incentive plans may be used throughout the entire organization, profit-based plans are typically limited to executives. In this case, *executive* is defined as those managers who can in some way affect the policies of the organization. The philosophy is that those policy decisions have an impact on the success of the organization. The group covered by executive incentive plans is generally much narrower than the group involved in the type of bonus plans discussed above.

The classification of an individual as being an executive is not necessarily simple. Some plans use a salary cutoff for determining eligibility. It is important to index such salary levels upward each year to avoid having an ever-increasing number of eligible managers.

Organizational level (who each manager reports to) can be used as a classification approach. If the chains of command are clearly drawn, this may be an appropriate approach. Often, this turns out to be complicated by the reality of how organizations have changed over time and the tangled webs that really exist as opposed to neat, theoretical organizational structures.

In large corporations that have had executive compensation plans for a number of years, most use either position title or salary grade level as the key indicators for eligibility.

Profit-Sharing Plans

Profit-sharing plans are generally centered around some target profit for a year. If the target is reached or exceeded, a portion of profits are distributed to the executives involved. However, setting the amount of the profit-sharing pool and determining how that pool will be allocated to specific individuals require a fair amount of forethought before the plan is actually put into action.

The Pool Size. One of the most important elements of profit-sharing plans is determination of how much of the profits earned will be given to the executives as a group. The amount ideally would be as small as possible, yet large enough to give executives a strong incentive to do their absolute best to manage the organization well.

Often, one of the key elements in determining the size of the pool is the competitive environment. The very best managers are in high demand, which tends to bid up their salary requests. If the manager is so effective that the financial well-being of the organization improves, a high salary may be justified. However, if the manager is hired but does not manage the firm as skillfully as expected, the high salary may make the organization suffer.

Furthermore, once hired at a high salary, the executive may relax. He or she has worked hard enough at previous positions to achieve a position with a high salary—and that salary is irrespective of performance. The use instead of a profit-sharing plan tells the executive that there will be high rewards for continued hard work and success, but essentially no rewards for resting on one's laurels.

Thus, the total compensation packages must be determined in a way that they are potentially lucrative enough to attract the best managers, but also weighted heavily enough toward profit sharing so that the executives have the desired incentives. Because the profit-sharing amount will vary from year to year, the trustees of the organization must determine what the pool should be in a reasonably good year so that, combined with the rest of the compensation package, they achieve the desired end. Suppose that the trustees of a hospital decide that the executives' incentive pool should be $100,000 in a moderately good year. The hospital now needs a mechanism so that the profit-sharing pool will automatically increase if the executives manage the hospital in such a way that there is a particularly good year, and so that the pool will decline if the hospital has a poor year.

Establishing such a mechanism is far from being a trivial problem. Suppose that the hospital is expected to make a $2 million profit in a reasonably good year. The most obvious method for establishing a profit share would be to compare the $100,000 with the $2 million, which would give a 5 percent result. Thus, we could establish the pool each year at 5 percent of profits.

One problem with this approach is that it awards a bonus even in years with relatively poor (although profitable) performance. If profits are needed for replacement of old equipment and buildings and for expansion, a $500,000 profit may not be a satisfactory result, and the trustees may not wish to use a formula that would award a bonus in such a situation.

One way to avoid this problem is to set a minimum ROA, with a bonus calculated only above that minimum. For instance, suppose that it is felt that no bonus should be paid unless the hospital earns at least $1 million but that an attractive bonus should be paid if the profits exceed $2 million. The $100,000 bonus desired at $2 million represents 10 percent of the profits in excess of $1 million.

$$\frac{\$100,000}{\$2,000,000 - \$1,000,000} \times 100\% = 10\%$$

If we use that as a basis for the bonus (i.e., 10 percent of the amount above $1 million), the bonus would be zero if the profits were only $500,000. On the other hand, they would be $200,000 at a profit of $3 million.

$$(\$3,000,000 - \$1,000,000) \times 10\% = \$200,000$$

Another approach would be to establish a sliding scale, such as 0 percent of profits up to $1 million; 2 percent of the next $500,000; 4 percent of the next $500,000; and so on up to some maximum percentage.

Alternative approaches ignore the absolute profits and focus instead on improvement over prior periods. It may be difficult to attract a top executive if results have been very poor for a number of years. It might take a long period to reach the results that would generate a significant profit-sharing pool. However, with a pool based on improved performance, executives will realize that a bonus is not totally out of reach.

Another way to determine a profit-sharing pool is based on industry results. An organization may be compared with some reasonably similar group, and the bonus can depend on the organization's performance relative to that group, based on one measure or a series of measures.

Dividing the Pool. The total incentive pool in a given year can be compared with the total salary level of all eligible employees and a ratio found. That ratio can then be used to divvy up the entire pool on the basis of relative salaries. The problem with that approach is that it fails to reward individual performance directly. That, in turn, weakens the incentive system that the plan is supposed to generate. Thus, many incentive systems rely on some measure of individual performance.

Generally, such measures require specific individual performance evaluation. Each individual is scored, along a variety of dimensions, and the total score is used to determine the relative share of the pool. According to Channon, selection of those methods should adhere to the following guidelines:

- Useful: Can the measure appraise the most important results? Does the measure isolate problems related to productivity?
- Easy to calculate: Are the measures easy to compile and calculate? Would different individuals make the same calculation?
- Controllable: Can the eligible participants have a significant effect on the performance being measured?
- Understandable: Is it likely that the majority of the participants can clearly grasp the measure?
- Fair: Is the measure perceived to be a fair and unbiased reflection of performance?
- Timely: Can the measure be calculated shortly after the end of the reporting period?
- Comparable: Can the measure be related to past performances?
- Flexible: Can the calculation be changed in order to meet rapidly changing economic conditions?
- Auditable: Can the calculation of the performance measure resist sabotage or manipulation?

- Sensitive: Is the measure sensitive enough to adequately reflect changes in performance from one period to the next?[2]

Using the above characteristics, a scoring system may be developed that will allow differentiation of performance among the various eligible managers. Although such an annual review may seem time-consuming and laborious, review of performance is an essential element in a management control system, and the effort will probably lead to valuable increases in overall managerial efficiency.

Stock Plans

Corporate health care systems have another option open to them in developing executive incentive systems: a *stock option plan*. In such plans, the executives receive at least part of their incentive compensation in the form of options to buy shares of stock at specified prices. If the corporation's performance is good enough to drive up the value of the stock, the managers will benefit because they will be able to exercise their options (buy shares of stock) at low prices and then sell them on the market at higher prices.

Since a corporation is trying to maximize the well-being of its stockholders, this tends to be an approach that can result in excellent goal congruence between the managers and the owners of the corporation. The managers are better off if they drive up the stock price, which is exactly what makes the owners better off, too.

Stock option plans are very complex, and give rise to a number of tax issues. A qualified stock option plan that meets certain conditions is accorded favorable tax treatment for the executives. A nonqualified plan has fewer restrictions but may be subject to a greater amount of tax.

Advantageous tax treatment is also available for "incentive stock options." These options allow managers to have some of their compensation taxed at long-term capital gains rates, which are lower than ordinary tax rates.

Stock options represent a complex area of federal tax law. Any corporate health care organization considering using stock options as part of its executive compensation plan should seek competent legal and/or tax counsel.

The Quality of Care Issue

The use of profit sharing and stock option plans creates problems because of the mixed mission of health care organizations. On the one hand, a profit is clearly desirable, because it helps to ensure the continued financial viability of the institution. On the other hand, it is desirable to make the profit as a result of managerial efficiencies rather than deteriorations in quality of care.

As with bonus systems, some fear that a profit-sharing mechanism may lead executives to cut costs regardless of the impact on quality. Generally, quality assurance mechanisms are at work. However, it remains a burden on the board of trustees or directors to make certain that monitoring controls are in place to ensure that cost cutting is not affecting quality beyond a specified, acceptable limit.

NOTES

1. J. Barfield, et al., *Cost Accounting: Traditions and Innovations* (New York: West Publishing Company, 1991), 646.
2. B. Channon, Executive incentive plans for hospitals, *Topics in Health Care Financing* (Summer 1986): 36.

SUGGESTED READING

Browdy, J.D., ed. 1989. Incentive compensation. *Topics in Health Care Financing* 16, no. 2.

Cleverley, W.O. 1990. ROI: Its role in voluntary hospital planning. *Hospital & Health Services Administration* 35, no. 1: 71–82.

Finkler, S.A. 1986. Evaluating investment centers and their managers. *Hospital Cost Accounting Advisor* 2, no. 6: 1–3, 6.

———. 1986. Executive incentive compensation. *Hospital Cost Accounting Advisor* 2, no. 6: 1, 5–8.

Lawrence, L., et al. July 1989. Compensation strategy motivates executives to achieve goals. *Healthcare Financial Management* 42–46.

Waller, W.S., and R.A. Bishop. October 1990. An experimental study of incentive pay schemes, communication, and intrafirm resource allocation. *The Accounting Review*, 812–836.

Williams, F.G., and G. Pearl. 1989. Employee incentive systems. In *Handbook of health care accounting and finance,* 2nd ed., ed. W.O. Cleverley, 349–372. Gaithersburg, Md.: Aspen Publishers, Inc.

EXERCISES

QUESTIONS FOR DISCUSSION

1. Why do we have responsibility centers?
2. What are some advantages of decentralization?
3. What are some weaknesses of decentralization?
4. What is responsibility accounting?
5. What are the four types of responsibility centers?
6. What are several characteristics of good performance measures?
7. What are the three key measures of an investment center? What are their relative merits?
8. Is the highest residual income reflective of the best manager or the best unit?
9. Why would a health care organization use a bonus system?
10. What are the advantages and problems of a bonus system based on individual merit?
11. What is the principal weakness of a bonus system based on an organization-wide sharing arrangement?
12. What is an alternative to a bonus system that still gives incentive to managers?
13. Why have an executive incentive plan?

PROBLEM

1. HCAA Hospital last year appointed Max Wealth as Director of Nonhospital Investments. In his first year, Wealth did an excellent job of investing hospital endowment funds. He opened a physician referral service, bought an ambulance company, and arranged several joint ventures in the ambulatory area. These initiatives were all quite profitable.

   In total, the hospital put up $10 million of its own money and borrowed $10 million of additional money for the investments. The preinterest income from all the ventures was $4 million. The interest rate was 10 percent, and the loan was outstanding for one full year.

   HCAA Hospital is now faced with specifying the basis for Wealth's evaluation for the next year. They want to be sure to give him incentives to continue his good performance. Wealth has no control over whether money invested comes from existing hospital funds or is borrowed by the hospital from a bank.

   a. Calculate the ROI.
   b. Calculate the ROA.
   c. Calculate the RI, assuming the hospital demands a 15 percent return on all assets invested, before consideration of interest cost.
   d. Suppose that next year projects will be available that will earn a profit of $1.8 million on an investment of $10 million. Which of the above methods will be the most appropriate for next year's evaluation of Max Wealth? The hospital would like to undertake projects with a 15 percent or better preinterest return.

   Ignore the effect of income taxes in this problem.

Note: Solutions to the Exercises can be found in Appendix A.

Application 16-1

A Review of "Accounting Systems, Participation in Budgeting, and Performance Evaluation"

Steven A. Finkler, PhD, CPA

Penno's article reports the results of his study into the relationship between accounting systems, performance evaluation, and budgetary participation. The focus of the study is on the economic value of participation in the budgeting process.

The author cites prior studies with varying conclusions regarding whether or not budgetary participation has an impact on employee performance. However, while the earlier studies examined participation and performance, they did not directly associate those factors with any specifics about the accounting system in place. Since performance is measured by the organization's accounting system, it seems reasonable to take Penno's approach, and examine the accounting system to determine its linkage with budgeting and performance.

The framework for the study is the principal-agent model. This is a common approach employed by accounting researchers to establish a model for economic analysis. It assumes that there is an owner (the principal) and a worker (the agent). The owner is unable to observe all

activities of the worker due to the large size of the organization. Therefore a system of motivating forces must be put into place to give the agent incentives to work in the owner's best interest. The owner must also have some measurement tools to be able to determine what the worker has achieved. This model is a reasonable one to employ in the hospital industry, even though it is difficult in some instances to define the owner. One can think of the hospital's Board as serving in that ownership role in its interactions with management of the hospital.[1]

Penno proposes that employees can do tasks that directly or indirectly influence the reported accounting results of the organization. An indirect activity is required for production to take place, but once done does not directly manifest itself in the financial results of the organization. Let's consider staffing for a nursing unit, to translate Penno's model into a hospital setting. A hospital nurse manager might spend time planning the staffing for a unit for the coming week. This might be done quite quickly, or might require significant effort. However, the accounting system will measure the amount of staffing used for the patients. If the acuity level is high, and staff consumed per patient day is great, the costs will be high even if the nurse manager made a significant effort to staff in a way to control costs.

Source: Reprinted from Steven A. Finkler, Review of "Accounting Systems, Participation in Budgeting, and Performance Evaluation," by Mark Penno, *The Accounting Review,* Vol. 65, No. 2, April 1990, pp. 303–314, reviewed in *Hospital Cost Management and Accounting,* Vol. 3, No. 3, pp. 7–8. Copyright 1991, Aspen Publishers, Inc.

If the accounting system in place simply compares the actual unit total cost to the budget, or even if it measures the actual cost per patient day to the budgeted cost per patient day, it won't capture the manager's effort. On the other hand, an accounting system which measures the cost per patient day adjusted for acuity might capture the fact that due to the manager's extra efforts, the cost per patient day, while higher than expected, was low considering the acuity level of the patients.

Thus, the basic theme of this article is interesting. Are accounting systems capturing the indirect efforts of managers, which have an impact on organizational results? If they do not, then managers will be frustrated. It is important to find ways to measure the efforts of managers that have a positive impact on the outcomes of the organization.

However, Penno loses track of this theme as he moves forward to develop his model. He considers that there are eight dimensions of managerial performance: planning, investigating, coordinating, evaluating, supervising, staffing, negotiating, and representing.[2] He asserts that it is likely that many activities within these dimensions are poorly measured by accounting systems. This is no doubt the case.

The mathematical model used by Penno to proceed in his analysis is rigorous but limited. It forces him to assume that indirect activities must be undertaken for production to proceed, but that varying levels of effort have no impact on production costs. Take away too much effort and there will be no production. However, above that threshold at which production takes place, additional effort has no impact on costs.

Little wonder then that he concludes that managers will not make an extra effort. Managers cannot be rewarded for extra effort, because the accounting system will not capture extra effort in indirect activities. Therefore managers will not provide extra effort, even if they are participating in the budget process. Penno goes on to indicate that "If top-down budgeting (no participation) is less expensive to administer than bottom-up budgeting (participation), showing a zero value to participation is equivalent to

showing a negative net value when administrative costs are also considered." (pp. 307–308)

One of the problems with modeling behavior mathematically is that one sometimes loses track of common sense. If more effort has no impact on cost containment, why would the principal want managers to make that extra effort? Of course they are not rewarded; the behavior is not doing anything one would want to reward. Penno has lost his theme. One does not want to reward hard work. One only wants to reward hard work that leads to some beneficial outcome. To accept the model as posed, one must believe that much of what managers do is wasted effort. Their efforts have no impact on results.

That is a strange argument. Most of what managers do may be indirect, but should lead to good results for the organization. If managers' efforts don't result in a measurable difference in outcomes, then did their efforts really have any effect? Should managers be encouraged to do things that don't lead to improved results? In order to model the problem, Penno establishes the fact that managers' actions have no impact on results, and then he triumphantly proves that managers won't work hard under those conditions.

The real question is whether they will work hard to do things that do improve outcomes, but that appear only indirectly in the results of the organization. The implications of this article are that it will be hard to motivate managers if much of their effort goes into tasks that have no direct impact on the results measured by the accounting system. That implication is reasonable, and would dictate a need to make the accounting system more sensitive to the actions of managers.

The author misses one other essential point. Participatory budgeting is not only a tool for improved motivation, but also tends to improve the accuracy of budgets. Line managers have more knowledge and expertise in their areas. Participation not only results in motivation, but also in preparation of a more sensible, workable budget.

NOTES

1. One could in turn think of the Board as being the agent for the ultimate owners. That raises the question of what ways the ultimate owners of a hospital have to provide motivation to the Board and to measure the performance of the Board. That, however, is beyond the scope of the present discussion.

2. These eight measures are based on an article by T. Mahoney et al., "The Job(s) of Management," *Industrial Relations,* February 1965, pp. 97–110.

Part IV

Cost Accounting for the 1990s and Beyond

For the last decade, there has been a growing literature critical of current cost accounting practices throughout all United States industries. The concern is that costing has evolved primarily into a tool for external reporting of financial results, rather than for the management of the organization. The concern has led to a movement to revise cost accounting practices drastically to make them more relevant. The criticisms of cost accounting and a number of suggested approaches for improvement are discussed in the first chapter in this part of the book.

One new technique that has received great attention is activity-based costing. This technique is also explained and discussed in Chapter 17. The underlying focus of activity costing is that overhead has become a major component of costs, and it is possible to improve significantly the accuracy of product costing by more closely considering the activities that cause overhead to be incurred.

The second chapter in this section, Chapter 18, looks at total quality management. Toward the end of the 1980s, businesses in this country, based on their observations of international industry, found that better quality does not necessarily mean higher costs. In fact, doing things right the first time, every time, might not only lead to a better product, but also save costs in the long run. Chapter 18 considers the various facets of quality management that are related to cost accounting in health care organizations.

Chapter 19 addresses the future of costing. There has been a growing focus on the costing and management of product lines in health care organizations. With this ever-increasing focus on product-line costs, what will happen to the traditional health care organization revenue center? What will happen to cost allocation in a product-line costing environment? These and other questions concerning the future of health care cost accounting are the topic of Chapter 19.

17

New Approaches to Cost Accounting

Goals of This Chapter

1. Discuss whether there is a problem with traditional cost accounting, and if so, determine its nature and cause.
2. Discuss the main proposals that have been made for modifying traditional cost accounting.
3. Explain the lessons learned from examining the Japanese approach to costing.
4. Explain what activity-based costing is and how it can be applied to health care organizations.

Key Terms Used in This Chapter

Activity-based costing; cost driver; job order costing; life-cycle accounting; process costing; technology costing.

Note: Key terms appear in italics when first used in the chapter. All key terms are defined in the Glossary.

IS THERE A PROBLEM WITH TRADITIONAL COST ACCOUNTING?

For the last few years, there has been a growing literature critical of current cost accounting practices throughout all industries. The concern is that costing has evolved primarily into a tool for external reporting of financial results rather than for the management of the organization. The concern has led to a movement to revise cost accounting practice drastically to make it more relevant. The question is whether such a revision is warranted, and if so, what approach is the proper one to take.

This issue is of particular importance to health care firms. The growing use of prospective payment systems has made an understanding of costs critical. Health care organizations have started to move toward better costing. For example, Application 17-1 at the end of this chapter notes that more than 70 percent of a group of surveyed hospitals had installed automated costing systems. However, the majority of the hospitals surveyed were still basing costs on ratio of cost to charges (RCC) rather than on a more specific procedure-level costing, such as that proposed by Cleverley (see Application 3-3 at the end of Chapter 3). Clearly, there is still room for further improvements in health care costing. However, such improvements cannot be made without a clear understanding of the current debate concerning problems with industrial cost accounting in America.

William Ferrara summarizes the academic's view of this current focus on cost accounting quite succinctly:

> Those of us who have spent a great portion of our lives studying, teaching, consulting, and working with cost/management accounting are both pleased and troubled by the attention focused on us and our discipline. We are pleased because it's always been obvious to us that our discipline is worthy of greater attention. On the other hand, we are troubled because we have difficulty believing that we are so out-of-date and in need of so much retraining.[1]

There is no doubt that industry has evolved over time. Organizations are more complex. They also have more sophisticated tools (e.g., advanced computer systems) to deal with the complexity. Accounting has not stood idly by for the last 50 years. In the last two decades, there has been a growing shift in cost accounting textbooks toward discussion of the elements of planning and control. Some textbooks have strongly admonished readers that cost accounting should perceive the requirements of external reporting as merely a peripheral function rather than the major purpose of costing.

Anyone can pick up a cost accounting text and find chapters on standard costing, cost behavior, breakeven analysis, capital budgeting, flexible budgeting, and variance analysis—all topics oriented toward the management of the organization. Yet the critics persist in saying that it is product costing for external reporting that has become the tail wagging the dog.

External reporting is not a new issue. For many decades, managers have been generating information not only to run their companies, but to report the results as well. However, several additional factors have come into play. One factor is the increasing competition from other countries faced by many American manufacturers. Why are we not competitive? For several decades, the primary argument was that our labor was more expensive, which it is. However, more recently, labor costs abroad have been rising, and less labor is used in the manufacturing process. These two factors should have reversed the trend of weakened U.S. competitiveness. However, now cost accounting has been accused of providing inadequate information for making product decisions appropriate to keep American firms competitive.

Another factor is the recent increase in the proportion of fixed costs and overhead costs relative to the direct materials and direct labor costs of making a product. In a situation with relatively more overhead, cost allocation issues become critical to product costing. Misallocations caused by cost allocation approaches used for external reporting may not be critical for external reports. However, if cost allocation focuses on external reporting requirements, management may be left without the accurate product-line information it needs to make wise decisions.

Ever since the introduction of Medicare some 25 years ago, the health care industry's costing practices have revolved around the Medicare cost report. The introduction of Diagnosis Related Groups (DRGs) presented most hospitals with a rude awakening. They really did not have much of an idea of what it really cost to treat different types of patients. This is not an accusation of the industry, because to a great extent, it had no need to know its true costs; it is simply a statement of the way things were.

Other industries are just beginning to catch up to the health care industry in their realization of the weaknesses of their internal cost accounting systems. This is an important development for health care organizations. The newly developed focus of industry at large on this problem, even if largely oriented toward the problems of manufacturing, can only help in developing alternatives that will aid the health care industry in the long run.

KAPLAN'S FOUR-STAGE COST MODEL

Robert Kaplan has been a leading proponent of the philosophy that one cost accounting system is inadequate for the needs of most modern organizations. Cost accounting systems become overly focused on generating data for external financial reporting and lose the necessary internal focus needed to provide information to help managers work more efficiently. For several years, Kaplan has argued that the current cost accounting systems in place should exist side by side with a new costing approach focused more directly on providing managers with the information they need to really understand what each of their products costs.

In a recent article, Kaplan reconsiders this concept, trying to answer the questions of those managers who feel it would be inappropriate to have more than one official cost accounting system.[2] The framework Kaplan uses is the development of a model of four stages of cost systems development.

The basic concept that Kaplan espouses is that it makes sense to have a cost accounting system to generate information for financial statements, another to collect cost information needed to motivate and evaluate managers, and a third system to use for making key management decisions. (See Figure 17-1.) Different costs for different purposes is an old accounting theme. However, the concept of using entirely separate costing systems has been proposed by academics only relatively recently. Kaplan argues that currently the best way to meet all three needs is probably with three systems, rather than with one system that serves at least two of the needs poorly.

Kaplan contends that the desire of concrete-minded individuals to have one complete cost system and to install it immediately is doomed to fail. We cannot move directly to the "promised land." According to Kaplan, any attempt to leap directly to "an entirely new, managerially relevant financial system almost surely will lead to a system with serious limitations for operational control or for strategic profitability analysis, perhaps both."[3]

Therefore he discusses the stages that organizations must move through in their efforts to achieve a workable, integrated cost system. The first stage is one of poor data quality. The second stage has a focus on external reporting. The third stage is one of innovation and managerial

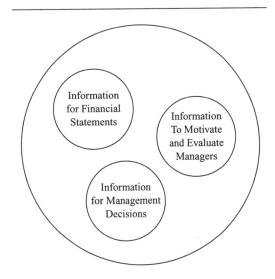

Figure 17-1 The Three Cost Accounting Needs

relevance. The fourth and final stage is that of the integrated cost system. (See Figure 17-2.) Most organizations are currently at Stage 2.

The Stage 1 level of poor data quality is generally found in new organizations. The data are not compiled accurately, resulting in data errors, math errors, large variances, and significant year-end adjustments. Most organizations have overcome such Stage 1 problems.

Stage 2, with its focus on external reporting, is generally represented by competent data collection. Data are not overly error-prone and tend to meet the standards and requirements for the various required external reports. At one time, costing systems may have been designed to provide management with information, but as external reporting requirements have increased, over time, the systems have been modified to meet the external needs. According to Kaplan, today such systems tend to have serious limitations with respect to product costing and profitability analysis.

Specifically, Kaplan feels that such systems are not timely, are overly aggregated, and are contaminated by cost allocations. Reporting on a month's operating results several weeks after the month has ended is too slow, according to Kaplan. Modern computer information systems should allow for a much more continuous flow of data needed for control actions. The departmental approach to costing yields too little information on what is happening with respect to each of the organization's product lines. This is not to say that departmental information is not valuable, just that it is not sufficient. Allocations of cost, although often needed for external reporting, serve little purpose but obfuscation when they are assigned to products or units that have no control over them.

Not only do allocations interfere with effective evaluation of units and managers, they create significant problems with the decisions that managers must make about individual products or product lines. This is especially true when costs really vary in some way other than that described by the cost allocations being used. For example, suppose that an operating room assigns costs to patients based on hours. The depreciation costs of the open heart surgery equipment will be assigned to all patients, even though that equipment is product-line specific. Decisions about all surgical product lines become questionable because all of the surgical cost data are tainted by the inclusion of costs for the open heart surgery equipment.

Kaplan's Stage 3 is a transitional, evolutionary stage. In this stage, all of the information from Stage 2 would be retained. External reporting would continue using the same information in an uninterrupted manner. However, an added focus would be placed on product costing with an activity-based cost system and on operational control with development of an operational performance measurement system. Activity-based costing systems are discussed later in this chapter.

Stage 3 has a focus on direct measures of operations such as quality, timeliness, flexibility, and customer service. Information is available on a more current and frequent basis. Information is presented in graphs rather than numbers. According to Kaplan, "The goal of these short-run financial summaries is not to control employees but to provide information to guide their learning and improvement activities."[4]

Stage 3 is not presented as a *fait accompli.* Stage 3 is the immediate goal that Kaplan feels organizations should be striving to achieve. The essence is to develop a system that will generate superior information for use by internal managers. The concepts he suggests are somewhat hazy. He has an outline, but it is up to the vari-

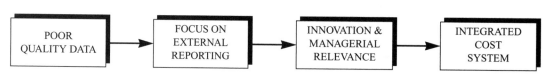

Figure 17-2 Kaplan's Four-Stage Model

ous organizations that take the step forward to do the hard work of determining the specifics of such systems.

Stage 4 is one of integration. In this future stage, the old costing systems of Stage 2 would be phased out. Data collected under Stage 3 primarily for management purposes would be reconciled to generate the external reports. In Kaplan's vision, this will be a reversal of the current situation. Costing now collects data for external reporting. Managers try to squeeze relevant information from that data. In Stage 4, costing will collect information for managers. External reports will be made by modifying the managerial data as best as possible.

It seems almost as if Stage 4 is simply Stage 2 with a different attitude. If we decide that management comes before reporting, it should be possible simply to tinker with existing systems to reach Stage 4 rapidly. Kaplan disagrees. He notes, "At this time, and with our present state of knowledge of what is possible and beneficial from newly designed operational control and activity-based systems, I am skeptical that we can develop the detailed systems specifications for a Stage 4 system."[5] Any attempts to bypass the full Stage 3 development will only result in a Stage 2 system operating on a fast, accurate 1990s computer, but not yielding useful information for management. Perhaps this explains the results reported in Application 17-1. That application found that hospitals were installing sophisticated computerized costing systems but were not really generating and using sophisticated cost information.

AN ALTERNATIVE: NEW GENERALLY ACCEPTED ACCOUNTING PRINCIPLES FOR ONE UNIFIED SYSTEM

Kaplan's voice is not the only one being heard on the issue of revising costing approaches. Not all agree with the vision Kaplan has for multiple costing systems, working in parallel until some undefined future point when Stage 4 (nirvana?)

is achieved. Dennis Peavey is one such researcher.

Peavey agrees with the growing number of researchers who are claiming that current costing does not provide a good measurement of profits, nor does it provide managers with the information they need for decision making.[6] However, while Peavey acknowledges the possibility of solutions such as the Kaplan approach of having a second cost accounting system working parallel with the current system, he does not believe that is the best approach. Instead, he proposes that the accounting industry adopt a set of new methods for accounting for product cost that would become Generally Accepted Accounting Principles (GAAP).

The trend of the 1980s into the 1990s has been for organizations to use more sophisticated technology. One by-product, at least in industry, is that the elements of cost in making products are proportionately changing. Direct labor costs are becoming a decreasing percentage of overall production cost, whereas costs that are generally considered to be overhead have been increasing as a percentage of the total.

The result is that product costing based on direct labor plus direct material plus overhead allocations is becoming increasingly more difficult. More and more of the product cost is based on indirect cost allocations, and less and less on direct costs. Unfortunately, indirect allocations are not very product-specific. They are based on broad averages of costs, assigned based on some general measure, such as direct labor hours. Such indirect costs may not vary in a reasonably direct proportion to direct labor hours.

While this trend may not be affecting health care organizations as severely as manufacturing industries, the issue is still a relevant one. Labor is not a very good measure for allocating many types of health care organization costs. Many measures used as a basis for allocations of health care organization costs are weak cause-and-effect measures at best. Cost accounting advances that can replace the key role labor has in cost allocations are of significant interest in the health care field.

According to Peavey, *technology costing* and *life-cycle accounting* have become sufficiently developed to be incorporated into standard, generally accepted accounting. Further, they are capable of providing cost information both for management use and for external reporting. The first of these techniques, technology costing, is oriented toward the control of costs and the avoidance of cost allocation problems. This approach could be incorporated into current accounting for an organization, according to Peavey, although the auditor's letter would probably have to indicate a change in accounting principles used by the organization. Life-cycle accounting might yield good costing and a better matching of revenues and expenses, but would in all likelihood require a change in acceptable GAAP. Each of these two costing approaches will be discussed.

Technology Accounting

The technology accounting (or technology costing) approach treats plant, equipment, and information systems as direct costs, as opposed to having depreciation costs simply thrown into overhead.

The philosophy behind this change is that depreciation is generally time-oriented instead of production-oriented. In a slow year, each unit of product (patient) is assigned more depreciation, and in a busy year, less. Nevertheless, the patients do not require differing amounts of plant or equipment depending on how busy the health care organization is. The alternative is an approach such as units of production allocation of depreciation cost.

For example, an electrocardiogram (EKG) machine may get old and wear out. Does it wear out, however, simply from getting old? Perhaps the machine can be used 5,000 times before it needs to be replaced. Suppose that we expect it to have a useful life of 5 years, and it costs $25,000 to buy. Traditional costing would probably assign depreciation based on an annual allocation, as follows:

$$\text{Annual depreciation} = \frac{\text{Cost}}{\text{Expected life}}$$

$$= \frac{\$25,000}{5 \text{ years}}$$

$$= \$5,000 \text{ per year}$$

Technology accounting would argue that it makes more sense to assign depreciation based on use, as follows:

$$\text{Annual depreciation} = \frac{\text{Cost}}{\text{Expected production life}}$$

$$= \frac{\$25,000}{5,000 \text{ uses}}$$

$$= \$5 \text{ per use}$$

In a year that the machine is used 1,000 times, we would still assign $5,000 of depreciation. However, in a slow year, with only 500 uses, only $2,500 would be charged. In a busy year, with 2,000 uses, $10,000 of depreciation would be charged.

Trying to adapt this to health care organization accounting will not be without its challenges. Does one allocate the depreciation cost of a health care organization building based on its desired occupancy over its lifetime, or based on some lower conservative guess at its occupancy? Will the EKG machine really wear out after 5,000 uses, or will we decide that it is obsolete, and replace it with a new model after five years, regardless of how often it has been used?

Life-Cycle Accounting

One approach to the costing problem that is receiving growing attention is life-cycle accounting. This has been defined as the "accumulation of costs for activities that occur over the entire life cycle of a product, from inception to abandonment by the manufacturer and consumer."[7] This approach is a significant departure from current GAAP.

First of all, it requires allocation of all revenues and expenses over the lifetime of the product. Thus, any start-up development costs, most of which would normally be expensed as research and development (R and D), would be amortized over the number of units of product expected. GAAP is more conservative in its immediate write-off approach.

According to Peavey, this conservatism creates a distortion in product costing. By writing costs off immediately, even though they generate future benefits, profits are understated initially and overstated in future years. Not only is the matching of revenues and expenses thrown off, but other problems may result as well. Development costs may become part of overhead, effectively being allocated to all products and distorting their true costs. The costs may be written off as general costs, not assigned to the cost of products at all. Because the R and D costs cannot be deferred, this may also be a factor depressing the level of R and D in the United States.

Traditionally, accountants have opposed an approach such as this because it may report unrealistically high profits in earlier years. If management is unduly optimistic about the number of units to be sold over a product's lifetime, they will defer costs to future periods when no revenues will turn out to be available.

For example, suppose that we spend $1 million today on research to develop a product that we believe will sell 1,000 units a year for five years. We would assign depreciation of $200,000 per year to each of the five years. However, what if we sell 1,000 units a year in the first and second years, but no units in the third, fourth, or fifth years? At the end of Year 2, our balance sheet would indicate an asset (investment in development) of $600,000. However, it will turn out that the asset is worthless. Users of the financial statements are misled, thinking there is a valuable asset.

Currently, financial statements are also misleading. The development costs would have been written off at the time of development. At the beginning of the first year following development, financial statements would reflect that no asset exists, because its costs have all already been expensed. In reality, however, we have the valuable development asset that will lead to sales in the future.

Accountants historically have chosen to err on the side of being conservative, at least partly because there is less room for manipulation. If R and D costs are expensed over the product's lifetime rather than as incurred, unscrupulous managers could intentionally overestimate the expected lifetime to make the organization appear more profitable than it is. Nevertheless, there are some proponents of the system who believe it is worth the risk, given the improved accuracy of reporting and the improved incentive for R and D.

Both of these methods, technology and life-cycle costing, can be integrated into existing systems and would not require two parallel systems, as advocated by Kaplan.

THE JAPANESE ALTERNATIVE

Interestingly, none of the various alternatives suggested so far come close to the costing approach used by the Japanese. It is worth considering their approach, because their competition has been cited as one of the primary reasons that current costing practice is felt to be inadequate.

Toshiro Hiromoto explained the Japanese costing system in an article several years ago.[8] According to Hiromoto, companies in Japan first assess the likely market price. Then they determine an acceptable cost based on that price. Production commences with the cost as a target, even if it is realized that the cost is unreasonably low. Over time, employees are encouraged to make improvements to bring costs down to the target. New processes are developed as needed to eventually meet the cost targets.

This approach is obviously opposite to the American approach of determining the cost and adding a mark-up to it. The Japanese cost allocation is set to motivate employees, rather than determine exact product costs. The managers want their accounting systems to be useful in creating a positive future position for the company, rather than determine the exact performance of a product at the current moment.

In such a system, the variances measured are between actual costs and allowable costs, rather than between actual costs and standard costs. Once allowable costs are within reach, there is a monthly cost reduction rate in the Japanese approach. This parallels a learning curve approach. Allowable costs are always being reduced. This creates a situation where American companies lose out if they are working toward meeting the same standard cost year after year.

Thirty years ago, there was a movement in this country toward direct costing and away from absorption costing. The idea at that time was that only those costs that are variable and that can be controlled directly by managers should be assigned to products. Responsibility accounting reigned supreme. Managers can be motivated only if they are assigned costs that they can control.

The proposed new technology and life-cycle costing techniques seem to be a movement in the reverse direction. Products are expected to absorb all costs that can possibly be assigned directly to them. It is argued that this may reduce the ability of costing to motivate managers, but it must be done to be competitive with the Japanese. Costs of products must be known exactly at any price. Isn't it ironic that, in Japan, the feeling is that accurate cost allocation is not so important, as long as workers are motivated?

ACTIVITY-BASED COSTING

One outgrowth of the focus on costing has been the rapid acceptance of activity-based costing (ABC) for manufacturing industries. The purpose of this section is to explain what ABC cost accounting is, why it has advantages, and how it can be applied to health care organizations.

What is ABC?

ABC is an approach to determining the cost of products (patients) or product lines (groups of similar patients). The approach improves the accuracy of costing different products or product lines by more accurately assigning overhead costs on a cause-and-effect basis. This is accomplished by using multiple overhead allocation bases. According to Peavey, "Activity accounting accumulates product costs and other financial and operational information based on the activities required to manufacture the product or achieve a financial or operational goal."[9] Activity accounting is primarily concerned with the determination of production and support activities. The reasoning is that, over time, direct labor will become less and less relevant, and a way is needed to capture indirect labor and other indirect costs and to assign them appropriately to different products.

The focus, then, is to look at departments such as purchasing. It may well be that a certain percentage of the costs of running the purchasing department relate to routine standing orders, and another percentage to special orders. Special orders may be extremely costly for a variety of reasons, such as the need to get bids. Are the costs of special orders ultimately being allocated to the right products (patients, in the case of a health care organization)? That depends on how purchasing department costs are allocated to purchases or departments. If such allocation is based on the cost of the items purchased, it may be a poor reflection.

The purchasing department is virtually always considered to be overhead; the costs of running that department would never be considered direct materials or direct labor in any production process. Therefore, those costs are almost always allocated to the revenue centers of the organization. A common allocation approach would be based on dollar value of items ordered. Thus, if the operating room of a hospital consumed 10 percent of the dollar value of all items ordered by purchasing, it would be allocated 10 percent of the cost of the purchasing department, in the step-down allocation process.

However, suppose that the operating room is also responsible for most of the special orders placed. If the special orders are typically for low-volume, specialized items, such as a particular porcine heart valve or a special type of suture, then the other departments may be effectively subsidizing the operating room.

The ABC solution to this problem is to analyze the activities of the purchasing department. First, it must be determined whether special orders are significantly different from routine orders. If so, then an estimate must be made of how much of the department's efforts relate to special orders and how much to routine orders. Assume that half of the department's costs of operations relate to special orders, and the other half to routine orders. Further assume that the cost of special orders is not dependent on the cost of the items ordered.

In that case, a new *cost driver* has been determined. A cost driver is simply some activity that is responsible for costs being incurred. More of that activity drives up costs. The cost driver in this case is special orders. Half of the purchasing department costs relate to special orders. That cost relates to the number of special orders. Under ABC, the purchasing department cost will now be allocated two ways. Half of the cost relates to routine orders and can be allocated by the old method. The other half relates to special orders and will be allocated on the basis of the number of special orders.

ABC considers overhead items that we generally take for granted as not having a cause-and-effect relationship. Activity costing proposes that often there is some specific activity that causes overhead costs to be incurred. Investigation will allow for identification of the crucial causal activity and determination of a volume measure that can be used to assign costs based on that activity ultimately to different product lines. The main difference from traditional costing would be the avoidance of allocating costs based on some simple algorithm, such as allocating purchasing costs based on equal shares per patient day or per dollar of purchase cost.

Not only does activity costing improve product costing, useful for decision making and for external reporting, it also provides information to help control costs. Once the true costs of special orders are considered and clearly identified in product costs, it may be more possible to get managers to avoid making such special orders.

This approach is allowable under current GAAP. It simply requires more sophisticated analysis of costs. If the impact of the change is significant, however, it may require a notation in the audit letter concerning a change in accounting method.

If activity costing is pushed to its ultimate, however, a change in GAAP would be required. Activity costing could be used to assign more accurately a variety of general and administrative expenses to specific patients or types of patients. If activities can be identified and measured, the organization could gain the advantage of better knowledge of what different products really cost by extending activity costing to these areas. This means that some costs that are currently period costs would become product costs that are assigned to inventory and do not become an expense until the product is sold. That, however, would not be acceptable for external reporting under existing accounting principles.

Why Use ABC?

There are two primary reasons for using such an approach. First, the cost information generated will be more accurate. Therefore, better decisions can be made. The general ABC argument is that most industries really do not have a good sense of which of their products or services are profitable and which lose money. The second reason is that employees will be more cost conscious and will spend less money if they use ABC information.

Consider the purchasing department/operating room example. The surgical patients who require special-ordered items are being undercosted by the historical system. It may appear that a particular type of surgery is profitable. However, there are always special orders associated with it. The true purchasing department cost of those orders has never accurately been associated with the departments and patients that caused the special orders.

Once the new cost driver is in place, that will change. The operating room will be directly charged for each special order. It can then assign the order to specific patients. This, in turn, will provide more accurate information about the cost of care for each type of patient. That, in turn, can lead the organization to revising its marketing strategy for different patient product lines.

It is also possible that ABC will directly reduce spending, even if the number and mix of patients is unchanged. Currently, the operating room in this example is a free rider. It benefits from getting special orders whenever it wants, without having to bear the burden. Once the purchasing department costs are directly assigned to the department that causes them to be incurred, there is likely to be a substantial reduction in the number of unnecessary orders.

Clearly, the methodology here does not apply only to the purchasing department and the operating room. Proponents of ABC would argue that every indirect cost within a department, and all indirect departments (i.e., nonrevenue cost centers), must be examined to determine a set of new cost drivers that can be used for allocations to patients. Those drivers, when taken as a whole, can result in dramatic improvements in the accuracy of the cost measurement for each product.

Allocation Principles

In order to understand fully the issue raised by ABC, one must consider some basic rudiments of product costing and cost allocation. The focus of product costing is on assignment of the costs the organization incurs to each unit of production (each patient) that causes the costs to be incurred. If we could do that with 100 percent accuracy, at no data collection cost, we would. In practice, we can never do it with 100 percent accuracy, and the more accurate we get, the more costly the data collection generally becomes.

This becomes most obvious when one considers whether to use *job-order costing, process costing,* or some in-between method. Job-order is generally considered the most accurate costing method. Specific, detailed records are kept for the actual resources consumed by each spe-

cific job. In contrast, process costing averages costs over a large number of jobs. If we use process costing for units (patients) that consume substantially different resources, our product costing will be very inaccurate.

Note that this is exactly what ABC hopes to avoid. Therefore, it is clear, with or without ABC, that a more specific, job-order approach should be used when there are different jobs or different types of product. In the health care industry, that is clearly the case. Each patient is unique. Therefore, the best costing (if data were free) would be total specification of the resources each patient consumed. Failing that, there should at least be highly accurate costing by product line (e.g., for each DRG or cluster of DRGs).

What does highly accurate costing mean? Certainly, it means that within each department, there should be some measure of the direct consumption of resources. Therefore, the labor and direct supplies used for each patient should be associated with each patient. That is what we expect to observe in a job-order system.

Such a system would not necessarily require direct observation of each patient. Special studies could be done and standards established. Therefore, each hernia patient could be assigned labor and materials costs according to the standard consumption expected, based on the special study.

If the study made a good estimate of the actual resources consumed on average by that type of patient, the results should be reasonable. Of course, special studies, although less expensive than direct observation of each patient, are still costly.

Furthermore, job-order type costing still does not address the issue of indirect costs or overhead. In fact, it is the indirect cost problem that has led to the nationwide movement to use an ABC approach.

Allocating Indirect Costs

What are *indirect costs*? Essentially, they are any costs that are not *direct costs*. Direct costs are those costs which can be directly traced to and associated with each unit of production on a cause-and-effect basis.

In other words, the major provision of care costs that any patient causes us to incur are direct costs. Clearly, the labor of nurses and technicians caring for the patient are direct costs. The clinical supplies used for the patient are direct costs. Anything that is not a direct cost is an indirect cost.

However, traditionally, many direct costs have been treated as indirect costs. This is at the heart of the ABC issue. Suppose that a folder is used for a patient medical record. The cost of the folder is generally treated as part of the indirect costs of the department, despite the fact that the cost could be traced directly to a patient. In all probability, that cost will become part of a per diem allocation to the patient. However, what if one patient stays two days, and another stays four days, yet they each require an identical medical record folder? Clearly, there will be an inaccuracy: one patient is charged twice as much as another for the same exact item, simply because of the longer length of stay.

It costs money to collect cost information. Is it worth the effort to assign specific costs to each patient for items that are very minor in expense or that are hard to associate with specific patients? For example, consider the costs of laundry. The laundry costs for each patient are far greater than the cost of the folder for the medical record. However, the cost of tracking each sheet and towel has been considered to be greater than the value of the information.

Health care organizations allocate the cost of laundry to departments based on the number of pounds used. The departments allocate the cost to their patients. The result is more accurate than simply an organization-wide per diem (process costing approach). However, it is less accurate than tracking the laundry per patient (job-order direct cost approach). So laundry becomes an indirect cost, not because there is no specific, patient-by-patient, cause-and-effect relationship, but rather because it is simply too expensive to track that relationship.

Thus, a direct cost is not simply one that can be tracked to each specific patient on a cause-and-effect basis. The determination of whether a cost is treated as direct or indirect must also be based on the relative costs of obtaining the information and the benefit of the more accurate information.

ABC advocates point out that over the twentieth century, for most manufacturing organizations, the indirect costs have become a larger and larger share of the total. Originally, when manufacturing was very labor-intensive, the vast majority of costs resided in direct labor and direct materials. Indirect costs, ranging from administration and supervision through lubricating oils and light bulbs, were a very minor part of the production cost. As such, any distortions created by the allocation of indirect costs were not serious problems. However, as automation creates production environments in which labor and materials become a smaller share of total costs, accurate allocation of indirect costs becomes more important for overall accuracy of costing.

ABC does not suggest that more costs be made direct. Rather, it advocates reexamination of the way that indirect costs are allocated. Currently, most departments allocate indirect costs on one basis. In general industry, direct labor hours or direct labor dollars are the most common allocation bases. Machine hours are another common base. These bases tend to focus on *volume*. How many units were produced? How many patients were treated? How many patient days were there?

Volume, however, may not be the most appropriate base for making accurate allocations. Costs may be driven primarily by a wide variety of activities that relate to the product in a cause-and-effect way. For example, as discussed above, special orders will affect purchasing.

Another common ABC example is set-up time. Set-ups are an example of an activity undertaken by supervisors to get a job into production. Most production overhead costs are allocated based on units of production. If 5,000 units are produced, and there is $10,000 of total department setup time, the cost is $2 per unit ($10,000/5,000 units = $2/unit).

Suppose, however, that there were ten jobs, each with one set-up, at a cost of $1,000 per set-up. If 1 job produced only 10 units, while 9 jobs produced around 550 units each, there is a severe misallocation. The low-volume job incurred $1,000 worth of supervisor time for its set-up for just 10 units, or $100 per unit. However, under traditional indirect cost allocation, those 10 units would be averaged with all the other units and be charged a set-up cost of only $2 per unit. The job is undercosted by $98 per unit.

In essence, even job-order companies allocate *indirect* costs on a process costing basis. If a distortion such as that described above occurs, the organization can be making products that cause it to lose enormous amounts of money without even knowing it. Elimination of such products would eliminate the set-up and reduce the organization's costs.

An ABC Example

Table 17-1 provides some basic information about a hypothetical (and obviously simplified) hospital pharmacy for one month. The pharmacy has dispensed 11,100 doses. The vast majority (10,000) was pills. The next largest volume related to simple drug reconstitutions. The lowest volume was for highly customized total parenteral nutrition (TPN) solutions. Table 17-1 indicates the number of pharmacist labor hours needed, the drug cost for each type of pharmaceutical, and the supplies for each.

Table 17-2 indicates the indirect costs for the pharmacy department. These are all costs incurred within the pharmacy itself. The administration costs include managerial, secretarial, clerical, and other internal administration costs.

Table 17-1 All Pharmacy Costs

Pharmaceutical Type	Labor Hours	Drug Cost ($)	Supplies ($)	Volume
A. Pills	500	10,000	2,000	10,000
B. Simple Reconstitution	100	10,000	1,000	1,000
C. Special TPN	20	3,000	500	100
Totals	620	23,000	3,500	11,100

Table 17-2 Overhead Costs

Cost Item	Overhead Cost
Administration	$12,000
Pharmacists	18,600
Supplies	3,500
Total	$34,100

The pharmacist costs are generally treated as indirect, even though one could classify them as direct labor. Historically, many hospitals felt it was not worthwhile to measure the amount of time spent by pharmacists dispensing specific medications. Therefore, the labor is an indirect cost.

Supplies are similarly treated as indirect. Some supplies are clearly indirect—such as office supplies used by secretaries and clerks. Those are included in the administration line. The supplies listed for $3,500 in Tables 17-1 and 17-2 refer to clinical supplies that could be directly associated with each dose. Again, this generally has not been done in pharmacy costing for most hospitals.

The goal of the allocation of indirect costs would be to attempt to charge each patient for the costs he or she causes to be incurred. The pharmacist labor cost and the supply cost, as well as the administrative costs of the department, must be allocated to the specific doses. A traditional approach would consist of dividing the total indirect costs by the total cost of the drugs to get an overhead rate as follows:

$$\frac{\$34,100 \text{ (Table 17-2)}}{\$23,000 \text{ (Table 17-1)}} = \$1.483$$

The $1.483 represents the amount of indirect overhead to be charged per dollar cost of pharmaceutical dispensed. Because the direct drug cost for pills was $10,000 (see Table 17-1), the indirect cost allocation to pills would be as follows:

$$\$10,000 \times \$1.483 = \$14,830$$

The same amount would be allocated to simple reconstitutions, because they also had a $10,000 direct cost for drugs. The TPN solutions had a direct drug cost of $3,000, so they would be assigned indirect costs of the following:

$$\$3,000 \times \$1.483 = \$4,449$$

Table 17-3 shows the resulting cost per drug dispensed, using this traditional approach. The direct drug cost for each type is added to the indirect cost to get a total for that type of drug. This total is divided by volume to get a cost per unit. The result is that the pill costs $2.48 per dose dispensed, the simple reconstituted drug costs $24.83, and the TPN costs $74.49. This appears to be a quite reasonable outcome.

However, activity-based costing would contest the notion that these results are reasonable. The allocation of the overhead was based on the dollar value of the drugs dispensed. Is that the factor that really drives the other costs in the pharmacy department?

The administrative costs are probably the hardest for which to determine a cost driver. Exactly what is related to supervisory costs and clerical costs? Do they rise with the number of prescriptions, the cost of the drugs, or some other factor? Generally, supervision costs tends to be related to the personnel being supervised. Therefore, we could hypothesize that the best cost driver available would be the number of hours worked by the pharmacists. The more hours of pharmacist work, the greater the need for supervision and other general administration.

What drives the cost of pharmacists? Is it the cost of the drugs they are dispensing? Is it pa-tient days? (Many pharmacy departments focus on department costs per patient day.) Clearly, the number of pharmacist hours is what drives pharmacist cost. If we can determine the hours spent on each type of drug dispensed, we can best assign pharmacist cost. Essentially, this implies allocating the indirect pharmacist cost the same way it would be assigned if it were treated as a direct cost on a job-order basis.

How should supplies be allocated? Given that administration and pharmacist time will be allocated based on pharmacist hours, should supplies be allocated in the same proportion? ABC would argue strongly against that. There is no reason to assume that the supplies are consumed in direct proportion with time spent. It might take a long time to reconstitute a drug, yet not take many supplies to do it. A better approach would be to do a special study of supplies used by different types of drugs and to develop a standard cost for each type of drug, independent of other factors, such as time.

Table 17-4 presents an ABC approach to allocating the pharmacy cost. The direct cost of drugs is unchanged. The indirect administrative cost is now allocated based on direct labor hours. Because the administration cost was $12,000 (from Table 17-2), and there were 620 pharmacist hours worked (from Table 17-1), the administrative allocation is $19.355 per hour:

$$\frac{\$12,000}{620 \text{ hours}} = \$19.355 \text{ per hour}$$

Similarly, the pharmacist time is allocated based on the hourly cost as follows:

Table 17-3 Traditional Costing

| Cost Item | Drug Type | | | |
	A. Pill	*B. Reconstitution*	*C. TPN*	*Total*
Drugs	$10,000	$10,000	$3,000	$23,000
Indirect cost	14,830	14,830	4,449	34,100
Total	$24,830	$24,830	$7,449	$57,100
Divided by volume	÷ 10,000	÷ 1,000	÷ 100	
Cost per Dose	$ 2.48	$ 24.83	$74.49	

Table 17-4 ABC Approach

| Cost Item | Drug Type | | | |
	A. Pill	B. Reconstitution	C. TPN	Total
Drugs	$10,000	$10,000	$3,000	$23,000
Administration	9,678	1,936	387	12,000
Pharmacists	15,000	3,000	600	18,600
Supplies	2,000	1,000	500	3,500
Total	$ 36,678	$15,936	$4,487	$57,100
Divided by volume	÷ 10,000	÷ 1,000	÷ 100	
Cost per Dose	$ 3.67	$ 15.94	$44.87	

$$\frac{\$18,600}{620 \text{ hours}} = \$30 \text{ per hour}$$

Table 17-1 indicated that 500 pharmacist hours were spent dispensing pills, so the total administrative cost related to pills is $9,678 (500 hours × $19.355). Similarly, the pharmacist cost is $15,000 (500 hours × $30).

The supplies would warrant a study to reveal the cost of supplies used per dose. Suppose that the study reveals the following costs, which are consistent with the information given in Table 17-1:

Drug Type	Supplies Cost/Dose
A. Pill	$ .20
B. Simple Reconstitution	1.00
C. TPN	5.00

The total supply cost for pills would then be $2,000 ($.20 × 10,000).

Looking at Table 17-4, we see that the newly calculated cost per item is substantially different from those calculated in Table 17-3. The cost per pill has risen nearly 50 percent from $2.48 to $3.67. The cost of reconstituting a drug is now measured as being $15.94 instead of $24.83. The most dramatic change is in the area of special TPN. In Table 17-3, it was calculated at $74.49 but is now shown to only cost $44.87.

Apparently, drugs of Type B and C use costly ingredients. Because of that, they were assigned large amounts of pharmacist labor, supply cost, and administrative cost. However, if the ABC approach is more accurate, then the true cost of those drugs is much less than had been thought.

If in fact the cost drivers selected to allocate the indirect costs make sense, then the ABC approach will be more accurate, and managers will be able to make better decisions. See Application 17-2 for another ABC example.

Does ABC Make Sense for Health Care Organizations?

The ABC approach has the potential to improve costing substantially. Because it still uses allocations of indirect costs rather than making them direct, in many cases, it can be done on a reasonably cost-effective basis.

ABC is not a new technique; it merely relies on a basic cost allocation principle. The more accurate we want costing to be, the greater the number of overhead application bases that are needed, because different costs vary based on different items. ABC introduces the language of cost drivers and activities to this basic allocation principle.

ABC does focus one's attention on the difference between volume-driven costs and activity-driven costs. It points out that there is a definite possibility of overallocating overhead to high-volume products and underallocating to low-volume products. This was the case in the set-up example. Caution is advised, however, for health care organizations. In the pharmacy example discussed above, just the reverse happened. The low-volume TPN received too great an allocation prior to ABC. In fact, ABC wound up allocating more cost to the high-volume type. This is because the traditional allocation was not based on volume. It was based on drug cost. The key lesson of ABC is that drug cost may be an inappropriate base for some overhead items, patient days may be inappropriate for some items, and pharmacist direct labor hours may be inappropriate for others.

Should health care organizations use this system? Bear in mind that its premise is that indirect costs have become a major factor. To the extent that costs are primarily labor and materials, ABC is not needed if those costs are assigned on a direct basis, because the error will not be large. To the extent that indirect costs make up a major share of the cost allocated to a patient, ABC becomes a more important tool.

One excellent example of the potential for ABC is in the area of costing nursing services. Instead of assigning nursing costs on a volume (patient day) basis, they could be assigned based on the cost of the different activities needed for patients at different classification levels. The level of patient acuity is the cost driver. Clearly, the current approach of treating each patient day as if it consumes the same amount of nursing cost is highly inaccurate. By using classification level as the cost driver, ABC would directly, and fairly inexpensively, have a dramatic impact on the quality of health care cost data.

NOTES

1. W.L. Ferrara, The new cost/management accounting: More questions than answers, *Management Accounting* 72, no. 4 (October 1990): 48.

2. R.S. Kaplan, The four-stage model of cost systems design, *Management Accounting* 71, no. 8 (February 1990): 22–26.

3. *Ibid.,* 22.

4. *Ibid.,* 24.

5. *Ibid.,* 26.

6. D.E. Peavey, Battle at the GAAP? It's time for a change, *Management Accounting* 71, no. 8 (February 1990): 31–35.

7. C. Berliner and J.A. Brimson, *Cost Management for Today's Advanced Manufacturing* (Boston: Harvard Business School Press, 1988), 341.

8. T. Hiromoto, Another hidden edge—Japanese management accounting, *Harvard Business Review* 66, no. 4 (July-August 1988): 22–28.

9. Peavey, Battle at the GAAP, 31.

SUGGESTED READING

Baptist, A., et al. January 1987. Developing a solid base for a cost accounting system. *Healthcare Financial Management* 42–48.

Baptist, A., and A. Stein. 1987. Keeping an eye on hospital costs. *Laventhol and Horwath Perspective* 13, no. 1:18–23, 48.

Berliner, C., and J.A. Brimson. 1988. *Cost Management for Today's Advanced Manufacturing.* Boston: Harvard Business School Press.

Cooper, R., and R.S. Kaplan. 1992. Activity-based systems: Measuring the cost of resource usage. *Accounting Horizons* 6, no. 3:1–13.

Ferrara, W.L. 1990. The new cost/management accounting: More questions than answers. *Management Accounting* 72, no. 4:48–52.

Harr, D.J. 1990. How activity accounting works in government. *Management Accounting* 72, no. 3:36–40.

Helmi, M.A., and M.N. Tanju. November 1991. Activity-based costing may reduce costs, aid planning. *Healthcare Financial Management* 95–96.

Johnson, H.T. 1990. Activity management: Reviewing the past and future of cost management. *Journal of Cost Management for the Manufacturing Industry* 3, no. 4:4–7.

_____. September 1992. It's time to stop overselling activity-based concepts. *Management Accounting* 26–35.

Kane, N. June 1985. Policy implications of hospital reporting practices. *Medical Care* 836–841.

Kaplan, R.S. 1990. The four-stage model of cost systems design. *Management Accounting* 71, no. 8:22–26.

Kaskiw, E.A., et al. 1987. Cost accounting in health care. *Hospital & Health Services Administration* 32, no. 4:457–474.

Krueger, D., and T. Davidson. 1987. Alternative approaches to cost accounting. *Topics in Health Care Financing* 13, no. 4:1–9.

Peavey, D.E. 1990. Battle at the GAAP? It's time for a change. *Management Accounting* 71, no. 8:31–35.

Shank, J., and V. Govindarajan. 1988. The perils of cost allocation based on production volumes. *Accounting Horizons* 2, no. 4:71–79.

Sharp, D., and L.F. Christensen. 1991. A new view of activity-based costing. *Management Accounting* 73, no. 3:32–34.

EXERCISES

QUESTIONS FOR DISCUSSION

1. What is the major concern about cost accounting, which has caused a reexamination of the entire field of cost accounting?
2. Is the current focus on changing cost accounting relevant to health care organizations? Why or why not?
3. What was largely responsible for the reexamination of traditional cost accounting?
4. What are the key elements of the model proposed by Kaplan?
5. Peavey discusses alternatives to the Kaplan approach for new costing. What are the methods, and what does each method advocate?
6. What is the focus of ABC (activity-based costing)?

PROBLEM

1. Wagner Hospital currently allocates all maintenance department costs based on departmental square feet. However, the manager of the pharmacy department has suggested that an ABC approach be used for the portion of the maintenance department costs that relate to repairing equipment. His contention is that the pharmacy has relatively little equipment that breaks.

However, it must subsidize many high-tech departments that require expensive equipment repairs. Using the data given below, calculate the maintenance cost assigned to the pharmacy using the existing method and using an ABC approach.

Data Table 1 All Maintenance Costs

	Routine Maintenance	Repairs	Total
Volume (sq. ft.)	100,000	800	
Labor hours	10,000	4,000	14,000
Labor cost/ hour	$12.00	$18.00	$13.71
Supplies	$20,000	$80,000	$100,000
Administration			$15,000

Data Table 2 Department Information

	Pharmacy	All Other Departments	Total
Square feet	2,000	98,000	100,000
Volume of repairs	3	797	800
Hours of repairs	6	3,994	4,000
Supplies used for repairs	$ 200	$79,800	$80,000

Note: Solutions to the Exercises can be found in Appendix A.

Application 17-1

Cost Accounting in Transition

Steven A. Finkler, PhD, CPA

Hospital Cost Management and Accounting attempts to take the lead in informing its readership about alternative possible approaches for cost accounting. However, we often lack the hard empirical data to determine which approaches are or are not being adopted. In an article by Orloff et al., in *Health Care Management Review,* an update has been provided that reviews "Who's Doing What and Why."[1]

Remaining competitive is not simply a matter of having the latest medical technology. Hospitals have learned over the last decade that they must be run efficiently. Costing data are crucial to making correct managerial decisions. But how accurate must costing data be? Are hospitals finding it essential to change their systems? Once changes are made, is the new information being used, or do managers continue to rely on tried and true techniques?

It is a long-standing principle in cost accounting that information is costly to collect, but that it isn't worth anything unless it directly impacts on decisions. If decisions are not likely to be influenced by the content of a report, then the money spent to generate the report is largely wasted. As new cost accounting techniques are being installed, are they being used? If they are not being used, why not?

The authors in the *Health Care Management Review* article note that the shift in reimbursement systems to prospective payment, and away from cost reimbursement could reasonably be expected to heighten hospital interest in costing systems. Specifically, it raises the importance of both monitoring and controlling patient costs. There is little controversy on that point, in the eyes of *Hospital Cost Management and Accounting.* When fixed prices are used for different types of patients, accurate knowledge of the cost of providing care to those different types of patients becomes important information.

However, that belief is not universally agreed upon. There are those who would argue that it is rare that prices are less than marginal costs. Therefore a hospital should want any patient it can get. Information about the true actual costs of different types of patients is valuable only to those who can afford to be choosy. A hospital that turns away many patients because of lack of space, may prefer to design an approach to accept only the most profitable patients.

However, such hospitals are not likely to be in financial difficulty to begin with. If they don't choose the right patients, they will still do well financially. They can afford to "satisfice." That

Source: Reprinted from Steven A. Finkler, "Cost Accounting in Transition," *Hospital Cost Management and Accounting,* Vol. 3, No. 4, July 1991, pp. 1–4. Copyright 1991, Aspen Publishers, Inc.

is, a satisfactory outcome to the managers of such an organization need not be the optimal or profit maximizing outcome.

Hospitals that are not in that position can ill afford to turn away any patient. Such hospitals need volume to help spread their fixed costs out over a larger patient base. They will accept the Prospective Payment System (PPS) fixed fee and be glad to get it. Knowing with extreme accuracy the cost of each type of patient may not help them.

A counter argument would claim that all hospitals must start to act competitively to survive. That means there must be the ability to negotiate prices, unless all patients are on a fixed fee system such as the federal PPS.

It is likely that each hospital's stance on adopting more sophisticated costing systems will depend partly on how difficult and costly it is to do so. In recent years, tremendous advances in technology have occurred, which make changes in costing systems feasible. *Hospital Cost Management and Accounting* has noted in the past that hospitals have the opportunity to upgrade their cost accounting in an era when computerization allows for far greater detail, precision, and accuracy than was available to industries that adopted more sophisticated costing systems in the past. The Orloff et al. article points out that vendors are offering a wide array of hospital cost accounting and case-mix reporting systems.

The conclusions of the Orloff article were based on a telephone survey of CEOs and financial managers from a national sample of 89 acute care hospitals, which they deemed to be representative. The survey was conducted in 1988 by SysteMetics/McGraw-Hill, Inc. (SMI) for the Prospective Payment Assessment Commission (ProPAC).

It is somewhat unfortunate that, as in most research studies, a fair amount of time passes from the actual research until it is compiled and submitted for publication, and then ultimately until it is published. As a result, we must content ourselves with considering information SMI collected in 1988. Nevertheless, the information should show the trends that were established well after the introduction of PPS.

It is also unfortunate that the sample size in that study was so small. Eighty-nine hospitals seem to be relatively few upon which to base conclusions about what percent of hospitals in each of a variety of groupings do or do not use certain cost accounting approaches. As a result the Orloff article is silent on many key issues, such as the impact of hospital ownership on costing systems used, the difference between for-profit and not-for-profit hospitals, and the differences between hospitals that are part of multihospital systems and those that are not.

The findings of the SMI study primarily separated hospitals by location and size. The study found that 72 percent of hospitals reported having an automated cost-accounting or case-mix system. Most of those were large urban hospitals (over 100 beds) or rural hospitals with 50 to 99 beds. The automated hospitals were reported to be more likely in areas with significant local competition and high proportions of Medicare revenues.

The bulk of hospitals with advanced costing systems have installed them since the advent of DRGs. The Orloff article reports that 80 percent of hospitals with automated systems implemented them since 1983. However, apparently PPS was just one factor in the decision to upgrade costing systems, with cost-containment efforts, improved quality and reliability of data for pricing and negotiations, performance evaluation, and performance standards also being cited.

The Orloff article breaks cost accounting into two categories: top-down, and bottom-up. The top-down approach uses ratio of cost to charges (RCCs) and is defined as the traditional approach. The authors noted that "[c]osts derived through this method are based on aggregate information and may not accurately reflect the actual costs of a particular procedure provided within a department."[2]

The alternatives to top-down costing are being increasingly adopted. These bottom-up approaches focus on the costs of procedures as the procedures are performed. They include actual costing, relative value units (RVUs), and standard costing. Orloff et al. refer to actual costing as the ideal form of costing, but note that in exchange for its high precision, there is the requirement of high effort, as well as high cost of data collection. The RVU method is cited as being a popular and growing approach. Standard costing is cited as having particular control advantages, since actual costs can be compared to standards, and actions taken to correct variances.

The benefits of the costing system used depend to a great extent on the level of detail of data collection. If data are collected within cost centers, focusing on the costs of procedures, the level of sophistication of resulting analyses increases. However, the SMI study found that 70 percent of hospitals collect department or cost center data as their most detailed level of investigation. Only 17 percent of hospitals collect procedure level cost data.

The much-criticized RCC method is still the dominant approach. The SMI study found that 66 percent of hospitals use RCCs alone, or a combination of approaches that include RCCs. Orloff et al. note that "[a] majority of hospitals, therefore, are making management decisions based on adjusted charge data rather than on actual costs incurred."[3]

However, we tend to view this conclusion with a degree of caution. The percentage of hospitals using RCC data alone for decision making would be of interest. That would indicate a high reliance on RCC data. The statistic of the use of RCC along with other methods doesn't tell us much. It is possible that the RCC method is just used for the DRGs that account for the bulk of categories, but the minority of costs.

Nevertheless, we tend to agree with the inference of the article that managers may be misleading themselves to the point of making harmful decisions by using highly inaccurate data for decision making. There is no question that RCC data do not accurately reflect resource consumption. A number of articles have documented that point. There has been little evidence, however, on whether the use of RCC data has actually led to any decisions which have financially hurt hospitals.

The authors of the SMI study developed a scale that rated hospitals as being less developed or more developed in terms of their costing precision and sophistication:

> Hospitals with less developed capabilities were defined either as having no automated cost accounting system or as using RCCs as their sole costing approach. Hospitals with more developed capabilities have automated cost accounting systems and use the actual costs method in combination with RVUs or RCCs. Within this category, the most developed hospitals regularly compare actual costs to standards for variance analysis.[4]

Given the findings of the SMI study that indicate that 72 percent of the hospitals reported having automated systems, it is surprising to note that only 21 percent of the hospitals were considered to be more developed. Apparently hospitals are adopting the technology, but not necessarily installing and using the more sophisticated costing approaches. However, Orloff notes that

> [i]ncreased financial pressure on hospitals and heightened competitiveness in local markets should support movement to more advanced methods and systems. Not only is it appropriate that hospitals' costing capabilities expand, such developments may be lagging behind hospitals' needs for information to respond effectively to their changing environment. For example, RCCs, currently the most prevalent costing method, cannot be used effectively when a hospital also employs creative pricing strategies. Under this scenario, hospital managers may in fact be making decisions on the basis of inaccurate information.[5]

There is one aspect of the *Health Care Management Review* article which we found to be quite disappointing. The title indicated that the article would not only tell who was doing what, but also why. The article doesn't adequately address the why question. Rather than explain why different hospitals use different costing approaches, Orloff et al. attempt to answer why cost information is needed.

The study found that 89 percent of the hospitals compare their cost data with DRG prices. In fact a surprisingly high 73 percent of the hospitals make quarterly or monthly comparisons of cost and price by DRG. It was found that 82 percent of hospitals perform profit and loss analysis by DRG, 71 percent measure profitability by physician, and 49 percent focus on the costs of PPS outlier cases. And, of noteworthy significance, a majority of hospitals use only charge information in the DRG analyses.[6]

Cost information is used for other purposes as well. A common area of use for cost information is physician education. Such education makes physicians aware of both the costs of care and how their practice of medicine compares with that of their peers. The SMI study also found that cost information is used for revising utilization review guidelines, identifying new potential markets, and making other management decisions.

Nevertheless, it isn't clear why some hospitals have retained "less developed" systems. Is it a result of poor management? Lack of resources to invest in cost accounting? A belief that the benefits of more sophisticated costing are offset by the costs of implementing a new system? Or is it because many managers believe that RCCs provide adequate cost information?

Note that the study found that 72 percent of the hospitals had in fact installed automated cost systems. Yet, 66 percent report heavy reliance on RCCs for cost derivation. This would seem to imply that even those with systems that can bypass RCCs still rely on them. Why? Orloff et al. finesse this issue by indicating that consultants tell them that it takes time to fully adjust to a new information system. They indicate that a phase-in period of 6 months to 2 years would not be unreasonable.

While that may be true, it still avoids directly trying to answer the question. Why do hospitals continue to rely heavily on traditional costing systems? It's not clear why the SMI study never posed that question to those hospitals with the presumably "less developed" systems. It seems that a critical element of the study should have been to validate the authors' preconceptions. Do hospitals with the "less developed" systems believe that their systems are inferior, but feel that they must live with them, or do they believe that their systems are just as good as "the high priced spread"?

NOTES

1. T.M. Orloff, et al. "Hospital Cost Accounting: Who's Doing What and Why?" *Health Care Management Review,* Fall 1990, pp. 73–78.
2. *Ibid.,* page 74.
3. *Ibid.,* page 75.
4. *Ibid.,* page 75.
5. *Ibid.,* page 78.
6. *Ibid.,* page 77.

Application 17-2

Improving Hospital Cost Accounting with Activity-Based Costing

Yee-Ching Lilian Chan, PhD, CPA, CMA, is currently Assistant Professor at the Michael G. DeGroote School of Business, McMaster University, Ontario, Canada.

Activity-based costing, a method designed for costing a product or service more accurately, has been implemented successfully in various manufacturing and service organizations.[1–5] By and large, the feedback from management is encouraging.

Better cost control and improved decision making are among the many benefits experienced by those who have adopted activity-based costing. In this article, activity-based costing is presented and recommended for hospital cost accounting, especially in determining the standard full-cost-per-service unit[6] provided by the hospital. Given the more accurate standard cost data, health care administrators should be able to plan and control costs more effectively as compared to their efforts in these areas with the conventional volume-based costing systems.

First, a conventional costing system for hospital accounting is presented. Next, the activity-based costing system is described, including an application in the health care industry as well as a discussion of its potential contributions and implementation concerns. Finally, some concluding remarks are provided.

Source: Reprinted from Yee-Ching Lilian Chan, "Improving Hospital Cost Accounting with Activity-Based Costing," *Health Care Management Review,* Vol. 18, No. 1, pp. 71–77, Aspen Publishers, Inc., © 1993.

CONVENTIONAL COSTING

Because revenues or payments are fixed per discrete episode of care on the basis of Diagnosis Related Group (DRG), per diem, or discharge, health care administrators have shifted their effort to managing the bottom line of their organization with an emphasis on cost control and management. Standard full costing, variance analysis, and bottom-line management are some of the tools recommended for planning and controlling the costs of servicing patients whose care comes under a DRG.[7] When these techniques are used in monitoring cost performance and assessing the profitability of the different types of treatments provided, the standard full-cost-per-service unit must be determined accurately for fair evaluation.

In general, three stages of cost allocation are used in determining the standard full-cost-per-service unit[8]:

1. Stage I allocation involves the tracing of direct costs to cost objects, which may include departments, divisions, territories, or products. (Cost object is any item for which a separate measurement of costs is desired, and direct cost is a cost that can be identified specifically with or traced to a given cost object in an economically feasible way.)

2. Stage II allocation involves allocating and reallocating costs from one cost object to another cost object (except a product cost object).
3. Stage III allocation involves allocating indirect costs to products (or services). (Indirect cost is a cost that cannot be identified specifically with or traced to the product [or service] in an economically feasible manner.)

Among these three stages of cost allocation, the tracing of direct costs to cost objects (Stage I allocation) is relatively simple as compared to the other two stages, which require the selection of an appropriate base for allocation. For instance, in determining the standard full cost per patient meal served by the dietary department, it is quite simple and straightforward to trace the direct costs of ingredients and labor to each patient meal. On the other hand, in allocating other support department costs (such as those of the maintenance department or administration) to the dietary department and applying the department's indirect costs (e.g., salaries and fringe benefits of the dietitian, costs of cooking utensils, allocated support department costs) to each patient meal, some allocation bases have to be selected. With conventional costing systems, one allocation base is generally selected for one cost pool. For example, in allocating the maintenance department costs to the dietary department, the use of maintenance hours provided as the allocation base is sufficient because a cause-effect relationship between the benefits received by the dietary department (as measured in maintenance hours) and the costs of operating the maintenance department is evident. On the other hand, if administrative costs, which include costs of operating the accounting, finance, personnel, and other administrative departments, are allocated to the dietary department on some bases (e.g., number of employees or total salaries paid), the resultant cost allocation can be misleading and unfair. This is because there is no direct cause-effect relationship between the accounting services provided to the dietary department and the number of employees (or total salaries paid) in that department. Also, this allocation scheme penalizes departments with a large number of employees (or a large amount of total salaries paid), and suboptimal decisions may result because these departments would try to reduce their share of the allocated costs by cutting headcounts and eventually reducing or eliminating certain essential services. Consequently, better schemes of cost allocation should be used in determining the standard full-cost-per-service unit.

ACTIVITY-BASED COSTING

During the late 1980s, many managers and accountants, especially those in the manufacturing industry, became discontented with their conventional costing systems. Many of these conventional systems can be described as volume-based cost accounting systems. That is, indirect costs are applied to products by using some volume-related allocation bases such as direct labor hours or machine hours. Consequently, low-volume products are consistently undercosted and high-volume products are consistently overcosted by such systems.[9] This observation was puzzling to most manufacturing managers who believed that high-volume products should enjoy a higher margin than low-volume products simply because of the greater efficiencies achieved through economies of scale. The dissatisfaction with the costing data manifested and led to the development of activity-based costing systems.

As the term indicates, an *activity-based costing system* focuses "on activities as the fundamental cost objects and uses the costs of these activities as building blocks for compiling the costs of other cost objects."[10] That is, costs are accumulated for each activity as a separate cost object and then applied to products as they undergo the various activities.

In an activity-based costing system, the allocation bases used for applying costs to products are called cost drivers, and they include any causal factor that increases the total costs of the activity. Both volume-related allocation bases (e.g., direct labor hours and machine hours) and other volume-unrelated allocation bases (e.g., the number of setups, material parts handled, and purchase orders processed) can be used as cost drivers in an activity-based costing system for applying costs to products.

For instance, when activity-based costing is used in determining the manufacturing cost of a product, the first task is to identify all activities that are required in its production. The amount of resources consumed by each activity and their costs are then traced and applied to the products. For example, in a factory that manufactures three different products, the machine has to be set up differently for each product. In this case, machine setup is an essential activity of the manufacturing process. If it can be assumed that setup labor time is the primary resource required, machine setup costs can be applied to the three products, as seen in Table 17-2-1. Therefore, by aggregating the costs of all activities required in its production, the manufacturing cost of a product is determined. Also, as illustrated in Table 17-2-1, there is no consistent overcosting of high-volume products (product A) and undercosting of low-volume products (product C) with activity-based costing.

Application of Activity-Based Costing in Health Care

Even though many of its applications deal with the costing of mass production of homogeneous units in the manufacturing sector, activity-based costing can also be applied in the health care sector in which patients are unique products themselves. This is because under activity-based costing, costs are accumulated for activities that consume resources and then ap-

plied to products (or patients) on the basis of the activities required in their production (or treatment). Therefore, regardless of whether we are manufacturing one million units of a product or treating one patient, the principle of cost application with activity-based costing remains unchanged.

As suggested by Cleverley,[6] the Standard Treatment Protocol can be used to account for the treatments and services provided to a patient with a specific disease. This protocol, in sum, consists of the list of services, including the standard full-cost-per-service unit and the estimated quality of service required, established for a specific DRG treatment. Therefore, by comparing the standard full cost data against the expected payment, the hospital administrator can determine if the specific DRG treatment contributes positively toward the hospital's bottom line or whether some corrective actions have to be taken to bring its cost down in line with the revenue generated. Also, a variance analysis of the standard full cost against actual cost provides the hospital administrator with insight into the operating efficiency of the service units.

The accuracy of the standard full cost data, clearly, is the backbone of the use of the Standard Treatment Protocol in hospital planning and cost control, and this is where activity-based costing may contribute. For instance, activity-based costing can be used in determining the standard full-cost-per-service unit, such as the standard full costs of the various tests conducted in a hospital laboratory, as given in Table 17-2-2. (A simple application, the costing of laboratory tests, is chosen over other more complicated examples, such as the costing of a surgical operation, to make the illustration of activity-based costing more effective.)

In applying activity-based costing to this hospital setting, the first task is to identify all activities required in performing the tests. These activities are simplified for illustration purposes and can be described as follows: This hospital laboratory is responsible for performing four different kinds of tests: P, Q, R, and S. Each test requires a specific setup of tools and equipment, which are maintained by the maintenance

---

Table 17-2-1 Determination of the Setup Cost of a Product with the Use of Activity-Based Costing

	Product		
	A	B	C
(Given: Wage rate per setup labor hour = $30)			
Setup labor time (hours)	0.5	1.2	0.8
Machine setup costs ($)	15	36	24
Units per run	100	50	20
Setup costs per unit ($)	0.15	0.72	1.20

Table 17-2-2 Standard Full Cost per Laboratory Test with the Use of Activity-Based Costing and Conventional Costing

Laboratory tests	Number of tests per year	Materials and supplies per test	Direct labor hour (DLH) per test	Machine (m/c) hour per test	Number of setups	Direct labor hour per setup
P	100,000	$ 5.00	0.05	0.220	5,000	0.05
Q	60,000	3.20	0.10	0.050	6,000	0.08
R	80,000	12.50	0.04	0.600	16,000	0.12
S	5,000	2.00	0.10	0.828	2,500	0.15
Wage rate			$30.00			$30.00
Department overhead*:						
Clerical support						$147,000
Setup						90,750
Tools and equipment						30,856
						$268,606
Allocated overhead†:						
Maintenance						$ 46,284
Supply processing and distribution						8,510
						$ 54,794
Total overhead						$323,400

(a) Activity-based costing

Overhead rates:

Clerical support	=	$147,000/245,000 tests	= $0.600 per test
Setup	=	$90,750/3,025 setup DLH	= $30.000 per setup DLH
Tools and equipment	=	$30,856/77,140 m/c hour	= $0.400 per m/c hour
Maintenance	=	46,284/77,140 m/c hour	= $0.600 per m/c hour
Supply processing and distribution	=	$8,510/$1,702,000	= $0.005 per material$

Laboratory tests	P	Q	R	S
Materials and supplies	$5.0000	$3.2000	$12.5000	$2.0000
Direct labor	1.5000	3.0000	1.2000	3.0000
Department overhead:				
Clerical support	0.6000	0.6000	0.6000	0.6000
Setup	0.0750	0.2400	0.7200	2.2500
Tools and equipment	0.0880	0.0200	0.2400	0.3312
Allocated overhead:				
Maintenance	0.1320	0.0300	0.3600	0.4968
Supply processing and distribution	0.0250	0.0160	0.0625	0.0100
Standard full cost per test	$7.4200	$7.1060	$15.6825	$8.6880

(b) Conventional costing

Overhead rate = $323,400/14,700 = $22.00 per DLH

Laboratory tests	P	Q	R	S
Materials and supplies	$5.0000	$3.2000	$12.5000	$2.0000
Direct labor	1.5000	3.0000	1.2000	3.0000
Overhead	1.1000	2.2000	0.8800	2.2000
Standard full cost per test	$7.6000	$8.4000	$14.5800	$7.2000

*The categories of department overhead have been greatly simplified for illustration.

†*Allocated overhead* refers to costs incurred by support departments that are charged to the laboratory for services provided. The categories of allocated overhead have also been greatly simplified for illustration.

department of the hospital. Once the tools and equipment are set up, the laboratory technicians use the materials and supplies delivered by the supply processing and distribution department to perform the tests. As the tests are conducted, the clerks must complete the required documents and distribute the test results to the appropriate party.

After identifying the activities, the amount of hospital resources required to carry out these activities is recorded, and a summary of the laboratory's cost and operating data is given in the upper panel of Table 17-2-2. That is, in addition to the costs of labor, materials, and supplies directly associated with each test, other expenses such as clerical support, setup, and tools and equipment are required in operating the laboratory. Also, because the laboratory requires services of both the maintenance department and the supply processing and distribution department, the costs of providing such support services are charged to the laboratory by using specific allocation bases. This allocated overhead, even though not directly incurred by the laboratory, is essential to the proper functioning of the laboratory. It must be included in determining the standard full costs for the four laboratory tests.

As the indirect costs of operating the laboratory are identified, they are applied to the four tests on the basis of the activities undertaken in performing each specific test. For instance, for each test performed there is a certain amount of documentation and paper work that has to be completed by the clerks. If the amount of time required for these functions is more or less the same for each test, it is appropriate to apply costs of clerical support to the tests on a per-test basis. Setup direct labor hours and machine hours, on the other hand, are more appropriate for applying costs of setup as well as tools and equipment to the laboratory tests respectively, because the cause–effect relationships are more transparent here. For the allocated overhead, two other cost drivers are used: machine hour for the maintenance department costs and material dollar for the supply processing and distribution department costs. This is because the longer the tools and equipment are used in laboratory tests,

the more maintenance is required. Also, the larger the amount of materials handled, the more service is required of the supply processing and distribution department. Therefore, with the use of activity-based costing the standard full costs for the four laboratory tests P, Q, R, and S are $7.4200, $7.1060, $15.6825, and $8.6880, respectively.

As illustrated in the previous example, various cost drivers can be chosen for applying indirect costs to cost objects under activity-based costing as long as a cause–effect relationship is evident. Conventional costing, on the other hand, usually uses one volume-related allocation base in cost application. For instance, if direct labor hour is chosen as the allocation base, the standard full costs for the four laboratory tests P, Q, R, and S are $7.60, $8.40, $14.58, and $7.20, respectively [Table 17-2-2(b)], which are quite different from the costs computed by using activity-based costing [Table 17-2-2(a)]. The difference is most significant with test Q (an increase of 18.21 percent) and test S (a decrease of 17.13 percent).

In fact, conventional costing has again overcosted the high-volume tests (P and Q) and undercosted the low-volume tests (R and S), as evidenced in the manufacturing sector. Activity-based costing, on the other hand, reports a more accurate computation of standard full costs by focusing on the activities of the laboratory and the resources those activities consume, as well as choosing cost drivers that exhibit a cause–effect relationship with the overhead charged to the laboratory.

Contributions of Activity-Based Costing

Activity-based costing is more accurate than conventional costing in determining product cost, not only when the products differ in their demand on various resources due to high diversity in volume, complexity, materials, and setup,[11] but also when there is a high proportion of volume-unrelated overhead costs.[11] Also, with the more informative product cost information generated from activity-based costing, managers can better identify the relevant costs and are likely to make better decisions in product or service pricing and abandonment, as well as in new product or service introduction.[12] As well, activity-based costing systems have assisted managers in implementing new strategic directions, such as identifying profitable orders for low-volume custom orders and setting competitive bid prices.[13]

In addition to reporting more accurate product cost and improving managerial decisions, activity-based costing can guide managers to effective cost reduction by focusing on non–value-added activities.[14] Costs can be reduced by decreasing the time or effort required to perform the activity or by eliminating the activity entirely if it does not add value to the company. For example, one way to reduce material handling overhead costs for the hospital is to decrease the distance between the supply processing and distribution department and its major user departments. In this way, materials can be delivered in the shortest time possible, thereby reducing handling costs. Another alternative is to have the suppliers deliver the materials directly to the user departments; in which case, material handling overhead costs are totally eliminated. Costs can also be reduced by selecting the low-cost activity from a set of design alternatives and sharing the activity with other products (or service units) to yield economies of scale.

Implementation Concerns of Activity-Based Costing

Despite the contributions of activity-based costing, the economic as well as technical feasibilities of implementing such a cost accounting system in an organization must be evaluated (that is, whether the benefits derived from activity-based costing more than offset its costs of implementation and whether it is feasible to identify the activities that consume resources, to accumulate costs per activity, and to select the appropriate cost drivers for cost application).

There are, in general, two kinds of costs associated with any cost system: (1) the costs of measurement and (2) the costs of errors.[15] The costs of measurement, which include the costs of routing the information to the cost system

and the costs of computation, are less with conventional costing than with activity-based costing. This is simply because more cost drivers are required with activity-based costing systems, thereby requiring greater efforts in data collection and measurement. The costs of errors, which include the costs of making a poor product, capital investment, and budgeting decisions, however, are greater with the conventional costing systems than with the activity-based costing systems, because less accurate product cost information is generated by the former. Thus the activity-based costing system should be implemented only when the decrease in cost of errors far exceeds the increase in cost of measurement. In fact, activity-based costing provides the most benefits to organizations facing severe competition, because the cost of errors attributed to conventional costing is very high.

In the development of activity-based costing systems, an activity analysis has to be conducted to identify activities that consume resources. This involves a detailed study of the organization's logistics and accounting information systems, and it is an expensive project in itself. Besides, it can be quite difficult and time consuming to identify and trace resource consumption to a specific activity because of the complexities involved. Thus it may be technically infeasible for some organizations to implement activity-based costing.

If the economic and technical feasibilities of an activity-based costing system are confirmed, the system designer must (1) decide on the number of cost drivers required by the system and (2) select the drivers from the alternatives available.[16] In general, the higher the desired accuracy of product costing, the larger the number of cost drivers required. Also, the greater the degree of product diversity, especially volume diversity, the more cost drivers are required. In addition, when a significant proportion of the total costs of the products is represented by a large number of activities, more cost drivers are required. Finally, when there is a low correlation between the cost drivers and the activities' consumption of resources, more cost drivers are needed. The designer, therefore, must trade off the desirability of having a large number of cost drivers with the costs of measurement and the increased complexity of the activity-based costing system.

In summary, the designer should focus on activities that represent a significant proportion of the total costs of products and select cost drivers that have a high correlation with the activities' consumption of resources, as long as the costs of measurement are within acceptable limits. On the other hand, for activities that have insignificant costs, it is appropriate to aggregate these activities and cost pools into one, and select a cost driver that is reasonable according to the designer's professional judgment.

As in any new system development, activity-based costing should only be implemented if its benefits far outweigh its costs. Also, management support and communication of the development plan to employees are essential to a successful implementation of activity-based costing in an organization.

As described in this article, activity-based costing provides more accurate product cost information than do conventional costing systems. The former approach is especially important in the health care industry in which planning and controlling the costs of services provided are the key to maintaining a healthy financial status for the organization. Combining activity-based costing with the development of Standard Cost Profile per service unit[6] and Standard Treatment Protocol per DRG allows health care administrators to identify unprofitable treatments, the costs of which are greater than the fixed payments received from Medicare. Once the costly treatments are identified, actions can be taken to either reduce or eliminate the nonessential activities of the treatments. Another alternative is to change the mix of health services provided to the public; that is, to reduce the costly services as much as possible. Thus activity-based costing provides more accurate product costing and more informative product cost information, both of which can assist health care administrators in making improved decisions.

Activity-based costing, however, is not a panacea to all problems within a hospital or any organization. If the organization is operating inefficiently, activity-based costing can assist managers in identifying activities that are costly or non–value-added. Nevertheless, it is still up to management to decide on the remedial actions that need to be taken to reduce the costs of such expensive activities and, eventually, to eliminate all non–value-added activities. Also, as indicated earlier, both the economic and the technical feasibilities of an activity-based costing system must be assessed before management approves its development and implementation in an organization.

An activity-based costing system is an invention of the Western world and has been implemented quite successfully in a number of manufacturing and service organizations. There are management consultants whose expertise is in developing activity-based costing systems for their clients. Also, a number of software packages are available, ranging from the more expensive package ACTIVA of Price Waterhouse to the cheapest package EasyABC designed by ABC Technologies Inc. (about U.S. $1,000), providing good support for the implementation of activity-based costing systems in various organizations. For health care organizations that are facing shrinking revenue sources and spiraling expenses, activity-based costing can be a valuable tool to administrators in controlling costs and making strategic decisions.

NOTES

1. J.Y. Lee, "Activity-Based Costing at Cal Electronic Circuits." *Management Accounting,* October 1990, 36–38.

2. T.E. Steimer, "Activity-Based Accounting for Total Quality." *Management Accounting,* October 1990, 39–42.

3. B.M. Chaffman and J. Talbott, "Activity-Based Costing in a Service Organization." *CMA* 64, no. 10 (1990): 15–18.

4. D.J. Harr, "How Activity Accounting Works in Government." *Management Accounting,* September 1990, 36–40.

5. R.J. Lewis, "Activity-Based Costing for Marketing." *Management Accounting,* November 1991, 33–35, 38.

6. W.O. Cleverley, "Product Costing for Health Care Firms." *Health Care Management Review* 12, no. 4 (1987): 39–48.

7. D.H. Schroeder, "Toward a Departmental Bottom-Line Perspective." *Health Care Management Review* 14, no. 1 (1989): 25–40.

8. C.T. Horngren and G. Foster, "Cost Allocation I." In *Cost Accounting: A Managerial Emphasis.* 7th ed. Englewood Cliffs, N.J.: Prentice Hall, 1991.

9. R. Cooper and R.S. Kaplan, "How Cost Accounting Systematically Distorts Product Costs." In *Accounting & Management: Field Study Perspectives,* edited by W.J. Bruns and R.S. Kaplan. Boston, Mass.: Harvard Business School Press, 1987.

10. C.T. Horngren and G. Foster, "Job Costing for Services, Process Costing and Activity-Based Costing." In *Cost Accounting: A Managerial Emphasis.* 7th ed. Englewood Cliffs, N.J.: Prentice Hall, 1991.

11. R. Cooper, "The Rise of Activity-Based Costing—Part One: What Is an Activity-Based Cost System?" *Journal of Cost Management* 1, no. 2 (1988): 45–54.

12. R. Cooper, "Cost Classification in Unit-Based and Activity-Based Manufacturing Cost Systems." *Journal of Cost Management* 4, no. 3 (1990): 4–14.

13. R. Cooper, "How Activity-Based Cost Systems Help Managers Implement New Strategic Directions." Working paper, Harvard Business School (January 1990).

14. P.B.B. Turney, "How Activity-Based Costing Helps Reduce Cost." *Journal of Cost Management* 4, no. 4 (1991): 29–35.

15. R. Cooper, "The Rise of Activity-Based Costing—Part Two: When Do I Need an Activity-Based Cost System?" *Journal of Cost Management* 1, no. 3 (1988): 41–48.

16. R. Cooper, "The Rise of Activity-Based Costing—Part Three: How Many Cost Drivers Do You Need, and How Do You Select Them?" *Journal of Cost Management* 1, no. 4 (1988):34–46.

18

Total Quality Management

Key Terms Used in This Chapter

Appraisal costs; continuous quality improvement (CQI); cost driver; external failure costs; internal failure costs; prevention costs; time driver; total quality management (TQM); quality driver.

Note: Key terms appear in italics when first used in the chapter. All key terms are defined in the Glossary.

COST ACCOUNTING AND QUALITY MANAGEMENT

In recent years, there has been a broad reexamination of the techniques of industrial management. The focus on cost accounting discussed in the previous chapter is just one manifestation of this reappraisal. Another major aspect of the reexamination is a focus on quality in all aspects of an organization's operations. This focus has commonly become referred to as *total quality management (TQM).*

TQM presents a philosophy for business that parallels a philosophy for health care. Simply stated, prevention is cheaper than cure. TQM focuses on doing things right initially and avoiding having to do them a second time. It is a broad concept that views high quality as a key to low cost. This is contradictory to the usual belief that low quality is cheap. Under TQM, we start to consider the high costs related to shoddy workmanship.

This does not simply relate to the quality of patient care. One could consider activity-based costing (ABC), discussed in the previous chapter, to be an example of TQM. ABC states that we will make more cost-effective decisions if we have more accurate data. It may cost a bit more to collect information on an ABC basis, but those costs will be more than recovered as a result of better decisions made based on more accurate information. Therefore, TQM is not simply an approach for improving the operations of an organization. It can also apply to improving the cost accounting methods of organizations.

TQM may represent a significant break in the traditional approach to management. By refocusing organizational attention on the quality aspects of production, many of the ingrained "business as usual" norms start to collapse. We may see a shift in accounting from a strong emphasis on control, to an even stronger emphasis on service. In the future, the finance function may not revolve around being a collector of cost information for top management so much as a dispenser of cost information needed by all levels of management.

All health care organizations attempt to provide the highest possible quality of care. However, quality has many dimensions. There is not only clinical quality, but also quality in administrative functions and other nonclinical elements of a health care organization's operations.

During 1992, the United States and Japan got into a war of words over the quality of American workmanship. The Prime Minister of Japan accused American workers of being inefficient on Mondays and Fridays. To what extent are such arguments stereotypes?

An article by Garvin in the *Columbia Journal of World Business* provides some evidence. In a study which compared American and Japanese manufacture of air conditioners, the findings were as follows:[1]

	United States Companies (%)	Japanese Companies (%)
Percentage of incoming parts and materials failing to meet specifications	3.30	0.15
Fabrication: Coil leaks per 100 units	4.4	0.1
Assembly line: Defects per 100 units	63.5	0.9
Service: Call rate per 100 units under first-year warranty coverage	10.5	0.6

The results of the study are clearly dramatic. It is likely that most health care managers are quite sure that 63.5 percent of their health care organization's patients do not receive defective care. However, it does say something about American attitudes toward the acceptability of errors.

Horngren and Foster have used the expression *quality driver* for any factor that is critical to the level of quality of a product or service.[2] This is similar to the concept of *cost drivers,* which are elements that can have a critical impact on the cost of a product or service. There are, of course, interrelationships between quality and cost drivers, given that improved quality may mean less repetition of activities and therefore lower costs.

Quality and Revenue

Quality can have a bearing on both revenues and expenses. The revenue side takes a long time for a payoff. Reputations for high quality are resilient and will last for a period of time after quality starts to deteriorate. Even one or two scandalous incidents (highly publicized cases of gross negligence) can often be absorbed with only minimal impact on patient flow.

Poor reputations are more difficult to overcome. However, they can be overcome gradually over time. Unfortunately, health care organizations under financial pressure are more likely to find that they can get a reputation improvement faster by perceived quality improvements rather than by real ones. The addition of a glamorous or technologically sophisticated service may do more for the short-run improvement in reputation and patient flow than fundamental changes designed to improve patient care gradually throughout the institution.

In the long run, however, it is that investment in basic quality for all patients that will gradually build a reputation as an outstanding health care organization. Health care organizations need to work not only on answering the immediate demands of the day, but also on positioning themselves for long-term health as an organization. This will occur by investing in quality now for the dividends it will yield later.

Quality and Cost

Nevertheless, many health care organizations are under intense financial pressure today. The concept of investing today for the dividends of tomorrow may not appeal to a health care organization that feels it has no available financial resources to make investments. Therefore, for many health care organizations, the focus on quality as a competitive tool must have at least some bearing on costs.

An approach to quality and costs should have two sides. First, one must consider the costs of improving quality. Second, one should consider the potential cost savings resulting from that quality improvement. This chapter will focus on both the costs of providing quality and the resulting cost savings.

AN INTRODUCTION TO TQM

When is good enough, good enough? Never, under the TQM approach to management. As good as we are, we can always get better. Any organization that becomes satisfied with where they are just asks to be by-passed by the competition. All organizations can work to be better than they already are.

A theme for the provision of health services in the 1990s has become TQM and *continuous quality improvement (CQI)*. These represent philosophies concerning the production of an organization's goods and services. Arikian notes, "TQM emphasizes a preventive approach to management, one that addresses problems before they arise, and handles concerns with a studied, long-term commitment to continuous improvement in product and service."[3] From a strategic management perspective, production in America has been dominated by an attitude of getting it done, and then fixing it if it's wrong. Observations of the Japanese production process, however, have taught us that if more time is spent on planning, less will be done wrong, and less will have to be fixed.

Many American corporations learned this lesson throughout the 1980s, as they lost some of their competitive edge. To regain that edge, corporations have adopted procedures that focus on avoiding the costs associated with poor quality. Examples of the change in attitude are apparent in the slogans adopted by corporations. For example, Ethicon, a manufacturer of sutures, adopted the policy, "Get it right the first time, every time."

Where is the key to the avoidance of errors? According to many theorists, it lies not with the workers, but with the processes or structures of organizations. All workers are inherently subject to failure ("to err is human"). The question is whether the organization designs a process to prevent that failure.

This is a concept very familiar to most accountants. When organizations are audited, whether by an internal accountant or by an outside, independent, Certified Public Accounting firm, the primary goal is to test the systems, not the employees. All individuals are expected to make errors. Accountants attempt to establish accounting systems that will catch and correct errors as they happen. The TQM approach extends this philosophy throughout the organization. Even further, it advocates developing systems that minimize the likelihood of errors occurring. Prevention is stressed over error detection and correction.

Organizations must decide that it is okay to spend time and money developing processes to reduce loss. Quality costs money. However, so does lack of quality. TQM focuses on the issue of being responsive to the needs of customers while reducing waste. Kirk notes that in examinations of Japanese firms,

> The most significant discovery related to their determination to *build quality into the product (or service)* rather than to inspect for errors and assume that error removal would lead to quality. Many Japanese managers bought into the concept of planning and followed through on it—unlike many American managers who avoid this concept like the plague, in preference to the ready-fire-aim approach. "We don't have time to plan," some American managers say. Contrarily, many Japanese businessmen say "we don't have time *not* to plan."[4]

Various authors have identified different elements of TQM and CQI. Deming, the pathbreaker in the field, established 14 points related to TQM.[5] These include such factors as focusing on education and training of employees, viewing employees not only as providers but also as customers, ensuring quality, and constantly focusing on finding ways to improve quality continuously. One of the essential elements is that it makes sense to avoid doing things wrong, rather than spending money correcting what was done wrong.

TQM and CQI are not cost accounting tools *per se.* However, TQM and CQI have cost accounting implications. Historically, health care organizations have minimized planning and maximized control over day-to-day operations. The lesson of TQM and CQI is that all health care managers will be more likely to achieve their objectives if they can redesign their work to allow much more time for planning and innovating. Such activities should not be occasional, but rather should be viewed as a major element of the management function. We must learn to focus on improving the service we provide rather than simply making sure we get it provided, whether it is patient care or the generation of cost information. In the long run, such increased focus on improvement and quality may well lead to more satisfied staff and patients, higher quality of care, more effective cost information, and lower costs.

There are several essential keys to implementing a TQM approach. First, the implementation must have the strong support and participation of the organization's top management. If there is a lack of commitment or involvement by those at the top, then the effort will likely be considered to be without true substance. Employees will make only half-hearted attempts that will likely be doomed to failure.

It is important to bear in mind the degree to which TQM represents an organizational culture. True, TQM is implemented by evaluating and changing processes within the organization. However, in many instances, processes can only be changed if there is an interdepartmental level of cooperation. Teamwork is essential to TQM.

The attitude of "it's not my problem" cannot exist if TQM is to be successful. Each employee must become focused on the concept that any problem is his or her problem. At the same time, each employee must understand that an individual cannot impose a solution to the problem— he or she must build a team consensus. Members of the team must all agree that a problem exists and must find a compromise solution to the problem that is agreeable to all.

For example, in the preparation of this book, the author observed a classic example of the dysfunctional behavior TQM tries to address.

The author's secretary sent four chapters of this book to an internal reprographics department for copying, attached to a "quick copy" form. Quick copy requires clean originals, the same size, meeting several other criteria. Copies are made immediately, with turnaround no more than 24 hours.

The reprographics department returned the originals 48 hours later, not copied, with a note saying that because the chapters were separately paper-clipped, they did not qualify for quick copy. The secretary was supposed to remove the four paper clips, and return the copying in one unseparated stack. The secretary was extremely annoyed and indicated, "I'll show those lazy jerks." He then proceeded to separate the chapters into four separate quick copy jobs. Although this required filling out one form for each job (expanding his time spent on ordering the copies), it was worth it to him, because he knew it would make more work for the copying department. In the process, both the secretary and the reprographics department had little concern for the customer, waiting for the copies.

This example is not provided to indicate who was right; they were both wrong. Worse, they had clearly adopted adversarial positions. Making life miserable for anyone who did not make their life pleasant became the primary objective. The wasted efforts and extra costs were irrelevant to the parties involved. The TQM approach to such a problem is to have meetings between all parties involved in the process. The author, as customer, should be involved so that his needs are known. The secretary, as customer, should be involved. The reprographics staff should be involved.

Such meetings and teamwork can result in significant benefits. As ultimate customer I did not really need quick copy service in this case and had not requested it. However, neither my secretary nor I had much interest in the fact that it is more efficient for the reprographics department if orders that are not rushes are not treated as rushes.

On the contrary, my concern is that rush jobs often do not get completed on a timely basis. Rush jobs are not done on a timely basis because too many nonrush jobs are ordered on a rush basis, clogging the system. Secretaries order nonrush jobs on a rush basis because everyone knows that copying jobs are often returned late, so they are afraid to order anything on a nonrush basis. The system becomes destined to low quality, high failure rates, and high cost.

A TQM effort could allow the different points of view to be shared, including an explanation of the constraints and true needs of all players. From a cost accounting perspective, the costs of different ways of ordering and processing can also be considered. This includes the costs of producing rush jobs versus routine jobs. It can also include the costs to the customer of a *bona fide* rush job arriving late. In some cases, such failures result in costly missed deadlines. Over the long term, such failures result in customers going outside the system at a higher cost to ensure receipt of reliable service.

To break this downward spiral, there must be clear signals of the seriousness of management about making the effort throughout the organization to cure its inefficiencies. There must be an effort from the top down to the bottom to work together at finding ways to improve customer satisfaction by improving quality of services and products.

A FOCUS ON TIME

The TQM philosophy suggests improving quality in all areas each year. As one example of the types of areas that TQM can address, this section discusses timeliness. This can take a number of forms—how long do patients have to wait to be treated in your emergency department? How long does it take the health care organization to make service additions? How far in advance must one schedule surgery?

One area that many health care organizations have focused on to gain a competitive edge is the introduction of new services. However, many organizations potentially lose the advantage they seek if they are slow at introducing new ventures. The time from the initial suggestion of a new service until it is actually introduced is an essential *time driver.*

If the purpose of the new service is at least partially to gain market share in an area before the competition, then speed of introduction becomes critical to success. This raises the question of the process that health care organizations take to get to new services. Health care organizations rely to a great extent on process in providing clinical care, because they often cannot measure the improved health output they produce. Yet, the introduction of new services may not follow a clearly specified process.

In many health care organizations, the process is haphazard. An advocate for a new idea develops it partly on his or her own, and then partly with help. The project may have to await the normal budget cycle for approval. In addition, it probably will have to be developed by managers who have other supervisory responsibilities as their primary jobs.

An alternative approach would be to have project managers who have as their primary responsibility the introduction of new ventures and innovations. Once the idea is first suggested, it can be triaged by these new project managers. A decision can be made regarding which projects have potential merit and can most benefit by fast-tracking, while other projects can be put in line for subsequent attention. In this way, the projects that most need quick introduction to gain a competitive advantage can be acted on much more expeditiously.

Another way that health care organizations can use time to gain a competitive advantage is to determine what types of services patients resent waiting for, and move to reduce the waiting time for those services.

In many industries, there has been a focus on reducing waiting time. For instance, Toys   Us now uses a gun-like device to read the uniform price codes (UPCs) at its check-out counters. This reduces the time for check-out, making customers more likely to use the store. Health care organizations need to work to modify their activities continuously so that patients will leave talking positively about the organization.

Avoiding long waits prior to admission makes scheduling a bit harder for the admissions department and will probably increase staffing cost, but will lead to more admissions in the future. In some cases, what is needed is simply management attention on reducing time. More thoughtful scheduling can work wonders. Instead of having 12 people arrive at 10 A.M., two patients can be told to arrive at 10, 2 at 10:10, 2 at 10:20, and so forth. Perhaps waiting could be reduced by doing most of the admission process through a preadmission telephone call.

In some cases, all such efforts already have been employed, and the only way to get further reductions in admission waiting times is to hire more staff. Unfortunately, it is very difficult to tie together the cause and effect of such an improvement. How does one determine how many more patients come to your organization because of a reputation for efficient service during admission?

Some health care organizations may find it hard to justify adding two full-time equivalents (FTEs) to the admissions department to reduce waiting time. However, if those two FTEs cost a combined $50,000 with benefits, then how many extra patients must be generated to justify that cost? Health care organizations are tremendously volume-driven organizations. Much of the cost of running the health care organization is fixed. An extra 30 or 40 patients a year may generate more than $50,000 in added contribution margin. If a hospital has 10,000 patients who are more satisfied this year, how many extra patients will there be next year?

Of course, this issue also applies to physicians. What time-driven irritants are there that discourage physicians from admitting patients to your organization? Are there any changes that can be made to reduce those irritants? How do the costs of those changes translate into the number of extra patients required to cover those additional costs?

Another element of time relates to patient length of stay. Despite the decade of experience with prospective payment, many hospitals cling to patient flow approaches that prolong rather than reduce length of stay. Length of stay relates to the number of patients a hospital can treat. If a hospital has occasion to turn patients away, then shorter lengths of stay would free beds for more patients. The same concept holds true for an emergency department. If emergency departments divert ambulances because they are full, then improving patient through-put would increase hospital revenues. Also, by reducing lengths of stay, the hospital reduces its costs.

How can length of stay be reduced? There are a number of articles that have been written on this topic. They range from case management—making someone responsible for moving the patient through the hospital in an expeditious manner—to analysis of physician treatment patterns to find which physicians are doing what that extends lengths of stay.

These examples all relate to just one issue: time. In each case, a TQM approach could result in improvements that would lead to better customer satisfaction and improved organizational success.

A FOCUS ON COST

Cost can be an extremely strong competitive tool. By being a low-cost producer, the health care organization is in a better position to earn a profit on fixed-price patients, such as Medicare patients paid on a Diagnosis Related Group (DRG) basis. It also is better able to compete for health maintenance organization (HMO) and preferred provider organization (PPO) business. Finally, it is in a better position to weather down-turns in volume.

A TQM approach to becoming a low-cost producer is to focus on costs as being value-added or non–value-added. Value-added costs are only those that directly affect the quality of the patient's care. In all likelihood, most activities are neither one extreme nor the other. They all contribute somewhat to patient care, but some elements could be removed from many activities without a specific, measurable decline in the quality of patient care. TQM advocates that we improve quality in the things that matter, the value-added areas. At the same time, we remove expenditures from areas where they do not matter, the non–value-added areas.

Patients do not really care about how often inventory is ordered or how much is kept on hand, as long as the items they require are there when they need them. Therefore, having appropriate clinical supplies when needed is a value-added item. Spending money on warehousing inventory or losing interest because of high inventory levels is not value-added.

Having the walls look cleanly painted is value-added. Painting them every three years instead of every six years is not. Providing clinical staff with access to up-to-date published information is value-added. The decision to have a central library versus individual department libraries is not value-added. Having timely reporting of test results is value-added. Repeating tests because test results have not been reported is not value-added.

The determination of all non–value-added activities is a difficult one. It takes a strong will, given that each non–value-added item has its own constituency supporting its continuation. However, in the long run, eliminating non–value-added costs is a much healthier process than putting freezes on spending or making across-the-board cuts. Health care organizations have already been put under so much financial pressure that there are many areas where further cuts will affect the lean. Therefore, cuts must be selective—aiming only at the fat. Categorization of the extent to which activities represent value-added or non–value-added can help health care organizations make additional cost reductions in a more rational manner.

TOTAL COST MANAGEMENT

As TQM has progressed, an area known as total cost management (TCM) has begun to emerge. This area focuses on developing the cost information needed in a TQM environment. A recent text notes,

> An effective cost management system should provide the necessary information through effective reporting that enables managers to make better decisions. To accomplish this goal, the emphasis on cost accounting

which is basically a reactive system based on past financial results must be changed to a proactive system which includes incorporating information or impact assessment of the organizational environment and operational technology.[6]

Although that definition is somewhat cumbersome, the key element surfaces. We must change cost accounting from being reactive to being proactive in order to aid in the process of TQM.

Being proactive is a good start. Clearly, managers need information before the fact, not after decisions are made. However, hasn't cost accounting historically focused on taking information about costs in the *past,* primarily so that information could be used to make better decisions about the *future?* This is a "which came first: the chicken or the egg" scenario. Can cost accounting information ever be proactive, or is it always necessary to use information about prior costs and then be reactive?

We can get out of that loop by realizing that the philosophy of TQM is more important than the semantics involved. One can think in terms of aggressively going out and collecting cost information that might be useful to managers in their TQM and CQI efforts. Such an aggressive stance is proactive, regardless of whether the information collected is historical data (and therefore its use, by nature, reactive). The question is, how can we be proactive? What data should we be attempting to collect to aid in TQM?

In order to make a start in answering those questions, we need to recall the theme of TQM and CQI. The orientation is to move away from having a fixed goal that we try to achieve year-in and year-out. Instead, we need to recognize the need constantly to try to be responsive to customers and to improve each year. In doing so, costs should actually be saved because we stop doing the activities that are not really responsive to the needs of our customers. The elimination of wasted, non–value-added activities makes the organization a more efficient producer of a superior product.

How do we currently measure the costs of an operating room (OR)? We look at the total dollars spent by line item: salaries, clinical supplies, and so forth. We probably also look at volume of output (hours of surgeries or numbers of procedures). That could be defined as a reactive approach. It does not generate data in a form most helpful to managers in their TQM efforts.

TQM would want to know how to make that department operate in a superior manner. That requires an understanding of the *process* in the department as well as a summary of its costs. What process is undertaken, and what outcomes are achieved? The OR does not just incur costs and generate revenues. It also provides service to physicians and patients.

An examination of the process by which this occurs might show that the OR has a significant amount of down time between procedures. During that time, staff are paid but are not fully productive. The capacity of the OR is substantially less than it could be if the down time were reduced. Why does the down time occur? What is its cost?

If nurses, surgeons, and anesthetists were each asked to design an ideal scheduling of the OR, they probably would come up with very different desired usage patterns. That inherently means that there will be a tension and a tug and pull between the individuals involved. Because the schedule established will not be that which best suits all participants, different individuals will each try to make reality conform to his or her desires instead of the official schedule. This is similar to the anecdote regarding the secretary and the reprographics department, discussed earlier. TQM requires that the various parties involved sit down and recognize the problem. Each person's interests should be considered, as should those of the organization as a whole. An agreement should be reached on a scheduling approach that is deemed to be the best compromise, and the various parties need to buy into that solution. Then everyone can have as a goal the continuous improvement in decreasing down time. Achieving movement in that direction becomes something toward which all parties involved strive.

Decreasing down time will improve the efficiency of the OR. It will be able to do more cases, and it will be paying staff for less down time. It will probably also improve patient quality perceptions. Patients will not have to wait as long to get in the OR. Physicians will be able to get more OR time. Quality has a number of different dimensions, all of which must be considered.

Where do costs come in? Clearly, having down time creates unneeded costs. TCM requires designing the cost information tools to collect information and show the costs of different alternative scheduling approaches and of the likely down time under each approach. Developing such information moves the focus away from tracking historical results and directly on proactively providing the information needed to make optimal decisions.

TCM is a critical element of planning. Basically, it calls for a broadening of our horizons in looking at what types of costs to consider in our decision making. It calls for allowing creativity to enter the process of attempting to understand what something will cost.

On a broader level, TCM must be prepared to be the watch dog balancing the competing costs of failure with the costs of prevention of failures. TQM argues that organizations do fail but that they could spend money to reduce failure, and in the process save wasted costs related to failure. As quality improves from low to high, failures are reduced. The costs of preventing the failures rise, as do the savings from fewer failures. At some point, the costs of extra quality may exceed the savings from reduced failure. TCM has an obligation to determine that point.

Cost Accounting and the Quality of Patient Care

Measurement of the quality of medical care has long been a perplexing problem for the health services industry. This problem is becoming more serious in the current cost control environment. As shown in Figure 18-1, higher quality is generally associated with higher costs.

Figure 18-1 Costs of Quality

In the figure, we can see that as one moves to higher levels of quality, costs of providing quality increase. At some point in Figure 18-1, the costs of quality may exceed any possible revenue from providing a service.

However, lowering the quality of care also has its costs to the organization. For example, lower quality is related to both declining reputation and rising numbers of malpractice cases. Balancing the costs of highest quality care against the costs of somewhat lowered quality poses an important challenge for health care organization managers. Figure 18-2 demonstrates the costs of low quality. Note that as quality decreases, certain costs are rising. At very low levels of quality, these costs, such as malpractice losses, may be extremely high. Health care organizations

Figure 18-2 Costs Related to Low Quality

should be starting to consider explicit ways that the cost accounting system can track the impacts of changes in the quality of care provided.

Health care organizations are in a particularly difficult position, because American society has been moving in a direction of greater quality demands at the same time that cost constraint on health care organizations has grown. Nowhere are Americans as likely to be willing to pay extra for quality as in their health care system. Nevertheless, there are restraints on most health care organizations that fight against maximizing the quality of care regardless of cost. Society is focusing more and more on the high and rising costs of health care.

TQM seeks to improve quality while restraining costs. Consider Figure 18-3. Suppose that this graph represents costs related to the pharmacy. High quality could take on many different aspects. One aspect might be more labor time to ensure that the patient has no drug allergies. Further quality is provided if the pharmacist checks all drugs prescribed for the patient to determine if there are dangerous drug interaction effects. Additional quality would be represented by taking the time to double-check that the medications dispensed are those ordered. Still additional quality might be provided if pharmacists examine patient charts to determine if medications ordered make sense, given the patient's diagnosis.

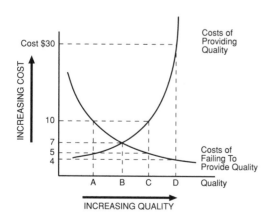

Figure 18-3 Tradeoff of Costs of Providing High Quality versus Costs Related to Low Quality

Suppose that making sure the patient has no known drug allergies is Quality Level A in Figure 18-3. Additionally checking for drug interaction effects represents Quality Level B. Level C represents a double-check that the medications dispensed are those ordered. Having the pharmacists examine patient charts to determine if medications ordered make sense, given the patient's diagnosis, is represented by Level D.

Under a TQM approach, we are always striving to do better. We need to find ways to improve quality. However, do patients need the "highest" level of quality? Should we insert pacemakers with a guaranteed 20-year life in 95-year-old patients? When does higher quality represent waste?

Striving for higher quality must be balanced against the costs of providing that quality and the benefits of providing it. In Figure 18-3, the average cost of providing Quality Level A is $5 (exclusive of the cost of the drug and its basic dispensation cost). However, because of failure to provide the highest level of quality, there are some costs related to low quality, such as adverse patient reactions to drugs, extending their length of stay, and/or malpractice losses. On average, these losses are $10 if we are at Quality Level A.

Moving to Quality Level B, these costs become $7 for providing quality and $7 related to failure to provide quality. This total of $14 represents a minimum cost. Had we provided Quality Level C, the total costs would have been $15, and at Level D, the total costs would have been $34. Therefore, it would make sense for the organization to choose Level B care, until we can determine ways to provide Levels C and D at a lower cost.

We still have a problem, which relates to developing an accounting system that can measure all of the costs. What are the costs of providing quality and the costs related to not providing quality?

Measuring Costs of Quality

The measurement of quality, while particularly difficult for health care organizations, is a problem in many industries. Quality brings to mind words like *superior, high-level,* and *excellent.* However, decision-making information needs require that quality be converted into a dollar measurement.

For example, salaries for personnel time spent in quality review activities directly relate to quality. If actions are taken that reduce quality, they may ultimately require increased time spent by review committees, offsetting some of the savings that were realized by reduced quality in the first place. Additionally, increases in malpractice suits, whether justified or not, create costs for the health care organization.

Essentially, the accounting system does not require the measurement of quality of patient care. That measurement might place an insurmountable obstacle in front of us. What we really need to be able to measure are the costs of actions that affect the quality of care.

Simpson and Muthler have identified four different types of costs related to quality:[7]

1. external failure costs,
2. internal failure costs,
3. appraisal costs, and
4. prevention costs.

The Simpson–Muthler model was designed for manufacturing industries, so it cannot be immediately applied to health care organizations without translation and modification. It does, however, present many opportunities for useful adaptation. We can view the curve in Figure 18-1 as representing appraisal costs combined with prevention costs. The curve in Figure 18-2 represents external failure costs combined with internal failure costs. Application 18-1 at the end of this chapter provides a specific health care example where this model was applied to a clinic setting.

External Failure Costs

For Simpson and Muthler, external failure costs refer to the need for repairs, shipping and handling, and warranty adjustments to repair or replace a defective product. The administration

costs related to a recall are also considered, as is product liability, including both legal fees and other costs that result from lawsuits. Additionally, goodwill cost is involved.

In health care organizations, similar types of costs may arise, particularly under prospective payment systems. Because there is a fixed payment for a patient, there is an incentive to discharge as soon as feasible. However, if a patient is discharged too early and must be readmitted to the hospital, it is unlikely that the hospital will be paid for that readmission. The product liability issues translate directly into hospital malpractice concerns. Goodwill is an issue regardless of industry. For any health care organizations located in areas with effective competition, word of mouth can reduce volume and have a long-term negative impact on the organization.

Suppose that a hospital were applying TQM to the problem of radiology retakes. That is, for some reason, it is determined that the x-ray taken is not adequate, and another image is needed. How should an external failure be defined for radiology retakes? One approach would be to argue that if a patient is discharged from the hospital and has to return, the costs associated with the return visit would be classified as external failure costs. Alternatively, bearing in mind the view that there are internal customers in addition to the patient, we might argue that if the patient has left the radiology area, any costs that arise are external.

If the patient returns to his or her room, and several hours later it is determined by a radiologist that the x-ray cannot be read and a retake is needed, all associated costs can be treated as external costs. There is no right or wrong decision concerning the classification of such a cost as an external failure or an internal failure. Each organization must make its own determination regarding what classification would be considered most useful.

Let's assume that this organization considers such retakes to fall under the external failure cost category. Exhibit 18-1 summarizes the annual external failure costs for radiology retakes. This is a simplified, hypothetical example. Note that the volume of retakes, according to the ta-

Exhibit 18-1 TQM Cost Worksheet: External Failure Costs

Date: 2/12/95

Subject of TQM Analysis _____ Radiology Department Retakes _____

Part A: External Failure Costs

Volume of Failures __650__ instances per annum; __840__ images

Type of Cost	Labor Hours	×	Average Rate ($)	=	Labor Costs ($)	+	Supply Costs ($)	+	Other Costs ($)	=	Total Costs ($)
Transport patient to radiology	420		12		5,040						5,040
Take x-ray machine to patient	340		25		8,500						8,500
Retake image and develop film	210		25		5,250		12,600		8,400		26,250
Read image and report	84		200		16,800		420				17,220
Order retake	32		200		6,400		420				6,820
System delays											
Total					41,990		13,440		8,400		63,830

Cost per failure instance: Total failure cost/instances = $63,830/650 = $98.20

---

ble, was 650 instances, but 840 images. Apparently, in some cases, more than one image was taken, and more than one image had to be retaken.

Each line in the worksheet represents one type of action needed to correct problems caused by the retakes. The labor hours for each row are multiplied by the average hourly rate to find the labor cost. This is added to the supply costs and any other costs to find the total cost for each activity. The columns are summed to find the total for each type of cost (e.g., labor, supplies, etc.).

In the worksheet, note the various costs being considered. Some patients had to be retransported back to radiology. The patients also would have to be transported back to their rooms. The round-trip time would need to be considered. This could be done by orderlies or transport clerks at a rate of $12 per labor hour, or a total cost of $5,040. Other patients could not be moved. A technician would have to take a portable x-ray machine back to the room. The technician is paid $25 per hour, so retakes requiring that the image be taken on a portable machine are most costly. The total technician

cost for transporting the machine was $8,500, according to Exhibit 18-1.

Note that these data should be based on the best available information. Some organizations will already have information on how long it takes to get patients, bring them to radiology, and return them. Others may have to perform special studies to get such information. Similarly, supply costs would have to be based on study of the costs of variable supplies likely to be used on average.

The largest cost involved, as one might expect, is the time of the x-ray technician retaking the images, plus the cost of the film and of developing it. The costs include not only the time of the x-ray technician ($5,250), but also the supply costs ($12,600) for film and developing solution, and other costs of $8,400. These other costs would include an allocation of machine cost, if the machines have a physical lifetime based on the frequency of use.

Less obvious, but important, costs are those related to the radiologist. This physician must place an order for a new image and must spend time reading an extra set of x-rays. Because physicians earn a high hourly rate, even a low number of hours translates into a high cost in these areas ($17,220 for reading the images and $6,820 for ordering new images, according to Exhibit 18-1).

It is important to capture as much of the relevant costs as possible. The relevant costs are only those that would change as a result of having to do retakes. On the other hand, it is important not to be frozen by a lack of complete data. Some cost information may not be available. We should at least try to gather as much information as is feasible. Clearly, the inconvenience to patients should be considered but would be extremely difficult to quantify.

The overall system delays should also be considered. If a patient needs a retake, the health care organization often cannot proceed with treatment. This may mean an extended stay, or it may delay an operation, causing a number of other patients, like dominoes, each to be delayed in turn. In Exhibit 18-1, system delays have been indicated, but not estimated. It is likely that a first attempt at TCM for retakes would not measure such costs. Over time, as the system is refined, there would be an attempt to assess the likely organization-wide impacts of the retakes and to place a cost estimate on the delays.

Internal Failure Costs

Internal failure costs are those defects that the organization discovers before the product is received by the customer. In industrial organizations, such costs include scrap (raw materials that have been ruined as well as labor and overhead) and the reworking of defects. In health care organizations, such internal failure typically occurs during the treatment of the patient.

For health care organizations under cost reimbursement, there was little impact resulting from these costs. Suppose that an x-ray were taken improperly, and the results could not be read for a definitive diagnosis. A patient often could be charged for both the original x-ray and the follow-up one. Of course, that is not the case under DRGs. Thus, there should be some tracking or estimation of the additional costs incurred when a task is not done right in the first place.

So-called scrap also includes the cost of supplies opened that should not have been, with a resulting loss of sterility and discarding of the supply item. Such costs also should be estimated and accounted for. If cost control results in less equipment maintenance, that also results in an internal failure cost. Equipment failure may require the postponement of procedures. For a busy computed tomography (CT) scan or magnetic resonance imaging (MRI), such postponement may mean either that all procedures are pushed off, and income is lost for the year, or that increased numbers of procedures during overtime hours are required. Such lost revenue or increased overtime costs are also quality costs that should be considered.

In the radiology retake example, errors that are detected before the patient leaves the radiology area would be considered to be internal failures. For example, if the film is developed, and the technician sees that it is cloudy or missed the target area, the patient immediately can have another x-ray taken.

It is likely that internal failure costs are less expensive than external ones. At a minimum, we can avoid the extra round-trip transportation of the patient or equipment. Even more significantly, in many cases, an internal error may be discovered before the radiologist reads the x-ray and orders a retake. Exhibit 18-2 provides hypothetical information regarding internal failures.

From this worksheet, it is apparent that internal failures are not expected to result in any need for additional transportation. By definition, these failures are detected before the patient has left the radiology area or before the machine has been removed from where the patient is. There are $52,530 of total costs related to retaking 1,480 images from 1,220 instances of failure.

Apparently, some of the images are not deemed inadequate until viewed by the physician, since there are still some costs for ordering retakes and reading images. However, they are relatively smaller than they were in the case of the external failures.

Exhibit 18-2 TQM Cost Worksheet: Internal Failure Costs

Date: <u>2/12/95</u>

Subject of TQM Analysis _____<u>Radiology Department Retakes</u>_____

Part B: Internal Failure Costs
Volume of Failures <u>1,220</u> instances per annum; <u>1,480</u> images

Type of Cost	Labor Hours	×	Average Rate ($)	=	Labor Costs ($)	+	Supply Costs ($)	+	Other Costs ($)	=	Total Costs ($)
Retake image and develop film	370		25		9,250		22,200		14,800		46,250
Read image and report	23		200		4,600		40				4,640
Order retake	8		200		1,600		40				1,640
System delays											
Total					15,450		22,280		14,800		52,530

Cost per failure instance: Total failure cost/instances = $52,530/1,220 = <u>$43.06</u>

The system delay line still appears on the worksheet. However, if the failure is internal, we generally would expect that it would be rectified much sooner and be less likely to have ripple effects throughout the organization.

Appraisal Costs

Simpson and Muthler's third type of quality cost refers to appraisal costs. They define such costs as those incurred from inspecting a product to be certain that the customer's requirements are met. They define the customer as both internal and external. An internal customer is the next employee in the organization to use a department's output. In a hospital, a radiologist might use the output of an x-ray technician. An internist might use the output of a laboratory technician.

Essentially, quality audits can take place from the arrival of supplies—inspection of the quality of items purchased—to a post-discharge chart review. The cost of such reviews must include both the labor involved and any equipment and supplies required for the review process.

Unlike the external and internal failure costs, which assess the costs of failing to provide high quality, the appraisal costs are a cost of providing quality. They represent money spent in an effort to minimize the two earlier types of costs.

For example, suppose that radiology could somehow examine samples from each batch of film before use. This might reduce the number of images taken with bad film, reducing subsequent internal and external failure costs. However, it might be necessary to expose some film to examine it. Once exposed, the film cannot be used. The cost of regularly exposing some film must be weighed against the cost of taking imaging using bad batches of film.

In the radiology retake example, another appraisal cost might be to have the technician examine the film as soon as it is developed. Although the technician may not be qualified to read the film and make a diagnosis, such examination should disclose whether the image captured the desired area and whether the image is clouded or clear. If such appraisal finds a problem, it is too late to avoid an internal failure; that has already occurred. On the other hand, it can prevent an external failure. Note from Exhibits 18-1 and 18-2 that the average cost per internal failure is only $43.06, whereas the cost per external failure is $98.20. By examining each x-ray, the technicians could reduce the

Exhibit 18-3 TQM Cost Worksheet: Appraisal Costs

Date: 2/12/95

Subject of TQM Analysis _____ Radiology Department Retakes _____
Total Volume: 60,000 images

Part C: Appraisal Costs

Type of Cost	Labor Hours	× Average Rate ($)	= Labor Costs ($)	+ Supply Costs ($)	+ Other Costs ($)	= Total Costs ($)
Examine samples from film batch	50	25	1,250	2,000		3,250
Examine each developed x-ray	500	25	12,500			12,500
Total			13,750	2,000	0	15,750

number of high-cost external failures. Exhibit 18-3 provides an example of appraisal costs.

In this example, it is assumed that there are two primary activities aimed at providing appraisals to reduce the cost of failures. The first is to sample film from batches for quality. From the worksheet, it appears that the organization has a technician spend about one hour per week on this task. The supply cost would be based largely on the cost of film made unusable by the examination process and any logs needed to record results. Presumably, bad batches of film would be returned to the supplier.

The second activity is to examine each developed x-ray. In contrast with the first appraisal task, which just takes a sample, this step calls for every developed x-ray to be reviewed by a technician before being sent to a radiologist. This is probably a quick process—they expect that it adds only 500 hours to technician time over a total of 60,000 images taken.

How well is this step done? From Exhibit 18-1, we know that there are a significant number of hours of physician time spent on rereading images and ordering retakes. The organization might want to evaluate whether its system is working. Are the physician hours related to retakes occurring because those images needed a physician to determine a retake was necessary or because the technician did not appraise the developed x-ray carefully enough?

Prevention Costs

The fourth type of quality costs is prevention costs. These costs are incurred by the organization in an effort to make sure that external and internal failure costs do not arise. These primarily consist of the costs of establishing a quality operating system. TQM stresses attempting to expand prevention to reduce failure costs and to reduce the need for appraisals.

In attempting to cut costs while not hurting patient outcomes, it likely will be necessary for health care organizations to establish already thought-out plans regarding where cuts should take place. Systems will have to be designed to ensure patient safety. For example, the time devoted to establishing a system in your hospital's OR to prevent sponges from being left in the patient is an example of the cost of establishing a quality control. That cost is a prevention cost. It locks in a level of quality to prevent future external or internal failure costs. The OR example is a long-standing practice at most hospitals, and it is likely that much effort will have to go into additional controls of that type. Managers should account for the cost of that effort.

It is quite difficult to determine how much effort and cost currently goes into preventing sponges from being left behind in patients. However, if we accept the current position as a base, we can assess the cost of changes. If TQM dictates that we need to work harder on keeping sponges out of patients, we can make some specific process change to check one extra time to see that all sponges are accounted for before patients are closed. The amount of time required for that check can be measured and the resources involved (such as labor) costed. It requires a great deal of care, however. It may be that everyone in the OR waits while the check is done. In that case, the cost includes the labor cost of all individuals waiting.

An additional cost in this area is that of training personnel. For example, many health care organizations are considering increased use of flexible nurse staffing. That is, it may become necessary to staff all units at lower levels on a regular basis and then to float nurses from low-occupancy units to high-occupancy units as the need arises. Such float staffing has long been resisted for a variety of reasons. One reason is that nurses claim that patient safety is compromised when nurses must work on units with which they are not familiar.

A solution to the lack of expertise and familiarity is to cross-train the nurses and to have a regular exchange program, moving nurses back and forth on a regular basis to ensure they maintain skills for at least two or three units. The money saved from the lower staffing levels is a benefit to the health care organization. At the same time, one should consider the increased prevention costs that are incurred in the cross-training of the nurses and in the administration of a program to rotate the nursing assignments to maintain the skills developed.

Exhibit 18-4 provides an example of prevention costs in the instance of the radiology retakes. Three types of prevention costs are considered to be designed to prevent failures requiring retakes: (1) staff training, (2) checking of the machine settings, and (3) machine overhauls.

Staff training costs are $4,000 for labor and $2,000 other. It is likely that the $2,000 represents workshop fees or the cost of conducting seminars to train employees. The labor cost represents the time of staff attending training sessions oriented at learning how to avoid the need for retakes.

Checking the machine settings for each use is a relatively minor cost. It only is estimated to require 100 hours of time, spread over 60,000 images taken, or just a few seconds per image. However, this is a critical prevention cost. Not only does it reduce the chance of an under- or overexposed film, it also reduces the risk of an overexposed patient. TQM would likely focus in on the benefit to patient quality of care that can be gained while reducing the failure costs related to poor quality.

Exhibit 18-4 TQM Cost Worksheet: Prevention Costs

Date: 2/12/95

Subject of TQM Analysis _____ Radiology Department Retakes _____

Total Volume: 60,000 images

Part D: Prevention Costs

Type of Cost	Labor Hours	× Average Rate ($)	= Labor Costs ($)	+ Supply Costs ($)	+ Other Costs ($)	= Total Costs ($)
Staff training	160	25	4,000		2,000	6,000
Checking of machine settings each use	100	25	2,500			2,500
Semi-annual machine overhauls	600	18	10,800	15,000		25,800
Total			17,300	15,000	2,000	34,300

Semi-annual machine overhauls require maintenance department labor and replacement parts (supplies). The benefit of such overhauls is that by keeping the x-ray equipment well maintained, there is less chance of poor images and also less patient radiation risk.

Total Quality-Related Costs

Exhibit 18-5 presents a summary of Exhibits 18-1 through 18-4. As in most activities of a health care organization, there is some money spent on correction of failures, and there is some money spent on appraisal and prevention of failures. If small, additional prevention costs could result in large reductions in failure costs, then such additional prevention should be undertaken.

Managers need to know the costs of undertaking CQI and the costs of not undertaking such programs. Often, they are at a loss on how even to begin to measure the implications of not implementing TQM or CQI. The structure of the worksheets presented here should be a significant aid. The cost of undertaking a program can be assessed by determining how the program will affect the amount spent on appraisal and prevention costs. Its benefits can be assessed by its impact on reducing the internal and external failure costs.

The cost of not undertaking such a program can be measured by the extent to which the program could reduce the failure costs. Managers can balance the increased prevention and appraisal costs of doing the program with the reduced failure costs to determine the feasibility of the program.

The worksheets in this section do not represent ideals. The ideal would show zero internal and external failure costs. Nor do they represent all possible appraisal and prevention activities. Instead, they are designed to measure what the organization is currently doing. This establishes a baseline or benchmark of quality costs. Over time, as changes are made, the organization can track the increase or decrease in each of the categories shown on Exhibit 18-5.

The organization can use this type of information to determine if it is worthwhile to spend more on appraisal and prevention to reduce internal and external failures. This, however, requires an evaluation of trade-offs, as discussed below.

Trade-offs

It is unrealistic to expect to have a system of such high quality that neither internal nor external failure costs will be incurred. To achieve such a result would require tremendous expen-

---

Exhibit 18-5 TQM Cost Worksheet: Summary

Date: 2/12/95

Subject of TQM Analysis _____ Radiology Department Retakes _____

Summary

Type of Cost	Labor Costs ($)	+	Supply Costs ($)	+	Other Costs ($)	=	Total Costs ($)
External failure costs (from Part A)	41,990		13,440		8,400		63,830
Internal failure costs (from Part B)	15,450		22,280		14,800		52,530
Appraisal costs (from Part C)	13,750		2,000		0		15,750
Prevention costs (from Part D)	17,300		15,000		2,000		34,300
Total costs	88,490		52,720		25,200		166,410

ditures on prevention and appraisal. Even with such expenditures, total elimination of external and internal failures might not be possible.

However, that does not present a reason not to measure all such costs. There is a definite relationship between the amount expended on prevention and appraisal on the one hand and the costs due to internal and external failures on the other. We should expect that as spending on prevention and appraisal rises, the costs due to internal and external failure decline.

It is likely that the first efforts at prevention and appraisal will have a very high payoff. Rather minor expenditures can eliminate the most glaring and costly potential problems. Additional expenditures result in somewhat less savings. Ultimately, a point will be reached where an extra dollar spent on prevention and appraisal will yield less than a dollar saved in internal and external failure.

This can be represented by a graph such as that shown in Figure 18-4. Moving to the right on the horizontal axis represents increasing quality. Moving up the vertical axis represents increasing cost. One line on the graph represents the costs associated with internal and external failures. As quality improves, failure costs decline. The other line of the graph reflects the costs of prevention and appraisal. As quality increases, these costs rise.

Note that the minimum total cost is not readily apparent. We *cannot* assume that the minimum total cost occurs where the two lines

intersect. It is possible, for example, that additional quality can be obtained for small increases in prevention costs. Those small increases might obtain the benefit of substantial declines in failure costs. Note, for example, in Figure 18-5, that a point well to the right of the intersection is superior to the intersection point. At the intersection, Point A on the horizontal axis, both failure and prevention costs are $10,000. At Point B on the horizontal axis, the prevention costs have only risen to $11,000, but the failure costs have fallen to $5,000. The total costs at Point A are $20,000 (i.e., $10,000 plus $10,000), whereas the total costs at Point B are only $16,000 (i.e., $11,000 plus $5,000).

It is important not to confuse total and marginal costs. Figure 18-5 demonstrates that an optimal level of quality does not necessarily exist at the intersection of *total* failure costs with *total* prevention and appraisal costs. However, it would exist at the intersection of *marginal* failure costs with *marginal* prevention and appraisal costs. The implication of this is that one should continue to improve quality as long as the marginal reduction in failure costs is greater than or equal to the marginal increase in appraisal and prevention costs. If quality were increased beyond that intersection, the reduction in failure costs would be less than the marginal increase in appraisal and prevention costs. It

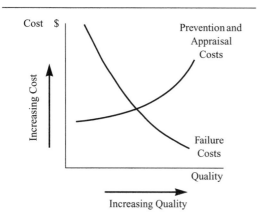

Figure 18-4 Relationship of Prevention and Appraisal and Failure Costs to Quality

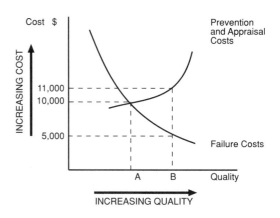

Figure 18-5 Failure Costs versus Prevention and Appraisal Costs: A Numerical Example

would not financially pay to improve quality further.

On the other hand, TQM stresses that new approaches to improve quality and reduce failure costs should constantly be sought. TQM is a continuous process, rather than simply a short movement from one level of quality to another.

Figure 18-5 indicates that it is appropriate for managers to start by developing a set of worksheets such as Exhibits 18-1 through 18-5. Such an approach can allow the manager to see the cost impact of making quality changes. For example, if x-ray machines were overhauled four times a year instead of twice a year, it would increase prevention costs. The increase could be compared with the expected decrease in failure costs.

If an attempt is made to measure or estimate each of the four types of quality costs, then the trade-offs can be evaluated. In practicality, it will probably not be possible, nor is it necessary, to find the exact point at which a dollar spent on prevention and appraisal will actually yield a dollar saved in terms of failures. The types of TQM initiatives available in practice are not likely to be so refined.

However, we can very easily envision a scenario such as the following. In an effort to reduce costs, all inventory levels are reduced to half their prior levels. If the health care organization has a $1 million inventory and a 10 percent cost of capital, the reduction in inventory size to $500,000 will save approximately $50,000 in interest costs alone. Additionally, the lower inventory will reduce the chance of obsolescence and inventory damage, saving perhaps another $10,000 a year (an arbitrary 1 percent of the old inventory level is used here, but in practice it should be estimated as accurately as possible). Thus, there is a potential to save $60,000 per year due to the new inventory policy.

However, if that policy is put in place without adequate planning and attention to implementation, it is likely that external and internal failure costs will rise. There will be times when the inventory on hand is inadequate to meet health care organization needs. Potentially, patient outcomes could be negatively affected, which, unchecked, could have detrimental financial impacts that would easily swamp the savings. Furthermore, it is not clear that without additional controls, the departments will all hold to the lower inventory levels.

On the other hand, if there is a clear view toward all aspects of quality costs, a beneficial outcome is more likely. First of all, careful prevention planning is required to determine which inventory items are crucial to patient well-being. If two types of bandage tape are kept on hand, and either one could replace the other without serious implications for the patient, the risk of running out is not serious. On the other hand, if an item is unique, and running out would have grave consequences, it makes a less attractive candidate for inventory reduction from the start.

Does that mean we should not reduce inventory for the critical items? Not necessarily. Again, the health care organization should balance the potential savings from inventory reduction for that particular item against the cost of ensuring that the supply of that item is adequate. Such assurances could come from monthly, weekly, or daily inventory counts, or could come from a computerized inventory system such as that used by supermarkets. Such a system keeps a perpetual inventory and quickly highlights items that need to be reordered.

Obviously, the monitoring system is a quality cost that could be expensive. On the other hand, overstocking is also expensive. Certainly, running out of a crucial item is expensive. The various costs must be balanced so that the health care organization gains more than it spends.

The key to the entire issue of quality costs is to look beyond the costs of a quality improvement and beyond the savings from an operational change. Too often, a health care organization will reject an improved inventory monitoring system on the grounds that it is a costly quality improvement with no specific payoff. That is not true. There is a payoff in reduced failure costs and in the ability to reduce inventory levels safely and earn a savings. Similarly, too often, a health care organization will jump at the opportunity to reduce inventory and save money, without realizing the exposure in additional failure costs. Quality costs are simply a way to ensure that we are considering both sides of the coin when there are proposals to enhance quality or when there are proposals to reduce costs.

Reporting Systems

To make quality costs a working part of the health care organization management framework, a cost accounting system must be in place that will gather the information and report it on an ongoing basis. Not only should there be a systematic approach but also an individual responsible for the system to ensure the implementation of the approach. In many health care organizations, that person might well be the director of quality assurance.

The person designated as responsible for quality costs must have the responsibility to

> identify and define what quality cost elements are needed to ensure that the resulting data adequately meet the needs of management....The accounting department must then devise a system for identifying the cost elements. Both departments should keep in mind that the raw data are usually provided by other departments and, as such, should be obtained with a minimum of inconvenience to regular operations.[8]

In order to operationalize a quality cost system, a health care organization must have not only an individual with primary responsibility, but also a system for reporting. The starting point for such a system is a set of source documents. Although only some of the costs may actually be measurable, source documents also should be prepared for estimates. There should be reporting of labor hours devoted to activities that relate to quality costs, as well as data sheets for other resources consumed. Such a system will provide information on issues such as the amount of supplies used when there was improper waste or the amount of labor consumed

when something had to be repeated because it was not done properly the first time.

The value of such reporting is clear. It may well be that when the quality cost reporting system is first established, management will have little idea of how much cost is incurred because of a lack of quality control. Health care organization quality control systems have been oriented far more toward patient outcomes than toward the resource implications of patient quality. The new information generated will point the direction for measures of appraisal and prevention that can save more money than they cost. The system will also generate the information needed to evaluate the likely impact of changes such as movement toward a greater degree of float and flexible staffing among nurses.

As the sophistication level within the health care organization quality cost reporting system grows, reports will ultimately parallel many other health care organization retrospective reports, with monthly and year-to-date budget and actual information, and variances, for each type of quality cost. Trends over time can be observed and slippages quickly flagged and corrected.

This book earlier recommended that health care organizations be innovative in the development of cost accounting ratios (Chapter 11). Quality costs represent a good example of an area for the development and use of cost accounting ratios. Once quality costs have been measured, it is possible to generate such cost accounting ratios. For example, quality costs (the sum of external failure, internal failure, appraisal costs and prevention costs) as a percentage of total health care organization costs or as a percentage of total revenues (hopefully both of these ratios will be decreasing over time) would likely provide very useful information.

Extensions

The uses of quality cost information are not limited to aggregate analysis. For example, it may well be possible as health care organization accounting systems move toward product-line information to collect quality cost information by product line, such as by DRG. If it turns out that most of the failure costs are related to just a few of the product lines, it will become a simpler matter to attempt to improve prevention or take other necessary actions. Certainly, such information will at least help us to zero in on the cause of the failures.

This is not to imply that quality costs are easy to implement. Making a system work is a major challenge because of the difficulty in measuring the impact of the status quo in terms of failures or the impact of changes in terms of benefits. The lack of existing data for comparisons with other health care organizations also makes the implementation of a quality cost system more challenging. What percentage of revenues should quality costs be? How low can a health care organization drive its overall quality costs through the expansion of prevention and appraisal? These are clearly unknowns in the health care organization industry. There are some individuals who object to TQM, arguing that it places too much emphasis on zero defects. (For example, see the discussion in Application 18-2.) However, the potential benefits of such a system, even if it takes several years to implement, are great. As we move toward the next century, TQM is a concept that is likely to become an everyday part of management and to have growing implications for cost accounting.

THE QUALITY OF COST DATA

To this point, this chapter has focused on what TQM is and how cost accounting data can aid managers in implementing TQM throughout the organization. However, this falls short in one respect. The cost accounting system itself must undergo CQI. That is the subject of this section.

Health care organization managers are frequently called upon to make cost estimates for both new and ongoing activities. Frequently, the raw data needed by someone in the health care organization are not impossibly difficult to obtain, and financial managers may be tempted to tell the end users of the information to collect it themselves.

However, financial managers are often aware of the limitations of raw data. Therefore, they should exercise care to make sure that all data used throughout the health care organization are collected and adjusted to be suitable to the analysis at hand. It is an old accounting saying that there are different costs for different purposes. The average cost used for one analysis would be inappropriate for a decision that needed marginal cost information.

Similarly, there are times when cost data being used for an analysis must be carefully reviewed for the following:

- to ensure the data are properly matched,
- to eliminate the effect of changing prices,
- to ensure it is based on constant technology,
- to eliminate clerical errors,
- to eliminate unrepresentative periods, and
- to balance the costs and benefits of more accurate information.

Each of these elements is discussed below.

Ensure Data Are Properly Matched

A common complaint about health care accounting is that there is a failure to match information adequately. For example, a nurse may be attempting to determine whether a specific unit is using more supplies than necessary for the number of patients treated. Unfortunately, the supply expense shown on the monthly variance report may not relate directly to supplies used.

Rather, it might indicate the amount of supplies received for that unit or the supplies that were bought. To use supply cost data for the analysis, a study of inventory levels may be necessary to determine exactly how much was used for the month.

Similarly, special studies may require cutoff adjustments for labor or utilities to make sure that the patients in a period are being compared with costs incurred to treat those patients, rather than earlier or later ones. Essentially, this means that sometimes accruals must be made within a year that normally we would only bother with at the end of a year.

This may seem cumbersome and unnecessary to some. However, if variance analysis is to be useful, it must compare accurate measures of actual costs to budgeted costs. If the actual costs reported on a monthly basis represent purchases instead of consumption, how can a department or unit manager determine if the department is consuming too much of a specific resource? Health care organizations place heavy emphasis on using variance analysis as a tool for control. Unfortunately, historically they have placed much less emphasis on ensuring that the data used for variance analysis are adequate for that internal managerial use.

Eliminate the Effect of Changing Prices

When managers are using cost information to make projections about coming-year costs, we must be concerned with the impact of changing prices. Simplistic approaches to this often assume that because inflation is built into any one estimate, there is no need to work actively to get inflation into our future projections.

If we are dealing with just one number being used to project a future number, that obviously would be incorrect. The fact that a current number reflects past inflation does not mean that it reflects future inflation.

On a more subtle basis, however, a similar problem affects a series of historical data points. Given that inflation over time has affected the past costs, one could argue that by trending the costs forward, inflation will be factored into the estimate—and it will. However, this is a haphazard approach, because the rate of inflation is not constant. Simply projecting a trend into the future is misleading.

A more reasonable approach is to use a relevant inflation index to adjust each historical value to a current value. Then the future cost projection can be made. That estimate will be devoid of an adjustment for inflation. The specific inflation rate anticipated for the coming year can then be used to adjust the forecast. The specific rate may well be higher or lower than the average rate over the preceding years.

Techniques for adjusting historical costs for the impact of inflation were discussed in Chapter 7.

Ensure Data Are Based on Constant Technology

Most industries have changes in technology that can directly affect cost estimates. Health care organizations certainly fall into that category. Cost information that is collected in a period with one type of technology is not directly usable for decision making as technology changes.

However, individuals who are not financial managers may not take note of this fact when they use historical cost information as the basis for their decisions. Cost managers should make every effort to determine how significant the impact of changing technology is in any particular instance. Small changes over time may well be impossible to track accurately. Managers should do their best, however, to consider the impact of such changes on the estimates.

If technological changes are substantial in the area of the cost estimate, it may be impossible to use historical data for a meaningful forecast. Although that is unfortunate, use of and reliance upon poor information is often worse than having no information at all.

Eliminate Clerical Errors

It is a very rare accounting system that has so many checks and balances that it is totally free from clerical error. As Moriarity and Allen note,

> no matter how good the accounting system, clerical errors occur. Numbers are added wrong, a cost that should be charged to Department A gets charged to Department B, an item is charged as a cost of operations when it should have been capitalized as an asset, and some items are capitalized that should be expensed.[9]

Many health care organization managers may be unaware of the inadequacies of accounting information. Two plus two is four. The books must balance. With those simple concepts in mind, many managers will fail to see the inherent approximate nature of accounting data. Although the cost accountant cannot make data perfect for use by nonaccountants, there are several things that can be done.

First, nonfinancial managers should be advised of the approximate nature of accounting information. There is no need for managers to have an unduly high confidence in the accuracy of accounting data that they use.

Second, the financial manager should, when possible, review specific data to be used as the basis for a decision to ensure to the extent possible that it is free of clerical errors. Some errors may be buried so deep into the specific numbers being used (having occurred in other numbers that formed the basis for numbers that formed the basis for the current calculations) that they cannot be uncovered without an unduly expensive investigation. On the other hand, a simple review of the numbers to be directly used in an analysis can at least eliminate some of the clerical or computational errors.

Eliminate Unrepresentative Periods

Many health care organizations encounter unusual circumstances from time to time that would make data collected during that time period particularly unrepresentative. For instance, a unit may be remodeled but remain open during the remodeling. This would severely suppress occupancy. There may be a small fire, putting part of a unit out of commission. Breakdowns in equipment might reduce the volume of a particular type of patient during the period when the equipment is out of service. Employee strikes are another circumstance that will result in severely distorted data for the period of the strike.

Cost data collected during such unrepresentative periods can be misleading to the user of the information. When several years of monthly data are being used, managers may easily forget that one month, several years earlier, was atypical. Financial managers should attempt to keep a record of unusual situations as they arise. Then they can refer back to that record before using data, to see if the data are likely to contain aberrant information.

Data from unrepresentative periods should be excluded from analyses whenever possible. If the analysis requires data from each time period, it may be advisable to replace the distorted data with dummy data that fits the existing data pattern. Statistical methods used for forecasting generally can adequately incorporate the random fluctuations health care organizations encounter. There are unusually busy or slow months. Outlier data points should not automatically be excluded. Such exclusion implies that such outliers cannot occur again in the future, even though it is likely that they might. However, specific, rare events that are truly unrepresentative will cloud the results rather than provide useful information.

Balance the Costs and Benefits of More Accurate Data

Cost information costs money. Managers are wasting the health care organization's resources if they spend more on collecting refined, precise data than is necessary for a specific analysis. Many nonfinancial managers find it difficult to accept any data that they believe is less than perfectly correct. The financial manager must make clear, however, that sometimes data need only be good enough for the decision at hand.

Managers must always consider the purpose of the data being collected. For what purpose are the data going to be used? How likely are small variations in the raw data to change the management decision based on the data? The more sensitive the decision is to changes in the data, the more reliable the information must be. The cost of better information must be balanced with the benefits of more accurate estimates.

Data are often taken for granted. A decision requires a certain type of cost information, so that information is collected. Financial managers, however, note that there are many answers to the same question about costs. The specific cost information provided may be critical in making a correct managerial decision.

Financial managers have a responsibility to help nonfinancial managers base their decisions on useful, relevant information. When raw data can be easily improved, financial managers should step forward and adjust the data. When improvements are too costly, financial managers should at a minimum inform the users of the data of their limitations and whether they are still the appropriate data to use, despite those limitations.

A FOCUS ON CUSTOMERS

One of the hallmarks of TQM is the importance of considering the needs and expectations of customers. Cost accountants must carefully consider the implications of this. Who are the customers of the cost accountant? Clearly, not only are patients customers; there are many internal customers as well. Nurses must realize that physicians are customers. After all, physicians admit patients. Pharmacists must realize that nurses are customers. After all, nurses administer medications. In addition, financial managers must realize that users of cost information are customers.

That is why the inherent focus of financial management is starting to shift from control to service. Certainly, finance retains its "scorekeeper" function. It must measure the movement of the organization, its managers, and its departments toward achieving its CQI goals. However, just as important is the need to teach managers what cost information is available, or could be available, and how to use that information.

Front-line managers and mid-level managers are customers. Inherently, by definition, line managers are customers and staff managers, such as finance managers, represent service departments. However, in many health care organizations, finance is perceived as a department of gatherers of information, controllers, and evaluators, but not as helpers: not as individuals who primarily are available to offer assistance.

TQM generates a need to be able to answer questions such as, "Why is Dr. A more (or less) costly than the other physicians with similar patients?" In order to improve clinical outcomes, efficiency, and effectiveness, cost accountants must respond to such a need by providing their customers (the organization's line managers) with relevant cost data.

Under a TQM approach to management, managers need to know the cost implications of potential decisions and the cost outcomes of approaches as they are implemented. Cost accountants must meet those needs of their customers.

NOTES

1. D. Garvin, Japanese quality management, *Columbia Journal of World Business* 19, no. 3:4, as cited by C.T. Horngren and G. Foster, *Cost Accounting: A Managerial Emphasis,* 7th ed. (Englewood Cliffs, N.J.: Prentice-Hall, 1991), 912.

2. C.T. Horngren and G. Foster, *Cost Accounting: A Managerial Emphasis,* 7th ed. (Englewood Cliffs, N.J.: Prentice-Hall, 1991), 913.

3. V. Arikian, Total quality management: Applications to nursing service, *Journal of Nursing Administration* 21, no. 6 (June 1991): 46.

4. R. Kirk, The big picture: Total quality management and continuous quality improvement, *Journal of Nursing Administration* 22, no. 4 (April 1992): 24.

5. T. Gillem, Deming's 14 points and hospital quality: Responding to the consumer's demand for the best

value in health care, *Nursing Quality Assurance* 2, no. 3 (1988): 70.

6. J.D. Suver et al., *Management Accounting for Healthcare Organizations,* 3rd ed. (Chicago: Healthcare Financial Management Association and Pluribus Press, Inc., 1992), 476–477.

7. J.B. Simpson and D.L. Muthler, Quality costs: Facilitating the quality initiative, *Journal of Cost Management for the Manufacturing Industry* 1, no. 1 (Spring 1987): 25–34.

8. *Ibid.,* 29–30.

9. S. Moriarity and C.P. Allen, *Cost Accounting,* 3rd ed. (New York: John Wiley & Sons, 1991), 70.

SUGGESTED READING

Anderson, C.A., and R.D. Daigh. February 1991. Quality mind-set overcomes barriers to success. *Healthcare Financial Management* 21–32.

Anonymous. 1992. Task force for quality in financial management. *Management Accounting* 74, no. 4:26.

Arikian, V. 1991. Total quality management: Applications to nursing service. *Journal of Nursing Administration* 21, no. 6:46–50.

Baptist, A., et al. 1987. Developing a solid base for a cost accounting system. *Healthcare Financial Management* 42–48.

Daigh, R.D. 1991. Financial implications of a quality improvement process. *Topics in Health Care Financing* 17, no. 3:42–52.

Gillem, T. 1988. Deming's 14 points and hospital quality: Responding to the consumer's demand for the best value in health care. *Nursing Quality Assurance* 2, no. 3:70–78.

Gitlow, H., and S. Gitlow. 1987. *The Deming guide to quality and competitive position*. Englewood Cliffs, N.J.: Prentice-Hall.

Horngren, C.T., and G. Foster. 1991. *Cost accounting: A managerial emphasis*. 7th ed. Englewood Cliffs, N.J.: Prentice-Hall.

Kirk, R. 1992. The big picture: Total quality management and continuous quality improvement. *Journal of Nursing Administration* 22, no. 4:24–31.

Lynn, M.L., and D.P. Osborn. 1991. Deming's quality principles: A health care application. *Hospitals and Health Services Administration* 36, no. 2:111–119.

McLaughlin, C.P., and A.D. Kaluzny. 1990. Total quality management. *Health Care Management Review* 15, no. 3:7–14.

McNair, C.J., et al. 1989. *Beyond the bottom line: Measuring world class performance*. Homewood, Ill.: Dow Jones-Irwin.

Milakovich, M.E. 1991. Creating a total quality health care environment. *Health Care Management Review* 16, no. 2:9–20.

Moriarity, S., and C.P. Allen. 1991. *Cost accounting*. 3rd ed. New York: John Wiley & Sons.

Omachonu, V.K. 1991. *Total quality and productivity management in health care organizations*. Norcross, Ga.: Industrial Engineering and Management Press, Institute of Industrial Engineers.

Riley, J.F., and S.R. Heath. 1992. Quality improvement means better productivity. *Healthcare Executive* 7, no. 3:19–21.

Schimmel, R.E., ed. 1991. Measuring quality of care. *Topics in Health Care Financing* 18, no. 2.

Simpson, J.B., and D.L. Muthler. 1987. Quality costs: Facilitating the quality initiative. *Journal of Cost Management for the Manufacturing Industry* 1, no. 1:25–34.

Steimer, T.E. 1990. Activity-based accounting for total quality. *Management Accounting* 72, no. 1:39–42.

Stodolak, F., and J. Carr. June 1992. Systems must be compatible with quality efforts. *Healthcare Financial Management* 72–77.

Suver, J.D., et al. September 1992. Accounting for the costs of quality. *Healthcare Financial Management* 29–37.

EXERCISES

QUESTIONS FOR DISCUSSION

1. Does higher quality necessarily require higher costs?

2. When one speaks of higher quality for health care organizations, does this refer to patient care quality?

3. What are some factors that managers should consider when reviewing the quality of cost accounting data?

4. What dilemma are most health care organizations facing with respect to the quality of patient care?

5. Is it essential that accounting departments be able to measure quality and the cost of improvements in quality?

PROBLEM

1. Develop an example of quality cost accounting. Follow the model presented in the chapter for radiology retakes. Make tables (with hypothetical data) for internal failure costs, external failure costs, appraisal costs, and prevention costs. Then suggest a change that would improve quality. Show how each of the four tables and the total costs change as a result of the proposed quality change.

Note: Solutions to the Exercises can be found in Appendix A.

Application 18-1

Using Cost Accounting Techniques in the Total Quality Management Framework

Donna S. Windemuth, RN, MPA,
is currently Associate Director, Administration at
The Hospital for Special Surgery, New York, New York.

Total Quality Management (TQM) means continuous quality improvement. Planning efforts are concentrated in the management of daily operations to minimize the costs of organizational quality failures. A Total Cost Management system is a natural part of the TQM approach. Increasing the efficacy and effectiveness of the cost accounting system results in better quality data, which improves management's overall decision-making process. To achieve this goal, the cost accounting system must be proactive, not reactive.[1]

Traditional financial reports that contain historical cost information are often used in the organizational decision-making process. The cost of quality is often hidden in these types of reports, and it is difficult to see the true costs of providing quality. A Total Cost Management system that is in alignment with TQM principles will continually create new cost accounting techniques to help improve data quality, which provides positive support to the management decision-making process.

TQM demonstrates that poor quality is expensive. Higher quality does not have to be expensive—in fact, quality improvements can achieve increased revenues and/or decreased costs, both of which have a positive impact on the institution's bottom line.[2] For example, improved client satisfaction can increase operating revenues as existing patients keep their health care appointments. The word-of-mouth spread of approval in the community improves market share, which adds to a positive revenue stream. When institutional procedures are improved to eliminate ancillary testing errors and repeat tests, the cost of these failures declines, as the costs for added labor and test materiel for repeat indices decrease.

Figure 18-1-1 depicts trade-offs experienced in the cost of quality. As preventative and ap-

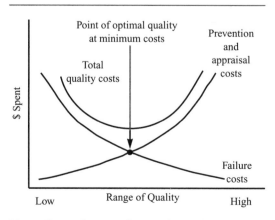

Figure 18-1-1 The Costs of Quality in Standard Operations

praisal costs increase, higher measures of quality are observed. As the number of preventative costs incurred rises, the number of failures declines. Lower quality yields a higher number of failures, which increases costs. The minimum point on the total cost line represents optimal quality at minimal costs.[3] Movement in this direction describes the total cost management journey within the TQM framework.

AN APPLICATION

Several methods may be used to calculate the cost of quality in a health care setting, including the preventative, appraisal, and failure costs models. A focused study was performed to illustrate the process and identify and resolve problems reported by the patients and nursing and clerical staff in an outpatient setting. Specifically, the concept was applied in the Gold Therapy outpatient clinic of a hospital. The Bethesda Inc. model outlines the TQM process steps.[4]

1. Review the Current Situation

Gold therapy is a treatment modality used for patients with rheumatic disease. In this setting, each patient receives a series of gold serum injections to ameliorate the anti-inflammatory process and relieve pain. Patients are scheduled for treatments on a weekly basis. The medication is given by the nursing staff based on blood test results from the previous week. The nurse reviews the medication precautions with the patient and, if appropriate, administers the medication. Before leaving the clinic setting, the patient schedules an appointment for a return visit. A high incidence of patient complaints led to an effort to identify reasons for service delays in the Gold Therapy Clinic. A team composed of the outpatient nurse manager, a laboratory technologist, a medical records manager, and the outpatient administrator was assembled to address the problem.

2. Describe the Process

The team developed a flow chart showing the patient flow process for gold therapy services.

The flow chart demonstrated how patient waiting time increased if laboratory reports were not available when the patient arrived for the clinic visit (see Figure 18-1-2). A cost-of-quality worksheet (see Exhibit 18-1-1) was used to develop estimates of non–value-added time or waste time.[5] A special study was conducted to measure the time spent in the various activities of the Gold Therapy Clinic procedure.

3. Explore Cause Theories

The team theorized that patient documentation was not properly prepared prior to the Gold Therapy Clinic visit date. Patients who were not registered in advance of their appointment times experienced longer waiting times before receiving their medication. The unavailability of medical records and laboratory reports added to patient waiting times. To revitalize staff morale and improve patient satisfaction, gold therapy clinic waiting times must be reduced.

4. Collect and Analyze Data

The patient process was studied for a period of six weeks. Preventative, appraisal, and failure quality cost areas were documented (see Table 18-1-1) on a Cost of Quality Calculation Table.[6] Each patient visit required an average of six minutes of preparation prior to gold therapy treatment. The following quality process failures were found to add to patient waiting times:

- lack of pre-registration—20 percent
- lack of medical records at visit—20 percent
- lack of available laboratory report—20 percent
- repeated laboratory test—5 percent
- no-show for gold therapy clinic—5 percent

The annual cost of poor quality was defined as the sum of the internal and external failures. These costs are shown in Table 18-1-1. Before the existing procedure was revised, the total cost of failure for the Gold Therapy Clinic was $8,066 annually. Note that this is substantially more than the $3,620 cost of prevention and appraisal (Table 18-1-1).

5. Generate Potential Solutions

The following process revisions were recommended:

- pre-register all patients by telephone before they arrive at the clinic
- have nursing perform chart review of all medical records for patients scheduled for gold therapy visits 24 hours before the appointment date
- identify at chart review patients who require repeat laboratory testing, and send them to the laboratory at clinic check-in
- develop patient satisfaction questionnaire for gold therapy patients

TQM is a system for meeting and exceeding client needs and expectations. To implement TQM at the Gold Therapy Clinic, the Shewhart model of the "Plan, Do, Check, and Act" cycle was used.[7]

a. Plan

A system to update all Gold Therapy Clinic registrations by telephone prior to the visit date was developed. Pre-visit chart review was added to the nursing assignment. A patient routing slip was completed and left at the check-in desk to expedite processing for patients who require repeat laboratory testing.

b. Do

The changes were implemented.

c. Check

The patient flow process was studied again two weeks after the new procedures were implemented, and the following results were noted.

Exhibit 18-1-1 Cost of Quality Worksheet

Department: _____   Date: _____

Internal Failure Costs

Descrip-tion	No. Hours per Month	$ Rate per Hour	$ Labor per Month	$ Supply per Month	$ Oth. Exp. per Month	$ Qual. Cost per Month	$ Qual. Cost per Year
(1)	(2)	(3)	(4) (2)×(3)	(5)	(6)	(7) (4)+(5)+(6)	(8) (7)×12
Total							

External Failure Costs

Descrip-tion	No. Hours per Month	$ Rate per Hour	$ Labor per Month	$ Supply per Month	$ Oth. Exp. per Month	$ Qual. Cost per Month	$ Qual. Cost per Year
(1)	(2)	(3)	(4) (2)×(3)	(5)	(6)	(7) (4)+(5)+(6)	(8) (7)×12
Total							

Department: _____   Date: _____

Prevention Costs

Descrip-tion	No. Hours per Month	$ Rate per Hour	$ Labor per Month	$ Supply per Month	$ Oth. Exp. per Month	$ Qual. Cost per Month	$ Qual. Cost per Year
(1)	(2)	(3)	(4) (2)×(3)	(5)	(6)	(7) (4)+(5)+(6)	(8) (7)×12
Total							

Appraisal Costs

Descrip-tion	No. Hours per Month	$ Rate per Hour	$ Labor per Month	$ Supply per Month	$ Oth. Exp. per Month	$ Qual. Cost per Month	$ Qual. Cost per Year
(1)	(2)	(3)	(4) (2)×(3)	(5)	(6)	(7) (4)+(5)+(6)	(8) (7)×12
Total							

Source: Reprinted from Robin D. Daigh, "Financial Implications of a Quality Improvement Process," *Topics in Health Care Financing,* Vol. 17(3), 1991, pp. 47–48. Copyright 1991, Aspen Publishers, Inc.

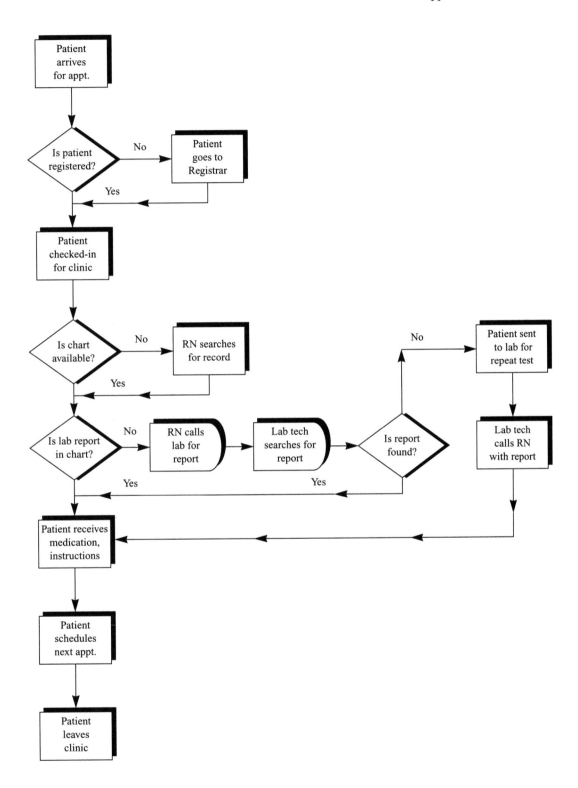

Figure 18-1-2 Gold Therapy Patient Flow Chart

Table 18-1-1 Cost of Quality Calculation, Gold Therapy Outpatient Clinic

Type	Description	Estimated Volume	Annual Volume	Staff Position	Minutes per Episode	Annual Hours	Hourly Wage ($)	Salary Expense ($)	Benefits (25%) ($)	Estimated Cost of Quality ($)
Prevention										
	Train RNs in GTC protocol	1 hour/year × 4 RNs	4	RN	—	4	22	88	22	100
	Train clerks in registration process	8 hour/year × 3 clerks	24	Reg. Clerk	—	24	14	336	84	420
Appraisal										
	Check registration for proper info.	100% of GTC pts. 1,200 vs./year	1,200	Reg. Clerk	1	20	14	280	70	350
	Chart review for lab report	100% of GTC pts. 1,200 vs./year	1,200	RN	5	100	22	2,200	550	2,750
Total Prevention and Appraisal Costs										3,620
Internal Failure										
	Face-to-face registration for patients not pre-registered	5 patients/week × 52 wks.	260	Reg. Clerk	20	87	14	1,218	305	1,523
	Locate chart not in GTC	5 patients/week × 52 wks.	260	RN	15	65	22	1,430	358	1,788
	Locate lab report not in GTC	5 patients/week × 52 wks.	260	RN	10	43	22	946	237	1,183
	Repeat lab test	1 patient/week × 52 wks.	260	Lab Tech	5	22	17	374	94	468
			52	Labor/machine/ supply cost per test run	—	—	2	104	—	104
External Failure										
	Loss of patient volume	5% of 1,200 pts. annually	60	Clinic revenue $50/vs.	—	—	—	—	—	3,000
Total Internal and External Failure Costs										8,066

- Face-to-face registration decreased by 40 percent, to three patients per week, resulting in an annual cost savings of $609.

- The length of time spent locating the medical record on the visit date was reduced by 80 percent, to one patient record/week. Patient waiting time was improved, but chart location time was displaced to 24 hours prior to the clinic visit date. Cost savings for this index was $0.

- The length of time spent locating laboratory reports on the clinic visit day was reduced to less than one patient/week. Cost savings were not actualized for this step because the labor effort was displaced to 24 hours prior to the clinic visit date.

- Repeat laboratory tests decreased to less than one patient/month, with a cost savings of $80.

- The patient no-show rate decreased by 40 percent, or by two patients/month. The increased revenues added $1,200 annually to clinic revenues.

Process improvements resulted in total cost savings of $1,889 annually. Patient satisfaction increased, due to greater expediency in clinic processing and decreased clinic waiting time.

d. Act

The new procedural changes were standardized and implemented throughout all clinics. Total cost savings for pre-registration and pre-visit chart review is expected to exceed $35,000 in labor dollars alone. These new processes are monitored on a monthly basis. Quality improvements to the medical record retrieval process for all clinic visits have also been required; a working team will be assembled for further investigation.

As referenced in the literature, the costs of quality prior to any improvement methodologies are 20 to 30 percent of net revenue.[8] In the outpatient clinic study, failure costs were reduced from 69 percent of pre-improvement quality costs to 63 percent of post-improvement quality costs. Additional cost savings are expected as the TQM team for outpatient services continues quality planning.

CONCLUSION

The Total Cost Management process is a natural part of the TQM process. Poor quality must be identified and eliminated in an industry that is challenged to exist and compete in an environment of scarce resources. Many creative avenues for obtaining cost information to improve the quality of management's decision-making process exist in the clinical setting. The cost of special studies and the appropriate resources to achieve such improvements must be weighed against the usefulness of the data obtained.[9] As health care organizations strive to satisfy their many customers, Total Cost Management methods will support their efforts to identify and resolve problems.

NOTES

1. J.D. Suver, B.R. Neumann, and K. Boles. *Management Accounting for Healthcare Organizations,* 3rd. ed., pp. 477–83. Chicago, Ill.: Healthcare Financial Management Association and Pluribus Press, Inc., 1992.

2. *Ibid.*

3. J.H. Atkinson, Jr., et al., *Current Trends in Cost of Quality.* NJ: NAA, 1991.

4. G. Kaminski, "Total Quality Management at Bethesda, Inc." *Journal for Healthcare Quality* 14, No. 6 (1992).

5. R.D. Daigh, "Financial Implications of a Quality Improvement Process." *Topics in Health Care Financing* 17, No. 3 (1991): 47–48.

6. C.A. Anderson and R.D. Daigh, "Quality Mind-Set Overcomes Barriers to Success." *Healthcare Financial Management* (February 1991): 31.

7. U.K. Sahney and G.L. Warden, "The Quest for Quality and Productivity in Health Services." *Frontiers of Health Services Management* 7, No. 4 (1991): 4–7.

8. D.L. Muthler and J.B. Simpson, "Quality Costs: Facilitating the Quality Initiative." *Journal of Cost Management for the Manufacturing Industry* 1, No. 1 (1987).

9. S.A. Finkler, *Cost Accounting for Health Care Organizations: Concepts and Applications.* Gaithersburg, MD: Aspen Publishers, 1993.

Application 18-2

A Review of "Supporting Manufacturing Management"

Steven A. Finkler, PhD, CPA

Elsewhere in this issue of *Hospital Cost Accounting Advisor* is a discussion of the benefits of a quality cost system. This article, by Larry Utzig, argues that the use of quality costs measurements leads to an overemphasis on defect-reduction and does little to raise product performance.

According to Utzig, pursuit of perfection in the form of zero defects has become a common view of quality. This leads to a focus on reducing failure costs rather than on building a reputation among customers for high quality. As a result, managers fail to consider the value of quality for achieving higher market share, higher prices, or both.

Essentially the problem Utzig sees stems from a different perception of high quality by managers and customers. According to the author, a customer would measure quality in terms of such factors as customer service, employee attitudes, and customer communication as well as product quality.

The author uses an example of electrical wall switches. For a contractor, ease of installation is

the key requirement, while for a homeowner appearance, quiet operation, and reliability are the key quality factors. This can easily be viewed from the hospital perspective. Are the customers the physicians who admit the patients, or are they the patients themselves? The answer in the hospital is probably "both." Quality measures should consider that as decisions are made regarding changes in hospital operations. Clearly, knowing who your customer is can impact on what is considered good quality.

The author stresses that customer-based measures are needed to know the relative importance of various aspects of the product to the consumer and the customer's current view of the organization's product relative to that of its competition. As the author puts it, "Quality leadership or parity with the leaders is achieved only through customer recognition. Internal quality measurements, including competitive product analyses, are insignificant" (page 68).

The author's points are well taken in general. There is no question that a hospital that buries itself in its own notion of quality may indeed miss the point. If we wish to reduce costs without unduly creating failures which are in turn more costly, we must understand what failures are likely to arise. Suppose that a hospital is used to using only the very best of a certain type of supply. It may bother hospital staff to switch to a lower quality product, but the patient may

Source: Reprinted from Steven A. Finkler, Review of "Supporting Manufacturing Management" by Larry V. Utzig, in the *Journal of Cost Management for the Manufacturing Industry,* Vol. 1, No. 1, Spring 1987, pp. 66–69. Review published in *Hospital Cost Accounting Advisor,* Vol. 3, No. 5, October 1987, p. 6. Copyright 1987, Aspen Publishers, Inc.

not know the difference, unless it impacts on the final patient outcome. If it will not affect the outcome, then use of the lower quality supply will not impact on the perceived treatment offered by the hospital. In that case the reduced costs may well be worthwhile.

However, it is our view that the quality cost approach, as described elsewhere in this issue of *Hospital Cost Accounting Advisor,* is not incompatible with these notions. Quality cost measurement doesn't require zero defects, but rather that the cost of defects be less than the cost of correcting or avoiding them. As Utzig notes, "Today's highly competitive environment requires an understanding of both the customer and internal views of quality. Total productivity improvement means increasing sales without increasing resources used or, better yet, increasing sales and decreasing resources used. Improved customer-perceived quality increases sales, and improved internal quality drives manufacturing capability" (page 69). We have no argument with that concept, and we believe that it is quite complementary to the establishment of a quality cost accounting and reporting system.

19

Summary and Issues for the Future

Goals of This Chapter

---

1. Introduce the notion that cost accounting is a dynamic field, changing in response to the cost information needs of health care organizations.
2. Address the current status and likely future directions of product-line costing.
3. Consider the possibly decreasing role of revenue centers and changing role of cost allocation for health care organizations in the coming years.
4. Provide a closing summary of the text, and of the importance of cost accounting development.

Key Terms Used in This Chapter

Distribution; market management; strategic business unit.

Note: Key terms appear in italics when first used in the chapter. All key terms are defined in the Glossary.

INTRODUCTION

Cost accounting is a well-developed field, built on a solid conceptual foundation. However, that does not mean that the field is static. That is far from the case, as the reader should have sensed from the topics covered in the preceding two chapters.

Health care is a dynamic field. As the needs of health care organizations change over time, cost accounting must be flexible, adjusting adequately to provide the information managers need. This chapter provides a summary of the text and looks at a few issues that are likely to be focal points of health care cost accounting debate in the coming years.

The era of prospective payment is expected to lead health care organizations to begin to do more accurate product costing. The 1990s and beyond will focus to an ever-greater extent on managed care. Such an approach will require more detailed product costing. Information must be available on what the costs are for each health care organization product or product line, with the product typically being identified as the patient, but detailed information is also desired concerning the intermediate products required to treat each type of patient.

COST ACCOUNTING FOUNDATIONS

Exhibit 19-1 outlines some of the major uses of cost accounting data. From a narrow perspective, cost accounting is an element of financial management that generates information about the costs of an organization. As such, cost accounting is a subset of accounting in general; accounting generates financial information. From a broader perspective, cost accounting encompasses the development and provision of a wide range of financial information that is useful to managers in their organizational roles. This includes all of managerial accounting, plus those elements of financial accounting related to the external reporting of cost information.

In particular, cost accounting is especially useful in the areas of planning and control, nonroutine decision making, inventory valuation and income determination, and preparation of required cost reports.

In general, costs are not measured in a way that provides an exact measure of resource consumption. Such measurement would be extremely costly. Rather, trade-offs are made between the accuracy of cost information and the costliness of collecting the information. A benefit/cost criterion is employed, which requires that the benefit of information always exceed the cost of its generation.

Exhibit 19-2 reviews the structure of the first section of this book.

As discussed in Chapter 1, a conflict arises in cost accounting between the dual roles of collecting cost information for external reports versus collecting information for use by managers. The focus and types of information for these two purposes often conflict. The last decade has seen a dramatic shift in health care and industry at large toward placing more emphasis on generating useful information for internal decision making.

Cost accounting focuses not only on generating cost information but also on using informa-

---

Exhibit 19-1 Some Uses of Cost Accounting

Cost accounting . . .
1. Generates information about the costs of an organization;
2. Encompasses the development and provision of financial information useful to managers;
3. Is especially helpful in the areas of
   - planning and control,
   - nonroutine decisions,
   - inventory valuation,
   - income determination,
   - preparation of required cost reports, and
   - decision making in general.

Exhibit 19-2 Summary of Part I

COST ACCOUNTING FOUNDATIONS

Cost Definitions
Product Costing
Cost Allocation
Cost–Volume–Profit (Breakeven) Analysis
Costing for Nonroutine Decisions

tion for control purposes. Control requires the active participation and cooperation of the individuals working for the organization. Therefore, the role of human beings in cost accounting cannot be overstated. Cost accounting must always consider the impact of accounting on motivation and incentives within the organization.

The foundations of cost accounting require an understanding of the basic definitions related to cost, the approaches organizations can take to costing their product, the methods that can be used for cost allocation, the tool of breakeven analysis, and the approach health care organizations can take for making nonroutine decisions.

Cost Definitions

A truism of cost accounting is that there are different measurements of cost for different purposes. The question, "What does it cost?" cannot be answered simply. First, one must respond, "It depends. Why do you want to know?"

Chapter 2 discussed the definitions and characteristics of

- full costs,
- average costs,
- cost objectives,
- direct costs,
- indirect costs,
- fixed costs,
- variable costs,
- joint costs, and
- marginal costs.

True costs, economic costs, and accounting costs were contrasted, as were long-term costs versus short-term costs. However, the definitions are merely a jumping-off point. The user of cost accounting information must carefully assess which measurement of cost is most appropriate for a particular problem or decision.

Product Costing

Ultimately, all health care organizations need to assign a cost to each patient treated. This is generally accomplished through some form of job-order or process costing system. Job-order costing is an approach that measures specifically the direct labor and materials used for an individual patient or a type of patient. In contrast, process costing is based on a broad averaging of costs across patients. Standard costing approaches attempt to determine, in advance, the likely costs of treating different types of patients, and in some cases, the individual intermediate products produced for the treatment of patients.

Regardless of which approach to product costing is chosen, there are a number of decisions that managers must make that require information about the cost of treating patients:

- Should a service be offered?
- Can we offer the service as cheaply as the competitor down the block?
- What is the minimum acceptable price for a product if it is to contribute to organizational profits?

These are the types of questions health care managers are asking today. Product costing provides the data to answer these questions.

Product costing is also needed for external reporting. There has been a growing interest by parties external to the organization to know what it costs the organization to treat different types of patients. For example, health maintenance organizations (HMOs) would like to know hospital costs for each type of patient so that they can negotiate more effectively. The federal government would like to know costs by type of patient so that it can set Medicare Diagnosis Related Group (DRG) rates more effectively.

Cost Allocation

Cost allocation represents taking costs from one area or cost objective and allocating them to others. There are two primary types of cost allocation that apply. The first is the allocation of indirect costs within a department to specific, individual patients. For example, how much of the head nurse's salary should be assigned to each patient on a medical/surgical unit of a hospital? The second type of allocation is from one department or cost center to another. For example, in a hospital, housekeeping might allocate its costs to the various departments and cost centers that use its services. The housekeeping costs, once allocated to other departments, can eventually be allocated to specific patients.

Many allocated costs are referred to as overhead. Overhead represents costs that are generally indirect, and cannot easily be associated with individual patients, even by a job-order type of detailed observation and measurement. Overhead costs therefore require some form of aggregation and then allocation to patients.

The goal of cost allocation is to associate costs as closely as possible with the patients that cause them to be incurred. Cost allocation was discussed in Chapter 4.

Cost–Volume–Profit Analysis

The relationship of costs, volume, and profits is one of the most essential in financial management. Why is this important? When organizations examine their total operations or any given program or service, managers must also be able to estimate how great the profits or losses are likely to be. Financial solvency of the organization requires that there be an understanding of what losses are expected to be encountered and how they will be offset. That information can be used by those who are in a position to weigh all factors in deciding what activities the organization should undertake or maintain.

If costs were a constant amount per patient, determining profitability for any existing or proposed service would be quite straightforward. The revenue per patient could be compared with the cost per patient. If the revenue is greater than the cost, a profit will result. However, since the average cost depends on volume, the revenue per patient may be greater or less than the cost per patient, depending on the volume of service attained, so profitability is uncertain. Breakeven analysis provides a tool that

allows managers to assess the volume at which any service moves from a loss position to a profit position. Chapter 5 addressed breakeven analysis and its limitations.

Costing for Nonroutine Decisions

Much of the management of an organization is concerned with the planning and control of routine operations. However, a significant portion of management effort also focuses on the nonroutine. Examples of nonroutine decisions include adding or dropping a service or program, expanding or scaling back a service or program, weighing the make versus buy decision, and handling short-run pricing concerns. In many cases, decisions related to nonroutine events are more difficult, if only because managers do not have the experience of dealing with the specific decisions on a day-to-day basis.

In addressing nonroutine decisions, managers must first identify alternative options. Next, the relevant costs for the decision must be ascertained. Nonfinancial issues related to the decision should also be considered. The approach to making nonroutine decisions was addressed in Chapter 6.

COST ACCOUNTING INFORMATION FOR PLANNING AND CONTROL

The second major part of this book considered the essential elements of cost accounting for the purposes of planning and control. Exhibit 19-3 summarizes the contents of this part. Chapter 7 focused on the prediction of future costs, Chapter 8 considered budgeting, Chapter 9 was pri-

Exhibit 19-3 Summary of Part II

COST ACCOUNTING INFORMATION FOR PLANNING AND CONTROL
Predicting Future Costs Budgeting Variance Analysis Management Control

marily concerned with variance analysis, and Chapter 10 discussed management control.

Predicting Future Costs

There are a number of different ways that future costs can be predicted. Where historical information is lacking, groups can be used to estimate costs. The nominal group technique and Delphi technique are the two most popular of these approaches. When historical data are available for the cost objective to be forecast, sophisticated statistical techniques can be used to furnish management with highly accurate projections.

Linear regression is one of the most widely used statistical techniques for cost estimation. Based on the equation for a straight line, linear regression allows one to estimate the slope and intercept of a line that is the best linear predictor based on historical data. The slope represents the variable cost, and the intercept represents the fixed cost. This allows one to estimate the future cost at any expected volume of activity.

Regression, however, is limited by the constraints of linearity. In recent years, computer technology has made curvilinear forecasting an accessible tool for health care managers. Such approaches allow the manager to make forecasts in situations in which a straight line does not adequately describe the historical patterns. This is especially true in cases where seasonality exists—a very common occurrence in the provision of health care services.

Another valuable tool for forecasting is learning curve analysis. Learning curves are a forecasting tool that have been in use for over 50 years. However, they have not been widely applied in the health care sector. As we start to focus more and more on total quality management and continuous quality improvement, tools such as the learning curve can provide substantial help.

Budgeting

A budget is a plan. Budgets are generally formalized written documents. Budgeting is the process of developing a plan, implementing it, and attempting to control outcomes so that they conform to or exceed the results called for by the plan. Budgeting is an element of cost accounting, because much of the planning relates to costs the organization expects to incur.

Planning is an essential process for the efficient management of organizations. It allows one to think ahead about potential problems and either avoid them or develop potential solutions. Planning requires an ongoing effort, with plans being made and carried out, then the results evaluated, and the information from what actually happens incorporated into future plans to improve the accuracy of the planning process. As such, it forms a continuous loop of information.

Organizations have many different types of budgets. These include long-range or strategic budgets, program budgets, operating budgets, capital budgets, cash budgets, and special-purpose budgets.

Specifically, we can think of the budget process as serving the roles of

- forcing managers to plan ahead and consider alternatives;
- improving organizational communication and coordination; and
- providing a basis for evaluation of unit and managerial performance.

Variance Analysis

Once a budget is made, an organization has a plan. However, reality rarely follows plans exactly. The variances between actual results and plans must be examined on a timely basis. If there are favorable variances that represent a positive result for the organization, we need to find out why, so that the actions that led to those variances can be encouraged and continued. If there are unfavorable results, we must try to determine if they are caused by controllable or noncontrollable events. Controllable events call for management action to get spending back within budget guidelines.

Traditional variance analysis compares the costs with the budget for each budget line for each cost center. Without significant time investment in investigation, such analysis provides only limited information to managers. Flexible budget variance analysis is an approach that focuses on what costs would have been budgeted to be if actual workload levels had been accurately forecast. This allows each line's variance to be segregated into the portion caused by changes in the price of resources, the portion caused by the change in the amount of resource used for each unit of service provided, and the portion caused by the change in the total amount of work done. With this added information, managers can make more informed decisions regarding whether variance investigation is required, and if so, can more easily focus that investigation.

Management Control

Control is the process of attempting to ensure that desired results are achieved. Management control systems are formalized systems used by an organization's management to ensure that its mission and specific goals are accomplished as effectively and efficiently as possible.

There are many elements of a control system designed to keep control over the organization and its results. Checks and balances exist to prevent fraud and embezzlement. Computer security controls exist to prevent alterations or accidental loss of critical information. As mentioned above, variance reporting systems exist to report on the organization's ability to keep actual results close to the budget.

Management control systems include such topics as systems for collecting accurate financial and cost information, systems to resolve conflict among needs, the programming process and program analysis, budgets, control of operations, measurement of output, reporting on performance, and evaluation of performance. Management control systems attempt to make what is in the best interests of the organization also be in the best interests of the individuals working for the organization.

One element of a management control system is the identification and monitoring of a set of key variables. These variables represent things that can change rapidly and have a significant impact on the results of the organization. Health care financial managers should attempt to establish and monitor a set of such variables. For example, under DRGs, each hospital may well have some particular DRGs that make money and some that lose money. A measure of the hospital's case-mix would be a key variable.

ADDITIONAL COST ACCOUNTING TOOLS TO AID IN DECISION MAKING

One of the most important roles of managers is to make decisions. The third part of this book provided additional tools of cost accounting aimed at helping managers in their decision-making role. Specifically, this section of the book considered aspects of cost accounting ratios, productivity measurement, inventory measurement, uncertainty, information systems, and performance evaluation and incentive compensation. This part of the book is summarized in Exhibit 19-4.

Cost Accounting Ratios

Ratio analysis is a tool that has long been used in financial management. However, it generally focuses on values taken from financial statements. Cost accounting ratios can be developed from internal data that are not available on financial statements. Such data can provide

Exhibit 19-4 Summary of Part III

ADDITIONAL COST ACCOUNTING TOOLS TO AID IN DECISION MAKING

Cost Accounting Ratios
Measuring Productivity
Inventory
Dealing with Uncertainty
Information Systems for Costing
Performance Evaluation and Incentive Compensation

managers with extremely valuable trend information.

There is virtually no limit to the specific cost accounting ratios that can be developed. Any comparison of two numbers that generates an insight or perspective not available from either number individually is potentially worthwhile. Chapter 11 proposed three major classes of cost accounting ratios: (1) general information ratios, (2) monitoring and control ratios, and (3) decision ratios.

Measuring Productivity

One concern of many hospitals today is that of productivity. As financial resources become more and more constrained, productivity improvements represent one way of cutting fat rather than lean. Productivity is an example of the use of cost accounting ratios to provide information for improved management of health care organizations. As financial constraints continue to mount, productivity becomes an ever-increasing concern for health care organizations. Cost accounting, as a field oriented toward generating information for decision making and performance measurement, has begun to focus attention on the problems related to productivity measurement.

As Chapter 12 noted, productivity represents the measurement of inputs required to produce an output. However, outputs always have been difficult to define in health care. Proxies such as visits, treatments, patient days, and discharges have been used. The most common productivity measure is output per labor hour. That is, for each hour of labor input, what quantity of goods or services is produced? This will measure just part of the organization's productivity. It fails, for example, to account for the amount of capital equipment used in producing the output.

In more general terms, we can define productivity as simply being the ratio of any given measure of output to any given measure of input, over a specified time period. Thus, we can look at total productivity as follows:

$$\text{Total productivity} = \frac{\text{Total outputs}}{\text{Total inputs}}$$

We can look at a partial productivity subpart of that total as follows:

$$\text{Partial productivity} = \frac{\text{Total outputs}}{\text{Partial inputs}}$$

It should be noted, however, that there is no correct result for these ratios. There is no absolute standard for the correct level of productivity. Therefore, these ratios must be used as a basis for comparison. A health care organization can compare itself with others but would probably do best to focus on the changes in its own productivity ratios over time.

Inventory

Inventory represents one of the areas where cost accounting is concerned with both internal and external reporting. The health care organization needs to know the cost of its inventory so that it can appropriately manage that resource and so that it can report the inventory asset on the balance sheet and the cost of patients treated on the income statement.

These reporting requirements result in a need to determine which costs are period costs and which costs are product costs. Period costs are all expensed in the current period, whereas product costs remain as assets until a product is sold. This is of particular importance to manufacturing organizations that have raw materials, work in process, and finished goods inventories.

From an internal management perspective, inventory is important because it causes the organization to tie up resources in nonproductive assets. Therefore, Chapter 13 also focuses on the issue of minimization of inventory costs. This requires an understanding of the economic order quantity (EOQ) technique, logistics issues, and to some extent, the just-in-time inventory approach.

Dealing with Uncertainty

In an ideal world, we would always know what will happen with certainty. The reality, of course, is that the future is highly uncertain. Cost accounting generates information that managers use to make plans for the future. Uncertainty can result in poor outcomes for the organization, when things do not happen according to expectations. What can be done about this problem?

To attempt to combat the potential for poor outcomes, a variety of techniques can be employed. Of specific value to health care organizations are the expected value technique, simulation analysis, network cost budgeting, and linear programming. All of these approaches were discussed in Chapter 14.

The goal of these approaches is to assess better the range of possible future events and the likelihood of each event occurring. Subjective probability estimates and constraints can be considered. That information can then be taken into account in the planning process. The resulting estimates of cost may still result in undesired outcomes. However, the decisions will have taken those possibilities into account, and weighed them against the potential benefits of the decision.

Information Systems for Costing

Cost accounting at one time was a manual process. However, the advent of computers allowed for the processing of more information at high speeds. The result is that most health care organizations now use automated systems for cost accounting. Such cost accounting systems have the potential of providing managers with the information they need to make decisions.

In designing a cost accounting system, however, there are many potential problems, as noted in Chapter 15. Often, health care organizations are dissatisfied with systems that they have spent millions of dollars installing. To reduce the chances of having such problems, managers should consider a number of questions before the system is developed. These questions should include the following at a minimum:

- When is information needed?

- How much detail is needed?
- How should information be presented?

Finally, the organization must decide whether it wishes to purchase a standard package or a customized package, or to develop its own software package. Each of the three alternatives has advantages and disadvantages.

Performance Evaluation and Incentive Compensation

Health care organizations have long recognized the need for performance evaluation. The development of revenue and cost centers in health care provides a responsibility center focus in which managers can be held accountable. It also provides the foundation for developing a set of incentives for managers.

There are a number of approaches to evaluating both responsibility centers and their managers, as was discussed in Chapter 16. These include the following:

- expenses,
- revenues,
- profits,
- return on investment (ROI),
- return on assets (ROA), and
- residual income (RI).

Each of these methods has advantages and limitations.

A growing area of interest in health care is that of incentive compensation. Such systems generally focus around either a bonus system or an executive incentive plan. Bonus systems have been used on a limited basis for top-level managers only, on a somewhat broader basis for all managers, and on a very broad basis for all employees. Executive compensation plans tend to focus only on the top levels of management.

These plans tend to fall within the domain of cost accounting largely because of the interrelationship between the incentive and the control of costs. Some measures of cost are essential.

They fall within the decision-making realm of cost accounting because the design of the system, to gain the best possible advantages for all concerned, is an important decision that the organization must make.

COST ACCOUNTING FOR THE 1990s AND BEYOND

The final section of this book has dealt with the breaking trends in cost accounting. In this section of the book, the goal has been to address the elements of cost accounting that are changing and that represent the future of cost accounting. This section is summarized in Exhibit 19-5.

New Approaches to Cost Accounting

Is there a problem with traditional cost accounting? According to Chapter 17, many cost accountants—both professors and practitioners—would agree that there is. Kaplan has strongly argued that the problems are so severe that we cannot develop one compromise cost accounting system that can serve the needs of both internal and external users. Others have taken a less severe approach, suggesting that there be a switch from traditional costing to a greater focus on technology accounting or life-cycle accounting.

The approach to modifying cost accounting that has received the greatest attention in recent years is activity-based costing (ABC). Curiously enough, there is nothing really new about ABC. It is merely a reapplication of the basic rudiments of cost accounting. Cost accounting dictates that all costs that have a cause-and-effect relationship be assigned to products based on

---

Exhibit 19-5 Summary of Part IV

COST ACCOUNTING FOR THE 1990s AND BEYOND
New Approaches to Cost Accounting Total Quality Management Summary and Issues for the Future

that relationship. Based on that premise, materials and labor are generally directly associated with products, whereas overhead is allocated.

Allocations tend to be broad averages. If the overhead has no cause-and-effect relationship, that is fine. If there is a strong cause-and-effect relationship, then the overhead allocation base chosen should take that into account.

If the total amount of overhead is small, however, then most organizations will not be overly concerned about whether they have the very best allocation base. Furthermore, they will be unlikely to use multiple allocation bases. After all, if the overhead is small, then any distortion caused by the allocation base will also be small.

ABC is based on the "discovery" that in recent years, overhead has represented a substantially growing portion of total costs. Therefore, to the extent that a cause-and-effect relationship exists, it is important to determine that relationship. The distortion from a bad allocation base may be substantial. ABC calls for examination of what drives costs. In other words, what is the source of the "cause" in a cause-and-effect relationship. Further, ABC recognizes that there may be more than one such cost driver. Purchasing costs may be driven to some extent by routine orders and to some extent by special orders. Therefore, two allocation bases are needed (the number of routine orders and the number of special orders). Further, the new bases may differ substantially from the good-enough bases (e.g., dollars of goods purchased) used in the past.

Health care does not have the same problem with rising overhead that many manufacturing industries have. Labor still makes up a substantial portion of the cost of health care services. Nevertheless, the lesson of ABC can serve the health care industry as well. Too many costs are allocated per patient day, or per x-ray, or per laboratory test. The costing of the future in health care organizations will undoubtedly be based on a better use of cost drivers.

In part, this will occur because the introduction of computerized cost accounting systems will make such data collection easier. In part, it will occur because, as the financial environment for health care providers becomes tougher and tougher, it will become increasingly important to understand the costs of different types of patients. That increased focus on product costing (discussed later in this chapter) will necessitate use of techniques such as ABC.

Total Quality Management

Chapter 18 has addressed the other dramatic movement in health care cost accounting today. That movement is in the area of total quality management (TQM). At this time, the relationship between TQM and cost accounting is not well refined.

Certainly, the basic principles of TQM have clear cost implications. The concept that the cost of high quality may be less than the cost of poor quality, when all factors are considered, is a topic for cost accounting measurement. However, the tools that will be used for that measurement have not been fully developed and refined. Much of the data needed for such assessments are not routinely collected.

A major theme for the remainder of this decade—one that will move us into the next century—will be ensuring that cost accounting plays its role in the TQM movement. That theme will evidence itself both in terms of the data cost accounting generates to assess TQM throughout the organization, and in terms of the way that TQM is applied to improving all cost accounting data generated by the organization.

ADDITIONAL FUTURE ISSUES

In addition to activity costing and TQM, there are several themes that will likely be a focus of cost accounting in the coming years. These themes are discussed below and are summarized in Exhibit 19-6.

Product-Line Costing

Health care cost accounting has been shifting more and more to focus on specific groups of patients, or product lines. The shift from a de-

Exhibit 19-6 Additional Future Issues

PRODUCT-LINE COSTING

Product-line origins
The future of product-line management

REVENUE CENTERS AND COST ALLOCATION

Revenue centers and cost centers
Argument for eliminating the revenue center concept
The future of revenue centers and cost allocation

---

partmental costing focus to a product-line focus was discussed in Chapter 2. There are two major approaches for providing the cost information management needs. One approach focuses on the near term and an evolution in cost data. The latter approach is more revolutionary.

The evolutionary approach has been prominently offered by a number of consulting firms. The formula consists primarily of using a grouper to divide a hospital's patients into DRGs. Next, the ratio of cost to charges is applied to the bills of patients in each DRG to calculate the cost of each DRG.

The next step in the evolutionary process would be gradually to revamp elements of the stepdown allocation procedure to improve the cost estimate by product. This consists primarily of shifting the cost accounting orientation from departments to products. For instance, some hospitals are starting to calculate a standard cost for each operating room (OR) procedure based on resources typically consumed by that procedure. This requires special studies of each procedure. Instead of time being the basis for allocation of OR costs, standard costs become the basis, greatly improving managerial information.

A more revolutionary approach is to start from scratch, tracking the costs of resources consumed by each patient. The most extreme of these approaches is to put a computer terminal next to each patient bed for collecting cost information. In addition to providing the patient care information that such systems commonly provide today, they would also collect resource consumption information. Each time nurses enter patient rooms, they would insert their identification card into the terminal. Nurses would do the same again as they leave. The computer would then have information on how much nursing time the patient consumed. It could even associate the hourly rate of the specific nurse with the patient to get more precise resource consumption information.

Consider a chest x-ray. We know that an ambulatory patient is much easier to x-ray than a postoperative coronary bypass patient. Nevertheless, we often have a standard chest x-ray fee. With a system such as this, we would associate with each patient his or her consumption of both x-ray technician time and radiology equipment time.

Product-Line Origins

What progress has been made in moving toward the evolutionary and revolutionary approaches to product costing and product-line management? Has product-line management really fulfilled its potential? Can product-line management be used as a tool to control costs, or is it simply going to add a new layer of bureaucracy and cost into health care administration?

The notion of product-line management has been used by manufacturers since before World War II. Its original concept was that each product would be assigned an advocate. That advocate would be responsible for doing everything possible for the product. The advocate would have to ensure that the product line was effectively marketed. The advocate was also responsible for getting the product effectively manufactured.

In such a system, the advocate is generally a staff person, without line authority. As Bowers notes, the advocate is one who "cajoles and persuades functional managers to cooperate in providing needed resources for the product."[1] At General Motors, the Chevette manager must compete with the Chevrolet and Cadillac managers to get radiators from the radiator department. From the health care administration perspective, the problem with this approach is that it leads to competition within the organization

for resources. A heart surgery manager would compete with the gall bladder manager for OR time. That does not necessarily mean that resources wind up going where they are most needed. Even worse, it does not place a very high emphasis on constraining the use of resources.

Not all manufacturing firms still use product-line management. Many firms discontinued its use because of conflict and frustration it created within the organization. Furthermore, product-line management often supplements existing functional management, adding another layer of costs. There must still be managers of departments, in addition to the product-line managers. In health care, the addition of such costs must be justified for organizations to be willing to incur them.

The Future of Product-Line Management

There has been some discussion in the literature of the way that hospitals organize themselves for product-line management. According to Patterson and Thompson, there are three approaches that a hospital could choose to take.[2] These approaches are:

1. market management
2. distribution
3. strategic business unit.

The market management model, as its name suggests, focuses mostly on creating an increased external market. The distribution model requires working on increasing the market from within (referring physicians) and from outside the organization. The strategic business approach would have managers look at not only marketing, but also allocation of resources and profitability.

For product-line management to make a difference in hospitals, it would seem that use of the strategic model is essential. The other two models do not substantially change the hospital's operations. They focus instead on slight modifications in the marketing activities. Advances in product-line management require a more global perspective, with a renewed emphasis on cost control.

Historically, health care organizations have managed the production of the intermediate products. Management has centered on efficient production of x-rays and patient days. No matter how efficiently a hospital or nursing home produces a patient day, it cannot afford to provide a fixed-fee patient with extra x-rays and extra patient days. The focus of product-line management must change to looking at the appropriate resources (x-rays, patient days) for patients in specific DRGs or clusters of DRGs.

Each product line must be examined for variations in the way it is provided. Variations should be considered both among clinicians practicing within the organization and, if possible, among practice patterns for that product line at a wide variety of other organizations. Then there should be concerted efforts to eliminate wasteful approaches to providing care to patients within the product line.

This is not a shocking revelation. People have been saying it since DRGs arrived in 1983. However, over the last several decades, whenever possible, hospitals have focused their attention on increasing revenues, as opposed to understanding and reducing costs. Adding programs, adding services, and finding ways to maximize the revenue stream from the existing patient pool are less painful than cost-cutting.

Even so, it is still surprising to find that hospitals that have undertaken product-line management do not seem to focus on an examination of the way the product is produced in order to reduce costs. With health industry costs continuing to rise, and the federal and state governments, as well as private insurers, coming under ever-increasing cost pressures, it would seem that using product-line management in this way should commence as quickly as possible.

The product-line cost information needed is not impossible to generate. The principles of cost accounting discussed in this book provide the reader with the needed tools to aggregate and measure costs on a product-line basis. However, such data collection is itself costly.

Recent developments, however, have begun to make it more practical. There is a definite movement toward greater and greater computerization of patient medical records. As the records become computerized, it becomes easier to extract information about individual patients. Comparisons of cost with treatments become easier for both providers and payers.

The degree to which health care organizations pursue product-line information will ultimately rest on the cost/benefit principle of cost accounting. It will not take place as a matter of course in health care organizations until the managers determine that the benefits of such data are greater than the costs of collecting the data.

Revenue Centers and Cost Allocation

Revenue centers are used both for rate setting and for Medicare and other payer cost reports. The introduction of prospective payment systems (particularly DRGs) ten years ago creates serious questions about the appropriateness of the revenue center system in use in health care organizations today. Efficient management decisions are neither a goal nor a byproduct of the revenue center approach. Some contend that a more rational approach for health care organization management would be to use a cost center approach exclusively instead of a mix of support cost centers and revenue centers.

In an exclusive cost center system, the traditional revenue centers of health care organizations would no longer have responsibility for profits, but simply for producing their output at an efficient cost. To think about this issue, we should start by considering the rationale behind revenue centers.

Revenue Centers and Cost Centers

Health care cost centers are divided into revenue and nonrevenue centers. Although it is often stated that patient care departments are revenue centers and non–patient-care departments are support cost centers (nonrevenue centers), that is not really true. For example, the largest patient care department, nursing, is rarely a revenue center. In addition, there is no specific accounting reason that prevents dietary from being a revenue center.

A more useful distinction between revenue and nonrevenue centers is the ability to charge patients, on a cause-and-effect basis, for differing consumption of resources. If all patients consume exactly the same amount of a resource each day, there is no need to go to the trouble of measuring that consumption for each patient. The cost can be logically put into a per diem that is equal for each patient. If different patients consume different amounts of a resource, equity indicates that we should charge them differentially, and a revenue center arises.

Some patients have surgery and some do not, so the OR is a revenue center and not only differentiates between those that have surgery and those that do not, but also among those who have surgery. Those with longer operations are charged more than those with shorter operations. On the other hand, we cannot tell who is really consuming what portion of the chief executive officer's time, so we do not attempt to make administration a revenue center and assign costs directly to patients in different amounts.

Some departments do have a cause-and-effect relationship and theoretically should be revenue centers, but are not for pragmatic reasons. For example, laundry is not used in equal proportions by all patients. However, the cost of observing how much laundry each patient consumes and charging for differential consumption would exceed the cost of doing the laundry. Thus, laundry is not a revenue center.

The same situation applied to nursing departments prior to the widespread use of patient classification systems. Historically, it was not feasible to charge different patients on the same unit different amounts for nursing care, even though they obviously did not all consume the same amount of nursing resources. However, measuring the nursing time spent on each patient would be extremely expensive.

The advent of patient classification systems makes it possible for nursing departments to be a revenue center because nursing can now mea-sure differential consumption by different patients and therefore charge accordingly. However, rather than making nursing a revenue center, some are now arguing that all revenue centers should be eliminated.

Argument for Eliminating the Revenue Center Concept

As long as some inpatient payments are not based on a prospective payment system, revenue centers will probably persist. However, if more states move to all-payer prospective payment systems, an argument for the elimination of revenue centers would exist. This would also be the case under some proposals for national health care financing reform.

The revenue center system allows for all costs, including nonrevenue center costs, to be accumulated in the revenue centers and allocated to patients in order to be reimbursed. Under cost reimbursement, this approach is required. However, if payments are not mere reimbursement of costs, the revenue centers can be dropped, simplifying the system dramatically and making it much more sensible at the same time.

Consider any industrial producer. An auto manufacturer is a good example. Under cost reimbursement, you would buy a car from a parts counter, ordering a steering wheel, four tires, an engine, and so forth. (In the hospital setting, you buy an x-ray, four laboratory tests, etc.) In that case, it makes sense to have revenue centers. If the parts salesman sells you an extra steering wheel (you never know when you might need one) for extra money, it benefits the automaker, and the steering wheel department has generated more revenue by providing two steering wheels instead of one. However, what if you buy the entire car for a fixed total price of $10,000 (like paying for a hospital stay at a fixed DRG payment rate)? Would the automaker benefit if it throws an extra steering wheel in the trunk? No, it generates more cost and no more revenue.

If a hospital, under a prospective payment system (PPS), provides an extra x-ray, will revenue increase? No. Should we reward the radiology department by saying that as a revenue center it gets more allocated revenue for more x-rays even though total revenue for the patient is fixed? No, that sends the wrong incentive.

Is it logical to believe that an automaker takes the $10,000 of revenue and starts to allocate that revenue among the fender department, radiator department, engine department, and so forth? How would it do it? How do you assess the portion of the $10,000 that should go to each department? Do we care if the buyer felt the engine was worth $8,000 and the body only $2,000 or vice versa? Would the buyer have purchased just the engine or just the body?

If PPS aims to get away from the concept of encouraging overprovision of health services, then there is no reason to encourage the perpetuation of a revenue center concept. This issue is discussed further in Application 19-1.

Similarly, some proposals for national health care financing reform call for approaches such as budgeted total payments per health care organization. If a skilled nursing facility were to receive a total lump sum, there would once again be no need to assign shares of that revenue to individual cost centers.

The Future of Revenue Centers and Cost Allocation

A new, innovative approach is simply to do away with the revenue center notion and the entire cost allocation process. Instead, the health care organization would report costs for a greater number of departments. Thus, the radiology department, now a nonrevenue center, would still report the cost per x-ray, but those costs would be the direct radiology department costs plus any indirect costs that have a clear cause-and-effect basis, such as meals and laundry. The cost centers that previously would have been allocated now stand on their own. Thus, there would be an administration department with costs, a legal affairs department, a telecommunications department, and so forth.

How Medicare should view the joint overhead costs in setting rates is primarily a policy issue. There will be many approaches to decide how much to include for each patient to cover joint overhead costs. However, although that will create policy decisions to be made, hiding the costs in the allocation quagmire just means that the decisions are made implicitly. It also tends to mislead us into thinking we know the cost to treat different types of patients, when, in fact, that is not the case.

Given poor statistical allocation bases, manipulated ordering of departmental allocation, allocation of joint costs, and conceptual problems related to how costs are assigned to patients within departments, we have such a tangled web today, woven over the many years of payment regulation, that it is doubtful that we know much at all about costs once the step-down process has been completed. It is true that the alternative of reporting costs for more departments (because none are eliminated through the closing part of the step-down) may seem more complicated. However, avoiding most inter–cost-center allocations creates substantial simplicity.

Also, it should be noted that just because a nonrevenue department is not allocated to other departments does not mean that every patient will wind up being assigned an equal share. We may decide that administration should be simply assigned on a patient day basis. Nursing, on the other hand, could develop a detailed costing system using patient classification to allocate its own costs differently to different patients, just as radiology currently does and will continue to do. The goal will be to look at the direct costs of each department and decide how to allocate them directly to patients, rather than to each other.

In other words, rather than perpetuating the existing cost allocation system which allocates costs to departments, allocation could be done directly to patients using more of an activity-based costing approach (see Chapter 17). For each department, the true cost drivers could be identified. The result would enhance the organization's ability to do product-line costing.

Even eliminating interdepartmental allocation of joint costs will not solve all of the product costing problems in health care organizations. We will still have distortions that need to be worked out by improved cost accounting systems. For example, often hospitals assign the cost of the operating room on the basis of the length of the procedure. The total costs of the operating room are divided by the number of hours of operations to get a cost per hour. This is a tremendous distortion, because many short procedures may use a large number of nurses and technicians and much expensive equipment, whereas a longer operation may be both less labor- and less capital-intensive. Nevertheless, the longer procedure will be charged more.

The solution to problems such as this is to begin having departments focus more specifically on the resources consumed by different types of patients. Many health care organizations have already begun to move in this direction on their own. The more cause-and-effect-related the allocation to patients by each department, the better.

The reader of this book should not be discouraged. Clearly, the problems related to costing in health care have not yet all been resolved. However, rather than bemoan that fact, the reader should recognize it as an opportunity. The health care field is ready for a revolution in cost accounting. Those who take up the challenge to apply the fundamental concepts of this book have the potential to make a significant difference in the efficiency with which their organizations operate.

NOTES

1. M.R. Bowers, Product line management in hospitals: An exploratory study of managing change, *Hospital and Health Services Administration* 35, no. 3 (Fall 1990): 367.

2. D.J. Patterson and K.A. Thompson, Product line management: Organization makes the difference, *Healthcare Financial Management* (January 1987): 66–72.

SUGGESTED READING

Baptist, A., et al. January 1987. Developing a solid base for a cost accounting system. *Healthcare Financial Management,* 42–48.

Bowers, M.R. 1990. Product line management in hospitals: An exploratory study of managing change. *Hospital and Health Services Administration* 35, no. 3:365–375.

Burik, D., and T.J. Duvall. May 1985. Hospital cost accounting: Implementing the system successfully. *Healthcare Financial Management* 74–88.

Finkler, S.A. 1980. Cost finding for high-technology high-cost services: Current practice and a possible alternative. *Health Care Management Review* 5, no. 3:17–29.

Kane, N. 1985. Policy implications of hospital reporting practices. *Medical Care* 23, no. 6:836–841.

Krueger, D., and T. Davidson. 1987. Alternative approaches to cost accounting. *Topics in Health Care Financing* 13, no. 4:1–9.

Lamont, D.P. 1988. A product line costing approach to admitting management. *Journal of Hospital Admitting Management* 13, no. 3:6–7, 28.

Orloff, T.M., et al. 1990. Hospital cost accounting: Who's doing what and why. *Health Care Management Review* 15, no. 4:73–78.

Patterson, D.J., and K.A. Thompson. January 1987. Product line management: Organization makes the difference. *Healthcare Financial Management,* 66–72.

Zelman, W.N., and D.L. Parham. 1990. Strategic, operational, and marketing concerns of product-line management in health care. *Health Care Management Review* 15, no. 1:29–35.

EXERCISES

QUESTIONS FOR DISCUSSION

1. How would you characterize the two major approaches to product-line costing?

Note: Solutions to the Exercises can be found in Appendix A.

2. What surprising results have been found in terms of implementation of product-line management?

3. Why have revenue centers lost much of their usefulness?

Departmental Bottom Lines

Steven A. Finkler, PhD, CPA

THE BASIC PROBLEM

How can things change and yet be made to be the same? This seems to be the theme behind a recent movement toward finding a way to assign revenues to units and departments under DRGs. The basic philosophy is that the value of revenue centers has been reduced by fixed fee payments which are not readily assignable to the various revenue centers.

Clearly, DRGs and other changes in payment systems have made things change. As a result, there are some strange paradoxes within hospital accounting systems. For example, the revenue assigned to each department based on the services it provides and the charges it generates does not necessarily add up to the total DRG payment received by the hospital. How can we now develop a system to put things back the way they were for department managers; to show them how much profit they are contributing to the organization? This would put things back the way they were before DRGs.

One recent article in particular by David Schroeder presented a mechanism for performing such revenue assignment.[1] The premise of

Source: Reprinted from Steven A. Finkler, "Departmental Bottom Lines," *Hospital Cost Management and Accounting,* Vol. 2, No. 12, March 1991, pp. 1–4. Copyright 1991, Aspen Publishers, Inc.

the article is not one that we particularly agree with. Essentially the theme is that "we used to have profit centers where the revenues that a department generated could be matched with its expenses. Managers knew where they were. The only problem with the old days was that the overhead departments were not assigned revenue." The problem with this line of reasoning is that it assumes that managers of departments and the performance of the departments were the key to generating profits or losses.

In fact, reimbursement systems have been at the heart of profits and losses for decades. If per diems were capped, but ancillary reimbursement at cost was unlimited, accountants moved more cost to ancillaries, raising their revenues. If competitive conditions allowed hospitals to increase prices for heart surgery, but forced them to reduce prices for physical therapy, they did so. These financial manipulations were the result of an effort to legally (or nearly legally) maximize reimbursement within a constrained environment. Often, however, the profit of a department resulted from the nature of reimbursement for that type of department, rather than on the efforts of the department and its manager.

Now, with DRGs, things have changed. Is it appropriate to strive for more accurate departmental profit calculations? Perhaps we are better off to consider how to react to the change in order to move forward, rather than how to make the change go away as much as possible. First let's consider how and why one might want to assign DRG revenues to departments.

WHY ASSIGN REVENUE?

The essence of Schroeder's argument was that hospitals should develop supplemental accounting reporting, with "[s]ystematic and rational determination of individual department bottom line [as] the principal objective." According to Schroeder, the advantages of this is that, "Providing the individual unit manager with bottom line (1) emphasizes accountability as opposed to accounting and (2) substitutes macro payment system perplexity with micro perspective. Intradependence replaces independence in traditional overhead departments. Cost quality analysis and comparability of intraorganizational effort is facilitated by recasting hidden fixed cost into visible surrogate market price. Secondary objectives center around the development of an entrepreneurial organizational model. Departments become strategic business units within a conglomerate."

We have a hard time digesting these concepts. How is there to be a systematic and rational determination of individual department bottom line? If we are talking about a wholly contained clinic, complete with its own lab and radiology unit, we can imagine it rationally being a profit center. On the other hand, for the vast majority of hospital departments, only a portion of the patient is treated. Shall the radiology department gloat over the huge profits it generates on a patient for whom every other department is losing money? Do we want a system where the radiology department is punished in terms of reduced profits if we discontinue a product line that is killing the profits of every other department?

As a general rule, departmental profit calculations can only generate ill will with few if any benefits, from our perspective. The problems start with the initial allocation of revenue. How can one take a single price per patient for a spe- cific DRG and allocate that among various departments? Is there some formula to tell us how much of the revenue to assign to each?

ASSIGNING DEPARTMENT'S REVENUE

Schroeder has developed such a formula for allocation of revenues to departments. He believes that things are screwy if you assign revenues to departments based on a charge per unit of service, when payment is made in a fixed lump sum manner. And he is certainly correct in that view. However, Schroeder's approach is to allocate DRG revenue to departments by reversing the step-down cost allocation approach. It is not clear that this method will not have its own problems.

By doing such a reverse step down, we can find the portion of each DRG that stemmed from costs in each revenue producing department, and use that information to allocate revenue back to those departments. Further, by determining the indirect costs that have been allocated to each revenue center by nonrevenue centers, we can take a share of revenue and allocate it back to the nonrevenue centers. For example, if 25 percent of lab cost is indirect allocated overhead, we can allocate 25 percent of the lab's share of total revenue for a patient back to the various overhead departments that generated the indirect cost.

IMPLICATIONS OF REVENUE ALLOCATION TO DEPARTMENTS

Clearly, a reverse step-down calculation can be performed. However, we must try to think about where such calculations will lead us. How will this process help rather than hinder us?

Suppose that physical therapy decides that their profit share is not great enough on a particular type of patient. However, if they double the number of hours of therapy that type of patient receives, their cost will be a larger percent of the overall cost of treating the patients. When revenues are stepped back into the revenue producing departments, physical therapy will be entitled to a bigger piece of the pie.

Have overall hospital revenues increased? No. Have costs increased? Yes. An accounting system which generates information that leads to perverse actions by various departments is not aiding in the overall process of efficient management. This is just one example of the problems that arise when revenue is assigned to departments under a DRG fixed fee reimbursement system.

Suppose that maintenance decides that it is losing money on patients treated by radiology, but making a fortune on neonatal intensive care. Will the hospital benefit or suffer if maintenance shifts its attention away from radiology toward neonatal intensive care? The cost of neonatal intensive care, including allocated indirect costs, will rise. Furthermore, as radiology equipment breaks down, certain patients will be diverted to other hospitals, causing the hospital to lose all revenues from those patients.

The key issue is that we are treating a whole patient. At General Motors, a car's selling price is compared closely to the total cost of making the car. However, it makes little business sense to take that price and divvy it up among the radiator, steering wheel, and fender departments. Any decisions related to the car must be made based on its profitability as a whole.

If we think about this a bit more it makes even less sense. If we allocate profits to departments, those departments which are losing money will work hard to be efficient and cut their losses. It may turn out, however, that some aspects of treating a patient just cannot be done without a loss. The hospital is still in good shape if the profits from the other departments offset these losses. But the departments that have profits will not have any reason to control costs carefully. They will logically feel that they can afford to spend some extra money—after all, they are a profit maker.

The result is that there will be financial pressure on the hospital resulting from the fact that some departments lose money, while other departments don't necessarily maximize their profits. Overall losses may well be the result. Certainly some departments will argue to discontinue unprofitable lines, while other departments are fighting to keep those same patients.

Schroeder has argued that "Effectiveness of decision making, planning, and control is inversely related to the management level at which it is exercised. One day of operation in the hospital is made up of thousands of individual transactions, originating at the department level. It is reasonable to design a system in which operations are managed at this level." There are some weaknesses to this philosophy. Not all decision making should be done at the lowest level. No department will ever have the entire hospital picture, and therefore decisions such as elimination of a product line can only be made at a higher level. But, to a great extent, this quote makes sense. Certainly, moving many decisions down to a level where there is more information, and more accurate information, can increase effectiveness.

However, revenue information does not start at that level. Cost information does. Departments should be experts at what it costs them to produce their product. They should be making decisions on reducing cost without reducing quality of care.

Earlier we noted the argument that department bottom lines emphasize accountability rather than accounting. This is not the case. Accountability does not require one to show a level of profits. Providing a cost budget (preferably flexible for volume changes) and holding one responsible for that budget provides a high degree of accountability. Requiring profit measures from departments that lose money due to the nature of things, rather than due to performance, will not increase accountability, just demoralization.

The key to moving forward and improving management, it seems, is not to try to patch up the old revenue center system, so that department heads can focus on how their department contributes toward profits. Rather the focus should be a team spirited approach to minimizing costs of production.

Realistically, few departments in the hospital can have any impact on the revenues of the hospital from its DRG based inpatients. If there can be no impact on revenues, we shouldn't devote great amounts of management attention to it. Therefore the focus should not be on how to fix revenue allocations. The focus should be strictly on cost and quality management. It is such an approach which is more likely to lead to im-proved efficiency, and greater hospitalwide financial success.

NOTE

1. D.H. Schroeder, "Toward a Departmental Bottom Line Perspective," by D.H. Schroeder, in *Health Care Management Review,* Vol. 14, No. 1, Winter 1989, pp. 25–40.

Glossary

Absorption costing—An inventory costing method in which all direct and indirect manufacturing costs, both variable and fixed, are product rather than period costs. (See *Product costs* and *Period costs*.)

Acceptance ratio—The number of candidates who accept job offers divided by the number of jobs offered.

Accounting—A system for keeping track of the financial status of an organization and the financial results of its activities; provides financial information for decision making.

Accounting control—The methods and procedures for the authorization of transactions, safeguarding of assets, and accuracy of accounting records (sometimes referred to as "preventive" controls).

Accounting cost—A measure of cost based on a number of simplifications, such as an assumed useful life for a piece of equipment.

Accounting rate of return (ARR)—The profitability of an investment calculated by considering the profits it generates, as compared with the amount of money invested.

Accrual accounting—An accounting system that matches revenues and related expenses in the same fiscal year by recording revenues in the year in which they become earned (whether received or not) and the expenses related to generating those revenues in the same year.

Accumulated depreciation—The cumulative amount of depreciation related to a fixed asset that has been charged over the years the organization has owned that asset.

Activity accounting—A method of tracking costs and other information by focusing on the activities undertaken to produce the good or service.

Activity-based costing (ABC)—An approach to determining the cost of products or product lines using multiple overhead allocation bases that relate to the activities that generate overhead costs.

Actual costing—A cost allocation approach that uses actual costs for labor, supplies, and overhead.

Acuity—A measurement of patient severity of illness that is related to the amount of resources required to care for the patient.

Acuity subcategory—The amount that would have been budgeted for the actual output level if the actual acuity level had been correctly forecast.

Acuity variance—The variance resulting from the difference between the actual acuity level and the budgeted level; the difference between the flexible budget and the value of the acuity subcategory.

ADC—See *Average daily census*.

Administrative control—The plan of organization and all methods and procedures that help management planning and control of operations—often referred to as feedback systems. Generally viewed more with respect to inefficiency than intentional misuse of resources.

Algebraic distribution—A cost allocation approach that uses simultaneous equations to allocate nonrevenue cost center costs to both nonrevenue and revenue cost centers in a manner that does not create distortions. Also called reciprocal distribution or matrix distribution.

Allowances—Discounts from the amount normally charged for patient care services. These discounts are sometimes negotiated (e.g., with Blue Cross) and other times mandated by law (e.g., Medicare and Medicaid).

ALOS—See *Average length of stay*.

Amortization—The allocation of the cost of an intangible asset over its lifetime.

Annuity—A series of payments or receipts each in the same amount and spaced at even time periods. For example: $127.48 paid monthly for 3 years.

Annuity payments (PMT)—See *Annuity*.

Application of overhead—See *Overhead application*.

Appraisal costs—Those costs incurred for inspecting a product to be certain that the customer's requirements are met.

Assets—Valuable resources. May be either physical, having substance and form, such as a table or building, or intangible, such as the reputation the organization has gained for providing high-quality health care services.

Audit—An examination of the financial records of the organization to discover material errors, to evaluate the internal control system, and to determine if financial statements have been prepared in accordance with Generally Accepted Accounting Principles.

Audit trail—A set of references that allows an individual to trace back through accounting documents to the source of each number used.

Auditor—A person who performs an audit.

Average costs—Full costs divided by the number of units of service.

Average daily census (ADC)—The average number of inpatients on any given day; patient days in a given time period divided by the number of days in the time period.

Average length of stay (ALOS)—The average number of patient days for each patient discharged; the number of patient days in a given time period divided by the number of discharges in that time period.

Bad debts—An operating expense related to the care provided for which payment is never received, even though the customer was expected to pay.

Balance sheet—See *Statement of Financial Position*.

Benefit/cost philosophy—The viewpoint that one should never spend more to collect cost information than the value of the information.

Best linear unbiased estimate—Result of a simple linear regression if regression data meet requirements of linearity, constant variance, independence, and normality.

Blue Cross—A major provider of hospitalization insurance to both individuals and groups. For most hospitals, one of the largest sources of revenue.

Bond payable—A formal borrowing arrangement between one borrower and a number of lenders. The lender may sell the financial obligation, in which case, the liability is owed to the new owner.

Bondholder—A creditor of the organization who owns one of the organization's outstanding bonds payable.

Bonding of employees—Insurance policy protecting the organization against embezzlement and fraud by employees.

Bonus systems—A method to provide an incentive for employees to improve their performance. Employees receive a financial payment or shares of stock if certain targets are achieved or exceeded.

Breakeven analysis—A technique for determining the minimum volume of output (e.g., patient days of care) necessary in order for a program or service to be financially self-sufficient.

Breakeven point—See *Breakeven volume*.

Breakeven time (BT)—The amount of time before the present value of cash inflows is at least equal to the present value of cash outflows.

Breakeven volume—The volume just needed to break even. Losses would be incurred at lower volumes and profits at higher volumes.

Budget—A plan that provides a formal, quantitative expression of management's plans and intentions or expectations.

Budgeting—A process whereby plans are made, and then an effort is made to meet or exceed the goals of the plans.

Business plan—A detailed plan for a proposed program, project, or service, including information to be used to assess the venture's financial feasibility.

Capital acquisitions—See *Capital assets.*

Capital assets—Buildings or equipment with useful lives extending beyond the year in which they are purchased or put into service. Also referred to as long-term investments, capital items, capital investments, or capital acquisitions.

Capital budget—A plan for the acquisition of capital assets.

Capital budgeting—The process of proposing the purchase of capital assets, analyzing the proposal for economic or other justification, and encompassing the financial implications of accepted capital items into the master budget.

Capital equipment—See *Capital assets.*

Capital investments—See *Capital assets.*

Capital items—See *Capital assets.*

Carrying costs of inventory—Capital costs and out-of-pocket costs related to holding inventory. Capital cost represents the lost interest because money is tied up in inventory. Out-of-pocket costs include such expenses as insurance on the value of inventory, annual inspections, and obsolescence of inventory.

Case-mix—The mix of different types of patients treated by a health care organization.

Case-mix index—A measurement of the average complexity or severity of illness of patients treated by a health care organization.

Cash budget—A plan for the cash receipts and cash disbursements of the organization.

Cash budgeting—Preparation of a cash budget.

Cash disbursement—The outflow of cash from the organization.

Cash flow—A measure of the amount of cash received or disbursed over a given period of time, as opposed to revenues or income that frequently are recorded at a time other than when the actual cash receipt or payment occurs.

Cash management—An active process of planning for borrowing and repayment of cash, or investment of excess cash on hand in order to optimize the organization's benefit from its cash balances.

Cash payment—See *Cash disbursement.*

Cash receipt—The inflow of cash into the organization.

Causal variable—An independent variable that is responsible for changes in the dependent variable.

Census—The number of patients occupying beds at a specific time of day (usually midnight).

Ceteris paribus—All other things being equal.

Charge master—A list of the organization's prices for each of its services.

Charity care—The care provided to individuals who are not expected to be able to pay because of limited personal financial resources and lack of insurance.

Chief financial officer (CFO)—The manager responsible for all of the financial functions in the organization.

Coefficient of determination—A measure of the goodness of fit of a regression, generally referred to as the "*R*-squared."

Committed costs—Those costs that cannot be changed in the short run.

Compound interest—A method of calculating interest that recognizes interest not only on the amount of the original investment, but also on the interest earned in interim periods of time.

Congruent goals—See *Goal congruence.*

Conservatism principle—The idea that financial statements must give adequate consideration to the risks faced by the organization. Therefore, conservative assumptions are often made in the presentation of financial information.

Constant dollars—Dollar amounts that have been adjusted for the impact of inflation.

Constant variance—Uniformity in the scatter of actual historical data points around an estimated line.

Contingency—An event that may or may not occur.

Continuous budgeting—See *Rolling budget.*

Continuous quality improvement (CQI)—A philosophy concerning the production of an organization's goods and services that proposes that there should be a constant focus on improvement in the quality of the product or service.

Contractual allowances—Discounts from full charges, available to governments and some other third-party payers, based on contractual agreement or government regulation.

Contribution from operations—The contribution margin from the routine annual operations of the organization.

Contribution margin—The amount by which the price per unit of service exceeds its variable cost. If the contribution margin is positive, it means that each extra unit of activity makes the organization better off by that amount.

Control—An attempt to ensure that actual results come as close to the plan as possible.

Control chart—A graph of variances that indicates upper and lower limits. A variance should be investigated if either of the limits is exceeded.

Control limit—An amount beyond which a variance should be investigated.

Controllable—Those items over which a manager can exercise a degree of control.

Conversion cost—The cost of converting raw materials inventory into the final service or product; labor plus overhead costs.

Corporation—A business owned by a group of individuals (shareholders or stockholders) that has limited liability; that is, the owners are not liable for more than the amount they invested in the firm.

Cost—The amount spent to acquire an asset. Costs have two stages: acquisition cost and ex-

pired cost. When some asset or service is purchased, the resources given in exchange represent the acquisition cost. Once the asset is fully consumed, it becomes an expired cost, or an expense.

Cost accounting—A subset of accounting related to measuring costs to generate cost information for reporting and making management decisions.

Cost accounting ratios—Ratios developed from internal financial information that does not appear on the organization's audited financial statements.

Cost accounting system—Any coherent system designed to gather and report cost information to the management of an organization.

Cost allocation—The process of taking costs from one area or cost objective and allocating them to others.

Cost base—The statistic used as a basis for allocation of overhead; for example, patient days or labor hours.

Cost behavior—The way that costs change in reaction to events within the organization, such as changes in the volume of units of service.

Cost–benefit analysis—Measurement of the relative costs and benefits associated with a particular project or task.

Cost center—A unit or department in an organization for which a manager is assigned responsibility for costs.

Cost driver—An activity that causes costs to be incurred.

Cost-effective—An approach that provides care that is as good as any other approach, but costs less, or an approach that provides the best possible care for a given level of cost.

Cost-effectiveness—A measure of whether costs are minimized for the desired outcome.

Cost-effectiveness analysis—A technique that measures the cost of alternatives that generate the same outcome. See *Cost-effective.*

Cost estimation—The process of using historical cost information to segregate mixed costs into their fixed and variable components, and then using that information to estimate future costs.

Cost finding—A process that finds the costs of units of service, such as laboratory tests, x-rays, or routine patient days, based on an allocation of nonrevenue cost center costs to revenue centers.

Cost measurement—The process of assessing resources consumed and assigning a value to those resources.

Cost objective—Any particular item, program, or organizational unit for which we wish to know the cost.

Cost of capital—The cost to the organization of the money used for capital acquisitions. Often represented by the interest rate that the organization pays on borrowed money.

Cost of goods sold (CGS)—The expense related to the sale of inventory.

Cost pass-through—A payment by a third party that reimburses the health care organization for the amount of costs it incurred in providing care to patients.

Cost-per-hire ratio—The costs related to advertising vacancies, using placement firms, interviewing and processing potential candidates, traveling, and moving, all divided by the number of individuals hired.

Cost pool—Any grouping of costs.

Cost reimbursement—Revenue based on paying the organization the costs incurred in providing care to the patient.

Cost reporting—The process of conveying information about the cost of resources consumed as related to a specific cost objective.

Cost–volume–profit relationship—The relationship of how costs, volume, and profits are interrelated.

CPM—See *Critical path method.*

Critical path—An indication in the critical path method of essential steps, a delay in which causes a delay in the entire project.

Critical path method (CPM)—A program technique that indicates the cost and time for each element of a complex project and indicates cost/time trade-offs where applicable.

Cross-subsidization of costs—A situation in which some patients are assigned more costs than they cause the organization to incur, and others are assigned less.

Current ratio—Current assets divided by current liabilities.

Curvilinear—A curved line.

Curvilinear forecasting—Forecasting using curved lines to make estimates of future values.

Decentralization—Delegation of decision-making autonomy downward within the organization.

Decision package—A zero-based budgeting term referring to a package of all of the information to be used in ranking alternatives and making a final decision.

Decision ratios—Cost accounting ratios that generate information to aid managers in making decisions.

Decision variables—Factors controllable by the organization that can affect volume.

Decreasing returns to scale—Increasing cost per unit at large volume levels due to capacity constraints or shortages of labor or supplies.

Deficit—An excess of expenses over revenues. Sometimes refers to the current year or budgeted year, and sometimes to the deficit accumulated over a period of years.

Delphi technique—An approach sometimes used for forecasting in which an expert group (which never meets) generates written forecasts that form the basis for making a decision. Each member's written forecast is distributed to all members of the group, along with the reasoning behind it. This process is repeated several times, and eventually a group decision is made.

Department—Any cost or revenue center.

Dependent variable—The item the value of which is being predicted.

Depreciate—Decline in value or productive capability; allocation of a portion of the original cost of an asset as an expense to each of the years of the asset's expected useful life.

Depreciation expense—The amount of the original cost of a fixed asset allocated as an expense each year.

Diagnosis Related Groups (DRGs)—A system that categorizes patients into specific groups based on their medical diagnosis and other characteristics, such as age and type of surgery, if any. Currently used by Medicare and some other hospital payers as a basis for payment.

Differential costs—See *Incremental costs.*

Direct costing—An approach to manufacturing accounting that assigns only variable costs to products. All fixed costs are treated as period costs rather than product costs. (See *Period costs* and *Product costs.*)

Direct costs—Those costs that are clearly and directly associated with the cost objective. They are generally under the control of the manager who has overall responsibility for the cost objective.

Direct distribution—Allocation of nonrevenue center costs directly and only to revenue centers.

Direct expenses—See *Direct costs.*

Direct labor—Labor that is a direct cost element.

Direct labor cost—The cost of direct labor.

Direct labor dollars—See *Direct labor cost.*

Direct labor hours—The number of hours of direct labor consumed in making a product or providing a service.

Direct method—Method for measuring cash flows that considers the inflows and outflows related to each of the organization's accounts.

Disbursement—Cash payment.

Discount rate—The interest rate used in discounting.

Discounted cash flow—A method that allows comparisons of amounts of money paid at different points of time by discounting all amounts to the present.

Discounting—The reverse of compound interest; a process in which interest that could be earned over time is deducted from a future payment to determine how much the future payment is worth in the present time.

Discretionary costs—Costs for which there is no clear-cut relationship between inputs and outputs. The treatment of more patients would not necessarily require more of this input; use of more of this input would not necessarily allow for treatment of more patients.

Distribution—An approach to product-line management that requires working on increasing the market from within (referring physicians) as well as from outside the organization.

Divergent goals—See *Goal divergence.*

Double distribution—An allocation approach in which all nonrevenue centers allocate their costs to all other cost centers once, and then a second allocation takes place using either step-down or direct distribution.

DRGs—See *Diagnosis Related Groups.*

Economic cost—The amount of money required to obtain the use of a resource.

Economic order quantity (EOQ)—A widely used quantitative technique for finding the optimal level of inventory to order and the optimal number of orders to place each year.

Economies of scale—The degree to which the cost of providing a good or service falls as quantity increases because fixed costs are shared by the larger volume of units.

Effectiveness—A measure of the degree to which the organization accomplishes its desired goals.

Efficiency—A measure of how close an organization comes to minimizing the amount of resources used to accomplish a result.

Efficiency variance—See *Quantity variance.*

Engineered costs—Costs for which there is a specific input–output relationship.

Equivalent units of production—A conversion of a number of partially completed units of work in process inventory into an equivalent number of completed units. For example, 100 half-completed units would be equivalent to 50 completed units.

Evaluative budgeting—An approach to allocating resources based on the idea that each element of expenditure for each unit or department is explained and justified.

Event—Occurrence that is beyond the control of managers; often referred to as a *state of nature.*

Exception report—A list of only those individual items, such as variances, that exceed a specified limit.

Expected value—The weighted average of the possible outcomes, using known or subjective probabilities as weights.

Expenditure—Payment. Often used interchangeably with expense.

Expense centers—See *Cost centers.*

Expenses—The costs of services provided; expired cost.

Expired cost—See *Cost.*

External accountant—An accountant who is hired by the organization but is not an employee of it.

External costs—The costs imposed on individuals and organizations resulting from the actions of an unrelated individual or organization. (See *Externality.*)

External failure costs—All costs related to having provided a good or service that turns out to be defective.

External reports—Reports prepared primarily for the use of individuals outside of the organization.

Externality—A side-effect impact on someone not party to an action that results from that action.

Favorable variance—A variance where less was spent than the budgeted amount. This does not necessarily imply something good happened.

Fee-for-service—A system in which there is a charge for each additional service provided (as opposed to a prepaid system in which all services are included in exchange for one flat payment).

Feedback—Use of information about actual results to shape future plans, in order to avoid past mistakes and improve future outcomes.

Financial accounting—A system that records historical financial information and provides summary reports to individuals outside of the organization of what financial events have occurred and of what the financial impact of those events has been.

Financial ratios—Ratios developed using data from the organization's financial statements prepared for external users.

Finished goods inventory (FGI)—Units of production that are complete and ready for sale.

First-in, first-out (FIFO)—Method of accounting for inventory that assumes we always use up the oldest inventory first.

Fiscal year—A one-year period defined for financial purposes. It may start at any point during the calendar year, and finishes one year later. For example, "Fiscal Year 1995 with a June 30 year end" refers to the period from July 1, 1994 through June 30, 1995.

Fixed costs—Costs that do not vary in total as the volume of units of service changes.

Flexible budget—A budget that is adjusted for volume of output.

Flexible budget variance—The difference between actual results and the flexible budget.

Float—(1) The interim period from when a check is written until the check is cashed and clears the bank; (2) movement of staff from one unit or department to another.

For-profit—An organization the mission of which includes earning a profit that may be distributed to its owners.

Forecast—A prediction of some future value, such as patient days, chest tubes used, or nursing care hours per patient day.

Forecast interval—A range of values surrounding a forecast for which there is a specified probability that the actual result will fall within the range.

Forecasting—The process of making forecasts.

FTE—See *Full-time equivalent.*

Full cost—All costs of a cost objective, including both direct costs and an allocated fair share of indirect costs.

Full-time equivalent (FTE)—The equivalent of one full-time employee paid for one year, including both productive and nonproductive (vacation, sick, holiday, education, etc.) time. Two employees each working half-time for one year would be the same as one FTE.

Future value (FV)—The amount a present amount of money will grow to be worth at some point in the future.

General information ratios—Cost accounting ratios that provide general background information to managers.

Goal congruence—A situation in which the goals, desires, and wants of the employees become the same as those of their employer.

Goal divergence—The natural differences between the goals, desires, and needs of the organization and those of its employees.

Goodness of fit—The ability of one variable to explain the variations in another.

Hash total—A control number. It has no inherent information content and is used only for control.

Health Care Financing Administration (HCFA)—Federal agency that administers the Medicare program.

Health maintenance organization (HMO)—An organization that provides health care services to individuals or groups in exchange for a predetermined monthly payment.

HMO—See *Health Maintenance Organization.*

Hourly rate—An allocation method that assigns costs to units of service based on the amount of time required to provide a treatment or procedure.

Hurdle rate—See *Required rate of return.*

Hybrid approaches—A mixture of two extreme approaches, such as job-order and process costing.

Incentives—Activities, rewards, or punishments used to make it in the individual's interest to act in a desired manner.

Income determination—The measurement of income, generally by subtracting expenses (expired costs) from revenues.

Incremental budgeting—An approach to resource allocation that simply adds an additional percentage or amount onto the prior year's budget allocation, without investigation of whether the continuation of the amounts authorized in the prior-year budget are warranted.

Incremental costs—The additional costs that will be incurred if a decision is made that would not otherwise be incurred.

Independence—With respect to specification analysis, a condition where each of the residuals is not related to the value of any of the others. The residuals are a measure of the distance from the regression line to each of the actual historical points.

Independent variable—The variable used to predict the dependent variable. The causal variable that is responsible for changes in the dependent variable.

Index of labor hours—Productivity measurement that divides actual labor hours by baseline labor hours.

Index of output—Productivity measurement that divides actual output by baseline output.

Index of output per labor hour—Productivity measurement that divides index of output by index of labor hours.

Indexing for inflation—Adjustment of historical information for the impact of changes in price levels.

Indirect costs—Costs that are not directly associated with a cost objective.

Indirect expenses—See *Indirect costs.*

Indirect method—Method for measuring cash flows that starts with the operating revenues and expenses and reconciles to actual cash flows.

Inputs—Resources used for treating patients or otherwise producing output. Examples of inputs include paid nursing hours, chest tubes, and intravenous (I.V.) solutions.

Institutional cost report—A document prepared by many health care organizations for submission, as required, to third-party payers such as Medicare, Medicaid, and Blue Cross.

Internal accountant—An accountant who works for the organization.

Internal control—A system of accounting checks and balances designed to minimize both clerical errors and the possibility of fraud or embezzlement; the process and systems that ensure that decisions made in the organization are appropriate and receive appropriate authorization. Requires a system of accounting and administrative controls.

Internal failure costs—Those costs related to correcting defects that the organization discovers before the product is received by the customer.

Internal rate of return (IRR)—A discounted cash flow technique that calculates the rate of return earned by a specific project or program.

Inventory—Materials and supplies held for use in providing services or making a product.

Inventory carrying costs—See *Carrying costs of inventory.*

Inventory costing—The process of determining the cost to be assigned to each unit of inventory, generally for financial statement purposes.

Inventory management—The appropriate ordering and storage of supplies.

Inventory ordering costs—See *Ordering costs.*

Inventory valuation—The process of determining the cost of inventory used and the value of inventory assets.

Investment centers—A responsibility center that not only controls its revenues and expenses but the level of capital investment as well.

IRR—See *Internal rate of return.*

Job-cost sheet—A management document used to accumulate all of the materials and labor used for a specific job.

Job-order costing—An approach to product costing that directly associates the specific resources used for each job with that job.

Joint costs—Fixed costs that are required for the treatment of several different types of patients. Elimination of any one of those types of patients would have no impact on these costs.

Just-in-time (JIT) inventory—An approach to inventory management that calls for the arrival of inventory just as it is needed, resulting in zero inventory levels.

Key variables—Things that can change rapidly and have a significant impact on the results of the organization.

Last-in, first-out (LIFO)—Inventory valuation method that accounts for inventory as if the very most recent acquisitions are always used prior to inventory acquired at an earlier date and still on hand.

Learning curve—See *Learning curve effect.*

Learning curve effect—Hypothesis that with each doubling of output, the cost per unit falls systematically.

Lease—An agreement providing for the use of an asset in exchange for rental payments.

Length of stay (LOS)—The number of days a patient is an inpatient. This is generally measured by the number of times the patient is an inpatient at midnight.

Life-cycle accounting—Accounting for all costs related to a product over its entire cycle from inception to abandonment.

Line item—Any resource that is listed as a separate line on a budget.

Linear programming (LP)—A mathematical technique that allows the user to maximize or minimize the value of a specific objective in a constrained environment.

Linearity—A straight-line relationship.

Logistics—The management of inventories, including their acquisition, transportation, storage, and distribution.

Long-range budget—A plan that covers a period of time longer than one year (typically three, five, or ten years), and provides the general direction that the organization will take to accomplish its mission.

Long-range planning—A planning process that focuses on general objectives to be achieved by the organization over a period of typically three to five years. Often referred to as strategic planning.

Long run—See *Long term.*

Long term—The period of time when fixed costs become variable and can be adjusted for any given output level.

Long-term assets—See *Capital assets.*

Long-term investment—See *Capital assets.*

LOS—See *Length of stay.*

MACRS—See *Modified Accelerated Cost Recovery System.*

Management control systems—Formalized systems used by an organization's management to ensure that the organization's mission and specific goals are accomplished as effectively and efficiently as possible.

Management information system—A system designed to generate information for managers. This term is commonly used for computerized systems for generating information.

Managerial accounting—Generation of any financial information that can help managers to manage better.

Managerial reports—Reports that provide information to help managers run the organization more efficiently.

Marginal cost analysis—A process for making decisions about changes based on the marginal costs of the change, rather than on full or average costs.

Marginal costs—The change in cost related to a change in activity. Includes variable costs and any additional fixed costs incurred because the volume change exceeds the relevant range for existing fixed costs.

Market management—An approach to product-line management that focuses mostly on creating an increased external market.

Market share variance—Variance caused by not actually realizing the percentage of total community admissions that were expected.

Market size variance—Variance caused by the existence of a greater or smaller number of patients in the community than was expected.

Master budget—A set of all of the major budgets in the organization. It generally includes the operating budget, long-range budget, programs budgets, capital budget, and cash budget.

Matrix distribution—See *Algebraic distribution.*

Matrix management—See *Matrix structure.*

Matrix structure—An organizational relationship in which a manager must draw upon a variety of the organization's personnel that do not directly report to that manager.

Medicare Cost Report—Institutional cost report prepared for Medicare.

Microcosting—The process of closely examining the actual resources consumed by a particular patient or service. Microcosting tends to be extremely costly and is generally done only for special studies.

Mixed costs—Costs that contain an element of fixed costs and an element of variable costs, such as electricity.

Modified Accelerated Cost Recovery System (MACRS)—Depreciation approach for federal income taxes that allows for greater

write-offs in earlier years and smaller ones in later years of the asset's life.

Monitoring and control ratios—Cost accounting ratios that can be used to generate information that aids managers in monitoring and controlling various aspects of the organization's operations.

Multiple distribution—The *double distribution* and the *algebraic* or *matrix distribution* approaches to cost allocation.

Multiple regression—Regression analysis that uses more than one independent variable.

Negotiative budgeting—Approach to resource allocation in which the amount allocated to a unit or department is based on a process of negotiation.

Net cash flow—The difference between cash receipts and cash payments.

Net present cost—The aggregate present value of a series of payments to be made in the future.

Net present value (NPV)—The present value of a series of receipts less the present value of a series of payments.

Network cost budgeting—Combining the techniques of network analysis with cost accounting to generate the most cost-effective approach to carrying out a project.

Nominal group technique—A forecasting technique in which a group of individuals are brought together in a structured meeting and arrive at a group consensus forecast.

Noncontrollable—Those items that a manager does not have the authority or ability to control.

Nonproductive time—Sick, vacation, holiday, and other paid, nonworked time.

Nonrevenue cost center—A cost center that does not charge directly for its services. Its costs must be allocated to a revenue center in order to be included in the organization's rates.

Nonroutine decisions—Management decisions that are not made on a routine, regularly scheduled basis.

Normal costing—A cost allocation approach in which actual costs are assigned for labor and supplies, and a budgeted rate is used to allocate overhead costs.

Normality—An element of specification analysis that requires that there be a normal distribution of historical points around the regression line.

Not-for-profit—An organization the mission of which does not include earning a profit for distribution to owners. A not-for-profit organization may earn a profit, but such profit must be reinvested for replacement of facilities and equipment or for expansion of services offered.

NPV—See *Net present value.*

Objective function—The equation that states the relationship between the objective in a linear programming problem and the other variables in the process. The objective is the item, the value of which we wish to optimize.

One-shot budget—A budget that is prepared only once, rather than on a regular, periodic basis, such as monthly or annually.

Operating budget—The plan for the day-in and day-out operating revenues and expenses of the organization. It is generally prepared for a period of one year.

Opportunity cost—A measure of cost based on the value of the alternatives that are given up in order to use the resource as the organization has chosen.

Ordering costs—Costs associated with an order, such as clerk time for preparation of a purchase order and shipping and handling charges.

OTPS—Other than personnel services.

Out-of-pocket costs—See *Incremental costs.*

Outcome—A result. Can be affected by management actions, in contrast to events, which are defined as occurrences that are beyond the control of managers.

Outputs—The product or service being produced, for example, patients, patient days, visits, or operations.

Over- or underapplied overhead—The amount that the actual overhead costs differ from the amount of overhead applied to units of service.

Overhead—Indirect costs. Often cannot be easily associated with individual patients, even by a job-order type of detailed observation and measurement. Overhead costs therefore require some form of aggregation and then allocation to units, departments, and ultimately patients or other units of service.

Overhead application—The process of charging overhead costs to units of service based on a standard overhead application rate.

Overhead application rate—The amount charged per unit of service for overhead, calculated using a cost base.

Overhead costs—See *Overhead.*

Partial productivity—A portion of the total productivity; total outputs divided by some subpart of total inputs.

Pass-through costs—See *Cost pass-through.*

Patient care variance—The extent to which paid, worked, productive time is actually consumed in the process of direct patient care as opposed to other activities.

Patient classification system—System for distinguishing among different patients based on their functional ability and resource needs.

Patient day—One patient occupying one bed for one day.

Patient mix—See *Case-mix.*

Patient-mix variance—Variance from the organization's expected patient case-mix.

Patient revenue per day—Total patient revenue divided by the number of days in the year.

Payback—A capital budgeting approach that calculates how long it takes for a project's cash inflows to equal or exceed its cash outflows.

Payer—An individual or organization that provides money to pay for health care services.

Per diem—Daily charge. Refers to (1) the charge per day for routine care, and (2) agency nurses who work day to day.

Per diem method—Approach used to allocate department costs to units of service, if the surcharge, hourly rate, and relative value unit methods do not reasonably apply.

Performance budget—A plan that relates the various objectives of a cost center with the planned costs of accomplishing those activities.

Period costs—Costs that are treated as expense in the accounting period that they are incurred, regardless of when the organization's goods or services are sold.

Periodic inventory—See *Perpetual versus periodic inventory.*

Perpetual versus periodic inventory—Under the perpetual inventory method, the organization keeps a record of each inventory acquisition and sale, so it always knows how much has been sold and how much is supposed to be in inventory, whereas under the periodic method, the organization records only purchases and uses a count of inventory to determine how much has been sold and how much is left on hand.

Personnel—Persons employed by the organization.

PERT—See *Program Evaluation and Review Technique.*

Planning—Deciding upon goals and objectives, considering alternative options for achieving those goals and objectives, and selecting a course of action from the range of possible alternatives.

Plant—The building.

Position—One person working one job, regardless of the number of hours that the person works.

PPO—See *Preferred provider organization.*

Preferred provider organization (PPO)—A health care provider organization that is recommended by an insurer or employer as being a preferred provider of services. PPOs generally offer the insurer or employer discounts, and employees or insured individuals who use the PPO generally pay less for their medical care than if they do not use the PPO.

Present costs—See *Net present costs.*

Present value—The value of cash flows to be received in the future, discounted to the present.

Prevention costs—Costs incurred by the organization in an effort to ensure that external and internal failure costs do not arise.

Preventive controls—See *Accounting controls.*

Price variance—(1) The portion of the total expense variance for any line item that is caused by spending a different amount per unit of resource than had been anticipated; (2) the portion of the total revenue variance caused by charging a different price for services than had been anticipated.

Prime cost—The direct costs of a product or service; raw materials plus labor costs.

Principal—The amount of money borrowed on a loan.

Private insurers—Insurance companies that are not part of the government.

Pro forma financial statements—Financial statements that present a prediction of what the financial statements for a project, program, or organization will look like at some point in the future.

Probabilistic estimate—An estimate that is based on a manager's subjective estimate of what is most likely to occur.

Process costing—Approach to product costing based on broad averages of costs over a large volume of units of service.

Product costing—Determination of the cost per unit of service. Job-order costing measures separately the cost of producing each job, whereas process costing is based on costs averaged across a large number of units of service. An individual patient or a group of patients of a similar type may be considered to be a job.

Product costs—Costs that are treated as part of the product and do not become expenses until the product is sold.

Product line—A group of patients that have some commonality that allows them to be grouped together, such as a common diagnosis.

Product-line costing—The determination of the cost of providing care to specific product lines.

Productive time—Straight time and overtime worked.

Productive versus nonproductive variance—The variance caused by an unexpected amount of nonproductive hours.

Productivity—The ratio of any given measure of output to any given measure of input over a specified time period.

Productivity measurement—The measurement of productivity.

Profit—The amount by which an organization's revenues exceed its expenses.

Profit center—A responsibility unit that is responsible for both revenues and expenses.

Health care organizations have referred to profit centers as revenue centers, emphasizing the fact that a specific charge for such centers will appear on patient bills.

Profit margin—Excess of revenue over expense divided by total revenue; an indication of the amount of profits generated by each dollar of revenue.

Profit-sharing plan—An incentive arrangement under which executives receive a portion of an organization's profits that exceed a certain threshold.

Profitability analysis—Analysis of the profits related to a specific program, project, or service under existing conditions or under a specific set of assumptions.

Program budget—A plan that looks at all aspects of a program across departments and over the long term.

Program Evaluation and Review Technique (PERT)—A multibranch programming technique designed to predict total project completion time for large-scale projects and to identify paths that have available slack.

Program stability—Ability of a software template to remain valid over time.

Programming—(1) The process of deciding what major programs the organization will commence in the future; (2) the development of computer software instructions.

Promotion-to-manager ratio—The total number of employees hired in a given year who have been promoted divided by the total number of employees hired in that year.

Proprietary—See *For-profit.*

Prospective payment—Payment based on a predetermined price for any particular category of patient (such as a particular Diagnosis Related Group [DRG]), as opposed to reimbursement based on a retrospective measure of the costs of care provided to the patient.

Prospective payment system (PPS)—An approach to paying for health care services based on predetermined prices.

Quality costs—Those costs incurred to ensure that a product is of the required quality. May include costs such as inspection or replacement, or harm to the patient created by using a low-quality item.

Quality driver—Any factor that is critical to the level of quality of a product or service.

Quantity variance—The portion of the total variance for any line item that is caused by using a different amount of input per unit of output (e.g., patient day) than had been budgeted.

Quick ratio—Cash plus marketable securities plus accounts receivable, all divided by current liabilities.

R-squared (R^2)—A regression analysis statistic that can range from a low of zero to a high of 1.0. The closer it is to 1.0, the more of the variability in the dependent variable that has been explained by the independent variable.

Rate—See *Overhead application rate.*

Rate variance—A price variance that relates to labor resources. In such cases, it is typically the hourly rate that has varied from expectations. See *Price variance.*

Ratio—One number divided by another.

Ratio analysis—A widely used managerial tool that compares one number to another to gain insights that would not arise from looking at either of the numbers separately.

Ratio of cost to charges (RCC)—A method used to convert charges from patient bills to costs by applying the ratio of the organization's costs to its charges.

Raw materials inventory (RMI)—Materials on hand that have been purchased for use in the productive process but that have not yet entered into that process.

Reciprocal distribution—See *Algebraic distribution.*

Regression analysis—A statistical model that measures the average change in a dependent variable associated with a one-unit change in one or more independent variables.

Regulation—A government rule that has the force of law.

Relative value unit (RVU) scale—An arbitrary unit scale in which each patient is assigned a number of RVUs based on the relative costs of different types of patients. For example, if nursing care costs twice as much for Type A patients as for Type B patients, then Type A patients will be assigned a number of relative value units that is twice as high as that assigned to Type B patients.

Relevant costs—Only those costs that are subject to change as a result of a decision.

Relevant range—The expected range of volume over which fixed costs are fixed and variable costs vary in direct proportion.

Required rate of return—The interest rate that must be achieved for a capital project to be considered financially worthwhile. Also called the hurdle rate.

Residual income (RI)—The profits from a project in excess of the amount necessary to provide a desired minimum rate of return.

Residuals—A measure of the distance from the regression line to each of the actual historical points.

Responsibility accounting—An attempt to measure financial outcomes and assign those outcomes to the individual or department responsible for them.

Responsibility center—A part of the organization, such as a department or a unit, for which a manager is assigned responsibility. Health care organizations generally have cost centers and revenue centers.

Return on assets (ROA)—Profit divided by total assets; a measure of the amount of profit earned for each dollar invested in the organization's assets.

Return on investment (ROI)—A ratio that divides the amount of profit by the amount of the investment. Just as an individual would measure the success of a personal investment, so an organization would use ROI to measure the yield received relative to an amount of money invested.

Revenue—Amounts of money that the organization has received or is entitled to receive in exchange for goods and/or services that it has provided.

Revenue center—A unit or department that is responsible and accountable not only for costs of providing services, but also for revenues generated by those services.

Revenue variances—Assessment of how much of the variance between expected and actual revenues results from changes in the total health care organization demand in a given geographic region, a health care organization's share of that total demand, its mix of patients, and the prices for each class of patient.

Rolling budget—A system in which a budget is prepared each month for a month one year in the future. For example, once the actual results for this January are known, a budget for January of the next year is prepared.

RVU—See *Relative Value Unit scale*.

Safety stock—Minimum level of inventory that an organization would attempt always to maintain on hand. Would be dipped into only when an event arises that would, in the absence of a safety stock, have resulted in a stockout.

Satisfice—Work hard enough to get by but not hard enough to obtain an optimal outcome.

Seasonality—A predictable pattern of monthly, quarterly, or other periodic variation in historical data within each year.

Seasonalization—Adjustment of the annual budget for month-to-month seasonality.

Self-pay patients—Patients who are responsible for the payment of their own health care bills because they do not have private insurance and are not covered by either Medicare or Medicaid.

Semi-fixed cost—See *Step-fixed*.

Semi-variable cost—See *Mixed cost*.

Sensitivity analysis—A process whereby the financial results are recalculated under a series of varying assumptions and predictions. Often referred to as "what if" analysis.

Service unit—A basic measure of the item being produced by the organization, such as patient days, home care visits, or hours of operation.

Short run—See *Short term*.

Short term—Period of time shorter than the long term. See *Long-term*.

Simple linear regression—Regression analysis that uses one dependent and one independent variable, and which produces predictions along a straight line.

Simulation—A mathematical approach that processes a number of different estimates a large number of times and projects the likelihood of various aggregate outcomes.

Sinking fund—Segregated assets to be used for replacement of plant and equipment.

Slack time—Waiting time between activities in a network analysis.

Social costs—See *External costs.*

Special-purpose budget—Any plan that does not fall into one of the other specific categories of budgets.

Specific identification—Inventory valuation method that identifies each unit of inventory and tracks which specific units are on hand and which have been sold.

Specification analysis—Requirements for regression analysis. If all four of the specification analysis factors are met, then the resulting estimates are considered to be the best linear, unbiased estimates.

Spending variance—The equivalent of the price or rate variance for fixed and variable overhead costs.

Spreadsheet—Large ledger sheets often used by accountants for financial calculations; computer software programs designed to provide automated spreadsheet calculations.

Standard cost profile—The costs, fixed and variable, direct and indirect, of producing each service unit.

Standard costs—Predetermined estimates of what it should cost to produce one unit of a product. Standards are determined by using historical results, time-and-motion observations, or industrial engineering calculations.

Standard treatment protocol—The set of intermediate products, or service units, consumed by a patient in each product line.

State of nature—See *Event.*

Statement of Financial Position—A financial report that indicates the financial position of the organization at a specific point in time. Often referred to as the balance sheet.

Step-down allocation—A method of cost allocation in which nonrevenue centers allocate their costs to all cost centers, both revenue and nonrevenue, that have not yet allocated their costs. Once a nonrevenue center allocates its costs, no costs can be allocated to it.

Step-fixed—A cost that is fixed over short ranges of volume but varies within the relevant range (sometimes referred to as step-variable).

Step-variable—See *Step-fixed.*

Stock option plan—See *Stock plan.*

Stock plan—Bonus arrangement that provides shares of stock as part of an executive incentive system.

Stockout costs—Costs incurred when a supply is not available but is needed and must be purchased immediately at a higher price from a local vendor.

Strategic budget—See *Long-range budget.*

Strategic business unit—An approach to product-line management that has managers look not only at marketing but also at allocation of resources and profitability.

Strategic management—The process of setting the goals and objectives of the organization, determining the resources to be allocated to achieve those goals and objectives, and establishing policies concerning getting and using those resources.

Strategic planning—See *Long-range planning.*

Subcategory—A device to allow separation of the flexible budget variance into the price variance and the quantity variance; the actual quantity of input per unit of output, multiplied by the budgeted price of the input, times the actual output level.

Subjective probability—A probability that is based on a manager's estimate rather than known odds.

Sunk costs—Costs that already have been incurred and will not be affected by future actions.

Support cost center—A cost center that is not a revenue center.

Surcharge method—Approach to cost allocation in which a revenue center compares its costs excluding inventory to the inventory cost and determines a proportional surcharge.

Surplus—See *Profit.*

t-test—A statistical test performed to ascertain that the value for the slope is indeed significantly different from zero. If the *t*-value is greater than 2.00, then the slope is assumed to be statistically different from zero.

Technology accounting—Approach to cost measurement in which plant, equipment, and information systems are treated as direct costs, as opposed to having depreciation costs simply thrown into overhead.

Technology costing—See *Technology accounting.*

Template—Customized computer program application that gives a framework to which managers can add variables to perform computerized analysis.

Third-party payer—Someone other than the patient who pays the health care provider for the patient's care. The most common third-party payers are Medicare, Medicaid, Blue Cross, and other private insurance companies.

Time and motion studies—Industrial engineering observations of the specific time and resources consumed for some activity.

Time driver—The time from an initial suggestion for a new service until it is actually introduced.

Time-series analysis—Use of historical values of a variable to predict future values for that variable without the use of any other variable, other than the passage of time.

Time value of money—Recognition of the fact that money can earn compound interest; therefore, a given amount of money paid at different points in time has a different value. The further into the future an amount is paid, the less valuable it is.

Total costs—The sum of all costs related to a cost objective.

Total productivity—The ratio of total outputs to total inputs; the amount of output per unit of input.

Total quality management (TQM)—A philosophy that prevention of defects is cheaper than cure. TQM focuses on doing things right initially and avoiding having to do them a second time.

Total variance—The sum of the price, quantity, and volume variances; the difference between the actual results and the original budgeted amount.

Transfer prices—The amounts charged to one responsibility center for goods or services acquired from another responsibility center in the same organization.

Trend—Patterns related to the passage of time.

True costs—Actual resources consumed. Measurement of unique true costs is rarely possible. No matter how accurate accounting information is, there always will be different assessments of cost in different situations. Even beyond this, however, true costs do not exist because accounting can never do more than approximate economic cost.

Uncontrollable—See *Noncontrollable.*

Unfavorable variance—A variance in which more was spent than the budgeted amount. That does not necessarily mean that the manager or unit performed badly. Nor does it mean that the variance was bad for the organization.

Uniform reporting—Proposed approaches to improve comparability of financial information among health care organizations.

Unit of service—See *Service unit.*

Use variance—Another name for the quantity variance. So-called because the quantity variance focuses on how much of a resource has been used. See *Quantity variance.*

Variable costing—See *Direct costing.*

Variable costs—Those costs that vary in direct proportion to patient volume.

Variance—The difference between the budget and the actual results.

Variance analysis—A comparison of actual results as compared with the budget, followed by investigation to determine why the variance(s) occurred.

Vendor—Supplier, such as a pharmaceutical company or hospital supply company.

Volume variance—The amount of the variance in any line item that is caused simply by the fact that the workload level has changed.

Weighted average method—Inventory valuation method that accounts for inventory as if the inventory all gets mixed together, and each unit is unidentifiable.

Weighted procedure method—An approach to allocating a cost center's costs to units of service based upon a special study that establishes the relative costliness of each type of service the center performs.

Winters' forecasting method—A statistical forecasting method that predicts seasonal patterns particularly well.

Work in process (WIP)—Inventory that has entered into the manufacturing process but has not yet been completed.

Work measurement—A technique that evaluates what a group of workers is doing and attempts to assess the number of workers needed to accomplish the tasks efficiently.

Work sampling—An approach to determining time and resources used for an activity based on observations at intervals of time rather than continuous observation.

Worked versus paid variance—The portion of the quantity variance that results from an unexpected level of paid but not worked time.

Working capital—The organization's current assets and current liabilities.

Working capital management—The management of the current assets and current liabilities of the organization.

Working capital method—Method for measuring cash flows that emphasizes a focus on working capital.

Workload—The volume of work for a unit or department.

Year-to-date—The sum of the budget and/or actual values for all months from the beginning of the year through the most recent period for which data are available.

Zero balance accounts—A system in which separate accounts are maintained at a bank for each major source of cash receipt and for major types of payments; at the close of each day, the bank, using computer technology, automatically transfers all balances, positive or negative, into one master concentration account. Any borrowing or investing of cash can then be done against that one account.

ZBB—See **Zero-base budgeting.**

Zero-base budgeting (ZBB)—A program-budgeting approach that requires an examination and justification of all costs rather than just the incremental costs and that requires examination of alternatives rather than just one approach.

Appendix A

Solutions to Exercises

CHAPTER 1

Questions for Discussion

1. The prime reason for undertaking any information-generating activity is so that an effective decision can be made.

2. Financial accounting provides information primarily for individuals or entities that are outside of, or external to, the organization. This includes banks, suppliers, in some cases owners, the government, and a range of others interested in the finances of a particular organization.

   Managerial accounting is the part of accounting related to providing information for internal users. Internal managers need a broad range of financial information to run the organization effectively. Managerial accounting generates any financial information that can help managers to manage better.

   Cost accounting includes all of managerial accounting, but it also focuses on certain elements of financial accounting that are closely related to cost measurement and control. For example, the Medicare cost report is part of financial accounting because it is prepared for outsiders. However, it is part of cost accounting because of its focus on cost measurement.

3. Planning means that the managers of the organization think through the implications of their actions before they act. By planning ahead, advantageous opportunities can be undertaken and problematic ones avoided.

   Will the plans actually work? That depends largely on how well the employees of the organization work to control operations and keep to the plan. The tools that allow managers to control ongoing activities and to respond in an effective manner when either controllable or uncontrollable

events occur make up the control elements of cost accounting.

4. The question of whether to add or delete a health care service or whether to expand a health care facility can have significant financial implications for the organization.

5. Application 1-2 is a review of an article by Robert Kaplan. The theme of that article is that one cost accounting system may be insufficient. Rather than trying to develop a perfect cost accounting system, Kaplan proposes the use of several parallel systems providing cost information for different purposes.

6. A good cost accounting system is one that is based on a knowledge of what information is needed, why it is needed, and what will be done with it once it is available.

7. False. A good cost accounting system should generate information that is more valuable than the cost of the system itself. Accuracy in cost measurement is desired but must be balanced against the cost of acquiring the information. Often, managers desire to use extremely accurate accounting information for making decisions. From an idealistic point of view, that makes perfect sense; from a pragmatic point of view, it is not always a sensible option. Wise use of the limited resources of an organization calls for the use of the least expensive adequate data for making a decision.

8. Often, approaches to recording expense information for reporting purposes are inadequate for efficient management. For example, managers can best control their department costs if they know the costs incurred each month. For reporting purposes, it is less important to record expenses in the specific month the resource was actually used, as long as total costs for the year are correct. Often, financial man-

agers will allow the external reporting needs to predominate the information-generation process.

9. Cost accounting is a field in which we often become buried in the numbers. If we do not closely consider the individual people involved in the cost accounting process, we may calculate accurate costs, but we may be causing things to cost more than they should.

It is the basic nature of individuals that their own personal goals will generally be divergent from the goals of the organization for which they work. To a great extent, it is the accountants of the health care organization who have to deal with this divergence and develop means of creating congruency. Cost accounting systems can be designed to provide incentives that will motivate employees to work in the organization's best interests.

CHAPTER 2

Questions for Discussion

1. False. The treatment of clerks would depend on the cost objective. If the objective is the costs of a department, a clerk in that department would be a direct cost. If the cost objective is the direct care cost, the clerk would be an indirect cost.

2. False. The cost objective is the unit (department, patient, etc.) the cost of which you want to measure.

3. False. The relevant range refers to the volume for which an analysis applies. For example, one might be budgeting with an expected volume of 1,000 patients. If fixed costs would remain fixed over any range of patients from 700 to 1,300, that would be the relevant range. Outside of the relevant range, one cannot assume that fixed costs would remain fixed. For example, a unit might be closed down, relieving the need for the fixed cost of a unit manager.

4. The cost to treat a patient is very situational. It depends on volume. It depends on the decision to which the cost information relates. Additionally, it depends on the specific situation of an individual institution, such as whether it has substantial excess capacity or is near its full capacity.

5. Over the long run, average revenues must at least equal average costs for an institution to be able to replace its facilities and capital equipment; in the short run, decisions should be made based on marginal costs. Marginal costs are defined as the change in cost related to a change in activity. If the added revenues exceed the added costs of treating additional patients, the health care organization will be in a better position.

6. Because true costs cannot ever be measured, it is likely that there will always be some cross-subsidization that will never be known nor be subject to measurement. Even with accounting costs, the effort required to avoid all cross-subsidization is greater than most organizations would be willing to undertake. It would be too costly. The issue is really one of degree. How substantial and significant is the degree of cross-subsidization, and how does it affect managerial decisions?

7. Quality assurance is a joint cost. The efforts of this department are intended to benefit all patients. However, the addition or deletion of a patient or class of patients would not likely affect the existence or costs of this department.

8. Both of these applications stress that more detailed costing focusing on specific types of patients can reduce the extent of cross-subsidization. This will provide managers with better information for decision making.

Problems

1. Applications 2-1 and 2-2 should be used as a basis for evaluating solutions.

2. Application 2-3 should be used as a basis for evaluating solutions.

3. The first step is to determine the total amount of RVUs of work performed.

Acuity Level	Patient Days	×	RVUs	=	Total RVUs
1	120		1.00		120.0
2	170		1.25		212.5
3	300		1.61		483.0
4	170		2.14		363.8
5	50		3.04		152.0
					1,331.3

Next, determine the cost per RVU:

$$\$167,744/1,331.3 = \$126.00/\text{RVU}$$

Finally, determine the RVUs for an average
DRG 174 patient:

Acuity Level	Patient Days	×	RVUs	=	Total RVUs
1	2		1.00		2.00
2	1		1.25		1.25
3	1		1.61		1.61
4	1		2.14		2.14
5	0		3.04		0.00
					7.00
					× $126.00
					$882.00

CHAPTER 3

Questions for Discussion

1. Process costing uses average information and assigns the same cost to each unit of output within a broad range of production. For example, all cans of cola have the same production cost under process costing. Job-order costing treats each job as unique and separately accumulates the costs of resources consumed for each job.

2. The use of the same cost per x-ray is process costing because it probably takes more resources to x-ray some types of patients than other types. However, to the extent that only patients who have x-rays are assigned x-ray cost, it is a job-order approach. Therefore, it is a hybrid of process and job order.

3. Job-order costing provides extremely detailed and accurate information about each individual job but tends to be very expensive. Process costing is very inexpensive, but its information is all broad averages across all patients.

4. From a point of view of the nature of the product produced, job-order costing is clearly more appropriate. Each individual patient is unique. The treatment for different patients with the same basic illness can vary widely. On the other hand, it is inappropriate to spend more money on collecting cost data than they are worth.

   Historically, the type of costing done in health care has been a mixture of process and job order. Assigning operating room costs only to patients who had surgery is a job-order approach. Operating room costs could be assigned in equal shares to all patients whether they had surgery or not.

On the other hand, assigning the same operating room cost per patient for each hour of surgery is clearly a process-costing approach.

As it becomes more important to have more accurate information for each different group of patients, there will likely be a shift toward more job-order type costing and less process costing.

5. Standards are predetermined estimates of what it should cost to treat a patient. General product-costing is concerned with aggregated costs that have been incurred to provide care to patients.

6. Cleverley proposed that health care organizations cost their products using a standard costing approach that is centered around service units (SUs), standard cost profiles (SCPs), and standard treatment protocols (STPs). In his system, he defines the treated patient as the product.

   Each patient is treated by being given a variety of intermediate products, or SUs. A particular type of laboratory test would be one SU. A day of nursing care at a certain intensity level would be another SU. For any given type of patient, we could design an STP that would list all the SUs necessary to treat the patient.

   The SUs, in turn, each have an SCP. This SCP would indicate specific information about labor, materials, departmental overhead, and allocated overhead. To the extent possible, these items should also be categorized as fixed or variable costs.

   By looking at an STP for a patient, we can see all of the predicted SUs required for treatment of the patient. By considering the SCP for each SU, we can build a total standard cost for treating a patient of a given type.

Problem

1. Each answer will be unique. Follow the Cleverley article in Application 3-3 as a guide.

CHAPTER 4

Questions for Discussion

1. There are two primary types of cost allocation. The first is the allocation of indirect costs within a department to specific individual patients. For example, how much of the head nurse's salary should be assigned to each patient on a medical/surgical unit of a hospital? The second type of allocation is from one department or cost center to another.

2. Yes. Job-order costing will associate direct costs with patients. Many indirect costs either cannot be assigned directly to individual patients, or else it would be too costly to do so. These costs become overhead items and must be allocated to patients.

3. In order to assign costs from one objective to another, it is necessary that there be a base. For example, we could choose to allocate costs based on patient days. In that case, the number of patient days would be the base. Alternatively, costs could be allocated based on hours. It is common to allocate housekeeping costs based on hours of service provided. The total number of hours of housekeeping service becomes the base. If this base is divided into the total cost for providing housekeeping services, the result is an overhead application rate—in this case, a cost per hour of service.

4. This allows for a determination of each patient's cost on an ongoing basis. Direct labor and supplies can often be observed on an ongoing basis. However, determination of the actual amount and cost of overhead consumed as it is consumed is much more difficult. Overhead might include costs such as heat and electricity, which cannot be determined exactly for a number of weeks at the earliest. Having a predetermined rate substantially simplifies the process of accumulating all the costs associated with a specific patient.

Further, suppose that patient census varies from month to month. Fixed costs will remain constant. The result is that in months of low census, there will be fewer direct hours of care over which to spread fixed costs. In high-occupancy months, there will be more direct hours over which to spread fixed costs. Thus, an actual costing overhead rate will vary substantially from month to month. It will appear that the cost of treating similar patients is changing, when what we are really observing is the impact of a change in volume. This problem is avoided if budgeted rates are used.

5. For health care organizations we can think of these six steps as

   - selecting a base for assigning costs to patients;
   - determining budgeted cost and volume;
   - computing overhead rate;
   - measuring actual base;
   - applying the budgeted overhead application rate to the actual volume; and
   - accounting for year-end differences between actual total overhead and the amount of overhead applied throughout the year.

6. This can happen because the fixed housekeeping costs will be allocated to departments based on hours of service used. If one cost center consumes fewer hours than expected, the fixed costs allocated to other cost centers will rise. This can be avoided by assigning fixed costs based on long-term budgets and variable costs based on current consumption of services.

7. Joint costs are inherently needed for treatment of different types of patients. If decisions are made based on cost information that contains joint costs, incorrect decisions may be made. This is because one might

overestimate the possible cost-savings from eliminating a service or might overestimate the added costs of a new service. See Chapter 6 for a discussion of related issues.

8. Traditional cost-finding starts with allocation bases that are often imprecise estimates. For example, pounds of laundry are used instead of the more accurate (but costly) pieces base. Next, step-down allocation is used instead of multiple apportionment. This inherently creates some distortion. That distortion may be significant if the order of allocation is manipulated to maximize reimbursement.

Once costs are assigned to revenue centers, they must be allocated to units of service. The methods used for this—hours of service, surcharge, per diem, and relative value units—all have problems that create potential inaccuracies in assigning costs to patients.

Problems

1. One base is the number of patients. The rate would be $50,000/1,000 = $50 per patient.

A second possible base would be admitting department hours consumed in processing patients. The rate would be $50,000/2,500 = $20 per hour.

2. a. Calculation of normal overhead rate on direct–labor-hour basis:

$$\text{Overhead rate} = \frac{\text{Expected overhead cost}}{\text{Expected direct labor hours}}$$

$$= \frac{\$810,000}{90,000 \text{ hours}}$$

$$= \$9 \text{ per hour}$$

Overhead applied
to Mr. Sic Lee = Direct labor hours × rate
= 20 hours × $9 per hour
= $180

b. Calculation of normal overhead rate on direct–labor-dollar basis:

$$\text{Overhead rate} = \frac{\text{Expected overhead cost}}{\text{Expected direct labor dollars}}$$

$$= \frac{\$810,000}{\$1,350,000}$$

$$= \$.60 \text{ per direct labor dollar}$$

Overhead applied
to Mr. Sic Lee = direct labor dollars × rate
= 380 direct labor dollars × .60
= $228

The results differed under the two different bases of normal costing. The probable reason for this difference is that some patients consume labor hours from more highly skilled individuals.

A direct labor hour basis system will assign a patient just as much overhead for having consumed an hour of licensed practical nurse (L.P.N.) labor as it will for having consumed an hour of registered nurse (R.N.) labor.

A system that assigns overhead on the basis of direct labor cost will assign more overhead for the consumption of an hour of a more highly paid worker's time.

Which basis is preferable? That depends on whether the overhead items in question are more closely related to the amount of labor an individual patient consumes or to the type of labor consumed.

3. Direct distribution.

		Allocation		
	Direct Cost	Maintenance Hours	Telecommunication # of Phones	Total Costs
Nonrevenue cost centers				
Maintenance	$80,000	($80,000)		$ 0
Telecommunications	40,000		($40,000)	0
Revenue cost centers				
Per diem	900,000	37,647	37,895	975,542
Operating room	300,000	42,353	2,105	344,458
Total cost	$1,320,000	$ 0	$ 0	$1,320,000

4. Step-down distribution.

5. Step-down distribution—changed order of allocation.

	Direct Cost	Allocation Mainte-nance Hours	Sub-total	Allocation Telecom-munication # of Phones	Total Costs
Nonrevenue cost centers					
Maintenance	$80,000	($80,000)			$ 0
Telecommuni-cations	40,000	12,000	$52,000	($52,000)	0
Revenue cost centers					
Per diem	900,000	32,000	932,000	49,263	981,263
Operating room	300,000	36,000	336,000	2,737	338,737
Total cost	$1,320,000	$ 0	$1,320,000	$ 0	$1,320,000

	Direct Cost	Allocation Telecom-munication # of Phones	Sub-total	Allocation Mainte-nance Hours	Total Costs
Nonrevenue cost centers					
Maintenance	$80,000	$ 2,000	$ 82,000	($82,000)	$ 0
Telecommuni-cations	40,000	(40,000)	0		0
Revenue cost centers					
Per diem	900,000	36,000	936,000	38,588	974,588
Operating room	300,000	2,000	302,000	43,412	345,412
Total cost	$1,320,000	$ 0	$1,320,000	$ 0	$1,320,000

CHAPTER 5

Questions for Discussion

1. True. The more patients there are to share the fixed costs, the lower the fixed costs per patient, and therefore the lower the average cost.

2. False. If the revenue equals the variable cost, the service will never break even because it will not recover its fixed costs. Further, even if the revenue exceeds the variable cost, the service will only break even if the volume is high enough for all of the fixed costs to be recovered. Therefore, one must determine the breakeven quantity.

3. False. If the entire organization is being evaluated, the joint costs should be included. However, if only one particular product, program, or service is being evaluated, any costs that are joint with other products or programs should be ignored in the calculation. That is because those costs will be encountered even if this product or program is not undertaken.

4. The use of a weighted average for determining the price and variable costs in the breakeven formula.

5. Prices may not be constant. The proportion of patients in each product category may not be constant. Predictions of fixed costs, variable costs, prices, and volumes may turn out to be inaccurate. Costs may be affected by factors other than volume.

6. This is because at low volumes, fixed costs are high for each patient, making average costs high and profitability less likely. If high volume can be ensured, fixed costs per patient will be low, keeping average costs low, and improving the chances of profits.

7. Contribution margin per unit of the most constrained resource (see Application 5-2).

Revenue as the sole measure is irrelevant, because we would not want to attract patients who have high revenues but even higher costs. Contribution margin is better, but is not sufficient if some resource is constrained. In the case where the organization nears capacity of any critical resource, it must consider the contribution margin per unit of the constrained resource.

Problems

1. (1) Find proportion of patients in each Diagnosis Related Group (DRG).

Estimated # of Patients	DRG #	Percentage of Patients
150	4	$\frac{150}{500} \times 100\% = 30\%$
100	5	$\frac{100}{500} \times 100\% = 20\%$
250	6	$\frac{250}{500} \times 100\% = 50\%$

(2) Find weighted average price and variable cost.

Weighted Average Price		Weighted Average Variable Cost	
$30\% \times \$400 =$	$120	$30\% \times \$100 =$	$ 30
$20\% \times\ 600 =$	120	$20\% \times\ 500 =$	100
$50\% \times\ 200 =$	100	$50\% \times\ 100 =$	50
Weighted price	$340	Weighted variable cost	$180

(3) Find total patients for new service to break even.

$$Q = \frac{FC}{P - VC} = \frac{\$25,000}{\$340 - \$180}$$

$$= \frac{\$25,000}{\$160}$$

$$= 156.25 \text{ breakeven number of patients}$$

(4) Find breakeven quantity for each DRG.

DRG 4	DRG 5	DRG 6
156.25	156.25	156.25
× 30%	× 20%	× 50%
47	31	78

Note that the $500,000 overhead costs exist whether or not we add this service with its three DRGs. The new service does not have to cover any of that cost to break even. If the new service can bring in one patient more than its breakeven point, the hospital will be better off, because there then will be some additional contribution toward the $500,000 overhead.

2. The salary of nurses is a step-fixed cost. The general approach of this solution is to compute the minimum breakeven point assuming the existence of the "basic" fixed expenses. The cost of nurses is then considered, and the breakeven point is raised accordingly.

Revenue for the year ended June 30, 1994, divided by the average revenue per operation equals the number of operations for the year:

$2,656,500 / $1,650 = 1,610

Total expenses allocated by operations divided by the total number of operations equals the variable expense per operation:

$563,500 / 1,610 = $350

Revenue per operation	$1,650
Less variable expense per operation	− 350
Contribution per operation	$1,300

Fixed costs	$ 953,000
Salary of supervising nurses	137,000
Total fixed costs	$1,090,000

Because maximum capacity in the operating room (OR) is 2,000 operations, the number of supervising nurses is fixed at two regardless of actual volume!

Salary expense of scrub and circulating nurses at minimum 800 operations:

Scrub nurses (11 × $59,000)	$649,000
Circulating nurses (6 × $54,000)	324,000
Total	$973,000

Total fixed expenses	$1,090,000
Salaries at 800 operations	973,000
Total fixed and step-fixed costs to be covered	$2,063,000
Divided by contribution margin	÷ 1,300
Breakeven number of operations	1,587

We have calculated costs at 800 operations, but would not break even at less than 1,587. However, at 1,587 operations, our costs would be higher! We would need an additional scrub nurse at that level.

Salary expense of nurses at 1,587 operations:

Scrub nurses (12 × $59,000)	$ 708,000
Circulating nurses (6 × $54,000)	324,000
Total	$1,032,000

Total fixed expenses	$1,090,000
Salaries at 1,587 operations	1,032,000
Total fixed and step-fixed costs to be covered	$2,122,000
Divided by contribution margin	÷ 1,300
Breakeven number of operations	1,632

Referring back to the staffing guide, we find that 1,632 operations could be handled by the same staff as 1,587, so this is a feasible breakeven point.

By having started with the costs for 800 operations and then having moved costs up until a feasible solution was found, we have assured ourselves of finding the lowest possible breakeven point.

3.

	Price	Variable Cost	Contribution Margin	Average Length of Stay
DRG 1	$8,000	$7,700	$ 300	2
DRG 2	2,000	1,000	1,000	3
DRG 3	5,000	3,000	2,000	8

	Contribution Margin per Day	Average Length of OR Procedure	Contribution Margin per OR Hour
DRG 1	$150	1	$300
DRG 2	333	4	250
DRG 3	250	7	286

a. Although DRG 1 has the highest revenue, it is not the most profitable. DRG 3 is the most attractive type of patient because of its $2,000 contribution margin per patient.

b. If patient days are constrained, then the best type of patient would be the one that yields the highest contribution margin per patient day. This would be DRG 2 with its contribution margin per patient day of $333.

c. If available OR time is limited, then the optimal patient would have the highest contribution margin per hour of OR time. That would be DRG 1 patients with a contribution margin of $300 per OR hour.

CHAPTER 6

Questions for Discussion

1. Adding a new service; dropping an old service; expanding or cutting back a program or service; performing certain tasks, such as laboratory tests, in-house versus purchasing them from an outside company; establishing charges for services to health maintenance organizations (HMOs) and preferred provider organizations (PPOs).

2. The goal of using relevant cost information is to show how financial results would differ for each of the alternatives. This will allow managers to select the best possible alternative. The first step is to consider what would happen if no action occurs and things continue as they are. That gives a baseline set of revenues and expenses.

   Next, the revenues and expenses that would likely occur under each other alternative must be considered. This may seem to be an overwhelming task. However, it is substantially simplified by the fact that some revenues and costs will remain the same regardless of what alternative is chosen. One key to understanding relevant costing is that costs and revenues that are common to all alternatives can be ignored. Selection of a superior alternative is based on the differences among alternatives, rather than the common costs or revenues.

   Sunk costs should be excluded. The only important information relates to what the organization will receive and will spend in the future under each available alternative. Past costs have been spent and are exactly the same for all alternatives, no matter which alternative is selected for the future.

3. Cost-benefit (CBA) and cost effectiveness (CEA) analysis are both approaches for comparing alternatives. CBA measures the ratio of the benefits of an alternative to its costs. A project is acceptable if it has a positive benefit/cost ratio. However, this requires assigning values to both the costs and the benefits in monetary terms. In practice, it is difficult to assign monetary values to health care outcomes.

   CEA is not as ambitious as CBA, in that it does not require a measurement of the value of the benefits. Rather, it relies on using comparisons. One considers whether a project achieves at least the same outcome for a lower cost. Such a project would be deemed to be cost-effective.

Problems

1. Struggling is better off without the open-heart surgery unit. The open-heart patients would generate a loss of $2,000 per patient, or a total loss of $200,000 for 100 expected patients.

   The additional non–open-heart patients resulting from additional affiliated physicians would generate revenue of $2,800,000. This is based on average revenue of $14,000 per patient times the 200 patients generated by 10 physicians at 20 patients per physician.

   The average cost of these patients would be $2,780,000 (200 patients × $13,900 per patient). However, that is not an appropriate measure for the decision faced by Struggling. It has excess capacity and undoubtedly has fixed costs that will be incurred whether or not it adds these 200 additional patients. The added revenue should be compared with only the added costs. Thus, the marginal cost information is appropriate. The marginal cost for the additional 200 patients would be $2,640,000 (200 patients × $13,200 per patient).

   The additional 200 patients yield an incremental profit of $160,000 ($2,800,000 revenue − $2,640,000 cost). However, the loss leader is generating a loss of $200,000. Thus, Struggling should not open an open-heart surgery unit, because the result will still be a loss, even after considering the benefits from an increased number of patients in other Diagnosis Related Groups (DRGs) ($160,000 added profit – $200,000 open-heart loss = –$40,000).

Furthermore, there may be medical reasons for not adding open-heart surgery. It is generally agreed by medical authorities that volumes below 150 or 200 patients per year result in poor quality and high mortality rates. Such medical factors should be considered in making decisions regarding new product lines, in addition to the financial factors.

2. Part a.

Fixed cost = $3,000,000
Variable cost/
  patient day = $150 per patient day

Variable cost = variable cost/patient day × patient days
Variable cost for 50,000 patient days
  = $150 × 50,000
  = $7,500,000
Variable cost for 60,000 patient days
  = $150 × 60,000
  = $9,000,000

Total cost = fixed cost + variable cost
  Total cost for 50,000 patient days
    = $3,000,000 + $7,500,000
    = $10,500,000
  Total cost for 60,000 patient days
    = $3,000,000 + $9,000,000
    = $12,000,000

Average cost = total cost/patient days
  Average cost for 50,000 patient days
    $$= \frac{\$10,500,000}{50,000}$$
    = $210

  Average cost for 60,000 patient days
    $$= \frac{\$12,000,000}{60,000}$$
    = $200

Part b.

The HMO has offered only $180 per patient day, whereas our average cost is currently $210. Even with the extra 10,000 patient days, our average cost only falls to $200. Nevertheless, we should accept this business.

The only relevant costs are those that would change. In going from 50,000 to 60,000 patient days, the fixed costs of this hospital (which has excess capacity) will not change. The variable costs are only $150 per patient day, which is less than the price offered by the HMO.

If we look at the total costs of the hospital, we see that the extra 10,000 patient days increase costs by only $1,500,000. The extra revenue of $180 per patient day will add $1,800,000. The hospital will thus be $300,000 better off if they accept the HMO offer.

The result is dependent on a number of factors. First, we must have excess capacity. If we had to incur additional fixed costs to have sufficient capacity, those incremental fixed costs would become relevant costs in the calculation. Second, we have assumed that acuity of the additional patients is similar to that of the current patient population. If the HMO patients are more acutely ill, they will consume more variable costs. Finally, we assume that giving a preferential price to the HMO will not cause the price paid by other patients and third-party payers to decrease. If it did, that might more than offset the benefit of the extra HMO patients.

CHAPTER 7

Questions for Discussion

1. Nominal group technique brings the individuals together in a meeting. In Delphi, the group never meets. The nominal group approach is quicker but is burdened by politics and personalities. The Delphi method is less influenced by such factors but is more cumbersome and time consuming.

2. If we were assuming that volume changed at a constant rate, and inflation changed at a constant rate, then a regression analysis could predict future costs, including the impact of inflation. However, because the rate of inflation varies from year to year, its impact must be identified separately first. Then the future costs can be estimated based on the expected change in volume.

3. The goal is to divide past costs into their fixed and variable components. Fixed costs can then be assumed to remain the same in the future, as volume changes. Those fixed costs can be added to the variable cost per unit for the expected number of units (e.g., patients) in the future, to arrive at a prediction of total costs in the future.

4. Because the technique uses only two extreme points, there is the risk that these points will not be representative. If one or both of the points are outliers, they will generate a predicted future cost that is not a reliable estimate.

5. Simple regression relies on one independent variable, such as the number of patients days, to be the predictor of the dependent variable, cost. In multiple regression, information from a number of different independent variables, such as patients days, severity of illness, and the number of cases by Dr. Smith, are used as predictors of the dependent variable. This is

likely to improve the accuracy of the prediction.

6. No. The problem is that there may be trends or seasonality. If so, the average of the high and low values will obfuscate such variability.

7. The closer a forecast line is to historical data points, the closer it is likely to be to future results. By fitting historical data to a curved line rather than a straight line, they are likely to be closer to that line. Projecting that curved line into the future is therefore likely to produce a more accurate prediction of the actual future results.

8. False. Computers fail to take into account what people know. Managers may have information about why the future is unlikely to be a reflection of the past. Such managerial information should be used to modify computer-generated predictions.

9. Both. According to the theory, even with turnover among employees, the organization itself will incorporate improvements over time that will reduce the labor needed to carry out a specific process or provide a specific service.

Problems

1. In this problem, the case-mix-adjusted admissions are the independent variable and the electricity cost is the dependent variable. The results of the regression should indicate that total electricity costs would be $223,167.

   The fixed cost is $69,000, and the variable cost is $20.83 per admission of case-mix equal to 1. The unadjusted R-squared is .879.

   These estimates differ from those obtained using patient days. Based on the R-squared and the standard error, it appears that patient days were a better predictor than case-mix-adjusted admissions in this hypothetical problem.

It is unlikely that using case-mix-adjusted admissions alone would be adequate. Diagnosis Related Groups (DRGs) are probably shortening length of stay for patients within any DRG. Fewer patient days would likely reduce electricity consumption somewhat. On the other hand, the average patient acuity is probably rising because the reduction in length of stay eliminates days of low acuity. Thus, each patient day likely consumes a greater amount of electricity. For example, days with computed tomography (CT) scans will not likely be eliminated, whereas days without CT scans will be, raising the average patient day electricity consumption. A preferable approach would be to use a multiple regression that uses as independent variables the case-mix-adjusted admissions as well as patient days and average acuity levels.

2. The fact that the last 128 tests each took 51.3 minutes immediately tells us that the laboratory manager is asking for too high a budget. His budget request of $12,257 is based on an average time of 56.3 minutes. His request assumes that some tests took more time and some took less time, but without any pattern.

In fact, there was a learning pattern, with the tests taking less and less time as we became more familiar with the technique. It is likely that over time, our technicians were able to specialize on various parts of the test or in some other way gain economies of scale and of learning.

Certainly, the budget should in no case be greater than $11,163, based on the 51.3 minutes per test for the last 128 tests of last year, multiplied by the projected 768 tests, divided by 60 minutes an hour, and multiplied by $17 per hour.

However, it is likely that the process is still being improved and that further learning economies will be achieved by the coming year's quadrupling of volume. We note

that the time taken for the second test was 92 minutes, or 92 percent of the 100 minutes for the first test. Based on this, we will prepare a graph for learning curves with 91, 92, and 93 percent rates, and plot the actual times given in the problem on that graph (see Figure A-7-1). It may be that the 92 percent will be misleading, but it is a good place to begin.

In order to construct the graph, we can start with the 100 minutes it took for the first test. The 91 percent curve would be constructed by plotting 100 minutes (vertical axis) for a volume of 1, then doubling the volume and multiplying the minutes by 91 percent again and again. The points for this curve would be as follows:

Volume	Minutes
1	100.0
2	$100.0 \times 91\% = 91.0$
4	$91.0 \times 91\% = 82.8$
8	$82.8 \times 91\% = 75.4$
16	$75.4 \times 91\% = 68.6$
32	$68.6 \times 91\% = 62.4$

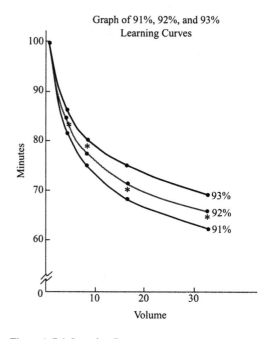

Figure A-7-1 Learning Curves

After plotting these points, the process would be repeated for 92 percent and 93 percent. That will give us a graph with three curves. We next plot the actual average times it took for these volumes, given in the problem as 100, 92, 85, 79, 71, and 66. Then we try to determine which curve the actual results most closely parallel.

It is readily apparent from the figure that this particular test has roughly a 92 percent learning curve rate. At such a rate, the technician time would be 100 minutes for the first test, 92 percent of that or 92 minutes for the next test, 92 percent of that or 84.6

minutes for each of the next two, and so on, as follows:

Number of Tests	Cumulative Total	Average Time
1	1	100
1	2	92
2	4	84.6
4	8	77.9
8	16	71.6
16	32	65.9
32	64	60.6
64	128	55.8
128	256	51.3
256	512	47.2
512	1,024	43.4

From this table, it also becomes apparent that having already done 256 tests, the next 256 should take 47.2 minutes each, and the following 512 tests should take 43.4 minutes each. Therefore, the total time allowed for next year should be 34,304 minutes ($[256 \times 47.2] + [512 \times 43.4]$), or 572 hours. At $17 per hour, this should require a budget of only $9,724. Thus, the correct budget would be 20.6 percent below the budget that was requested.

CHAPTER 8

Questions for Discussion

1. Specifically, we can think of the budget process as serving the roles of

    1. forcing managers to plan ahead and consider alternatives;
    2. improving organizational communication and coordination; and
    3. providing a basis for evaluation of unit and managerial performance.

2. The role of human beings cannot be underestimated. It is people who will either carry out or not carry out the plan as budgeted. It is important that the budget system provide motivation and incentives to carry out the plan and that the budget be perceived as being fair.

3. There are four primary problem areas in the traditional approach of preparing budgets once a year:

    1. time-management concerns,
    2. attitudes toward the budget process,
    3. accuracy, and
    4. increasing myopia with respect to the future.

    Continuous budgeting requires a small amount of time on a regular basis instead of a large amount at one time, making the process more manageable. Attitudes improve if the overwhelming burden of the task is reduced. Preparation of budgets is more accurate because there is less reliance on hazy memories. Finally, there is less myopia because there is always about a one-year planning horizon.

4. The long-range plan should focus not only on major program additions, but also on the services and programs that already exist. Expanding a service, contracting one, or even deleting a program or service require the same consideration and planning as the addition of a program or service does.

5. Zero-base budgeting (ZBB) is attractive because it requires evaluation of all costs, rather than just the coming year's increment. This helps prevent budgets from becoming "fat" over time. Many organizations use ZBB analysis to see exactly how money is being spent within a unit or department. Such an approach requires existing programs to justify their continued existence and spending habits. Additionally, ZBB requires a close focus on alternatives. Examination of alternative volumes, quality, and methods of production creates an opportunity for cost-savings and the introduction of innovative approaches to providing care.

6. The operating budget is the plan for day-in and day-out operating revenues and expenses for the organization, usually for a period of one year.

7. Many changes in an organization require a long lead time and take a number of years to be fully implemented. A long-range budget allows management to examine where the organization is relative to its peer group; what improvements can be made over the next three, five, or ten years; and what must be done each year to move toward those goals. The long-range plan allows managers to put aside day-to-day problems and to develop a vision for where the organization should be headed and how it can get there.

8. Program budgets are special budgeting efforts analyzing specific programs. Generally, the orientation is toward evaluation of a planned new program or a close examination of an existing program, rather than a mere plan of the revenues and expenses for the program for the coming year. The purpose of the program budget is to make a decision: Should the new program be undertaken or not?

9. Because program budgets often cut across departments, they generally must be developed with committee input from at least the major departments that will be affected by the service. Program budgets also cut across years. The financial impact of the service needs to be assessed not just in the coming year, but over a reasonably long period of time. Because the operating budget is a one-year budget, special budget treatment is needed to evaluate new programs or services.

10. A capital expenditure is an expenditure for the acquisition of items that will last for more than the year they are placed into service. Capital expenditures are made to purchase items that will provide benefits for a number of years into the future. If capital items are only evaluated based on their benefits for the coming year, their value to the organization will be understated. The operating budget only has the capability to look at one coming year's revenues and expenses. Therefore, capital items must be put into a separate budget that can evaluate their benefits over their entire useful lifetime.

11. No. It is possible for an organization to run out of cash and go out of business even if it is not losing money. Many of the expenses that an organization incurs are paid currently. Wages are typically paid at least monthly and frequently biweekly or weekly. However, revenues may take several months to collect because of the internal lags in processing patient bills and the external lags before payment. Thus, an organization can literally run out of cash even though it is making a profit! This is why having a cash budget is critical.

12. When cash is received or spent is just as important as how much is received or spent. The timing of payments is critical to the outcome of that analysis. If an organization has a choice of paying $10,000 today or $2,000 per year for 5 years, the latter

alternative is superior. The same total amount of dollars is being spent. However, by making the payments in the future, the organization can earn interest on some of the money in the interim. Time value of money indicates that the same amount of money spent or received at different points in time is not equally valuable.

13. The payback method ignores what happens after the payback period is over, and it ignores the time value of money.

14. For most organizations, revenues and expenses are not recorded in the accounting records at the time cash is received or paid. Revenue is usually recorded when patients are billed. It may be weeks or months before the patients or a third-party payer such as Medicaid pays the bills.

15. In order to pay employees and meet other obligations on a timely basis, the organization's managers must know how much cash is expected to be on hand at any given time. The amount and timing of the cash flowing into and out of the organization can affect substantially the ability of the organization to meet its current cash obligations. Therefore, a distinct, separate, cash budgeting process exists.

Problems

1. Decision package for open heart surgery (abridged):

    (1) **Program:** Open heart surgery
    Principal department: Cardiology and operating room
    (2) **Statement of activity:** To provide coronary artery bypass graft surgery, valve surgery, and correction of congenital heart defects to community patients.
    (3) **Objective:** To reduce levels of mortality and morbidity currently experienced

in the community due to inadequate heart surgery facilities.

(4) **Activity description:** Acquisition, installation, and operation of heart surgery equipment and attraction of a top-quality cardiac surgery team.

(5) **Activity benefit**: Reduction or elimination of mortality and morbidity in the community; revenues.

(6) **Resources:** Bypass pump and related equipment; surgeons, cardiologists, nurses; supplies; and one or two operating room (OR) suites.

(7) **Alternatives**—Levels of effort:

(a) Dedicate two surgical suites; this would satisfy entire community demand now and for the foreseeable future. Total estimated cost $4 million.

(b) Dedicate one surgical suite and equip a second suite that would be used for other operations as well; this would eliminate all mortality and 60 percent of morbidity resulting from lack of equipment and facilities. Estimated annual cost $3,600,000.

(c) Dedicate one surgical suite; this would eliminate all mortality and 15 percent of morbidity. Estimated annual cost of $3 million.

(d) Equip one suite, but allow other operations to take place in this suite as well; this would eliminate only 80 percent of mortality. Estimated annual cost $2,600,000.

2. a. 6% per year, $N = 5$ years, present value (PV) = $10,000, future value (FV) = $13,382.

b. .5% per month, $N = 60$ months, PV = $10,000, FV = $13,489.

3. Cash now = $100,000. Cash later = $300,000 = FV, $N = 12$ years, 12% per year interest. Value of cash later in today's dollars = PV = $77,003. Take the $100,000 today!

4. Annual payment (PMT) = $10,000, $N = 25$ years, 12% interest per month, PV = $78,431.

5. PMT = $5, 10% interest, 20 years. Extra outlay for double pane = $50. Present value of fuel savings = $42.57. Do not get double pane.

PMT = $5, 6% interest, 20 years. Extra outlay for double pane = $50. Present value of fuel savings = $57.35. Buy double pane.

At higher interest rates, it is more costly to lay out the $150. By spending only $100, the remaining $50 would earn a high rate of interest. At 6 percent, the $50 earns less interest, so it is not as worthwhile to pay less today and higher fuel costs in the future.

6. Note that it must be assumed that the revenues and costs in this problem represent cash flows. Present value analysis is based on cash, not revenues or expenses.

Costs: PMT = 150,000, $N = 4$, interest = 12%. PV = $455,602.

Revenue:

FV = 100,000, $N = 1$, interest = 12%. PV =	$ 89,286
FV = 150,000, $N = 2$, interest = 12%. PV =	119,579
FV = 200,000, $N = 3$, interest = 12%. PV =	142,356
FV = 250,000, $N = 4$, interest = 12%. PV =	158,880
Total PV revenues:	$510,101

Net Present Value (NPV)
= Present Value Revenue – Present Value Cost
= $510,101 – $455,602 = $54,499

The NPV is positive, so this program earns $54,499 more than 12 percent. Accept the program.

7. Cash Budget for *Care for the Homeless*:

Cash Receipts	January	February	March
Unified Path	$93,000		
City (24,000/12 with 1 month lag)		$ 2,000	$ 2,000
State (50% in Month 1 and 1/11 of balance			
ance			
each following month)	44,000		
88,000 × 50% = 44,000 January			
88,000 – 44,000 = 44,000 balance		4,000	4,000
44,000/11 = 4,000 monthly			
County (10% of outstanding balance each			
month)			
50,000 × 10% = 5,000 January	5,000		
50,000 – 5,000 = 45,000 balance			
45,000 × 10% = 4,500 February		4,500	
45,000 – 4,500 = 40,500 balance			
40,500 × 10% = 4,050 March			4,050
	$142,000	$10,500	$10,050

CHAPTER 9

Questions for Discussion

1. If the variance is significant and unfavorable, managerial action may be necessary. If the organization cannot afford to have such a large unfavorable result, it may have to revise spending plans elsewhere in the organization. Just because the variance is out of the control of the organization does not mean we can passively accept its negative implications for the organization.

2. False. The problem with traditional variance analysis is that it does not account for changes in volume. It assumes that one would expect to spend the budgeted amount, regardless of the actual number of patients treated. Further, it does not do a very good job of showing managers where to look for the underlying causes of variances, such as whether they are attributable to the price of inputs or the amount of inputs used.

3. A flexible budget is one that is adjusted for volume. An initial budget is based on an anticipated volume of activity. In preparing the budget, one could also prepare alternate budgets based on a range of possible volume outcomes. Thus, we could plan a budget assuming 1,000 patients but also create alternate budgets showing the expected costs for 800, 900, 1,100, or 1,200 patients. Each of these would be considered to be a flexible budget, based on the costs that we would expect to incur at the specified volume.

4. Essentially, we can break down the cause of any variance into three main factors. Either it is caused by more or fewer units of activity (patients, laboratory tests, etc.) than expected (the volume variance), or by a higher or lower price paid for resources consumed (the price variance), or by more or fewer resources consumed per unit of activity (the quantity variance).

5. It will always total to the same amount. The price, quantity, and volume variances are simply the total variance divided into three components.

6. True. Small, random variances need not be investigated. Managers must decide how small a variance they will investigate. This decision can be made on formal statistical upper and lower limits, or based on trends observed, or based on the manager's judgment. Another approach is to assess how costly it will be to investigate the variance and what the potential cost implications are of not investigating it.

7. The quantity variance could be divided into an acuity variance, worked versus paid variance, productive versus nonproductive variance, and a new quantity variance. The acuity variance would indicate the portion of the quantity variance resulting from a different actual mix of patients from that expected. The worked versus paid variance focuses on the portion of the quantity variance that arises because of a change in the amount of paid but nonworked time. The productive versus nonproductive variance considers changes in the amount of time worked, but in nonproductive activities, such as education. This should not imply that educational activity is not valued. However, unexpected time spent on education implies a need for additional paid time to provide care to patients.

Problems

1. We must first calculate the original budget contribution margin, the volume flexible budget contribution margin, the patient mix flexible budget contribution margin, and

the actual contribution margin as follows (contribution margin = CM):

Original Budget Contribution Margin

DRG 1:	Budget Patient Volume	×	Budget DRG 1 Proportion	×	Budget DRG 1 CM
DRG 2:	Budget Patient Volume	×	Budget DRG 2 Proportion	×	Budget DRG 2 CM
+DRG 3:	Budget Patient Volume	×	Budget DRG 3 Proportion	×	Budget DRG 3 CM

DRG 1: 500 × 50% × $500 =	$125,000
DRG 2: 500 × 30% × $200 =	30,000
+DRG 3: 500 × 20% × $400 =	40,000
Original budget CM	$195,000

Volume Flexible Budget Contribution Margin

DRG 1:	Actual Patient Volume	×	Budget DRG 1 Proportion	×	Budget DRG 1 CM
DRG 2:	Actual Patient Volume	×	Budget DRG 2 Proportion	×	Budget DRG 2 CM
+DRG 3:	Actual Patient Volume	×	Budget DRG 3 Proportion	×	Budget DRG 3 CM

DRG 1: 450 × 50% × $500 =	$112,500
DRG 2: 450 × 30% × $200 =	27,000
+DRG 3: 450 × 20% × $400 =	36,000
Volume Flexible budget CM	$175,500

Patient Mix Flexible Budget Contribution Margin

DRG 1:	Actual Patient Volume	×	Actual DRG 1 Proportion	×	Budget DRG 1 CM
DRG 2:	Actual Patient Volume	×	Actual DRG 2 Proportion	×	Budget DRG 2 CM
+DRG 3:	Actual Patient Volume	×	Actual DRG 3 Proportion	×	Budget DRG 3 CM

DRG 1: 450 × 65% × $500 =	$146,250
DRG 2: 450 × 20% × $200 =	18,000
+DRG 3: 450 × 15% × $400 =	27,000
Patient mix flexible budget CM	$191,250

Actual Contribution Margin

DRG 1:	Actual Patient Volume	×	Actual DRG 1 Proportion	×	Actual DRG 1 CM
DRG 2:	Actual Patient Volume	×	Actual DRG 2 Proportion	×	Actual DRG 2 CM
+DRG 3:	Actual Patient Volume	×	Actual DRG 3 Proportion	×	Actual DRG 3 CM

DRG 1: 450 × 65% × $475 =	$138,938
DRG 2: 450 × 20% × $250 =	22,500
+DRG 3: 450 × 15% × $470 =	31,725
Actual CM	$193,163

Using the results calculated above, our variances are as follows:

The Volume Variance

Static budget contribution margin	$195,000
− Volume flexible budget CM	−175,500
Volume variance	$ 19,500 U

The Patient Mix Variance

Volume flexible budget CM	$175,500
− Patient mix flexible budget CM	−191,250
Patient mix variance	$ 15,750 F

The Price Variance

Patient mix flexible budget CM	$191,250
− Actual CM	−193,163
Price variance	$ 1,913 F

The Total Variance

Volume variance	$19,500 U
Patient mix variance	15,750 F
+ Price variance	+ 1,913 F
Total variance	$ 1,837 U

The original budgeted contribution margin was $195,000, and the actual result was $193,163, a difference of only $1,837. That difference represents the total variance. It is minor and would appear not to warrant investigation.

However, our individual variances provide a substantially different picture. There was a small positive price variance. Investigation yields the fact that this resulted from substantial price increases in DRGs 2 and 3, but a price decrease in DRG 1. Because DRG 1 is our largest volume service, we need to be especially vigilant regarding its price.

As we investigate further, other interesting results are also apparent. Our number of admissions suffered a significant drop, a fact that we find from the volume variance. On the other hand, the contribution margin lost by this drop in patients was made up for by the shift in our patient mix toward our most profitable patients. However, we should be concerned, because the profit margin on those patients appears to be falling.

On the other hand, it is possible that we lowered our price for DRG 1 in order to attract more patients in our most profitable area. While that might make sense, we should still be quite concerned about the overall decrease in patient admissions.

2. The case-mix variance is the current volume times the current cost, less the prior volume times the current cost, as follows:

	Current Volume	×	Current Cost	
DRG A	6	×	$4,600	= $27,600
DRG B	7	×	$9,300	= 65,100
				$92,700

	Prior Volume	×	Current Cost	
DRG A	5	×	$4,600	= $23,000
DRG B	8	×	$9,300	= 74,400
				$97,400

Case-mix variance		favorable	$ 4,700

The shift by Dr. Jones from high-cost DRG B patients toward lower cost DRG A patients resulted in a $4,700 decrease in the cost of treating his patients. Thus, we are observing a strong case-mix change.

The cost variance is the prior volume times the current cost, less the prior volume times the prior cost, as follows:

	Prior Volume	×	Current Cost	
DRG A	5	×	$4,600	= $23,000
DRG B	8	×	$9,300	= 74,400
				$97,400

	Prior Volume	×	Prior Cost	
DRG A	5	×	$4,200	= $21,000
DRG B	8	×	$9,500	= 76,000
				$97,000

Cost variance		unfavorable	$ 400

As we can see from the cost variance, once we have adjusted for the change in case mix, Dr. Jones' cost of treating patients has actually risen, not fallen!

In addition to these variances, it would also be quite helpful to have the reimbursement rate for DRG A and DRG B. Suppose that in both March and April, we receive $6,000 for each patient in DRG A and $9,500 for each patient in DRG B. The March revenue ($5 \times \$6,000 + 8 \times \$9,500$) is $106,000, while the April revenue ($6 \times \$6,000 + 7 \times \$9,500$) is $102,500. Revenue has fallen $3,500, while costs have fallen $4,300. Perhaps we should tolerate Jones' cost variance and encourage him to shift his practice even further toward high-margin DRG A.

3. The first step in solving this problem is to calculate the standard error, as follows:

Patient #	(X) Number of Tests	(X–X̄) Deviation from Mean	(X–X̄)^2
1	15	–13	169
2	28	0	0
3	21	– 7	49
4	40	12	144
5	33	5	25
6	29	1	1
7	22	– 6	36
8	36	8	64
Total	224	0	488

$$\text{Mean} = \bar{X} = \frac{\text{Sum of observations}}{\text{Number of observations}}$$

$$= \frac{224}{8}$$

$$= 28$$

$$\text{Standard deviation} = \sqrt{\frac{(X - \overline{X})^2}{(\text{Number of observations} - 1)}}$$

$$= \sqrt{\frac{488}{(8 - 1)}}$$

$$= \sqrt{\frac{488}{7}}$$

$$= 8.35$$

$$\text{Standard error} = \frac{\text{Standard deviation}}{\sqrt{\text{Number of observations}}}$$

$$= \frac{8.35}{\sqrt{8}}$$

$$= 2.95$$

Two standard errors would be twice the 2.95 standard error calculated above, or 5.90. In this problem, last month's observed mean of 35 results in a deviation of 7 from the standard test mean of 28. Since 7 is greater than 5.90, the deviation is more than two standard errors.

Two standard errors encompass all normal events with a 95 percent probability. That is, we are 95 percent confident that if the process of controlling ancillary usage is working properly, the observed mean for any month should not be more than two standard errors greater or fewer than the test mean.

In this case, two standard errors is 5.90. There is only a 2.5 percent chance that we are controlling ancillary tests properly, but that patients require 5.90 more tests than the test mean of 28; and there is only a 2.5 percent chance that we are controlling ancillary tests properly, but that patients require 5.90 fewer tests than the test mean of 28.

Thus, given that the mean last month of 35 is more than two standard errors from the test mean of 28, it is very unlikely that ancillary tests were being appropriately controlled last month. Investigation should take place.

CHAPTER 10

Questions for Discussion

1. According to two noted authors in the field of management control, Anthony and Young,

   management control principles are tentative, incomplete, inconclusive, vague, sometimes contradictory, and inadequately supported by experimental or other evidence. Some of them will probably turn out to be wrong. Nevertheless, they seem to have sufficient validity so that it is better for managers to take them into account than to ignore them. Most importantly, they seem to work in a considerable number of actual organizations.[1]

   Thus, management control is hardly a science. It requires common sense and flexibility. However, there has been enough evidence of the value of such systems that health care managers should learn about them, and consider in what cases they might prove useful.

2. To achieve the best results for the organization, we need to develop a set of control systems that assign responsibility to each center based on that which it is uniquely in a position to control. In order to accomplish this, responsibility centers are classified as being revenue centers, expense centers, profit centers, and investment centers.

3. Management control systems focus on human beings. To a great extent, it is the actions of people that are monitored by such systems to ensure that errors are minimized and that people's actions are congruent with the goals of the organization.

The focus on people is not exclusive. For example, keeping track of the values of key variables is also a major management control concern. However, the essence of management control does revolve around ensuring that people are acting in a fashion to optimize the results of the organization. For instance, deciding on what the key variables are is inadequate by itself, unless someone monitors those variables on a regular basis and takes remedial actions in response to the value of the variables, when appropriate.

4. Time cards represent a formal management control. A supervisor who drops by each employee to say hello at the beginning of the shift is an informal control.

5. Key variables for an emergency department might include the number of hours per week that ambulances are diverted, inpatient admissions from the emergency department, and deaths in the emergency department.

6. Internal control systems have two primary purposes. The first of these is to provide systems to protect the assets of the organization. The second purpose is to promote efficiency so that resources are used as effectively as possible.

7. There are a variety of elements that, added together, provide an organization with a good system of internal control. The first critical element is that there be a workable audit trail. Additionally, Horngren and Foster have noted that an internal control system should have reliable personnel with clear responsibilities; separation of duties; proper authorization; adequate documents; proper procedures; physical safeguards; bonding, vacations, and rotation of duties; independent checks; and cost/benefit analysis.[2]

Problem

1.

Approach	Transfer Price	University's Profit	Women's Profit	Combined Profit
1. Full charges	$300	$ 40	$ 70	$110
2. Variable costs	200	–60	170	110
3. Market price	250	–10	120	110
4. Negotiated price	?	?	?	110
5. Use of outside laboratory	250	–60	120	60

As long as a transfer price is set, and the lab work is done at University, the two hospitals in total will earn $110. Even if the negotiated-price approach is taken, the issue is merely how to split the profits between the two hospitals—the total profit does not change.

However, if an outside laboratory is used, Women's would benefit as compared with the full charge it is currently paying. The overall profits for the two hospitals combined, however, would fall. Thus, it is very much in the overall interest to find a price that will keep the laboratory work internal. The difficulty is in finding a price all sides will consider fair and using a method that is not too time consuming. For example, a system that requires negotiation for every test would be very time consuming.

The market price might be the easiest to justify in this case. Using a transfer price of $250, the market price, Women's will do just as well as if they went outside to the competing laboratory. At this price, University will lose $10 per test when it considers its full costs. However, if it loses the business to an outside laboratory, it will lose $60 per test because of the unavoidable overhead. In other words, even at the market price of $250, University will be better off by $50 per test than if it loses the business, because it will recover all of its variable costs and receive a $50 contribution toward overhead.

NOTES

1. R. Anthony and D. Young, *Management Control in Nonprofit Organizations,* 3rd. ed. (Homewood, Ill.: Irwin Press, 1984), 3.

2. C.T. Horngren and G. Foster, *Cost Accounting: A Managerial Emphasis,* 7th ed. (Englewood Cliffs, N.J.: Prentice-Hall), 919–922.

CHAPTER 11

Questions for Discussion

1. Any one ratio provides limited information. Knowing that the current ratio is 2 (implying $2 of current assets for every dollar of current liabilities) may be more informative than knowing that current assets are $1,832,000 while current liabilities are $916,000. However, it would be even more helpful if there were something against which to compare that value of 2.

   Organizations compare their own ratio values for trends over time. They also compare their values with those of specific close competitors. It is also common to compare values with groups of other organizations or even the industry as a whole.

2. Financial statement data are limited in many respects. First, they must comply with Generally Accepted Accounting Principles. They do not handle problems such as inflation and alternative accounting principles well. More importantly, a much wider range of information is available to managers internally than is available in financial statements.

3. Cost ratios can be used to give general information about the organization. They can also be used to provide specific infor-mation for monitoring and controlling operations. Finally, they can provide data that can be especially helpful for making decisions.

4. • Pharmacy revenue per patient day.
   • Pharmacy revenue per discharge.
   • Drug cost per patient day.
   • Salary cost per patient day.
   • Pharmacist hours per discharge.
   • Management support hours per patient day.

Problems

1. This is an open-ended question. Each answer will be unique.

2. Costs were higher than expected.

$$\text{Cost per case-mix-adjusted discharge} = \frac{\text{Cost per discharge}}{\text{Case-mix index}}$$

$$= \frac{\$6,000,000 \text{ cost}/2,000 \text{ discharges}}{1.4}$$

$$= \frac{\$3,000}{1.4}$$

$$= \$2,143$$

Costs adjusted for case-mix were $2,143 per discharge, or $143 more per discharge than anticipated.

CHAPTER 12

Questions for Discussion

1. The most common productivity measure is output per labor hour. That is, for each hour of labor input, what quantity of goods or services is produced? This will measure just part of the organization's productivity. It fails, for example, to account for the amount of capital equipment used in producing the output. In more general terms, we can define productivity as simply being the ratio of any given measure of output to any given measure of input over a specified time period.

2. Total productivity compares all outputs to all inputs to determine the amount of output per unit of input. Partial productivity compares total outputs to certain specific inputs. The resulting output/unit of input does not reflect all the costs of producing that output.

3. First, the product varies considerably. A hospital will likely treat patients from several hundred different Diagnosis Related Groups (DRGs), and within DRGs there is substantial variation among patients. Furthermore, we do not just keep producing. If we have extra labor and materials at a slow point in a factory operation, we can produce some extra units to lower the cost per unit. In a health care organization, we can only work with the patients we have. That sometimes means unavoidable downtime (and lost resources) waiting for the next patient.

   Additionally, it is difficult to assign costs of most departments directly to patients of any given type. Although cost accounting systems are moving in the direction of direct association of costs with patients, it is not clear that resource inputs will ever be assigned to patients with the same degree of accuracy and detail as is possible in a factory process that produces only one given type of product.

Thus, we run into problems of productivity measurement. Should we measure productivity as the cost per patient day, or the cost per discharge, or the cost per hour of surgery? All of these measures are flawed in the same way. They are unlikely to tell us how our productivity is changing because there is no assurance that the output measure is constant. As the clinical mix of patients changes, the inputs required for patient days, discharges, or hours of surgery also change.

Another difficult problem concerns the potential for changes in quality. Productivity measures implicitly assume that quality is held constant. Obviously, it is incorrect to consider a reduction in hours per treatment to be a productivity gain if it was accomplished by reducing quality. Similarly, the basic total productivity ratio is inadequate to segregate the impact of case-mix changes from the impact of productivity changes.

4. The question is whether there is a relationship between the hours of direct patient care time and indirect but productive time. If there is, then we can monitor the relationship on a monthly basis to ascertain whether productivity is being improved, or at least maintained.

   For example, suppose that we found that respiratory (inhalation) therapists needed 30 minutes of indirect time for each 1 hour of therapy. The indirect time might include reviewing the patient chart, gathering supplies and/or equipment, walking to the patient room, walking from the patient room, making entries in the patient chart, and replacing and restocking supplies and equipment. Additional indirect time might include scheduling and other necessary administrative activities.

   If we divide the required indirect time by the direct time, we determine that the expected indirect time is 50 percent (i.e., 30 minutes divided by 60 minutes). If we performed a study of what our inhalation therapists do, and found that the 30 minutes of indirect time was a reasonable level for a 1-hour therapy session, then we could set it up as a standard.

Suppose that we have in fact done that. Our indirect standard rate would be 50 percent of our direct rate. In future months, we could add 50 percent to the direct patient care hours to determine the total care hours. Then we could examine the actual total hours to assess our productivity.

5. One approach is to monitor some productivity measure of direct costs. For example, we could keep track of the average hours of surgery per patient or average hours of respiratory therapy per treatment. If these measures start to fall, that is a sign of increasing productivity in the area of direct costs. However, it also is an indication that the indirect cost relationship to direct costs should be reevaluated.

Alternatively, some health care organizations will likely start to have their clinicians log their hours for various activities. The benefit of such logging would be that not only would we have a continuously updated relationship between direct and indirect productive hours, but we would also have a continuously updated relationship between worked hours that are direct, indirect, and nonproductive.

6. Examples of such departments include personnel, marketing, legal, finance, administration, housekeeping, security, and plant operations.

7. Engineered costs are those for which there is a specific input–output relationship. More patient days require more meals from the dietary department. More x-rays require more sheets of x-ray film. Generally, such relationships can be readily observed. Engineered costs normally include the direct materials and direct labor cost.

Committed costs are those costs that cannot be changed in the short run, such as during the coming year. An example would be the depreciation cost on the hospital building. Similarly, long-term leases, depreciation on equipment, insurance, and some interest are costs over which managers have little current control. Costs that will become committed require careful scrutiny by the organization. Generally, they are reviewed as part of the capital budget process. Once committed to, however, they do not tend to vary from year to year. Fluctuations in the volume of services provided will often have no effect on such committed costs.

Discretionary costs are those that are incurred, typically each year, in an amount that is approved as part of the normal budget process. However, there is not a clear relationship between the volume of services and the amount of cost that must be incurred. Managers must make a decision regarding the level that is deemed to be appropriate. As a result, these costs are sometimes referred to as managed costs.

8. The productive process in discretionary departments is similar to a black box, with activities being nonroutine, nonrepetitive, and hard to quantify.

Just as the process of discretionary departments may be hard to define clearly, so are the outputs. Whereas an engineered cost department produces some measurable output capable of being evaluated in terms of revenue production and, to some extent, quality, the discretionary cost departments often are producing information. The outputs of such departments defy measurement and are hard to value. Quality measurement may pose a problem as well.

For example, if the legal department loses a malpractice law case, is it because it did a poor job or because the case was not winnable? Was the decision to go to court rather than to settle a good decision with a bad outcome or a decision based on poor judgment on the part of the department? Were the legal resources devoted to the case too little to be able to make a winning case or too much for a case that could not be won in any event?

9. The definition of effectiveness is whether or not the organization accomplishes its desired goal. A set of goals or objectives should be established for a discretionary cost center. After the fact, there should be measurement to see if those goals and objectives were met. If so, then the department is effective. On the other hand, efficiency refers to the amount of resources used to accomplish the result. For any given result that occurs, the organization should be attempting to minimize the cost of resources required.

Efficiency and effectiveness ratios can help monitor the productivity of such a discretionary cost center or department. For example, to monitor the productivity of the hiring function of a personnel department, one could use the cost per hire, the acceptance ratio, and the average time to fill each vacant position.

10. Each answer will be a unique response to this question.

Problems

1.

	Baseline		
Meal Type	Labor Hours per Meal	Number of Meals	Total Hours
Standard	.25	200,000	50,000
Low-sodium	.30	40,000	12,000
Special	.40	50,000	20,000
		290,000	82,000

	Current Period		
Meal Type	Actual Number of Meals	Actual Labor Hours	Current Volume × Base Period Hours
Standard	170,000	N/A	170,000 × .25 = 42,500
Low-sodium	45,000	N/A	45,000 × .30 = 13,500
Special	60,000	N/A	60,000 × .40 = 24,000
	275,000	76,500	80,000

Equivalents used: 15 minutes = .25 hours, 18 minutes = .3 hours, 24 minutes = .40 hours.

Index of output: $80,000/82,000 \times 100$	$= 97.56\%$.
Index of labor hours: $76,500/82,000 \times 100$	$= 93.29\%$.
Index of output per labor hour:	
$97.56\%/93.29\% \times 100$	$=104.58\%$.
Productivity gain: $104.58\% - 100\%$	$= 4.58\%$.

The productivity gain was slightly less than the desired 5 percent.

2. $33\% \times 27,000 = \$8,910$ expected indirect costs

$27,000	direct costs
+ 8,910	indirect costs
$35,910	productive time – direct and indirect

$$\frac{35,910 \text{ productive time}}{40,000 \text{ paid time}} \times 100\% = 90\% \text{ productivity}$$

Presumably, the remaining 10 percent or $4,000 represents a combination of sick leave, slack time between work activities, and inefficiency. If those items are reduced, the productivity rate would rise.

CHAPTER 13

Questions for Discussion

1. The perpetual inventory method requires the organization to keep a running, continuous record of the receipt of inventory items and their use. On a daily basis, items are counted when they enter the inventory, and they are counted when they are used. A physical count of inventory is taken once a year to confirm the perpetual records and to allow adjustments for any losses that have occurred due to breakage, shrinkage, obsolescence, or theft.

   The alternative to the perpetual system is the periodic system of inventory accounting. In this system, a specific tracking of inventory does not take place. From a reporting perspective, the accountant simply adds the beginning amount of inventory to the purchases of inventory to find the total amount that was available for use. At the end of an accounting period, the remaining inventory is counted. This amount is subtracted from the amount available in order to calculate how much inventory was used.

   The periodic system of accounting for inventory is generally less expensive than is perpetual inventory accounting and is also less accurate and useful to managers.

2. It will lead to increased cash inflows if some patients are paid on a cost reimbursement basis and/or will reduce tax payments for for-profit organizations.

3. No. Inventory flow is unchanged. Clearly, there is a fiction with last in, first out (LIFO). How can we use up units before we have even acquired them? Physically, this would not be possible. However, from an accounting point of view, it is perfectly possible. We simply wait until the end of the year, then apply the LIFO inventory method by *assuming* that those items

bought closest to the end of the year were the first ones consumed during the year.

   Thus, health care organizations can continue to use their regular inventory processing methods. Inventory can flow through the health care organization in its normal manner, which will generally mean that we physically use up the oldest inventory first.

4. The more inventory acquired at one time, the greater the investment (and therefore interest cost) and other carrying costs (such as storage). On the other hand, keeping only a small amount of inventory on hand increases the number of times we must order inventory and increases the related ordering costs. It is the fact that the ordering costs and carrying costs tend to work in opposite directions that dictates the need for a formalized quantitative approach. Economic order quantity (EOQ) finds the number of orders and size of each order, which results in minimizing the combined total of carrying and ordering costs.

5. The relevant costs are those that we would expect to vary with the amount of inventory on hand at any time, the costs that would vary with the number of units purchased, and the costs that would vary with the number of orders placed in a year.

   For example, inventory taxes (where applicable) and insurance on inventory are items that would vary with the number of units in inventory at any time. The capital cost, which depends on the purchase price, would vary with the size of the order, as would shipping and handling. The costs of the telephone call to place the order and the purchasing agent's time would vary with the number of orders.

6. The EOQ model is complicated by factors such as restrictions on order size, quantity discounts, uncertain conditions, stockouts, and storage constraints.

   The EOQ model assumes that units can be acquired individually. That is not always the case. Some items may well be packaged in such a way that the supplier will only provide round quantities or even dozens.

The model generally assumes that there is one price for each type of inventory. Realistically, volume discounts may apply. The impact of such discounts is to reduce the costs of buying larger quantities because the higher carrying costs are offset by lower prices for the inventory itself.

Uneven patterns of usage might result in an increase in the rate that we use inventory, which might cause us to run out. There is also the possibility that, for some reason, the supplier will have a delay in delivering the items we order.

An uncommon, but possible, problem that might arise would be an EOQ that is so large that we have no room to store the inventory. If we are constrained in that way, it would pay to order as close to the EOQ as possible.

7. The area of logistics includes the costs related to acquiring inventories, transporting them, storing or warehousing them, distributing them, and carrying them. It also includes a variety of decisions regarding the capacity levels for which the organization prepares itself.

8. There are a variety of trade-offs that must be considered. Often reducing one logistics cost results in increasing another. A balance must be established.

9. No. Just-in-time (JIT) inventory represents more of a target toward which to work. It would be nearly impossible actually to achieve zero inventories in most health care organizations.

10. No matter how hard an industry works to coordinate its needs with its supplier, there will invariably be problems with implementing a JIT system. Whether in industry or hospitals, the workflow will not necessarily proceed in an orderly manner. Failure to anticipate peaks perfectly will mean that

some orders will not be filled because of lack of inventory.

In the health care industry, this may result in loss of life. Therefore, health organizations will always have to maintain at least some inventories of some items. However, not all inventory items are critical to life. It is likely that a careful review of all health care inventory and supply purchases would indicate that a large percentage of items—perhaps over 90 percent—are not life-essential.

It is important to bear in mind that the ideal of JIT is never achieved in reality. Virtually all organizations do maintain at least small levels of safety stock. Health care organizations that choose to implement some version of JIT must be aware of the problem of outages and must make careful plans.

11. The original supplies are referred to as raw materials inventory (RMI). These materials enter into the production process. If units of product are started but are unfinished at the end of an accounting period, they are referred to as work in process (WIP). When the WIP is completed, it becomes finished goods inventory (FGI).

12. All manufacturing costs are divided into either period costs or product costs. A period cost is one that is automatically considered to be an expense relating to the accounting period in which it is incurred. A product cost is associated with the product being sold. It does not become an expense until the product is sold. Product costs are those costs that are directly related to the production of the product, whereas period costs are all other costs.

13. No. The issue concerns whether fixed overhead costs will reside in units of finished goods inventory. Given that most health care providers sell services, rather than manufactured products, this issue is of little importance. However, for those organizations that do make a product, some of

which is in inventory at year-end, this is relevant.

Problems

1. Economic order quantity problem:

(A) $$EOQ = \sqrt{\frac{2AP}{S}}$$

A = 2,000 bedpans/year

P = $16 + $20 + $4 = $40

S = (10% × $4) + $.60 = $1

$$EOQ = \sqrt{\frac{2 \times 2,000 \times 40}{1}}$$

$$= \sqrt{160,000}$$

$$= 400$$

(B) At the EOQ of 400, the total costs (TC) would be as follows:

$$TC = \frac{QS}{2} + \frac{AP}{Q}$$

$$= \frac{400 \times \$1}{2} + \frac{2,000 \times \$40}{400}$$

$$= \$200 + \$200$$

$$= \$400$$

At the discount volume of 1,000, the total cost capital cost would be 10 percent of $3.90, or $.39, as opposed to $.40 at a price of $4. This means the carrying cost would be $.01 lower. The total cost would then be as follows:

$$TC = \frac{QS}{2} + \frac{AP}{Q}$$

$$= \frac{1,000 \times \$.99}{2} + \frac{2,000 \times \$40}{1,000}$$

$$= \$495 + \$80$$

$$= \$575$$

However, this $575 should be reduced by the savings of $.10 per unit for 2,000 units, or a total of $200. In this case, the cost when buying 1,000 at a time would then be $375, as compared with the EOQ cost of $400. It should be noted, however, that 1,000 bedpans will take up a lot of storage space, and the cost of extra storage space required, if any, would have to be considered prior to making a final decision.

2. The answer depends on what inventory costing system the nursing home is using. If it uses LIFO, then the 500 syringes at $9 each were used, becoming a $4,500 expense, and the value of inventory is $4,000. If first in, first out (FIFO) is used, then the expense is $4,000, and the inventory is valued at $4,500. A weighted average approach would yield a $4,250 value for both expense and inventory. The key is that inventory costing is based on an assumption. It does not matter which units were actually used. The system determines how we ascertain the cost to be assigned to the ending inventory.

3. Absorption costing assigns all overhead to product produced. Therefore, in 1993, the following applies:

$500,000/10,000 = $50 per tray
$50/tray overhead + $600 other = $650
$650 is the cost of goods sold (CGS) per unit and the FGI value per unit.
9,000 units sold × $650 = $5,850,000 total CGS.

For 1994,

$500,000/14,000 = $35.71 per tray
$35.71/tray overhead + $600 other = $635.71
$635.71 is the CGS per unit and the FGI value per unit for 1994 production.

During 1994, assuming FIFO, the following applies:

1,000 units from 1993 sold with a cost of $650 each.
8,000 units from 1994 sold with a cost of $635.71 each.

Total CGS is $5,735,680 (1,000 × 650 + 8,000 × 635.71).

Under variable costing, the entire $500,000 of overhead would be charged as an expense each year. The additional CGS would be the $600 variable cost per unit. In both years, that would be 9,000 @ $600 or $5,400,000. The total cost of goods sold would therefore be $5,900,000 in both years.

Cost of Goods Sold Table

	Absorption	**Variable**
1993	$5,850,000	$5,900,000
1994	$5,735,680	$5,900,000

Under absorption costing, they appear to have lower costs and therefore higher profits in 1994 than in 1993. However, that is an illusion. The costs are lower because pro-duction was higher, and more 1994 costs were assigned to FGI than was the case in 1993. One must question whether and when the FGI of 6,000 units will be sold. At that time, the inventoried overhead costs will become an expense.

4.

Volume	% Complete Labor	Labor Equivalent Units	% Complete Supplies	Supply Equivalent Units
100	25	25	50	50
100	75	75	90	90
		100		140

	Equivalent Units	Cost Per Unit	WIP Inventory Cost
Labor	100	$ 20	$ 2,000
Supplies	140	580	81,200
Total Inventory WIP Cost			$83,200

CHAPTER 14

Questions for Discussion

1. Managers can take actions to affect outcomes, but events are defined as occurrences that are beyond the control of managers. For that reason, events are sometimes referred to as states of nature.

2. No. It represents a weighted average of possible outcomes. In all likelihood, the expected value will never be the actual result. It will sometimes be higher and sometimes lower. Over the long run, if the subjective probabilities are estimated correctly, the expected average would represent the average of the outcomes.

3. False. The expected value approach assumes that investors are risk-neutral. Essentially, it assumes that you do not mind losing if you are likely to win an equal amount. Also, the potential size of the loss is assumed to not be a major concern. Some managers may be reluctant to risk a large potential loss for such a small potential reward, even if the reward is much more likely than the loss. Certainly, with a large enough number of investments (bets), things should even out. However, we may not invest enough times. We may run a series of losses and be fired before the laws of chance turn our way.

4. We must recognize the fact that all of these estimates are based on subjective probability. When we roll a die, we know that there is a 1/6 chance of each side showing. Assuming it is a fair die, the probabilities are known with certainty. In situations facing managers, we often do not know with certainty what the probabilities are.

   One reason that managers demand a risk premium—a positive rather than zero expected value—is because of the nature of subjective probabilities. We might have the odds wrong.

5. Additional information removes uncertainty from the process. This is likely to result in an increase in expected value. This occurs because we can avoid bad investments if we know in advance that they will be bad. Therefore, the amount that you would pay for information is anything up to the amount that the expected value will rise because you are using that information.

6. Absolutely. The more passes, the better the accuracy. The greater the number of variables involved, the more important it is to run the simulation many times.

7. Many analyses that managers undertake require a number of assumptions. If several of these assumptions are wrong, the compounded effect can be quite significant. A 20 percent error on each of four variables may mean that the total estimate is off not just by 20 percent, but potentially by much more than 20 percent. Simulation analysis can be used to understand the likely range of outcomes better. It is a sophisticated form of sensitivity analysis.

8. There are three primary concerns about the use of simulation analysis. The first is that it might be prohibitively costly. The second is that the model may be built incorrectly. The third is that the probability estimates may be incorrect.

   In recent years, however, computer power has increased in a geometric fashion. It has now become relatively inexpensive to run simulations, and there are many software programs available that simplify the process.

   The need to set up the model correctly is important but really does not add to the complexity of planning a new venture or preparing a budget. The specific calculations that need to be made must be carefully laid out in any case to result in a correct analysis.

   A greater concern is the subjectivity of the projections. Ultimately, we cannot get around the fact that the simulation analysis rests on the subjective probabilities assigned by the person developing the simulation.

Despite these limitations of simulation, simulation avoids ignoring the possibility of unfavorable outcomes compounding other unfavorable outcomes. At the same time, it improves on sensitivity analysis by not treating the "all things go wrong" situation as if it was just as likely to occur as the original projected result.

9. A network uses a diagram to show the relationships in a complex project. Arrows are used to represent specific activities that must be done. It is possible to start from one point and have many activities that all begin from that point and take place at the same time. The crucial aspect of network analysis is identifying those activities that must be completed before some other activity or activities can commence. Generally a critical path is determined. Any delay along the critical path will delay the entire project. Some delays that are not along the critical path can occur without slowing the entire project.

10. Network cost budgeting refers to combining the techniques of network analysis with cost accounting to generate the most cost-effective approach to the project. In network analysis, it is often assumed that the network is laid out in an optimal fashion. However, it is clear that networks do not indicate the *only* timelines that are possible. Using overtime or extra staff, it is often possible to reduce the amount of time needed. Such time reductions are often associated with extra cost. That extra cost may be justified if other benefits result. Network cost budgeting can be used to decide when it pays to spend money to reduce elements on the critical path.

11. Linear programming is a mathematical technique that allows the user to maximize or minimize the value of a specific objective in a constrained environment. For example, one might want to maximize profits or minimize costs.

Unconstrained maximization or minimization is rarely a realistic goal. Minimized costs would be zero. However, we never expect an organization's costs to be zero. We want to minimize the costs, given that the organization treats a certain number of patients of a certain type.

Constraints generally exist and must be considered as we attempt to maximize or minimize our objective. Linear programming finds an optimal solution for the goal subject to the various constraints that exist.

12. Not anymore. Computers now make linear programming a practical tool for many health care organizations.

Problems

1. We are planning the staff level for the emergency department (ED). The ED managers know that it is most economical to staff the ED at just the level needed to provide care to all patients who arrive. Extra staff would mean wasted resources. However, if the ED is short of staff, it will likely need to call in agency help or put some staff members on overtime shifts, creating more cost than if adequate staffing had originally been planned.

The problem assumed the following distribution and payoff:

| | | Cost/Patient | | |
| | | Low | Medium | High |
ED Cases	Probability	Staff	Staff	Staff
20,000–25,000	.10	$50	$60	$70
25,001–30,000	.40	55	50	60
30,001–35,000	.35	60	50	55
35,001–40,000	.15	70	60	50

The problem was to determine the optimal staffing pattern, using expected value analysis.

There are three possible actions that we are considering taking: we can staff low, medium, or high. For each of the three actions, there are four possible results. Tables A-14-1, A-14-2, and A-14-3 provide the expected value for each alternative staffing pattern.

The key to the solution is to recognize that the probability of each possible volume is independent of our staffing, so it is the same in each table. However, the cost per patient at each volume will depend on the staffing level. Therefore, it must be changed in each table. The expected value is the product of the probability of each volume multiplied by the cost per patient for that volume for that staffing level.

The low staffing pattern has an expected value of $58.50 per patient, the medium staffing pattern has an expected value of $52.50 per patient, and the high staffing pattern has an expected value of $57.75 per patient.

Given that the ED wants to minimize the average cost per patient treated, this information indicates that the medium staffing pattern should be chosen, even though there is a risk of high volume occurring, requiring overtime, and low volume occurring, resulting in underutilized staff.

Table A-14-1 Expected Value for Low Staffing Pattern

Patient Volume	Probability	Cost per Patient	Expected Value
20,000–25,000	.10	$50	$ 5.00
25,001–30,000	.40	55	22.00
30,001–35,000	.35	60	21.00
35,001–40,000	.15	70	10.50
			$58.50

Table A-14-2 Expected Value for Medium Staffing Pattern

Patient Volume	Probability	Cost per Patient	Expected Value
20,000–25,000	.10	$60	$ 6.00
25,001–30,000	.40	50	20.00
30,001–35,000	.35	50	17.50
35,001–40,000	.15	60	9.00
			$52.50

Table A-14-3 Expected Value for High Staffing Pattern

Patient Volume	Probability	Cost per Patient	Expected Value
20,000–25,000	.10	$70	$ 7.00
25,001–30,000	.40	60	24.00
30,001–35,000	.35	55	19.25
35,001–40,000	.15	50	7.50
			$57.75

2.

Outcome	Probability	Value
150,000	3%	$ 4,500
75,000	14%	10,500
37,500	25%	9,375
17,500	16%	2,800
5,000	13%	650
– 5,000	11%	–550
– 17,500	9%	–1,575
– 37,500	6%	–2,250
– 75,000	3%	–2,250
–150,000	0%	–270
Expected Value		$20,930

3. Many possible answers, each unique.

CHAPTER 15

Questions for Discussion

1. Failure to determine what questions need to be answered in advance. You must decide what information is needed from the system before the system is designed.

2. Although there cannot be a large number of people who have final approval on a system, all managers should be involved in its design. If they are not, there is a good chance that the system will not respond adequately to their costing needs. Further, the support needed during the system installation and implementation will not be readily forthcoming.

3. When information is needed, the level of detail of the information that will be generated and the types of reports to be generated.

4. Dangers include lack of adequate quality control, lack of generalizability, program instability over time, and lack of organizational access to the template.

CHAPTER 16

Questions for Discussion

1. The use of responsibility centers arises because of the need to decentralize authority within every large organization. Some degree of autonomy must be delegated downward within health care organizations in order for them to be able to run efficiently. It is impossible for top management of most health care organizations to make all of the decisions that are needed to carry out the organization's activities.

2. One of the most prominent advantages of decentralization is that it enhances the development of management talents within the hospital. Managers in a decentralized environment are forced to develop skills as decision makers and problem solvers. Another key reason for having high degrees of decentralization is that it puts the power for decision making at the level where the best information is available. As information about individual units and departments moves up through the hospital, it tends to become distorted and dated. The manager on the scene is the most likely to be able to make a timely and informed decision. A final significant advantage of decentralization is that it allows the health care organization to manage by exception rather than by the rule.

3. Decentralization is not without its weaknesses. One weakness relates to the costs of training managers to handle authority. Another problem relates to the need for communication channels. Decentralization must also deal with errors made by managers. Another problem relates to conflicting goals and interests. Finally, decentralization requires a sophisticated reporting system.

4. Responsibility accounting is an approach in which specific units are established. Accounting information is then gathered for each unit. That information is then used to report on the performance of each specific unit and its manager. Reports are generated in a responsibility accounting system. The reports generally reflect the costs and possibly the revenues and profits of a unit.

   In some responsibility accounting systems, a single report is issued for each unit, which includes all costs. In other systems, two reports are issued: one for the performance of the unit and one for the performance of the manager. In either case, the key focal point for managerial performance evaluation is the portion of the unit's costs that are controllable.

5. To achieve the goal of providing proper incentives, responsibility centers are generally divided into cost centers, revenue centers, profit centers, and investment centers. Cost centers are responsible for costs only. Revenue centers are responsible for revenues only. Profit centers are responsible for both costs and revenues. Investment centers are also responsible for the sourcing of funds used by the center.

6. According to Barfield and colleagues,

   performance measurements should have the following characteristics: (1) they must be designed to reflect organizational goals and objectives; (2) they must be specific and understandable; (3) they must promote harmonious operations between and among units; and (4) if financial they must reflect an understanding of accounting information.[1]

   A number of qualitative measures, although subjective, may also be useful. Such measures can evaluate general competence, decision-making ability, problem solving, and so forth, based on a supervisor's observations. Nevertheless, many managers are likely to respond better to concrete, quantitative measures of performance. Such measures create a specific goal to work toward and allow managers always to know how well they are doing.

7. Three common measures used to bring the investment into the evaluation are return on investment (ROI), return on assets (ROA), and residual income (RI). ROI is the most frequently referred-to measure of performance for an investment. This measure is a ratio that divides the amount of the profit by the amount of the investment. This measure can be a good indicator of how successful a particular investment is. However, whenever a manager is given a set of resources with which to work but does not control the source of those resources, ROI will not be an appropriate measure of performance because the result will differ depending on how much money is borrowed.

ROA is an alternative that avoids the problems of interest and the appropriate investment amount. The method is superior to ROI for the evaluation of the manager who does not control investment decisions but otherwise is responsible for the venture. However, both ROI and ROA discourage managers from undertaking ventures that are lucrative but not quite as lucrative as current investments.

RI is an approach developed to overcome that problem. In this approach, the health care organization would define a minimum desired return, such as 15 percent. All potential investments would be "charged" that 15 percent as a condition to determine whether the investment should be undertaken. Any profits left after that 15 percent charge would be accumulated as the "residual" income. The manager must maximize the residual income.

8. The highest RI may simply reflect a more lucrative investment. Managers should be rewarded for their results relative to a budgeted goal. Other objectives should also be included in any final evaluation. Thus, there should be at least a qualitative assess-

ment of whether a manager is sacrificing the long-run well-being of the organization for short-run results.

9. Bonuses are often used in organizations because they can give individuals incentives to take actions that are in the interests of the organization.

10. The use of a system based on individual merit presents the opportunity for the greatest increases in efficiency. Such a system gives employees a clear signal that what they do counts.

One of the principal problems with such a system is that a great administrative burden is placed on the organization if each individual (or even just each manager) is to be evaluated. Not only is it quite time consuming, it also opens the organization up to significant morale problems if the bonuses assigned are not deemed to be fair.

11. Since the direct link between one person's performance and that person's reward is removed, each individual can relax more and rely on the efforts of others. When each individual feels that his or her actions can have little, if any, impact on the ultimate bonus, all individuals have less incentive to find more efficient methods for the organization.

12. Probably the simplest of these would be to have each individual in the organization who has responsibility for a budget be evaluated in the form of a letter from his or her direct superior. Such a letter need merely indicate an awareness that a particularly good job, or poor job, was done with respect to controlling costs and meeting the budget. This approach is obvious, simple, and usually highly effective.

13. Once hired at a high salary, the executive may relax. He or she has worked hard enough at previous positions to achieve a position with a high salary which is irrespective of performance. The use instead of

a profit-sharing plan tells the executive that there will be high rewards for continued hard work and success but essentially no rewards for resting on one's laurels.

Problem

1. a. ROI. Profits before interest were given as $4 million. The interest charge of 10 percent on $10 million will be $1 million, reducing net income to $3 million. The hospital invested $10 million of its own money. Therefore, the ROI is $3 million divided by $10 million, or 30 percent.

   b. ROA. This measures the profit, ignoring interest cost, compared with the total assets employed, regardless of source. Therefore, the entire $4 million profit (before interest expense) is compared with the $20 million total investment. The result is an ROA of 20 percent ($4/$20 × 100%).

   c. RI. This evaluates income left after applying a base charge. In this case, $20,000,000 was employed, and the base charge is 15 percent. Therefore, the charge is $3 million. Given that the pre-interest profit was $4 million, the RI is the difference of $1 million.

   d. The new investments will yield a profit of $1.8 million on an investment of $10 million. Using ROA, the new investment would lower the existing 20 percent value. However, the hospital would like this investment, which has an 18 percent return ($1.8/$10).

   If we use ROI, the result depends on how much we choose to borrow. If no money is borrowed, the 18 percent return will lower the evaluation of Mr. Wealth, based on the current 30 percent ROI. However, if the hospital borrows $8 million at 10 percent, the after-interest profit will fall to $1 million (because there is $800,000 of interest). However, the resulting $1 million of profit on a hospital investment of $2,000,000 is an ROI of 50 percent. Mr. Wealth can look good or bad depending on how much is borrowed—a factor over which he has no control.

   The RI approach would require a base charge of $1.5 million (15 percent of the $10 million investment). The excess would be an RI of $300,000. This is an increase in total RI over the previous year. The result is an incentive system that causes Mr. Wealth to do what the hospital would want. RI is the approach that should be chosen.

REFERENCE

1. J. Barfield, et al., *Cost Accounting: Traditions and Innovations* (New York: West Publishing Company, 1991), 646.

CHAPTER 17

Questions for Discussion

1. The concern is that costing has evolved primarily into a tool for external reporting of financial results rather than for the management of the organization.

2. Yes. This issue is of particular importance to health care firms. The growing use of prospective payment systems has made an understanding of costs critical. Rather than being reimbursed total costs, more and more health care is being paid for on a fixed-price basis. Organizations must be able to determine if they are making or losing money on different types of patients.

3. The prime motivator has been the fact that American industry has lost its competitive edge on a global basis. Other countries are making products better and less expensively than the United States, even after accounting for the lower wage rates overseas.

4. The basic concept that Kaplan espouses is that it makes sense to have a cost accounting system that generates information for financial statements, another to collect cost information needed to motivate and evaluate managers, and still a third system to use for making key management decisions.

   He discusses the stages that organizations must move through in their efforts finally to achieve a workable, integrated cost system. The first stage is one of poor data quality. The second stage is a focus on external reporting. The third stage is one of innovation and managerial relevance. The fourth and final stage is that of the integrated cost system. Most organizations are currently at Stage 2.

5. According to Peavey, technology and life-cycle accounting have become sufficiently developed to be incorporated into standard, generally accepted accounting.

The technology accounting approach treats plant, equipment, and information systems as direct costs rather than simply treating depreciation costs as overhead. The philosophy behind this change is that depreciation is generally time-oriented instead of production-oriented. In a slow year, each unit of product (patient) is assigned more depreciation, and in a busy year, less. Yet the patients do not require differing amounts of plant or equipment depending on how busy the health care organization is. The alternative is an approach such as units of production allocation of depreciation cost.

Life-cycle accounting has been defined as the "accumulation of costs for activities that occur over the entire life cycle of a product, from inception to abandonment by the manufacturer and consumer."[1] This approach is a significant departure from current Generally Accepted Accounting Principles (GAAP). It requires allocation of all revenues and expenses over the lifetime of the product. Thus, any start-up development costs, most of which would normally be expensed as research and development, would be amortized over the number of units of product expected. GAAP is more conservative in its immediate write-off approach.

6. Activity-based costing (ABC) considers that volume is not the only generator of cost. Often, activities with low volume may generate significant amounts of cost. If indirect costs are allocated based on volume, they will be overassigned to some patients and underassigned to others. A more accurate approach would be to allocate indirect costs based on the activities that drive them.

Problem

1. The first step would be to determine the total costs of the maintenance department.

These consist of the $100,000 spent on supplies, the $15,000 spent on administration, and the labor cost of $192,000 (i.e., 10,000 hours @ $12 plus 4,000 hours @ $18, or 14,000 hours @ $13.71 per hour). This is a total cost of $307,000. The traditional application rate would be as follows:

$$\frac{\$307,000}{100,000 \text{ square feet}} = \$3.07/\text{square foot}$$

That rate would cover both routine maintenance and repairs. Because the pharmacy has 2,000 square feet, it would be assigned a cost of $6,140. Alternatively, since the pharmacy is 2 percent of the total square feet (2,000/100,000 × 100%), we could simply multiply the total maintenance department cost of $307,000 by 2 percent to get the $6,140 in the traditional step-down approach.

What allocation would an ABC approach yield? First, we must make some choices about allocation bases. Given that administration is supervising personnel, we can allocate the administrative cost based on direct labor hours.

What about the labor cost? First consider labor for repairs. The cost could be allocated based on square feet, or on the number of repairs, or on the length of the repair. The cost for labor is driven by the number of hours the workers work. It is not the volume of repairs, but rather how long they take that is critical to an accurate allocation. Therefore, repair labor should be allocated based on direct labor hours.

One could argue that routine labor should also be allocated in that fashion. However, is it worthwhile to gather that information? In the example, hours spent on routine maintenance in the pharmacy department were not supplied. Therefore, one must allocate routine labor based on square feet. However, one must consider whether the extra accuracy would justify the collection of additional data on where workers spend their time.

Similarly, supplies used for routine maintenance will have to be allocated based on square feet. Supplies for repairs could be allocated based on the number of repairs, how long they take, or the specific supplies used. In actuality, it is likely that major supplies (repair parts) could be assigned specifically to each repair based on actual costs. Other supplies (nuts, nails, etc.) would probably be assigned based on direct labor hours, assuming that workers use supplies fairly evenly over the time they work. In this case, we have been given actual costs for supplies used.

The actual allocation becomes somewhat tricky, because routine maintenance is being allocated using different cost drivers from repairs. First, consider administration. The total cost is $15,000. There were 14,000 labor hours, so the rate would be $1.071 per hour. The pharmacy had 6 hours of repairs, and would be charged $6.43. Repairs in other departments took 3,994 hours and would be charged $4,279.29.

However, what about the remaining $10,714.28 of administrative cost? The administration related to routine work cannot be charged based on hours because we do not know the hours for each department, as discussed above. The pharmacy is 2 percent of the square feet, so it will be allocated 2 percent of this remaining administrative cost, or $214.29, with the balance of $10,499.99 being charged to other departments.

The pharmacy department consumed repairs that required 6 hours of labor at $18 per hour, or a total of $108. The other departments consumed 3,994 hours at $18 per hour, or $71,892. The remaining 10,000 hours at $12 per hour, or $120,000, are allocated based on square feet; 2 percent of $120,000 is $2,400, and 98 percent of $120,000 is $117,600.

The supplies used for repairs can be allocated directly as given in the solution below, $200 for pharmacy and $79,800 for other departments, based on actual costs incurred and assigned to repair projects directly. The remaining $20,000 of routine supplies would be allocated based on square feet; 2 percent of $20,000 is $400, and the remaining 98 percent is $19,600.

In sum, the total pharmacy costs under the ABC approach are as follows:

Pharmacy Total	
Routine	$3,014
Repairs	314
Total	$3,328

This total of $3,328 is only a little more than half the original allocation of $6,140. Clearly, the more accurate costing approach does have a significant impact in this instance.

The solution table is as follows:

Pharmacy	Routine	Repairs
Administration	$ 214	$ 6
Labor	2,400	108
Supplies	400	200
Total	$3,014	$314

All Other Departments	Routine	Repairs	Total
Administration	$ 10,500	$ 4,279	$ 15,000
Labor	117,600	71,892	192,000
Supplies	19,600	79,800	100,000
Total	$147,700	$155,971	$307,000

REFERENCE

1. C. Berliner and J.A. Brimson, *Cost Management for Today's Advanced Manufacturing* (Boston: Harvard Business School Press, 1988), 241.

CHAPTER 18

Questions for Discussion

1. No. By avoiding costs related to errors and doing things over, it is possible that doing things better initially will be less expensive.

2. Not necessarily. In addition to patient care, one can think of the quality of accounting information. Accountants can practice total quality management (TQM) by constantly working to improve the quality of the information they provide to the organization's managers.

3. Cost data being used for an analysis must be carefully reviewed for the following:

   • to ensure the data are properly matched,
   • to eliminate the effect of changing prices,
   • to ensure they are based on constant technology,
   • to eliminate clerical errors,
   • to eliminate unrepresentative periods, and

   • to balance the costs and benefits of more accurate information.

4. Patient care costs have been rising dramatically for the last quarter century. There is now great pressure to control costs. Placing limits on quality is one approach that is sometimes presented. We cannot afford the highest quality. However, TQM indicates that costs can actually be reduced by raising quality rather than lowering it.

5. Essentially, it is not the measurement of quality of patient care that is required by the accounting system. That measurement might place an insurmountable obstacle in front of us. What we really need to be able to measure are the costs of *actions* that affect the quality of care.

Problem

1. Each answer will be unique. See Application 18-1 and the radiology retake example in Chapter 18 for guidance.

CHAPTER 19

Questions for Discussion

1. One can think of these as evolutionary and revolutionary. The evolutionary approach relies heavily on existing cost information—grouping patients and applying the ratio of cost to charges to their bills to approximate product-line costs. However, step-down-generated data are quite poor when used to approximate the costs actually incurred to treat different patients. The revolutionary approach is more of a micro-costing technique. Under such an approach, specific studies would have to be undertaken to estimate the actual resources consumed by different types of patients. Hybrid approaches, such as patient classification systems used to determine nursing costs of different types of patients, are also possible.

2. The major surprise was that obtaining improved cost data has apparently not been a key motivating factor in the development of product-line management systems.

3. Under prospective payment, the health care organization does not receive extra payment for extra individual services. For example, a hospital will not receive any extra payment from Medicare for an inpatient who receives an extra laboratory test or x-ray. Assigning revenues to departments gives them an incentive to increase volume. That, in turn, increases costs. However, if revenue does not increase with volume, then the incentive given is detrimental to the organization's financial well-being.

Index

D

About the Author

Steven A. Finkler, PhD, CPA, is professor of public and health administration, accounting, and financial management at New York University's (NYU) Robert F. Wagner Graduate School of Public Service. At NYU, Professor Finkler directs the financial management specialization in the Program in Health Policy and Management. He is also the editor of Aspen Publishers, Inc.'s, *Hospital Cost Management and Accounting,* a monthly publication, and is a member of the editorial boards of *Health Services Research* and *Health Care Management Review.*

Professor Finkler received a B.S. in economics and an M.S. in accounting from the Wharton School. His master's degree in economics and doctorate in business administration were awarded by Stanford University. An award-winning teacher and author, Dr. Finkler, who is also a CPA, worked for several years as an auditor with Ernst and Young and was on the faculty of the Wharton School before joining NYU.

Among his publications are three other books: *Finance and Accounting for Nonfinancial Managers* (Revised Edition, Prentice-Hall, 1992), *Budgeting Concepts for Nurse Managers* (Second Edition, W.B. Saunders, 1992), and *Financial Management for Nurse Managers and Executives,* co-authored with Christine Kovner (W.B. Saunders, 1993).

He has published over 200 articles in many journals, including *Healthcare Financial Management, Health Care Management Review, New England Journal of Medicine, Health Services Research, Inquiry, Medical Care, Nursing Economics,* and *The Journal of Nursing Administration.*

Professor Finkler has consulted extensively and has worked on a wide variety of costing studies in the field of health services research. He conducts seminars on health services financial management, both around the country and abroad.